THE OXFORD H

METAPHYSICS

THE OXFORD HANDBOOK OF

METAPHYSICS

Edited by

MICHAEL J. LOUX

AND

DEAN W. ZIMMERMAN

OXFORD

UNIVERSITY PRESS

OXFORD

UNIVERSITY PRESS

Great Clarendon Street, Oxford OX2 6DP

Oxford University Press is a department of the University of Oxford.
It furthers the University's objective of excellence in research, scholarship,
and education by publishing worldwide in

Oxford New York

Auckland Cape Town Dar es Salaam Hong Kong Karachi
Kuala Lumpur Madrid Melbourne Mexico City Nairobi
New Delhi Shanghai Taipei Toronto
With offices in
Argentina Austria Brazil Chile Czech Republic France Greece
Guatemala Hungary Italy Japan South Korea Poland Portugal
Singapore Switzerland Thailand Turkey Ukraine Vietnam

Oxford is a registered trade mark of Oxford University Press
in the UK and in certain other countries

Published in the United States
by Oxford University Press Inc., New York

ISBN 978-0-19-928422-1

Printed in the United Kingdom by
Lightning Source UK Ltd., Milton Keynes

ACKNOWLEDGEMENTS

Thanks are due to Peter Momtchiloff, who provided help and encouragement at every stage of this project. Thanks also to Margaret Jasiewicz, Cheryl Reed, Tina Elkins, Linda Lange, and David Manley, who worked on the preparation of the manuscript. And special thanks to Noell Birondo, who handled the page proofs and oversaw the final stages of the project.

Contents

PART VI PERSONS AND THE NATURE OF MIND

PART VII FREEDOM OF THE WILL

PART VIII ANTI-REALISM AND VAGUENESS

Notes on the Contributors

Thomas M. Crisp, Assistant Professor of Philosophy at Florida State University.

Hartry Field, Professor of Philosophy at New York University.

Kit Fine, Professor of Philosophy at New York University.

Carl Ginet, Professor of Philosophy Emeritus at Cornell University.

Sally Haslanger, Associate Professor of Philosophy at the Massachusetts Institute of Technology.

John Hawthorne, Professor of Philosophy at Rutgers University.

Joshua Hoffman, Professor of Philosophy at the University of North Carolina at Greensboro.

Jaegwon Kim, Founce Professor of Philosophy at Brown University.

Michael J. Loux, Schuster Professor of Philosophy at the University of Notre Dame.

E. J. Lowe, Professor of Philosophy at Durham University.

Tim Maudlin, Professor of Philosophy at Rutgers University.

Graham Nerlich, Professor of Philosophy at Adelaide University.

Michael C. Rea, Associate Professor of Philosophy at the University of Notre Dame.

Howard Robinson, Member of the Faculty of Philosophy at the Central European University.

Gary S. Rosenkrantz, Professor of Philosophy at the University of North Carolina at Greensboro.

Theodore Sider, Associate Professor of Philosophy at Rutgers University.

Peter Simons, Professor of Philosophy at Leeds University.

Ernest Sosa, Elton Professor of Natural Theology and Professor of Philosophy at Brown University.

Zoltán Gendler Szabó, Associate Professor of Philosophy at Cornell University.

Michael Tooley, Professor of Philosophy at the University of Colorado at Boulder.

Peter van Inwagen, O'Hara Professor of Philosophy at the University of Notre Dame.

Ted Warfield, Associate Professor of Philosophy at the University of Notre Dame.

Timothy Williamson, Professor of Philosophy at Oxford University and Fellow of New College.

Dean W. Zimmerman, Associate Professor of Philosophy at Rutgers University.

INTRODUCTION

MICHAEL J. LOUX

DEAN W. ZIMMERMAN

ITS detractors often characterize analytical philosophy as anti-metaphysical. After all, we are told, it was born at the hands of Moore and Russell, who were reacting against the metaphysical systems of idealists like Bosanquet and Bradley; and subsequent movements in the analytic tradition—logical positivism and ordinary language philosophy—made the elimination of metaphysics the cornerstone of their respective philosophical agendas. The characterization is not, however, completely accurate. For one thing, the earliest movement in the tradition—the logical atomism of Russell and the early Wittgenstein—was thoroughly metaphysical in its orientation. To be sure, the metaphysics at work there was conservative, lacking the speculative excesses and obscurantist jargon of the idealists; but no less than the idealists, the logical atomists were concerned to provide a comprehensive account of the ontological structure of reality. For another, while card-carrying positivists and ordinary language philosophers were officially committed to the view that the claims of the traditional metaphysician are somehow problematic (perhaps meaningless; perhaps, just confused), the fact is that philosophers from both movements continued to deal with the problems confronting traditional metaphysics. Of course, they were anxious to conceal this fact, parading their work as talk about logical syntax or as conceptual analysis; but no one was fooled; and in any case, their attacks on metaphysics were themselves anchored in theses (typically theses expressing a radical form of anti-realism) that were no less metaphysical than the views they sought to undermine.

Still, it remains true that for much of its early history analytic philosophy was inhospitable to traditional metaphysics; and it cannot be denied that in the heyday of logical positivism in the 1930s and 1940s or in the post-war period when the ordinary language philosophy of the later Wittgenstein was most influential, it was not fashionable to bill oneself as a metaphysician. But by the early 1960s prejudices against metaphysics were beginning to soften. This change in attitude was due to the work of philosophers who were willing to address metaphysical questions in spite of the long-standing prejudices. Philosophers like Arthur Prior, Roderick Chisholm, and Wilfrid Sellars come to mind here; but two philosophers were especially influential in the rehabilitation of metaphysics—W. V. O. Quine and P. F. Strawson. They had their roots in the anti-metaphysical traditions they helped undermine. Quine came out of the tradition of logical positivism, and Strawson was originally a representative of the ordinary language tradition. Both attempted to show that there is a project in metaphysics responsible philosophers can in good conscience undertake. For Strawson, the project was what he called 'descriptive metaphysics'. According to Strawson, the aim of descriptive metaphysics is the systematic characterization of the most general categorial or structural features of the conceptual scheme in terms of which we talk and think about the world. Quine, by contrast, focused on the ontological commitments associated with accepting a body of discourse. His famous slogan 'To be is to be the value of a bound variable' was supposed to provide a criterion by which the metaphysician can determine just which kinds of entities we commit ourselves to by endorsing a given body of statements. Both philosophers were highly influential, each on his respective side of the Atlantic. Strawson's conception of descriptive metaphysics was attractive to philosophers—typically British philosophers—who grew up in the tradition of conceptual analysis; whereas Quine's notion of ontological commitment appealed to philosophers—typically American philosophers—schooled in the more formal logistic approaches characteristic of the logical positivist tradition.

The upshot was that philosophers no longer felt the need to conceal their interest in metaphysical issues, and there was something like a revival of traditional metaphysics. In Britain the revival had a distinctively Kantian flavour. Philosophers posed metaphysical questions by asking about the presuppositions of this or that conceptual practice—our identification and reidentification of particulars, our ascription of spatio-temporal location, our use of the classificatory concepts at work in predication. Questions about the objectivity of the concepts structuring those practices were central here, and those questions naturally unfolded into more general questions about the nature of realism and the possibility of anti-realist theories of meaning and truth.

In the United States the revival of interest in metaphysics was expressed in the more self-consciously ontological idiom of categories. Initially, philosophers followed Quine's lead in asking whether our beliefs (either those expressed in our best scientific theories or those at work in our day-to-day confrontation with the world) commit us to the existence of abstract entities. And if they do, are those abstract entities things like sets whose identity conditions can be given in straightforwardly extensional terms, or are we committed to things like properties and propositions? And these questions led to others. Those who endorsed the existence of properties faced questions about individuation. If there are such things as properties, how are they related to familiar concrete particulars? Are the latter just bundles of properties, or do particulars constitute an irreducible ontological category? And since propositions are the sorts of things that are said to be necessary, possible, contingent, and impossible, those who endorsed the existence of propositions found themselves forced to confront questions about modality. Do we need to follow Leibniz and appeal to a special category of objects—possible worlds—to explain how modal claims can be true or false? And if so, how do particulars figure in the story? Are they the sorts of things that can exist in different possible worlds? And what does that tell us about their ontological structure? The range of legitimate metaphysical questions kept expanding, and soon philosophers in this tradition were asking all the old questions. What is the nature of time? What is it for an ordinary object to persist through time? What is the nature of space? Do events constitute an irreducibly basic kind of object? If so, what are they like and what are their identity conditions? What is causation? Are there any uncaused events?

In both Britain and the United States the revival of metaphysics was gradual. At first, there was a piecemeal character to work in the field. With rare exceptions, philosophers were wary of large-scale metaphysical theories—the construction of comprehensive ontological schemes, theories about the nature of and relations among the most abstract categories under which absolutely *everything* falls, and the use of this ontological machinery to settle issues about mind–body relations, causation, philosophy of religion, and so on. Comprehensive, ontology-driven metaphysics was associated with the names of the idealists whom Russell and Moore had effectively defeated—McTaggart, Bosanquet, Bradley, Royce, Joachim. The systematic *realist* metaphysics of Russell and Moore themselves (the Moore of *Some Main Problems of Philosophy*), and of other realists like Samuel Alexander, Roy Wood Sellars, H. H. Price, D. C. Williams, and C. D. Broad, had been made to seem misguided and outdated first by the arguments of the logical empiricists, then by the harangues of Wittgensteinians and other ordinary language philosophers; and so an impressive body of non-idealist systematic metaphysics was ignored and then forgotten.

We suspect that, past mid-century, few philosophers really believed that the standard verificationist arguments against the meaningfulness of metaphysical claims were any good. Nevertheless, systematic metaphysics continued to languish. It was typical of those who began to raise the old metaphysical questions during the 1960s and 1970s to proceed cautiously, addressing now this metaphysical problem, now that. Their caution was understandable; after the idealists were routed, the most prominent builders of metaphysical systems were Whitehead, Bergson, and Paul Weiss. Despite their evident genius, whatever insights they had into metaphysical problems were invisible to analytic philosophers. Indeed, they seemed to many to serve as an object lesson: This is what happens when you try to do metaphysics in the grand manner. They and their admirers produced bodies of work that followed the same recipe used by the nineteenth-century idealists: (i) set forth your own baroque ontological scheme in a new, peculiar jargon; (ii) claim that it is radically opposed to all preceding metaphysical systems; and (iii) explain its intricacies in a series of ever longer books, introducing as many undefined technical terms as possible.

By the mid-1980s a new generation of philosophers was coming to the study of metaphysics. These philosophers had no first-hand knowledge of the positivist or ordinary language attacks on metaphysics. For them, the attacks were quaint episodes from a distant past rather than serious theoretical challenges. Accordingly, they were not in the least apologetic about doing metaphysics, nor were they content with a piecemeal approach to metaphysics. Unlike many of their predecessors, they were willing to attempt the construction of comprehensive ontological theories, building upon the work of such trailblazers in the rehabilitation of systematic metaphysics as Roderick Chisholm, David Armstrong, and David Lewis.

Quine's criterion of ontological commitment was very important to philosophers like Chisholm and Lewis. Both are rightly regarded as champions of a chastened approach to metaphysics, one that neither shies away from the traditional problems of ontology, nor falls back into the arcane, untethered system-building that had given metaphysics a bad name; and both regarded Quine's criterion as an antidote to the besetting sins of traditional metaphysicians.

The approach to questions of ontological commitment defended by Quine in 'On What There Is' (1948) was already in place by 1939, when Chisholm and Quine overlapped at Harvard (Chisholm a graduate student, Quine a young professor). In the hands of Chisholm, Lewis, and their heirs, Quine's criterion of ontological commitment is understood to be something like this: If one affirms a statement using a name or other singular term, or an initial phrase of 'existential quantification', like 'There are some so-and-sos', then one must either (1) admit that one is committed to the existence of things answering to the singular term or satisfying the description, or (2) provide a 'paraphrase' of the statement that eschews singular terms and quantification over so-and-sos. So interpreted, Quine's criterion can be seen as a logical development of the methods of Russell and Moore, who assumed that one must accept the existence of entities corresponding to the singular terms used in statements one accepts, unless and until one finds systematic methods of paraphrase that eliminate these terms.

The metaphysics of Chisholm and, later, Lewis look nothing like Quine's, however. For Quine, it is the deliverances of science alone that should determine our ontological commitments. As Chisholm saw it, this was the decisive point at which he departed from Quine and took inspiration from Moore: Why not assume, in the seminar room, the same things we take ourselves to know in everyday life? Why are we suddenly not entitled to them? Lewis, and the younger generation of metaphysicians who came into their own in the 1980s, by and large side with Chisholm and Moore. Once all our ordinary convictions are taken into account, the traditional problems of metaphysics return with a vengeance, as they do not for Quine. As a result, ontology must be responsive to other areas of philosophy; a particular ontological scheme shows its adequacy by its usefulness in the resolution of problems elsewhere. Desiderata for an ontological scheme include both simplicity (a point about which Quine would agree) and scope. One metaphysical system is superior to another in scope in so far as it allows for the statement of satisfactory philosophical theories on more subjects—theories that preserve, in the face of puzzle and apparent contradiction, most of what we take ourselves to know.

One presupposition of the version of Quineanism invoked by Chisholm and Lewis is that the nature of the ontological categories is somewhat opaque to us. There is still hope for ontology, however, since our fallible intuitions about the subject can be tethered in this way to success elsewhere, in the resolution of philosophical problems concerning better-known matters.

The differences between Quine's starting point and that of Chisholm, Lewis, and the rest lead to greater differences down the line. With only (a small subset of) the sciences yielding truths for the ontologist to consider, Quine can rest content with an austere naturalism: although one cannot accept the mathematics needed for science without set theory, no further 'queer entities' need be recognized; there is only space-time and its particular contents, and sets of such things. Chisholm, Lewis, and company have many more truths to consider, and more apparent paradoxes to resolve. They have generally found it very difficult to arrive at metaphysical theories satisfying both desiderata of simplicity and scope without giving up Quine's insistence upon a purely extensional language and logic. Lewis was able to retain extensionality, but at great cost—the positing of an extravagant ontology of concrete, spatio-temporally disconnected universes, which he defended by an explicit appeal to Quinean principles of ontological commitment. His attitude toward the contents of *our* world, however, remained staunchly materialist, and not substantially different from that of Quine. Chisholm, unlike Lewis, rejects Quine's logical scruples, taking at least one intentional (mental) and intensional (non-extensional) notion as a primitive. He also concludes that the only way to retain most of what we think we know about persons is to admit that they are very special: they have causal powers unlike those found elsewhere in nature, they can 'grasp' or conceive of abstract objects, and their persistence conditions are mysteriously different from those of ordinary physical objects. Such conclusions make his metaphysics unacceptable to Quine and other naturalistically inclined philosophers. Although there is much in the metaphysics of both Chisholm and Lewis that their critics find mysterious or unbelievable, both systems include solutions to a host of philosophical puzzles, and stand as a challenge to be met by anyone who would defend metaphysical naturalism and nominalism while rejecting Lewis's vastly enlarged physical ontology.

Most philosophers today who identify themselves as metaphysicians are in basic agreement with the Quinean approach to systematic metaphysics exemplified in the work of Chisholm and Lewis. Indeed, it is probably not much of an exaggeration to say that today's crop of metaphysicians can be divided fairly exhaustively into those most influenced by the one or the other. That division is reflected in the debates discussed in the chapters that follow. Those chapters approach the field topically. Each focuses on a fundamental metaphysical issue; the aim is to provide an account of the nature and structure of the debate over the issue. But the chapters are not merely *about* metaphysics; they are also exercises *in* metaphysics with authors attempting to advance the debate over the relevant issues. The first three focus on the traditional dichotomy of universal and particular. Zoltán Szabó discusses nominalistic accounts of the phenomena central to the debate over universals; whereas Joshua Hoffman and Gary Rosenkrantz focus on Platonistic accounts of universals. E. J. Lowe closes Part I by discussing problems surrounding the individuation of particulars. Next, there follows a pair of chapters on very general ontological issues. John Hawthorne deals with the concept of identity, and Peter van Inwagen discusses the phenomenon of ontological commitment and attempts to show how the case of fictional discourse is to be accommodated.

Modal issues have been pivotal in recent analytic metaphysics. Here, the central debate has been between those endorsing non-reductive theories of modality and those insisting on reductive accounts of modal phenomena. In his contribution Kit Fine deals with approaches of the first sort; whereas Ted Sider examines approaches of the second sort. In addition, discussion of non-reductive theories can be found in Hoffman and Rosenkrantz's chapter on Platonistic theories of universals.

Part IV focuses on issues bearing on the metaphysics of time and space. One important debate on the nature of time pits what are called presentists against those who construe time as a fourth dimension on a par with the three spatial dimensions. Thomas Crisp examines presentist theorists; whereas Michael Rea discusses four-dimensionalism. In his chapter, Graham Nerlich discusses issues bearing on the debate over the status of space-time. Finally, Sally Haslanger discusses the different approaches to questions about persistence through time and their theoretical roots in the metaphysics of time.

Part V deals with a series of interrelated issues about events, causation, and physical theory. In the first chapter Peter Simons discusses recent debates about the existence and nature of events. Michael Tooley and Hartry Field each contribute a chapter on causation. Tooley focuses on broader issues about the analysis of our concept of causation; whereas Field examines the more particular case of causation in physical theory. Finally, we have a chapter by Tim Maudlin on the metaphysical implications of quantum mechanics.

The next three chapters focus on questions about the metaphysics of persons and the mental. Dean Zimmerman examines materialist accounts of persons. His chapter is followed by two more general discussions of the metaphysical status of the mental. The first, by Howard Robinson, focuses on general ontological questions about the nature and structure of perceptual and conceptual episodes. The second, by Jaegwon Kim, considers the way questions about supervenience and reduction have come together in recent attempts at providing materialist accounts of intentional phenomena. Then we have two chapters on the problem of freedom of the will. Carl Ginet examines libertarian approaches; whereas Ted Warfield discusses compatibilist accounts of freedom.

Part VII bears broadly on realism and attempts to delineate alternatives to realism. Michael Loux discusses the very influential debates over realism and anti-realism that originated with Michael Dummett and dominated the British philosophical scene in the 1970s, 1980s, and early 1990s. Ernest Sosa considers approaches to questions about realism that have their origin in facts bearing on ontological relativity. Finally, Timothy Williamson attempts to lay out the central features of metaphysical debates over the nature of vagueness.

PART I

UNIVERSALS AND PARTICULARS

CHAPTER 1

NOMINALISM

ZOLTÁN GENDLER SZABÓ

1. INTRODUCTION

ARE there numbers? What about directions, sets, shapes, animal species, properties, relations, propositions, linguistic expressions, meanings, concepts, rights, values, or any other abstract entities? There are two sorts of answers to such questions: straight ones and oblique ones. The straight answers are typically introduced by the expression 'of course', as in 'Of course there are, otherwise how could sentences like "2 + 2 = 4" and "There is something Napoleon and Alexander have in common" be true?' and 'Of course there aren't, for how could we even know or speak of things that are causally inert?' The oblique answers are usually headed by the locution 'well, you know', as in 'Well, you know that really depends on whether you take this to be an internal or external question' and 'Well, you know that actually depends on whether you mean "exist" in a thick or thin sense'. Analytic philosophers tend to feel a strong inclination towards the clear-cut. But ontology—and especially the ontology of the abstract—is an area in which it is hard to dismiss oblique lines.

The *nominalist* sticks with straight negative answers: she unqualifiedly rejects abstract entities of any sort whatsoever.[1] The nominalist's equally straight opponent

Thanks to Tamar Szabó Gendler, Benj Hellie, Harold Hodes, Ted Sider, and Scott Spiker for comments and criticism.

[1] 'Nominalism' is often used in another sense as referring to the doctrine that there are no universals. In the traditional medieval sense of the word, nominalism is the doctrine that whatever

is the *anti-nominalist,*[2] who accepts at least one type of abstracta. On the face of it, their views are clear opposites. Nonetheless, both expend a good deal of effort fending off a variety of oblique answers seeking a middle ground between their views.

Nominalism is certainly not the most surprising eliminativist thesis—there are some who deny the existence of ordinary material objects, mental states, or persons—but it is among the most radical of those widely held. Nominalism does away with so many kinds of putative entities that the ontology it yields may not even be properly described as a desert landscape. After all, aren't landscapes, at least in one of the perfectly legitimate senses of this word, abstract?

Nominalism is a divisive doctrine. Proponents often concede that they are fighting an uphill battle, but justify their insistence with an appeal to ontological conscience; opponents tend to be sceptical about the sincerity of such appeals. They suspect that nominalism is indeed much like a desert: an uncomfortable place whose main attraction is that it is hard to be there. Some of this clash is no doubt the result of a genuine conflict in philosophical temperament, but there is another source as well. Contemporary nominalism grows out of a number of different traditions, each contributing its distinct understanding of the key terms of the nominalist thesis. The intensity of many philosophers' belief in the *absurdity* of nominalism is partly the result of the seeming simplicity and underlying ambiguity of the position.

To bring out the perplexing character of nominalism, consider the often voiced concern that the view appears to be a self-undermining. For suppose that a nominalist—call him Nelson—just told you that there are no abstract entities. How should Nelson describe what he did? Did he say something? Certainly not, if saying something amounts to expressing a proposition. Did he utter something? Clearly not, if uttering something requires the articulation of a sentence type. Did he try to bring you to share his belief? Obviously not, if sharing a belief requires being in identical mental states.

Of course, Nelson is not likely to be moved by all this. After all, there is a nominalistically acceptable way of describing what happened: he produced meaningful noises and thereby attempted to bring you into a mental state relevantly similar to one of his own. There is no mention of propositions, sentences, or shareable beliefs here, and still, in an important sense, we are told precisely what was going on. Nevertheless, that we can find such an alternative way of talking is by no means

---

exists is particular, and nothing but particular. According to nominalists, generality belongs to certain *nominal expressions* alone, and it belongs to them only in the sense that they may apply to more than one particular. The origin of the term 'nominalism' is subject to serious scholarly dispute; cf. Courteney (1992).

[2] The term 'Platonism' is occasionally used in the literature in the sense I employ 'anti-nominalism'. Unfortunately, it is also often used in a richer sense, when it carries additional commitment to the mind-independence of abstract entities. Since neither sense of 'Platonism' has much to do with Plato's metaphysics, I have opted for a neutral term.

a *complete* response to the concern about self-undermining. For the questions raised were merely bypassed, not answered. We can raise them again: When Nelson produced those meaningful noises, did he say something? did he utter something? did he try to bring you to share his belief? If the answer is no, Nelson must tell us just how we ended up in a massive error in thinking the commonplace thought that Nelson *did* say something by uttering a sentence and that we might have ended up sharing his belief. If the answer is yes, he has to explain how that concession is supposed to be compatible with his renunciation of abstracta. How Nelson answers this challenge is crucial for a full understanding of his position.

I will begin (Section 2) with a good deal of clarification. Participants in contemporary debates surrounding nominalism tend to share certain assumptions about what ontological commitment amounts to, how the abstract and the concrete are to be distinguished, and what objects in general are. It is good to have these assumptions on the table. Then (Section 3) I turn to a discussion of nominalist attitudes towards the apparent commitment ordinary thinking and speech carry to abstracta. This is followed by a survey of some of the most influential arguments for nominalism (Section 4) and against it (Section 5). The chapter ends (Section 6) with a brief look at some oblique answers to the ontological question about abstracta. I will make no attempt to resolve the issues here, but my anti-nominalist inclination will no doubt show throughout.

2. THE NOMINALIST THESIS

The debate about nominalism concerns the question whether there are abstract entities. The terms of this question—'there are', 'abstract', and 'entity'—are all subject to interpretative disagreements. I will start by examining them one by one.

2.1 Are There . . .

The standard view nowadays is that we can adequately capture the meaning of sentences like 'There are *F*s', 'Some things are *F*s', or '*F*s exist' through existential quantification. As a result, not much credence is given to the idea that we must distinguish between different kinds or degrees of existence.[3] When we talk

---

[3] Commitment to a univocal quantificational analysis of existence claims need not be taken as entailing the rejection of fundamental categories in metaphysics. But the distinction cannot be ontological: entities in the different categories exist in the same sense of the word.

about whether there are cheap hotels in New York and when we talk about whether possible worlds exist, there is no fundamental difference in logical form between the claims at stake. If this much is agreed upon, alternative conceptions of ontological commitment must be presented as alternative views about quantification.[4]

There are all sorts of exotic existential quantifiers in formal languages: some are interpreted substitutionally; some can bind predicate-, function-, or sentence-variables; some bind all variables within their scope unselectively. There are formal languages, for example those of intuitionistic, free, and quantum logic, where certain classical inferences are invalid. There is no serious question about the coherence of the semantic rules governing such languages.[5] But this does not settle the deeper question whether these formal devices have anything to do with anything we ordinarily think or say.

The usual line of defence against employing non-standard quantification to capture our existential idioms goes back to Quine. It relies on two claims. First, that the interpretation *given* to the classical objectual first-order existential quantifier is just this: there are things that are thus and so. Secondly, that the ordinary existential idioms are *univocal*: there is only stylistic difference between saying that there are things that are thus and so and saying that thus and sos exist (Quine 1969: 106). Both claims are widely endorsed, both are plausible, both are nonetheless questionable. We do tend to say when elucidating the meaning of the material conditional that we interpret $\varphi \rightarrow \psi$ as *if φ then ψ*, but there is good reason to suspect that we are wrong about that. The English 'if ... then' seems to have a different semantics. This shows that the ordinary language glosses we give for sentences of first-order logic may not capture their correct interpretations. We do not bestow meaning upon our logical symbolism simply by insisting on a canonical paraphrase.[6] The univocality of our ordinary existential idioms is no less problematic. After all, it is a fact of ordinary language use that it is fairly *natural* to say that there is a good chance that the Supreme Court won't choose a president again and it is fairly *unnatural* to say that something is such that it is a good chance that the Supreme Court won't choose a president again. It is also a fact that many native speakers of English would baulk at the inference from the first claim to the second. Is it really obvious, prior to any empirical

---

[4] For reservations regarding the view that quantification and ontology are inextricably bound together, see Azzouni (1998) and Szabó (forthcoming).

[5] Although claims of incoherence occasionally do surface in the philosophical literature. To get a sense how the coherence of non-standard quantification is to be defended, see e.g. Dummett (1973a), Boolos (1975), and Kripke (1976).

[6] It is of course true that we did not learn quantificational theory as our mother tongue. But this does not mean that its acquisition proceeds simply by establishing a translation manual from ordinary language to the language of first-order logic. It would be hard to deny that the meaning of the standard existential quantifier is fixed by the way we use it. But it does not follow from this that a tiny aspect of this use—our willingness to offer the ordinary existential idioms as adequate translation—is by itself sufficient to determine what it means.

investigation, that the proper explanation of this fact will not involve the postulation of ambiguity?

Quine has another argument for adopting his strategy of regimenting ontological disputes: just as he thinks we should believe in the existence of those things our *best theory* says there are, he also thinks we should interpret 'exist' to mean what our *best logic* says it means. And Quine thinks our best logic is classical first-order logic: he often praises it for its 'extraordinary combination of depth and simplicity, beauty and utility' (Quine 1969: 112–13). No doubt, classical first-order logic is the best-understood quantificational logic and it has remarkable meta-logical features, which distinguish it sharply from its alternatives. Still, it is by no means clear that this is enough to make sense of the claim that classical first-order logic is *better* than the rest. And even if it is, couldn't it be that by regimenting our ordinary speech using our best logic, we end up misinterpreting it? Those of us who—unlike Quine—believe that typically there is a fact of the matter regarding the truth-conditions of sentences in ordinary language cannot simply dismiss this possibility.

Whether our ordinary existential idioms are well represented by the standard existential quantifier is an open empirical problem of linguistics. But this fact need not paralyse ontology. For even if it turned out that ordinary language does not employ the devices of classical first-order logic, there is no reason to doubt that we do *understand* those devices, and that we do find the use of '∃' illuminating in articulating ontological problems. We want to know whether the sentence '∃x (x is an abstract entity)' is true,[7] and we are prepared to say that the correct answer to this question would resolve the debate about nominalism. Once the semantic questions are bracketed, there is presumably no harm in the continued use of ordinary language. Even if it turns out that 'there are' or 'exist' mean something slightly different from what '∃' does in classical first-order logic, the difference now appears immaterial to the debate at hand.[8]

2.2 . . . Abstract . . .

There is no generally accepted way to draw the distinction between the abstract and the concrete. Still, there is a rough agreement on the paradigms. Concrete entities are in some important aspect like pebbles (or donkeys, or protons), whereas abstracta are like numbers (or shapes, or propositions). To characterize the distinction this way is vague and unprincipled, but it is the natural starting point; discussions of the

---

[7] This, of course, is not a sentence in English. But we seem to have a pretty good grasp of its meaning anyway.

[8] No doubt this quick argument will not convince everyone. In Sect. 6 I will briefly return to this issue.

distinctions between the physical and the mental and between the descriptive and the normative begin the same way.

Tradition says that abstract entities are *abstractions* from concrete ones. Abstract entities lack specificity in the sense that an incomplete characterization of a complete entity may serve as a complete characterization of a correlated abstract entity. Geometrical shapes provide an obvious example: if we describe a large red wet circular patch of paint on a piece of paper in purely geometrical terms, we give, on the one hand, an incomplete description of the paint patch and, on the other, a unique specification of an abstract entity, a circle of a certain size.

Those who prefer to distinguish between the abstract and the concrete in this way will often say that abstract entities are *given to us* through abstraction, a mental process whereby we selectively attend to some, but not other, features of a concrete thing.[9] But this should not be taken as an invitation to psychologism. Even if one thinks that abstraction is nothing but the formation of abstract ideas, those abstract ideas themselves will not be abstract entities. They are concrete representational states of concrete minds. If there *are* abstract entities, they are things that are *uniquely* represented by abstract ideas. Like John Locke, one can believe in abstract ideas and be a wholehearted nominalist.

Even if one steers clear of the psychologistic connotations of the traditional distinction, it is hard not to read some sort of ontological dependence into the doctrine that certain entities are abstractions from others. It is natural to think that a length is necessarily a length *of* something, that a direction is necessarily the direction *of* something, that a set is necessarily the set *of* some things, etc. Following up on this insight, one might suggest that *criteria of identity* for abstract entities must be spelled out in terms of concrete ones. The length of *a* is identical to the length of *b* iff a Euclidean transformation maps the endpoints of *a* to the endpoints of *b*; the direction of *a* is identical to the direction of *b* iff *a* and *b* are parallel; the set of Fs is identical to the set of Gs iff all Fs are Gs and all Gs are Fs, etc. It has even been suggested that we could bypass the traditional notion of abstraction and *define* the distinction between abstract and concrete in terms of the sort of criteria of identity associated with them.[10] But if we do so, we commit ourselves to a

---

[9] There is another, closely related mental process often referred to as 'abstraction'. Abstraction of this second kind is a kind of generalization: we attend to features that a number of distinct concrete things have in common. For a criticism of the idea that certain concepts are acquired through the mental process of abstraction, see Geach (1957).

[10] Chapter 14 of Dummett (1973b) makes the proposal that an abstract object is such that it is essential to the understanding of any of its names that the referent be recognized as lying within the range of a functional expression, such as 'shape of . . .' or 'direction of . . .'. Dummett recognizes that his distinction is not precise, but he insists on the importance of the insight behind it. He claims that the sense in which a shape or direction must be 'of' something is 'very akin to the conception of logical dependence which Aristotle expresses by the preposition "in" when he gives as part of his characterization of a substance that it is not "in" anything else' (1973b: 487). Dummett's distinction has been contested on the grounds that it characterizes abstract entities purely extrinsically, and hence does

modal claim: that abstract entities could not exist without their concrete correlates. (How could 'the direction of a' denote something if a does not refer?) This sounds plausible in some cases; if there were no lions, there would not be such a thing as the genus *Panthera leo*, if the earth didn't exist, there would not be such a thing as the equator, and if there were no tokens of the English word 'house', then the word itself would fail to exist. But not all abstracta seem to be like this. Should we really believe that if there were no circular patches, circular geometrical shapes would also fail to exist? If we say that propositions are abstractions from sentences, which are, in turn, abstractions from pencil marks and human noises, should we also insist that before there were those marks and noises there were no propositions either? It seems better not to include in the definition of abstract entities that they ontologically depend on their concrete correlates.[11]

The real problem with the traditional way of drawing the line between abstract and concrete is not that talk about abstraction carries dubious connotations. One can resist those connotations: the core of the traditional division is nothing more than the claim that abstract entities can be fully characterized in a vocabulary that would be insufficient to fully characterize concrete entities. The vocabulary of geometry is sufficient to identify the circle, but could not be used to identify any circular paint patch. If this is so, the reason must be that the circle *lacks* certain properties that can distinguish paint patches from one another. But the traditional story fails to tell us what these properties are. Photons don't have rest mass, black holes don't emit light, points in space don't have extension, so they all lack properties that are standardly used to distinguish among concrete things.[12] Nonetheless, they are all classified as concrete. It is hard to see how the traditional division can explain this.

This leads us to the way abstract and concrete entities are usually distinguished in current discussions. Abstract entities are supposed to lack observational, causal, and spatio-temporal properties, i.e. they are (i) in principle imperceptible, (ii) incapable

---

not tell us about their nature (cf. Lewis 1986: 82). Even if it is true that we could not understand the name of a direction unless we recognize that the direction is a direction of some line, one could raise the question why this is so. One answer to this, suggested in chapter 3 of Hale (1987), is that in order to understand a name of a direction we must understand the sortal predicate '. . . is a direction', in order to understand this predicate we must know the criterion of identity for directions, and the criterion of identity of directions is spelled out in terms of the relation of parallelism between lines.

[11] Rejecting the idea that abstract entities ontologically depend on *their concrete correlates* is not the same as rejecting that they ontologically depend on the *totality of concreta*. Rosen (1993) calls this latter claim 'the supervenience of the abstract', and he argues that it is part of the commitments of ordinary thought. He also notes that the asymmetry of this dependence cannot be adequately captured modally: the relevant global supervenience claim holds in the opposite direction as well.

[12] One might argue that photons have zero rest mass, that black holes emit light of zero intensity, and points have zero extension, and so they all possess properties abstract entities lack. But the difference between lacking a property and possessing it to degree zero is even less clear than the difference between abstract and concrete.

of causal interaction, and (iii) not located in space-time. These features are typically not taken to be independent; in fact the first is often explained through the second, which in turn is explained by the third. These explanations are not beyond doubt. One might certainly hold that one could see that a cat is on a mat, that 'that cat is on the mat' is a singular term referring to a proposition, and that propositions do not enter into causal relations. Or one might hold that in understanding the English word 'cat' we must enter into a causal relation with the word, while denying that the word 'cat' occupies some region (or regions) of space-time. Of course, those who deny that we must be causally related to what we perceive or that causal relations must hold between spatio-temporally located entities may well be wrong. It is, nevertheless, a good idea not to try to smuggle substantive doctrines into the explication of a distinction. So, I will simply drop the first two criteria and stick with the third: an entity is abstract just in case it is not in space-time.[13]

2.3 . . . Entities?

It is best to understand 'entity' as it occurs in the nominalist thesis as a predicate whose extension is all-encompassing. Given that 'there is' is construed as the first-order existential quantifier, this decision amounts to taking the quantification in the nominalist thesis to be absolutely unrestricted.[14]

For some, the debate over nominalism is not about the existence of abstract *entities*, but about the existence of abstract *objects*. Such a distinction is usually motivated on broadly Fregean grounds: objects can be referents of genuine singular terms, functions can be the referents only to other kinds of expressions (cf. Dummett 1973b; Wright 1983; Hale 1987). Since it is usually emphasized that genuine singular terms are all and only those expressions that can flank the identity sign

---

[13] There are putative entities that are intuitively in time, but not in space. It is, for example, quite natural to say that words or animal species came to being and will cease to exist, though they are nowhere. Vendler (1967) claims that events fall in this category. (Compare: 'The collapse of the Germans was sudden' and 'The collapse of the Germans was 2000 miles long'.) Disembodied spirits might be another example. If these proposals are coherent, we must recognize an ambiguity in the above characterization of abstract entities. Not having spatio-temporal location can be construed as lacking *both* spatial *and* temporal properties, or as lacking *either* spatial *or* temporal properties.

According to some, impure sets (if they exist) are where their members are; according to some, God is outside space and time. Given the spatio-temporal characterization of the abstract–concrete distinction, these views entail respectively that impure sets are concrete and that God is abstract. These conclusions are no doubt in conflict with our initial intuitions. But I would be reluctant to blame the definition for the conflict.

[14] Whether wholly unrestricted quantification even makes sense is a matter of some controversy. For arguments against the coherence unrestricted quantification, see Dummett (1973b: 530–1, 567–9; 1991: 232–5, 313–19). For a response to Dummett, see Cartwright (1994).

in a meaningful sentence, this distinction is closely connected with another one, according to which objects are entities that possess determinate identity conditions (cf. Lowe 1995).[15]

Why think that the distinction between objects and non-objects drawn *within* the category of entities bears ontological significance? Because not all existential quantification appears to have the same kind of ontological significance. The inferences from 'Peter kicked a stone' to 'Peter kicked something' and 'Peter did something' are equally irresistible. But while 'This thing Peter kicked in the morning is identical to that thing Peter kicked in the evening' makes perfect sense, 'This thing Peter did in the morning is identical to that thing Peter did in the evening' is rather dubious. Perhaps we can have entities without identity, but surely not objects without identity.[16]

The intuition that 'Peter did something' does not have the same ontological significance as 'Peter kicked something' is worth taking seriously. But it is not clear that the best way to accommodate it involves distinguishing objects from other sorts of entities. The second-order formula '$\exists X$ (Peter Xed)' has plausibly the same content as the sentence 'There are some agents and Peter is one of them', and if this is so it only entails the existence of agents. The sentence involves plural quantification, and hence it ought to be distinguished from its singular counterparts: 'There is something whose instances are agents and Peter is an instance', 'There is something whose members are agents and Peter is a member', and 'There is something some of whose parts are agents and Peter is such a part'.[17] That there are true sentences apparently expressing higher-order existential quantification does not show that we must distinguish between two kinds of entities; rather it indicates that some existential quantification carries no commitment to a value (as opposed to value*s*) of its bound variable.[18]

If the decision made in Section 2.1 to interpret the nominalist thesis as involving classical first-order existential quantification was correct, considerations about the ontological commitments of higher-order quantification are beside the point

---

[15] Lowe's distinction does not coincide with the way Fregeans draw the line between objects and non-objects. Lowe believes that there are vague entities (e.g. elementary particles or ordinary waves) that can be referred to by expressions, that may well pass all the syntactic tests Fregeans might posit for genuine singular terms. Identity statements involving such terms would be meaningful, but would lack determinate truth-value. Cf. Lowe (1994).

[16] Although followers of Davidson (1967) do tend to point to the validity of such inferences as providing support for postulating quantification over events in the logical form of action sentences, they do not regard this as a decisive issue. The crucial evidence comes from the logic of adverbial modification.

[17] The quickest way to see the need for distinguishing between plural and singular quantification is to compare the sentences 'There are some sets of which every set that is not a member of itself is one' and 'There is a set of which every set that is not a member of itself is a member'. The first is a truism, the second a contradiction. Cf. Boolos (1984: 66).

[18] For a detailed argument that monadic second-order quantification is ontologically innocent, see Boolos (1985). For a dissent, see Resnik (1988).

anyway. The sentence '∃x (x is an abstract entity)' is true just in case an abstract entity is included in the domain of quantification. If the domain is unrestricted, an internal division in it cannot make a difference for ontology, no matter how metaphysically important it is.

3. How to be a Nominalist

Nominalism is nothing more than the thesis that there are no abstract entities. But to be a nominalist is more than to accept nominalism. Despite their occasional rhetoric, no nominalist thinks that abstracta are *exactly* on a par with ghosts, sea serpents, and other figments of our imagination. Since there are no ghosts or sea serpents, stories that are told about them are plainly false and should not be propounded as factual. But nobody—well, almost nobody—thinks that we should demote our talk about numbers, probabilities, languages, species, concepts, or virtues to that of fairy tales. What is the difference?

3.1 'Speak with the Vulgar . . .'

According to most nominalists, there is *nothing wrong* with serious utterances of sentences like 'Caesar uttered the same sentence over and over again', 'The number of planets in the solar system is nine', or 'After the Jurassic period many dinosaur species went extinct', *despite the fact* that there are no sentences to be uttered twice, no numbers to count planets, and no species to go extinct. To bolster their case, they might point out, for example, that there is similarly nothing wrong with saying that the sun rises, sets, or moves above the meridian. We all say such things, even though most of us are no longer in the grips of Ptolemaic astronomy. We can 'think with the learned, and speak with the vulgar'.[19]

But things cannot be left at this. Like any radical eliminativist, a nominalist owes us a story of why we can speak in just about any setting—except for the one of philosophical inquiry—as if there were certain entities out there to be referred to when we believe no such thing. As Carnap puts it, a philosopher with such a disposition seems to speak with an uneasy conscience, 'like a man who in his everyday life does with qualms many things which are not in accord with the high

---

[19] The phrase and the example are from Berkeley's *Principles of Human Knowledge* (1711), §51. There they serve to defend his immaterialism against the charge of verbal impropriety.

moral principles he professes on Sundays' (Carnap 1950: 205). Now we have analogy set against analogy: the nominalist insists that his talk about abstracta is like everyone else's talk about the rising and the setting of the sun, while his opponent contends that it is more like the faint hypocrisy of a Sunday Christian's prayers. Which analogy is more apt?

When pressed about this matter, nominalists tend to invoke the notion of a *paraphrase*. When we say that the sun is rising, our words could be paraphrased roughly as 'The sun appears to be rising' or, perhaps, as 'Some straight lines between our eyes and points on the surface of the sun no longer intersect with the surface of the earth'. Since the paraphrases clearly do not require the truth of Ptolemaic astronomy, we may go ahead and use the original, less clumsy sentences in our speech. Similarly, the story goes, since (1) can be paraphrased as (2), and since (2) does not carry ontological commitment to chances, talk about possibilities in (1) is unproblematic, even for the nominalist.

(1) There is a good chance that it will snow tomorrow.
(2) It will most likely snow tomorrow.

As it stands, this line of defence is rather murky.[20] Although it is intuitively clear that the existence of a paraphrase somehow legitimizes the use of a sentence that appears to carry an unacceptable commitment, it is unclear both what this legitimization amounts to and how it is accomplished. This is because the very notion of a paraphrase involves a crucial ambiguity. One can think of a paraphrase either as a way of bringing out what a sentence really means by providing an approximate synonym, or as a way of replacing the sentence with another that has quite a different meaning but could nonetheless be reasonably employed in its stead. I will call the first type of paraphrase *semantic*, the second *pragmatic*.[21]

How semantic paraphrases are supposed to legitimize sentences like (1) is fairly clear. If what (1) really means is something like (2), then perhaps it does not, after all, commit us to the existence of chances. The trouble is that it is not easy to believe that (1) and (2) are near-synonyms. The nominalist claims there are no such things as chances. If she is right, it sure *seems like* (1) would have to be false, but (2) could still be true. But how could semantic paraphrases differ so obviously in their truth-conditions? In ordinary contexts, where we don't much care whether our words carry commitments to chances and other abstracta, (2) may count as a semantic paraphrase, but how can we sustain such a judgement once we shift our attention to the problem of nominalism? Furthermore, even if we grant that (2) is an adequate

---

[20] Things are not helped by the fact that Quine, the source of the paraphrase defence, is often rather elusive on what he means by paraphrase. In Quine (1948) he uses all of the following expressions to characterize the relationship between an expression and its paraphrase: 'translate', 'explain', 'rephrase', 'analyse', 'identify', 'interpret', and 'expand'.

[21] Burgess and Rosen (1997) call a nominalist strategy that provides semantic paraphrases *hermeneutic*, and a nominalist strategy that is aimed at pragmatic paraphrases *revolutionary*.

semantic paraphrase of (1) in any context, and that consequently the intuitions that (1) entails the existence of a chance and that (2) does not *both* cannot be correct, we still don't know which one to jettison. Why interpret the alleged equivalence in a deflationary rather than an inflationary way; why assume that *neither* of them entails the existence of chances, rather than that *both* of them do? (cf. Alston 1957; Wright 1983: 31–2).

These worries are by no means decisive against nominalists who wish to make use of semantic paraphrase. The usual answer to the first worry is that our willingness to explain the meaning of either of these sentences with the other is sufficient evidence for the claim that they are near-synonyms. In responding to the second worry, nominalists may suggest that we break the symmetry by appeal to intuition, or the principle that *ceteris paribus* ontology ought to be as slender as possible. Whether the claims that (2) is a near-synonym of (1) and that neither entails that there are chances is ultimately acceptable depends on whether they can find their place among the consequences of our best and most comprehensive semantic theory. In matters of meaning, it is hard to see how there could be a higher authority to appeal to.

Semantic paraphrases are usually given in a piecemeal fashion. The anti-nominalist throws a number of sentences at her opponent, each of which apparently quantifies over abstracta. The nominalist throws his semantic paraphrases back. As the anti-nominalist's sentences get more sophisticated, so do the nominalist's para-phrases. (For example: 'There are more cats than dogs' is paraphrased by Goodman and Quine as follows: 'Every individual that contains a bit of each cat is larger than some individual that contains a bit of each dog'. A bit of something is defined as a part of that thing whose size equals that of the smallest of the cats and dogs; officially: x is a bit of z iff for every y, if y is a cat or a dog and is bigger than no other cat and dog, neither is x bigger than y nor is y bigger than x and x is part of z; Goodman and Quine 1947: 180.) As the game advances, the claim that these paraphrases do nothing more than uncover what the ordinary sentences *really* mean becomes more and more baffling. Given the unsystematic character of the project, the idea that the real meaning of a large (probably infinite) set of sentences of our language is given this way is a threat to systematic semantics. Still, it is possible that semantic theory will come up with truth-conditions of the relevant sentences that match the truth-conditions of their suggested paraphrases. Whether we should *expect* this could only be assessed on a case-by-case basis.

Pragmatic paraphrases work very differently. Semantic paraphrases are approx-imate synonyms, and hence can hardly diverge in truth-value. But if paraphrases are nothing more than suitable replacements, all we need to insist on is that *most ordinary consequences* of pragmatic paraphrases have the same truth-values. So, we can concede that if there are no such things as chances, (1) is false even though (2) may well be true, without thereby undermining the claim that typically (2) is a good replacement for (1). The existence of a pragmatic paraphrase does not legitimize the use of the original sentence in *all* contexts, but it may do so in *some* where we are not concerned about certain entailments. The question is, how?

At this point *fictionalism* comes to the rescue. Philosophers who are fictionalists about Fs believe that sentences that entail 'There are Fs' are literally false but fictionally true.[22] When we use literally false but fictionally true sentences, our practice is legitimate, as long as it is clear in the context that we are immersed in the fiction, that we do not intend to question the constitutive assumptions of the fiction. When I utter 'Odysseus was set ashore at Ithaca while sound asleep', my utterance is unobjectionable as long as it is clear that I merely recount how things are according to Homer's epic. The same sort of thing occurs, according to the fictionalist nominalist, when we utter 'There are prime numbers larger than 100'. The appropriate pragmatic paraphrase for the first sentence is 'According to Homer's *Odyssey*, Odysseus was set ashore at Ithaca while sound asleep'; for the second sentence 'According to the Peano arithmetic, there are prime numbers larger than 100'.

The fictionalist can even provide paraphrases in a reasonably uniform fashion. The algorithm is roughly as follows: Suppose S is a sentence that carries commitment to abstract entities of a certain type. Suppose further that our best theory about entities of that type is T. Then the pragmatic paraphrase of S is 'According to T, S'. There are, of course, a number of problems with this. We don't know how to select T, we are not told what we should do if S carries commitment to more than one type of abstract entity, and—most importantly—we don't have a precise understanding of 'according to T' for arbitrary T.[23] Nonetheless, the approach looks promising.

Non-literal use is an unquestionably pervasive feature of natural language. Even in the middle of our most serious theoretical discussions, even when we are using straightforward declarative sentences in a way that is indistinguishable from their assertoric use, we *may* in fact speak metaphorically and we *may* in fact convey the content of some fiction.[24] Still, when we do this, we tend to be aware, or at least easily made aware, that we are speaking figuratively. The surprising suggestion here is that in the philosophically interesting cases this is not so: we are *wholly* immersed

---

[22] This is not *the* standard definition of fictionalism, because there is no standard definition. Mine is fairly narrow. Some would regard fictionalism about Fs to be compatible with the claim that 'There are Fs' lacks truth-value (e.g. Field 1989: 4 n. 4); others think fictionalists can be agnostic regarding the existence of Fs (e.g. the 'third grade of metaphorical involvement' in Yablo 2000).

[23] If we take T to occupy referential position in 'According to T' the paraphrases will carry commitment to theories. If theories are taken to be abstracta, this does not help the nominalist. If they are taken to be contingent concrete entities (e.g. linguistic tokens), we face the problem that our paraphrases will be contingent truths. This is a problem if we are paraphrasing sentences about mathematical entities, which according to most exist necessarily. So, it seems that the fictionalist nominalist should not accept that T occupies a referential position in 'according to T'. Also, we must surely insist that 'According to Frege's *Basic Laws of Arithmetic*, there are numbers' is true and 'According to Frege's *Basic Laws of Arithmetic*, there are unicorns' is false, even though the system of Frege's *Basic Laws of Arithmetic* is inconsistent. These facts make a semantic theory about 'according to T' hard to come by.

[24] In fact, exploiting non-literal talk can be theoretically advantageous; cf. Melia (1995), Balaguer (1998), and especially Yablo (1998).

in a fiction and it takes serious reflection to notice that our words are not to be taken literally. According to the fictionalist nominalist, with regard to mathematics and other disciplines deep into commitment to abstracta, we are much like children lost in the game of make-believe.[25]

3.2 '... Think with the Learned'

Suppose we have nominalistically acceptable paraphrases for every sentence we would wish to maintain in our ordinary and scientific discourse. This does not mean that nominalism has won the debate about abstract entities. After all, as Quine remarks, we could paraphrase each closed sentence S of a theory T as 'True (n)', where n is the Gödel number of S and 'True' is the truth-predicate for T, and in this way reduce our ontology to that of the natural numbers (Quine 1964).[26] But not even a modern day Pythagorean would believe that this *shows* that there is nothing beyond the world of numbers. By itself, paraphrase settles no ontological question. Still, one might suggest, even if the nominalist has not won the debate, by providing paraphrases he has certainly done enough to *explain* what his position is.

Not so. For the nominalist must face a query regarding the status of the nominalist principle itself. If ordinary sentences about abstracta are in need of paraphrase, it seems that we could paraphrase the nominalist thesis as well. According to the nominalist, when someone says that there are prime numbers larger than 100 she should not be taken as quantifying over numbers. Why then should she be taken as quantifying over abstracta were she to say that there are abstract entities? But if she is not, why on earth would the nominalist object? Nominalist paraphrase, when applied across the board, does not help the nominalist. Rather, it leads to a thorough elimination of the metaphysical debate concerning abstracta.

So, nominalists need a story about *when* paraphrase is to be applied. One rather dismissive but nonetheless widespread reaction to this worry is to say that nominalist paraphrase is to be applied when we conduct serious business. Mathematics is the queen of sciences, so we must strive to interpret the results of mathematics as truths; metaphysics is the handmaid of the sciences, so we need not bother.

But this response is unsatisfactory. First of all, defenders of semantic paraphrases cannot simply say that the anti-nominalist credo 'There are abstract entities' *need*

---

[25] Stanley (2001) argues that this consequence of fictionalism sits badly with what we know about the way children acquire the ability to comprehend mathematical discourse and the way they learn about games of make-believe.

[26] There is a catch: to be able to define the truth-predicate, the language of paraphrases would typically need higher-order quantification. This, in turn, depending on one's views on ontological commitments of higher-order logic, may bring extra commitments to properties, sets, or whatever one thinks predicate-variables are assigned as semantic values. Still, we would have here an ontological reduction of the concrete to the abstract.

not undergo nominalist paraphrase; they must insist that it *should not*. Otherwise, the anti-nominalist credo is nominalistically acceptable. Secondly (and this applies to defenders of semantic and pragmatic paraphrases alike), if the anti-nominalist's claim that there are numbers is to be rejected, so is his argument that there must be numbers because there are primes over 100 and primes are numbers. And this argument cannot be rejected unless the nominalist is willing to concede that *in this context*, mathematical sentences are not to be paraphrased.

The obvious retreat is that sentences should only be paraphrased in contexts where such a paraphrase does not defeat the very purpose of their utterance. When the anti-nominalist says that there are abstract entities, the aim of his utterance is to make an *assertion* that is true just in case there are abstract entities. When the mathematician says that there are prime numbers that are larger than 100, her purpose must be something else. Either she does not assert anything (she only *quasi-asserts*[27] that there are prime numbers that are larger than 100), or if she does assert something, it must be something nominalistically acceptable (for example, the nominalistic paraphrase itself). Or so the nominalist must believe.

This is a significant empirical hypothesis about what mathematicians actually do when they make sincere utterances in the context of doing mathematics. One way it can be defended is by asking mathematicians what they think they are doing when they make those utterances. If this yields a result unfavourable for the nominalist (as I suspect it will), the nominalist must insist that the real purpose of the mathematician's utterance is hidden from her. If she insists that all she ever wanted to do in uttering sentences like 'There are primes that are larger than 100' is to assert the existence of primes larger than 100, she is in error about her own speech acts. This proposal boils down to the suggestion that there are numerous truths about the way we *should* interpret each other's ordinary utterances that are hidden from linguistically unsophisticated but otherwise well-informed and able native speakers. In other words, interpretation—the process whereby a competent hearer determines what a particular utterance of the speaker is supposed to convey—is a radically *non-transparent* matter.[28]

If the non-transparency of interpretation is too hard to swallow, the nominalist may opt for a different strategy. He may concede that mathematicians really do intend to assert things that entail the existence of abstract entities, but insist that the aims of individual mathematicians should not be confused with the aim of mathematics. Perhaps, when individual mathematicians make their utterances, they really do intend to commit themselves to abstracta. But that does not mean that they do this *qua* mathematicians. If, for example, we could say that the aim of mathematics is not truth, only the enhancement of empirical science, and that

---

[27] The term is from Rosen (1994). He introduces it in discussing van Fraassen's notion of acceptance. Quasi-assertion stands to genuine assertion as acceptance in van Fraassen's sense stands to genuine belief.   [28] This concern is raised in Szabó (2001).

the aim of empirical science is also not truth, only empirical adequacy, we could maintain that in going beyond the aim of their discipline, mathematicians who intend to make genuine assertions in doing mathematics are trespassing outside the bounds of their trade.[29] And there might be other, less radical, ways to argue that the aims of science would not be frustrated by nominalist paraphrase.

To be a nominalist one must do two things besides accepting the truth of the nominalist thesis. One must explain why speaking *as if* there were abstracta is an innocent thing to do, and one must also explain why the innocence of such speech does not entail the innocence of anti-nominalism.

4. Arguments for Nominalism

There are a number of considerations that had been advanced in favour of nominalism. But before they are surveyed, it is useful to remember what Goodman and Quine have to say about their own motives for refusing to admit abstract entities in their ontology: 'Fundamentally this refusal is based on a philosophical intuition that cannot be justified by an appeal to anything more ultimate' (Goodman and Quine 1947: 174). If the arguments seem weak, that may be because they are not the real grounds for the *horror abstractae*.

4.1 Intelligibility, Physicalism, and Economy

Goodman has argued that sets are unintelligible because set theory embraces a distinction between entities without a genuine difference. The metaphysical principle (he calls it the principle of nominalism) violation of which is supposed to result in unintelligibility is this: if a and b are *made up* of the same constituents, then $a = b$ (cf. Goodman 1956). This is a fairly restrictive principle. Besides sets, it also excludes linguistic types (the sentence types 'Nelson admires Van' and 'Van admires Nelson' are distinct, even though they are made up of the same word types), Russellian propositions (the Russellian propositions expressed by 'Nelson admires Van' and 'Van admires Nelson' are also distinct, despite the fact that they are made up of the same individuals and the same relation), and events (the event of Nelson's admiring Van and Van's admiring Nelson are distinct, despite the sameness of their participants), etc. It also forces us to give up the distinction between the statue and the

---

[29] van Fraassen (1980) advocates such a view. For his discussion of the relation between the aims of science and the intentions of individual scientists, see van Fraassen (1994).

clay it is made of. So, how can anyone believe not only that Goodman's principle is true, but that putative entities that violate it are unintelligible?

One reason Goodman cites is the connection between his principle of nominalism and the principle of extensionality. Let $\in^*$ be the ancestral of $\in$; then the principle of extensionality can be stated as (3), and Goodman's nominalist principle as (4):[30]

(3) $\forall x \forall y \forall z((x \in y \leftrightarrow x \in z) \rightarrow y = z)$

(4) $\forall x \forall y \forall z((x \in^* y \leftrightarrow x \in^* z) \rightarrow y = z)$.

So, Goodman's nominalism is nothing more than a consequence of Quine's strictures against intensional entities. Of course, this may not be a lot of help nowadays: contemporary philosophers who reject properties, relations, or propositions typically do not do so on account of the mere fact that they violate extensionality.

There is another way to get a feel for nominalistic qualms about set theory. Set theory dictates that we must distinguish between an object and the singleton set containing that object. As David Lewis has argued, if we have a primitive singleton function, plural quantification, and mereology, then we have set theory in its full glory (Lewis 1991, ch. 3). Since everyone agrees that plural quantification and mereology together cannot generate abstracta from concreta, the culprit must be the singleton function. And the relationship between an object and its singleton is indeed puzzling. Our intuitive conception of a set is that it is a collection of *objects*— if we have but a single object, what are we to make of the collection constituted by *that object alone*?[31]

Even if we accept unintelligibility as a good prima facie reason to deny existence, we are still far from nominalism in the contemporary sense. Rejecting sets, sentence types, and propositions is not the same as rejecting *all* abstracta. There are all sorts of putative abstract entities that are intuitively atomic (e.g. numbers, word types, basic properties, etc.), and Goodman-style reasons are insufficient for rejecting them.[32]

Will physicalism come to the nominalist's help? Some have felt that the real problem with abstracta is that their existence conflicts with the view that everything is physical. Unfortunately, although it is quite intuitive to say that spatio-temporal location is a *sine qua non* of physicality, it is not clear how this intuition can be

---

[30] For Goodman, the constituents of a set are exactly the members of its transitive closure. One might protest that Goodman confuses '⊆' and '∈', but since the issue is precisely whether we can fully understand set-theoretic membership as a non-mereological notion, this objection would not be dialectically helpful.

[31] Couldn't we use the lasso metaphor and say that a set is what one gets by 'lassoing' a number of objects together? Singleton sets would then be single objects with a 'lasso' around them. The problem, of course, is exactly how to make sense of this metaphor. Lewis himself is deeply puzzled by singletons, but refrains from rejecting set theory on account of metaphysical misgivings. See esp. Lewis (1991: 57–9).

[32] Goodman (1956: 156) insists that the ordinary distinction between abstract and concrete is vague and unstable, and claims that for him nominalism is nothing beyond the rejection of classes.

backed up. If we say that physical entities are the ones whose existence is guaranteed by contemporary physical theories, then—as proponents of indispensability
arguments tirelessly emphasize—a wide array of mathematical entities turn out to
be physical. If we say that physical entities are the ones that are subject to physical
laws, abstracta may or may not qualify depending on how the laws are stated. For
example, if the law of gravity implies that gravitational force is exerted on absolutely everything, then the number 2 is probably not physical; if the law of gravity
only implies that gravitational force is exerted on everything *that has mass*, it may
well be. If physical entities are those capable of entering into causal interactions,
abstracta will count as non-physical depending on how strict we are on what 'entering' amounts to. If entering into causal relations requires being actually causally
related to something, then plausibly nothing but events will qualify as physical.
If it means something weaker, then material objects and elementary particles are
physical, but so are perhaps lots of abstracta. Why could one not say, for example,
that properties can be involved in causal relations because they can be instantiated
and their instances can participate in events that are causally related to others? If
physical entities are those that are made up of elementary particles, abstracta would
probably not qualify as physical, but then neither would concrete events. Even if
Brutus and Caesar are constituted by elementary particles, it is hard to see how
Brutus' killing of Caesar could be. And if causal relata are events, this sort of view
paves the road to causal nihilism.

I am not saying that it would be impossible to define 'physical' in a non ad hoc
manner that justifies the intuition that abstracta are non-physical without causing
trouble elsewhere. But I do think that the failure of the most obvious definitions
is indicative of a serious difficulty with this line of thinking. There are two ways
in which the existence of entities of a certain sort may be in conflict with a world-
view based on physics. The entity may get in the way of physical explanations,
or it may be superfluous for physical explanations. But abstract entities are not
likely to get in the way: unlike phlogiston, ether, angels, or the unmoved mover,
they are not used in physical explanations as providing the casual source of some
observable phenomenon. They may be superfluous, but they are not obviously so.
And *if* they are superfluous, they are superfluous not only for physical explanations, but for all sorts of blatantly non-physical ones as well. Why would a theist,
a phenomenalist, or an idealist need properties or numbers any more than a
physicalist in trying to explain natural phenomena? The source of the intuition
that there is a conflict between the acceptance of abstract entities and physicalism may have nothing to do with physics and everything to do with ontological
economy.

Is there a powerful argument from ontological economy to nominalism? There
might be. Why multiply entities beyond necessity? If abstracta are indeed superfluous for explanatory purposes, most of us would gladly banish them from our

ontology.[33] The problem is that most scientific theories do appear to quantify over abstracta, and consequently, the claim that they are superfluous in explanation is rather shaky. Even if we can reconstruct our usual theories in such a way that they are no longer committed to anything but concrete entities, it remains a serious question whether the explanations provided by the reconstructed theory are *all things considered* preferable to the explanations we had before. Ontological economy is not a free lunch: typically theories with slimmer ontologies are vastly more complex in other regards. This sort of complexity cannot always be dismissed as inessential. Otherwise what should we say to those who stubbornly maintain their belief in the Ptolemaic astronomy arguing that by postulating enough epicycles all the experimental evidence supporting the heliocentric view could be accommodated?

Besides, ontological economy does not clearly favour the nominalist. If the size of one's ontology is such a powerful concern, why not try to reconstruct our scientific theories so that they no longer quantify over concreta? Reducing the physical world to the world of numbers is technically no harder than proceeding the other way round. If we are to prefer nominalism to Pythagoreanism, there must be something besides a desire for desert landscapes that motivates us.

4.2 Causal Isolation

The arguments from intelligibility, physicalism, or ontological economy are not at the centre of contemporary debates about the ontological status of abstract entities. The arguments that move most contemporary nominalists tend to be variations on a single theme. Since abstract entities lack spatio-temporal location, they cannot have any sort of causal impact on us. Their causal isolation makes our *access* to them deeply problematic. Without causal links, nominalists contend, our knowledge about and reference to abstract entities become mysterious. This sort of consideration against abstract entities of one kind or another is probably very old, but contemporary versions go back only to Paul Benacerraf's paper 'Mathematical Truth' (Benacerraf 1973).

Even before considering how to state this objection more precisely a caveat is required. This sort of argument is applied all the time across the board against all sorts of abstracta, but the fact that it was originally presented in the context of the philosophy of mathematics is of utmost importance. For, as I noted in Section 2.2, it is by no means clear that all abstract entities are causally isolated from us. The novel *The Good Soldier Šweik* is presumably an abstract entity, but one that is causally

---

[33] Not everyone, though. Prior (1954: 31) writes: 'I simply do not possess the sheer zeal for waving Ockham's razor about which seems to burn within so many of my contemporaries; my motto is *entia non sunt subtahenda praeter necessitatem*, and even the property of non-self-inherence I have given up with a sigh and only under extreme compulsion.'

dependent on a host of concrete ones. It could never have existed without the efforts of the Czech writer Jaroslav Hašek, and he would never have written it were it not for the involvement of the army of the Austro-Hungarian monarchy in the First World War. Furthermore, there are a host of other concrete events—among them the writing of this very passage—that causally depend on the novel itself. Entities of this sort are often called *dependent abstracta*. If they exist, the argument from causal isolation cannot establish nominalism.[34]

Let us set dependent abstracta aside and focus on the preferred targets of the causal argument: abstract entities that exist independently of how the concrete world happens to be. To state the argument from causal isolation properly, we would need to spell out the exact sense in which causal connection is required for knowledge and reference. This is not a trivial task; simple versions of the causal constraint are likely to exclude future events from what is knowable or available for reference. The nominalist may bite the bullet and accept presentism or the growing block model of time, but intuitively, the case against abstracta is stronger than the case against the reality of the future. After all, even if future events cannot cause anything in the present, they will be causally *connected* with events occurring now. Whatever meteorologists know about the weather tomorrow, they know it because they know about past events, which are likely to contribute causally to future events.

Although the epistemological and the semantic challenges to anti-nominalism are both based on the causal isolation of (non-dependent) abstracta, it is important to keep them apart. The claim that some appropriate causal connection is required for knowledge is more secure than the claim that it is required for reference.

Causation may enter the theory of reference at two points: at initial baptism and at the chain of reference-preserving uses. The problem for the anti-nominalist is presumably at the first of these points: abstract entities, not being in space or time, cannot be objects of initial baptisms. But an initial baptism, at least as Kripke originally conceived it, does not require causal contact.[35] We can introduce a name by means of a meaningful description that uniquely fits the object to be named. A frequent response to this is that predicates we could use in constructing the appropriate reference-fixing description for an abstract object are as problematic as the names themselves (cf. Jubien 1977). To fix the reference of '9' through 'the number of planets' or the reference of 'sphere' through 'the shape of the tennis

---

[34] It seems plausible that linguistic expressions, if they exist, are dependent abstracta. I assume that we speak truthfully when we say that Lewis Carroll coined many words and I assume that we are also correct in thinking that coining is a matter of creation, not of discovery. Had Lewis Carroll not written 'Jabberwocky' the English word 'chortle' would not exist. Many philosophers reject this common-sense view and regard linguistic expressions as existing eternally and necessarily.

[35] Kripke (1972) explicitly allows for the introduction of names through initial reference-fixing via descriptions. Versions of the causal theory of reference that disallow this would have a difficult time explaining how the name 'Neptune' came to refer.

ball' works only if the predicates 'number' and 'shape' stand in appropriate causal connections to entities they apply to. But how could they, given the abstract character of numbers and shapes?

As it stands, this argument is not convincing. First of all, couldn't the anti-nominalist drop the problematic predicate? What if we say that '9' refers to the result of counting all the planets and 'sphere' refers to what the end of a stick can touch when the other end is fixed? One might object that these descriptions can only be properly interpreted by someone who already knows that their intended denotations are a number or a shape, respectively. I have no idea whether this hypothesis is true, but it is in sharp conflict with our common experience with young children. Secondly, it is far from clear what exactly the causal requirement for predicates amounts to. Clearly, there are meaningful predicates with empty extensions, so we cannot demand that *all* meaningful predicates be causally connected to things they apply to. One might explicitly restrict the requirement to non-empty predicates, but this seems arbitrary. Why couldn't non-empty predicates be meaningful in virtue of the same sort of facts—whatever they might be—that account for the meaningfulness of empty predicates?[36] Finally, even if this line of argument is correct, it is hard to see how it could help the nominalist. If, owing to the lack of causal connections between the numbers and us, the predicate 'number' lacks a semantic value, then presumably so do the sentences 'There are numbers' and 'There are no numbers.' So, instead of establishing his thesis, the nominalist pushing the semantic challenge has made a great step towards dissolving the metaphysical debate.[37]

So, nominalists must agree that we can at the very least *describe* abstract entities, otherwise their own view is inexpressible. But even if semantic considerations are

---

[36] A possible suggestion is that all semantically simple predicates are causally connected to what they apply to and insist that all empty predicates are semantically complex; e.g. 'unicorn' is equivalent to 'horse-shaped animal with a horn on its forehead' or something like that. But the failure of earlier proposals involving lexical decomposition should give us a pause. See Fodor (1998) for an argument that we are unlikely to find such equivalencies.

[37] Hodes (1984) argues along a different line that no definite description we can come up with could adequately fix the reference of numerals. Benacerraf (1965) and Putnam (1967) already argued that reference-fixing via descriptions is problematic in mathematics. The idea behind Hodes's argument is that reference-fixing through a description cannot work, because we can systematically reinterpret whatever we can say about the natural numbers in such a way that (i) we preserve the truth-values of all our claims, but (ii) the numerals will now pick out different objects. The argument is similar to Putnam's 'model-theoretic' argument, so at first it seems that the anti-nominalist can claim that whatever move saves radical indeterminacy in the general case can be applied in the mathematical case as well. But, according to Hodes, what saves the determinacy of reference in the general case is some sort of causal relation, and since that is unavailable when the referent is a number, the anti-nominalist does have a real problem here. This argument is immune to the first two objections above. As an argument *against anti-nominalism*, it is also immune to the third: the opponent of anti-nominalism may opt for an oblique answer to the question whether there are numbers, as opposed to embracing the straight nominalist line. This is exactly the view taken in Hodes (1990).

of little use for them, nominalists can still make a strong case against abstracta on epistemological grounds. Typically the argument assumes that knowledge requires causal connection, and if stated this way the disagreements may well get bogged down in disagreements about what exactly constitutes knowledge. But the most treacherous minefields of epistemology can be bypassed, as Hartry Field (1988, 1989) has emphasized. All the argument requires is two rather obvious premises: that mathematicians have by and large *reliable* beliefs about mathematics (i.e. that if they believe a mathematical theorem then that theorem is *ceteris paribus* true[38]), and that this is not a brute fact resisting all explanation. If these are granted, the epistemological challenge is to give the rough outlines of what this explanation could be. This is a hard task: for the nominalist, the claim that despite the lack of causal connections there are reliability links between the beliefs of mathematicians and the entities those beliefs are supposed to be about is as mysterious as if someone claimed to have reliable beliefs about 'the daily happenings in a remote village in Nepal' (Field 1989: 26).

The analogy is gripping, but suspicious. Clearly, we could not have reliable beliefs about the happenings in remote places without being somehow causally linked with the events that take place there. But the world of abstracta is not remote—its denizens are not in space and time at all. More importantly, it is not a world where anything happens, for (non-dependent) abstract entities do not undergo change. The predictable reaction to Field's charge from anti-nominalists is that although causal connections are required to track daily happenings, their role is less clear when we are talking about beliefs whose subject-matter is eternal and necessary.[39] This should not be taken as a full-blown response to the epistemological challenge, though. The point is merely that the reliability of mathematical beliefs is on a par with the reliability of other beliefs of necessary truths.

There is, however, a legitimate concern about declaring the epistemology of mathematics a mere chapter in an as yet undeveloped general modal epistemology. Mathematical necessity seems importantly different from both physical and logical necessity. On the one hand, most philosophers regard physical necessity as necessity given the fundamental but contingent laws of physics. In other words, they believe that what is physically necessary could still have been otherwise. A similar view about mathematics would not be very plausible. On the other hand, most philosophers regard logical necessity as absolute, but not existence-involving. Logic tells

---

[38] As Field has pointed out, this way of spelling out the claim that mathematicians are by and large reliable in forming mathematical beliefs does not require an inflationary notion of truth. The claim boils down to nothing more than that the schema 'If mathematicians accept "*p*" then *p*' holds in nearly all its instances whenever '*p*' is a mathematical sentence.

[39] If one believes, as David Lewis does, that causal influence requires counterfactual dependence, one must conclude that necessary facts are all causally inefficacious. Counterfactuals with necessary antecedents are vacuous. This is one of the reasons Lewis rejects this sort of epistemological argument against mathematical entities as well as possible worlds. Cf. Lewis (1986: 111).

us nothing about what sort of things there are, or even about how many things there are.[40] By contrast, assuming standard semantics for mathematical theories, mathematics does require the existence of an enormous number of entities. And because mathematical necessity is *sui generis* in this way, concerns about explaining the reliability of our mathematical beliefs may well be more severe. We can think of physical necessities as physical facts of maximal generality, and if we do so we can perhaps still make sense of the idea that in forming beliefs about them we are causally influenced by those facts themselves. And we can think of logical necessity as arising from the meanings of logical constants and explain the reliability of our logical beliefs by an appeal to our conceptual mastery. But these explanations will not easily carry over to the mathematical case.

It is worth pointing out that although Field often talks as if the task of explaining the reliability of mathematical beliefs required giving an account of a pervasive correlation, this is certainly an overstatement. We could account for the reliability of mathematical beliefs by pointing out that mathematical theories tend to be axiomatized and hence belief in the theories is reliable if belief in the axioms is. So the epistemological challenge boils down to a demand for an explanation of how belief in the axioms can be reliable.

Anti-nominalists have three ways to counter this challenge. They can follow Gödel, accept the apparent *sui generis* character of mathematical necessity, and postulate an equally *sui generis* faculty we have that ensures the reliability of our beliefs in the axioms of mathematics.[41] They can follow Frege in epistemologically assimilating the axioms of mathematics to the truths of logic[42] and swallow the consequence that our knowledge of the meanings of key mathematical terms somehow guarantees that they successfully refer. Or they can follow Quine in epistemologically assimilating mathematical and physical truth and downplaying key modal intuitions, perhaps rejecting the idea of absolute necessity altogether.[43]

In the end, what considerations of causal isolation give to the nominalist is an important epistemological challenge for the mathematical anti-nominalist. It boils down to the demand to account for the epistemic credentials of our beliefs in the fundamental axioms of mathematics. The force of this challenge is somewhat weakened by the fact that we don't have particularly convincing views about why other general beliefs—beliefs in the laws of physics and logic—are reliable, so it is

[40] Classical logic, as it is usually stated, requires the non-emptiness of the domain of quantification and hence it is not ontologically innocent. The common view nowadays seems to be that this is only a matter of convenience, not of substance.

[41] Such a view need not follow Gödel (1947) in thinking that this rational faculty is relevantly similar to perception.

[42] Of course, Frege proposed such assimilation only for the truths of arithmetic, not for all mathematical truths.

[43] Again, this need not involve acceptance of Quine's epistemological holism or a wholesale denial that there are important differences in how we assess mathematical claims and the claims of empirical sciences.

hard to see whether mathematics really poses special difficulties. Nonetheless, to the extent that we find mathematical axioms to be different from other claims of maximal generality, the challenge stands.

5. Arguments against Nominalism

The most popular objection to nominalism stresses the extent to which rejection of all abstract entities flies in the face of common sense. A nominalist must either deny that the sentence '2 is a prime number' is true, or must insist that it does not commit one who believes in its truth to the existence of the number 2. Either way, she must reject a well-entrenched belief. Those who are firmly convinced that philosophy can never hold surprises will no doubt find this objection decisive. Those of us who have doubts about the ultimate wisdom of the folk may need arguments.

5.1 Indispensability

But what if we replace the folk with the experts of the scientific community? Then we arrive at what is currently the most influential argument against nominalism, the *indispensability argument*. Versions of the argument go back to Quine and Putnam.[44] It can be stated as follows: Certain mathematical theories, such as arithmetic or real analysis, are indispensable for modern physics in the sense that the physical theories cannot be stated in a form that would be compatible with the falsehood of those mathematical theories. But these mathematical theories are ontologically committed to abstract entities: the quantifiers used in stating them range over domains that must include mathematical entities that are not in space or time. So the physical theories themselves carry commitment to abstracta. And since we have no adequate grounds for rejecting these physical theories—they are part of our overall best theory of the world—we should acquiesce to the existence of abstracta.

There is an easy way for the nominalist to reject such considerations. He could simply deny that we must believe what our best scientific theory says. This need not involve an outright rejection of the results of science, only suspension of belief. One might suggest, for example, that it is enough if we *accept* our best scientific theory, where acceptance is an attitude that requires that we act, at least when we

---

[44] The standard references are Quine (1951) and Putnam (1971).

theorize, as if we believed.[45] But the easy way out is not very popular nowadays. It requires a willingness to override the usual standards by which our scientific theories are evaluated, and hence it is in conflict with *naturalism*, even in the least demanding sense of that word. Most analytic philosophers (and certainly the overwhelming majority of the usually scientifically hard-nosed nominalists) are reluctant to announce that the best scientific theory we have is unworthy of belief, unless they can point at reasons that would be recognizably scientific.[46] So, most nominalists tend to look elsewhere for a reply to the indispensability argument.

If one takes the indispensability argument seriously, there are only two strategies for resisting its conclusion: one could deny either that mathematical theories are committed to the existence of abstracta, or that they are indispensable for physics. The former involves a programme in semantics: show that despite appearances mathematical theories could be true without there being mathematical entities that they are true of. The latter involves a programme in physics: develop new physical theories that fail to entail the existence of mathematical entities, but nonetheless have the level of empirical adequacy and explanatory power that our current theories do.[47]

Those who take the former route typically introduce modality into their interpretation of mathematical theories. The key idea goes back to Hilary Putnam, who suggests that mathematical claims could be interpreted as involving modality, where the relevant notion of possibility is taken as a primitive (Putnam 1967). Mathematical existence claims are then to be understood as claiming not that there are mathematical entities of one kind or another, but only that the existence of such entities is possible.

There are many ways this basic idea can be turned into a full-blown sentence-by-sentence reinterpretation of mathematical theories.[48] For the sake of illustration, let me sketch briefly and informally a particular example of such an approach,

[45] Van Fraassen (1980) advocates such a shift of attitudes towards empirical science that would do away with ontological commitments to unobservables.

[46] Although note that almost no physicist would argue that the fact that we employ standard analysis in our theories about most physical quantities *settles* the question whether these entities are in fact continuous. There *might be* scientific arguments against the claim that our best scientific theory is strictly speaking true. Cf. Cartwright (1983).

[47] It is important to notice that in so far as a nominalist is attempting to respond to the indispensability argument, she need not be concerned with the entirety of mathematics. For it is arguable that only a small fragment of contemporary mathematics has any application outside of mathematics. As a result, nominalists tend to focus primarily on the theory of real numbers, which is undoubtedly widely employed in the empirical sciences.

[48] The first idea one might pursue is to reinterpret mathematical sentences as making claims not about what sorts of mathematical entities there are, but about what sorts of physical marks there could be; e.g. 'There are prime numbers larger than 100' would be rendered roughly as 'There could be numerals for prime numbers larger than 100'. Such a strategy is pursued in Chihara (1990). For a survey of modal strategies in reinterpreting mathematical theories, see Burgess and Rosen (1997, sects. II.B and c).

the so-called *modal structuralist* line (due to Hellman 1989; for more details see ch. 1). Consider a sentence S of second-order Peano arithmetic. We will provide a new interpretation for S by associating it with another sentence S' of second-order Peano arithmetic and declaring that the new interpretation of S is identical to the old interpretation of S'. S' is a conjunction of a hypothetical claim and a categorical one. The categorical component ensures that it is possible that there is an ω-sequence, i.e. a set isomorphic to the natural numbers.[49] The hypothetical component tells us that if there were such a thing as an ω-sequence, then S would hold in it. Given the usual rendering of subjunctive conditionals, this latter claim says that necessarily, if X is an ω-sequence, then S holds in X.

The proposal that arithmetical sentences have such elaborate semantics is a radical claim. This fact is often overlooked because nominalists are often vague about the status of such reinterpretations. Saying that arithmetic *could be* interpreted in a nominalistically acceptable fashion is not the same as saying that such an interpretation captures what arithmetical sentences *mean*. (We can all agree with Quine that 'Lo, rabbit!' could be interpreted as 'Lo, undetached rabbit-parts!', but we can also reject semantic nihilism and insist that these sentences don't mean the same thing.) Besides working out the precise details of these nominalistic interpretations, nominalists must also provide some reason for us to believe that these interpretations are correct.

Let us now consider the prospects of the other nominalist programme aimed at responding to the indispensability argument. Proponents of this second programme concede that there is no mathematics without numbers (or other mathematical entities) and that consequently current scientific theories are nominalistically unacceptable. Their aim is to show that we could do science without numbers (or other mathematical entities). The most prominent advocate of this idea is Hartry Field (1980).

Field's strategy for nominalizing science has two components. First, he suggests that we can develop alternatives to current scientific theories that are nominalistically acceptable. In support of this claim he develops a version of the Newtonian gravitational theory, where no quantifier ranges over mathematical entities. The entities that play the role of surrogates for real numbers are space-time points and regions. He argues that this is not a violation of nominalism: parts of space-time are concrete entities instantiating contingent physical properties and participating in causal interactions.[50] The ontology of the theory is not small: the axioms entail that there are continuum many space-time points and the powerset of continuum

---

[49] Since the nominalist does not want to conclude from $\Diamond \exists x(x$ is an ω-sequence) that $\exists x \Diamond (x$ is an ω-sequence), she has to employ a modal logic without the Barcan formula.

[50] Of course, talk about 'properties' and 'instantiation' here are not to be taken seriously. Field regards the eliminability of apparent reference to properties from the language of science as a foregone result.

many space-time regions, and hence that there are this many concrete physical objects. Secondly, he argues that adding mathematical theories to a nominalistically acceptable scientific theory has no bad effect on the nominalistic portion of the resulting theory. That is, mathematical theories are *conservative* over nominalistically acceptable theories in the sense that if a sentence within the nominalistic language of the original theory was not a theorem of the original theory, then neither is it a theorem of the expanded theory. This means that although mathematical theories are *false* (owing to their commitment to the existence of abstract mathematical entities), they are nonetheless instrumentally *good*, for we can use them to provide short cuts for tedious deductions within nominalistically acceptable theories.

Both steps of Field's programme have been subjected to detailed criticism. It is an open question whether all scientific theories are amenable to the sort of nominalization Field performs on Newtonian gravitational theory.[51] And it is a matter of controversy whether informal statements of the conservativity of mathematics over nominalistically acceptable theories adequately capture the technically much more involved results given in the appendix to Field's book (cf. Shapiro 1983; Field 1985; Burgess and Rosen 1997, sect. III.B.i.).

5.2 The Context Principle

There is a simple but influential argument against nominalism, which is sometimes referred to as the 'Fregean argument'. It goes as follows (cf. Hale 1987: 11). Consider a simple sentence of arithmetic, say, the sentence '2 + 2 = 4'. Observe two things about this sentence. First, that it is an obvious truth. Secondly, that the numeral '2' functions as a singular term within this sentence. But if an expression functions as a singular term within a sentence, then there must be an object denoted by the singular term, if the sentence is true. Therefore, there is an object denoted by '2', or in other words, the number 2 exists.

The crucial step in this argument is supported by Frege's context principle, the thesis that only in the context of a sentence does a word have meaning. This principle has been subject to a variety of interpretations; the one that this premiss derives from was motivated by a reading of §60 of the *Foundations of Arithmetic* developed by Michael Dummett and Crispin Wright (see Dummett 1973*b*: 494 ff.; Wright 1983, sect. iii). The main ideas behind this reading are as follows: (i) the principle should be construed to be about reference,[52] (ii) it denies that once we settle on how

---

[51] Malament (1982) argues that the strategy does not extend to quantum mechanics. Balaguer (1998) attempts to give a nominalistic version of quantum mechanics.

[52] What makes the interpretation of Frege's dictum particularly difficult is that the *Foundations* pre-date the distinction between sense and reference. The word actually used by Frege is *Bedeutung*, which normally means 'meaning' but will come to mean 'reference' in Frege's later writings.

a certain expression contributes to the truth-conditions of sentences in which it occurs, we can have any further questions about the semantic value of the expression, and hence (iii) it subordinates questions of ontology to questions of truth and logical form.

As stated the context principle appears too strong: it neglects the possibility of expressive limitations. For it is plainly possible for a language to have non-codesignating singular terms that are intersubstitutable in every sentence without change of truth-value. But it seems that the current reading of the context principle excludes this: since there is no difference in how they affect the truth or falsity of any sentence in the language, there should be no difference in their semantic values either. Demanding that the language under consideration pass certain minimal criteria of expressive power (e.g. requiring that it should contain the identity predicate) can eliminate the problem. Alternatively, we can weaken the principle. Perhaps settling all questions about how an expression contributes to the truth-conditions of sentences in which it occurs does not settle *all* questions about the semantic value of the expression, but it may well settle the question whether the expression *has* a semantic value. For the purposes of the Fregean argument, this is all we need. The idea is that by determining that a certain expression functions as a singular term within a true atomic sentence we have settled how it contributes to the truth of that sentence, and so given the context principle, we can no longer hesitate in accepting that it has the appropriate semantic value.

Once the justification for the crucial step in the Fregean argument is made clear, one possible reaction from the nominalist is to say something like this: 'I agree that if "2" were a *genuine* singular term, then there would be no denying that it purports to refer to the number 2. And if we grant that $2 + 2 = 4$, there is no way to banish numbers from our ontology. But why say that "2" functions as a genuine singular term? Why not insist that, despite superficial appearances, its real work in the semantics of this sentence is something quite different?' In defence of the claim that '2' is really a singular term, the anti-nominalist appeals to formal—syntactic and inferential—criteria. Since numerals as they occur in arithmetical sentences are noun phrases, and since they support the right kinds of inferences, they are singular terms by ordinary criteria. And these cannot be overridden by extraordinary criteria formulated by an appeal to intuitions about what there *really* is. Syntax over ontology, as the spirit of the context principle dictates.

Ordinary criteria exclude from the class of singular terms a variety of idiomatic or quasi-idiomatic expressions, and so anti-nominalists who take the Fregean argument on board are not saddled with ontological commitment to sakes and their kin. Nonetheless, there are plenty of expressions that are troublesome: 'the existence of a proof', 'the identity of the murderer', 'the occurrence of the explosion', and 'the whereabouts of every student' are just a few. In response to these, proponents of the Fregean argument must refine their criteria or bite the ontological bullet.[53] This is a genuine balancing act, and it may well prompt doubts about the viability of the whole programme. Are we really sure that our intuitions about the validity of certain arguments are independent of our intuitions about the referential status of expressions within those arguments? If not, there is a danger that our judgements used in determining whether an expression passes all the tests for singular termhood are already tainted by our views on whether the expression purports to designate.[54] And if this is so, nothing is left of the primacy of broadly formal considerations over ontological ones.

Let us set these concerns aside and assume that the balancing act can succeed. Can the nominalist then resist the force of the Fregean argument? Well, he can do so by denying that the sentence '2 + 2 = 4' is true. This certainly amounts to going against one of the best-entrenched beliefs we have, but as Hartry Field has shown, one can make a case. The question is whether there is any way the anti-nominalist can bypass a direct appeal to intuition here, whether he could make an argument that could rationally compel a nominalist of Field's stripe.

Here is an attempt. Forget about sentences of pure arithmetic and concentrate on the arrangement of plates and forks on a big dining-room table. Suppose you see that the forks and the plates are paired perfectly: each fork is immediately adjacent to exactly one plate and there is no plate without a fork immediately adjacent to it. Then you can immediately conclude that the number of forks is identical to the number of plates. But if this inference is indeed valid, then the sentence 'If the plates and the forks are perfectly paired, then the number of plates is identical to the number of forks' must be true. And since expressions like 'the number of plates' pass the formal tests for singular termhood as well as '2' does, this sentence can replace '2 + 2 = 4' in the Fregean argument.

But what if the nominalist disputes the validity of this inference? Couldn't he argue that since a claim about perfect pairing of plates and forks does not commit one to the existence of numbers, but the claim that the number of plates is identical to the number of forks does, the inference is illegitimate?[55] Well, the anti-nominalist can point to the fact that the relevant conditional is simply one direction of an instance of Hume's principle, the claim that the number of Fs = the number of Gs iff there is a one-to-one correspondence between the Fs and the Gs. And Hume's

---

[53] For a detailed discussion, see Hale (1987, ch. 2).

[54] There is another concern here worth mentioning: one might worry whether the intuitions regarding the validity of the relevant inferences are reliable. In Szabó (2000) I argue against the Russellian view that definite descriptions carry semantic uniqueness implications. If the semantic contribution of the definite article is simply existential quantification and if uniqueness implications associated with many uses of sentences containing definite descriptions arise pragmatically, then definite descriptions *tout court* fail the inferential tests for singular termhood. They appear to pass them owing to a pragmatic illusion.   [55] This is the line taken in Field (1985).

principle is something that is arguably constitutive of our grasp of the concept of a natural number, so rejecting it is tantamount to embracing conceptual confusion. In other words, the anti-nominalist may insist that this principle is analytic.

The nominalist is going to resist this move. He may concede that the conditional 'if natural numbers exist then Hume's principle is true' is analytic, or at least (in case he is an opponent of the analytic–synthetic distinction) that it is obvious to the point of indisputability. But he will not yield on the categorical formulation. After all, we know that second-order logic together with Hume's principle entails the Peano axioms,[56] and consequently the existence of infinitely many objects. Should we really believe that *analytic consequences of pure logic* exclude a finitistic ontology?[57]

One way to strengthen the anti-nominalist argument is to drop the talk of analytic connections and resort to *explicit stipulation*. Here is the idea.[58] (The case is much easier to make for directions than it is for numbers, so I will here switch examples.) Start with a classical first-order language L with a restricted vocabulary understood as talking only about concrete inscriptions of lines, not about their directions. Then extend this language into L^* in such a way that all the sentences of L retain their meanings in L^*. In addition to the vocabulary of L, L^* contains a unary primitive function symbol 'the direction of' and new predicates 'F^*', 'G^*', . . . indexed to the old ones 'F', 'G', . . . We give meaning to the sentences of L^* containing new symbols by stipulating that they are synonymous with certain sentences of L. For example, we stipulate that 'the direction of a = the direction of b' means in L^* what 'a is parallel to b' does, that if it is true that whenever 'F' applies to a line, it applies to every line parallel to it, then 'the direction of a is F^*' means in L^* what 'a is F' does, and otherwise it is meaningless, etc. By making the appropriate stipulations, we can ensure both that '$\exists x$ (x = the direction of a)' is true in L^* and that expressions of the form 'the direction of x' pass the inferential tests for singular termhood. If the context principle is correct, this entails that we now have bona fide singular terms in true atomic sentences, so we must accept ontological commitment to directions.[59]

Now, it is probably best not to think that we can expand a theory's ontology through appropriate linguistic stipulation. It's the other way round: the argument is best construed as an attempt to show that languages that apparently carry no commitment to abstracta are actually up to their necks in that sort of commitment. Still, this is a striking conclusion, a result that not only nominalists find puzzling. The natural suspicion is that the nominalist cannot have it both ways: he cannot insist that 'the direction of a' functions as a genuine singular term in 'the direction

---

[56] This fact was first noted in Parsons (1965) and independently rediscovered in Wright (1983).

[57] For an enlightening exchange on the question whether it makes sense to declare Hume's principle analytic, see Boolos (1997) and Wright (1997).   [58] The argument is from Rosen (1993).

[59] Actually, all we get is ontological commitment to *something* all concrete line inscriptions have and all and only parallel line inscriptions share. There is a further step in concluding that these entities are directions. But this step is probably not particularly controversial.

of $a =$ the direction of b' *and* that this sentence means by stipulation nothing more nor less than 'a is parallel to b'. But it is not clear how exactly the conclusion is to be resisted without giving up on the context principle. To bolster his case here, the anti-nominalist needs only a special case of the principle, according to which there is nothing more to being a classical first-order language with identity than behaving in all inferential respects like such a language (Rosen 1993: 162).[60]

The moral is that the fate of the Fregean argument rests on a thorough defence of a precisely stated version of the context principle. No anti-nominalist believes that this is an easy task, or that it has been done. But some hope that it can be done.[61]

6. A MIDDLE WAY?

None of the arguments for or against nominalism is, it seems to me, conclusive. By itself, this is not surprising: philosophical arguments rarely have that character. But the elusiveness of the problem has tempted some philosophers to entertain less than straightforward answers to the question whether there are abstract entities. The first and most famous of these oblique answers is due to Rudolf Carnap (1950).

According to Carnap, to understand the problem of the existence of abstract entities, we need to distinguish between two kinds of questions, or more precisely, between two ways of interpreting a question. We can construe a question as *internal* or *external* with respect to a particular linguistic framework. A linguistic framework is the totality of conventions specifying the syntax and semantics of a language together with certain rules of confirmation; a question is taken as internal with respect to it just in case it is interpreted as asking for an answer to be established within that framework. Carnap's verdict is that questions regarding the existence of abstracta tend to be trivial when taken as internal and deeply problematic when taken as external. The problematic character of external questions of existence is supposed to be the result of our lack of established rules for providing an answer. For example, if we construe the question 'Are there numbers?' as internal to the framework of arithmetic, the answer is a straightforward yes. But an interpretation of this question that is external to any particular linguistic framework can only be regarded as a query about whether we should adopt the framework of arithmetic.

---

[60] Rosen continues the argument by showing that there is a way out for the nominalist even if he accepts the context principle. The escape works when the existence of directions is at stake, but unfortunately fails when the Fregean argument is run for sets or numbers.

[61] For criticism and ultimate rejection of the Context Principle, see e.g. Hodes (1990) and Lowe (1995).

For Carnap, this is not a theoretical question. It is a practical issue to be settled on the basis of considerations of expediency and fruitfulness.

Carnap's view has been out of fashion for a while. This is largely due to the fact that philosophers were convinced by the gist of Quine's famous criticism. There is something deeply unappealing about the thought that means of rational justification arise from limited frameworks we might adopt and that consequently there is no rational way to justify the choice of any one of these particular frameworks. For a naturalist of Quine's stripe, there is no sharp boundary between theoretical questions and practical ones. Every question must be answered as part of a project of designing the best overall theory of the world, where the criteria of evaluation *include* Carnap's expediency and fruitfulness along with other considerations normally used in comparing scientific theories. But the aspect of Carnap's view Quine so forcefully criticized could be separated from the rest. One could maintain the idea that ontological questions are in some way fundamentally ambiguous, while giving up on Carnap's insistence that one of their readings is rationally unapproachable.

One can ask the question 'Are there infinitely many prime numbers?' or the question 'Are there *really* numbers?' One would be naturally inclined to regard the former as a sort of question that is appropriately raised in the context of a high school mathematics class and fully answered by the Euclidean proof. One would not be naturally inclined to think that the Euclidean proof together with the fact that prime numbers are numbers answers the second question. The word 'really' seems to be doing some sort of work in the latter question; it indicates somehow that we are looking for a different sort of answer. This is the source of Carnap's intuition. He then goes on, analyses the difference in a conventionalist way, and repudiates the latter question as asking for a sort of answer that could not be given. One might abandon his solution to the problem, while respecting the underlying insight.

What sort of alternative explanation could there be for the alleged fundamental ambiguity in ontological questions? There are a number of possibilities. The one that departs least from Carnap's original thought is the fictionalist line. According to a fictionalist about abstracta, when we speak about numbers, models, properties, and the rest we immerse ourselves in pretence. *Within* this fiction all those entities exist, but *outside* the fiction in the real world they don't. When we ask a question like 'Are there infinitely many prime numbers?' we are not looking for a true answer, only for an answer that is true in the mathematical fiction. The word 'really' marks that we wish to drop the curtains and go after truth *simpliciter* (cf. Yablo 1998, 2000).

Now, this is not really an oblique answer: it is only fictional worlds that have abstracta; the real one is just as the nominalist thinks it is. But there are other ways to argue for a fundamental ambiguity in ontological questions, which make it harder to say whether the adopted view is a version of nominalism or anti-nominalism. One might, for example, argue that we have two notions of *reference*—one requiring full-blown epistemic contact and another one that does not—and that terms for certain abstracta refer in one, but not the other, sense. Or one might claim that there is no unique *structure* associated with sentences talking about certain abstracta and that the truth-conditions determined through one of these structures commit one to the existence of those entities, while the truth-conditions determined through the other don't. Or one might insist that we have two notions of *belief*—believing that *F*s exist and believing in *F*s—and that these two beliefs involve different kinds of commitment, one appropriate for certain abstracta, while the other inappropriate.[62]

It may be that each of these attempts to strike a middle ground between straight-forward acceptance and straightforward rejection of abstract entities fails. With enough foot-stamping one can usually convince people that there is no conceiv-able source of ambiguity in asking the simple question 'Are there abstract entities?' (I myself performed some of the foot-stamping at the end of Section 2.1 above.) Be it as it may, a convincing answer does not seem to loom large on the horizon.[63]

References

Alston, William (1957). 'Ontological Commitments'. *Philosophical Studies*, 9: 8–17.

Azzouni, Jody (1994). *Metaphysical Myth, Mathematical Practice: The Ontology and Epistemology of Exact Sciences*. New York: Cambridge University Press.

—— (1997). 'Thick Epistemic Access: Distinguishing the Mathematical from the Empirical'. *Journal of Philosophy*, 94: 427–84.

—— (1998). 'On "On What There Is"'. *Pacific Philosophical Quarterly*, 79: 1–18.

Balaguer, Mark (1998). *Platonism and Anti-Platonism in Mathematics*. Oxford: Oxford University Press.

Benacerraf, Paul (1965). 'What Numbers could not Be'. *Philosophical Review*, 74: 47–73.

—— (1973). 'Mathematical Truth'. *Journal of Philosophy*, 70: 661–79.

Berkeley, George (1711). *A Treatise concerning the Principles of Human Knowledge*, in *The Works of George Berkeley, Bishop of Cloyne*, ed. A. A. Luce and T. E. Jessop, 9 vols. London: Thomas Nelson, 1948–57.

Boolos, George (1975). 'On Second-Order Logic'. *Journal of Philosophy*, 72: 509–27.

—— (1984). 'To be is to be a Value of a Variable (or to be Some Values of Some Variables)'. *Journal of Philosophy*, 81: 430–49.

—— (1985). 'Nominalist Platonism'. *Philosophical Review*, 94: 327–44.

—— (1997). 'Is Hume's Principle Analytic?', in Richard Heck (ed.), *Language, Truth and Logic: Essays in Honour of Michael Dummett*. Oxford: Clarendon Press, 245–62.

Burgess, John, and Gideon Rosen (1997). *A Subject with No Object*. Oxford: Clarendon Press.

Carnap, Rudolf (1950). 'Empiricism, Semantics, and Ontology'. Repr. as appendix to Carnap, *Meaning and Necessity: A Study in Semantics and Modal Logic*, 2nd edn. Chicago: University of Chicago Press, 1956, 205–21.

[62] For the first view, see Azzouni (1994, 1997), for the second, Hodes (1984, 1990, 1991), for the third Szabó (2003).

[63] For the record: Balaguer (1998) argues that the question is univocal, that there is an optimal version of nominalism and an optimal version of anti-nominalism, that these versions are immune from refutation, and that the best way to think of this is to admit that there is no fact of the matter.

Cartwright, Nancy (1983). *How the Laws of Physics Lie*. Oxford: Oxford University Press.

Cartwright, Richard (1994). 'Speaking of Everything'. *Nous*, 28: 1–20.

Chihara, Charles (1990). *Constructibility and Mathematical Existence*. Oxford: Clarendon Press.

Courteney, William J. (ed.) (1992). *Vivarium*, 30. Special issue devoted to the conference 'The Origin and Meaning of Medieval Nominalism' held at the University of Wisconsin-Madison, 3–5 Oct. 1991.

Davidson, Donald (1967). 'The Logical Form of Action Sentences', in Davidson, *Essays on Actions and Events*. Oxford: Clarendon Press, 1980, 105–23.

Dummett, Michael (1973*a*). 'The Philosophical Basis of Intuitionistic Logic', in Dummett, *Truth and Other Enigmas*. Cambridge, Mass.: Harvard University Press, 1978, 215–47.

—— (1973*b*). *Frege: Philosophy of Language*. Cambridge, Mass.: Harvard University Press.

—— (1991). *Frege: Philosophy of Mathematics*. Cambridge, Mass.: Harvard University Press.

Field, Hartry (1980). *Science without Numbers: A Defense of Nominalism*. Oxford: Basil Blackwell.

—— (1984). 'Platonism for Cheap? Crispin Wright on Frege's Context Principle', in Field, *Realism, Mathematics and Modality*. Oxford: Basil Blackwell, 1989, 147–70.

—— (1985). 'On Conservativeness and Incompleteness', in Field, *Realism, Mathematics and Modality*. Oxford: Basil Blackwell, 1989, 125–46.

—— (1988). 'Realism, Mathematics and Modality'. *Philosophical Topics*, 19: 57–107.

—— (1989). 'Fictionalism, Epistemology and Modality', in Field, *Realism, Mathematics and Modality*. Oxford: Basil Blackwell, 1989, 1–52.

Fodor, Jerry (1998). *Concepts: Where Cognitive Science Went Wrong?* Oxford: Clarendon Press.

Geach, Peter (1957). *Mental Acts: Their Content and their Objects*. London: Routledge & Kegan Paul.

Gödel, Kurt (1947). 'What is Cantor's Continuum Problem?' Rev. in Paul Benacerraf and Hilary Putnam (eds.), *Philosophy of Mathematics: Selected Readings*, 2nd edn. Cambridge: Cambridge University Press, 1983, 470–85.

Goodman, Nelson (1956). 'A World of Individuals', in Goodman, *Problems and Projects*. Indianapolis: Bobbs-Merrill, 1972, 155–72.

—— and W. V. O. Quine (1947). 'Steps towards Constructive Nominalism'. *Journal of Symbolic Logic*, 12: 97–122. Repr. in Nelson Goodman, *Problems and Projects*. Indianapolis: Bobbs-Merrill, 1972, 173–99.

Hale, Bob (1987). *Abstract Objects*. Oxford: Basil Blackwell.

Hellman, Geoffrey (1989). *Mathematics without Numbers*. Oxford: Clarendon Press.

Hodes, Harold (1984). 'Logicism and the Ontological Commitments of Arithmetic'. *Journal of Philosophy*, 81: 123–49.

—— (1990). 'Ontological Commitment: Thick and Thin', in G. Boolos (ed.), *Essays in Honor of Hilary Putnam*. Cambridge: Cambridge University Press, 235–60.

—— (1991). 'Where do Sets Come From?' and 'Corrections to "Where do Sets Come From?"' *Journal of Symbolic Logic*, 66: 150–75, 1486.

Jubien, Michael (1977). 'Ontology and Mathematical Truth'. *Nous*, 11: 133–50.

Kripke, Saul (1972). *Naming and Necessity*. Cambridge, Mass.: Harvard University Press.

—— (1976). 'Is there a Problem about Substitutional Quantification?', in Gareth Evans and John McDowell (eds.), *Truth and Meaning*. Oxford: Clarendon Press, 325–419.

Lewis, David (1986). *On the Plurality of Worlds*. Oxford: Basil Blackwell.

—— (1991). *Parts of Classes*. Oxford: Basil Blackwell.

Lowe, E. J. (1994). 'Vague Objects and Quantum Indeterminacy'. *Analysis*, 45: 110–14.

—— (1995). 'The Metaphysics of Abstract Objects'. *Journal of Philosophy*, 92: 509–24.

Malament, David (1982). Review of Hartry Field's *Science without Numbers*. *Journal of Philosophy*, 79: 523–34.

Melia, Joseph (1995). 'On What There Isn't'. *Analysis*, 55: 223–9.

Parsons, Charles (1965). 'Frege's Theory of Number', in Parsons, *Mathematics in Philosophy*. Ithaca, NY: Cornell University Press, 1983, 150–72.

Prior, Arthur (1954). 'Entities', in Prior, *Papers in Logic and Ethics*. Amherst, Mass.: University of Massachusetts Press, 1976.

Putnam, Hilary (1967). 'Mathematics without Foundations'. *Journal of Philosophy*, 64: 5–22.

—— (1971). *Philosophy of Logic*. New York: Harper.

Quine, W. V. O. (1948). 'On What There Is'. *Review of Metaphysics*, 2: 21–38.

—— (1951). 'Two Dogmas of Empiricism'. *Philosophical Review*, 60: 20–43.

—— (1964). 'Ontological Reduction and the World of Numbers', in Quine, *The Ways of Paradox*. Rev. and enlarged. Cambridge, Mass.: Harvard University Press, 1976, 212–20.

—— (1969). 'Existence and Quantification', in Quine, *Ontological Relativity and Other Essays*. New York: Columbia University Press, 91–113.

Resnik, Michael (1988). 'Second-Order Logic Still Wild'. *Journal of Philosophy*, 85: 75–87.

Rosen, Gideon (1993). 'The Refutation of Nominalism(?)' *Philosophical Topics*, 21: 149–86.

—— (1994). 'What is Constructive Empiricism?' *Philosophical Studies*, 74: 143–78.

Shapiro, Stewart (1983). 'Conservativeness and Incompleteness'. *Journal of Philosophy*, 80: 521–31.

Stanley, Jason (2001). 'Hermeneutic Fictionalism', in H. Wettstein and P. French, (eds.), *Midwest Studies in Philosophy*, xxv: *Figurative Language*. Oxford: Basil Blackwell, 36–71.

Szabó, Zoltán Gendler (2000). 'Descriptions and Uniqueness'. *Philosophical Studies*, 101: 29–57.

—— (2001). 'Fictionalism and Moore's Paradox'. *Canadian Journal of Philosophy*, 31: 293–308.

—— (2003). 'Believing in Things'. *Philosophy and Phenomenological Research*, 66: 584–611.

van Fraassen, Bas (1980). *The Scientific Image*. Oxford: Clarendon Press.

—— (1994). 'Gideon Rosen on Constructive Empiricism'. *Philosophical Studies*, 74: 179–92.

Vendler, Zeno (1967). 'Facts and Events', in Vendler, *Linguistics in Philosophy*. Ithaca, NY: Cornell University Press, 122–46.

Wright, Crispin (1983). *Frege's Conception of Numbers as Objects*. Aberdeen: Aberdeen University Press.

—— (1997). 'On the Philosophical Significance of Frege's Theorem', in Richard Heck (ed.), *Language, Truth and Logic: Essays in Honour of Michael Dummett*. Oxford: Clarendon Press, 201–44.

Yablo, Steven (1998). 'Does Ontology Rest on a Mistake?' *Proceedings of the Aristotelian Society*, suppl. vol. 72: 229–61.

—— (2000). 'A Paradox of Existence', in A. J. Everett and T. Hofweber (eds.), *Empty Names, Fiction, and the Puzzles of Non-Existence*. Palo Alto: CSLI, 275–312.

CHAPTER 2

PLATONISTIC THEORIES OF UNIVERSALS

JOSHUA HOFFMAN
GARY S. ROSENKRANTZ

1. THE ABSTRACT–CONCRETE DISTINCTION

PLATONIC realism asserts the existence of one or more kinds of *abstract entities*. Necessarily, a Platonic realist is a realist about abstract entities. However, as we shall see, some (but not all) Platonic realists are realists about *universals*. Thus, a thorough defence of Platonic realism calls for, as a preliminary, an adequate exposition or analysis of the notion of an abstract entity, and an adequate exposition or analysis of the notion of a universal.

The distinction between abstract and concrete entities is, we believe, a fundamental categorial distinction, in that every entity is either concrete or abstract, and no entity is both. We believe that the abstract–concrete distinction is, in fact, the *most fundamental* categorial distinction.[1]

---

[1] It might be held that *being an entity* is an ontological category, but if it is, then it is a *universal* category, or one under which everything falls. Hence, *being an entity* does not distinguish one kind of being from another; it draws no categorial *distinctions*.

How is the abstract–concrete distinction to be understood? To begin, let us stipulate that *places*, *times*, and *individual substances* are uncontroversial instances of concreta, while *shareable properties* and *sets* are uncontroversial instances of abstracta. In what follows we outline some of the most important attempts to analyse the abstract–concrete distinction and what we take to be their inadequacies.

(1) Concrete entities are *in space*, while abstract entities are not.

There are at least two objections to this analysis. First, since a Cartesian soul is by definition not in space, that is, since it does not *occupy any place*,[2] (1) implies that a Cartesian soul is abstract. This is incorrect, because a Cartesian soul is an individual substance, and as such it is concrete. Secondly, since places are not themselves *in* space (they do not occupy any places), (1) implies that places are abstract, when, as we have noted, they are concrete. Thirdly, since times are not *in* space (do not occupy places), (1) implies falsely that times are abstract. Thus, (1) does not provide a logically necessary condition for being a concrete entity.

(2) Concrete entities are *in space or in time*, while abstract entities are not.

This analysis avoids the problems concerning Cartesian souls and places if it is necessarily true that absolute time exists. For on that assumption, necessarily, a Cartesian soul or a place is in time. On the other hand, it might be assumed that, possibly, time is relational. In that case, (2) does seem to have problems with Cartesian souls. In particular, if it is possible that time is relational, then, apparently, there could be a *static* world containing a non-spatial thinking substance engaged in an *atemporal* contemplation of necessary truths. Yet, it seems that a possible soul of this sort may possess (unrealized) *potentialities* to undergo intrinsic psychic changes or (unexercised) *powers* to bring about changes. Although an atemporal, non-spatial, thinking substance having such potentialities or causal powers would surely be a concretum, it obviously would *not* stand in spatial or temporal relations. Hence, (2) appears to have the undesirable implication that a possible soul of this kind would be an abstractum. So, arguably, (2) does not provide a logically necessary condition for being a concrete entity. Furthermore, (2) implies that no abstract entity exists in time. This assertion is highly questionable, and in any case, an analysis of the abstract–concrete distinction that did not rely upon this assertion would be superior to one that did, other things being equal. Thus, it is questionable that (2) provides a logically sufficient condition for being a concrete entity.[3]

---

[2] We equate *being in space* with *occupying a place*, and we equate *being in time* with *occurring at a time (or times) or existing at a time (or times)*. Thus, being in space is not the same as *having or standing in spatial relations*. A place stands in spatial relations to various other entities, but does not occupy a place. If a place occupied a place, then an absurd infinite regress of places would be generated. Moreover, arguably, parallel considerations apply to times. Below, we consider a definition of abstracta in terms of having spatial relations or temporal relations, rather than in terms of being in space or in time.

[3] See below for further discussion of our claim that abstract entities exist in time.

(3) Concrete entities are *in space-time*, while abstract entities are not.

There are at least three objections to this analysis. Like (1), (3) falsely implies that Cartesian souls are abstract. Secondly, just as places cannot be said to be in space, so they cannot be said to be in, that is, they do not occupy, space-time. Thus, (3) does not provide a logically necessary condition for being a concrete entity. Finally, (3) commits one to the *impossibility* of there being a three-dimensional space and a separate temporal dimension. If three-dimensional space is even *possible*, then one cannot analyse the abstract–concrete distinction in terms of space-time, for if three-dimensional space is possible, then various concrete entities could be in space but not in space-time. No analysis of the abstract–concrete distinction should commit one to the impossibility of a three-dimensional space and a separate temporal dimension.

(4) Concrete entities *enter into spatial and temporal relations*, while abstract entities do not.[4]

The first difficulty is that while souls *do not* enter into spatial relations, they are concrete. A second difficulty is that while places *do* enter into spatial and temporal relations, times *do not* enter into spatial relations. Thus, (4) falsely implies that times are abstract. So (4) does not provide a logically necessary condition for being a concrete entity.

(5) Concrete entities *enter into spatial or temporal relations*, while abstract entities do not.[5]

This account avoids the problems about spaces and times, for spaces enter into spatial relations, and times enter into temporal relations. However, any difficulties with Cartesian souls that affect (2) also affect (5). Moreover, various abstract entities *do* enter into temporal relations. For example, at noon there are various humans who exemplify Wakefulness, a shareable property. And Hoffman and Rosenkrantz assert at 2 p.m. that the empty set is peculiar, in which case, at 2 p.m. the empty set is asserted by them to be peculiar. And of course, if abstract entities exist in time, then they enter into temporal relations, for example, the relation of existing at the same time as Abraham Lincoln. Another reason to suppose that abstracta enter into temporal relations is that properties undergo relational change. Consider, for instance, an abstractum such as Wakefulness. Of course, this property cannot undergo *intrinsic change*, unlike, for example, Socrates, who intrinsically changes when he falls asleep. But an entity *e* can enter into temporal relations by undergoing *relational change*, even though *e* does *not* intrinsically change. Thus, an entity's

---

[4] Here we assume that space is three-dimensional and that time is a separate dimension.

[5] See e.g. Lowe (1998). While Lowe actually states his definition of *being concrete* in terms of 'being in space or time', he sometimes states his analysis in terms of entering into spatial or temporal relations. Furthermore, Lowe holds, for example, that it is a trivial truth that a particular space is in or occupies itself. This seems to us to confuse the relation of Identity with that of Occupation. It is likely, therefore, that Lowe believes (2) and (5) to be equivalent, while we think that, properly understood, they are not equivalent.

being (intrinsically) immutable is compatible with its undergoing relational change. Necessarily, if an entity *e* changes its relations to other entities, then *e* enters into temporal relations. For example, a basic particle which does *not* intrinsically change, but which is orbited by other particles over some interval of time, enters into temporal relations with these other particles. Similarly, since Wakefulness is exemplified by Socrates at one time and not at another, this property undergoes relational change. Thus, Wakefulness *does* enter into temporal relations. It follows that (5) has the erroneous implication that Wakefulness is a concretum. Moreover, on some views of universals (certain Aristotelian or neo-Aristotelian views, e.g. Armstrong 1989), a universal is both abstract and has spatial location or locations. (See below for an exposition of this sort of view about universals.) For example, on such views, Squareness is located wherever there is a square object. Thus, (5) does not provide a logically sufficient condition for being a concrete entity.

(6) Concrete entities are *capable of motion or intrinsic change*, but abstract entities are not.

Since Cartesian souls can undergo intrinsic change, (6) correctly implies that they are concrete. However, neither places nor times are capable of motion or intrinsic change. Thus, according to (6), places and times are abstract, and (6) does not provide a logically sufficient condition for being an abstract entity.

(7) Concrete entities have *contingent existence*, while abstract entities have *necessary existence*.

First, (7) implies that a necessary God would be abstract, when such a being would be concrete. Secondly, if space, time, space-time, or mass-energy have necessary existence, then (7) implies that they are abstract, when they are concrete. So (7) has the undesirable feature of not being neutral about the modal status of such entities. Thirdly, an Aristotelian universal such as Humanity has contingent existence (because its existence depends upon the existence of human beings), but this sort of universal (and every universal) is abstract. Finally, a *set* of contingent, concrete entities, e.g. the set of American League baseball players, appears to be an abstract entity that has contingent existence. Thus, (7) provides neither a logically necessary nor a logically sufficient condition for being a concrete entity.

(8) Abstract entities are *exemplifiable or instantiable*, while concrete entities are not.

As we have said, it does seem that all universals are abstracta, but the problem with (8) is that there are other sorts of abstracta that are *not* exemplifiable, for example, sets and propositions. Hence, (8) does not provide a logically necessary condition for being an abstract entity.

(9) Abstracta are (intellectually) *graspable*, while concreta are not.

While it does seem to be true that no concrete entity is graspable, it does not seem to be the case that all abstract entities are. For example, it does not seem to be true that a *set* of concrete entities is graspable. Moreover, if haecceities exist, then the haecceity of a necessarily unconscious body is not graspable.[6] Thus, (9) does not provide a logically necessary condition for being an abstract entity.

(10) Concreta can be causes or effects, but abstracta cannot.

Many philosophers hold that while concrete events can be causes or effects, individual substances cannot. If this is correct, then (10) falsely implies that individual substances are abstract. Moreover, there are similar difficulties with regard to times, places, mereological sums, and other sorts of concreta. It might be replied that concreta can be *involved* in causes and effects, while abstracta cannot. However, it is difficult to understand in what sense of 'involvement' this is so. For example, if the concrete event *Jones's being angry* is a cause of Jones's turning red in the face, then why isn't Jones's anger (arguably, an abstract entity) also involved in this cause? Furthermore, according to some ontologies, facts are causes but are abstracta.[7] Thus, (10) does not seem to provide either a logically sufficient or a logically necessary condition for being a concrete entity.

Despite the failure of all of the attempts discussed,[8] we believe that it is possible to analyse the abstract–concrete distinction by shifting the focus somewhat and by employing certain additional ontological concepts.

To begin, we take the concept of an ontological category as undefined, and note that any comprehensive understanding of the world presupposes the use of such categories. A crucial component of our analysis of the abstract–concrete distinction is an intuitive notion of a class of ontological categories that are at a certain level of

---

[6] The haecceity of an entity *a* is the property of being identical with *a*. See Rosenkrantz (1993: 56–68).

[7] These observations provide a reply to a recent well-known argument for scepticism about abstract entities. According to this sceptical argument, (i) an abstract entity cannot enter into causal relations; (ii) we have knowledge about an entity only if that entity enters into causal relations; therefore, (iii) we cannot have knowledge about an abstract entity. In the light of the aforementioned observations, it would seem that either (i) or (ii) is false. That is, either (i) is false because facts or the like are abstract and can enter into causal relations, or (ii) is false for either of the following two reasons. First, we have knowledge about material substances even though they cannot enter into causal relations. Secondly, although abstracta cannot enter into causal relations, there is a sense in which abstracta are involved in causal relations, and we can have knowledge about an entity if it is involved in causal relations in that sense. Cf. Kim (1981: 339–54).

[8] It seems that such failures have led other philosophers to doubt whether there is such a thing as the abstract–concrete distinction at all. For example, Kim (1981: 348) writes as follows. 'The force of saying that something is "abstract" or "platonic" has never been made clear. One sense sometimes attached to "abstract" is that of "eternal"; an abstract object in this sense neither comes into being nor perishes. Another closely related sense is that of not being in space and time. Abstract entities in this sense are atemporal and nonspatial: they lack location in space-time. A third sense is that of "necessary"; abstract entities in this sense are said to "exist necessarily". It is by no means obvious that these three senses are equivalent: for example, one traditional concept of God makes him abstract in the first and third sense but not in the second'. Kim's scepticism about the very existence of the abstract–concrete distinction will prove to be unwarranted if we can provide an adequate analysis of this distinction that accommodates the relevant intuitive data.

generality. Intuitively, the ontological categories on the following list, L, appear to be at the same level of generality.

(L) Event, Place, Time, Boundary, Mereological Sum, Property, Relation, Substance, Set, and Proposition.

Examples of ontological categories which also seem to be at this level of generality, but which we have not included on L, are Number and Trope.

As we have said, Entity might be said to be the most general ontological category. And as we have argued, Entity subdivides into the ontological categories of Concrete Entity and Abstract Entity. Concrete Entity subdivides into the ontological categories of Substance, Place, Time, Event, Trope, Boundary, Absence, Mereological Sum, and so on. Abstract Entity subdivides into the ontological categories of Property, Relation, Proposition, Set, and so forth. Accordingly, we can say that Entity is at the highest level of generality (level A), Concrete Entity and Abstract Entity are at the next highest level of generality (level B), and the subdivisions of Concrete Entity and the subdivisions of Abstract Entity are at the next lower level of generality (level C). Furthermore, there are level D ontological categories which are subdivisions of level C ontological categories, and so on. For example, Physical Object and Non-physical Soul are subdivisions of Substance; Surface, Edge, and Corner are subdivisions of Boundary; Shadow and Hole are subdivisions of Absence, and so forth.

Intuitively speaking, to say that an ontological category is at level C is to say that it is of the same level of generality as the categories on L. This idea can be explained in a simplified fashion as follows. Assume for the sake of argument that there could be entities belonging to each of the ontological categories on L. In that case, an ontological category is at level C if and only if (i) that category neither subsumes nor is subsumed by a category on L, and (ii) that category is not subsumed by an ontological category which is not on L and which satisfies (i). (The relevant notion of category subsumption can be understood in terms of this example: Boundary *subsumes* Surface just because, first, necessarily, a surface is a boundary, and secondly, possibly, some boundary is not a surface.)[9]

The abstract–concrete distinction can now be analysed as follows. An entity x is concrete if and only if x is an instance of a level C category which could be instantiated by some entity y which has spatial or temporal parts; and an entity z is abstract if and only if z is not concrete. We take the general concept of a *part* as undefined. Examples of *spatial* parts are the right and left halves of a physical object, and examples of *temporal* parts are the first and second halves of an hour. Proper parts of these kinds are concrete. Perhaps there are also *logical* parts, for instance,

[9] For a more detailed and formal account of the notion of an ontological category's being at level C, see Hoffman and Rosenkrantz (1994: 182–7). This account does not depend upon the simplifying assumption that there could be entities of each of the categories on L and implies that an ontological category is at level C only if there could be an entity belonging to that category.

the properties that are the conjuncts of the compound property of being a man *and* being unmarried. Any such proper parts are abstract.

This account of the abstract–concrete distinction gives the correct result in all of the problem cases discussed earlier. First, even if a Cartesian soul lacks spatial and temporal parts, a Cartesian soul is an instance of a level C category, namely, Substance, which could have some (other) instance with spatial parts, for example, a tree. Hence, our analysis of the abstract–concrete distinction has the desired implication that a Cartesian soul is a concrete entity. Our analysis also has the desired consequence that because some places and times have spatial or temporal parts, respectively, places and times are concreta. Wakefulness, an instance of the level C category Property, is an abstract entity. This follows from the fact that there could not be an abstract property that has spatial or temporal *parts*, even if there could be a property that enters into spatial or temporal relations.

It should also be noted that our analysis of the abstract–concrete distinction has the important virtue of being *ontologically neutral* about many of the issues that other attempted analyses are not neutral about. For example, whether one thinks that universals are Platonic or Aristotelian, on our analysis they are abstracta. On our analysis, even if one thinks that Cartesian souls are possible, they are concreta. On our analysis, one does not have to assert that all necessary beings are abstract, for whether or not a substance or time or space or space-time are contingent or necessary, they are all concreta. Finally, our account of the abstract–concrete distinction has the desired implication that a set qualifies as an abstractum, even if that set has spatio-temporal location in virtue of having spatio-temporally located *elements*. For a set belongs to the level C category Set, and no possible instance of Set has spatial or temporal *parts*. Note that because Parthood is a transitive relation, and Elementhood is not, elements of sets are *not* parts of them. (To suppose that a set has spatial or temporal parts is probably to confuse a set with a mereological sum, namely, a concrete collection that has parts.)

However, Jonathan Lowe has written about this analysis that he finds it 'somewhat odd to suppose that the concreteness of an entity should depend upon the features of *other* entities which happen to belong to the same ontological category and from which it differs precisely in *lacking* these features' (Lowe 1995: 203). But it is misleading to say that these entities 'happen' to belong to the same ontological category, since this suggests that their belonging to the same ontological category is an *accidental* fact about them. Indeed, because the entities in question belong to the same *ontological category*, they essentially have an ontologically significant resemblance that is *sufficient* for their belonging to that category, even if they *differ* in some ontologically significant respect. Moreover, because ontological categories are *fundamental* to metaphysics, it is entirely appropriate that in addition to their *classificatory* function, they have a significant role to play in *analysing* important metaphysical notions. Thus, there is no apparent reason to doubt that the concreteness of an entity depends upon 'the kind of company it keeps' within an ontological category at level C.

2. Universals and Particulars

To begin, let us ask what a universal is. A universal is an entity that is possibly such that it has two or more instances.[10] A particular is an entity that is not a universal.

An instance of a universal instantiates or exemplifies that universal. We believe that instantiation is primitive and unanalysable. If there are instantiable universals, then it appears that any attempt to analyse instantiation must do so in terms of the *instantiation* of one or more other universals. Thus, it seems that any attempted analysis of instantiation would suffer from the fatal flaw of vicious circularity. But if instantiation connects substances and their properties across the *fundamental ontological division*, i.e. the division between concreta and abstracta, then it is not surprising that instantiation is primitive and unanalysable.

There appear to be at least two basic kinds of universals: *properties* and *relations*.[11] So, if there are three cubes at some time, then each of these cubes exemplifies or instantiates the property of Cubicalness at that time. Another sort of example is provided by the instantiation of the relation of Betweenness. In this example a trio or ordered triple of items instantiates this relation. Thus, while a property is expressed by a one-place predicate, e.g. 'x is cubical', a relation is expressed by a multi-place predicate, e.g. 'x is between y and z'.[12] Betweenness, like Cubicalness, qualifies as a universal: much as there can be two or more objects at a single time such that each of these objects exemplifies the property of Cubicalness at that time, there can be two or more trios of objects at a single time such that each of these trios exemplifies the relation of Betweenness at that time.

---

[10] This statement is ambiguous. First, it might mean that for any universal U, U is possibly such that it has two or more instances at a single time. Secondly, it might mean that for any universal U, U is possibly such that it has an instance x, and U is possibly such that it has an instance y, where x is not identical with y. An example of each kind of universal is *being the president of an organization* and *being the first president of the United States*, respectively. (Note that the first sense is stronger than the second, so that any universal that satisfies the first definition will satisfy the second, but not vice versa.) What we mean by a universal for the purposes of this chapter is to be understood in terms of the first sense of 'is possibly such that it has two or more instances'. We think that this is the standard notion of a universal.

[11] Sentence types might be another sort of universal. However, arguably, a sentence type is identical with a sign-design property.

[12] As others have argued, not every predicate expresses a genuine universal. For example, the one-place predicate 'non-self-instantiating' fails to express a genuine property. The proof parallels Russell's demonstration that there is no such set as the set of all and only those sets that are not members of themselves. In particular, if there were such a property as being non-self-instantiating, then it would have either to instantiate itself or not to instantiate itself. The former entails that such a property would be non-self-instantiating, and the latter entails that such a property would be self-instantiating. It follows that being non-self-instantiating would have both to instantiate itself and not to instantiate itself. Since this is absurd, it is impossible that there be such a property as being non-self-instantiating. Thus, the one-place predicate 'non-self-instantiating' does not express a genuine property.

We assume that, possibly, there are abstract universals, abstract particulars, and/or concrete particulars. An example of an *abstract universal* is a Platonic property such as Squareness. Squareness in this sense is an entity that exists independently of any square entity, that is, independently of any square. Moreover, Squareness of this sort is a necessary being, and is eternal (having no beginning or end), (intrinsically) immutable, mind-independent,[13] and non-spatial. It is not perceptible (being outside of space), though instances of it are. However, as we hold that all entities (other than times themselves) are in time, we believe that Platonic abstract entities are in time.

On an Aristotelian conception of universals, (at least some) universals have contingent existence, and every universal depends for its existence upon its having one or more instances. According to some versions of Aristotelianism, if two square entities exist at a given time, then there are two places such that Squareness is wholly located at each of those places at that time. If there are no square entities, then Squareness does not exist. On the other hand, suppose that non-physical (i.e. Cartesian) souls are possible. And suppose that there are two such souls, each of which is angry. Then each soul exemplifies Anger, but Anger is not wholly located in each place that the souls occupy, since by hypothesis such souls do not occupy any places. So, on certain versions of Aristotelianism, some universals are located and some are not, but in every case a universal depends for its existence upon its having one or more instances.

We have said that all universals are abstract entities and that no abstract entity can have spatial or temporal parts. It might be thought that the Aristotelian conception of universals is incompatible with these claims, for the following reasons. Suppose that there are three square entities, and that Squareness, an Aristotelian universal, exists where the three square entities exist. Then doesn't Squareness have spatial parts, namely, three parts, corresponding to the three square entities? In answer to this criticism, we reply that this inference is mistaken, and confuses an Aristotelian universal with a different sort of entity, namely, a mereological sum. In our example, Squareness does not exist *partly* in each of the three places it exists; rather it exists *wholly* in each of those three places. On the other hand, if we collect or sum those three square entities, then what we have is not an abstract entity, something belonging to the kind Universal, but a different sort of entity, one that is concrete not abstract, and that falls under the category *Mereological Sum*.

We have provided examples of two sorts of abstract universals. An example of an *abstract particular* is an entity e such that (i) e could not have two or more instances, and (ii) e belongs to a level C category that is not capable of having

---

[13] To say that a universal U is mind-independent is to say that U does not exist in virtue of one or more minds grasping U or thinking about U.

an instance with spatial or temporal parts. Examples of such abstract particulars seem to be sets and propositions. Sets, unlike properties and relations, cannot be instantiated.[14] And although sets have *elements*, the elements of a set are not *parts* of that set: as we have argued, the having-an-element relation is not the same relation as (and has different logical properties from) the part–whole relation. (See Section 1.) Propositions, like sets, properties, and relations, cannot have spatial or temporal parts. And while there are different instances of one or more *sentence types* that express the same proposition, the proposition itself does not have instances, and so is a particular.

Finally, examples of *concrete particulars* are individual substances, times, places, and (on at least one understanding of them) tropes. Since there are substances, times, and places that have spatial or temporal parts, all substances, times, and places are concrete. Moreover, as none of them can have instances, they all are particulars. A trope, e.g. the particular wisdom of Socrates, is an entity that cannot have more than one instance; indeed, it is not correct to speak of a trope as having any instances at all. Tropes are particulars. One way, and perhaps the standard way, to understand tropes is as entities which (in some cases) have spatial parts, and hence, as concreta.[15]

What emerges from this discussion of universals and particulars with respect to Platonic realism is that this form of realism postulates abstracta that have necessary existence, are (intrinsically) immutable, and exist 'outside of' space. Putative examples of such Platonic abstracta include unexemplified universals, e.g. the property of being a horned horse, false propositions, e.g. the proposition that there are horned horses, and sets that do not have a contingently existing element, e.g. the empty set. It should be noted that a Platonic realist can consistently postulate the existence of Platonic universals, or Platonic particulars, or both. For example, one can postulate Platonic propositions but not Platonic universals, or postulate Platonic universals but not Platonic sets, propositions, or any other sort of Platonic particulars, or postulate Platonic sets but neither Platonic universals nor propositions.

---

[14] Many philosophers have thought that elementary arithmetic is best understood as ultimately concerning sets. If elementary arithmetic were best understood in this way, then this would be a good reason for accepting the existence of sets. An alternative view is that elementary arithmetic is best understood as ultimately concerning universals, for example, quantitative properties. If elementary arithmetic were best understood as ultimately concerning universals, then that would be a good reason for accepting the existence of universals.

[15] Another way to understand tropes is as particulars that cannot have spatial (or temporal) parts. So understood, tropes are *abstract* particulars rather than concrete particulars. Some trope theorists hold that tropes necessarily belong only to the objects that have them at any given time, and cannot be shared by different objects at other times. Other trope theorists hold that a given trope can be had by one object at one time and by a different object at another time. This difference in the understanding of tropes does not affect the issue of whether or not they are abstract or concrete entities.

3. AN ARGUMENT FOR UNIVERSALS

As we have stated, Platonic realists about universals hold that universals are intrinsically immutable, eternal, necessarily existent, mind-independent, and non-spatial. On the other hand, Aristotelian realists about universals hold that universals, though intrinsically immutable and mind-independent, are not necessarily existent, and, on some versions, hold that at least some universals are spatial and not eternal.

The opponent of the realist about universals argues that only concreta exist. Such an opponent can allow for the existence of entities such as substances, times, places, events, and tropes, but cannot accept the existence of abstracta such as universals (for example, properties or relations), sets, and propositions. This position is known as nominalism.

There are two main motivations for nominalism. First, there is the admirable commitment to Ockham's razor or a principle of ontological parsimony, a principle that requires one to postulate no more entities than are necessary to explain the data. Secondly, there is a queasiness about postulating entities that are unobservable or non-empirical, existing in a non-physical realm. The first motivates nominalists to oppose all forms of realism about universals. The second motivates nominalists to oppose any Platonistic version of realism about universals, and to oppose some Aristotelian versions of realism about universals.

The realist about universals counters that in order to account for a variety of data, one must postulate the existence of universals. What are these data? There are many statements that occur in our discourse which at least appear to be about shareable properties, for example:

(1) Morris has the property of being a cat.

The realist argues that at least some of these statements actually are about such properties, on the ground that these statements cannot be translated into equivalent ones that are not about shareable properties. If such an argument is sound, then shareable properties actually exist.

But according to the nominalist, there are no true statements about shareable properties, and any true statement apparently about such a property, such as (1), can be translated into one that is not about such a property. For example, (1) is just another way of saying that

(1a) Morris is a cat,

and (1a) is not about any shareable property.

A successful ontological translation may be held to have the same meaning as the original statement, but it must at least be necessarily equivalent to the original statement. If a translation is *not* synonymous with the original statement, then it must be an *analysis* of the original statement. Necessary equivalence is necessary but not sufficient for an analysis.[16]

The nominalist argues that because (1) is translatable as (1a), the truth of (1) does not actually commit us to the existence of shareable properties. After all, (1a) refers merely to a cat, i.e. Morris, and *a cat*, unlike *the property of being a cat*, is a concretum. As Quine would put the matter, when we put (1a) into quantified form, i.e. $(\exists x) (x =$ Morris & x is a cat), we do not quantify over shareable properties, but only over a concrete entity, namely, Morris. Since (1) is translatable as (1a), (1) does not require us to postulate the existence of shareable properties, and since an ontology of only concrete entities is more parsimonious than an ontology of both concrete and abstract entities, the nominalist concludes that we should not postulate the existence of abstract entities on the basis of truths like (1).

The realist believes that there are other true statements about shareable properties that are not so easily translated as (1). The ensuing discussion will follow this pattern. The realist will put forward various true statements, statements that apparently refer to shareable properties, and the nominalist will attempt to translate such statements without making any such references. In each case the realist's example will occur first, to be followed by one or more proposed nominalistic translations.

Before proceeding to our discussion of the realist's examples, it should be observed that nominalists have adopted at least three different strategies for translating the statements in question.[17] The 'meta-linguistic nominalist' attempts to translate these statements in terms of discourse about language. The 'trope nominalist' accepts the existence of tropes and offers translations that quantify over or refer to such concrete entities. The 'austere nominalist' offers translations that refer neither to language nor to tropes, but to such familiar concreta as substances, events, or states. We regard metalinguistic nominalism as the weakest approach. For example, this approach cannot even deal with (1). The metalinguistic nominalist would seek to translate (1) as *The predicate 'is a cat' applies to Morris*. This proposed translation is not equivalent to (1), for (1) can be true whether or not there is any language containing the predicate 'is a cat'. The same sort of difficulty always applies to any proposed metalinguistic translation.[18] For this reason, we will ignore all such proposals in what follows. However, we will discuss trope-nominalist translations in those cases where the difference between them and the austere-nominalist

---

[16] For example, *Red is a colour* is necessarily equivalent to *a bachelor is unmarried*, but the latter is not an analysis, and so not an adequate translation, of the former. A plausible translation of *Red is a colour* is discussed in the text below.

[17] For a detailed discussion of these three strategies, see Loux (1998, ch. 2).

[18] Similar remarks apply if a nominalist adopts a conceptualist translation strategy. For example, such a conceptualist would propose to translate (1) as *The concept of a cat applies to Morris*. But this proposed translation does not appear to be equivalent to (1), for it is not apparent that (1) entails the existence of a mind containing the concept of a cat. Similar difficulties affect conceptualist models of possible worlds. See our criticisms of such models in Sect. 4 below.

translation is of particular interest. One reason for adopting this procedure is that if all other things are equal, austere nominalism is ontologically more parsimonious than trope nominalism, and thus is preferable.

(2) Red is a colour.

A nominalist may plausibly hold that (2) can be translated as:

(2*a*) All red things are coloured things.

Notice that unlike (2), (2*a*) does not refer to *Red* (an abstract colour), but only to *red things* and *coloured things* (which are concreta).

(3) The property of being a horned horse is unexemplified.

(3), too, can be readily translated in a nominalistic fashion as:

(3*a*) There does not exist a horned horse.
(4)   Red resembles Orange more than it resembles Green.

A nominalist may try to translate (4) as

(4*a*) Red things resemble orange things more than they resemble green things.

But while (4) is necessarily true, (4*a*) is false. For example, a red Subaru resembles a green Subaru more than it resembles an orange fruit. Thus, (4) cannot be translated as (4*a*). Or a nominalist may attempt to translate (4) as

(4*b*) Red things resemble orange things in colour more than they resemble green things in colour.

But the phrase 'in colour' seems to refer to colours, for example, Red, Orange, Green, and so on, which are abstract entities. Thus, (4*b*) appears not to be a satisfactory nominalistic translation of (4). Similar difficulties apply to an attempted translation of (4) such as *The way in which red things are coloured resembles the way in which orange things are coloured more than it resembles the way in which green things are coloured.*

Nevertheless, a nominalist can apparently translate (4) as

(4*c*) If x is a red thing, y is an orange thing, and z is a green thing, and if x, y, and z are otherwise as similar as a red, orange, and green thing can be, then x resembles y more than x resembles z.

Although (4*c*) talks about what things *can be*, and 'can be' is a modal term, (4*c*) does not involve any explicit quantification over abstract entities. Thus, in the context of the present debate, (4*c*) suffices as a nominalistic translation of (4). However, later we will argue that modalities presuppose the existence of abstract entities, such as properties or propositions. Until then, we will not object to nominalistic translations that employ modalities provided that they make no explicit reference to abstract entities.

On the other hand, the trope nominalist might argue that (4) can be translated without employing modalities as

(4*d*) A trope of red intrinsically resembles a trope of orange more than it intrinsically resembles a trope of green.

(5)   Courage is a moral virtue.

(5) cannot be translated along the same lines as the superficially similar (2), namely, as

(5*a*) All courageous people are morally virtuous people.

While (5) is true, (5*a*) is false, since there are courageous Nazis who are not morally virtuous. That is, being courageous does not automatically make one morally virtuous *tout court*.[19] Note that since (5*a*) is false, an attempt to translate (5) as *All courageous people are morally good people* is doomed to failure. Similar criticisms apply to both of the following proposed translations of (5): *All courageous people tend to be morally virtuous people, All courageous actions are morally right,* and *All courageous actions are morally good*. Another possible translation is:

(5*b*) All other things being equal, a courageous person is a morally virtuous person.[20]

The realist might object to (5*b*) on the ground that it employs a *ceteris paribus* notion whose meaning is neither defined nor well understood. To this a nominalist can rejoin that the meaning of such a notion is clear but primitive and unanalysable. This debate over (5*b*) appears to end in a stalemate, but, of course, it is preferable for a nominalist to have a translation that does not employ an unanalysable primitive notion of this kind.

A similar attempt to translate (5) is:

(5*c*) If *x* is courageous, then to that extent, *x* is morally virtuous.

Similar comments apply to the notion of *to that extent* as apply to the notion of *other things being equal*.

(5*d*) Be courageous!

This proposed translation assumes that (5) is neither true nor false, but really a disguised imperative or prescription. Notice that this proposed translation commits one to an extreme form of anti-realism in ethics (and in value theory more generally). To many, this is too high a price to pay for a defence of nominalism, and,

---

[19] According to the Socratic conception of moral virtue, one cannot possess a particular moral virtue unless one possesses *every* moral virtue, and hence one cannot be courageous unless one is virtuous *tout court*. Assuming that a Nazi cannot be virtuous *tout court*, on the Socratic conception of moral virtue it follows that there could not be a courageous Nazi. We (and most contemporary moral philosophers) reject the Socratic conception of moral virtue.

[20] Michael Loux suggests that this is the best that an 'austere nominalist' can do to translate (5). See Loux (1998, ch. 2).

in any case, a defence of a nominalistic translation that is neutral about the moral realism–moral irrealism debate is much to be preferred over one that is not.

(5e) A courage trope is a virtue trope.

(5e) implies that when someone is courageous, that person possesses a particular courageousness, and that this particular courageousness possesses a trope of being a particular virtue. Given this commitment to an ontology of tropes, we can find no fault with this proposed translation. But as we noted earlier, *ceteris paribus*, austere nominalism is preferable to trope nominalism.

(5f) If *x* is courageous and *y* is not, and if *x* and *y* are otherwise as similar as a courageous person and a non-courageous person can be, then it is *at least* probable that *x* is more morally virtuous than *y*.

(5f) is compatible with a controversial view about the original (5), namely, that courage is only contingently a moral virtue. If this is correct, then (5) is not a necessary truth. This controversial claim might be supported by the earlier example of the courageous Nazi, who, it appears, is not made more virtuous by being courageous, but, arguably, more vicious. Thus, if most persons were, in some possible world, consistently Nazi-like, then in that world, arguably, courage would not be a moral virtue. But given the actual nature of all known moral agents, namely, human beings, the possession of courage is at least likely to increase the virtue of its possessors. (5f) is also compatible with the view that (5) is necessarily true, since in that case, it is *at least* probable, namely, it is *necessary*, that under the conditions in question, *x* is more morally virtuous than *y*. We conclude that (5f) is a fairly plausible austere-nominalist translation of (5), and all other things being equal, preferable to (5e), the trope-nominalist translation.

(6) The tomato and the fire engine have the same colour.[21]

A nominalist can plausibly translate (6) as

(6a) The tomato and the fire engine are coloured the same as one another.

Note that while an adverbial expression such as '*x* is coloured the same as *y*' *relates* a concrete *coloured thing*, *x*, to a concrete *coloured thing*, *y*, an adverbial expression of this kind does not seem to refer to abstract *colours*. Moreover, since the meaning of such an adverbial expression is *intuitively clear*, a nominalist does not seem to be obliged to *define* the adverbial expression in question.

(7) That shape has been exemplified many times.[22]

A plausible nominalistic translation of (7) is

(7a) That shaped thing (or anything shaped exactly like it) is such that many shaped things have been shaped the same as it is.

(8) Some characteristics of physical objects are as yet undiscovered by us.

---

[21] This example is from Loux (1998: 66).   [22] This example is from Loux (1998: 67).

A nominalist can plausibly translate (8) as

(8a) Some physical objects are characterized differently than any of us, as of yet, has discovered any physical object to be characterized.

Notice (8a), unlike (8), does not quantify over hitherto undiscovered abstract *characteristics* of physical objects, but instead merely describes *concrete physical objects* as *characterized* differently than we have discovered any physical object to be characterized. Thus, (8a), unlike (8), does not appear to quantify over (or refer to) abstract properties.

(9) The property of being a horned dinosaur is other than the property of being a feathered quadruped.

A nominalist may try to translate (9) as

(9a) Every concrete thing is such that it is not both a horned dinosaur and a feathered quadruped.

But, *possibly*, some horned dinosaur is a feathered quadruped. Since (9) is *necessarily true*, it follows that, possibly, (9) is true and (9a) is false. Thus, (9a) is not equivalent to (9). So, (9a) is not an adequate translation of (9). Similar remarks apply to an attempted nominalistic translation of (9) as *Every concrete thing is such that it is not either a horned dinosaur or a feathered quadruped.*

A plausible austere-nominalist translation of (9) is

(9b) Possibly, there is a horned dinosaur that is not a feathered quadruped (or a feathered quadruped that is not a horned dinosaur).

But it also seems to be true that

(10) Being a triangle is other than being a trilateral.

(10) cannot be translated along the lines that (9) was, since it is impossible for there to be a triangle that is not a trilateral, or for there to be a trilateral that is not a triangle. Examples such as (10) are important because an austere nominalist cannot translate them without introducing psychologically intensional contexts (of belief, thought, conception, knowledge, etc.). For example, one promising translation of (10) appears to be

(10a) Possibly, someone thinks that something is a triangle without thinking that something is a trilateral (or thinks that something is a trilateral without thinking that something is a triangle).

The realist might object to (10a) as a *nominalistic translation* on the ground that the objects of thought are abstract entities, such as properties or propositions, so that (10a) implicitly commits us to abstracta. Although this is a serious rejoinder, we will not address this issue any further in this chapter.

On the other hand, a trope nominalist can translate both (9) and (10) without employing modalities. For example, a trope nominalist can translate (9) as

(9c) A trope of being a horned dinosaur is other than a trope of being a feathered quadruped, and a trope nominalist can translate (10) as

(10*b*) A trope of triangularity is other than a trope of trilaterality.

Our final example presents the most serious challenge, we believe, to nominalism.[23]

(11) There are shapes that are never exemplified.

Plato argued that the natural world does not contain a perfect triangle or a perfect square on the ground that no natural object ever has sides that are perfectly straight. Since a perfect triangle and a perfect square are possible, if Plato is right, then it seems that *perfect triangularity* and *perfect squareness* are shapes that are never exemplified, and hence that (11) is true. In any case, it appears that the natural world does not ever contain either a regular polygon having a googolplex of sides or a 114-dimensional analogue of a cube. Nonetheless, shaped objects of these kinds are geometrically possible. Thus, it appears that *being a regular polygon having a googolplex of sides* and *being a 114-dimensional analogue of a cube* are examples of shapes that are never exemplified. And there seem to be infinitely many other examples of such unexemplified shapes. Hence, it appears that (11) is true.

A nominalist might offer the following translation of (11):

(11*a*) Possibly, there are shaped objects *x* and *y* such that (i) *x* is shaped differently from *y*, and (ii) *x* and *y* are shaped differently from anything that ever exists.

However, it is self-contradictory to say that *there are* shaped objects that are shaped differently from anything that *ever exists*. Thus, it is *not* possible that there are such shaped objects, and so (11*a*) is *necessarily false*. Since (11) is true, and (11*a*) is false, we conclude that (11) cannot be translated as (11*a*).

Obviously, parallel remarks apply if 'objects' in (11*a*) is replaced with 'tropes'. So, (11) cannot be translated in such a way by the trope nominalist.

(11*a*) is incoherent because it attributes possibility to a dictum or proposition that is impossible, i.e. *that there are shaped objects that are shaped differently from anything that ever exists*. However, possibility may also be attributed to a *res*, or a *thing*. Thus, we should distinguish *de dicto* possibility, e.g. the possibility of a proposition's being true, from *de re* possibility, e.g. a thing's possibly having a property. For instance, although *de dicto* the proposition *that a man who is sitting now is not sitting now* is certainly impossible, it is true *de re* that a man who is sitting now is possibly not sitting now. After all, while the *proposition* in question is self-contradictory, it is surely the case that a *man* who is sitting now could have been standing now instead.

---

[23] This example is due to Chisholm (1996: 21).

Accordingly, a nominalist might attempt to translate (11) by using *de re* possibility as follows.

(11*b*) For any physical objects *x* and *y*, *x* and *y* are possibly such that they are shaped differently from any physical object and differently from one another.

(11*b*) entails (11). Moreover, unlike (11*a*), (11*b*) is not self-contradictory, or obviously impossible. But (11*b*) is a translation of (11) only if it is also the case that (11) entails (11*b*). However, (11) does *not* entail (11*b*). One way to see this is in terms of the possibility of intrinsically immutable shaped objects, for example, Democritean atoms. Such atoms have their shapes *necessarily* (or *essentially*), and so are not possibly shaped differently. Since (11) is true in some possible worlds containing Democritean atoms, but (11*b*) is false in all such worlds, (11) and (11*b*) are not equivalent. Thus, (11) cannot be translated as (11*b*).

Parallel remarks apply to an attempt to translate (11) as *For any shape trope T, T is possibly shaped differently from any shape trope*. After all, a shape trope, like a Democritean atom, is not possibly shaped differently from the way it is shaped.

Nor does replacing 'any' in (11*b*) with 'some' result in a translation of (11). Clearly, there are possible worlds containing Democritean atoms in which this latest proposal is *false* and (11) is *true*. Moreover, such a proposal entails the existence of physical objects, while (11) does not seem to do so.

Next, a nominalist may propose to translate (11) as

(11*c*) Either there are never any round things and never any triangular things, or there are never any round things and never any square things, or there are never any triangular things and never any square things, or there are never any round things and never any pentagonal things, or there are never any square things and never any pentagonal things, or there are never any triangular things and never any pentagonal things . . .

Notice that (11) does *not* entail a finitely long version of (11*c*) that *omits* the concluding ellipsis. For example, *possibly*, (11) is *true*, because *being a regular polygon with a googolplex of sides* is never exemplified, but (11*c*) without the ellipsis is *false*, because there *are* round things, triangular things, square things, and pentagonal things. Considerations of the same kind apply to any finitely long version of (11*c*) that omits the concluding ellipsis. So, no finitely long version of (11*c*) of this kind can serve as a nominalistic translation of (11). Moreover, we cannot set forth an *infinitely long* version of (11*c*), one that *replaces* the ellipsis with an *uncountable infinity* of conjunctive disjuncts. Thus, for the purposes of a proposed translation such as (11*c*) the concluding ellipsis is *indispensable*.

It follows that (11*c*) can serve as a nominalistic translation of (11) only if we can nominalistically define the concluding ellipsis in (11*c*). But it is very doubtful that we can do this. Although (11) is *true*, it is obvious that any version of (11*c*) that refers to (or quantifies over) just *actually existing* shaped things (or kinds of them) is *false*. So, it seems that (11*c*) is equivalent to (11) only if the ellipsis in (11*c*) is spelled out in terms of quantification over *all possible kinds of shaped things*. In particular, it appears that (11*c*) is equivalent to (11) only if the ellipsis in (11*c*) is shorthand for *continue so as to include, for any two possible kinds of shaped things, a disjunct (consisting of two conjuncts) which entails that those two kinds of shaped things never exist*.[24] But a *possible kind of shaped thing* sounds suspiciously like an abstract entity, and arguably can be identified with a shape universal. And to quantify instead over all *possible* shape tropes would not seem to help the trope nominalist to translate (11). After all, it is far from clear that we can coherently quantify over *non-existent* possible tropes without being committed to quantifying over abstracta. Since it is not apparent that the ellipsis in (11*c*) can be spelled out without quantifying over, or referring to, abstracta, it does not seem that (11*c*) can serve as a nominalistic translation of (11).

Some nominalists might now be tempted to reply that (11) is actually *false* on the ground that an unexemplified shape does not exist. If such a reply were justified, then a nominalist would be entitled to reject (11) without translating it. But in the light of the apparent truth of (11), any nominalist who makes this reply assumes the burden of proof. Moreover, consistency apparently requires that such a nominalist also hold that (1)–(10) are false on the ground that (1)–(10) fail genuinely to refer to existing properties. But, unfortunately for this sort of nominalist, it seems to be undeniable that at least many of (1)–(10) are *true*. For example, surely, it is (contingently) true both that *Morris has the property of being a cat* and that *the tomato and the fire-engine have the same colour*. Moreover, *Red is a colour* is known to be (necessarily) true a priori (and likewise, it appears, for *Red resembles Orange more than it resembles Green*). Since it seems undeniable that the foregoing examples are true, and since it would be ad hoc for a nominalist to accept these examples and to reject (11), the nominalist reply under discussion appears to be unsound.

Given our discussion of (11) up to this point, it appears that *even with the introduction of modalities* the trope nominalist has no advantage over the austere nominalist in translating (11).

At this juncture it may be observed that (11) is equivalent to

(11*d*) In some possible world, there are things that are shaped differently from one another and differently from anything that ever exists in the actual world.

Can (11*d*) serve as a nominalistic translation of (11)? The important thing about (11*d*) is that it introduces quantification over (or reference to) *possible worlds*.[25] The nature of possible worlds is a matter of controversy. According to the most widely

---

[24] While earlier proposed translations of (11) such as (11*a*) and (11*b*) made use of *possibility*, they did *not* explicitly quantify over all *possible kinds of shaped things*.

[25] Although earlier proposed translations of (11) such as (11*a*) and (11*b*) made use of *possibility*, they did *not* explicitly quantify over *possible worlds*.

held accounts of their nature, possible worlds are abstract entities such as properties or propositions (or sets of them). But according to an important alternative account, possible worlds are concreta. Evidently, if possible worlds are abstracta, then (11*d*) cannot serve as a nominalistic translation of (11). On the other hand, if possible worlds are concreta, then it seems that (11*d*) can serve as such a translation. In the final section of this chapter, we will defend the idea that possible worlds are abstract entities such as properties or propositions (or sets of them). Thus, assuming that we are right, a nominalist cannot translate (11) as (11*d*). In the light of our earlier discussion of proposed translations of (11), if (11) cannot be translated as (11*d*), then it appears that a nominalist's prospects for translating (11) are not good. To the extent that a nominalist is unable to translate (11), the existence of Platonic universals, i.e. unexemplified shapes, seems to be plausible. Moreover, we remind the reader that several of our earlier examples appear to be translatable (for an austere nominalist) only by employing modality, for example, possibility. The examples in question are (4), (5), (9), and (10). Since we share the widely accepted view that modalities, i.e. possibility, necessity, impossibility, and contingency, need to be understood in terms of a possible worlds semantics, we conclude that if our argument in the next section is correct, (11) poses a serious challenge to nominalism of any sort,[26] and (4), (5), (9), and (10) all pose a serious challenge to austere nominalism.

4. Modality and Platonic Realism

According to one traditional argument for Platonic realism, an adequate account of the nature of possibility implies the existence of Platonic abstract entities. This argument (call it Argument A) may be stated as follows.

(A1) There are non-obtaining possibilities, e.g. *there being winged quadrupeds.*

(A2) A non-obtaining possibility is not a concrete entity.

(A3) Everything is either abstract or concrete.

(A4) Therefore, there are abstract non-obtaining possibilities.

(A5) These abstract non-obtaining possibilities have necessary existence.

(A6) If there are abstract non-obtaining possibilities that have necessary existence, then Platonic realism is true.

(A7) Hence, Platonic realism is true.

---

[26] For a defence of the thesis that geometry is best understood as the study of geometrical Platonic universals, see Rosenkrantz (1981: 101–10).

Clearly, Argument A is logically valid. Thus, if all of the premisses of Argument A are true, then Platonic realism is true. But are all the premisses of Argument A true? Notice that since (A4) is incompatible with nominalism, a nominalist must reject either (A1), (A2), or (A3). However, (A1) and (A3) are extremely plausible, and most nominalists would accept them. Moreover, (A2) strikes us as intuitively plausible. For example, it seems to us that a non-obtaining possibility such as *there being winged quadrupeds* is *not* a concrete entity. If non-obtaining possibilities are abstract entities, then possible worlds also are abstract entities. Yet, some contemporary philosophers have rejected (A2) on the ground that possible worlds are *concrete entities*. If these philosophers are correct, then (A2) is false and Argument A is unsound. In that case Argument A does *not* justify the acceptance of Platonic realism. Thus, whether Argument A justifies the acceptance of abstract non-obtaining possibilities depends upon the ontological status of possible worlds, and in particular, upon whether possible worlds are abstracta or concreta.

In what follows, we defend Argument A by arguing for the view that possible worlds are abstracta. That is, we shall argue that an adequate conception of the ontological status of possible worlds implies that possible worlds are *abstract* necessary beings such as propositions or properties (or sets of them).

There are four general positions on the ontological status of possible worlds that need to be considered: the *conceptualist model*, the *combinatorial model*, the *abstract worlds model*, and the *concrete worlds model*.

According to the conceptualist model, possible worlds are *mental constructions*, for instance, complexes of thoughts or concepts (see e.g. Rescher 1975). The conceptualist model implies that for any x, if x is possible, then x is possible *because* there are one or more thinkers who have an idea of x. But then the thinkers *themselves* are possible *because* they have *reflective ideas*, that is, ideas of *themselves*. This seems to get things backwards: it appears that reflective ideas are possible *because* thinkers are possible. Thus, it seems that there is an explanatory incoherence at the very heart of the conceptualist model.[27] If this is correct, then the conceptual model is unacceptable.

Furthermore, the conceptualist model implies that if there are never any reflective thinkers, then there are never any possibilities at all. Thus, if it is *possible* that there are never any reflective thinkers, then the conceptualist model has the absurd consequence that *it is possible that there are never any possibilities at all*. The conceptualist model can avoid this absurdity only by presupposing that it is *necessary* that there is a reflective being, for example, God. But it is not clear to us that there is sufficient

---

[27]   The conceptualist model of possibility is subject to this difficulty because it implies that possibility is a *subjective* matter. It should be observed that a similar criticism applies to a subjective theory of truth, for example, the theory that a proposition p is true for us if and only if we believe p. This theory of truth implies that the proposition *that there are beliefs* is true because we *believe* that there are beliefs. Since nothing can be explanatorily prior to itself, such an explanation of the truth of this proposition is absurd.

epistemic justification for accepting this controversial presupposition. (A practitioner of *rational theology* should accept the presupposition in question only if he or she has sufficient epistemic justification for accepting it.) Thus, we have doubts about any model of possible worlds that depends upon such a presupposition.

According to the combinatorial model, the actual world is the set or collection of everything there is, and the other possible worlds consist of all of the possible combinations of the basic entities that exist in the actual world (see e.g. Cresswell 1972: 1–13). Unfortunately, though, this model cannot accommodate possible worlds containing fundamental particles or souls that do not exist in the actual world. We assume that a model of possible worlds should allow for such worlds. However, since fundamental particles and souls are not compound things, possible fundamental particles or souls which do not exist in the actual world cannot be understood in terms of possible combinations of basic entities that exist in the actual world. We regard this as a rather serious shortcoming of the combinatorial model.

According to the abstract worlds model (AWM), a possible world is an *abstract entity*, for instance, a very large conjunction of propositions, a conjunction which is *maximal* or *suitably complete*, and which does not imply a contradiction. Such an infinite conjunction of propositions is itself a possible proposition. AWM is associated with Alvin Plantinga (1974). AWM presupposes the classic logical law of excluded middle, i.e. that every proposition is either true or false, and also that every proposition has necessary existence. According to AWM, the actual world includes only *true* propositions.[28] There are infinitely many other possible worlds, and each of them includes one or more *false* propositions.

On the other hand, according to the concrete worlds model (CWM), a possible world is a *concrete entity*, for example, a causally isolated collection of concrete things. This model is associated with David Lewis (1968: 113–26). According to CWM, each of the infinitely many concrete worlds is causally inaccessible to all of the others. *The actual world* is the collection of concrete things of which *we* are a part. Some *other* possible worlds are collections of concrete things of which *we* are *not* a part. It follows that no single thing exists in more than one possible world, though each thing has *counterparts* in other worlds that resemble it. *Transworld identity* is rejected on the ground that no formal criterion of transworld identity is available.

It might be argued that CWM is unacceptable because it implies that *all* of a concrete entity's *dated properties* are essential to it. On this model concrete entities are 'world-bound'; each of them exists in just *one* possible world. Moreover, necessarily, if an entity *e* has a property at some time *t*, then at *every* time it is true that *e* has

---

[28] There are variations upon AWM, depending upon the precise ontology of abstract entities employed, for example, *conjunctions of properties* may be substituted for *conjunctions of propositions*, or *sets* of properties or propositions may be substituted for *conjunctions* of them. Since for our purposes these variations are not particularly important, we ignore them in the text and take Plantinga's version of AWM as representative.

that property at t. Hence, CWM implies that for any concrete entity x, any property F, and any time t, if x has F at t, then it is literally impossible for x to lack F at t. For example, if Jones is sitting at t, then CWM implies that it is literally impossible that *Jones* is not sitting at t. Thus, CWM appears to imply that Jones is *essentially* sitting at t. But this implication of CWM is extremely unintuitive: it certainly seems literally possible for *Jones* to be standing at t rather than sitting at t. It follows that there is an intuitive sense in which Jones appears to be *accidentally* sitting at t. So, it seems that by implying that Jones is essentially sitting at t, CWM is guilty of a kind of *excessive essentialism*. Lewis seeks to escape this charge of excessive essentialism by *redefining* an essential property of a concrete entity as a property of a concrete entity which *every* counterpart of that concrete entity possesses; and by *redefining* an accidental property of a concrete entity as a property of a concrete entity which *some* counterpart of that concrete entity lacks. In particular, Lewis would argue that since there is a possible world in which a counterpart of Jones is standing at t, Jones is accidentally sitting at t. Still, because a counterpart of Jones is someone *other than* Jones, this alleged sense of Jones's accidentally sitting at t is a rather unintuitive one. Moreover, AWM sustains a much more intuitive understanding of Jones's accidentally sitting at t, an understanding which implies that in some possible world *Jones* is not sitting at t. Is there a good reason why we should settle for CWM and the unintuitive understanding of Jones's accidentally sitting at t that it requires?

Ontological parsimony is often given as a reason for preferring CWM to AWM. The contention is that CWM posits only concrete entities, whereas AWM posits both concrete entities and abstract entities.[29] It is claimed that by positing abstract entities AWM multiplies entities unnecessarily. Since one should not multiply entities unnecessarily, it can be argued that CWM is preferable to AWM.

Nevertheless, ontological parsimony is a good reason for preferring CWM to AWM only if CWM accommodates the data. Indeed, if a theory T_1 accommodates the data, and another theory T_2 does not, then T_1 is preferable to T_2 even if T_2 is ontologically more parsimonious than T_1. AWM accommodates the intuitive datum that it is literally possible for *Jones* to be standing at t rather than sitting at t, but it seems that CWM does not. Thus, it appears that *even if* CWM is ontologically more parsimonious than AWM, AWM is preferable to CWM.

In any case there are good reasons to deny that ontological parsimony favours CWM over AWM. To begin with, Lewis accepts the existence of sets. In particular, Lewis reduces a property F-ness to the set containing all sets of Fs in all possible worlds, where each of the contained sets has as its elements all of the entities that are F in a given possible world. But sets are *abstract* entities.[30] Thus, it seems that AWM does not enable us to avoid postulating abstract entities after all.

---

[29] For an account of the abstract–concrete distinction, see Sect. 1.

[30] Our account of the notion of an abstract entity in sect. 1 is consistent with the intuition that a set is an abstract entity. We have argued that while sets can have members, they cannot have parts. (Parthood

Indeed, it can even be argued plausibly that ontological parsimony favours AWM over CWM. To see this, notice that there are two relevant ways in which entities can be multiplied unnecessarily: (i) by multiplying unnecessarily the number of *explanatory categories*, and (ii) by multiplying unnecessarily the number of entities *within* an explanatory category. When nominalists argue that their ontology of concrete entities is more parsimonious than the realist's ontology of concrete and abstract entities, their argument is that realism multiplies entities unnecessarily in the *first* of these two ways. On the other hand, when Copernicus argues that his heliocentric theory of the solar system is more parsimonious than Ptolemy's geocentric theory on the ground that it utilizes far fewer epicycles, Copernicus' argument is that Ptolemy's theory of the solar system multiplies entities unnecessarily in the *second* of the two ways. Since the proponents of CWM postulate the existence of abstract sets, and since there are an uncountable infinity of abstract sets, it seems that CWM is just as committed as AWM to an uncountable infinity of abstract entities. But unlike AWM, CWM is also committed to an uncountable infinity of concrete individual things. Hence, proponents of AWM can argue plausibly that CWM multiplies *concrete entities* unnecessarily. This is to multiply entities unnecessarily in the second of the two ways specified earlier.

But there are two replies that might be offered on behalf of Lewis. First, it might be argued that if propositions are abstract entities of an irreducible category, then there are abstract entities of *another* irreducible category, for example, properties or sets.[31] However, such a reply presupposes that sets are abstract entities of an irreducible category and that *their* existence does *not* imply that there are abstract entities of another irreducible category. But then it cannot be assumed that the existence of irreducible propositions (or properties) implies that there are irreducible abstract entities of another category, e.g. sets.[32] So, it does not seem to be true that AWM must reduce properties or propositions to sets in order to avoid being committed to abstract entities of more irreducible categories than CWM. We conclude that this first reply is problematic.

Secondly, it might be argued that abstract properties and propositions are suspect because they lack a formal criterion of identity, while abstract sets are *not*

is a transitive relation, but Membership is not.) Since a set cannot have spatial or temporal parts, a set qualifies as an abstract entity on our account.

[31] An *irreducible category* is an ontological category that cannot be reduced to another ontological category; and a *reducible category* is an ontological category that can be reduced to another ontological category. Positing entities of *reducible* categories multiplies entities unnecessarily only if positing entities of the irreducible categories to which they ultimately can be reduced multiplies entities unnecessarily. Thus, what fundamentally needs to be considered in this case is the number of *irreducible categories* of abstract entities.

[32] Although Plantinga's possible worlds take propositions as irreducible, alternative schemes define abstract possible worlds in terms of properties, taken as irreducible. So, given our argument in the text, arguably, there are abstract properties, but there are not abstract entities of another irreducible category.

suspect in this respect. Sets, it is argued, have a formal criterion of identity in terms of their membership: a set $S_1 =$ a set S_2 if and only if S_1 and S_2 have the same members. This reply presupposes that a category of entity that lacks a formal criterion of identity is suspect. But we shall argue that this presupposition is false. If there is a formal criterion of identity for entities of some category, then this criterion must refer to entities that belong to one or more *other* categories. For instance, sets cannot be identified unless there is reference to entities which belong to other categories and which are members of sets; and arguably, substances are identified by reference to attributes, places are identified by reference to bodies, times are identified by reference to events, and so on. Hence, in each such case either (i) there is an *infinite regress* of these references, (ii) there is a *circle* of these references, or (iii) there is a *stopping place*: a reference to an entity which has *primitive* identity, i.e. which lacks a formal criterion of identity and which is therefore not identified by reference to anything else. Of these three alternatives it is the third and final one that is by far the most plausible. Thus, it is very likely that there are entities that have primitive identity. And propositions (or properties) are as good candidates as any for entities with primitive identity. Therefore, the lack of a formal criterion of identity for propositions (or properties) should not place them under suspicion. Consequently, the second reply on behalf of Lewis does not succeed.

In a related vein, it may be noted that scepticism about transworld identity is fuelled by doubts about the possibility of a formal criterion of transworld identity for concrete entities.[33] But the demand for a formal criterion of *transworld identity* for concrete entities is no more reasonable than the demand for a formal criterion of *identity* for propositions (or properties). Primitive identities are acceptable in both of these cases.

Further criticisms of CWM raise doubts about the intelligibility and intuitiveness of its ontological presuppositions. First, CWM postulates the existence of infinitely many causally isolated concrete worlds. That is, according to CWM, no entity in one possible concrete world can interact with, or even be located within the same space-time continuum as an entity in another possible concrete world. But the intelligibility of radically isolated, spatio-temporally discontinuous physical systems of this kind is questionable.[34] Secondly, even if CWM is intelligible,

---

[33] For an argument that implies that a formal criterion of transworld identity for concrete entities can be formulated in terms of their haecceities, see Rosenkrantz (1993).

[34] Although we would concede the intelligibility of discontinuities in the spatial or temporal paths that an object follows within space or time, such discontinuities are different in kind from the ones whose intelligibility we do not countenance. Only the latter involves discontinuities between one space-time continuum and another, and the causal inaccessibility of one continuum from another. We are also sceptical of the intelligibility of speculative theories in contemporary physics that posit radically isolated, spatio-temporally discontinuous physical systems, e.g. the many-worlds interpretation of quantum mechanics.

the ontology it postulates is wildly unintuitive. No ordinary language-user who understands modal discourse has the faintest idea that by using such terms he is thereby committed to the existence of infinitely many causally isolated concrete universes. Such an ordinary language-user would be astonished to hear that his modal discourse implies the existence of infinitely many 'counterparts' to himself and to every other actual object. Lewis might reply that the same language-user would be as astonished to learn that his modal discourse implied the existence of infinitely many causally inaccessible abstract entities, as AWM implies. But, as we saw earlier, there are a great many terms in ordinary language that certainly appear to be the names of abstract entities, abstract singular terms such as 'Courage', 'Redness', 'Squareness', and so forth. On the other hand, there are no terms in ordinary language that appear to name one's counterparts. Moreover, as discussed earlier, CWM itself postulates the existence of infinitely many causally inaccessible abstract entities, namely, sets. For these reasons, it certainly looks as though CWM's ontological presuppositions are less intuitive than AWM's.

Our conclusion, based upon the foregoing considerations, is that AWM is preferable to CWM.[35] Moreover, since AWM provides an account of possible worlds that is objective, AWM is free of the defects of the conceptualist model. In addition, unlike the combinatorial model, AWM allows for the possibility of fundamental particles and/or souls that do not exist in the actual world. AWM allows for the possibility of these simple substances because AWM implies that for any possible substance, actual or non-actual, simple or compound, there is a proposition of the form 'a exists' which is necessarily such that it is true (false) just in case the possible substance in question exists (does not exist). It can be argued that a singular proposition of this kind involves a haecceity or individual essence that is either exemplified (when the possible substance exists) or unexemplified (when the possible substance does not exist). So, AWM identifies a possible world in which there is a simple substance that does not exist in the actual world with a maximal conjunctive proposition that has as a conjunct an appropriate contingently *false* singular contingent proposition of the aforementioned sort. Hence, AWM does not have the drawback of the combinatorial model (of ruling out non-actual possible simple substances).

Thus, of the four models of possible worlds considered, AWM appears to be the best. Since AWM implies that there are (true and false) abstract propositions that are necessary beings or (exemplified and unexemplified) abstract properties that are necessary beings, there are reasons for accepting the existence of abstract necessary beings of at least one of these kinds. (The actual world consists of only true propositions or only exemplified properties, and each one of the non-actual possible worlds

---

[35] For additional considerations that favour AWM, see Rosenkrantz (1983, ch. 3).

partly consists of some false propositions, e.g. *there being winged quadrupeds*, or some unexemplified properties, e.g. *being a winged quadruped*.)[36]

To conclude, we have argued that there is an unavoidable employment of modalities in the translation of many truths apparently about universals. We have also argued that the only adequate semantics for such modalities is provided by AWM, and that AWM commits us to the existence of Platonic abstract entities. In other words, we have made a plausible case, we believe, that Argument A is sound, and that Platonic realism is true.

However, to this point, our argument establishes at most that either propositions or Platonic universals exist. It might be argued on behalf of a Platonism of properties and relations without propositions that any truth seemingly about propositions can be translated into one about properties and/or relations. Similarly, one might argue on behalf of a Platonism of propositions without properties or relations that any truth apparently about properties or relations can be translated into one about propositions. It may very well be that if one considers only translation arguments, there is no reason for preferring one of these Platonic ontologies to the other. However, there is a consideration of another kind that lends support to an ontology that includes Platonic universals. In particular, it is intuitive to suppose that any proposition has one or more properties or relations as constituents. A plausible argument in support of this supposition is that any proposition can be analysed in terms of quantifiers, properties and/or relations, and logical or modal connectives and operators.[37] For example, the proposition that all men are mortal can be analysed as (x) (if x has the property of being a man, then x has the property of being mortal), the proposition that Rosenkrantz exists can be analysed either as $(\exists x)$ $(x = \text{Rosenkrantz})$, or as $(\exists x)$ (x has the property of being identical with Rosenkrantz),[38] and the proposition that something is non-self-instantiating can be analysed as $(\exists x)$ (x lacks the property of being self-instantiating).[39] Examples of this kind support the idea that all propositions have a degree of *structural complexity* that

---

[36] Recall that on some variants of AWM, possible worlds are properties (or sets or conjunctions of them). See n. 28.

[37] This argument is suggested by a remark of Bertrand Russell (1959: 93): 'It will be seen that no sentence can be made up without at least one word which denotes a universal ... Thus all truths involve universals, and all knowledge of truths involves acquaintance with universals.'

[38] By the proposition that Rosenkrantz exists, we mean the proposition that *he* would express by saying 'I exist'. Note that '=' signifies a (two-term) relation, namely, Identity. Since Identity is a relation that *everything* bears to itself, but to nothing else, Identity is a universal. On the other hand, *being identical with Rosenkrantz*, that is to say, his haecceity, is an individual essence. An individual essence of an entity *e* is an essential property of *e* that is necessarily repugnant to anything else. So, although Rosenkrantz's haecceity is a property, it is not a universal. Nothing in this chapter requires us to prefer one of the two analyses of *Rosenkrantz exists* to the other.

[39] See n. 12, where it is shown that there is no such property as *being non-self-instantiating*, since to suppose otherwise entails a logical contradiction. However, it appears to be logically consistent to suppose both that there is such a proposition as *something is non-self-instantiating*, and that there is such a property as *being self-instantiating*.

can be understood in terms of their constitutive properties and/or relations. On the other hand, it is clearly not the case that a property or relation such as Redness or Betweenness has a *proposition* as a constituent.[40] Since it seems that *every* proposition has one or more properties or relations as constituents, but it is *not* generally the case that a property or a relation has a proposition as a constituent, it seems that properties and relations are *ontologically prior* to propositions. The foregoing line of reasoning gives us reason to prefer an ontology of Platonic universals without propositions to one of propositions without Platonic universals. Thus, the considerations in Section 3 concerning the unavoidability of modalities in ontological translations lead us to accept an ontology that includes at least Platonic universals. Whether or not an adequate ontology would include propositions (and/or sets) as well as Platonic properties and relations is an issue worth further exploration, but one that falls outside the scope of this chapter.

References

Armstrong, D. M. (1978*a*). *Nominalism and Realism*, vol. i of Armstrong, *Universals and Scientific Realism*. Cambridge: Cambridge University Press.

—— (1978*b*). *A Theory of Universals*, vol. ii of Armstrong, *Universals and Scientific Realism*. Cambridge: Cambridge University Press.

—— (1989). *Universals: An Opinionated Introduction*. Boulder, Colo.: Westview Press.

Campbell, Keith (1990). *Abstract Particulars*. Oxford: Basil Blackwell.

Chisholm, Roderick (1976). *Person and Object: A Metaphysical Study*. LaSalle, Ill.: Open Court.

—— (1996). *A Realistic Theory of Categories*. Cambridge: Cambridge University Press.

Cresswell, Hugh (1972). 'The World is Everything that is the Case'. *Australasian Journal of Philosophy*, 50: 1–13.

Hoffman, Joshua, and Gary Rosenkrantz (1994). *Substance among Other Categories*. Cambridge: Cambridge University Press.

Kim, Jaegwon (1981). 'The Role of Perception in *A Priori* Knowledge: Some Remarks'. *Philosophical Studies*, 40: 339–54.

Lewis, David (1968). 'Counter-part Theory and Quantified Modal Logic'. *Journal of Philosophy*, 65: 113–26.

—— (1983). 'New Work for a Theory of Universals'. *Australasian Journal of Philosophy*, 61: 343–77.

—— (1986). *On the Plurality of Worlds*. Oxford: Basil Blackwell.

Loux, Michael (1978). *Substance and Attribute*. Dordrecht: Reidel.

—— (1979). *The Possible and the Actual*. Notre Dame, Ind.: University of Notre Dame Press.

—— (1998). *Metaphysics: A Contemporary Introduction*. London: Routledge.

Lowe, E. J. (1989). *Kinds of Being*. Oxford: Basil Blackwell.

---

[40] On the other hand, it appears that a *special* property like *being such that* $2 + 2 = 4$ does have a proposition as a constituent, namely, the proposition that $2 + 2 = 4$.

Lowe, E. J. (1995). Review of *Haecceity: An Ontological Essay*. *Mind*, 413: 202–5.
—— (1998). *The Possibility of Metaphysics*. Oxford: Oxford University Press.
Plantinga, Alvin (1974). *The Nature of Necessity*. Oxford: Oxford University Press.
Quine, W. V. O. (1953). *From a Logical Point of View*. Cambridge, Mass.: Harvard University Press.
—— (1960). *Word and Object*. Cambridge, Mass.: Harvard University Press.
Rescher, Nicholas (1975). *A Theory of Possibility*. Pittsburgh: University of Pittsburgh Press.
Rosenkrantz, Gary (1981). 'The Nature of Geometry'. *American Philosophical Quarterly*, 18: 101–10.
—— (1993). *Haecceity: An Ontological Essay*. Dordrecht: Reidel.
Russell, Bertrand (1959). *The Problems of Philosophy*. Oxford: Oxford University Press.
Stout, G. F. (1921). *The Nature of Universals and Propositions*. Oxford: Oxford University Press.

CHAPTER 3

....

INDIVIDUATION

....

E. J. LOWE

1. TWO SENSES OF 'INDIVIDUATE'

....

THE term 'individuation' has both a metaphysical and an epistemic or cognitive sense, although these two senses are closely related. In the epistemic sense, individuation is a cognitive activity—something that we, or intelligent beings in general, can *do*. For someone to *individuate* an object, in this sense, is for that person to 'single out' that object as a distinct object of perception, thought, or linguistic reference. Different people clearly have different powers of individuation in this sense. Thus, an expert naturalist, upon entering some unexplored patch of jungle, may well be able to single out individual living organisms there which I am unable to differentiate from their environment, lacking as I do the appropriate biological concepts. But individuation in this epistemic sense presupposes individuation in the metaphysical sense. One can only 'single out' objects which are there to be singled out, that is, parts of reality which constitute single objects. Individuation in the metaphysical sense is an ontological relationship between entities: what 'individuates' an object, in this sense, is whatever it is that makes it the single object that it is—whatever it is that makes it *one* object, distinct from others, and the very object that it is as opposed to any other thing.

   Philosophers of an anti-metaphysical bent may look askance at this second notion of individuation, doubting its utility and perhaps even its coherence. They may want to echo Bishop Butler's famous dictum 'Everything is what it is and not another thing' with the suggestion that nothing more need or can be said on the subject. Does it, they may ask, really make much sense to pose the question of what *makes* an object one object and the very object that it is? Is it not in the very nature of an individual object to be one and the same as itself? Isn't our question rather like asking what makes a horse a horse, or what makes the number 2 the number 2? Well, it is true enough that nothing could *be* an individual object that wasn't one and the same as itself, but it is not incontestable that everything whatever is an individual object or thing. And while some philosophers do indeed seem to believe that every existing entity is an individual (see e.g. Locke 1975: III. iii; Quine 1961), even they must admit to understanding the thesis that they deny—that there are *non*-individuals—and do for the most part acknowledge that metaphysical questions of individuation are substantive rather than just trivial in character. Classic examples of putative non-individuals are properties and relations (conceived as universals rather than as particulars, or tropes). We might also cite such entities as quantities of homogeneous matter—which, it seems, could exist, even if modern atomic physics excludes their actual existence—and the 'particles' of quantum theory. I shall say more about such entities in a moment.

In the light of these remarks, a brief word of caution is called for, because some philosophers offer what they call 'principles of individuation' for categories of entities which they would be loath to describe as 'individual objects' (e.g. *events*; see Davidson 1969). Very often what they have in mind may better be described as *criteria of identity*, variously conceived as 'synchronic', 'diachronic', or even 'transworld' in scope. It is sometimes even assumed that there must be a criterion of identity for every kind of entities K that we can intelligibly talk about—an assumption that I shall challenge later. Such a criterion is generally conceived to be an informative and non-circular principle of the form 'If x and y are Ks, then x is identical with y if and only if x and y stand in relation R to one another'—where R may be different for different kinds K. The precise character and role of such criteria are matters that I shall return to in due course, when I shall argue that, even where individuals are concerned, criteria of identity are only obliquely related to questions of individuation in the metaphysical sense. But for the moment I shall simply observe that it seems at best misleading to speak of 'individuation' where the existence and nature of individuals are not at issue.

An apparently more weighty objection to the metaphysical concept of individuation, at least as I have characterized it, is that it should not be presupposed that what makes an object *one* object is also what makes it the very object that it is. That is to say, it may be objected that the concept, as I have characterized it, comprises two distinct and potentially separable elements. Accordingly, it may be urged that we really need to distinguish two different metaphysical concepts of individuation, each comprising just one of these elements. However, given that something does indeed qualify as a single object of some kind, it is hard to see how what makes it the very object that it is could fail to be what also makes it *one* object, for such an entity could not be the very object that it is without thereby being one object. In other words, where *individual objects* are concerned, it does not appear that the two elements comprised in my characterization of the metaphysical concept of individuation are separable in the way suggested. They may indeed be separable where other categories of entities are concerned—as we shall shortly see—but since such entities are precisely not *individuals*, it would once again be at best misleading to speak of their being 'individuated' in any sense.

2. Some Terminological Distinctions

Before proceeding further, I need to clarify my terminology in certain respects. There are three key terms whose applications may easily be conflated and which I have not so far been entirely careful to distinguish myself: 'individual', 'object', and 'particular'. None of these terms has an application as general as the perfectly general term 'entity' (or 'item'), which can be used to denote anything whatever that does or could exist. The term 'particular' is generally used in opposition to the term 'universal'—particulars being entities which instantiate (are instances of) universals, on the assumption that universals do indeed exist. The term 'object' (or 'thing') is generally used in opposition to the term 'property'—objects 'possessing', or being 'bearers' of, properties and properties being 'borne' by objects. Properties, however, may either be conceived to be particulars (when they are commonly called 'tropes') or else be conceived to be universals. Finally, the term 'individual' denotes something that has 'individuality' or, in other words, something that is 'individuated', in the metaphysical sense explained above. Hence, although my focus so far has been on individual *objects*, one might easily suppose there to be individuals which do not qualify as 'objects', in the sense of being property-bearers. In what follows, I shall try to keep an open mind about this issue, while continuing to focus on the individuation of objects.

3. Individuality, Identity, and Countability

If earlier remarks of mine are correct, it is questionable to assume that identity and *countability* are mutually inseparable—that items can constitute a countable plurality if and only if they are determinately distinct from one another. Quantities of matter—especially if homogeneous in nature—and the 'particles' of quantum theory plausibly provide, in different ways, counter-examples to this assumption (see Lowe 1998, ch. 3; but for another view of quantities of matter, or 'masses', see Zimmerman 1995). On the one hand, quantities of matter would seem to be determinately identical with or distinct from one another, and yet are apparently not countable entities. One can sensibly ask *how much* gold or water there is in a certain location, but not, it seems, *how many* quantities of gold or water there are. A question of the latter sort, I suggest, is pointless not merely in the epistemic sense that we could never hope to discover a correct answer to it, but in the more fundamental semantic or metaphysical sense that nothing could unproblematically qualify as a 'correct' answer to it. This, at bottom, is because quantities of matter lack intrinsic unity, being decomposable by indefinitely many different principles of division into smaller quantities of the same kind and requiring no spatial connectedness among their parts. The very same quantity of matter may be scattered over a wide region of space, or gathered together into a compact mass. Consequently, there is no clear sense in saying that it is a 'one' or a 'many', in advance of specifying its spatial distribution: and even then, what *counts* as 'one' or 'many' are the *pieces* or *parcels* of matter into which it is divided, not the quantity of matter as such. On the other hand, the 'particles' of quantum theory—for example, the two electrons orbiting the nucleus of a helium atom—are evidently countable entities, but apparently ones which may lack determinate identity. For in the case of two such electrons there is, it seems, no fact of the matter as to which electron is which, because they are mutually 'entangled' in virtue of their state of 'superposition'.

If these suggestions are correct—and here I advance them merely to illustrate how the assumption now at issue might be challenged—it follows that quantities of matter and quantum particles are not properly described as 'individuals'. This accords with my earlier characterization of the metaphysical concept of individuation, which implies that entities of these kinds cannot be said to be 'individuated'. For I said that what individuates, in the metaphysical sense, is whatever it is that makes an entity *one* entity, distinct from others, and *the very entity that it is*, as opposed to any other. But while an electron is *one* entity of a certain kind, there may apparently be no fact of the matter as to *which* electron an electron is and consequently nothing which 'makes it the very electron that it is'. Conversely, while something may make a quantity of matter the very quantity of matter that it is, nothing necessarily makes it *one* quantity, if quantities of matter lack intrinsic unity and are consequently not countable entities in their own right.

These points being granted, it may none the less be insisted that, for many kinds of entity, identity and countability are indeed inseparable—and it is these entities that may properly be described as being 'individuals' or as having 'individuality'. Traditionally, individual *substances* fall paradigmatically into this class, which may help to explain—given the long historical dominance, until fairly recent times, of substance ontologies—why identity and countability have seemed to many philosophers to be absolutely inseparable. It is on the individuation of substances that I shall concentrate in what follows, partly because this has received the most attention in the literature on individuation and partly because of its intrinsic interest. A preliminary task, however, is to say more exactly what the term 'individual substance' should be understood to denote.

Roughly, an individual substance is conceived to be an individual object which is capable of independent existence—one which could exist even in the absence of any other such object (in the sense of 'could' in which this expresses metaphysical possibility). This will hardly do as a *definition* of 'individual substance', not least because it is implicitly circular—but it may suffice as a loose characterization of the notion or criterion for its application (see further Hoffman and Rosenkrantz 1994; Lowe 1998, ch. 6). Thus, for example, it seems that an individual material sphere could exist as a solitary occupant of space. Of course, it would not literally be the *sole* occupant of space, since it is composed of quantities of matter which occupy space and has a surface which occupies space. But, given that these quantities of matter, the sphere's surface, and space itself do not themselves qualify as individual substances (because, apparently, they are not even individual objects), it seems we can say that the sphere would be the *only* individual substance occupying space in these circumstances and hence that it satisfies our criterion for something's being an 'individual substance'— namely, that it should be an object which requires the existence of no other individual substance in order to exist. Note, however, that if we want to allow, as we arguably should, that there can be composite substances possessing substantial parts, then we should more precisely say that an individual substance is an object which requires the existence of no other *wholly distinct* individual substance in order to exist (where by two 'wholly distinct' individual substances I mean two individual substances which have no substantial part in common). This will permit us to say, for instance, that living organisms are individual substances, even while accepting that their internal organs and cells are individual substances in their own right. For although it is, of course, *causally* impossible for an organism to survive for any appreciable length of time in isolation from other, wholly distinct substances—because of the demands of its metabolic processes—it does not appear to be *metaphysically* impossible for an organism to be a solitary occupant of space throughout its existence, however brief, and this suffices for it to qualify as an individual substance according to the independence criterion that I have just proposed.

4. RELATIONS, PROPERTIES, AND INDIVIDUATION

So what individuates an individual substance: what makes it *one* individual substance of a certain kind and the very individual substance that it is? Not, apparently, any *relation* that the substance may bear to any other, wholly distinct substance—because, being a substance, it could exist as the very substance that it is even in the absence of any other, wholly distinct substance. This, incidentally, appears to exclude one currently popular view about the individuation of living organisms which normally reproduce sexually—assuming that such organisms qualify as individual substances—namely, the view that such organisms are individuated by the gametes from which they originated (see especially Kripke 1980: 112 ff.). For the gametes are wholly distinct from the mature organism and it is surely not metaphysically necessary that such an organism should have had such a causal origin. However, even if an individual substance cannot be individuated by any relation that it bears to other substances, alternative proposals are available, many of which have a lengthy philosophical pedigree (for historical surveys, see Gracia 1994; Barber and Gracia 1994).

It may be suggested, for instance, that a substance is individuated by its intrinsic (non-relational) properties, conceived as universals. This might be advanced in conjunction with the thesis that a substance just *is* (identical with) a 'bundle' of coinstantiated universals (for discussion, see van Cleve 1985). However, this would imply that an implausibly strong version of Leibniz's principle of the identity of indiscernibles is a metaphysically necessary truth. We can surely conceive, with Max Black, a world containing *two* material spheres qualitatively exactly similar to one another in every respect (see Black 1952; and, for recent discussion, O'Leary-Hawthorne 1995; Zimmerman 1997; Hughes 1999). But if the two spheres, being individual substances, are therefore determinately distinct entities (unlike the two orbital electrons of a helium atom), the universals that it exemplifies cannot be what make one of the spheres the very sphere that it is as opposed to the other sphere. So an individual substance cannot, apparently, be individuated by its intrinsic properties, nor, a fortiori, can it simply be constituted by those properties (i.e. it cannot simply *be* a 'bundle' of coinstantiated universals).

5. MATTER, FORM, AND INDIVIDUATION

Another suggestion is that an individual substance is individuated by its constituent *matter*. This, of course, presupposes that all individual substances are material substances, which might be queried (e.g. by those who think that immaterial Cartesian egos do or could exist and are or would be individual substances). But even setting aside this query, there are problems with this proposal (see further Lowe 1998, ch. 9). The thought would be that what makes one of our two exactly similar material spheres the one that it is is the particular matter of which it is composed—the assumption being that the very same matter cannot exist in two different places at once. However, a sphere's matter surely could not be what makes the sphere *one* sphere, because matter, as we have observed, lacks intrinsic unity. The very same matter which composes the sphere *could* instead compose a number of different spheres, or an object of non-spherical shape, or even be scattered haphazardly across the universe. Consequently, given that what individuates a material sphere must be what makes it one sphere, it cannot be individuated purely by its matter. Equally, on the other hand, the sphere's *form*—its spherical shape or sphericity, assuming this to be a universal—cannot be what individuates it: for its sphericity cannot be what makes the sphere the very sphere that it is, given that there may be another exactly similar sphere which exemplifies the same universal.

So, it seems, it could at best only be a *combination* of matter and form that fully individuates something like an individual material sphere. But what do or should we mean by a 'combination' of matter and form here? We surely cannot just mean a pair of items, one of which is a particular quantity of matter and the other of which is a certain universal, such as sphericity. For such a pair consisting, say, of a haphazardly scattered quantity of matter and sphericity will not serve to individuate any material sphere at all, since the pair could apparently exist even in a universe devoid of individual material spheres. (In such a universe, sphericity might be exemplified by something non-material, such as a region of space, or might exist unexemplified, if there can be unexemplified universals.) Rather, by a 'combination' of matter and form we must apparently mean some matter *exemplifying* that form—in the case under discussion, a spherical piece of matter.

But, it might well seem, a spherical piece of matter *just is* a material sphere, so that if what individuates a material sphere is a spherical piece of matter, then a material sphere is simply individuated *by itself*. This is not, however, an unintelligible answer to the question of what individuates a material sphere. Perhaps, indeed, all that we can say of the individuation of substances is that individual substances *individuate themselves*—or, at least, that they are not individuated by any entity or entities distinct from themselves (cf. Loux 1978, ch. IX; 1998a: 117 ff.; 1998b). I shall return to this suggestion shortly.

Conceivably, however, it will be questioned whether a material sphere *just is* (identical with) a spherical piece of matter. If we allow that a material sphere could undergo change in respect of its constituent matter—and, clearly, in one sense of the term 'material sphere', we do want to allow this—then we cannot identify a material sphere with the piece of matter constituting it at any given time. That being so, however, a material sphere (in the currently understood sense) will not be individuated solely by a certain combination of matter and form. After all, if material spheres can undergo a change of their constituent matter, we can in principle envisage circumstances in which two different material spheres undergo a complete exchange of their constituent matter, so that the piece of matter constituting one of the spheres at an earlier time later comes to constitute the other sphere.

6. Space, Time, and Individuation

The foregoing sort of consideration may suggest that what individuates material substances is neither their matter nor their form nor the combination of both, but quite simply their spatio-temporal circumstances. For instance, it may now be suggested that what makes one of our two spheres, in the imagined two-sphere universe, one sphere and the very sphere that it is is the set of spatial locations or regions that it occupies throughout its history—these regions, themselves being spherical in form, giving the sphere its material unity as a single spherical object and its identity as the very sphere that it is. However, this seems to presuppose that space itself has substantival status, in which case material spheres and other material bodies are not, after all, individual substances—rather, space itself is an individual substance and material bodies are non-substantial individuals which exist in virtue of the successive occupancy by matter of contiguous regions of space. (Thus, on this view, what we ordinarily think of as the continuous movement through space of an individual material sphere really just amounts to some matter's successively occupying the members of a continuous series of spherical regions of space.) But, in that case, we have not really addressed the question of what individuates individual substances by saying what individuates such things as material spheres, these turning out not to be individual substances after all. If space itself is the only individual substance, it would seem that it would again have to be self-individuating. The upshot is that, so far, we have found no way to conceive of individual substances other than as being individuated by themselves.

7. Tropes and Individuation

We saw earlier that it is difficult to hold that individual substances are individuated by their intrinsic properties, conceived as universals, because there can apparently be a plurality of individual substances which are qualitatively identical with one another. But it may seem more promising to propose that individual substances are individuated by their intrinsic properties where these are conceived of not as universals, but as *particulars*—more specifically, as the entities that have variously been called 'individual accidents', 'modes', 'property instances', or 'tropes' (see Campbell 1990). Two individual substances cannot, apparently, share the very same property instance or trope—the very same particular sphericity or redness, say. So, although the two material spheres in our imaginary example are exactly similar to one another, it may be urged that what makes each one the individual sphere that it is is *its* particular sphericity and other tropes. Each trope of one of the spheres exactly resembles some trope of the other, but such perfectly matching tropes are none the less numerically distinct, being properties of different objects.

However, the obvious objection to saying that individual substances are individuated by their tropes is that this is to put the cart before the horse. That is to say, it may be urged that tropes themselves are at least partly individuated by the substances to which they belong—a particular redness, say, by the individual red object of which it is a property—in which case it would apparently involve one in a vicious circularity to say that individual substances are in turn individuated by their tropes. Here it may be asked why such a circularity would have to be vicious, given that it apparently even makes sense to suppose that an individual substance might be individuated by *itself*. The answer is that individuation, it seems, cannot be a symmetrical relation, although it may well be an anti-symmetrical relation. (A relation R is anti-symmetrical just in case, for any things x and y, if x is R to y and y is R to x, then x is identical with y.) That is to say, two different entities cannot each individuate, or help to individuate, the other, even though some entities might be self-individuating. Discussion of this claim is, however, something that I shall postpone until later.

But, even accepting that individuation is not a symmetrical relation, it might be denied that tropes are in fact individuated even in part by the individual substances to which they belong, in which case the foregoing charge of circularity could be avoided. However, if tropes are not individuated at least in part by the individual substances to which they belong, why shouldn't a particular trope—say, a particular redness or sphericity—belong to more than one individual substance, either at the same time or at successive times? Why shouldn't tropes 'migrate' from one individual substance to another? But if tropes can do that, then why shouldn't the two different material spheres of our imaginary example undergo a complete exchange of their tropes? And if they can do that, then, clearly, the spheres cannot be individuated by their tropes. It emerges, thus, that there is a dilemma for those who would say that objects such as material spheres are individuated by their intrinsic properties, even where the latter are conceived as particulars, that is, as tropes. For either such particular properties are individuated at least in part by the objects to which they belong or they are not so individuated. In the former case, a circularity ensues if we say that the objects are in turn individuated by the properties. And in the latter case, nothing seems to prevent objects from exchanging their properties, in which case they cannot, after all, be individuated by those properties. Either way, an object cannot, it seems, be individuated by its particular properties or tropes.

But perhaps this argument is too quick. For it may be urged that objects such as material spheres are in fact nothing more than the tropes which belong to them—that they are, in other words, just 'bundles' of compresent tropes (see Campbell 1990; Simons 1994). We rejected earlier the proposal that objects are bundles of coinstantiated *universals*, because this was incompatible with the plausible contention that two exactly similar material spheres might exist in an otherwise empty universe. But since exactly similar tropes may be numerically distinct, nothing prevents there being two distinct bundles of exactly similar tropes, which is what our two material spheres would be, according to the latest proposal. Now, if objects are just bundles of tropes, perhaps we should say that, strictly speaking, if a trope departs from a given trope-bundle, then that very trope-bundle ceases to exist, in which case trope-bundles—and hence our material spheres—cannot, after all, exchange their tropes. In that case, the earlier objection to saying that objects are individuated by their tropes falls down. Nevertheless, this seems, on the face of it, an implausible way to avoid the objection in question, because it commits its advocates to the view that an object, such as a material sphere, cannot undergo any change of its intrinsic properties.

To this it may be replied that there are, in any case, other reasons to regard as problematic the common-sense idea that objects such as material spheres can undergo changes of their intrinsic properties. I refer especially to the notorious 'problem of intrinsic change' (see Lewis 1986: 202 ff.; Lowe 1998: 127 ff.). Perhaps we should regard something such as a material sphere not as a *single* trope-bundle, but rather as a 'four-dimensional' entity whose momentary temporal parts are single trope-bundles. In that case, what it really means to say that a material sphere has different properties at different times is that its earlier and later temporal parts are different trope-bundles. If tropes themselves can persist and belong to different trope-bundles at different times, then, indeed, two material spheres could, in principle, undergo a complete exchange of their tropes over a period of time: each could have, although only at different times, the very same trope-bundle as a temporal part. But no two material spheres could have exactly the same temporal parts at all times. Hence, it seems, we could now say, without threat of circularity, that an individual material sphere is individuated by its complete trope-history—that is, by the complete temporal sequence of tropes belonging to it at successive times throughout its existence.

However, this proposal is viable only if we can make appropriate sense of the notion of a momentary trope-bundle which it invokes. What 'ties together' the tropes of a momentary trope-bundle? Perhaps the relation of 'compresence' is supposed to do this all by itself. However, compresence alone apparently cannot serve this purpose if, as seems plausible to many philosophers, it is possible to have coinciding objects that are numerically distinct—such as a bronze statue and the lump of bronze which composes it (see Lowe 1989a, ch. 5; 1998, ch. 9; but see also Zimmerman 1995: 85 ff.). For, in that case, it seems that we would need to have two distinct trope-bundles residing in exactly the same place at the same time, consisting of the statue's tropes and the lump's tropes respectively. Against this, it may be urged that since the statue's tropes and the lump's tropes at any given time during their coincidence would be exactly similar and co-located, their tropes would not in fact be numerically distinct and we would have, in reality, only a single trope-bundle—and from this it might further be inferred that the statue and the lump could not be numerically distinct objects after all. This presupposes, however, that numerically distinct but exactly similar tropes cannot be co-located. Why should that be so? After all, tropes are not like quantities of matter, which exclude one another from the same place at the same time in virtue of matter's impenetrability. If tropes can persist, why shouldn't two distinct but exactly similar tropes 'merge' with one another temporarily? At this point our discussion unfortunately runs into the difficulty that there is very little consensus among trope theorists themselves concerning the persistence conditions and individuation of tropes—and, indeed, little prospect of their achieving a consensus on principled grounds.

8. Substrata and Individuation

Some philosophers who are sympathetic to the idea of particular properties may diagnose the foregoing difficulty as arising from a misconceived tendency to think of tropes as individual objects in their own right, when in reality they are not objects at all, but, rather, *ways* objects are—and, hence, more appropriately described as 'modes' or 'accidents'. If particular properties are modes of objects (including individual substances), then such objects cannot, after all, be nothing over and above their properties—they cannot be bundles of particular properties, nor even four-dimensional entities whose momentary temporal parts are bundles of particular properties. On this view of the matter, the 'bundle' approach is guilty of confusing the *properties* of objects with their constituent *parts* (cf. Martin 1980). But if an object is more than just the sum of its properties, what additional element does objecthood involve, over and above the possession of properties?

One historically important answer to this question is that an individual object—or, at least, an individual substance—possesses a 'substratum', in which its various properties 'inhere' (see Locke 1975: II. xxiii; and, for discussion, Lowe 2000). The substratum may be conceived to be a 'bare particular', devoid of any qualitative character of its own, because the properties which it 'supports' are the properties of the object whose substratum it is, rather than of the substratum in its own right (on 'bare particulars', see Allaire 1963, 1965; Chappell 1964; Moreland 1998). Such a substratum may be held to perform a dual ontological role. On the one hand, it may be held to 'tie together' various particular properties as the properties of a single object—something which the relation of compresence or co-location cannot apparently do. On the other hand, it may be held to *individuate* the object, by making the object the particular object that it is—again, something which the object's particular properties cannot apparently do, because (on this view of the matter) those properties owe their very identity to the object, being 'ways' *it* is. Bare particulars, it seems, will have to be self-individuating, for although there are supposedly many of them, they are all qualitatively indistinguishable from one another (lacking as they do any qualitative character whatever), nor can they apparently be individuated spatio-temporally. But they will be extremely strange entities, if indeed we can really make sense of them at all. They will be individuals, but not individual *objects*, since they lack properties of their own. Lacking properties of their own, it is something of a mystery how they manage to 'support' the properties of the objects whose substrata they are. Perhaps the best we can say about them is that they are non-qualitative *aspects* of objects—the *property-bearing* aspects of objects, as opposed to the qualitative aspects, which are the properties borne (cf. Martin 1980; and, for discussion, Lowe 2000).

Few philosophers now think that bare particulars, or substrata, are theoretically fruitful additions to our ontology. Such entities 'solve' the problem of the individuation of objects by fiat, but at the expense of generating impenetrable mysteries. The element of truth in substratum theory is that an object, or individual substance, is not just the sum of its particular properties and consequently that trope-bundle theories are inadequate. But we should not conclude from this that an object is somehow *more* than just the sum of its particular properties, in the sense of being a complex which somehow consists of those properties plus an extra non-qualitative ingredient, the elusive 'substratum'. (Such a 'complex' would have to be something other than a simple mereological sum of its constituents, be it noted.) Rather, the lesson is just that objects are ontologically prior to their properties, with the latter being dependent for their existence and identity upon the former. In no sense is a property a 'constituent' of an object: it is merely a 'facet' or 'aspect' of an object— something which we can talk about or think of separately from that object only by an act of abstraction. It is unnecessary and extravagant to invoke self-individuating substrata or bare particulars to solve the problem of the individuation of objects or individual substances: if we are going to have to appeal to self-individuating entities for this purpose, we might as well resort to the doctrine that ordinary individual substances themselves are self-individuating.

9. HAECCEITIES AND INDIVIDUATION

So far, we have found little promise in the idea that individual substances are individuated by their intrinsic properties, whether we conceive of the latter as universals or as particulars. But perhaps that is because we have been assuming that properties, conceived as universals, are necessarily *shareable* by numerically distinct objects. Properties such as sphericity and redness are indeed multiply shareable, but, conceivably, there are other properties that are not. A preliminary point worth emphasizing here, however, is that we cannot assume that every meaningful predicate necessarily expresses a property that some entity could possess. We know this as a matter of pure logic, because the predicate 'is non-self-exemplifying' is meaningful—and yet there cannot, on pain of contradiction, be any such property as the property of being non-self-exemplifying (cf. Loux 1998*a*: 34 ff.; Lowe 1999). (Suppose there were such a property: then either it would exemplify itself or it would not—but if it *did* exemplify itself, then it would be non-self-exemplifying and so would *not* exemplify itself; and if it did *not* exemplify itself, then it would be non-self-exemplifying and so *would* exemplify itself. This, of course, is just a version of Russell's famous paradox, applied to properties rather than to sets.)

Consider, then, the predicate 'is identical with *O*', where *O* is some object or individual substance. Is there such a property as the property of being identical with *O*? Perhaps there is: but if so, it is a property which is unshareable, since it is a property which only one object, *O* itself, can possess. Such putative properties are sometimes called 'individual essences' or 'haecceities' (literally, 'thisnesses') (see Adams 1979; Rosenkrantz 1993). If individual substances possess haecceities, then, plausibly, they are individuated by their haecceities. For instance, the two qualitatively exactly similar material spheres of our imaginary example will each be so individuated: sphere *A* will be individuated by its property of being identical with sphere *A*, a property which it does not share with sphere *B*. This may seem like a mere linguistic trick, perhaps—and maybe, indeed, it is—but we should not too lightly assume this.

It may be objected that it is blatantly circular to say that sphere *A* is individuated by its property of being identical with sphere *A*, for isn't that property itself individuated by *A*—isn't *A*, the property's only possible possessor, at least partly what makes the property of being identical with *A* the very property that it is (assuming that such a property really exists at all)? Now, of course, it is questionable whether we should really speak of properties—in the sense of universals—being *individuated* at all, since universals, arguably, are precisely *not* individuals. But let us set aside that doubt for present purposes. Even so, just because the property of being identical with *A*—assuming that it exists—has been introduced to us by means of the predicate 'is identical with *A*', we should not uncritically assume that this predicate captures the intrinsic nature of the property. After all, it would seem that one and the same property can often be expressed by quite different predicates, which may even convey different concepts. For instance, the properties expressed by the predicates 'triangular rectilinear figure' and 'trilateral rectilinear figure' are arguably one and the same (see further Lowe 1999). (After all, it is metaphysically necessary that anything which exemplifies one of these properties also exemplifies the 'other'.) So, there may in principle be a predicate which expresses the property of being identical with *A* which makes no reference to *A*. It may perhaps be that there is no humanly learnable language which contains such a predicate, but that would only imply something about our cognitive limitations, not anything about the property itself. The upshot is that we cannot automatically assume that there would be anything circular in saying that an individual substance is individuated by its haecceity, assuming that it has one.

It would seem that haecceities, if they exist, are non-qualitative properties, since qualities appear by their very nature to be shareable between objects. This may make haecceities seem rather like the bare particulars that we discussed earlier, for both haecceities and bare particulars are items that are non-qualitative non-objects. However, whereas bare particulars are, obviously, particulars, haecceities, we have been supposing, are universals, albeit unshareable ones. Both will no doubt strike their critics as being extravagant metaphysical fictions, dreamed up merely in order to 'solve' a difficult ontological problem but otherwise serving no useful purpose. It may be wondered, though, why—if one is going to invoke such esoteric entities—one shouldn't equally invoke a category of entity which is at once a *particular* property, like a trope, and yet also like a haecceity in being non-qualitative. Assuming that all particular properties are necessarily unshareable, such a property would be so too. But it would also be the case that no two objects could possess *exactly similar* particular properties of this kind, since exact similarity is a relation in which only qualitative properties can stand to one another. How might we refer to such a putative particular property, say of material sphere *A*? Presumably, we might refer to one such property, if nowise else, as *A*'s particular property of being identical with *A*. But how would this entity differ from *A*'s substratum, assuming that to exist too? Both would be non-objects and non-qualitative particulars. If the question is unanswerable, as I suspect it probably is—other than by mere stipulation—then perhaps this reflects badly on any ontology which includes either sort of entity. We do metaphysics and ourselves no service by inventing mysterious entities to solve deep ontological problems, such as the problems of individuation.

There is one kind of object for which the notion of a haecceity has some genuine intuitive appeal, however—namely, *persons* or, more generally, subjects of experience, such as you or I (see further Swinburne 1995). One may easily be persuaded that, even if there were another person just like oneself in every qualitative respect, possessing exactly similar thoughts and feelings, then that other person would nevertheless differ from oneself precisely in not being *oneself*—in not being *me*, in my case. This clearly has something to do with the 'first-person perspective' that any subject of experience may adopt towards him- or herself but not towards anyone else. The property of being me, if it exists, might indeed be called a 'perspectival' property—a property which something has in virtue of being thought of or grasped from a particular 'point of view' (its own). It would be extravagant to suppose that *all* individual substances somehow 'grasp themselves' from their own point of view, in the manner perhaps of Leibnizian monads, but any substance that does so might well be described as being 'self-individuating', in the cognitive sense of individuation as well as the metaphysical (on Leibniz and individuation, see Cover and O'Leary-Hawthorne 1999). However, these thoughts take us away from more fundamental issues of individuation which deserve exploration.

10. SORTAL CONCEPTS AND INDIVIDUATION

One point about individuation that has so far received little explicit attention in our discussions is the alleged *sortal relativity* of individuation. It is often maintained that objects cannot be individuated merely *qua* objects, but only *qua* objects of this or that *sort* or *kind* (see Geach 1980; Wiggins 1980; Lowe 1989*a*, ch. 2). Sometimes the thesis is meant to concern individuation in the cognitive sense, sometimes individuation in both the cognitive and the metaphysical senses. As far as individuation in the cognitive sense is concerned, it is certainly plausible to say that one can only 'single out' an individual object of thought or reference as an object of some kind, not barely as an object (see Wiggins 1986). This is because singling out an object in this sense seems to require the cognizer to think of that object as falling under some sortal concept. Merely to point in a certain direction and assert, for example, 'That object is red' always invites the question 'Which object?', to which an appropriate reply might be something like 'that *book*' or 'that *flower*', in which a sortal term is invoked. Sortal terms are general terms that convey sortal—or, as we may also call them, individuative—concepts. These can be contrasted with what may be called *adjectival* or *characterizing* concepts, which are conveyed by such general terms as 'red' and 'square'. It is often contended that what fundamentally distinguishes sortal from characterizing concepts is that while both have criteria of *application*, only the former have associated with them a criterion of *identity* for the items to which they can properly be applied (see Strawson 1959: 168; Dummett 1981, ch. 16). Thus, for something to qualify as being *square*, it must have four equal rectilinear sides set at right angles to one another. But for something to be a *tiger*, say, it must not only have an appropriate range of characteristics (e.g. of colour, shape, and size) at any given time, but must also satisfy certain identity conditions which determine, *inter alia*, what changes in its characteristics it may undergo over time. Objects falling under different sortal concepts often satisfy different identity conditions. For example, tigers and other living organisms may undergo considerable variations in their size and material constitution over time, whereas this is not possible for something like an individual grain of sand. As these examples show, however, the thesis that individuative concepts impose certain identity conditions on the objects to which they apply has metaphysical implications. The sense in which a tiger *can*, but a grain of sand *cannot*, grow bigger or change its shape is the sense in which 'can' expresses metaphysical possibility.

11. CRITERIA OF IDENTITY AND INDIVIDUATION

Mention of identity conditions brings us back to the topic of criteria of identity, which was touched upon earlier. A criterion of identity for things of a sort or kind K is a principle purporting to state, in an informative and non-circular way, the identity conditions for individual Ks (see further Lowe 1989a, ch. 2; 1989b; 1998, ch. 2). In other words, such a criterion purports to state, informatively and non-circularly, the truth-conditions of canonical identity statements concerning individual Ks—statements such as 'This K is identical with that K'. Such statements may concern identity *over* time—diachronic identity—or identity *at* a time—synchronic identity. As we shall shortly see, they may also concern identity *across possible worlds*, that is, so-called 'transworld' identity. For an example concerning synchronic identity, imagine seeing the head of a tiger protrude from one side of a tree and the tail of a tiger protrude from the other side of the same tree. One might point first towards the head and then towards the tail and ask 'Is *that* tiger (numerically) the same as *this* tiger?' A satisfactory identity criterion for tigers should specify, informatively and non-circularly, the conditions which must obtain for a positive answer to this question. It will imply, for instance, that the answer is yes only if the head and the tail in question are appropriately connected so as to form parts of a single living organism. For an example concerning diachronic identity, by contrast, imagine seeing a tiger beside a certain tree on one day and a tiger beside the same tree on the next day and asking 'Is *this* (today's) tiger the same as *that* (yesterday's) tiger?' Once again, a satisfactory identity criterion for tigers should specify, informatively and non-circularly, the conditions which must obtain for a positive answer to this question. It will imply, for instance, that the answer is yes only if today's tiger is spatio-temporally continuous with yesterday's tiger.

What do these issues have to do with the topic of individuation, in the metaphysical sense? Some philosophers speak and write as if individuation in this sense simply has to do with the question of synchronic identity conditions, but matters are not as simple as this (see Woods 1965). Certainly, an object's synchronic identity conditions are germane to the question of what individuates it, in the metaphysical sense. We can see this from our foregoing tiger example. As I have formulated it earlier, the question of what individuates an object is the question of what makes it one object of its kind and the very object of its kind that it is. However, where—as in the case of our tiger—an object of a certain kind must have proper parts of certain kinds which must be arranged in appropriate ways, its being *one* object of that kind will certainly involve its having suitably integrated parts. The tiger head and tiger tail of our example are parts of *one* tiger because they belong to a set of such suitably integrated parts. However, even so, it seems incorrect to say that the tiger's parts are *what individuate it*, not least because a tiger can lose or exchange some of its parts: for instance, it can lose its tail or it may receive a new heart by way of organ transplantation. What makes a tiger one object of the tiger kind is, no doubt, at least partly its possession of suitably arranged tiger parts, but *which* individual objects those parts are is not, it seems, germane to the tiger's individuation.

It does not seem possible, even in principle, to state identity conditions for every kind of individual object in an informative and non-circular way: not every sortal term, it seems, can be supplied with an identity criterion for the items to which it applies. Recall that the general form of an identity criterion for Ks is this: 'If x and y are Ks, then x is identical with y if and only if x and y stand in relation R to one another.' To avoid circularity, relation R must be specifiable without reference to facts involving the identity of things of kind K. It may indeed be specified with reference to facts involving the identity of things of *another* kind, K^*, but in that case the question arises as to whether there is an informative and non-circular identity criterion for K^*s. If there is, it must not, again on pain of circularity, invoke a relation R^* which cannot be specified without reference to facts involving the identity of things of the first kind, K. We see, then, that we have set out here upon a regress which can only be terminated without circularity by a criterion of identity invoking a relation which can be specified without reference to facts involving the identity of things of *any* kind. Can there be a criterion of identity meeting this condition, however? It seems unlikely, even if the impossibility cannot be formally proved. Paradigm examples of identity criteria do all fail to meet this condition, it seems. In set theory, for instance, the criterion of identity for sets (the so-called axiom of extensionality) states that sets are identical if and only if they have the same members—and the relation of having the same members obviously cannot be specified without reference to facts involving the identity of those members.

The implication appears to be, then, that in any system of ontology objects of certain kinds must be included for which no informative and non-circular identity criterion can be supplied (cf. Lowe 1989a, ch. 2; 1998, ch. 7). These objects may be said to have primitive or unanalysable identity conditions. It appears that they will also have to be self-individuating. However, the converse does not necessarily hold: an object may conceivably be self-individuating without therefore having primitive or unanalysable identity conditions. Living organisms may perhaps be a case in point. It may be that living organisms—and perhaps, indeed, individual substances quite generally—are individuated by nothing but themselves (a possibility that we envisaged earlier). But even if this is so, we can still acknowledge that living organisms of various kinds satisfy distinctive identity criteria which help us to answer questions concerning the identity of such organisms both at a time and over time of the sort illustrated earlier. The key point to appreciate here is that an answer to a question of the form 'Is this K the same as that K?' (an identity question) may draw on different resources from those drawn on by an answer to a question of the form 'What makes an individual K the very individual K that it is?' (an individuation question, in the metaphysical sense of individuation). Of course, if we know how to answer the individuation question for Ks, we *may* thereby be in a position to formulate an identity criterion for Ks which will enable us to answer identity questions concerning Ks. But the answers are not guaranteed to be so intimately related.

Here one might be tempted to suggest, utilizing the language of possible worlds, that a principle of individuation for Ks is a *transworld* criterion of identity, whereas synchronic and diachronic criteria of identity are only 'intraworld' principles. A transworld identity criterion tells us, as it were, how to identify an individual K in any world in which it exists, whereas an intraworld identity criterion only tells us which Ks are numerically the same or different within a single world. On the basis of the latter sort of criterion we might affirm, for instance, that material substances of the same kind which share the same spatial location at some time during their histories are numerically identical: but this does not help us to identify a material substance in every possible world in which it exists, given that it is contingent what locations a material substance may occupy during its career. In fact, however, there is no more reason why a transworld identity criterion for Ks should be deemed to qualify as a 'principle of individuation' for Ks than either a synchronic or a diachronic identity criterion should. For it is a precondition of *identifying* an individual 'across' possible worlds that it should already be individuated in each of the worlds in which it exists. Presumably, an individual will be individuated in the same way in each possible world in which it exists, so that, for instance, if an individual substance is individuated in *this* world—the actual world—by its haecceity, assuming it to possess one, it will be individuated by its haecceity (which will presumably be the *same* haecceity) in every possible world in which it exists. But, obviously, this does not imply that we may identify that individual substance 'across' possible worlds only as the individual substance possessing that haecceity, any more than the corresponding thing is implied in the diachronic case.

12. INDIVIDUATION AND EXPLANATION

This is an appropriate point to conclude with a return to a claim I made earlier, that although individuation may be an anti-symmetric relation, it is not a symmetrical one (cf. Lowe 1998, ch. 6). That is to say, individual objects of at least some kinds may be self-individuating, but two different individuals cannot both individuate, or help to individuate, each other. This is because individuation, in the metaphysical sense, is a determination relation: an individual object's individuator is the entity, or set of entities, which determines—makes it the case—that that individual object is the very object that it is. As such, individuation is an *explanatory* relation: an individual object's individuator *explains* why that individual object is the very object that it is. But it would seem that explanatory relations, quite generally, cannot be symmetrical in character (for discussion, see Ruben 1990, ch. VII). That is to say, two distinct entities or states of affairs cannot each explain the other, in the very same sense of 'explain'. For instance, the height of a flagpole may causally explain the length of the shadow it casts, but, for that very reason, the length of the shadow cannot causally explain the height of the flagpole—although it may, of course, be used to *predict* the latter.

It is true that, in the *cognitive* sense of 'explain' in which this means, roughly, 'render intelligible', fact F_1 may explain fact F_2—render it intelligible—to a person P_1 even though, conversely, fact F_2 explains fact F_1 to another person P_2. For instance, the fact that Smith's enemy was in the house on the day of Smith's death may render intelligible to the detective the fact that Smith was murdered, whereas the fact that Smith was murdered may render intelligible to Smith's neighbour the fact that Smith's enemy was in the house on that day. However, even here there is no genuine symmetry of explanation, because the beneficiaries of the two explanations are two different people. And, in any case, the kind of explanation provided by an object's individuator is not essentially cognitive in nature, nor is it person-relative. Rather, it is metaphysical or ontological in nature: to 'explain', in this sense, is not to 'render intelligible' (to someone), but to *account for*. But the notion of a '*self*-explanatory' state of affairs, in this sense of the expression, appears to be perfectly coherent—and is perhaps even required by any adequate theory of explanation in order to provide a terminus to explanatory regresses. Certainly, it seems that any satisfactory ontology will have to include self-individuating elements, the only question being which entities have this status—space-time points, bare particulars, tropes, and individual substances all being among the possible candidates. The remaining individuals of the system will then be individuated, ultimately, via the relations they bear to the self-individuating elements, making the system as a whole well-founded in respect of the facts of individuation obtaining in it. While I have tried to keep an open mind about which entities do in fact have self-individuating status, it will be evident that my sympathies lie with the candidacy of ordinary individual substances, if only because other candidates seem to create more problems than they solve.

References

Adams, R. (1979). 'Primitive Thisness and Primitive Identity'. *Journal of Philosophy*, 76: 5–26.

Allaire, E. B. (1963). 'Bare Particulars'. *Philosophical Studies*, 14: 1–8. Repr. in Laurence and Macdonald (1998: 248–54).

Allaire, E. B. (1965). 'Another Look at Bare Particulars'. *Philosophical Studies*, 16: 16–21. Repr. in Laurence and Macdonald (1998: 259–63).

Barber, K. F., and J. J. E. Gracia (eds.) (1994). *Individuation and Identity in Early Modern Philosophy*. Albany: State University of New York Press.

Black, M. (1952). 'The Identity of Indiscernibles'. *Mind*, 61: 152–64. Repr. in Black (1954: 80–92).

—— (1954). *Problems of Analysis: Philosophical Essays*. London: Routledge & Kegan Paul.

Butler, R. J. (ed.) (1965). *Analytical Philosophy*, 2nd series. Oxford: Basil Blackwell.

Campbell, K. (1990). *Abstract Particulars*. Oxford: Basil Blackwell.

Chappell, V. C. (1964). 'Particulars Re-clothed'. *Philosophical Studies*, 15: 60–4. Repr. in Laurence and Macdonald (1998: 255–8).

Cover, J. A., and J. O'Leary-Hawthorne (1999). *Substance and Individuation in Leibniz*. Cambridge: Cambridge University Press.

Davidson, D. (1969). 'The Individuation of Events', in N. Rescher (ed.), *Essays in Honor of Carl G. Hempel*. Dordrecht: Reidel, 216–34. Repr. in Davidson (1980: 163–80).

—— (1980). *Essays on Actions and Events*. Oxford: Clarendon Press.

Dummett, M. A. E. (1981). *Frege: Philosophy of Language*, 2nd edn. London: Duckworth.

Geach, P. T. (1980). *Reference and Generality*, 3rd edn. Ithaca: Cornell University Press.

Gracia, J. J. E. (ed.) (1994). *Individuation in Scholasticism, the Later Middle Ages and the Counter-Reformation, 1150–1650*. Albany: State University of New York Press.

Hoffman, J., and G. S. Rosenkrantz (1994). *Substance among Other Categories*. Cambridge: Cambridge University Press.

Hughes, C. (1999). 'Bundle Theory from A to B'. *Mind*, 108: 149–56.

Kripke, S. A. (1980). *Naming and Necessity*. Oxford: Basil Blackwell.

Laurence, S., and C. Macdonald (eds.) (1998). *Contemporary Readings in the Foundations of Metaphysics*. Oxford: Basil Blackwell.

Lewis, D. K. (1986). *On the Plurality of Worlds*. Oxford: Basil Blackwell.

Locke, J. (1975). *An Essay concerning Human Understanding*, ed. P. H. Nidditch. Oxford: Clarendon Press.

Loux, M. J. (1978). *Substance and Attribute*. Dordrecht: Reidel.

—— (1998a). *Metaphysics: A Contemporary Introduction*. London: Routledge.

—— (1998b). 'Beyond Substrata and Bundles: A Prolegomenon to a Substance Ontology', in Laurence and Macdonald (1998: 233–47).

Lowe, E. J. (1989a). *Kinds of Being: A Study of Individuation, Identity and the Logic of Sortal Terms*. Oxford: Basil Blackwell.

—— (1989b). 'What is a Criterion of Identity?' *Philosophical Quarterly*, 39: 1–21.

—— (1998). *The Possibility of Metaphysics: Substance, Identity, and Time*. Oxford: Clarendon Press.

—— (1999). 'Abstraction, Properties, and Immanent Realism', in Rockmore (1999: 195–205).

—— (2000). 'Locke, Martin and Substance'. *Philosophical Quarterly*, 50: 499–514.

Martin, C. B. (1980). 'Substance Substantiated'. *Australasian Journal of Philosophy*, 58: 3–10.

Moreland, J. P. (1998). 'Theories of Individuation: A Reconsideration of Bare Particulars'. *Pacific Philosophical Quarterly*, 79: 51–63.

O'Leary-Hawthorne, J. (1995). 'The Bundle Theory of Substance and the Identity of Indiscernibles'. *Analysis*, 55: 191–6.

Pettit, P., and J. McDowell (eds.) (1986). *Subject, Thought, and Context*. Oxford: Clarendon Press.

Quine, W. V. O. (1961). 'On What There Is', in Quine, *From a Logical Point of View*, 2nd edn. Cambridge, Mass.: Harvard University Press.

Rockmore, T. (ed.) (1999). *Proceedings of the Twentieth World Congress of Philosophy, ii: Metaphysics*. Bowling Green, Ohio: Philosophy Documentation Center.

Rosenkrantz, G. S. (1993). *Haecceity: An Ontological Essay*. Dordrecht: Kluwer.

Ruben, D.-H. (1990). *Explaining Explanation*. London: Routledge.

Simons, P. M. (1994). 'Particulars in Particular Clothing: Three Trope Theories of Substance'. *Philosophy and Phenomenological Research*, 54: 553–75. Repr. in Laurence and Macdonald (1998: 364–84).

Strawson, P. F. (1959). *Individuals: An Essay in Descriptive Metaphysics*. London: Methuen.

Swinburne, R. (1995). 'Thisness'. *Australasian Journal of Philosophy*, 73: 389–400.

van Cleve, J. (1985). 'Three Versions of the Bundle Theory'. *Philosophical Studies*, 47: 95–107. Repr. in Laurence and Macdonald (1998: 264–74).

Wiggins, D. (1980). *Sameness and Substance*. Oxford: Basil Blackwell.

——(1986). 'On Singling Out an Object Determinately', in Pettit and McDowell (1986: 169–80).

Woods, M. J. (1965). 'Identity and Individuation', in Butler (1965: 120–30).

Zimmerman, D. W. (1995). 'Theories of Masses and Problems of Constitution'. *Philosophical Review*, 104: 53–110.

——(1997). 'Distinct Indiscernibles and the Bundle Theory'. *Mind*, 106: 305–9.

PART II

EXISTENCE AND IDENTITY

CHAPTER 4

....

IDENTITY

....

JOHN HAWTHORNE

1. INTRODUCTION

....

THE topic of identity seems to many of us to be philosophically unproblematic. Identity, we will say, is the relation that each thing has to itself and to nothing else. Of course, there are many disputable claims that one can make using a predicate that expresses the identity relation. For example: there is something that was a man and is identical to God; there is something that might have been a poached egg that is identical to some philosopher. But puzzling as these claims may be, it is not the identity relation that is causing the trouble. The lesson appears to be a general one. Puzzles that are articulated using the word 'identity' are not puzzles about the identity relation itself.

One may have noticed that our gloss on identity as 'the relation that each thing has to itself and to nothing else' was not really an analysis of the concept of identity in any reasonable sense of 'analysis', since an understanding of 'itself' and 'to nothing else' already requires a mastery of what identity amounts to. But the appropriate response, it would seem, is not to search for a 'real analysis' of identity; rather, it is to admit that the concept of identity is so basic to our conceptual scheme that it is hopeless to attempt to analyse it in terms of more basic concepts.

Thanks to Kit Fine, Daniel Nolan, Brian Weatherson, Timothy Williamson, Dean Zimmerman, an audience at the 2001 Mighty Metaphysical Mayhem conference at Syracuse, and especially Tamar Gendler and Ted Sider for helpful comments and discussion.

Why is the concept of identity so basic? The point is not that we have inevitable need for an 'is' of identity in our language. Our need for the concept of identity far outstrips our need to make explicit claims of identity and difference. Consider, for example the following two simple sentences of first-order predicate logic:

$$\exists x\, \exists y(Fx \text{ and } Gy)$$
$$\exists x(Fx \text{ and } Gx).$$

Both require that there be at least one thing in the domain of the existential quantifier that is F and that there be at least one thing in the domain of the existential quantifier that is G. But the second sentence makes an additional requirement: that one of the things in the domain that is F be identical to one of the things in the domain that is G. Without mastery of the concept of identity it is not clear how we would understand the significance of the recurrence of a variable within the scope of a quantifier. In this vein, Quine observes that 'Quantification depends upon there being values of variables, same or different absolutely. . .' (Quine 1964: 101). Similar remarks apply to sentences of natural language. By way of bringing out the ubiquity of the notion of identity in our language, Peter Geach notes of the pair of sentences 'Jim wounded a lion and Bill shot it' and 'Jim wounded a lion and Bill shot another (lion) dead' that the first expresses identity and the second diversity (Geach 1991: 285).

2. CHARACTERIZING IDENTITY

Even if the concept of identity is basic for us, that does not mean that we can say nothing by way of characterizing identity. In what follows, I shall begin with some relatively informal remarks about identity as it relates to logic, some understanding of which is crucial to any metaphysical inquiry into the identity relation. I shall then go on to discuss various ideas associated with Leibniz's law and the principle of the identity of indiscernibles. These preliminaries will leave us well placed to usefully examine some unorthodox views concerning identity.

2.1 *I*-Predicates and Identity

It will help us to begin by imagining a tribe that speaks a language, L, that takes the form described by first-order predicate logic. So let us suppose that L contains individual constants, quantifiers, variables, truth-functional connectives, together with a stock of one-place predicates, two-place predicates, and so on. The individual constants in the tribe's language (which serve as the names in that language) each have a particular referent, the predicates particular extensions, and so on. Let us thus assume that there is a particular interpretation function, INT, from individual constants to bearers (selected from a universe of discourse that comprises the domain of objects that fall within the range of the quantifiers of L) and from predicates to extensions (a set of objects from the universe of discourse for a one-place predicate, a set of ordered pairs for a two-place predicate, and so on[1]) that correctly characterizes the extensions of the individual constants and predicates that are deployed in L. Assume there is a binary predicate 'I' in L for which the following generalizations hold:

(1) $\ulcorner \alpha I \alpha \urcorner$ is true for any interpretation INT^* of L that differs from INT at most in respect of how the individual constants of L are interpreted.[2]

(2) $\ulcorner (F\alpha \text{ and } \alpha I\beta) \supset F\beta \urcorner$ is true for any interpretation INT^* of L that differs from INT at most in respect of how the individual constants are interpreted. (F may be a simple or a complex predicate.)

(1) guarantees that 'I' expresses a reflexive relation:[3] (1) and (2) guarantee that 'I' is transitive and symmetric. Postponing the question of whether 'I' expresses the identity relation, we can say that, given its behaviour in L, 'I' behaves just as one would expect of a predicate that did express the identity relation. Let us say that a binary predicate of a language that obeys requirements (1) and (2) is an I-predicate for that language.

Quine has pointed out that, so long as a first-order language has a finite stock of predicates, one can stipulatively introduce a binary predicate that will be an I-predicate for that language:

The method of definition is evident from the following example. Consider a standard language whose lexicon of predicates consists of a one-place predicate 'A', two-place predicate 'B' and 'C' and a three-place predicate 'D'. We then define '$x = y$' as short for:

(A) $Ax \equiv Ay \cdot \forall z(Bzx \equiv Bzy \cdot Bxz \equiv Byz \cdot Czx \equiv Czy \cdot Cxz \equiv Cyz \cdot \forall z'(Dzz'x \equiv Dzz'y \cdot Dzxz' \equiv Dzyz' \cdot Dxzz' \equiv Dyzz'))$

Note the plan: the exhaustion of combinations. What '$x = y$' tells us, according to this definition, is that the objects x and y are indistinguishable by the four predicates; that they

---

[1] I shall not here try to deal with difficult questions that arise from the possibility that the universe of discourse, and, indeed, the range of application of certain predicates, are too big to form a set (and hence for which talk of a predicate's extension is problematic). I do not thereby pretend that these issues are irrelevant to philosophical discussions of identity, as shall be clear from the discussion of Geach.

[2] α, β are metalinguistic variables ranging over individual constants; F, G metalinguistic variables ranging over predicates. I am using standard corner quote conventions.

It might be that some particular object x has no name in L. (1) requires that $\ulcorner \alpha R \alpha \urcorner$ be true on the deviant interpretation that assigns the same extension to 'I' as INT but that assigns x as the referent of α.

[3] Though of course it is silent on whether it is a necessary truth that everything is I to itself.

are indistinguishable from each other even in their relations to any other objects z and z' insofar as these relations are expressed in simple sentences. Now it can be shown that, when [A] holds, the objects x and y will be indistinguishable by any sentences whether simple or not, that can be phrased in the language. (Quine 1970: 63)

Of course, if there is not a finite stock of basic predicates in the first-order language L, then an I-predicate for L cannot be mechanically introduced by stipulation in the manner prescribed. But assuming a finite stock, it is coherent to suppose that our tribe had introduced their binary predicate 'I' in this manner. That is not, obviously, to say that where there is an infinite stock, there will be no I-predicate: it is just that its method of introduction could not be the brute-force method that Quine describes.[4]

It is worth noting the way in which the use of variables in the stipulation imposes considerable discriminatory power upon I-predicates that are introduced by Quine's method. Suppose we have two predicates 'is 2 miles from' and 'is a sphere'. Consider a world of two spheres, call them 'sphere 1' and 'sphere 2', that are 5 feet from each other.[5] An I-predicate introduced by Quine's technique will not be satisfied by an ordered pair consisting of distinct spheres. One of the clauses in the definition of 'xIy' will be '$\forall z(z$ is 2 miles from $x \equiv z$ is 2 miles from $y)$. But this is not satisfied by the ordered pair ⟨sphere 1, sphere 2⟩. (This can be seen, for example, by letting z be sphere 1.) So, given the stipulative definition, it follows that '$\exists x \, \exists y(x$ is a sphere and y is a sphere and $\sim xIy)$' is true. (Similarly, if there are two angels that don't love themselves but do love each other and for which the tribe has no name, an I-predicate introduced using, *inter alia*, the predicate 'loves' will not be satisfied by an ordered pair of distinct angels.)

Isn't there some robust sense—and one that is not merely epistemic—in which the spheres are indiscernible with respect to that tribe's language? Quine acknowledges a notion of 'absolute discernibility' with respect to a language which holds of two objects just in case some open sentence in that language with one free variable is satisfied by only one of those two objects. Two objects are, meanwhile, 'relatively discernible' just in case there is some open sentence with two free variables that is not satisfied when one of the pair is assigned as the value of each variable but is satisfied when distinct members of the pair are assigned as the respective values of the two free variables (or vice versa). (See Quine 1960: 230.) The two spheres are absolutely indiscernible relative to the simple language just envisaged: Any open sentence with just one free variable will be satisfied by both or neither of the spheres. But they are relatively discernible: consider the open sentence 'x is 2 miles from y'.

As Quine himself is well aware, that a predicate is an I-predicate for some language L provides no logical guarantee that it expresses the identity relation itself, nor even

---

[4] I leave aside Zeno-style thought experiments in which a tribe makes infinitely many stipulations in a finite space of time by taking increasingly less time to make each stipulation.

[5] I have Black (1999) in mind here.

that the extension of the I-predicate, relative to the domain of discourse of L, be all and only those ordered pairs from the domain whose first and second members are identical. Suppose L is so impoverished as to have only two predicates, 'F' and 'G', that somehow manage to express the properties of being a dog and being happy respectively.[6] If speakers of L introduce an I-predicate by Quine's technique, then it will hold for all things that are alike with respect to whether they are dogs and whether they are happy. Of course, if a binary predicate expressing the identity relation already existed in the object language, then an I-predicate so introduced would be guaranteed to express[7] the identity relation too. More generally, we can say that if an I-predicate satisfies the following additional condition (3), then it will be guaranteed to hold of all and only those pairs in the domain of discourse that are identical (assuming L contains at least one predicate letter other than 'I').

(3) $\ulcorner(F\alpha \text{ and } \alpha I\beta) \supset F\beta\urcorner$ is true for any interpretation INT^* of L that differs from INT only in respect of how the individual constants and predicates other than 'I' are interpreted.[8]

But the point remains that it is not a logically sufficient condition for a binary predicate in some language L's expressing the identity relation that it be an I-predicate in L: when an I-predicate is introduced by Quine's machinery, there will be a way of interpreting the non-logical vocabulary[9] in such a way that the definition for the I-predicate is validated (and, correlatively, (1) and (2) hold relative to that interpretation) but where 'I' is not satisfied by all and only those ordered pairs of objects (drawn from the domain of discourse) whose first and second members are identical.

Let us now imagine our tribe to have the machinery to speak about properties. One can imagine this feat to be accomplished in two ways: First, by the apparatus of second-order quantification, whence the tribe has the capacity to quantify into the predicate position. Alternatively, we can imagine that the tribe's language has properties within the domain of its first-order variables, and that the tribe has such predicates as 'is a property' and 'instantiates' in its stock, as well as some principles about properties that belong to some segment of their conception of the world that

---

[6] Of course Quine himself will only tolerate properties when they are treated as sets. Most of the points made in the text do not turn on this. Note, though, that if one gives an extension construal of relations, then any difference in quantificational domains will make for a difference in the 'relation' picked out by an I-predicate. Note also that an extensional conception of the identity relation does not sit well with views that preclude certain entities—say, proper classes—from being members of sets, but which claim of those entities that they are self-identical. Note, finally, that an extensional account of the identity relation will preclude us from certain natural modal claims about the identity relation (assuming the world could have contained different objects).

[7] Or at least extensionally coincide with.

[8] Assuming L has at least one basic predicate other than 'I'.

[9] Where in this context, the predicate 'is identical to', if it exists in the language, counts as non-logical vocabulary.

encodes their theory of properties. Either way, the tribe will now have extra expressive resources.[10] First, even given an infinite stock of basic predicates, they could stipulatively introduce a predicate R that will be an 'I'-predicate for their language L. Supposing we opt for second-order machinery, and that the language contains only unary, binary, and ternary basic predicates, we can stipulatively introduce R after the manner Quine suggested. Thus we define '$x = y$' as short for:

$$\forall F \forall R_2 \forall R_3 (Fx \leftrightarrow Fy) \cdot \forall z (R_2zx \leftrightarrow R_2zy) \cdot (R_2zy \leftrightarrow R_2zy) \cdot$$
$$\forall z'(R_3zz'x \leftrightarrow R_3zz'y) \cdot (R_3zxz' \leftrightarrow R_3zyz' \cdot R_3xzz' \leftrightarrow R_3yzz'),$$

where the domain of 'F' are the properties expressed by the basic monadic predicates, where the domain of 'R_2' are the properties expressed by the basic binary predicates, and so on. The point would still remain that a predicate so introduced is not logically guaranteed to express the identity relation: The second-order machinery guarantees that the predicate so introduced will behave like an I-predicate with respect to the infinite stock of predicates in the language, but if there are plenty of properties and relations unexpressed by the infinite stock (and thus outside the domain of the second-order quantifiers characterized above), that is consistent with the I-predicate's failing to express the identity relation.

But what if we allow the tribe not merely to have the resources to speak about the properties and relations expressible in their current ideology, but to be enlightened enough to speak in a general way about all properties and relations whatsoever? Let us suppose that they are liberal about what counts as a property and what counts as a relation. (This is not a conception of properties and relations according to which only a small subset of one's predicates—the elite vocabulary—gets to express properties and relations.) This would give them yet more expressive power, indeed enough expressive power to stipulatively introduce a predicate that holds of all and only identical pairs (in the domain of discourse). The following definition would do:

(D1) $xIy \leftrightarrow \forall R \forall z(xRz \leftrightarrow yRz)$

as would

(D2) $xIy \leftrightarrow \forall F(Fx \supset Fy)$,

where D2 corresponds to the standard definition of identity within second-order logic. Assuming, then, that the tribe has the appropriate second-order machinery available, it can stipulatively introduce a predicate that is logically guaranteed to hold of all and only identical pairs (drawn from their domain of discourse).

With suitably enriched expressive resources, the tribe might, relatedly, make some stipulations about how their I-predicate is to behave with respect to extensions of

---

[10] I shall not pursue here the question of whether the need for a second-order variables is a deep one.

their language, L, or else interpretations of their language other than INT.[11] For example, the tribe might stipulate of 'I' that $\ulcorner(F\alpha$ and $\alpha I\beta) \supset F\beta\urcorner$ is true for any interpretation of L that agrees with INT with regard to the extension of 'I' and with regard to the logical vocabulary and the universe of discourse (but which may differ in any other respect).[12] Alternatively, the tribe might stipulate that $\ulcorner(F\alpha$ and $\alpha I\beta) \supset F\beta\urcorner$ is true for any extension $L+$ of their language that contains additional constants and/or predicates (whose interpretation agrees with that of L for those constants and predicates common to L and $L+$). Both of these stipulations require that the extension of 'I' be the class of identical pairs.[13] Any interpretation of L that assigned 'I' an extension other than the class of identical pairs would be one for which $\ulcorner(F\alpha$ and $\alpha I\beta) \supset F\beta\urcorner$ would be false under some interpretation of the relevant non-logical vocabulary. (If 'I' is true of some distinct x and y, then let the interpretation assign x and y to the respective individual constants and let it assign the singleton set containing x to the predicate.) Thus any interpretation of L that assigned a relation extensionally different from identity to 'I' would be one to which one could add predicates which under some interpretation would generate a language $L+$ for which the schema did not hold. Hence the tribe's stipulations could only be respected by interpreting 'I' to hold between any x and any y iff x is identical to y. As with second-order machinery, the capacity to talk about extensions of the language brings with it the capacity to place stipulative constraints upon an I-predicate that can only be satisfied if the predicate holds of all and only identical pairs (in the domain of discourse).

Does this discussion conflict with the idea that identity is a basic concept and cannot be analysed? No. That a predicate expressing identity *could be* explicitly introduced by one of the mechanisms stated does not imply that the concept of identity is dispensable or parasitic: the point remains that mastery of the apparatus of quantification would appear to require an implicit grasp of identity and difference (even where there is no machinery available by means of which to effect some explicit characterization of identity). Someone who used second-order machinery

[11] There is, of course, a complex web of issues connected with the threat of paradox generated by semantic machinery, including the question of which expressive resources force a sharp distinction between object and meta-language. Such issues are not irrelevant, as we shall see, to certain deviant approaches to identity: but they cannot be engaged with here.

[12] I assume once again that 'I' is not the only basic predicate in L.

[13] Cf. Williamson (1987/88). It is perhaps worth emphasizing the following point: if the domain of the tribe's quantifiers is, say, smaller than ours, then we could not, strictly, say that the extension of 'I' was the class of identical pairs—since the extension of 'is identical to' in our language would include ordered pairs of objects that fell outside the tribe's universe of discourse. Our sense of a single identity relation that can serve as the target of philosophical discourse is tied to our sense of being able to deploy utterly unrestricted quantification. And, as Jose Benardete remarked to me, it seems that our visceral sense that we understand exactly what we mean by 'identity' seems, on the face of it, to be jeopardized somewhat by those philosophical positions that deny the possibility of utterly unrestricted quantification. The issues raised here are beyond the scope of the current chapter.

to introduce an identity predicate would, by this reckoning, already have some tacit mastery of what the identity relation came to (whether or not a predicate expressing identity was already present in the language.) Nor is there any presumption above that in order to grasp the concept of identity, one *must* be in a position to provide some sort of explicit characterization of the identity relation in terms of extensions of one's language, or second-order machinery, or property theory, or whatever.

2.2 The Identity of Indiscernibles

Philosophers often give the name 'Leibniz's law' to the first of the following principles, and the 'identity of indiscernibles' to the second:

(LL) For all x and y, if $x = y$, then x and y have the same properties

(II)   For all x and y, if x and y have the same properties, then $x = y$.

It is sometimes said, furthermore, that while the first principle is uncontroversial, the second principle is very controversial. Such claims are often driven by a certain picture of what a property is. Consider, for example, the set-theoretic gloss on properties that is standardly used for the purposes of formal semantics. On this rather deflationary conception of properties, the property expressed by a predicate is the set of things of which that predicate is true (the 'extension' of that predicate). (Philosophers who baulk at an ontology of properties—construed as entities that can be distinct even though their instances are the same—frequently have less trouble with the purely extensional notion of a set.) On this conception, the principles can be given a set-theoretic gloss, namely:

(LL) $\forall x \forall y (x = y \supset \forall z (x$ is a member of $z \supset y$ is a member of $z))$.

(II) $\forall x \forall y ((\forall z (x$ is a member of z iff y is a member of $z)) \supset x = y)$.

Assuming our set theory takes it as axiomatic that everything has a unit set,[14] then, quite obviously, we will be committed to regarding the identity of indiscernibles as a fairly trivial truth. This is because it is crucial to the very conception of a set that x and y are the same set if and only if they have the same members.[15] We may note, relatedly, that in second-order logic, the identity of indiscernibles is normally conceived of in a way that reckons it no more controversial that the set-theoretic gloss.[16] Indeed, any conception of properties according to which it is axiomatic

---

[14] The issue of 'proper classes' complicates matters here. On some versions of set theory, there exist entities that are not members of any set, this being one device to help steer set theory clear of paradox.

[15] Once again there is no point in complaining that, so construed, the identity of indiscernibles cannot now be an 'analysis' of identity, since that ought never to have been the project in any case.

[16] Thus Shapiro (1991) writes of the 'identity of indiscernibles' principle '$t = u : \forall X (Xt$ iff $Xu)$' that it is not intended as 'a deep philosophical thesis about identity... As will be seen, on the standard semantics, for each object m in the range of the first-order variables, there is a property which applies to m, and m alone. It can be taken as the singleton set $\{m\}$' (1991: 63).

that there is, for each thing, at least one property, instantiated by it and it alone (the property of being identical to that thing, for example), will be a conception on which LL and II are equally unproblematic.

To make a controversial metaphysical thesis out of II, one has to provide some appropriate restriction on what can be considered as a property. For example, some philosophers employ a 'sparse' conception of properties according to which only a few privileged predicates get to express properties. (If identity isn't in the elite group, then it may, strictly speaking, be illegitimate even to speak of 'the identity relation', since there is no such entity even though 'is identical to' is a meaningful predicate.[17]) With a sparse conception in place, one might reasonably wonder whether, if x and y have the same sparse properties, then x and y are identical. Another example: One might wonder whether if x and y share every 'non-haecceitistic property', then x and y are identical (where haecceitistic properties—such as *being identical to John* or *being the daughter of Jim*—are those which, in some intuitive way, make direct reference to a particular individual(s)). One may be so interested because one thinks that there are not, strictly speaking, haecceitistic properties in reality (cf. Black 1999, discussed below); but even if one tolerates haecceitistic properties, one might think it an interesting metaphysical question whether the restricted thesis is true.

For any restricted class of properties, we can usefully imagine a target language in which there are only predicates for the restricted class of properties under consideration, plus quantifiers, an identity predicate, variables, and truth-functional connectives. We can now ask two questions. First, for any pair of objects x and y, will there be some predicate in the language that is true of one of them but not the other? This, in effect, is a test for the relevant restricted identity of indiscernibles thesis. Secondly, we can ask whether an I-predicate introduced by Quine's brute force method, using the vocabulary of that language (minus the identity predicate), would have as its extension all and only identical pairs. We need only recall Quine's distinction between things that are 'absolutely discernible' and things that are 'relatively discernible' to realize that the questions are distinct. To illustrate: Suppose there are two angels, Jack and Jill. Each is holy. Each loves him- or herself and the other angel. Consider a first-order language L containing the monadic predicates 'is an angel', 'is holy', and the diadic predicate 'loves'. Consider also a first-order language $L+$ that contains the predicates of L and, in addition, the predicate 'is a member of'. Neither L nor $L+$ contains individual constants. Nor do they contain an identity predicate. The angels are not absolutely discernible relative to L. That is, there is no open sentence with one free variable constructible in L such that Jack satisfies it but Jill doesn't. Nor are the angels relatively discernible in L. There is no

---

[17] Of course, the nominalist goes further and says that all ontologically serious talk of properties is illegitimate. Such a nominalist will owe us a nominalistically acceptable version of Leibniz's law. If that version is to apply to natural languages, the context-dependence of certain predicates should not be ignored.

relational truth of the form '$\exists x \exists y(x$ is an angel and y is an angel and $\exists z(xRz$ and $\sim yRz$))' that is constructible in L. How about $L+$? Relative to $L+$, the angels are not absolutely discernible. But they are relatively discernible. After all, $L+$ has the resources to express the truth: '$\exists x \exists y(x$ is an angel and y is an angel and $\exists z(x$ is a member of z and $\sim y$ is a member of z))'.

When we are in a position only to discern relatively but not to discern absolutely a certain pair of objects, that should not makes us queasy about our commitment to the existence of the pair. In his famous 'The Identity of Indiscernibles' Max Black seems on occasion to think otherwise. At a crucial juncture he has one of his interlocutors question whether it makes sense to speak of the haecceitistic properties of unnamed things. One of his interlocutors suggests of two duplicate spheres that are 2 miles from each other that they have the properties *being at a distance of 2 miles from Castor* and *being at a distance of 2 miles from Pollux*. Black's other interlocutor responds: 'What can this mean? The traveller has not visited the spheres, and the spheres have no names—neither "Castor", nor "Pollux", nor "a", nor "b", nor any others. Yet you still want to say they have certain properties which cannot be referred to without using names for the spheres' (Black 1999: 69). Black makes a fair point— which in Quine's lingo is the observation that the properties cannot be absolutely discerned using the resources of our language. That is not to say that they cannot be relatively discerned. To deny the existence of the pair of properties in such a world on the basis of our inability to discern them absolutely is no better, it would seem, than to deny the existence of the pair of spheres in the world on the basis of the fact that we cannot absolutely discern them. Analogously,[18] the singleton sets of spheres cannot be absolutely discerned, but that is not to say that they cannot be relatively discerned; and it would be utterly misguided to reject the claim that each thing has a singleton set on the basis of the fact that, for some pairs, we cannot absolutely discern the sets using our language (or any readily available extension of it).[19] The thought experiment of two lonely duplicate spheres works well to illustrate the thesis that it is possible that there be two things that cannot be absolutely discerned using a language with a rich range of qualitative, non-haecceitistic predicates. But it is not an effective way to make trouble for a liberal view of properties, one that allows the properties instantiated by each sphere to differ.

2.3 Substitutivity, Identity, Leibniz's Law

When we imagined a tribe that used a first-order language, we imagined that single predicates of their language were not such as to enjoy different extensions

---

[18] And on the set-theoretic gloss of properties, it is more than an analogy.
[19] I leave it open whether some other argument against haecceitistic properties might work.

on different occasions of use. If some predicate of their language 'F' expressed the property of being tall on its first occasion of use in a sentence and of being not tall on its second occasion of use, then 'Either a is F or it is not the case that a is F' could hardly be validated by first-order logic. Any language to which the schemas of first-order logic can be mechanically applied will not be a language with predicates whose extension is context-dependent in this way.

When it comes to natural languages with which we are familiar, matters are thus more complicated. We are forced to dismiss the metalinguistic principle that if an English sentence of the form 'a is identical to b' is true, then 'a' can be substituted *salva veritate* for 'b' in any sentence of English. This substitutivity principle, as a thesis about English, is false. The pair of sentences 'Giorgione was so called because of his size' and 'Barbarelli was so called because of his size' are counter-examples to the principle as it stands.[20] Here the predicate 'is so called because of his size' expresses different properties in different contexts, the key contextual parameter being the proper name that it attaches to.[21]

It was natural to envisage our earlier tribe as operating with the following inference rule:

(LL*) $\alpha I \beta \vdash P \supset Q$ (where P and Q are formulae that differ at most in that one or more occurrences of α in P are replaced by β in Q).

As we have just seen, this principle, with 'is identical to' substituted for 'I', cannot govern natural languages. So it seems very unlikely that our grip on the concept of identity is underwritten by that principle. In the context of discussing first-order languages, logicians often refer to LL* as Leibniz's law. One feels that *something like* that axiom governs our own understanding. But it can't be that axiom itself. So what is the correct understanding of Leibniz's law?

We have, in effect, touched on two alternative approaches. First, we have a property-theoretic conception of Leibniz's law:

(LL1)   If $x = y$, then every property possessed by x is a property possessed by y.

A closely related approach is set-theoretic:

(LL2)   If $x = y$, then every set that x belongs to is a set that y belongs to.

---

[20] As Cartwright (1987a) points out, the observation that 'the occurrence of "Giorgione"... is not purely referential... far from saving the Principle of Substitutivity... only acknowledges that the pair... is indeed a counterexample to it' (1987a: 138). As he goes on to point out, the example makes no trouble for a property-theoretic version of Leibniz's law. Also relevant here is Williamson's version of Leibniz's law, discussed below.

[21] Hence it is plausible to maintain that 'is so called because of his size' expresses the property 'is called "Giorgione" because of his size' when combined with the name 'Giorgione' and the property 'is called "Barbarelli" because of his size' when combined with the name 'Barbarelli'.

Both approaches have their limitations. If one has nominalist scruples against abstract objects, one will dislike both.[22] More importantly, the principles will have no direct bite in certain cases: If the semantic value of a predicate is context-dependent, then we cannot use these principles to test straightforwardly for non-identity. 'is so called because of his size' is one such predicate: one cannot say which property or set it expresses independently of the proper name it is combined with (unlike 'is called "Giorgione" because of his size'). This in turn makes for a possible strategy of response when confronted with an argument for non-identity using Leibniz's law: one might try claiming that the predicate in question expresses different properties (or has different extensions) depending on the proper name it is combined with (claiming that either the morphological features of the name or else the mode of presentation attaching to the name or some other crucial contextual parameter is relevant to the extension of the predicate).

Timothy Williamson has offered a third conception of Leibniz's law, which is avowedly metalinguistic, and which will be helpful to our later discussions:

[LL3]   Let an assignment A assign an object o to a variable v, an assignment A^* assign an object o^* to v, and A^* be exactly like A in every other way. Suppose that a sentence s is true relative to A and not true relative to A^*. Then o and o^* are not identical. (Williamson, forthcoming)

This principle can obviously be extended to cover individual constants:

Let an interpretation A assign an object o to a constant α, an interpretation A^* assign an object o^* to α, and A^* be exactly like A in every other way. Suppose that a sentence s is true relative to A and not true relative to A^*. Then o and o^* are not identical.

Return to 'Giorgione was so called because of his size'. An interpretation of this sentence that assigned Giorgione as the referent of 'Giorgione' will agree in truth-value with an interpretation of this sentence that assigned Barbarelli as the referent of 'Giorgione' and which in every other respect agreed with the first interpretation. This brings out an intended virtue of the metalinguistic conception: its application need not be restricted to a purely extensional language. And, as Williamson is aware, it promises to be especially useful as a test where the defensive strategy just gestured at is deployed. Suppose one defends the identity of x and y, pleading context-dependence in the face of a pair of true sentences 'Fa' and '$\sim Fb$', where 'a' refers to x, 'b' refers to y. The cogency of the plea can be tested by considering whether 'Fa' gets the same truth-value relative to a pair of assignments A and A^* such that A assigns x to 'a', A^* assigns y to 'a', A being exactly like A^* in every other way.[23]

---

[22] And even if one believes in abstract objects, they may not be the ones required by the relevant principle (for example, we may not believe in sets).

[23] As for its ontological commitments: that depends, of course, on how the notion of 'assignment' is cashed out. The standard model-theoretic approach will of course require sets.

3. Deviant Views: Relative, Time-Indexed, and Contingent Identity

3.1 Relative Identity

Famously, Peter Geach argued that the notion of absolute identity should be abandoned.[24] Suppose a lump that is also a statue exists at $t1$. Call it George. The lump gets squashed. A new statue (made by a new craftsman) is fashioned out of the squashed lump at $t2$. Call it Harry. Is George Harry? Geach's framework provides an answer with some intuitive appeal:

(A) George is the same lump as Harry.
(B) George is a different statue from Harry.

Statements of the form 'a is the same F as b' cannot, on this view, be analysed as 'a is an F, b is an F, and a is identical to b'. If such statements as 'Harry is the same lump as George' and 'Harry is the same statue as George' could be so analysed, then A and B, in conjunction with fact that George and Harry are both statues, would yield contradiction.[25] Relative identity predicates of the form 'is the same F as' are thus taken as semantically basic.

What then of the question 'Is George the very same thing as Harry?' On Geach's view, this question makes no sense. We can and must make sense of the world without the notion of absolute identity. Instead, we slice up reality with the aid of various basic sortal-relative identity predicates which, when 'derelativized', yield basic count nouns: 'is a statue', 'is a lump', and so on. On Geach's view, we can only grasp the meaning of a count noun when we associate with it a criterion of identity—expressed by particular relative identity sortal. The predicate 'is a thing' is not admitted as a sortal, and thus does not provide a basis for asking and answering questions of identity.

The 'count' in 'count noun' deserves particular attention. Geach notes the intimate tie between the concept of identity and the concept of number: non-identity between x and y makes for at least two; non-identity between x and y, y and z, and x and z makes for at least three; and so on. If judgements of identity are sortal-relative, so for judgements of number. Just as the question 'Is George identical to Harry' lacks sense, so does the question 'How many statue-shaped things were there present during the process?' (even if we strip the predicate 'statue-shaped' of all

---

[24] For valuable discussions of Geach's views, see Dummett (1993) and Noonan (1997).

[25] This point occasionally gets clouded by a use of the term 'diachronic identity' as if it were the name for a relation that is very intimate but not quite the same as identity. Any such use is likely to generate confusion.

vagueness[26]). Relative identity predicates are the basis for any given count. If asked to count statues, I will gather things together under the relation 'is the same statue as'. If asked to count lumps, I will gather things together under the relation 'is the same lump as'. (It is, then, obviously crucial to Geach's approach that relative identity predicates be symmetric and transitive.[27])[28]

In this connection, it should be noted that Geach's approach throws set theory into jeopardy. Our conceptual grip on the notion of a set is founded on the axiom of extensionality: a set x is the same as a set y iff x and y have the same members. But this axiom deploys the notion of absolute identity ('same members'). Eschew that notion and the notion of a set has to be rethought. In so far as the notion of a set is to be preserved at all, then identity and difference between sets has to be relativized: The question whether the set containing George is the same set as the set containing Harry cannot be answered in a straightforward fashion. Other concepts central to logic and semantics will also have to be significantly rethought. What, for example, is to count as an

---

[26] The predicate 'statue-shaped' does not have a criterion of identity associated with it and thus is not, by Geach's lights, a sortal.

[27] A relative identity relation R—say, being the same lump—is not reflexive, since it is not true that everything has R to itself (after all, some things aren't lumps), though any such relation will be such that if $x\ R$ some y then xRx.

[28] Geach often invokes Frege (1953) in support of his relative identity approach. As far as I can see, Frege's thesis that number concepts are second-order offers little support for Geach's approach. Frege's idea was that such concepts as 'at least two in number' are second-order concepts of first-level concepts, not first-level concepts that apply to objects. The most straightforward argument offered by Frege for this thesis is that it allows us to make excellent sense of claims of the form 'The Fs are zero in number', a claim that would be unintelligible if 'are zero' had to be a predicate of the things that satisfy 'F'. No Geachian conclusions should be drawn from Frege's remarks. In particular, Frege had no trouble with a simple binary relation of absolute identity. And his doctrines are perfectly consistent with the thesis that some number attaches to the concept 'x is identical to x' and that there is thus an absolute count on the number of objects in the world. Frege does say of the concept red, 'To a concept of this kind no finite number will belong', on account of the fact that 'We can . . . divide up something falling under the concept "red" into parts in a variety of ways, without the parts thereby ceasing to fall under the same concept "red".' But this is a long way from Geach's thesis that 'the trouble about counting the red things in a room is not that you cannot make an end of counting them, but that you cannot make a beginning; you never know whether you have counted one already, because "the same red thing" supplies no criterion of identity' (Geach 1980: 63). Frege's point seems to precisely be that you cannot make an end of counting them, and this for a boring reason: every red thing has red parts, this ensuring that 'no *finite* number' will belong to the number of red things. Frege does say that 'if I place a pile of playing cards in [someone's] hands with the words: Find the Number of these, this does not tell him whether I wish to know the number of cards, or of complete packs of cards, or even say of points in the game of skat. To have given him the pile in his hands is not yet to have given him completely the object he is to investigate.' Once again, this does not demonstrate a commitment to a radical view. After all, the proponent of absolute identity and difference would hardly be disposed to read an instruction of the form 'Find the number of these' as 'Find the number of objects in my hand'. As Frege reminds us, such instructions as the former are typically elliptical for an instruction far more mundane than the latter.

'extensional context'? What is it to mean to say that two terms 'corefer'? All of these notions are built upon the notions of simple identity and difference. Abandon those notions and the intelligibility of a large range of logico-semantic concepts is cast into doubt.

Current wisdom about proper names would also need rethinking were Geach's approach to be accepted. According to Geach, in order for a proper name to have a legitimate place in the language, it must have a criterion of identity associated with it—given by a relative identity predicate. The popular view (see Kripke 1972) that a name can be cogently introduced by either demonstration—'Let "Bill" name that thing (pointing)'—or else by a reference-fixing description (that need not encode a sortal in Geach's sense)—'Let "Bill" name the largest red thing in Alaska'—is thus anathema to Geach. Notice that, strictly speaking, the story with which I began this section did not, by Geach's standards, deploy legitimate proper names. I introduced 'George' as a name of the thing at $t1$ which is both a lump and a statue. But I didn't specify a relative identity predicate that is to govern the use of 'George'. Thus my mode of introduction left it undetermined whether the thing at $t2$ is to count as 'George', and thus how such sentences as 'George is statue-shaped at $t2$' are to be evaluated. Relative to the statue criterion, the latter sentence will be reckoned false—for nothing at $t2$ is the same statue as the statue at $t1$. Relative to the lump criterion, the sentence will be reckoned true—for the lump at $t1$ is the same lump as something that is statue-shaped at $t2$. Geach does not want sentences embedding a proper name that attribute a property to a thing at a time to be largely indeterminate in truth-value: hence the insistence on an associated criterion of identity. Return to the original case. We can introduce 'George' as the name for the lump at $t1$. Since the lump at $t1$ is also a statue, it is also true that 'George' is the name of a statue. But since 'George' has entered the language as a name for a lump, the rule for 'George' is that everything (at whatever time) that is the same lump as the lump at $t1$ shall count as deserving the name 'George'. Hence, it is the name *of* a statue, but not *for* a statue. (What if we instead insisted that George is not a statue at all? According to this suggestion, George is a lump but is not the same statue as any statue, being not a statue at all. This undercuts the motivation of the approach, one which is supposed to provide an alternative to a metaphysics that postulates distinct but wholly coincident objects. A standard metaphysics of coincident objects can allow that some statue-shaped lump can be the same lump as some statue-shaped lump at a later time without being the same statue as that lump: but it will explain this fact not by invoking a deviant view of identity but by simply pointing out that some statue-shaped lump can fail to be the same statue as anything whatsoever on account of the fact that statue-shaped lumps are not identical to the statues that they constitute.)

Notice that, on Geach's view, one does not come to understand a count noun merely by acquiring the ability to recognize, in any given case, whether or not the count noun applies to it.[29] Let us suppose that 'is a living thing' is true of a quantity of matter iff it has organic-biological characteristics F, G, and H. This may enable one to say of any quantity of matter whether or not it is a living thing. But this criterion of application would not enable one to discern of any pair of quantities of matter whether or not they counted as the same living thing. If the meaning of 'is the same living thing' is to fix the meaning of 'is a living thing', then a criterion of application will not in general provide the basis for understanding a count noun.[30]

Geach's approach is not merely designed (as the lump and statue example brings out) to give a distinctive treatment of diachronic questions about identity. He has also deployed it to give a distinctive treatment of certain synchronic questions. Consider his treatment of the so-called 'problem of the many': When we truly say 'There is a cat on the mat', there are a plentitude of overlapping cat-shaped quantities of 'feline tissue' that differ ever so slightly with respect to their boundaries. Which of them is the cat? Are we forced to the absurd conclusion that, contrary to common sense, there are many cats on the mat? Geach answers:

Everything falls into place if we realize that the number of cats on the mat is the number of different cats on the mat and $c13$, $c279$, and c [where $c13$, $c279$, and c are three cat-shaped quantities of feline tissue] are not three different cats, they are one and the same cat. Though none of these 1,001 lumps of feline tissue is the same lump of feline tissue as another, each is the same cat as any other: each of them, then, is a cat, but there is only one cat on the mat, and our original story stands.[31] (Geach 1980: 216)

It is easy enough to see a key drawback of Geach's approach here. Let 'Tabby' name $c13$, and 'Samantha' $c279$, and suppose that Samantha but not Tabby has some white bit of feline tissue, call it 'Freddy'. Suppose every other bit of Samantha is black (at least near the surface) and that every bit of Tabby is black. By hypothesis, Tabby is the same cat as Samantha and yet, at the time we are considering, the following truths hold:

> Samantha has Freddy as a part
> Tabby does not have Freddy as a part
> Tabby is black all over
> Samantha is not black all over

If I tell you that a certain cat is black all over and that Samantha is the very same cat as the aforementioned cat, wouldn't the inference to 'Samantha is black all

---

[29] Of course, it is not strictly true that mastery requires such recognitional capacities either. We should learn to live without verificationism. We may note that Geach's discussions of criteria of identity suggests that, on the matter of diachronic identity, he is rather too much in the grip of a verificationist picture.   [30] Wright (1983) was helpful to me here.

[31] This style of treatment, as a number of authors have noticed, offers one gloss on the mystery of the Trinity: There are three persons: Christ is not the same person as God the Father (and so on). There is one divinity: Christ is the same God as the Father.

over' be utterly compelling? Within the current framework, though, the inference schema

> α is black all over at t
> α is the same cat as β
> β is black all over at t

is invalid.

A vital feature of the notion of identity is its amenability to Leibniz's law. Within an extensional language, inferences of the form

> α is F
> α is identical to β
> Therefore, β is F

are valid. But inferences of that form are not in general valid within the current framework, even when the predicates are paradigmatically extensional from the standpoint of orthodoxy. (Consider instead Williamson's version of Leibniz's law, ready-made even for languages with intensional predicates. Given Geach's conception, the analogous version for 'is the same cat as', is wrong. 'Tabby is black all over' is true on the intended interpretation. Tabby is the same cat as Samantha. But if we were to assign Samantha as the referent of 'Tabby', keeping the interpretation otherwise unchanged, then on that assignment 'Tabby is black all over' would have to be reckoned false.)

Geach's relative identity predicates do not behave in the way Leibniz's law requires. We shouldn't, however, conclude that *all* inferences of the form

> α is F
> α is the same G as β
> Therefore, β is F

are invalid. After all, there may be some particular pair of predicates for which this inference *is* always truth-preserving. For example, instances of the schema

> α is not a duck
> α is the same cat as β
> Therefore, β is not a duck

are always truth-preserving. Following Peter van Inwagen, let us say that a particular relative identity predicate R 'dominates' a particular predicate F if and only if it is a necessary truth that $\ulcorner \forall x \, \forall y (\, (xRy$ and x is $F) \supset y$ is $G)\urcorner$ (see van Inwagen 1995). van Inwagen notes that, within this kind of framework, there will be plenty of substantive, non-trivial, questions concerning which predicates are dominated by which relative identity predicates. We have just noted, for example, that predicates of the form 'being black all over at t' may well not be dominated by 'is the same cat as'. And we noted earlier, in effect, that predicates of the form 'being a statue at t', while dominated by the predicate 'is the same statue as', are not dominated by predicates of the form 'is the same lump as'.

Consider now one of Geach's examples of a relative identity predicate, 'is a sur-man'. The idea is this: x is to count as the same surman as y iff x is a man, y is a man, and x and y have the same surname. My father, Patrick Hawthorne, is thus the same surman as me. Clearly 'is the same surman as' does not dominate 'was born in 1964', since that is true of me and not of my father. On the other hand, one would suppose that it does dominate 'is a man'. Relative identity predicates are supposed to be legitimate bases for the introduction of a proper name. Thus let us introduce 'Bob' as the name for (and not merely of) the surman that is the same surman as me. Thus anything that is the same surman as me will merit that name. Assuming 'is the same surman as' dominates both 'is a man' and 'has the surname "Hawthorne"', Bob's surname is 'Hawthorne' and Bob is a man.

But if my hair is brown and my father's black, which colour is Bob's hair?[32] Are we to say that there is a man—Bob—with no hair?[33] The criterion of identity does not seem to be an adequate basis upon which to discern which predicates are applicable to Bob.

There are two reactions here. One is the tack of Geach's later self, namely, to renounce 'is the same surman as' as a legitimate basis for the introduction of a proper name:

The question is whether I could go on to construct propositions of the forms 'F(some surman)' and 'F(every surman)'. By my account of the quantifying words 'every' and 'some', this would be legitimate only if there could also be propositions of the form '$F(a)$', where 'a' is a proper name for a surman, a name with its built-in criterion of identity given by 'is the same surman as'. But without the unrestricted assumption that any old non-empty equivalence relation founds a class of proper names, there is not the faintest reason to believe such proper names could be given. Dummett and others have hotly attacked the poor surmen; I must abandon them to their doom. (Geach 1991: 295)

One might instead try to show that, with suitable inventiveness, a proper name for a surman can be given some discipline. We are familiar with the tack of time-indexing predicates. The lump is spherical at $t1$, flat at $t2$, and so on. This handles predication for things that are present at different times. Bob would appear to be present at different places. So perhaps predications need to be place-indexed. Bob, like myself, is brown-haired at p at t (the place where I am at t), and is black-haired at $p2$ at t (the place where my father is at t). The trouble is that this approach runs into trouble with various platitudes. We want to say that no man could be in two places at the same time. Bob is, by hypothesis, a man, and yet Bob is at $p1$ and at $p2$. Even more awkward is the question of how many men there are.[34] We know that Bob is a man and that Bob is the same surman as John and the same surman

---

[32] This problem is raised in Dummett (1993: 321).

[33] Granted, it is not absurd to suppose that there is a hairless man. But this seems like a very dubious basis for thinking that a hairless man exists.

[34] Similarly, suppose I have changed my name from 'Hawthorne' to 'O'Leary-Hawthorne' and then back again. There are two surman. Which of them am I the same surman as?

as Patrick. But given that 'same man is' is transitive, we cannot say that Bob is the same man as John and the same man as Patrick. So are Bob, Patrick, and John to count as three different men? That will make a hash of our ordinary methods for counting men.

So perhaps we would do better to follow the original tack of jettisoning the idea that 'surman' is a suitable basis for a proper name. But doesn't the problem generalize? Suppose a clay statue is at $t1$ made of a lump, call it 'Lump1' and at $t2$ made of a slightly different lump (through erosion or small replacements), call it 'Lump2'. Let 'Jerry' name the clay statue that endures throughout the period from $t1$ to $t2$. (I didn't use a particular time, you will note, when introducing 'Jerry' as the name for a clay statue.) Is Jerry the same lump of clay as Lump1? Is Jerry the same lump of clay as Lump2? We don't want to say that Jerry is not a lump of clay at all, since it would be strange to allow that some clay statues are lumps of clay, others not. And since 'is the same lump as' is transitive, we cannot give an affirmative answer to both of the questions just raised. Given the symmetry, we had better give a negative answer to both. So is it, then, the case that at $t1$ there exists a statue that is the same lump of clay as Lump1 and another statue—Jerry—which is not the same lump of clay as Lump1? The original intuitiveness of the approach has evaporated. The problem is structurally analogous to the concern just raised about surmen. But one has no temptation in this case to respond by admitting that the sortal 'is a statue' is an unacceptable foundation for a proper name.

The most promising approach here, I suggest, is to make use of the notion of semantic indeterminacy: It is determinate that Jerry is a statue and determinate that Jerry is either the same lump as Lump1 or the same lump as Lump2, but it is indeterminate whether Jerry is the same lump as Lump1 and indeterminate whether Jerry is the same lump as Lump2.[35] Rampant indeterminacy of this sort will have to be tolerated by the proponent of the approach. But perhaps it is not so damaging.

I shall not inquire further into the depth of this problem as there are even more pressing concerns about Geach's approach. I express four such concerns below.

1. There is something altogether absurd, it would seem, with the following pair of claims:

> Jim is black all over at t
>
> It is not the case that Jim is black all over at t.

How is Geach to explain the patent absurdity? It is natural to appeal to the relative identity sortal that governs the proper name 'Jim'. Perhaps that relative identity sortal dominates the predicate 'black all over', and this fact explains why we cannot endorse both claims. But suppose 'Jim' is the name for a cat and that, for reasons we have just seen, 'is the same cat as' does not dominate 'black all over'.

---

[35] Cf. standard supervaluationist treatments of vagueness.

Then we cannot offer that style of explanation. Meanwhile, the style of explanation that is most natural is forbidden, namely: That the reason that the pair of claims cannot be true is that one and the same object cannot be such that it is both black all over and not black all over at the same time. That style of explanation makes use of the rejected notion of identity. Even if we could begin to bring ourselves to live with the idea that Jim is the same cat as Jack and that Jim but not Jack is black all over, it is much harder to live with the cogency of the above pair of claims. Are we to learn to live with that pair too? And if not, what is the mechanism for ruling them out? There would appear to be an especially intimate relationship between Jim and Jim that precludes Jim being black all over and Jim not being black all over that fails between, say, Tabby and Samantha in our earlier example. Geach seems to lack the resources to explain this.

What, then, if Geach simply claims that the pair are logically contradictory, refusing to explain matters further? Note, though, that the two sentences are not contradictory if the first occurrence of 'Jim' names a cat in Blackpool and the second a quite different cat in Coventry. Some condition has to be satisfied in order for there to be a genuine contradiction here. Orthodoxy has a very easy time saying what the condition is, namely, that the two name tokens are names for the very same thing. The problem is that this story is not available to Geach: and it is utterly unclear what story is to take its place.

2. The proposals concerning the use of a proper name, as I have understood them, are not in fact coherent. Return to the Tabby and Samantha example. Suppose we agree that there is a cat composed of certain parts that exclude Freddy (which you may recall, is a particular candidate cat part). I stipulate that 'Samantha' is the name for that cat, and not merely of that cat. That is to say, I insist on associating the criterion of identity of cathood (as opposed, say, to feline tissue) with 'Samantha'. Having so associated that criterion, one would presume that, suitably informed, I would be able to evaluate claims using 'Samantha'. But how would I do it? Suppose I find that some cat is F. How do I then determine whether that fact is sufficient for the truth of 'Samantha is F'? Well, it would appear that by associating the cat criterion with 'Samantha' I have thereby given myself a procedure: What I do in the case at hand is to determine whether the thing in question is the same cat as Samantha. If it turns out that it is, then I will come to accept the claim that Samantha is F. (Of course, if I had associated a feline tissue criterion with 'Samantha', then the discovery that the F thing was the same cat as Samantha wouldn't have sufficed.) The trouble is that this cannot be the procedure that Geach has in mind. For recall that (a) Samantha has Freddy as a part, (b) Tabby lacks Freddy as a part, and (c) Samantha is the same cat as Freddy. By the proposed procedure, we will now be committed to claiming that Samantha lacks Freddy as a part (since 'Samantha' has the cat criterion associated with it and 'Samantha' picks out a cat that is the same cat as a cat that lacks Freddy as a part). That is intolerable, given (a). So how exactly

does a criterion of identity ground our competence in a proper name? I remain uncertain.[36]

3. I earlier noted the apparent need for the concept of absolute identity in order to understand the significance of recurring variables in first-order predicate logic. Consider, for example, the claim '$\exists x(x$ is perfectly round and x is red all over)'. How, if we are Geach, are we to understand the truth-conditions for a claim like this? We can make the worry a little more precise.[37] Suppose a tribe comes along and uses what appears to be a first-order language without the identity symbol. We can imagine, then, that the tribe writes down sentences like

(S1) $\exists x(x$ is red and x is round).

This tribe then declares that they have read Geach and have been convinced that there is no such thing as absolute identity. The tribe notices our inclination to take S1 in their mouths as expressing the claim that there is a red thing that is identical to some round thing. The tribe insists that this would be to misconstrue the content of what they were saying. They insist that S1 encodes no claim about identity. We have misunderstood. We ask them to explain to us the semantics of S1. We notice that the tribe is careful to use a meta-language without an identity predicate. Our failure to get the hang of what the tribe is supposed to be saying by S then simply recurs when we encounter such semantic claims as

(S2) '$\exists x(x$ is red and x is round)' is true iff $\exists x(x$ satisfies 'is red' and x satisfies 'is round').

For the tribe will claim that we have misunderstood when we take S2 to be equivalent to the claim that S1 is true iff something that satisfies 'is red' is identical to something that satisfies 'is round'. It is not that we can show such a tribe that their own rules of inference lead to what is, by their standards, absurdity. In that sense, there is no incoherence charge that we can level against them. But we may justly complain that such a tribe is unintelligible to us. We are simply at a loss to make sense of the variables at work in the tribe's language. In that sense, we may justly worry that a proponent of Geach's views is ultimately unintelligible in just the same way.

Perhaps the proponent of Geach's framework would respond to all this by claiming that S1 is somehow incomplete, and that a relative identity predicate appropriate

---

[36] There are also puzzles concerning how to evaluate definite descriptions. Suppose an artefact is composed of Lump1 and is the same artefact as one composed of Lump2. How do we evaluate 'The artefact is composed of Lump1'? Do we reckon it false because even though there is an artefact that is composed of Lump1 and every artefact (in the relevant domain) is the same artefact as it, there is some artefact that is the same artefact as it that is not composed of Lump1? Such questions point to further difficulties for a Geachian semantics.   [37] I am grateful to Kit Fine here.

to the variable needs to be supplied to complete it.[38] First-order predicate logic, even without identity, would then need rewriting. The relevant work remains to be done.

4. A pressing issue for the defender of Geach is to explain *why* the concept of absolute identity is incoherent. Suppose we begin with a language L devoid of a sign of absolute identity, containing only relative identity predicates, proper names, variables, predicates, and so on. What would be wrong with adding a predicate 'I' that is governed by a reflexivity axiom—so that any claim $\ulcorner \alpha R \alpha \urcorner$ is true—and by Leibniz's law (recall generalizations (i) and (ii) earlier)?[39] Apply it to the problem of the many: We would now be able to extract the conclusion that while Tabby I Tabby (by reflexivity) and Samantha I Samantha (by reflexivity), it is not the case that Tabby I Samantha (by Leibniz's law).[40] Suppose we continue to maintain that 'Tabby is the same cat as Samantha' is true. We shall then wish to observe that, as the predicate 'is the same cat as' is being used, it does not require that the relation expressed by 'I' obtains between Tabby and Samantha. It seems that 'I' will now express genuine identity and that 'is the same cat as' is being used to express a relation that can hold between non-identical pairs. Apply this perspective to the problem of the Trinity: Suppose that 'Christ is the same divinity as the Father' and 'Christ is a different person from the Father' both express truths. The natural diagnosis is that since 'Christ is a different person from the Father' becomes false when 'Christ' is reinterpreted as referring to the Father, then, by Leibniz's law,[41] Christ is not identical with the Father. If the relevant sentences are both true, 'is the same divinity as' will have to be treated as expressing a transitive and symmetric relation that can hold between non-identical pairs.

Geach has recognized the possibility of introducing an I-predicate into a language that lacked an identity predicate. But he claims that one is never thereby in a position to claim of one's I-predicate that it expresses absolute identity:

No criterion has been given, or, I think, could be given for a predicable's being used in a language L to express absolute identity. The familiar axiom schemata for identity could at most guarantee, if satisfied, that the relative term under investigation will be true in L only of pairs that are indiscernible by descriptions framed in terms of the other predicables of L.

---

[38] Further radicalizations are possible: perhaps it is a sortal relative matter whether any two given predicate tokens express the same property or not. (It would, after all, be unfortunate if it turned out that Geach was tacitly using a semantics in which the identity and difference of properties is absolute.) This in turn will complicate the matter of assessing various property-theoretic versions of Leibniz's law, as applied to various identity sortals. What would we make of a believer in the Trinity who introduced a 'same-God-property as' sortal and claimed that if a person x has a property F and that person is the same God as some person y, then that person will have some property which is the same God-property as F? One might claim that something rather in the spirit of Leibniz's law is salvageable by this finesse. It is not within the scope of this chapter to explore such proposals as this one.

[39] One method of introduction would be to apply Quine's method, described earlier, to L, assuming its basic stock of predicates is finite and that it is extensional. If L merely has an extensional fragment, one could apply Quine's method to that fragment.

[40] Assuming suitable expressive resources for L.   [41] I am using Williamson's version here.

This cannot guarantee that there is no proper extension of L, with extra predicables, that makes possible the discrimination of things which were indiscernible by the resources of L. (Geach 1991: 297)

What Geach is trading on, then, is a point already noted: the mere fact that a predicate is an I-predicate for a language is of itself no guarantee that the predicate expresses the identity relation.

What of the attempt to define identity outright using the resources of second-order logic? Here is Geach again:

Sometimes we are told identity is definable in second-order logic: for any F, $F(x)$ iff $F(y)$. But it is gravely doubtful whether such quantification is admissible if quite unrestricted: can a quantification cover *all* properties or concepts, including such as would be expressed by this very style of quantification? (Geach 1991: 297)

and elsewhere:

'For real identity', we may wish to say, 'we need not bring in the ideology of a definite theory T. For real identity, *whatever* is true of something identical with a is true of a and conversely, regardless of which theory this can be expressed in; and a two-place predicable signifying real identity must be an I-predicable no matter what other predicables occur along with it in the theory.' But if we wish to talk this way, we shall soon fall into contradictions; such unrestrained language about 'whatever is true of a', not made relative to the definite ideology of a theory T, will land us in such notorious paradoxes as Grelling's and Richard's. If, however, we restrict ourselves to the ideology of a theory T, then, as I said, an I-predicable need not express strict identity, but only indiscernibility within the ideology of T. (Geach 1972: 240)

If we assume (*per impossibile* for Geach) that there is such a relation as strict identity, the worry isn't that our imagined I-predicate is false of pairs that are strictly identical. We can all agree that if x and y are identical, then the relation expressed by an I-predicate will hold between x and y. The worry is that the converse does not hold and that, moreover, there is no device available by means of which we can stipulatively ensure that it does hold. We cannot, says Geach, legitimately quantify over all extensions of our language or over all properties and relations. But without the ability to do that, it is not clear how we can ensure that some binary predicate will express strict identity.

I have a number of concerns about this line of resistance.[42]

First, once one realizes that there is at least an I-predicate of English[43]—call it 'English-identity'—that is available, much of the intuitive interest of the original approach disappears. We agree that if there is such a thing as strict identity, then English non-identity guarantees strict non-identity (whether or not English-identity

[42] Much of what follows reiterates points made in Dummett (1993).

[43] Of course, since English is not an extensional language, we should strictly say that 'English-identity' is merely an I-predicate with respect to some extensional fragment of English, perhaps idealized to remove elements of context-dependence. Geach, wisely, does not fuss over such issues; neither shall we.

is or isn't the same relation as strict identity). Consider, for example, the treatment of the Trinity: It is certain that Christ is not English-identical to the Father and thus certain that if there *is* strict identity, it fails to obtain between the Father and Christ. The requirements of 'English-identity' *are no more* demanding than strict identity. Christ and the Father fail even to pass those standards.

Secondly, one presumes that Geach will offer an argument to the effect that the concept of absolute identity is incoherent. But what we really find instead is an argument to the effect that there is no straightforward mechanism for defining absolute identity that is provided by the resources of logic (without an identity predicate) alone, nor even by a second-order logic that provides the means for quantifying over a (restricted) domain of properties. But since the concept of identity is plausibly a basic one, it is not clear how to move from these remarks about definition to a conclusion that asserts the incoherence of the concept of absolute identity.

Thirdly, Geach would appear to be trying to have it both ways. Suppose we allow ourselves the English predicate 'is identical to'. We announce the reflexivity of the property it expresses by claiming: 'Everything is identical to itself.' And we announce commitment to Leibniz's law: If x is identical to y, then the truth-value of any English sentence with a name that refers to x will be unaltered on an otherwise similar interpretation that interprets that name as referring to y. If we hadn't read Geach, we would go on and deploy 'is identical to' in mandatory ways: Tabby is not identical to Samantha. Christ is not identical to the Father. But now we are supposed to worry that just maybe 'is identical to' fails to express 'strict identity'. How were we supposed to be convinced that there is a worry here? Geach points out that, just perhaps, there are extensions of English such that predicates of that extended language will distribute differently with regard to some pair that satisfies the ordinary English 'is identical to'. Now it seems we have a ready answer: let us stipulate that 'is identical to' will satisfy Leibniz's law not merely when it comes to English but, moreover, for any extension of English. But in response Geach argues that it is incoherent to quantify over any extension of English in this way. But didn't Geach have to quantify over extensions of English in order to raise the worry in the first place? Either talk of extensions of English is incoherent, in which case a worry that 'is identical to' doesn't express absolute identity cannot be raised, or else we can raise quantify over a domain of extensions of English, relative to which we can point out that perhaps an I-predicate of English will not express identity proper. But in so far as one can coherently quantify over a domain of extensions, one can stipulatively introduce a predicate that will be immune to the relevant worry: with such quantificational apparatus in place, one can introduce a predicate 'is identical to' stipulating that it is an I-predicate relative to any extension. The apparatus required for raising the worry is the very apparatus needed for solving it. It is as if Geach allows himself unrestricted quantification over extensions of our language in order to get the worry going on and subsequently points out that only restricted quantification over extensions of the language is coherent.[44]

Fourthly,[45] even granting for the moment that quantification over absolutely all properties makes no sense,[46] there remains the possibility that it is perfectly coherent to quantify over all relative identity relations (of which the relations expressed by, say, 'is the same cat as' is an example). The threat of paradox raised by quantification over absolutely all properties does not so clearly arise when one's domain is restricted in this way. At the same time, this domain can form the basis, even by Geach's lights it would seem, of a perfectly serviceable notion of 'absolute identity': x is identical to y iff for all relative identity relations R, xRy.

In sum: it is no mere artefact of philosophical fashion that Geach's relative identity approach has few adherents.

3.2 Time-Indexed Identity

A lump of clay (call the lump 'Clay') is fashioned into a statue (call it 'Statue') at $t1$. At $t2$ it is refashioned into a jug (call it 'Jug'). What is the relationship between Clay, Statue, and Jug? One feels intuitive pressure towards admitting that Statue no longer exists at $t2$. One feels intuitive pressure against thinking there are two things in the same place at the same time at $t1$. And one feels intuitive pressure towards allowing that Clay exists at $t1$ and $t2$. Many standard accounts simply resist along one or more dimensions of intuitive pressure. Geach's relative identity approach attempts to accommodate all these intuitions. Another approach similarly designed is that which insists that identity is time-indexed. Begin by noting that ordinary predications intuitively need a time index. If Clay changes colour from red to blue, we would appear to need a time index to capture the relevant truths: Clay is red with respect to such-and-such a time, and blue with respect to a later time. If the truths about colour need time-indexing, then why not the truths about identity?

---

[44] There is certainly more to say here on this particular point. The most promising version of Geach's objection will allow that there are larger and larger domains of properties available for properties variables, but no maximal domain (or at least so to speak—it is not clear that such a metasemantic claim as the one just made will be strictly allowable). For any I-predicate introduced by appeal to one domain of properties $D1$, one would then always be able to cite a larger domain $D2$ relative to which it is intelligible that a pair of objects satisfy the original I-predicate but nevertheless differ with respect to certain properties in $D2$. It is beyond the scope of this chapter to evaluate this particular semantic perspective. We should be clear, though, that the mere impossibility of utterly unrestricted quantification hardly serves to vindicate Geach. Even if some ordinary English claims of the form 'Some F is identical to some G' involve restricted quantification, that does not at all by itself imply that, from a perspective in which a more inclusive domain is in view, we can make a speech like '$o1$ (which is F) and $o2$ (which is G) make true the ordinary English sentence "Some F is identical to some G" even though they are not really identical.' (Thanks to Ted Sider here.)

[45] I am grateful to Kit Fine here.

[46] Whether unrestricted quantification of this sort is possible is not an issue I can pursue here.

Why not say that Clay is identical to Statue with respect to such-and-such a time and that Clay is not identical to Statue but instead to Jug at a later time? Following some ideas of Paul Grice, this view was developed by George Myro:

I think that we should not regard this as a 'new notion of identity, relativized, identity-at-a-time—any more than we should in dealing with an object changing from being red to being green, regard ourselves as needing a 'new' notion of being red, relativized, being-red-at-a-time. The idea is simply that we should regard statements—*not excluding statements of identity*—as subject to temporal qualifications in a systematic and uniform way. Thus, we are to envisage having in a 'regimented' sort of way:

> at t, A is red
> at t', A is green (not red)

and:

> at t, $A = B$
> at t', $A \neq B$

such that in suitable circumstances, *both* members of each pair are true. (Myro 1997: 155–6)

Note that there are certain puzzle cases for which this approach will yield distinctive results where Geach has nothing to offer. Suppose I exist at $t1$ and at $t2$ undergo fission into two individuals, John1 and John2. Geach cannot say that I am the same person as John1 and am the same person as John2, since relative identity predicates are suppose to be symmetric and transitive.[47] Nor can the intuitive difficulties of the case be traced to a vacillation between a pair of relative identity predicates. Geach's account has no new ideas to offer on fission cases. By contrast, Myro's approach is ready-made for this case:

> At $t1$ John1 $=$ John2
> At $t2$ it is not the case that John1 $=$ John2.

By contrast, those cases where Geach's approach offers distinctive approaches to synchronic questions about identity (the problem of the many, the Trinity, and so on) are cases where Myro's approach has nothing distinctive to offer.

Myro is well aware of the pressure from Leibniz's law. Consider first the property-theoretic version. Return to the fission case. Let us suppose that at $t2$ John2 is in Paris and John1 is in Rome. It then seems that at $t1$ John1 has the property of being such that he will be in Rome at $t2$, and that at $t1$ John2 lacks that property. But can't we then fairly conclude that at $t1$ John1 is not John2?

---

[47] See also Prior (1957), which treats fission in a way that adapts the time-relative identity approach to a presentist perspective (where a presentist is one who thinks that only presently existing individuals exist, so that facts about the future and past expressed by primitive tense operators no more require the existence of merely past and future beings than modal operators require the existence of merely possible beings).

Myro himself focuses on the property-theoretic version of Leibniz's law. He insists that all statements must, like colour attributions, be temporally qualified. He thus insists that Leibniz's law first be temporally qualified thus:

At all times, if $A = B$, then A is F if and only if B is F

(where 'F' expresses a property). Aware that this does not, by itself, solve the problem with which we are currently concerned, he goes on to add the following suggested qualification to the law:

So the general way of dealing with the complication is to divide properties into those which are '*time-free*'—like being on the mantelpiece—which are represented by open sentences *not* containing temporal qualifications, and those which are '*time-bound*'—like being on the mantelpiece on Tuesday—which are represented by open sentences which do contain temporal qualifications. And what must be done is that 'Leibniz's Law subject (like other statements) to temporal qualification' is to be, in addition *restricted* to properties which are '*time-free*'— properly represented by open sentences (or 'predicates') which do not (relevantly) contain temporal qualifications. (Myro 1997: 157)

There is a natural worry. Suppose we concede to Myro his predicate 'is identical to'. We then introduce our own predicate 'is really identical to', which is governed by Leibniz's law in its unrestricted version.[48] Perhaps Myro will complain: 'But then you will count John1 and John2 as two at $t1$ when they are really one at $t1$.' Given the intimate connection between the identity predicate and counting, it is easy to see through the complaint. Myro is using the relation he expresses by 'is identical to' as a basis for a count at $t1$. But we intend to count by the relation expressed by 'is really identical to'. From the perspective of the latter, Myro will be reckoned to be counting certain equivalence classes of really distinct objects that are bundled together under an equivalence relation of 'have the same time-free properties'.

But perhaps the proponent of time-indexed identity can resist. Let us begin by noting that, following Williamson, we can avoid the detour through properties. Suppose it is now $t1$. By hypothesis, now, John1 = John2. Further now, John1 will be in Rome at $t2$. But if John1 is identical to John2, then an interpretation of 'John1 will be in Rome at $t2$' which assigned John2 as the reference of 'John1' but which was in other respects the same as the original ought to preserve truth-value (recall the applicability of Williamson's test to intensional contexts). Myro's best tack would be to allow that such an interpretation *would* preserve truth-value, just as an interpretation of 'Giorgione is so-called because of his size' is true on an interpretation that assigns Barbarelli as the referent of 'Giorgione'. ('is so called because of his size' generates an intensional context, with the result that substituting the name 'Giorgione' for the name 'Barbarelli' will not preserve truth-value. However, that by itself is no threat to the metalinguistic version of Leibniz's law.) Myro's approach stands or falls at this point, I suspect. Concede that interpreting 'John1' as

---

[48] Note that this move parallels one made earlier in connection with Geach.

referring to John2 makes the sentence 'John1 will be in Rome' false, and one is left with no alternative but to suppose that there are two objects in play and that Myro is appropriating 'is identical to' in order to express a relation other than identity.

Let us persist with the Giorgione–Barbarelli analogy.

(1) Giorgione is so called because of his size

is perfectly acceptable. But the existence of an intensional context renders dubious the use of existential instantiation to deliver

(2) There is someone who is so called because of his size.

The inference is unacceptable, since the content of 'is so called because of his size' is context-dependent. In particular, its content depends upon the particular lexical items that precede it.[49] The premiss says that Giorgione was called 'Giorgione' because of his size. The conclusion says, in effect, that someone is called 'someone' because of his size, a claim that hardly follows from the premiss.

The approach we are considering on behalf of Myro allows that

(3) It is now the case that John1 will be in Rome

and

(4) It is now not the case that John2 will be in Rome

are both true, even though the truth-value of (3) is the same on any pair of assignments that assign John1 and John2 respectively to 'John1' (where those assignments are otherwise exactly the same). This can only be so if the content of 'will be in Rome' is context-dependent, so that it has a different meaning (and a different extension) according to the subject term it is combined with. Since, by hypothesis, the referent of 'John1' and 'John2' are the same, and since their superficial orthographic features seem irrelevant in this case, it seems likely that the proponent of the view we are exploring will think that 'John1' and 'John2' have different *meanings*—call them with Frege 'modes of presentation'—which determine a different meaning (and thus extension) for 'will be in Rome' as it occurs in (3) and (4). Thus even though 'John1' and 'John2' now refer to the very same object, 'John1 will be in Rome' is true and 'John2 will be in Rome' is false, since the pair of tokenings of 'will be in Rome' in (3) and (4) are not true of the same objects. Let us imagine, then, that the extension of a given token of 'will be in Rome' depends upon a contextual parameter that is fixed either by the mode of presentation of the subject term (or else by some rule that is not explicitly articulated). In effect, 'John1' and 'John2', while agreeing in referent, fix the relevant contextual parameter in different ways, owing to the different modes of presentation associated with them.[50]

---

[49] As Brian Weatherson pointed out to me, the relevant piece of semantics would have to be complicated further to handle such sentences as 'Giorgione is so called because of his size and so is Tiny Tim'.

[50] The analogy with the 'Giorgione' case is not perfect, of course. In the latter case, what matters to the content of 'is so called because of his size' is the lexical make-up of the noun phrase or determiner

If the modes of presentation associated with 'John1' and 'John2' are crucial to the meaning of 'will be in Rome' in (3) and (4), then we should expect to be more than a little troubled by the use of existential instantiation on (3) and (4) to deliver:

(5) It is now the case that $\exists x(x$ will be in Rome)

(6) It is now that case that $\exists x(\sim x$ will be in Rome).

On the approach we are considering, (5) and (6) will be incomplete as they stand. We shall only be able to make sense of (5) and (6) by treating them as elliptical for some such claims as the following:

(7) It is now the case that $\exists x(x$ *qua* such and such (for example, *qua* John1) will be in Rome)[51]

and

(8) It is now the case that $\exists x(x$ *qua* so and so (for example, *qua* John2) will not be in Rome).

That the unqualified (5) and (6) should be reckoned incomplete is a claim that seems hard to defend, to say the least.[52] Note in any case that we are now, in effect, exploring an approach to 'time-indexed identity' that is not so far from orthodoxy about *identity* as may first be imagined.[53] After all, on the approach currently being considered, 'will be in Rome' does not have a property associated with it *simpliciter*, since it is incomplete. The real future-describing properties, on the view now being explored, are properties like *being such that qua John1 one will be in Rome*. Adopt that perspective on the nature of temporal properties and the restriction of Leibniz's law to 'time-free properties' can, after all, be lifted.[54]

phrase that precedes the predicate. In the current case what plausibly matters (for one who adopts Myro's perspective) is the sense or mode of presentation of the lexical item that precedes the predicate. (I do not by any means intend myself to be *endorsing* the idea that proper names have modes of presentation associated with them.)

[51] I do not pretend that the '*qua F*' construction has been suitably explained. Indeed, I leave it to proponents of the view to make it maximally intelligible. As a first pass, though, we should think of 'will be' as expressing a three-place relation between an object, a mode of presentation, and a property. If the relevant mode of presentation is not explicitly supplied, it will have to be supplied by the context of conversation. Otherwise, a 'will be' utterance will not determinately express a proposition.

[52] Similarly, the view would have it that 'He will be in Rome' (pointing) is incomplete unless some parameter-fixing mode of presentation is supplied.

[53] It should be noted that there is a very different way of handling the issue, suggested by Gallois (1998). The worry about John1 and John2 proceeded via a very natural assumption: Some x is at $t1$ such that it will be F at $t2$ iff at $t2$ x is F. Gallois rejects that assumption. We are thus denied the licence to use the fact that at $t2$ John1 is in Rome and at $t2$ John2 isn't in Rome as a basis for inferring that at $t1$ John1 will be in Rome at $t2$ and at $t1$ it is not the case that John2 will be in Rome at $t2$. The approach is offered as a way of combining temporary identity with Leibniz's law (at least in the 'temporally qualified' form). The intuitive oddity of the view should, however, be evident. Though I shall pursue the point here, it also seems that the cogency of this approach requires the unavailability of a description of the world that deploys timeless quantifiers and various relations of objects to times.

[54] Another deviant approach to tensed claims that leaves orthodoxy about identity undisturbed is provided by Sider (1996), who adapts counterpart theory to diachronic issues.

Let me finally remark on Myro's first qualification of Leibniz's law. Instead of

> For all x and y, if $x = y$, x has some property F if and only if y has some property F

he opts for the temporally qualified

> At all times, if $x = y$ then Fx iff Fy.

One would think that we can assimilate the second version to the first. What is it for a claim of the form 'At t α is red' to be true? A natural suggestion is that to be red is to stand in a certain relation to a time.[55] Orthodoxy tells us, indeed, that the truths about the world can thus be expressed with a timeless quantifier and no temporal prefix. From this perspective 'At t something is red' has the following logical form:

$$\exists x(xRt)$$

(where 't' picks out a time and 'R' expresses a relation that can hold between objects and times).[56] From this perspective, the time-indexed approach to identity becomes particularly strained. No one can reasonably suppose that 'a is red at $t1$' is an intensional context, forbidding existential instantiation. Suppose John1 is red at $t1$ and is red at $t2$, and that John2 is red at $t1$ and not red at $t2$.

The following claims are now unproblematically licensed:

> $\exists x(x$ is red at $t1$ and x is red at $t2)$
> $\exists x(x$ is red at $t1$ and is not red at $t2)$.

But now the inference to

> $\exists x(x$ is red at $t1$ and $\exists y(y$ is red at $t1$ and x is not $y))$

is irresistible. The cogency of Myro's approach depends, it would seem, on the unavailability of a description of the world that deploys timeless quantifiers and various relations of objects to times.

3.3 Contingent Identity

In *Naming and Necessity* Saul Kripke wrote:

Waiving fussy considerations deriving from the fact that x need not have necessary existence, it was clear from $(x)\Box(x = x)$ and Leibniz's Law that identity is an 'internal' relation: $(x)(y)(x = y \supset \Box x = y)$. (Kripke 1972: 3)

---

[55] Perhaps primitive, perhaps reducible to having a temporal part that is red *simpliciter* that exists at that time.

[56] An alternative view holds that the copula expresses a three-place relation between a thing, a property, and a time. The point that follows could be easily adapted to fit that view. For further discussion, see Sally Haslanger ch. 11 in this volume.

Some have argued, by contrast, that identity is contingent. But coherent versions of the contingent identity view do not present us with a novel conception of identity, and in particular, do not invoke some alternative to Leibniz's law (in either its property-theoretic or else metalinguistic versions). Rather, they attempt to reconcile the contingent identity thesis with an utterly orthodox conception of the identity relation itself. An excellent case in point is provided by David Lewis's defence of the contingent identity view.[57] Lewis defends a counterpart-theoretic approach to modality according to which $\ulcorner\alpha$ is possibly $F\urcorner$ is true just in case there is some appropriately similar entity to the thing designated by α—a 'counterpart' in another possible world—that satisfies F, and $\ulcorner\alpha$ is necessarily $F\urcorner$ is true just in case every appropriately similar entity in modal space satisfies F. He explicitly allows that a thing may have more than one counterpart in another world. A rigorous presentation of this view requires a translation scheme that translates the sentences of quantified modal logic into counterpart-theoretic language. Lewis's suggested translation scheme recommends that we treat the claims that $(x)\Box(x = x)$ as the claim that everything is such that every counterpart of it is self-identical. So translated, the claim comes out as true. Meanwhile, it recommends that we treat $(x)(y)(x = y \supset \Box x = y)$ as the claim that if x is identical to y, then for all worlds w, if some z is the counterpart of x in w and some v is the counterpart of y in w, then z is identical to v. The full quantificational structure of the latter claim is disguised by the 'perversely abbreviated language of quantified modal logic' (Lewis 1983: 46). Given that, on Lewis's view, a thing may have a pair of counterparts in another world, this claim comes out false. One may quibble with the translation. But grant the translation and that the counterpart relation is sometimes one–many, and one can scarcely think that a suitable version of Leibniz's law will vindicate the truth of the necessity of identity thesis.[58]

This is how it should be. Interesting philosophical doctrines would do well, it seems, to exploit and not challenge our mastery of the concept of identity. It remains unlikely that there really are any serious philosophical puzzles about identity as such. And here we return to the theme with which we began. Puzzles

---

[57] See Lewis (1983). Another excellent case in point is Gibbard (1975). The key idea there is one borrowed from Carnap, namely that while in non-modal contexts proper names denote objects and variables range over objects, in modal contexts proper names denote individual concepts and variables range over individual concepts. Suppose (i) $A = B$. Still it may be (ii) Possibly A is not identical to B and it is not the case that possibly A is not identical to A. This will be because in (ii) 'A' and 'B' refer to distinct individual concepts. We are in no way forced to concede that there is a pair of assignments which yield differing truth-values for (ii) differing only in that one assigns A to 'A', and that the other assigns B to 'A'. Presumably, if (ii) is otherwise understood normally, then an assignment of either A or B to (ii) will yield falsity. Analogous remarks apply in connection with the property-theoretic version of Leibniz's law, in connection with which the reader should consult Gibbard (1975, sects. v, vi). I should note that there may be little of substance that separates Gibbard and Lewis on these issues.

[58] For more on this, see Lewis (1983, postscript).

that are articulated using the word 'identity' are almost certainly puzzles about something else.

REFERENCES

Black, Max (1999). 'The Identity of Indiscernibles', in J. Kim and E. Sosa (eds.), *Metaphysics: An Anthology*. Oxford: Basil Blackwell. First pub. in *Mind*, 51 (1952), 153–64.

Cartwright, Richard (1987*a*). 'Identity and Substitutivity', in Cartwright, *Philosophical Essays*. Cambridge, Mass.: MIT Press, 135–48.

—— (1987*b*). 'On the Logical Problem of the Trinity', in Cartwright, *Philosophical Essays*. Cambridge, Mass.: MIT Press, 187–200.

Dummett, Michael (1993). 'Does Quantification Involve Identity?', in Dummett, *The Seas of Language*. Oxford: Oxford University Press, 308–27.

Frege, Gottlob (1953). *The Foundations of Arithmetic* (1884), trans. J. L. Austin, 2nd edn. Oxford: Basil Blackwell.

Gallois, André (1998). *Occasions of Identity*. Oxford: Clarendon Press.

Geach, P. T. (1967). 'Identity'. *Review of Metaphysics*, 21: 2–12.

—— (1972). *Logic Matters*. Berkeley: University of California Press.

—— (1980). *Reference and Generality*, 3rd edn. Ithaca, NY: Cornell University Press.

—— (1991). 'Replies', in Geach, *Philosophical Encounters*, ed. H. A. Lewis. Dordrecht: Kluwer.

Gibbard, Allan (1975). 'Contingent Identity'. *Journal of Philosophical Logic*, 4: 187–221.

Griffin, Nicholas (1977). *Relative Identity*. Oxford: Clarendon Press.

Kripke, Saul (1972). *Naming and Necessity*. Cambridge, Mass.: Harvard University Press.

Lewis, David (1983). 'Counterpart Theory and Quantified Modal Logic', in *Philosophical Papers vol. i*, Oxford: Oxford University Press, 39–46.

Myro, G. (1997). 'Identity and Time' (1986), in Michael Rea (ed.), *Material Constitution*. Lanham, Md.: Rowman & Littlefield, 148–72.

Noonan, Harold (1997). 'Relative Identity' in Bob Halen and Crispin Wright (eds.), *Companion to the Philosophy of Language*. Oxford: Basil Blackwell, 634–52.

Prior, Arthur (1957). 'Opposite Number'. *Review of Metaphysics*, 11: 196–201.

Quine, W. V. O. (1960). *Word and Object*. Cambridge, Mass.: MIT Press.

—— (1964). Review of P. T. Geach, *Reference and Generality*. *Philosophical Review*, 73: 100–4.

—— (1970). *Philosophy of Logic*. Cambridge, Mass.: Harvard University Press.

Shapiro, Stewart (1991). *Foundations without Foundationalism*. Oxford: Oxford University Press.

Sider, Theodore (1996). 'All the World's a Stage'. *Australasian Journal of Philosophy*, 74: 433–53.

van Inwagen, Peter (1995). 'And yet they are not Three Gods but One God', in van Inwagen, *God, Knowledge and Mystery*. Ithaca, NY: Cornell University Press, 222–59.

Williamson, Timothy (1987/88). 'Equivocation and Existence' in *Proceedings of the Aristotelian Society*, 88: 109–27.

—— (forthcoming). 'Vagueness, Identity and Leibniz's Law' in Giaretta, Bottani, and Carrera (eds.), *Individuals, Essence and Identity: Themes of Analytic Metaphysics*. Dordrecht: Kluwer.

Wright, Crispin (1983). *Frege's Conception of Numbers as Objects*. New York: Humanities Press.

CHAPTER 5

···

EXISTENCE, ONTOLOGICAL COMMITMENT, AND FICTIONAL ENTITIES

···

PETER VAN INWAGEN

MEINONG has famously (or notoriously) said, 'There are objects of which it is true that there are no such objects.'[1] What could have led him to make such an extraordinary statement? He was, or so he saw matters, driven to say that there were objects of which it was true that there were no such objects by data for which only the truth of this extraordinary statement could account. These data were of two sorts: linguistic and psychological.[2] The linguistic data

---

[1] '...es gibt Gegenstände, von denen gilt, dass es dergleichen Gegenstände nicht gibt' (Meinong 1969: 490). I will take it to be uncontroversial that for Meinong everything, without exception, is an 'object' (*Gegenstand*). I am aware that Meinong distinguished objects from 'objectives' (*Objective*). If, for example, the thought crosses my mind that golf is a popular sport, golf is the *Gegenstand* of my thought, and the popularity of golf is its *Objectiv*. But objectives are objects: if I believe that the popularity of golf is regrettable, the object of my belief is the popularity of golf. Since, at least in Meinong's sense of the word, everything is an object—since 'object', in Meinong's usage, is the most general count noun—I will take it to be uncontroversial that 'Every object is *F*' is equivalent to 'Everything is *F*' and that 'Some object is *F*' is equivalent to 'Something is *F*'.

[2] The psychological data pertain to the phenomenon of intentionality. I will not discuss these data. One of the unstated assumptions of this chapter (unstated outside this note) is that all human

consisted of sentences like the following and what seemed to be obvious facts about them:

> The Cheshire Cat spoke to Alice
> The round square is an impossible object
> Pegasus was the winged horse captured by Bellerophon.

The obvious facts were these: first, each of these sentences is or expresses a truth; secondly, the result of writing 'There is no such thing as' and then the subject of any of these sentences is, or expresses, a truth. (I so use 'subject' that the subject of 'the Taj Mahal is white' is 'the Taj Mahal' and not the Taj Mahal. I use 'there is no such thing as' to mean 'there is no such thing as, and there never was or will be any such thing as'.) Thus, for example, it is true that the Cheshire Cat spoke to Alice, and it is also true that there is no such thing as the Cheshire Cat. We have, therefore, the following general truth:

> There are true subject–predicate sentences (i.e. subject–predicate sentences that express truths when uttered in appropriate contexts) such that the result of writing 'there is no such thing as' and following this phrase with the subject of any of these sentences is true.

These are the linguistic data. Reflection on these data suggests the following question. The proposition expressed by the offset sentence, the proposition that summarizes the linguistic data, is a *semantical* generalization, a proposition that asserts that there are linguistic items of a certain description ('sentence') that possess a certain semantical property (truth); How can we express this same generalization in the 'material mode'? How can we state it as a thesis not about the semantical properties of linguistic items but about the things those linguistic items purport to refer to? Well, strictly speaking, we *can't* do this: 'Rome is populous' and ' "Rome is populous" is true' are not, strictly speaking, two ways of expressing the same proposition. Perhaps we should instead ask this: how can we express in a single sentence the general fact that is expressed collectively by the 'whole' infinite class of sentences of which the sentences

> The Cheshire Cat spoke to Alice and there is no such thing as the Cheshire Cat
> The round square is an impossible object and there is no such thing as the round square
> Pegasus was the winged horse captured by Bellerophon and there is no such thing as Pegasus

psychological phenomena can be adequately described and accounted for without any appeal to 'objects of which it is true that there are no such objects'.

are three representatives? (This 'single sentence' would not be a semantical sentence, for sentences of the type illustrated by our three examples are not semantical sentences; they do not ascribe semantical properties like truth or reference to linguistic items.) The sentence 'There are objects of which it is true that there are no such objects' represents an attempt at an answer to this question, but Meinong obviously recognizes that there is something unsatisfactory about this attempt, since he does not baldly say that there are objects of which it is true that there are no such objects; rather, he says, 'Those who were fond of a paradoxical mode of expression could very well say, "There are objects of which it is true that there are no such objects".' Um . . . yes—but suppose one was *not* one of those who were fond of a paradoxical mode of expression; what non-paradoxical mode of expression would one use in its place?

One obvious suggestion is: 'There are objects that do not exist'. But Meinong would object to this suggestion on grounds that are related to a peculiarity of his metaphysical terminology, for he holds that things that are not in space and time—the ideal figures the geometer studies, for example—do not 'exist' (*existieren*), but rather 'subsist' (*bestehen*), another thing entirely, or almost entirely, for subsistence is, like existence, a species of being. And this terminological red herring (in my view it is a terminological red herring) confuses matters. We had better leave the word 'exists' alone for the moment. But if we do not allow ourselves the use of the word 'exists', our question is unanswered: What shall we use in place of 'There are objects of which it is true that there are no such objects'? Perhaps we should turn to the question, What, exactly, *is* wrong with this sentence? What grounds did I have for calling it an 'extraordinary' sentence; why did Meinong suggest that this sentence was paradoxical? The answer to this question seems to *me* to be simple enough: there could not possibly be objects of which it was true that there were no such objects: if there *were* an object of which it was true that there was no such object (as it), that object would *be*; and if it *were* (if I may so phrase my point), it would not be true of it that there was no such object as it. This point is inescapable—*unless*, of course, 'there are' has (and 'es gibt' has and 'il y a' has) more than one sense. For suppose 'there are' has two senses; let the phrase itself represent one of these two senses, and let the same phrase in bold-face represent the other: there will be no contradiction in saying that there are objects of which it is true that **there are** no such objects. Or, at any rate, no contradiction that can be displayed by the simple argument I have just set out. (This simple argument can be phrased very neatly in the formal quantifier–variable idiom, in what Quine has called the canonical notation of quantification: 'There are objects of which it is true that there are no such objects' is equivalent to '$\exists x$ there is no such object as x'; 'there is no such object as x' is equivalent to 'Nothing is x' or '$\sim \exists y \ y = x$'; 'There are objects of which it is true that there are no such objects' is therefore equivalent to '$\exists x \sim \exists y \ y = x$'; and this formula is in its turn equivalent to '$\exists x \sim x = x$'—that is, 'Something is not identical with itself'. The force of this argument, of course, depends on the assumption that only one sense can be given to '∃'. For suppose this symbol is ambiguous; suppose there are two senses it might have. If we allow the symbol itself to represent one of these two senses, and 'E' to represent the other, then we are forced to admit nothing more than that 'There are objects of which it is true that there are no such objects' is equivalent either to '$\exists x \sim Ey\ y = x$' or to '$Ex \sim \exists y\ y = x$'. And this thing, we are forced to admit, is not obviously self-contradictory. To deduce an absurdity like '$\exists x \sim x = x$' or '$Ex \sim x = x$' from either of these formulae, one would have to make use of some principle that governed the relations between the 'two' existential quantifiers, some principle along the lines of '$\exists \alpha F\alpha \vdash E\alpha F\alpha$' or its converse, and a Meinongian is unlikely to assent to the validity of any such principle.) But it is not evident that 'there is' can plausibly be regarded as having two senses. Whether this is so is a question to which we shall return. For the moment, it seems safe to say that a strong prima facie case can be made for the logical equivalence of 'There are objects of which it is true that there are no such objects' and 'Some objects are not identical with themselves'.

Meinong, so far as I know, was not aware of the strong prima facie case for the equivalence of 'There are objects of which it is true that there are no such objects' and 'Some objects are not identical with themselves', but, as we have seen, he was obviously aware that there was something logically unsatisfactory about the former sentence. Meinong and I agree, therefore, that the sentence 'There are objects of which it is true that there are no such objects' must, in the last analysis, be replaced with some other sentence. But what sentence? Chisholm has made some suggestions:

Meinong wrote 'There are objects of which it is true that there are no such objects'. But he was well aware that this statement of his doctrine of *Aussersein* was needlessly paradoxical. Other statements were: ' "The non-real" is not a "mere nothing"', and 'The object as such . . . stands beyond being and non-being.' Perhaps the clearest statement was provided by Meinong's follower, Ernst Mally: '*Sosein* is independent of *Sein*.' We could paraphrase Mally's statement by saying: 'An object may have a set of characteristics whether or not it exists and whether or not it has any other kind of being.'[3] (Chisholm 1972: 15)

Let us follow Chisholm and use 'the doctrine of *Aussersein*' as a name for the thesis such that the words 'There are objects of which it is true that there are no such objects' is a needlessly paradoxical formulation of that thesis. Our problem is this: How is the doctrine of *Aussersein* to be formulated without paradox? (Is this the same problem as: 'How are we to express, in a single general sentence—not a semantical generalization—the fact that is expressed collectively by the infinite class of sentences of which our three sample sentences are representatives?' The answer is a qualified yes: if, as Meinong believed, 'Pegasus' denotes an object of which it is true both that it was a winged horse and that it has no kind of being, the answer is yes; otherwise, it is no. Cf. n. 6.) It seems to me that the alternative formulations

---

[3] '*Aussersein*' may be translated as 'independence [*sc.* of objects] of being'. '*Sosein*' may be translated as 'being-thus' or 'predication' or 'having characteristics'. '*Sein*' means 'being' (the mass term, not the count noun).

Chisholm mentions fare no better than the original. Let us first consider Chisholm's paraphrase of Mally's suggestion.

What does 'an object may' mean when it is followed by a predicate? It is clear that it is not Chisholm's intention to use 'an *F* may *G*' to express epistemic possibility—as in 'A disgruntled employee may be the murderer'. Chisholm's use of 'an *F* may *G*' is rather illustrated by sentences like 'A quadratic equation may have only one solution' and 'A Bengal tiger may weigh over 600 pounds'. That is to say, 'an object may *G*' (in this sense) means just exactly 'some objects *G*'. And an object that has no kind of being must be just our old friend 'an object of which it is true that there is no such object (as it)'. (For if there *is* such an object as *x*, then—surely?—*x* must have some kind of being.) Chisholm's paraphrase, therefore, is equivalent to 'Some objects are such that there are no such objects as they'—that is to say, 'There are objects of which it is true that there are no such objects'.

Let us turn to Mally's actual words, or to Chisholm's semi-translation of his actual words: '*Sosein* is independent of *Sein*'. Suppose one said, 'Mathematical ability is independent of sex.' This *could* mean that there was no 'lawlike' connection between mathematical ability and being male or being female, a thesis logically compatible with the proposition that every mathematically able person is a woman. But, surely, Mally does not mean the doctrine of *Aussersein* to be consistent with the following statement: 'Every object of predication *in fact* is (has being), but there's no nomic necessity in that; if the course of history had gone otherwise, it might well have turned out that there were objects of predication that were not (had no being).' No, Mally's words are certainly meant to be a way of saying that the class of objects of predication that have no being is *in fact* non-empty; that is to say, his words must mean or be equivalent to 'Some objects of predication are not (have no being)'. That is to say: 'There are objects [of predication] of which it is true that there are no such objects'. The reader who agrees with what I have said so far in this paragraph will almost certainly agree with me when I say, as I do, that 'The non-real is not a mere nothing' and 'The object as such stands beyond being and non-being' are also essentially equivalent to 'There are objects of which it is true that there are no such objects'. The problem of finding a non-paradoxical expression of the doctrine of *Aussersein* is therefore so far unsolved. The problem of expressing in full generality the (non-semantical) thesis of which

> The round square is an impossible object and there is no such thing as the round square

and

> Pegasus was the winged horse captured by Bellerophon and there is no such thing as Pegasus

are particular cases is therefore so far unsolved.

Many philosophers would be perfectly content to say that this problem is unsolved for the same reason that the problem of trisecting the angle by Euclidean means is unsolved: it has no solution. *I* should be perfectly content to say this, at any rate.

In my view, the only generalization that has these two sentences as particular cases is a semantical generalization, something like the semantical generalization set out in the first paragraph of this chapter as a summary of the 'linguistic data.'

And here, I think, the matter would stand if the linguistic data that supported the doctrine of *Aussersein* consisted only of sentences of the form 'F*x* and there is no such thing as *x*'. But there are other linguistic data that support the doctrine of *Aussersein*, sentences not of this form that seem to be true and whose truth seems to imply that there are objects of which it is true that there are no such objects. (And, as we shall see, it is not easy to understand these sentences as supporting only some 'harmless' semantical thesis.) The most persuasive of these data, the only ones that are really hard for the anti-Meinongian to deal with, belong to what I shall call *fictional discourse*. (I will not attempt to defend this judgement.) By fictional discourse I mean not the sentences that are contained in works of fiction but rather sentences spoken or written *about* works of fiction—whether they issue from the pen of F. R. Leavis or from the mouth of the fellow sitting beside you on the plane who is providing you with an interminable defence of his conviction that Stephen King is the greatest living novelist. The sentences of fictional discourse that I mean to call attention to are those that have the following four features: (i) they are existential quantifications, or at least look as if they were; (ii) they have complex quantificational structures (e.g. ∃∀∃)—or look as if they did; (iii) the inferences from these sentences that standard quantifier logic endorses for sentences that have the quantificational structures these sentences appear to have are valid—or at least *appear* to be; (iv) they contain not only predicates such as you and I and our friends might satisfy (predicates like 'is fat', 'is thin', 'is bald', 'is the mother of') but also 'literary' predicates like 'is a character', 'first appears in chapter 6', 'provides comic relief', 'is partly modelled on', 'is described by means of the same narrative device the author earlier used in her more successful depiction of', and so on. Here is an example:

> There is a fictional character who, for every novel, either appears in that novel or is a model for a character who does.

(This sentence would express a truth if, for example, Sancho Panza served as a model for at least one character in every novel but *Don Quixote* itself.) This sentence is (i) an apparent existential quantification; (ii) complex in its apparent quantificational structure; (iv) contains literary predicates: 'is a fictional character', 'appears in', and 'is a model for'. Moreover, (iii) it certainly appears that the inferences licensed by quantifier logic for sentences with the apparent quantificational structure of the above sentence are valid. It appears, for example, that we can validly deduce from the above sentence the sentence

> If no character appears in every novel, then some character is modelled on another character.

And this inference is, or appears to be, endorsed by quantifier logic, for it seems that its premiss and conclusion can be correctly translated into the quantifier–variable idiom as follows:

$\exists x(x$ is a fictional character & $\forall y(y$ is a novel $\rightarrow$ (x appears in $y \vee \exists z(z$ is a fictional character & z appears in y & x is a model for $z)))$)

$\sim\exists x(x$ is a fictional character & $\forall y(y$ is a novel $\rightarrow$ x appears in $y)) \rightarrow \exists x \exists y$ y is a model for x.

And the second sentence is a formal consequence of the first. (And the thesis that these two translations are correct does not seem to be in any way implausible or far-fetched. They certainly *look* correct. And, really, what alternative is there? Surely these translations *are* correct? Surely the inference *is* valid?) Now note a second formal consequence of the first sentence: '$\exists x$ x is a fictional character'—that is to say: 'There are fictional characters'. It seems, therefore, that the logical relations among certain sentences of fictional discourse can be accounted for only on the assumption that there are fictional characters.[4] (It is not to the point that the first of our sentences does not express a truth. The two sentences were chosen to provide

---

[4] For an extremely interesting reply to this argument, see Walton (1990: 416–19). Walton's reply—which is in aid of his thesis that there is nothing about works of fiction that threatens to force fictional entities upon us—is very complex and resists compression. At the centre of this very complex reply is the thesis that someone who utters (assertively; in a literary discussion; in ideal circumstances) the sentence 'If no character appears in every novel, then some character is modelled on another character' is using language in a very different way from someone who utters (assertively and so on) the sentence 'If no one is a citizen of every country, then someone is carrying someone else's passport'. The latter speaker is simply making an assertion about nations and their citizens and certain of the relations that hold among these things. The former speaker is *not* making an assertion about novels and the characters that occur in them and the relations that hold among these things. He is rather engaged in a certain game of pretence. It is a part of this game of pretence that the real universe is 'divided into realms corresponding to the various novels', and that each realm and its inhabitants were literally created by the author of the novel to which it corresponds. In uttering the sentence 'If no character appears in every novel, then some character is modelled on another character', he is pretending to describe this universe and the actions and motives of the creators of its several realms. He is not, in fact, saying something that has the logical structure that 'If no character appears in every novel, then some character is modelled on another character' has; he is, rather, *pretending* to say something that has that logical structure (which is why he uses that sentence). My main objection to this theory—to the theory of which I have given an incomplete and inadequate account: the reader is directed to the original—is that it simply does not seem to me to be *true* that the speaker who utters 'If no character appears in every novel, then some character is modelled on another character' (assertively and so on) is engaged in any sort of pretence. I would assimilate his case to the case of the speaker who says 'Some novels are longer than others'—a case of simple description of how things stand in the world if ever there was one. I would ask: is it really plausible to suppose that the speaker who says 'Some novels contain more chapters than others' and the speaker who says 'Some novels contain more characters than others' are engaged in radically different kinds of speech act? Isn't it much more plausible to suppose that each speaker is making the same *sort* of assertion and that their assertions differ only in *content*? Isn't it much more plausible to suppose that each speaker is simply making an assertion about the relations that hold among novels, relations that are grounded in various features of the internal structures of these novels?

an example of a formal inference that was simple but nevertheless subtle enough that the utility of quantifier logic in demonstrating its validity was evident. But there are plenty of true sentences of fictional discourse whose obvious translations into canonical notation allow the immediate deduction of '∃x x is a fictional character'. One example among thousands of possible examples would be: 'In some novels, there are important characters who are not introduced by the author till more than halfway through the work'.)

Suppose, then, that there are fictional characters—objects of thought and reference like Tom Sawyer and Mr Pickwick. If this supposition is correct, how can we avoid the conclusion that there are objects of which it is true that there are no such objects? For is it not evident that Tom Sawyer and Mr Pickwick do not exist and never did exist? And if they do not exist (I continue to respect Meinong's attempt to distinguish between two modes of being, existence and subsistence, ill-judged though I believe it to be), there are no such things as they, for, if there are such things as they, they are human beings, and human beings can participate in being only by existing.

We have reached this conclusion, that there are fictional characters, on the basis of certain linguistic data; primarily this datum: that the first of our sentences allows the formal deduction of the second. More generally, we have argued that if the obvious logical consequences of certain sentences of fictional discourse are accounted for in what seems the only possible way, there will be (true) sentences of fictional discourse from which 'There are fictional characters' can be validly deduced. But could these data perhaps be interpreted semantically (following our earlier model, following the way I proposed dealing with data like the apparent truth of 'The Cheshire Cat spoke to Alice and there is no such thing as the Cheshire Cat'), and thus rendered 'harmless'? Could they not be given some semantical interpretation that would have no consequences about fictional characters 'themselves,' but only such semantical consequences as 'There are character-*names* that occur in works of fiction that can be used in sentences of fictional discourse that express truths'? I can say only that I see no way to do this. If there is indeed no way to do this, then the data of fictional discourse I have adduced constitute stronger support for Meinongianism than the linguistic data that Meinong and his followers appeal to.

We seem, therefore, to have a strong argument for the doctrine of *Aussersein*. But, as we have seen, there is a strong argument against this doctrine, an argument that we have not seen how to deal with: The doctrine of *Aussersein* entails, or seems to entail, that something is not identical with itself—a *reductio ad absurdum* if ever there was one. But if we have not seen how to deal with this argument, we have at least mentioned in passing what will seem to many to be a promising way of dealing with it: the 'way of the two quantifiers.'

Suppose, then, that we have two 'existential' quantifiers (but we must read nothing ontological into the label 'existential quantifier'), '∃' and 'E'. Let us propose the following two readings for these quantifiers (when we earlier touched on the possibility of there being two existential quantifiers, we did not propose readings for them). Suppose we read 'E' as an existential quantifier whose range is restricted to those objects that participate in being, to the objects that are. And suppose we read '∃' as an existential quantifier whose range is absolutely unrestricted, whose range comprises *all* objects, even those that are not. It is easy enough to see that if we allow ourselves this distinction, and if we suppose that fictional characters fall within the range of the wider existential quantifier and do not fall within the range of the narrower, we may interpret our linguistic data in a way that entails no paradoxical consequence. Our data would support only this conclusion: '∃x x is a fictional character'. And nothing paradoxical follows from this conclusion. We cannot deduce from it either that something that lacks any sort of being (some fictional character, say) is not identical with itself, or that something that has being is not identical with itself. We can come no closer to this conclusion than what we supposed at the outset, that something that lacks being is not identical with anything that has being. And this miss is a good deal better than a mile; it is, in fact, not paradoxical at all.

These reflections on what Meinong must do if he is to state the doctrine of *Aussersein* without paradox are not very profound. I do not think it is controversial that the doctrine of *Aussersein* requires a kind of quantification that 'goes beyond being'. The important question is this: *can* there be a kind of quantification that goes beyond being? It is my contention that there cannot be, that the idea of quantifying beyond being simply does not make sense. I can hardly hope to demonstrate this to the satisfaction of the committed Meinongian, however: any argument I can present for this position must be an argument the Meinongian has already considered— or, at best, a technical refinement of an argument the Meinongian has already considered. I will do what I can, however: I will explain why the idea of quantifying beyond being does not make sense to *me*.

I begin by examining the idea of universal quantification, an idea expressed by a large variety of words and phrases, the most important of which are 'all', 'everything', and 'there is no'.[5] More exactly, I begin by examining the idea of *unrestricted* universal quantification. (It is a commonplace of the philosophy of language that when one uses the idiom of universal quantification, one often, one perhaps usually, has some tacit restriction in mind. 'We've sold everything,' says the sales clerk after a particularly busy day behind the counter, and we who hear this assertion do not protest that the number 510, the Taj Mahal, and the counter—a concrete object right there in the shop—remain unsold.) We all, I believe understand the idea of universal quantification, and it does not require much philosophical instruction for us pass from an understanding of this idea to an understanding of the idea of unrestricted universal quantification. Now it seems to me that the idea of unrestricted universal quantification is a pellucid and wholly unambiguous idea. And it seems to me that

---

[5] The argument that follows in the text is deeply influenced by Lewis (1990). But Lewis is not to be held responsible for the way I have formulated the argument.

everyone, everyone including the Meinongian and me, means the same thing by the phrase 'unrestricted universal quantification'—although the Meinongian and I will certainly disagree about which unrestricted universal quantifications are *true*. Let us use the symbol '∀' to express absolutely unrestricted universal quantification (in other words, let us use this symbol in its usual sense). I say this:

$\forall x \sim x$ is a unicorn.

The Meinongian says this:

$\sim\forall x \sim x$ is a unicorn.

(In fact, the Meinongian says this is a necessary truth.) I say I don't see how the Meinongian's assertion could be true. The world being as it is, the Meinongian's assertion seems to be false (if Kripke is right, necessarily false). If the Meinongian's assertion were true—this is what I want to say—and if I were made free of all space and all time, I ought to be able to find, encounter, or observe a unicorn. But this I should *not* be able to do: no magic carpet or starship or time machine could take me to a place where there was a unicorn. The Meinongian will reply that the truth of '$\sim \forall x \sim x$ is a unicorn' does not entail the 'findability' of unicorns. Not everything [an absolutely unrestricted 'everything'] is a non-unicorn, the Meinongian says— and yet unicorns are nowhere to be found. (More precisely: they *are* to be found in certain places, but I cannot visit these places because they do not exist.) Unicorns are nowhere to be found because they lack *being*. But when the Meinongian says this, I must protest that either he contradicts himself or I do not understand him. (He will no doubt respond to this protest as Chisholm once responded to a similar protest: 'I accept the disjunction.') In my view, on my understanding of being, each statement (after the first) in the following sequence is a consequence of—and is in fact equivalent to—the preceding statement in the sequence:

All unicorns lack being.

For every object that is a unicorn, it is true of it that there is no such object (as it).

Every unicorn is such that everything [an unrestricted 'everything'] is not it.

$\forall x(x$ is a unicorn $\rightarrow \forall y \sim y = x)$.

$\forall x \sim x$ is a unicorn.

Thus, according to *my* understanding of 'lacks being', the Meinongian says both that all unicorns lack being and that it is false that all unicorns lack being ('$\sim\forall x \sim x$ is a unicorn'). It would therefore seem that—since the Meinongian obviously does not mean to embrace a straightforward formal contradiction—the Meinongian must mean something different by 'has being' and 'lacks being' from what I mean by these phrases. But what *does* he mean by them? I do not know. I say 'x has being' means '$\sim\forall y \sim y = x$'; the Meinongian denies this. Apparently, he takes 'has being' to be a primitive, an indefinable term, whereas I think that 'has being' can be defined in terms of 'all' and 'not'. (And I take definability in terms of 'all' and 'not' to be important, because I am sure that the Meinongian means exactly what I do by 'all' and 'not'—and thus he understands what *I* mean by 'has being' and is therefore an authority on the question whether he and I mean the same.) And there the matter must rest. The Meinongian believes that 'has being' has a meaning that cannot be explained in terms of unrestricted universal quantification and negation. He therefore believes in two kinds of quantification where I believe in one. I have two quantifiers—'∀' and '∃' (that is '~∀ ~')—and he has four: the two I have and two others: 'A' and 'E'. These two quantifiers may be defined as follows:

$$\mathsf{A}xFx =_{df} \forall x(x \text{ has being} \rightarrow Fx)$$
$$\mathsf{E}xFx =_{df} \exists x(x \text{ has being} \mathrel{\&} Fx).$$

Or so they may be defined for the benefit of someone who knows what the Meinongian means by 'has being'. But not for my benefit, for, as I have said, I do not know what the Meinongian means by 'has being'.

I therefore cannot accept the Meinongian doctrine of *Aussersein*. But what then of our strong argument *for* the doctrine of *Aussersein*?—the argument based on the data of fictional discourse? Since I do not understand the idea of objects of which it is true that there are no such objects, nothing can be (for me) an argument for the existence or reality or being (none of these is the right word, of course, but what would be the right word?) of objects of which it is true that there are no such objects. What is for the Meinongian an argument for the doctrine of *Aussersein* becomes for someone like me a *problem*: What are those of us who cannot understand objects that lack being to say about fictional discourse, which appears to be a vast repository of evidence for the [insert proper verb-stem here]-ing of such objects? *We* must understand fictional discourse in a way that does not presuppose the doctrine of *Aussersein*. *We* must adopt a non-Meinongian analysis of, or account of, or theory of, fictional discourse. And what might such a theory be?[6] What are the available

---

[6] One sort of non-Meinongian analysis of fictional discourse might make use of the idea of 'substitutional quantification'. (I take it that no one can properly say, 'I am a Meinongian because I have two sorts of existential quantifier that bind variables in nominal positions, the objectual or the referential—that's the narrow one—and the substitutional—that's the wide one.' A Meinongian, surely, is a philosopher who thinks there are two kinds of *objectual* quantifier, a wide objectual quantifier whose range comprises all objects and a narrow one whose range is restricted to the objects that are. Essentially the same point can be made in terms of reference. One does not qualify as a Meinongian in virtue of saying that the sentence 'Pegasus is a winged horse' is true despite the fact that 'Pegasus' does not refer to anything. A Meinongian must say that 'Pegasus is a winged horse' is true because 'Pegasus' refers to a winged horse, and is true despite the fact that the horse 'Pegasus' refers to does not exist.) I will not discuss analyses of fictional discourse based on substitutional quantification in this chapter. I refer the reader to van Inwagen (1981).

non-Meinongian theories of fictional discourse? This question is the subject of the remainder of this chapter.[7]

I begin with a brief exposition of a theory I have presented in various publications (van Inwagen 1997, 1983, 1985) When I have set out this theory, I will describe two other non-Meinongian theories of the ontology of fiction, those of Nicholas Wolterstorff and Amie Thomasson. Wolterstorff and Thomasson's theories are, in a sense I shall try to make clear, in substantial agreement with mine; they differ from mine in being much more specific than I care to be about the metaphysical nature of fictional characters.[8]

A non-Meinongian theory of fiction (that is, a theory of fiction that allows only one sort of existential quantifier) must answer the following question: How are we to deal with the fact (or is it a fact?) that when fictional discourse is translated into the quantifier–variable idiom, it can be seen to imply that fictional characters like Tom Sawyer and Mr Pickwick *are* or *have being*, that they *exist*? (In the remainder of this chapter, I will use 'exist' to mean the same as 'are' and 'have being', for I need no longer attend to Meinong's spurious distinction between existence and subsistence; I need no longer pretend to respect the idea that existence is one of two

---

[7] For Meinongian theories of fiction, see Routley (1980, esp. ch. 7); Parsons (1975, 1980); Castañeda (1979).

Edward Zalta's 'object theory' (see n. 18) can be given a Meinongian interpretation, and 'encoding', a fundamental concept of object theory, depends to a large degree for its intuitive content on examples drawn from fiction.

I am aware of two other theories of fictional objects that *might* be described as Meinongian. According to Robert Howell (1979: 130), fictional objects are 'non-actual but well-individuated objects that exist in a variety of fictional worlds'. (Howell would repudiate the suggestion that his theory is appropriately described as Meinongian; he describes Meinongian theories as 'quasi-actualist'.) Howell does not explicitly say what a 'non-actual object' is, but it seems clear from what he says about them that they are objects that exist in non-actual worlds and do not exist in the actual world. In my view, there are no non-actual objects (in this sense)—despite the fact that there are non-actual worlds in which everything that exists in the actual world exists, and other things as well. (See Plantinga 1974, ch. VII and VIII.) The theory presented in Charles Crittenden's *Unreality: The Metaphysics of Fictional Objects* (Crittenden 1991) is pretty clearly a Meinongian theory in *some* sense, but Crittenden, despite his title, adopts a resolutely anti-metaphysical attitude that leads him to avoid any attempt to give a systematic account of the nature of 'grammatical objects' (in which category he places fictional objects). What he says about the nature of grammatical objects is haphazard in the extreme, and I can't help thinking that he says things in some places that flatly contradict things he says in other places. But I am not sure of this, because I do not really understand the scattered remarks that are supposed to explain the notion of a grammatical object.

[8] Kendall Walton's theory, the theory described in n. 4, is also a non-Meinongian theory of the ontology of fiction. But Walton's theory is wholly different from Wolterstorff's and Thomasson's and mine. Walton's theory denies the existence of fictional characters—and not in the subtle way (or the unintelligible way: take your pick) in which the Meinongian denies the existence, and even the being, of fictional characters. Walton denies the existence of fictional characters in the same straightforward sense as that in which the naturalist denies the existence of supernatural beings and the nominalist the existence of universals. The Meinongian says that 'Tom Sawyer' names something that lacks being; Wolterstorff, Thomasson, and I say that 'Tom Sawyer' names something that has being; Walton says that 'Tom Sawyer' names nothing at all.

modes of being.) I propose that we simply accept this implication. I propose that we adopt a theory according to which fictional characters exist. I propose, in fact, that the existence of fictional characters is just what our examination of fictional discourse has demonstrated. More exactly, I hold that our examination of fictional discourse has demonstrated that this follows from two assumptions: that what is said by those engaged in fictional discourse is (often) true, and that there is no way to rewrite or paraphrase the true sentences of fictional discourse so as not to allow the deduction of '$\exists x$ x is a fictional character' from the obvious and proper translations of these sentences into the 'canonical notation of quantification'. The first of these assumptions seems obviously right: 'In some novels there are important characters who are not introduced by the author till more than halfway through the work' seems to be, without qualification, *true*. As to the second, it may be possible to understand sentences like 'In some novels there are important characters who are not introduced by the author till more than halfway through the work' in a way that allows their truth to be consistent with there being no fictional characters, but I have never been able to think of any way to do this and I have never seen any workable suggestion about how it might be done. Since, therefore, I think there are true sentences of fictional discourse (vast numbers of them, in fact) that entail 'There are fictional characters' (which I take to be equivalent to 'Fictional characters exist'), and since I think one should accept the perceived logical implications of that which one believes,[9] I conclude—tentatively, perhaps, but all philosophical conclusions should be tentative—that fictional characters exist.

The preceding paragraph and the preceding passages to which it alludes illustrate a certain style of reasoning concerning matters of existence. This importance of this style of reasoning in ontological disputes, trivial though it may seem, was not appreciated by philosophers till Quine's very persuasive writings on ontological method forced them to attend to it. The reasons I have given for thinking that fictional characters exist are, in fact, an application of what is sometimes called 'Quine's criterion of ontological commitment.'[10] Having said this, I must immediately record my conviction that there is an important sense in which there is no such thing as Quine's criterion of ontological commitment. That is, there is no proposition, no *thesis*, that can be called 'Quine's criterion of ontological commitment'—and this despite the fact that several acute and able philosophers (see e.g. Church 1958; Cartwright 1954) have attempted to formulate, or to examine possible alternative

---

[9] Unless, of course, these perceived logical implications are so incredible as to lead one to withdraw one's assent from the proposition that has been seen to imply them. This reservation does not seem to me to apply in the present case. 'Fictional characters exist' does not seem to me to be so incredible that it should lead me to withdraw my assent from 'In some novels there are important characters who are not introduced by the author until more than halfway through the work'.

[10] See his classic essay 'On What There Is', in Quine (1961: 1-19) and *Word and Object* (Quine 1960, ch. VII). Quine soon came to prefer 'ontic commitment' to 'ontological commitment', but few philosophers have followed his example; we seem to be stuck with the more cumbersome phrase.

formulations of, 'Quine's criterion of ontological commitment.' In so far as there is anything that deserves the name 'Quine's criterion of ontological commitment,' it is a strategy or technique, not a thesis. This matter is important enough to warrant a brief digression on ontological commitment.

Strategies and techniques can be applied in various contexts. Let us concentrate on the context supplied by a debate, an ontological debate, a debate between two philosophers about what there is. Argle, let us say, contends that there are only concrete material objects. Bargle points out that Argle has asserted that there are a great many holes in this piece of cheese, and calls Argle's attention to the fact that a hole does not seem to be describable as a 'concrete material object.' I trust you know how this story goes.[11] It is, as its authors intended it be, a paradigm of the application of Quine's strategy. It has, however, a special feature. One of the characters in the dialogue (Bargle) is, as we might say, forcing the application of the strategy; but the other character (Argle) *cooperates*; Argle does not dispute the legitimacy of the questions Bargle puts to him. But some philosophers might not be so cooperative as Argle. Consider, for example, the late Ernest Gellner. In a review essay on Quine's contributions to philosophy Gellner gave a very nice description of Quine's ontological strategy, and, having paused briefly to identify himself as a nominalist, went on to say:

The dreadful thing is, I haven't even tried to be a serious, card-carrying nominalist. I have never tried to eliminate 'quantification' over abstract objects from my discourse. I shamelessly 'quantify over' abstractions *and* deny their existence! I do not try to put what I say into canonical notation, and do not care what the notation looks like if someone else does it for me, and do not feel in the very least bound by whatever ontic commitments such a translation may disclose. (Gellner 1979: 203)

In an ontological debate with someone like Gellner one would have to apply different strategies from those that are appropriate in a debate with someone like the admirable Argle. But I shall not further consider philosophers like Gellner. I have a lot to say to them, but I will not say it in this chapter. Here I will simply assume that Gellner's confession comes down to this: I don't mind contradicting myself—I don't mind both saying things that imply that there are abstractions (for to quantify over abstractions is *inter alia* to say things that imply that there are abstractions) and saying that there are no abstractions—if figuring out how to avoid contradicting myself would require intellectual effort.

Those philosophers who, like Argle, admit the legitimacy of Quine's strategy in ontological debate will, I think, mostly be willing to accept the following thesis: The history of ontological debates in which all parties admit the legitimacy of Quine's strategy shows that it is harder to avoid tacitly asserting the existence of things like numbers, sets, properties, propositions, and unrealized possibilities than one might

---

[11] I allude, of course, to David and Stephanie Lewis's classic paper 'Holes' (Lewis and Lewis 1970).

have thought it would be. If, for example, you think there are no numbers, you will find it difficult to recast all you want to say in the quantifier–variable idiom (and to do so in sufficient 'depth' that all the inferences you regard as valid will be valid according to the rules of first-order logic) without finding that the sentence

$\exists x$ x is a number

is a formal consequence of 'all you want to say'. It may be possible in the end for you to do this—for you to 'avoid ontological commitment to numbers'—but you will not find it a trivial undertaking.

What I have said about numbers I say about fictional characters: If you think there are no fictional characters, you will find it difficult to recast all you want to say in the quantifier–variable idiom (and to do so in sufficient 'depth' that all the inferences you regard as valid will be valid according to the rules of first-order logic) without finding that the sentence

$\exists x$ x is a fictional character

is a formal consequence of 'all you want to say'. It may be possible in the end for you to do this—for you to 'avoid ontological commitment to fictional characters'—but you will not find it a trivial undertaking. (I am inclined to think you will find it an impossible undertaking.)

It seems, therefore, that much of what we say in fictional discourse is true and that the truths of fictional discourse carry ontological commitment to fictional characters. That is to say, it seems that fictional characters exist. And, since the names that occur in works of fiction, names like 'Mr Pickwick' and 'Tom Sawyer' (when they occur not in works of fiction, but in discourse *about* works of fiction, in what I am calling fictional discourse), denote fictional characters if fictional characters are there to be denoted, Mr Pickwick and Tom Sawyer are among the things that are—an assertion that we anti-Meinongians regard as equivalent to the assertion that Mr Pickwick and Tom Sawyer are among the things that exist. (It should be noted that, at least in certain circumstances, ordinary speakers are perfectly willing to apply the word 'exist' to fictional characters. Consider: 'To hear some people talk, you would think that all Dickens's working-class characters were comic grotesques; although such characters certainly exist, there are fewer of them than is commonly supposed'; 'Sarah just ignores those characters that don't fit her theory of fiction. She persists in writing as if Anna Karenina, Tristram Shandy, and Mrs Dalloway simply didn't exist'.)

There is an obvious objection to any theory of fiction that implies that fictional characters exist. It might be stated as follows. There are characters in some novels who are witches—for example, in John Updike's *The Witches of Eastwick*. If the characters of this novel exist, therefore, it follows that witches exist—and, as we all know, witches don't exist. For an adequate reply to this objection I must refer you elsewhere. (See van Inwagen 1977, 1983, 1985.) The essence of the reply is that we must distinguish between those properties that fictional characters *have* and those that they *hold*.[12] Fictional characters *have* only (*a*) 'logical' or 'high-category' properties like existence and self-identity, (*b*) properties expressed by what I have called 'literary' predicates—being a character in a novel, being introduced in chapter 6, being a comic villainess, having been created by Mark Twain, being modelled on Sancho Panza . . .[13] Properties that strictly entail the property 'being human'—being a resident of Hannibal, Missouri, being an orphan who has a mysterious benefactor, being a witch—they do not have but *hold*. (Of course, if a fictional character holds the property *F*, then it *has* the literary property 'holding the property *F*'.) It is therefore not true in, as they say, the strict and philosophical sense that any fictional characters are witches—or that any of them are human, female, or a widow who lives in Eastwick, Rhode Island. What we should say in, as they say, the philosophy room is this: some of them *hold* the properties expressed by these predicates.

But what about our firm conviction—everyone's firm conviction—that Tom Sawyer and Mr Pickwick and Sherlock Holmes do not exist? Let us consider two cases in which someone might use the sentence 'Sherlock Holmes does not exist'. Consider, first, a frustrated detective who says in exasperation, 'It would take Sherlock Holmes to solve this case, and unfortunately Sherlock Holmes doesn't exist.' Consider, next, an amused London cop who is responding to a flustered tourist who can't find 221B Baker Street ('You know, Officer—where Sherlock Holmes lived'). 'Lord bless you, sir, Sherlock Holmes doesn't exist and never did. He's just a chap in a story made up by someone called Conan Doyle.' It seems to me that the first use of 'Sherlock Holmes does not exist' expresses the proposition

> No one has all the properties the fictional character Sherlock Holmes holds (nor has anyone very many of the most salient and striking of these properties).

The second use of 'Sherlock Holmes does not exist' expresses—I would argue— something like the following proposition.

> Your use of the name 'Sherlock Holmes' rests on a mistake. If you trace back the use of this name to its origin, you'll find that it first occurs in a work of fiction, and that it was not introduced into our discourse by an 'initial baptism'. That is, its origin lies in the fact that Conan Doyle wrote a story in which one of the characters held the property 'being named "Sherlock Holmes"', and we

---

[12] Holding, like having, is a two-place relation. In 'Creatures of Fiction' (van Inwagen 1977) I employed instead of this two-place relation the three-place relation 'ascription', a relation that holds among a character, a property, and a 'place' in a work of fiction. This is a technically more satisfactory device, since it allows us to represent the fact that one and the same character may be, say, unmarried in one 'place' (chapter 4, for example), and married in another 'place', such as the second half of chapter 6.

[13] Or, rather, these are the only properties they have other than those that may be prescribed by a specific theory of the nature of fictional characters. Compare: 'Numbers have only logical properties like self-identity and arithmetical properties like being prime or being the successor of 6'. There is no doubt a sense in which this is true, but we must recognize that a specific theory about the nature of numbers may ascribe further properties to them—like being an abstract object or being a set.

customarily refer to fictional characters by their fictional names. (That is to say: if *x* is a name, and if a fictional character holds the property of being named *x*, we customarily use *x* as a name of that character.) You have mistaken this story for a history or have mistaken discourse about a fictional character for discourse about an historical figure—or both.

The difference between these two examples is this: In the first example both the speaker and the audience know that Holmes is fictional and the speaker is making a comment that presupposes this knowledge in the audience; in the second, only the speaker knows that Holmes is fictional, and is, in effect, informing the audience of this fact. The lesson I mean to convey by these examples is that the non-existence of Holmes is not an ontological datum; the ontological datum is rather that we can use the *sentence* 'Sherlock Holmes does not exist' to say something true. (Or something false. I can imagine cases in which it was used to say something false.[14]) Different theories of the ontology of fiction will account for this datum in different ways. According to one ontology of fiction, the reason we can use this sentence to say something true is that 'Sherlock Holmes' does not denote anything. According to another, the reason is that 'Sherlock Holmes' denotes something non-existent. I prefer a third account, the rather more complicated account I have briefly outlined. These ontologies should be compared and evaluated not simply by seeing how well they explain our reactions to special and isolated sentences like 'Sherlock Holmes does not exist'; they should be compared and evaluated by seeing how well they explain our reactions to the whole range of sentences we use to talk about fiction— and our ability to integrate these explanations with an acceptable philosophy of the quantifier and an acceptable general ontology.

Here, then, is a non-Meinongian theory of fictional characters, non-Meinongian in that it rejects the thesis that fictional characters lack being, and hence does not allow the deduction of the Meinongian conclusion that it is false that everything [unrestricted] has being. What other non-Meinongian theories are possible? I will attempt to categorize the possible non-Meinongian theories of fictional characters. I will begin by isolating the two central assumptions of the theory I have just set out. They are:

1. Fictional characters exist or have being. (And this despite the fact that a sentence formed by prefixing the name of a fictional character to 'does not exist' can often be used to express a truth.)

---

[14] It is a hundred years in the future. Sally is being examined on her Ph.D. thesis, 'The Detective in British Popular Fiction before the First World War'. A pompous (and ill-informed) examiner speaks as follows: 'This thesis appears most impressive. But it is concerned largely with the appropriation by the popular imagination of a fictional detective called Sherlock Holmes. I know the popular fiction of the period well, and I'm sorry to have to tell you that Sherlock Holmes does not exist. Conan Doyle never created any such character. The author simply made him and his supposed popularity with the public up. Apparently she believed that no one on this committee would know the period well enough to expose her fraud.'

2. What appears to be the apparatus of predication in 'fictional discourse' is ambiguous. Sometimes it expresses actual predication, and sometimes an entirely different relation. When, for example, we say, 'Tom Sawyer was created by Mark Twain,' we are using the copula 'was' to assert that the property expressed by the predicate 'created by Mark Twain' actually belongs to the fictional character Tom Sawyer. When we[15] say (and say truly), 'Tom Sawyer was a boy who grew up along the banks of the Mississippi River in the 1840s', we use the copula 'was' to express that other, 'entirely different', relation to which I have given the name 'holding'. Tom Sawyer, in other words, belongs to the extension of the property expressed by 'created by Mark Twain'. But if we look, or God looks, at all the members of the extension of the property expressed by 'boy who grew up along the banks of the Mississippi River in the 1840s', we, or he, will not come upon Tom Sawyer. We, or he, will come upon no one but the inhabitants of man-shaped regions of space-time who are spatio-temporally related to you and me. There is a particular number of such filled, man-shaped regions (now for ever fixed), and the size of this number cannot be, and never could have been, affected by purely literary creation of the sort Mark Twain was engaged in. Tom Sawyer, therefore, does not *have* the property expressed by 'boy who grew up along the banks of the Mississippi River in the 1840s'. And yet he bears some intimate relation to it—a relation he does not bear to any of its 'competitors' (for example: the property expressed by 'boy who grew up along the banks of the Rhine in the 1680s'). And this relation is such that when we say,

---

[15] 'We' who are engaged in fictional discourse. If Mark Twain had been so artless as to include the sentence 'Tom Sawyer was a boy who grew up along the banks of the Mississippi River in the 1840s' in *The Adventures of Tom Sawyer*, he would not have been engaged in fictional discourse—discourse *about* fiction—and would not have expressed the proposition that we should express if we used this sentence as, say, a part of a summary of the plot of *Tom Sawyer*. If he had included this sentence in the book, it would there have been a sentence of fiction, not of fictional discourse, and would have expressed no proposition at all, for, when a writer of fiction writes a sentence (even a straightforward declarative sentence like this one), he makes no assertion. If someone had been looking over Mark Twain's shoulder when he wrote the sentence 'Tom Sawyer was a boy who grew up along the banks of the Mississippi River in the 1840', and had said, 'That's true' or 'That's false', this person could only have misunderstood what Mark Twain was doing; this person must have thought that Mark Twain was writing not fiction but history. What then was Mark Twain doing (or what would he have been doing if this imaginary literary episode were actual) when he wrote 'Tom Sawyer was a boy who grew up along the banks of the Mississippi River in the 1840s'? Well, this is a question for the philosopher of fiction. It is a question I need not answer in the present chapter, for its correct answer is irrelevant to my purposes. I will say just this: in this matter, I am a 'Waltonian'. Despite my disagreement with Kendall Walton about the existence of characters (see n. 4), I am in general agreement with him about the nature of fiction. Mark Twain was engaged in crafting a literary object that he intended to be usable as a prop in a certain game of pretence it would authorize, an object a reader could use, in a special, technical sense, as a prop in a game in which the reader pretended to be reading a history—and to understand what a novel or story *is* is to understand that, like a hobby-horse, its purpose is to be so used as a prop in a game of pretence. (As with most rules, there are exceptions. Authors do sometimes make assertions in works of fiction: in 'asides to the reader', asides that are general observations on human life and not comments on the events in the fiction, by 'omniscient' third-person narrators—that is, third-person narrators who are not themselves inhabitants of the world of the story.)

'Tom Sawyer was a boy who grew up along the banks of the Mississippi River in the 1840s', we say something that is true *because* Tom Sawyer bears that relation to that property; and it is such that if anyone said, 'Tom Sawyer was a boy who grew up along the banks of the Rhine in the 1680s', what that person said would be false *because* Tom Sawyer failed to bear it to the property expressed by the predicate of that sentence. It is possible for a character to hold inconsistent properties—to have first met her only lover in London *and* to have first met her only lover in Buenos Aires, for example— but this is normally due to authorial inadvertence. A Meinongian object can be an impossible object, an object that literally *has* inconsistent properties (witness the round square), and Meinong would say that a fictional character who first met her only lover in London and who first met her only lover in Buenos Aires was an impossible object in just this sense. But for the non-Meinongian, for the philosopher who recognizes only one existential quantifier, this is not an option. The fact that an author can, by inexplicable accident or Borgesian design, compose a story one of whose characters first met her only lover in London and first met her only lover in Buenos Aires, is by itself enough to show that a non-Meinongian theory of fiction must distinguish having and holding (or must at any rate distinguish having from something that does the same work as holding). I am not able to define holding (unless to specify the role the concept plays in our talk about fiction is to define it: I mean I am unable to provide a Chisholm-style 'replacement definition' of holding, one whose definiens contains only unproblematic, perfectly clear terms), or even to find a good name for it. (My choice of the word 'hold' has *no* basis other than the familiar phrase in the wedding service, 'to have and to hold'.[16]) But 'holding' makes sense if fictional discourse makes sense. And fictional discourse, for the most part, makes sense.

I will regard any theory of the ontology of fictional characters that endorses both these 'central assumptions' as in fundamental agreement with mine. (I include, as part of the second assumption, the point made in note 15: 'typical' declarative sentences in works of fiction are not the vehicles of assertions made by the authors of those works.)

Three philosophers have presented theories of fiction I regard as in fundamental agreement with mine: Saul A. Kripke, in his as yet unpublished Locke Lectures (delivered in 1973), Nicholas Wolterstorff in his book *Worlds and Works of Art* (Wolterstorff 1980), and Amie Thomasson in her book *Fiction and Metaphysics* (Thomasson 1999).

Wolterstorff's and Thomasson's theories are, as I say, in fundamental agreement with mine: they endorse my two central assumptions. But Wolterstorff and Thomasson are more specific about the nature of fictional characters than I have

---

[16] For a discussion of the inadequacies of the other word I have used for this relation, 'ascription', see van Inwagen (1977: 50–1).

been.[17] (I will not discuss Kripke's Locke Lectures because they have not been published.) My own theory has nothing to say about what larger ontological categories (other than, perhaps, 'abstract object') fictional characters belong to, and I do nothing to explain 'holding' beyond giving examples and hoping for the best. Wolterstorff and Thomasson, however, say a great deal about these matters, and their theories stand in instructive opposition.[18]

I will first discuss Wolterstorff's theory. According to Wolterstorff, characters are *kinds*.[19] They are kinds 'maximal within a work' (or, as with Sherlock Holmes and Huckleberry Finn, maximal within two or more works). I will explain this idea through a series of definitions. (They are rough and could be refined. I do not always use Wolterstorff's technical terms.) Suppose we know what it is for a proposition to be 'true in' a work of fiction.[20] We can agree, perhaps, that it is true in *War and Peace* that there are human beings, that some early nineteenth-century Russian aristocrats

[17] Compare what is said about 'the property role' versus 'the nature of properties' in the discussion of the problem of universals in van Inwagen (1998). I have argued for the conclusion that 'the character role' is filled, and I have made only a few very abstract remarks about the nature of the things that fill it. Wolterstorff and Thomasson also argue for the conclusion that the character role is filled; they go on to present theories about the nature of the things that fill it.

[18] There are two other theories, at least, that might be described as in essential agreement with mine. One is the theory of fictional objects that Edward Zalta presents as one of the fruits of 'object theory' (see Zalta 1983, 1988). According to Zalta, there are two kinds of predication, 'exemplification' and 'encoding'. Exemplification corresponds roughly to what I call 'having' and 'encoding' to what I call 'holding'. But I do not regard having and holding as two sorts of predication. In my view having is predication—and predication is predication, full stop. I regard 'holding' as a special-purpose relation peculiar to literary discourse, a relation that happens to be expressed in ordinary speech by the words that, in their primary use, express the general logical relation of predication. It must be said, however, that Zalta's 'object theory' is an immensely powerful and ambitious theory of abstract objects. If I were convinced that object theory succeeded as a general, comprehensive theory of abstract objects, I should agree that what I had called 'holding' was just encoding in application to one very special sort of abstract object—fictional characters—and was therefore a species of predication. An evaluation of the general claims of 'object theory', however, would take us far beyond the scope of this chapter.

The second theory is that presented by Nathan Salmon in Salmon (1998). Salmon's theory of fictional objects is certainly in fundamental agreement with mine. His theory of fiction, however, endorses a thesis I reject: that typical sentences contained in a work of fiction (as opposed to fictional discourse) express propositions—in almost all cases false, and necessarily false, propositions—about fictional characters. According to Salmon, the sentence '"The game's afoot, Watson!" cried Holmes', written by Conan Doyle, expresses the necessarily false proposition that a certain fictional character has (not holds but has) the property of having cried out the words 'The game's afoot, Watson!' (But Salmon does not maintain that Doyle, in writing this sentence, asserted the proposition it expresses.) Cf. n. 15.

[19] Kinds, according to Wolterstorff, correspond one–one to properties (and, Russellian monsters aside, a property is given by every open sentence or condition on objects, however complex), but are apparently a distinct ontological category. The kind 'Neanderthal man', for example, a kind of human being, is an abstraction, a universal—membership in it is what is universal among Neanderthals and among the members of no more inclusive class—and it is an eternal, necessarily existent Platonic object that would exist not only if there were no Neanderthals but if there were no physical world. It is intimately related to the property 'being a Neanderthal', but is numerically distinct from it and from every other property.

[20] This is a marvellously subtle notion. See David Lewis's marvellously subtle Lewis (1978).

spoke French better than Russian, and that there is a man named 'Pierre Bezúkhov'. The conjunction of all the propositions true in a work we call its *world*. A proposition may *include* a kind: it does so if its truth entails that that kind has members. Thus, the proposition that some Greeks are wise includes the kinds 'human being', 'Greek', and 'wise Greek'. A kind may *incorporate* a kind: kind A incorporates kind B if it is impossible for something of kind A not to be of kind B. Thus, 'Greek' incorporates 'human being'. If a kind is included in the world of a work, and if no other kind included in that world incorporates it, it is maximal within that work—this being the term we set out to define. It is, I should think, intuitively evident that there is a kind that incorporates 'man named "Pierre Bezúkhov"' and is maximal within *War and Peace*.

To be a character in a given work, Wolterstorff holds, is just exactly to be a person-kind (a kind that incorporates 'person') maximal within that work. (Thus, since there are kinds, since kinds exist—and since person-kinds maximal within works exist—fictional characters exist.) Consider the fictional character Pierre Bezúkhov—that kind maximal within *War and Peace* that incorporates 'man named "Pierre Bezúkhov"'. As every object must, Pierre Bezúkhov has a 'complete' set of properties: for every property, he has either that property or its complement. He has such properties as being self-identical, being a kind, being an eternal object, being an important character in *War and Peace*, and not being a human being. He does *not* have such properties as being human, being the son of Count Cyril Bezúkhov, or having lived in the nineteenth century. But, of course, he does *incorporate* these properties (we may say that a character incorporates a *property* if it incorporates the kind associated with that property).[21] Wolterstorff and I, of course, mean the same thing by 'have', and 'incorporation' (this is not a term he actually uses) plays the role in his theory that 'holding' plays in mine. That is to say: if I

---

[21] Certain conventions are on display in this paragraph: 'A character may, without any explanation or baptismal ceremony, be referred to by a name if it incorporates the kind associated with the property of having that name'; 'A character is normally referred to as "he" if it incorporates the kind "male"'

It should be remarked that similar conventions apply in my own theory: in particular, this one: a name can be applied to a character in critical discourse if the property of having that name is held by or ascribed to that character. (See the second paraphrase of 'Sherlock Holmes does not exist' in the text.) And such a name will be a full-fledged proper name. Some have apparently thought that my appeal to the existence of such a convention to explain the fact that, for example, 'Tom Sawyer' names a certain fictional character is inconsistent with the thesis that a full-bodied Kripkean theory of proper names applies to the names of fictional characters. It is not. It does not even appear to be, as far as I am able to judge. By way of analogy, imagine the following convention, another 'automatic naming' convention: in a certain culture any male baby with green eyes automatically receives, and *must* receive, the name 'Robin' (but females and non-green-eyed males can also be given the name 'Robin' if their parents are so inclined). Imagine that Sally, a woman of that culture, hears that the Smiths have had a green-eyed male baby, and proceeds, without giving any thought to what she is doing, to refer to the new arrival as 'Robin Smith', despite the fact that no one has performed a ceremony in which a name was conferred on the baby. It is obvious that 'Robin Smith' in Sally's mouth is functioning as a proper name for the new child, and that nothing in this case contradicts Kripke's theory of proper names.

were to decide that characters were kinds, I would also decide that holding was incorporation.

By being specific about the ontology of fictional characters, and by (in effect) replacing my vague, ostensively explained notion of 'holding' with the relatively precise and explicitly defined notion of incorporation, Wolterstorff lays his theory open to many difficulties that my theory avoids (or puts itself in a position to respond to more easily) by the clever expedient of being vague. I will mention five.

First, there is the 'Joe DiMaggio' difficulty: persons casually referred to in a story (whether, to speak the language of everyday fictional discourse, they are real people like DiMaggio or fictional people) become characters in the story. Thus, since the world of *The Old Man and the Sea* includes (in virtue of some casual thoughts of old Santiago's about baseball) a person-kind, maximal in that novel, that includes the kind 'famous ball player named "Joe DiMaggio"' (if there is such a kind as 'Joe DiMaggio', the kind-analogue of the property *being Joe DiMaggio*, it includes that kind, too). Thus, it follows from Wolterstorff's theory that Joe DiMaggio is a character in *The Old Man and the Sea*. Or suppose that, as seems plausible, it is true in the world of *War and Peace* that everyone has a paternal grandfather. Then a person-kind that incorporates 'paternal grandfather of a man named "Count Cyril Bezúkhov"' is maximal in the novel; that is to say, one of Pierre's great-grandfathers is a character in the novel, even though he is never explicitly mentioned in the novel.

Secondly, there is the 'Robinson twins' difficulty.[22] Suppose a story contains a reference to 'the Robinson twins', but says nothing to differentiate them. Then there is *one* person-kind, maximal in the story, that incorporates the kind 'being one of a pair of twins named "Robinson"'. That is to say, *one and only one* of the characters in the story is named 'Robinson' and has a twin.

Thirdly, there is the fact that, if Wolterstorff is right, every property incorporated by a character is *essentially* incorporated by that character. So, for example, Lewis Carroll could not have so arranged literary matters that the character we in fact call 'Alice' was asked the riddle 'Why is a raven like a rolling-pin?' instead of 'Why is a raven like a writing-desk?'; a character who was asked the former riddle would have been a different character, even if the *Alice* books were changed in no other way. And, assuming that characters exist in unfinished stories, the characters in unfinished stories change (not 'descriptively' but 'numerically': they do not come to incorporate new properties—which would be impossible; rather, they vanish from the unfinished work and are replaced by distinct characters) almost every time the author adds to or revises his or her manuscript.

---

[22] See Walton (1983, esp. 187–8). I believe it was Robert Howell who first discussed cases of this general kind. See Howell (1979).

Fourthly, there is the fact that a character who incorporates inconsistent properties (which a character certainly might; I have been told that one of the characters in *War and Peace* is in two places at once) incorporates all properties.[23]

Finally, Wolterstorff's characters are eternal, necessarily existent objects. They are thus not literally created by the authors who are normally described as their creators. Mr Pickwick, for example, exists at all times and in all possible worlds. In writing *The Pickwick Papers*, Dickens perhaps caused the entity we call 'Mr Pickwick' to have the property *being a fictional character*, but he did not bring it into existence. A corollary is: the same character could, in principle, occur in causally independent works by different authors.

I now turn to Thomasson. Her theory, like Wolterstorff's, shares my two central assumptions, and, like his theory, is much more specific than mine about the nature of fictional characters. Her theory is, as one might say, the mirror image of Wolterstorff's. According to Thomasson, fictional characters are not necessary and eternal; they are, rather, in the most literal sense, created—brought into existence—by their authors. They hold the properties they hold ('hold' is my word, not Thomasson's) for the most part accidentally: 'Tom Sawyer', the very character that is in fact called 'Tom Sawyer', might have had only nine toes; Alice, she and not another, might have grown taller before she grew smaller. Fictional characters, Thomasson tells us, are 'abstract artifacts' and seem to differ from ordinary or concrete, material artefacts mainly in being abstract: their causal, temporal, and modal features are remarkably like those of concrete works of art, such as paintings and statues. When we compare Thomasson's Tom Sawyer with Wolterstorff's, the advantages seem to be all on Thomasson's side. The way she tells us is the literally correct way to talk about fictional characters is the way we do talk about fictional characters, for we talk of Mark Twain's creating Tom Sawyer, and we talk as if Tom did not exist before Mark Twain created him and would not have existed if Mark Twain had not created him. In Thomasson's view, the creativity of an author is literally creativity; in Wolterstorff's view (as in the Meinongian's), the creativity of an author is something more like an ability to find interesting regions of logical space, regions that exist independently of the author and, indeed, independently of the whole of concrete reality. Wolterstorff's authors bring us news from Plato's heaven; Thomasson's authors *make* things.

The only problem I can see with this appealing theory is that it is not at all clear that it is metaphysically possible. Can there really be abstract things that are made? Some might find it implausible to suppose that even God could literally

---

[23] My own theory, at least as it is presented in 'Creatures of Fiction' (van Inwagen 1977), faces the same difficulty, owing to my perhaps unwise stipulation that 'ascription' is closed under entailment. But I could have avoided the difficulty by refraining from making the stipulation, or restricting it in some way. It would not be at all easy for Wolterstorff to modify his theory in such a way that it does not have this feature.

create an abstract object. Only God can make a tree, granted, but can even God make a poem—that is, cause the object that is the poem to begin to exist? (I think it is clear that Thomasson has no special problem in this area as regards fictional characters; if an author can bring a poem or a novel—as opposed to a manuscript—into existence, there would seem to be no reason to suppose an author could not bring a character into existence.) One very plausible argument for the conclusion that it is possible to bring abstract objects into existence is provided by sets. If I can bring any objects into existence, it would seem that I can bring sets into existence. If I bring A and B into existence, then, surely, (if there are sets at all) I bring the set $\{A, \{A, B\}\}$ into existence, for the existence of that set supervenes on the existence of A and B. And that set is certainly an abstract object. (To adapt a point of Nelson Goodman's, nothing in the world of 'nominalistically acceptable things' could ground or explain the non-identity of the set $\{A, \{A, B\}\}$ with the set $\{B, \{A, B\}\}$.) Similarly, one might suppose, if the existence of characters supervenes on the existence of, say, manuscripts, and if an author can bring a manuscript into existence, then the author can thereby—*must* thereby—bring certain characters into existence.

But this analogy is not decisive. Uncontroversial examples of abstract objects other than sets (not themselves wholly uncontroversial) that can be brought into existence might be hard to find, and Thomasson's abstract artefacts are nothing like sets. (Sets have the wrong properties. If a character were, say, a set of linguistic items of some sort, characters would have properties more like those Wolterstorff's theory ascribes to characters than those Thomasson's theory ascribes to characters.) Thomasson, in fact, appeals to another sort of analogy:

> ... it is a common feature of many cultural and institutional entities that they can be brought into existence merely by being represented as existing. Just as marriages, contracts, and promises may be created through the performance of linguistic acts that represent them as existing, a fictional character is created by being represented in a work of literature. (Thomasson 1998)

But is it evident that when two people marry, or when a contract or a promise is made, an object called a 'marriage' or a 'promise' or a 'contract' thereby comes into existence? It seems to me to be much more plausible to say that in such cases 'all that happens' is that things already in existence acquire new properties or come to stand in new relations: the property *having promised to teach Alice to drive*, for example, or the relation *is married to*. If I say that this is 'all that happens'—that no new things come into existence in such cases—I commit myself to the thesis that quantificational sentences like 'Some marriages are happier than others' or 'A contract made under duress is not binding' can be paraphrased as sentences whose variables range only over people, properties, relations, times, and such other things as we were probably going to have to 'quantify over' in any case. It seems to me very plausible to suppose that the required paraphrases are possible. And if they are not possible, if we find that we must quantify over, say, marriages, what would be so objectionable about regarding a marriage as an abstract object?—a set, say, that contained one man and one woman and nothing else: a 'marriage' would be said to be 'in force', or to 'have been entered into', or some such suitable phrase, at a moment just in the case that its members then became married to each other. I certainly have no strong tendency to believe that when Alice and James marry, a new object called 'their marriage' comes into existence. If no such new object does come into existence, this might be because there *never* is any such object as their marriage, or it might be because, although there is such an object as their marriage, it existed before they were married and 'was entered into' by them at the moment they were married. I'm not sure whether there is a 'right' or 'wrong' in these matters, and if there is, I have a hard time seeing why it would be of any great philosophical importance what was right and what was wrong. What is of some philosophical importance is this: it is not a philosophical datum that 'many cultural and institutional entities. . .can be brought into existence merely by being represented as existing'. And we are therefore left without any strong reason for believing that it is metaphysically possible for anything to have the properties Thomasson ascribes to 'abstract artifacts'. I hasten to add that I know of no strong reason for thinking that it is *not* possible for anything to have these properties.

Wolterstorff's theory is unintuitive in many respects (it cannot be reconciled with many of things we are naturally inclined to believe about fictional entities), but it asks us to believe only in things that we, or the Platonists among us, were going to believe in anyway. Thomasson's theory respects what we are naturally inclined to believe about fictional entities, but it achieves its intuitive character by, as it were, brute force: by postulating objects that have the features we are naturally inclined to think fictional entities have. The metaphysical possibility of objects having the requisite combination of properties is supported only by analogy to 'cultural and institutional entities', and I have given reasons for being sceptical about whether there really are any such things, and reasons for at least some uncertainty about whether, if there are, they have the properties they must have to serve as the other term in Thomasson's analogy.

If what I have said is correct, then, although there are good reasons for believing that there are such things as fictional characters, existent objects that bear some relation that is not 'having' to properties like *committed suicide by throwing herself under a train* and *was born on the banks of the Mississippi in the 1830s*, the question of the metaphysical nature of these objects (whether, for example, they are eternal and necessarily existent) is very far from having been given a decisive answer.

References

Cartwright, Richard (1954). 'Ontology and the Theory of Meaning'. *Philosophy of Science*, 21: 316–25. Repr. in Cartwright, *Philosophical Essays*. Cambridge, Mass.: MIT Press, 1987, 1–12.

Castañeda, Hector-Neri (1979). 'Fiction and Reality: Their Relations and Connections'. *Poetics*, 8: 31–62.

Chisholm, Roderick M. (1972). 'Beyond Being and Non-Being', in Herbert Feigl, Wilfrid Sellars, and Keith Lehrer (eds.), *New Readings in Philosophical Analysis*. New York: Appleton-Century-Crofts, 1972, 15–22.

Church, Alonzo (1958). 'Ontological Commitment'. *Journal of Philosophy*, 55: 1008–14.

Crittenden, Charles (1991). *Unreality: The Metaphysics of Fictional Objects*. Ithaca: Cornell University Press.

Gellner, Ernest (1979). 'The Last Pragmatist, or the Behaviourist Platonist', in Gellner, *Spectacles and Predicaments: Essays in Social Theory*. Cambridge: Cambridge University Press, 199–208.

Haller, Rudolf, and Rudolf Kindinger (eds.) (in collaboration with Roderick M. Chisholm) (1969–73). *Alexius Meinong Gesamtausgabe*. Graz: Akademische Druck- und Verlagsanstalt.

Howell, Robert (1979). 'Fictional Objects: How they Are and How they Aren't'. *Poetics*, 8: 129–77.

Laurence, Stephen, and Cynthia Macdonald (eds.) (1998). *Contemporary Readings in the Foundations of Metaphysics*. Oxford: Basil Blackwell.

Lewis, David (1978). 'Truth in Fiction'. *American Philosophical Quarterly*, 15: 37–46.

—— (1983). *Philosophical Papers*, vol. i. New York: Oxford University Press.

—— (1990). 'Noneism and Allism'. *Mind*, 99: 23–31.

—— and Stephanie Lewis (1970). 'Holes'. *Australasian Journal of Philosophy*, 48: 206–12. Repr. in Lewis (1983: 3–9).

Meinong, Alexius (1969). 'Über Gegenstandstheorie', in Haller and Kindinger (1969–73).

Parsons, Terence (1975). 'A Meinongian Analysis of Fictional Objects'. *Grazer Philosophische Studien*, 1: 73–86.

—— (1980). *Non-Existent Objects*. New Haven: Yale University Press.

Plantinga, Alvin (1974). *The Nature of Necessity*. Oxford: Clarendon Press.

Quine, W. V. O. (1960). *Word and Object*. Cambridge, Mass.: MIT Press.

—— (1961). *From a Logical Point of View*, 2nd edn. Cambridge, Mass.: Harvard University Press.

Routley, Richard (1980). *Exploring Meinong's Jungle and Beyond: An Investigation of Noneism and the Theory of Items*, Departmental Monograph no. 3. Canberra: Philosophy Department, Research School of Social Sciences, Australian National University.

Salmon, Nathan (1998). 'Nonexistence'. *Nous*, 32: 277–319.

Thomasson, Amie L. (1998). 'The Artifactual Theory of Fiction'. Paper presented at the CSLI Conference 'Empty Names, Fiction, and the Puzzles of Non-Existence', Stanford University, Mar. 1998.

—— (1999). *Fiction and Metaphysics*. Cambridge: Cambridge University Press.

van Inwagen, Peter (1977). 'Creatures of Fiction'. *American Philosophical Quarterly*, 14: 299–308. Repr. in van Inwagen (2001: 37–56).

—— (1981). 'Why I don't Understand Substitutional Quantification'. *Philosophical Studies*, 39: 281–5. Repr. in van Inwagen (2001: 32–6).

—— (1983). 'Fiction and Metaphysics'. *Philosophy and Literature*, 7: 67–77.

—— (1985). 'Pretense and Paraphrase', in Peter J. McCormick (ed.), *The Reasons of Art*. Ottawa: University of Ottawa Press, 1985, 414–22.

—— (1998). 'The Nature of Metaphysics', in Laurence and Macdonald (1998: 11–21).

—— (2001). *Ontology, Identity, and Modality: Essays in Metaphysics.* Cambridge: Cambridge University Press.

Walton, Kendall L. (1983). Review of Wolterstorff (1980). *Journal of Philosophy*, 80: 179–93.

—— (1990). *Mimesis as Make-Believe: On the Foundations of the Representational Arts.* Cambridge, Mass.: Harvard University Press.

Wolterstorff, Nicholas (1980). *Worlds and Works of Art.* Oxford: Clarendon Press.

Zalta, Edward (1983). *Abstract Objects.* Dordrecht: Reidel.

—— (1988). *Intensional Logic and the Metaphysics of Intensionality.* Cambridge, Mass.: MIT Press.

PART III

MODALITY AND POSSIBLE WORLDS

CHAPTER 6

THE PROBLEM OF POSSIBILIA

KIT FINE

1. INTRODUCTION

ARE there, in addition to the various actual objects that make up the world, various possible objects? Are there merely possible people, for example, or merely possible electrons, or even merely possible kinds?

We certainly talk as if there were such things. Given a particular sperm and egg, I may wonder whether that particular child which would result from their union would have blue eyes. But if the sperm and egg are never in fact brought together, then there is no actual object that my thought is about. (Cf. Gupta 1980: 20 n. 15.) Or again, in the semantics for modal logic we presuppose an ontology of possibilia twice over.[1] For first, we countenance various possible worlds, in addition to the actual world; and second, each of these worlds is taken to be endowed with its own domain of objects. These will be the actual objects of the world in question, but they need not be actual *simpliciter*, i.e. actual objects of *our* world.

What are we to make of such discourse? There are four options: (i) the discourse is taken to be unintelligible; (ii) it is taken to be intelligible but non-factual, i.e. as

I should like to thank Roderick Batchelor, Michael Loux, and Chris Peacocke for many helpful comments.

[1] See Kripke (1963) for a standard exposition of the semantics.

not in the business of stating facts; (iii) it is taken to be factual but reducible to discourse involving no reference to possibilia; (iv) it is taken to be both factual and irreducible.[2] These options range from a full-blooded form of actualism at one extreme to a full-blooded form of possibilism at the other. The two intermediate positions are possibilist in that they accept the intelligibility of possibilist discourse but actualist in that they attempt to dispense with its prima facie commitment to possibilia. All four positions have found advocates in the literature. Quine, in his less irenic moments, favours option (i); Forbes (1985: 94) advocates option (ii), at least for certain parts of possibilist discourse; many philosophers, including Adams (1974) and myself, opt for (iii); while Lewis (1986) and Stalnaker (1976) have endorsed versions of (iv) that differ in how full-blooded they take the possible objects to be.

My focus in the present chapter is on the third option. I wish to see to what extent reference to possibilia might be understood in other terms. Can we regard talk of possibilia as a mere *façon de parler*, perhaps somewhat in the same manner as talk of the average man or of infinitesimals?[3] I shall not be concerned to argue directly against any of the other options. However, any argument for the viability of (iii) is indirectly an argument against their plausibility. For (iv), especially in its more extreme forms, offends against what Russell has called our 'robust sense of reality', (i) offends against our even more robust sense of what is intelligible, while (ii) offends against our somewhat less robust sense of what is factual. It is therefore preferable to go with the third option, if we possibly can.

2. PROBLEMS WITH PROXY REDUCTION

The most obvious way to make sense of possibilist discourse is in terms of surrogates or proxies. With each possible x is associated another entity x', acceptable to the actualist, and any statement $\phi(a, b, \ldots)$ about the possibles $a, b, \ldots$ is then understood in terms of a corresponding statement $\phi'(a', b', \ldots)$ about the associated entities $a', b', \ldots$ As a model for such a reduction, we may take the logicist-style reduction of numbers to sets: each number is associated with a 'representative' set, and a statement about numbers is then understood in terms of a corresponding statement about the associated sets.[4]

---

[2] See Fine (2001) for a general discussion of what these various options amount to.

[3] As should be clear from Fine (2001), the viability of any reduction will also depend upon its success in accounting for our understanding of modal discourse and our knowledge of modal truth. See Peacocke (2001) for a broader discussion along these lines.

[4] For more on the general approach, see Quine (1964, 1969).

But what is the relationship between a possible object and its surrogate? For which entities are the possibilia traded in? The simplest view on the matter is that the relationship is one of identity; each entity is traded in for itself. But such a 'reduction', if it may be called that, is *always* available to us. And so how can it serve to alleviate ontological qualms in any particular case? The answer is that the significance of such a reduction must lie in the way the entities are described. We have a domain of entities that is characterized in problematic terms. It is then shown how each entity from this domain is identical to an entity from a domain that is characterized in relatively unproblematic terms; and doubts about the entities, *qua* members of the problematic domain, are thereby laid to rest. A physicalist's doubts about the ontological status of mental events, for example, might be put to rest in this way if he comes to believe that every mental event is in fact a physical event.

Is a similar kind of view available to the actualist? Can he maintain that possibilia are really just Ys, for some actualistically acceptable description Y (i.e. for some description that makes no reference to merely possible objects)? After all, the possible winners of a race consist of the actual losers. So could not something similar be true in the case of possibilia? Could not every possible X be identical to an actual Y, for some actualistically acceptable description Y?

It seems to me that no view of this sort can be correct. Suppose, to fix our ideas, that it is maintained that every (merely) possible person is identical to an actual property—one perhaps that specifies its 'essence'. Consider now a possible person. Then it is possibly a person. But no property is possibly a person and so no possible person is identical to a property: for there is a possibility for the one, namely that of being a person, which is not a possibility for the other.

A similar difficulty besets many other identifications of this sort that have been proposed. Possible states of affairs, for example, have often been taken to be propositions. But this cannot be correct, since any possible state of affairs is possibly a state of affairs but no proposition is possibly a state of affairs. Or again, Stalnaker (1976: 230) and Plantinga (1974: 44) have suggested that we might think of a possible world as a way the world might have been. But a possible world is possibly the world, just as a possible person is possibly a person, yet no way the world might have been is possibly the world, just as no way I might have been is possibly me. Thus it is not just that the actual world is not a way things might be, as emphasized by Stalnaker (1976: 228) and van Inwagen (1980: 407); no possible world is such a way either.

Whatever the merits of reduction via identity in other contexts, it is of no avail here. If there is to be a proxy reduction, it had better be achieved by means of proxies that are distinct from the possibilia themselves.

But again, an obvious solution suggests itself. For why not 'identify' each possible world with a proposition that is true in that world alone (or, if we wish to pick out a particular proposition, with the conjunction of all propositions that are true in the world)? And why not identify each possible object with a property that is necessarily borne by that object alone (or with the conjunction of all properties that are necessarily borne by the individual)? Each possible, be it world or object, is in effect identified with a description by which it might be specified.[5]

The main difficulty with this proposal is that there can be no assurance, from an actualist point of view, that distinct possible objects or worlds can be identified with distinct surrogates. Let us provide a simple illustration of the difficulty. Suppose there is some radioactive material in the actual world w_0 that just happens not to emit any particles from a certain time on but that *might* have emitted two particles of the same type at that time. These two particles, call them α and β, are presumably merely possible; they are not identical to any actual particles. And it is plausible to suppose that there is no actualistically acceptable means by which they might be distinguished. Of course, there is a possible world w_1 in which α is distinguished by one trajectory and β another. But if there is such a world, then there is presumably another world w_2 just like it in which the trajectories are interchanged. For what is so special about α as opposed to β that it is destined to have the one trajectory rather than the other?[6] Thus we will be as unable to distinguish between the worlds as we are to distinguish between the particles themselves.

If we pretend that w_1 and w_2 and the actual world w_0 are the only worlds that there are, then we might depict the scenario as follows:

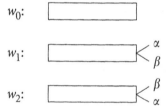

Here, in this miniature 'pluriverse', the worlds w_1 and w_2 are actualistically indiscernible, as are the particles α and β. Given that there is no actualistically acceptable means by which the particles or worlds might be distinguished, they will be associated with the very same surrogates, since any actualistically acceptable means of associating them with distinct surrogates would provide us with an actualistically acceptable means of distinguishing between the particles or worlds themselves; and given that this is so, the reduction must fail, since it will not even be capable of representing the fact that the particles or worlds are distinct.

Another kind of problem case arises from the possibility of there being indiscernible individuals *within* a world. Imagine a universe of eternal recurrence

---

[5] A view of this sort was originally proposed by Prior (1977, ch. 2), though only for the case of worlds. Essentially the same account was later given by Adams (1974: 204). The extension to possible individuals was proposed by Fine in Prior and Fine (1977) and possibly by Plantinga (1976) (though not if his disclaimers in Plantinga 1985: 330–2 are to be heeded).

[6] We might even suppose that there were convincing scientific reasons for allowing both possibilities in determining the probability of emission.

(with respect to both past and future) in which a new messiah appears in every epoch. There are then infinitely many possible messiahs; and presumably each of them will be actualistically indiscernible from the others.

A third kind of case arises from the possibility of there being indiscernible natural properties or kinds. (See Bricker 1987: 349–53; Lewis 1986: 158–65; McMichael 1983, for examples of this sort.) There are two subcases here, just as in the case of individuals, depending upon whether the indiscernibilities are *intra*world or *inter*world. Pure cases of interworld indiscernibility might always be disputed on the grounds that the identity of a kind, in these cases, is to be tied to role (as on the views of Swoyer 1982; Shoemaker 1980, 1998). Thus given that the kinds are indiscernible in their respective worlds, their roles will be the same and hence the kinds themselves must be the same. However, intraworld cases are not so readily disposed of. Suppose, for example, that there are two fundamental kinds of matter in the universe, positive and negative, governed by such laws as: like matter attracts; unlike matter repels. The two kinds of matter would then have completely symmetric roles and so as long as they are 'alien' kinds, not of this world, there would again appear to be no actualistically acceptable way in which they might be distinguished.

There are two main responses to these arguments. One is to dispute the possibilities upon which they are based. It has sometimes been denied, for example, that there can be worlds that are qualitatively, or actualistically, alike and yet differ merely in the identity of the individuals that they contain (e.g. by Lewis 1986, sect. 4.4; Adams 1981); and, under such views, there would only be one possibility for α and β depicted by w_1 and w_2 in the picture above, not two. But there is something unsatisfactory about making the reduction dependent upon such views—both because they are controversial and because we wish to explain what sense might be given to possibilist discourse by someone who did not accept them. It would be preferable, if at all feasible, to provide a reduction which was free from any substantive assumption about what was or was not possible.

The second response to the cases is to accept the putative possibilities and yet deny that they involve genuine actualist indiscernibilities. Despite our claims to the contrary, it will be maintained that the particles or the messiahs or the kinds of matter can be actualistically distinguished after all. For let x be any given possible object. Then associated with this object will be a certain identity property, the property of being identical to x. But in contrast to the object x itself, this property—like all properties—will exist necessarily. It will therefore be an actual object; and so we may use it, in an actualistically acceptable way, to distinguish x from all other objects (see Plantinga 1976). (Of course, when x itself is a property or the like, we may proceed directly, by this line of reasoning, to the conclusion that it necessarily exists.)

One way of dealing with this response is to deny the claims of necessary existence upon which it depends. The property of being identical to Socrates, it might be countered, can only exist when Socrates exists; and the kind *positive matter* can only exist in a world in which there is positive matter.[7] But there is, I believe, a more fundamental objection to be made. Let us suppose that an actualist comes to the view that (necessarily) properties necessarily exist. Should the properties that he previously took to be problematic because they were merely possible now be regarded as unproblematic? I think not. Rather, they should still be taken to be problematic, though for reasons that no longer turn on their being merely possible.

For a more fundamental way to understand the actualist's position is that he objects to the idea that general possibilities might be the source of a distinctive ontology of objects that instantiate those possibilities. Consider the possibility that there is a talking donkey ($\Diamond \exists x Px$). The possibilist will claim that it follows from this possibility that there really is an object, possible if not actual, that instantiates it; there is an object, that is to say, that is possibly a talking donkey ($\exists x \Diamond Px$). The actualist will deny that there need be any such object (except as a mere *façon de parler*) and, in general, he will be suspicious of any object whose existence would appear to depend upon its being the instantiator in this way of a general possibility.

But the identity properties of merely possible objects and the alien kinds are just of this sort. It is only because of the possibility of there being an identity property for such-and-such a possible object and it is only because of the possibility of there being a kind which plays such-and-such a role that we are led to believe that there *are* such properties or kinds. Without the belief in the general possibilities, we would have no reason to believe that there were such things. On this understanding of what lies behind the actualist's position, then, he will remain suspicious of these properties and kinds on account of their possibilist origins, even though he accepts that they exist. He will think of them, like other problematic existents, of standing in need of analysis in terms of existents of another sort.[8]

3. The Possibility of Proxy Reduction

As a result of these difficulties, many philosophers have given up on the idea of proxy reduction; and, indeed, the difficulties in the particular reduction proposed above might appear to extend to any reduction whatever. For consider again our miniature pluriverse with its three worlds w_0, w_1, w_2 and its two particles α and β;

---

[7] Fine in Prior and Fine (1977, sect. 4) and McMichael (1983: 60–1) develop objections along these lines.

[8] A related objection is made in Fine (1985, sect. 2) and an altogether different objection to the necessary existence of alien properties is developed by Lewis (1986: 160–1).

and suppose that a represents, or goes proxy for, α. Then, as we have seen, it must also represent β. For a must be an actual object (or, at least, actualistically acceptable); and so, if it failed to represent β, we could distinguish between α and β in an actualistically acceptable manner, since α would have the property of being represented by a while β would not. This therefore suggests that it will in general be impossible to obtain a unique proxy for each possible individual and that any acceptable form of proxy reduction must therefore fail.

Uniqueness of proxies is not, however, necessary for a proxy reduction to succeed.[9] We may reduce three-dimensional Euclidean geometry to real analysis by identifying each point with a triple of real numbers. But the identification is far from unique. Indeed, any given point might be associated with any given triple. But the ambiguity will not matter as long as it does not result in any ambiguity in truth-value of the sentences to be reduced. This therefore suggests that we may let a represent α and b represent β under one scheme of representation as long as we are also prepared to allow that a represents β and b represents α under another. The previous difficulty then disappears since, given the symmetric nature of the representations (which cannot themselves be actualistically distinguished), we will be left with no way to distinguish between α and β.[10]

A problem remains, however. For a similar story should be told about w_1 and w_2. There will be two proxies, say w and v, that indifferently represent w_1 and w_2 or w_2 and w_1. Suppose now that we pick on a particular scheme of representation, say that in which a represents α, b represents β, w represents w_1, and v represents w_2. Then how are we to determine which paths for a and b are to be assigned in w? Whatever we say, the paths assigned in v must be the reverse. But there seems to be no basis for taking the paths to go one way rather than the other. Thus even when we pick on a particular scheme of representation, there appear to be irresolvable indeterminacies in how it is to be applied.

In order to solve this further difficulty, we must somehow 'coordinate' the representation of individuals and worlds. Let me indicate one way in which this might be done. (The less technically minded reader may skip the details.)[11] Let us suppose that we use the distinct actual entities w_1, w_2, ... as proxies for the possible worlds and the distinct actual entities i_1, i_2, ... as proxies for the possible individuals, both actual and merely possible. We assume that each actual individual i_k goes proxy for itself. Thus it is the actual entities that are not individuals that will go proxy for what we take to be the merely possible individuals. Coordination may now be achieved by means of a *proxy pluriverse*. This consists of three items: the class W of

---

[9] Contrary to what the criticisms in Lewis (1986: 158, 163–4) might appear to suggest.

[10] Curiously, similar difficulties arise in understanding Cantor's account of cardinal numbers as sets of units (Fine 1998a).

[11] The basic idea behind the method is presented in Fine in Prior and Fine (1977: 148), and a related approach has been developed by Sider (2001, sect. 5).

world-proxies; the class I of individual-proxies; and a class of proxy relationships. Each proxy relationship is of the form $\langle w, R, i_1, i_2, \ldots, i_n \rangle$, where w is a proxy world, R is an (actual) n-adic relation, and $i_1, i_2, \ldots, i_n$ are proxy individuals. Intuitively, a proxy relationship indicates that the relation R holds of the possible individuals represented by $i_1, i_2, \ldots, i_n$ in the possible world represented by w. Thus a proxy pluriverse represents how the pluriverse might be; it provides an explicit tabulation or model, via the proxies, of the relationships that hold of the possible individuals in each of the worlds.[12]

A proxy pluriverse will not in general be 'realistic'; it will not represent the way the pluriverse really is. How then are such proxy pluriverses to be singled out? In order to answer this question, let us suppose that we are given a list (or well-ordering) $i_1, i_2, \ldots$ of all the proxy individuals. We may then define in a natural way what it is for the proxy world w of the proxy pluriverse to be *realized by* a corresponding list of individuals $x_1, x_2, \ldots$ For this requires that R hold of $x_{k_1}, x_{k_2}, \ldots, x_{k_n}$ just in case $\langle w, R, i_{k_1}, i_{k_2}, \ldots, i_{k_n} \rangle$ is a proxy relationship of the proxy pluriverse. Thus a proxy world will be realized by an assignment of individuals to proxy individuals if it correctly represents the relations that hold among those individuals. A proxy pluriverse may now be said to be *realistic* (given a list of its proxy individuals) if possibly there is an x_1, possibly there is an $x_2, \ldots$ such that:

(1) each $x_k = l_k$, when l_k is an actual individual (taken to go proxy for itself);
(2) x_j and x_k are distinct for $j \neq k$;
(3) necessarily any individual is identical to x_1 or x_2 or $\ldots$;
(4) each proxy world is possibly realized by $x_1, x_2, \ldots$;
(5) it is necessarily the case that some proxy world is realized by $x_1, x_2, \ldots$

Clauses (1)–(3) say that $x_1, x_2, \ldots$ are pairwise distinct and together constitute the domain of possibilia; clause (4) says that each of the proxy worlds represents a genuine possibility (under the given assignment of individuals to proxy individuals); and clause (5) says that the proxy worlds exhaust the genuine possibilities.[13]

Given a realistic proxy pluriverse, we may then quantify over the proxy worlds and the proxy individuals as if they were the possible worlds and the possible individuals of the real pluriverse. Thus instead of saying that R holds of a pair of possible individuals in a given possible world, we may say that $\langle w, R, i, j \rangle$ is a proxy relationship within the given proxy pluriverse. There will of course be many realistic pluriverses (and many ways of ordering their proxy individuals). But the ambiguity will not matter, since different realistic pluriverses are isomorphic and hence will yield the same truth-value for any given possibilist claim.

---

[12] We shall suppose that distinct proxy worlds enter into different relationships—so that if $w \neq v$ then there is a relation R and proxy individuals $i_1, i_2, \ldots, i_n$ such that $\langle w, R, i_1, i_2, \ldots, i_n \rangle$ is a proxy relationship within the proxy pluriverse while $\langle v, R, i_1, i_2, \ldots, i_n \rangle$ is not, or vice versa.

[13] A similar modal description of the pluriverse is given in Prior and Fine (1977: 147).

The resulting reduction is highly inelegant. It requires enormous expressive resources in order to capture a relatively modest extension in expressive power. For whether a given proxy pluriverse is realistic depends upon the truth of the infinitary proposition given by the clauses (1)–(5) above. And so, in stating any given reduction, we must either possess the means to express this infinitary proposition, in which case the language of the reduction must itself be infinitary, or we must possess the means to refer to this proposition (or to a corresponding sentence), in which case the language of the reduction must be capable of describing the structure and semantics of an infinitary language or ontology of propositions.

But there is a more serious problem. For how can we be sure that there *is* a realistic proxy pluriverse? The problem is essentially one of cardinality. For in order for a proxy pluriverse to be realistic there must possibly be an x_1, possibly be an $x_2, \ldots$ such that $x_1, x_2, \ldots$ are all the possible individuals that there are. There must therefore be as many variables 'x_1', 'x_2', $\ldots$—or operators 'possibly an x_1', 'possibly an x_2',$\ldots$—as there are possible objects. But suppose there are c such operators, for some cardinal number c. It is then arguable that there could be a greater, infinite number d of possibilia. For there could be a possible world that contained d 'parallel' universes, each with its own particles; and since there are presumably only finitely many actual particles (and since, necessarily, each particle is necessarily a particle), at least d of these particles from the parallel universes will be non-actual.

There are perhaps ways in which this latter problem might be solved.[14] But a general form of the cardinality worry remains. For if a proxy reduction is to succeed, there must be a one–one correspondence between the possible individuals and worlds of the pluriverse, on the one side, and the objects of the actual world on the other (or perhaps we should say, more cautiously, between the possible individuals and worlds of the pluriverse and the objects of some *possible* world, since one might carry out the reduction from the perspective of some possible world, viewed as actual, rather than from the perspective of the actual world itself).

But is such an assumption reasonable? Will there be a world within the pluriverse of the same 'size' as the pluriverse itself? This is a difficult question (and of some interest in itself). But I am inclined to think the answer is no. For there is a puzzle whose solution appears to require that we give up the assumption.[15] I shall state the puzzle for the case of 'communicating egos', though there are other forms it might take.

---

[14] One solution, suggested in Prior and Fine (1977: 148), is to use so-called 'quasi-classes' to set up a one–one correspondence between the possibilia and the actualia (a great gain in elegance and simplicity is thereby also achieved). Quasi-classes are the possibilist counterpart of plural quantification (in the sense of Boolos 1984) and were introduced, along with the general idea of plural quantification, in Prior and Fine (1977: 146–7).

[15] Some related arguments, based on diagonal considerations, have been discussed by Forrest and Armstrong (1984), Bringsjord (1985), Menzel (1986*a*), and Kaplan (1995).

We imagine ourselves attempting to ascertain how many possible Cartesian egos there are. Now even if there are no actual Cartesian egos, there could be one. That is:

(1) There is at least one possible ego.

It is also plausible that:

(2) Given any possible world containing one or more egos, there is a possible world in which those egos exist and in which, for any subclass of those egos, there is an ego which is in telepathic communication with just those of the given egos that are members of the subclass.

Finally, we may wish to maintain that:

(3) Given any class of possible egos, there is some possible world in which they all exist.

Although each of these assumptions is individually plausible, together they are inconsistent. For from (3) (letting the class be the class of all possible egos), it follows that:

(4) There is a possible world (call it Descartes's world) in which all possible egos exist.

From (1), it follows that

(5) Descartes's world contains some egos.

And from (2), it follows that:

(6) Given any possible world which contains some egos, there is a possible world which contains more egos,

since in the world with telepathic communication there will be more communicating egos than egos with which they communicate. But (4) and (6) are incompatible with one another, since there can be no possible world which contains more egos than the class of them all.

What are we to say? Which of the assumptions (1)–(3) should be given up? It is natural to suppose that it should be (3). But we would like this principle for the most part to be true. And if we ask what is it about the class of all possible egos that prevents them from all existing, the only acceptable answer would appear to be that the class is too large. In other words, the domains of each possible world will be subject to a 'limitation of size'; and even though the pluriverse may be capable of exceeding this size, the worlds within the pluriverse will not be. Each such world will possess an 'actual' or 'actualizable' infinity of objects and be incapable of accommodating the 'potential' infinity of possible objects that belong to the pluriverse as a whole.[16]

---

[16] This is a distinction that may be easier for the actualist rather than for the possibilist to maintain. For the actualist may argue that just as there is no perspective (one transcending all ordinals) from

But if this is our motivation for rejecting the possible existence of all possible egos, then we are obliged to conclude that there are more possible egos than there are objects in any possible world, since it is only this that prevents them all from possibly existing.

If this is right, then the assumption that there could be as many actuals as possibles is untenable and the whole idea of a proxy reduction should be abandoned.[17] But even if it is not right and another solution to the puzzle is discovered, there is still something unsatisfactory, for the reasons already given, about having the adequacy of the reduction depend upon such substantive metaphysical views; and it would be desirable if some other way of reducing possibilist discourse could be found.

4. REDUCTION WITHOUT PROXIES

It is important to bear in mind that a reduction need not proceed via proxies. The mother of all reductions, Russell's theory of descriptions, cannot readily be regarded as one in which entity gives way to entity, and another example, more pertinent to our present concerns, is that in which quantification over pairs is replaced by quantification pairs. Instead of saying 'there is a pair x such that . . .', one says 'there is an x_1 and an x_2 such that . . .'. Here there is no single entity that goes proxy for a pair.

Many philosophers seem to have followed Lewis (1986: 141) in supposing that they must either go with *proxy* reduction ('ersatzism') or accept possible worlds realism. But this is a false dilemma. For as I have indicated in previous work,[18] it is possible to provide a straightforward nonproxy reduction of possibilist discourse.

The basic idea is to take modality as primitive and to treat the possibilist quantifier 'there is a possible object x' as equivalent to 'possibly there is an object x'—where the second quantifier (in the scope of the possibility operator) is actualist, ranging in each world over the actual objects of that world. Thus to say that there is a possible object that is possibly a talking donkey is to say that possibly there is an object that is possibly a talking donkey.

Unfortunately, the above method does not work in all cases. To say that there is a possible object that is not actual is not to say that possibly there is an (actual) object

which the class of all sets is given, so there is no perspective (one transcending all possible worlds) from which the class of all possibilia is given. (In this connection, see Menzel 1986*a,b*; Grim 1986.)

[17] There is a related problem over cardinality in representing Fregean abstracts as sets within the cumulative hierarchy (Fine 1998*b* or 2002: 14).

[18] Beginning with Fine in Prior and Fine (1977: 130–9). A comparison with the standard proxy reduction is made in Fine (1985: 180–3) and some technical details can be found in Fine (1979, 1981, 1982).

that is not actual, since the latter claim is necessarily false while the former claim is presumably true. The method must therefore be modified.

The difficulty is that the possibility operator takes us to another world, whereas we wish to evaluate the statement governed by the possibilist quantifier in the original world. We therefore need some device to take us back to the original world. There are various ways in which this might be done, but let me here present just one. Back-reference is to be achieved, in the most direct and straightforward manner, by means of reference to the actual world. Thus to say that there is a possible object that is not actual will be to say that the actual world is such that it is possible that there is an object whose non-existence is compatible with that world being actual. And, in general, to say that some possible object ϕs is to say that the actual world is such that it is possible that there is an object whose ϕ-ing is compatible with that world being actual.

The reduction of possible worlds is now merely the special case of the reduction of possible individuals in which the individuals are taken to be the worlds. Thus to say 'for some possible world' will be to say 'possibly for some (actual) world' in the simplest case; and back-reference can be achieved in the general case in the same way as before. (Thus worlds will now play a double role, as the objects of quantification and as the means for securing back-reference.)

Of course, we do not get rid of the world on this approach—merely *possible* worlds. But the problem for the actualist is not with the actual world, but with possible entities, whether they be worlds or of some other kind. If we also wish to get rid of the actual world and treat it as a special kind of fact, say, or proposition, then this is something that might be tacked onto the present reduction but is of no concern to the actualist as such.

The beauty of the method is that it does not require any addition to the ontology. Quantification over possibilia, be they worlds or individuals, is eliminated in favour of the corresponding quantification over actualia. There is a direct trade between the ontology of possibilia, on the one hand, and the ideology of modality, on the other. Moreover, the assumptions upon which the reduction depends are minimal. It need only be assumed that:

(1) necessarily there is a world; and
(2) necessarily, for any world and true proposition, the truth of the proposition is implied by the existence of the world.[19]

Once these assumptions are granted, the adequacy of the reduction is guaranteed.

The main difficulty with this approach is that it is not clear how it is to be extended to quantification over sets of possibles (Fine in Prior and Fine 1977: 145). We could try

---

[19] If we wish to take care of questions concerning the identity of worlds, then it should also be assumed that there is necessarily at most one world.

to understand such quantification as quantification over possible sets. But a possible set can only consist of compossibles, i.e. of objects that can possibly all exist, whereas we should also allow for quantification over all sets of non-compossible objects.

A uniform solution to this problem is available in the case of any proxy reduction, since a set of the objects from the class of objects to be reduced can always be identified with the set of their proxies; and it would be desirable if a uniform solution could also be obtained in the case of any non-proxy reduction. One possibility here is to treat quantification over sets as a certain form of plural quantification. To say that there is a set X is to say, in effect, that there are certain individuals $x_1, x_2, \ldots$; and to say that $x \in X$ is to say, in effect, that x is one of the individuals $x_1, x_2, \ldots$ Let us be a little more precise. (Again, the less technically minded reader may skip the details.) Suppose that we are somehow equipped with an understanding of a first-order language L_1 in which the quantifiers range over individuals; and let it be granted that our understanding extends, in principle, to sentences of infinitary length (we could equally well work with propositions rather than sentences). Suppose that we now introduce a quantifier $\exists X$ over sets of individuals; and consider any sentence ϕ of the resulting language. We wish to extend the truth-predicate to the resulting language, though without quantifying over sets. This may be done inductively on the logical complexity of the sentence to which the truth-predicate is applied. The clauses in the case of the truth-functional connectives and the quantifier $\exists x$ over individuals are straightforward. And so that leaves sentences of the form $\exists X \phi$. Intuitively, we wish to say that such a sentence is true iff an instance is true, but we have no straightforward way of saying what an instance is. What we may do instead is to find a first-order counterpart of an instance. This can be obtained in two steps. First we replace each free occurrence of the set-variable 'X' in ϕ by a term '$\{x_1, x_2, \ldots\}$' with a given number of distinct new variables 'x_1', 'x_2', $\ldots$ (sets give way to individuals); and then we replace each atomic subformula '$x \varepsilon \{x_1, x_2, \ldots\}$' in the resulting formula by '$x = x_1 \vee x = x_2 \vee \ldots$' (membership gives way to identity), and similarly for all other atomic subformula involving $\{x_1, x_2, \ldots\}$.[20] Let the resulting sentence be 'ϕ'. Then an instance of $\exists X \phi$ may be taken to be a sentence of the form '$\exists x_1, x_2, \ldots, \phi$'.

We thereby obtain truth-conditions for a language L_2 with variables for both individuals and sets of individuals. The same general method can be extended to a language L_3 with quantifiers that range over sets of 'rank' ≤ 2, i.e. over sets whose members are either individuals or sets of individuals; and the construction may then be continued into the transfinite. We thereby obtain truth-conditions for a language

---

[20] Atomic formulae of the form $\{x_1, x_2, \ldots\} \in x, x \in y$ and $x = \{x_1, x_2, \ldots\}$ are replaced by $\perp$; and $X = Y$ is treated as definitionally equivalent to $\forall x(x \in X \equiv x \in Y)$. Special provision should be made for the null class.

L_α of arbitrary order α; and so, as long as we are able to identify the sets we wish to quantify over as those whose rank is less than a given ordinal α, we are in a position to account for quantification over such sets in terms of our understanding of the base language.

This reduction does not allow us to eliminate reference to sets altogether, since the definition of truth requires the full resources of set theory.[21] But the reduction does show how we may extend our understanding of quantification over sets of arbitrary rank to the ontology of any infinitary first-order language. And since our non-proxy reduction of possibilist discourse extends straightforwardly to the infinitary quantifier 'there are possible objects $x_1, x_2, \ldots$', we are thereby able to account for higher-order quantification over sets of possible individuals, sets of such sets, and so on throughout the cumulative hierarchy.[22]

5. FICTIONALISM

We have argued against any proxy reduction of the possible to the actual and in favour of a certain form of non-proxy reduction. But are there any other acceptable forms of non-proxy reduction?

One candidate is the modal fictionalism of Rosen (1990).[23] The possibilist wishes to assert:

(e) possibly there are talking donkeys iff there is a possible world in which donkeys talk.

And, in general, where ϕ is a modal claim and ϕ^* is its possibilist translation, the possibilist will maintain:

(E) ϕ iff ϕ^*.

But, given that he accepts the possibility of talking donkeys and other such modal claims, he is thereby committed to a plethora of possible worlds. The fictionalist,

---

[21] Indeed, it also requires that we be able to treat the domain of sets in the object language as a set within the meta-language. But this set-theoretic 'ascent' is something which one might argue is always available to us.

[22] The idea behind this reduction derives from Gödel's reconstruction of Russell's no-class theory in Gödel (1944: 132).

[23] A related form of fictionalism, to which similar criticisms apply, is that of Armstrong (1989). An altogether different approach, which I shall not discuss, is that of Forbes (1985: 89–95). The view is critically examined in Cresswell (1990: 47–62) and Chihara (1998, ch. 4).

by contrast, will think of the possibilist's views of the pluriverse as constituting a fiction and will therefore replace (e) with:

(e′) possibly there are talking donkeys iff it is true according to the fictional account of the pluriverse that there is some possible world in which there are talking donkeys;

and, more generally, he will replace (E) with:

(E′) ϕ iff it is true in PW that ϕ^*,

where PW is the fictional account of the pluriverse. In this way, he can take advantage of the possible world semantics for modal discourse without committing himself to its ontology. In making the transition from ordinary modal claims to their possibilist translation, we enter a fictional realm of possible worlds and their inhabitants, according to the fictionalist, rather than one that is genuinely there.

The view, as stated, would appear to fall flat on its face. For on any account of the fiction PW that might reasonably be proposed, there will presumably be possibilist translations ϕ^* of modal claims ϕ whose truth-value is not settled within PW. Perhaps ϕ^* is the claim that there is a possible world in which there are more than $\aleph_{17}$ individuals. It is not then implausible to suppose that

(I) it is not true in PW that some possible world contains more than $\aleph_{17}$ individuals and it is not true in PW that every possible world contains at most $\aleph_{17}$ individuals.

But, from the modified equivalence (E′) above and the first part of (I), it follows that it is not possible that there are more than $\aleph_{17}$ individuals and, from (E′) and the second part of (I), it follows that it is not necessary that there are at most $\aleph_{17}$ individuals. And this is a contradiction.

In the face of this difficulty, Rosen (1990: 341–3) has suggested that modal claims ϕ like the one above should be taken to be indeterminate, i.e. to be neither true nor false. But this is of no help in avoiding the contradiction unless principle (E′) is somehow modified. Presumably, the intent is that it should take the form:

(E″) it is true that ϕ iff it is true in PW that ϕ^*,

where 'it is true that' is an operator that converts an indeterminate statement into one that is false. But the scope of the view is now seriously compromised, for we lack any account of what it is in general for a modal statement ϕ to hold. Where ϕ is indeterminate, we would like there to be a possibilist or quasi-possibilist translation that is correspondingly indeterminate. But the fictionalist is unable to provide any such translation, since ϕ^* and 'In PW, ϕ^*' are both false. Thus the fictionalist is unable adequately to represent the question 'Is it possible that there are more than $\aleph_{17}$ individuals?' He can only provide a question to which the answer is no, whereas we want a question to which the answer is neither yes nor no.

Numerous other difficulties for the view have been raised (see Rosen 1990, 1993, 1995; Brock 1993; Noonan 1994; Divers 1995; Hale 1995; Nolan and Hawthorne 1996; Chihara 1998; Sider 2002). Three strike me as especially serious. First, the account depends upon a problematic notion of what it is to be true in a fiction. For can we understand this notion in the required way without already presupposing an understanding of modality? Second, it is not clear how to specify an adequate fiction PW, one that will deliver the right truth-values, without already presupposing the truth of the modal statements whose truth-conditions are in question. Third, the account does not adequately represent the content of modal claims even should it get their truth-value right. To make the controversial claim that things are necessarily spatio-temporally connected is not to claim that it is true in a fiction, in which every possible world is taken to be spatio-temporally connected, that every possible world is spatio-temporally connected, even should the claim be true. (To some extent, these difficulties are interdependent. We might solve the first difficulty, for example, by taking truth-in-a-fiction to be strict logical implication, but the second difficulty then becomes more acute.)

From our own point of view, Rosen's fictionalism involves a large element of overkill. For it attempts to get rid of the ordinary modal idioms in addition to the ontology of possible worlds and individuals. But suppose we are happy with the modal idioms and merely wish to rid ourselves of possibilia. A much more satisfactory form of fictionalism can then be maintained. For we can take the possible worlds semantics itself to constitute a fiction. Thus among the basic postulates of the fiction will be the following:

(1) A statement is true iff it is true in the actual world;
(2) Possibly A is true in a world iff A is true in some world;
(3) Something ϕs is true in a world w iff some individual of w ϕs in w.

We also import all truths into the fiction as long as their quantifiers are restricted to what is actual.[24]

There are three major differences between our fictionalism and Rosen's. First, instead of telling a metaphysical story about the constitution of the pluriverse, as with Rosen's account, our fiction tells a semantical story about the connection of the pluriverse with the modal facts. Second, truth-in-a-fiction is not a new substantive notion for us; it is simply logical implication (in the strict sense). Third, the connection between modal and possibilist claims is reconceived. Instead of modifying the original equivalence (E) to (E′) (or to (E″)), we modify it to:

(E‴) it is true in the fiction that (ϕ iff ϕ^*).

---

[24] This corresponds to Rosen's 'encyclopedia' (1990: 335). We need the restriction to prevent the importation of something like 'everything is actual'.

Thus the original equivalence (E) is itself taken to be assertible within the given fiction and reasoning can proceed within the fiction as if we were bona fide possibilists.

It is clear, in the light of these differences, that our account is not subject to the difficulties mentioned above. Since we do not insist upon (E'), the difficulty over indeterminacy does not arise. But should the actualist statement ϕ be true, there is no difficulty in showing that ϕ^* is true in the fiction. For (ϕ iff ϕ^*) will be true in the fiction by the semantical postulates, ϕ will be true in the fiction by importation, and so ϕ^* will be true in the fiction as a logical consequence. Thus (E') will never fail when ϕ is either true or false; and there will be no unwanted gaps. Since the imported modal truths may be used in this way to deliver the correct possibilist consequences, there is no special difficulty in providing an adequate non-circular account of what the fiction is. Finally, there will be no difficulty over according the correct content to modal claims, since no attempt is made to ascribe a content to them. Our aim is simply to adopt a fictionalist simulacrum of possibilist discourse.[25]

The new form of fictionalism is analogous to if–then-ism in the philosophy of mathematics[26] and is not without its attractions. It is still subject to difficulties, however. For we have substantive views about the nature of possible worlds—we do not think of them as mere ciphers. We are inclined to think, for example, that no two worlds can be exactly alike or that what is true at a world cannot be different from what it is. These views should not, of course, be understood as being literally true of how things are for the fictionalist, since he does not believe in many worlds, but it should be possible for him to understand them as being true of how things are in the fiction. Thus he should take it to be true in the fiction that no two worlds are exactly alike or that what is true in a world cannot be different from what it is. However, under the most natural construal of what the fiction is, these various questions concerning the content of the fiction will not be settled one way or the other. The worlds serve merely as pegs upon which to hang the modal truths and nothing beyond their serving this structural role need be said about their nature. So the view will suffer from a problem of incompleteness after all, not with respect to ordinary modal claims but with respect to the superstructure of worlds within which they are embedded.

How might this incompleteness be repaired? There are two main options. The first is to add postulates to the fiction that explicitly describe the nature of the worlds. Thus there may be a postulate stipulating that no two worlds are exactly alike. But we then face a variant of the third of the objections listed above. For to claim, in the intended sense, that no two worlds are exactly alike is not to claim that this is true in a fiction in which it has been stipulated to hold. The other option is to have these

---

[25] I might note that the objections made by Brock (1993) and Hale (1995) are also inapplicable to the present version of fictionalism.

[26] As characterized in Putnam (1967, sect. 3), for example.

various claims follow from actualist modal truths in much the same way that the existence of worlds with talking donkeys follows from the possibility that donkeys talk. Thus suppose we take it to be true that necessarily for any (actual) world w and necessarily for any distinct world v there is some elementary fact holding in v but not in w (or vice versa). Then the rest of the fiction might be so set up that, once this modal truth is imported into the fiction, the desired possibilist truth concerning the discernibility of distinct worlds will follow. But in this case, the fictionalism does no work, for, given that our actualist modal language already contains quantification over worlds, possibilist quantification over worlds and individuals will be uncontroversially definable in the manner of our own reduction. Thus fictionalism of the supra-modal sort is either inadequate or redundant.

REFERENCES

Adams, R. M. (1974). 'Theories of Actuality'. *Noûs*, 8: 211–31. Repr. in Loux (1979: 190–209).
—— (1981). 'Actualism and Thisness'. *Synthese*, 49: 3–41.
Armstrong, D. M. (1989). *A Combinatorial Theory of Possibility*. Cambridge: Cambridge University Press.
Boolos, G. (1984). 'To be is to be the Value of a Variable (or Some Values of Some Variables)'. *Journal of Philosophy*, 81: 430–50. Repr. in *Logic, Logic, Logic*. Cambridge, Mass.: Harvard University Press, 54–72.
Bricker, P. (1987). 'Reducing Possible Worlds to Language'. *Philosophical Studies*, 52: 331–55.
Bringsjord, S. (1985). 'Are there Set-Theoretic Possible Worlds?' *Analysis*, 451: 64.
Brock, S. (1993). 'Modal Fictionalism: A Reply to Rosen'. *Mind*, 102: 147–50.
Chihara, C. S. (1998). *The Worlds of Possibility*. Oxford: Clarendon Press.
Cresswell, M. J. (1990). *Entities and Indices*. Dordrecht: Kluwer.
Divers, J. (1995). 'Modal Fictionalism cannot Deliver Possible Worlds Semantics'. *Analysis*, 55: 81–88.
Fine, K. (1979). 'First-Order Modal Theories II—Propositions'. *Studia Logica*, 39: 159–202.
—— (1981). 'First-Order Modal Theories I—Sets'. *Noûs*, 15: 117–206.
—— (1982). 'First-Order Modal Theories III—Facts'. *Synthese*, 53: 43–122.
—— (1985). 'Plantinga on the Reduction of Possibilist Discourse', in J. E. Tomberlin and Peter van Inwagen (eds.), *Profiles: Alvin Plantinga*. Dordrecht: Reidel, 145–86.
—— (1998a). 'A Defence of Cantorian Abstraction'. *Journal of Philosophy*, 95/12: 599–634.
—— (1998b). 'The Limits of Abstraction', in M. Schirn (ed.), *The Philosophy of Mathematics Today*. Oxford: Clarendon Press, 503–630.
—— (2001). 'The Question of Realism'. *Philosophers Imprint* [electronic journal], 1/1: 1–30.
—— (2002). *The Limits of Abstraction*. Oxford: Oxford University Press.
Forbes, G. (1985). *The Metaphysics of Modality*. Oxford: Oxford University Press.
—— (1989). *Languages of Possibility*. Oxford: Basil Blackwell.
Forrest, P., and D. M. Armstrong (1984). 'An Argument against David Lewis' Theory of Possible Worlds'. *Australasian Journal of Philosophy*, 62: 164–8.
Gödel, K. (1944). 'Russell's Mathematical Logic', in P. A. Schilpp (ed.), *The Philosophy of Bertrand Russell*. Evanston, Ill.: Northwestern University. Repr. in Kurt Gödel, *Collected Works*, vol. ii. Oxford: Oxford University Press, 1990.

Grim, P. (1986). 'On Sets and Worlds: A Reply to Menzel'. *Analysis*, 46: 186–91.

Gupta, A. (1980). *The Logic of Common Nouns*. New Haven, Conn.: Yale University Press.

Hale, B. (1995). 'Modal Fictionalism—A Simple Dilemma'. *Analysis*, 55: 63–7.

Kaplan, D. (1975). 'How to Russell a Frege–Church'. *Journal of Philosophy*, 72: 716–29. Repr. in Loux (1979: 210–24).

——(1995). 'A Problem in Possible-World Semantics', in W. Sinnot-Armstrong (ed.), *Modality, Morality and Belief: Essays in Honor of Ruth Barcan Marcus*. Cambridge: Cambridge University Press.

Kripke, S. (1963). 'Semantical Considerations on Modal Logic', *Acta Philosophica Fennica*, 16: 83–94. Repr. in L. Linsky (ed.), *Reference and Modality*. Oxford: Oxford University Press, 1971.

Lewis, D. (1986). *On the Plurality of Worlds*. Oxford: Basil Blackwell.

Loux, M. (1979) (ed.). *The Possible and the Actual*. Ithaca, NY: Cornell University Press.

McMichael, A. (1983). 'A Problem for Actualism about Possible Worlds'. *Philosophical Review*, 92: 49–66.

Menzel, C. (1986*a*). 'On Set-Theoretic Possible Worlds'. *Analysis*, 46: 68–72.

——(1986*b*). 'On the Iterative Explanation of the Paradoxes'. *Philosophical Studies*, 49: 37–61.

Nolan, H., and J. O. Hawthorne (1996). 'Reflexive Fictionalism'. *Analysis*, 54: 23–32.

Noonan, H. (1994). 'In Defence of the Letter of Fictionalism'. *Analysis*, 54: 133–9.

Peacocke, C. (2002). 'Principles for Possibilia', *Noûs*, 36/3 (Sept.), 486–508; also to appear in A. O'Hear (ed.), *Logic, Thought and Language*, Royal Institute of Philosophy, Suppl. 51 (2002), 155–81.

Plantinga, A. (1974). *The Nature of Necessity*. Oxford: Clarendon Press.

——(1976). 'Actualism and Possible Worlds'. *Theoria*, 42: 139–60. Repr. in Loux (1979: 253–73).

——(1985). 'Response to Fine', in J. E. Tomberlin and P. van Inwagen (eds.), *Profiles: Alvin Plantinga*. Dordrecht: Reidei.

Prior, A. N. (1977). 'Egocentric Logic'. Repr. in Prior and Fine (1977: 28–45).

Prior, A. N., and K. Fine (1977). *Worlds, Times and Selves*. London: Duckworth.

Putnam, H. (1967). 'The Thesis that Mathematics is Logic', in R. Schoenman (ed.), *Bertrand Russell: Philosopher of the Century*. London: Allen & Unwin, 273–303.

Quine, W. V. O. (1964). 'Ontological Reduction and the World of Numbers'. *Journal of Philosophy*, 61: 209–16. Repr. in Quine, *The Ways of Paradox*. New York: Random House, 1966.

——(1969). *Ontological Relativity*. New York: Columbia University Press.

Rosen, G. (1990). 'Modal Fictionalism'. *Mind*, 99: 327–54.

——(1993). 'A Problem for Fictionalism about Possible Worlds'. *Analysis*, 53: 71–81.

——(1995). 'Modal Fictionalism Fixed'. *Analysis*, 55: 67–73.

Shoemaker, S. (1980). 'Causality and Properties', in Peter van Inwagen (ed.), *Time and Cause*. Dordrecht: Reidel. Repr. in Shoemaker, *Identity, Cause and Mind: Philosophical Essays*. Cambridge: Cambridge University Press.

——(1998). 'Causal and Metaphysical Necessity'. *Pacific Philosophical Quarterly*, 79: 59–77.

Sider, T. (2002). 'The Ersatz Pluriverse', *Journal of Philosophy*, 99: 279–315.

Stalnaker, R. C. (1976). 'Possible Worlds'. *Noûs*, 10: 65–75. Repr. in Loux (1979: 225–34).

Swoyer, C. (1982). 'The Nature of Causal Laws'. *Australasian Journal of Philosophy*, 60: 203–23.

van Inwagen, P. (1980). 'Indexicality and Actuality'. *Philosophical Review*, 89: 403–26.

Williamson, T. (1998). 'Bare Possibilia', *Erkenntnis*, 48: 257–73.

CHAPTER 7

REDUCTIVE THEORIES OF MODALITY

THEODORE SIDER

1. MODALITY

LOGIC begins but does not end with the study of truth and falsity. Within truth there are the *mode*s of truth, ways of being true: necessary truth and contingent truth. When a proposition is true, we may ask whether it *could* have been false. If so, then it is contingently true. If not, then it is necessarily true; it *must* be true; it could not have been false. Falsity has modes as well: a false proposition that could not have been true is *impossible* or necessarily false; one that could have been true is merely contingently false. The proposition that some humans are over 7 feet tall is contingently true; the proposition that all humans over 7 feet tall are over 6 feet tall is necessarily true; the proposition that some humans are over 7 feet tall and under 6 feet tall is impossible, and the proposition that some humans are over 9 feet tall is contingently false.

Of these four modes of truth, let us focus on necessity, plus a fifth: possibility. A proposition is possible if it is or could have been true; hence propositions that are either necessarily true, contingently true, or contingently false are possible.

Thanks to Karen Bennett, Phillip Bricker, John Hawthorne, Michael Loux, Peter Momtchiloff, Daniel Nolan, John Louis Schwenkler, Brian Weatherson, and Dean Zimmerman for helpful comments.

Notions like the modes of truth in being concerned with what might have been are called modal. Dispositions are modal notions, for example the disposition of fragility. Relatedly, there are counterfactual conditionals, for example 'If this glass were dropped, it would break'. And the notion of supervenience is modal. (See Kim 1993, pt. I; David Lewis 1986: 14–17.) But let us focus here on necessity and possibility.

Modal words are notoriously ambiguous (or at least context-sensitive; see Kratzer 1977).[1] I may reply to an invitation to give a talk in England by saying 'I can't come; I have to give a talk in California the day before'. This use of 'can't' is perfectly appropriate. But it would be equally appropriate for me to say that I *could* cancel my talk in California (although that would be rude) and give the talk in England instead. What I cannot do is give both talks. But wait: it also seems appropriate to say, in another context, that given contemporary transportation, one can give a talk in California one day and England the next. It may be very exhausting, but one *can* do it. What one cannot do is give a talk in California and then give a talk in England the next *hour*. But in yet another context one could say the following: 'Given the limits on travel faster than the speed of light, one cannot give a talk on earth, and then another on Alpha Centauri an hour later. But one *could* give a talk in California and then an hour later give a talk in England.' Finally, even this performance seems appropriate: 'The laws of nature could have been different. Supraluminal travel might have been permitted by the laws of nature. One could (if the laws had indeed allowed supraluminal travel) have given a talk on earth, and then another an hour later on Alpha Centauri, 4.12×10^{13} km. away. What is impossible is giving talks on earth and Alpha Centauri at the very same time.'

There are, therefore, different 'strengths' of necessity and possibility, which can be signified by modal words (like 'can') in different contexts. Philosophers have tended to concentrate on a very broad sort, so-called 'metaphysical' possibility and necessity. According to many, it is metaphysically possible that the laws of nature be different, that the past be different from what it actually was, and so on.[2] All of the scenarios in the last paragraph—giving a talk in England, giving a talk in California one day and England the next, giving a talk in California at one moment and a talk in England an hour later, giving a talk on earth one moment and on Alpha Centauri an hour later—are metaphysically possible. What is *not* metaphysically possible? Almost everyone agrees that contradictions are metaphysically impossible—it is metaphysically impossible to both give a talk in California and also not give a talk in California. And everyone who accepts the legitimacy of the notion of analyticity— of truth that is in some sense guaranteed by meaning—agrees that the negations of analytic sentences like 'All bachelors are unmarried' are impossible. But it is usually thought that there exist further impossibilities. Examples might include the existence of a round square, someone's being taller than himself, someone's being in

---

[1] There are also epistemic modals, which I will ignore.

[2] Although see Kneale (1949) and Shoemaker (1998) on the necessity of the laws of nature, and Prior (1955) on the necessity of the past.

two places at once, George W. Bush's being a donkey, there existing no numbers, and there existing some water that is not made up of H_2O. Exactly what is metaphysically impossible beyond logical and analytic contradictions is unclear; this unclarity is what makes the analysis of metaphysical possibility and necessity so difficult. But it is metaphysical possibility and necessity that most concern philosophers, and so from now on it is on the metaphysical sense of the modal notions that I will focus.

It is common to distinguish between *de re* and *de dicto* modality. The contrast may be brought out with this example:

(*De dicto*)   Necessarily, the number of the planets is odd
              ($\Box$ (the x: Nx) Ox)

(*De re*)   The number of the planets is such that it is necessarily odd
              (The x: Nx) $\Box$ (Ox)

The *de dicto* sentence is false. It claims that it is necessary that the number of the planets is odd, whereas there clearly might have been six or eight planets. The *de re* sentence, however, is presumably true. It claims *of* the number that actually numbers the planets—namely, 9—that it is necessarily odd. Assuming with orthodoxy that mathematical facts are necessary, this is true: the number 9 itself is necessarily odd. The *de dicto* sentence claims that a certain *descriptive* claim is necessary: it is necessary that the number picked out by the description 'the number of the planets', whatever that might turn out to be, is odd. In each possible world, whatever number is the number of the planets in that world must be odd. In contrast, the *de re* sentence uses the description 'the number of the planets' to single out a certain individual, the number 9, but then goes on to make a modal claim about that number itself; the description used to single out 9 plays no role in evaluating the modal claim about 9. In each possible world, 9 itself must be odd, never mind whether 9 is the number of the planets in that world.

There is a grammatical contrast between the *de re* and the *de dicto* sentences that is made clearer by the symbolically regimented versions of those sentences. In the *de re* sentence there is a variable in the scope of the modal operator $\Box$ (symbolizing 'it is necessary that') that is bound to a quantifier outside the scope of the $\Box$, whereas in the *de dicto* sentence no quantification into the scope of modal operators occurs. A further example: the false sentence 'Possibly, some bachelor is unmarried', or '$\Diamond \exists x(Bx \,\&\, \sim Mx)$' is *de dicto*, whereas the true sentence 'Some bachelor is possibly unmarried', or '$\exists x(Bx \,\&\, \Diamond \sim Mx)$' is *de re*, since the variable x occurs inside the scope of the $\Diamond$ but is bound to the quantifier $\exists x$, which occurs outside the scope of the $\Diamond$. This grammatical or syntactic way of drawing the *de re–de dicto* distinction is common, and can be extended to natural language given the existence of natural language analogues of modal operators and variable-binding. However, for present purposes it will be useful to (somewhat stipulatively) draw the distinction slightly differently. Specifically, in addition to sentences with quantification into modal contexts, let us also count as *de re* modal sentences in which 'directly referential terms' occur within the scope of modal operators. Directly referential terms are terms whose propositional contributions are simply their referents, for example proper names and indexicals. The reason for counting these sentences as *de re* is that they attribute modal properties to objects *simpliciter*, rather than under descriptions.[3]

Modality is important to philosophy for many reasons. A first reason derives from philosophy's traditional association with logic. Advances in modal logic in the middle of the twentieth century provided a reason to be interested in the modalities. Moreover, propositions that are logically true seem necessarily true. Another source of modality's importance is that necessary truth, according to one tradition, demarcates philosophical from empirical inquiry. Science identifies contingent aspects of the world, whereas philosophical inquiry reveals the essential nature of its objects; philosophical propositions are therefore necessarily true when true at all.

But the most important source of importance derives from modality's connections with epistemology and philosophy of language. These connections are at the core of analytic philosophy. The propositions identified by traditional epistemology as those that can be known a priori, independent of sensory experience, seem necessary. These are generally agreed to include the propositions of logic as well as analytic truths. Whether there are other a priori propositions was one of the great questions of seventeenth- and eighteenth-century epistemology, and the debate continues to this day. But it was generally agreed until recently that all a priori propositions are necessarily true. Indeed, before the publication of Saul Kripke's *Naming and Necessity* (Kripke 1972), it was not uncommon to identify aprioricity with necessity.

Given the compelling examples of necessary a posteriori propositions given by Kripke, and by Hilary Putnam (1975), as well as Kripke's examples of contingent a priori propositions, this identification is no longer made. And given W. V. O. Quine's (1951) critique of analyticity, some have doubted the connection between analyticity and necessity, others the sense of the notion of necessity itself. But despite this, many of the important traditional connections remain. It is still relatively common to claim that *some* necessary propositions are a priori; thus, the nature of necessity is relevant to epistemology, for what is necessary truth, that it can be ascertained without sensory input? And despite Quine, there remains an overwhelming temptation to think that the notion of linguistic convention has *some* legitimate application, and *some* connection with the traditional notion of necessity.

---

[3] *De re* modal claims are often explained etymologically as those that attribute necessity to an object, a *res*, e.g. the number 9, rather than to a proposition, a dictum, e.g. the proposition that the number of the planets is odd. But this way of drawing the distinction is misleading. In a perfectly good sense of 'object', propositions are objects. Moreover, modal sentences containing directly referential terms inside the scopes of modal operators would attribute modal properties to (singular) propositions, but would nevertheless be *de re* on my usage.

2. REDUCTION

Our topic is the reduction of modality, whether modal notions can be reductively defined. Certainly some modal notions can be defined in terms of other modal notions. Take as undefined any of the five modalities of truth discussed above, and the rest may be defined in terms of it. For example, symbolizing ⌜It is necessary that ϕ⌝ as ⌜$\Box\phi$⌝, one can define the other modalities thus:

it is possible that ϕ:	$\sim\Box\sim\phi$
it is contingently true that ϕ:	$\phi \,\&\, \sim\Box\phi$
it is contingently false that ϕ:	$\sim\phi \,\&\, \sim\Box\sim\phi$
it is impossible that ϕ:	$\Box\sim\phi$
it is contingent whether ϕ:	$\sim\Box\phi \,\&\, \sim\Box\sim\phi$

But these definitions are not reductive, since necessity is utilized without being defined. The more interesting question is whether a *reductive* definition of modality is possible, a definition of the modal in terms of the non-modal.

Why seek such a thing? One traditional motivation lies in modality's connection to epistemology. Many modal claims are known a priori, and it is a puzzle how this is possible, how we manage to know modal claims without the benefit of sensory experience. The epistemology of the modal can be secured if modal notions are defined in terms of notions whose epistemology is secure.

There are also reasons from metaphysics to seek reduction. Reductionism is required by any ontology that claims to give a comprehensive account of reality in terms of primitive entities and notions that do not include modal notions. And some metaphysical programmes without quite so high ambitions require reductionism, for example, the extensionalism of Quine and Davidson.[4]

It is easy to get into a frame of mind according to which modal notions should not be taken as 'rock bottom', ontologically speaking. The frame of mind is not unlike Hume's when he confronted causation. One can see the prior event, and also the later one, but where is the causation? Likewise: I can see that this coloured thing is extended, and indeed that all coloured things I have examined are extended, but where is the necessity, that coloured things *must* be extended? Part of the puzzlement here is of course epistemic, and epistemic reasons for reductionism have already been mentioned. But there is a particularly metaphysical puzzlement here as well. In metaphysics one seeks an account of the world in intelligible terms, and there is something elusive about modal notions. Whether something *is* a certain way seems unproblematic, but that things might be otherwise, or must be as they are, seems to call out for explanation.

---

[4] See e.g. Quine (1951) and Davidson (1967). Of course, many extensionalists prefer eliminativism to reductionism.

Accepting necessity or possibility as a primitive feature of reality would be like accepting tensed facts as primitive, or accepting dispositions as primitive, or accepting counterfactuals as primitive. While some are willing to make these posits, others seek to reduce 'hypothetical' notions to 'categorical' notions—notions which are in a sense 'self-contained' and do not 'point beyond themselves' as the hypothetical notions do (see Sider 2001a, ch. 2, sect. 3).

Parsimony is a final metaphysical reason to seek reduction. The metaphysician prefers desert landscapes when she can get them; when it is possible to reduce, we should. Of course the reduction might fail; parsimony gives us reason to search but does not guarantee success. *Primitivism*, the view that modality is unanalysable, is an important and legitimate alternative to reductionism, and is favoured by many because of the difficulty of finding an adequate reduction. But reduction is the topic of the present chapter.

Primitivism and reductionism are not exhaustive alternatives: one might prefer *eliminativism* to each.[5] The eliminativist denies that there is any such thing as modality. I will not take on eliminativism here except to say that it is a position of last resort, given the embedding of modality in ordinary and philosophical talk and practice. At any rate, the availability of the eliminativist position is no reason to bypass our inquiry into reductionism, for if a tenable reduction does exist, then there is no reason to be an eliminativist.

A reduction of modality is an analysis of modal propositions in certain other terms. By analysis I mean identity: if the proposition that *it is necessary that everything coloured is extended* is analysed as the proposition that *p*, then the proposition that *it is necessary that everything coloured is extended* just is the proposition that *p*. A proposed reduction must at least be extensionally adequate in that the modal propositions and the reducing propositions must have the same truth-values. In addition, to be non-circular, or genuinely reductive, the terms in which the reducing propositions are expressed must be 'non-modal'. But there is a bit of awkwardness here: in a sense the reducing terms must indeed be modal if the reduction is successful, since if the reduction is successful then the reducing propositions *are* modal propositions, given that analysis is identity. The awkwardness should be resolved as follows. Any reductionist programme takes certain notions as being 'acceptable'. What acceptability amounts to depends on what is driving the reduction—it may be epistemic acceptability, or categoricity, or extensionality, or something else. 'Non-modal', then, means 'acceptable'—a reduction is non-circular or genuinely reductive if the notions it employs are acceptable according to its standards, whatever those may be.

---

[5] Perhaps we can classify Simon Blackburn (1993), Hartry Field (1989: 38–45), and Quine (1951, 1953a) as eliminativists about metaphysical necessity and possibility.

There are several strategies for reduction. In Section 3 I discuss reductions based on possible worlds, both abstract (Sections 3.1–3.4) and concrete (Sections 3.5–3.10); in Section 4 I discuss conventionalism.[6]

3. POSSIBLE WORLDS

The analysis foremost in the contemporary consciousness is the possible worlds analysis, which reduces possibility and necessity via the Leibnizian biconditionals:[7]

A proposition is necessary iff it is true in all possible worlds

A proposition is possible iff it is true in some possible world.

A possible world is a complete possible history of the entire universe. One possible world is actual—this is the totality of what actually occurs. The other worlds are merely possible—they are non-actual ways things might have been.[8]

3.1 Reductionism about Modality and the Ontology of Possible Worlds

Provided one believes in possible worlds at all, the *truth* of the Leibnizian biconditionals is hard to question. But if talk of truth in possible worlds must itself be defined in terms of possibility and necessity, then these biconditionals will not constitute reductive analyses. One might still employ possible worlds in a reduction of some of the other modal notions, thus providing a partial reduction of some modal notions to possibility and necessity. One could give definitions of counterfactuals, statements about dispositions, claims of supervenience, and so on, in terms of possible worlds, even if talk of possible worlds must ultimately be understood in terms of possibility and necessity. But if the possible worlds reduction of modality is to be

---

[6] This survey of reductive strategies is incomplete in at least two ways: it concentrates exclusively on recent theories, and it ignores the quasi-epistemic theory of modality currently being developed by David Chalmers.

[7] These are characterizations of metaphysical possibility and necessity. Narrower sorts of possibility and necessity may be characterized by restricting the quantifier over possible worlds in various ways. For example, a proposition is nomically possible iff it is true in some possible world that obeys the laws of the actual world.

[8] Concerning possible worlds, in addition to the following section, see Kit Fine's contribution to this volume (ch. 6).

complete, the notion of truth in possible worlds must be non-modal. And whether this is so depends on the ontological status of possible worlds.

It is important to separate the general contemporary interest in possible worlds from their use in reducing modality. Possible worlds are ubiquitous in metaphysics, and are frequently utilized in semantics (see Carnap 1947; Dowty's exposition of Montague grammar in Dowty *et al.* 1981; Lewis 1970; Cresswell 1973), ethics (see Feldman 1986), probability theory (see Lewis 1980), philosophy of mind (see Chalmers 1996), and many other contexts.[9] The suitability of possible worlds for these other purposes is largely independent of their ontological status. Not so for their use in reducing modality.

According to David Lewis, the most prominent defender of the possible worlds analysis of modality, possible worlds are 'concrete' entities of a kind with the world we live in.[10] The totality of cows that are spatio-temporally related to us does not exhaust the totality of cows in existence. There are in addition all the cows that exist in other possible worlds. Thus, for Lewis, reality includes purple cows, talking cows, flying cows, and so on: purple, talking, and flying cows are possible, and so by the Leibnizian biconditionals exist in other possible worlds, and so according to Lewis's metaphysics of possible worlds exist *simpliciter*. In calling these cows 'cows', Lewis means to be speaking completely literally; they are no less real or concrete or cow-ey than actual cows. The actual world is just one world among many, and has no privileged ontological status. Its actuality consists merely in being *our* world. Inhabitants of other worlds call their worlds actual and they speak truly as well: 'actual', according to Lewis, is an indexical word that refers to the possible world of the speaker.

For most of us this is too much to take. Those who wish nevertheless to speak of possible worlds must therefore provide some kind of reduction of possible worlds talk that does not require ontological commitment to the Lewisian multiverse. But, as we will see, this is difficult to achieve without presupposing modality. Many accept this limitation, and consequently do not attempt to reduce the modal to the non-modal.

3.2 Linguistic Ersatzism

Many of the leading reductions of possible worlds talk identify possible worlds with certain abstract entities. The abstract possible worlds of these so-called

---

[9] The purely formal 'possible worlds' in the model theory for modal logic (see Hughes and Cresswell 1996; Chihara 1998) must be distinguished from the genuine possible worlds useful in metaphysics, semantics, philosophy of mind, and so on. See Lewis (1986: 17–20), Sider (2001c), and the beginning of Sider (2002).

[10] The main defence of this theory is in Lewis (1986); see also Lewis (1968, 1970, 1971). Lewis has reservations about the term 'concrete' (see Lewis 1986, sect. 1.7).

'abstractionist' views are allegedly much easier to believe in than Lewis's concrete worlds. One proposal, which Lewis labels 'linguistic ersatzism', identifies worlds with sets of sentences.[11] A possible world in which donkeys talk and fish walk would be identified with a set that includes the sentences 'Donkeys talk' and 'Fish walk', in addition to other sentences describing the rest of what occurs in this possible world. Possible individuals inhabiting these possible worlds may be constructed as well—as sets of formulae containing free variables. For example, a talking donkey might be constructed as a set containing, among others, the formulae 'x is a donkey' and 'x talks'.

The problem then becomes how to distinguish sets of sentences that describe possible worlds from sets of sentences that describe states of affairs that could not possibly occur. Call a set, S, of sentences an *ersatz world* iff S is *maximal* in that, for each sentence, either it or its negation is a member of S. We cannot say that a proposition is possible iff it is expressed by some sentence in some ersatz world, for this would count *every* (expressible) proposition as possible—every sentence is a member of the set of *all* sentences, which is obviously maximal.[12] The proposition that some fish are not fish would turn out possible. We must, it seems, restrict our attention to the *ersatz possible worlds*, where an ersatz world is *possible* iff it would be possible for all the members of the set to be true together. But this characterization of an ersatz possible world makes use of the notion of possibility. Therefore, a possible worlds analysis of modality that makes use of ersatz possible worlds in this way is circular.[13]

Many other abstractionist theories have the same limitation. I will illustrate the point by discussing the reduction of worlds to states of affairs proposed by Alvin Plantinga (1974, 1976), but parallel points can be made about similar theories defended by Robert M. Adams (1974) and Robert Stalnaker (1976).[14] Plantinga's states of affairs are abstract entities much like propositions (indeed, it is hard to see how they differ from propositions). States of affairs are to be distinguished from sentences since distinct sentences in different languages may all assert that the very same state of affairs obtains. States of affairs are abstract, necessarily existing

---

[11] See e.g. Jeffrey (1965: 196–7). Probably the clearest statement is in Lewis (1986, ch. 3), which criticizes linguistic ersatzism as well as other reductions of possible worlds. Subsequent literature on this topic has been largely a reaction to Lewis's critique. My discussion of abstractionist theories of possible worlds is heavily indebted to Lewis. See Bricker (1987) for a further critique; see Heller (1998), Roy (1995), and Sider (2002) for responses. Terminological note: what I call linguistic ersatzism is what Lewis calls linguistic ersatzism with a *rich* world-making language; what I call 'combinatorial' conceptions of possible worlds are what Lewis calls versions of linguistic ersatzism with a poor world-making language.

[12] Let us here ignore Cantorian problems with the existence of a set of all sentences.

[13] Even setting aside the reduction of modality, linguistic ersatzism (like most other reductive theories of worlds) has trouble accounting for possibilities involving non-actual individuals. See Bricker (1987: 349–53), Fine's contribution to this volume (ch. 6), Lewis (1986: 157–65), McMichael (1983), and Sider (2002).

[14] See Lewis (1986, sect. 3.4), for criticisms of these views; see van Inwagen (1986) for a response.

entities. A given state of affairs may 'obtain', or it may fail to obtain: the state of affairs *Plantinga's being tall* obtains since Plantinga is indeed tall; the state of affairs *Plantinga's being an atheist* does not obtain since Plantinga is not, in fact, an atheist. (Thus, Plantinga's conception of states of affairs is unlike another conception according to which there are no false or non-obtaining states of affairs or facts. See e.g. Wittgenstein 1921; Armstrong 1977.) Some definitions: say that a state of affairs, *S*, is *possible* iff it is (metaphysically) possible for *S* to obtain; say that *S includes T* when it is impossible for *S* to obtain without *T* obtaining; say that *S precludes T* when it is impossible for *S* and *T* to both obtain; finally, say that *S* is *maximal* iff for any state of affairs, *T*, either *S* includes *T* or *S* precludes *T*. Given these definitions, Plantinga identifies the possible worlds with the maximal possible states of affairs. Various objections can be raised against this account, for example to the assumptions that states of affairs exist necessarily and that maximal states of affairs exist (see Fine 1985; Chihara 1998: 120–41). But the main point to notice here is that Plantinga's possible worlds cannot be utilized in a completely reductive account of modality since Plantinga uses the notion of possibility in defining his possible worlds. Plantinga does not pretend otherwise; he accepts that possibility and necessity must remain unanalysed.

3.3 Combinatorialism

Some abstractionists avoid circularity by giving a combinatorial definition of a possible world. Consider, for example, the identification of possible worlds with sets of space-time points, each set representing the possibility that all and only the points in the set are occupied by matter. (Cf. Cresswell 1972; Heller 1998; Quine 1969; Lewis 1986: 146–8.) I call this a 'combinatorial' conception of possible worlds because the multiplicity of worlds results from the combinatorial nature of set theory: for any combination of space-time points there exists a set containing all and only those points. This definition of 'possible world' is clearly non-modal. Modality is not needed to rule out impossible representations of worlds because it is intuitively plausible that any pattern of occupation of space-time points is possible.

Recall the Leibnizian biconditionals used to define possibility and necessity: 'a proposition is necessary iff it is true in all possible worlds' and 'a proposition is possible iff it is true in some possible world'. In addition to the notion of a possible world, these biconditionals make use of the notion of propositions being *true in* possible worlds. Identifying worlds with sets of space-time points may eliminate modality from the definition of 'possible world,' but, as Lewis has argued, modality reappears in the definition of 'true in' (see Lewis 1986: 150–7; 1992). What would it mean to say that it is true in a certain set, *S*, of space-time points that there exists a talking donkey? The set does not literally contain a talking donkey; rather, it in some sense 'represents' the existence of a talking donkey. But 'represents' is as in need of explanation as is 'true in'.

If we could analyse 'talking donkey' in terms of occupied points of space-time, then we could determine precisely which patterns of occupation would suffice for the existence of a talking donkey, and then we could say that it is true in S that there is a talking donkey iff S contains one of these patterns. But no one knows how to provide this sort of analysis of 'talking donkey'. Moreover, a *general* analysis of modality requires a general definition of 'proposition p is true in set S' for arbitrary propositions p; a series of one-off definitions for a few chosen propositions is no progress towards a general analysis.

We might define 'p is true in possible world w' as meaning 'necessarily: if all and only the points in w are occupied by matter, then p is true'. But this definition uses necessity. No other definition seems available; 'true in', therefore, renders the account of modality circular.

Similar remarks apply to other combinatorial accounts of possible worlds. On one proposal, possible worlds are combinations (sets) of fundamental states of affairs (compare Armstrong 1989, 1997; Skyrms 1981; Wittgenstein 1921). On another, worlds are combinations of primitive atomic sentences, where a primitive atomic sentence is an atomic sentence involving only primitive vocabulary (compare Carnap 1947). Each of these theories has the following form: a possible world is a combination of 'elements'. The hope is that 'elements' may be construed so that *all* combinations of elements are possible, thus eliminating the need for a modal definition of a *possible* combination of elements. But the problem is then how to say when a *non-element* is true in a possible world. Suppose that a donkey's talking is not itself a fundamental state of affairs and that 'donkey' and 'talk' are not primitive predicates; in virtue of what, then, does a donkey talk *in* a set of elements? Only the circular modal definition suggests itself: a donkey talks relative to a set of elements iff, necessarily: if all and only the elements of that set are true, then a donkey talks.

The combinatorialist might enrich the conception of elements, and allow an element corresponding to 'a donkey talks'. But then it will no longer be true that all combinations of elements are possible. The presence of some elements that concern occurrences at the micro-level will be incompatible with the presence of certain other elements that concern talking and donkeys, and modality will again be needed to define 'possible world' (see Lewis 1986: 150–7).

I have argued that abstractionists about possible worlds must appeal to modal notions in order to define 'possible world' and 'true in'. One might instead appeal to logical consequence and analyticity in these definitions. A linguistic ersatzer might, for example, define a possible world as a maximal set of sentences that does not logically imply any sentence that is analytically false. But there are commonly thought to exist impossibilities beyond those that are analytically false (see Section 4.2 below). The definition thus counts certain sets of sentences as being ersatz possible worlds despite the impossibility of those sentences being true together. Perhaps one could appeal to other notions in addition to analyticity. But anyone able to do this is well along the way to a reduction of possibility and necessity that doesn't require possible worlds at all. (Of course one might use worlds to analyse other modal notions.) The theory we are considering is thus morphing into a theory of the sort to be discussed in Section 4.2.

3.4 Fictionalism

A somewhat different reductive theory of worlds talk is Gideon Rosen's (1990) modal fictionalism. Unlike the theorists discussed so far, Rosen does not identify possible worlds with abstract entities. He rather regards talk of possible worlds as being like talk of characters in works of fiction. We speak of Sherlock Holmes despite his non-existence: we say things like 'Sherlock Holmes is a detective'. This is legitimate because in uttering such a sentence one does not *really* intend to discuss a real person; one really means something like this: 'According to the Doyle stories, Sherlock Holmes is a detective'. Rosen views talk of possible worlds as being like talk of fictional characters: a sentence, *P*, about possible worlds should be regarded as meaning that 'according to the fiction of possible worlds, *P*'. Rosen goes on to suggest an analysis of modality. For any modal sentence, *P*, let *P** be the possible worlds analysis of *P*. For example, if *P* is 'possibly, there are talking donkeys', then *P** would be 'in some possible world there are talking donkeys'. Rosen's analysis of the modal sentence *P* is then this: according to the fiction of possible worlds, *P**.

The status of this account as a *reduction* of modality is doubtful, since it is plausible that the locution 'according to' occurring in Rosen's analysis expresses a modal notion (see Rosen 1990, sect. 8). Rosen's analysis mentions a 'fiction of possible worlds'. This fiction is set out in Rosen's paper, and is in effect a short summary of David Lewis's theory of possible worlds given in *On the Plurality of Worlds* (Lewis 1986). But this summary, and indeed the entirety of *On the Plurality of Worlds*, falls far short of an exhaustive description of a plurality of worlds. This is entirely unsurprising (and not just because of limitations of finitude). If it were possible to explicitly lay out a description, *D*, of the possible worlds, then the theorists discussed above who identified worlds with abstract entities would not have needed modal notions to define their possible worlds. The linguistic ersatzer, for example, could simply have defined the possible worlds as all and only the sets of sentences describing worlds in *D*. Explicitly constructing *D* is difficult precisely because of the difficulty of reductively analysing modality. Metaphysical possibility is narrower than logical and analytical possibility, but exactly how much narrower is unclear. This is the fundamental obstacle to the reduction of modality, and it remains an obstacle whether one is telling a fiction about possible worlds or trying to construct worlds from abstract entities.

Rosen's fiction, therefore, falls far short of a complete description of the totality of possible worlds. Why, then, does Rosen suppose his reduction of worlds talk adequate? According to Rosen, given the everyday notion of truth according to a fiction, much more is true in a fiction than what the fiction explicitly states. For example, it is presumably true in the Sherlock Holmes stories that Holmes had a liver, even though this is never explicitly mentioned. Likewise, Rosen claims, much more is true in his fiction of worlds beyond what he explicitly builds into it. But now, let P be any true modal sentence such that P^* (P's worlds analysis) is not explicitly entailed by Rosen's fiction. If Rosen's account is to be adequate, then despite his fiction not explicitly entailing P^*, it must nevertheless be true according to that fiction that P^*. Thus, Rosen's 'according to' is doing much of the work of analysing modality; accepting 'according to' without definition seems tantamount to accepting unreduced modality. (For more details, see Sider 2002, sect. v.)

Another important reduction of worlds talk is defended by Kit Fine (1977; see also his 1980, 1981, 1982, and his contribution to this volume, ch. 6). Like Rosen, Fine does not identify worlds with abstract entities; but Fine makes no use of fictions. Rather, he translates sentences about possible worlds directly into a modal language. The rough idea is to interpret ⌜there is a possible individual such that ϕ⌝ as meaning ⌜possibly, there exists an individual such that ϕ⌝. Clearly, this account of talk about possible worlds cannot be used in a reductive theory of modality since it overtly employs modal notions. Fine, of course, intends no such reduction; his goal is to reduce talk of possible *worlds*, not modal talk generally.

3.5 Lewisian, 'Concrete' Possible Worlds

Hard as they are to accept, Lewisian possible worlds allow a non-circular analysis of possibility and necessity; that is their great advantage. So for the remainder of this section I consider Lewisian possible worlds.

The possible worlds analysis of modality via the Leibnizian biconditionals is reductive only if the terms 'possible world' and 'true in' are non-modal. As we have seen, a Lewisian possible world is a concrete entity of the same kind as our own world. Such a possible world is simply the mereological sum or fusion of all the entities it contains. So our own world is the mereological sum of our surroundings and us. A possible world in which donkeys fly and pigs talk would be an object containing flying donkeys and talking pigs. But which fusions of possible objects count as possible worlds? How are Lewisian possible worlds individuated? If no answer could be given, the Lewisian analysis would not be reductive after all, for the predicate 'possible world' as applied to pieces of Lewis's multiverse would remain a modal primitive.

Lewis's answer is to define possible worlds spatio-temporally: x is a possible world iff (roughly) x is a *maximal spatio-temporally interrelated whole*, in that (i) any two parts of x are spatio-temporally related to each other, and (ii) anything that is spatio-temporally related to any part of x is itself part of x (Lewis 1986, sect. 1.6). This is a non-modal definition of a possible world.

We are now in a position to give the Lewisian reduction of *de dicto* necessity. Consider any sentence, ϕ, with no free variables or directly referential terms. Say that ϕ is *true in* a possible world, w, iff ϕ is true when all its quantifiers are restricted to parts of w. Then, we can say that ⌜Necessarily, ϕ⌝ is true iff ϕ is true in every possible world w.[15]

According to Lewis, possible worlds do not overlap—no possible individual is (wholly) present in more than one possible world.[16] Therefore, the account just given of *de dicto* necessity cannot be straightforwardly carried over to *de re* necessity. For to decide whether, for example, George W. Bush is necessarily human we would have to ask whether the sentence 'Bush is human' is true in other possible worlds. But Bush exists only in the actual world and not in any other possible world. Instead, Lewis defends a *counterpart theory* of *de re* modal claims. To say that Bush is necessarily human is not to say that Bush himself exists in other possible worlds and is human in those worlds; rather, it is to say that all of Bush's *counterparts* are human. And to say that Bush is possibly human is to say that some of Bush's counterparts are human. A counterpart of Bush in a world, w, is an object in w that is similar enough to Bush, and which is at least as similar to Bush as are other objects in w. Exactly what sort of similarity is relevant can vary depending on the interests of the person uttering the *de re* modal sentence and her conversational audience. Thus, Lewis achieves a reduction of *de re* modality to the non-modal notion of similarity plus Lewisian possible worlds.[17]

3.6 The Incredulous Stare

Lewis's analysis of modality is compelling and comprehensive. Nevertheless, almost no one other than Lewis himself accepts it in its entirety. The chief reason is that most philosophers regard the existence of Lewisian possible worlds as being extremely implausible. According to Lewis, there exist golden mountains, unicorns, talking donkeys, and fire-breathing dragons. You've got to be kidding me! Lewis calls this reaction the incredulous stare, and takes it seriously, but argues that the intrinsic implausibility of his possible worlds are outweighed by the theoretical benefits of

[15] Sorts of necessity narrower than metaphysical necessity may be analysed by restricting the quantifier over worlds in various ways.

[16] See Lewis (1986, ch. 4), for an extensive defence of this view.

[17] See Lewis (1968; 1971; 1986, sect. 1.2 and ch. 4 on counterpart theory). Lewis gives possible worlds analyses of other modal notions in Lewis (1986, ch. 1; 1973).

positing them. Here Lewis follows Quine's (1948) conception of ontological commitment: it is reasonable to postulate the entities over which one's best overall theory quantifies. According to Lewis, his theory of possible worlds provides the best systematic account of modal and other phenomena; its ontology is therefore reasonable (Lewis 1986, ch. 1). Lewis's argument is deliberately parallel to Quine's famous argument for the existence of sets: our best overall empirical theory, mathematical physics, quantifies over real numbers; therefore, we have reason to posit real numbers, or the sets to which they may be reduced. (See Putnam 1971; Quine 1951, sect. 6; 1960, ch. 7.)

It is an interesting question why most philosophers so vehemently reject Lewisian worlds, especially since many accept the Quinean conception of ontological commitment and take the Quinean argument for sets seriously. Some may regard Quinean indispensability arguments as only being successful when applied to scientific theories; Lewis's argument concerns a theory whose alleged benefits are largely philosophical rather than empirical. This probably was Quine's reaction. But many philosophers have a more sympathetic attitude towards philosophy than did Quine, and yet regard Lewis's argument as a non-starter. Perhaps they reject Lewis's claim that his modal realism provides the most powerful systematic account of modal and other phenomena. Perhaps I speak for the majority when I say that I do not really know why I find the incredulous stare compelling; I only know that I do.[18]

3.7 The Objection from Actualism

Like the incredulous stare, the objection from actualism is directed against the existence of Lewisian possibilia. But whereas the objection behind the incredulous stare is that Lewisian worlds are *unlikely* (for reasons of parsimony), the objection from actualism is that Lewis's ontology is conceptually incoherent. It is not incoherent that there exist fire-breathing dragons and talking donkeys; and it is arguably not incoherent that there exist fire-breathing dragons and talking donkeys that are not spatio-temporally related to me. What is incoherent, according to the objection, is the existence of anything at all that is *non-actual*. The objector upholds *actualism*, the claim that it is a conceptual truth that everything is actual. According to the actualist, Lewis's *possibilism*, his acceptance of the existence of non-actual things, is conceptually incoherent since 'actual' is simply a blanket term for absolutely everything (see Lycan 1979, sect. VI; Lewis 1986, ch. 2.1). If Lewisian worlds— concrete entities spatio-temporally unrelated to us—really did exist, they would simply be part of actuality (since the actual includes absolutely everything), and would have nothing to do with possibility and necessity.

---

[18] For more on the incredulous stare, see Bigelow and Pargetter (1987, sect. 2).

Lewis's own response to this objection is powerful. Lewis considers three claims:

(1) Everything is actual
(2) Actuality consists of everything that is spatio-temporally related to us, and nothing more.
(3) Possibilities are not parts of actuality, they are alternatives to it.

According to Lewis, the actualist claims that (1) is analytically true, and that (2) is synthetic (i.e. non-analytic) and probably false, whereas Lewis's view commits him to (2) and the denial of (1). Lewis replies as follows: '. . . I think [all three theses] are on an equal footing. Together they fix the meaning of "actual," but they go far beyond just fixing meanings. I don't see any evidence that the analyticity is concentrated more in some of them than in others' (1986: 99–100). I would expand on this reply by appeal to the following familiar picture of content determination. Linguistic convention supplies *defeasible* constraints on meaning, constraints that may be defeated by what candidate meanings exist. Example: convention supplies the defeasible constraint that things that are in *contact* have absolutely no space between them; in fact there is no relation of this sort between material bodies (at least, none that fits with other things we say about contact); as a consequence, the meaning of the term 'contact' is a relation that does not satisfy this conventional constraint. So in a sense, the sentence 'Things that are in contact have absolutely no space between them' is analytic but false! It is something like analytic since it is a conventional constraint on the meaning of 'contact', but it is false since this constraint is outweighed by other considerations; consequently, 'contact' means something that does not obey the constraint. Arguably, the claim that a person has free will only if her actions are causally undetermined is another such claim. Given this picture of meaning, Lewis's reply could be that (1), (2), and (3) are all partial conventional constraints on the meaning of 'actual'. In fact, the best candidate meaning for 'actual' (and other modal terms) is given by Lewis's theory of modality, which vindicates (2) and (3) but not (1). So Lewis can grant the objector that (1) is in a sense analytic; it is nevertheless false.

3.8 Island Universes

Other objections to Lewis's modal realism may be raised, objections that focus on Lewis's definition of a possible world as a spatio-temporally interrelated whole. This definition rules out the possibility of an absolutely empty possible world (though, as Lewis notes, it allows the possibility of a world containing nothing but empty spacetime; Lewis 1986: 73). More worrisome is that the definition rules out the existence of a single possible world containing two disconnected space-times, for Lewis's definition counts two disconnected space-times as two worlds rather than one. Intuitively, one would have thought it possible that there exist disconnected space-times, that there exist pairs of things that are in no way spatio-temporally related to each other.[19]

One could modify Lewis's definition of a possible world to avoid this difficulty. Suppose Lewis counted *every* individual as a possible world—even individuals containing parts from different maximal spatio-temporally interrelated sums. Possible worlds, on this definition, would overlap extensively. I myself would count as a possible world, as would the aggregate of me plus the Eiffel Tower, as would the aggregate of me, the Eiffel Tower, and the Empire State Building, and so on. Now consider two maximal spatio-temporally interrelated sums—two Lewis-worlds. On the new definition the sum of these two possible individuals itself counts as a possible world. Hence there are possible worlds with disconnected space-times, and we have avoided the undesirable consequence that disconnected space-times are impossible.

On this view, I inhabit a possible world that contains a talking donkey—take any fusion of me, any possible talking donkey, and zero or more other things. And yet we certainly do not want it to turn out that an everyday utterance by me of the sentence 'There exists a talking donkey' would be true. Thus, we should add to the view the claim that in non-modal sentences, quantifiers are typically restricted in some way. (Most of us believe this anyway.) For Lewis, the quantifiers in non-modal sentences are restricted (at least) to objects in the actual world—i.e. the world of the speaker—but on this new view there is no such thing as *the* world of the speaker. Instead the view ought to be that the quantifiers in a non-modal sentence should be restricted (at least) to things spatio-temporally related to the speaker. Everyday utterances of 'There exists a talking donkey' no longer turn out true. But now there is a different odd consequence. Although the sentence 'It is possible that there exist disconnected space-times' turns out true, in no possible world could one truly utter 'There (actually) exist disconnected space-times'. I leave it to the reader to judge whether this is worse than the implausible consequence facing Lewis's original theory that we were trying to avoid.

3.9 Shalkowski's Objection

An interesting objection of a rather different sort has been raised by Scott Shalkowski (1994). (See also McGinn 2000, ch. 4.) Lewis's analysis is that a (*de dicto*) proposition is possible iff it is true in all Lewis-worlds. But suppose that Lewis-worlds containing 9-feet-tall humans, or purple cows, are simply absent from Lewis's multiverse. Then certain propositions will incorrectly turn out impossible. To rule out these 'gaps in logical space', Shalkowski argues, Lewis must require that there exists a Lewis-world for every possible way things could have been. But then his account would become

---

[19] For arguments that this is possible, see Bigelow and Pargetter (1987, sect. 3) and Bricker (2001: 33–9). Bricker also discusses empty worlds.

circular, for he would need modal notions to characterize his multiverse. Relatedly, suppose a round square, or a box both empty and full, were present in Lewis's multiverse. Then certain impossible propositions would be judged possible by Lewis's analysis. To rule out impossibilia in his multiverse, so the objection goes, Lewis must again make circular use of modal notions—he must claim that his multiverse contains only *possible* objects.

To evaluate this objection we must be clear about the nature of circularity and the aims of analysis. Suppose reality is just the way Lewis thinks it is. That is, suppose that Lewis's multiverse exists, and that there is a possible world for all and only the possible ways things might have been. Never mind what reason there would be for thinking reality to be this way; just suppose for the moment that it does. There is then the question of whether there is room in this reality for modality. Within this multiverse, is there a candidate property we can identify with the property of being a possible proposition? The answer seems to be *yes*—it is the property of being a proposition that is true at some Lewis-world. As shown above, this property can be defined in entirely non-modal terms (in terms of spatio-temporal notions and the restriction of quantifiers). Thus, an adequate non-modal definition of 'possible' can be given, *if* Lewis's ontology is indeed correct. There is then the question of whether it is reasonable to believe that Lewis's ontology is correct. But here Lewis has his Quinean answer—we ought to believe in his ontology because of its theoretical utility. So: if reality is as Lewis says it is, then a reductive analysis of modality is possible; moreover, Lewis has an argument that reality is indeed this way.

A reductive analysis of modality must be (i) genuinely reductive, and (ii) materially adequate. An analysis is genuinely reductive if the terms in the analysans are non-modal; it is materially adequate if the truth-values it assigns to modal sentences are the correct ones. Since all that is required for an analysis to be genuinely reductive is that its analysans not contain modal notions, and since Lewis's analysans involves only spatio-temporal notions and quantifier restriction, Lewis's analysis is genuinely reductive, contrary to Shalkowski's claim that it is circular. It is certainly true that there are modal conditions Lewis's multiverse must obey if his analysis is to be materially adequate—as Shalkowski says, the multiverse must contain a maximal spatio-temporally interrelated whole for each possibility, and it must contain no impossible objects. But the existence of this modal condition of material adequacy does not compromise the genuinely reductive character of the analysis. If the existence of an F-condition of adequacy on an analysis of F-ness would render that analysis circular, then no analysis of *anything* would be non-circular. It is an adequacy condition on the analysis of F-ness as G-ness that all and only Fs are Gs. I think, therefore, that Shalkowski's objection should be rejected.

3.10 The Humphrey Objection to Counterpart Theory

Any argument against Lewisian possible worlds is also an argument against the reductive theory of *de dicto* modality that presupposes them. But rejecting Lewisian possible worlds does not require rejecting the counterpart-theoretic analysis of *de re* modality. One could reject Lewis's theory of possible worlds and individuals, supply some other reduction of *de dicto* modality or take it as primitive, and then utilize *de dicto* modality in a construction of ersatz possible worlds and individuals as discussed above. A counterpart relation could then be introduced over these ersatz possible individuals, and something very much like Lewis's analysis of *de re* modality could then be given. (see Stalnaker 1986; Sider 2002.)

But there are arguments against counterpart theory that do not turn on the Lewisian conception of the nature of possible individuals, the most famous of which is Saul Kripke's 'Humphrey objection'. After losing the 1972 presidential election to Richard Nixon, imagine Hubert Humphrey saying to himself 'I might have won the election if only I had done such and such.' According to counterpart theory, the analysis of Humphrey's claim 'I might have won' is that a counterpart of Humphrey's in another possible world wins the election. But, Kripke argues, while Humphrey cares very much that he might have won, surely Humphrey 'could not care less whether someone *else*, no matter how much resembling him, would have been victorious in another possible world' (1972: 45 n. 13). On one interpretation, the objection is that the counterpart-theoretic analysis of *de re* modal statements is inconsistent with the significance we invest in modal judgements. Another way of taking the objection is simply that counterpart theory gives an intuitively implausible analysis of everyday modal judgements.

I find these objections unconvincing. It must be granted that the average non-philosopher might find the counterpart-theoretic analysis unfamiliar, and perhaps surprising, but if this were an obstacle then few philosophical analyses of any sort would be possible. We must not demand of a correct analysis that it be immediately recognized as such by any competent speaker—we learned this from the paradox of analysis. Our demands must be more modest: the analysis must fit most of our usage of the term being analysed, it must not be too ad hoc, it must presuppose no objectionable ontology or primitive notions, and so on. Whether counterpart theory best fits these desiderata is something that must be settled on the basis of a philosophical investigation into its merits and the merits of competing theories; counterpart theory should not be dismissed out of hand simply because of the intuitions behind the Humphrey objection. (see Hazen 1979: 320–4; Forbes 1987: 143; Sider 2001*a*: 194–6.)

4. CONVENTIONALISM

4.1 Truth by Convention

The old 'linguistic' or 'conventionalist' theory of necessity has few contemporary adherents, for the most part with good reason. In *Language, Truth and Logic*, A. J. Ayer gives a bald statement of conventionalism. Note that necessity and apriority are apparently equated, as was not atypical at the time (Ayer's index entry for 'Necessary propositions' reads 'See *A priori* propositions'):

> The views which are put forward in this treatise derive from the doctrines of Bertrand Russell and Wittgenstein, which are themselves the logical outcome of the empiricism of Berkeley and David Hume. Like Hume, I divide all genuine propositions into two classes: those which, in his terminology, concern 'relations of ideas,' and those which concern 'matters of fact.' The former class comprises the *a priori* propositions of logic and pure mathematics, and these I allow to be necessary and certain only because they are analytic. That is, I maintain that the reason why these propositions cannot be confuted in experience is that they do not make any assertion about the empirical world, but simply record our determination to use symbols in a certain fashion. (Ayer 1952: 31)

A proposition is analytic, Ayer goes on to say, 'when its validity depends solely on the definitions of the symbols it contains...' (1952: 78). Analytic propositions can be known a priori because they are 'devoid of factual content' (1952: 78), because they merely 'record our determination to use words in a certain fashion'.

Though Ayer is mostly concerned with epistemology, with claiming that logic and mathematics are a priori because analytic, he also says that a truth is necessary iff it is analytic in this sense. Analytic truths, for Ayer, 'say nothing about the world'; this theory of necessity might, therefore, be thought congenial to metaphysical as well as epistemological reductionists.

Something like this view of necessity was once widely held, both by logical positivists and by ordinary language philosophers.[20] A language comes equipped with certain rules, which language-users conventionally adopt. Certain sentences, analytic sentences, will be true purely in virtue of these rules. Language-users *make these sentences true* by adopting the relevant conventions. The sentence ⌜It is necessary that ϕ⌝ is true iff sentence ϕ is one of these analytic sentences.

Some criticisms are familiar. Ayer says that an analytic statement 'records our determination to use symbols in a certain way'; if this means that analytic statements are actually *about* language use, then analytic statements would seem to be contingent, since it is contingent that we use language the way we do (Broad

---

[20] Among conventionalists, see Carnap (1937, sect. 69; 1950) and Malcolm (1940). For thorough (critical) discussion and references to conventionalists and their critics, see Pap (1958, ch. 7); see also Lewy (1976, esp. ch. 5), and Boghossian (1997).

1936: 107). A related argument may be based on the work of Casimir Lewy (1976: 9). The conventionalist supposes that something like (1) gives the meaning of (2):

(1) 'Vixen' means the same as 'female fox'.
(2) Necessarily, something is a vixen if and only if it is a female fox.

However, it is arguably possible for (2) to be true while (1) is false; imagine that we used 'vixen' as we actually do but used 'female fox' to refer to a kind of ice cream.[21]

But the most profound objections, I think, are those that challenge the very idea of something's being 'true by convention'. In what sense is the truth of the following due to convention?

(B) All bachelors are men.

(B) is true in part because of the meanings we assign to the terms 'bachelor' and 'men,' and indeed, to 'all' and 'are'. But all sentences, however contingent and empirical, share this debt to convention: 'The acceleration due to gravity is 9.8m/s^2' would not be true if we used '9' to mean 8 or 'gravity' to mean rocket propulsion. As Quine says in 'Truth by Convention', 'definitions are available only for transforming truths, not for founding them' (1966b: 81). When one defines 'bachelor' as meaning the same as 'unmarried man', one provides a new linguistic vehicle for expressing the (logical) truth that all unmarried men are men, namely sentence (B). But this does not make (B) true, for this explanation of its truth depended on the 'prior' truth that all unmarried men are men. One can call (B) 'analytic', if this means just that it may be transformed into a logical truth by substituting synonyms for synonyms, but it has not been shown to be conventionally true unless logical truths can be shown to be conventionally true. And, as Quine famously goes on to argue, logical truths do not in any important sense owe their truth to conventions.

Quine's argument that logical truths are not true by convention is ingenious and extremely influential. Nevertheless, I think there is a more compelling case to be made.[22] What could it mean to say that we make logical truths true by convention? Imagine an attempt to legislate truth: 'Let every sentence of the form "If P then P" be true'. What would this accomplish? The legislator could be resolving to use the word 'true' in a new way; he could be listing the sentences to which this new term 'true' applies. But this isn't making logic true by convention; it is legislating a new

---

[21] For further discussion, see Ibberson (1979).

[22] Arguments somewhat similar to mine are given by the critics of conventionalism mentioned in n. 38. Quine's arguments in 'Truth by Convention' (Quine 1966b) were two. First, he shows that the conventionalist about logic can be aped by an obviously wrong-headed conventionalist about empirical science. This shows that *something* is wrong about logical conventionalism, but doesn't show exactly what that is. Secondly, Quine argues that since there are infinitely many logical truths, but we can only give conventions in a finite way; logic itself will be required to infer non-basic logical truths from our conventions. But (i) Quine has no adequate response to the claim that our conventions are implicit in our societal linguistic behaviour, and (ii) Quine has no adequate response to a finitary conventionalist who tries to introduce conventional truth in a language whose set of well-formed formulae is finite, nor to a conventionalist with an infinitary mind who legislates all the truths of logic individually.

sense of 'true'. On the other hand, the legislator could be singling out a meaning for 'if . . . then': 'if . . . then' is to stand for a relation, R, between propositions, such that for any proposition, p, the proposition that $R(p, p)$ is true. But this does not amount to logical truth by convention either, for it appeals to an antecedent notion of propositional truth. The propositions $R(p, p)$ are assumed to 'already' be true; they are then used to pick out the desired relation R.

There are a number of ways I can cause the proposition that my computer monitor has been thrown out of the window to be true. I could throw the monitor out myself, pay or incite someone else to do it, and so on. I cannot, however, cause this proposition to be true simply by pronouncing. I can pronounce until I am blue in the face, and the monitor will remain on my desk; my pronouncements do not affect the truth-values of statements about computer monitors. Statements about conventions are different. These we, or at least our linguistic community, *can* make true by pronouncement. A convention consists of the activities of language-users; that is why we can so easily make it true that conventions exist. (It is hard to say how explicit, recognized, or unanimous the pronouncement must be; indeed, 'pronouncement' is stretched.) Only statements *about pronouncements*, for example statements about conventions, seem to be made true by our pronouncements.[23] Statements about monitors, or bachelors, or rain, are about a part of the world we cannot affect simply by pronouncement. That it is either raining or not raining is about rain; I cannot affect the world in the matter of rain simply by pronouncement; therefore, I cannot make it the case that either it will rain or it will not rain simply by pronouncement.

A related argument is this. I cannot make it the case that it rains simply by pronouncing, nor can I make it the case that it does not rain simply by pronouncing. But if I cannot make it the case that p simply by pronouncement, nor can I make it the case that q simply by pronouncement, then I cannot make it the case that p or q simply by pronouncement.[24] Therefore, I cannot make it the case that either it rains or it doesn't rain, simply by pronouncement. Similarly for other logical truths. If ϕ expresses a logical truth, then I cannot in general make it the case that ϕ simply by pronouncement.

Seen in this light, Ayer's claims that logical truths 'depend solely on meaning' and 'say nothing about the world' look misleading at best. In what sense does the truth of 'It is raining or it is not raining' depend solely on the meanings of its terms? Certainly, its truth depends on the fact that 'or' means disjunction and 'not' means negation; but doesn't it also depend on a fact about disjunction and negation, to the

---

[23] As Karen Bennett pointed out, there are mixed cases, e.g. a president's appointing an ambassador or a preacher's pronouncing a couple husband and wife. The contents of these pronouncements are partly about conventions, and are in part made true by the pronouncements.

[24] It is not true of all sentential operators O that $\sim O (p \text{ or } q)$ follows from $\sim Op$ and $\sim Oq$; the argument merely assumes this to be the case for the operator 'I can make it the case simply by pronouncement that'.

effect that any disjunction of a proposition with its negation is true?[25] In what sense do logical truths 'lack factual content'? 'It is raining or it is not raining' concerns the world, specifically concerning the matter of rain. After all, 'It is raining' and 'It is not raining' each concerns the world on the subject of rain, and the disjunction says that one or the other will hold. And how could 'All bachelors are male' not say anything about the world? It contains a quantifier over bachelors, and says of them that they are male. So it says something about the properties of bachelors—as worldly entities as one could ask for.

4.2 Beyond Truth by Convention

Truth by convention should be rejected, along with conventionalist theories of modality based on that notion. But reductions similar in spirit to conventionalism may yet survive. For example, the claim that necessity is analyticity is separable from the claim that analytic truths are true by convention. One could reject the latter while accepting the former, as did C. I. Lewis (1946, bk. 1).[26] This identification of necessity with analyticity was once very popular (though many defenders also subscribed to truth by convention).[27] Carnap (1947) held a hybrid view that granted an important role to analyticity, but which also appealed to possible worlds construed as sets of atomic sentences. A related view is that necessity is to be identified with some sort of logical truth or provability, the only meaning for 'necessary' to which Quine (1953a) was friendly. (This was, of course, a consequence of his unfriendliness towards analyticity.) Note that it is probably inaccurate to describe these philosophers as identifying what I have been calling metaphysical necessity with analyticity. It would be better to say that these philosophers rejected, or did not possess, the contemporary concept of metaphysical necessity; their claim was that analytic necessity is the only sensible sort of necessity in the neighbourhood.[28]

Few nowadays would identify necessity with analyticity, given the now well-known synthetic sentences that express necessary truths; it is from these cases that the contemporary notion of 'metaphysical necessity' springs (see Plantinga 1974: 2).

What are these synthetic necessary truths? Many would cite mathematical examples. On some conceptions of mathematical truth, the sentences of mathematics are not analytic, but are nevertheless necessarily true.

---

[25] It might be said that the truth of 'It is raining or it is not raining' does not *modally* depend on anything other than the meaning of this sentence, since it is necessarily true that if the sentence has its actual meaning then it is true. But this modal conception of truth by convention could not play a part in reducing modality.

[26] Lewis does not distinguish a priori from necessary truth. See also Lewis and Langford (1959, ch. vi), in which '◇' is interpreted as 'self-consistency', meaning analytic consistency (see Lewis 1918, ch. v for an earlier presentation).   [27] See Pap (1958, pt. 2) for an excellent discussion.

[28] See Neale (2000) on the history of modal logic and the concept of necessity.

I would cite also the laws of mereology, whatever those are. There are some conditions, C, such that it is necessarily true that whenever objects satisfy conditions C, there exists an object that is composed of those objects, a 'fusion' of those objects. I myself would claim that the conditions C are vacuous, that objects *always* have a fusion; but even defenders of restrictive mereology will want to claim that there are *some* conditions that necessarily suffice for fusion. However, it is very difficult to see how the sentence 'If some objects are in conditions C, then there exists something that is composed of those objects' could be analytic, for it conditionally asserts the *existence* of a thing, and how could such a statement be analytic?[29]

Claims about the essences of particular things seem not to be analytic, but are necessary. That George W. Bush is human seems synthetic since names like 'George W. Bush' seem to lack definitions, but many would claim it is necessarily true that Bush is human. Likewise, Kripke and Putnam's cases of the necessary a posteriori seem synthetic. Putnam (1975), for example, argues that any liquid not made of H_2O would not be water, and concludes that it is necessary that all water is made of H_2O. But it is not part of the meaning of 'water' that water is made of H_2O, since 'water' was used long before anyone knew of the chemical make-up of water, and surely 'water' has not since changed its meaning.

A final obstacle to the identification of necessity with analyticity is *de re* modality. If $\ulcorner\Box\phi\urcorner$ means that the sentence ϕ is an analytic truth, then it is hard to make sense of quantification into modal contexts. Given the usual Tarskian treatment of quantification, $\ulcorner\exists x\Box Fx\urcorner$ is true iff there is some object, o, such that $\ulcorner\Box Fx\urcorner$ is true relative to an assignment of o to the variable 'x'; $\ulcorner\forall x\Box Fx\urcorner$ is true iff for every o, $\ulcorner\Box Fx\urcorner$ is true relative to an assignment of o to the variable 'x'. In each case we must make sense of the application of '$\Box$' to $\ulcorner Fx\urcorner$—a sentence with a free variable. Given necessity as analyticity, $\ulcorner\Box Fx\urcorner$ is true relative to an assignment of o to the variable 'x' iff $\ulcorner Fx\urcorner$ is analytic, relative to an assignment of o to the variable 'x'. But how could $\ulcorner Fx\urcorner$ be analytic, relative to an assignment of o to 'x'? Analyticity is a function of meaning, not merely reference, whereas with open sentences relative to assignments we have only reference. This (together with scepticism about a more metaphysical conception of modality, under which quantification into modal contexts *would* make sense) was the heart of Quine's attack on *de re* modality (see Quine 1953*b*; Burgess 1997; Neale 2000).

For these reasons many doubt the identification of necessity with analyticity; and, as mentioned above, many reject the conventionalist theory of necessity as well. Nevertheless, analyticity and convention may yet play an important role in the reduction of modality. I take it that logical, analytic, and mathematical truths do not owe their truth to convention, except in the uninteresting sense in which every true sentence partly owes its truth to the conventions that give that sentence its meaning.

---

[29] On mereology, see Lewis (1986: 212–13), Sider (2001*a*, ch. 4, sect. 9.1), and van Inwagen (1990). For an argument that statements of existence are not analytic, see Sider (2001*b*) and the introduction to Sider (2001*a*). The chief opposing view is that of Carnap (1950).

It might still be a convention to call logical, analytic, and mathematical truths necessary. It would be analytic to 'necessary' that logical, analytic, and mathematical truths are necessary. 'Necessary' would be a word used for truths of certain kinds.

Pretend for the moment that only logical, analytic, and mathematical truths are necessary. One could then hold that 'necessary' just means 'is either a logical, analytic, or mathematical truth'. This theory is reductive, and similar in spirit to conventionalism, but it makes no objectionable assumptions about 'truth by convention'. On this theory, there is a convention to call logical, analytic, and mathematical truths necessary. So, provided '2 + 2 = 4' is a mathematical truth, the following sentence will be true:

Necessarily, 2 + 2 = 4.

Convention can do this much. It need not play any role in making it true that 2 + 2 = 4, or in making this be a mathematical truth. '2 + 2 = 4' is made true by whatever makes mathematical truths true generally (perhaps facts about numbers in Platonic heaven); its status as a *mathematical* truth is made true by whatever generally makes mathematical truths mathematical (perhaps the fact that its subject matter is mathematics).

The contingency objection was that conventionalism turns statements about logic and mathematics into statements *about* conventions, which then inherit the contingency of conventions. The present theory has no such consequence, nor does it imply that statements that logical, analytic, or mathematical truths are necessary are about conventions, nor does it imply that such statements are mind-dependent. It is a convention to call logical, analytic, and mathematical truths necessary, but the *content* of a statement of, say, mathematics is just mathematical, and the content of a statement of necessity is just that a certain sentence or proposition is a logical, analytic, or mathematical truth, which has nothing to do with convention.

Conventionalists granted a special status to convention as a source of truth. This was an essential part of the epistemology of many conventionalists. Ayer, for instance, used it to explain our knowledge of logical and mathematical truths. But if we are not trying to fit modality into an overly demanding epistemology, we do not need convention to play this role.

Conventionalists also seemed to regard truth by convention as an essential ingredient to a reductive theory of necessity. As Paul Boghossian (1997: 336) puts it: 'Guided by the fear that objective, language-independent, necessary connections would be metaphysically odd, [the positivists] attempted to show that all necessities could be understood to consist in linguistic necessities . . . Linguistic meaning, by itself, was supposed to generate necessary truth; *a fortiori*, linguistic meaning, by itself, was supposed to generate truth.' But the theory just sketched shows that we do not need truth by convention to account for modality without appealing to anything 'metaphysically odd'. Moreover, truth by convention would not have demystified modality on its own anyway. Like many writers, Boghossian seems to presuppose that if linguistic meaning generates truth, then it automatically generates *necessary* truth. This does not follow without further assumptions about necessity. Some account of necessity is still required to bridge the gap between 'true by convention' and 'necessary'. If necessity were truth in all Lewisian worlds, then the gap would be bridged, for then conventional truth would suffice for necessary truth (provided that the same conventions were adopted for talk about worlds other than our own). But no positivist had *this* in mind. The thought must rather have been to bridge the gap by a convention involving 'necessary': 'necessary' just means 'made true by convention'. But now it is clear that truth by convention was never needed, for 'necessary' could just as well be regarded as obeying a different convention, one that does not require truth by convention, for example the convention that 'necessary' applies to the truths of mathematics and logic, and to analytic truths.

The theory just sketched is far too simple to be plausible. Some necessities are neither logical nor mathematical nor analytic; moreover, the theory as stated has nothing to say about *de re* modality. Its existence nevertheless makes a point: theories that claim that necessary truths are truths *of a certain kind* enjoy some of the virtues of traditional conventionalism while avoiding many of the standard objections. Whether a workable theory of this sort can be developed thus becomes an interesting and important question. There are obstacles, but I believe that this approach should be taken seriously by reductionist-minded philosophers of modality.[30]

REFERENCES

Adams, R. H. (1974). 'Theories of Actuality'. *Noûs*, 8: 211–31. Repr. in Loux (1979: 190–209).

Armstrong, D. M. (1989). *A Combinatorial Theory of Possibility*. New York: Cambridge University Press.

—— (1997). *A World of States of Affairs*. New York: Cambridge University Press.

Ayer, A. J. (1952). *Language, Truth and Logic*, 2nd edn. New York: Dover.

Bigelow, John, and Robert Pargetter (1987). 'Beyond the Blank Stare'. *Theoria*, 53: 97–114.

Blackburn, Simon (1993). 'Morals and Modals', in his *Essays in Quasi-Realism*. New York: Oxford University Press, 52–74.

Boghossian, Paul (1997). 'Analyticity', in B. Hale and C. Wright (eds.), *A Companion to the Philosophy of Language*. Oxford: Basil Blackwell.

Bricker, P. (1987). 'Reducing Possible Worlds to Language'. *Philosophical Studies*, 52: 331–55.

—— (2001). 'Island Universes and the Analysis of Modality', in Gerhard Preyer and Frank Siebelt (eds.), *Reality and Humean Supervenience: Essays on the Philosophy of David Lewis*. Lanham, Md.: Rowman & Littlefield, 27–55.

Broad, C. D. (1936). 'Are there Synthetic *A Priori* Truths?', *Proceedings of the Aristotelian Society*, suppl. vol. 15: 102–17.

---

[30] I hope to pursue this strategy in a future paper. A somewhat related reductive account is defended by Christopher Peacocke (1997, 1999).

Burgess, John P. (1997). 'Quinus ab Omni Naevo Vindicatus', in Ali A. Kazmi (ed.), *Meaning and Reference. Canadian Journal of Philosophy*, suppl. vol. 23: 25–65.

Carnap, Rudolf (1937). *The Logical Syntax of Language*. London: Routledge & Kegan Paul.

—— (1947). *Meaning and Necessity: A Study in Semantics and Modal Logic*. Chicago: University of Chicago Press.

—— (1950). 'Empiricism, Semantics and Ontology'. *Revue Internationale de Philosophie*, 4: 20–40. Repr. as an appendix to Carnap, *Meaning and Necessity: A Study in Semantics and Modal Logic*, 2nd edn. Chicago: University of Chicago Press, 1956, 205–21.

Chalmers, David (1996). *The Conscious Mind*. Oxford: Oxford University Press.

Chihara, C. S. (1998). *The Worlds of Possibility*. Oxford: Clarendon Press.

Cresswell, M. J. (1972). 'The World is Everything that is the Case'. *Australian Journal of Philosophy*, 50: 1–13. Repr. in Loux (1979).

—— (1973). *Logics and Languages*. London: Methuen.

Davidson, Donald (1967). 'Truth and Meaning'. *Synthese*, 17: 304–23.

Dowty, David R., Robert E. Wall, and Stanley Peters (1981). *Introduction to Montague Semantics*. Dordrecht: Kluwer.

Feldman, Fred (1986). *Doing the Best we Can*. Dordrecht: Reidel.

Field, Hartry (1989). *Realism, Mathematics and Modality*. Oxford: Basil Blackwell.

Fine, Kit (1977). Postscript to Fine, *Worlds, Times and Selves*. London: Duckworth.

—— (1980). 'First-Order Modal Theories, Part II—Propositions'. *Studia Logica*, 39: 159–202.

—— (1981). 'First-Order Modal Theories, Part I—Sets'. *Noûs*, 15: 117–206.

—— (1982). 'First-Order Modal Theories, Part III—Facts'. *Synthese*, 53: 43–122.

—— (1985). 'Plantinga on the Reduction of Possibilist Discourse', in J. E. Tomberlin and P. van Inwagen (eds.), *Alvin Plantinga*. Dordrecht: Reidel, 145–86.

Forbes, Graham (1987). 'Is there a Problem about Persistence?'. *Proceedings of the Aristotelian Society*, suppl. vol. 61: 137–55.

Hazen, Allen (1979). 'Counterpart-Theoretic Semantics for Modal Logic'. *Journal of Philosophy*, 76: 319–38.

Heller, Mark (1998). 'Property Counterparts in Ersatz Worlds'. *Journal of Philosophy*, 95: 293–316.

Hughes, G. E., and M. J. Cresswell (1996). *A New Introduction to Modal Logic*. London: Routledge.

Ibberson, John (1979). 'Necessity by Convention'. *Mind*, 88: 554–71.

Jeffrey, Richard (1965). *The Logic of Decision*. New York: McGraw-Hill.

Kim, Jaegwon (1993). *Supervenience and Mind*. Cambridge: Cambridge University Press.

Kneale, W. C. (1949). *Probability and Induction*. Oxford: Clarendon Press.

Kratzer, Angelika (1977). 'What "Must" and "Can" Must and Can Mean'. *Linguistics and Philosophy*, 1: 337–55.

Kripke, Saul (1972). *Naming and Necessity*. Cambridge, Mass.: Harvard University Press.

Lewis, C. I. (1918). *A Survey of Symbolic Logic*. Berkeley: University of California Press.

—— (1946). *An Analysis of Knowledge and Valuation*. LaSalle, Il.: Open Court.

—— and C. H. Langford (1959). *Symbolic Logic* (1932), 2nd edn. New York: Dover.

Lewis, David (1968). 'Counterpart Theory and Quantified Modal Logic'. *Journal of Philosophy*, 65: 113–26.

—— (1970). 'General Semantics'. *Synthese*, 22: 18–67.

—— (1971). 'Counterparts of Persons and their Bodies'. *Journal of Philosophy*, 68: 203–11.

—— (1973). *Counterfactuals*. Cambridge, Mass.: Harvard University Press.

Lewis, David (1980). 'A Subjectivist's Guide to Objective Chance', in Richard C. Jeffrey (ed.), *Studies in Inductive Logic and Probability*, vol. ii (Berkeley: University of California Press). Repr. with added postscripts in Lewis, *Philosophical Papers*, vol. ii. New York: Oxford University Press, 1986, 83–132.

—— (1986). *On the Plurality of Worlds*. Oxford: Basil Blackwell.

—— (1992). 'Critical Notice of D. M. Armstrong, *A Combinatorial Theory of Possibility*'. *Australasian Journal of Philosophy*, 70: 211–224.

Lewy, Casimir (1976). *Meaning and Modality*. Cambridge: Cambridge University Press.

Loux, Michael J. (ed.) (1979). *The Possible and the Actual*. Ithaca, NY: Cornell University Press.

Lycan, William (1979). 'The Trouble with Possible Worlds', in Loux (1979: 274–316).

McGinn, Colin (2000). *Logical Properties*. Oxford: Oxford University Press.

McMichael, Alan (1983). 'A Problem for Actualism about Possible Worlds'. *Philosophical Review*, 92: 49–66.

Malcolm, Norman (1940). 'Are Necessary Propositions Really Verbal?', *Mind*, 49: 189–203.

Merricks, Trenton (2001). *Objects and Persons*. Oxford: Clarendon Press.

Neale, Stephen (2000). 'On a Milestone of Empiricism', in Alex Orenstein and Petr Kotatko (eds.), *Knowledge, Language and Logic*. Dordrecht: Kluwer, 237–346.

Pap, Arthur (1958). *Semantics and Necessary Truth*. New Haven: Yale University Press.

Peacocke, Christopher (1997). 'Metaphysical Necessity: Understanding, Truth and Epistemology'. *Mind*, 106: 521–74.

—— (1999). *Being Known*. Oxford: Clarendon Press.

Plantinga, Alvin (1974). *The Nature of Necessity*. Oxford: Oxford University Press.

—— (1976). 'Actualism and Possible Worlds'. *Theoria*, 42: 139–60. Repr. in Loux (1979: 253–73).

Prior, A. N. (1955). 'Diodoran Modalities'. *Philosophical Quarterly*, 5: 205–13.

Putnam, Hilary (1975). 'The Meaning of "Meaning"' in K. Gunderson (ed.), *Language, Mind and Knowledge*, Minnesota Studies in the Philosophy of Science vol. 7. Minneapolis: University of Minnesota Press. Repr. in Hilary Putnam, *Mind, Language and Reality: Philosophical Papers*, vol. ii. Cambridge: Cambridge University Press, 1975, 215–71.

—— (1971). *Philosophy of Logic*. New York: Harper & Row.

Quine, W. V. O. (1948). 'On What There Is'. *Review of Metaphysics*, 2: 21–38. Repr. in Quine (1953c: 1–19).

—— (1951). 'Two Dogmas of Empiricism'. *Philosophical Review*, 60: 20–43. Repr. in Quine (1953c: 20–46).

—— (1953a). 'Three Grades of Modal Involvement'. *Proceedings of the XIth International Congress of Philosophy*, 14. Amsterdam: North-Holland. Repr. in Quine (1966a: 156–74).

—— (1953b). 'Reference and Modality'. in Quine (1953c: 139–59).

—— (1953c). *From a Logical Point of View*. New York: Harper & Row.

—— (1960). *Word and Object*. Cambridge: MIT Press.

—— (1966a). *The Ways of Paradox*. New York: Random House.

—— (1966b). 'Truth by Convention', in Quine (1966a: 70–99). in O. H. Lee (ed.) First pub., *Philosophical Essays for A. N. Whitehead*. New York: Longmans.

—— (1969). 'Propositional Objects', in his *Ontological Relativity and Other Essays*. New York: Columbia University Press, 139–60.

Rosen, Gideon (1990). 'Modal Fictionalism'. *Mind*, 99: 327–54.

Roy, Tony (1995). 'In Defense of Linguistic Ersatzism'. *Philosophical Studies*, 80: 217–42.

Shalkowski, Scott A. (1994). 'The Ontological Ground of the Alethic Modality'. *Philosophical Review*, 103: 669–88.

Shoemaker, Sydney (1998). 'Causal and Metaphysical Necessity'. *Pacific Philosophical Quarterly*, 79: 59–77.

Sider, Theodore (2001*a*). *Four-Dimensionalism: An Ontology of Persistence and Time*. Oxford: Clarendon Press.

—— (2001*b*). 'Criteria of Personal Identity and the Limits of Conceptual Analysis', in J. E. Tomberlin (ed.), *Philosophical Perspectives, XV: Metaphysics*. Cambridge, Mass.: Basil Blackwell, 189–209.

—— (2001*c*). Review of Charles Chihara, *The Worlds of Possibility*. *Philosophical Review*, 110: 88–91.

—— (2002). 'The Ersatz Pluriverse'. *Journal of Philosophy*, 99: 279–315.

Skyrms, Brian (1981). 'Tractarian Nominalism'. *Philosophical Studies*, 40: 199–206. Repr. as appendix to D. M. Armstrong, *A Combinatorial Theory of Possibility*. New York: Cambridge University Press, 1989, 145–52.

Stalnaker, Robert (1976). 'Possible Worlds'. *Noûs*, 10: 65–75. Repr. in Loux (1979: 225–34).

—— (1986). 'Counterparts and Identity', in P. French, T. Uehling, and H. Wettstein (eds.), *Midwest Studies in Philosophy, xi*. Minneapolis: University of Minnesota Press, 121–40.

van Inwagen, Peter (1986). 'Two Concepts of Possible Worlds', in P. French, T. Uehling, and H. Wettstein (eds.), *Midwest Studies in Philosophy, xi*. Minneapolis: University of Minnesota Press, 185–213.

—— (1990). *Material Beings*. Ithaca: NY: Cornell University Press.

Wittgenstein, Ludwig (1921). *Tractatus Logico-Philosophicus*, trans. D. F. Pears and B. F. McGuinness. London: Routledge & Kegan Paul, 1974.

PART IV

TIME, SPACE-TIME, AND PERSISTENCE

CHAPTER 8

PRESENTISM

THOMAS M. CRISP

PRESENTISM, roughly, is the thesis that only the present is real. The opposite view is *eternalism* or *four-dimensionalism*, the thesis that reality consists of past, present, and future entities.[1] After spelling out the presentist's thesis more carefully, I shall say something about why one might think it true. Finally, I'll develop four prominent objections to presentism and say something about how the presentist might reply to each.

1. PRESENTISM EXPLAINED

Presentism is a thesis about what there is, about the range of things to which we're ontologically committed. Simply put, it's the thesis that *everything* is present.

Thanks to Hans Halverson, Alvin Plantinga, Michael Rea, Donald Smith, Ted Warfield, and Dean Zimmerman for helpful comments and conversation.

[1] The term 'four-dimensionalism' is sometimes used as a name for the thesis that things persist through time by having temporal parts or stages located at different times. I'll use the term 'perdurantism' as a name for that thesis and reserve 'four-dimensionalism' as a name for the thesis that there are past, present, and future entities. Also, 'eternalism' is sometimes used as a name for the view that all propositions have their truth-values *eternally* (a proposition has its truth-value eternally if it is either always true or never true). I shall not use it in this way. The thesis named by my 'eternalism'—the thesis that reality includes past, present, and future entities—is interestingly independent of the thesis that propositions have their truth-values eternally.

Though we'll eventually need a refinement or two, we can put it thus:

(Pr) For every x, x is present,

where an object x is present iff x *occupies* or *exists at* the present time. Four comments. First, (Pr)'s quantifier is to be taken as *unrestricted*, one which ranges over *everything*. Its domain is our most inclusive domain of quantification rather than some subdomain of our most inclusive domain.

Secondly, we shall think of *the present time* as follows. Say that an object x is *slim* iff, for any y and z, if y and z are parts of x, then there is either no temporal distance or a temporal distance of *zero* between y and z. A *time*, let us say, is a maximal slim object: an object such that the mereological sum of it and anything which isn't a part of it is not slim.[2] The present time, intuitively, is the maximal slim object that includes as a part every event[3] that occurs *now*.

Thirdly, say that something *exists at* or *occupies* the present time iff it is a part of the present time. And finally, I leave undefined the notion of temporal distance, though the intuitive idea should be clear enough. If our most inclusive domain of quantification includes past as well as present entities, it presumably includes Lincoln and his assassination. The temporal distance between his assassination and the present is a little over 137 years.

Some will complain that (Pr), as it stands, is either trivially true or manifestly false.[4] Since the universal and the existential quantifiers are duals, (Pr) can be re-expressed as

(Pr$_e$) $\sim$ (there exists something x such that $\sim$ (x is present)).

Now, what is the tense of the verb 'exists' in the above quantifier phrase 'there exists something x such that ...'? Is it present-tensed? If so, (Pr$_e$) amounts to the denial of the claim that something which exists now (i.e. at the present time) is such that it is not present. But, trivially, nothing which exists at the present time isn't present. (Pr$_e$), so read, amounts to a trivial truth.

Perhaps 'exist' here is to be read *disjunctively*, yielding:

(Pr$'_e$) $\sim$ (there existed, exists, or will exist something x such that $\sim$ (x is present)).

But this doesn't look promising since (Pr$'_e$) amounts to the denial of the claim that there existed, exists, or will exist something which isn't present. But surely there existed something which isn't present. Who can deny that there existed something

---

[2] For purposes of this chapter, I shall presuppose an unrestricted mereology. On this view, very roughly, any objects, the xs, no matter their relations to one another, compose another object y such that y is the mereological sum or fusion of the xs.

[3] I shall assume that, necessarily, there are *events*, things which *happen*, *occur*, or *take place*. I'll say more below about what I take these to be.

[4] Lawrence Lombard makes this complaint (or something very close to it) in Lombard (1999: 254–5), as does Craig Callender (2000, S588–9). For discussion, see Sider (1999: 325–7); Zimmerman (1998b: 209–10); Merricks (1995: 523; 1999: 421–2); Hinchliff (2000, S576–7); and Rea, Ch. 9 in this volume.

identical with the Roman empire which is no longer present? If (Pr$_e'$) forces us to deny this, it is a trivial falsehood.

Maybe the verb should be read *tenselessly*:

(Pr$_e''$) $\sim$ (there exists (tenselessly) something x such that $\sim$(x is present)).

Those who 'take tense seriously' will object that there *are* no tenseless verbs (see e.g. Smith 1993, ch. 6; Tichy 1980: 177–9). But even if they're wrong, (Pr$_e''$) doesn't fare any better than its predecessors. It's a simple matter of logic that (Pr$_e''$) implies

(Pr$_e'''$) $\sim$ (there exists (tenselessly) a past, present, or future thing x such that $\sim$ (x is present)).

But the latter, presumably, is true iff it is false that there existed, exists, or will exist something x such that $\sim$(x is present)—iff (Pr$_e'$) is true. The upshot: (Pr$_e''$) implies (Pr$_e'''$), which is logically equivalent to a trivial falsehood. Since it's obvious that this is so, it's obvious that (Pr$_e''$) is false.

In sum: if (Pr$_e$)'s 'exist' is present-tensed, it is a trivial truism. If disjunctively tensed or tenseless, it is manifestly false. Since it's hard to see how else to read it, it looks as if (Pr$_e$) is either trivially true or manifestly false. And, since (Pr) is presumably equivalent to one or another of these readings of (Pr$_e$), (Pr) fares no better. Presentism is either a trivial truism or a manifest falsehood.

I reply that the foregoing complaint—call it the *triviality complaint*—trades on a *de re–de dicto* ambiguity. Take the disjunctively tensed reading of (Pr$_e$), the denial of

(4Dism) There existed, exists, or will exist something x such that $\sim$(x is present).

(4Dism) admits of a *de re* and a *de dicto* reading. Read *de re*, its quantifier phrase 'there existed, exists, or will exist' expresses quantification over the domain of temporal things, the domain of things which existed, exist, or will exist. (4Dism), on this reading, comes to something like:

(4Dism$_r$) Quantifying over all temporal things, for some x, x was, is, or will be such that it doesn't exist in t_α,

where 't_α' names the present time. Presentism ((Pr)) is logically equivalent to the denial of this claim.

Read *de dicto*, (4Dism) says something like:

(4Dism$_d$) It was, is, or will be the case that: something is such that it doesn't exist in t_α.

(4Dism$_d$) is a *de dicto* claim predicating of the dictum or proposition *something is such that it doesn't exist in t_α* the property of either having been true, being true now, or being such as to be true in the future. (Pr) is not logically equivalent to the denial of (4Dism$_d$): it's possible both that (*a*) for every x, x is present, and (*b*) the proposition *something doesn't exist in t_α* was, is, or will be true.

Now, the triviality complainer proposes that (4Dism) is trivially true on the grounds that there existed something *x*—viz. the Roman empire—such that *x* existed, and *x* isn't present. Take the *de re* reading of (4Dism) first. Does the past existence of the Roman empire render (4Dism)—so construed—trivially true? No. It is not a trivial truth that the open sentence following the quantifier in (4Dism$_r$) is satisfied by the Roman empire. This is because it's not a trivial truth that our most inclusive domain of quantification is still populated by something identical with the Roman empire. Were it trivially true that the four-dimensional view of space and time is correct—that our most inclusive domain of quantification includes past, present, and future entities—I suppose it would be obvious that our widest quantificational domain still includes the Roman empire. But four-dimensionalism *isn't* trivially true. It may *be* true, but if it is, we require serious argument to see that it is.

Construed *de dicto*—that is, read as (4Dism$_d$)—(4Dism) is trivially true all right, and this because it's an obvious fact of history that

WAS (something identical with the Roman empire will not exist in t_α).[5]

But nothing interesting follows. The preceding argument presupposed

(P1) (Pr$_e$), read disjunctively, is a trivial falsehood because it is the denial of (4Dism), a trivial truth.

Read *de dicto*—as (4Dism$_d$)—(4Dism) is a trivial truth and (P1) comes out true. But this helps the triviality complainer's case only if it's also true that

(P2) (Pr$_e$), read disjunctively, is logically equivalent to (Pr)

(her strategy, remember, is to claim that (Pr) fares only as well as (Pr$_e$) since the two are logically equivalent). Here there's trouble. (Pr$_e$), construed as the denial of (4Dism$_d$), is *not* logically equivalent to (Pr) since (4Dism$_d$) is compossible with (Pr). Read *de re*—as (4Dism$_r$)—the denial of (4Dism) (aka Pr$_e$) is logically equivalent to (Pr) and (P2) comes out true. But so read, (4Dism) is not a trivial truth and (P1) comes out false.

Summarizing: (4Dism) admits of two plausible readings, a *de re* and a *de dicto* reading. Read it *de re* and (P1) comes out false; read it *de dicto* and (P2) comes out false. Since the triviality complainer requires the truth of both (P1) and (P2), I conclude that her complaint can be adequately answered. Presentism, construed as (Pr), is neither trivially true nor trivially false.

That said, presentism probably shouldn't be construed as (Pr). To arrive at a proper statement of the thesis, we need one—maybe two—emendations. First, presentism is better construed as the claim that it's *always* the case that, for every *x*, *x* is present. Some philosophers (e.g. C. D. Broad 1923 and Michael Tooley 1997)

---

[5] Here and in the sequel I employ the past-tense operator of tense logic. ⌜WAS(S)⌝ abbreviates ⌜it was the case that S⌝.

think of the spatio-temporal world as a growing four-dimensional block. On this view, the world includes past and present entities but no future entities. As time passes, new entities come into existence and the four-dimensional universe grows by accretion. Presentists reject this view of time. Note, though, that if time has a first moment and the growing-block view is right, for a brief moment at the dawn of time (Pr) is true. Better, then, to think of presentism as the claim that it's always the case that, for every *x*, *x* is present. And secondly, most presentists think of their theory as necessarily true if true. I shall reserve judgement about this latter emendation. The reasons I know of for being a presentist offer no reason at all for thinking presentism a necessary truth.

For purposes of this chapter, then, let us think of presentism as the following thesis:

Presentism. It is always the case that, for every *x*, *x* is present.

2. Why Presentism?

There are no knock-down arguments for presentism, like most other substantive theses in philosophy, it cannot be established conclusively. It is, however, a natural position to take given certain metaphysical and linguistic commitments, commitments which I (and many others I suspect) find attractive. I shall now lay out those commitments and say a few words about why one might think them plausible. I shall not offer conclusive arguments for them. Though I take these commitments to accord well with the deliverances of 'common sense,' I don't think conclusive arguments are to be had. I'll close this section by arguing that presentism is the only metaphysic of time consistent with these commitments.

2.1 First Metaphysical Commitment: Endurantism

Endurantists think that spatio-temporal continuants persist through time by *enduring.*[6] A thing persists through time, loosely speaking, when it exists at various times. A thing *x* endures, we'll say, iff (i) it never has a *temporal extent* (i.e. it is not 'spread out' in time in the way that my desk is 'spread out' in space) and

---

[6] Recent endurantists include Haslanger (1989*a,b*, 1994); Hinchliff (1996, 2000); Johnston (1987, 1992); Lowe (1987, 1988); Mellor (1981, 1998); Merricks (1994, 1999); Rea (1995, 1998, 2000); van Inwagen (1990); and Zimmerman (1997, 1998*a,b*, 1999). For discussion, see Sider (2001).

(ii) for some $m \neq n$, it was (will be) the case n units of time ago (hence) that, for some y, $x = y$, and it was (will be) the case m units of time ago (hence) that, for some z, $x = z$.[7] The opposite of this view is *perdurantism*: roughly, the thesis that spatio-temporal continuants persist through time by being spread out in time in the way that things like my desk are spread out through space. Perdurantism comes in two main varieties. Worm-theoretic perdurantism says that spatio-temporal continuants like you and me are spatio-temporal 'worms': mereological fusions of *instantaneous temporal parts* or *stages*[8] located at different times.[9] Stage-theoretic perdurantism is the view that the spatio-temporal continuants recognized by common sense, continuants like you and me, are instantaneous temporal stages.[10] (A brief word of explanation about the latter view. One might be tempted to ask: if the spatio-temporal continuants of ordinary belief—desks, chairs, and the like—are to be identified with instantaneous temporal stages, in what sense are they continuants? A continuant, one thinks, is something with a history, something which lasts longer than an instant. Theodore Sider, a contemporary defender of the stage view, answers that *de re* predication of temporal properties like *being such as to exist in the past* should be analysed in terms of a temporal version of modal counterpart theory. On this view, to say that my desk has the property of existing in the past is to say that it has a counterpart in the past. So to the question whether, on his view, my desk is really a persisting thing, Sider answers yes, since after all, it has the property of existing now and of existing in the past (it occupies the present time and has counterparts which occupy past times).)

Thus far endurantism and its main alternatives. Why might one endorse endurantism over its rivals as an account of persistence? Here is one reason. Whereas endurantism comports nicely with certain obviously true claims, its competitors don't. Consider the distinction between having a property *directly* and having a property *indirectly*. I have a property F *indirectly*, let us say, iff I have F in virtue of the fact that one of my proper parts has F. For example, I am seated at present. Given worm-theoretic perdurantism, I have the property of being seated at present by virtue of the fact that one of my proper temporal parts is seated at present. I have a property F *directly*, say, iff I have F but nothing is, was, or will be such that (a) it is a proper part of me and (b) it has F. For example, I have a headache. But, one

---

[7] This way of putting the notion of endurance is fine for present purposes. But, one might wonder, what is it for a thing to have no temporal extent, not to be 'spread out' in time in the way that the spatio-temporal objects of common sense are 'spread out' in space? Answering this question turns out to be surprisingly difficult. For discussion, see Merricks (1999) and Sider (2001).

[8] An *instantaneous temporal part* or *stage* of a thing x, roughly, is a part of x such that (i) it is located at and only at an instant t, and (ii) it overlaps everything which is a part of x at t. (Here I follow Sider 2001, ch. 3.)

[9] Recent adherents include Armstrong (1980); Balashov (1999, 2000); Heller (1984, 1990, 1992, 1993); Hudson (1999, 2001); Lewis (1983a, 1986, 1988); and Quine (1960, 1963, 1976, 1981). For discussion, see Sider (2001).

[10] This view has been defended recently by Theodore Sider (1996, 2000, 2001).

thinks, I do not have the property of having a headache by virtue of the fact that any proper part of mine has this property: though I have a headache, presumably none of my proper parts does.

Now, I take it as obviously true that I have my headaches directly rather than indirectly. Endurantism implies nothing to the contrary. Not so, however, with worm-theoretic perdurantism. On this view, my having a headache at present is a matter of one of my proper temporal parts having a headache at present. The upshot: on the worm view, I have my headaches indirectly rather than directly. So much the worse, I say, for worm-theoretic perdurantism.

I also take it as obviously true that it was someone numerically identical with me who began typing this sentence. The stage-theoretic perdurantist denies this: on her view, the person who began the previous sentence was someone numerically distinct from the person who ended it, though similar in many ways. The endurantist, on the other hand, is free to suppose that one and the same person, strictly speaking, started and ended the sentence.

So endurantism comports well with certain obvious truths, truths which its rivals must deny. I find it attractive for this reason. I realize that these remarks will persuade few non-endurantists. For one thing, not everyone will agree that it is obviously true that I have my headaches directly or that one and the same person, strictly speaking, started this sentence as ended it. And for another, many will agree that non-endurantist theories of persistence have counter-intuitive consequences, but they'll think of the benefits of these theories as outweighing their costs. So I don't pretend to have given a serious argument for endurantism. As advertised, I'm offering only brief comments on why one might find it attractive.

2.2 Second Metaphysical Commitment: The Change Thesis

Things change. A complete description of the present moment will describe me differently than a complete description of the world as it was ten years ago. According to the first, I'll have properties and stand in relations such that, according to the second, I don't. We might put the point as follows. Say that successive instants of time are exhaustively described by *instant-descriptions* (*i-descriptions* for short): propositions which express maximally detailed descriptions of an instantaneous state of the world. One i-description describes the present moment; i-descriptions of the past describe what was; i-descriptions of the future describe what will be.

Again, a complete description of the present moment will describe me differently than a complete description of the world as it was ten years ago. More generally and in terms of i-descriptions:

> *Change Thesis.* According to i-descriptions of the past, I have properties and stand in relations which, according to the present i-description, I do not have and do not stand in. I-descriptions of the past represent me as having properties

and entering into relations distinct from those I'm represented as having and entering into by the present i-description.

What can be said on behalf of the Change Thesis? Other than that it seems obviously true, I have no idea.

2.3 Linguistic Commitment: The Univocality of Tense

Were you to insist that there are two equally good candidates for the meaning of the word 'was' such that, given the first, it was true that Lincoln is president, but given the second, it was never true that Lincoln is president, I should think you'd been corrupted by philosophy. No doubt one can think of outré meanings of 'was' on which it was never true that Lincoln is president. But there is no plausible candidate for its ordinary language meaning on which it was never true that Lincoln is president. This is because there is just *one* plausible candidate for the meaning of our ordinary language 'was', and given this meaning, it was true that Lincoln is president. So too with other tensed expressions. The words 'will' in 'the meeting will start at noon' and 'has been' in 'my watch has been malfunctioning' are univocal: linguistic convention together with whatever else it is that fixes meaning[11] has affixed just one semantic value to each of these ordinary language tensed expressions (presumably, a different one for each). What *is* the semantic value of these expressions as deployed in ordinary language? This is not an easy question. More important for present purposes is that they are univocal. In a slogan: tense is univocal. Call this the Univocality Thesis.

What can be said on behalf of this thesis? Here again, other than that it seems obviously true, I'm not sure.

2.4 The Argument for Presentism

The best reason for being a presentist, I think, is that presentism is the only metaphysic of time consistent with the foregoing metaphysical and linguistic commitments. I shall now try to show that, among the main alternative metaphysics of time, presentism alone satisfies these constraints.

My argument takes for granted that the following theories exhaust the options: presentism, static eternalism, and dynamic eternalism. Let me briefly explain the latter two positions. Eternalism, again, is the view that reality includes past, present, and future entities. Better: it's the thesis that our most inclusive domain of quantification includes entities at non-zero temporal distance from one another. Thus understood,

---

[11] For discussion of what, besides linguistic convention, fixes meaning, see Lewis (1983*b*, 1984) and Sider (2001, introd.).

eternalism is the opposite of presentism. Dynamic eternalism is the conjunction of eternalism and a dynamic or A-theoretic view of time.[12] Static eternalism is the conjunction of eternalism and a static or B-theoretic view of time. One holds a dynamic or A-theoretic view of time, I shall say, iff one subscribes to the following thesis:

> *Absolute Change Thesis.* Where *C* is the most inclusive class of events, either it was false that *C* is the most inclusive class of events or it will be false that *C* is the most inclusive class of events.

On the dynamic conception of time, then, the totality of events in existence changes over time. Not so on the static or B-theoretic conception. A static or B-theoretic conception of time, as I shall think of it, is any conception of time on which the Absolute Change Thesis is false.

My argument has three parts. First, I'll argue that static eternalism is inconsistent with the conjunction of endurantism and the Change Thesis. Then I'll argue that dynamic eternalism is inconsistent with the Univocality Thesis. Finally, I'll suggest that presentism is consistent with the conjunction of all three.

2.4.1 *Static Eternalism is Inconsistent with Endurantism and the Change Thesis*

Suppose for *reductio* that static eternalism, endurantism, and the Change Thesis are all true. The Change Thesis says, again, that according to i-descriptions of the past, I have properties and stand in relations which, according to the i-description of the present, I do not have and do not stand in. To fix ideas, let us think of i-descriptions of 'the past' and 'the present' in the following way. Let us suppose that the eternalist's past, present, and future entities are embedded in a *space-time*, a four-dimensional manifold of point-sized entities which contains or embeds all the objects and events of our spatio-temporal world. (We presuppose, then, a *substantival* view of space-time: the view that the quantifiers of the physicists' space-time theories range over an entity, space-time, which contains or embeds the objects and events of the physical world. Nothing crucial hangs on this: everything I say is easily recast in terms of a *relationalist* view of space-time, the view that all talk about space-time in our scientific theories is reducible to talk about the spatio-temporal properties of and relations among physical objects.) Say, then, that an i-description of 'the past' ('the present') is a maximally detailed description of the objects and events embedded in a past (present) *time-slice*, where a time-slice is a global three-dimensional spacelike hypersurface of space-time. (Set aside for now questions arising from relativistic physics like: past with respect to *whom*?)

---

[12] Broad's growing block theory (1923) is a version of dynamic eternalism. See, too, Tooley (1997) and McCall (1994).

A note about endurantism in the context of our space-time construal of eternalism. Endurantism says that spatio-temporal continuants persist through time but have no temporal extent. In the context of space-time eternalism, this amounts to the thesis that spatio-temporal continuants are three-dimensional objects which persist through space-time by exactly occupying or overlapping disjointed three-dimensional subregions of space-time at timelike separation from one another. Continuants, on this picture, are *multiply located* entities since they exactly occupy or overlap multiple, disjointed regions of space-time. (So continuants on this view are like David Armstrong's recurring universals which, if they exist, are multiply located constituents of spatio-temporal things; see Armstrong 1978a,b).

The Change Thesis, then, amounts to the claim that for some relation R[13] and for some i-descriptions d_1 and d_2 such that d_1 and d_2 exhaustively describe time-slices t_1 and t_2 respectively, according to d_1, I exist and stand in R, and according to d_2, I exist but do not stand in R. Suppose this claim true. Say too that I am an enduring object, multiply located at non-overlapping three-dimensional regions of space-time at timelike separation from one another. If so, then d_1 describes t_1 as containing a three-dimensional object identical with me which stands in R, and d_2 describes t_2 as containing a three-dimensional object identical with me which does not stand in R. If d_1 describes t_1 as containing something identical with me which stands in R, then quantifying over the occupants of t_1, something identical with me stands in R. Likewise, if d_2 describes t_2 as containing something identical with me which does not stand in R, then quantifying over the occupants of t_2, something identical with me does not stand in R. From this it follows that, quantifying over the occupants of both t_1 and t_2, something identical with me both stands in R and does not stand in R. But nothing could manage that! Static eternalism conjoined with endurantism and the Change Thesis yields contradiction.

Here I expect two rejoinders. First, you might object that this argument pays insufficient attention to *tense*. Suppose that t_2 is the present time and t_1 a past time. If d_1 describes t_1 as containing something which is identical with me and stands in R, then given that t_1 is past, we are entitled to infer only that, quantifying over the occupants of t_1, something identical with me *stood* in R. And if d_2 describes t_2 as containing something identical with me which does not stand in R, then given that t_2 is present, we can infer only that, quantifying over the occupants of t_2, something identical with me does not now stand in R. So from d_1 and d_2, we can infer only that, quantifying over the occupants of t_1 and t_2, something identical with me stood in R but does no longer. Since there's nothing contradictory about this, we see how to avoid the contradiction: simply take the tense of our verbs seriously.

But how does taking the tense of our verbs seriously help here? If I *stood* in R but do no longer, then given the Change Thesis and static eternalism, d_1, the

---

[13] For simplicity, I'll put the Change Thesis in terms of relations and drop talk of monadic properties.

i-description of a past time-slice t_1, describes me as a relatum of R, and d_2, the i-description of the present time-slice t_2, doesn't. Since (given endurantism) I occupy or overlap both t_1 and t_2 (or, for those worried that I'm not being sufficiently attentive to the tense of my verbs: I presently stand in the *occupies* or *overlaps* relation to both t_1 and t_2), we get the bizarre result that a maximally detailed description of t_1 describes me, *qua* overlapper of t_1, as a relatum of R, but a maximally detailed description of t_2 describes me, *qua* overlapper of t_2, as not standing in R. But how could this be? Conjoined twins Abby and Brittany share their legs in common. Let A be a maximally detailed description of Abby. A describes a shared leg as the right leg of Abby. Let B be a maximally detailed description of Brittany. Could it be that, according to B, the leg in question is *not* the right leg of Abby? Of course not. (Cf. Lewis 1986: 201.) Likewise, then, with d_1 and d_2.

Second rejoinder. Static eternalism *is* compatible with change. For, you might think, to change is to be F at some times and not at others, where F is a schematic term replaceable by any monadic predicate expression. But it's perfectly compatible with static endurantism that things endure and undergo change in this sense. For instance, some think that being F at a time-slice t is simply a matter of occupying t and bearing the F-at relation to it.[14] According to this proposal, to be fat at a time-slice t_1 and not at a time-slice t_2 is to occupy both t_1 and t_2 and bear the *fat-at* relation to the first but not the second. Since there is nothing contradictory about a thing's wholly occupying two time-slices and being, in this sense, fat at the one and not at the other, we see that static eternalism conjoined with endurantism is compatible with change.

But this argument is an *ignoratio elenchi*. For I did not argue that the conjunction of static eternalism with endurantism is inconsistent with the sort of change described in the previous paragraph. I argued, rather, that the conjunction of static eternalism and endurantism is incompatible with the Change Thesis. And a thing could occupy both t_1 and t_2 and bear the *fat-at* relation to the first but not to the second without changing in the sense specified by the Change Thesis.

Perhaps you'll reply that change, at least the sort given us by common sense, the sort one undergoes when one is F at one time and not at another, does not require the sort of change specified by the Change Thesis. If I occupy t_1 and t_2, bear the *fat-at* relation to one but not the other, then I change, even if there is no property F or relation R such that, according to a maximally detailed description of t_1, I have F or stand in R, but according to a maximally detailed description of t_2, I don't. Since change—the common-sense sort of change—is perfectly compatible with the

---

[14] See e.g. Mellor (1981: 111). There are other options. You might think that a thing is F at t iff it has the relativized or time-indexed property *being-F-at-t* (cf. van Inwagen 1990: 247; for discussion, see Hinchliff 1996; Merricks 1994; Rea 1998). Others propose that a thing is F at t iff it bears the three-term instantiation relation to *being F* and t (cf. van Inwagen 1990: 247 and Johnston 1987: 127–9; for discussion, see Hinchliff 1996; Merricks 1994; Lewis 1988; Haslanger 1989a; and Rea 1998).

conjunction of static eternalism and endurantism, it's of little interest that change *à la* the Change Thesis isn't.

I disagree. Give a maximally detailed description of any 1972 time-slice that contains a toddler-shaped region of space-time exactly filled by me. Compare that description with the i-description of the present time-slice. To my mind, it is simply incredible to suppose that these descriptions will represent me as having just the same properties and standing in just the same relations. Accordingly, I can make no sense of the idea that the Change Thesis is false. Given that I find endurantism an attractive theory of persistence, it's of great interest to me, anyway, that static eternalism, endurantism, and the Change Thesis are jointly incompatible.

2.4.2 *Dynamic Eternalism is Incompatible with the Univocality Thesis*

I make various assumptions. First, I shall suppose for conditional proof that dynamic eternalism is true. If so, then (i) the totality of events in existence changes over time in the sense specified by the Absolute Change Thesis and (ii) the spatio-temporal world is embedded in a space-time manifold and at least some parts of that world are at non-zero temporal distance from one another.

Next, I shall follow Roderick Chisholm (1990) in thinking of events as concrete things which occur iff something instantiates a property. We'll say that, for any x, the event x-being-F occurs at (is located at, exists at) a region R of space-time iff x is located at R and bears the having relation to F. Given the eternalist's picture and this account of events, the following seems hard to deny:

> *Event Thesis.* If for some y located at a past time-slice t, $y = x$-being-F, then x-being-F occurred at t.

To illustrate, the event *Lincoln-being-assassinated* is part of our past: something located in a past time-slice t is identical with it. It seems quite natural to say, then, that it occurred at t, where here (and in the statement of the thesis), we use the 'occurred' of ordinary language, as in 'the meeting occurred yesterday'.

Now, according to the dynamic eternalist, the totality of events in existence changes over time. Let C be the class which is presently the most inclusive class of events. Then dynamic eternalism says that it was false or will be false that C is the most inclusive class of events. Suppose it was false that C is the most inclusive class of events because it was false that C exists. It was false that C exists, say, because events which are now members of C have come into existence recently. (An event e has come into existence recently iff something is identical with e but it was the case not long ago that nothing in our most inclusive domain of quantification is, was, or will be identical with e.) Since (we shall suppose) classes have their members essentially, if events which are now members of C have come into existence recently, we get that it was false that C exists. To fix ideas, say that it was false exactly ten years ago that C exists.

Something x is *lonely*, say, iff x does not coexist with C—iff, for some y in our most inclusive domain of quantification, $y = x$, but for no z in that domain is it true that $z = C$. ('C', again, names that class which is presently the most inclusive class of events.) Something is *accompanied* iff it is false that it is lonely. So everything—quantifier wide open—is accompanied. But if we assume with the dynamic eternalist that it was false exactly ten years ago that C exists, we may infer that exactly ten years ago everything—quantifying unrestrictedly—was lonely.

Now, let Fred be some wholly past object which occupies a past time-slice t located exactly ten years before the present. (Say too that Fred is short-lived: he occupies *only t*.) Since everything, quantifying unrestrictedly, is accompanied, Fred is accompanied. That is, the having relation links Fred and the property *being accompanied*. Given our Chisholmian theory of events, we may infer that the event *Fred-being-accompanied* is located at t, exactly ten years in the past. Given this and the Event Thesis, we may infer that *Fred-being-accompanied* occurred exactly ten years ago.

But if, exactly ten years ago, everything was lonely (see the paragraph before last), then exactly ten years ago Fred was lonely. And if Fred was lonely exactly ten years ago—if, exactly ten years ago, Fred had the property of *being lonely*—then from our Chisholmian theory of events we may infer that exactly ten years ago there occurred the event *Fred-being-lonely*. So we get this: exactly ten years ago the events *Fred-being-lonely* and *Fred-being-accompanied* both occurred. But it should be clear that this is impossible. You might as well say that exactly ten years ago *the-stick-S-being-bent* occurred, as did *the-stick-S-being-straight*. What's to do?

I see two options. First option: postulate two tenses. *Fred-being-lonely* occurred exactly ten years ago; so did *Fred-being-accompanied*. That is, it was the case exactly ten years ago that *Fred-being-lonely* occurs; and it was the case exactly ten years ago that *Fred-being-accompanied* occurs. Both claims are true. In both cases, we use an ordinary language 'was'. But 'was' in ordinary language is equivocal (more generally, tense in ordinary language is equivocal). There's the 'was' we use—was$_1$—when we say truly that it was the case ten years ago that *Fred-being-lonely* occurs, and there's the 'was' we use—was$_2$—when we say truly that it was the case ten years ago that *Fred-being-accompanied* occurs. Each 'was' means something different, and they work in such a way that it is perfectly sensible to suppose both that it was$_1$ the case exactly ten ago that *Fred-being-lonely* occurs, and it was$_2$ the case exactly ten years ago that *Fred-being-accompanied* occurs. In brief, the Univocality Thesis is false.

Second option: reject the Event Thesis. We've supposed that if something located at a past time-slice t is the event *x-being-F*, then *x-being-F* occurred at t, where the 'occurred' in play here is the 'occurred' of ordinary language, as in 'the meeting occurred yesterday'. We avoid contradiction and the need for two tenses in ordinary language if we simply deny the inference from 'there is something identical with *x-being-F* located ten years ago' to '*x-being-F* occurred ten years ago'. There might be a technical, philosopher's sense of 'occurred' on which this inference holds, but given ordinary language use of the word, the inference fails.

I find the latter suggestion to be misguided. If an event is located in the past, then it follows quite obviously, I think, that this event occurred, in the ordinary sense of the word. How could there be past events which never occurred (in that ordinary sense of 'occurred')? By my lights, anyway, denying the Event Thesis is not a serious option.

This leaves the first option.[15] I can't see any other way for the dynamic eternalist to avoid contradiction. Thus I conclude that dynamic eternalism is incompatible with the Univocality Thesis.

2.4.3 *Presentism is Consistent with Endurantism, the Change Thesis, and the Univocality Thesis*

The presentist has no difficulty accommodating the conjunction of endurantism, the Change Thesis, and the Univocality Thesis. First, nothing about presentism implies that tensed expressions aren't univocal. Secondly, the presentist is free to suppose that among the present things are i-descriptions which presently misrepresent the world but *were* or *will be* such as to accurately represent it. The Change Thesis says that among the i-descriptions which were accurate descriptions of the world are i-descriptions that represent me as having properties and entering into relations distinct from those I'm represented as having and entering into by the i-description which now represents the world. Presentism implies nothing to the contrary. Finally, the thesis of endurantism says that a present thing *x* has persisted iff (i) *x* has no temporal extent (and never has), and (ii) for some *n*, it was the case *n* units of time ago that something is identical with *x*. Given presentism, nothing ever has a temporal extent. And it's perfectly consistent with presentism that the proposition that something is identical with me both is and was true.

The upshot: unlike its alternatives, presentism comports nicely with our foregoing metaphysical and linguistic commitments. For those of us who find these commitments attractive, this is good reason for believing presentism to be true. Not conclusive reason, however, since presentism's costs may be severe enough to outweigh this advantage. Many philosophers suppose that presentism's costs are severe indeed. In the next section I lay out what I take to be the strongest reasons for thinking so. I'll urge that presentism's costs have been greatly exaggerated.

---

[15] An option I do not consider is rejecting Chisholm's theory of events. I set this option aside since essentially the same argument can be run without Chisholm's theory. See e.g. Sider (2001; ch. 2).

3. The Price of Presentism

3.1 Presentism and Singular Propositions

Some propositions are *about* me. For example, the propositions *Crisp is a lousy chess player*, and *Alison married Crisp* are about me. So too with *the husband of Alison is a lousy chess player*: it is also about me. But the first propositions seem importantly different from the last. The first two, as it is sometimes put, are more *directly* about me than the last. What's to say here? What makes the first two propositions more directly about me than the last? It's not at all easy to specify. Rather than trying, let us take the distinction between these sorts of propositions as primitive and call a proposition which is directly about an individual—in the way that *Fischer is a good chess player* is directly about Fischer—a *singular* proposition.

Some philosophers suspect that singular propositions—some of them at any rate—spell trouble for presentism.[16] Call something *wholly past* if it used to exist, does not now exist, and won't exist. (The notion of *wholly future* is defined likewise.) Presentism entails that there are neither wholly past nor wholly future objects. But, it would appear, there are singular propositions about wholly past objects—e.g. *Lincoln was tall*—and maybe wholly future objects too—e.g. *Newman₁ is human*, where we stipulate that 'Newman₁' shall name the first person born next century.

This poses a problem for the presentist if we accept a widely held thesis about singular propositions. Following Alvin Plantinga (1983), let us think of *existentialism* as the thesis that singular propositions depend for their existence on the individuals they are about. We can put the thesis more precisely as follows. I shall follow George Bealer (1982) in thinking of '$[Fx]$' as a singular term such that (i) its referent is the singular proposition that x is F, and (ii) it can contain externally quantifiable variables—e.g. $\exists x\, \exists y(x = [Fy])$. I'll say too that the standard modal operators '$\Box$' and '$\diamond$' are one-place predicates which apply to singular terms like '$[Fx]$'. Thus armed, we can state existentialism more precisely as follows:

$Existentialism$ $\Box[\forall F\; \forall y\; \forall x_1, x_2, \ldots (y = [Fx_1, x_2, \ldots]) \rightarrow \Box[\exists z(z = y) \rightarrow$
$.\exists v_1(v_1 = x_1)\,.\,\exists v_2(v_2 = x_2)\,.\,\ldots])].$

In English: necessarily, for every F and y and every $x_1, x_2, \ldots$ such that y is the proposition that $Fx_1, x_2, \ldots$, necessarily, y exists only if $x_1, x_2, \ldots$ also exist.[17]

To see why the presentist has trouble if existentialism is true, suppose that no present object is Lincoln. Given presentism, this is to say that *nothing* is Lincoln. Though it was the case that something is identical with Lincoln, this is true no longer. But given existentialism, if this is so, it follows that *there are no singular propositions*

---

[16] See e.g. Fitch (1994). For discussion, see Markosian (forthcoming), Sider (1999), and Rea, Ch. 9 in this volume.

[17] For ease of exposition, I employ second-order quantification (quantification into the predicate position), but everything I say is easily recast in terms of a first-order language.

about Lincoln. And isn't this absurd? Surely there *are* singular propositions about Lincoln; I've just expressed several of them. We believe that Lincoln was the sixteenth president, that he was wise, that he was tall, etc. In so believing, we grasp singular propositions about him (or, at any rate, singular propositions which were about him). This is utterly obvious. So the presentist faces a dilemma. Either she must deny that there are singular propositions about wholly past and wholly future objects, or she must reject existentialism. The first horn of the dilemma is unattractive: surely there are singular propositions about the wholly past, e.g. *Lincoln was tall.* But the second horn is no better. Existentialism, these days, is de rigueur. This is because, on the usual account of singular propositions, they are non-mereological fusions which contain as *constituents* the objects they are about. Like sets, they are thought to depend for their existence on their constituents.

Philosophers have responded in different ways.[18] Theodore Sider (not himself a presentist) thinks that the presentist should grant that there are no singular propositions about the wholly past and that sentences like 'Lincoln was tall' do not express truth. Though the presentist can't help herself to the *truth* of sentences like 'Lincoln was tall', says Sider, she can regard them as *quasi-true* ('Lincoln is tall' is quasi-true if there is a true proposition that would have been true and would have entailed the truth of 'Lincoln is tall' had four-dimensionalism been true; Sider 1999: 332–3). It's a good thing for a philosophical theory if it can 'save' the truth of our ordinary talk and thought about the world. Theories which can't pay a theoretical price. The price isn't high, though, if they can at least save the quasi-truth of our ordinary talk and thought. And, thinks Sider, presentism does the latter.

I offer the presentist a different (and I think better[19]) reply. I grant that the presentist must either reject singular propositions about the wholly past and future or reject existentialism. And I grant that doing the former is costly. But I deny that rejection of existentialism is costly. De rigueur or not, existentialism is surely false.

---

[18] See e.g. Markosian (forthcoming) and (for a non-presentist reply on behalf of the present) Sider (1999).

[19] Sider's notion of quasi-truth raises interesting questions. For instance, he seems to suggest that a sentence S is quasi-true iff it satisfies an instance of the following schema:

> S is quasi-true iff there is a true proposition p such that, were O true, p would have been true and would have entailed the truth of S,

where O states some thesis of ontology like presentism, four-dimensionalism, or realism about propositions (Sider 1999: 343–7). But consider this thesis of ontology: goblinism, the thesis that there are necessary, nefarious beings—goblins—bent on the destruction of humanity. Goblinism is, if true, necessarily true. Consider the proposition that goblins would have existed were goblinism true. This proposition is true, would have been true had goblinism been true, and would have entailed the truth of 'Goblins exist'. Thus, by Sider's definition, 'Goblins exist' is quasi-true.

Now I'm unclear on what the benefits of quasi-truth are. The idea is supposed to be that ordinary thought and talk are respected if we show them to be quasi-true. But do we really respect ordinary talk and thought if they turn out on our theory to be no better off than claims like 'Goblins exist'? You tell me that 'Lincoln was more than an inch tall' is not true. How does it help assuage my incredulity by reassuring me that, although this sentence isn't true, it is quasi-true, in just the same way that 'Goblins exist' is?

This is because it has the outrageous implication that there are no contingent objects. But you and I are contingent objects—we might not have existed; so existentialism is to be rejected.

Why think that existentialism has this implication? Here is one reason.[20] Suppose for *reductio* that there is a contingent object c. Let 'F' name some property had by c so that $[Fc]$ is a true, singular proposition about c. Existentialism, recall, says that:

$$\Box[\forall F \; \forall y \; \forall x_1, x_2, \ldots (y \; = \; [Fx_1, x_2, \ldots] \; \rightarrow \; \Box[\exists z(z \; = \; y) \; \rightarrow \; . \, \exists v_1(v_1 \; = \; x_1) \; . \, \exists v_2(v_2 = x_2) \ldots .])].$$

Together with a few truths of modal and quantificational logic, it implies:

(1) $\Box[\exists z(z = [Fc]) \rightarrow \exists v(v = c)]$.

And (1) together with a thesis I'll call the Necessity Thesis implies

(2) $[\exists z(z = [Fc]) \rightarrow \exists v(v = c)]$ is true in every possible world.

The Necessity Thesis says that, for any proposition p, if $\Box p$ then p is true in every possible world—where p is true in a world W iff, necessarily, were W actual, p would be true. As we'll see below, this initially plausible thesis is contentious. But let us accept it for now and move on.

(2) together with a thesis I'll call the Truth Thesis implies

(3) $\Box[\exists y(y = [\exists z(z = [Fc]) \rightarrow \exists v(v = c)])]$.

The Truth Thesis says that for any world W and any proposition p, if p is true in W then p exists in W. This thesis is very plausible. For a proposition p is true in W iff, necessarily, were W actual, p would be true. But it's exceedingly hard to see how a proposition could be true without existing. So it seems that, necessarily, were p true, p would exist, and hence that p is true in W iff, necessarily, were W actual, p would exist. That is, p is true in W iff p exists in W. So, if $[\exists z(z = [Fc]) \rightarrow \exists v(v = c)]$ is true in every world, then by the Truth Thesis, we get that it exists in every world—or, alternatively, that, necessarily, it exists.

Now, notice that $[\exists z(z = [Fc]) \rightarrow \exists v(v = c)]$ is a singular proposition about c. Application of existentialism to it yields

(4) $\Box[\exists w(w = [\exists z(z = [Fc]) \rightarrow \exists v(v = c)]) \rightarrow \exists v(v = c)]$.

And (4) together with (3) implies

(5) $\Box[\exists v(v = c)]$,

the denial of our assumption that c is an object which exists but might not have. This completes our *reductio*.

---

[20] The essentials of the argument to follow are found in Plantinga (1983); see, too, Bealer (1993, 1998).

There is a standard objection to this sort of argument.[21] It starts from the idea that there are two types of necessity, weak and strong. Strong necessity attaches to a proposition p when p is true in every possible world—when p is such that every way things could have turned out is a way in which p is true. A proposition p can be weakly necessary even if it's not the case that no matter how things should have gone, p would have been true—even if it's not the case that p is true in every possible world.

Armed with these two types of necessity, the objector puts the following dilemma against our anti-existentialism argument. The necessity in premiss (1)—the claim that $\Box[\exists z(z = [Fc]) \rightarrow \exists v(v = c)]$—is either weak or strong. If weak, then the move to premiss (2) is illegitimate, since the Necessity Thesis is false interpreted in terms of weak necessity. Again, it says that for any proposition p, if $\Box p$ then p is true in every world. This is true only when interpreted in terms of strong necessity. But if the necessity in premiss (1) is strong necessity, then we've no justification for asserting it. I say that (1) is implied by existentialism. But which necessity is expressed by the embedded '$\Box$' in existentialism? My opponent is likely to insist that it is weak necessity. So read, existentialism does not imply (1).

In brief: (1)'s necessity is either strong or weak. If weak, the inference to premiss (2) is illegitimate; if strong, (1) is unmotivated. Either way, the argument is no good.

How strong is this reply to our anti-existentialism argument? *Very* strong, if there is a viable notion of weak necessity in the offing. Thus far we've said only that a proposition can be weakly necessary even if it's not true in every world. But more needs to be said. What exactly is weak necessity?

Here I think my opponent is in trouble. So far as I'm aware, no one has been able to produce an informative analysis of weak necessity. We could take the notion of weak necessity as primitive, but this seems to me a bad way to proceed. A reasonable requirement on the introduction of primitives into the ideology of our theories is that we *understand* them, that we have some grasp on what they are to mean. But I do not understand the notion of primitive weak necessity. I think I understand well enough primitive strong necessity, the sort that attaches to a proposition p when, no matter how things should have gone, p would have been true. Primitive weak necessity, on the other hand, is mysterious to me—and I suspect I'm not alone here.

The usual approach is to analyse weak necessity in terms of Kit Fine's distinction between *inner* and *outer* truth or Robert Adams's distinction between truth *in* a world and truth *at* a world (see Fine 1981: 196–201; 1985: 163; Adams 1981). (Fine and Adams seem to be talking about precisely the same distinction. I'll use Adams's terminology.) A proposition p is true *in* a world W iff it is strongly necessarily that W obtains only if p exists and is true. But consider the proposition *Socrates does not exist* and let W_s be a world according to which there is no Socrates. Given

---

[21] For a formidable version of this objection, see Fine (1985).

existentialism, *Socrates does not exist* is not true *in* W_s. But still, we want to say, there's a sense in which it accurately describes what goes on in W_s. The language of truth *at* a world is intended to express the relationship which holds between a proposition p and a world W when, whether or not p is true *in* W, it accurately describes what goes on in W in the way that *Socrates does not exist* accurately describes what goes on in W_s.

The true in–true at distinction in hand, we can analyse weak necessity as truth *at* every world and think of strong necessity as truth *in* every world. The trouble is that, thus far, we *don't* have the true in–true at distinction in hand. In particular, we don't have a clear concept of truth *at* a world. I suggested that p is true at W when it accurately describes what goes on in W, in the way that *Socrates does not exist* accurately describes what goes on in W_s. But this isn't terribly informative. The most obvious sense in which *Socrates does not exist* accurately describes what goes on in W_s is that, were W_s to be actual, *Socrates does not exist* would be true. But the existentialist denies that *Socrates does not exist* would be true were W_s actual.[22] What else might it mean to claim of *Socrates does not exist* that it accurately describes what goes on in W_s? I have no idea.

What we need, then, is an informative analysis of truth *at* a world. And this we do not have. All attempts to analyse the notion of truth at a world I'm aware of either presuppose the notion of weak necessity or yield wildly counter-intuitive results. We could take the notion of truth at a world as primitive, but here again, this seems to me a bad way to proceed: I, at any rate, haven't the slightest idea what the notion means.

By my lights, the prospects for a reductive account of weak necessity are bleak. Since I don't understand the notion of weak necessity taken as a primitive (and I suspect no one else does either), I think we're justified in rejecting the foregoing objection to our anti-existentialist argument on the grounds that no one understands its central concept.

There are other ways of replying to our anti-existentialism argument, but none, I think, fares any better than the above line of reply. Existentialism has the outrageous implication that there are no contingent objects. The presentist pays no steep price by rejecting it.[23]

---

[22] Well, at any rate, the existentialist *should* deny that *Socrates does not exist* would be true were W_s actual. She does deny that this proposition would *exist* were W_s actual. I suppose she could think, however, that *Socrates does not exist* would be true but non-existent were W_s actual. But this is a counter-intuitive view—*very* counter-intuitive. How could a proposition manage to be true but fail to exist? Isn't this like supposing that Fred could fail to exist but nevertheless manage to be fat?

[23] What's to say, then, about the popular view of singular propositions on which they are complexes built up out of properties, relations, and the objects they are about? Though there are various approaches one could take, the best way to be an anti-existentialist, I think, is found in Bealer (1998). On this view, propositions—singular or no—are *sui generis* abstract entities which have no parts, members, or constituents. They do not represent by virtue of their structure; they have none. Rather, they represent by virtue of various primitive logical relations—e.g. singular predication—they bear

3.2 Presentism and True Singular Propositions about the Past

Here is a truism: the singular proposition that John is tall predicates of John the property *being tall*. As we might put it, the proposition that John is tall bears the *singular predication* relation to John and the property *being tall*. Likewise, the proposition that John is taller than Mary bears the singular predication relation to John, Mary, and the *is taller than* relation. I shall take this relation as undefined and presuppose that it is governed by the following principle of singular predication:

(PSP) $\Box[\forall p \forall xs \forall R(p$ singularly predicates R of the $xs \rightarrow \Box[p \rightarrow \exists zs$ (the zs are the $xs)])]$.[24]

PSP is an exceedingly plausible principle. Could *John is tall* have been true if there were no John? Could John be taller than Mary if there were no John or no Mary? Of course not! (What about *John has the property of non-existence*? Isn't this a counter-example to PSP? I think not. Though it might have been false that John exists, John could not have had the property of non-existence.) PSP is plausible so I shall take it as true. I offer no argument on its behalf since (*a*) I don't know of any, and (*b*) if it is false, the objection to presentism I'm about to develop is a non-starter.

PSP makes trouble for the presentist. Consider *Lincoln was tall*. The presentist who rejects existentialism can countenance the *existence* of such a proposition. But given PSP, she can't countenance its *truth*. For *Lincoln was tall*, one thinks, singularly predicates *having been tall* of Lincoln—or if it doesn't now, it did. But then given PSP, it entails the existence of Lincoln. Since the presentist does not believe in Lincoln, she must therefore deny that Lincoln was tall. But isn't this crazy? Lincoln was, after all, tall. By the same line of reasoning, the presentist is committed to rejecting all manner of obviously true singular propositions: e.g. *Lincoln was taller than an inch*, *Caroline was born to JFK and Jackie*, *Clinton belongs to the party to which FDR belonged*. If presentism requires us to give up such obvious truths, then so much the worse for presentism.[25]

---

to *inter alia* one another, concrete objects, properties, and relations. See Bealer (1998) for further discussion.

[24] Here I employ *plural* quantification. For the uninitiated, '$\forall xs(Fxs)$' may be thought of as an abbreviation for 'it is true of any things whatsoever that they are such that they are F'; '$\forall xs \forall y(xsRy)$' may be read as 'it is true of any things$_x$ whatsoever that they$_x$ are such that it is true of any thing$_y$ whatsoever that it$_y$ is such that they$_x$ bear R to it$_y$'. (In the latter case, we index variables to our pronouns to make clear which pronouns go together.) For discussion, see van Inwagen (1990: 25–8).

[25] A similar argument can be run with non-singular propositions like *the fourteenth president of the United States was inaugurated before the twenty-third president of the United States* and an analogue of PSP built for descriptive propositions. I'll treat only the singular proposition version of the argument; what I say in the sequel applies equally well, I think, to the argument framed in terms of descriptive propositions.

I reply by denying that the singular propositions of the previous paragraph are obvious truths. Take *Lincoln was tall*. There are two closely related propositions here:

(6) Lincoln was such as to be tall,

where (6) singularly predicates the property of having been tall of Lincoln; and

(7) *WAS* (Lincoln is tall),

where (7) is a *de dicto* proposition predicating past truth of the proposition *Lincoln is tall*. (Note that (7) predicates no property of Lincoln, and given the denial of existentialism, is perfectly compatible with his non-existence.) Since the presentist thinks that our most inclusive domain of quantification no longer includes Lincoln, she must reject (6). But she need not reject (7): given that she denies existentialism, it is perfectly compatible with her ontology.

(7), let us agree, is obviously true, something for which we have prodigious historical evidence. We've many photographs of Lincoln and written records about him which, taken together, make (7) highly likely. What of (6)? Do our many photos of Lincoln and written records about him make *it* highly likely? They do not. Let *E* be an exhaustive description of those photos and written records which together make it highly likely that (7) is true. Since (6) entails

(8) for some x, x is, was, or will be identical with Lincoln,

we know that (6) is no more likely on *E* than (8). So the question is: how likely is (8) on *E*? It is not likely at all. Suppose I, a presentist, and you, a four-dimensionalist, have the following philosophical dispute. I grant that it was the case that Lincoln exists, but I deny that he is still included in our most inclusive domain of quantification. That domain, I say, includes only present things; since Lincoln ceased to exist some time ago, our widest quantificational domain no longer includes him. You disagree, insisting that our most inclusive domain of quantification *does* still include Lincoln. Our most inclusive domain includes past, present, and future things, you argue, and thus still includes Lincoln.

Now, would it shed any light whatsoever on our dispute to learn of the photos and written records which together make it highly likely that (7) is true? That is, would the truth of *E* confirm your thesis over mine, or vice versa? I should think not. *E* isn't the right sort of evidence for resolving a dispute like ours. It is good evidence indeed for (7). But that claim is not under dispute; we both grant it. Our dispute is over (8), and *E* isn't evidence one way or the other about this. *E*, as we might put it, is evidentially neutral with respect to (8): (8) is as likely as not on *E*. If so, then since (6) entails (8), it follows that (6) is not likely on *E*.

Similar reasoning applies to the other singular propositions considered above. So we've plenty of historical evidence for

(9) Caroline is such that *WAS*(she is born to JFK and Jackie),

where (9) predicates of Caroline the property of being an x such that the proposition that x is born to JFK and Jackie was true. ((9), notice, is perfectly compatible with presentism. It entails the existence of Caroline and *Caroline is born to JFK and Jackie*, but—given the denial of existentialism—does not entail the existence of JFK and Jackie.) We don't have good evidence, however, for

(10) Caroline bears R to JFK and Jackie,

where R is the relation x bears to y and z iff x was born to y and z. Likewise, we've excellent evidence for

(11) Clinton belongs to a party P such that WAS(FDR belongs to P).

But we don't have good evidence at all for

(12) Clinton bears R^* to FDR,

where R^* is the relation x bears to y iff x belongs to a political party to which y belonged.

As best I can tell, PSP does not commit the presentist to the denial of any obviously true singular propositions about the wholly past or future.

3.3 Presentism and Relativity Physics

It is widely believed that presentism is incompatible with special and general relativity.[26] Since these are paradigmatically successful scientific theories, if presentism *is* incompatible with them, its price is high indeed.

So is there an incompatibility here? Sadly enough, it seems so. Special and general relativity, as usually construed, are space-time theories: theories which attempt to describe the trajectories of various sorts of physical particle—e.g. free particles, particles acted on by gravity, particles acted by electromagnetic forces—in terms of four-dimensional space-time models. We can think of a space-time theory T as having two parts. First, there's a set of equations describing the trajectories of various types of physical particle. These determine a class of space-time models, where each model of T is an n-tuple $\langle M, \Phi_1, \ldots, \Phi_m \rangle$ such that M is a four-dimensional manifold of points and $\Phi_1, \ldots, \Phi_m$ are *geometrical objects* (set-theoretical mappings) defined on M which represent the geometrical structure of M. Secondly, there's a set of propositions—following van Fraasen (e.g. 1987), the *theoretical hypotheses* of T—which describe the relationship between the models of T and the spatio-temporal world. On the usual approach, special and general

---

[26] For discussion, see Godfrey-Smith (1979); Sider (2001: 42–52); Monton (2001); Putnam (1967); Rietdijk (1966, 1976); Maxwell (1985); Sklar (1974, 1981); Rea (1998); Stein (1968, 1970, 1991); Savitt (1994, 2000); Hinchliff (1996, 2000); and Callender (2000).

relativity include a four-dimensionalist theoretical hypothesis,[27] a proposition to the effect that the models of the theory are either (*a*) isomorphic representations of space-time, the four-dimensional manifold of places-at-a-time in which all spatio-temporal entities—past, present, and future—are embedded, or (*b*) isomorphs of physically possible space-times.

There is an obvious sense, then, in which presentism is incompatible with special and general relativity as usually construed: on the standard construal, they postulate the existence of a four-dimensional space-time embedding past, present, and future entities. The presentist denies there is such a thing.

But is this a substantive incompatibility? Could we just alter the theoretical hypotheses of special and general relativity, replacing their four-dimensionalist theoretical hypotheses with a presentist alternative? The idea would be this. Instead of thinking of the space-time models of relativity as isomorphic representations of a four-dimensional spatio-temporal world, we suppose that only a *part* of each model represents by isomorphism. For each model, we suppose a foliation or slicing of the model's manifold into a series of three-dimensional spacelike hypersurfaces. We then construe *one* member of this series as an isomorph of the *three*-dimensional world; other members of the series are construed as representations of past and future states of this 3-world. The entire series represents the evolution of the 3-world through time.

To be sure, this is not the usual way of proceeding, but is it a *substantive* departure from orthodox relativity? Most philosophers and physicists, I think, would answer this question in the affirmative. Adding a presentist theoretical hypothesis to relativity requires adding a privileged foliation to our space-time models: for each model, recall, we specify a particular slicing of the model's manifold into a series of spacelike hyperspaces and think of the resulting series of 3-spaces as uniquely representing the evolution of our 3-world through time. But many would say that adding a preferred foliation to relativity means rejecting both the letter and the spirit of the theory. Einstein's most important insight, it is commonly thought, is the idea that there *is* no privileged foliation of space-time (or our models thereof), no distinguished way of carving it (them) into spaces and times. Adding a presentist theoretical hypothesis to relativity means rejecting this core insight of Einsteinian relativity.

The upshot: presentism is incompatible with relativity at both a surface and a deeper level. Most philosophers, I think, regard this as a knockdown argument against presentism. If being a presentist requires the rejection of orthodox relativity, then being a presentist is simply too costly.

But what exactly *is* the cost paid by the presentist who adds to relativity a presentist theoretical hypothesis in the way described above? I grant that doing so amounts to

---

[27] I borrow this way of putting things from Monton (2001).

the introduction of a preferred foliation, and that this requires abandoning a central principle of relativity. But what precisely is the cost of abandoning this principle? What price do we pay if we add a preferred foliation to our space-time models?

One worry is that such a foliation is empirically undetectable.[28] Let $\langle M, \Phi_1, \ldots, \Phi_m \rangle$ be the general relativistic model that (together with a preferred foliation) represents the evolution of our three-dimensional universe through time. The trouble is that we have no way of determining empirically which 3-slice of M represents the present state of the world, and hence which foliation of M represents the evolution of the world through time. But, some might suggest, if we've no way of detecting a preferred foliation, we've no business postulating its existence.

But why think this? The suggestion is that there's something untoward about postulating the existence of something we have no way of detecting empirically. But in these post-positivism days, why think that?

One might worry that the postulation of a preferred foliation amounts to the postulation of an explanatorily superfluous entity, since we can formulate kinematic and dynamic laws of motion without recourse to this extra space-time structure. The price of adding a preferred foliation to relativity, then, is the price paid by any theory which postulates explanatorily superfluous entities.

I reply that even if it were true that the evolution of all physical quantities can be described without recourse to a preferred foliation,[29] it wouldn't follow that a preferred foliation is superfluous *tout court*. For the presentist, a primary function of our space-time models is to represent the historical development of the three-dimensional universe through time. But they can play this role only if they contain a preferred foliation.

Another worry: relativistic physics and its egalitarianism about reference frames has been highly successful as a physical theory. Doesn't this strongly suggest that it gives us an accurate picture of the structure of space-time? (See Maudlin 1996: 296–8.)

By way of reply, this much seems plausible: the success of relativity at predicting and explaining various phenomena strongly suggests that it gives us an accurate picture of the temporal and spatial metrical structure of the universe. But the presentist need not deny this. Let $\langle M, \Phi_1, \ldots, \Phi_m \rangle$ be a general relativistic space-time model which (together with a preferred foliation) represents the evolution of our 3-world through time. The presentist might suppose (a) that the material world is embedded in an evolving, variably curved 3-space constituted by points at spacelike separation from one another, and (b) that this 3-space successively takes on

---

[28] For discussion, see Maudlin (1996: 295–6).

[29] Whether the evolution of *all* physical quantities can be described without appeal to a preferred foliation is a matter of controversy. If the Bohmians are right, or if some version of fixed foliation quantum gravity turns out to be right (see Monton 2001), the evolution of at least some quantities *does* depend on a privileged foliation.

a metrical structure isomorphic to successive 3-slices of M. She can suppose further that temporal duration in our 3-world is trajectory-relative in the way suggested by general relativity, so that the lapse of time measured by any particle p is given by the timelike distance along the curve through M representing p's history. Given these assumptions, the spatial and temporal metrical properties of the presentist's evolving 3-world will be exactly those predicted by general relativity.

So the success of relativity suggests that it gives us an accurate picture of the metrical structure of the universe. Thus far, the presentist can agree. But does it likewise suggest that the correct theoretical hypothesis for relativity is a four-dimensionalist rather than a presentist hypothesis? I can't see why it would. Adding a presentist hypothesis (and thus a preferred foliation) to relativity yields a theory which, given current science, is empirically equivalent to standard relativity. It's hard to see why the modified theory would differ from the standard version in predictive or explanatory power. But if there is no difference on this point between the two theories, then the predictive and explanatory success of standard relativity is no argument against presentistic relativity.

And a final worry: the discussion thus far assumes that relativistic space-time models can be foliated, that they can be 'sliced' into a family of global spacelike hypersurface. But it's a well-known fact about general relativity that not all of its models are capable of foliation. (Gödel 1949, for instance, proposed a widely discussed model of general relativity which cannot be foliated.) Since adding a presentist theoretical hypothesis to general relativity requires that its models be foliatable, don't we have a problem here?

We do not. For we need not suppose that adding a presentist theoretical hypo-thesis to general relativity requires that *all* of its models be foliatable. The sensible presentist won't be dogmatic about the logical or even the physical necessity of pre-sentism. She can grant with equanimity that there are logically and even physically possible worlds in which four-dimensionalism is true, and that some of the latter are constituted by space-times which can't be sliced into a family of global spacelike hypersurfaces. In such worlds, presentism is false. So what? There would be trouble for the presentist if the space-time models of *our* world couldn't be foliated. But the usual assumption among physicists is that the models of our world *can* be foliated.[30]

I can't see any reason for thinking that the cost of adding a presentist theoretical hypothesis to relativity is high. Doing so changes the theory in important ways, I grant. But the resulting theory is empirically equivalent to the old theory, and, as best I can tell, carries no unacceptable implications.[31]

---

[30] The reader should note that most presentists think of presentism as necessarily true if true. If they're right, my response to the previous paragraph's worry is in trouble. Since I am not inclined to regard presentism as a necessary truth, however, I shall not worry about this.

[31] For a related approach to these issues, see Craig (2001).

3.4 Presentism and the Grounding Objection

It is sometimes charged against the presentist that her ontology lacks the resources to *ground* past and future truths.[32] It is a plausible principle that contingent truths like *Lincoln existed* require the existence of some thing or things in the world which *account for, ground,* or *make true* the truths in question. But what among the present things—which, according to the presentist, exhaust reality—grounds a truth like *Lincoln existed*? Says the objector: nothing. So presentists face an uncomfortable dilemma: reject the principle that contingent truths need grounding or give up truths like *Lincoln existed*. Either way, presentism is pricey.

Says the objector: truths require grounding! But what does this talk of *grounding* amount to? What is it for a truth to be grounded and why do truths need grounding anyway?

A standard answer to these questions proceeds from the *truthmaker axiom*. John Fox states the principle nicely: 'By the truthmaker axiom I mean the axiom that for every truth there is a truthmaker; by a truthmaker for A, I mean something whose very existence entails A' (Fox 1987: 189). Some comments. First, to say of a thing x that its existence entails some proposition p is to say that every possible world where x exists is a world where p is true. Secondly, not every truthmaker theorist will think that each truth requires a *single* truthmaker. As Greg Restall points out, it's difficult to see what single thing could make true the proposition that Arvo Pärt's *Magnificat* has been performed at least three times (Restall 1996: 332). Better to say that each truth has a truthmaker or *truthmakers*. And thirdly, the role of truthmaker is typically filled by Russellian facts or states of affairs—non-mereological[33] complexes built up out of properties, relations, and particulars.[34]

These points noted, we can tighten up Fox's formulation of the truthmaker axiom by stating it thus:

> *Truthmaker.* $\Box[\forall p(p \rightarrow \exists xs \Box[\text{the } xs \text{ exist} \rightarrow p])]$.

A truth is *grounded*, then, when it has a truthmaker, some thing or things whose existence entails the truth in question. According to Truthmaker, all truths need truthmakers. Why think this? Why subscribe to Truthmaker? This is a hard question. Typically, I think, philosophers endorse it because they're committed to a certain version of the correspondence theory of truth. On this version of the theory, whenever something is true, some thing or things in the world make it true. Truthmaker, you might suppose, is a natural way of fleshing this doctrine out.

---

[32] See e.g. Sider (2001, ch. 2). For discussion, see Keller (forthcoming); Bigelow (1996); and Rea, Ch. 9 in this volume.

[33] So Armstrong: 'States of affairs hold their constituents together in a non-mereological form of composition, a form of composition that even allows the possibility of having different states of affairs with identical constituents' (1997: 118).

[34] Though, for an alternative ontology for truthmakers, see Mulligan *et al.* (1984).

Given plausible assumptions, Truthmaker spells trouble for the presentist. It is an exceedingly plausible truth about the past that woolly mammoths existed. But, says the objector, what among the present things is such that its existence entails this proposition? Isn't it *possible* that things have been just as they presently are and there have been no woolly mammoths? (For example, isn't it possible that things be just as they presently are except that God created the world five minutes ago?) Of course it is. It follows that nothing among the present things ensures the truth of the proposition that woolly mammoths existed. Given Truthmaker and the presentist's claim that the present things exhaust reality, then, it must not be true that woolly mammoths existed. Indeed, most of what we ordinarily take to be true about the past and future looks to be called into question by this line of reasoning. If the presentist must reject most of what we hold true about the past and future, so much the worse for presentism.

As it stands, however, Truthmaker is controversial. What of truths like *all ravens are black* or *there are no unicorns*? Is there some thing whose existence entails the truth of these claims? Many join David Lewis in supposing that such truths 'are true not because things of some kind *do* exist, but rather because counterexamples *don't* exist' (Lewis 1992: 216).

Consider, too, truths like *John is tall*. John's existence doesn't entail it; nor does the joint existence of John and the property *being tall*. So what does? The usual story has it that the fact *John's being tall*—the non-mereological fusion of John and the property *being tall*—does the job. But what could these non-mereological fusions be? It's not at all obvious that there are such things. Without them, though, the truth that John is tall looks to be a counter-instance to Truthmaker.

So Truthmaker is controversial. Should the presentist reject it? I don't know, but it doesn't really matter since there is a less controversial version of Truthmaker, one which works just as well in an objection to presentism and is vastly more difficult to deny.

David Lewis (2001: 609 ff.) and John Bigelow (1988: 133) formulate this weaker version of Truthmaker as the claim that *truth supervenes on being*, where this means that truth supervenes on what things there are, the properties they instantiate, and the relations they enter into. Put differently: there could be no difference in what is true without there also being a difference in what things exist and which properties and relations they instantiate. Regimented in terms of possible worlds, this principle becomes

> *Supervenience.* For any proposition p and worlds w and w^*, if p is true in w and not in w^*, then (a) according to w, something exists in it but not in w^* (or vice versa), or (b) according to w, some objects instantiate a property or relation in it but not in w^* (or vice versa). (Cf. Lewis 2001: 612.)

Supervenience looks, on reflection, to be obviously true—so obvious as to be trivial. Consider what it would take for the principle to be false. It would fail if (*a*) there were distinct worlds w_1 and w_2 such that, according to each, the very same things exist in w_1 as in w_2 and instantiate the very same relations and properties in w_1 as they do in w_2, but (*b*) for some proposition p, p is true in w_1 but not in w_2. But are two worlds in which the very same things exist, exemplifying the same properties and relations, really *two*? It's a plausible principle, I think, that for any possible worlds w_1 and w_2, w_1 is distinct from w_2 iff w_1 represents what things exist and which properties and relations they instantiate differently than w_2.[35] Given this principle, Supervenience is trivial since no possible world w and no proposition p is such that p is true and not true in w.

So Supervenience is plausible, indeed trivial. But presentism looks to contravene it. Again, it's an obvious truth that woolly mammoths existed. Since present things could have been just as they are and woolly mammoths not have existed, this truth does not supervene on what present things there are and which properties and relations they instantiate. But according to presentism, the present things exhaust reality. So this truth does not supervene on what things there are and which properties and relations they instantiate. So given presentism, Supervenience is false. So much the worse, then, for presentism.

Let us say that the foregoing bit of reasoning captures the grounding objection to presentism. As stated, the objection depends on two principles, Supervenience and a principle I shall call *Temporal Combinatorialism*, the principle that

> Things could have been just as they are at present and the past have been different.

Presentists will likely object to the latter. Let me briefly say something about two ways of doing so.

First way: *Obviously* things could not have been just as they are and the past have been different because among the present things are propositions about the past— e.g. *dinosaurs roamed the earth*—and among their properties are properties like *being true*. Surely things couldn't have been presently such that this very proposition has the truth-value it does and dinosaurs not have roamed the earth. Likewise for all other truths about the past. Temporal Combinatorialism is trivially false.

True enough. But this isn't a very satisfying objection. Temporal Combinatorialism is easily reformulated so as to avoid this problem. When the sceptic proposes that things could have been just as they are and the past different, she presumably does not mean to suggest that propositions about the past could have had the same truth-values and the past have been different. The principle she has in mind is something more like

> *Temporal Combinatorialism'*. Things could have been just as they are at present (ignoring the present distribution of truth and falsity and grue-like properties

---

[35] Alternatively: it's a plausible principle that no two worlds are logically equivalent.

defined from truth and falsity using quantifiers, Boolean operators, and the like[36]) and the past have been different.

Though I think this principle is false, it's not obviously false in the way that Temporal Combinatorialism is.

Recall the logic of the grounding objection: things could have been just as they are and the past different (Temporal Combinatorialism); so past truths (or many of them at any rate) don't supervene on the present things, their properties, and relations; so, given presentism, they don't supervene on being; so, given presentism, Supervenience is false. But given our reformulated principle of Temporal Combinatorialism, this argument no longer works. The trouble occurs 'at the step from Temporal Combinatorialism' to the claim that past truths don't supervene on present things, their properties, and relations ('the present', for short). It's of course consistent with Temporal Combinatorialism' that past truths *do* supervene on the present (Temporal Combinatorialism' only gives us that past truths don't supervene on the present *ignoring the present distribution of truth and falsity and grue-like properties built from them*).

No deep problem here, though; the argument is easily repaired. The guiding intuition behind Supervenience is that possible worlds which disagree about which propositions are true won't disagree *only* about which propositions are true. Worlds that disagree about truths, one thinks, will also disagree about which things exist and/or which properties (other than *being true*, *being false*, and the like) they instantiate. We might restate the principle, then, as something like:

> *Supervenience'*. For any proposition p and worlds w and w^*, if p is true in w and not in w^*, then (a) according to w, something exists in it but not in w^* (or vice versa), or (b) according to w, some objects instantiate a property or relation (other than truth and falsity and grue-like properties built from them) in it but not in w^* (or vice versa).

This principle is a bit more contentious than Supervenience. Some might suppose that there are *brute* truths: roughly, true propositions such that there are worlds which disagree with ours, grue-like properties aside, only about the truth of these propositions. For example, maybe there are worlds which differ from ours just in the truth-values they assign brute counterfactuals of chance, or brute counterfactuals of freedom.

I don't know of a good argument that there aren't such brute truths. It does seem exceedingly strange, though, that truths about the past and future should be such truths. The truth that I have hair is not brute—worlds in which it is false that I have hair will represent various of my properties differently than does the actual world.

---

[36] Why include grue-like (grue: for some future time t, the property of being observed to be green before t or observed to be blue after t) properties built from truth and falsity using quantifiers, Boolean operators, and the like? Else we get obvious counter-examples to our restricted version of Temporal Combinatorialism involving properties like *being true or a round square*.

A hundred years from now it will be true that I had hair. Isn't it odd that *that* truth should be brute?

Maybe you're a presentist and see no problem with past and future truths being brute in this way. I know of no good argument that you're wrong. Since I don't share your views, though, and I should like to remain neutral on the question whether there are brute truths, it would be nice for me if there were a way for the presentist to reject our revised Temporal Combinatorialism while accepting Supervenience'. And, there is.

Second way: Presentists with certain metaphysical commitments have a well-motivated objection to Temporal Combinatorialism' (henceforth, 'Temporal Combinatorialism'). A few comments about the sort of metaphysical commitments I have in mind. Start with the possible worlds picture of things. Realists about possible worlds take possible worlds talk literally in that they believe reality to be populated by *possible worlds*. Talk of such things is not merely heuristic; it is literal truth. Possible worlds realists of course disagree about what these things are: some say maximal possible states of affairs or propositions, others, maximal consistent sets of propositions; at least one philosopher, famously, thinks of them as maximally spatio-temporally connected physical objects.[37]

Let us call the philosopher who takes possible worlds talk literally a *possible worlds realist*. To sharpen the view, I'll set aside that brand of possible worlds realism peculiar to Lewis according to which possible worlds are big physical objects. We'll think of the possible worlds realist as one committed to the existence of *abstract* possible worlds.

Those who take possible worlds talk literally often talk of a binary *logical accessibility* relation defined on the set of possible worlds. The idea here is that a proposition is possible iff it is true in some world *logically accessible* from ours. There is disagreement, of course, about the formal properties of this accessibility relation. Let us set those aside, though, and add to our characterization of possible worlds realism commitment to a binary logical accessibility relation defined on the possible worlds.

A. N. Prior (Prior and Fine 1977), Roderick Chisholm (1979), and Edward Zalta (1987) think of *moments of time* as abstract objects. Times, on this view, are, like possible worlds, abstract representations: intuitively, they are abstract representations of an instantaneous state of the world. Thinking of times in this way will be very attractive to the presentist, especially to the presentist who is also a possible worlds realist. Supposing that there are such things, like supposing that there are possible worlds, offers the presentist great gain in, to borrow David Lewis's phrase, unity and economy of theory. As worlds enable us to give an economical theory of modal talk, times enable us to give an economical theory of temporal talk, and much more

[37] Here, of course, I speak of Lewis (see e.g. 1986).

besides. If you're a presentistic possible worlds realist because you like the theoretical pay-offs of your possible worlds realism, then you'll likely be attracted to abstract time realism for the same reasons.

Of the many times there are, one has the distinction of being the present time. (Just as, of the many possible worlds there are, one has the distinction of being the actual world.) Among the times which aren't present, some are past and some are future. What makes for a time's being past or being future? The possible worlds realist, impressed by the similarities between worlds and times, might suppose that what makes for a time's being past is similar to what makes for a world's being possible. A world is possible for us when it bears the *logical* accessibility relation to our world. So too, we can say, a time is past or future for us when it bears the *temporal* accessibility relation to our time. If we take this relation to carry a direction, we can say that a time is past when it is *backwardly* temporally accessible and future when it is *forwardly* temporally accessible. More simply, we can say that a time is past when it is *earlier than* the present time and future when it is *later than* the present time.

Let us call the philosopher who believes in such abstract times and an earlier–later relation linking them an *abstract time realist.* Now, notice this crucial point. The abstract time realist will deny Temporal Combinatorialism. This principle, recall, says that things could have been just as they are at present (ignoring the distribution of truth, falsity, and the like) and the past different. Not so, if you're an abstract time realist: you believe that among the present things are abstract times standing in their earlier–later relations to one another. But these things could not have been just as they are, bearing just the earlier–later relations they bear to one another, and the past have been different. According to the abstract time realist, for any proposition p, necessarily, it was the case that p iff, according to a past (i.e. earlier) time, p. (Truths about the past, on this view, are similar to modal truths: for any p, it's possibly the case that p iff, according to a possible world, p.) So, for example, it was the case that I graduated from college. Says the abstract time realist: this iff, according to an earlier time t, I graduated from college. Since the way things presently are includes t's bearing the earlier relation to the present time (and, we shall assume, times, like worlds, have their representational properties essentially), it follows that things could not have been just as they presently are and its not be the case that I graduated from college.

So the presentistic abstract time realist will reject Temporal Combinatorialism and be unimpressed by the grounding objection. Moreover, if you're already a possible worlds realist, abstract time realism costs you almost nothing in ontology. True, you need times and the temporal accessibility relation, but for the possible worlds realist, these represent little by way of theoretical outlay. If you believe in worlds, you probably already believe in times: if you're ontologically committed to maximal ways things could be, then you're likely also committed to maximal ways things were, are, or will be. Temporal accessibility represents a real addition to the possible worlds picture, but not, I think, a costly one. This relation, recall, is merely an earlier–later relation defined on abstract times. Almost any ontology suitable to our temporal world will include some sort of primitive temporal ordering relation. True, my earlier–later relation is defined on abstract times; the usual story casts the earlier–later relation as a relation on *concrete* times (or maybe events). But this isn't obviously a demerit for my relation.

In conclusion, then, presentists with room enough in their ontologies for abstract worlds and times will be unimpressed by the grounding objection.

4. Conclusion

The foregoing objections to presentism are, I think, the most damaging. On balance, they fail to demonstrate much by way of theoretical cost. Presentism is not a costly doctrine. Since it's the only metaphysic of time consistent with the metaphysical and linguistic commitments adumbrated in the second section of this chapter, those who find these commitments attractive have good reason for being presentists.

References

Adams, R. M. (1981). 'Actualism and Thisness'. *Synthese*, 49: 3–41.

Armstrong, D. M. (1978a). *A Theory of Universals, Universals and Scientific Realism*, vol. i. Cambridge: Cambridge University Press.

——(1978b). *A Theory of Universals, Universals and Scientific Realism*, vol. ii. Cambridge: Cambridge University Press.

——(1980). 'Identity through Time', in Peter van Inwagen (ed.), *Time and Cause: Essays Presented to Richard Taylor*. Dordrecht: Reidel, 67–78.

——(1997). *A World of States of Affairs*. Cambridge: Cambridge University Press.

Balashov, Yuri (1999). 'Relativistic Objects'. *Noûs*, 33: 644–62.

——(2000). 'Enduring and Perduring Objects in Minkowski Space-Time'. *Philosophical Studies*, 99: 129–66.

Bealer, George (1982). *Concept and Quality*. Oxford: Clarendon Press.

——(1993). 'Universals'. *Journal of Philosophy*, 90: 5–32.

——(1998). 'Propositions'. *Mind*, 107: 1–32.

Bigelow, John (1988). *The Reality of Numbers: A Physicalist's Philosophy of Mathematics*. Oxford: Oxford University Press.

——(1996). 'Presentism and Properties'. *Philosophical Perspectives*, 10: 35–52.

Broad, C. D. (1923). *Scientific Thought*. London: Kegan Paul.

Callender, Craig (2000). 'Shedding Light on Time'. *Philosophy of Science*, 67 (Proceedings), S587–99.

Chisholm, Roderick M. (1979). 'Objects and Persons: Revisions and Replies'. *Grazer Philosophische Studien*, 7/8: 317–61.

—— (1990). 'Events without Times: An Essay on Ontology', *Noûs*. 24: 413–28.

Craig, William Lane (2001). *Time and the Metaphysics of Relativity*. Dordrecht: Kluwer.

Fine, Kit (1981). 'First-Order Modal Theories II—Propositions'. *Studia Logica*, 39: 159–202.

—— (1985). 'Plantinga on the Reduction of Possibilist Discourse', in J. E. Tomberlin and Peter van Inwagen (eds.), *Alvin Plantinga*. Dordrecht: Reidel, 145–86.

Fitch, Greg W. (1994). 'Singular Propositions in Time'. *Philosophical Studies*, 73: 181–7.

Fox, John F. (1987). 'Truthmaker'. *Australasian Journal of Philosophy*, 65: 188–207.

Gödel, Kurt (1949). 'A Remark about the Relationship between Relativity Theory and Idealistic Philosophy', in P. Schilpp (ed.), *Albert Einstein: Philosopher-Scientist*. La Salle, Ill.: Open Court, 557–62.

Godfrey-Smith, William (1979). 'Special Relativity and the Present'. *Philosophical Studies*, 36: 233–44.

Haslanger, Sally (1989*a*). 'Endurance and Temporary Intrinsics'. *Analysis*, 49: 119–25.

—— (1989*b*). 'Persistence, Change, and Explanation'. *Philosophical Studies*, 56: 1–28.

—— (1994). 'Humean Supervenience and Enduring Things'. *Australasian Journal of Philosophy*, 72: 339–59.

Heller, Mark (1984). 'Temporal Parts of Four Dimensional Objects'. *Philosophical Studies*, 46: 323–34.

—— (1990). *The Ontology of Physical Objects: Four Dimensional Hunks of Matter*. Cambridge: Cambridge University Press.

—— (1992). 'Things Change'. *Philosophy and Phenomenological Research*, 52: 695–704.

—— (1993). 'Varieties of Four Dimensionalism'. *Australasian Journal of Philosophy*, 71: 47–59.

Hinchliff, Mark (1996). 'The Puzzle of Change', in J. E. Tomberlin (ed.), *Philosophical Perspectives*, x: *Metaphysics*. Cambridge, Mass.: Basil Blackwell, 119–36.

—— (2000). 'A Defense of Presentism in a Relativistic Setting'. *Philosophy of Science*, 67 (Proceedings), S575–86.

Hudson, Hud (1999). 'Temporal Parts and Moral Personhood'. *Philosophical Studies*, 93: 299–316.

—— (2001). *A Materialist Metaphysics of the Human Person*. Ithaca, NY: Cornell University Press.

Johnston, Mark (1987). 'Is there a Problem about Persistence?' *Proceedings of the Aristotelian Society*, suppl. vol. 61: 107–35.

—— (1992). 'Constitution is not Identity'. *Mind*, 101: 89–105.

Keller, Simon (forthcoming). 'Presentism and Truthmaking', in Dean Zimmerman (ed.), *Oxford Studies in Metaphysics*, vol. i. Oxford: Oxford University Press.

Lewis, David (1983*a*) 'Survival and Identity', in Lewis, *Philosophical Papers*, vol. i. Oxford: Oxford University Press.

—— (1983*b*). 'New Work for a Theory of Universals'. *Australasian Journal of Philosophy*, 61: 343–77.

—— (1984). 'Putnam's Paradox'. *Australasian Journal of Philosophy*, 62: 221–36.

—— (1986). *On the Plurality of Worlds*. Oxford: Basil Blackwell.

—— (1988). 'Rearrangement of Particles: Reply to Lowe'. *Analysis*, 48: 65–72.

—— (1992). Review of D. M. Armstrong, *A Combinatorial Theory of Possibility*. *Australasian Journal of Philosophy*, 70: 211–24.

—— (2001). 'Truthmaking and Difference-Making'. *Noûs*. 35: 602–15.

Lombard, Lawrence (1999). 'On the Alleged Incompatibility of Presentism and Temporal Parts'. *Philosophia*, 27: 253–60.

Lowe, E. J. (1987). 'Lewis on Perdurance versus Endurance'. *Analysis*, 47: 152–4.

—— (1988). 'The Problems of Intrinsic Change: Rejoinder to Lewis'. *Analysis*, 48: 72–7.

McCall, Storrs (1994). *A Model of the Universe*. Oxford: Clarendon Press.

Markosian, Ned (forthcoming). 'A Defense of Presentism', in Dean Zimmerman (ed.), *Oxford Studies in Metaphysics*, vol. i. Oxford: Oxford University Press.

Maudlin, Tim (1996). 'Space-Time in the Quantum World', in James T. Cushing, Arthur Fine, and Sheldon Goldstein (eds.), *Bohmian Mechanics and Quantum Theory: An Appraisal*. Dordrecht: Kluwer, 285–307.

Maxwell, N. (1985). 'Are Probabilism and Special Relativity Incompatible?' *Philosophy of Science*, 52: 23–43.

Mellor, D. H. (1981). *Real Time*. Cambridge: Cambridge University Press.

—— (1998). *Real Time II*. London: Routledge.

Merricks, Trenton (1994). 'Endurance and Indiscernibility'. *Journal of Philosophy*, 91: 165–84.

—— (1995). 'On the Incompatibility of Enduring and Perduring Entities'. *Mind*, 104: 523–31.

—— (1999). 'Persistence, Parts and Presentism'. *Noûs*, 33: 421–38.

Monton, Bradley (2001). 'Presentism and Quantum Gravity'.

Mulligan, Kevin, Peter Simons, and Barry Smith (1984). 'Truth-Makers'. *Philosophy and Phenomenological Research*, 44: 287–321.

Plantinga, Alvin (1983). 'On Existentialism'. *Philosophical Studies*, 44: 1–20.

Prior, A. N., and Kit Fine, (1977). *Worlds, Times and Selves*. Amherst: University of Massachusetts Press.

Putnam, Hilary (1967). 'Time and Physical Geometry'. *Journal of Philosophy*, 64: 240–7.

Quine, W. V. O. (1960). *Word and Object*. Cambridge, Mass.: MIT Press.

—— (1963). 'Identity, Ostension, and Hypostasis', in Quine, *From a Logical Point of View*, 2nd edn., rev. Evanston, Ill.: Harper & Row, 65–79.

—— (1976). 'Whither Physical Objects', in R. S. Cohen, P. K. Feyerabend, and M. W. Wartofsky (eds.), *Essays in Memory of Imre Lakatos*. Dordrecht: Reidel, 497–504.

—— (1981). *Theories and Things*. Cambridge, Mass.: Harvard University Press.

Rea, Michael (1995). 'The Problem of Material Constitution'. *Philosophical Review*, 104: 525–52.

—— (1998). 'Temporal Parts Unmotivated'. *Philosophical Review*, 107: 225–60.

—— (2000). 'Constitution and Kind Membership'. *Philosophical Studies*, 97: 169–93.

Restall, Gregg (1996). 'Truthmakers, Entailment and Necessity'. *Australasian Journal of Philosophy*, 74: 331–40.

Rietdijk, C. W. (1966). 'A Rigorous Proof of Determinism Derived from the Special Theory of Relativity'. *Philosophy of Science*, 33: 341–4.

—— (1976). 'Special Relativity and Determinism'. *Philosophy of Science*, 43: 598–609.

Savitt, Steve (1994). 'The Replacement of Time'. *Australasian Journal of Philosophy*, 72: 463–74.

—— (2000). 'There's no Time Like the Present (in Minkowski Spacetime)'. *Philosophy of Science*, 67 (Proceedings), S563–74.

Sider, Theodore (1996). 'All the World's a Stage'. *Australasian Journal of Philosophy*, 74: 433–53.

—— (1999). 'Presentism and Ontological Commitment'. *Journal of Philosophy*, 96: 325–47.

—— (2000). 'The Stage View and Temporary Intrinsics'. *Analysis*, 60: 84–8.

—— (2001). *Four-Dimensionalism: An Ontology of Persistence and Time*. Oxford: Clarendon Press.

Sklar, Lawrence (1974). *Space, Time and Spacetime*. Berkeley: University of California Press.

—— (1981). 'Time, Reality, and Relativity', in Richard Healy (ed.), *Reduction, Time, and Reality*. New York: Cambridge University Press, 129–42.

Smith, Quentin (1993). *Language and Time*. Oxford: Oxford University Press.

Stein, Howard (1968). 'On Einstein–Minkowski Space-Time'. *Journal of Philosophy*, 65: 5–23.

—— (1970). 'A Note on Time and Relativity Theory'. *Journal of Philosophy*, 67: 289–94.

—— (1991). 'On Relativity Theory and Openness of the Future'. *Philosophy of Science*, 58: 147–67.

Tichy, Pavel (1980). 'The Transiency of Truth'. *Theoria*, 46: 165–82.

Tooley, Michael (1997). *Time, Tense & Causation*. Oxford: Oxford University Press.

van Fraassen, Bas (1987). 'The Semantic Approach to Scientific Theories', in Nancy Nersessian (ed.), *The Process of Science*. Dordrecht: Kluwer, 105–24.

van Inwagen, Peter (1990). 'Four-Dimensional Objects'. *Noûs*, 24: 245–55.

Zalta, Edward N. (1987). 'On the Structural Similarities between Worlds and Times'. *Philosophical Studies*, 51: 213–39.

Zimmerman, Dean W. (1997). 'Immanent Causation', in J. E. Tomberlin (ed.), *Philosophical Perspectives*, vol. xi: *Mind, Causation and World*. Cambridge, Mass.: Basil Blackwell.

—— (1998a). 'Temporal Parts and Supervenient Causation: The Incompatibility of Two Humean Doctrines'. *Australasian Journal of Philosophy*, 76: 265–88.

—— (1998b). 'Temporary Intrinsics and Presentism', in Peter van Inwagen and Dean W. Zimmerman (eds.), *Metaphysics: The Big Questions*. Malden, Mass.: Basil Blackwell, 206–19.

—— (1999). 'One Really Big Liquid Sphere: Reply to Lewis'. *Australasian Journal of Philosophy*, 77: 213–15.

CHAPTER 9

FOUR-DIMENSIONALISM

MICHAEL C. REA

1. INTRODUCTION

FOUR-DIMENSIONALISM, as it will be understood in this chapter, is a view about the ontological status of non-present objects. *Presentists* say that only present objects exist. There are no dinosaurs, though there were such things; there are no cities on Mars, though perhaps there will be such things.[1] *Four-dimensionalists*, on the other hand, say that there are past or future objects (or both); and in saying this, they mean to put such things ontologically on a par with present objects. According to the four-dimensionalist, non-present objects are like spatially distant objects: they exist, just not here, where we are.

The term 'four-dimensionalism' is sometimes applied to a very different sort of view (see e.g. Heller 1990, 1993; Sider 1997, 2001). Consider a man, Fred, who was born in 1975, went to kindergarten in 1980, and graduated from high school in 1993. One very natural way to think about this progression is to think that Fred *moves*,

I would like to thank Tom Crisp, Curt Andrew DeKoning, Richard Hanley, Trenton Merricks, and Ted Sider for very helpful (and timely) comments on an earlier draft. Thanks also to Corrie Maxwell, Marty Strachan, and Katie Weber for valuable research assistance.

[1] Presentism is compatible with the view that there neither were nor will be objects other than those present; but I am not aware of any presentists who endorse such a view. Defenders of presentism include Bigelow (1996); Chisholm (1990); Merricks (1994, 1995, 1999); Hinchliff (1996, 2000); Markosian (2002); Prior (1959, 1967, 1968*b,c*, 1970, 1996); Zimmerman (1996, 1997, 1998). Sider (1999) offers important arguments on behalf of presentism, though he himself does not endorse it. See also Crisp's contribution to this volume, Ch. 8.

whole and complete, through each of these times in his career. Admittedly, he is different at each time: he grows taller, more independent, more knowledgeable, and so on as time passes. But one and the same man exists in his entirety at each of these different times. This view is sometimes called 'three-dimensionalism' because it holds that ordinary objects are three-dimensional, temporally non-extended entities. It is also called 'endurantism', because objects are said to *endure* if and only if they last over time by being wholly present at every moment at which they exist.[2] Some philosophers, however, believe that objects *perdure*—that they last over time without being wholly present at every moment at which they exist. So, for example, in the case of Fred such philosophers would say that the infant, the kindergartener, and the graduate are distinct *temporal parts* of a four-dimensionally extended whole. This view is variously called 'four-dimensionalism', 'perdurantism', or 'the doctrine of temporal parts'.[3] Some think that four-dimensionalism understood as the denial of presentism implies four-dimensionalism understood as perdurantism.[4] But whether or not that is true, the important thing to recognize is that these are two very different views. To avoid confusion, I will in this chapter reserve the term 'four-dimensionalism' exclusively for the view that presentism is false, and I will use the term 'perdurantism' to refer to the view that objects last over time without being wholly present at every time at which they exist.

Four-dimensionalism comes in several varieties. The two main varieties are *eternalism* and the *growing block theory*. Eternalists believe that all past and future objects exist (i.e. there are some past objects, there are some future objects, and there neither were nor will be objects that do not exist).[5] Growing block theorists believe that all past objects exist, but future objects do not.[6] There are also further options. For example, Storrs McCall (1976, 1994) endorses a *shrinking tree* theory. On his view, at the beginning of the universe every physically possible future exists, so that from every time not just one but many physically possible futures branch

---

[2] In support of endurantism, see Chisholm (1976, app. A); Haslanger (1989); Hinchliff (1996); Johnston (1987); Merricks (1994); Rea (1998); van Inwagen (1990); Zimmerman (1998).

[3] In support of perdurantism, see Armstrong (1980); Heller (1990, 1993); Lewis (1986: 202–4; 2002a); Sider (1997, 2001). Whereas orthodox perdurantism says that familiar objects persist by having distinct temporal *parts* at different times, there is a variation on perdurantism according to which familiar objects persist by having distinct *counterparts* standing in for, or representing, them at various times. This view is described and defended in Sider (1996, 2000, 2001).

[4] See e.g. Armstrong (1980); Balashov (2000); Broad (1927, ch. 2); Carter and Hestevold (1994); Christensen (1981); Gödel (1979); Merricks (1995, 1999); Quine (1960, sect. 36); Smart (1963). Note too that some think the implication goes the other way: perdurantism implies the denial of presentism. See e.g. Carter and Hestevold (1994); Merricks (1995, 1999); Oaklander (1992). In Rea (1998) I argue against the view that four-dimensionalism implies perdurantism. However, the argument works only if WP (1998: 234) is amended so that condition (*b*) reads as follows: (*b*) it is not the case that the *x*s t-compose a proper part of *y*.

[5] See e.g. Grünbaum (1963); LePoidevin (1991); Mellor (1981a, 1998); Minkowski (1952); Quine (1960, sect. 36); Russell (1915); Smart (1963); Sider (2001); and D. C. Williams (1951).

[6] See Adams (1986); Broad (1927, ch. 2); Rakic (1997); Tooley (1997); and Zeilicovici (1989).

off. But, as the universe ages, branches disappear, thus producing a successively shrinking tree whose trunk represents the fixed past and whose branches represent remaining physically possible futures. Alternatively, one might endorse a *shrinking block* theory, according to which all future objects but no past objects and no objects belonging to 'merely possible' futures exist. Or one might believe that only some but not all past objects, only some but not all future objects, or some but not all of both, exist. All of these varieties except eternalism entail that time is in some sense dynamic. Eternalism is compatible with the idea that the structure of space-time is ever changing if we are willing to understand change as simply a matter of exemplifying different properties at different locations in space-time. It is also at least prima facie compatible with the idea that time *passes*, if we are prepared to view the property of presentness as a sort of 'spotlight' moving along an eternally existing series of events.[7] But the four-dimensionalist alternatives to eternalism seem, at least initially, to allow for more robust changes in the structure of space-time. Most notably, these views, like presentism, hold that events, times, and objects may come into or pass out of existence.

I said above that presentists deny the existence of past and future objects whereas four-dimensionalists accept the existence of non-present objects. This way of drawing the distinction will do for rough-and-ready purposes, but attention to the different varieties of four-dimensionalism makes it clear that official formulations will need to be more careful. For example, if the growing block theory is true, and if there was a *first* time in the block, then that first time would have been one at which it was true that there exist no past or future objects. The same goes for the last time in a shrinking block. But it seems implausible to say that these two theories imply, respectively, that presentism was or will be true, but only for a moment. Furthermore, we must also keep in mind that presentism and four-dimensionalism are views about the ontological status of past and future objects in the *actual* world, and, properly speaking, have no implications for the ontological status of objects in other *possible worlds* if such there be.[8] So, in light of these considerations, we should officially characterize presentism as follows. Presentism is the view that it always has been and always will be the case that there are no actual but non-present (spatio-temporal) objects. Four-dimensionalism will be officially characterized as the view that presentism is false. As with our rough-and-ready characterization, this one leaves open the question whether presentism and its denial are *necessarily* true if true at all; but it rules out the unwelcome possibility that presentism might only be temporarily true.[9]

---

[7] The 'moving spotlight' or 'policeman's bullseye' metaphor is due to, but not endorsed by, C. D. Broad (1927, ch. 2).

[8] Thanks to Richard Hanley for this point. More on possible worlds in Sect. 2 below.

[9] Some characterize presentism as the view that, *necessarily*, no non-present objects exist. (See e.g. Bergmann 1999; Sider 2001.) However, I see no reason to dismiss at the outset the possibility that presentism and its denial are contingent.

At this point, some assumptions should be made explicit. First, I assume, for ease of exposition, that the word 'object' applies to *events* as well as to familiar particulars like horses and trees. Second, as indicated by the parenthetical qualifier in the official formulation of presentism, I assume that in denying the existence of non-present objects, the presentist does not thereby commit herself to the repudiation of objects like numbers, properties, or other non-spatio-temporal items. Third, I assume that times are concrete sums of events. Thus, on my view, presentists and four-dimensionalists also differ about the existence of past and future times. All three assumptions are harmless. The first two are merely terminological; dropping them would just add awkwardness to our formulations. The third is more substantial; but it too could be dropped at the expense of complicating our discussion a bit. Those who deny that times are events or sums thereof typically take them to be abstract states of affairs. A presentist who endorses this sort of view will admit that past and future times *exist*, but she will deny that they *obtain*. Thus, our formulations would need to take account of this difference. But, again, nothing hinges on the issue; so, except where the view that times are abstract is explicitly under consideration, I'll proceed on the assumption that times are concrete. One might worry that talk of times is unacceptable altogether from the point of view of contemporary physics. The reason is that such talk might seem to presuppose that time as we know it is an absolute, observer-independent feature of reality, whereas the special theory of relativity seems to imply that space and time are both mere appearances of a more fundamental reality—namely, space-time. However, there are ways of understanding talk of times that get round this concern. For example, we may say that a concrete time is a plane of simultaneity in a frame of reference or the sum of all of the events that share such a plane, and we may take an abstract time to be the total state of the universe on such a plane.[10]

This chapter will provide a critical overview of the main arguments in favour of four-dimensionalism. I will begin in Section 2 by discussing several issues that will help us better to understand the nature of the debate between presentists and four-dimensionalists. Sections 3–5 will then discuss in detail the three main arguments in support of four-dimensionalism: the argument from the impossibility of temporal passage, the truthmaker argument, and the argument from special relativity. We'll see that the first two arguments on their own pose no serious threat to presentism. However, we'll also see that the options available to presentists for replying to the third argument are extremely implausible, and that the considerations commonly cited in favour of presentism are generally outweighed by those arising out of the first and third arguments taken together. Thus, I'll conclude that, as the debate currently stands in the literature, four-dimensionalism has the upper hand.

---

[10] For a characterization of planes of simultaneity and frames of reference, see Sect. 5 below. Alternative ways of characterizing times in a relativistic context correspond to the various alternatives for defining 'the present time' that are discussed in Sect. 5.

2. UNDERSTANDING THE DEBATE

Before turning to arguments in support of four-dimensionalism, it is important first to be sure that we understand the terms of the debate. There are two ways in which the current literature threatens to obscure our understanding. One is by tempting us to conflate the presentism–four-dimensionalism debate with 'A-theory–B-theory' debate or with the 'tenser–detenser' debate. The other is by tempting us to think that there really is no meaningful debate in the neighbourhood at all—that four-dimensionalism is either trivially true or trivially false. I'll discuss each of these issues in turn.

Let us begin with the temptation to conflate the presentism–four-dimensionalism debate with the A-theory–B-theory controversy.[11] In presenting his famous argument for the conclusion that time is unreal, J. M. E. McTaggart (1908, 1921) introduces a distinction between three kinds of ordered series of events. Working backward alphabetically, a 'C-series' is one whose members are ordered, but not necessarily in a temporal manner; a 'B-series' is one whose members are ordered by earlier-than and later-than relations; and an 'A-series' is one whose members each may be characterized as past, present, or future, but not all three at once. In rejecting the idea that an event may be characterized as past, present, and future all at once, McTaggart assumes that A-determinations are not reducible to B-relations. McTaggart also explicitly assumes that A-determinations are transitory.[12] In the literature these two assumptions have been preserved, so that it is generally held that an A-series exists only if pastness, presentness, and futurity are transitory and not reducible to B-relations. However, there are two further assumptions lurking in McTaggart's characterization of an A-series, both of which may be dispensed with. One is that A-determinations are either properties or relations; the other is that there are three of them. The latter assumption would be rejected by a presentist who believes that times are concrete sums of events (for, on her view, there would be no past and future times to have the properties of pastness and futurity). The former assumption would be rejected by one who thinks that presentness is reducible to existence, and that existence is neither a property nor a relation (see e.g. Craig 1997). Nevertheless, most participants in the A-theory–B-theory debate would agree that one who rejects these two assumptions may nonetheless count as an A-theorist so

---

[11] See C. Williams (1996) for references illustrating how the two debates have been conflated in the literature. After exposing various ways in which the A-theory–B-theory debate has been misunderstood, and after showing how various ways of characterizing the debate fail, Williams challenges subsequent workers on the issue to find in the debate a 'genuine contrast of believable theories'. Below I characterize the debate in a way that I think provides a satisfactory answer to this challenge.

[12] Following Sosa (1979), I say that a property is transitory iff it may be exemplified by some entity without being eternally exemplified by that entity. Thus, a property may count as transitory even if it is had essentially by the things that have it.

long as she holds (*a*) that some things were or will be present which are not in fact present, and (*b*) that facts about what was or will be the case cannot be reduced to B-relations holding between existing things. Every version of presentism entails (*b*), and (*a*) is trivially entailed by what we might call *common-sense presentism* (the view that presentism is true and that there were or will be objects other than those present). So, as an official characterization we will say that an A-series exists just in case both (*a*) and (*b*) are true. In what follows, I will speak as if this is equivalent to the claim that an A-series exists just in case presentness is an *irreducible transitory property*. In doing this, I ignore the fact that presentness might be reducible to something like existence, and I also ignore the possibility that presentness and existence might not be properties. We could do away with these assumptions without substantially affecting the arguments below, but only at the price of severely complicating the discussion.

In the literature on McTaggart's argument the C-series is often ignored. Furthermore, it is generally taken for granted that the series of events that constitutes our world's history is at least a B-series.[13] Thus, the three main questions in the A-theory–B-theory debate are (i) whether an A-series is possible, (ii) whether our world's history constitutes an A-series, and (iii) whether a mere B-series can count as a temporal series. As far as I know, everyone who believes that an A-series is possible also believes that our world's history *is* an A-series. Hence, the term 'A-theory' is used in the literature mainly to refer either to the view that our world's history is an A-series or to the view that no series counts as a temporal series unless it is an A-series. On the former way of using the term, McTaggart does not qualify as an A-theorist; on the latter way of using the term, he does. For purposes here, I will use the term in the former way.

People often speak as if the question whether an A-theory is true is just equivalent to the question whether presentism is true. But from what has just been said, it should be clear that it is not. McTaggart characterized the A-theory under the presupposition that eternalism is true. Furthermore, growing block theorists like Broad and Tooley, as well as shrinking tree theorists like McCall, explicitly reject presentism while at the same time endorsing the claim that presentness is irreducible and transitory.[14] So one should not simply assume that accepting an A-theory commits one to presentism. Furthermore, accepting presentism does not commit

---

[13] There is some debate about whether a B-series could exist without an A-series; but we'll leave that debate aside. Also, some—e.g. Craig (1998)—differentiate between a 'pure A-theory', a 'pure B-theory', and a 'hybrid A–B theory'. On this view, presentism is a pure A-theory, eternalism is a pure B-theory, and dynamic versions of four-dimensionalism are the hybrids. However, I see no reason to deny that presentism is an A–B hybrid. Presentists face a prima facie problem of explaining how present events could stand in B-relations with non-present events (there being no such things). But any plausible presentism will have to find *some* way to make sense of cross-time relations; and once this is done, presentism will have the resources to accommodate B-relations.

[14] See Broad (1927, ch. 2); McCall (1976, 1994); Tooley (1997). Others who have (apparently) accepted an A-theory without accepting presentism include Bigelow (1991) and Smith (1995). Bigelow has more

one to an A-theory. For example, one might believe that only the present exists *and* that there neither have been nor will be times other than the present. On this view, presentness might be irreducible, but it would not be transitory; hence there would be no A-series.

So the presentism–four-dimensionalism debate is not equivalent to the A-theory–B-theory debate. Nevertheless, there is at least this connection between the two: *Common-sense presentism*, as we observed above, does imply that an A-theory is true. Furthermore, some think that the implication goes in the reverse direction as well (see e.g. Craig 1997; cf. also Zimmerman 1998). Thus, the success of various arguments in the A-theory–B-theory debate will have direct bearing on the presentism–four-dimensionalism debate, even if the two debates are not to be identified with one another.

Related to the A-theory–B-theory debate is the controversy between *tensers* and *detensers*. Detensers are those who think that tensed language is somehow reducible to tenseless language; tensers are those who think that it is not. At the heart of the debate is the question whether tensed sentences can be true even if events in the world fail to constitute an A-series. For example: Suppose Jones was tall but is now short owing to an unfortunate error during knee surgery. Tensers want to say that part of what makes the sentence 'Jones was tall but is now short' true is the fact that Jones's being short occurs at a time which has the irreducible transitory property of being present. On their view, the meanings of words like 'now', 'was', 'will be', and so on can't be cashed out in terms of earlier-than, later-than, and simultaneity relations; and the truth of sentences containing such words is not guaranteed by the mere holding of B-relations among various times. On this way of looking at things, the tenser–detenser debate is closely related to the A-theory–B-theory controversy. Indeed, the B-theory is generally taken to be a *tenseless* theory of time, and the A-theory is generally taken to be a *tensed* theory of time. Thus, in so far as we can see how one might conflate the presentism–four-dimensionalism debate with the A-theory–B-theory debate, so too we can see how one might conflate it with the tenser–detenser debate. But, as before, it is possible to accept presentism without taking tense seriously; and it at least appears to be possible to take tense seriously without accepting presentism.[15]

So much, then, for the temptation to conflate our debate with others in the philosophy of time. What, now, of the temptation to see our debate as empty? The worry arises as follows: Consider the four-dimensionalist claim that some time other than the present exists. In this claim, the predicate 'exists' is either tensed or tenseless. If it is tensed, then to affirm that some time other than the present exists is to say that some such time exists *now*, which is false. Thus,

---

recently accepted presentism (Bigelow 1996). Smith accepts a doctrine which he *calls* presentism but which differs from what presentism is ordinarily taken to be.

[15] See references in n. 14.

four-dimensionalism appears absurd. On the other hand, if 'exists' is tenseless, then it would appear to be equivalent to the predicate 'did, does, or will exist'. But no one denies that non-present times did or will exist. Hence, four-dimensionalism appears trivial.[16]

A common response is to compare the presentism–four-dimensionalism debate with the actualism–possibilism debate.[17] Most of us believe that there are other ways the world could have been. Taking this belief seriously has led many to think that, in addition to the actual world and its concrete inhabitants, there are also countless *possible* worlds. But if there are such things, *where* are they? Two alternatives suggest themselves: they are right here in the actual world, or they are somewhere else. *Actualists* believe that everything there is exists in the actual world; so, since there aren't any concrete things in the actual world that are plausibly taken to be possible worlds (total ways the universe might have been), actualists tend to believe that possible worlds are abstract items like propositions or states of affairs (cf. Plantinga 1974, 1976). *Possibilists*, on the other hand, believe that some things exist that do not exist in the actual world; thus, they are free to say that other possible worlds are concrete things just like ours (cf. Lewis 1986). At first blush, however, their thesis is puzzling. Plausibly, the actual world is just the total way things are; and, plausibly, anything that exists would have to be included in the total way things are. But then anything that exists must exist in the actual world, which is what the possibilist denies. Still, we can understand the debate. One way to understand it is to see it as a debate precisely over the question whether *existence* trivially entails *existence in the actual world*. Actualists say yes; possibilists say no. Another way to understand it (or perhaps the same way in different guise) is to see it as a debate over whether our *unrestricted* quantifiers range over non-actual things. That quantifiers can be restricted is evident in ordinary discourse. Are all the students in the room? Yes, for most contexts, just in case all the students enrolled in the course are present; no, however, for someone who happens to be wondering whether every student that exists has somehow managed to squeeze into her lecture hall. In most contexts, then, the quantifier in the question 'Are all the students in the room?' is restricted; but it is also possible to drop the restrictions. Thus, the debate between actualists and possibilists might be seen as a debate over the question whether, all restrictions dropped, there exist any objects that don't exist in the actual world. Actualists say no; possibilists say yes.

The analogy is obvious. Other times are like other worlds; they are just ways things were or will be rather than ways things might have been. Presentists hold

---

[16] Cf. Larry Lombard's remarks on the apparent triviality of presentism in Lombard (1999: 254). For responses to this sort of worry, see Zimmerman (1996, 1998); Sider (1999). My own responses below mirror and borrow examples from theirs.

[17] Cf. Adams (1986); Markosian (2002); and Sider (2001, ch. 2).

that *existence* trivially implies *present existence*; four-dimensionalists disagree.[18] Four-dimensionalists believe that the unrestricted quantifier ranges over past and future things as well as present things; presentists disagree. Four-dimensionalists will affirm claims like 'there are dinosaurs and computers'; presentists will not. Assuming that sets exist only when their members do, a four-dimensionalist can believe that there is a set containing a dinosaur and a computer; a presentist cannot. Thus, the debate is not empty.

3. TEMPORAL PASSAGE

In the last section I said that common-sense presentism implies that presentness is irreducible and transitory. But if presentness is transitory, then time passes. Virtually no one is willing to deny that there were or will be times other than the present. Thus, debate about whether temporal passage is possible has direct bearing on the question whether presentism is true.

The most well-known arguments against the possibility of temporal passage are those given by J. M. E. McTaggart (1908, 1921) and D. C. Williams (1951). Interestingly enough, however, both start with the assumption that four-dimensionalism is true. In the case of Williams, this assumption renders his argument completely sterile with respect to the presentism–four-dimensionalism debate. The crucial premiss is that there is no distinction to be drawn between an event's *existing* and its *happening*. Thus, he argues, since past and future events exist, they are (in a tenseless sense) also happening; so there is no ontologically relevant difference between those events and present events that could give sense to the claim that presentness is a temporary property. But presentists needn't be concerned about whether four-dimensionalism is incompatible with temporal passage. What the presentist needs to worry about is whether temporal passage is compatible with presentism. If it isn't, then her view is in deep trouble. Williams does not speak to this question. Ultimately, neither does McTaggart; but this fact is not immediately obvious. Thus, McTaggart's argument merits closer consideration.[19] As I have already mentioned, McTaggart's goal was to

---

[18] More carefully: Presentists hold that *actual* existence trivially implies present existence. After all, a presentist who accepts a Lewisian brand of possibilism might think that there are other concrete *worlds* (that don't exist at the present time), but not other concrete *times*. Since most presentists are actualists, however, I'll ignore this complication in what follows. Except where possibilism is explicitly under discussion, I'll assume that the unrestricted quantifier ranges only over actual things.

[19] Important treatments of McTaggart's argument may be found in Broad (1927; 1938, bk. 7, ch. 35); Christensen (1974); Craig (1998); Dummett (1978); Gale (1968); Horwich (1987); Lowe (1987, 1992); McCall (1994); Mellor (1981a, 1998); Prior (1967); Schlesinger (1980); Shorter (1984); Smith (1995);

defend the striking thesis that time is unreal. His argument for this conclusion has two main premisses. The first is that a series of events counts as a temporal series only if it is an A-series; the second is that an A-series is impossible. I will not discuss the first premiss since only the second has direct bearing on the main topic of this chapter.

There is some dispute about the structure of McTaggart's defence of the second premiss. Everyone agrees that McTaggart thinks that a contradiction can be derived from the supposition that an A-series exists (because he says so explicitly). What people disagree about is the question of *how* he thinks it can be derived. The interpretation I prefer is the one that sees McTaggart's argument as parallel to the so-called 'problem of temporary intrinsics' (see Craig 1998; cf. also Broad 1927, ch. 2). Since the purpose of this chapter is not to settle exegetical debates but only to provide an overview of the main arguments in support of four-dimensionalism, and since I think that the interpretation of McTaggart that I favour is the one that sets his argument on strongest ground, I will not take the time to discuss other interpretations here.

The problem of temporary intrinsics is an alleged problem about the possibility of intrinsic change.[20] To illustrate, let us consider a putative example of intrinsic change: Philip is drunk in the evening, sober the next morning.[21] In order to understand this scenario as a case involving genuine change, we need somehow to be able to say that one and the same person is drunk in the evening and sober in the morning. But there is prima facie reason for thinking that we can't say this. Let the name 'Philip-drunk' refer to Philip when he is drunk; let the name 'Philip-sober' refer to Philip when he is sober. We then have:

(1) Philip-drunk is drunk.
(2) Philip-sober is sober.

But 'Philip-drunk' and 'Philip-sober' are supposed to be just alternative names for Philip; and, indeed, it appears that, in order for Philip to have *changed*, it would have to be the case that Philip-drunk = Philip-sober = Philip. Thus, it apparently follows that:

(3) Philip is both drunk and sober.

But (obviously) being drunk and being sober are mutually incompatible properties. Thus, it appears that the supposition that intrinsic change occurs involves a contradiction: it implies that one and the same thing can be both φ and not-φ, for some property φ.

Tooley (1997); Zeilicovici (1986, 1989). See also Sosa (1979) for a brief critical survey of the main options in explaining the phenomenon of temporal passage.

   20 The most famous recent statement is in Lewis (1986: 202–3). But see also Broad (1927, ch. 2).
   21 The example is due to C. S. Peirce, quoted in Chisholm (1976, app. A).

The problem of temporary intrinsics is generated by the following tacit assumption:

(A) For any x and φ, if x is, was, or will be φ, then x is φ.

Once this is clear, there is no need to resort to using funny names for Philip in order to raise the problem. We may simply reason directly from the assumption: If Philip is drunk at one time and sober at another, then Philip is drunk and sober; but being drunk and being sober are mutually incompatible; thus, intrinsic change involves a contradiction. But once matters are put thus baldly, we can see that intrinsic change is not the culprit. The culprit is the assumption, which raises problems not only for intrinsic change, but for other sorts of change as well. If Philip is at one time the tallest man in Boston and at another time not, then Philip both is and is not the tallest man in Boston, which is contradictory; if Philip exists at one time but not at another, then Philip both does and does not exist, which is contradictory; and so on. The problem is very general, and is therefore more aptly described not as a problem about temporary intrinsics but simply as a problem about change.

Like the problem of temporary intrinsics, McTaggart's argument is just a special case of this very general problem about change. According to McTaggart, an A-series is incoherent because, on the one hand, A-determinations are mutually incompatible but, on the other hand, every event in an A-series must have every A-determination. The reason every event must have every A-determination is as follows. There exists an A-series only if A-determinations are transitory. But if they are transitory, then it must be possible for one and the same event to have one A-determination and then another in succession. So suppose this happens: event E is present, was future, and will be past. From (A), it follows directly that E *is* past, present, and future, which is contradictory. Note that in formulating this puzzle we needn't assume that pastness and futurity are properties. Presentists will deny that anything has the *property* of being past or future since past and future events do not exist. But they will admit that present events now exemplify the property of being present and will later fail to exemplify it by failing to exist; and this is all that is needed, in conjunction with (A), to generate a contradiction.[22]

It is possible to solve the problem of temporary intrinsics without rejecting (A). For example, we might say that Philip manages to be both drunk and sober by having distinct temporal parts, one of which is drunk and the other of which is sober. Or we might deny that Philip manages to be both drunk and sober at all—rather, he is both *drunk-at-t_1* and *sober-at-t_2* for some distinct times t_1 and t_2.[23] However,

---

[22] We could even do away with the assumption that *presentness* is a property. But, again, for the sake of convenience I am ignoring such complications.

[23] Lewis (1986, 2002a) recommends the first solution; Mellor (1981a, ch. 7; 1998, ch. 9) and van Inwagen (1990) recommend the second. For other, somewhat more complicated solutions, see e.g. Haslanger (1989); Johnston (1987); Paul (2002); Sider (2000).

such solutions do not carry over well as responses to McTaggart's argument. The first solution fails because everyone who believes that time passes believes that events can be wholly future, then wholly present, and then wholly past; but the temporal parts solution makes no provision for change which cannot be analysed as the having of different parts with different properties. The second solution fails because applying it would involve treating A-determinations as permanent relational properties which, *ex hypothesi*, they aren't. The other solutions in the literature compatible with (A) suffer from similar defects. Thus, it would appear that the only responses available to McTaggart's argument are either to grant the conclusion—that A-determinations are not transitory—or to reject (A).

Rejecting (A) amounts to denying that tense is appropriately disregarded in the formulation of the puzzle. For this reason, I'll call any solution to McTaggart's problem which involves rejecting (A) a *tenser* solution. There are at least two different kinds of tenser solution. The *strong* tenser solution denies that there are any tenseless facts at all. On this view, there is no meaningful sense at all in which something is F which is not presently F. If Philip was drunk and is now sober, there is no way of analysing this fact in the manner of (1) and (2). Philip-drunk, in so far as he is just Philip, is not drunk; he was drunk. Similarly, there is no time *t* such that he is drunk at *t* (unless *t* is present). On this view, (A) is equivalent to the obviously false assumption that if an object *x* has ever been *F*, it is presently *F*. The *weak* tenser solution, on the other hand, grants that there are tenseless facts but simply denies that facts about A-determinations are reducible to such facts. This view offers no general solution to the problem of change; for it does not rule out the following restricted version of (A):

(A*) For any *x* and φ (such that φ is not an A-determination), if *x* is, was, or will be φ, then *x* is φ.

(A*) will suffice to generate the problem of temporary intrinsics and various other instances of the problem of change. However, rejecting (A) without rejecting (A*) will at least solve McTaggart's problem since that problem is specifically about A-determinations.

As should already be clear, presentism solves McTaggart's problem by entailing the strong tenser solution. Given presentism, there are no past or future objects; thus, it is trivially true that something is φ just in case it is presently φ. Still, two questions linger. First: Is a tenser solution coherent? If not, then presentism is skewered by McTaggart after all. Second: Can a non-presentist accept a tenser solution? If not, then for those who find it counter-intuitive to reject the idea of temporal passage, presentism offers a distinct advantage over four-dimensionalism.

In presenting his argument, McTaggart considers and rejects a response that superficially resembles a tenser solution. He observes that the natural reply to his argument is to deny that *E is* past, present, and future and to insist instead that tense be retained: *E was* future, *is* present, and *will be* past. But, he argues, making this reply launches an infinite regress. The regress arises as follows. Suppose E is present and will be past. One way to understand this is to suppose that (a) past and future times exist, (b) every event is (tenselessly) present at every time at which it exists, (c) every event is (tenselessly) past from the point of view of times later than those at which they exist, and (d) our point of view is from a time at which E exists rather than from a time later than all times at which E exists. But, of course, this is not something that a *tenser* could endorse; for it takes A-determinations to be permanent properties which are reducible to B-relations, and it explicitly allows that every event is (tenselessly) past, present, and future. Apparently, however, the only other way of understanding it is to suppose that there exists a time t_1 at which E is present and that there *will* exist a time t_2 at which E will be past. This avoids committing us to the idea that E is both present and past. But it seems to leave us right back where we started. After all, an event E is present if and only if the time at which it exists is present; thus, to say that there is a time t_1 at which E is present and there will be a time t_2 at which E will be past entails that t_1 is present and will be past. But now from (A) it follows that t_1 is both present and past—contradiction again. McTaggart notes that we can try to understand the claim that t_1 is present and will be past by saying that there is a time T_1 in some higher-level time series at which t_1 is present, and there *will be* a time T_2 at which t_1 will be past. But this, in turn, entails that T_1 is present and will be past, and so we face the same problem all over again. Hence our regress.

Of course, in saying all this, McTaggart is simply taking it for granted that (A) is true and presupposing that it is unacceptable to dodge the regress by saying that tensed facts are unanalysable. Thus, in the end, McTaggart fails to rebut the tenser solution because he fails even to consider it as a serious option. For this reason, C. D. Broad and others have characterized his argument as a 'howler'.[24] Broad writes: 'The fallacy in McTaggart's argument consists in treating absolute becoming as if it were a species of qualitative change, and in trying to replace temporal copulas by non-temporal copulas and temporal adjectives' (Broad 1938: 317). On his view, an event's coming to be present isn't a matter of its acquiring some qualitative property. Rather, an event's coming to be present is just its *coming to be*—absolutely, independently of any relations to external times. Temporal becoming (and therefore tense) is not reducible to tenseless facts about properties had at different times.

Two features of Broad's response are worth attending to. First, Broad takes it for granted that there is a real distinction to be drawn between becoming on the one hand and change on the other. Second, he takes it for granted that it is a fallacy to treat becoming as if it were an essentially temporal process. Both claims are suspect, however. As Aristotle famously observed, when substances are generated, qualitative

---

[24] Broad (1938: 316); Sider (2001, ch. 2 n. 29); see also Prior (1967: 4–7); Christensen (1974).

change *is* involved; and the generation takes place in time. When a horse comes into existence, some matter changes from being arranged non-horse-wise at one time to being arranged horse-wise at some other time. Similarly for any other case of substantial generation. So why think that matters could be any different for times and events? Given my own acquaintance with familiar cases of generation, I find it absolutely impossible to understand the view that times are generated without being generated *at a time* in some higher-level temporal series. Broad's notion of absolute becoming seems unintelligible.[25]

But should a presentist be moved by this? I doubt it. For the intuition that absolute becoming is unintelligible just boils down to an intuition that tensed facts are reducible to tenseless ones. Thus, it boils down to an intuition that presentism is false (which, presumably, a presentist either won't share or, for independent reasons, will find unmoving). If asked for a reason why I find absolute becoming unintelligible, all I could offer is the brute intuition that part of what it means to say that something is present and will be past is that there is some time at which the thing is present and some later time at which it is past. To say this is just to engage in the same 'fallacy' as McTaggart; only it is *not* a fallacy, but a difference of intuitions. And, if the literature is any guide, once we have uncovered this difference, there is little else to be said on either side.

Let us now waive worries about absolute becoming and focus on our second question: the question whether, if coherent, a tenser solution is available to non-presentists. Initially, one might think that it is not. For example, Dean Zimmerman (1998) argues that the primary motivation for taking tense seriously is 'the desire to do justice to the feeling that what's in the past is over and done with, and what's in the future only matters because it will eventually be present' (Zimmerman 1998: 212). But, he says, on the supposition that past or future objects (or both) exist, we have no resources for doing justice to this claim. 'If yesterday's headache still exists and remains as painful as ever,' he asks, 'why should I be relieved now?' (Zimmerman 1998: 212). And if we try to avoid this consequence by admitting tenseless quantification but not tenseless predication—e.g. if we allow that the headache exists but deny that it is dull, sharp, painful, painless, or anything else— then we end up with a view according to which past objects are like bare particulars: they exist, but they have no properties. (Cf. Zimmerman 1998; Sider 2001, ch. 4.)

I agree that it is a bad idea to admit tenseless quantification without tenseless predication; and so I am also inclined at least tentatively to agree that four-dimensionalist tensers will need some further solution to the problem of temporary intrinsics. If Philip exists, and if we admit tenseless predication, then we are committed to saying that he is both drunk and sober. Hence, our contradiction remains. A tenser *might* try to respond by saying that tenseless contradictions are okay; it's

---

[25] Smart (1949, 1987a) also offers criticism of the notion of absolute becoming.

the tensed ones that we want to avoid. This is certainly one way of taking tense seriously. But it is also a very hard pill to swallow. Most four-dimensionalist tensers seem to prefer the doctrine of temporal parts (cf. Broad 1927, ch. 2).

But I don't think that these considerations on their own show that a weak tenser solution to McTaggart's problem is untenable. For one thing, they do not at all challenge the coherence of the solution; and, indeed, there's good reason to think that presentists *can't* challenge its coherence. Presentism requires absolute generation; but once absolute generation is admitted, there's no reason to doubt that a growing block theory is coherent. Thus, the weak tenser solution is on no worse a footing than presentism with respect to coherence. Furthermore, even if we grant that four-dimensionalist tensers can't meet Prior's famous challenge to explain what we are thanking goodness for when we say 'Thank goodness that's over!', there are other motivations for being a tenser besides the desire to meet that challenge—foremost among them being the intuition that time passes.[26] Moreover, Prior's challenge seems overrated. No one asks who or what we are thanking when we say 'Thank goodness that's over!'; and no one thinks that there is a sound argument for theism or Platonism lurking in the neighbourhood. But our feelings of gratitude at the passing of a headache are just as much—or as little!—in need of philosophical explanation as our feelings of relief.

So the weak tenser solution, if coherent at all, is readily available to four-dimensionalists. Growing block theorists may follow Broad in characterizing the passage of presentness as the absolute generation of times. Shrinking block or shrinking tree theorists may characterize it as the absolute destruction of times. And eternalists may characterize it as absolute qualitative change in times. Broad himself would baulk at the idea of absolute qualitative change; but given that substantial generation always occurs in time and always involves qualitative change, it is hard to see what grounds one could have for objecting to such change that would not also be grounds for objecting to absolute generation.[27]

Presentism, then, offers no special advantage over four-dimensionalism with respect to solving McTaggart's problem. On the other hand, presentism solves McTaggart's problem only if the strong tenser solution is coherent; and, for some, there are strong intuitive grounds for thinking that that solution is not coherent. As we have already seen, however, the intuition that the tenser solution is incoherent is equivalent to the intuition that presentism is false; hence, it is not an intuition that presentists can reasonably be expected to share. The argument from the impossibility of temporal passage thus concludes in stalemate.

---

[26] Prior's challenge appears in Prior (1959). Garrett (1988), MacBeath (1983), Mellor (1981*b*, 1983) offer responses compatible with four-dimensionalism.

[27] Craig (1997) argues that an A-theory can't be accepted by a four-dimensionalist who regards A-properties as intrinsic properties. But, as I see it, his argument fails because, like Broad, he fails to take seriously the very close connection between absolute becoming and absolute qualitative change.

4. TRUTHMAKERS

Many philosophers are attracted to the idea that *truth supervenes on being*, or that *every truth has a truthmaker*.[28] To say that truth supervenes on being is just to say that any world that duplicates ours with respect to what there is and how things are also duplicates ours with respect to what is true. Whether this is sufficient for every truth's having a truthmaker will depend in part upon what you think truthmakers are and what you think the relation of truthmaking amounts to. Typically, the claim that truth supervenes on being is taken to be weaker than the truthmaker principle (the claim that every truth has a truthmaker). But for present purposes I'll ignore this fact and simply talk as if the truthmaker principle is satisfied if and only if truth supervenes on being. Our focus will be on the question whether the truthmaker principle thus conceived offers any convincing reason to reject presentism in favour of four-dimensionalism. I'll argue that it doesn't.

Ignoring details for the moment, there is a very quick way of seeing why the truthmaker principle won't be an effective weapon against presentism. In describing the principle, David Lewis concedes that it might take different forms for different philosophers. Which form it takes depends on what sorts of objects, events, properties, and relations the philosopher in question countenances. So, for example, Armstrong (1997) requires that truth be grounded in states of affairs; Lewis (1999a) requires that it be grounded in 'things and which perfectly natural properties and relations they instantiate'. Others might impose different requirements, depending on their particular ontological views. But now it should be clear why the principle will be dialectically impotent. Targets of truthmaker objections may simply respond by expanding the class of objects, events, properties, and relations that are taken to serve as truthmakers. And once such a response is given, reviving the objection is difficult. One can call it a cheat; or one can heap disparagement upon the newly introduced class of entities; but, if the literature is any guide, such further objections are typically (and rightly) taken with a grain of salt.[29] Such, in fact, has been the fate of the truthmaker objection against presentism.

That said, however, let us now explore in some detail the truthmaker objection against presentism and some of the replies that are available. The objection takes the form of a *reductio ad absurdum*: (i) Suppose presentism is true. Then (ii) our world doesn't include past or future objects or events. But (iii) if our world doesn't include past or future objects or events, then there is nothing in the world that could ground propositions about the past or future. Therefore, (iv) propositions about the

---

[28] For starters, see Armstrong (1989, 1997); Bigelow (1988: 122, 132–3); Lewis (1999a,b, 2002b).

[29] An abundance of examples illustrating this point may be found in the literature on modal realism, realism about universals, and truthmakers for counterfactuals.

past and future lack truthmakers. Therefore, (v) if the truthmaker principle is true, then propositions about the past and future are not true. But (vi) the truthmaker principle is true, and (vii) at least some propositions about the past and future are true. Therefore, (viii) presentism must be false.[30]

If we grant the truthmaker principle, the crucial premises in this argument are (iii) and (vii). The choice between the two is essentially a choice between supplying truthmakers for propositions about the past and future or somehow making plausible the claim that many or all of those propositions are false. Happily (for presentists) there are strategies available for accomplishing each of these tasks that do not exact a high ontological or intuitive price.

Towards understanding how presentists might supply truthmakers for truths about the past and future, it will be instructive briefly to consider another domain of truths for which we might be thought to face some sort of grounding problem: the domain of modal truths. As in the temporal case, the problem in the modal case is that there seems to be no object or event in the actual world that could ground truths about what *could have been* the case or about what *must be* the case. But, of course, there are many such truths. There could have been a tenth planet in our solar system; there couldn't have been a round square automobile on top of the number 7. David Lewis could have been shorter; he couldn't have been a golf ball. Therefore, we have a problem.

One response to this modal problem is to follow David Lewis (1986) in taking the modal operators 'possibly' and 'necessarily' to be quantifiers over concrete possible worlds. On Lewis's view, to say that there could have been a tenth planet is just to say that there exists a concrete world spatio-temporally disconnected from ours that includes a counterpart of our solar system which has a tenth planet. This response is the analogue of four-dimensionalism, which takes the temporal operators 'was' and 'will be' to be quantifiers over concrete times. Thus, there is nothing in this response that will be of use to presentists.[31]

Another response to the modal problem is to suppose that true modal propositions are grounded in irreducible modal properties of material objects.[32] On this view, what makes it true that (e.g.) David Lewis could not have been a golf ball is just the exemplification by Lewis of the primitive property *being essentially something*

[30] This way of putting it generalizes a variety of more specific truthmaker objections, the most significant of which are discussed below. Among the most important discussions of these objections and related issues are Adams (1986); Bigelow (1996); Chisholm (1990); Fitch (1994); LePoidevin (1991); Markosian (2002); Prior (1967, 1968b); Sider (1999, 2001). See also Gale (1968) and Sprigge (1992).

[31] Well, there is this much: A presentist might say to a four-dimensionalist: 'Look how incredible the Lewisian response is in the modal case! Are you sure you want to embrace it in the temporal case?' This is surely to be taken seriously, but it is far from decisive.

[32] Alvin Plantinga (1974) is plausibly read as endorsing a view like this; however, one must be careful about attributing it to him since elsewhere (Plantinga 1985: 374) he explicitly expresses hesitation about the truthmaker principle.

other than a golf ball (or, more likely: *being essentially a human being*). What makes it true that our solar system could have included a tenth planet is either the exemplification by our solar system of the primitive property *being possibly such as to include an additional planet*, or some combination of simpler irreducible modal properties exemplified by objects in our solar system and in relevant other places throughout the universe. Likewise, then, a presentist might respond to the temporal problem by saying that truths about the past and future are grounded in irreducibly *tensed* properties of material objects.[33] Some philosophers will be uneasy with the idea that there are irreducible modal properties and irreducible tenses. But common-sense presentists should not be. As we saw in Section 3, common-sense presentists avoid McTaggart's problem only by taking tense as irreducible. Thus, irreducibly tensed properties are already built into the common-sense presentist's view; and if irreducible tenses are unproblematic, irreducible modal properties should not be either.

So far, then, it appears that the presentist can dodge the truthmaker objection without incurring any ontological cost that is not already built into her view. Still, we are not out of the woods yet. For there is the further problem of accounting for the truth of singular propositions involving past objects. Various examples have been raised to illustrate this problem. Two that are particularly worthy of attention are the following, both borrowed from Sider (1999):

(7) Abraham Lincoln was tall.

(8) David Lewis admires Frank Ramsey.

Dualism and other immortality-entailing theories aside, (7) attributes a property to a past object, and (8) implied, at the time it was published, that past objects can be related to present objects. The trouble is that, if presentism is true, then past objects don't exist and so they aren't available to have properties or to stand in relations. The names 'Abraham Lincoln' and 'Frank Ramsey' would appear to be non-referring, since there is nothing in the universe of a contemporary presentist to which they *could* refer. But if the names are non-referring, then it is hard to see how the sentences could be true.[34]

Once again, however, we have a (rough) modal parallel. It is possible that David Lewis does not exist. So there is a world in which David Lewis does not exist and in which the following proposition is true:

(9) David Lewis does not exist.

[33] This sort of view is endorsed by Bigelow (1996); Chisholm (1990); Markosian (2002); Prior (1967, 1968b). Cf. also Zimmerman (1997: 91–2). Sider (1999) offers important critical discussion and expansion of the view.

[34] All of the references in n. 30 discuss the problem of referring to past objects, the problem of attributing properties to past objects, the problem of cross-temporal relations, or all three.

But if David Lewis does not exist in that world, then he's not around to occur in or be the subject of the proposition that he does not exist; so how could (9) possibly be true? The answer, according to some, is that, strictly speaking, Lewis himself isn't the subject of (9). Rather, Lewis's *essence* (the property of being identical to Lewis) is the subject. On this view, (9) does not predicate non-existence of Lewis. Rather, it predicates the property of being non-exemplified of Lewis's essence. Since Lewis's essence exists necessarily, (9) can be true in worlds where Lewis doesn't exist.[35] Thus, on the very plausible assumption that there could have been things that don't exist, our world also contains essences that could have been exemplified but aren't; and if only we were acquainted with those essences, we could truthfully assert propositions like (9) without (absurdly) committing ourselves to the conclusion that things presently non-existent can nonetheless presently have properties.

A presentist, then, might say that we *are* acquainted (by virtue of causal relations to past events) with some of the essences of non-existent objects, and this is what explains our apparent ability to attribute properties and relations to those objects. On this view, (7) and (8) are equivalent to something like the following:

(10) The property of being identical to Lincoln was co-exemplified with the property of being tall.

(11) The property of being identical to Ramsey was co-exemplified with various other properties in such a way as to give rise (through some complex causal chain) to feelings of admiration in David Lewis.

Lincoln and Ramsey don't occur in these propositions; so there is no problem arising from the fact that *they* do not exist. The properties *being identical to Lincoln* and *being identical to Ramsey* do occur in these propositions and are presently unexemplified; but, again, our acquaintance with them can be explained by the causal connections between present events and the past exemplifications of those properties. Of course, it might seem a little odd to suppose that (7) is really about Lincoln's *essence* rather than about Lincoln himself. And the alleged equivalence of (8) and (11) might seem to have the even worse consequence that Lewis's feelings of admiration, rather than being *about* or *directed towards* Ramsey, are instead about or directed towards either nothing or Ramsey's essence (which would be absurd). But concerns about these consequences are misplaced. Even if Lincoln is not strictly the subject of (7), there is a clear intuitive sense in which (7) and (10) are *about* Lincoln. (7) and (10) tell us about a property that was co-exemplified with Lincoln's essence; and in so doing, they tell us about Lincoln himself, albeit without referring to him. Similarly, it is quite plausible to think that feelings of admiration are about or directed towards an individual just in case they are, in the right sort of way, *caused by* that individual; but (11) is consistent with—indeed, entails—that Lewis's feelings are caused by Ramsey.

---

[35] Or so says Plantinga (1976). For disagreement, see Adams (1981).

Thus, there seems to be no obstacle to saying that Lewis's feelings of admiration are about Ramsey, even though Ramsey himself isn't available as an object of reference.

One might object that we haven't really solved the problem yet because we are simply taking it for granted that non-existing things can stand in relations to existing things. Causal relations *are* relations, after all; and, quite plausibly, they are existence-entailing—i.e. it is plausible to think that, necessarily, only existing things are causally related. Perhaps a presentist could simply abandon this idea.[36] But even if she doesn't, there are other ways around the problem. One is to suppose that causal relations hold not between objects but between propositions or states of affairs. Another is to suppose that causal relations hold between irreducibly tensed properties of the world (e.g. the property of having had a certain sort of past, or the property of being pregnant with a certain sort of future), each of which presently exists and is presently exemplified.[37] Either way, the presentist can maintain the view that causal relations obtain only between existing things; for propositions, properties, and the world all presently exist. But she can also give sense to the claim that we are causally related to past objects like Lincoln and Ramsey and that such causal relations explain our ability to assert truths about their essences. The way to do it is just to reconstruct the causal chains leading from Lincoln and Ramsey to us in terms of true tensed propositions involving relations between their essences and ours, or in terms of tensed world properties involving their essences and ours.

The cost of embracing the package of views just described is a commitment to individual essences which exist even when the individuals of which they are essences do not exist, and a commitment to the claim that causal relations are relations among things other than concrete objects or events. Since there is independent motivation from other quarters for accepting individual essences which exist even in *worlds* in which the corresponding individuals fail to exist, I see no reason to think that the former cost is one that a presentist should be worried about.[38] And the latter cost does not seem especially objectionable either.

So, presentists are committed to irreducible tenses in any case; and in light of the foregoing, it would appear that, at most, the only other commitment they would need to incur in order to solve their truthmaker problem is a commitment to necessarily existing individual essences. Perhaps they could even get by with less. After all, there are other, ostensibly more conservative strategies for solving the modal problem; and perhaps those strategies will have coherent temporal parallels.[39]

---

[36] Hinchliff (1996: 124–5) appears to be content with this suggestion.

[37] Bigelow (1996) discusses both alternatives and endorses the latter. Cf. also Prior (1967, ch. 8; 1968b); Zimmerman (1997: 91–2).

[38] See Plantinga (1976) for the relevant motivation. See Markosian (2002) for objections about the cost. Adams (1986) also objects to the claim that individual essences can pre-exist the objects of which they are essences; but unlike Markosian, he allows that essences of past objects continue to exist.

[39] See Sider's contribution to this volume, Ch. 7, for some of the available options.

But the modal strategies described above strike me as eminently plausible and acceptable, and so it is hard to see why presentists should not be able to adapt them for their own purposes.

However, one might think that the truthmaker problem doesn't *need* to be solved. Or, at any rate, it is not clear that it needs to be solved in a way that supplies truthmakers for *all* of the tensed propositions we take to be true. Theodore Sider (1999), for example, has recently argued that irreducible tenses alone will suffice to supply truthmakers for many tensed propositions (in particular: propositions describing purely qualitative states of affairs not involving spatio-temporal positions or relationships), and that the rest may plausibly be regarded as strictly false, but nonetheless *quasi-true*.[40] On his view, a tensed sentence *S* is quasi-true just in case there is some true proposition that would have been true and would have entailed *S* had eternalism been true.[41] That true proposition is an *underlying truth* for *S*. Thus, the basic idea is that sentences like (7) and (8) are strictly false, but are nonetheless close enough to the truth for presentist purposes so long as there are underlying truths for them. Though it initially seems counter-intuitive to say that (7) and (8) are false, Sider points out that, in general, quasi-truths are simpler to assert than their more accurate underliers, and empirical evidence alone won't distinguish between the two. Thus, he argues, there is a plausible psychological explanation for why quasi-truths might appear to us to be genuinely true, and presentists who endorse this solution aren't committed to rejecting the claim that we have empirical justification for our (merely quasi-true) beliefs about the past.

As Sider himself notes, it is not obvious that the quasi-truth strategy for defending presentism will take the presentist all the way home. He argues persuasively that sticky problems arise in accounting for cross-time spatio-temporal relations and causal relations (Sider 1999, 2001). But the approach is at least promising. Still, there is an important cost associated with the strategy. Underlying truths are *purely qualitative*—i.e. they make reference only to properties and relations that can be multiply exemplified. But underlying truths in conjunction with eternalism are supposed to entail the truth of sentences like (7) and (8), which refer to specific individuals. Thus, the view implies that the exemplification of some set of purely qualitative properties might, in conjunction with eternalism, be sufficient for the existence of some specific individual (e.g. Abraham Lincoln). But many philosophers find this implausible. Suppose we managed to create a perfect atom-for-atom duplicate of Abraham Lincoln just as he was ten minutes before his death. Would our technological activity be sufficient to re-create *Lincoln himself*? If we did

---

[40] See also Markosian (2002) for a different but related approach.

[41] For those who think that eternalism and presentism are necessarily true if true at all, there are prima facie problems about counter-possibles that crop up here. Sider addresses those concerns, but for purposes here we'll just leave them aside.

it twice, would we re-create him twice over? Presumably not. But if not, then why think that a purely qualitative underlier in conjunction with eternalism would *entail* that *Lincoln* was tall? Plausibly it would only entail that someone exactly like Lincoln was tall.

Of course, this objection assumes what Sider would deny—namely, that it is implausible to suppose that there are no individual essences (Sider 1999: 335 n. 13). But once this is clear, we can see that, for present purposes, the objection in no way damages the presentist arsenal. What we have now is a reply to the truthmaker objection that will suit those who like individual essences, and a different reply that will suit those who don't. Each has its cost; but the important thing to see is that those who are troubled by the costs of one solution are extremely unlikely to be troubled by the costs of the other.

So there are various ways in which presentists might resist the truthmaker objection without paying a substantial intuitive or ontological price. Thus, I see no reason to think that the truthmaker objection on its own lends any great support to four-dimensionalism. Before closing this section, however, I should like to observe that there is another side to this coin. Thus far, I have focused exclusively on the four-dimensionalist challenge that presentists cannot supply truthmakers for tensed truths. But I would be remiss if I did not mention the fact that there are resources in the literature for presentists to raise precisely the same challenge against four-dimensionalists.

To appreciate this fact, one must first understand in a little more detail the central issue in the tenser–detenser debate. Earlier in this century the debate between tensers and detensers concerned the question whether tensed sentences were *translatable* by tenseless sentences.[42] For example, detensers held that sentences like (R1) below were synonymous with sentences like (R2) (where the words in parentheses represent various options for finishing the sentence that were offered by different theories):

(R1) It is now raining.
(R2) The occurrence of rain is simultaneous with (this utterance/the tokening of (R1)/this sense datum/etc.)

Similarly, sentences like (R3) below were taken to be synonymous with sentences like (R4):

(R3) It was raining yesterday.
(R4) The occurrence of rain is a day earlier than (this utterance/the tokening of (R3)/this sense datum/etc.).

Tensers, on the other hand, disagreed.

---

[42] See e.g. Smart (1949, 1963); Grünbaum (1963); Prior (1968a); Gale (1968).

The tensers won this particular debate. The view that tensed sentences can be translated by tenseless sentences is now referred to as the *Old* Tenseless Theory of Time—old because it is now generally agreed to have been refuted.[43] But detensers have regrouped in support of the *New* Tenseless Theory of Time, according to which tensed sentences aren't translatable by tenseless sentences but can, nevertheless, be given tenseless truth-conditions.[44] As with the old theory, the underlying idea is that there is no need to regard tense as a real, intrinsic feature of the world in order to account for the truth of tensed sentences. Tensers, on the other hand, continue to press for the conclusion that tense *must* be taken to be an intrinsic feature of the world if tensed sentences are to come out true.[45] In effect, then, tensers are raising a truthmaker objection.

Well, not quite. Truth-conditions are different from truthmakers. Truthmakers provide a sufficient condition for a proposition's truth; but truth-conditions are necessary and sufficient conditions. Still, I think it is reasonable to see the issue in terms of truthmaking because if tenseless truthmakers can be supplied for tensed truths, the tensers' position is vitiated—and this regardless of whether the truthmakers happen also to qualify as truth-conditions.

So if we agree with the tensers that a tenseless world lacks truthmakers for tensed truths, then we have a truthmaker objection against any theory that postulates a tenseless world. This isn't quite a truthmaker objection against four-dimensionalism, since growing block, shrinking block, shrinking tree, and moving spotlight theories are all four-dimensionalist theories that recognize tense as an intrinsic feature of the world. But if we add the premiss (which many seem to find plausible) that four-dimensionalism is incompatible with the thesis that presentness is an irreducible transitory property of events, then our truthmaker objection will rule out four-dimensionalism after all.

I am inclined to think that the detensers have the better of the tenser–detenser debate, and that tensed sentences can have tenseless truthmakers after all. But whether I am right about this does not really matter for present purposes; for I have already argued that it is a mistake to think that presentism is coherent *and* that four-dimensionalism is incompatible with the thesis that presentness is an irreducible transitory property. If I am right, then the truthmaker objection against four-dimensionalism is a non-starter and, indeed, the whole tenser–detenser debate is irrelevant to the question whether four-dimensionalism is true. This is a significant point in its own right since it might otherwise be tempting to think that an argument for the conclusion that tense is irreducible is *ipso facto* an argument for presentism. But that is incorrect.

---

[43] See the introductory chapters of Oaklander and Smith (1994) for a concise summary of the history of this debate.

[44] See esp. Smart (1987*a*); Mellor (1981*a*, 1998); and the essays by Oaklander, Beer, and Williams in Oaklander and Smith (1994).

[45] See esp. Smith (1995) and the essays by Smith in Oaklander and Smith (1994).

5. RELATIVITY

By far the most well-known and widely discussed claim advanced on behalf of four-dimensionalism is the claim that presentism is incompatible with the special theory of relativity (SR for short).[46] Towards justifying this claim, I'll first provide a brief intuitive explanation of the central claims of SR and the reasons why one might think those claims conflict with presentism. I'll then present a somewhat more formal argument for the conclusion that SR conflicts with presentism.

In short, SR is the thesis that the laws of physics are constant in every inertial frame of reference One consequence of this thesis is that the speed of light is constant in every inertial frame of reference. A frame of reference is a coordinate system defined with respect to a particular object in space-time. An inertial frame of reference is a coordinate system that is not accelerated. For example: imagine two particles A and B floating past one another in outer space at a constant rate of 10 km./hr.; and imagine further that each particle is at the origin of its own distinct coordinate system. The coordinate systems will then be frames of reference defined with respect to each particle; and they will be *inertial* frames of reference because neither particle (and hence neither coordinate system) is accelerated. If particle A accelerates, say because it comes under the gravitational influence of a nearby asteroid, then the corresponding frame of reference accelerates and so ceases to qualify as an inertial frame of reference. To appreciate the significance of the thesis that the laws of physics are constant in every inertial frame of reference, it will help to consider a pair of examples.

First example (borrowed from Geroch 1978): There are certain particles called *mu mesons* which, when produced under laboratory conditions, have a lifespan of 1 microsecond. The same sorts of particles, however, are produced in nature by the collision of cosmic rays with atoms in the upper atmosphere. The mu mesons that are thus produced naturally travel towards the earth at high speeds and have a lifespan of 10 microseconds. According to SR, however, the laws of physics are the same in every frame of reference; thus (contrary to appearances) mu mesons produced in a lab and mu mesons produced in nature decay at the *same* rate in their respective frames of reference. The upshot is striking. If SR is true, it follows that observers at rest with respect to naturally produced mu mesons would observe those particles to have a lifespan of 1 microsecond whereas we would observe the very same particles to have a lifespan of 10. Thus, SR entails that different observers in different frames of reference may disagree about durations.

Second example (adapted from Einstein 1961): Suppose you are travelling on a very long train (a train that is 1 light-second long, as measured by someone on

---

[46] See esp. Christensen (1981, 1993); Putnam (1967); Rietdijk (1966); Sider (2001); Sklar (1985a); Smith (1995). See also references listed in nn. 50–61. Further arguments arise out of general relativity. Perhaps the most well known is that presented in Gödel (1979). I will not discuss this argument here; but see Savitt (1994) and Yourgrau (1991) for discussion and further references.

the train) which is moving at a speed of 1,000 m./sec. relative to its track. Suppose further that, at time t_1, the rear end of the train is at point A on the track, and that at time t_2 (1 second later than t_1) the front end of the train is at point B on the track. Standing at point A at time t_1, you emit a light signal. Now, if the laws of physics are constant in every inertial frame of reference, then the speed of light is constant in every inertial frame of reference. Given this, and given that the length of the train as measured by someone on the train is 1 light-second, it follows that the signal takes exactly 1 second to reach the front end of the train, which would then be at point B on the track. But notice: if, as seems plausible, the length of the train as measured by someone on the train is the *same* as the length of the train as measured by someone on the track, it follows that the distance between point A and point B is 1,000 metres *more* than 1 light-second. But if that is right, then we are committed to saying either that the light signal travelled, relative to the track, a distance greater than 1 light-second in 1 second, or that, relative to the track, the trip taken by the light signal took more than 1 second. The thesis that light travels with constant velocity in all frames of reference rules out the first alternative; thus, if we accept SR we are forced to affirm one or both of the following claims: (i) a trip that takes 1 second in the train's frame of reference takes longer in the track's frame of reference, or (ii) an object 1 light-second long in the train's frame of reference is shorter in the track's frame of reference. In other words, SR commits us to the conclusion that observers in different frames of reference may disagree about distances, durations, or both.

In Newtonian physics, distances and durations are invariant across inertial frames of reference. In SR, they are not. SR entails that observers in different inertial frames of reference will disagree about distances and durations; but they will agree about a quantity called the 'interval' between two events. The interval is a kind of combination of distance and duration, including as 'components' all three spatial dimensions and the temporal dimension. What it measures is a separation in *space-time* rather than a separation in space or time. Still, physicists do speak of *spacelike* separations and *timelike* separations between events; and since the facts about such separations depend exclusively on facts about the interval between the separated events, those facts too are invariant across inertial frames of reference. Events are spacelike-separated when the interval between them is positive, timelike-separated when the interval is negative, and *lightlike*-separated when the interval is null. Timelike-separated events are events such that signals travelling slower than light could reach one from the other; spacelike-separated events are events such that only signals travelling faster than light could reach one from the other; and lightlike-separated events are events such that only signals travelling at the speed of light could reach one from the other. For example, suppose you watch a batter at a distance hit a baseball. You see the hit; a moment later you hear the crack. Intuitively, what you see (like what you hear) occurs some time *after* the actual hitting itself. So: let E1 be whatever event in your life happened simultaneously (in your frame of reference) with the hitting of the baseball; let E2 be your seeing the hit; let E3 be your hearing the crack. The actual hitting of the ball was spacelike-separated from E1; no causal signal slower than or equal to the speed of light could have put E1 in touch with that event. But the hitting of the ball was perhaps lightlike-separated from E2 (since it is the light signals coming from that event that are responsible for your seeing it), and it was clearly timelike-separated from E3 (since slower-than-light signals could and did travel from that event to E3). We should note that it is a mistake simply to equate spacelike and timelike separation respectively with our intuitive notions of spatial and temporal separation in a frame of reference. But timelike separation does seem to *entail* temporal separation in a frame of reference. At any rate, events that are timelike-separated are typically said to be in each other's absolute past or absolute future; and it is hard to see how those descriptions could possibly be inappropriate.

Geometrically, the explanation for why observers in different frames of reference disagree about distances and durations while agreeing about intervals is that such observers are rotated with respect to one another. In other words, SR implies that uniform relative motion *just is* rotation in spacetime. But now it is easy to see why SR poses a problem for presentism. Earlier I said that in a relativistic context times are plausibly taken to be sums of events sharing a plane of simultaneity in a frame of reference (or, alternatively, the state of the universe on such a plane).[47] So far so good; but the fact is, given common-sense assumptions about what other objects exist in the world, there are objects that share a plane of simultaneity with me which are also in relative motion (and thus rotated) with respect to me. But this implies that a plane of simultaneity defined relative to my frame of reference will *intersect* (rather than completely overlap) a plane of simultaneity defined relative to their frame of reference. So consider some such object X. X will be on my plane of simultaneity, but I will not be on X's. Furthermore, events that are in my absolute past or my absolute future might be on X's plane of simultaneity. Thus, if I define 'the present time' as the sum of all of the events that share a plane of simultaneity with me in my frame of reference, and if I also say that only present events exist, then I arbitrarily privilege my own frame of reference over X's. Furthermore, if someone in X's frame of reference offers the same sort of definition and then goes on to accept presentism, her view will have the (obviously false) consequence that I don't exist. Thus, it would appear that SR is inconsistent with presentism.

There are, of course, various ways of resisting this argument. But before presenting those, I would like first to offer a somewhat more formal presentation of it. The argument runs as follows:[48]

(1) SR is true. (Premiss)

---

[47] As Einstein defines it, two events x and y are simultaneous in a frame of reference S just in case light signals travelling from x and y would be observed at the same time by a detector which is at rest in S and equidistant from x and y. A plane of simultaneity in S passing through an event x is just the set of all events in space-time which are simultaneous (by the above definition) with x in S.

[48] This formulation supersedes my earlier formulation in Rea (1998). As formulated there, the argument begs the question against the presentist.

(2) The present time relative to an event x on the worldline of an object O is the sum of all of the events that share a plane of simultaneity with x in O's frame of reference. (Premiss)

(3) There is at least one event E that (a) exists at the present time in my frame of reference and (b) is on the worldline of an object in motion relative to me. (Premiss)

(4) Therefore: There is at least one event E such that the present time relative to E is not identical to the present time relative to me. (From 1, 2, 3)

(5) Presentism is true only if there is a unique present time. (Premiss)

(6) Therefore: Presentism is false. (4, 6)

No one denies that the sub-argument for (4) is valid. Given this, there should be no question that the rest of the argument is valid either. Thus, all that is left for a presentist to do is to reject one of the unsupported premisses: (1), (2), (3), or (5). I'll briefly consider each of these alternatives, beginning with the denial of (2).

First response: Deny that the present time relative to an event x in the career of an object is to be defined as the sum of all of the events sharing a plane of simultaneity with x in the object's frame of reference. One who endorses this response (and who believes that she exists at the present time) rejects the general view that a time is to be identified with a sum of events on a plane of simultaneity in some frame of reference.[49] This seems sensible enough at first glance. On presentism, the present time is ontologically privileged (by virtue of being the only time that exists). But SR countenances no privileged planes of simultaneity or frames of reference. Therefore, on presentism, the present time should not be identified with a sum of events on a plane of simultaneity in a frame of reference. But what are the alternatives? Broadly speaking, three have been taken seriously in the literature: define the present time relative to an event E as the sum of all or some of the events that are spacelike-separated from E; define it as the sum of all or some of the events that are either timelike- or lightlike-separated from E; or define it as including nothing more than E itself.[50] The trouble is that all of these suggestions imply one or more of the following claims: (a) what events count as present vary from observer to observer; (b) for some observers, past or future objects exist; or (c) there are no objects which are present but not coincident with E. Which of these claims are implied depends on the way in which the various suggestions are developed; but the important thing to notice is that the first conflicts with premiss (5), the second

---

[49] She also rejects the general view that a time is to be identified with an abstract state of affairs corresponding to the total state of the universe on such a plane. Henceforth, I'll continue to ignore the view that times might be thought of as states of affairs; but the reader should keep in mind that, for every claim I make about concrete times, there are parallel claims that could be made about abstract times.

[50] See e.g. Christensen (1981, 1993); Fitzgerald (1969); Godfrey-Smith (1979); Hinchliff (2000); McCall (1976, 1994); Maxwell (1985); Mellor (1974); Rakić (1997); Savitt (2000); Sider (2001); Sklar (1974, ch. IV; 1985a); Smith (1995); Stein (1968, 1991).

conflicts with the fundamental presentist thesis that past and future objects don't exist, and the third conflicts with premiss (3). What we need, then, to escape the argument is some plausible way of defining 'the present time' that will not imply any of (a)–(c). Unfortunately, contemporary physics seems utterly devoid of resources for doing this.

Second response: Deny that there exists at the present time at least one other event on the worldline of an object in motion relative to me. One who endorses this view *might* accept the fact that other objects exist but (bizarrely) deny that any of them are in motion. More likely, one who accepts this view will simply deny that there are any other objects in the world at all. In other words, the rejection of (3) is most naturally accompanied by a very extreme form of solipsism. (Not only are there no other minds; there are no other *things*.) Surprisingly enough, this response has been recommended in the literature, though generally in conjunction with the relative-existence response discussed below.[51] But most, I think, will agree that if this is the best that can be done to save presentism, four-dimensionalism comes out the clear winner.

Third response: Deny that presentism implies that there is a unique present time. Presentism, again, is the view that no times other than the present exist. But, in light of the above considerations, there are at least two ways of understanding this. So far I have been understanding presentism as equivalent to the claim that, always, there exists exactly one time. But one might instead take presentists to be asserting that, always, there exists *relative to them* exactly one time. In other words, one might take presentism as implying that existence is observer-relative.[52] If 'the present time' is defined in terms of simultaneity, this view will imply that existence is *frame*-relative; if 'the present time' is defined in terms of spacelike, timelike, or lightlike separation, it will imply that presentness is *event*-relative; and if 'the present time' is identified with the single event which is 'here and now', it will imply a 'pluralistic solipsism'.[53] Admittedly, embracing relative existence avoids the conflict between presentism and SR. But is presentism really *so* powerfully intuitive that we should be willing to relativize existence in order to save it? My own inclination is to say no—mainly because I find the notion of relative existence wholly unintelligible. Moreover, even if this relative-existence brand of presentism were intelligible, it is not at all clear that it would offer any real advantage over four-dimensionalism. After all, in some sense it actually *preserves* the four-dimensionalist intuition that all events in space-time are ontologically on a par.[54] The main difference is that instead of all existing *simpliciter*, they all exist from some points of view but not from others.

---

[51] See esp. Stein (1968, 1991). For criticism, see Rietdijk (1976).

[52] See esp. Fitzgerald (1969); Godfrey-Smith (1979); Hinchliff (2000); McCall (1994); Sklar (1974: 274–5; 1985a).   [53] Cf. Stein (1968: 18); Godfrey-Smith (1979: 242–3).

[54] Cf. Sklar (1985: 297).

Final response: Reject SR. This is by far the most popular response; and, though I am not convinced that it is an especially reasonable response, I do think that it is at least *much more* sensible than any of the alternatives we have just considered. There are various arguments in the literature for the conclusion that it is reasonable to reject SR. Among the more well-known claims that have been made (individually or jointly) on behalf of rejecting it are the following:

(A) The thesis that there is a privileged reference frame was rejected by Einstein for verificationist reasons. But verificationist reasons are not good reasons.[55]

(B) It is possible to construct theories that are empirically equivalent to SR and according to which there is a privileged frame of reference.[56]

(C) The thesis that there is a privileged frame of reference is actually favoured by other scientific theories (e.g. general relativity and quantum mechanics).[57]

(D) SR is not really a theory about *time* at all. Rather, it is a theory about observable luminal relations among physical events, and nothing more. Construed as such, it may be true; but construed as a theory about time, it is false.[58]

It is beyond the scope of this chapter to assess the merits of these claims. But we should notice that, apart from endorsing (D), anyone who pursues this route in replying to the argument from SR has effectively *conceded* that SR conflicts with presentism. The only question once this has been conceded is whether SR itself should be the victor in the conflict.

For the moment, let's ignore option (D) and take it for granted that SR *is* a theory about time. Obviously if the empirical evidence ultimately goes against SR, the threat it poses for presentism will evaporate. The more interesting question is what we should say if it turns out that the empirical evidence does not favour SR over some non-relativistic rival. One might think that pragmatic considerations (appeals to elegance, ease of exposition, ontological economy, and so on) should guide our choice. But, though there may well be non-relativistic rivals to SR, it is doubtful that any extant rival would be favoured over SR by such criteria as these. Indeed, part of the complaint against SR is that pragmatic criteria seem to play *too much* of a role in explaining why it is favoured over its rivals.

Alternatively, one might try to settle the matter by an appeal to intuition.[59] This, in fact, is the most common sort of appeal made on behalf of presentism. Intuition speaks strongly in favour of the conclusion that presentness is a temporary intrinsic property. It also speaks strongly in favour of the conclusion that there aren't any

---

[55] See e.g. Craig (1990) and Swinburne (1983). Sklar (1985a) also observes that verificationism lies at the foundations of relativity theory; but he stops short of recommending that the theory be dropped or amended.   [56] See e.g. Craig (1990); Tooley (1997, ch. 11).

[57] See e.g. Craig (1990); Swinburne (1983); Tooley (1997, ch. 11).

[58] See e.g. Craig (1990); Prior (1996); Smith (1995).

[59] Here and throughout I am thinking of intuitions simply as pre-theoretical beliefs about *either* contingent or necessary matters.

dinosaurs, that Julius Caesar is no more rather than very far away, that we who are alive today are not in any sense unborn or already dead, and so on. Furthermore, many of our ordinary attitudes towards time—for example, our tendency to experience indifference towards events we believe to be in the distant future and relief or nostalgic longing towards various events that are in our past—seem to reflect a belief that past and future events don't exist.[60] So one might think that, in so far as presentism is not decisively ruled out by empirical evidence, these sorts of intuitions may and should take the lead. But here too I think that presentists are on shaky ground. For one thing, many of us have intuitions that conflict with presentism (for example: the intuition that absolute becoming is unintelligible). For another thing, both SR *and* its non-relativistic rivals entail that space and time are very different from what ordinary intuition takes them to be. Nobody, pre-theoretically, thinks that objects shrink when they go very fast or that time speeds up as objects slow down. But, so far as we can tell now, these consequences (or relevantly similar ones) will be implied by *any* physical theory consistent with the empirical data. These considerations do not all by themselves reveal that our intuitions about space and time are worthless. But they should give us pause about trusting them too far.

As I mentioned above, some philosophers think that the problem with SR lies not in its claims about the observable behaviour of light, rigid bodies, and other physical objects, but rather in its claim to tell us something about *time*. The motivation for thinking that SR is not a theory about time comes in large part from the idea that objects not existing in our space-time might nonetheless stand in temporal relations. Thus, for example, Quentin Smith (1995) argues that propositions and mental states are not in physical space-time but nonetheless stand in temporal relations; and William Lane Craig (1990) argues that God is in time without being in physical space-time.[61] One who accepts this sort of view can deny what I said in the previous paragraph about physical theories implying that time is not what we imagine it to be; for (as I understand it) their view implies that the nature of 'real' or 'metaphysical' time is not described by physical theory.

I have some sympathy with this sort of view. I am somewhat attracted to the idea that God is in time, but that his time is not physical time. I also think that mind–body dualism ought to be taken seriously. (For those inclined to scoff at mind–body dualism, see Rea (2002), where I argue that even naturalists are committed to it.) But both of these views seem to imply that there are events that are in time but not in physical space-time. Still, I see no reason to think that adopting the view that SR is not a theory about time will be of any real help to the presentist. Admittedly, she dodges the conclusion that past and future *times* exist by going this route. But even on a non-temporal construal, SR will still imply that past and future *physical objects and events* exist. Thus, one who accepts such a construal of SR will still be committed

[60] On this, see esp. Prior (1959) and Cockburn (1997). But see also references in n. 26.
[61] For criticism of Smith's view, see Nerlich (1998).

to the claim that dinosaurs, Julius Caesar, our births and deaths, and everything else that ever was or will be all exist just as we do. So it is not at all clear that, in going this route, the presentist manages to save anything that is worth saving. She will preserve the intuition that time passes and that tense is an objective feature of the world. She may also preserve the bare claim that non-present times (whatever times might be, on this view) do not exist. But, as we saw in Section 3, presentism offers no special advantage over four-dimensionalism with respect to accommodating tense and the passage of time; and once we have conceded the existence of all past and future physical objects and events, it is hard to see why we should care about, or be motivated to accept the view that, there are no times other than the present. Denying that physical time is real time saves presentism only by stripping it of all that makes it attractive.

6. Conclusion

Ultimately, then, presentism has very little going for it. It is committed to what some take to be an incoherent notion of absolute becoming; it offers no advantage over four-dimensionalism with respect to accommodating tense or temporal passage; and the only viable alternatives to admitting that it conflicts with SR involve a commitment to extreme solipsism, relative existence, or both. Furthermore, even if SR is false, there is no reason to think that intuition will generally favour presentism over four-dimensionalism. As I see it, then, all of this together constitutes a strong cumulative case in favour of four-dimensionalism.

REFERENCES

Adams, R. M. (1981). 'Actualism and Thisness.' *Synthese*, 57: 3–42.

—— (1986). 'Time and Thisness', in P. French, T. Uehling, and H. Wettstein (eds.), *Midwest Studies in Philosophy*, xi. Minneapolis: University of Minnesota Press, 315–30.

Armstrong, D. M. (1980). 'Identity through Time', in Peter van Inwagen (ed.), *Time and Cause: Essays in Honor of Richard Taylor*. Dordrecht: Reidel, 67–78.

—— (1989). *A Combinatorial Theory of Possibility*. New York: Cambridge University Press.

—— (1997). *A World of States of Affairs*. Cambridge: Cambridge University Press.

Balashov, Yuri (2000). 'Enduring and Perduring Objects in Minkowski Space-Time'. *Philosophical Studies*, 99: 129–66.

Bergmann, Michael (1999). '(Serious) Actualism and (Serious) Presentism'. *Noûs*, 33: 118–32.

Bigelow, John (1988). *The Reality of Numbers*. Oxford: Oxford University Press.

—— (1991). 'Worlds Enough for Time'. *Noûs*, 25: 1–19.

—— (1996). 'Presentism and Properties'. *Philosophical Perspectives*, 10: 35–52.

Broad, C. D. (1927). *Scientific Thought*. New York: Harcourt, Brace.

—— (1938). *Examination of McTaggart's Philosophy*, vol. ii, pt. 1. Cambridge: Cambridge University Press.

Carter, William, and H. Scott Hestevold (1994). 'On Passage and Persistence'. *American Philosophical Quarterly*, 31: 269–83.

Chisholm, Roderick (1976). *Person and Object*. Lasalle, Ill.: Open Court.

—— (1990). 'Referring to Things that No Longer Exist'. *Philosophical Perspectives* 4: 545–56.

Christensen, Ferrell (1974). 'McTaggart's Paradox and the Nature of Time'. *Philosophical Quarterly*, 24: 289–98.

—— (1981). 'Special Relativity and Space-Like Time'. *British Journal for the Philosophy of Science*, 32: 37–53.

—— (1993). *Space-Like Time*. Toronto: University of Toronto Press.

Cockburn, David (1997). *Other Times*. Cambridge: Cambridge University Press.

Craig, William Lane (1990). 'God and Real Time'. *Religious Studies*, 26: 335–47.

—— (1997). 'Is Presentness a Property?' *American Philosophical Quarterly*, 34: 27–40.

—— (1998). 'McTaggart's Paradox and the Problem of Temporary Intrinsics'. *Analysis*, 58: 122–7.

Dummett, Michael (1978). 'A Defense of McTaggart's Proof of the Unreality of Time' (1960), in Dummett, *Truth and Other Enigmas*. Cambridge, Mass.: Harvard University Press.

Einstein, Albert (1961). *Relativity: The Special and the General Theory*, trans. R. W. Lawson. New York: Crown.

Fitch, Greg (1994). 'Singular Propositions in Time'. *Philosophical Studies*, 73: 181–7.

Fitzgerald, Paul (1969). 'The Truth about Tomorrow's Sea Fight'. *Journal of Philosophy*, 66: 307–29.

Gale, Richard (1968). *The Language of Time*. London: Routledge & Kegan Paul.

Garrett, Brian (1988). ' "Thank Goodness that's Over" Revisited'. *Philosophical Quarterly* 38: 201–5.

Geroch, Robert (1978). *General Relativity: From A to B*. Chicago: University of Chicago Press.

Gödel, Kurt (1949). 'A Remark about the Relationship between Relativity and Idealistic Philosophy' (1949), in Paul Arthur Schilpp (ed.), *Albert Einstein: Philosopher-Scientist*. LaSalle, Ill.: Open Court, 1979, 55–62.

Godfrey-Smith, William (1979). 'Special Relativity and the Present'. *Philosophical Studies*, 36: 233–44.

Grünbaum, Adolf (1963). *Philosophical Problems of Space and Time*. New York: Alfred A. Knopf.

Haslanger, Sally (1989). 'Endurance and Temporary Intrinsics'. *Analysis*, 49: 119–25.

Heller, Mark (1990). *The Ontology of Physical Objects*. Cambridge: Cambridge University Press.

—— (1993). 'Varieties of Four Dimensionalism'. *Australasian Journal of Philosophy*, 71: 47–59.

Hinchliff, Mark (1996). 'The Puzzle of Change'. *Philosophical Perspectives* 10: 119–36.

—— (2000). 'A Defense of Presentism in a Relativistic Setting'. *Philosophy of Science*, 67 (Proceedings), S575–86.

Horwich, Paul (1987). *Asymmetries in Time: Problems in the Philosophy of Science*. Cambridge, Mass.: MIT Press.

Johnston, Mark (1987). 'Is there a Problem about Persistence?' *Proceedings of the Aristotelian Society* suppl. vol. 61: 107–35.

LePoidevin, Robin (1991). *Change, Cause, and Contradiction*. New York: St Martin's Press.

LePoidevin, Robin (ed.) (1998). *Questions of Time and Tense*. Oxford: Clarendon Press.

Lewis, David (1986). *On the Plurality of Worlds*. Oxford: Basil Blackwell.

—— (1999*a*). 'Armstrong on Combinatorial Possibility' (1992), in Lewis (1999*c*: 196–214).

—— (1999*b*). 'A World of Truthmakers?' (1998), in Lewis (1999*c*: 215–20).

—— (1999*c*). *Papers in Metaphysics and Epistemology*. Cambridge: Cambridge University Press.

—— (2002*a*). 'Tensing the Copula'. *Mind*, 111: 1–14.

—— (2002*b*). 'Truthmaking and Difference-Making'. *Noûs*, 35: 602–15.

Lombard, Lawrence (1999). 'On the Alleged Incompatibility of Presentism and Temporal Parts'. *Philosophia*, 27: 253–60.

Lowe, E. J. (1992). 'McTaggart's Paradox Revisited'. *Mind*, 101: 323–6.

—— (1987). 'The Indexical Fallacy in McTaggart's Proof of the Unreality of Time'. *Mind*, 96: 62–70.

MacBeath, Murray (1983). 'Mellor's Emeritus Headache'. *Ratio*, 25: 81–8.

McCall, Storrs (1976). 'Objective Time Flow'. *Philosophy of Science*, 43: 337–62.

—— (1994). *A Model of the Universe*. Oxford: Clarendon Press.

McTaggart, J. M. E. (1908). 'The Unreality of Time'. *Mind*, 18: 457–84.

—— (1921). *The Nature of Existence*, vol. ii. Cambridge: Cambridge University Press.

Markosian, Ned (2002). 'A Defense of Presentism', in Dean Zimmerman (ed.), *Oxford Studies in Metaphysics*, vol. i.

Maxwell, Nicholas (1985). 'Are Probabilism and Special Relativity Incompatible?' *Philosophy of Science*, 52: 23–43.

Mellor, D. H. (1974). 'Special Relativity and Present Truth'. *Analysis* 34: 74–8.

—— (1981*a*). *Real Time*. Cambridge: Cambridge University Press.

—— (1981*b*). 'Thank Goodness that's Over!' *Ratio*, 23: 20–30.

—— (1983). 'MacBeath's Soluble Aspirin'. *Ratio*, 25: 89–92.

—— (1998). *Real Time II*. London: Routledge.

Merricks, Trenton (1994). 'Endurance and Indiscernibility'. *Journal of Philosophy*, 91: 165–84.

—— (1995). 'On the Incompatibility of Enduring and Perduring Entities'. *Mind*, 104: 523–31.

—— (1999). 'Persistence, Parts, and Presentism'. *Noûs*, 33: 421–38.

Minkowski, H. (1952). 'Space and Time' (1908), in H. A. Lorentz, A. Einstein, H. Minkowski, and H. Weyl, *The Principle of Relativity*. New York: Dover, 1952, 73–91.

Nerlich, Graham (1998). 'Time as Spacetime', in LePoidevin (1998: 119–34).

Oaklander, L. Nathan (1992). 'Temporal Passage and Temporal Parts'. *Noûs*, 26: 79–84.

—— and Quentin Smith (eds.) (1994). *The New Theory of Time*. New Haven: Yale University Press.

Paul, L. A. (2002). 'Logical Parts'. *Noûs*, 36: 578–96.

Plantinga, Alvin (1974). *The Nature of Necessity*. New York: Clarendon Press.

—— (1976). 'Actualism and Possible Worlds'. *Theoria*, 42: 139–60. Repr. in Michael J. Loux (ed.), *The Possible and the Actual*, Ithaca, NY: Cornell University Press, 1979, 253–73.

—— (1985). 'Replies to my Colleagues', in J. E. Tomberlin and Peter van Inwagen (eds.), *Alvin Plantinga*. Dordrecht: Reidel, 313–96.

Prior, A. N. (1959). 'Thank Goodness that's Over'. *Philosophy*, 34: 12–17.

—— (1967). *Past, Present, and Future*. Oxford: Clarendon Press.

—— (1968*a*). 'Spurious Egocentricity' (1967), in Prior (1968*c*: 15–25).

—— (1968*b*). 'Changes in Events and Changes in Things' (1962), in Prior (1968*c*: 1–14).

—— (1968*c*). *Papers on Time and Tense*. London: Oxford University Press.

—— (1970). 'The Notion of the Present'. *Studium Generale*, 23: 245–8.

—— (1996). 'Some Free Thinking about Time', in B. J. Copeland (ed.), *Logic and Reality: Essays on the Legacy of Arthur Prior*. Oxford: Oxford University Press, 47–51.

Putnam, Hilary (1967). 'Time and Physical Geometry'. *Journal of Philosophy*, 64: 240–7.

Quine, W. V. O. (1960). *Word and Object*. Cambridge, Mass.: MIT Press.

Rakić, Nataša (1997). 'Past, Present, Future, and Special Relativity'. *British Journal for the Philosophy of Science*, 48: 257–80.

Rea, Michael (1998). 'Temporal Parts Unmotivated'. *Philosophical Review*, 107: 225–60.

—— (2002). *World Without Design: The Ontological Consequences of Naturalism*. Oxford: Clarendon Press.

Rietdijk, C. W. (1966). 'A Rigorous Proof of Determinism Derived from the Special Theory of Relativity'. *Philosophy of Science*, 33: 341–4.

—— (1976). 'Special Relativity and Determinism'. *Philosophy of Science*, 43: 598–609.

Russell, Bertrand (1915). 'On the Experience of Time'. *The Monist*, 25: 212–33.

Savitt, Steven (1994). 'The Replacement of Time'. *Australasian Journal of Philosophy*, 72: 463–74.

—— (2000). 'There's No Time Like the Present (in Minkowski Spacetime)'. *Philosophy of Science*, 67 (Proceedings), S563–74.

Schlesinger, George (1980). *Aspects of Time*. Indianapolis: Hackett.

Shorter, J. M. (1984). 'The Reality of Time'. *Philosophia*, 14: 321–39.

Sider, Theodore (1996). 'All the World's a Stage'. *Australasian Journal of Philosophy*, 74: 433–53.

—— (1997). 'Four-Dimensionalism'. *Philosophical Review*, 106: 197–231.

—— (1999). 'Presentism and Ontological Commitment'. *Journal of Philosophy*, 96: 325–47.

—— (2000). 'The Stage View and Temporary Intrinsics'. *Analysis*, 60: 84–8.

—— (2001). *Four-Dimensionalism*. Oxford: Oxford University Press.

Sklar, Lawrence (1974). *Space, Time, and Spacetime*. Berkeley: University of California Press.

—— (1985*a*). 'Time, Reality, and Relativity' (1981), in Sklar (1985*b*: 289–304).

—— (1985*b*). *Philosophy and Spacetime Physics*. Berkeley: University of California Press.

Smart, J. J. C. (1949). 'The River of Time'. *Mind*, 58: 483–94.

—— (1963). *Philosophy and Scientific Realism*. London: Routledge & Kegan Paul.

—— (1987*a*). 'Time and Becoming' (1980), in Smart (1987*b*: 78–90).

—— (1987*b*). *Essays Metaphysical and Moral*. Oxford: Blackwell.

Smith, Quentin. 1995. *Language and Time*. New York: Oxford University Press.

Sosa, Ernest (1979). 'The Status of Temporal Becoming: What is Happening Now?' *Journal of Philosophy*, 76: 26–42.

Sprigge, T. L. S. (1992). 'The Unreality of Time'. *Proceedings of the Aristotelian Society*, 92: 1–19.

Stein, Howard (1968). 'On Einstein-Minkowski Space-Time'. *Journal of Philosophy*, 65: 5–23.

—— (1970). 'A Note on Time and Relativity Theory'. *Journal of Philosophy*, 67: 289–94.

—— (1991). 'On Relativity Theory and the Openness of the Future'. *Philosophy of Science*, 58: 147–67.

Swinburne, Richard (1983). 'Verificationism and Theories of Space-Time'. in Swinburne (ed.), *Space, Time, and Causality*. Dordrecht: Reidel, 63–78.

Tooley, Michael (1997). *Time, Tense, and Causation*. Oxford: Clarendon Press.

van Inwagen, Peter (1990). 'Four-Dimensional Objects'. *Noûs*, 24: 245–55.

Williams, Clifford (1996). 'The Metaphysics of A- and B- Time'. *Philosophical Quarterly*, 46: 371–81.

Williams, D. C. (1951). 'The Myth of Passage'. *Journal of Philosophy*, 48: 457–72.

Yourgrau, Palle (1991). *The Disappearance of Time*. Cambridge: Cambridge University Press.

Zeilicovici, David (1986). 'A (Dis)solution of McTaggart's Paradox'. *Ratio*, 28: 175–95.

—— (1989). 'Temporal Becoming Minus the Moving Now'. *Noûs*, 23: 505–24.

Zimmerman, Dean (1996). 'Persistence and Presentism'. *Philosophical Papers*, 25: 115–26.

—— (1997). 'Chisholm on the Essences of Events', in L. E. Hahn (ed.), *The Philosophy of Roderick M. Chisholm*. Chicago: Open Court, 73–100.

—— (1998). 'Temporary Intrinsics and Presentism', in Dean Zimmerman and Peter van Inwagen (eds.), *Metaphysics: The Big Questions*. Cambridge: Mass.: Basil Blackwell. 206–20.

CHAPTER 10

SPACE-TIME SUBSTANTIVALISM

GRAHAM NERLICH

1. INTRODUCTION

1.1 Space-Time and Relativity Theory

SPACE-TIME evolved from space and time. Newton never formally defined either of them, but his penetrating Scholium to the Definitions is the classic source of substantivalism (Newton 1999). Einstein reshaped both concepts in the special theory of relativity (STR) of 1905, so that both temporal and spatial intervals vary with a change of reference frame. In 1908 Minkowski's interpretation of STR introduced a four-dimensional space-time in which differences in uniform motion correspond to differences of *direction* among time like lines and only force-free worldlines are straight. In the general theory of relativity (GTR) Einstein banished gravity as a force acting across space on bodies, recasting it as the curved semi-Riemannian geometry of space-time. The trajectories of freely falling objects are geodesics ('straightest' paths) of space-time (Einstein 1923).

If space-time is real, it should be among the ontic commitments of our best scientific theory—GTR. In standard developments of GTR, the commitment to space-time looks straightforward. A basic account of flat space-time structure usually precedes the introduction of the apparatus (tensors) for presenting matter in various ways in arbitrary coordinates. Thereafter geometric and physical developments standardly go hand in hand.

It was early argued that this approach misleads us about the structure of reality, for there is no such thing as space-time, existing independently of matter, yet shaping it and shaped by it. Some reasons are classical. There are no reasons of current *science* which demand our rewriting the straightforward conclusion.

Theories may not wear their best delineations on their faces. Analysis of GTR lies beyond our present scope. Nevertheless, significant metaphysical themes can be extricated fairly well from the technical difficulties which entangle them.[1]

A cloud obscures this prospect for both substantivalist and relationist. Theories of motion usually progress conservatively. Much of Newton remains in GTR. However, quantum theory and GTR cannot both be true as they stand. Reconciling them is a major problem for contemporary physics. A quantum theory of gravity is expected to change the face of GTR radically and unforeseeably. The metaphysical themes which have dominated space-time metaphysics may change markedly, too.

1.2 Space and Time by Themselves

Space and time held a central place in metaphysics from its beginning in Plato. It is easy to see why. Everything real is somewhere, sometime. That claim, though not absolutely compelling, is plausible. Thus space and time suggest themselves to metaphysics as touchstones of reality. The advent of space-time has done little to change this. Indeed the metaphysics of space-time and of space are significantly alike and their problems largely interchangeable (as I shall take for granted). Nevertheless, space-time is not at all simply related to classical concepts: for example, it may even resist division into a time and a space (Earman 1970*a*).

We can rewrite the plausible claim. Everything real is *related*, spatio-temporally, to every other real thing (i.e. bodies). This deletes reference to places and times. But does it delete space and time themselves? To answer that question is to take up a perspective on the debate between space-time substantivalists and their main opponents, relationists.

Many grumble at the ambiguous 'substantivalism' as a name for space-time realism. Realism's core theses are that space and space-time exist independently (in some interesting sense) of their contents; they are not reducible to bodies and relations among them; space-time is a *type* of entity different from the type of physical things or physical quantities. Space-time is metaphysically peculiar, perhaps even bizarre (immaterial yet with concrete relations to concrete things and, most worrying, elusive to perception). So, if it fills a central role in a serious modern theory then, even though GTR might turn out false, it would remain of substantial metaphysical interest.

---

[1] The books that form the main canopy over the forest of relevant work are Sklar (1974); Friedman (1983); Torretti (1983); Earman (1989*b*). Dainton (2001) is a useful and informal account of many aspects of the area.

'Absolute' is ambiguous, too. Most commonly, it contrasts with 'relative' in theories of motion. It also opposes 'relational' in ontology, and 'dynamic' applied to certain structures in GTR (see Section 4).

1.3 Relationism

There are many delineations of relationism (Lucas 1984, app.).[2] Earman (1989*b*: 12) lists three claims:

R1 All motion is the relative motion of bodies . . . space-time . . . cannot have structures which support absolute quantities of motion.

R2 Spatiotemporal relations among bodies are direct . . . not parasitic upon relations among . . . spatial points.

R3 There are no irreducible, monadic spatial properties, like 'is located at space-time point p'.

R1 is discussed in Section 5. R2's appeal depends on our countenancing symmetrical relations which are not grounded in the qualities of the objects they relate, nor mediated by matter connections. That looks promising in flat space-time (Mundy 1983) where vectors can be understood as bilocal objects, reaching from one point to another. But in curved space-time we must use *pointwise* located *tangent* vectors. Length then measures a *path* from point to point. That requires relations among things to be mediated by points between them (Nerlich 1994*a*; Bricker 1993).

The classical contrast between relationism and substantivalism fits best with a metaphysics of atoms and the void. It accommodates itself to modern field physics rather differently (for details, see Hooker 1971; Friedman 1983, ch. VI, sect. 1; Earman 1989*b*, ch. 8; Rynasiewicz 1996*a*; Belot 2000). In the seventeenth century extension and shape were primitive properties of bodies. Even atoms were assumed to be primitively shaped and sized. It seemed right to construe distances, for instance, as simply measures of the number of possible bodies—atoms or, later, metre rules—that could extend across 'empty space' from one body to another. That began relationism's appeal to possibilia to mediate spatial relations.

Entities which serve to reduce space to relations among them should, arguably, not themselves be essentially spatial, but somehow pre-spatial. Leibniz's monads purport to achieve that. I know of no other attempt at it.

The birth of relativity physics invigorated a relationism confident of full vindication in science. However, the last three decades have seen a resurgence of substantivalism, a renewed respect for Newton's philosophy of science, and a clearer grasp of what GTR implies. It is this resurgence which is mainly described here, although relationists make major contributions to understanding space-time

---

[2] Hooker (1971) considers the resources available to relationism.

metaphysics (Reichenbach 1958; Grünbaum 1973; Barbour 1982) and recent work brightens relationism's prospects. Supersubstantivalism, the theory that everything may be reduced to variably curved space-time, is omitted (Graves 1971; Grünbaum in Suppes 1973). So is Foster's interesting idealist critique of space and time (Foster 1982).

This sketches a background for this chapter, which describes the ongoing debate between substantivalists and relationists. It begins with the clash between Newton and Leibniz, graduates to a setting in modern relativity theory, considering several themes in that light: the relativity of motion; a modern variant of Leibniz's classic objection to the reality of space (the hole argument); the role of observationally underdetermined theory in the quest to reduce space-time to mere relations; the role of convention in space-time theories. Finally, there is a brief account of Kant's elegant argument for substantivalism based on the difference between left and right.

2. THE CLASSICAL DEBATE

Controversy about how motion is relative began the classical debate over the reality of space. Galileo was the first to articulate anything like a principle of relative uniform motion. The first half of our century saw a consensus that relativists had won that controversy; the present consensus sees Newton as clearer-sighted, gaining a victory on points. When Newton's unpublished work appeared in 1962 his essay 'De Gravitatione' shed stronger light on his views. Since then both philosophers and historians have reevaluated the documents of the controversy. Stein (1967), a landmark paper, began (in philosophy) a more anachronistic process, recasting classical theories in modern dress (i.e. as generally covariant space-time theories) resulting in a significant and favourable reappraisal of realism.

Newton (1999) presents the classic statement of spatial and temporal realism in the famous Scholium and, more explicitly, in 'De Gravitatione'. Space is a necessary being, a disposition of all being. Extension is 'exceptionally' clearly conceivable even without bodies. It is not (strictly) a substance, since it affects nothing, but is closer to substance than to accident (Newton 1962: 132).

Newton's space is absolute. It is immovable for a metaphysical reason. Parts of space and time have no 'hint of individuality apart from . . . order and position' (Newton 1962: 136); so it makes no sense to think they could swap places and keep their identity in doing so. The argument reappears in the Scholium:

Just as the order of the parts of time is immutable, so is the order of the parts of space. Suppose those parts to be moved out of their places, and they will be moved (if the expression be allowed) out of themselves. For times and places are, as it were, the places as well of themselves as of all other things . . . and that the primary places of things should be moved is absurd. (Newton 1999: 410)

Newton is concerned with spatial relations, as any realist must be; not at all with relation*ism*. His relations are place-to-place spatial relations, not thing-to-thing.[3]

But the Scholium takes its absolutist turn most forcibly in two graphic examples: that the surface of rotating water in a bucket is curved, regardless of any relative motion between water and bucket; that two rotating globes joined by a cord would betray their motion, even in otherwise empty space, by a tension in the cord. Newton's immediate aim was to refute Descartes, but his arguments extend to a case for absolute place and motion by assuming that if acceleration (change in velocity) is an absolute quantity, then velocity (change of place) and place itself must be absolute, too.

Newton foresaw Mach's famous objection to the bucket argument—it overlooks the possibility that water in the bucket remains still while the rest of the universe rotates round it, causing the water's surface to curve. The suggestion is rejected as absurd (Newton 1962: 128).

Newton and Leibniz share at least a verbal formula: motion is change of place and place consists of relations to other things. For Leibniz, but plainly not for Newton, the things must be material objects, which makes 'x moves with respect to y' a symmetrical relation.

Leibniz, like Berkeley and others, is not an ideally consistent relativist. Both believed that 'x moves' is non-relational and somehow causal. Neither produced a theory of motion which approached the power and clarity of Newton's.[4]

3. LEIBNIZ EQUIVALENCE: THE CLASSICAL ARGUMENT

3.1 An Objection to Realism

Leibniz proposed the most salient of all metaphysical objections to realism. It underpins R2: spatial relations are not mediated. It supports, thereby, the relationist

---

[3] The passage has been frequently cited, e.g. Stein (1967); DiSalle (1994); Rynasciewicz (1995); Torretti (1999).

[4] Excellent discussions of the themes touched on here may be found in Stein (1967, 1977, 1993); Lacey (1970); Sklar (1974: 161–93); Earman (1979; 1989*b*, ch. 1, ch. 4, sects. 1–5); Friedman (1983: 227–9); Lucas (1984: 119–34); Bricker and Hughes (1990); Rynasiewicz (1995).

contention that space is a mere representation.[5] Leibniz's 'static shift' argument runs thus:

Space is something absolutely uniform; and, without the things placed in it, one point of space does not absolutely differ in any respect whatsoever from another point of space. Now from hence it follows (supposing space to be something in itself, besides the order of bodies among themselves) that 'tis impossible there should be a reason why God, preserving the same situation of bodies among themselves, should have placed them in space after one particular manner.... But ... those two states ... would not at all differ from one another ... they being absolutely indiscernible.[6] (Alexander 1984: 26)

The 'kinematic shift' (Alexander 1984: 38) runs: If God added to each object the same uniform velocity as to every other (relative to their existing states of motion), then, since we could not discern the difference, the two supposed states are the same.

Leibniz aims to reduce to absurdity the 'supposing space to be something in itself'. He grants space to the absolutist and defies him to find any way of using it. He implicates the indiscernibility of *points* in this absurdity. The thesis that indiscernible descriptions refer to just one state of affairs is called *Leibniz equivalence*.

There are familiar parallels. If everything were to double in size instantaneously ('overnight') then we could not perceive the alleged expansion (Grünbaum 1973).

3.2 Leibniz's Principles

Leibniz derives all this from two deeper principles: of the identity of indiscernibles and sufficient reason. Neither is straightforward.

The first (and main) principle presupposes a privileged set of properties, since, by hypothesis, differences (in place, in size, in motion) between the states plainly distinguish them in *under*privileged ways. Of course, just that is to be reduced to absurdity (Earman 1989*b*: 118–20; Nerlich 1994*b*: 148; but see Friedman 1983: 218 ff.). Earman suggests the privilege lies in observability. However, the relationist may prefer to star something ontic: the relations must be thing–thing. This yields an indiscernibility principle:

(IP) Properties or relations which make no privileged differences are not real properties or relations.

This bids us detach underprivileged thing–space, or space–space (point–point) relations. They are idle: space is *absurd*—an intellectual monster. This yields R2, the directness thesis of relationism.

---

[5] A modern descendant, the Hole Argument, dominated the literature in the 1990s.
[6] The useful names 'static' and 'kinematic shift' I take from Maudlin (1993: 188–9).

3.3 The Role of Points

Leibniz gets the equivalence of the states from the absolute similarity of spatial points. This is dubious in two ways.

First, Newton's realism stresses order of situation as individuating places. While this is not flatly at odds with Leibniz's diagnosis, it is different.

Secondly, points miss the point. Euclidean space is homogeneous and isotropic: that is what offends against the principles. But Euclidean points and their distance relations are no different, ontically, from those in exotic spaces. It is not the points but the geometric structure that permits or forbids Leibniz shifts as indiscernible by thing–thing spatial relations. In Euclidean space a group of particles *can* each have the same uniform velocity as every other, for they can move on parallel trajectories. But if space forbids parallels, they can't: the particles will converge or diverge as they move, thus betraying their motion. It is false that space can do nothing. We only need to change its geometry to see that (Earman 1970*b*, 1989*a,b*; Friedman 1983; Nerlich 1994*b*, ch. 6).

It is worth noting that Leibniz's 'static shift' employs indexicals (suppose God had created everything 10 miles from *here*) and cannot properly claim indiscernibility but only empirical indeterminacy. The 'kinematic shift' concerns some actual but unknowable state of affairs—the absolute velocity which, according to Newton, the material universe as a whole has (Maudlin 1993; Earman 1989*b*, ch. 6).

3.4 Non-Euclidean Geometry

Few geometries have the symmetries exploited in Leibniz-style objections. Euclidean geometry is a special case. Spaces are alike ontologically; thus Leibniz never establishes a *metaphysical* objection. The realist makes perfectly intelligible use of the Euclidean indiscernibles as *symmetries*, not *identities*. Euclidean space falls squarely within the context of theories where geometries do observable, explanatory work (Nerlich 1994*b*, *passim*; DiSalle 1994).

The realist can use the indiscernibility principle's highly plausible converse against Leibniz. Since (in spaces of non-zero constant curvature) an object's shape, for example, differs depending on how much space it fills, then the quantity of space occupied by a body[7] matters for thing–thing relations among its material parts. Therefore, such differences are mediated by real, not ideal, space. R2 and R3 are false (Nerlich 1994*b*: 156–7).

Relationists may argue that to double the space as well as the object will restore the indiscernibility. But that misses the point. The realist need only show that space

---

[7] Relative to space's radius of curvature.

or space-time standardly does observable work, not that it always must in every weird example.

4. Representing GTR: General Covariance

4.1 The Apparatus of Representation

Before GTR, models of dynamically possible worlds were founded on a particular *manifold*—an abstract, mathematical, basis space: Euclidean space (or flat space-time). It could be peopled with dynamically interesting things (discovered or postulated). The manifold was among the *absolute objects* of the theory, indifferent to what it contained and the same in every model.[8] *Dynamical objects* vary among models and are affected by the absolute (and other) objects.

Euclidean space admits coordinates which encode rich information. Cartesian expressions neatly identify distances, straight lines, angle sizes, and so on. These implications are the elegant gift of those coordinates, possible *only* in Euclidean space.

But in GTR, space-time geometry and matter distribution constrain each other at each point in accordance with a fundamental law written $G = kT$ (roughly, G encodes geometric structure and T describes matter and energy). The distribution of mass and energy in space-time is largely unknown, so we must be able to model possible worlds where metric and matter both vary from point to point and from world to world, as the contingencies of matter and energy dictate. In GTR, space-time is a *dynamical* object.

For a space with wildly varying geometry, we have no synoptic, metrically direct way to represent it on analogy with our global view of Euclidean geometry. We have to construct it piecemeal, by placing all the structures in *tangent* spaces; that is, (Euclidean) vector spaces. Roughly, one of these touches at each point of the (virtually formless) basic manifold space and the richer structures (vectors and tensors) are defined only within tangent spaces. These are then related to each other by the affine connection. Perhaps creatures brighter than we are could see curved spaces immediately as metric wholes. We do not know how far this reflects our limitations and how far it reflects the nature of space-time.

These problems forbid beginning with a metrical manifold. They demand a particular style of representation, a *generally covariant* one. That has proved seriously

---

[8] This sketches the classic Anderson (1967); see also Friedman (1983 sect. II.2); Norton (1987, 1992); Earman (1989*b*: 47).

confusing. It is unclear how far metaphysical debate about GTR has addressed merely this style of representation rather than the worlds it presents.

What follows is naive but sketches the core of general covariance.

We start with a *differential* manifold. Using a visualizable analogy, differential geometry concerns the properties constant in a (rubber) block, infinitely, but smoothly, deformable. No cutting, no joining. Any closed surface inside the block, for instance, deforms smoothly into any other, destroying shape and size but not closedness. Differential geometry doesn't just ignore what its deformations destroy: in it, there *is no* size, shape, straightness, or definite angle. All that is true of a closed surface in differential space is that it is closed. To visualize is to assign size and shape, and is false to differential spaces; nevertheless, we can *understand* a space in which figures have just those meagre structures and no more. The more, in GTR, arrives only when matter and richer geometry are specified together.

We add coordinates to this meagre space, since smoothly naming the points must precede spreading any structure-bestowing properties smoothly among them. Coordinates are assigned on the back of a meshwork of curves which are merely smooth. They imply nothing about lengths, straightness, or angularity since the manifold *has* no such properties. Coordinate numbering reflects only smoothness.

A GTR model may use several differential spaces, each equivalent (in these meagre structures) to a patch of four-dimensional Euclidean space. They can be sewn together, smoothly again, to make a manifold of any desired global topology, however exotic.

Matter is fed into this, not in lumps but pointwise: mass–density, momentum, pressure, electromagnetic properties, and so on. These are specified in *tensors*—complexes of vectors, i.e. complexes of magnitude and direction. These, too, vary smoothly from point to point, yielding *tensor fields*. Geometry enters at the same time, not strictly on the back of the matter entries, but by mutual constraint, since we can't specify a distribution of the matter properties independently of a suitable space to spread them in. (You can't distribute continents as they are terrestrially arranged independently of having a spherical surface.) Mass and matter tensors fix the geometry of geodesics (straightest trajectories) and curvature; electromagnetic properties fix metrical, including conformal (angle-defining), features. Tensors do their geometric and other work just by being smoothly distributed; coordinate expressions tell us only that the distribution is smooth. The information, *implicit* in Cartesian coordinates for earlier formulated theories, is now made *explicit* in tensors. These tensors, of whatever kind, tend to be described as *geometrical objects* in (not properties of) the manifold, a suggestive, possibly a misleading, usage (see Sections 6.1, and 7.7 below).

None of this mimics creation. It is simply *a style of representation* of dynamically possible worlds. Its relation to an aboriginal order of structures or to an order of ontic depth is another and a contentious issue. A differential manifold models what every space-time shares with every other—a local smoothness and continuity.

4.2 Defining General Covariance

Having made generally covariant representation a little intuitive, there are two rather different ways to define it formally, one through coordinates, the other through the differential manifold. Both convey the message that the theory is formulated so that everything is told by the tensors and the tensor fields.

Envisage a fully structured model of space-time, with all the information about matter and metric set out in a field of tensors (each with four coordinate numbers). First, a *passive* (coordinate) *diffeomorphism* is any smooth distortion of the coordinates used to assign the tensors to their points. Then:

> A theory, T, is *generally covariant* iff the laws of T remain the same in form under any passive diffeomorphism.

Against the background sketched, this is trivial. If the coordinates encode only smoothness, it can make no odds to smoothly change their *numbering*, since it leaves tensors fixed at their points. Everything structural is encoded in them.

The second approach to the same message is more confusing, but deeper. An *active diffeomorphism* is analogous to a smooth distortion of the manifold, though it is not metrical. A visual analogy is helpful, but the reader must be alert to subtract the metric element.

Consider a fully metrical space-time. Imagine that you can 'switch off' all the tensors, so that everything 'goes limp'. 'Peel off' a *copy* of this base space, with all the (inactive) tensors. Now drag the copy across the original, 'distorting' it randomly but smoothly, carrying all the idle tensors tagged to their copy-points, and set it down again on the original. The copy-tensors will have been dragged onto new points of the original. Now switch all the tensors back on to restore the metric and the matter distribution. The tensors act as before since their *smooth distribution* is unchanged. The *metric* structure of the copy will be identical with the original. But the tensors are now attached to different points of the manifold by the dragging.

That is an active diffeomorphism. Now for a definition:

> A theory, T, is *generally covariant* iff every active diffeomorphism of a model of T yields another model of T.

The background sketched makes this trivial, too. Indeed the dragged model (although a distinct *model* from the original) seems to picture the very same possible world. But this is contested (see Section 6).

We can define various properties of transformations through active diffeomorphisms, such as isometry. Useful later (and illustrative of intuition unfriendliness) is:

> A diffeomorphism $d_s : M \rightarrow M$ is a *dynamical symmetry of* T iff for any dynamically possible model $\langle M, A_1, \ldots, A_n, D_1, \ldots, D_n \rangle$ (where the A_i are T's absolute objects, D_i its dynamical objects) $\langle M, A_1, \ldots, A_n, d_s^* D_1, \ldots, d_s^* D_n \rangle$ is also a dynamically possible model ($d_s^* D_1$ is a dragged object).

Roughly, some transformation is a dynamical symmetry iff it 'replaces' the whole matter-contents (tensors) of the universe (in an absolute space-time) so that no discernible dynamical difference results. It is a kind of static shift.

Absolute objects (which feature again here) are intended to be fixed space-times[9], like Minkowski's, fixed for all STR models; or the absolute simultaneity classes (Euclidean spatial hypersheets) of Newtonian space-time. In GTR, there are no absolute objects, since space-time is dynamic, the metric varying from place to place and model to model.[10]

4.3 Covariant Formulations and Symmetry Principles

Classical descriptions of space-time can be rewritten in the style of general covariance, provided we define appropriate tensors on the manifold (Stein 1967; Sklar 1974; Friedman 1983; Torretti 1983). Earman (1989*b*, ch. 2) arranges some in order of progressive geometrical richness. The space-times are classical in that all of them divide into spacelike sheets of absolutely simultaneous events, each with a Euclidean spatial geometry. The sheets are ordered in time. Tensor fields induce this and richer geometric structure. Add an appropriate geometry tensor to move from Machian space-time to Leibnizian; add a rigging vector field to produce Newton's unique frame; and so on. These additions enrich the *purely geometric* structures of the space-times.

Material point-trajectories lie on timelike curves of the manifold. To assert, relative to theory *T*'s space-time, that an object has uniform speed refers one to the geometric structure defined to settle whether the assertion is meaningful in *T*, and, if meaningful, whether or not true. The various space-times are named for those committed just to the structure provided in it. The series begins with Mach's space-time and ends with Aristotle's.

Friedman (1983) begins with a helpful account of the structure of generally covariant space-time theories. Newtonian and neo-Newtonian space-times are described (including a curved classical space-time interpretation of Newtonian gravity). Then follow STR and GTR, providing an extensive comparison among the theories. Some sophistication in mathematics and physics is required to follow this (and much else in the field), but Friedman provides many penetrating comments on the metaphysical aspects of all the theories. (More specifically philosophical matters are dealt with in the last two chapters of this illuminating book.)

---

  [9] But the definition does not quite behave itself. See Friedman (1983: 59); Earman (1989*b*: 38–40).
  [10] See Sklar (1974, sect. iiiD); Angel (1980, ch. 10); Friedman (1983, ch. ii, sects. 2,3, ch. v, sect. 5, ch. vi, sect. 1); Torretti (1983); Earman (1974, 1989*b*); Stachel (1993); Belot (2000); and esp. Norton (1987, 1989*a*, 1992) on these often confusing topics.

Earman and Friedman (1973) examines Newtonian gravitation in curved classical space-time, arguing from it for space-time realism. Sklar (1985, sect. 6) argues that the paper is inconsistent in its methodology. The point is moot and subtle.

There are anachronisms in this approach, as is well recognized, but also advantages of clarity, decisiveness, and ease of comparison with covariant formulations of modern relativity theories. For instance, one sees clearly that even so deeply dyed a relativist as Mach assumed at least a minimal (yet not trivial) space-time structure.

5. THE RELATIVITY OF MOTION

Articulate discussion of the relativity of motion began against the background of a picture of force-free motion. Galileo foreshadowed the principle which became Newton's first law of motion, but Descartes was first to state that only *changes* in states of rest or steady motion in a straight line may be explained causally. It gave something tangible to both sides of the debate about motion (R1).

There were early identifications with how things worked 'at rest' and how, for example, in a steadily moving ship. This is intuitive but inexact.

5.1 Reference Frames and Symmetry

Einstein believed, at first, that the general covariance of GTR yielded the Holy Grail: a full relativity of motion. But we just saw that even the most absolutist theories can be so formulated. A relativity of motion must rest on some feature of reality itself, not on a mode of portraying it. Let us begin by assuming that any such feature lies in metrical space-time and consider, later, whether relativists can shed that ontic commitment.

Assume that an adequate theory requires that motion must be related to something. Call this something a *frame of reference*; in space-times, that is a congruence of timelike (inertial) lines, which means, in turn, a set of paths which free-fall point particles would trace, such that exactly one passes through each space-time point and none intersect. Relative motion demands that many reference frames be allowed in dynamics. Notoriously, Newton argued for just one, absolute space itself. To transform one's vantage point from one frame to another (equivalent to some motion) requires, mathematically, a *group* of transitive and symmetrical transformations. Dynamically allowed symmetry is the core of relativity.

We should look for these symmetries in the structure of space-time itself and in the structure of dynamics. Classical physics after Newton admits an infinite class of *inertial* frames of reference linked by the group of Galilean transformations (its symmetry group). But not just any frame. Leibniz insisted that arbitrary systems of bodies constitute acceptable frames of reference. So did Mach and Einstein, in the early days of GTR. But free fall remains distinguished from forced motion.

If space-time has certain symmetries, then relative motion may make *geometric* sense. For instance, Euclidean space is the same wherever you are and in whatever direction you look. Minkowski space-time is symmetrical in that change from one congruence of timelike lines to another leaves the geometry identical. So motion is relative among them because of that symmetry. Not so if you change to accelerating timelike lines, for that swaps straights for curves and the geometry is not at all the same. And if space or space-time are variably curved, as in GTR, the geometry may differ at different times and places, so there are no (interesting) symmetries and the relativity of motion is not sustained. In general, relativity (or lack of it) gets defined via the results of active transformations, against the background, not always of diffeomorphisms of a bare manifold, but, for example, by rigid transformations of, say, Minkowski space-time. The transformation yields something identical (or not) with what is transformed. Essentially, it is *groups* of transformations that define relevant symmetries.

Dynamical symmetries similarly envisage dynamical identities under transformations of some sort. Roughly, dynamical symmetry transformations envisage the matter of the universe being repositioned by the transformation without dynamically discernible differences. Leibniz's static shift is such a transformation (a rigid translation).

In an adequate theory, space-time symmetries should coincide with dynamical ones (Earman 1989*b*: 46, 48–55). Newton's theory fails the test: change in uniform motion is a dynamical symmetry but not a space-time symmetry. While tensors may supply the geometrical structure which absolute space demands, the structure fails to do any real work. Thus Newtonian space-time gave place to neo-Newtonian space-time in which acceleration, but not motion, is absolute.

There is no doubt that the focus on symmetries has deepened our understanding of relative motion. But the rather formidable apparatus used does not give us what we want in the ship examples. Budden (1997) identifies nautical (intuitive) relativity as follows: 'repetitions of isolated experiments performed in different states of inertial motion yield the same results'.

Modern relativity, defined by means of symmetries (see Budden 1997: 488; cf. Norton 1989*a*; Earman 1974; Friedman 1983, ch. IV, sect. 5) of a theory, *T*, is neither necessary nor sufficient for nautical relativity, giving rise to counter-intuitive and unwanted instances.

5.2 Rotation

Newton showed that acceleration and especially rotation are not relative. This led him to conclude that uniform motion and place are also absolute. The objections to his inference are decisive. Absolute acceleration does not entail differences in absolute velocities (Stein 1967; Sklar 1974, sect. IIIC).

Newton's Scholium placed rotation at the core of relativity's difficulties. Earman (1989b, ch. 4) specifically stresses rotation as the nemesis of theories of relative motion. In terms available to classical physics, rotation resists relativist analysis because angular momentum is conserved, so that rotation needs no force external to the rotating object to sustain it.

The most famous, and perhaps the most confident, attempt to solve the problem of rotation is Ernst Mach's (already mentioned). It captured Einstein's imagination. However, recent literature abounds in rejections of Mach's strictures on Newton (Sklar 1974, sect. IIIE; Angel 1980: 180–2; Stein 1977; Friedman 1983, ch. II, sect. 3, ch. V, sect. 5; Earman 1989b, ch. 4, sect. 8; Torretti 1983, ch. 6.3). There is fairly wide agreement, then, that there is no adequate classical theory of the relativity of motion.

Maudlin (1993) sketches a range of relationist positions. A fully Newtonian relationist, for example, may exploit both spatial and temporal metrical relations among the parts of four-dimensional objects since both are defined in Newtonian space-time.

This agreement rests, perhaps, on confining attention to particle theories. Wilson (1993) argues (roughly) that continuum mechanics, by describing states of extended substances which depend on their histories (as in metal fatigue etc.), permits a fully workable mechanics, which includes rotation, in Leibnizian space-time. Leibniz was not the rampant verificationist he seems.

Wilson is not alone. Since the universe has no measurable total angular momentum, it looks legitimate, on relativist grounds, to ignore it and seek a deterministic classical physics within the constraint of zero universal rotation. Various attempts to do so have been developed. One (characteristically abstract) tactic is to set the problem in the phase space of the Hamiltonian approach to classical physics, rather than in space or space-time directly. One is then free to fix the dimensions of phase space by distance relations among particles and by degrees of freedom acceptable to relativist and relationist metaphysics.[11]

5.3 Special Theory of Relativity

In modern relativity theory, relativism seems to fare rather worse. Very briefly for STR, while there is no preferred frame of reference and so no preferred velocity for

---

[11] See Barbour (1982); Bertotti and Easthope (1978). The project is criticized in Earman (1989b, ch. 5, sect. 2) and explained (at greater length, but still fairly accessibly) and defended in Belot (2000).

timelike worldlines, there is a distinction between straight and curved worldlines which corresponds to the difference between uniform and accelerated motion. This does not depend on dynamical concepts. Each acceleration vector, like the null or light cone structure, relates the geometry of a worldline to the Minkowski structure itself. It is a *spacelike* vector, whereas a velocity vector is timelike. There is an absolute velocity, the same with respect to every frame, that of light. These distinctions are definable within the geometry of Minkowski space-time (Sklar 1974: 206–9; Winnie 1977; Friedman 1983: 149–59; Maudlin 1993; Earman 1989*b*, ch. 5, sects. 4–6 and pp. 128–30). Malament (1985) shows that for any relativistic space-time which meets fairly weak and intuitive conditions on light cone (conformal, angle-determining) structure, rotation is well defined. See also Friedman (1983: 223–36).

Nevertheless, in Minkowski space-time, spatio-temporal relations among material events can also distinguish rotation from non-rotation metrically, without regard to any dynamical effects. The worldlines of particles of a rotating body of water, for instance, are not geodesical. Spatio-temporal relations among events on them characterize their curvature (Maudlin 1993; Earman 1989*b*: 128–30).

5.4 General Theory of Relativity

GTR permits an immense variety of models and is less hospitable to the relativity of motion than either STR or classical physics. As in STR, rotation is a conformal (angle-defining) invariant, defined in the geometry itself (unless the light cone structure is bizarre) (Malament 1985). Acceleration in general is geometrically defined (non-geodesical timelike path), but more open to relationist treatment since there should always be a push-or-pull matter source.

Yet GTR contains no absolute objects (no fixed space-time). All the geometric objects are constrained by mass–energy distribution, since the metric tensor is so constrained. So it may seem that, even though free-fall paths are geometrically distinguished from accelerations, the whole structure is caused by the matter distribution, and thus properly relativist (Lariviere 1987).

However, that is not a one-way constraint nor a clearly causal one. A particular distribution of mass–energy presupposes a particular space-time structure, whether we consider this as an initial value problem or dependent on a total content of space-time. Minkowski space-time admits only a distribution of matter consistent with zero space-time curvature, and so on (Sklar 1974: 75; Earman 1989*a*,*b*, ch. 5, sect. 8).

5.5 Lapse of the Debate?

Rynasiewicz (2000) argues that we cannot usefully project the classical debate into a modern context. Indeed, the early debate itself fails to conform neatly to standard metaphysical views of relativism (R1–R3 of Section 1.2 above) and absolutism. Newton, Leibniz, and Descartes all take some motions to be true and others apparent. A main issue of the Scholium is whether true motion requires absolute space. In the modern context, relativity principles and definitions ought to spring from the methods sketched in Section 4, especially symmetry considerations. For various technical reasons, Rynasiewicz argues that clear boundaries between relative and absolute motions cannot be drawn within GTR. Some plausible-seeming criteria bring even Mach into doubt as a bona fide relativist (cf. Friedman 1983, ch. v, sect. 5, ch. vi, sect. 2; Field 1980, 1985; Earman 1989b, ch. 8, sect. 5).

Sklar speculates that we may drop our beginning assumption that motion must be related to something, but does not adopt the speculation. That would bypass the usual debate by ascribing the inertial properties as unanalysed primitives to the objects themselves. But that cuts the long-lived fruitful link between issues of force and acceleration (Friedman 1983: 232–3; Earman 1989b, ch. 6, sect. 9).

6. THE HOLE ARGUMENT

6.1 The Problem

Earman and Norton raise an objection which, if sound, commits substantivalists to an absurd indeterminism (Earman and Norton 1987; see also Earman 1986, 1989b; Norton 1987, 1989b, 1992). They liken the objection to Leibniz's 'static shift' argument of Section 3. But the objection calls on the subtleties of general covariance and resists brief, accessible treatment.

Earman and Norton exploit the feature that we may define its geometric and matter objects (tensors) anywhere on the manifold since the manifold is merely smooth. So any diffeomorphism of a model of T is another model of T. A diffeomorphism is thus like a Leibniz 'static shift' since it drags the geometric objects (tensors) of the model to new manifold places. The diffeomorphism changes only which manifold points they are 'painted on'.

Perhaps this reflects just the fact that a theory cannot determine its models beyond isomorphism. But worse follows (Earman 1989b: 190).

For any model M, of T, we can find a diffeomorphism d which takes us to a model, M^*, identical with M, *except* within a region (hole) where d drags the tensors to different manifold points of the region. Picture it as before. 'Switch off' the tensors, so that all is merely smooth. Within a confined region (hole) of the model, 'distort' a copy, so that the tensors in the hole are all dragged to different points of the original. Then 'switch on' again. The dragged tensors do exactly what they did before; they produce the same metric and dynamics within the hole, based on different manifold points. Worse still, let M^* be identical with M up to a time, t, but diverge (in terms of which manifold points have which tensors) thereafter. The pasts of the two models are identical, their futures different (though, metrically and dynamically, the models are identical before *and after t*). The *total* state of affairs before t fails to determine later total states. But this mere variation in properties attached to *manifold* points gives no *physical* reason for indeterminism. Determinism is trivially robbed of the 'fighting chance' it deserves (Earman 1989*b*: 180–1).

Intuitively, these two models represent the same *world* and should be identified in an equivalence class. M and M^* are Leibniz equivalent, but not 'real manifold' equivalent. Consequently, the manifold does not represent a real space-time, since manifold differences are unreal. It is a *mere* representation.

Even so, the best candidate for space-time may well be the manifold. Rather, the best candidate is a structure fully represented by differential manifolds. The ambiguity of terms like 'manifold' (mathematical object in the model—its physical world correlate) makes reading the literature confusing. The metric field, then, is seen, not as a *property* of space-time, but as an alien *object* contained in it. It behaves just like matter fields. Nor is this merely a formal resemblance, for it carries the energy of gravitational radiation (encoded as a pseudo-tensor) (Earman 1989*b*, ch. 1, sect. 6; Hoefer 1996, sect. 11; Rynasiewicz 1996*a*, sect. 5).

The hole argument springs most naturally from GTR, where the metric standardly varies from point to point, so that the manifold provides the only fixed geometric background. But diffeomorphisms will still breed indeterminism in more richly endowed background space-times, so long as there are significant symmetries (translational symmetries, for instance) (Norton 1989*b*).

Earman and Norton credit Einstein with first advancing the objection (Norton 1987).[12] The interpretation of Einstein's view in 1916 is problematic (Norton 1987 on the problems; pp. 173–4 for Einstein's letter). Drawings in a letter to Ehrenfest portray diffeomorphisms as *metrical distortions*. Einstein *appears* to base the powerful claim that only point coincidences are observable, on that interpretation. If so, it testifies again to the power of general covariance to confuse. Diagrams of diffeomorphically related situations in recent work (Butterfield 1989; Teller 1991; Norton 1992) need to be interpreted cautiously.

Earman has proposed eliminating points but deriving the manifold structure from a Leibniz algebra (Earman 1977, 1989*b*), which would permit a less objectionable identification, in his view, of structures common to diffeomorphic

---

[12] The attribution is contested in Maudlin (1990).

models. The efficacy of this (quite technical) proposal is contested (Rynasiewicz 1992).

Various defences of substantivalism have been pursued. Most of these oppose either the claimed variety of indiscernible possible worlds or the consequence of indeterminism; some that the objection really shows nothing at all.

6.2 First Responses

That T is deterministic might seem to mean that every pair of worlds which model T and which share duplicate segments of an appropriate kind (initial segments, slices, etc.) are duplicates throughout (cf. Lewis 1986).

Butterfield (1987, 1989) argues, first, for a modified determinism. If two models share duplicate parts appropriate to raising the determinist question, we need not require that they are also global duplicates in *manifold* points, but only metrically and dynamically. This weaker requirement neutralizes the models which differ only in the hole, for they are alike metrically. That is plausible, surely. Butterfield canvasses a number of advantages in this account of determinism.

Substantivalism must also reject Leibniz equivalence: that any two isomorphic models represent the same possible world. Butterfield[13] argues that only one of the models can represent a world, for the points of the base set can exist only in one world.

Maudlin (1990) offers, for different reasons, a simpler solution in which, again, just one of the metrically similar models of T represents a possible world.[14] Manifold points hold their metric properties essentially and models which assign them other metric properties (via diffeomorphisms) can represent nothing possible. Metric essentialism has one immediate attraction. It plausibly disqualifies any merely differential space as a candidate for real space-time. There must be a metric before there can be a physical world at all (Stachel 1993).

These escape routes are rejected (Norton 1989b; Earman 1989b, ch. 9, sects. 13, 14): first, nothing can distinguish, on either route, which model represents a possible world and which is an 'impostor', representing nothing possible; secondly, metric essentialism disallows plausible modal and counterfactual statements, such as 'The space-time curvature at this point would have been different if. . .'; lastly, the metric, as a dynamical object of GTR, should belong with other dynamical objects in models of the theory.[15]

---

[13] Again following Lewis (1986) counterpart theory.

[14] A variation on this theme is presented in Bartels (1996). A weaker thesis, that the *determinable* property 'has a metric' is essential to space-time, is perhaps more plausible.

[15] Earman (1989b: 159–63) argues that the manifold 'functions as a kind of dematerialised ether in GTR' and is space-time itself.

6.3 Identity of Points

Perhaps the different models don't represent different possible worlds because the manifold points are really identical on some criterion acceptable to substantivalism. For instance, no two things can swap all their properties and retain their numerical difference.[16]

But this may bring out, as deterministic, possible worlds which are indeterministic (for example, it is determined that one of many indistinguishable things gains a property but not *which* one; Wilson 1993; Belot 1995; reply in Brighouse 1997). But a plausible haecceitism allows theories to be indeterministic even if all the different possible futures open to any world which make the theory true are qualitatively identical (Melia 1999). Determinism requires also that each of the *parts* of each world which match qualitatively before *t* match qualitatively throughout. This leads to a determinism which escapes the hole argument.

6.4 Other Essentialisms

Healey (1995) leaps from the hole with an attractive picture of substantivalism. He distinguishes between space-time realism and substantivalism. To bare realism, the hole argument presents no difficulty, for every diffeomorphism of a model of the real world also models it via another representation function (via a reverse diffeomorphism and the first representation). But substantivalism is a modal view, an entity being more substantial the more its properties and parts may differ without its ceasing to be what it is.

Healey argues that space-time may differ from its constituent points in the degree to which it is substantial. Points need a Minimal Essence: a space-time point *p* cannot be *usurped*: *q* may have all *p*'s geometric and matter-related location properties in some other possible world, but *p* must also have them there. The hole diffeomorphism plainly usurps, so does not represent a possible world. This constraint on transworld identity for points renders them less robustly substantive than space-time itself, for that could have been built from quite different points with quite different properties.

6.5 Dismissing the Hole Argument

Can the argument be simply dismissed as yet another misunderstanding of general covariance?

---

[16] Variations on roughly this theme are pursued in Horwich (1978); Brighouse (1994); Hoefer (1996).

Perhaps proper attention to the deductive structure of GTR reveals that determinism is about which theorems are deducible from a properly axiomatized theory (Mundy 1992; Leeds 1995). This would show that substantivalism and determinism are not opposed. However, that view is contested (Rynasiewicz 1994, 1996b).[17]

Rynasiewicz interprets the hole argument as reflecting, in common with several quite different indeterminisms, that a theory can fix its models only up to isomorphism. He provides helpful examples.

If the intended thrust of the hole argument really is to mimic Leibniz's 'static shift', the analogy is imperfect. Leibniz blamed the indiscernibility of spatial points; the manifold points are indeed indiscernibly different, too. But Leibniz misdiagnosed his objection. The blandness of Euclidean geometry floats his example: the identity of points has nothing to do with it. In other geometries we saw that the shifts falter: they are symmetries, not identities. Analogously, despite the trivial structure of differential manifolds, it is not inevitable that GTR should choose a basis that is smooth and continuous. Especially not if one considers a merger with quantum mechanics. But then the diffeomorphic shifts would no longer be available. (But one still needs to gain determinism.)

Let me gesture, very crudely, at a stronger, objection. The classic shifts correspond to differences which can (in principle) be brought about by causes. We begin to see how God might do all of it, because we know how to do some of it ourselves. So the changes start off looking like real causal changes and the Leibniz *reductio* hooks onto something. But the smooth motions over the manifold correspond to nothing causal, nothing we can conceive how actually to do. Thus the problem looks tied to a particular apparatus of representation. True, unlike other theories that can be represented covariantly, there is no option to proceed otherwise with GTR. But it is far from clear what the significance of that fact is.

Perhaps the *mandatory* general covariance of GTR has a rather different significance, namely that it is a gauge theory. This refers to the symmetries in the tangent space at any point, which are the same for every tangent space. These local symmetries do not link up to yield a global symmetry in the simple way Euclidean geometry has made familiar. This feature suggests a significant analogy with gauge symmetries in quantum field theory, although how to pursue the analogy more deeply remain obscure (Belot and Earman 1999; Belot 1999, 2000).

---

[17] Wilson (1993) raises a somewhat similar objection.

7. REDUCTION, THEORY EQUIVALENCE, AND CONVENTION

7.1 The General Problem

The awkwardness that syntactically conflicting theories may be observationally equivalent, underdetermined by all actual and possible observations, looms large in space-time theory. To show observationally equivalent theories factually equivalent would take a long stride towards realizing relationist ambitions. A main focus has been on a reduction of space-time relations to causal ones. This presupposes some satisfactory distinction between the observable and the theoretical (Friedman 1983, ch. vii; Sklar 1985, *passim*).

Poincaré (1952) argued that science need never abandon the simplest geometry (Euclid's). He considers a Euclidean disk on which a force field distorts measuring rods differently in different places. They deliver a non-Euclidean metric, though, by hypothesis, the space is Euclidean. Here the very same observations are consistent with and support both geometries for the disk. Assuming freedom to posit or neglect undetectable distorting forces, Poincaré concludes that we may always choose Euclid's simplest geometry. It is now a short step to deeming such syntactically conflicting theories observationally, and therefore factually, equivalent (Sklar 1974: 88–94; Friedman 1983: 20–2, 294–6).

In the first 1905 paper on STR (Einstein 1923) Einstein argued that simultaneity in an inertial frame is *stipulated*, consistently with the observably constant round-trip speed of light but constrained by no other fact. Giving light the same one-way speed in *all* directions is merely the simplest stipulation. Thus, simultaneity is fixed by arbitrary convention. The equivalence principle, which filled an especially prominent role in early expositions of GTR, appeared to equate acceleration with rest in a gravitational field. (But both the field and the acceleration must be uniform, or else equivalence holds only in the limit.)

Thus convention appeared to be at the core of scientific progress. Conventions invaded metaphysics both in avoiding scepticism about which of the observationally equivalent theories is true and in offering a means of banishing unwanted structures, like space-time, from ontology.[18] Two principal conventionalist themes are, first, that apparent spatial and space-time structures (metrical and even topological ones) are pervaded by conventions, and so non-factual; secondly, that there is no fact of matters, in STR, about simultaneity with respect to a frame of reference.

Lucas (1976) argues for spatial and temporal structures being fixed a priori by stipulation based on, for example, requirements of communication. But this is a unique style of argument, not conventionalism in a quasi-reductive sense.

---

[18] The two classics of conventionalism are Reichenbach (1958) and Grünbaum (1973).

7.2 Conventions in Metric and Topology

Reichenbach saw geometry as testable only in conjunction with the arbitrary specification of a *universal* force—one which affects (distorts) all bodies (however constituted) identically, admitting no insulating walls. Reichenbach noted that gravitation is a universal force. This opened the door to freely postulating other such forces, even when they do not destroy coincidences—even when they have no source. The crucial metrical issue is to determine congruence: whether a rod retains its length in transport. Reichenbach argued that this can be settled only by an arbitrary coordinative definition, stipulatively linking the concept 'congruent' with a physical structure (transportable rod). Thus there is no matter of fact as to which metric is the true one.

An extension of this approach led him to argue that the topology of space and space-time were also conventional, not factual structures.

This somewhat standard sketch of Reichenbach has been reassessed (Shapiro 1994). Most notable, perhaps, is the argument (Shapiro 1994, sect. 5) that Reichenbach accepts the constraint that a definition of congruence must permit *ordinary* judgements about space to prevail as an aspect of 'descriptive simplicity'. This seems to concede in advance the objection raised by Putnam (1975*a*, *b*) and to require retracting conventionalism's more astonishing claims.

If conventionalists escape the scepticism threatened by observationally equivalent theories, they must do so by rendering syntactic inconsistencies non-factual. This evacuates space-times of much of their geometric structure.

Grünbaum (1973, chs. 3, 16) purges the epistemic flavour of Reichenbach's universal forces. Drawing (contentiously) on Riemann, he argues that if space has a continuous topology it cannot also have an intrinsic metric, since that would need to be constructed (impossibly) from topology.[19] Metric enters by convention. Thus there is no basis for factual mistakes about metrical matters. Grünbaum's exposition of conventionalism is its landmark work.

Conventionalism in respect of metric and topology has been extensively and effectively criticized. The highly simplified story told above passes over the serious methodological issues which are unavoidable in any proper treatment. The debate is impartially examined in this regard (and taxonomized) in Sklar (1974).

If metrical judgements really are conventions, they grossly mislead. We would do best to drop them altogether. No methodological advantage can compensate for the widespread delusion that golf balls are *really* small. Yet no one proposes *doing without* metrical language, though no conventionalist account gives them a clear, positive role (Nerlich 1994*a*, ch. 7).

---

[19] That step has seemed gratuitous to many; see Friedman in Suppes (1973).

Friedman describes conventionalism as ideological relationism (Friedman 1983, ch. VII): it aims to prune the theoretical properties and relations with which space-time theories structure the world, rather than prune their domains of quantification. The methodological issues raised by underdetermination by observation are carefully examined. Friedman contrasts convention with relativity. The latter leads to a wider class of equivalent descriptions, but the ideology is correspondingly narrowed, cancelling structures which lack unifying explanatory force. Thus neo-Newtonian physics cancels the ideology which described absolute space, substituting an equivalence class of inertial frames, because absolute space had no greater power to explain or unify phenomena. Conventionalism also widens the class of descriptions deemed semantically equivalent, yet it paradoxically retains the ideology, while dismissing its structure-reporting (e.g. its metric) role. A metric has unifying force, but only if we take it as a real structure. Friedman goes on to argue that a relativized theory, without conventional elements, must be better confirmed because of its unifying, explanatory role.

Torretti (1983) is strongly critical of conventionalism, especially of Reichenbach's claims about universal forces. Glymour (1972, 1977) examines the topological and evidential questions, arguing persuasively that a theory invoking universal forces will be less well confirmed than one which does not.[20]

7.3 Causal Reduction

Leibniz argued that temporal relations are really causal ones. Robb (1914) claims to define explicitly all the spatio-temporal relations of Minkowski space-time (up to congruence) in terms of an 'after' relation. Robb explicates 'after'—it is directly given in consciousness (1914: 4) and, if e is after f, then e can produce an effect at f. Robb's primitive relation is standardly written 'causality' or 'causal connectibility', following Leibniz, despite Robb's choice.

Winnie (1977) demonstrates that the whole metrical congruence structure of Minkowski space-time coincides with this causal structure. That suggests that the geometry *is* the causal structure, effecting a very explicit reduction. Sklar (1985, ch. 3) considers this in depth. He points out the difficulties in extending it to curved space-times and raises a number of serious objections to the claim that, even in the case of STR, the coincidence is an identity. Sklar presents many-sided, impartial, and ingenious analyses of the methodological problems which beset attempts to gain a well-defined picture of the metaphysics and epistemology of space-time. Various theses about theory equivalence, and theories of confirmation and language-meaning, tend to topple into unwanted forms under pressure of striving for a stable

---

[20] Angel (1980) also examines the issue illuminatingly.

non-sceptical perspective on space-time. No account emerges from Sklar's critique as fully satisfactory.

The identification of 'after' with causal connectibility is dubious. Speculative theories (within STR) have been pursued which reject the null cone as defining the limit of causal connectibility (the photon may be massive, for example). If so, the core thesis of STR is not the principle that light is the fastest signal. It is the Lorentz invariance of STR laws; that is, it is the structure of Minkowski space-time (Nerlich 1994*b*, chs. 2,3).

7.4 Simultaneity and Convention

Einstein's claim that (with respect to any inertial frame) simultaneity of distant events can only be stipulated sparked an enduring controversy. It forms an imperfectly clear part of the relationist programme to reduce space-time structure to causal connectibility. The Lorentz transformation (the symmetry group of Minkowski space-time) makes standard synchrony (a constant speed for light in every direction) natural. But, if space-time is just a representation, perhaps only causal connectibility is available to determine simultaneity. The conventionality of simultaneity has been strongly supported.[21]

In the first challenge to this (Ellis and Bowman 1967 following Bridgman 1962), clocks, transported ideally slowly from one spatial point in a frame to others, afford a unique global (relative) simultaneity. The result is standard simultaneity—a constant speed for light in all directions. Since transported clocks are continuants, the procedure is impeccably causal.

This was hotly disputed.[22] Salmon's careful and convincing critique of attempts to measure the speed of light in one direction shows that all are doomed to circularity. Later literature endorses slow clock transport in a near consensus (e.g. Friedman 1983, ch. VII, sect. 4; Torretti 1983). Bridgman's proposal is widely accepted as both relational and factual.

But Malament (1977) presents the most salient criticism of simultaneity conventionalism. He argues that standard simultaneity is explicitly (and uniquely) definable in causal (i.e. Robbian) terms. Given an inertial worldline O and two temporally separated events on it, a and b, the two light cones (one through each event) intersect in a sphere, which defines a spacelike hyperplane. This is both orthogonal to O and intersects it at p, midway between a and b. It thus causally defines a set of events simultaneous with p.[23]

---

[21] Most notably in Reichenbach (1958) and Grünbaum (1973).

[22] See a panel discussion in Grünbaum *et al.* (1969). Ellis (1971) replies.

[23] The construction is illustrated and discussed in Norton (1992: 222–6); see also Friedman (1983: 310–12). The crucial uniqueness claim is contested (Sarkar and Stachel 1999), arguing that Malament improperly requires a condition of time symmetry.

It is not entirely clear what the issue is. Trivially, since STR admits a generally covariant formulation, it admits *coordinates* with spacelike hyperplanes not orthogonal to its timelike curves. Indeed, it admits some which are not even flat. All this without offence to any causal physics. It is unclear why free choice of t-constant hypersurfaces is conventional (non-factual) whereas choice of *timelike* coordinate curves sets up a relation, not a convention. Perhaps choosing a frame of reference (a time and a space) takes us into another ideology and ontology (but this remains to be clarified). If so, is it a mere convention that one chooses an isotropic space (Winnie 1970; Torretti 1983)?

Causality as defined in the literature coincides with mere *possible* causal connections. Appeal to possibilia as part of relationism's general reductive armoury, here and throughout relationist analyses, is frequently employed (Sklar 1974, 1985, ch. 8; Manders 1982). Its use appears open to strong objections of circularity: the possibilities are founded in what they aspire to reduce (Nerlich 1994a, ch. 2; Lacey and Anderson 1980; Butterfield 1984).

7.5 Observation and Theory

What is an observational base for GTR? Einstein claimed that nothing is observable but material point coincidences (Einstein 1923: 117–18).[24] That impoverishes observation severely. Because it is coloured by Einstein's views on general covariance at the time, it is not entirely clear what he intended.

Various proposals have been made about key observables for space-time theories. The most obvious is that the observables are clocks and rods, but the physics of clocks and rods falls within the physics of matter (quantum theory) rather than within GTR. How to correct them for perturbations lies outside the relativity theories. But light rays and free-fall particles are satisfactory observables. These still need correction, but the theory of these distortions lies within GTR (Ehlers *et al.* 1972; Carrier 1990).

DiSalle reads relativistic space-times as physical geometries (DiSalle 1995). Space-time is not a hidden entity to be inferred from the best causal explanation. It is arrived at by coordinative definitions, stipulative to some degree, which identify geometric concepts with physical ones. The observation of physical processes, then, is observation of the geometry itself. Nerlich (1994a) sketches distantly similar view, that (the set of all possible) light-particle interactions inscribe the geometry observationally through physical 'tracings'. Unlike DiSalle, Nerlich (1994a) argues at length for space-time's role as an explanatory, though non-causal, entity. It explains,

---

[24] The issue is discussed in Stachel (1980); Norton (1987, sect. 4; 1989a, sect. 5.2).

for example, why the force-free (uncaused) motion of a dust cloud in exotic spaces may betray itself (Nerlich 1994a; see Section 3.3 above).

7.6 Space-Time as a Representation

Consider the set of space-time points 'occupied' by some physical event, and all spatio-temporal relations among them. Let the relations be expressed in vector form by appropriate n-tuples of numbers. Realists and relationists alike agree that this collection of events and relations is real. But the structure can be embedded in the richer structure of space-time and point–point relations. Relationists, following Leibniz, take the richer embedding as a mere (conventional) representation, conveniently visualizing the real material structure embedded in it. Thus space-time is a mere picture, a representation.

Friedman suggests that the embodied structure may be embedded in space-time either as submodel of a realist model or as space-time's *representing* the material structure (Friedman 1983, ch. VI, sect. 3). In the first case space-time must play an explanatory role; in the second case it is merely pictorial. Friedman defends the first option on the ground that the realist interpretation not only unifies and explains the material relations, but is better confirmed by a wide range of evidence than any mere conjunction of representations would be.

Mundy (1983, 1986a,b) rigorously develops a somewhat similar strategy for STR, undertaking to give the physical content of Minkowski space-time as the material structure, then embedding it uniquely in space-time as a representation.[25]

To admit space-time as a useful fiction surely concedes that space-time is not an absurdity. The question about its reality has become purely one of theoretic economy.

7.7 Field and Plenum

Field physics requires a real space-time, since space-time points are the objects to which field properties (tensors) are ascribed (Field 1980, 1985). We need them to define even the most elementary of quantitative spatial relations. It does indeed seem that, whereas the shapes and sizes of objects could be regarded as their primitive properties, there is no parallel way to regard fields as objects providing their own primitive extendedness.

---

[25] See also Catton and Solomon (1988) (whether a relation is definable depends on the ideology and ontology of the theory); Earman (1989b) (the tactic presupposes a greater degree of success for the relationist programme than is at all warranted).

However, if there are a non-zero tensors at every space-time point, perhaps all spatial relations hold relative to them, thus delivering relationism. In GTR this condition seems to hold if the metric is, metaphysically, an *object* contained in the manifold, as generally covariant language suggests (see Section 6.1 above). Less trivially, it carries energy—in the form of gravitational radiation, for example. So if we take it to be, therefore, a not purely spatial object, the plenum hypothesis is fulfilled—there is matter at every space-time point.

Does this spell the end of substantivalism's view of the independence of space-time from matter? Friedman concludes that the debate survives because it can only be the vanishing (non-vanishing) of the true *matter* tensors which is crucial for a true plenum (Friedman 1983: 221–2). Earman argues that the concrete *events* acceptable to the relationist are not strictly identical with space-time *points* which are occupied (Earman 1989b: 163–4; see also Maudlin 1993, sect. 6).

Rynasiewicz (1996a) regards the substantivalist/relationist debate as outmoded. The concepts of space-time and matter are too vague to allow us to settle whether field physics favours the one at the expense of the other. In particular, nothing can clearly settle the question whether electromagnetism leaves us with a kind of relativisitic ether or whether the field quantities are properly ascribed to space-time points. Hoefer (1998) replies that the debate, far from outmoded, is settled in favour of substantivalism. Field physics commits us to a real space-time.

8. Incongruent Counterparts

Incongruent counterparts are alike but different.[26] That a left hand exactly mirrors a right captures the likeness. That left gloves don't fit right hands captures the difference. Kant offered diverse comments on this.[27] He argued from incongruent counterparts to substantival space in a graphic example. Suppose no object exists apart from a single hand. It must be either left or right. We quickly see that no twisting, turning, or other rigid motion can transform the hand into the space of its reflection. Its handedness (enantiomorphy) cannot depend on its relation to another

[26] All references in this section are to van Cleve and Frederick (1991). The editors' introductory papers (pp. 1–26) provide an excellent survey of the area.

[27] In his 1768 'On the First Ground of the Distinction of Regions in Space' (pp. 27–33). Kant's later thoughts on incongruent counterparts raise the question whether the difference between left and right can be explicated without appeal to other chiral concepts and without pointing to examples. That question is not considered here. Martin Gardner (pp. 61–95) draws together a range of topics and examples, and sides, without close examination of the metaphysical question, with the relationists against Kant.

object, since there *is* none. Its leftness (rightness) must rest on its relationship to space as a whole, considered as a unity. This argument is not repeated in Kant's later work.

The argument is a challenge. It is strongly intuitive. It deftly robs the relationist of material to work with. The outline of Kant's argument is simple, yet the precise role of space in it is puzzling. Few have followed Kant to his realist conclusion. Flat denial of the claims is self-consistent but implausible.

Möbius noted (pp. 39–41) that the problem exists in dimensions other than three. If one can turn an n-dimensional enantiomorph over in an $n + 1$-dimensional space, it can be brought into congruence with its counterpart. Finally, in a space of suitable topology (non-orientable), counterparts can always be rigidly moved into coincidence and congruence with each other.

Earman examines the question with characteristic penetration. Touching Kant's somewhat mysterious remark that the left–right difference rests on an 'inner principle', he suggests positing primitive internal relations such as standing-in-a-left-configuration (pp. 131–49). This may seem plausible in that we could transform right hand into left by reconfiguring its parts. Van Cleve suggests that the difference lies in the direction, the orientation of parts, since we could transform right to left by, for example, reorienting how fingers bend (pp. 203–34).

Nerlich supports Kant's reasoning in contexts other than Euclidean space (pp. 151–72). Four things must be noticed once we widen the kind of space in which the lone hand might reside. First, since hands are spatial objects, the hand will always be in a space, even if only its own space. Secondly, if it inhabits a space which, unlike Euclidean space, is non-orientable (e.g. the 2-space of the Möbius strip), then it will be rigidly movable into its own reflection (homomorphic). Therefore, thirdly, whatever character the hand has (left or right) consists in how it is 'entered' in orientable space, in much the way Kant argued. Fourthly, there is no intrinsic difference among hands which would serve to differentiate left from right.

This has been contested by most of the ensuing contributors to the debate.

Sklar raises several objections (pp. 173–86). Principally, it neglects the relationist's reference to possible relations, including possible rigid motions along which a hand might move.[28] Van Cleve offers useful distinctions (pp. 203–34). Internalism seeks to ground enantiomorphy in internal structures; externalism grounds it on external object-relations, while absolutism grounds it on relations to space. Relations grounded in the nature of their terms differ from ungrounded ones. This allows us to rewrite incongruent counterparthood: it is grounded *internally* in the asymmetry of a hand, but also grounded *absolutely* in the way it is embedded in orientable space. Thus hands are *internally* congruent (counterparts) by virtue of internal relations of distance and angle, yet may be *externally* incongruent, if the global character

---

[28] The relationist's use of modals is mentioned at the end of Sect. 7.4 above.

of space will (won't) allow rigid motion of one into the space occupied by its mirror image. External incongruence is then a relation which can arise out of the permitted motions and the embedding (i.e. out of the space) which contains hands.

Earman dismisses Nerlich's explication of Kant (pp. 235–55). First, rather than refer to space globally, one can define a local enantiomorphy in terms of rigid motions confined just to the neighbourhood of a hand. (Better, perhaps, a hand is handed relative to its own hand space (p. 162).) This enables us to distinguish handed from non-handed objects, e.g. visually. (However, 'no plane of symmetry' does that job; and the outcome of *global* rigid motions will surely trump local ones in respect of handedness.) Secondly, if relationism fails, it will fail for some other reason—perhaps that it cannot deal with the orientability of space. But if the question is what the relationist can do given such meagre resources *in this example*, his successes elsewhere are another matter. Of course, failure here might say little about why relationism is wrong in principle.

If relationists can sustain the thesis that space is a mere representation, then a lone hand will always be *represented* as handed (or not).[29] This concedes something to Kant's intuitive claim.

Earman also argues that if reflection symmetry fails *in the laws of physics* (as in parity non-conservation), then only realism has the analytical resources to express the fact. Van Cleve argues that orientation must be *intrinsic* if parity fails as a matter of law (pp. 21–2).

Walker notes, entertainingly, that we can surely see the difference between right and left hands without being enantiomorphic perceivers (pp. 187–201).[30] If a traveller were to pursue a glove round the circuit of some suitably finite non-orientable space, then the glove would not change its appearance for the traveller as he follows it. On completing the circuit, stay-at-home gloves would appear handed oppositely to their former appearance.

9. CONCLUSION

The debate has achieved no decisive consensus. But space-time is no longer reproached as unintelligible and it ought no longer to be regarded as perceptually elusive or a necessarily idle postulate. It plays a fruitful and an elegant role in modern realist explanation of the world.

---

[29] Harper (p. 276) suggests some such gloss on Earman.
[30] The topic is expanded interestingly in Earman's paper and also in an acute and imaginative treatment by Harper (pp. 263–313).

The advantages of relationism seem now to lie wholly in its ontic economy and its epistemic immediacy. These now look like matters of rather fine detail. DiSalle (1995) argues interestingly that the relevant relations are not immediate at all, for example, since all the spatial ones depend on a judgements of simultaneity and presuppose a space-time metric. Relationists have tended to focus less on the immediacy of relations and more on their adequacy for various tasks. I believe that relationism's tendency to postulate whatever objects are needed for its work remains dubious, as does the postulation of space-time as a useful fiction.

The relativity theories revolutionized space-time metaphysics with a wealth of examples which pure imagination could never match. But the increasingly technical load on metaphysical argument is sometimes unhelpful.

Nevertheless, I regard two formidably technical questions as of clear, immediate importance. What, precisely, is the significance of the mandatory status of general covariance in GTR? What is the ontological significance of the fact that space-time metric carries energy of gravitational radiation?

References

Alexander, H. G. (ed.) (1984). *The Leibniz–Clarke Correspondence*. New York: Barnes & Noble.

Anderson, J. L. (1967). *Principles of Relativity Physics*. New York: Academic Press.

Angel, R. (1980). *Relativity: The Theory and its Philosophy*. Oxford: Pergamon Press.

Arthur, Richard (1994). 'Space and Relativity in Newton and Leibniz'. *British Journal for the Philosophy of Science*, 45: 219–40.

Barbour, J. B. (1982). 'Relational Concepts of Space and Time'. *British Journal for the Philosophy of Science*, 33: 251–74.

Bartels, Andreas (1996). 'Modern Essentialism and the Problem of Individuation of Space-time Points'. *Erkenntnis*, 45: 25–43.

Belot, Gordon (1995). 'New Work for Counterpart Theorists: Determinism'. *British Journal for the Philosophy of Science*, 46: 185–95.

—— (1999). 'Understanding Electromagnetism'. *British Journal for the Philosophy of Science*, 49: 531–55.

—— (2000). 'Geometry and Motion'. *British Journal for the Philosophy of Science*, 51: 561–95.

—— and John Earman (1999). 'From Physics to Metaphysics', in J. Butterfield and C. Pagonis (eds.), *From Physics to Philosophy*. Cambridge: Cambridge University Press, 166–86.

Bertotti, B., and P. Easthope (1978). 'The Equivalence Principle according to Mach'. *International Journal of Theoretical Physics*, 17: 309–18.

Bricker, Phillip (1993). 'The Fabric of Space: Intrinsic vs. Extrinsic Distance Relations', in P. French, T. Uehling, Jr., and H. Wettstein (eds.), *Midwest Studies in Philosophy*, xviii: *Philosophy of Science*. Notre Dame: University of Notre Dame Press, 271–94.

—— and R. I. G. Hughes (1990). *Philosophical Perspectives on Newtonian Science*. Cambridge, Mass.: MIT Press.

Bridgman, P. W. (1962). *A Sophisticate's Primer of Relativity*. Middletown, Conn.: Wesleyan University Press, 64–7.

Brighouse, Carolyn (1994). 'Space-time and Holes'. *Proceedings of the Philosophy of Science Association*, 1: 117–25.

—— (1997). 'Determinism and Modality'. *British Journal for the Philosophy of Science*, 48: 465–81.

Budden, Tim (1997). 'Galileo's Ship and Space-time Symmetry'. *British Journal for the Philosophy of Science*, 48: 483–516.

Butterfield, Jeremy (1984). 'Relationism and Possible Worlds'. *British Journal for the Philosophy of Science*, 40: 101–13.

—— (1987). 'Substantivalism and Determinism'. *International Studies in the Philosophy of Science*, 2: 10–32.

—— (1989). 'The Hole Truth'. *British Journal for the Philosophy of Science*, 40: 1–28.

Carrier, Martin (1990). 'Constructing or Completing Physical Geometry: On the Relation between Theory and Evidence in Accounts of Space-Time Structure'. *Philosophy of Science*, 37: 369–94.

Catton, Philip, and Graham Solomon (1988). 'Uniqueness of Embedding and Space-Time Relationism'. *Philosophy of Science*, 55: 280–91.

Dainton, Barry (2001). *Time and Space*. Chesham: Acumen.

DiSalle, Robert (1994). 'On Dynamics, Indiscernibility and Space-time Ontology'. *British Journal for the Philosophy of Science*, 45: 265–87.

—— (1995). 'Space-time Theory as Physical Geometry'. *Erkenntnis*, 42: 317–37.

Earman, John (1970*a*). 'Space-Time; or, How to Solve Philosophical Problems and Dissolve Philosophical Muddles without Really Trying'. *Journal of Philosophy*, 67: 259–77.

—— (1970*b*). 'Who's Afraid of Absolute Space'. *Australasian Journal of Philosophy*, 48: 287–317.

—— (1974). 'Covariance, Invariance and the Equivalence of Frames'. *Foundations of Physics*, 4: 267–89.

—— (1977). 'Leibnizian Space-Times and Leibnizian Algebras', in R. E. Butts and J. Hintikka (eds.), *Historical and Philosophical Dimensions of Logic, Methodology and Philosophy of Science*. Dordrecht: Reidel, 93–112.

—— (1979). 'Was Leibniz a Relationist?', in P. French, T. Uehling, Jr., and H. Wettstein (eds.), *Midwest Studies in Philosophy*, iv: *Studies in Metaphysics*. Minneapolis: University of Minnesota Press, 212–30.

—— (1986). 'Why Space is not a Substance (at least not to First Degree)'. *Pacific Philosophical Quarterly*, 67: 225–44.

—— (1989*a*). 'Remarks on Relational Theories of Motion'. *Canadian Journal of Philosophy*, 19: 83–7.

—— (1989*b*). *World Enough and Space-Time: Absolute versus Relational Theories of Space and Time*. Cambridge, Mass.: MIT Press.

—— and M. Friedman (1973). 'The Meaning and Status of Newton's Law of Inertia'. *Philosophy of Science*, 40: 329–59.

—— and John Norton (1987). 'What Price Space-time Substantivalism? The Hole Story'. *British Journal for the Philosophy of Science*, 38: 515–25.

Ehlers, J., F. Pirani, and A. Schild (1972). 'The Geometry of Free Fall and Light Propagation', in L. O'Raifeartaigh (ed.), *General Relativity: Papers in Honour of J. L. Synge*. Oxford: Clarendon Press, 63–84.

Einstein, Albert (1923). *The Principle of Relativity: A Collection of Original Memoirs on the Special and General Theory of Relativity*. London: Dover.

Ellis, B. (1971). 'On Conventionality and Simultaneity—a Reply'. *Australasian Journal of Philosophy*, 49: 177–203.

—— and P. Bowman (1967). 'Conventionality in Distant Simultaneity'. *Philosophy of Science*, 34: 116–36.

Field, Hartry (1980). *Science without Numbers: A Defence of Nominalism*. Princeton: Princeton University Press.

—— (1985). 'Can we Dispense with Space-Time?' *Proceedings of the Philosophy of Science Association*, 2: 33–90.

Foster, John (1982). *The Case for Idealism*. London: Routledge & Kegan Paul.

Friedman, Michael (1983). *Foundations of Space-Time Theories: Relativistic Physics and Philosophy of Science*. Princeton: Princeton University Press.

Glymour, Clark (1972). 'Topology, Cosmology and Convention'. *Synthese*, 24: 195–218.

—— (1977). 'The Epistemology of Geometry'. *Noûs*, 11: 227–51.

Graves, John (1971). *The Conceptual Foundations of Contemporary Relativity Theory*. Cambridge, Mass.: MIT Press.

Grünbaum, Adolf (1973). *Philosophical Problems of Space and Time*, 2nd edn. Dordrecht: Reidel.

——, W. C. Salmon, B. C. van Fraassen, and A. I. Janis (1969). 'A Panel Discussion of Simultaneity by Slow Clock Transport in the Special and General Theories of Relativity'. *Philosophy of Science*, 36: 331–99.

Healey, Richard (1995). 'Substance, Modality and Space-time'. *Erkenntnis*, 42: 287–316.

Hoefer, Carl (1996). 'The Metaphysics of Space-Time Substantivalism'. *Journal of Philosophy*, 93: 5–27.

—— (1998). 'Absolute versus Relational Space-time: For Better or Worse, the Debate Goes On'. *British Journal for the Philosophy of Science*, 49: 451–67.

Hooker, Clifford (1971). 'The Relational Doctrines of Space and Time'. *British Journal for the Philosophy of Science*, 23: 97–130.

Horwich, Paul (1978). 'On the Existence of Time, Space and Space-Time'. *Noûs*, 12: 397–419.

Lacey, Hugh M. (1970). 'The Scientific Intelligibility of Absolute Space'. *British Journal for the Philosophy of Science*, 21: 317–42.

—— and Elizabeth Anderson (1980). 'Spatial Ontology and Physical Modalities'. *Philosophical Studies*, 38: 261–85.

Lariviere, B. (1987). 'Leibnizian Relationism and the Problem of Inertia'. *Canadian Journal of Philosophy*, 52: 437–8.

Leeds, Stephen (1995). 'Holes and Determinism: Another Look'. *Philosophy of Science*, 62: 425–37.

Lewis, David (1986). *On the Plurality of Worlds*. Oxford: Basil Blackwell.

Lucas, J. R. (1976). *A Treatise on Time and Space*. London: Methuen.

—— (1984). *Space, Time and Causality*. Oxford: Clarendon Press.

Malament, David (1977). 'Causal Theories of Time and the Conventionality of Simultaneity'. *Noûs*, 11: 293–300.

—— (1985). 'A Modest Remark about Reichenbach, Rotation and General Relativity'. *Philosophy of Science*, 52: 615–20.

Manders, Kenneth (1982). 'On the Space-Time Ontology of Physical Theories'. *Philosophy of Science*, 49: 575–90.

Maudlin, Tim (1990). 'Substances and Space-Time: What Aristotle would have Said to Einstein'. *Studies in the History and Philosophy of Science*, 21: 531–61.

—— (1993). 'Buckets of Water and Waves of Space: Why Space-time is Probably a Substance'. *Philosophy of Science*, 60: 183–203.

Melia, Joseph (1999). 'Holes, Haecceitism and Two Conceptions of Determinism'. *British Journal for the Philosophy of Science*, 50: 639–64.

Mundy, Brent (1983). 'Relational Theories of Euclidean Space and Minkowski Space-time'. *Philosophy of Science*, 50: 205–26.

—— (1986a). 'Embedding and Uniqueness in Relational Theories of Space'. *Synthese*, 67: 383–90.

—— (1986b). 'The Physical Content of Minkowski Geometry'. *British Journal for the Philosophy of Science*, 37: 25–54.

—— (1992). 'Space-Time and Isomorphism'. *Proceedings of the Philosophy of Science Association*, 1: 515–27.

Nerlich, Graham (1994a). *The Shape of Space*, 2nd edn. Cambridge: Cambridge University Press.

—— (1994b). *What Spacetime Explains: Metaphysical Essays on Space and Time*. Cambridge: Cambridge University Press.

Newton, Isaac (1962). 'De Gravitatione', in *Unpublished Scientific Papers of Isaac Newton*, ed. and trans. A. Hall, and M. Hall. Cambridge: Cambridge University Press, 121–56.

—— (1999). Scholium to the Definitions, in Newton, *The Principia: Mathematical Principles of Natural Philosophy*, trans. Bernard Cohen and Anne Whitman. Berkeley: University of California Press, 408–15.

Norton, John (1987). 'Einstein, the Hole Argument and the Reality of Space', in John Forge (ed.), *Measurement, Realism and Objectivity*. Dordrecht: Reidel, 153–88.

—— (1989a). 'Coordinates and Covariance: Einstein's View of Space-Time and the Modern View'. *Foundations of Physics*, 19: 1215–63.

—— (1989b). 'The Hole Argument'. *Proceedings of the Philosophy of Science Association*, 2: 56–64.

—— (1992). 'Philosophy of Space and Time', in Merrilee Salmon *et al. Introduction to the Philosophy of Science*. Englewood Cliffs, NJ: Prentice Hall, 179–231.

Poincare, Henri (1952). *Science and Hypothesis*, trans. W. J. Greenstreet. New York: Dover.

Putnam, Hilary (1975a). 'An Examination of Grünbaum's Philosophy of Geometry', in Putnam, *Philosophical Papers, Mathematics, Matter and Method*. Cambridge: Cambridge University Press, 93–129.

—— (1975b). 'The Refutation of Conventionalism', in Putnam, *Philosophical Papers, Mind, Language and Reality*. Cambridge: Cambridge University Press, 153–61.

Reichenbach, Hans (1958). *The Philosophy of Space and Time*. New York: Dover.

Robb, A. A. (1914). *A Theory of Time and Space*. Cambridge: Cambridge University Press.

Rynasiewicz, Robert (1992). 'Rings, Holes and Substantivalism: On the Program of Leibniz Algebras'. *Philosophy of Science*, 59: 572–89.

—— (1994). 'The Lessons of the Hole Argument'. *British Journal for the Philosophy of Science*, 45: 407–36.

—— (1995). 'By their Properties, Causes and Effects: Newton's Scholium on Time, Space, Place and Motion—I. The Text—II. The Context'. *Studies in History and Philosophy Science*, 26: 133–53, 295–321.

Rynasiewicz, Robert (1996a). 'Absolute vs. Relational Space-time: An Outmoded Debate?' *Journal of Philosophy*, 93: 279–306.

—— (1996b). 'Is there a Syntactic Solution to the Hole Problem?' *Proceedings of the Philosophy of Science Association*, 3, suppl., S55–S62.

—— (2000). 'On the Distinction between Absolute and Relative Motion'. *Philosophy of Science*, 67: 70–93.

Sarkar, Sahotra, and John Stachel (1999). 'Did Malament Prove the Non-Conventionality of Simultaneity in the Special Theory of Relativity?' *Philosophy of Science*, 66: 208–20.

Shapiro, Lionel S. (1994). ' "Coordinative Definition" and Reichenbach's Semantic Framework: A Reassessment'. *Erkenntnis*, 41: 287–323.

Sklar, Lawrence (1974). *Space, Time and Space-time*. Berkeley: University of California Press.

—— (1985). *Philosophy and Space-time Physics*. Berkeley: University of California Press.

Stachel, John (1980). 'Einstein's Search for General Covariance'. Paper presented to the Ninth International Conference on General Relativity and Gravitation, Jena. Repr. in D. Howard, and J. Stachel (eds.), *Einstein and the History of General Relativity*, Einstein Studies, 1. Birkhauser.

—— (1993). 'The Meaning of General Covariance', in John Earman, Clark N. Glymour, and John J. Stachel (eds.), *Philosophical Problems of the Internal and External Worlds: Essays on the Philosophy of Adolf Grünbaum*. Pittsburgh: University of Pittsburgh Press.

Stein, Howard (1967). 'Newtonian Space-Time'. *Texas Quarterly*, 10: 174–200.

—— (1977). 'Some Pre-History of General Relativity', in John Earman, Clark N. Glymour, and John J. Stachel (eds.), *Foundations of Space-Time Theories*. Minneapolis: University of Minnesota Press, 3–49.

—— (1993). 'On Philosophy and Natural Philosophy in the Seventeenth Century', in P. French, T. Uehling, Jr., and H. Wettstein (eds.), *Midwest Studies in Philosophy*, xviii: *Philosophy of Science*. Notre Dame: University of Notre Dame Press, 177–201.

Suppes, Patrick (ed.) (1973). *Space, Time and Geometry*. Dordrecht: Reidel.

Teller, Paul (1991). 'Substance, Relations, and Arguments about the Nature of Space-Time'. *Philosophical Review*, 50: 363–97.

Torretti, Roberto (1983). *Relativity and Geometry*. Oxford: Pergamon Press.

—— (1999). *The Philosophy of Physics*. Cambridge: Cambridge University Press.

van Cleve, James, and Robert Frederick (eds.) (1991). *The Philosophy of Left and Right: Incongruent Counterparts and the Nature of Space*. Dordrecht: Kluwer.

Wilson, Mark (1993). 'There's a Hole and a Bucket, Dear Leibniz', in P. French, T. Uehling, Jr., and H. Wettstein (eds.), *Midwest Studies in Philosophy*, xviii: *Philosophy of Science*. Notre Dame: University of Notre Dame Press, 201–41.

Winnie, John (1970). 'Special Relativity without One-Way Velocity Assumptions'. *Philosophy of Science*, 37: 81–99; 223–38.

—— (1977). 'The Causal Theory of Space-Time', in John Earman, Clark N. Glymour, and John J. Stachel (eds.), *Foundations of Space-Time Theories*. Minneapolis: University of Minnesota Press, 134–205.

CHAPTER 11

··

PERSISTENCE
THROUGH TIME

··

SALLY HASLANGER

1. THE PUZZLE(S)

··

THINGS change: objects come into existence, last for awhile, go out of existence, move through space, change their parts, change their qualities, change in their relations to things. All this would seem to be uncontroversial. But philosophical attention to any of these phenomena can generate perplexity and has resulted in a number of long-standing puzzles.[1]

One of the most famous puzzles about change threatens to demonstrate that nothing can persist through time, that all existence is momentary at best. Let's use the term 'alteration' for the sort of change that occurs when a persisting object changes its properties, e.g. when a tomato ripens and turns red, when a candle shortens as it burns, when someone's face brightens with a smile. Suppose I put a new 7-inch taper on the table before dinner and light it. At the end of dinner when I blow it out, it is only 5 inches long. We know that a single object cannot have incompatible properties, and being 7 inches long and being 5 inches long are

Thanks to Roxanne Fay, Ned Hall, and Steve Yablo for comments on earlier drafts. Special thanks to Dean Zimmerman for his ongoing patience in addition to his excellent comments and editorial advice. This chapter is dedicated to the memory of David Lewis.

[1] There are puzzles concerning motion (e.g. Zeno's paradoxes; Sainsbury 1995, ch. 1), constitution (Rea 1996), generation and destruction (Parmenides; Haslanger 1989b), growth (Aristotle), and the replacement of parts (the Ship of Theseus; Hobbes 1839, ch. 2, sect. 7; Chisholm 1970, 1973, 1975).

incompatible. So instead of there being one candle that was on the table before dinner and also after, there must be two distinct candles: the 7-inch taper and the 5-inch taper. But of course the candle didn't shrink instantaneously from 7 inches long to 5 inches long: during the soup course it was 6.5 inches long; during the main course it was 6 inches long; during dessert it was 5.5 inches long. Following the thought that no object can have incompatible lengths, we must conclude, it seems, that during dinner there were several (actually many more than just several!) candles on the table in succession.

It is not hard to see that the heart of this puzzle concerns the very concept of alteration. Alteration involves a change of properties: the object has a property before the change that is incompatible with one it has after the change. But objects cannot have incompatible properties. So no object can persist through a change in its properties, i.e. alteration is impossible. Add the straightforward assumption that the passage of time involves change (for example, if something persists through time, then at the very least it is older at the later time than it was at the earlier time), and it seems we must conclude that nothing persists through time at all. This result is paradoxical because it contradicts what we take to be obvious, namely, that some things persist through time and through change.

It will be helpful to articulate some of the principles that work together to generate the problem. Let's start with these:

(1) *Persistence condition.* Objects, such as a candle, persist through change.
(2) *Incompatibility condition.* The properties involved in a change are incompatible.
(3) *Law of non-contradiction.* Nothing can have incompatible properties, i.e. nothing can be both P and not-P.

Fortunately, these three principles, on their own, do not yet generate a contradiction. This is because we have left unspecified what it is for something to 'persist' through change and what it is for a property to be 'involved' in a change, and there are interpretations of these notions that render (1)–(3) consistent. So we should be optimistic that there are solutions to the problem that allow us to preserve (1)–(3). But if the problem does not lie in accepting (1)–(3), where exactly is it, and how can we avoid it?

Two further principles elaborate what seem to be additional essential features of alteration:[2]

(4) *Identity condition.* If an object persists through a change, then the object existing before the change is one and the same object as the one existing after the change; that is, the original object continues to exist through the change.

---

[2] Note that these principles are stated in what I hope to be a form that is not committal with respect to one's account of time, or tense, or the details of one's ontology. In fact, the strategies I will consider to avoid the paradox will involve providing more specific (and controversial) interpretations of these principles.

(5) *Proper subject condition.* The object undergoing the change is itself the proper subject of the properties involved in the change; for example, the persisting candle is itself the proper subject of the incompatible properties.

Now it seems we have the makings of a contradiction. To simplify the example, suppose one morning, in preparation for dinner that evening, I put my new 7-inch taper in the candlestick and set it on a shelf next to the window. The day is unexpectedly hot, and when I return from work I find that the sun has softened the wax and my taper is bent. Suppose that the candle persists through the change from straight to bent. That is to say that there is *one thing*, the candle, that is the *proper subject* of the property straightness and of the property bentness. But straightness and bentness are incompatible: nothing can be both straight and bent. In the face of this contradiction, there are a number of possible conclusions to draw. Contrary to appearances, one of the principles we started with must be false. So either:

(not-1) Objects such as the candle do not persist through change; or

(not-2) The properties involved in the change are compatible after all; or

(not-3) Objects can have incompatible properties, i.e. things can be both P and not-P; or

(not-4) An object may persist without continuing to exist; or

(not-5) An object undergoing change, such as the candle, is not the proper subject of the incompatible properties involved in the change.

Let us consider some of these options more carefully.

2. PERSISTENCE: PERDURANCE, ENDURANCE, AND EXDURANCE

Although one possible response to the puzzle is to maintain that in fact nothing persists through time, this is usually seen as a course of last resort. The idea that objects persist is so deeply rooted in our ordinary conception of things, it has taken on the status of a Moorean fact which all parties to the debate must accommodate.

It is controversial, however, what exactly is required for something to persist through a stretch of time. Several conceptions of persistence have been developed in recent literature. Two prominent ones are: *endurance* and *perdurance* (Lewis 1986: 202).[3] Roughly, an object persists by *enduring* iff it is *wholly present* at different times.[4] For example, the candle endures iff the candle itself is wholly present at

---

[3] I will return to a third conception of persistence, *exdurance*, below.

[4] Some have argued that this definition of endurance is unclear or untenable and have proposed alternative definitions. See Sider (1997); Merricks (1999).

t (in the morning when I set it on the shelf), and it is also wholly present at a distinct time t' (in the afternoon when I return... and presumably in the intervening times). The notion of being 'wholly present' may become clearer by contrast with the perdurantist's notion of being 'partly present'. On the perdurantist's conception of persistence, an object persists through time in a way analogous to how an object is extended through space. The candle is spatially extended through its 7-inch length not by being wholly present at each spatial region it occupies, but by having parts at the different regions. Likewise, according to the perdurantist, the candle is extended through time not by being wholly present at different times, but by having parts or stages at different times. So the candle persists by *perduring* iff the candle has a part at t (in the morning when I set it on the shelf), and a part at a distinct time t' (in the afternoon when I return... and presumably in the intervening times).

The notion of perdurance provides the resources for a relatively straightforward account of alteration (e.g. Quine 1963; Hirsch 1982; Lewis 1983; Heller 1993; Sider 2001): the persisting candle is composed of temporal parts or stages that only briefly exist; distinct *candle-stages* are the proper subjects of the incompatible properties, *being straight* and *being bent*, and the temporal composite which consists of the stages is the subject of persistence (understood as perdurance). On the perdurance account, the persisting object does not undergo alteration by 'gaining' or 'losing' properties; instead, it changes in a way analogous to how a painting changes colour across the canvas. The canvas is green at this part and blue at another; the candle is straight at this part and bent at another. Contradiction is avoided by modifying the proper subject condition: the persisting thing (the composite) is not the proper subject of the properties 'gained' and 'lost' (the stages are), but the proper subjects of the properties are at least parts of the persisting thing. For the perdurantist, this is close enough.

On this account, persisting things are temporally extended composites, also known as a space-time worms. But given the ontology of worms and stages, the option of yet another account of persistence arises. According to the *stage theory*, ordinary persisting objects are stages that persist not by enduring or perduring, but by having distinct stage counterparts at other times. Stage theory says that in the afternoon when I find my bent candle on the shelf, the candle is the bent-stage coexisting with me then, but that stage persisted from before (in the relevant sense) by virtue of having a (straight) counterpart stage on the shelf in the morning. (Sider 1996: 446; 2000: 86–7; Hawley 2001, esp. ch. 2). Although on this view ordinary objects are stages and so (strictly speaking) only exist momentarily, they can nonetheless persist by virtue of having counterpart antecedent and/or successor stages.

The idea behind this view is to treat identity over time as analogous to identity across possible worlds in modal counterpart theory. Consider: David Lewis might not have been a philosopher. On a counterpart theory this is true not because *Lewis* exists in a different possible world in which he never takes up philosophy, but because there is a world in which a *counterpart of Lewis* never takes up philosophy (Lewis 1986: 9–11 and ch. 4). Similarly, the morning's straight candle(-stage) persists as the afternoon's bent candle(-stage) not by the earlier entity *itself* existing at the later time, but by virtue of the latter stage being a counterpart of the earlier one.[5] Let's call this form of persistence *exduring* (duration via the object's relation to entities other than or outside of it).

It is important to emphasize that the current defenders of the stage theory do not disagree with perdurantists over ontology: both views agree that there are stages and composites of stages ('worms'). Stage theory differs from the perdurance view in two important respects: (i) it allows exdurance to count as a form of persistence, and (ii) it maintains that *ordinary* things are stages that persist by exduring, rather than composites that persist by perduring. In principle there could be a version of the stage theory which denies that there are perduring things and claims instead that there are only stages and the only way for something to persist is by exduring. (This might be a promising strategy for someone who favours an ontology without enduring things but is also opposed to unrestricted mereological composition.) But, as it stands, the debate between the perdurance and exdurance theorists does not concern the existence of perduring things.

In sum, we so far have three views of persistence to consider:

> *Perdurance theory.* Objects persist only by perduring. There are perduring, but no enduring or exduring, particulars.

> *Exdurance theory (aka stage theory).* Ordinary objects persist by exduring. There are (weird) perduring particulars, and no enduring particulars.

> *Endurance theory.* Ordinary objects persist by enduring. There are enduring particulars, and there may or may not be perduring or exduring particulars as well.

Cast in these terms, it appears that the original puzzle has faded into the background: the issue is not whether it is coherent to claim that some things persist through time and through change. All parties to the debate at this point can allow that there are perduring things, so if perdurance counts as a form of persistence, there are things that persist. The question is *how* things persist. More specifically, bracketing the question of what sort of persistence might be enjoyed by weird objects, the question is: Do ordinary objects—particulars such as apples and bananas, candles and daffodils—persist by perduring, exduring, or enduring?[6]

---

[5] Theorists differ in what they take the relevant counterpart relations for persisting objects to be. For example, Katherine Hawley argues that the relations between stages that constitute an ordinary ('natural') object will be 'non-supervienient', i.e. they are not wholly determined by the intrinsic properties of the relata, and are not spatio-temporal relations (Hawley 2001, ch. 3, esp. sects. 3.1, 3.6). Sider, however, is not committed to this (Sider 1996).

[6] Some have found it tempting to claim that the disagreements between these options is only 'verbal' or 'terminological' and not ontological. I argue in Haslanger (1994) that there is a substantive

However, one might reasonably resist this reframing of the problem. If the original challenge was to show how *alteration* is possible, not just *persistence*, then it isn't clear that this has yet been accomplished. On neither the perdurance theory nor stage theory is there a single thing which is the proper subject of the incompatible properties involved in the change: in both cases distinct stages are the proper subject of the changing properties; perduring and exduring things do not in any obvious way alter. The appearance of alteration is accounted for, strictly speaking, by a succession of stages. It seems that the promise of genuine alteration is held out by the endurance theory, but we have not yet seen how an endurance theory avoids the original puzzle. Following this line of thought the question remains: Is alteration *really* possible?

Although there is something important to this concern (and I will return to discuss elements of it further below when I consider further the *proper subject condition*), it isn't entirely fair to the perdurantist and exdurantist. Remember that the puzzle presents us with what at least appears to be an inconsistent set of claims. One cannot 'solve' such a puzzle without rejecting or reinterpreting one or another (or several) of the claims at issue. None of the theories before us will be able to preserve exactly what we started with. What counts as a 'solution', then, and what criteria we should use to evaluate different solutions is, at this point, somewhat unclear; for example, are some of the principles more important to preserve than others? Have we misstated or stated too vaguely any of the intuitions at issue? How concerned should we be to preserve our initial intuitions? Pausing here to address these methodological questions would be useful, but also distracting; in particular, it could easily pre-empt an open exploration of the options still before us. So I shall continue to lay out a range of options worth considering. But we should keep in mind that there may be background disagreements between the different parties to the debate about what exactly are the goals and priorities of our inquiry. We shall return to some of the methodological questions along the way.

3. PRESENTISM, NON-PRESENTISM (OR ETERNALISM), AND SERIOUS TENSING

In the previous section I suggested that debate between the perdurantist, endurantist, and exdurantist is not over the existence of perduring things; the perdurantists'

---

disagreement between the perdurance and endurance theories, and the argument could be extended to show that there is a substantive disagreement between the endurance and exdurance theories. I leave the task of showing that there is a substantive disagreement between perdurantism and exdurantism to others.

ontology of stages and worms can be accepted by stage theorists and endurantists. Rather, ontologically speaking, the issue is whether there are enduring things *in addition to* stages and worms. Recently, however, some have maintained that the background ontologies of perdurance and endurance are incompatible: it is not possible for a world to have both perduring and enduring particulars. If this is the case, then we cannot set aside so quickly the question whether there are perduring things to focus on how ordinary things persist, for commitment to perduring (or exduring) things would rule out endurance.

Those who hold that perdurance and endurance are incompatible maintain that each entails different understandings of time (Carter and Hestevold 1994; Markosian 1994; Merricks 1995; Lombard 1999; cf. Parsons 2000; Simons 2000*a*). More specifically, the suggestion is that perdurantism is committed to a four-dimensional ontology on which all times equally exist, and endurantism is committed to a three-dimensional ontology on which only the present and presently existing things are real. This debate is valuable to consider because it highlights how the views of persistence we've considered so far are related to other significant theses about time and tense, and also because it introduces one endurantist model for addressing the original puzzle.

To begin, we need to distinguish a presentist from a non-presentist account of time.[7] According to the presentist, only the present exists, and consequently only present objects exist. Socrates *existed*, and future objects *will exist*, but because they do not presently exist, we cannot truly claim that they exist (e.g. Hinchliff 1996; Bigelow 1996; Zimmerman 1998*a*; Markosian forthcoming). The presentist's ontological claims are often connected to a semantic thesis asserting the irreducibility of tensed to untensed predication.[8] On this view, to say that something exists, or walks, or is red, is to say something about how it is in the present, not 'timelessly'. A non-presentist (also called an 'eternalist' (Sider 1999: 326) and sometimes a 'four-dimensionalist' (Rea, Chapter 9 in this volume)),[9] denies that only the present exists, and allows that there are things that do not presently exist, i.e. there are entirely

---

[7] Note that there are different forms of presentism and non-presentism. Presentists may differ not only in their account of the semantics of tensed statements, but also in their ontologies (cf. Hinchliff 1996; Simons 2000*b*). Non-presentists may differ substantially also in their semantics and their accounts of time; for example, some non-presentists claim that no time is ontologically privileged, while others deny this (existence and non-existence are not the only forms of ontological privilege). For example, on the 'flashlight' or 'moving spotlight' view of time, all times exist, but one is privileged by being present (it is the one on which the spotlight of the present shines).

[8] Note that an eternalist may also maintain that tensed discourse is irreducible to untensed discourse, for tense may be essentially indexical. So the semantic thesis does not distinguish the presentist from non-presentist. I will consider related metaphysical commitments to tense below. For useful discussion of the interwoven claims of presentism and serious tensing, see Sider (2001, ch. 2); Zimmerman (1998*a*).

[9] Note that the term 'four-dimensionalism' is used in different ways by different authors, and is sometimes used to refer simply to perdurantists. Ted Sider offers one clear statement of 'four-dimensionalism' that takes its central idea to be that 'for any way of dividing up the lifetime of an object into separate intervals of time, there is a corresponding way of dividing the object into temporal parts

past or entirely future things: According to eternalism, Socrates exists, but does not presently exist; to say that Socrates was wise is to say something true of an existing but non-present thing.[10]

Presentism is also closely allied with, though distinguishable from, a metaphysical claim asserting that propositions (or whatever one takes the bearers of truth to be) are tensed entities that concern how things were, are, and will be rather than how things timelessly *are*. On this view, because propositions are tensed entities, they are not timelessly true or false, but are, were, or will be true or false, i.e. their truth or falsity is a tensed matter (Zimmerman 1998a, 208–9). This approach, sometimes called the 'serious tenser' approach, allows in principle that there are non-present things, so must be distinguished from presentism (see Zimmerman 1998a; Markosian 2001; for an example, Smith 1993).[11] Presentism is a view about what exists (only the present and things existing in the present); in contrast, serious tensing is a view concerning what is true or false about the things that exist (only tensed propositions).

What does it mean to say that propositions (or what some might prefer to call states of affairs) are tensed entities?[12] Consider:

(*a*) The apple is (presently) green.
(*b*) The apple was green.

According to the serious tenser, (*a*) and (*b*) express distinct propositions. Suppose the apple starts out green, in which case (*a*) is true; but as the apple turns red the proposition (*a*), that the apple is (presently) green, becomes false, though now (*b*) is true. (Speaking of states of affairs, the apple's being (presently) green ceases to obtain, as it turns red.) On this view, one's having a property is, metaphysically speaking, always something that occurs in the present: what obtains is what presently

that are confined to those intervals of time.' (Sider 1997: 204). Because of the potential misunderstandings, I prefer to avoid the term 'four-dimensionalism' and disaggregate the theses at issue, speaking instead of presentists–eternalists, perdurantists–endurantists, serious tensers–non-tensers, etc.

[10] Note that how one understands time and how ones understands the semantics of tensed discourse are to some extent separable. One might hold an eternalist account of time, and yet hold that tensed discourse is not reducible to untensed discourse (see Sider 2001, esp. ch. 2). Those who believe that tensed discourse is not reducible to untensed discourse are also sometimes called 'tensers', sometimes those 'who take tense seriously' (Zimmerman 1998a). Early influential discussions of the ontology of tense include McTaggart (1908); Prior (1959).

[11] Thanks to Dean Zimmerman for helping me understand better the distinction between presentism and serious tensing. Zimmerman (1998a) is very valuable in clarifying the issues.

[12] Although serious tensers tend to claim that all predication is tensed, so all propositions are tensed, it isn't clear to me why one couldn't hold the weaker view that there is both tensed and untensed predication, and some propositions are tensed and others are untensed. Simply allowing untensed predication (and tenseless facts) does not commit one to saying that tensed predication can be analysed in terms of tenseless predication, or that the untensed facts are primitive. But I admit a certain amount of confusion on these issues.

obtains, but what presently obtains captures the sequence of past, present, and future in different sorts of tensed facts. Socrates *was* wise; the Dalai Lama *is* wise. These two statements attribute wisdom to Socrates and the Dalai Lama respectively, from the point of view of the present, so to speak. But on the serious tenser approach there are two different predicative relations to wisdom at issue: being (presently) wise and having been wise.[13] One way to capture this would be to say that instantiation comes in three flavours: past ('was'), present ('is'), and future ('will be'), and apparently 'tenseless' instantiation must be understood in terms of these other three.[14] I will return to the issue of taking tense seriously below. But it is important to recognize that although a presentist who wants to make claims about the past and future is committed to serious tensing, at least in principle, serious tensing is an option for non-presentists as well.

With a clearer differentiation of views, let's return to the argument that perdurance and endurance are incompatible. The crucial claim is that perdurance entails non-presentism and endurance entails presentism. Because, the argument goes, presentism and non-presentism are incompatible, it is not possible for there to be both perduring and enduring things. The endurance side of the argument is this: Suppose some things endure through change. If all times are equally real, and if a changing object is wholly present at different times, then the object must have incompatible properties. But this is impossible. (Note that, in effect, this is just the original puzzle.) So if a changing object is wholly present at different times, then not all times are equally real; only the present exists. Thus endurance entails presentism. (See e.g. Merricks 1995: 526–7.)

This argument, however, is unconvincing because it ignores a number of controversial issues. The allegation is that an object cannot be wholly present at different times while undergoing change. But why not? Looking back at the premises we identified in setting up the puzzle, there are several that might be revised in order to accommodate endurance without presentism. In particular, we have yet to consider what it is for an object to be a subject of properties (so we could reject or modify the *proper subject condition*), and what sort of properties are instantiated in objects that undergo change (so we could reject or modify the incompatibility condition).

---

[13] Although I suggest here that serious tensing involves more than one predication relation, another option would be to postulate one basic predication relation (*being (presently) F*), and introduce past- and future-tense operators.

[14] As I understand the serious tenser approach, the core thesis is the metaphysical claim that instantiation is always tensed. It follows from this that propositions stating a tensed claim can change their truth-value as time passes: *the apple is green* becomes false. This, then, is captured by saying that truth or falsity (obtaining–not obtaining) is a tensed matter. Note, however, that one may maintain that propositions are true at some times and not others, i.e. that propositions are not eternally true or false, without being a serious tenser. One may, for example, hold that propositions are true at times in a way analogous to propositions being true at worlds.

Hence, the argument that endurance entails presentism construes the endurantist's options too narrowly.[15]

Thus far, it appears that there are presentist and eternalist versions of endurantism:

> *Presentist endurantism.* Only presently existing objects exist; ordinary objects persist by enduring;[16] and
>
> *Non-presentist (eternalist) endurantism.* Past, present, and future objects all exist; ordinary objects persist by enduring (allowing that there are both enduring, exduring, and perduring particulars).

So far it appears that the existence of enduring things is compatible with both understandings of time. The temporal parts ontology, however, is typically articulated in an eternalist framework. Is such an ontology committed to eternalism? Is it possible to be a presentist and also accept an ontology of temporal parts? Recall the views to consider:

> *Perdurance theory.* Objects persist only by perduring. There are no enduring or exduring particulars.
>
> *Stage theory.* Ordinary objects persist by exduring.

By venturing a bit further into the details it becomes clear, I believe, that the issues of persistence and presentism cross-cut each other. Let us begin with the stage theory: Is the stage theory compatible with presentism, or is it committed to eternalism? According to presentism, only the present exists. So, if all objects are stages, only present stages exist. But it is possible for a present stage to persist by *exduring* if it has counterpart stages at other times. Rearticulating this in a way compatible with presentism, one could maintain that a present stage persists by virtue of the fact that a (distinct) counterpart stage *will replace* it, or that it *replaced* an earlier (distinct) counterpart stage. On this view, the present (aka what exists) contains a 'flow' of short-lived entities, linked into persisting things through tense-sensitive counterpart relations.

One might object to this view by claiming that existing things cannot bear relations to non-existing things. However, if presentism is to be tenable at all, it must provide an account of statements that appear to assert cross-temporal relations (Markosian forthcoming). Consider:

I am the daughter of Anne and Robert Haslanger.

---

[15] Merricks (1995) acknowledges that there might appear to be other options open to an endurantist besides opting for presentism, but argues that the other options, e.g. modifying the incompatibility or proper subject conditions, are untenable.

[16] I will discuss below whether perdurantism and exdurantism are compatible with presentism. I argue that they are. If this is correct, then the presentist endurantist can also allow that there are stages and perduring things, but will claim that ordinary things persist by enduring.

(Neither of them (on the presentist's view) exists.) Or more basic to the view:

Yesterday occurred before today.

(Keep in mind that on the presentist's view, yesterday does not exist.) Whether the presentist can provide an interpretation (or an 'underlier'; Sider 1999; cf. Markosian forthcoming) of cross-temporal statements that avoids relations between existing and non-existing things is controversial; however, if such a strategy is available, there is no reason to think it could not handle counterpart relations sufficient for exdurance. In short, if presentism is tenable at all, it has the resources to accommodate exduring things.

But given a way to accommodate exdurance, can a presentist also accommodate perdurance? It depends on how one articulates the notion of perdurance. If to perdure an object must *exist at different times* by having parts at those times, then perdurance is not compatible with presentism. But a presentist could say that a persisting candle consists of the present candle-stage and those stages of it that already *were* and those that *will be*. Although some have claimed that one cannot have as a part something that doesn't exist (Merricks 1995: 524), again, this intuition is biased against the presentist. If a presentist has the resources to account for cross-temporal relations, there does not appear to be any special reason to baulk at cross-temporal relations between parts: my maternal grandmother is part of my extended family even though she does not (presently) exist. A presentist should be able to accommodate claims such as this. If so, then there are resources available to the presentist—including, for example, serious tensing—to articulate a version of the perdurance theory.[17]

However, it appears to be implicit in some understandings of presentism that things existing in the present are wholly present, and the properties they instantiate are only those they presently instantiate. (Neither of these claims follows from the thesis that only the present and presently existing things exist; but presentism is sometimes construed as a cluster of related theses.) If this is the case, then the perdurance theorist could not maintain that the candle exists (is wholly present in the present) in a way consistent both with its perduring and presentism (Oaklander 1992: 81–2). In any case, all perdurance and exdurance theorists to date prefer to state their positions in a form that favours non-presentism, and there is no reason to think that the presentist version is preferable.[18]

In light of the issues just raised, it appears that there is a broader range of accounts than is ordinarily considered; i.e. each of the perdurance, endurance, and exdurance

---

[17] It may be more plausible to think of events as perduring within a presentist framework than objects; there is some evidence that Chisholm looked favourably on such a view (in correspondence with Dean Zimmerman). See also Simons (2000a).

[18] However, it is instructive to note that the statements of both perdurance and endurance are in a form suited to eternalism rather than presentism, so more will need to be said about a presentist's account of persistence.

accounts can be developed within either a presentist or eternalist account of time. In other words, one's commitment to presentism or eternalism does not force a commitment to a particular account of persistence (though it may constrain how one articulates it). I will return to consider the role of time in competing solutions to the puzzle, but so far I have simply laid out a set of views based on their accounts of *persistence*. I have not yet considered how these accounts accommodate or fail to accommodate the other principles used to generate the original puzzle. For example, I have not discussed in detail how or whether the different views can capture the idea that an object undergoing alteration changes with respect to *its* properties. We should turn, then, to consider whether the other assumptions I started with provide a basis for thinking that ordinary objects perdure, endure, or exdure.

4. Methodological Interlude

But should we move on so easily? It might seem that we should pause at this point in the discussion to consider whether perdurance, endurance, or exdurance provides a plausible account of *persistence*. After all, if it is a 'Moorean' fact that things persist, shouldn't we be sure we have captured this fact and haven't misconstrued what persistence *really is*?

But how should we decide 'what persistence really is'? Should we rely on introspective evidence about our concept of persistence (list the standard platitudes about persistence), with the goal of understanding the ontological commitments of our everyday conceptual scheme (if so, whose conceptual scheme exactly are we interested in, and why)? Should we decide by working out a semantics of tensed discourse (Ludlow 1999), with the goal of understanding the ontological commitments of ordinary language? Or should we aim to determine what sorts of particulars there really are by working out a full metaphysical picture that best accommodates our needs in other areas (philosophy of language, epistemology, physics . . .), and then accept the account of persistence entailed by that picture? Each of these strategies suggests a different understanding of and approach to the problem.

Some have suggested that our ordinary term 'persistence' is indeterminate with respect to the ontological details we've been considering. The idea is that our semantical and analytical intuitions are not sufficient to distinguish among the accounts, so cannot provide a guide to which account is best (Johnston 1987). If this is the case, there are several different options: one might look to empirical science for answers; one might look for a priori considerations beyond reflection on our language or our concepts to settle the matter (Haslanger 1989*b*, 1992). Although there are methodological advantages to viewing the ordinary predicate 'persists' as ontologically indeterminate, I myself find it much more plausible to think that our ordinary notion of persistence is to be analysed as endurance than either of the alternatives. To suggest that exdurance captures our ordinary notion of persistence strikes me as bizarre; to interpret persistence as perdurance only slightly less so.

But even if our concepts of persistence, change, identity, etc. are better captured by some of the options we've considered than others, the question arises whether the main goal of the project is to provide an *analysis* of our concepts. After all, finding a satisfactory solution to the puzzle may require that we *revise* our concepts. It is certainly possible that a cluster of our everyday concepts commits us to paradox, in which case revision is called for; given the nature of the paradox, one or another plausible claim must be rejected. The question is which one? If the goal is to provide an account on which ordinary things undergo alteration, then what's important is to provide a metaphysical picture on which the claim that objects alter comes out true, or at least close to true. In this spirit, Ted Sider suggests, for example, that the goal ought to be to provide 'underliers', i.e., more specifically, quasi-truthmakers,[19] for our original assumptions rather than 'interpretations' (Sider 1999, esp. 330–3). It may well be that, in the end, what is meant by 'objects alter' is quite different from what we originally imagined when employing our ordinary pre-theoretic concepts. But this in itself is not an objection. It is likely that all the resolutions to the paradox require some revisionary notions, and such revisions can surely be made in the spirit of correction. But then, how do we decide between the options before us? In the end it may be that a number of different options are reasonable, depending on one's other commitments. I will return to these issues and to consider the trade-offs of the various views.

5. RELATIONALISM, INCOMPATIBILITY, AND TEMPORARY INTRINSICS

Where are we now? We have seen that there are several different options for accounting for the persistence of ordinary objects. The main contenders are perdurantism,

---

[19] Strictly speaking, we are looking not for 'truthmakers' but for 'quasi-truthmakers', since the account provided does not render the original claims—on their intended interpretations—true. Instead, roughly speaking, 'a sentence is quasi-true if the world is *similar enough* to the way it would have to be for the sentence to be genuinely true' (Sider 1999: 332). More precisely, with respect to the eternalist–presentist debate: 'If there is ... a "quasi-supervenience base" for a sentence S—to a first approximation, a true proposition P that would have been true and entailed the truth of S, if eternalism were true—then ... P is an *underlying truth* for S, and [is] ...*quasi-true*' (Sider 1999: 332–3).

exdurantism, and endurantism, each of which have, at least in principle, versions compatible with presentism and eternalism. It is not yet clear, however, how an eternalist endurantist can avoid the original puzzle. In other words, how can something be wholly present at different times—times that are equally real—and have incompatible properties?

The law of non-contradiction (3) is considered by all parties to the debate to be non-negotiable. However, another starting assumption is the incompatibility condition:

(2) *Incompatibility condition.* The properties involved in a change are incompatible.

This assumption appears to be called into question if one combines an endurantist account of persistence with what we'll call the *relational* approach to temporal qualification, namely, the approach that all properties are really relations to times.

Consider the facts that we are trying to accommodate.

(c) The candle is straight in the morning.
(d) The candle is bent in the afternoon.

Plausibly contradiction will be avoided if we can figure out a way to understand the temporal qualifications 'in the morning' and 'in the afternoon' so that *being straight* and *being bent* are not properties of the object at the same time. One straightforward way to understand the qualification is to treat the predicates 'is straight in the morning' and 'is bent in the afternoon' as expressing two-place relations: to say that the candle is straight at 8 a.m. is to say that the *being straight at* relation holds between the candle and 8 a.m. Correspondingly, to say that the candle is bent at 5 p.m. is to say that the *being bent at* relation holds between the candle and 5 p.m. (*Mutatis mutandis* for *n*-place relations: add a place for time.) Paradox is avoided because there is no inconsistency in standing in the *bent at* relation to one time and the *straight at* relation to another.[20] Yet because *being straight at t* and *being bent at t'* are compatible, there is a sense too in which the incompatibility condition has been sacrificed. This is meaningful because the incompatibility condition is what seems to capture the fact that change occurs.

A quick answer to this complaint is that we should be more sensitive to what the incompatibility condition requires. One way of thinking about incompatible relations is to take R and R^* to be incompatible just in case nothing can stand in both R and R^* to the same thing(s). So being shorter than and being taller than are incompatible, not because I cannot be both shorter than Michael Jordan and taller than Spike Lee, but because I cannot be both shorter than Michael Jordan and

---

[20] On the exdurance and perdurance accounts, straightness and bentness are attributed to different candle-stages, so each view is consistent with the claim that the properties involved in the change are incompatible. So, in so far as it solves the persistence problem, the 'relationalist' strategy appeals only to endurantists.

taller than Michael Jordan. Even though *being bent at t* and *being straight at t'* are compatible, *being bent at* and *being straight at* are incompatible in the sense that the candle could not stand in both relations to the same time. In other words, it may be that the *relations* in question are incompatible, even if the *relational properties*, i.e. the properties of *being straight at t* and *being bent at t'*, are compatible. The fact of change is captured because the candle cannot stand in both the *straight at* and *bent at* relations unless it persists through a change, represented by its different relations to the different times.

Given these observations, the combination of endurantism, eternalism, and relationalism looks quite appealing: some things are wholly present at different times, and they can undergo change by standing in incompatible relations to different times. [21]

The main objection to this account is that it fails to accommodate the phenomenon of *temporary intrinsics*. In fact, some have argued that temporary intrinsics lie at the heart of the puzzle about persistence through change (Lewis 1988). The intrinsic properties of an object are, roughly, those properties it has by virtue of itself alone, and not by virtue of its relations to other things; they are the properties that any duplicate of the object would have. According to David Lewis, relational changes, e.g. when my son grows to be taller than I am, can be accommodated by viewing them as being relativized to time. For example, although it might seem that in the case in question, *being taller than* is a relation between Isaac and me (I am currently taller than Isaac, but he will no doubt come to be taller than I am), Lewis sees no objection to treating it as a relation between Isaac, me, and a time: Sally is taller than Isaac on 1 August 2001; Sally is shorter than Isaac on 1 August 2009. Paradox is avoided because the relational properties (*being taller than Isaac on 1 August 2001, being shorter than Isaac on 1 August 2009*) are compatible. The problem, he maintains, arises if we attempt to account for all change by construing the properties involved as relational. Doing so would eliminate temporary monadic properties, i.e. temporary qualities, or temporary intrinsics, for apparently monadic properties (such as *being bent* or *being straight*) would have to be construed as relations to times.

Why the special concern with temporary intrinsics (Hawley 1998)? It can't be simply the worry that objects should not be 'bare' but must have *some* intrinsic properties, for things might be 'clothed' with permanent intrinsic properties (or even essential intrinsic properties). It can't be that our intuitions about what's monadic are stronger than about what's dyadic (as opposed to triadic etc.), for this isn't plausible: why should the idea that *being bent* is a monadic property of the candle (as opposed to being a dyadic relation between the candle and a time) be more important than the idea that *being taller than* is a dyadic relation between

[21] For a helpful discussion of the resources of this view, see Hawley (2001: 16–20). Although Hawley doesn't ultimately defend a relationalist account, she effectively explores its strengths.

Isaac and me (as opposed to a triadic relation between Isaac, me, and a time)? The motivation for focusing on temporary intrinsics seems to be simply that we *do* want to accommodate the phenomenon of intrinsic change, more specifically, to have an understanding of what it is to be a subject of properties that makes intrinsic change possible. Objects have some intrinsic properties: some of their properties are due just to how they are. But, surprisingly perhaps, objects sometimes change in these very respects—in shape, in their internal workings, in how they themselves are. How can we capture this?

One way is Lewis's way: deny that temporary intrinsics are in any way relational. But there are certainly others. The very notion of an 'intrinsic duplicate' needs clarification, and it is an open question whether being monadic is essential to the notion of intrinsic property (Zimmerman 1998a: 207–8; Haslanger 1989a; Lewis 2002: 3–4). Relations to times are exactly the sort of relations that may plausibly count as intrinsic. For example, consider two balls, b and b^*, that are intrinsic duplicates. Plausibly intrinsic duplicates can exist at different times, so suppose b exists at t and b^* exists at t^*. Now suppose b and b^* differ in their relational properties, e.g. b is red at t, but b^* is not red at t^*, or b is 3 inches in diameter at t but b^* is not 3 inches diameter at t^*. Surely, contrary to our original supposition, we should not count the balls as intrinsic duplicates even if they only vary in the relational ways just indicated; but if the balls must be alike in certain relational respects in order to be intrinsic duplicates, then it is plausible to say that their intrinsic nature is not captured by their monadic properties. Conversely, suppose that no temporary properties are monadic (namely, all temporary properties are relations to times), but x and y stand in all the same two-placed relations to their respective times (so where one is red at t, the other is red at t'; where one is 3 inches diameter at t, the other is 3 inches diameter at t', etc.). Is it not plausible that they are intrinsic duplicates?

Where, then, do we stand? Is the endurantist relationalist account tenable: can objects endure and change by standing in incompatible relations to different times? It seems yes. First, it is possible to develop an account of intrinsic property and intrinsic change which allows that not all intrinsic properties are monadic; so a relationalist could accommodate temporary intrinsics by claiming that when an object is bent at t and straight at t', it undergoes intrinsic change. Secondly, if one is uncomfortable toying with the notion of intrinsicness, the fact remains that there is nothing irrational in denying the phenomenon of intrinsic change and maintaining that all alteration is relational. An account that allows us to capture intrinsic change would be attractive, but we've seen no argument that giving up intrinsic change would be a disaster. Thirdly, in accepting a relational view it might appear that one compromises the assumption that change involves incompatible properties (that the properties *being bent at t* and *being straight at t'* are compatible is crucial to avoiding the puzzle), but there is a sense in which the relations in question are incompatible. So the relationalist account fares quite well so far.

One might reasonably ask, however, in what sense does the relationalist account really capture *change*? Does the fact that I am both taller than my son and shorter than my father indicate any sense in which I've changed? Surely not. How, then, does standing in incompatible relations to two different times capture change? I will return to this question below when we consider the 'no change' objection to the perdurance view.

6. Perdurance, Proper Subjects, and Change

I mentioned above that we would have to return to the question whether the perdurance account of persistence provided the resources to capture the notion of alteration, or whether perdurantists simply replace alteration with succession. With the problem of temporary intrinsics now before us we can ask more pointedly, does the perdurance account itself adequately capture intrinsic change?

After the persistence condition, the most controversial and difficult assumption in the puzzle is what we've been calling the *proper subject condition*, namely,

(5) *Proper subject condition.* The object undergoing the change is itself the proper subject of the properties involved in the change; for example, the persisting candle is itself the proper subject of the incompatible properties.

If the heart of the puzzle is in the phenomenon of temporary intrinsics, the proper subject condition is where the heart is truly exposed. Change is interesting in its own right and we have reason to look for an account that preserves some form of persistence, but problems about change have been central to metaphysics for millennia because they focus us on questions about predication and instantiation: What is it for an object to have a property? Especially: What is it to have an intrinsic property? And if a property is intrinsic, how can an object lose it (or gain it)?

It is a disadvantage of the perdurance account that it sacrifices the proper subject condition. How? Consider again the candle's change from straight to bent. On the perdurance view, the proper subject of straightness is the early candle-stage; the proper subject of bentness is the later candle-stage. The candle composed of these parts is not strictly speaking both straight and bent (otherwise we would be left again with a contradiction), but is only indirectly or derivatively straight and bent by virtue of having parts that are. Thus, the perdurantist tells us that the candle (namely, the candle-worm) is itself never the proper subject of *being bent* or *being straight*. The endurantist has no reason to make such a strange claim.

Note further that the perdurantist who stresses the importance of temporary intrinsics is in a somewhat awkward position, for by sacrificing the proper subject condition, we seem to get the wrong subjects for the intrinsic properties. Lewis emphasizes that *bentness* and *straightness* are intrinsic properties. That seems plausible. But what seems plausible is that they are intrinsic properties of ordinary objects such as candles and railroad tracks and persons. To capture this intuition by saying that *bentness* and *straightness* are properly speaking intrinsic properties of candle-stages, railroad-track-stages, and person-stages, and are derivatively intrinsic properties of candles, railroad tracks, and persons (by being intrinsic properties of their parts), compromises the insight we were aiming for (Haslanger 1989*a*: 119–20; Zimmerman 1998*a*: 215). This may seem too subtle for serious consideration. But it was Lewis—the arch-perdurantist—after all, who emphasized the issue of intrinsicness, so asking the perdurantist to pay attention to what counts as the proper subject of an intrinsic property is only fair.

However, are the benefits of the perdurance account so powerful that they outweigh concerns about whether it fully satisfies the proper subject condition? One can find a variety of objections to the metaphysic of temporal parts underlying the perdurance theory. For example, some have argued that the notion of temporal part is not intelligible (van Inwagen 1990, 2000); others have objected to the mereological assumptions seeming to underlie it (Thomson 1983; van Inwagen 1981); others have complained of its over-abundant ontology of momentary particulars popping into and out of existence (Thomson 1983); others have argued that it renders change inexplicable (Haslanger 1989*a*); others have suggested it cannot adequately account for motion (consider the rotating disk objections; Kripke 1978; Armstrong 1980; Zimmerman 1998*b*, 1999; Lewis 1999; Hawley 1999; Callender 2001); still others have argued that it is unmotivated (Rea 1998). However, the objection especially relevant to the problem of change we're considering is the 'no change' objection (McTaggart 1927, ch. 33; Lombard 1986: 108–9; Simons 1987: 34–7, 126; Mellor 1981: 110–11; Heller 1992).

There are two versions of the 'no change' objection, both of which assume an eternalist version of perdurantism.[22] According to the first version, the perdurance view is allegedly committed to a 'static' conception of time: time and all its occupants are stretched out 'timelessly' in four dimensions; stages, like dots in a pointillist painting, can bear the right sort of relations to each other to count as a persisting object, but nothing really moves; nothing even comes into or goes out of existence. Everything is just *there*. On the second version—we might call it the 'no alteration' objection to distinguish it from the first—stages are thought to come into and go out of existence instantaneously in succession. So it is granted that there is change

---

[22] The 'no change' challenge (in somewhat different forms) is one that arises not only for eternalist perdurantism, but for any eternalist view. We'll see that the perdurantist's strategy for response is parallel to ones available to other endurantists as well.

(indeed, almost nothing but), but because there is nothing that gains or loses one of *its* properties, there is no genuine alteration. The stages come and go, but do not alter; the persisting thing has different parts with different properties, but it too does not alter. So persistence (as perdurance) through time may be achieved, but genuine alteration is denied.

The perdurance theorist responds to both versions of the objection in the same way: although the perdurance account may not be adequate to capture every construal of what change or alteration involves, it does justice to the phenomena that must be accommodated. Any account of change must do justice to the facts we've already considered:

(c) The candle is straight in the morning.
(d) The candle is bent in the afternoon.

These facts are accommodated by the perdurantist's paraphrases or reconstruals:

(c*) The candle has as a part a morning-stage (or morning segment) that is straight.
(d*) The candle has as a part an afternoon-stage (or afternoon segment) that is bent.

Although both (c*) and (d*) are eternally true, this does not undermine the claim that change has occurred, for, the perdurantist maintains, change occurs when an object's temporal parts have incompatible properties. Nor do (c*) and (d*) undermine the claim that alteration is possible, for alteration can be understood simply as variation in the intrinsic qualities of a thing. According to the perdurantist, having a straight-stage and a bent-stage is our best account of such variation: bentness and straightness are incompatible intrinsic properties of the stages that are parts of the persisting thing.

Although I've sketched the 'no change' objection in response to the perdurance theory, there are versions of it that can arise for other eternalist accounts, including endurantist and exdurantist accounts. (Note in particular that I ended the previous section with a version of the 'no change' objection against the eternalist relationalist.) Because eternalism allows for a 'timeless' representation of the world, it is in danger of seeming entirely static. Admittedly, change may not appear familiar to us when considered from a timeless perspective, and yet we may be describing change nonetheless; after all, our experience of change is in time. In short, eternalists can allow that their models do not fully capture the phenomenology of change, but also maintain that they do capture the ontology underlying the phenomenology. So the 'no change' objection, by itself, does not force us to abandon the eternalist accounts of persistence.

Summarizing where we stand with the perdurance view: How can an object persist through change with respect to the way it is by virtue of itself alone? The perdurantist answers: it has parts with incompatible properties. What is the relation between the persisting object and the properties involved in such a change? The perdurantist answers: the persisting thing's relation to the properties is mediated by the parts which have them intrinsically, but a property intrinsic to the parts is intrinsic to the whole. So thus far it appears we have a couple of different options available for thinking about alteration: the perdurance theory (persisting things perdure with intrinsically different parts), and relationalism (persisting things endure and stand in incompatible (intrinsic) relations to different times). Stage theory and presentism remain on the table for further consideration: how do they fare with respect to the set of original principles? Are they viable options?

7. Stage Theory and Lasting Intrinsics

Note that the exdurance or stage view has many of the same benefits as the perdurance account, without some of its disadvantages. Remember, on the stage view, ordinary objects are stages that persist by *ex*during, i.e. by standing in counterpart relations to distinct stages at other times. As on the perdurance account, the stage view provides a simple way to avoid the predication of incompatible properties in cases of change: the subjects of the incompatible properties (different stages at different times) are distinct, so no contradiction arises. It also accommodates temporary intrinsics: intrinsic properties are instantiated in exduring objects (which are stages); the candle's *being bent* or *being straight* is not construed relationally (it is neither a relation to times, nor a relation to parts that have the intrinsics, as in Lewis's story). Moreover, the stage theory appeals to certain ontological minimalists by not needing to postulate sums of stages over and above the stages themselves. (For further advantages, see Hawley 2001; Sider 2001.)

Note, however, that the stage view does not appear to accommodate *history-dependent* intrinsics. If it is reasonable to insist that an adequate account of alteration do justice to temporary intrinsics, such as *being bent*, then it would seem that it should also do justice to history-dependent intrinsics such as being a horse or being a chair. Plausibly horses and chairs are horses and chairs not simply by virtue of their occurrent properties, but by virtue also of properties they have had and/or will have. In other words, something's currently being a horse is an intrinsic property that depends on how *it* is at other times. But on the exdurance account, strictly speaking there is no way that *it* (the stage) is at other times. *It* is some way or another at other times by virtue of counterparts at those times. So *its* being a horse is not intrinsic (to its proper subject, namely, the stage), but depends on how other things are. Having seen that there are numerous ways to rethink the notion of intrinsicness, there are no doubt ways for the exdurantist to respond. But the response will require some trade-off in our intuitions.

Moreover, the stage theory appears to reject the identity condition (4) outright. The identity condition requires that if an object persists through a change, then the object existing before the change is one and the same object as the one existing after the change. The stage theory asserts that objects persist without *themselves* being present (either wholly or partly) at different times; objects are short-lived and persist by having *counterparts* at different times.

As one might expect, there is a (by now familiar) strategy of response at hand. The idea is that statements expressing persistence facts must be systematically reconstrued. Although it is true to say that the candle that is straight in the morning is one and the same candle as the candle that is straight in the afternoon, the 'underlier' for this statement, what makes the statement true, is not an identity between the morning candle and the evening candle, but the fact that a certain counterpart relation holds between them. So at the level of ordinary speech the identity condition is preserved, even if at the ontological level the identity condition is violated. (This general strategy can be used to respond both to the problem of history-dependent intrinsics and to the alleged violation of the identity condition.)

To my mind, however, this strategy strains the limits of credibility. Nonetheless, it highlights a broader methodological question that has cropped up repeatedly in evaluating the various solutions to the puzzle. In articulating the original assumptions that gave rise to the puzzle, how philosophically laden, how ontologically committal, were the claims? Is our goal in solving the puzzle to provide 'analyses' of the key concepts, e.g. of persistence, change, property, etc. which demonstrate that the given set of claims employing these concepts are compatible? Or is our goal not to provide 'analyses', but 'underliers'—accounts of the underlying facts that make the claims true or 'quasi-true', but which don't in any traditional sense capture the 'meaning' of the original claims? If we are seeking 'analyses', then it isn't at all clear that our ordinary intuitions provide enough data to discriminate between the various options. But if we are seeking 'underliers', it isn't clear what is constraining our choice of interpretations. If an ontology on which nothing exists for any substantial length of time can be construed as satisfying the identity condition on persistence, namely, that things persist by continuing to exist through time, then it is hard to see how the identity condition has constrained our ontology at all.

A more appealing approach to the puzzle, I believe, is to interpret the initial assumptions as articulating considered judgements concerning ontology, and as employing at least some terms whose interpretation the various parties to the debate agree upon. Which terms they will be cannot be decided by fiat in advance, but must be decided as the debate unfolds. If we proceed in this way, I think at this stage we should agree to disagree about the term 'persistence', but agree to agree about the term 'identity'. If so, then the stage theory maintains that there is persistence without identity over time, and the other parties to the debate (both the perdurance and endurance theorists) maintain that persistence requires identity—either identity of the worm or of the subject of change. So, rather than saying that the exdurance account is compatible with the identity condition, the debate is better served by saying that the exdurantists bite the bullet and reject the identity condition. This, however, need not be fatal to the exdurantist if the main goal is to preserve persistence, for persistence is, at least in one sense, preserved.

8. PRESENTISM AND 'JUST HAVING' A PROPERTY

We have just considered three eternalist approaches in detail: relationalism, perdurantism, and exdurantism. But are there grounds for thinking that presentism offers a better alternative? If we make it a priority to preserve the *proper subject condition*, then some would maintain that our best candidate is a presentist approach, for the presentist's emphasis is certainly on capturing how, for example, an enduring object that *was straight* can *be bent*. But even more promising, the presentist endurance solution seems to provide a model on which the five conditions can be jointly satisfied (see Hinchliff 1996: Zimmerman 1996, 1998a). Although, as we saw above, the issue of presentism cross-cuts persistence (one can be a presentist and, with adjustments, maintain any of the views on persistence), presentism is especially appealing to endurantists who are unhappy with a relationalist account.[23]

Recall that the presentist maintains that only the present exists or is real. Combining this ontology with a serious approach to tense, the following view emerges. We satisfy the persistence condition and identity condition by allowing that the candle endures: it *is* wholly present now, it *was* wholly present before (and presumably *will be* later). Moreover, we make sense of the idea that the candle is the proper subject of the properties involved in the change by attending to tense: it (the candle itself) *was* straight, but that very candle *is* also bent. Further, the properties of being straight and bent are not relational: following terminology offered by Mark Hinchliff (1996), the properties are ones that the candle can *just have* (in other terms, the properties *being straight* and *being bent* are ones the candle has *simpliciter*). The candle *just is* straight, and then it *just is* bent. The properties of *bentness* and *straightness* are incompatible properties (nothing can *just have* both), as required by the incompatibility condition. And finally, we avoid contradiction by noting that the only

---

[23] As indicated above, the perdurantist and exdurantist have other ways of avoiding the puzzle, so they don't need presentism to do the work of providing a solution. They may choose to be presentists on other grounds, however.

properties the candle has *simpliciter* are the properties it presently has; even though it *had* the property of being straight, this does not conflict with its *just having* the property of being bent. (See also Craig 1998.)

Of course, all parties to the debate want to account for the possibility of genuine alteration by providing an account of temporal qualification. Because we need not be presentists to take tense seriously, we need to say more to clarify what is distinctive of the presentist's approach (Rea, Chapter 9 in this volume; Bigelow 1996). Let's consider two claims we want to make about the candle:

(e) The candle is bent.
(f) The candle was straight.

On the presentist's view, (e) expresses a primitive predication between the candle and the property of being bent. This primitive predication, which I have referred to as 'just having' or 'having *simpliciter*', is paradigmatically instantiated by an object and a property in the present. We must be clear, though, that the presentist does not define 'just having' as 'having now' or 'presently having'; it is a substantive metaphysical thesis that objects 'just have' the properties they have in the present. So we should understand (e) as:

(e^*) The candle *just has* bentness.

In contrast, (f), by virtue of the tense, can be understood by applying the tense operator 'it was the case that' to the primitive predication holding between the candle and straightness:

(f^*) It was the case that the candle *just has* straightness.

So, although it is not the case that the candle *is* straight, it *was* straight; it does not *just have* straightness, but it *just had* straightness.[24]

So far the approach addresses the problem of alteration by taking tense seriously, i.e. by treating the predicative elements in propositions as tensed rather than tenseless. Where does presentism fit in? How are these views about our tensed discourse related to the ontological commitments of presentism? As we've seen, according to the serious tenser, facts about how things 'are' are facts about the way they are, were, or will be. But one need not be a presentist to accept this view. An eternalist can maintain that there are wholly past things (Socrates) and wholly future things (my first grandchild) but any proposition concerning these things is temporally moored

---

[24] The fact that an object *just has* a property is not a fact that obtains eternally: some candles 'just have' straightness, but will fail to 'just have' straightness later. But there is no contradiction here, since the properties an object has and the properties the object will have may be incompatible. Note also that some may prefer to articulate the presentist position as committed to only one instantiation relation ('just having') and to accommodate past and future tense by operators: it was the case that x just has P; it will be the case that x just has P.

in the present.[25] For example, it is compatible with serious tensing that Socrates exists and stands in backward-looking relations to his past properties, e.g. Socrates has the property of *having been wise*, of *having been a social 'gadfly'*, of *having been executed*. But once we have the resources of serious tensing, these seem sufficient to address the problem of change, and the presentist ontology is not needed. In other words, on the strategy just outlined, it is the serious tenser's metaphysical commitment to tensed propositions that allows us to evade the contradiction, not the presentist ontology. We can say that there are ways the object *was* other than (and incompatible with) the way it *is*, but that's because *having had* a property is not the same as *just having* it.

So where do we stand? If we are drawn to endurantism but want to resist relationalism, then serious tensing seems to be a promising strategy to avoid the original puzzle. Serious tensing is compatible, at least in principle, with either presentism or eternalism, so one need not endorse presentism to pursue this strategy. This may come as a relief, for as we saw above for the perdurance view, there are a wide range of arguments against presentism that have nothing to do with change or alteration. (We've glimpsed before questions about the presentist's ability to handle cross-temporal relations and singular propositions about the past; there are others (Markosian forthcoming). These don't arise for the eternalist serious tenser.)

However, Zimmerman has argued that the combination of eternalism (some things exist that don't presently exist) and serious tensing is not an appealing position (Zimmerman 1998a). He argues: Consider my past headache. Suppose, with the eternalist, that it exists but does not presently exist.[26] Given serious tensing, we cannot say that it *is* painful, for that would mean that it is presently painful, and by hypothesis, it isn't (though it *was* painful). But doesn't this leave us with a rather ghostly non-painful headache? In fact on this view, all wholly past entities exist, but the only properties they *have* (read as tensed) are mere reflections of their past lives (e.g. they aren't in space but were in space; aren't shaped but were shaped; etc.). Although this is not an incoherent position (Smith 1993), its drawbacks have led most serious tensers to opt for presentism.

So what about the combination of presentism and serious tensing? Is it an appealing option? Setting aside complaints against presentism that stem from considerations outside of the debate over alteration, are there arguments against

---

[25] Here's another way to put the idea: it is possible to hold the view that quantifiers range over things existing at all times, and also that anything asserted of the things in the domain of the quantifier expresses a tensed fact.

[26] It is something of a question what sense to give the claim that the past headache exists. Is this to be understood as an untensed 'exists'? If so, then this seems incompatible with a serious tenser who rejects untensed predicates (though perhaps there are serious tensers who aren't *really* serious and allow that there are both tensed and untensed facts). Alternatively it could mean that the headache either existed, exists, or will exist, but if this is the right interpretation, then it isn't clear the headache is a 'ghostly' existing entity as suggested below.

its proposed analysis of change? There are places where David Lewis seems to suggest the following argument: Persistence requires that things be wholly present at different times. But on the presentist view, strictly speaking, there is only one time (the present). So the presentist cannot accommodate persistence.

If this is the argument, then Lewis's conception of persistence seems to beg the question against the presentist. For example, Lewis maintains that if I persist, then (as Zimmerman articulates it):

(PC) There are at least two different times; one at which I am bent, the other at which I'm straight. (Zimmerman 1998: 213)

Zimmerman argues that we can get the force of this on a presentist view, without the eternalist ontological commitment (Zimmerman 1998a: 212–16). He offers the following paraphrase:

(Z) Either I was bent and would become or had previously been straight; or I will be bent and will have been or be about to become straight, or I will be straight and will have been or be about to become bent. (Zimmerman 1998a: 215)

In short, the persistence of an entity does not require that more than one time exists, but only that other times *did exist* or *will exist* at which the entity *was* or *will be* wholly present. And this seems right.

However, there may be more to the objection. Lewis has also argued:

[According to the presentist, non-present times] are like fake stories; they are abstract representations, composed out of the materials of the present, which represent or misrepresent the way things are. When something has different intrinsic properties according to one of these ersatz other times, that does not mean that it, or any part of it, or anything else, just has them—no more so than when a man is crooked according to the *Times*, or honest according to the *News*. This is a solution that rejects endurance because it rejects persistence altogether. (Lewis 1986: 204; see also Lewis 2002: 2)

What is the argument here? Here's one interpretation: Suppose that the candle is now bent but was straight. If the presentist says,

(g) In the past, the candle is straight.

The embedded claim that the candle is straight is false, but it is allegedly 'made true' by adding the modifier 'In the past'. But Lewis asks, how does adding the modifier 'In the past' allow us to capture a truth? According to the presentist there is no straight candle—only presently existing things exist, and the candle now before us is bent. In short, there is no (existing) past by reference to which the claim (g) is true. Instead, (g) must be made true by a 'fake story'. So, he claims, the presentist does not provide us with the resources to capture persistence.

But again this argument seems to beg the question against the presentist. Lewis's idea seems to be that propositions must be evaluated as true or false within an eternalist framework: the facts are laid out timelessly and propositions are true iff they correspond to one of the (timeless) facts. But, as we've seen, this is not a model the presentist would or need endorse. The candle that was straight presently exists (but is bent now); the fact that the candle *was* straight is a present (past-tensed) fact about it and (*g*) is true in virtue of that present fact. It appears, then, that presentism offers an option to the endurantist.

If one insists on certain eternalist frameworks for understanding persistence, time, and tense, then the presentist alternative looks doomed. However, so far we haven't found compelling reasons to favour one background framework above all others. At moments it appears that the conversation is on the verge of breaking down because different parties to the debate are working with such different accounts of time and tense. However, rather than be discouraged by this, one might find the discussion is enriched by tracing the roots of the controversy over change to other metaphysical debates. The challenge, however, is to keep track of the various elements of the discussion and their relation to each other. At issue so far have been:

Time. Does only the present exist? (eternalism v. presentism)

Tense. Are there (primitively) tensed facts? (serious tensing v. non-serious tensing) If so, are all facts tensed, or only some? Semantic: Are grammatical tense and temporal indexicals eliminable, or do ordinary statements have an essential temporal indexical element? (Perry 1979)

Propositions. Do propositions change in their truth-value over time?

Persistence. What is required for persistence? (perdurance, endurance, exdurance)

Existence. What is it to exist 'at a time'? Are particulars 'wholly present' at different times in the same way that universals are 'wholly present' at different places?

Change. What constitutes genuine alteration? Is there genuine alteration (or only succession)? Is there really change in an eternalist framework?

Intrinsicness. Are all intrinsic properties monadic? Are some relations intrinsic to one of the relata?

Properties. Are all temporary properties 'disguised' relations to times? What are the proper subjects of non-occurrent (or lasting) properties?

Predication. What is the relation between an object and its properties? Is predication timeless or tensed? Are there several predication relations or one? (And we're about to consider: Can we temporally modify predication, and if so how? Is predication a relation involving time or non-relational?)

It may seem that there are already enough approaches on the table and we don't need to explore any others. But there is still a set of endurantist views worth considering.

9. Endurance: Temporally Qualified Instantiation?

Some endurantists are uncomfortable with a presentist ontology: they want to allow that times other than the present and things other than presently existing things exist. Among these, some are also uncomfortable with a relationalist account of temporal qualification. Initially the view that temporary properties are really relations to times was seen as sub-optimal because it appears to reject the premiss in our original puzzle which requires that the properties involved in the change be incompatible (though we considered strategies to reconstrue incompatibility). More importantly, it does not appear to be the best account of temporary *intrinsics* (though it can do fine if we allow that not all intrinsics are monadic). Are there still more options for an eternalist endurantist?

Many endurantists have toyed with the thought that an object's having a property at a time should be explicated so that it is *the object's having of the property* that is temporally qualified. Three strategies for spelling this out have emerged: copula-tensing, adverbialism, and what I'll call *SOFism*, (for 'state-of-'fairs-ism').

9.1 Copula-Tensing

According to the copula-tenser, objects *have* properties, and the *having* is open to temporal qualification: the candle *has* straightness *at t* and not *at t**. In other words, instantiation is taken to be a separable relation holding between an object, a property, and a time. This view avoids the claim that the properties involved in the change are relations; it can also say that they are incompatible (an object cannot *have* bentness *at* and *have* straightness *at* the same time). Contradiction is avoided by claiming that the candle is not straight and bent *simpliciter*, but *is-at-t* straight and *is-at-t** bent.

The standard response to this approach is that treating the copula as a separable relation lands one in Bradley's regress (Bradley 1897, ch. 3; Armstrong 1978: 106 ff.): if a separate copula is needed to bind an object to a property, then what binds an object to the copula itself (isn't the separate copula just a relation like others)? Do we need another copula to do that work? If so, then we will need an infinite number of copulas, each to bind the next; if not, then we don't need the copula to begin with and should treat the property as binding itself to the object. (Lewis 2002: 6–7). One response to this argument would be to suggest that the copula is *not* like other properties or relations and is uniquely able to bind (other) properties or relations to their subject(s); but such moves are not entirely appealing (Lewis 2002: 7, 10–11).

9.2 Adverbialism

The adverbialist solution attempts to sidestep the Bradley regress, while still capturing the insight that the object's *having* the property is what should be temporally
modified. The question is how to avoid ontological commitment to the copula as
a relation distinct from the instantiated property (Johnston 1987). The idea is that
having a property—understanding 'having' as some sort of 'non-relational tie'—is
something that can be temporary, and this temporary 'attachment' should be understood by analogy with other adverbial modifiers. For example, the following claims
are consistent:

(*h*) The candle is actually straight.

and

(*i*) The candle is possibly bent.

Of course, there are different ways to construe (*h*) and (*i*), but on one construal, the
adverbs 'actually' and 'possibly' are modifying the way in which the candle is straight
and bent respectively. Returning to the temporal case, we might construe:

(*c*) The candle is straight in the morning

as

(c_{adv}) The candle is *in-the-morningly* straight.

The adverbialist avoids contradiction as long as we are precluded from dropping
the adverbial qualifications, for (c_{adv}) is compatible with

(d_{adv}) The candle is *in-the-afternoonly* bent.

Unquestionably, this option is difficult to state elegantly, but the objective is
clear enough. But will it do as a solution to the persistence puzzle? The candle
persists, and changes by having—in temporally distinct 'ways'–incompatible properties. There may be some awkwardness in claiming that the object can, in some
sense, have incompatible properties (Merricks 1994: 169), but the adverbialist maintains that inconsistency arises only when an object has incompatible properties *in
the same way* (temporally speaking). And this makes sense. So the adverbialist is not
really in danger of forfeiting the principle of non-contradiction; rather, we must
simply restate the principle so that it makes explicit qualification to ways of having
properties.

9.3 SOFism

Another strategy for articulating the idea that it is the having of properties that
should be temporally qualified develops the idea that *what is the case* depends on

the time under consideration (Forbes 1987; Haslanger 1989*a*; Lowe 1988; Myro 1986). Graeme Forbes has offered an account along these lines employing states of affairs. Drawing on some of Forbes's suggestions, let us distinguish type and token states of affairs. A type state of affairs consists of a relation between an object and a property:[27] *x's being P*. A token state of affairs consists of such a type obtaining at a time: *x's being P obtaining at t*.[28] To say that the candle is bent in the afternoon is to say that the (type) state of affairs *the candle's being bent* obtains in the afternoon, or in other words, the type has a token instance: *the candle's being bent in the afternoon*.[29]

As it stands it isn't entirely clear how to interpret the view just sketched.[30] One way of fleshing it out, let's call this strategy *SOFism*, can again be usefully compared to an approach to modal discourse (e.g. Lewis 1986). For example, suppose that the candle in question is actually yellow. It might, however, have been blue. The (type) state of affairs *the candle's being blue* does not actually obtain, but possibly obtains, i.e. it does not obtain in the actual world but obtains in another possible world.[31] The candle's being (actually) yellow and the candle's being (possibly) blue are incompatible, but do not conflict, because the instantiations of the (type) states of affairs occur in different worlds. Likewise the candle's being (in the morning)

[27] For ease of exposition I'll speak of an object and a property, allowing that a more complete exposition would have to include relations as well.

[28] As noted above, it is open to an eternalist to opt for serious tensing. Rather than go through every possible option here (in a discussion that is already too complicated), I will focus on the non-serious tenser option, allowing that a serious tenser option could be articulated.

[29] A further question is what sense to make of the contrast between type and token states of affairs. Adopting a trope theory would be one option: token states of affairs consist of an object and a trope (Simons 2000*b*). Then we could understand (iii) as true just in case the candle and the straightness trope (the instantiation of straightness in the candle) constitute a token state of affairs in the morning. Some states of affairs types have no tokens at all; others have tokens but only at some times. But is the introduction of tropes extraneous? Could we simplify the picture by maintaining instead that each time consists of a collection of states of affairs, and to say that a state of affairs *S* obtains at some time *t* is to say that *S* is in the *t* collection? (Is this the ontological pay-off of what Merricks is really getting at in Merricks 1994?)

[30] Note that in my 'Endurance and Temporary Intrinsics' (Haslanger 1989*a*) I didn't defend the view that Hinchliff ascribes to me (Hinchliff 1996: 122). He suggests I opted for a temporalist account on which propositions are true at times (and not eternally); but in the same paragraph (1996: 121) I specifically suggest the eternalist option. Although my prose is far less clear than I would like, on the following page I attempt to descend semantically to speak of an object's instantiation of a property, holding at a time. My concern here was to argue that the instantiation of the property by the object was not problematically relational, so I was less clear on the relation between that instantiation and the time. But I think the best way to construe what I was getting at would be to opt for complex eternalist propositions whose semantic values are much like what Forbes suggests.

[31] In the modal case, modal realists believe that possible worlds other than the actual world are real; modal actualists believe that only the actual world is real. In the temporal analogue, eternalists believe that times other than the present are real; presentists believe that only the present is real. The actualist and presentist typically offer fictionalist or constructivist accounts of non-actual–non-present times. Fortunately for the eternalist, the existence of non-present times is usually taken to be more plausible than the existence of non-actual worlds.

straight and the candle's being (in the afternoon) bent do not conflict because the instantiations of the (type) states of affairs occur at different times.

If SOFism continues to borrow from Lewis's modal example (Lewis 1986: 5–6), tense would be explicated (though not necessarily eliminated) using quantification. For example,

> The candle was straight iff there is a past time t, such that at t the candle is straight.

Or in other words: iff there is a past time t such that at t the (type) state of affairs *the candle's being straight* obtains. The phrase 'at t' serves on this view to restrict names or quantifiers within its scope to the time in question. In ordinary present-tense claims such as 'The candle is straight' the domain[32] is restricted to the actual present. More complex statements must be treated with care. For example, Lewis (1986: 6) in

> Nowadays there are rulers more dangerous than any ancient Roman.

The 'nowadays' restricts the domain of the quantifier 'there are rulers' to within a few decades of the present, but it cannot plausibly be taken to so restrict the quantifier in 'any ancient Roman'. So more needs to be said in a full analysis to address such cases. However, an advantage of an account using restricted quantifiers is that it provides resources for understanding the various types of temporal qualification we regularly employ (e.g. 'nowadays', 'when I was young'. . .) beyond standard tenses.

Although suggestive, this strategy won't exactly work for a SOFist exploring endurance options, for in restricting quantifiers to a particular domain, one isn't necessarily restricting them to a particular time. For example, suppose again that the candle endures, is straight at t, and bent at t'. If 'at t' restricts the description 'The candle' to the domain of things existing at t, and the candle endures to t', then we have not avoided contradiction: the candle (which is in the domain of things at both t and at t') would be both bent and straight.

Instead what we need is a way to understand the temporal qualification 'at t' as restricting the context for the claim rather than the domain of the names, quantifiers (etc.). There are a number of ways one might accomplish this, but it is illuminating to consider what Barwise and Etchemendy call an 'Austinian' approach to propositions. They say:

According to Austin, a legitimate statement provides two things: a historical (or actual) situation s_A, and a type of situation T_A. The former is just some limited portion of the real world; the speaker refers to it using what Austin calls 'demonstrative conventions.' The latter is, roughly speaking, a property of situations determined from the statement by means of 'descriptive conventions' associated with the language. The statement A is true if s_A is of type T_A; otherwise it is false. (Barwise and Etchemendy 1987: 28–9)

---

[32] Taking 'the domain' in this context to be the domain of the quantifier in the analysis of the definite description 'the candle'.

They go on to suggest that the 'Austinian proposition' expressed by A is the claim that s_A is of type T_A (Austin 1950). So, on this view, every proposition is about a situation, and says of the situation that it is of a certain type. We determine what situation a statement is about by some combination of explicit and contextal cues.

How does this idea help us think about persistence through change? There are a number of ways to flesh this out, but one way is to maintain that both lexical and pragmatic cues function as 'demonstrative factors' that temporally restrict what situations a particular statement is about. So, for example, when I speak in the morning and say, 'The candle is straight', tense, together with contextual cues, indicate that I am speaking about a concrete situation in the present, and the 'descriptive factors' determine that I am saying of this situation that it is of the type *the candle's being straight*. When I speak in the afternoon and say, 'The candle is bent', I am saying of the concrete situation (then) that it is of the type *the candle's being bent*. I might also say then that 'The candle was straight'. If so, then again various cues indicate that I am speaking of a different (past) situation which is of the type *the candle's being straight*. There is no contradiction here. The type situations are incompatible (they cannot obtain at the same time), but there is no conflict in saying of distinct situations that they are of incompatible types. Although in drawing on the Austinian framework I've switched from talk of type–token states of affairs to type–token situations, for our purposes here the terminology can function as interchangeable.[33]

On this view, the statement 'The candle is straight' may appear to change in its truth-value as the candle bends, but the proposition expressed by a given utterance: that s_A is of type T_A does not change its truth-value.[34] This in itself raises a number of difficult issues; for example, how does this proposition's truth-value depend on the world at all? How are the indexical elements, including tense, to be treated? How do we account for propositions about non-real situations? (See Barwise and Etchemendy 1987: 129–30.) These are important issues, but they extend beyond the scope of this chapter. For the time being we will have to work with this sketch of only part of the view. (For further details, see e.g. Barwise and Etchemendy 1987; Barwise and Perry 1983.)

To summarize, then, the SOFist account of change seems to be this: There are enduring things wholly present in token states of affairs obtaining at different times

---

[33] On the Barwise and Etchemendy account, situations are sets of states of affairs (Barwise and Etchemendy 1987: 75, 123). Similarly in Barwise and Perry (1983). This terminological distinction is useful, but for our limited purposes here it is not essential to make the distinction.

[34] In my earlier essay (Haslanger 1989a) I pointed to an account along the lines I am suggesting here. However, there I suggested that on such a view propositions would obtain at times (and so change their truth-values). That suggestion has been criticized (e.g. Lewis 2002: 11–12), but, as I am indicating here, one can pursue the strategy without claiming that propositions vary in their truth-values over time. I see myself here as attempting to articulate the approach more fully and with a greater sensitivity to the many background issues. However, there is still much work to be done to sort out the view and its implications.

(endurantism); in states of affairs such as the candle's being straight and the candle's being bent, the properties *being straight* and *being bent* are qualities of the candle (not relations to times); and these properties are incompatible. There is no contradiction because the two states of affairs types involving incompatible properties (*the candle's being bent* and *the candle's being straight*) don't have tokens at the same time. This would seem to be an option that preserves many of our original intuitions: an object can endure through a change in its intrinsic properties.[35]

SOFism differs from the accounts I've so far considered by suggesting that the principal job of an ordinary subject–predicate sentence is not to express a primitive predication between an object and a property (either a temporally relativized predication, or a predication corresponding to the presentists (or perdurantists) *just having* or having *simpliciter*). Instead, it takes an ordinary statement to be making a claim about a state of affairs type obtaining, or alternatively about a token state of affairs being of a certain type.

Note, however, that there are potentially two predicational elements in this picture: first, whatever is going on between x and P such that they constitute a type state of affairs, and secondly, the realization of that type in the token. The relation between x and P in the type state of affairs is not temporally qualified; this is as close as one gets in the SOFist picture to 'just having' or *having simpliciter*. Yet the SOFist also maintains that an object's having a property (x's being F) is the sort of thing that—at least for some range of objects and some range of properties—occurs at times. So there also appears to be a temporally relativized element *obtaining at t* in the picture. Note, however, that what happens *at t* is that the type has a token; this is not a relation holding between the object undergoing change and its properties. So even if there may be reason to worry about temporally relativizing the copula (or making all temporary properties relations to times), these worries need not arise here.

10. HAVING A PROPERTY SIMPLICITER

Interestingly, perdurantists and presentists lodge the same complaint against those who seek to temporally qualify instantiation, whether adverbially or as qualifying

---

[35] Admittedly, Lewis argues that we should reject identity across possible worlds and opt for counterparts instead; he offers an analogue of this argument in defence of his perdurantism. However, many have rejected his argument against identity across possible worlds and take identity across time and across worlds to be the more crucial notions to preserve. In any case, the parallel to Lewis's view of modality ends before his commitment to counterparts.

states of affairs: temporary intrinsics are not had *simpliciter*, there is a gap, a medi-ation, a problematic externality between the object and its properties. Hinchliff argues, for example, that all the relativized instantiation views are, contrary to what I asserted at the end of the previous section, just versions of the relational solution, and so fail to show how objects undergo intrinsic change (Hinchliff 1996); Lewis makes the same complaint (Lewis 1988, 2002), as do others (Merricks 1994; Sider 2001).[36] The structure of the argument seems to be as follows:

(i) In order to accommodate intrinsic change, what's predicated of the object (and at issue in the change) must be a genuine monadic property (and not a 'disguised relation').

(ii) *P* is a genuine monadic property only if something can have *P simpliciter*.

(iii) On the various adverbialist accounts the objects don't have the properties *simpliciter*, i.e. they don't *just have* what are supposed to be their intrinsic properties.

(iv) So the various adverbialist accounts cannot accommodate temporary intrinsics.

At first glance, this argument seems simply to beg the question, since it specifies what it is to be an intrinsic property in terms of a particular primitive predica-tion relation *having simpliciter*. (It also assumes what was questioned earlier, that intrinsic properties must be monadic.) But why must we understand predication in just this way? If the primary concern is simply whether we can avoid treating intrinsic qualities as relational, all of the accounts that temporally qualify instanti-ation would seem to do fine. For example, on the SOFist account there is no reason whatsoever to think that the state of affairs type *the candle's being bent* involves a relational property. The bentness—which is the property at stake in the change—is nothing other than the property that the candle has when the type state of affairs obtains (in other words: it is the property *of the candle* in the token state of affairs).

Perhaps, however, the concern is about the nature of objects on a model that temporally relativizes instantiation.[37] If objects don't *just have* their properties, but their having is somehow mediated, distanced, then what is the nature of the enduring object? Does it have any intrinsic properties other than its essential properties? Even if it is not a 'bare' particular, is it stripped down too far to plausibly count as an

---

[36] I don't mean to suggest that this complaint is the only one lodged against those who seek to explicate change in a way that qualifies how things have their properties. See e.g. Hawley (2001, e.g. sect. 1.5).

[37] There are several ways of using the term 'nature'. Here I'm following Lewis in meaning not the essence, but the way the object is in itself. Something like how it is intrinsically. Though as before we must be cautious about making robust assumptions about what counts as intrinsic.

ordinary object, one of the apples and bananas, candles and daffodils, that make up our world? (See Lewis 1988; cf. Hawley 2001, sect. 1.4.)

The SOFist (and other eternalist endurantists) should, I believe, reject this question. Note that the competing views can also be forced to think of objects as stripped down to their essences. For example, we can ask the presentist: Tell me about this object that *was* wholly present and *is now* wholly present, the one that just has bentness now, and just had straightness before: what is *its* nature? If the presentist accepts the question, then he will have to face the same concerns about the 'thinness' of the object. Even the perdurantist will have trouble answering the question: Tell me more about the nature of the perduring thing, that persisting thing with a straight-stage and a bent-stage: what is *its* nature?

A presentist should answer: If you are interested in the object's nature, then you have to consider how it is now or how it was before . . . etc. There's no way to give an answer 'from nowhere' or more precisely 'no time'. A perdurantist should answer: If you are interested in a perduring thing's nature, you have to consider what its stages are like. But why should a SOFist (or any of the other eternalist endurantists) have to say more? Why can't the same strategy work? If you want to know what the object itself is like—what its nature is, how it is intrinsically—one can only answer from a point of view in time: one can say how it was in the morning, is now, or will be tomorrow. It exists eternally, but it doesn't follow that we can describe its nature from an eternal standpoint; we can describe some of the states of affairs it functions in, and these obtain at times, but it isn't as if we can talk about it outside of any state of affairs.

Setting this worry aside, though, there remains still a further way to develop the concern. As we've seen, there are at least two elements of the SOFist picture that might count as loosely predicative: the relation between the candle and bentness in the type state of affairs (the candle's *being* bent—in the type-constituting way), and the obtaining of the type state of affairs. Consider the first: the *being* that constitutes states of affairs types is unqualified: time doesn't play a role in their constitution. But if the enduring candle is an element of two (existing) states of affairs, namely, *the candle's being bent* and *the candle's being straight*, then these states of affairs must be compatible, otherwise we'd be faced with a contradiction. Recalling that we are concerned here with states of affairs *types*, one way to avoid contradiction would be to say that the property isn't being genuinely predicated of the object in the types; perhaps states of affairs types should be understood as ordered pairs or the like. But then the ontological force of predication must occur when the state of affairs type *obtains*: it is only in the token that the candle really *is* bent. Contradiction is avoided here because the instantiation of the type in the token, i.e. the type's obtaining, is temporally relativized: *the candle's being straight* obtains at t, *the candle's being bent* obtains at t'. So, the critic continues, the view must be that the type's being instantiated in a token consists in the property's being genuinely instantiated in the object *at a time*. In other words, the object can only really *have* its temporary properties if it has them at a time. But this just collapses into the relational account.[38]

There are two points to make in response to this objection. The first is to deny that the obtaining of a (type) state of affairs is a matter of a potential instantiation being, one might say, activated or implemented (at a time). After all, we don't normally think of the relation between types and tokens in this way; for example, I'm not even sure how to apply this suggestion to the relation between my token copy of *On the Plurality of Worlds* and the type. Admittedly more needs to be said about the type–token distinction for it to illuminate the relation between possible states of affairs and concrete (occurring) states of affairs. But the SOFist's suggestion is that, in saying that the candle is straight, one is claiming that the concrete state of affairs of *the candle's being straight* (delimited with respect to the present) is of the type *the candle's being straight*. Although it is possible to construe the token state of affairs as existing just when the relation *obtaining at* holds between a possible state of affairs and a time, it is equally possible to construe the token state of affairs as basic. If so, it would be wrong to construe the token state of affairs as somehow constituted by a relation between the type and the time.

However, *even if* a token state of affairs is a type state of affairs obtaining at a time, and so involves a kind of temporal relativization of the 'obtaining', the point of resisting temporal relativization was to preserve the intimate relation between the *persisting object* and the *properties* involved in intrinsic change. This is not the relation at issue in the obtaining of the state of affairs; so it isn't obvious why we can't allow the obtaining to be temporally qualified.

The second point is to challenge directly what seems to have been an underlying assumption throughout the debate, namely, that our fundamental ontology consists of objects and properties and these somehow constitute states of affairs. A different model takes token states of affairs to be the fundamental entities, and treats objects and properties as in an important sense derivative (Armstrong 1990, 1997; Barwise and Perry 1983: 58; Barwise and Etchemendy 1987). On such a view concrete (token) states of affairs such as *the candle's being bent at t* are the world's building blocks, and the candle, the property *being bent*, and the (type) state of affairs *the candle's being bent* are all, in a sense, abstractions; or, if not abstractions (which can suggest something 'in the mind'; cf. Fine 1998; Simons 2000*a*), then at the very least the token states of affairs are not constituted mereologically from objects and properties. Moreover, on this approach our ordinary judgements concern token states of affairs and their types. The tokens can be understood as the obtaining of state of affairs types at times, but this is not an 'analysis' of them.

---

[38] Thanks to Dean Zimmerman for helping me see the force of this objection. I've articulated it here in a way that collapses into the relational account because I've been explicating the SOFist view in eternalist–non-tenser form. But if one opted for a different form of SOFism, it might collapse into the presentist–serious tenser solution.

On this model, predication does not function as a way to build facts or states of affairs out of more basic entities (objects and properties), for the token states of affairs are basic. To charge, then, that the SOFist is relying on a 'disguised' relational model of predication is to insist that the SOFist frame her view in a substantivalist ontology, but this simply begs the question.

In other words, perhaps the underlying charge against the SOFist is that our ordinary subject–predicate statements must express a basic predication between object and property; this is what the SOFist is missing.

(6) *Unqualified predication condition.* To say that an object has a property (that x is F) is to say that there is an unqualified predication holding between the object and the property; (and similarly, what makes it the case that objects stand in a relation (that xRy) is an unqualified predication holding between the objects and the relation).

Note that this condition articulates both a semantic intuition and an ontological intuition. Is it fair to interpret this principle as what's at issue? Presumably the SOFist would deny that we need accommodate this condition. On the SOFist account, statements of this form do not express an unqualified predication relation between the object and the property in the sense that the presentist and perdurantist seem to want. But little, if anything, seems to be lost if the endurantist does not meet this demand. And without (6), the arguments against the SOFist are unconvincing.

11. Conclusion

So where do we stand? We've explored a broad range of views on the issue of persistence through time and the problem of alteration. In particular, we've considered in detail:

Perdurance theory. Objects persist only by perduring. There are perduring, but no enduring or exduring, particulars.

Exdurance theory (aka stage theory). Ordinary objects persist by exduring. There are (weird) perduring particulars, and no enduring particulars.

Endurance theory. Ordinary objects persist by enduring. There are enduring particulars, and there may or may not be perduring or exduring particulars as well.

Each of these views has versions that take different stands on the presentism–eternalism debate, and on the serious tensing question. Moreover, I've considered four different versions of the endurance theory (relationalism, copula-tensing, adverbialism, and SOFism) distinguished by their different approaches to predication. All of the views preserve the idea that, in some sense, ordinary things persist through change; and all of them require that we at least modify if not reject one of our original assumptions. I have not considered, although relevant and interesting, approaches to the puzzle that question underlying assumptions about identity, e.g. Leibniz's law (aka the principle of the indiscernibility of identicals) (Baxter 1988, 2001; Myro 1986), and objections drawing on results in contemporary physics (Balashov 2000a,b,c). The line had to be drawn somewhere.

At this stage of the debate I think we should conclude that the constraints on an acceptable account (especially if we confine ourselves to the agreed constraints) aren't enough to decide between several plausible options. There may well be a cluster of yet unarticulated 'Moorean facts' to which we all must do justice and yet only one view can handle. But we have not found such a cluster of facts that only one view can accommodate, and I have my doubts about whether the debate can be settled in this way even over the long run. Instead, I believe that a convincing argument for one view over the others will depend on pragmatic and contextual considerations. What we need is a clear articulation of what's at stake in our accounts of change, of predication, of intrinsic properties. Is there anything that hinges on which account of these notions we opt for? My own conviction is that a number of our practices and forms of self-understanding depend upon the idea that there are enduring things, and persons are among them. But I do not believe that there are arguments from neutral starting points that lead to this conclusion, nor do I believe that those who opt for different starting points from mine are being irrational. This is an area where, I suspect, there are a number of rationally acceptable alternatives, and figuring out what they are and what they each offer us is about the best we can do.

REFERENCES

Armstrong, David (1978). *Nominalism and Realism.* Cambridge: Cambridge University Press.

——— (1980). 'Identity through Time,' in P. van Inwagen (ed.), *Time and Cause.* Dordrecht: Reidel, 67–78.

——— (1990). *A Combinatorial Theory of Possibility.* Cambridge: Cambridge University Press.

——— (1997). *A World of States of Affairs.* Cambridge: Cambridge University Press.

Austin, John L. (1950). 'Truth,' *Proceedings of the Aristotelian Society*, suppl. vol. 24: 111–28. Repr. in Austin, *Philosophical Papers*, 2nd edn., ed. J. O. Urmson and G. J. Warnock. Oxford: Oxford University Press, 1961, 117–33.

Balashov, Yuri (2000a). 'Relativity and Persistence'. *Philosophy of Science*, 67: 549–62.

——— (2000b). 'Persistence and Space-Time: Philosophical Lessons of the Pole and Barn'. *The Monist*, 83: 321–40.

Balashov, Yuri (2000*c*). 'Enduring and Perduring Objects in Minkowski Space-Time'. *Philosophical Studies*, 99: 129–66.

Barwise, Jon, and John Etchemendy (1987). *The Liar: An Essay in Truth and Circularity*. Oxford: Oxford University Press.

—— and John Perry (1983). *Situations and Attitudes*. Cambridge, Mass.: MIT Press.

Baxter, Donald (1988). 'Identity in the Loose and Popular Sense'. *Mind*, 97: 575–82.

—— (2001). 'Loose Identity and Becoming Something Else'. *Noûs*, 35: 592–601.

Bigelow, John (1996). 'Presentism and Properties', in J. E. Tomberlin (ed.), *Philosophical Perspectives*, x. Cambridge: Basil Blackwell, 35–52.

Bradley, F. H. (1897). *Appearance and Reality*, 2nd edn. Oxford: Oxford University Press.

Callender, Craig (2001). 'Humean Supervenience and Rotating Homogeneous Matter'. *Mind*, 110: 25–43.

Carter, William, and H. S. Hestevold (1994). 'On Passage and Persistence'. *American Philosophical Quarterly*, 31: 269–83.

Cartwright, Richard (1975). 'Scattered Objects', in Keith Lehrer (ed.), *Analysis and Metaphysics*. Dordrecht: Reidel, 153–71.

Chisholm, Roderick (1970). 'Identity through Time', in H. Kiefer and M. Munitz (eds.), *Language, Belief, and Metaphysics*. Albany: State University of New York Press, 163–82. Repr. in van Inwagen and Zimmerman (1998: 173–85).

—— (1973). 'Parts as Essential to their Wholes'. *Review of Metaphysics*, 26: 581–603.

—— (1975). 'Mereological Essentialism: Further Considerations'. *Review of Metaphysics*, 28: 477–84.

Craig, William Lane (1998). 'McTaggart's Paradox and the Problem of Temporary Intrinsics'. *Analysis*, 58: 122–7.

Fine, Kit (1998). 'Cantorian Abstraction: A Reconstruction and a Defense'. *Journal of Philosophy*, 95: 599–634.

Forbes, Graham (1987). 'Is there a Problem about Persistence?' *Proceedings of the Aristotelian Society*, suppl. vol. 61: 137–55.

Haslanger, Sally (1989*a*). 'Endurance and Temporary Intrinsics'. *Analysis*, 49: 119–25.

—— (1989*b*). 'Persistence, Change, and Explanation'. *Philosophical Studies*, 56: 1–28.

—— (1992). 'Ontology and Pragmatic Paradox'. *Proceedings of the Aristotelian Society*, 92: 293–313.

—— (1994) 'Humean Supervenience and Enduring Things'. *Australasian Journal of Philosophy*, 72: 339–59.

Hawley, Katherine (1998). 'Why Temporary Properties are not Relations between Physical Objects and Times'. *Proceedings of the Aristotelian Society*, 98: 211–16.

—— (1999). 'Persistence and Non-Supervenient Relations'. *Mind*, 108: 53–67.

—— (2001). *How Things Persist*. Oxford: Oxford University Press.

Heller, Mark (1992). 'Things Change'. *Philosophy and Phenomenological Research*, 52: 695–704.

—— (1993). 'Varieties of Four-Dimensionalism'. *Australasian Journal of Philosophy*, 71: 47–59.

Hinchliff, Mark (1996). 'The Puzzle of Change'. J. E. Tomberlin (ed.), *Philosophical Perspectives*, x: *Metaphysics*. Atascadero, Calif.: Ridgeview, 19–36.

Hirsch, Eli (1982). *The Concept of Identity*. Oxford: Oxford University Press.

Hobbes, Thomas (1839). *De Corpore*, II. ii, in *The English Works of Thomas Hobbes*, ed. William Molesworth. London: Bohn, i. 136.

Johnston, Mark (1987). 'Is there a Problem about Persistence?' *Proceedings of the Aristotelian Society*, suppl. vol. 61: 107–35.

Kripke, Saul (1978). 'Identity and Time'. Unpub. lecture series.

Lewis, David (1983). 'Survival and Identity', plus postscripts, in Lewis, *Philosophical Papers*, vol. i. Oxford: Oxford University Press, 55–77.

—— (1986). *On the Plurality of Worlds*. Oxford: Basil Blackwell.

—— (1988). 'Rearrangement of Particles: Reply to Lowe'. *Analysis*, 48: 65–72.

—— (1999). 'Zimmerman and the Spinning Sphere'. *Australasian Journal of Philosophy*, 77: 209–12.

—— (2002). 'Tensing the Copula'. *Mind*, 111: 1–13.

Lombard, Lawrence (1986). *Events: A Metaphysical Study*. London: Routledge & Kegan Paul.

—— (1999). 'On the Alleged Incompatibility of Presentism and Temporal Parts'. *Philosophia*, 27: 253–60.

Lowe, E. J. (1987). 'Lewis on Perdurance versus Endurance'. *Analysis*, 47: 152–4.

—— (1988). 'The Problem of Intrinsic Change: Rejoinder to Lewis'. *Analysis*, 48: 72–7.

Ludlow, Peter (1999). *Semantics, Time, and Tense*. Cambridge, Mass.: MIT Press.

McTaggart, J. M. E. (1908). 'The Unreality of Time'. *Mind*, 18: 457–84.

—— (1927). *The Nature of Existence*, vol. ii. Cambridge: Cambridge University Press.

Markosian, Ned (1994). 'The 3D/4D Controversy and Non-Present Objects'. *Philosophical Papers*, 23: 243–9.

—— (2001). Review of Peter Ludlow, *Semantics, Tense and Time*. *Journal of Philosophy*, 98: 225–9.

—— (forthcoming). 'A Defense of Presentism'. *Oxford Studies in Metaphysics*.

Mellor, D. H. (1981). *Real Time*. Cambridge: Cambridge University Press.

Merricks, Trenton (1994). 'Endurance and Indiscernibility'. *Journal of Philosophy*, 91: 165–84.

—— (1995). 'On the Incompatibility of Enduring and Perduring Entities'. *Mind*, 104: 523–31.

—— (1999). 'Persistence, Parts, and Presentism'. *Noûs*, 33: 421–38.

Myro, George (1986). 'Identity and Time', in Richard Grandy and Richard Warner (eds.), *The Philosophical Grounds of Rationality*. New York: Clarendon Press, 383–409.

Oaklander, L. Nathan (1992). 'Temporal Passage and Temporal Parts'. *Noûs*, 26: 79–84.

Parsons, Josh (2000). 'Must a Four-Dimensionalist Believe in Temporal Parts?', *The Monist*, 83: 399–418.

Perry, John (1979). 'The Problem of the Essential Indexical'. *Noûs*, 13: 3–21.

Prior, A. N. (1959). 'Thank Goodness that's Over'. *Philosophy*, 34: 12–17.

Quine, W. V. O. (1963). 'Identity, Ostension, and Hypostasis', in Quine, *From a Logical Point of View*, 2nd edn. Evanston, Ill.: Harper & Row, 65–79.

Rea, Michael (1996). *Material Constitution*. Totowa, NJ: Rowman & Littlefield.

—— (1998). 'Temporal Parts Unmotivated'. *Philosophical Review*, 107: 225–60.

Sainsbury, R. M. (1995). *Paradoxes*. Cambridge: Cambridge University Press.

Sider, Theodore (1996). 'All the World's a Stage'. *Australasian Journal of Philosophy*, 74: 433–53.

—— (1997). 'Four Dimensionalism'. *Philosophical Review*, 106: 197–231.

—— (1999). 'Presentism and Ontological Commitment'. *Journal of Philosophy*, 96/7: 325–47.

—— (2000). 'The Stage View and Temporary Intrinsics'. *Analysis*, 60: 84–8.

—— (2001). *Four-Dimensionalism: An Ontology of Persistence and Time*. Oxford: Oxford University Press.

Simons, Peter (1987). *Parts: A Study in Ontology*. New York: Clarendon Press.

—— (2000*a*). 'How to Exist at Time when you have no Temporal Parts'. *The Monist*, 83: 419–36.

—— (2000*b*). 'Identity through Time and Trope Bundles'. *Topoi*, 19: 147–55

Smith, Quentin (1993). *Language and Time.* Oxford: Oxford University Press.

Thomson, Judith J. (1983). 'Parthood and Identity across Time'. *Journal of Philosophy*, 80: 201–20.

van Inwagen, Peter (1981). 'The Doctrine of Arbitrary Undetached Parts'. *Pacific Philosophical Quarterly*, 62: 123–37.

—— (1990). 'Four-Dimensional Objects'. *Noûs*, 24: 245–55.

—— (2000). 'Temporal Parts and Identity across Time'. *The Monist*, 83/3: 437–59.

—— and Dean Zimmerman (ed.), (1998). *Metaphysics: The Big Questions.* Oxford: Basil Blackwell.

Zimmerman, Dean (1996). 'Persistence and Presentism'. *Philosophical Papers*, 25: 115–26.

—— (1998a). 'Temporary Intrinsics and Presentism', in van Inwagen and Zimmerman (1998: 206–19).

—— (1998b). 'Temporal Parts and Supervenient Causation: The Incompatibility of Two Humean Doctrines'. *Australasian Journal of Philosophy*, 76: 265–88.

—— (1999). 'One Really Big Liquid Sphere: Reply to Lewis'. *Australasian Journal of Philosophy*, 77: 213–15.

PART V

EVENTS, CAUSATION, AND PHYSICS

CHAPTER 12

EVENTS

PETER SIMONS

Events, dear boy. Events.
(Reply attributed to Harold Macmillan on being
asked his greatest problem in politics)

PHILOSOPHICAL discussion of the ontological category of events is relatively young. There is no entry for 'event' in the 1967 *Encyclopedia of Philosophy*. Most philosophically mooted categories are old, but events come to full prominence only in the twentieth century, first in issues of the philosophy of science, then in the philosophies of mind, action, and language. Events are disputed entities on every point: whether there really are any; whether they are metaphysically basic or reducible; what their nature and structure is; how they are to be justified; what use they are. There is little agreement on any of these points, but in the light of discussion in the late twentieth century it seems that the ontological category of events is here to stay.

1. WHETHER THERE ARE EVENTS: EVIDENCE IN FAVOUR

According to dictionaries, an event is anything that happens, takes place, or occurs. The question whether there are events can then be answered quickly and positively. There are, for example, births, marriages, and deaths, like the birth, marriage, and death of Lenin. These three items are all events; therefore there are events. This is common sense: there are events just as there are things and places. We perceive, discuss, plan, are unwittingly involved in, and engineer events like football games, surprise parties, road accidents, and rocket launches. In the popular and uncomplicated sense of 'there are', undoubtedly there are events.

Philosophically, events are much less secure. Until the twentieth century most ontologists paid them little or no attention by contrast with substances, properties, relations, and states of affairs. There might be events in the loose and popular sense, but strictly and philosophically events might be nothing more than *façons de parler* whose basis lay in things, their properties, and the succession of different properties a thing might have at different times. On this view, a tennis ball's being squashed is no denizen of reality but simply a convenient phrase we use when confronted with a sequence of different shape characteristics of the one substance. At best an event is a logical construction, not part of the basic furniture of the world.

Much of the short philosophical history of the category of events is about the fight for their ontological respectability, presenting the evidence that there are events, in a strict and philosophical sense, and accompanying this with an account of their nature and structure. Without a clear consensus emerging on the subsidiary points, on the basic existential question events have gained widespread acceptance, indeed the emphasis has gradually shifted from the question whether there are events to the question whether there is anything *apart from* events.

Evidence that there are events in the unproblematic popular sense is legion and unsophisticated, consisting merely in adverting to the many occasions we perceive and participate in, identify, and speak about events. Dramatic and important events such as battles, assassinations, and catastrophes form the subject matter of countless books, films, investigations, and inquiries. The discipline of history is about events as much as it is about the participants in events; about Waterloo, the sinking of the *Titanic*, and the shooting of John F. Kennedy just as much as it is about the soldiers, the ship, the iceberg, the drowned passengers, the presidential victim. It is events that are chronicled and recorded. This need not impress someone for whom events are reducible to other categories: repetition of an error anchors rather than lessens it. So it is said we need specific *philosophical* reasons for believing in events. These come in three basic sorts: scientific, linguistic, and metaphysical.

1.1 Scientific

1.1.1 *Causality*

Most of science is about giving explanations for why things are as they are, and one very common kind of explanation is causal. We explain why the plane crashed by citing the loss of its rudder during turbulence. The two events are connected as cause and effect. The presence of an unobservable black hole is inferred from the observed effects of X-ray radiation caused by matter being rapidly accelerated into it. Similar explanation patterns are found all over science. On this view, events are not peripheral entities but those central to scientific theory. For metaphysicians inclined to naturalism, the view that our principal ontological categories are to be taken from natural science, this is evidence enough for there being events. This reason is relatively independent of difficulties about defining what causation is. As long as science needs causation, and causation is between events, science needs events and so metaphysics needs events.

This argument is strong but does not convince everyone. Some question whether causation is a relation between events. One alternative is that it is facts, not events, that are causally related. (Mellor 1995). Another is that the primary form of causation is so-called agent causation, which holds between an active substance such as a human agent, and an event, as when John raises his arm (Lowe 2001). This need not undermine events fully if they are retained as the second term.

Even if causation is a relation exclusively or partially between events, this does not anchor events irrevocably into ontology, if events are regarded as non-basic entities. It remains possible that event-relating causation be replaced by a more basic relation between the items in terms of which events are analysed. However, the centrality of causation in scientific explanation and the lack of consensus about what might replace or analyse it renders the argument from causation a stable and weighty one in favour of events as denizens of reality.

A logical difficulty about causal explanation is that it appears not to be extensional. If causality relates events and these are items in the world, then different terms for an event should be substitutable in explanations. If Lincoln died because Booth shot him, and Booth's shooting Lincoln was the same event as Booth's crooking his finger, then Lincoln died because Booth crooked his finger. As the complex discussion of event individuation below makes clear, not all who accept the first premiss accept the conclusion. The issue is helped by distinguishing causal *description*, which is extensional, from causal *explanation*, which is not, because causal explanation is a relation between propositions about events, rather than a relation between events.

1.1.2 *Physics and Cosmology*

The ontology of events rose in philosophy with the rise of relativity theory in physics. In propounding relativity in dynamics and electrodynamics, Einstein postulated the relativity of simultaneity to an observer's state of motion. The terms of the relation of simultaneity must be events or their parts, so physics uses events in one of its fundamental theories. In Minkowski's formulation of relativity, space and time are merged as four-dimensional space-time, and the analogue of a spatial point, something without extension, is a point-event, spatial points and regions being extended in the temporal dimension. In quantum mechanics the main conceptual problem is the so-called measurement problem, which concerns the relationship between on the one hand the continuous development of an extended dynamical system, as represented in Schrödinger's wave equation, and on the other hand the sudden localization in an event such as absorption and emission. In quantum field theory the dual wave–particle view of matter and energy can no longer be sustained and the ontology appears to contain only spatio-temporally extended fields and their various local and global values. Since the patterns of value variation across these regions have temporal as well as spatial parts, it seems from the point of view of fundamental physics that the fundamental physical entities are more event-like than thing-like (Bartels 2000).

Much of modern cosmology concerns the originary event of our universe, the big bang, whether is was punctual or extended, what traces it has left, and so on. The big bang, even more than other originary events, presents problems for those who see all events as changes, since there was nothing there beforehand to change.

Significantly, those philosophers who proposed events as an important ontological category early in the twentieth century were those closest to developments in modern physics such as Whitehead, Russell, and Carnap.

1.1.3 *Other Areas of Science*

In the theory of evolution biologists are interested in the origin and extinction of species, which happen in what are called speciation and extinction events. Such events are typically quite extended, though in some cases, such as the supposedly catastrophic extinction of dinosaurs at the end of the Cretaceous, the temporal extension is very short. Other events of strong theoretical interest to biologists are cell division in meiosis and mitosis.

In psychology, physiology, and the philosophy of mind, the issue of materialism most often takes the form of questions about events: are mental events physical events in the brain, and if not, how are the two kinds of events related? Most solutions to the mind–body problem can be characterized by how they approach the relationship between mental and physical events, from identity through supervenience and unilateral causation to independence (see Section 7.1).

1.2 Linguistic

The twentieth century was the heyday of the linguistic turn in philosophy, and the status of events in ontology in that century was characteristically enhanced less by the evidence from science than by arguments from the philosophy of language. Of these the most famous and influential is due to Donald Davidson (1967).

1.2.1 *The Logical Form of Action (and Other) Sentences*

A sentence may describe an action (or other event) in greater or less detail. Suppose, to take Davidson's example, Jones slowly butters a piece of toast with a knife in the bathroom at midnight. Then, when said after the event, all of the following sentences truly apply:

> Jones slowly buttered a piece of toast with a knife in the bathroom at midnight.
> Jones buttered a piece of toast in the bathroom at midnight.
> Jones buttered a piece of toast in the bathroom.
> Jones buttered a piece of toast at midnight.
> Jones slowly buttered a piece of toast.
> Jones buttered a piece of toast.
> Jones buttered something with a knife.
> Jones did something with a knife in the bathroom at midnight.

The problem with representing all of these sentences with their different layers of adverbial modification as atomic sentences in standard first-order predicate logic, being variously about Jones, the bathroom, the knife, etc., and using a predicate *buttered*, is that the predicate is required to take different arguments, sometimes a different number of arguments, in different sentences. This leads to one of two consequences regarded as unpleasant: either there is a plurality of logically unrelated atomic predicates *butter*, with different numbers of arguments, or there is one predicate *butter* which is multigrade, i.e. whose number and type of arguments must vary. The latter alternative had been pointed out earlier by Anthony Kenny (1963, ch. 7) as a problem for predications about actions.

In 1927 Frank Ramsey (1990: 37) suggested that the correct logical form of the sentence *Caesar died* is not atomic, but in fact it is an existential quantification, roughly:

> For some e(e is a death of Caesar).

Davidson proposes an extension of Ramsey's idea, to cope with the multiplicity of valid inferences from the complete buttering sentence. If, slightly modifying Davidson's original suggestion, and ignoring tense, we represent this as

> For some e and for some x(e is a buttering of x & x is a piece of toast & e is done by Jones & e takes place at midnight & e is done with a knife & e takes place in the bathroom & e is slow),

then all of the sentences that can validly be inferred from the first drop out as valid-predicate logical inferences by conjunction elimination under an existential quantifier, assuming plausibly that their logical forms uniformly contain similar implicit quantifiers. What would otherwise require a multiplicity of ad hoc explanations become instances of a familiar and simple valid inferential form. The theory means that instead of needing to postulate a host of ad hoc inference principles or meaning postulates to account for the logical behaviour of verbs and adverbs in the natural language, the inference is handled by standard logic, the detailed variation being relegated to the question of how logically to represent particular lexical items and phrases from the natural language. This is a considerable theoretical gain and means that, invoking Quine's criterion that a theory is ontologically committed to those entities over which its sentences quantify, the analysis provides good evidence for the entities quantified over in it, namely events. Since true adverbially modifying vernacular sentences about actions and other events are legion in any natural language, the analysis entails that in speaking any natural language we are up to our ears in ontological commitment to events.

Davidson's argument, minor issues of detail aside, was a watershed: it rapidly gained widespread acceptance, and as a result contributed more to the habilitation of events as bona fide entities in ontology than any other single piece. Prior to that time, despite their transient popularity with scientifically minded philosophers, events were generally regarded with suspicion by philosophers of language and those of traditional leanings. Whereas Strawson (1959) in Aristotelian fashion took individual substances as the prime particulars, since Davidson the issue has rather shifted to the question whether there *are* any individual substances, and not just events.

Davidson's argument for events was not uniformly accepted. Not all adverbs allow of clause-dropping, e.g. *allegedly*, and the effects Davidson notes may be obtained without quantification over events if a logic of predicate-modifiers is adopted (as advocated, for example, by Clark 1974). A general offensive against events is mounted by Terence Horgan (1978). In semantics, the issue may be one of a trade-off between logical simplicity (extensional first-order logic with events) and ontological simplicity (intensional logic with predicate operators); for a statement of this view, see Quine (1985).

1.2.2 *Further Evidence for Davidson's Hypothesis*

Additional linguistic evidence for Davidson's analysis of many predications as quantifying over events comes not just from sentences about events other than actions, but also from other linguistic phenomena. *Naked infinitive* constructions such as

John saw Mary cry

cannot be correctly paraphrased using a full clause, as in 'John saw that Mary cried', but may be analysed employing events (Higginbotham 1983):

For some $e(e$ was a crying by Mary & John saw $e)$.

Terence Parsons has extended Davidson's analysis to account for phenomena about the progressive aspect in English, and used the analogy with Davidson's quantification over events to argue that an analysis of the logical form of English sentences suggests we are also ontologically committed to states and processes (Parsons 1990).

1.2.3 *Designata for Certain Noun Phrases*

Verbs describing what things do can usually be nominalized in two ways: one as a gerund, as *marry* becomes *marrying*; the other, which varies morphologically, produces a non-verbal noun as in *marriage*. The former are called *imperfect nominals*, the latter *perfect nominals* (Bennett 1988: 4 ff.). Sentences can be thus nominalized in two ways, as *John marries Mary* becomes either *John's marrying Mary* or *John's marriage to Mary*. This distinction was made prominent by Zeno Vendler (1957). Perfect nominals behave more like normal nouns than do imperfect nominals: they can take articles, be pluralized, take adjectives, and resist modalization, whereas imperfect nominals resist articles and pluralization, take adverbs, and accept modal modification (Bennett 1988: 4–5). Sentences based on imperfect nominals are much more akin to those framed using *that*-clauses. The suggestion is that corresponding to the linguistic distinction is the ontological one: whereas imperfect nominals stand for propositions or states of affairs, perfect nominals stand for events, and since the perfect nominal subjects of some true sentences stand for something rather than nothing, there are events. John's marriage to Mary took place last Saturday, John's marriage to Mary is an event, therefore there are events. That in the vernacular events are typically said to 'occur', 'happen', or 'take place' whereas things are said to 'exist' is sometimes adduced as a reason for regarding the philosophical proposition 'Events exist' as nonsense rather than false (Hacker 1982), but the general sense of 'there are', often also rendered 'exist', rises above such parochialisms of idiom. That there are perfect nominals standing for processes (the earth's rotation) and states (Mary's contentment) suggests again that the categories of state, process, and event blur into one another.

1.2.4 *Events as Truthmakers*

Whereas imperfect nominals seem to stand for states of affairs or propositions, which are items expressed or projected by language and are true or false, perfect nominals stand for items outside language which may be named and quantified over, and whose third semantic role is to make sentences or other truth-bearers true. Perhaps the first to highlight the truthmaking role of events was Russell. In his *Philosophy of Logical Atomism* he says 'If I say "Socrates is dead", my statement will be true owing to a certain physiological occurrence which happened in Athens long ago' (Russell 1986: 163; that Russell calls his truthmakers 'facts' is just part of the terminological and oftentimes conceptual chaos which threatens in this field). Russell's laconic examples, where conditions, occurrences, and states are all mentioned as facts or truthmakers, anticipate Ramsey and Davidson.

The truthmaking role is different from that described by Davidson. Whereas Davidson sees the need to quantify over events as arising from an analysis of a sentence's logical form, giving its truth-*conditions*, truthmakers arise not through logical analysis but reflection on what by existing grounds the truth of a truth-bearer, the sentence's *truthmakers*. What makes it true that Socrates is dead (modulo tense again) is what the perfect nominal *the death of Socrates* names, that unique and complex event. The truthmaking role is, however, connected with Davidson's analysis in that for a sentence like *John kissed Mary* to be true, *any* event which is a (past) kissing of Mary by John may serve as a truthmaker for the sentence, thereby reinforcing Davidson's quantificational analysis, which says there *is* (was) just such an event, or indeed more than one.

To the extent that the semantics of truth is regarded as requiring truthmakers for some or all true sentences (Armstrong 1987, ch. 8), events commend themselves as strong candidates for the role in many cases, and their ontological respectability is enhanced thereby.

1.3 Lewis's Argument from Change

Following Aristotle, most philosophers have analysed change as involving (in the simplest case) four components: the substratum or object changing, the property or state the object has before the change, the property or state it has afterwards, and the time of change. The substratum is typically taken to be a continuant, that is, an object without temporal parts, which *endures*, and so unlike an event, which does have temporal parts unless it is instantaneous, and so *perdures*. David Lewis (1986a: 202–5) proposed an argument that all changing things have temporal parts. For example, if a stick is straight and then bent, the stick is the substratum, being straight and being bent are the initial and final properties. Lewis argues that being straight and being bent are intrinsic properties of the stick and are incompatible. To explain how one thing can have incompatible properties, there are three possibilities. Either being straight is not an intrinsic property but a relation between the stick and one or more times; or only the present is real (presentism) and the stick only has its present property, or finally the stick has temporal parts, earlier ones being straight and later ones being bent. Of the three, Lewis argues that the third is the only acceptable one, so all things which change have temporal parts. One way of taking Lewis's conclusion is to say that he makes all temporal objects into events, or at least objects like events in lasting by perduring.

Lewis's argument has not gained universal support, some commentators believing there is an attractive fourth possibility maintaining the status of the substratum as a continuant (e.g. Haslanger 1989). Nevertheless, the doctrine of temporal parts, which had previously been espoused mainly by logicians such as Bolzano, Leśniewski, Carnap, and Quine, has thereby gained much support, to the extent that the defenders of continuants are now metaphysically on the defensive. (See further Section 6.3 below.)

2. The Metaphysical Nature of Events

General philosophical acceptance that there are events does not imply unity among philosophers about what they are, and there have been many proposals, of which the principal ones are discussed in this section.

2.1 Events as Attribute Exemplifications

This theory is primarily associated with Jaegwon Kim (1966, 1969, 1976), but has been anticipated or endorsed with variations by other writers, notably Richard Martin (1969), Alvin Goldman (1971), and Jonathan Bennett (1988). The view, which takes the Aristotelian conception of change as its starting point, sees an event as the exemplification by an object or several objects of an attribute (property or relation) at a time or over a period. Schematically, if we consider P to be the attribute, s the object, and t the time, we can specify the event of s's having P at t as the triple $[s, P, t]$. For example, if a person shouts, the person is the object, *shouting* is the property, and the time of the shout is the time. For a dyadic attribute event, consider the collision of the *Titanic* with the iceberg. This has as its two objects the ship and the unnamed iceberg, as its property *colliding with*, and as its time a period of around ten seconds on the fateful night.

This theory has in its favour that it corresponds closely to a standard way of referring to events, using perfect nominals with the nominalized verb for the attribute, names for the participatory objects, and an adverbial for the time, as in *the collision of the Titanic with the iceberg on 14 April 1912*. It does not make events basic entities, as the three constituents are more basic, but it does yield straightforward identity conditions for events (Kim 1976: 161), namely

$$[s, P, t] = [s^*, P^*, t^*] \text{ if and only if } s = s^* \ \& \ P = P^* \ \& \ t = t^*.$$

However, as I shall discuss below, these conditions lead to a questionably fine-grained differentiation of events. At times Kim has spoken of the event $[s, P, t]$ as if it simply *were* the ordered triple $\langle s, P, t \rangle$, but this cannot be correct, since the triple exists if its constituents exist, whereas many triples of constituents do not yield events, e.g. the triple ⟨Socrates, playing tennis, 1 June 1984⟩. Kim recognizes this (Kim 1976: 160) by making it an existence condition that

$$[s, P, t] \text{ exists (occurs) if and only if } s \text{ has } P \text{ at } t.$$

Another problem with the triple view is that triples are standardly conceived as abstract entities, usually sets, whereas events are concretely located in space and time. When this is taken into account, it seems that events are after all something distinctive, albeit supervenient, and that Kim's analysis and notation are meant to highlight their subvenient basis, consisting of their essential constituents.

Additional problems arise in discerning suitable attributes to be constituents of events. Some tautologously universal properties such as self-identity or being such that $2+2 = 4$ apply to all things at all times, and to suppose they constitute events is to stretch that term too far. So there needs to be some way of realistically restricting candidate properties, and it is not clear what this should be. Also some properties are static, for instance being white. A piece of paper may remain white for years, yet this hardly constitutes an event in standard parlance. Kim accommodates this by stretching the term 'event' so that it covers states as well. As a piece of terminological legislation this moves the problem elsewhere, but the question of what distinguishes states from events in the narrower sense, whether it is a deep metaphysical distinction or not, remains.

2.2 Events as Tropes

A modification of Kim's account of events is proposed by Jonathan Bennett (1988: 88), according to which an event is the instantiation of a property at a spatio-temporal region, what Bennett calls a *zone*. The variation is to take account of events where the subjects are not obvious. Bennett in fact considers that properties in general are best regarded as fundamentally instantiated by zones rather than substances (Bennett 1988: 117), which is an interesting metaphysical thesis but going beyond what we can discuss. The events are individual because the instantiation of a property is an individual, what the Scholastics and Leibniz called an individual accident and what is now known, following D. C. Williams, as a *trope* (Williams 1953). Each trope is an individual instance of a repeatable property, so to that extent the account is similar to Kim's. But Bennett does not subscribe to Kim's connection between the metaphysics and the semantics of events (Bennett 1988: 93), so is subject to fewer of the strictures against Kim's view.

Carol Cleland (1991) also regards events as involving tropes—in her view events are changes *in* tropes (see Section 2.5)—but unlike Bennett she does not consider tropes to be individuated by their regions of instantiation, because she wishes to leave open the possibility of tropes that have no spatial location (Strawsonian sounds, Cartesian mental events). Cleland's suggestion to use tropes in the theory of events antedates Bennett's (Cleland 1991: 252).

2.3 Events as States of Affairs

Kim's attributes with their subjects are closely related to what some philosophers would call 'states of affairs'. Rather than say [s, P, t] exists when s has P at t, we might say that the state of affairs of s having P exists at t, and that it is this state of affairs—we might write it [s, P]—that is the event which exists (occurs) at t. This is the view put forward by Roderick Chisholm (1970). Chisholm's view makes events akin to propositions: for him a proposition is a state of affairs that necessarily either always obtains or always does not, whereas an event is a state of affairs which sometimes obtains and sometimes does not, and which implies change (Chisholm 1970: 20). Chisholm's theory allows, indeed requires one to say, that events can recur, or re-occur, that is, obtain at times between which they do not obtain. Every morning John wakes up the states of affairs of John waking up recurs.

An advantage of Chisholm's account is that it yields propositions and events as subspecies of a single category, namely states of affairs. However, most commentators have found it has greater disadvantages. Events are generally viewed as concrete particular things which are unique, do not recur, and can be counted. On Chisholm's view there is no such event as John's waking up on Tuesday 1 August 2000: if we leave the time out we get the recurrent event of John's waking up, if we put it in we get the state of affairs of John's waking up on 1 August 2000 and that is a true proposition, not an event. Davidson, who criticizes Chisholm's view (Davidson 1970), points out that adverbial modification is also difficult for Chisholm: if John woke up abruptly on 1 August 2000, then because he doesn't always wake up abruptly his waking up and his waking up abruptly are two different events which co-occur on 1 August 2000, whereas common sense would see them as one event, John's waking being the same as his abrupt waking. Another difficulty mentioned by Davidson is that Chisholm has great difficulty in explaining how we may count individual events, or say that one event preceded another. In the face of such difficulties, the view that events are concrete particulars has generally prevailed over Chisholm's alternative, and Chisholm himself subsequently changed his mind, viewing events as 'contingent states of contingent things' (Chisholm 1994).

2.4 Events as Concrete Particulars

Davidson's view of events as what we quantify over in action and other event predications gives us little to go on concerning the metaphysical nature of events, and in view of the difficulties attending the more structured accounts of Kim and Chisholm this may be regarded as a positive feature. A more liberal view would be that events are those denizens of space and time which occur at particular times and places and come in different kinds, but that there is no single metaphysical structure or kind of structure that all events possess, rather that they are variously structured and related according to kind. While unspecific and unexciting, the view might be closer to the truth. The effect is to blur the distinction between events and other kinds of spatio-temporal particulars such as substances. The most extreme view of this kind is found in Quine (1960: 131): 'Physical objects . . . are not to be distinguished from events, or ... processes. Each comprises simply the content, however heterogeneous, of some portion of space-time, however disconnected or gerrymandered.' Any space-time region on this view contains or specifies just one event, which goes contrary to intuitions supported by language. To use an example from Davidson (1969: 230) a sphere's rotating and its getting warmer may coincide. In each case we have the same region, but arguably two events. Quine is happy to accept and live with his divergence from ordinary ways of speaking (Quine 1985: 167). A similar theory to Quine's is put forward by, E. J. Lemmon (1967).

A theory which like Quine's take events to be spatio-temporal particulars but offers a different and more discriminating account of when events are identical is due to Myles Brand (1976), according to which events are identical only if they *necessarily* occupy the same spatio-temporal region (see Section 4.2 below).

If more than one event can be going on at once in a region, then something other than position must distinguish them. Davidson's suggestion (discussed below, Section 4.3) is that different events have different causes and/or effects. Elizabeth Anscombe, who rejects this general condition but whose views in other ways come close to Davidson, rejects the idea of a general recipe for identifying events and considers it to be part of the semantics of the particular sortal terms used to pick out different event kinds (Anscombe 1979: 225, 229). One may notice the approach to Kim here: if instead of Kim's attribute one substitutes an event sortal, then a canonical *description* of an event may be given which besides this sortal evokes just the other kinds of mentioned items that Kim and Bennett evoke, namely subjects and times or spatio-temporal regions: *John's kissing of Mary at 6 p.m. on 23 December 2001.* The difference is that this is no longer taken as a constitutive *definition* of an event, merely a reflection of our extant practice in conceptualizing events of all sorts.

2.5 Events as Changes

Kim's events involve just a single attribute, and in this respect do not count as changes, which require there to be at least two attributes, between which the substrata of change move. However, to avoid anomalous 'static events', and to remain closer to the intuitive idea of an event as requiring change, Lawrence Lombard (1986, ch. 7) *defines* events as changes, building on and explicating the traditional Aristotelian account of change. Specifically, for Lombard, an *atomic event* is a certain kind of non-repetitive continuous change of an atomic object through a continuous quantity space (Lombard 1986: 171), and an event is either an atomic event, or a synchronic non-atomic event, i.e. an event composed of simultaneous atomic events, or a diachronic event, one composed of a temporal sequence of atomic or synchronic non-atomic events (Lombard 1980: 172). This constructive account leaves hostages to fortune over the definition of an atomic participant object as well as over discontinuous events in quantum mechanics, and boundary events, if there are such (see Section 5.1 below), though these tend to be problems for everyone. It also illustrates again, as do the other theories, how difficult it is to marry general metaphysical views on events with the examples thrown up in natural and scientific discourse.

Cleland (1991) takes events to be changes not in things but in what she calls 'existential conditions', which are tropes, such as having a temperature, which are determinable rather than determinate. (A determinate trope would be, for example, *this temperature of* 90°, while the determinable trope would be *this temperature.*) Tropes—or at least some tropes—in Cleland's view are ultimate individuals which derive their individuality neither from their subjects nor from their location. She criticizes Lombard's view as requiring that all changes be changes in things (see Section 4.4), and criticizes Bennett's view as requiring all tropes to be spatial. In favour of Cleland's view is that her account accords closely with the way physicists specify the states of physical systems in terms of the values of variable quantities. Also her theory, unlike Bennett's, does not require space-time to be substantive, and is compatible with relationism about space and time. Against it is the reification of determinable tropes in addition to determinate ones, and the relatively weak instances of non-spatial tropes (Cartesian and Strawsonian events).

3. METAPHYSICAL DISPUTES
ABOUT EVENTS

3.1 Whether Events are Ontologically Basic or Derived

Assuming there are events, the question remains whether they form a basic category or are derived or constructible in terms of other more basic categories. Among others, Whitehead, Quine, Anscombe, and Davidson take events to be basic denizens of reality, irreducible to others. On the other hand some philosophers (Kim 1976; Bennett 1988) who are happy to accept events see them as constructed from or supervenient upon more basic entities, such as objects, properties, and times. Bennett states trenchantly, 'Events are not basic items in the universe; they should not be included in any fundamental ontology. . . . all the truths about them are entailed by and *explained* or *made true* by truths that do not involve the event concept' (Bennett 1988: 12). This does not mean we can eliminate event discourse. If events are not basic, then the identity of events is determined by the identities of the more basic entities on which they supervene or out of which they are constructed. If events are basic, then their identity conditions are *sui generis* and may be either given by a single general recipe, or again not (see below, Section 4).

3.2 Whether Events are Particular or Universal

Because events are closely connected to time and space, namely the time and place of their occurrence, it is generally held that they are particulars, indeed for many they are the paradigm particulars. A minority of philosophers, comprising principally Richard Montague and Roderick, M. Chisholm, have argued that events are universal or repeatable entities. The principal rationale for this is that we speak of actions or events as being repeated, as when we say

John ran a mile yesterday and he did it again today.

Chisholm's view on events was discussed in Section 2.2. Montague (1969) takes events to be properties of times, while Lewis (1986b) takes them to be properties of spatio-temporal regions. Assuming properties to be universals, this makes events universals, and talk of their repetition or recurrence literal.

Most philosophical proponents of events, however, have taken them to be particulars which are unrepeatable. On this view John did not repeat yesterday's run today, but did a new run today which was like yesterday's in being a mile run. The two runs are related by resemblance and/or by belonging to the one kind. What one party calls an event the other calls an instance of an event; what they call events the first party calls an event kind. The dispute between the proponents of events as particulars and those of events as universals is thus to some extent a fight for priority in using the term 'event'. Even where events are taken to be properties, they may be taken as particulars, as in Bennett's trope theory. For a comprehensive discussion of repeatability, see Brandl (2000).

3.3 Whether All Events are Changes

Typical events with which we are familiar are changes. A leaf falls to the ground, a person shifts position to get more comfortable, a marksman's bullet hits its target and punches a hole. Some changes are slow and continuous and are called 'processes' rather than 'events'; the growth of a tree or the greying of John's hair, for example. Some events are much more than a single change; a race or a battle, for instance. Nevertheless, the thought is that every event is or involves at least one change in an object or between objects, with complications required to take account of more complex events. Thus Lawrence Lombard defines an event as a certain simple change or complex of changes (Lombard 1986: 171–2; see above, Section 2.5).

This account goes some way to illuminating the various forms of complexity that events may exhibit, but it fails as a definition of event if some events are not changes, and it seems some are not. The standard Aristotelian account of change requires there to be a substratum which exists throughout the change, from beginning to end, pre-existing and surviving it, just as the leaf pre-exists, exists throughout, and survives its fall. But some events are the creation or annihilation of entities, whether something small like a particle, something medium-sized like a house, or something large like a star or the material universe. If an object is created, it does not pre-exist its creation, and if an object is destroyed it cannot survive its destruction.

It may be objected that such existential changes are parasitic upon changes in other things, such as constituent matter. Nothing is created from nothing or destroyed totally. When a star explodes in a supernova, what happens is that its constitutive matter and energy is rapidly scattered as energy and matter, and this (by conservation laws) survives the change. *Ex nihilo nihil, in nihilum nil posse reverti*. Against this it may be replied that creation *ex nihilo* and destruction *in nihilum* appear to be not only conceptually possible but actually commonplace according to quantum physics, that the big bang is a prominent case, and that there may be destructions (of material or non-material things) which nothing survives.

3.4 Whether all Events have Participants

If, as proposed by Kim, Goldman, Bennett, and others, events are instantiations of properties and relations, then all events have participants or subjects: the leaf that falls, the person that moves, the bullet and target that collide. This would apply even if not all events are changes, provided the participant is involved in some way, e.g. by coming into existence or ceasing to exist in the event. The death of Socrates is the death *of Socrates*. It would also apply if some events are changes in other events (are 'higher-order' events), e.g. its coming about today that John's birth was exactly sixty years ago.

Against this it has been suggested by Myles Brand (1977) that there are events without participants, such as a change of intensity in a field. Meteorological changes have often been linked to sentences without genuine subjects, as in 'It is getting warmer', and the sounds of Strawson's disembodied sound-world (Strawson 1959, ch. 2) would also qualify as participantless events. A response to these examples is that such events indeed have participants, but more subtle ones than the gross bodies of more familiar examples. A temperature changes in the invisible air, the charge increases in an intangible field, and Strawson's world only makes physical sense if there is a medium in which the sounds travel. Bennett, who accepts with Kim and Goldman that events are attribute instantiations, regards the subject of events as spatio-temporal regions rather than objects and times. The problem with this kind of response is that it risks reifying items such as fields and regions which we might have other reasons, for example of ontological parsimony or their lack of causal powers, to resist reifying. If the *only* reason to reify fields or regions came from the metaphysical requirement that all events have participants, it would be weak indeed, but there are usually other though not undisputed reasons to take such entities seriously. On the other hand if, as many metaphysicians believe, events and their ilk are the primary constituents of the physical world, then there is good reason to suppose that they ultimately have no participants more basic than themselves, but rather that such participants, whether tangible like bodies or intangible like fields and regions, are themselves abstracted from or constructed out of events.

3.5 Whether there is a Distinction between Real and Cambridge Events

Following Geach (1969: 71; 1972: 321), an object is said to undergo a *Cambridge change* when some proposition about it changes its truth-value. The epithet derives from the fact that many Cambridge philosophers including McTaggart and Russell defined change thus. Many Cambridge changes are not real changes in their subject but changes in its relation to other things, which may or may not themselves change. For instance, I become shorter than my son when he outgrows me, while I stay the same height. The real change is in him, not in me. Likewise a married woman becomes a widow when her husband dies. Sometimes a Cambridge change is constituted by real change in neither object. When two objects move towards one another, neither changes intrinsically thereby (though there is a concomitant change in their mutual gravitational attraction, this is a consequence of their approach, not constitutive of it). When a person attains the age of 18 on her birthday, this is not a real change, though it is often accompanied by many such, rather she simply lives through a time which is eighteen years later than her birth. Another odd aspect of Cambridge change is that it can occur in the absence of its subject: in 2021 Napoleon will come to have been dead 200 years, while in 1569 he became 200 years short of birth. Likewise events seem to be able to undergo Cambridge change: in 2021 Napoleon's death will become 200 years past. Yet arguably, events, being (wholly or mostly) changes in or among things, are not themselves subjects of change (extending the argument of Dretske 1967 that events cannot move).

   To distinguish a real event from a Cambridge event there needs to be a robust notion of intrinsic property, such that a real change in an object, a real event involving it, consists in the object's losing one such a property and gaining another from the same determinable family. Although the idea of an intrinsic property seems intuitive, it is hard to pin down exactly. The mutual approach of two bodies, while an intrinsic change in neither, does appear to be a real process, one whose subject is not either of the bodies separately but the system consisting of them both. The change in distance between the two is thus a real change, but of the pair, not of either individual. There is a fairly strong intuition that real changes are distinguishable from mere Cambridge changes, but as yet no clear way to demarcate the former from the latter. (For a suggestion on how to tell relational from non-relational change, see Lombard 1986: 97.)

4. IDENTITY CONDITIONS FOR EVENTS

Following the strictures of Quine's thesis 'No entity without identity', it has been held that if we accept events into our ontology then we should be prepared to state under what conditions events are the same event, that is, to give identity conditions for events. Consideration of this issue has occupied a large part of the literature on events, and it has been particularly prevalent in the discussion of action theory. The debate has strung out a series of positions between those who have relatively few events and those who have relatively many. Irving Thalberg (1971) has dubbed the former 'unifiers' and the latter 'multipliers'. Roughly speaking, unifiers tend to find one event under two descriptions where multipliers consider there to be two events. A minority of philosophers (Anscombe 1979; Bennett 1988: 93 ff.) have rejected the call for a general account of identity conditions as leading at best to unenlightening truisms. Identity conditions say when events are the same. They are not necessarily identity *criteria*, which are recipes we can apply to *tell* when events are the same. Identity conditions have the general form

For all e and e^*: $e = e^*$ iff $R(e, e^*)$,

where 'e' and 'e^*' range over events, and R is some condition on events which, to avoid triviality or circularity, is not itself identity and does not presuppose identity. In giving schematic identity conditions below I shall elide the preposed universal quantifier.

4.1 Coincidence: Quine

According to Quine's view of events, there is only one event per spatio-temporal region:

$e = e^*$ iff for some r, e is the total content of r & e^* is the total content of r.

There are still many events because there are many regions, but not more than one event per region. This avoids triviality and circularity, but it depends on having regions and identity conditions for them, and, more substantively, it fails to account for cases where we do seem to have more than one event per region. It also depends on the idea of total contents of a region. The same idea is put forward by E. J. Lemmon (1967).

4.2 Necessary Coincidence: Brand

To account for the fact that we distinguish events which occupy the same region, such as the sphere's rotating and its warming, Myles Brand (1977) proposes to sharpen

Quine's condition from coincidence to necessary coincidence. Events are identical if and only if it is necessary that they occupy the same region:

$e = e^*$ iff necessarily: for all r, e occupies r iff e^* occupies r.

This allows the rotating and warming to be discerned, since one might occur without the other, or they might both occur but be displaced temporally with respect to one another. Brand contrasts this condition with that for material objects, which *are* identical if they occupy the same region.

Brand's account uses modal concepts that Quine would find objectionable, though that objection would not worry everyone. It is, however, questionable whether material objects can only be present one per region. Also, if its location is essential to an event, which is by no means implausible, then accidentally coincident events would after all be necessarily coincident, undermining the condition. Clearly the condition cannot be used to tell events apart, since we only observe the actual world, so our confidence that coincident events are distinct cannot come from inspecting different worlds and their contents, but from some other source, which suggests that the condition, even if correct, is a by-product of event identification rather than constitutive thereof.

4.3 Co-Causality: Davidson

Davidson (1969) proposes to identify events that have the same causes and effects:

$e = e^*$ iff for all f, f causes e iff f causes e^* & e causes f iff e causes f.

This condition has been objected to on two grounds, one substantive, one formal. Substantively, the question concerns events which lack causes and lack effects. For all we know, there may be such events. If there are such events, then Davidson's condition would identify them all. But if there are many such events with different spatio-temporal locations, then Davidson's condition is materially inadequate (Brand 1977).

The formal objection is that the right-hand side of Davidson's condition itself quantifies over events and so is circular, presupposing event identity for there to be well-defined values for the event-variable f to range over (among others Wilson 1974; Brand 1977). This objection is difficult to adjudicate, because as stated it depends on whether quantification over some items presupposes identity conditions for those items, and this question is far from straightforward. Davidson defends his condition against formal circularity since the right-hand side does not contain the identity predicate. The condition is certainly impredicative, however, and the question arises whether this is a defect. Impredicativity in general, despite the strictures of early Russell and Poincaré, does not as such appear objectionable. Quine, however, who has no difficulty with impredicativity as such, warns that 'we can define impredicatively but we cannot individuate impredicatively' (Quine

1985: 166). In response, Davidson (1985) backed away from his condition, adopting Quine's own.

4.4 Identification by Constituent: Kim

Kim's constituent theory of events readily yields identity conditions for them: they are identical iff their constituents are:

$$[s, P, t] = [s^*, P^*, t^*] \text{ iff } s = s^* \ \& \ P = P^* \ \& \ t = t^*.$$

This is as clear as the identity conditions for the constituents, of which perhaps the most insecure are those for properties. The criticism most frequently levelled against Kim's theory is that it results in an unacceptable plurality of finely differentiated events, because of the requirement for identity of the constituent property. In particular in sentences with adverbial modification which goes over into adjectival description of an event, as *John woke abruptly* goes over into *John's abrupt waking*, untutored intuition would tell us that John's waking and John's abrupt waking are one and the same event, but the properties of waking and of waking abruptly are not identical, because some wakings are abrupt and others are not. So according to Kim's view as standardly understood these would be two events, not one. A similar argument applies in countless other cases. Also if, by virtue of their different life histories, the ball and its constituting metal are different, then so should the ball's rotating and the metal's rotating. But these are clearly one event, not two (Gjelsvik 1988).

It has been argued by Alvin Goldman that there are reasons to suppose fine-grained discrimination is needed in action theory to account for the 'by'-locution (Section 7.2), but that would not apply in this case. Thus the very reason which Davidson gives for there being events, namely efficacy in giving the logic of adverbial modification, is a stumbling block for Kim's theory. For further discussion on the unifier–multiplier controversy as it applies to action theory see Section 7.2.

A reply which Kim makes to the accusation that his theory makes too many ontological distinctions is that one must distinguish the constituent property of an event, which is had by its subject (or subjects), from properties which the event itself has (Kim 1976: 168–9.) Thus John's waking abruptly yesterday is John's waking, which event has the property of being abrupt. What Kim must do is block the transference of the adjective to an adverbial which becomes the constituent property of a distinct event, or what Kim calls a *generic event*. This he considers, so that predicate modifiers expressing manners, means, and methods (Kim 1976: 169) would be regarded as expressing properties of events not constituent properties in them. In general, however, he prefers there to be many events at one place and time and to claim that the proliferation is relatively harmless.

4.5 Mereological Compromise: Thalberg, Thomson

The opposition between unifiers like Davidson and Anscombe on the one hand and multipliers like Kim and Goldman on the other led several philosophers to propose a compromise between the two positions, whereby events seen as one by unifiers and as two wholly distinct events by multipliers are seen as distinct but closely related, in particular by part–whole relations. Where unifiers would take Booth's shooting Lincoln to be the same event as Booth's killing Lincoln, and multipliers would take them to be two events with different constituent properties, the same participants and slightly different times, the compromise position, suggested by Irving Thalberg (1971) and Judith Jarvis Thomson (1971, 1977), is that we have two events, one of which is part of the other: the killing includes the shooting as a part, but also includes the subsequent death as a part, which the shooting does not. They are thus neither wholly distinct nor wholly identical. The suggestion is that many (not all) of the disputed cases of event identity would turn out to concern events which are distinct but mereologically related (e.g. through overlap). On this view events are identical if and only if their parts coincide:

$$e = e^* \text{ iff for all } f: f \text{ is part of } e \text{ iff } f \text{ is part of } e^*.$$

This condition of *mereological extensionality*, while it is probably true for events, does not advance anything specific about events if other things satisfy it. And since arguably the only parts of events are events, the principle by quantifying over events suffers from the same kind of circularity as Davidson's causal condition (Section 4.3) if regarded as a principle of individuation.

5. SUBCATEGORIES OF EVENTS

Everyone who accepts events agrees that they come in multifarious kinds, as reflected in the nominal expressions describing them. It may be asked whether there are philosophically important subcategories of events. Leaving aside actions and mental events for later, I focus here on size and complexity as dimensions of variation.

5.1 Momentary and Punctual Events

If events have to last for a time, or are changes from one state to another, then there can be no such thing as an instantaneous or strictly momentary event. At best some events (such as the fission of a single atomic nucleus) might be extremely short in temporal extent. In physics it appears that the minimum time-span below which no events or changes can be registered or make a difference is the so-called *Planck time* of approximately 10^{-43} seconds. If this restriction governs the physical universe, then no natural event could be instantaneous. However, philosophers have speculated since the Presocratics that some changes are instantaneous, because suppositions to the contrary are more problematic. If an object comes into existence or ceases to exist, begins to move or comes to a stop, then it appears paradoxical to say that the object comes into existence or ceases to exist gradually or over a period: it could only do so 'at a stroke'. An object ceasing to move cannot be ceasing to move over an interval; there must be either a last instant of movement or a first instant of rest.

While natural events might perhaps not have mathematical sharpness of extent, perhaps notional or conventional events do: the New Year begins at a place on the stroke of midnight there, and while this is a boundary rather than a natural event, it is in time and sandwiched between temporal extents nevertheless. Just as there are spatial boundaries having no thickness like that between France and Germany, or the equator bounding the northern and southern hemispheres, so there might be temporal boundaries like that between 1999 and 2000 or the moment when John and Mary become man and wife, which have no temporal thickness and which we do name, so it would be churlish to deny these the epithet 'event'.

By extension of this thought, events typically have spatial extent, but perhaps there are notional or conventional events with no extent at all. Quantum physics bids us consider a physically minimally meaningful Planck volume of approximately 10^{-105} m^3, which is tiny but not zero. If an event were lacking in spatial extent, it would fill an infinitesimal part of even this small volume. But again perhaps we might consider such events as limits or boundaries, for example the event of the earth's centre of gravity (a spatial point) entering the new millennium at 0000 hours GMT. Classical physics has traditionally operated with material particles of zero volume, and relativity physics with point-events whose spatio-temporal extent is zero.

The model for such considerations has always been classical geometry, joined latterly by the theory of real numbers, which envisages a continuum as being literally composed of points. In general philosophers have tended to one or other persuasion: either they are happy to see such mathematical structures exemplified—even if virtually—in natural reality, or they are queasy about anything real having zero size in any dimension.

5.2 Simple and Complex Events

Most or all events, being spatio-temporally extended, have segments or phases corresponding to subdivisions of their extents. In this bare geometrical sense, all events other than point-events have parts and are thus complex, or non-atomic.

A conceptually more interesting distinction between simple and complex pertains to an event's *natural* parts. A performance of Beethoven's *Eroica* Symphony by a standard-sized orchestra will consist of more than a million events of a musician's playing a note, spread among eighty or so players, each such event involving several coordinated hand movements, blowings, and so on, all (we hope) appropriately and beautifully synchronized and sequenced, coordinated by typically several thousand beats and other gestures by the conductor over the work's 1,856 bars. Each of these sub-events is, while not always discretely separated from its adjacent fellows, a natural unit demarcated well enough by changes of bowing, fingering, etc. We pronounce the whole performance a single event, and it has many parts: movements, sections, phrases, chords, as well as bits played by different players or sections of the orchestra. The individual note-playings out of which all these are built are atomic relative to these greater wholes, and they correspond in number roughly to notes in the score multiplied by the number of players per part. It would be perhaps possible to specify the whole performance as a single Kimian event with the orchestra as subject and a hugely complex property, but a far more natural analysis along these lines would be to take each individual note-playing by each individual player as a Kimian event, and regard the larger events as mereological fusions of the smaller ones.

In this case the summand events come from different regions. Are there cases of what Bennett (1988: 147) calls 'non-zonal fusions', where two or more events add up mereologically to a single event despite being based on the same region? It seems there are. If a top moves across the table and at the same time spins, its traversing the table is one event and its spinning the while is another, but its total movement, the spinning traverse of the table, is a third, made up of the other two (Bennett 1988: 145). If this procedure could be continued to exhaustion, then we should eventually reach an event which is the maximal event-like occupant of its region. Among *such* events, Quine's identity conditions would prevail.

A different kind of complexity arises if the constituent property of a Kimian event is logically complex. Some metaphysicians (not all) allow that there are negative, conjunctive, disjunctive, etc. properties, that is, they allow that properties may compound logically. If they can, then Kimian events may do so also. Let John dance and sing at the same time. Then [John, dancing and singing, from 10 until 10.05] is one event with two other events, given by the conjoint property's conjuncts, added together. Negative events are a more serious story, however. There may be a story to tell about why John did not react when struck by Mike, but it is arguably unacceptably stretching the notion of event to regard *John's not reacting* as an event on all fours with Mike's striking John. If *not reacting* is a bona fide property, then John's not reacting is a bona fide event. While things' not happening may figure in explanations, including causal ones (the dog's familiarity with the intruder caused it not to bark in the night), it is possible that such locutions trade on the use of nominals to stand for *facts* rather than *events* (a point stressed by Bennett 1988, *passim*). The idea that events may be compounded logically is exploited in Peterson (1989), but most ontologists regard negation as a logical, not an ontological, operator.

6. Events and other Categories

If events are part of our ontology, the question arises as to how they differ from other admitted items. As ever, for events the story is not simple. In what follows, we shall assume that events are spatio-temporally located particulars of some sort or other, leaving their nature otherwise open.

6.1 Events and States

Often the term 'event' is stretched by philosophers to cover any particular object in time which extends over time or has temporal parts. On this view states *are* events. However, there is some point in distinguishing events from states, as we do in ordinary language, so we may ask what the point is.

In general, as the name suggests, states are static, events are not. John's sitting up is an event; his remaining prone is a state. This suggests that events are changes, or imply change, while states do not. As a datum for further investigation, this is good as far as it goes. However, one man's state is another man's process. A sphere at an unchanging temperature is static in temperature variation, but that is only because its constituent molecules continue to move with the same mean kinetic energy. Jiggling around as those molecules do is no state. Again, a uniformly accelerating body is static with respect to the forces upon it and felt within it, but it may be speeding more in a direction or changing its direction, as is a body in orbit or free fall, which are hardly static conditions. This suggests that the notion of a state is often used relative to some condition or predicate as denoting lack of change in this regard, but that need not connote complete changelessness. This suggests that states and processes are so closely akin that we cannot drive a clear ontological wedge between them.

6.2 Events and Processes

Processes such as growth, ageing, steady motion, or rotation standardly involve change in some respect or other (though if they are steady they may be static in other respects, as just noted). If events are changes, and processes are steady changes, are not processes events also? Many philosophers have drawn this consequence, but not all. The vernacular distinction between processes and events is a stable if not precise one, and we may question further. One line of discussion goes right back to Aristotle's distinction among actions and other events between actions that have a goal or terminus (*kinesis*) and those which do not, but simply continue (*energeia*). In a ground-breaking work which set much of the discussion of events in train, Vendler (1957) distinguished verbs describing human conditions into four classes: those for activities (e.g. running), accomplishments (e.g. running a mile), achievements (e.g. finding), and states (e.g. wanting). Following Aristotle, Kenny (1963) likewise distinguishes activities such as snoring or walking, which have no terminus, from performances or actions with a goal, such as walking to the North Pole. The distinction is carried beyond actions (performances and activities) more generally to events and processes respectively by Dov Gabbay and Julius Moravcsik (1980).

A thorough discussion of the issues involved in classifying temporal items in this way is by Alexander Mourelatos (1978). An interesting aspect of the distinction is that there is arguably a parallel between the mass–count distinction among meanings of nouns and the process–event distinction among meanings of verbs. Processes, like stuff, do not connote criteria for counting, whereas events, like things, do.

6.3 Events and Continuants

Events are typically changes in or among things which are not themselves changes. Such things, which lack temporal parts, are three-dimensional in extent and exist as wholes at every time at which they exist, are traditionally called substances, but are more neutrally called *continuants* by, W. E. Johnson. (Events proper, processes, and states he together called *occurrents.*) Following Lewis's change argument and considerations from physics, may philosophers are inclined to think, against the Western tradition from Aristotle to Strawson, that continuants either in fact have temporal parts and so are really occurrents, or, what amounts to much the same, that there are only occurents, no continuants as strictly defined, the assumption that there are being just entrenched prejudice. Against this, defenders of continuants point out that if events are changes, and only continuants can change (e.g. Geach 1972: 304, and many others), then nothing changes so there are no changes after all, that what we call change is in effect replacement of one thing by another, much in the style of Heraclitus or Hume.

The debate among the various sides in this dispute is hugely involved and cannot be tracked here, but five metaphysical positions about objects in time and existing at different times may be differentiated: (1) pure perdurantism: that there are only occurrents; (2) pure endurantism: that there are only continuants; (3) duality of equals: that both continuants and occurrents exist and neither reduces to or is generally prior over the other; (4) priority endurantism: that both exist but continuants have ontological priority; (5) priority perdurantism: that both exist but occurrents have ontological priority. Each of these positions has had its adherents.

7. Some Philosophical Uses of Events

7.1 Mind–Body

A very natural way to put issues about mind and body is to talk of relations between mental and physical events. This framing of the traditional debate, which came to prominence in the 1950s, also helped to start the modern discussion of events in general. In the light of the foregoing discussion it will by now be clear how the debate can take its turn according to the various conceptions of event outlined. Three examples may suffice to illustrate. An epiphenomenalist Davidsonian will distinguish mental events from physical brain events by their effects: epiphenomenal mental events have no physical effects while physical events may cause other physical events as well as mental events. A Kimian will typically distinguish mental from physical events because they have different constitutive properties, for example mental events may be constituted by phenomenological properties which are distinct from neurophysiological properties. Of course a materialist may argue that this begs the question, and the debate will shift to questions of property dualism, but if there is a duality of properties there is also one of events. Finally, a materialist or identity theorist may well go along with Davidson, Quine, or Bennett and say that mental events are simply brain events under a different description, so that mental events have an actual but unperceived location in the brain. The distinctions among token and type identity theorists, anomalous monists, functionalists, and others may all be formulated in terms of events, their kinds, and the causal laws governing them. This has indeed become the standard way to approach the issue of mind and body.

7.2 Action

In the philosophy of action, which is one of the theoretical mainstays of ethics, the nature of action is debated, and the philosophy of action has been a rich source of debate and examples in event theory, especially in the unifier–multiplier controversy. Following Davidson (1967), most philosophers regard actions as a subclass of events, those where it makes sense to ask why the agent did what she did. Some philosophers (von Wright 1963; Bach 1980) regard actions not as events but as willings or bringings about of events by agents, employing a notion of agent causality distinct from that of event causality.

The principal contribution of action theory to event theory (rather than vice versa) has been as a rich source of example and controversy. An early foray is Anscombe (1957: 37–46), where a unifier account of actions sees many as being identical, but described by different descriptions. Booth's crooking his finger, Booth's pulling the trigger, Booth's firing the gun, Booth's shooting Lincoln, Booth's killing Lincoln, are all the same action and the same event. A multiplier such as Kim would see these as five actions constituted by different properties. Kim's account is given supplementary structure by Goldman (1971), who points out that the five actions are not merely distinct but linked by what he calls 'level-generation', expressed by the 'by' locution: Booth killed Lincoln *by* shooting him, he shot him *by* firing the gun, he fired the gun *by* pulling the trigger, he pulled the trigger *by* crooking his finger. All of these *by*-relations may hold, but critics have suggested that Goldman's view, like Kim's, multiplies events beyond reason, and that 'by' goes with facts and explanation rather than with events and ontology. The asymmetries of 'by' seem to tell against unification even on Davidson's account, because while the crooking of Booth's finger caused the gun to fire and Lincoln to be shot, Lincoln's being shot did not cause Booth's pulling the trigger. Booth's killing of Lincoln cannot be identical with his pulling the trigger, because Lincoln was not yet shot, let alone dead, when the trigger was pulled.

There is much that is confused and confusing in such examples, not least the prevalence of '-ing' gerunds which can stand now for facts, now for events (Bennett 1988: 6 and *passim*). A measured response to the problem is that of the mereological compromisers, for whom the relationship between earlier and later in the sequence of descriptions is that they describe a mereologically nested sequence of events: the crooking is part of the pulling is part of the firing is part of the shooting is part of the killing. The killing is only complete when Lincoln dies, some hours after the shooting. Against this Davidson can point out that Booth need do nothing further to ensure Lincoln's death once he has pulled the trigger, and that the various descriptions of the action, while not logically equivalent, do as things turned out describe the same event. A similar stance is taken by Anscombe and Bennett: the shooting is not a killing initially, but only becomes so subsequently, once Lincoln dies. This seems to imply that events change 'posthumously', which we saw was problematic. However, if the change is a Cambridge or relational one, the shooting's coming to have caused Lincoln's death, then the unifier defence may be admitted, the difference between the action's description as a shooting and its description as a killing being one of epistemological rather than ontological significance, just as we can describe the same woman relationally as the eldest granddaughter of George V or as the elder grandmother of Prince William of Wales, and name her as Elizabeth Windsor.

REFERENCES

Anscombe, E. (1957). *Intention*. Oxford: Basil Blackwell.

—— (1979). 'Under a Description'. *Noûs*, 13: 219–33. Repr. in Casati and Varzi (1996: 303–18).

Armstrong, D. M. (1987). *A World of States of Affairs*. Cambridge: Cambridge University Press.

Bach, K. (1980). 'Actions are not Events'. *Mind*, 89: 114–20. Repr. in Casati and Varzi (1996: 343–50).

Bartels, A. (2000). 'Quantum Field Theory: A Case for Event Ontologies?', in J. Faye, U. Scheffler, and M. Urchs (eds.), *Things, Facts and Events*. Amsterdam: Rodopi.

Bennett, J. (1988). *Events and their Names*. Cambridge: Cambridge University Press.

Brand, M. (1976). 'Particulars, Events, and Actions', in Brand and Walton (1976: 133–58).

—— (1977). 'Identity Conditions for Events'. *American Philosophical Quarterly*, 14: 329–37. Repr. in Casati and Varzi (1996: 363–72).

—— and D. Walton (eds.) (1976). *Action Theory*. Dordrecht: Reidel.

Brandl, J. (2000). 'Do Events Recur?', in Higginbotham *et al.* (2000: 95–104).

Casati, R., and A. Varzi (eds.) (1996). *Events*. Aldershot: Dartmouth.

Chisholm, R. M. (1970). 'Events and Propositions'. *Noûs*, 4: 15–24. Repr. in Casati and Varzi (1996: 89–98).

—— (1994). 'Ontologically Dependent Entities'. *Philosophy and Phenomenological Research*, 54: 499–507.

Clark, R. (1974). 'Adverbial Modifiers', in R. Severens (ed.), *Ontological Commitment*. Athens: University of Georgia Press, 22–36.

Cleland, C. (1991). 'On the Individuation of Events'. *Synthese*, 86: 229–54. Repr. in Casati and Varzi (1996: 373–400).

Davidson, D. (1967). 'The Logical Form of Action Sentences', in Rescher (1967: 81–95). Repr. in Davidson (1980: 105–21) and Casati and Varzi (1996: 3–18).

—— (1969). 'The Individuation of Events', in Rescher (1969: 216–34). Repr. in Davidson (1980: 163–80) and Casati and Varzi (1996: 265–84).

—— (1970). 'Events as Particulars'. *Noûs*, 4: 25–32. Repr. in Casati and Varzi (1996: 99–106).

—— (1980). *Essays on Actions and Events*. Oxford: Clarendon Press.

—— (1985). 'Reply to Quine on Events', in LePore and McLaughlin (1985: 172–5).

Dretske, F. (1967). 'Can Events Move?' *Mind*, 76: 476–92. Repr. in Casati and Varzi (1996: 415–28).

Gabbay, D. M., and J. Moravcsik (1980). 'Verbs, Events, and the Flow of Time', in C. Rohrer (ed.), *Time, Tense and Quantifiers*. Tübingen: Niemeyer, 59–83.

Geach, P. T. (1969). *God and the Soul*. London: Routledge & Kegan Paul.

—— (1972). *Logic Matters*. Oxford: Basil Blackwell.

Gjelsvik, J. (1988). 'A Note on Objects and Events'. *Analysis*, 48: 15–18.

Goldman, A. (1971). 'The Individuation of Action'. *Journal of Philosophy*, 68: 761–74. Repr. in Casati and Varzi (1996: 329–42).

Hacker, P. M. S. (1982). 'Events, Ontology and Grammar'. *Philosophy*, 57: 477–86. Repr. in Casati and Varzi (1996: 79–88).

Haslanger, S. (1989). 'Endurance and Temporary Intrinsics'. *Analysis*, 49: 119–25.

Higginbotham, J. (1983). 'The Logic of Perceptual Reports: An Extensional Alternative to Situation Semantics'. *Journal of Philosophy*, 80: 100–127. Repr. in Casati and Varzi (1996: 19–46).

Higginbotham, J. (1983). F. Pianesi, and A. Varzi (eds.) (2000). *Speaking of Events*. New York: Oxford University Press.

Horgan, T. (1978). 'The Case against Events'. *Philosophical Review*, 87: 28–47. Repr. in Casati and Varzi (1996: 243–64).

Kenny, A. J. P. (1963). *Action, Emotion and Will*. London: Routledge & Kegan Paul.

Kim, J. (1966). 'On the Psycho-physical Identity Theory'. *American Philosophical Quarterly*, 3: 277–85.

—— (1969). 'Events and their Descriptions: Some Considerations', in Rescher (1969: 198–215).

—— (1976). 'Events as Property Exemplifications', in Brand and Walton (1976: 159–77). Repr. in Casati and Varzi (1996: 117–36).

Lemmon, E. J. (1967). 'Comments on D. Davidson's "The Logical Form of Action Sentences"', in Rescher (1967: 96–103).

LePore, E., and B. P. McLaughlin (eds.) (1985). *Actions and Events: Perspectives in the Philosophy of Donald Davidson*. Oxford: Basil Blackwell.

Lewis, D. (1986a). *On the Plurality of Worlds*. Oxford: Basil Blackwell.

—— (1986b). 'Events', in Lewis, *Philosophical Papers*, vol. ii. New York: Oxford University Press, 241–69. Repr. in Casati and Varzi (1996: 213–42).

Lombard, L. B. (1986). *Events: A Metaphysical Study*. London: Routledge & Kegan Paul.

Lowe, E. J. (2001). 'Event Causation and Agent Causation'. *Grazer Philosophische Studien*, 61: 1–20.

Martin, R. M. (1969). 'On Events and Event-Descriptions', in J. Margolis (ed.), *Fact and Existence*. Oxford: Basil Blackwell, 63–73, 97–109.

Mellor, D. H. (1995). *The Facts of Causation*. London: Routledge.

Montague, R. (1969). 'On the Nature of Certain Philosophical Entities'. *The Monist*, 53: 159–94. Repr. in Montague, *Formal Philosophy*. New Haven: Yale University Press, 1974, 149–87.

Mourelatos, A. P. D. (1978). 'Events, Processes, and States'. *Linguistics and Philosophy*, 2: 415–34. Repr. in Casati and Varzi (1996: 457–75).

Parsons, T. (1990). *Events in the Semantics of English: A Study in Subatomic Semantics*. Cambridge, Mass.: MIT Press.

Peterson, P. L. (1989). 'Complex Events'. *Pacific Philosophical Quarterly*, 70: 19–41. Repr. in Casati and Varzi (1996: 153–77).

Quine, W. V. O. (1960). *Word and Object*. Cambridge, Mass.: MIT Press.

—— (1985). 'Events and Reification', in LePore and McLaughlin (1985: 162–71). Repr. in Casati and Varzi (1996: 107–16).

Ramsey, F. P. (1990). 'Facts and Propositions' (1927), in Ramsey, *Philosophical Papers*. Cambridge: Cambridge University Press. *First pub. in Proceedings of the Aristotelian Society*, suppl. vol. 7: 153–70.

Rescher, N. (ed.) (1967). *The Logic of Decision and Action*. Pittsburgh: University of Pittsburgh Press.

—— (ed.) (1969). *Essays in Honor of Carl G. Hempel*. Dordrecht: Reidel.

Russell, B. (1986). *Collected Papers, viii: The Philosophy of Logical Atomism and Other Essays, 1914–19*. London: Allen & Unwin.

Strawson, P. F. (1959). *Individuals: An Essay in Descriptive Metaphysics*. London: Methuen.

Taylor, B. (1985). *Modes of Occurrence: Verbs, Adverbs and Events*. Oxford: Basil Blackwell.

Thalberg, I. (1971). 'Singling Out Actions, their Properties and Components'. *Journal of Philosophy*, 68: 781–6.

Thomson, J. J. (1971). 'Individuating Actions'. *Journal of Philosophy*, 68: 771–81.

—— (1977). *Acts and Other Events*. Ithaca, NY: Cornell University Press.

Vendler, Z. (1957). 'Verbs and Times'. *Philosophical Review*, 66: 143–60. Repr. rev. in Vendler (1967: 97–121).

—— (1967). *Linguistics in Philosophy*. Ithaca, NY: Cornell University Press.

von Wright, G. H. (1963). *Norm and Action: A Logical Inquiry*. London: Routledge & Kegan Paul.

Williams, D. C. (1953). 'On the Elements of Being'. *Review of Metaphysics*, 7: 3–18, 171–92. Repr. as 'The Elements of Being', in Williams, *Principles of Empirical Realism*. Springfield: Thomas, 1966, 74–109.

Wilson, N. L. (1974). 'Facts, Events, and their Identity Conditions'. *Philosophical Studies*, 25: 303–21.

CHAPTER 13

CAUSATION AND SUPERVENIENCE

MICHAEL TOOLEY

1. THE BASIC ISSUES

THE fundamental questions that must be answered by any adequate theory of causation fall into three main groups. First, there are issues concerned with the nature of causation: What it is for two states of affairs to be causally connected, what is a causal law, and how are the two related? How are causal states of affairs related to non-causal states of affairs? Are the former logically supervenient upon the latter? What are the formal properties of causation? Is it necessarily an asymmetric relation? Does causation necessarily have a direction? If so, what is the basis of the direction of causation?

Secondly, there are questions concerning the epistemology of causation, including whether causal relations can be immediately perceived, and what account can be given of the confirmation of causal hypotheses on the basis of statistical information.

Thirdly, there are questions about the relations between causation on the one hand, and space and time on the other: Is it possible for there to be a temporal or spatial gap between a cause and its effect, with no intervening causal process? Can a cause be later than its effect, or else simultaneous with it? How is time related to causation? Is the direction of time to be defined in terms of the direction of causation, or vice versa, or neither?

2. ALTERNATIVE GENERAL APPROACHES TO THE NATURE OF CAUSATION

Questions concerning the nature of causation first came sharply into focus as a result of David Hume's famous discussions (1739–40, 1748), and, since his time, many different accounts have been advanced. It will be helpful, however, to divide these various approaches into four general types—which I shall refer to as direct realism, Humean reductionism, non-Humean reductionism, and indirect, or theoretical, realism—since, as we shall see, there are powerful general arguments that often bear upon all of the approaches within a given category.

This fourfold division rests upon the following three distinctions: first, that between reductionism and realism; secondly, that between Humean and non-Humean states of affairs; and, thirdly, that between states that are immediately observable and those that are not. So let us consider each of these distinctions in turn, starting with that between reductionism and realism.

The realism versus reductionism distinction in this area arises in connection with both causal laws, and causal relations between states of affairs. As regards causal laws, reductionists claim that causal laws are reducible to facts about the total history of the universe, while realists deny that this is so. Similarly, as regards causal relations, reductionists claim that causal relations between states of affairs are reducible to non-causal facts about states of affairs, including the non-causal properties of, and relations between, events, whereas realists claim that no such reduction is possible.

But what exactly does reduction come to in these cases? The answer is that reduction can take two forms. On the one hand, there are analytical reductions, where the relations in question hold as a matter of logical necessity, broadly understood. On the other, there are reductions that involve a contingent identification of causation with some other relation.

2.1 Analytic Reductionism

A traditional way of formulating the basic issue in the case of analytic reductionism is in terms of whether the relevant causal concepts are *analysable* in non-causal terms. It seems preferable, however, to formulate the relevant theses in terms of the slightly broader concept of *logical supervenience*. Thus, let us say that two worlds, W and W^*, agree with respect to all of the properties and relations in some set, S, if and only if there is some one-to-one mapping, f, between the individuals in the two worlds, such that (1) for any individual x in world W, and any property P in set S, x has property P if and only if the corresponding individual, x^*, in W^*, also has property P, and vice versa, and (2) for any n-tuple of individuals, $x_1, x_2, \ldots, x_n$ in W, and any relation R in set $S, x_1, x_2, \ldots, x_n$ stand in relation R if and only if the corresponding individuals, $x_1^*, x_2^*, \ldots, x_n^*$, in W^*, also stand in relation R, and vice versa. Then we can say that the properties and relations in some other set T that is completely distinct from S are logically supervenient upon the properties and relations in set S if and only if, for any two worlds W and W^*, if W and W^* agree with respect to the properties and relations in set S, they must also agree with respect to the properties and relations in set T.

Given these concepts, the relevant reductionist theses can be characterized as follows. First, reductionism with respect to causal relations. This comes, initially, in two forms, depending upon what the reduction base is claimed to be:

> *Strong reductionism with respect to causal relations.* Any two worlds that agree with respect to all of the non-causal properties of, and relations between, particulars, must also agree with respect to all of the causal relations between states of affairs. Causal relations are, in short, logically supervenient upon non-causal properties and relations.

> *Weak reductionism with respect to causal relations.* Any two worlds that agree both with respect to all of the non-causal properties of, and relations between, particulars, and with respect to all causal laws, must also agree with respect to all of the causal relations between states of affairs.

Secondly, reductionism with respect to causal laws. Here the central contention is that what causal laws there are is fixed by the total history of the world. That contention can also take, however, a stronger form and a weaker form:

> *Strong reductionism with respect to causal laws.* Any two worlds that agree with respect to all of the non-causal properties of, and relations between, particulars, must also agree with respect to causal laws.

> *Weak reductionism with respect to causal laws.* Any two worlds that agree both with respect to all of the non-causal properties of, and relations between, particulars, and with respect to all causal relations between states of affairs, must also agree with respect to causal laws.

There are some obvious interrelations here. Strong reductionism with respect to causal relations, when combined with weak reductionism with respect to causal laws, entails strong reductionism with respect to causal laws. Similarly, strong reductionism with respect to causal laws, combined with weak reductionism with respect to causal relations, entails strong reductionism with respect to causal relations.

Strong reductionism on either issue cannot, accordingly, be combined with only weak reductionism on the other. But what about being merely a weak reductionist with regard to both causal laws and causal relations? This combination also seems problematic. For, on the one hand, if causal laws are logically supervenient upon the non-causal properties of, and relations between, particular events, together with causal relations between events, then causal laws would seem to be ontologically less basic than causal relations, while if causal relations are logically supervenient upon causal laws plus the non-causal properties of, and relations between, particular events, then it would seem that causal laws are ontologically more basic than causal relations. It seems doubtful, therefore, whether one can have a coherent ontology if one attempts to embrace only weak reductionism both with respect to causal laws and with respect to causal relations. Accordingly, if one is going to be a reductionist with respect to *both* causal laws and causal relations, it would seem that it is the strong reductionist views that one should embrace.

2.2 Contingent Identity Theories

Analytic reductionism is not, however, the only reductionist possibility. For, just as in the case of the mental, where one can grant that mental states of affairs are not logically supervenient upon physical states of affairs, but then go on to claim that mental states of affairs are contingently identical with physical states of affairs, so one can reject analytic reductionism in the case of causation, but hold that causation in our world is, as a matter of fact, identical with some relation that can be characterized in non-causal terms. Thus David Fair (1979), for example, has proposed that causation in this world can be identified with the transference of energy and/or momentum, while other writers, such as Wesley Salmon (1997) and Phil Dowe (2000a,b), have suggested that causal processes can be identified with continuous processes in which quantities are conserved.

2.3 Realism

Finally, how is realism to be characterized? A realist with regard to causation holds that the obtaining of a causal relation between two states of affairs is not reducible to states of affairs that involve only non-causal properties and relations. A realist must, accordingly, reject all contingent identity theories of causation. Must he or she also reject analytic reductionism, with regard to both causal relations and causal laws? The answer is that the realist must certainly reject strong reductionism with regard to causal relations. On the other hand, the realist could accept weak reductionism with regard to causal relations, provided that that was combined with a rejection of both strong and weak reductionism with regard to causal laws. Alternatively, a realist might reject both strong and weak reductionism with regard to causal relations, while accepting weak reductionism with regard to causal laws.

2.4 Humean versus Non-Humean Reductionism

In addition to the gulf between reductionism and realism, there are also very important divides within both reductionism and realism. In the case of reductionism, the crucial division involves a distinction between what may be called Humean and non-Humean states of affairs. So let us now turn to that distinction.

A principle that Hume frequently appealed to was that there could not be logical connections between distinct existences. But what exactly are distinct existences? An existence, here, I think, is best viewed as a state of affairs. If so, the question is when two states of affairs are distinct. One answer that might be offered is that two monadic states of affairs, such as a's having property P and b's having property Q, are distinct if and only if either a is not identical with b or P is not identical with Q. But that analysis does not seem right, since distinct existences, so understood, could very well be logically related. In particular, if b were a part of a, then b's having a certain property might very well entail a's having a certain property.

The natural reaction to this problem is to shift from talk about things' not being identical to talk about things' not overlapping: two monadic states of affairs, such as a's having property P and b's having property Q, are distinct if and only if either a and b do not overlap, or properties P and Q do not overlap. (Overlap of properties would need, of course, further explanation, but the basic thought here is that if there are conjunctive properties, then any such property overlaps each of its conjuncts.)

The idea now is to explain the distinction between Humean and non-Humean states of affairs along roughly the following lines. First, any property or relation with which one can be directly acquainted—that is 'directly observable', that is 'immediately given' in experience—is *ipso facto* a Humean property or relation. Secondly, any state of affairs, all of whose constituent properties and relations are Humean, is a Humean state of affairs. Finally, any other state of affairs, S, is Humean if and only if there is no set, C, of Humean states of affairs such that C together with S entails the existence of a Humean state of affairs, T, that is distinct from S, and that is not entailed by C alone.

Given the concept of a Humean state of affairs, a reduction may be classified as Humean if the relevant reduction base consists entirely of Humean states of affairs. Otherwise, the reduction is non-Humean.

What would be an example of a non-Humean state of affairs? Suppose that P and Q are non-overlapping properties that are directly observable, and thus Humean properties, and consider the view that laws of nature are states of affairs that consist of properties' standing in certain second-order relations—including N, the relation of nomic necessitation—such that the second-order state of affairs entails the existence of a corresponding regularity. So, for example, the state of affairs that consists of P and Q standing in relation N would entail that everything that has property P also has property Q. Then that second-order state of affairs would seem, prima facie, to be non-Humean, since it together with the Humean state of affairs that consists of some particular, a, having property P entails the existence of the state of affairs that consists of a's having property Q, a state of affairs that appears to be distinct from the two states of affairs that together entail its existence.

An account of causal relations that accepted the thesis of weak reductionism with respect to causal relations, but then went on to offer an account of laws in terms of second-order relations between universals, would thus be a reductionist account of causal relations, albeit, presumably, a non-Humean one.

Why is it important to distinguish between these two types of reductionism? The reason is that one of the most crucial objections to realist approaches involves the claim that there cannot be logical connections between distinct states of affairs. But if this objection is sound, it also tells against non-Humean reductionism. In one respect, therefore, non-Humean, reductionist approaches are much closer to realist approaches than they are to Humean reductionist accounts, and this is philosophically very important.

The third and final distinction is that between direct realism and indirect, or theoretical, realism. According to direct realism, some causal states of affairs can be immediately given. Are these causal laws, or causal relations between states of affairs? Since it is not at all plausible that one can be directly acquainted with causal laws, the relevant states of affairs must consist of causal relations between states of affairs. Thus direct realism can be defined as a version of realism that claims that the relation of causation is immediately given in experience.

Indirect, or theoretical, realism rejects this claim, maintaining either that the relation of causation is itself an irreducible, theoretical relation, or, alternatively, that causal laws are irreducible, theoretical states of affairs, and that causal relations must be reduced to causal laws, plus non-causal properties and relations. Either way, then, the relation of causation is not directly observable.

3. DIRECT REALISM

I have suggested that a good way of categorizing different approaches to the nature of causation is in terms of the four alternatives of direct realism, Humean reductionism, non-Humean reductionism, and theoretical realism. Let us now consider each of these in turn.

Direct realism involves three main theses. First, the relation of causation is directly observable. Secondly, that relation is not reducible to non-causal properties and/or relations. Thirdly, the relation of causation is also not reducible to non-causal properties and/or relations together with causal laws—since such a reduction would entail that one could not be directly acquainted with the relation of causation. Fourthly, the concept of the relation of causation is analytically basic.

A number of philosophers have claimed that the relation of causation is observable, including David Armstrong (1968: 97; 1997: 211–16), Elizabeth Anscombe (1971: 92–3), and Evan Fales (1990: 11–25). Thus Anscombe argues that one acquires observational knowledge of causal states of affairs when, for example, one sees a stone break a window, or a knife cut through butter, while Fales, who offers the most detailed argument in support of the view that causation is observable, appeals especially to the impression of pressure upon one's body, and to one's introspective awareness of willing, together with the accompanying perception of the event whose occurrence one willed.

Suppose that it is granted that in such cases one does, in some straightforward sense, observe that one event causes another. Does this provide one with any reason for thinking that direct realism is true? For it to do so, one would have to be able to move from the claim that the relation of causation is thus observable to the conclusion that it is not necessary to offer any analysis of the concept of causation, that it can be taken as analytically basic. But observational knowledge, in this broad, everyday sense, would not seem to provide adequate grounds for concluding that the relevant concepts are analytically basic. One can, for example, quite properly speak of physicists as seeing electrons when they look into cloud chambers, even though the concept of an electron is certainly not analytically basic. Similarly, the fact, for example, that sodium chloride is observable, and that one can tell by simply looking and tasting that a substance is sodium chloride, does not mean that the expression 'sodium chloride' does not stand in need of analysis.

But might it not be argued in response, first, that, one can observe that two events are causally related in precisely the same sense in which one can observe that something is red; secondly, that the concept of being red is analytically basic, in virtue of the observability of redness; and therefore, thirdly, that the concept of causation must, for parallel reasons, also be analytically basic?

This response is open, however, to the following reply. If a concept is analytically basic, then one can acquire the concept in question only by being in perceptual or introspective contact with an instance of the property or relation in question that is picked out by the concept. One could, however, acquire the concept of being red in a world where there were no red things: it would suffice if things sometimes looked red, or if one had hallucinations of seeing red things, or experienced red after-images. The concept of red must, therefore, be definable, and so cannot be analytically basic.

What is required if a concept is to be analytically basic? The answer that is suggested by the case of the concept of redness is that for a concept to be analytically basic, the property or relation in virtue of which the concept applies to a given thing must be such that that property or relation is immediately given in experience, where a property or relation is immediately given in experience only if, for any two qualitatively indistinguishable experiences, the property must either be given in both or given in neither.

Is the relation of causation immediately given in experience? The answer is that it is not. For given any experience E whatever—be it a perception of external events, an awareness of pressure upon one's body, or an introspective awareness of some mental occurrence, such as an act of willing, or a process of thinking—it is logically possible that appropriate, direct stimulation of the brain might produce an experience, E^*, which was qualitatively indistinguishable from E, but which did not involve any causally related elements. So, for example, it might seem to one that one was engaging in a process of deductive reasoning, when, in fact, there was not really any direct connection at all between the thoughts themselves—all of them being caused instead by something outside of oneself. Causal relations cannot, therefore, be immediately given in experience in the sense that is required if the concept of causation is to be unanalysable.

Let us now turn to objections to direct realism. The first has, in effect, just been set out. For if, for any experience in which one is in perceptual or introspective contact with the relation of causation, there could be a qualitatively indistinguishable, hallucinatory experience in which one was not in contact with the relation of causation, it would be possible to acquire the concept of causation without ever being in contact with an instance of that relation. But such experiences are logically possible. So the concept of causation must be analysable, rather than being analytically basic.

Secondly, it seems plausible that there is a basic relation of causation that is necessarily irreflexive and asymmetric, even if this is not true of the ancestral of that relation. If either reductionism or indirect realism is correct, one may very well be able to explain the necessary truths in question, since the fact that causal concepts are, on either of those views, analysable means that those necessary truths may turn out to be analytic. Direct realism, by contrast, in holding that the concept of causation is analytically basic, is barred from offering such an explanation of the asymmetry and irreflexivity of the basic relation of causation.

Thirdly, direct realism encounters epistemological problems. Thus, features such as the direction of increase in entropy, or the direction of the transmission of order in non-entropic, irreversible processes, or the direction of open forks, often provide evidence concerning how events are causally connected. Similarly, causal beliefs are often established on the basis of statistical information—using methods that, especially within the social sciences, are very sophisticated. Given an appropriate analysis of the relation of causation, one can show why such features are epistemologically relevant, and why the statistical methods in question can serve to establish causal hypotheses, whereas if causation is a basic irreducible relation, it is not at all clear how either of these things can be the case.

4. HUMEAN REDUCTIONISM: GENERAL OBJECTIONS

Objections to Humean reductionist theories of causation are of two sorts. First, there are objections to the supervenience theses to which such theories are committed. Secondly, there are objections that are directed against specific theories. The former are the focus of the present section.

4.1 Reductionism with Respect to Causal Laws

The distinction between strong and weak reductionism with respect to causal laws is important for understanding what options are open when one is setting out an account of the nature of causation. It is not, however, crucial with respect to the choice between reductionist and realist approaches to laws, since strong and weak reductionist views are exposed to precisely the same objections.

Philosophers such as Dretske (1977), Tooley (1977; 1987, sect. 2.1.1), Armstrong (1983), and Carroll (1994) have argued that reductionist accounts of the nature of laws are exposed to several very strong objections. Let us briefly consider, then, some of the more important ones.

4.1.1 *Laws versus Accidental Regularities*

First, then, there is the familiar problem of distinguishing between laws and accidental regularities. For example, there may well be some number N such that, at no time or place in the total history of the universe is there ever a sphere of radius N metres that contains only electrons. But if there is such a number, does that mean that it is a *law* that no sphere of radius N metres can contain only electrons? Might it not, instead, be merely an accident that no such sphere exists? But if so, what serves to differentiate laws from mere cosmic regularities?[1]

4.1.2 *Basic Laws without Instances*

A second objection concerns the possibility of basic, uninstantiated laws, and may be put as follows. Suppose, for the sake of illustration, that our world contains psychophysical laws according to which various types of brain states causally give rise to emergent properties of experiences. Let us suppose, further, that at

---

[1] For a much fuller discussion of the problem of distinguishing between laws and accidental uniformities, see Armstrong (1983, ch. 2).

least some of these psychophysical laws connecting neurophysiological states to phenomenological states are basic—that is, incapable of being derived from any other laws, psychophysical or otherwise—and, for concreteness, let us suppose that the psychophysical law connecting a certain type of brain state to experiences involving a specific shade of purple is such a law. Finally, let us assume that the only instances of that particular law at any time in the history of the universe involve sentient beings on earth. Given these assumptions, consider what would have been the case if our world had been different in certain respects. Suppose, for example, that the earth had been destroyed by an explosion of the sun just before the point when, for the first time in history, a certain sentient being would have observed a purple flower, and would have had an experience with the corresponding emergent property. What counterfactuals are true in the alternative possible world just described? In particular, what would have been the case if the sun had not gone supernova when it did? Would it not then have been true that the sentient being in question would have looked at a purple flower, and thus have been stimulated in such a way as to go into a certain neurophysiological state, and then to have an experience with the relevant emergent property?

It seems to me very plausible that the counterfactual in question is true in that possible world. But that counterfactual cannot be true unless the appropriate psychophysical law obtains in that world. In the world where the sun explodes before any sentient being has looked at a purple flower, however, the law in question will not have any instances. So if the counterfactual is true in that world, it follows that there can be basic causal laws that lack all instances. But if that is so, then causal laws cannot be logically supervenient upon the total history of the universe.[2]

4.1.3 *Probabilistic Laws*

A third objection concerns a problem posed by probabilistic laws. Consider a world where it is a law that the probability that an event with property P has property Q is equal to one half. It does not follow that precisely one half of the events with property P will have property Q. Indeed, the proportion that have property Q need not be anywhere near one half: it can have absolutely any value from zero to one.

The existence of the law in question does have, of course, *probabilistic* implications with respect to the proportion that will have property Q. In particular, as the number of events with property P becomes larger and larger, the *probability* that the proportion of events with property P that also have property Q will be within any specified interval around the value one half approaches indefinitely close to one. But this is, of course, perfectly compatible with the fact that the existence of the

---

[2] I have discussed the question of the possibility of uninstantiated basic laws in more detail in Tooley (1987: 47–51).

law in question does not *entail* any restrictions upon the proportion of events with property *P* that have property *Q*.

More generally, any probabilistic law is compatible with *any* distribution of properties over events. In this respect, there is a sharp difference between probabilistic laws and non-probabilistic laws. Any non-probabilistic law imposes a constraint upon the total history of any world containing that law—namely, the corresponding regularity must obtain. But a probabilistic law, by contrast, imposes no constraint upon the total history of the world. Accordingly, unless one is prepared to supplement one's ontology in a very unHumean way—by postulating something like objective, ontologically ultimate, single-case chances—there would not seem to be even a potential reduction base in the case of probabilistic laws.[3]

4.1.4 *Justifying Beliefs about Cosmic Regularities*

The fourth and final objection that I shall mention concerns an epistemological problem that arises if one attempts to identify laws either with cosmic regularities in general, or with regularities that satisfy certain additional constraints. On the one hand, the evidence for any law consists of a finite number of observations. On the other, any law has a potentially infinite number of instances. Can such a finite body of evidence possibly justify one in believing that some law obtains, if laws are essentially just regularities? For if laws are merely certain kinds of regularities, with no further ontological backing, is it not in fact *likely* that the regularities that have held with respect to the cases that have been observed so far will break down at some point?

This objection can be formulated in a more rigorous way by appealing to some general, quantitative account of confirmation, according to which any generalization of the sort that expresses a possible law has a probability infinitesimally close to zero relative to any finite body of evidence. Carnap's system of confirmation, for example, has that property.[4] It is possible to argue, of course, that any system with this property is necessarily defective. But then the challenge is to construct a system that assigns non-zero probability to generalizations expressing possible laws, upon finite observational evidence, in an infinite universe, and while there have certainly been attempts to meet this challenge (see e.g. Hintikka 1966), I think it can be argued that they are ad hoc, and fail to appeal to independently plausible principles.

But how is the realist any better placed with respect to this epistemological problem? The answer is that a realist can view the existence of a causal law as constituted by a single, atomic state of affairs, rather than by a potentially infinite conjunction of states of affairs. Thus, for example, if laws are identified with certain second-order, atomic states of affairs involving irreducible relations between universals, it can be

---

[3] A fuller account of the problem posed by probabilistic laws can be found in Tooley (1987: 42–7).

[4] For a discussion of this, see Carnap (1962: 70–5).

argued that this type of realist account enables one to prove that quite a limited body of evidence may make it very probable that a given law obtains (Tooley 1987: 129–37).

To sum up. Reductionist accounts of causal laws face at least four serious objections. First, they appear unable to draw a satisfactory distinction between laws and accidental uniformities. Secondly, they cannot allow for the possibility of basic, uninstantiated laws. Thirdly, probabilistic laws seem to pose an intractable problem. Fourthly, it is difficult to see how one can ever be justified in believing that there are laws, if one adopts a reductionist account. A realist approach, by contrast, can provide satisfactory answers to all of these problems.

4.2 Reductionism with Respect to Causal Relations

General objections to reductionist approaches to causal relations fall into two groups. First, there are objections that centre upon the problem of giving an account of the direction of causal processes, and which claim that there are possible causal worlds where reductionist accounts of the direction of causation either do not apply at all, or else do apply, but generate the wrong answers. Secondly, there are objections involving what may be referred to as problems of underdetermination. For what these objections attempt to establish is that there can be worlds that agree with respect to, first, all of the non-causal properties of, and relations between, events, secondly, all causal laws, and thirdly, the direction of causation, but which disagree with respect to causal relations between corresponding events.

4.2.1 Direction of Causation Objections

Here I shall mention two objections. The thrust of the first is that there are possible causal worlds to which reductionist accounts of the direction of causation do not apply, while that of the second is that there are possible causal worlds for which reductionist accounts yield wrong answers with respect to the direction of causal processes.

4.2.1.1 Simple Worlds

Our world is a complex one, with a number of features that might be invoked as the basis of a reductionist account of the direction of causation. First of all, it is a world where the direction of increase in entropy is the same in the vast majority of isolated or quasi-isolated systems. Secondly, the temporal direction in which order is propagated—such as by the circular waves that result when a stone strikes a pond, or by the spherical wave fronts associated with a point source of light—is invariably the same. Thirdly, consider the causal forks that are involved when two events have either a common cause or a common effect. A fork may be described as open if it does not involve both a common cause and a common effect. Then it has been claimed that it is a fact about our world that all, or virtually all, open forks are open in the same direction—namely, towards the future.[5]

Can such features provide a satisfactory account of the direction of causation? One objection arises out of possible causal worlds that are much simpler than our own. In particular, consider a world that contains only a single particle, or a world that contains no fields, and nothing material except for two spheres, connected by a rod, that rotate endlessly about one another, on circular trajectories, in accordance with the laws of Newtonian physics. In the first world there are causal connections between the temporal parts of the single particle. In the second world each sphere will undergo acceleration of a constant magnitude, owing to the force exerted on it by the connecting rod. So both worlds certainly contain causal relations. But both worlds are also utterly devoid of changes of entropy, of propagation of order, and of open forks. So there is no hope of basing an account of the direction of causation upon any of those features.

What account can a reductionist give, then, of the direction of causation? The answer is that there is only one possibility. For, given that the simple worlds just described are completely symmetrical in time, events themselves do not exhibit any structure that serves to distinguish between the direction from cause to effect and the inverse one from effect to cause. So if the direction of causation is to be reduced to anything else, it can only be to the direction of time. But, then, in turn, one will have to be a realist with respect to the latter. There will be no possibility of reducing the direction of time to any structure present in the arrangement of events in time.

Could the reductionist instead respond by challenging the claim that such worlds contain causation? In the case of the rotating-spheres world, this could only be done by holding that it is logically impossible for Newton's second law of motion to be a causal law, while in the case of the single particle world, one would have to hold that identity over time is not logically supervenient upon causal relations between temporal parts. But, in addition, such a challenge would also involve a rejection of the following very plausible principle:

> *The intrinsicness of causation in a deterministic world.* If C_1 is a process in world W_1, and C_2 a process in world W_2, and if C_1 and C_2 are qualitatively identical, and if W_1 and W_2 are deterministic worlds with exactly the same laws of nature, then C_1 is a causal process if and only if C_2 is a causal process.

For consider a world that differs from the world with two rotating spheres by having additional objects that enter into causal interactions, and one of which collides with one of the spheres at some time t. In that world the process of the spheres rotating around one another during some interval when no object is colliding with them

---

[5] For the first, see Hans Reichenbach (1956: 117–43) and Adolf Grünbaum (1973: 254–64). For the second, see Karl Popper (1956: 538). For the third, see Reichenbach (1956: 161–3) and Wesley Salmon (1978: 696).

will be a causal process. But then, by the above principle, the rotation of the spheres about one another, during an interval of the same length, in the simple universe, must also be a causal process.

But is the principle of the intrinsicness of causation in a deterministic world correct? Some philosophers have claimed that it is not. In particular, it has been thought that a type of causal situation to which Jonathan Schaffer (2000: 165–81) has drawn attention—cases of 'trumping pre-emption'—show that the above principle must be rejected.

Here is a slight variant on a case described by Schaffer. Imagine a magical world where, first of all, spells can bring about their effects via direct action at a temporal distance, and secondly, earlier spells prevail over later ones. At noon Merlin casts a spell to turn a certain prince into a frog at midnight—a spell that is not preceded by any earlier, relevant spells. A bit later Morgana also casts a spell to turn the same prince into a frog at midnight. Schaffer argues, in a detailed and convincing way, that the simplest hypothesis concerning the relevant laws entails that the prince's turning into a frog is not a case of causal overdetermination: it is a case of pre-emption.

It differs, however, from more familiar cases of pre-emption, where one causal process pre-empts another by preventing the occurrence of some event that is crucial to the other process. In this action-at-a-temporal-distance case, both processes are fully present, since they consist simply of the casting of a spell plus the prince's turning into a frog at midnight.

A number of philosophers, including David Lewis (2000), have thought that the possibility of trumping pre-emption shows that the principle of the intrinsicness of causation in a deterministic world is false, the idea being that there could be two qualitatively identical processes, one of which is causal and the other not. For example, at time t_1 Morgana casts a spell that a person turn into a frog in one hour's time at a certain location. That person does turn into a frog, because there was no earlier, relevant spell. At time t_2 Morgana casts precisely the same type of spell. The person in question does turn into a frog, but the cause of this was not Morgana's spell, but an earlier, pre-empting spell.

Is this a counter-example to the intrinsicness principle? The answer is that it is not. Causes are states of affairs, and the state of affairs that, in the t_1 case, causes the person to turn into a frog is not simply Morgana's casting of the spell: it is that state of affairs together with the absence of earlier, relevant spells. So when the complete state of affairs that is the cause is focused upon, the two spell-casting cases are not qualitatively identical. Trumping pre-emption is not a counter-example to the principle of the intrinsicness of causation in a deterministic world.

4.2.1.2 Temporally 'Inverted' Worlds

It is the year 4004 BC. A Laplacean-style deity is about to create a world rather similar to ours, but one where Newtonian physics is true. Having selected the year AD 3000 as a good time for Armageddon, the deity works out what the world will be like at that point, down to the last detail. He then creates two spatially unrelated worlds: the one just mentioned, together with another whose initial state is a flipped-over version of the state of the first world immediately prior to Armageddon—i.e. the two states agree exactly, except that the velocities of the particles in the one state are exactly opposite to those in the other.

Consider, now, any two complete temporal slices of the first world, A and B, where A is earlier than B. Since the worlds are Newtonian ones, and since the laws of Newtonian physics are invariant with respect to time reversal, the world that starts off from the reversed, AD 3000-type state will go through corresponding states, B^* and A^*, where these are flipped-over versions of B and A respectively, and where B^* is earlier than A^*. So while the one world goes from a 4004 BC, Garden of Eden state to an AD 3000, pre-Armageddon state, the other world will move from a reversed, pre-Armageddon type of state to a reversed, Garden of Eden type of state.

In the first world the direction of causation will coincide with such things as the direction of increase in entropy, the direction of the propagation of order in non-entropically irreversible processes, and the direction defined by most open forks. But in the second world, where the direction of causation runs from the initial state created by the deity—that is, the flipped-over, AD 3000-type of state—through to the flipped-over, 4004 BC type of state, the direction in which entropy increases, the direction in which order is propagated, and the direction defined by open forks will all be the opposite one. So if any of the latter were used to define the direction of causation, it would generate the wrong result in the case of the second world.

As with the 'simple universes' argument, it is open to a reductionist to respond by holding that the direction of causation is to be defined in terms of the direction of time. But here, as before, this response is only available if one is prepared to adopt a realist view of the direction of time. For any reductionist account of the latter in terms of the structure exhibited by events in time cannot possibly generate the right results in both cases for two worlds that are 'inverted twins'—such as the two worlds just described.

4.2.2 Underdetermination Objections

A reductionist approach to causal relations is also exposed to a variety of 'underdetermination' objections, the thrust of which is that fixing all of the non-causal properties of, and relations between, events, all of the laws, both causal and non-causal, all of the dispositional properties, propensities, and objective chances, and, finally, the direction of causation for all possible causal relations that might obtain, does not always suffice to fix what causal relations there are between events.

The first of the two arguments that I shall set out here focuses upon a world with probabilistic laws, while the thrust of the second argument is that the same conclusion holds even in a fully deterministic world.

4.2.2.1 *The Argument from the Possibility of Uncaused Events plus Probabilistic, Causal Laws*

Three arguments that can be advanced against reductionist accounts of causation are variations on a single theme—all of them focusing upon problems that arise concerning causal relations in indeterministic worlds. However, they differ slightly in their assumptions. One argument assumes only that indeterministic causal laws are logically possible. A second argument, on the other hand, incorporates the further assumption that there is nothing incoherent in the idea of an uncaused event. The third argument—and the one that I shall set out here—also involves that assumption, plus the additional assumption that probabilistic laws are logically possible.[6]

The argument in question runs as follows. First, can statements of causal laws involve the concept of the relation of causation? Consider, for example, the following statement: 'It is a law that for any object x, the state of affairs that consists of x's having property F causes a state of affairs that consists of x's having property G'. Is this an acceptable way of formulating a possible causal law?

Some philosophers contend that it is not, and that the correct formulation is, instead, along the following lines:

(*) It is a causal law that for any object x, if x has property F at time t, then x has property G at $(t + \Delta t)$.

But what reason is there for thinking that it is the latter type of formulation that is correct? Certainly, as regards intuitions, there is no reason why there should not be laws that themselves involve the relation of causation. But in addition, the above claim is open to the following objection. First, the following two statements are logically equivalent:

(1) For any object x, if x has property F at time t, then x has property G at $(t + \Delta t)$;

(2) For any object x, if x lacks property G at time $(t + \Delta t)$, then x lacks property F at t.

Now replace the occurrence of (1) in (*) by an occurrence of (2), so that one has:

(**) It is a causal law that for any object x, if x lacks property G at time $(t + \Delta t)$, then x lacks property F at time t.

The problem now is that it may very well be the case that while (*) is true, (**) is false, since its being a causal law that for any object x, if x has property F at time t, then x has property G at $(t + \Delta t)$ certainly does not entail that there is a backward *causal* law to the effect that for any object x, if x lacks property G at time $(t + \Delta t)$, then x lacks property F at t. So anyone who holds that (*) is the

---

[6] All three arguments are set out in Tooley (1990*b*).

correct way to formulate causal laws needs to explain why substitution of logically equivalent statements in the relevant context does not preserve truth.

By contrast, no such problem arises if one holds that causal laws can instead be formulated as follows:

> It is a law that for any object x, the state of affairs that consists of x's having property F at time t causes a state of affairs that consists of x's having property G at time $(t + \Delta t)$.

Let us assume, then, that the natural way of formulating causal laws is acceptable. The next step in the argument involves the assumption that probabilistic laws are logically possible. Given these two assumptions, the following presumably expresses a possible causal law:

> (L_1)   It is a law that, for any object x, x's having property P for a time interval Δt causally brings it about, with probability 0.75, that x has property Q.

The final crucial assumption is that it is logically possible for there to be uncaused events.

Given these assumptions, consider a world, W, where objects that have property P for a time interval Δt go on to acquire property Q 76 per cent of the time, rather than 75 per cent of the time, and that this occurs even over the long term. Other things being equal, this would be grounds for thinking that the relevant law was not (L_1), but rather:

> (L_2)   It is a law that, for any object x, x's having property P for a time interval Δt causally brings it about, with probability 0.76, that x has property Q.

But other things might not be equal. In the first place, it might be the case that (L_1) was derivable from a very powerful, simple, and well-confirmed theory, whereas (L_2) was not. Secondly, one might have excellent evidence that there were totally uncaused events involving objects' acquiring property Q, and that the frequency with which that happened was precisely such as would lead to the expectation, given law (L_1), that situations in which an object had property P for a time interval Δt would be followed by the object's acquiring property Q 76 per cent of the time.

If that were the case, one would have reason for believing that, on average, over the long term, of the 76 cases out of a 100 where an object that has had property P for Δt and then acquires property Q, 75 of those cases will be ones where the acquisition of property Q is caused by the possession of property P, while 1 out of the 76 will be a case where property Q is spontaneously acquired.

There can, in short, be situations where there would be good reason for believing that not all cases where an object has property P for an interval Δt, and then acquires Q, are causally the same. There is, however, no hope of making sense of this, given a reductionist approach to causal relations. For the cases do not differ with respect to relevant non-causal properties and relations, nor with respect to causal or non-causal laws, nor with respect to the direction of causation in any potential causal relations. Moreover, if dispositional properties, propensities, and objective chances are logically supervenient upon causal laws plus non-causal states of affairs, then the cases do not differ with respect to dispositional properties, propensities, or objective chances. Alternatively, if one rejected the latter supervenience claim, and held that dispositions, propensities, and objective chances were ultimate, irreducible properties, that would not alter things, since the relevant dispositions, propensities, and objective chances would be the same in both cases. The conclusion, consequently, is a very strong one: causal relations between events are not logically supervenient upon the totality of states of affairs involving non-causal properties of, and relations between, events, all of the laws, both causal and non-causal, all of the dispositional properties, propensities, and objective chances, and, finally, the direction of causation for all possible causal relations that might obtain. But if causal relations are not logically supervenient upon these states of affairs, what can they be supervenient upon? It seems difficult to avoid the conclusion that causal relations must be ultimate and irreducible relations between states of affairs.

4.2.2.2 *The Argument from the Possibility of Exact Replicas*

The argument just set out appeals to the possibility of indeterministic worlds. The thrust of this second argument, by contrast, is that a reductionist approach to causation is exposed to counter-examples even in the case of deterministic worlds.

Suppose that event P causes event M. In general, there will certainly be nothing impossible about there also being an event, M^*, which has precisely the same properties[7] as M, both intrinsic and relational, but which is not caused by P. But what about relations? Is it logically possible for it also to be the case that either (1) the only relation between P and M is that of causation, or else (2) any other relation that holds between P and M also holds between P and M^*?

If either situation obtained, one would have a counter-example to a reductionist approach to causal relations. For on a reductionist view, P's causing M is logically supervenient upon the non-causal properties of, and the non-causal relations between, P and M, together with the causal laws. So if M^* has precisely the same non-causal properties as M, and also stands to P in the same non-causal relations as M does, then it follows, on a reductionist view, that P must also cause M^*, contrary to hypothesis.

But are such situations possible? In support of the claim that they are, consider the idea of a world, W, that satisfies the following two conditions. First, in W, the only *basic* external relations between different temporal slices of the world, or between parts of different temporal slices, are temporal relations and causal relations. Secondly, W possesses an appropriate sort of symmetry—specifically, rotational symmetry, such as characterized the simple Newtonian world, described

---

[7] The only restriction upon properties here is that they must not involve particulars—so that, for example, being 5 miles from the Grand Canyon does not count as a property.

earlier, that consisted of only two spheres, of the same type, connected by a rod, that rotated endlessly about one another on circular trajectories.

Are such worlds possible? The requirement of rotational symmetry seems unproblematic, but what about the requirement that the only basic external relations between different temporal slices of the world, or between parts of different temporal slices, are temporal relations and causal relations? Can one argue that, as a matter of logical necessity, there would have to be some other type of basic external relation that held between things at different times?

What might such a candidate be? About the only possibility that comes to mind is that of spatial relations between different objects at different times. But this suggestion seems problematic in two ways. First, it is not clear why a world need contain any basic, trans-temporal spatial relations. Secondly, such trans-temporal spatial relations are surely not such as could be immediately given in experience, and so some analysis of the concept of such relations is needed. The natural analysis, however, is in terms of spatial relations, at different times, to one and the same enduring frame of reference. But then the question arises of how the idea of an enduring frame of reference is to be explained. To bring in trans-temporal relations would render the analysis circular. But if one uses only temporal and causal relations, then the only basic external relations between things existing at different times will be temporal and causal relations.

Accordingly, the claim that worlds such as W are logically possible appears reasonable. If so, the argument proceeds as follows. Given that world W possesses rotational symmetry, there must be at least two particles that have precisely the same properties, both intrinsic and relational, in virtue of the rotational symmetry. Let A and A^* be two such particles, and let P be the extended temporal part of particle A that consists of all temporal parts of A which exist at times prior to some time t, and let M be the extended temporal part that consists of all the temporal parts of A that exist at t or later. Similarly, let P^* and M^* be the corresponding parts of the particle A^*.

The final assumption that the argument needs is that identity over time logically supervenes on causal relations between temporal parts. Given this assumption, it follows that P is causally related to M in a way that it is not to M^*. But M and M^* differ neither with respect to their non-causal properties, nor with regard to their non-causal relations to P, nor to anything that exists at intervening times. There is, therefore, no non-causal basis for P's being causally related to M but not to M^*.

Finally, as in the case of the previous argument, the situation is not changed if one also brings in dispositions, propensities, and objective chances: they cannot serve to make it the case that P is causally related to M in a way that it is not to M^*. Causal relations do not, therefore, logically supervene upon non-causal states of affairs, nor upon such states of affairs combined with causal laws, together with dispositions, propensities, and objective chances, plus facts about the direction of causation.

4.3 Summing Up

We have seen that reductionist accounts, both of causal laws and of causal relations, are open to very serious objections. In the case of laws, there are the problems posed by cosmic but accidental uniformities, by uninstantiated basic laws, and by probabilistic laws, together with the difficulty of showing that one is justified in believing that laws obtain, if one holds that laws are, basically, cosmic uniformities. In the case of causal relations, there are, first of all, the objections that turn upon the problem of explaining the direction of causation, as illustrated by the case of very simple universes, and the case of temporally 'inverted' universes. Secondly, there are the underdetermination objections, the thrust of which is that causal relations between events are not logically supervenient even upon the totality of all non-causal facts, together with all laws, both causal and non-causal, together with dispositions, propensities, and objective chances, plus the direction of causation in all potential causal processes.

5. Humean Reductionism

Many different accounts of causation, of a Humean reductionist sort, have been advanced, but four types are especially important. Of these, three involve analytic reductionism. First, there are approaches which start out from the general notion of a law of nature, then define the ideas of necessary, and sufficient, nomological conditions, and, finally, employ the latter concepts to explain what it is for one state of affairs to cause another. Secondly, there are approaches that employ subjunctive conditionals, either in an attempt to give a purely counterfactual analysis of causation (Lewis 1973b, 1986c), or as a supplement to other notions, such as that of agency (von Wright 1971). Thirdly, there are approaches that employ the idea of probability, either to formulate a purely probabilistic analysis (Reichenbach 1956; Good 1961–2; Suppes 1970; Eells 1991)—where the central idea is that a cause must, in some way, make its effect more likely—or as a supplement to other ideas, such as that of a continuous process (Salmon 1984). Finally, a fourth approach involves the idea of offering, not an analytic reduction of causation, but a contingent identification of causation, as it is *in this world*, with a relation whose only constituents are non-causal properties and relations. One idea, for example, is that causal processes can be identified with continuous processes in which relevant quantities are conserved (Salmon 1997, 1998; Dowe 2000a,b).

5.1 Causes and Nomological Conditions

One very familiar approach to causation involves attempting to analyse causation in terms of nomological concepts. Given the idea of a law of nature, one can define what it is for a state of affairs to be a nomologically necessary condition of some other state of affairs, or a nomologically sufficient condition of another state of affairs. Similarly, one can define what it is for a state of affairs to be nomologically necessary in the circumstances, or nomologically sufficient in the circumstances, for another state of affairs. The proposal is then that what it is for one state of affairs to cause another can be analysed in terms of these nomological concepts.

According to one version, a cause is a condition that is necessary in the circumstances for its effect, where to say that event c is necessary in the circumstances for event e is roughly to say that there is some law, l, and some circumstance, s, such that the non-occurrence of c, in circumstance s, together with law l, logically entails the non-occurrence of e. (Ignoring temporal constraints upon the relation between cause and effect, this answer is essentially that advanced by Ernest Nagel (1961: 559–60). It is also considered seriously, but rejected, by Michael Scriven (1966, esp. sect. 8, pp. 258–62), while a very similar view is defended by Raymond Martin (1972: 205–11).)

Alternatively it may be held instead that a cause is a condition that is sufficient in the circumstances for its effect, where to say that event c is sufficient in the circumstances for event e is to say that there is some law, l, and some circumstance, s, such that the occurrence of c, in circumstance s, together with law l, logically entails the occurrence of e. (If, once again, we ignore the addition of temporal constraints, this answer is essentially equivalent, for example, to views advanced by John Stuart Mill (1874: III. v), R. B. Braithwaite (1953: 315–18), H. L. A. Hart and A. M. Honoré (1959: 106–7), C. G. Hempel (1965: 349), and Karl Popper (1972: 91).)

Another possibility is that for one event to cause another is for its occurrence to be both necessary and sufficient in the circumstances for the occurrence of the other event—a view that was seriously entertained, but ultimately rejected, by Richard Taylor (1966, ch. 3).

These accounts, however, are open to a number of very serious objections. First, it seems very plausible, especially in view of quantum physics, that probabilistic causal laws are logically possible, and while such laws do not preclude there being nomologically necessary conditions for a given type of event, they do entail that there are no nomologically sufficient conditions. So if probabilistic causal laws are possible, all of the above accounts, except for the first, are ruled out.

Secondly, all of the above fall prey to the underdetermination problem, set out in the preceding section.

Thirdly, it would certainly seem that there could be laws that are not causal—such as, for example, Newton's third law of motion. But given that law, all of the above analyses have the unacceptable consequence that A's exerting a certain force on B at a given time causes B to exert an equal and opposite force on A at that very same time.

One way of attempting to escape this objection would be by reformulating the account in terms of basic laws, and then arguing that all non-causal laws must be derivable from causal laws. But it is not at all easy to see how one might establish the latter thesis.

Finally, and most seriously of all, no account of causation in terms of nomological relations alone can provide any account of the direction of causation. Thus, if our world were a Newtonian one, where the basic laws are time-symmetric, the total state of the universe in 1950 would have been both necessary and sufficient not only for the total state in 2050, but also for the total state in 1850. It would therefore follow, on any of the above accounts, that events in 1950 had caused events in 1850.

The only way to escape this problem within the context of this general approach is by adding the requirement that one event can be the cause of another event only if the one is temporally prior to the other. To make this part of the definition of a cause seems, however, unsatisfactory. For while it may be true that a cause necessarily precedes its effect, if this is true, it should be a deep analytical result, not an immediate consequence of the analysis of causation—given that readers and writers of science fiction have certainly thought that they could imagine scenarios involving backward causation.

5.2 Counterfactual Approaches

A second important reductionist approach attempts to analyse causation in terms of counterfactuals. One way of arriving at this approach is by analysing causation in terms of necessary and/or sufficient conditions, but then interpreting the latter, not in terms of nomological connections, as above, but in terms of subjunctive conditionals. Thus one can say that c is necessary in the circumstances for e if, and only if, had c not occurred, e would not have occurred, and that c is sufficient in the circumstances for e if, and only if, had e not occurred, c would not have occurred.

John Mackie took this tack in developing a more sophisticated analysis of causation in terms of necessary and sufficient conditions. Thus, after defining an INUS condition of an event as an insufficient but necessary part of a condition which is itself unnecessary but exclusively sufficient for the event, and then arguing that c's being a cause of e entails c's being at least an INUS condition of e, Mackie asked how necessary and sufficient conditions should be understood. For general causal statements, Mackie favoured a nomological account, but for singular causal statements, he argued for an analysis in terms of subjunctive conditionals (1965: 254).

The most fully worked-out counterfactual approach, however, is that of David Lewis (1973b).[8] His original, basic strategy involved analysing causation in terms of a narrower notion of causal dependence, and then analysing causal dependence counterfactually: (1) an event c causes an event e if and only if there is a chain of causally dependent events linking e with c; (2) an event g is causally dependent upon an event f if and only if, had f not occurred, g would not have occurred.

Causes, so construed, need not be necessary for their effects, since counterfactual dependence, and hence causal dependence, are not necessarily transitive. Nevertheless, Lewis's approach is very closely related to necessary condition analyses of causation, since the more basic relation of causal dependence is a matter of one event's being counterfactually necessary in the circumstances for another event.

How satisfactory are analyses of causation in terms of counterfactuals? One objection to Lewis's approach is that it is formulated in terms of events, and it then becomes a delicate matter to set out an account of the individuation of events that will not generate unwelcome consequences concerning causal relations (Lewis 1986b; Bennett 1998). A better approach, it would seem, would be to view the basic causal relata as states of affairs, and thus to regard the basic singular causal statements as those that explicitly specify the causally relevant factors, and that do not incorporate causally extraneous information. For not only does this seem metaphysically more perspicuous, it also enables one to avoid getting one's account of causation entangled in the problem of the individuation of events.

Of course, we certainly make causal statements that provide no information at all about what properties and/or relations enter into the causally relevant states of affairs—such as 'Mary's action caused an interesting occurrence'. But it is quite a straightforward matter to analyse such event statements in terms of metaphysically more basic statements concerning causal relations between states of affairs.

A second objection—originally advanced by Jaegwon Kim (1973b)—focuses upon the fact that there are a number of counterfactuals that have nothing to do with causation. If, for example, John and Mary are married at time t, it is true that if John had not existed at time t, then Mary would not have been married at time t. But John's existing at time t is not a cause of the simultaneous state of affairs that is Mary's being married at time t.

How might this objection be handled? There has been relatively little discussion of this problem, but it would seem that one will have to draw a line between counterfactuals whose truth depends upon laws of nature, and those whose truth does not so depend. Exactly how this is to be done, given the type of approach to counterfactuals that must be employed here, is not entirely clear.

A third objection is that some counterfactuals are based upon non-causal laws. Thus, for example, counterfactuals such as 'If A had not exerted force F upon object

---

[8] For later discussion, and some revisions, see Lewis (1986c).

B, then B would not have exerted a force G upon A' will be true in Newtonian worlds by virtue of Newton's third law of motion. On Lewis's counterfactual analysis, it follows that A's exerting force F on B causes B's exerting force G on A, and vice versa—which is not the case.

A fourth objection involves overdetermination, or redundant causation, where two events, C and D, are followed by an event E, and where each of C and D would have been causally sufficient, on its own, to produce E. If it is true that C causes E and that D causes E, then one has a counter-example to Lewis's counterfactual analysis. Lewis contends that we are uncertain what to say here. Do C and D each cause E, or do they jointly cause E? But is Lewis right about this? If, for example, Lewis (1973a: 73) were right in holding that 'a contingent generalization is a *law of nature* if and only if it appears as a theorem (or axiom) in each of the deductive systems that achieves a best combination of simplicity and strength', then it would seem that it would have to be the case that C causes E and D causes E, since more complicated generalizations are needed if one is to say instead that it is only the combination of C together with D that causes E. Similarly, if simplicity is, instead, epistemologically relevant, will not the conclusion be the same? So overdetermination is a problem.

A fifth objection involves cases of pre-emption—since here, too, one has causation without causal dependence. Until recently, the discussion of pre-emption had focused on cases where one causal process pre-empts another by blocking the occurrence of some state of affairs in the other process, and a number of ways of attempting to handle this type of pre-emption have been advanced—involving such notions as fragility of events, quasi-dependence, continuous processes, minimal-counterfactual sufficiency, and minimal-dependence sets (Lewis 1986c; Menzies 1989; McDermott 1995; Ramachandran 1997). But none of these approaches can handle the case of trumping pre-emption (Schaffer 2000), where, intuitively, pre-emption occurs, even though both processes are fully present.

David Lewis's own reaction to the problem posed by trumping pre-emption has been to replace his previous counterfactual accounts by a new, 'causation as influence', account:

Where C and E are distinct actual events, let us say that C *influences* E if and only if there is a substantial range $C_1, C_2, \ldots$ of different not-too-distant alterations of C (including the actual alteration of C) and there is a range $E_1, E_2, \ldots$ of alterations of E, at least some of which differ, such that if C_1 had occurred, E_1 would have occurred, and if C_2 had occurred, E_2 would have occurred, and so on. (Lewis 2000: 190)

But this account does not really provide an answer to the trumping pre-emption objection. For suppose that, contrary to what is required for Lewis's idea of causation as influence to be applicable, there is *not* a substantial range $C_1, C_2, \ldots$ of different not-too-distant alterations of C: there is only C, or its absence. Suppose further that there is a substantial range of alterations of D—D_1, D_2, and so on—and where, in the absence of C, D will give rise to E, D_1 to E_1, D_2 to E_2, and so on, and where E, E_1, E_2, etc. are all distinct. Suppose, finally, that if C accompanies any of D, D_1, D_2, etc., then it is always E that comes about. Then surely the simplest hypothesis will involve laws according to which C pre-empts all of D, D_1, D_2, etc. Consequently, there are cases of trumping pre-emption that Lewis's revised account cannot handle.

Finally, there is the most serious objection of all—an objection that applies to every attempt to analyse causation in terms of counterfactuals, regardless of the details. The thrust of this objection is that, on the one hand, classical analyses of counterfactuals—including ones that treat such conditionals as arguments, rather than as statements—invoke causal laws, and so such analyses cannot be employed on pain of circularity; and, on the other hand, the only alternative to such approaches is a Stalnaker–Lewis style of account in terms of similarity relations over possible worlds (Stalnaker 1968; Lewis 1973a), and accounts of the latter sort are exposed to decisive objections.

Consider, then, one way of formulating the latter sort of approach, according to which a counterfactual 'If p were the case, then q would be the case' is true in a given world, W, if and only if either there is a possible world in which both p and q are true that is more similar to W than any possible world in which p is true and q is false, or else there are no possible worlds where p is true (cf. Stalnaker 1968: 170; Lewis 1973a: 16). Such an account is exposed to a number of objections. To begin with, there is a slight variant on a type of objection originally advanced against a Stalnaker–Lewis style of account of counterfactuals by philosophers such as Jonathan Bennett (1974), Kit Fine (1975), and a number of other philosophers who contended that the Stalnaker–Lewis account generated the wrong truth-values for counterfactuals in which the consequent could only be true if the world were radically different from the actual world. Thus Fine, for example, argued that the following counterfactual would turn out to be false on a Stalnaker–Lewis approach:

If Nixon had pressed the button, there would have been a nuclear holocaust.

But Lewis was able (in Lewis 1979), by assigning certain weights to big miracles, to perfect matches of particular facts throughout a stretch of time, and to small miracles, to make it the case that the Nixon and the button counterfactual came out true, rather than false.

Lewis's escape, however, cannot handle the general problem that Fine, Bennett, and others raised. For his solution depends upon the fact that Nixon's pressing the button is an event which would have multiple effects, and which thus is such that it would require a very big miracle to remove all traces of that event, and so to achieve a perfect match with the future of the actual world. As a result, one needs only to construct a case involving an event that has only a single effect. Then Lewis's account of similarity will not block the counter-example.

Imagine, then, a world that is rather different from ours in certain respects. First, it is a world where it is possible to bring about physical events psychokinetically. Secondly, it is a world where an act of willing that something be brought about psychokinetically involves no physical change: it consists, instead, only of an appropriate state involving emergent qualia. Finally, such a qualia state is almost causally impotent: its only effect is the psychokinetic occurrence of the event that was willed; there is not even any memory trace of the relevant act of willing in the person who performed the act.

Alternatively, if the idea of a direct causal connection between the act of psychokinetic willing and the occurrence of the event willed is thought unacceptable, one can arrange a mechanism: there can be a non-branching causal chain that proceeds along a straight line to the location where the event occurs, and where no part of the intervening chain has any other effects.

A strange world! Yet surely logically possible. But, then, imagine Nixon—or a Nixon counterpart—in such a world, and one where he does not will that the button be pressed psychokinetically. What would be the case if Nixon, in such a world, *had* willed that the button be pressed psychokinetically? The correct answer, surely, is given by the following counterfactual:

> If Nixon had willed that the button be pressed psychokinetically, then that would have happened, and there would have been a nuclear holocaust.

But on Lewis's approach, this counterfactual will be false. For an act of willing that something happen psychokinetically, in the world that we are imagining, will have only one effect: the occurrence of the event that was willed to happen. There is no causal branching, and so only a single, small, localized miracle is required to bring it about that, although Nixon wills that the button be pressed psychokinetically, the button is nevertheless not pressed, and so, instead of a nuclear holocaust, there is a perfect match with the future of the original world in which Nixon does not will that the button be pressed psychokinetically. So if the absence of a small, localized, single miracle contributes less to similarity than does a perfect match with respect to all future states of affairs, then it follows that the above counterfactual is false, rather than true. So Lewis's escape does not work: it fails to handle a variation on the Nixon-and-the-button example.

There are many other objections to a Stalnaker–Lewis approach to the analysis of counterfactuals. Here I shall mention only two—connected with arguments set out above, in Section 4. First, a Stalnaker–Lewis account cannot handle the case of simple worlds. Lewis's version, for example, entails that there is no counterfactual dependence, and therefore no causation, and so no identity over time, in such worlds. Secondly, there are the temporally inverted twin worlds: a Stalnaker–Lewis approach will entail that there is counterfactual dependence in the flipped-over world, but it will assign the wrong direction to that dependence.

5.3 Probabilistic Approaches

One of the more significant developments in the philosophy of causation in this century has been the emergence of the idea that causation is not restricted to deterministic processes—a conclusion that appears to be strongly supported by quantum physics. What implications might this conclusion have with respect to the analysis of causal concepts? One suggestion, advanced by philosophers such as Reichenbach, Good, and Suppes, is that probabilistic notions should play a central role in the analysis of causal concepts.

This basic idea of analysing causation in probabilistic terms can be carried out in a variety of ways. At the heart of any such programme, however, is the idea that causes must, in some way, make their effects more likely. The traditional way of attempting to capture this idea within probabilistic approaches to causation has been in terms of the notion of *positive statistical relevance*, where an event of type B is positively relevant to an event of type A if and only if the conditional probability of an event of type A relative to an event of type B is greater than the unconditional probability of an event of type A. Thus Suppes (1984: 151), for example, introduces the notion of a prima facie cause, defined as follows: 'An event B is a prima facie cause of an event A if and only if (i) B occurs earlier than A, and (ii) the conditional probability of A occurring when B occurs is greater than the unconditional probability of A occurring.'

More recently, however, a number of philosophers have argued that the correct way to capture the idea that a cause makes its effect more likely is not in terms of a difference between the conditional and unconditional probabilities of a given type of event, but, rather, in terms of appropriate subjunctive conditionals concerning the objective chances of the individual event in question (Mellor 1986, 1995; Lewis 1986c; Menzies 1989). Briefly put, the basic idea is that a sufficient condition of C's being a cause of E is that C and E are actual, individual events such that the objective chance of E's occurring is greater given the occurrence of C than it would have been if C had not occurred.

While these two approaches are similar in many respects, there is nevertheless a very great metaphysical gulf between them, since the second approach has to invoke ontologically ultimate, objective chances, and, in doing so, it is embracing an ontology that involves non-Humean states of affairs. For this reason, a discussion of the latter approach will be left until the next section.

Perhaps the most crucial test for any theory of causation is whether it can provide a satisfactory account of the direction of causation. How does the present theory fare? The first thing to note is that the postulate that a cause raises the probability of its effect does not itself provide any direction for causal processes. For when the following equation for conditional probabilities

$$\text{Prob}(E/C) \times \text{Prob}(C) = \text{Prob}(E \,\&\, C) = \text{Prob}(C/E) \times \text{Prob}(E)$$

is rewritten as

$$\text{Prob}(E/C)/\text{Prob}(E) = \text{Prob}(C/E)/\text{Prob}(C),$$

one can see that $\text{Prob}(E/C) > \text{Prob}(E)$ if and only if $\text{Prob}(C/E) > \text{Prob}(C)$. So causes raise the probabilities of their effects only if effects also raise the probabilities of their causes.

How, then, can the direction of causation be analysed probabilistically? The most promising suggestion was set out by Reichenbach in his book *The Direction of Time* (1956). Reichenbach's proposal involves the following elements: first, what he referred to as 'the Principle of the Common Cause'; secondly, a probabilistic characterization of a 'conjunctive fork'; thirdly, a proof that correlations between event types can be explained via conjunctive forks; and, fourthly, a distinction between open forks and closed forks.

As regards the first element, Reichenbach's principle of the common cause is as follows: 'If an improbable coincidence has occurred, there must exist a common cause' (Reichenbach 1956: 157). Here the basic claim is that if events of type A, say, are more likely to occur given events of type B than in the absence of events of type B, and if the explanation of this is not that events of type A are caused by events of type B, or vice versa, then there must be some third type of event—say, C—such that events of type C cause both events of type A and events of type B.

Secondly, there is Reichenbach's characterization of the idea of a conjunctive fork, which—using a slightly different notation—can be put as follows (1956: 159): Events of types A, B, and C form a conjunctive fork if and only if:

(1) $\text{Prob}(A \& B/C) = \text{Prob}(A/C) \times \text{Prob}(B/C)$
(2) $\text{Prob}(A \& B/\text{not-}C) = \text{Prob}(A/\text{not-}C) \times \text{Prob}(B/\text{not-}C)$
(3) $\text{Prob}(A/C) > \text{Prob}(A/\text{not-}C)$
(4) $\text{Prob}(B/C) > \text{Prob}(B/\text{not-}C)$.

Thirdly, Reichenbach then shows that, provided that none of the relevant probabilities is equal to zero, equations (1)–(4) entail:

(5) $\text{Prob}(A \& B) > \text{Prob}(A) \times \text{Prob}(B)$.

This in turn entails:

(6) $\text{Prob}(A/B) > \text{Prob}(A)$
(7) $\text{Prob}(B/A) > \text{Prob}(B)$.

So we see that the existence of a conjunctive fork involving event types A, B, and C provides an explanation of a statistical correlation between the event types A and B.

Finally, Reichenbach distinguishes between open forks and closed forks. Suppose that events of types A, B, and C form a conjunctive fork, and that there is no other type of event—call it E—such that events of types A, B, and E form a conjunctive fork. Then A, B, and C form an open fork. On the other hand, if there is another type of event, E, such that events of types A, B, and E also form a conjunctive fork, what one has is a closed fork.

As Reichenbach emphasizes, there can certainly be conjunctive forks that involve common effects, rather than common causes (1956: 161–2). But since conjunctive forks can, as we have just seen, explain statistical correlations, if there were an *open* fork that involved a common effect, then the relevant statistical correlation would be explained, even though there was no common cause, and this would violate the principle of the common cause. Hence, conjunctive forks involving a common effect must always be closed forks. All open forks, therefore, must involve a common cause, and so the direction of causation is fixed by the direction given by open forks.

This is a subtle and ingenious attempt to offer a probabilistic analysis of the relation of causation, and one that appeals only to Humean states of affairs. Unfortunately, it appears to be open to a number of decisive objections.

In the first place, there are strong grounds for holding that Reichenbach's crucial claim that it is impossible for there to be open forks that involve a common effect rather than a common cause is mistaken. For one thing, if the laws of nature are time-symmetric, then, regardless of whether they are probabilistic or non-probabilistic, for every possible universe there must be a temporally inverted twin. So for every universe with time-symmetric laws that contains forks open to the future, there will be a possible universe that is a temporal mirror image, with forks open to the past.

Such temporally inverted universes may, of course, be extremely unlikely, but that does not matter, since Reichenbach's claim is that universes with forks open to the past are impossible.

In addition, however, one can also show, by a different argument, which runs as follows, that such forks are not, in fact, especially unlikely. Suppose that A and B are types of events that do not cause one another, and for which there is no common cause. Then it *might* be the case that the conditional probability of an event of type A given an event of type B was *exactly equal* to the unconditional probability of an event of type A, but surely this is not necessary. Indeed, it would be more likely that the two probabilities were at least slightly different, so that the conditional probability of an event of type A given an event of type B was either greater than or less than the unconditional probability of an event of type A.

Let us suppose, then, that the second of these alternatives is the case. Suppose, further, that the occurrence of an event of type A is a causally necessary condition for the occurrence of a slightly later event of type E, and, similarly, that the occurrence of an event of type B is a causally necessary condition for the occurrence of a slightly later event of type E.

Finally, let us suppose—as is perfectly compatible with the preceding assumptions—that the relative numbers of all possible combinations of events of types A, B, and E, throughout the whole history of the universe, are given by Table 13.1:

Table 13.1

	E		Not-E	
	A	Not-A	A	Not-A
B	1	0	18	12
Not-B	0	0	42	28

From this table, one can see that $\text{Prob}(A) = 61/101$, or about 0.604, while $\text{Prob}(A/B) = 19/31$, or slightly less than 0.613, so that, if the absolute numbers are not too large, there will not be anything especially remarkable about the fact that $\text{Prob}(A/B) > \text{Prob}(A)$.

Next, examining the numbers that fall under 'E', we can see that we have the following probabilities:

$\text{Prob}(A/E) = 1$

$\text{Prob}(B/E) = 1$

$\text{Prob}(A \& B/E) = 1.$

Hence the following is true:

(1) $\text{Prob}(A \& B/E) = \text{Prob}(A/E) \times \text{Prob}(B/E).$

Similarly, examining the numbers that fall under 'Not-E', we can see that we have the following probabilities:

$\text{Prob}(A/\text{Not-}E) = 60/100 = 0.6$

$\text{Prob}(B/\text{Not-}E) = 30/100 = 0.3$

$\text{Prob}(A \& B/\text{Not-}E) = 18/100 = 0.18.$

So the following three equations are also true:

(2) $\text{Prob}(A \& B/\text{not-}E) = \text{Prob}(A/\text{not-}E) \times \text{Prob}(B/\text{not-}E)$

(3) $\text{Prob}(A/E) > \text{Prob}(A/\text{not-}E)$

(4) $\text{Prob}(B/E) > \text{Prob}(B/\text{not-}E).$

Hence, in a universe of the sort just described, the three types of events A, B, and E form a conjunctive fork. Moreover, since there is, by hypothesis, no type of event, C, that is a common cause of events of types A and B, it is therefore the case that A, B, and E constitute an open fork. This open fork then defines the relevant direction of causation as the direction that runs from events of type E towards events of the two types, A and B, that are causally necessary conditions for the occurrence of an event of type E.

In short, not only is it logically possible to have an open fork that involves a common effect, rather than a common cause, but there need not be any significant unlikelihood associated with the occurrence of such an open fork. The direction of open forks cannot, therefore, serve to define the direction of causation.

The conclusion, accordingly, is that the type of probabilistic approach we are considering fails a crucial test: it is unable to provide a satisfactory account of the direction of causation. But the theory is also defective in a number of other ways. In particular, it runs afoul of all of the general objections to reductionist accounts of causation. Thus, it cannot handle the case of simple worlds; it assigns the wrong direction to causation in the case of temporally inverted worlds; and it fails to provide anything upon which causal relations can supervene in the underdetermination cases.

Another shortcoming is this. One of the most appealing approaches to the problem of offering an account of the direction of time is a causal theory. Other things being equal, then, one would prefer an account of causation that does not immediately rule out a causal analysis of the direction of time. Can one, then, combine a probabilistic account of causation with a causal theory of the direction of time? The answer is that it does not appear that one can. The reason is that the relevant statistical relations between types of events cannot simply be relations between two types of events, each of which can be located anywhere—since otherwise the probability of an event of type A given an event of type B would be either zero or one. So it looks as if the probabilities in question must concern, for example, the likelihood of there being an event of type A in the vicinity of an event of type B, and *slightly later*.[9] But if that is right, then probabilistic theories presuppose the earlier-than relation, so that the latter relation cannot be analysed in probabilistic terms.

We have not yet considered the most fundamental claim involved in probabilistic theories—the claim, namely, that causes always make their effects more likely than they would otherwise be. Is this true? The answer appears to be that it is not—as even some philosophers who are sympathetic to the general idea that there is some connection between causation and probability, such as Daniel Hausman (1998), have realized. For consider the following case. Assume that there are atoms of type T that satisfy the following conditions:

(1) any atom of type T must be in one of the three mutually exclusive states—A, B, and C;

(2) the probabilities that an atom of type T in states A, B, and C, respectively, will emit an electron are, respectively, 0.9, 0.7, and 0.2;

---

[9] One defender of a probabilistic approach to causation who is especially clear on this matter is Ellery Eells (1991, ch. 5).

(3) the probabilities that an atom of type T is in state A is 0.5; in state B, 0.4; in state C, 0.1.

Now, given that, for example, putting an atom of type T into state B would be quite an effective means of getting it to emit an electron, it is surely true that its being in state B is a probabilistic cause of its emitting an electron. But this would not be so if the above account were correct. For if D is the property of emitting an electron, the unconditional probability that an atom of type T will emit an electron is given by $\text{Prob}(D) = \text{Prob}(D/A) \times \text{Prob}(A) + \text{Prob}(D/B) \times \text{Prob}(B) + \text{Prob}(D/C) \times \text{Prob}(C) = (0.9)(0.5) + (0.7)(0.4) + (0.2)(0.1) = 0.75$. But the conditional probability of D given B was specified as 0.7. We have, therefore, that $\text{Prob}(D) > \text{Prob}(D/B)$. So if a cause had to raise the probability of its effect, it would follow that an atom of type T's being in state B could not be a probabilistic cause of its emitting an electron. This, however, is unacceptable. So the thesis that a cause must raise the probability of its effect, in the relevant sense, must be rejected.

The thesis that causes necessarily make their effects more likely is exposed, therefore, to a decisive objection. The basis of this objection is the possibility of there being one or more other causal factors that are incompatible with the given factor, and more efficacious than it. For, given such a possibility, events of type C may be the cause of events of type E even though the probability of an event of type E, given the occurrence of an event of type C, is less than the unconditional probability of an event of type E.

But is there nothing, then, in the rather widely shared intuition that causation is related to increase in probability? The answer is that causation may be related to increase in probability, but not in the way proposed by those who favour a probabilistic analysis of causation. For it would seem to be true, for example, that the logical probability of an event of type E, given that an event of type C has occurred, and that events of type C *causally* necessitate events of type E, will be higher than the a priori logical probability of an event of type E.[10] But this relation cannot, of course, be used as part of a probabilistic *analysis* of causation, since the relationship itself involves the concept of causation.

5.4 Conserved Quantities and Continuous Processes

The three Humean approaches considered so far all offer a reductionist *analysis* of causation. Analytic reductionism is not, however, the only form that reductionism with respect to causation can take. Thus, even if it does turn out to be the case that

---

[10] Or, at least, this will be so, provided that it is not the case either that the logical probability of an event of type E is equal to one, or that the logical probability of an event of type C is equal to zero. For a proof, see Tooley (1987: 277–8, 325–8).

causal facts are not logically supervenient upon non-causal ones, there is still the possibility of an a posteriori identification of causal and non-causal facts.

The idea of a non-analytic reduction of causation has been advanced over the past few years by a number of philosophers. Thus David Fair (1979), for example, proposed that basic causal relations can, as a consequence of our scientific knowledge, be identified with certain physicalistic relations between objects—relations that can be characterized in terms of the transference of either energy or momentum between the objects involved; while, more recently, Wesley Salmon (1997) and Phil Dowe (2000a,b) have proposed that causal processes are to be identified with continuous processes in which quantities are conserved. Thus Dowe (2000b: 173), for example, suggests the following account:

> *Causal connection.* Interactions I_1, I_2 are linked by a causal connection in virtue of causal process p only if some conserved quantity exchanged in I_2 is also exchanged in I_1, and transmitted by p.

What are the general prospects for a contingent identification of causation with such physicalistic relations? Perhaps the first point that needs to be made is that once one abandons the view that causal relations are logically supervenient upon non-causal states of affairs, and embraces an a posteriori reduction, one is left with the question of how the concept of causation is to be analysed.

But does someone who advances a contingent identity thesis really need to grapple with this issue? Can it not be left simply as an open question? Perhaps, but the situation in the case of contingent identity theses concerning the mind suggests that this may very well not be so. For until a satisfactory analysis has been offered, there is the possibility of an argument to the effect that it is *logically impossible* for causal relations to be identical with any physicalistic relations. In particular, might it not plausibly be argued that the concept of causation is the concept of a relation that possesses a certain *intrinsic* nature, so that causation must be one and the same relation in all possible worlds, just as what it is for something to be a law of nature cannot vary from one world to another? But if this is right, then one can appeal to the possibility of worlds that involve causation, but that do not contain the physicalistic relations in question, or that involve non-continuous causal connections between events, in order to draw the conclusion that causation cannot, even in this world, be *identical* with the relevant physicalistic relation.

What is needed, in short, if an a posteriori reduction is to be sustainable, is a satisfactory analysis of the concept of causation according to which causation, rather than having an intrinsic nature, is simply whatever relation happens to play a certain role in a given possible world. But at present, no such analysis seems to be at hand.

A second problem for any contingent identification of causation with a physicalistic relation arises from the fact that one needs to find a physicalistic relation that, like causation, has a direction, but where the direction of the physicalistic relation does not itself need to be cashed out in terms of causation. In Fair's account, for example, the appeal is to the direction of the *transference* of energy and/or momentum, and this is exposed to the immediate objection that the concept of transference itself involves the idea of causation.

Fair's response to this problem is that the direction of transference can be explained in temporal terms, rather than causal ones (1979: 240–1). But this response involves substantial assumptions concerning the relation between the direction of time and the direction of causation. In particular, many philosophers think that the direction of time is itself to be explained in terms of the direction of causation—a view that is immediately precluded by Fair's account.

If, on the other hand, one appeals to features such as the direction of the increase in entropy, or of open forks, etc., to supply the direction for causal processes, one encounters the problem that there are simple worlds, and temporally 'inverted' worlds, that have the same laws, and the same fundamental particles, as our world, but where the contingent identification being proposed generates either the wrong direction for causal processes, or none at all.

A third difficulty concerns the relation between brain states and the properties of experiences, or between thoughts and decisions and subsequent action. Thus, many philosophers hold that the phenomenal, qualitative properties of experiences cannot be reduced to non-emergent physicalistic properties. But if this is right, is it plausible that some quantity is conserved when a brain event gives rise to an experience, or that there is a transference of energy and/or momentum from the fundamental particles of physics to states of affairs involving qualia? Or is it plausible that when a thought results in behaviour, some conserved quantity was transmitted from the thought to the brain? If these suppositions are not plausible, then any identification of causation with physicalistic relations presupposes the highly controversial claim that the mind involves no properties other than those that are reducible to the properties and relations that enter into theories in physics.

In view of the above points, the prospects for a physicalistic reduction of causation do not appear bright.

6. NON-HUMEAN REDUCTIONISM

Humean states of affairs were characterized recursively in Section 2, the basic idea being that distinct Humean states of affairs cannot stand in logical relations to one another. A reduction can be defined, then, as non-Humean if the reduction base involves non-Humean states of affairs.

What are some possible examples of non-Humean states of affairs? The two that are especially important in the present context are the existence of strong laws—or, at least, non-probabilistic ones—and the possession, by individuals, of irreducible dispositional properties. Thus, as regards the former, strong laws, whether they are conceived of as second-order relations between universals, as by Dretske, Tooley, and Armstrong, or as structureless states of affairs, as by Carroll, are by definition states of affairs that entail the existence of certain Humean states of affairs—namely, cosmic regularities involving only Humean properties—which, it appears, they neither are identical with, nor overlap.

The idea that strong laws commit one to logical connections between distinct states of affairs has been especially emphasized by Bas van Fraassen (1989), who views it as a decisive objection to such a conception of laws. But whether strong laws do involve non-Humean states of affairs turns out to depend upon precisely what account is given of the ontology involved, since it can be shown that if transcendent universals are admitted, there are metaphysical hypotheses concerning the existence of such universals that do clearly and straightforwardly entail the existence of corresponding regularities (Tooley 1987: 123–9).

Secondly, dispositional properties, if they are conceived of as ontologically ultimate, irreducible properties, rather than as being logically supervenient upon non-dispositional properties plus causal laws, enter into non-Humean states of affairs. This can be seen most clearly if one considers a world where time is discrete. In such a world, if water-solubility were an irreducible dispositional property of an object, then an object's having that property at some time t, and being in (unsaturated) water at time t, together with the existence of the object and the water at the next instant, would logically entail that the object is dissolving at that next instant.

What are the most important types of non-Humean reductionist approaches to causation? I think that there are two. One involves the idea that causal states of affairs are logically supervenient upon non-causal properties and relations—including the earlier-than relation—plus strong laws. The other involves an account in which objective chances play a crucial role.

The first of these approaches is closely related, however, to one of the realist accounts of causation that will be considered in Section 7. In this section, accordingly, I shall focus upon accounts of the second sort.

6.1 Causation and Objective Chances

A number of philosophers—including Edward Madden and Rom Harré (1975), Nancy Cartwright (1989), and C. B. Martin (1993)—have both advocated an ontology in which irreducible dispositional properties, powers, propensities, chances, and the like occupy a central place, and maintained that such an ontology is relevant to causation. Often, however, the details have been rather sparse. But the basic idea of analysing causation in terms of objective chances was set out in 1986 both by D. H. Mellor and by David Lewis (1986c) and then, more recently, Mellor has offered a very detailed statement and defence of this general approach in his book *The Facts of Causation* (1995).

6.1.1 *Lewis's Account: Counterfactuals and Objective Chances*

This general approach to causation was briefly sketched by David Lewis in a postscript to his article 'Causation':

> there is a second case to be considered: c occurs, e has some chance x of occurring, and as it happens e does occur; if c had not occurred, e would still have had some chance y of occurring, but only a very slight chance since y would have been very much less than x. We cannot quite say that without the cause, the effect would not have occurred; but we can say that without the cause, the effect would have been very much less probable than it actually was. In this case also, I think we should say that e depends causally on c, and that c is a cause of e. (1986c: 176)

Lewis advanced this as an account of probabilistic causation. But, as Lewis notes, by employing chances where the probabilities are exactly one and exactly zero—as contrasted with infinitesimally close to one and zero—one can view this as a general account of causation that covers non-probabilistic causation as well as probabilistic causation.

A feature of this account that does not seem especially plausible is the requirement that, in the absence of the cause, the probability of the effect would have been much lower. If one drops that requirement, Lewis's account is as follows:

(1) an event c causes an event e if and only if there is a chain of causally dependent events linking e with c;

(2) an event e is causally dependent upon an event c if and only if events c and e exist, and there are numbers x and y, such that (a) if c were to occur, the chance of e occurring would be equal to x; (b) if c were not to occur, the chance of e occurring would be equal to y; and (c) x is greater than y.

6.1.2 *Mellor's Account of Causation: Objective Chances and Strong Laws*

A very closely related analysis was set out by D. H. Mellor in his book *The Facts of Causation* (Mellor 1995), but Mellor's account is much more detailed and wide-ranging, and he offers a host of arguments in support of central aspects of the analysis, including the crucial claim that a cause must raise the probability of its effect. Mellor also diverges from Lewis in rejecting a regularity account of laws in favour of a view according to which even basic laws of nature can exist without having instances.

Mellor's approach, in brief, is as follows. First, he embraces an ontology involving objective chances, where the latter are ultimate properties of states of affairs, rather than being logically supervenient upon causal laws together with non-dispositional properties, plus relations. Secondly, he proposes that chances can be defined as properties that satisfy three conditions: (1) the necessity condition: if the chance of P's obtaining is equal to one, then P is the case; (2) the evidence condition: if one's total evidence concerning P is that the chance of P is equal to k, then one's subjective probability that P is the case should be equal to k; (3) the frequency condition: the chance that P is the case is related to the corresponding relative frequency in the limit.[11] Thirdly, chances enter into basic laws of nature. Fourthly, Mellor holds that even basic laws of nature need not have instances, thereby rejecting reductionist accounts in favour of a realist view. Fifthly, any chance that P is the case must be a property of a state of affairs that temporally precedes the time at which P exists, or would exist. Finally, and as a very rough approximation, a state of affairs c causes a state of affairs e if and only if there are numbers x and y such that (1) the total state of affairs that exists at the time of c—including laws of nature—entails that the chance of e is x, (2) the total state of affairs that would exist at the time of c, if c did not exist, entails that the chance of e is y, and (3) x is greater than y.[12]

6.2 Objections

6.2.1 *Logical Connections between Temporally Distinct States of Affairs*

This approach is exposed to at least five serious objections. First, as noted above, if dispositions are irreducible properties of individuals at a time, then the world contains logical connections between *temporally* distinct states of affairs, and precisely the same is true in the case of extreme chances, where the probability in question is either exactly one or exactly zero. But this type of logical connection between temporally distinct states of affairs seems deeply problematic.

One might, of course, renounce such extreme chances, but it is not easy to see why objective chances with values between zero and one should be metaphysically acceptable entities, while chances with the values zero and one are not. In addition, if one rejects extreme chances, then one will have to offer a different account of causation in the deterministic case, and the idea that the concept of causation is disjunctive in that way does not seem very appealing.

---

[11] For a precise formulation of the last condition, see Mellor (1995: 38–43).
[12] Mellor's own formulation (1995: 175–9) is different, and considerably more complicated.

6.2.2 *Closest-Worlds Conditionals*

Secondly, in considering Lewis's analysis of causation in the deterministic case, we saw that it was exposed to a number of objections connected with the Stalnaker–Lewis-style account of counterfactuals on which it was based. Lewis's account of probabilistic causation falls prey to precisely the same objections, and the same is true of Mellor's account, since he too employs closest-worlds-style conditionals.

But is the use of such conditionals an essential feature of any analysis of causation in terms of objective chances? Initially, it might seem that it is. For the analysis must refer not just to the chance of the effect e at the time of the cause c, but to the chance that there *would* have been of e's occurring if c had not occurred. Accordingly, counterfactual conditionals are needed, and in the context of giving an analysis of causation, one can certainly not adopt a causal account of the truth-conditions of counterfactuals. So what alternative is there to a closest-worlds account?

The answer is that there is another alternative—namely, one that arises out of the idea that the chances that exist at a given time, rather than supervening on categorical states of affairs that exist at that time together with probabilistic causal laws, supervene instead upon categorical states of affairs together with non-probabilistic, non-causal laws linking categorical properties at a time to chances at that time. For if this view can be defended, then rather than asking about the chance that e would occur in the closest worlds where c does not occur, one can ignore past and future similarities, and ask instead about the chance that e would occur in those worlds where c does not occur and that are *most similar at the time of c* to the world where c occurs.

The idea, in short, is that one can shift from closest-worlds counterfactuals to closest-momentary-slices counterfactuals, thereby avoiding the objections to which the former are exposed.

6.2.3 *Underdetermination Objections*

Thirdly, an analysis of causation in terms of objective chances is also exposed to underdetermination objections since, as we saw in Section 4.2.2, the latter show that causal relations between events are not logically supervenient even upon non-causal states of affairs combined with causal laws, together with dispositions, propensities, and objective chances, plus facts about the direction of causation.

6.2.4 *The Objection to the Probability-Raising Condition*

Fourthly, as in the case of probabilistic accounts of a Humean reductionist sort, the present account is also exposed to the objection that causes need not raise the probability of their effects. For although it is possible, by adopting Lewis's distinction between causation and causal dependence, to argue—as Lewis does—that an analysis of causation in terms of objective chances does not entail that *causes* always raise the probabilities of their effects, the objection in question still applies, since one can show that a cause need not make its effect more likely than it would otherwise be even in the case of *direct* causation.

To establish that this is so, the argument that was offered earlier to show that a cause need not raise the probability of its effect needs to be modified slightly, both so that it deals with direct causal connections, and so that it refers to objective chances, rather than to conditional and unconditional probabilities. This can be done as follows. Suppose that there is a type of atom, T, and relevant laws of nature, that entail the following:

(1) any atom of type T must be in one of the four mutually exclusive states–A, B, C, D;

(2) an atom of type T in state A has an objective chance of 0.999 of moving directly into state D; an atom in state B has an objective chance of 0.99 of moving directly into state D; an atom in state C has an objective chance of 0 of moving directly into state D;

(3) there is a certain type of situation—S—such that any atom of type T in situation S must be in either state A or state B.

Suppose now that x is an atom of type T, in situation S, in state B, and that x moves directly into state D. Given that, for example, putting an atom of type T into state B would be quite an effective means of getting it into state D, it is surely true that x's being in state D was probably caused by x's having been in state B. But this would not be so if the above account were correct. For consider what would have been the case if x had not been in state B. Given that x was in situation S, x would, in view of (3), have been in state A. But then x's objective chance of moving directly into state D would have been 0.999, and so higher than what it is when the atom is in state B.

The point here, as before, is that a given type of state may be causally efficacious, but not as efficacious as alternative states, and, because of this, it is not true that even a direct cause need raise the probability of its effect, contrary to what would be required if the above analysis were sound.

6.2.5 *Objective Chances and a Causal Theory of Time*

The final objection starts out from the observation that if there is, at location s and time t, a certain objective chance of a state of affairs of type E, this is not, of course, equal to the probability that there is a state of affairs of type E somewhere in the universe: it is, rather, the probability that there is a state of affairs of type E in a location appropriately related to s and t.

What does this mean in the case of time? If backward causation is logically possible—as Lewis believes, and as Mellor does not—then it would seem that there could be an objective chance at location s and time t that was the chance that there is an event of type E at a certain temporal distance either before or after t. Such chances would be 'bidirectional'. But let us set those aside, and consider only the cases where a chance of there being an event of type E is either a chance of there being an event of type E at a later time, or else a chance of there being an event of type E at an earlier time. All such chances, then, would themselves incorporate a temporal direction—either the later-than direction, or the earlier-than direction. But this means that if one proceeds to analyse causation in terms of objective chances that are not of a bidirectional sort, one cannot, on pain of circularity, analyse the direction of time in terms of the direction of causation.

7. CAUSATION AS A THEORETICAL RELATION

Could causation be a theoretical relation between states of affairs? Serious exploration of this idea required two developments—one semantical, the other epistemological. As regards the former, one needed a non-reductionist account of the meaning of theoretical terms—something that was provided by R. M. Martin (1966) and David Lewis (1970). Then, as regards the epistemological side, one needed to have reason for thinking that theoretical statements, thus interpreted, could be confirmed. That this could not be done by induction based on instantial generalization had been shown by Hume (1739–40: IV. ii), so the question was whether there was some other legitimate form of non-deductive inference. Gradually, the idea of the method of hypothesis (hypothetico-deductive method, abduction, inference to the best explanation) emerged, and, although by no means uncontroversial, this alternative to instantial generalization is widely accepted by present-day philosophers.

These two developments opened the door to the idea of treating causation as a theoretical relation, and two main accounts have now been advanced. According to the one, all basic laws are causal laws, so that an account of the necessitation involved in basic laws of nature *ipso facto* provides an account of causal necessitation. According to the other account, by contrast, basic laws need not be causal laws, and consequently the relation of causation cannot be identified with a general relation of nomic necessitation. How, then, is causation to be defined? The answer offered by the second approach is, first, that causal laws must satisfy certain postulates involving probabilistic relations, and, secondly, that causation can then be defined as the relation that enters into such laws.

7.1 Causation and Nomic Necessitation

The idea that causal necessitation can be identified with nomic necessitation was advanced by David Armstrong and Adrian Heathcote (1991), and then developed in more detail by Armstrong in his book *A World of States of Affairs* (1997, esp. 216–33). As set out by Armstrong and Heathcote, the thought is that the identification of causal necessitation with nomic necessitation is necessary, but a posteriori. This presupposes that one has some independent grasp of the concept of causation, and here Armstrong and Heathcote appeal to the idea that causation is directly observable.

As noted earlier, the claim that causation is directly observable in a sense that entails that the concept of causation is semantically basic is open to very strong objections: causation would need to be immediately given in experience, and it is not. However, the basic approach here can be reformulated slightly to avoid this problem. The starting point is the idea that laws of nature cannot be identified with cosmic regularities, or any subset thereof: laws—or, at least, basic laws—are, instead, atomic states of affairs that involve certain second-order relations between universals. Let us suppose, then, for simplicity, that in the case of non-probabilistic, basic laws, there is one such relation—call it nomic necessitation. The central thesis can then be formulated as the proposition that causal necessitation is analytically identical with nomic necessitation, either just as a matter of definition, or else in virtue of a theorem—possibly a rather deep one—that follows from the correct analysis of causation. Two first-order states of affairs will then stand in the most fundamental causal relation when those two states of affairs are appropriately involved in an instance of a basic law—that is, when those two states of affairs are connected by the relation of nomic necessitation. The general relation of causation connecting states of affairs can then be defined as the ancestral of that basic relation.

This approach has a number of important advantages. In particular, it does not fall prey to any of the objections to Humean reductionist approaches set out earlier. Thus, neither the fact that causal relations need not supervene on causal laws together with the totality of non-causal states of affairs, nor the possibilities of simple worlds, or of 'inverted' worlds, poses any problem.

What objections, then, might be raised? First, this account presupposes the intelligibility of strong laws, in view of the postulation of the second-order relation of nomic necessitation. So one might object—as Bas van Fraassen (1989) has—that strong laws are impossible because they involve logical connections between distinct states of affairs. There are, however, good reasons for thinking that van Fraassen's argument is unsound (Tooley 1987: 123–9).

A second objection turns upon the claim that not all laws of nature need be causal, as is illustrated, for example, by Newton's third law of motion. For one object's exerting a force on another does not cause the other object to exert an equal and opposite force back on the first object. But if causal necessitation just is nomic necessitation, how are non-causal laws possible?

Armstrong's answer to this objection is that non-causal laws are supervenient upon causal laws. The case just mentioned shows, however, that this response will not work. What is true is that it follows, for example, from the law of gravitation that if object *A* exerts a *gravitational* force on object *B*, then *B* exerts an equal and opposite *gravitational* force on *A*, and similarly for forces of electrostatic attraction and repulsion, magnetic attraction and repulsion, and so on. But the obtaining of these specialized, derived laws does not entail Newton's third law: the latter is supervenient, not upon the force laws alone, but upon the force laws together with a 'totality fact' to the effect that such-and-such types of forces are the only ones found in our world. This totality fact, however, is not itself a law, let alone a causal law, and so Newton's third law of motion is not supervenient upon the causal laws found in a Newtonian world.

But this may not be a decisive objection. Perhaps the third law of motion is correctly viewed, in a Newtonian world, not as a law, but as a regularity that obtains in virtue of all of the force laws, together with the totality fact that there are no other types of forces.

A third objection is this. When causation is identified with nomic necessitation, one is really offering an account of what it is for one state of affairs to be a causally sufficient condition of another state of affairs. But one also needs an account of what it is for one state of affairs (or type of state of affairs) to be a causally *necessary* condition of another, and the thrust of the third objection is that it is not at all clear that a satisfactory account is available, given the Armstrong–Heathcote approach.

What account can be given, then, of the claim that states of affairs of type *C* are causally necessary for states of affairs of type *E*? One possibility is this:

(1) A state of affairs of type *C* is a causally necessary condition of a (corresponding) state of affairs of type *E* if and only if the absence of a state of affairs of type *C* is a causally sufficient condition for the absence of a (corresponding) state of affairs of type *E*.

But Armstrong would not find this approach very appealing, as he is reluctant to allow absences to function as causes.

One could avoid this problem by adopting, instead, the following analysis:

(2) A state of affairs of type *C* is a causally necessary condition of a (corresponding) state of affairs of type *E* if and only if a state of affairs of type *E* is a causally sufficient condition for a (corresponding) state of affairs of type *C*.

But this analysis is even more problematic, since it commits one to the existence of backward causation in situations where there is no warrant at all for such a postulation.

A fourth objection concerns the relation between causation and time, and this has two aspects. On the one hand, while a number of philosophers have attempted to prove that causes must precede their effects, the question of whether backward causation is possible remains deeply controversial. But if causal necessitation is simply nomic necessitation, then it would seem that it follows immediately that backward causation is logically possible, since there appears to be nothing impossible about its being a basic law that states of affairs of type A are always preceded by states of affairs of type B. Nor is there any problem about causal loops, where a state of affairs of type A causes a state of affairs of type B, and the latter causes the earlier state of affairs of type A.

The other, and closely related, aspect concerns the possibility of simultaneous causation. Given that there does not appear to be any reason for holding that laws of necessary coexistence are impossible, it would seem that Armstrong must allow that causes might be simultaneous with their effects. But if causes and effects can be simultaneous, then causal theories of the direction of time are absolutely precluded—as is not the case with the possibility of backward causation, since the latter is compatible with the view that the *local* direction of time is given by the direction of local causal processes.

Finally, and most importantly, Armstrong's account fails to forge any connection between causation and probability, and, because of this, it cannot provide an adequate account of the epistemology of causation. This can be illustrated by the following case. Consider some very simple type of state of affairs S, and some very complex type of state of affairs T. (S might be a momentary instance of redness, and T a state of affairs that is qualitatively identical with the total state of our solar system at the beginning of the present millennium.) In the absence of other evidence, one should surely view events of type S as much more likely than events of type T. Suppose that one learns, however, that events of type S and events of type T always occur together, and that this two-way connection is nomological. Then one's initial probabilities need to be adjusted, but exactly how this should be done is not clear. But what if one learns, instead, that events of type S are causally sufficient and causally necessary for events of type T? Then surely what one should do is to adjust the probability that one assigns to events of type T, equating it with the probability that one initially assigned to events of type S. Conversely, if one learns that events of type T are causally sufficient and causally necessary for events of type S, then surely what one should do is to adjust the probability that one assigns to events of type S, equating it with the probability that one initially assigned to events of type T.

If this is right, then in a case where events of type S and events of type T always occur together, the frequency with which they occur will provide very strong evidence concerning whether events of type T are caused by events of type S, or vice versa. Armstrong's account, however, can provide no reason why this should be so.

7.2 Causation and Asymmetric Probability Relations

The other main proposal for analysing causation as a theoretical relation is based upon the idea that there are connections between causation, on the one hand, and prior and posterior probabilities on the other. As set out by Tooley (1987, 1990*a*), the idea is that causation is defined as the unique relation between states of affairs that is such that any laws into which that relation enters in a certain way must satisfy certain postulates—two of the most crucial of which may be stated, in slightly simplified form, as follows, where $C(P, Q)$ is an abbreviation for 'It is a law that for all x, if x has property P, then x's having property P causes x to have property Q':

(P_1) $\text{Prob}(Px, C(P, Q)) = \text{Prob}(Px)$

(P_2) $\text{Prob}(Qx, C(P, Q)) = \text{Prob}(Px) + \text{Prob}(\sim Px) \times \text{Prob}(Qx, \sim Px)$.

These postulates are suggested in a very direct fashion by the example just mentioned involving states of affairs of types S and T. For what these two postulates say is that, given no additional information, the posterior probability of a state of affairs of type P, given the information that states of affairs of type P cause states of affairs of type Q, is precisely equal to the prior probability of states of affairs of type P, whereas, by contrast, the posterior probability of a state of affairs of type Q, given the information that states of affairs of type P cause states of affairs of type Q, is a function of the prior probability of states of affairs of type P. The posterior probability of an effect, accordingly, is a function of the prior probability of its cause, whereas the posterior probability of a cause is not a function of the prior probability of its effect.

This account has a number of advantages. First, like the Armstrong–Heathcote approach, it avoids all of the objections that confront Humean reductionist approaches. Simple worlds and 'inverted' worlds are not a problem, nor is the fact that causal relations need not supervene on causal laws together with the totality of non-causal states of affairs. Secondly, the connection between causation and probability that is introduced by postulates (P_1) and (P_2) explains how statistical information is relevant to the evaluation of competing causal hypotheses. Thirdly, the asymmetries with respect to probabilities that are introduced by postulates (P_1) and (P_2) explain both the asymmetry and the direction of causation.

What objections might be directed against this account? Sometimes it is objected that treating causation as a theoretical relation between states of affairs places causal claims outside the scope of confirmation (Price 1996: 154). But given the connection between causation and probability, this objection is clearly unsound.

A second objection—and one that would certainly be advanced by Bas van Fraassen—is that if causation is treated as a theoretical relation, one needs to employ inference to the best explanation to confirm causal hypotheses, and this is bad news, since inference to the best explanation is not a sound inductive method.

The thesis that inference to the best explanation is problematic certainly deserves serious discussion. At the same time, however, this is clearly not an objection that points to some special problem connected with causal realism, since if this objection were sound, it would undercut the vast majority of our knowledge claims.

A third objection arises if one interprets laws as strong laws, rather than as cosmic regularities of some sort. For then it can be argued that one is postulating non-Humean states of affairs. But unlike the Armstrong–Heathcote version of causal realism, strong laws are an optional extra in the case of this second account. Moreover, as noted earlier, it is also possible to argue that, if transcendent universals are admitted, one can establish that there can be logical connections between second-order relations between universals, on the one hand, and regularities on the other.

A fourth and final objection—and perhaps the most important—is that the present account makes ineliminable use of the idea of logical probability, and that the latter notion is deeply problematic. But in response it can be asked whether, if one rejects the idea of logical probability, one can offer any satisfactory answer to the challenge of inductive scepticism.

8. Summing Up: The Metaphysics of Causation

Traditionally, the main divide between accounts of the nature of causation has been viewed as that between reductionist accounts and realist accounts. We have seen, however, that there are also very great gulfs within realist accounts, between direct realism and indirect, theoretical-term realism, and within reductionist accounts, between Humean reductionist accounts and non-Humean ones. Indeed, non-Humean reductionist approaches to causation are, in some respects, closer to realist accounts than to Humean reductionist accounts.

What are the central advantages and disadvantages of the various approaches, and which seems most promising? As regards non-Humean reductionist accounts, the appeal is quite clear: the introduction of objective chances initially looks as if it may enable one to provide a satisfactory account of probabilistic laws, and of probabilistic causal connections—something that does not seem possible given a Humean, reductionist approach. The cost, however, appears very high, since the postulation of irreducible, objective chances commits one to the existence of logical connections between states of affairs that are distinct in the very strong sense of occupying different spatio-temporal locations.

If this latter idea is not acceptable, the choice is then between Humean reductionist approaches and realist accounts. The former are exposed to a number of objections, some of which vary from one Humean reductionist theory to another, and some of which are general, with the latter including various underdetermination objections, and objections based upon very simple universes, and 'temporally inverted' ones. None of these poses any problem, by contrast, for realist theories, where the most important objections centre, in the case of direct realism, upon the claim that the concept of causation is analytically basic, and, in the case of theoretical-term realism, upon the idea of strong laws, and the idea of logical probability.

The central objection to direct causal realism does seem strong. But, as regards the objections to theoretical-term realism, it is, in the first place, not at all clear that strong laws violate the thesis that there can be no logical connections between distinct existences; and, secondly, it can be argued that if the idea of logical probability were unsound, no beliefs at all could be inferentially justified. So there are grounds for thinking that there may very well be satisfactory answers to the crucial objections to the view that causation is a theoretically defined relation. By contrast, both the general objections to Humean, reductionist approaches, and many of the theory-specific objections, seem quite compelling.

REFERENCES

Anscombe, G. E. M. (1971). *Causality and Determination*. Cambridge: Cambridge University Press.

Armstrong, D. M. (1968). *A Materialist Theory of the Mind*. London: Routledge & Kegan Paul.

—— (1983). *What is a Law of Nature?* Cambridge: Cambridge University Press.

—— (1997). *A World of States of Affairs*. Cambridge: Cambridge University Press.

—— and Heathcote, Adrian (1991). 'Causes and Laws'. *Noûs*, 25: 63–73.

Bennett, Jonathan (1974). 'Counterfactuals and Possible Worlds'. *Canadian Journal of Philosophy*, 4: 381–402.

—— (1998). *Events and their Names*. Indianapolis: Hackett.

Braithwaite, R. B. (1953). *Scientific Explanation*. Cambridge: Cambridge University Press.

Bretzel, Philip von (1977). 'Concerning a Probabilistic Theory of Causation Adequate for the Causal Theory of Time'. *Synthese*, 35: 173–90.

Carnap, Rudolf (1962). *Logical Foundations of Probability*, 2nd edn. Chicago: University of Chicago Press.

Carroll, John W. (1994). *Laws of Nature*. Cambridge: Cambridge University Press.

Cartwright, Nancy (1979). 'Causal Laws and Effective Strategies'. *Noûs*, 13: 419–38. Repr. in Cartwright, *How the Laws of Physics Lie*. Oxford: Oxford University Press.

—— (1989). *Nature's Capacities and their Measurement*. Oxford: Clarendon Press.

Davis, Wayne (1988). 'Probabilistic Theories of Causation', in James H. Fetzer (ed.), *Probability and Causation: Essays in Honor of Wesley Salmon*. Dordrecht: Reidel, 133–60.

Dowe, Phil (2000a). *Physical Causation*. New York: Cambridge University Press.

Dowe, Phil (2000b). 'Causality and Explanation'. *British Journal for the Philosophy of Science*, 51: 165–74.

Dretske, Fred I. (1977). 'Laws of Nature'. *Philosophy of Science*, 44: 248–68.

—— and Snyder, Aaron (1972). 'Causal Irregularity'. *Philosophy of Science*, 39: 69–71.

Eells, Ellery (1991). *Probabilistic Causality*. Cambridge: Cambridge University Press.

Ehring, Douglas (1997). *Causation and Persistence*. New York: Oxford University Press.

Fair, David (1979). 'Causation and the Flow of Energy'. *Erkenntnis*, 14: 219–50.

Fales, Evan (1990). *Causation and Universals*. London: Routledge.

Fine, Kit (1975). 'Critical Notice—Counterfactuals'. *Mind*, 84: 451–8.

Good, I. J. (1961–2). 'A Causal Calculus I–II'. *British Journal for the Philosophy of Science*, 11: 305–18; 12: 43–51.

Grünbaum, Adolf (1973). *Philosophical Problems of Space and Time*, 2nd edn. Dordrecht: Reidel.

Hart, H. L. A., and Honoré, A. M. (1959). *Causation and the Law*. Oxford: Clarendon Press.

Hausman, Daniel M. (1998). *Causal Asymmetries*. Cambridge: Cambridge University Press.

Hempel, C. G. (1965). *Aspects of Scientific Explanation*. New York: Free Press.

Hesslow, Germund (1976). 'Two Notes on the Probabilistic Approach to Causation'. *Philosophy of Science*, 43: 290–2.

Hintikka, Jaakko (1966). 'A Two-Dimensional Continuum of Inductive Methods', in Jaakko Hintikka and Patrick Suppes (eds.), *Aspects of Inductive Logic*. Amsterdam: North-Holland, 113–32.

Hume, David (1739–40). *A Treatise of Human Nature*. London.

—— (1748). *An Enquiry concerning Human Understanding*. London.

Humphreys, Paul (1981). 'Probabilistic Causality and Multiple Causation', in Peter D. Asquith and Ronald N. Giere (eds.), *PSA 1980*. East Lansing, Mich.: Philosophy of Science Association, ii. 25–37.

Kim, Jaegwon (1973a). 'Causation, Nomic Subsumption, and the Concept of Event', *Journal of Philosophy*, 70: 217–36.

—— (1973b). 'Causes and Counterfactuals'. *Journal of Philosophy*, 70: 570–2. Repr. in Sosa and Tooley (1993: 205–7).

Lewis, David (1970). 'How to Define Theoretical Terms', *Journal of Philosophy*, 67: 427–46.

—— (1973a). *Counterfactuals*. Cambridge, Mass.: Harvard University Press.

—— (1973b). 'Causation'. *Journal of Philosophy*, 70: 556–67. Repr. with postscripts in Lewis (1986a).

—— (1979). 'Counterfactual Dependence and Time's Arrow'. *Noûs*, 13: 455–76. Repr. with postscripts in Lewis (1986a).

—— (1986a). *Philosophical Papers*, vol. ii. Oxford: Oxford University Press.

—— (1986b). 'Events', in Lewis (1986a: 241–69).

—— (1986c). 'Postscripts to "Causation"', in Lewis (1986a: 172–213).

—— (1986d). 'Postscripts to "Counterfactual Dependence and Time's Arrow"', in Lewis (1986a: 52–66).

—— (2000). 'Causation as Influence'. *Journal of Philosophy*, 97/4: 182–97.

McDermott, Michael (1995). 'Redundant Causation'. *British Journal for the Philosophy of Science*, 40: 523–44.

Mackie, John L. (1965). 'Causes and Conditions'. *American Philosophical Quarterly*, 2: 245–64. Repr. in Sosa and Tooley (1993: 33–55).

—— (1974). *The Cement of the Universe*. Oxford: Oxford University Press.

Madden, Edward H., and Rom Harré (1975). *Causal Powers*. Oxford: Basil Blackwell.

Martin, C. B. (1993). 'Power for Realists', in John Bacon, Keith Campbell, and Lloyd Reinhardt (eds.), *Ontology, Causality and Mind*. Cambridge: Cambridge University Press.

Martin, R. M. (1966). 'On Theoretical Constructs and Ramsey Constants'. *Philosophy of Science*, 33: 1–13.

—— (1972). 'The Sufficiency Thesis'. *Philosophical Studies*, 23: 205–11.

Mellor, D. H. (1986). 'Fixed Past, Unfixed Future', in Barry Taylor (ed.), *Contributions to Philosophy: Michael Dummett*. The Hague: Nijhoff, 166–86.

—— (1995). *The Facts of Causation*. London: Routledge.

Menzies, Peter (1989). 'Probabilistic Causation and Causal Processes: A Critique of Lewis'. *Philosophy of Science*, 56: 642–63.

Michotte, Albert (1963). *The Perception of Causality*. London: Methuen.

Mill, John Stuart (1874). *A System of Logic*. New York: Harper.

Nagel, Ernest (1961). *The Structure of Science*. New York: Harcourt, Brace, & World.

Popper, Karl (1956). 'The Arrow of Time'. *Nature*, 177: 538.

—— (1972). *Objective Knowledge: An Evolutionary Approach*. Oxford: Clarendon Press.

Price, Huw (1996). *Time's Arrow and Archimedes' Point*. Oxford: Oxford University Press.

Ramachandran, Murali (1997). 'A Counterfactual Analysis of Causation'. *Mind*, 106: 263–77.

Ramsey, F. P. (1929). 'Theories'. First pub. in R. B. Braithwaite (ed.), *The Foundations of Mathematics*. London: Routledge & Kegan Paul, 1931.

Reichenbach, Hans (1956). *The Direction of Time*. Berkeley and Los Angeles: University of California Press.

Salmon, Wesley (1978). 'Why Ask "Why?"?' *Proceedings and Addresses of the American Philosophical Association*, 51/6: 683–705.

—— (1980). 'Probabilistic Causality'. *Pacific Philosophical Quarterly*, 61: 50–74.

—— (1984). *Scientific Explanation and the Causal Structure of the World*. Princeton: Princeton University Press.

—— (1997). 'Causality and Explanation: A Reply to Two Critiques'. *Philosophy of Science*, 64: 461–77.

—— (1998). *Causality and Explanation*. New York: Oxford University Press.

Schaffer, Jonathan (2000). 'Trumping Preemption'. *Journal of Philosophy*, 97/4: 165–81.

Scriven, Michael (1956–7). 'Randomness and the Causal Order'. *Analysis*, 17: 5–9.

—— (1966). 'Causes, Connections, and Conditions in History', in William H. Dray (ed.), *Philosophical Analysis and History*. New York: Harper & Row.

Skyrms, Brian (1980). *Causal Necessity*. New Haven: Yale University Press.

Sosa, Ernest, and Michael Tooley (eds.) (1993). *Causation*. Oxford: Oxford University Press.

Stalnaker, Robert C. (1968). 'A Theory of Conditionals', in Nicholas Rescher (ed.), *Studies in Logical Theory*. Oxford: Basil Blackwell. Repr. in Ernest Sosa (ed.), *Causation and Conditionals*. Oxford: Oxford University Press, 1975, 165–79.

Strawson, Galen (1989). *The Secret Connexion: Causation, Realism, and David Hume*. Oxford: Oxford University Press.

Suppes, Patrick (1970). *A Probabilistic Theory of Causality*. Amsterdam: North-Holland.

—— (1984). 'Conflicting Intuitions about Causality', in P. French, T. Uehling, and H. Wettstein (eds.), *Midwest Studies in Philosophy*, ix. Minneapolis: University of Minnesota Press, 151-68.

Taylor, Richard (1966). *Action and Purpose*. Englewood Cliffs, NJ: Prentice-Hall.

Tooley, Michael (1977). 'The Nature of Laws'. *Canadian Journal of Philosophy*, 7/4: 667–98.

Tooley, Michael (1984). 'Laws and Causal Relations', in P. French, T. Uehling, and H. Wettstein (eds.), *Midwest Studies in Philosophy*, ix. Minneapolis: University of Minnesota Press, 93–112.

—— (1987). *Causation: A Realist Approach*. Oxford: Oxford University Press.

—— (1990*a*). 'The Nature of Causation: A Singularist Account', in David Copp (ed.), *Canadian Philosophers*, *Canadian Journal of Philosophy*, suppl. 16: 271–322. Repr. in Jaegwon Kim and Ernest Sosa (eds.), *Metaphysics: An Anthology*. Oxford: Basil Blackwell, 1999, 458–82.

—— (1990*b*). 'Causation: Reductionism versus Realism'. *Philosophy and Phenomenological Research*, 50: 215–36.

van Fraassen, Bas C (1989). *Laws and Symmetry*. Oxford: Clarendon Press.

von Wright, Georg Henrik (1971). *Explanation and Understanding*. Ithaca, NY: Cornell University Press.

CHAPTER 14

CAUSATION IN A PHYSICAL WORLD

HARTRY FIELD

1. CAUSAL ELIMINATIVISM

OF what use is the concept of causation? Bertrand Russell (1912–13) argued that it is not useful: it is 'a relic of a bygone age, surviving, like the monarchy, only because it is erroneously supposed to do no harm'. His argument for this was that the kind of physical theories that we have come to regard as fundamental leave no place for the notion of causation: not only does the word 'cause' not appear in the advanced sciences, but the laws that these sciences state are incompatible with causation as we normally understand it. But Nancy Cartwright has argued (1979) that abandoning the concept of causation would cripple science; her conclusion was based not on fundamental physics, but on more ordinary science such as the search for the causes of cancer. She argues that Russell was right that the fundamental theories of modern physics say nothing, even implicitly, about causation, and concludes on this basis that such theories are incomplete. It is with this cluster of issues that I will begin my discussion.

Russell's claim that the notion of causation is not needed in fundamental physics has been disputed by Earman (1976), but I think Russell is right and Earman wrong. Earman mentions various causal concepts in physics: determinism, causal signals,

Thanks to Ned Block, Cian Dorr, Christopher Hitchcock, Paul Horwich, Lisa Warenski, and the editors for comments on previous versions.

and microcausality. But determinism is explainable without the notion of causation, as both Russell in the above article and later Earman himself (1986) have observed. The notion of causal signal is needed in physics only on an operational construal of that; on a less operational view, notions like flow of energy-momentum and various temporal notions such as the light cone structure suffice for the purposes that talk of causal signals have been standardly put. As for microcausality, I'm not sure which of several things Earman had in mind, but I don't see any that support his case.

But of course from the non-appearance of the notion in fundamental physics it doesn't follow that fundamental physics doesn't provide the means to explain it; and it certainly doesn't follow that the whole idea of causation is incompatible with what fundamental physics tells us. But Russell had two arguments for these stronger conclusions.

One argument (not his main one) concerns directionality. The relation between cause and effect is supposed to have an important temporal asymmetry: causes normally or always precede their effects. This does not appear to be simply a matter of the earlier member of a cause–effect pair being conventionally called the cause; rather, it is connected with other temporal asymmetries that play an important role in our practices. For instance, we tend to *explain* later events in terms of earlier ones but not vice versa; and we think that it makes sense to stop smoking as a teenager so that one will not get cancer later, but that it does not make sense to take a cancer-preventative later in life so that one will not have smoked as a teenager (or to take a cancer-preventative in early childhood so that one won't smoke later on). Most people would defend these practices on the grounds that causes explain their effects but not conversely, and that it makes sense to prevent an effect by preventing its cause but not vice versa. The notion of cause is intimately bound up with these asymmetries of explanation and action, as well as with numerous other temporal asymmetries.

But at the level of fundamental physical law, it is hard to see any grounds for the evident directionality of causation. The point is sometimes put a bit contentiously, by claiming that (perhaps with a few minor exceptions) the fundamental physical laws are completely time-symmetric. If so, then if one is inclined to found causation on fundamental physical law, it isn't evident just how directionality gets in. But this is an unnecessarily contentious way to put the point: it is not obvious that the claim that the basic laws of physics are time-symmetric is correct; indeed, the notion of the time symmetry of a law itself is not as clear as it sounds.[1]

Russell put the point differently, in a way that doesn't rely on any claim of time symmetry. All the candidates for fundamental laws of physics known at the time he wrote had the characteristic of being *deterministic in both directions*. That is, from

---

[1] It depends on which of the other concepts involved in a law are treated as primitive and which as implicitly involving time: the latter but not the former may be allowed to shift in a transformation that reverses time. See Sklar (1974: 364–8).

a complete specification of the state of the universe at one time, plus the laws, it follows what the state of the universe is at any other time, *earlier or later*.[2] Russell noted that there seems to be no distinction within fundamental physics between the way in which the past determines the future and the way in which the future determines the past. This seems to be incompatible with the ordinary conception of causation, for part of that conception is that the past determines the future in a more fundamental and important way than any way in which the future might determine the past.

Three points about this argument. The first is that it needn't rely on the claim that the laws of physics are deterministic in both directions, but merely on the idea that they 'have essentially the same character in both directions'. Giving up determinism wouldn't in itself alter the situation very much, if the laws 'had the same indeterministic character in both directions' (to put it vaguely). But *certain kinds of* indeterministic laws might be such as to give rise to a fundamental distinction in temporal direction: for instance, those with well-defined probabilities only in the forward direction. (If one takes quantum mechanical laws to include 'the collapse of the wave packet', then the law governing the collapse would appear to be an example; but such 'collapse' interpretations of quantum mechanics are highly controversial.)

The second point is that even if one grants that the laws of physics are deterministic in both directions, there is still room in principle for arguing that their character in the forward direction is importantly different from their character in the backwards direction. For instance, Lewis (1986*d*) claims that there are many more determinants of an event at times after the event than there are determinants of it at times before it. I think this claim about an 'asymmetry of overdetermination' is wrong, and will discuss it later on.

Even if one can't make a distinction in direction at the level of fundamental law, one still might make it in physical terms, by bringing in the initial conditions that obtain at our world. Indeed, Lewis's approach was probably intended as an instance of this strategy. But my third point is that this strategy can be made more flexible if one brings in statistical considerations. That is, it might be that there tend to be statistical features of the initial conditions in which we typically apply fundamental physical laws that aren't shared by the final conditions; I will mention possible such features at the end of Section 2 and in Section 4. (The statistical features needn't be supposed to be global features of the universe; they need only be as pervasive as the 'directionality' that we observe. So it is no objection to the approach that there might turn out to be a future epoch or a distant region in which these regularities were reversed.) It is such statistical features of the initial conditions

---

[2] This requires a slight qualification, noticed by Earman (1986): unless one assumes a finite upper bound on the velocity of propagation of forces (thereby ruling out Newton's law of gravitation), one must make some further assumptions about boundary conditions. But whatever qualifications are required must be made in the forward direction as well as the backward, so I don't think they much affect the basic point.

that account for the dramatic directionality of the laws of thermodynamics; this gives some initial plausibility to the idea that it might account for the directionality of causation as well.

Price (1992) objects to using statistical considerations to found the directionality of causation, on the grounds that it doesn't give us *enough* asymmetry. In particular, Price argues that the statistical approach doesn't give rise to any important asymmetry in single interactions in conditions where statistical asymmetries are irrelevant—for instance, where only a few particles are involved and they are isolated from their environments (no waves coming in, etc.). I think that Price is partially correct: in such situations, there is no asymmetry that is intrinsic to the interaction itself. Still, if the earlier-than relation is associated with certain statistical regularities (even ones local to our epoch and our region of the universe), then in appealing to this relation in situations with no intrinsic statistical asymmetry one is still invoking an extrinsic statistical asymmetry; and I think that a defender of the statistical approach can say that this is the only temporal asymmetry there is reason to believe in. This would mean that, within certain systems, an explanation of the past state by means of the future state is intrinsically on par with an explanation of its future state by its past state: preference for the latter over the former could be justified only by appeal to other systems in which the statistical regularities matter. So the statistical approach may not give enough asymmetry *to validate our ordinary preconceptions*; but perhaps the problem is with the preconceptions, not with the statistical approach.[3]

If something like this is right, then Russell's first argument is problematic: although it is true that the notion of 'cause' is not needed in fundamental physics, even statistical physics, still directionality considerations don't preclude this notion from being consistently added to fundamental physics; and indeed, it may even be the case that the notion can be explained within statistical physics. Such an explanation would not capture our full intuitive preconceptions about the directionality of causation, but it could capture a good bit of them.

But Russell had another argument, on which he put more weight. He claimed that our causal way of thinking relies on the assumption that there are laws that tell us that when a finite number of quite localized things hold at one time, some other particular thing must happen a short time later. (When someone strikes a non-defective match and holds it to a flammable substance and there's oxygen present and a few other things hold, a fire must result.) Russell points out that no proposed 'law' of this sort has a chance of being correct,[4] and that physics

---

[3] As I will note later, the asymmetry in statistical relations doesn't hold among *all* variables; the claim is only that it holds among variables *salient to us*. So the directionality in causation has a surprising anthropomorphic aspect as well as a surprising extrinsic aspect.

[4] And the corresponding statements involving 'will' instead of 'must' are never *non-accidentally* correct: if they are exceptionless, it is only because the initial conditions required for an exception are never realized.

has progressed by replacing such alleged laws by differential equations. In some ways differential equations have a very different character: for instance, instead of directly connecting things at two different times (which leaves lots of opportunities for outside influences to make things go wrong), a differential equation involves a single time only: it determines the rate at which a quantity changes at a given time t from the value of it and other quantities at that very time; by giving the rate of change, it indirectly gives you the values at other times, though only when a very detailed description of the values at t are plugged in. In fact, even when one assumes that 'causal influence' can't exceed the speed of light, still one will need a description of an entire cross-section of the past light cone of an event to determine the event. Somewhat more precisely, *information about what happens at an earlier time can't suffice to determine the event unless it includes information about each point at that time that is within the past light cone*; only when there is information about each such point can the possibility of intervention from afar (e.g. by extremely powerful pulses of energy) be excluded. This seems to mean that (assuming determinism) facts about each part of the past light cone of an event are among the causes of the event.[5] (Of course, most such facts won't be salient enough to be worth mentioning in typical contexts where we are asked to cite causes, but like the presence of oxygen when (or a moment before) a fire starts, they are causes nonetheless.) Russell did not consider the possibility of indeterministic laws, but the point would be little changed if he had: the general point is that no reasonable laws of physics, whether deterministic or indeterministic, will make the probability of what happens at a time depend on only finitely many localized antecedent states; one will need an entire cross-section of the light cone to make the determination. Indeed, given quantum non-locality, one will need even more.

Perhaps all this shows is that an event has a lot more causes than we may naively assume; what's the big deal in that? But there would be a big deal if we had to conclude that if c_1 and c_2 are both in the past light cone of e then there is no way of regarding one of them as any more a cause of e than the other: then Sam's praying that the fire would go out would be no less a cause than Sara's aiming the water-hose at it, and the notion of causation would lose its whole point. *One* way to read Russell (possibly not the most interesting way) is as implicitly arguing that the form of our physical laws makes this conclusion inevitable; such an argument is explicitly discussed by Latham (1987), and I think it raises a serious problem for those, like Davidson (1967), who restrict causes to fairly concrete events.

More explicitly: what I take to be the clear truth behind the (Russell?)–Latham argument is that since there is always a possibility of interventions from afar, the

---

[5] This is certainly implied by views (Mackie 1965; Bennett 1988) on which any part of a minimal sufficient condition for something happening at t is one of its causes; or by weaker views that imply this only when all parts of that minimal sufficient condition involve the same time, and that time is earlier than t.

non-occurrence of those interventions must be included among the causes of an event. Instead of sitting there idly praying, Sam might have taken effective means to keep the fire going, say by shooting a hole in Sara's water-hose before it could put out the fire. His *not* shooting the hose should be included among the causes of the fire going out. Of course, this is the kind of cause that we wouldn't mention (unless there was some special reason to think he *might* shoot the hose); like the presence of oxygen in the lighting of a match, it is an extraordinarily non-salient cause, but it is a cause nonetheless, and virtually every serious account of causation will treat it as such. This is not in itself a problem. But it would become a problem if we thought that causes have to be events and that when Sam was sitting there praying instead of shooting the hose, there was only one event (a praying-and-not-shooting-the-hose event): for then we would have to conclude that his praying was a cause of the fire going out. And by extension of the reasoning, we would have to conclude that everything about the past light cone of the fire's going out was a cause of it. To avoid this, we had better avoid the Davidsonian view that only quite concrete events can serve as causes: we should instead say either that facts as well as events can serve as causes (Bennett 1988); or that the events that serve as causes can be highly unspecific, including 'omissions' like Sam's not shooting the hose (Lewis 1986a,c); or some such thing.[6]

I don't think Latham's argument is all that Russell was worried about when he stressed the difference between differential equations and simple pre-scientific laws about what happens when you strike a match. Whether his other worries are more troublesome I'm not sure. (I'll mention one or two of them later.) At any rate, Russell's conclusion was that the notion of causation is hard to make sense of in physical terms, and from this he drew the conclusion that it is a notion that we ought to abandon. Abandoning it would do no harm, he thought, because physics doesn't need it.

2. Effectiveness of Strategies and Causal Graphs

But, as Cartwright points out (Cartwright 1979), the cost of abandoning the notion of causation is intolerably high: for that notion is intimately connected with the distinction between effective and ineffective strategies. We all think that for the

---

[6] I suspect that the difference between Bennett and Lewis is mostly terminological, over what they mean by 'event'. Another variant with little if any substantive difference from the Bennett view is that 'is a cause of' isn't a relation at all, but rather, is part of a sentential connective.

goal of avoiding lung cancer, it's beneficial to stop smoking. Intuitively the reason is that smoking is a cause of lung cancer. The reason is *not* simply that there is a high statistical correlation between smoking and lung cancer. For correlation is symmetric: if there is a high statistical correlation between smoking and lung cancer, there is a high statistical correlation between lung cancer and smoking. But for the goal of stopping smoking, it is not in the least beneficial to take a cancer-preventing drug, because cancer isn't a cause of smoking. Similarly, there is a high statistical correlation between lung cancer and the foul breath that cigarettes produce, owing to the fact that both are caused by smoking. But for avoiding cancer, breath mints do no good; nor would a cancer-preventing drug be likely to be of use in avoiding bad breath.

The most dramatic illustrations of the point also illustrate something called 'Simpson's paradox', a surprising fact about statistics known since about the turn of the century, but which before Cartwright's article was not known as widely among philosophers as it should have been. The illustration that follows is not hers, but derives from a discussion of Ronald Fisher's of whether we have evidence that smoking causes cancer. (I've added a small twist.)

Imagine that we have performed a statistical study in which many people are randomly chosen and studied over the course of a lifetime; they are categorized in terms of whether they smoked heavily in their early years and whether they got lung cancer later in life. Imagine that the breakdown is as in Table 14.1. It looks as if, if you smoke, your chances of cancer are $49,501/100,000 = 0.49501$, whereas if you don't, your chances are only $9,980/900,000 = 0.01109$. 'Obviously you're much better off not smoking'. (By a factor of about 45 to 1.)

But to continue the fantasy, suppose we gather further information about these very same people, namely, information as to which ones possess a certain gene, Gene X. (This new information in no way alters the statistics above.) Let's pretend that this new information allows us to break down the original table to look like Table 14.2. Suppose you have Gene X. Then if you smoke, your chances of cancer are $49,500/99,000 = 0.5$, whereas if you don't, your chances are $990/1,000 = 0.99$. 'Obviously if you have Gene X, you're much better off smoking.' (By a factor of almost 2 to 1.) But suppose you don't have Gene X. Then if you smoke, your

Table 14.1

	Smokers (no.)	Non-smokers (no.)
Cancer	49,501	9,980
No cancer	50,499	890,020
TOTAL	100,000	900,000

Table 14.2

	Smokers with X (no.)	Smokers without X (no.)	Non-smokers with X (no.)	Non-smokers without X (no.)
Cancer	49,500	1	990	8,990
No cancer	49,500	999	10	890,010
TOTAL	99,000	1,000	1,000	899,000

chances of cancer are $1/1,000 = 0.001$, whereas if you don't your chances are $8,990/899,000 = 0.01$. 'Obviously if you don't have Gene X, you're also much better off smoking.' (By a factor of 10 to 1.) The information about the gene in no way alters the overwhelmingly high statistical correlation between smoking and cancer, but seems to dramatically alter its significance. For the natural conclusion from the second data is this: *Smoking is not a cause of cancer, and in fact tends strongly to prevent cancer; though there is a strong positive statistical correlation between smoking and cancer, that is because they have a common genetic cause.*[7] So from a health-conscious point of view, one ought to endure the disgusting habit of smoking because of its health benefits.[8] (Perhaps it even is a health benefit to all those other people who are forced to breathe your second-hand smoke.)

The example illustrates three points. First, it emphasizes what should have been a familiar point anyway, that correlation doesn't imply causation. (The earlier examples of lung cancer not causing smoking and of neither lung cancer nor nicotine breath causing the other already made this clear.) Secondly, it illustrates the initially surprising mathematical fact that *a variable S can be positively correlated with a variable C overall and yet be negatively correlated with C both conditional on a third variable X and also conditional on $\neg X$.* The example not only illustrates this, but shows how it can happen: it can happen if the causal situation is as pictured in the following 'causal graph' (where the labelled arrows indicate positive or negative influence),

---

[7] Of course, just as the natural causal conclusion to draw from the first set of data is undercut by the fuller data in the second set, so also the natural causal conclusion to draw from the fuller data in the second set could conceivably be undercut by still further data.

[8] At the same time, if you have no independent knowledge of whether you have the gene, it is bad news to find yourself smoking, since this is evidence that you have the gene and have a good chance of getting cancer as a result of it despite your best efforts to prevent it by smoking.

and if the positive correlation between S and C induced by their common cause X is sufficient to outweigh the negative correlation between them that results from the preventative effect of S on C. The third point that is illustrated is that it is the causal conclusions and not the correlations that we need to know in order to best achieve our ends. (Cartwright concedes that we might be able to make do with conditional probabilities instead of causal notions, but only on a conception of conditional probability that is 'causally loaded', i.e. that involves holding fixed all other causal factors not causally dependent on the condition.)

I think this makes a compelling case against Russell's view that we should do without causal notions. But Cartwright herself draws a much stronger conclusion, a kind of *causal hyper-realism*, according to which there are causal facts *that outrun the totality of 'non-causal facts'* (i.e. the facts that could be expressible in some language without using causal terminology). Indeed, her claim isn't simply that there is no reasonable way to explicitly define causation in non-causal terms; it seems to be that causal claims don't even supervene on the non-causal facts. Among the 'non-causal facts' she includes the basic laws of physics—e.g. Newton's law that an object accelerates in direct proportion to the force impressed on it and in inverse proportion to its mass. She holds that the causal fact that a force on an object *makes* the object go faster is not reducible to Newton's law, nor to other non-causal facts either, such as the equations of energy flow from the sources of fields to the fields themselves to the accelerating objects. (Such equations are just further parts of fundamental physics, which she regards as 'laws of association' rather than as causal.) Rather, the claim that a force on an object makes the object go faster states a further truth about the world that physics leaves out. Evidently there is some sort of causal fluid that is not taken account of in the equations of physics; just how it is that we are supposed to have access to its properties I am not sure.[9]

But despite the implausibility of the hyper-realist picture, we have a problem to solve: the problem of reconciling Cartwright's points about the need of causation in a theory of effective strategy with Russell's points about the limited role of causation in physics. This is probably the central problem in the metaphysics of causation.

One thing that needs to be noted about this problem is that the examples given of the need of the notion of causation (for instance, 'Teenage smoking tends to cause lung cancer') have concerned *general* causal claims among variables that are *fairly inexact* in the sense that they can be instantiated in many different ways. First, let's discuss the generality. The precise connection between such general causal claims and specific causal claims like 'Joe's teenage smoking was a cause of his lung cancer' is complex and controversial: some have thought that singular causal claims should be explained in terms of general causal claims; some have thought the order of explanation should be reversed; some have thought that both should be explained in terms of some third thing (for instance, objective probability); and some have

---

[9] I'm also not sure why the laws governing the causal fluid don't count as mere laws of association.

thought that we simply have two different kinds of causal claim that are only loosely connected with each other.

The view that takes general causal claims as primary is totally implausible if general causal claims include claims like 'Turning the left knob on radios clockwise causes the volume to increase'. That may be a true generalization, or may have been one at a time when radio cases had a certain design, but as a generalization over systems of different sorts it has little interest or robustness. General claims *about a given system*, such as 'Turning the left knob of *this* radio clockwise causes the volume to increase', might with more plausibility be regarded as prior to singular causal claims.

But 'singularist' views that take singular causal claims as primary and explain general claims in terms of singular seem at least equally plausible.[10] On such a view, 'Smoking is a cause of cancer' might mean something like 'The probability of a person's smoking being a significant cause of his getting cancer, given that he smokes and given an appropriate context, is not insubstantial'.[11] Should the fact that the motivation we have given for the need of causation involves general causal claims undermine this? I don't think so: for in fact what is important to know for deciding how to act isn't whether refraining from smoking is *generally* an effective strategy for avoiding cancer, but whether it would be an effective strategy *for me* to adopt. And so what I need to know is the chance that smoking will cause cancer in my own case. The focus on generalizations was really just a matter of convenience, justified only in circumstances where the agent can regard himself as a typical member of the population.[12]

[10] I'm not certain that the priority issue between singular claims and *system-restricted* general claims is ultimately a clear one.

[11] Note that there are three different ways in which this is interest-relative: interests determine the appropriate contexts, they determine how significant a causal role is being claimed for smoking in those contexts, and they determine how high the probability of causation needs to be to count.

[12] It might be thought that I shouldn't even really care about the chance of my smoking *causing* my cancer, but only about the conditional probability of my *getting* cancer on the assumption that I smoke and the conditional probability on the assumption that I don't smoke. If so, causation might seem irrelevant to effectiveness of strategy after all. I am sympathetic to the idea that what a person should be concerned about can be stated simply in terms of conditional probabilities; but this is defensible only on a special interpretation of the probabilities involved, and the required notion of probability is intimately bound up with the notion of causation.

The issues here have been more thoroughly discussed in the context of theories of rational decision rather than theories of effectiveness of strategy. A common claim (e.g. Skyrms 1980) has been that standard ('evidential') decision theory dictates the obviously unreasonable conclusion that even if one knows the Gene X story to be true one ought not smoke (if health is the only consideration), provided that one doesn't know whether one has Gene X. To avoid the conclusion, it is alleged that one must modify decision theory by building the notion of causation explicitly into one's rule of decision. But a number of authors have pointed out ways round the argument for replacing evidential decision theory by a causal decision theory. Some (e.g. Horwich 1987) rely on the controversial assumption that the only way for Gene X to lead us to smoke is to produce in us an introspectible desire to smoke (this is called the 'tickle defence'), but more recent authors avoid this: see e.g. Price (1986, 1991); Meek and Glymour (1994). Still, on the Price and Meek–Glymour accounts the agent's subjective probabilities are

But though it is probably not significant that our examples of the need of causation have concerned *general* causal claims, I think it is significant that they have concerned claims that involve *fairly inexact variables*. 'Inexact' here doesn't mean 'vague': rather, a variable is inexact if the claim that it assumes a given value on an occasion can be realized in many different ways that on a deeper level of analysis are importantly different. If I am deciding whether to smoke, then even if I have detailed information about the other factors that are relevant to whether I will get lung cancer, I certainly can be nowhere near having *enough* information: the outcome is bound to depend on fine details about the state of my body now and of the rest of the universe that I will interact with, and on the details of how I might carry out my decision to smoke or to refrain from smoking. (It will also depend on the outcomes of irreducibly chance processes, if the universe is indeterministic; but it is the kind of statistical probability that exists over and above any ultimate chanciness that there may be that is important to my current point.) This means that the predictions of interest to us could not be made on the basis of the underlying physics without the use of substantial statistical assumptions, of the general sort that are also required for thermodynamics. The notion of causation, like the notions of temperature and entropy, derives its value from contexts where statistical regularities not necessitated by the underlying physical laws are important. As noted before, that does not necessarily mean that the notion of causation can't be applied in contexts where such statistical regularities are absent; but it does make the point of causal talk in such contexts depend in a surprising way on factors extrinsic to the contexts.

I will conclude this section by mentioning a recent account of the empirical confirmation of causal generalizations by correlational data (Spirtes *et al.* 1993; see also Pearl 2000). The account in Spirtes, Glymour, and Scheines (1993) has a considerable bearing on the topics I have discussed. It makes clear that causal graphs like the one displayed several pages back play an important role in our thinking about causation and about how we expect the correlations to alter when we make decisions (or when the system is disturbed from the outside); and it makes explicit the assumptions we employ about how the causal structure of the graph constrains the assignment of objective probabilities to combinations of values of the variables. In doing so, it makes clear precisely *how* the notion of causation is directional. If Z is a common *cause* of X and Y, then that will tend to induce an *unconditional* probabilistic dependence between X and Y; though as long as there are no intermediate common causes, holding fixed the value of Z cancels the probabilistic dependence of X and Y.[13] If on the other hand Z is a common *effect* of X and Y, it is pretty much the other way around: the common effect *doesn't* induce

intimately bound up with her beliefs about causation, and some might argue that they need to be justified in terms of assumptions about causation (or about objective probability in some causally loaded sense). So the significance of avoiding explicit appeal to causation in the decision rule is controversial.

[13] Of course, these dependences and independences can be masked by other common causes of X and Y.

an *unconditional* dependence between X and Y, but holding the common effect fixed does induce a probabilistic dependence.[14] (The account of how probabilities are to be modified when the system is disturbed by a decision or by a 'natural' occurrence from the outside also involves directional elements, but this asymmetry seems to derive from the basic asymmetry in the way that causal graphs constrain probability. See the 'Manipulation Theorem' in Spirtes *et al.* 1993, sect. 3.7.2.)

This account of the asymmetry in causal graphs gives a way to make fairly precise the temporal asymmetry that underlies the concept of causation: the asymmetry consists in the pair of facts

> (M) that the variables we find salient tend to be probabilistically related in such a way that you can draw causal graphs among them in accordance with Spirtes *et al.*'s conditions (the ones roughly sketched in the preceding paragraph);

and

> (T) (around here anyway, and among salient variables) what are causes on the causal graph criterion nearly always precede their effects.

(This is similar to, though more comprehensive than, the 'fork asymmetry' discussed by many writers, e.g. Horwich 1987.) The salience condition needs emphasis: if the universe is two-way deterministic as in classical physics, one can find very unnatural variables for which the temporal orientation in (T) is reversed: see Arntzenius (1993, sects. 5 and 6). And with 'exact' variables in the sense explained above, the asymmetry completely disappears in classical physics. Quantum mechanics gives rise to more dramatic failures of (M) and (T) together: the much discussed non-local correlations between measurements of distant particles[15] cannot be given explanations that accord with (M) except with highly unnatural causal graphs (for instance, ones where the outcome of the measurement influences either the prior state of the particles or the prior choice of settings of the measurement instruments). But despite all these limitations on their scope, (M) and (T) together describe an overwhelmingly pervasive asymmetric regularity on the macroscopic scale. Interesting questions arise about how this regularity is to be explained, but I will not pursue them.

Even if there are extraordinarily non-salient variables for which what would count as a 'cause' by Spirtes *et al.*'s constraints comes later than what counts as an 'effect', it doesn't follow that we should take Spirtes *et al.*'s approach as dictating that some effects precede their causes. A better conclusion is that causes must always

---

[14] Whether the light switch at one end of the hall is up may be independent of whether the light switch at the other end is up, even though the positions are highly correlated given that the light is off (they must be in opposite positions, barring a burned-out bulb or melted wire), and almost perfectly correlated given that the light is on.

[15] See e.g. Maudlin (1994, ch. 1) or any of the essays in Cushing and McMullin (1989).

be temporally prior to their effects, but that this is non-arbitrary because of the empirical fact (T). (Horwich 1987 makes a similar suggestion.)

Spirtes *et al.*'s theory may confirm one of Russell's suspicions: the causal graphs that its authors employ involve only finitely many variables, and this fact[16] plays a key role in how they develop the theory. If the theory *can't* be developed independently of this assumption, Russell would appear to be right in holding that the methodology of testing *general* causal claims essentially requires a radical idealization of the underlying physics. And perhaps this conclusion could be transferred to singular claims too, if causal graphs play a substantial role in the theory of them (as I think is likely). However, I don't think it at all obvious that the causal graph approach can't be generalized. Intuitively, it seems (barring quantum non-locality and the like) that one should be able to think of the physical universe as a causal system with a node for each space-time point, with the value of the node expressing the totality of the values of physical quantities at that point; the light cone structure gives the dependence relations. The kind of simple causal systems we employ in practice seem as if they ought to have such a 'non-discrete causal system' as a limiting case. But of course the details of this vague suggestion would need to be worked out, and I wouldn't be surprised if some of our causal intuitions (e.g. about pre-emption, soon to be discussed) would fail to be validated in the limiting case.

3. CAUSATION AND COUNTERFACTUALS

I have emphasized the statistical underpinnings of the notion of causation, at least with regard to directionality; but that does not necessarily mean that an account of causation applicable to individual processes must make explicit reference to statistical facts. How else might an account of singular causation proceed?

An idea mentioned in passing by Hume (1748), and taken up by Lewis (1973), is that causation involves counterfactual dependence. Hume and Lewis use 'would' counterfactuals: the initial idea (before the bells and whistles are added) is that for John's smoking to have caused his cancer, it must be the case that if he hadn't smoked he wouldn't have gotten cancer.[17] An alternative (McDermott 1995a) uses 'might' counterfactuals: the initial idea is that for John's smoking to have caused his cancer,

---

[16] Or at least the fact that the causal ordering of the variables is backwards-discrete, i.e. that every node that has a non-immediate predecessor p has an immediate predecessor q of which p is a predecessor.

[17] If our interest is in contrastive causation (Hitchcock 1993, 1995), as it really should be, we need contrastive counterfactuals: the counterfactualist should say that for John's smoking cigarettes as opposed to his smoking cigars to have caused his cancer, it must be the case that if he had smoked cigars instead

it must be the case that if John hadn't smoked he might not have gotten cancer; that is, it must not be the case that if he hadn't smoked he would have gotten cancer.[18] There are also intermediate alternatives, e.g. 'would probably' counterfactuals and more complicated counterfactuals that involve comparisons of probability. The differences between these alternatives are not insignificant (and they arise under determinism as well as under indeterminism),[19] but will not be discussed here.

The counterfactual framework is broad enough to encompass many accounts of causation not often thought of as counterfactual accounts. For instance, Mackie (1965) has offered an account of causation under determinism in terms of which for C to cause E, there must be a minimal sufficient condition for E that includes C (minimally sufficient given the basic physical laws). Given determinism, the existence of a sufficient condition for E that includes C is trivial; what's crucial is the minimality, and what it says is that excluding C from the condition, the laws no longer guarantee E.[20] A natural way to put that is: if C hadn't occurred, E might not have either. On a suitable account of counterfactuals (basically, the Goodman account in terms of laws), Mackie's account is just an account in terms of 'might' counterfactuals.

Counterfactuals are of course notoriously context-dependent: much more so even than causal claims. It is perfectly within the bounds of ordinary counterfactual talk to say that if the barometer needle hadn't dropped, there wouldn't have been a storm a short time later; but no one wants to say that the dropping of the barometer

of cigarettes he would not have gotten cancer. The use of contrastive causal statements is especially important when we try to generalize to an account of causation for indeterministic contexts, but that lies outside the scope of this chapter. (See Menzies 1989 for a discussion of one important issue about it.)

[18] The distinction between 'would' counterfactuals and 'might' counterfactuals apparently collapses if, like Stalnaker, one takes the following to be a logical law:

(CEM) Either (if A were the case then B) or (if A were the case then not-B).

But even on Stalnaker's view such a distinction remains; it just must be drawn differently. For in defending (CEM) against apparent counter-examples, Stalnaker concedes that it is sometimes indeterminate which disjunct holds. In that case, there is a distinction between it being determinate that if John hadn't smoked he wouldn't have gotten cancer and it not being determinate that if John hadn't smoked he would have gotten cancer, and we could use that distinction instead of the distinction between 'would' counterfactuals and 'might' counterfactuals in our theory of causation.

[19] Even under determinism, there are various ways for John to have smoked and not to have smoked, ways not necessarily under John's powers to discriminate between, and whether cancer results is likely to depend on the way in which he smokes or fails to smoke. It is not out of the question to invoke a statistical probability measure over the ways of his not smoking, and perhaps the ways of his smoking as well; and it is worth distinguishing such a use of statistical probability from the use of any dynamic probability measure involved in fundamental indeterministic laws, because a theory might well invoke these different kinds of probability in different ways.

[20] It should be clear from the discussion of the Russell–Latham problem that such a minimal sufficient condition for E will have to be very big: if it includes only information about a specific time prior to E then it will have to include some information about each point at that time that is in the past light cone of E.

needle was a cause of the storm. Similarly, it is perfectly acceptable to say that if Jane's parents had both had blue eyes, Jane would have had blue eyes too; but most people who say that know that this is not a cause–effect relation but is owing to a common cause, the parental genotypes. Lewis recognizes that such counterfactuals must be discounted if causation is to be based on counterfactuals. Lewis says that the barometer counterfactual and the blue-eyes counterfactual are acceptable only in special contexts, contexts where we allow 'backtracking arguments'. If a backtracking argument is one where we reason from effects to causes, it is plausible to say that such counterfactuals do involve backtracking arguments: a scientifically knowledgeable person asked to defend the barometer counterfactual would do so by saying that if the barometer needle fell, that would most likely be owing to a region of low pressure that would be likely to cause a storm. It is also plausible that there are contexts in which we do not accept counterfactuals supported only by backtracking arguments. I don't know if Lewis is right that the latter contexts are 'the normal ones', but doubt that it much matters: it would be no serious threat to a counterfactual account of causation if it required a somewhat specialized kind of counterfactual. What does matter, though, is whether the distinction between the two kinds of context can be made without appeal to the notion of causation. If it can't, then there seems to be a circularity in a counterfactual theory that depends on the restriction to non-backtracking counterfactuals (counterfactuals that can be defended without appeal to backtracking arguments).

One possible way to avoid the use of the notion of causation in distinguishing backtracking counterfactuals from others is to use temporal order instead. Of course, in the above examples it can't be used directly: the barometer counterfactual and the blue-eyes counterfactual involve the same standard time order present in the case of non-backtracking counterfactuals (the time of the consequent is later than that of the antecedent).[21] But perhaps we could argue that these counterfactuals are only supportable by means of other counterfactuals (a barometer to low pressure counterfactual or a parental phenotype to parental genotype counterfactual) that involve reverse time order. We would have to argue this *without using causal notions* if this was to help the counterfactual theorist of causation; but maybe this could be done.

This approach is reasonably attractive, but it is not one that Lewis can use. For one of the main advantages that Lewis claims for his counterfactual approach to causation is that it *explains* the directionality of causation: more specifically, it explains why causes nearly always precede their effects (at least in our part of the universe in

---

[21] Lewis notes that counterfactuals in which the time order of consequent to antecedent is the reverse of this tend to be given special syntactic markers (Lewis 1986d: 34–5). Note though (contrary to what his discussion there suggests) that this syntactic 'peculiarity' is not present in all counterfactuals that depend on backtracking arguments: it isn't present in the barometer counterfactual or the blue-eyes counterfactual, since the time order there is standard.

the current epoch), and does so not merely as a result of stipulation that causes are always prior but in a fashion that illuminates the genuine directional asymmetry noted earlier. But he could not claim this advantage for the counterfactual account if his account of causation were to be based on a restriction to those counterfactuals in which the time of the antecedent precedes the time of the consequent: then causes would precede effects simply by fiat.

It is sometimes suggested that the 'peculiarity' of backtracking conditionals arises from their extreme indeterminacy or uncertainty. If this were so, perhaps excluding the extremely indeterminate or uncertain counterfactuals would suffice to exclude backtrackers without relying either on explicit fiat or on the notion of cause. But the claim that the peculiarity of backtrackers arises from their extreme indeterminacy or uncertainty appears to be false. Consider the following pair:

(1) If Oswald hadn't killed Kennedy in 1963, Kennedy would have won the 1964 election.
(2) If Kennedy had won the 1964 election, Oswald wouldn't have killed him in 1963.

Provided that we don't simply exclude backtracking conditionals, (2) seems more certain than (1) (and less likely to be indeterminate in truth-value than (1)): with (1), there's always a chance that the affair with Marilyn Monroe would have become public and that this would have outraged the American public so much that they preferred Goldwater (or whoever the Republican candidate might have been); a comparable story for (2) would have to be wilder (the government keeping his assassination secret; or the public being so outraged by the choice of Johnson and Goldwater that they preferred to write in a dead man; or whatever). I agree that many kinds of counterfactuals seem more indeterminate in the backwards direction than in the forward, but this and many other examples make it highly doubtful that our tendency to exclude backtrackers can be wholly explained as due to that fact.

Lewis makes a different attempt to found the distinction between backtracking and non-backtracking counterfactuals independently of both causation and time, but it too is a failure, as I will argue in the next section. Still, I think it may be possible to found the distinction using less than the full notion of singular causation, and in a way that allows for a serious explanation of directionality.[22] Let us put aside

---

[22] One approach that might do this would be based on the idea (mentioned earlier as a possibility) that system-specific general causal claims are prior to singular causal claims; if Spirtes *et al.*'s-style causal models could be used in an account of the general causal claims, the direction of the arrows in such models could be used in an account of singular causation.

Another approach would be to separate the explanation of directionality from the account of counterfactuals proper, by building explicitly into the latter that the time of the antecedent must precede that of the consequent but then going on to explain why an account with this feature is more explanatorily useful than one with the reverse time order built in. (This is the analogue for counterfactuals of something I suggested directly for causation in the penultimate paragraph of Sect. 2.) Of course,

any doubts we may have that this can be done, and return to how non-backtracking counterfactuals can be used in an account of causation.

Suppose C and E are true event-statements about disjoint regions. The simplest 'would'-counterfactual approach to singular causation would be to take causation to be counterfactual dependence (in a non-backtracking sense): (The fact that) C is a cause of (the fact that) E iff if C weren't the case, E wouldn't be the case either; or in symbols, $\neg C \,\square\!\!\rightarrow \neg E$.[23] This was essentially Hume's proposal. (Not his main view, of course, but a proposal he mentioned in passing.) Lewis (1973) weakened the account slightly: C is a cause of E iff there is some chain of true event statements $A_0, A_1, \ldots, A_n$, with $A_0 = C$ and $A_n = E$, such that for each $i < n$, $\neg A_i \,\square\!\!\rightarrow \neg A_{i+1}$. This modification of Hume guarantees that singular causation is transitive.

There is, however, reason to doubt that singular causation should be thought transitive. Consider a famous example from Cartwright (1979) (one that Cartwright uses for a different purpose). Suppose that Nancy sprays a fairly effective weedkiller on a weed in her garden; this triggers its 'immune system' to counter it, and as a result the plant survives to photosynthesize for years to come. The spraying of the weedkiller was a cause of the 'immune reaction'; the immune reaction was a cause of the survival, or of the future photosynthesis; so transitivity dictates that the spraying of the weedkiller should be a cause of the survival, or of the future photosynthesis. Pre-theoretically, this seems dubious. Further examples casting doubt on transitivity can be found in McDermott (1995b). The examples are probably not decisive, but they certainly have some force, and raise the question of whether there are good reasons to accept transitivity.

Lewis's reason for accepting transitivity (not only in 1973 but in two substantial revisions of his view: Lewis 1986e, 2000) was to deal with a certain sort of pre-emption. Suppose Joe throws a rock at a window, breaking it. Pete, closer to the window, was poised to throw an identical rock along the final segment of the same path that Joe's rock actually took, in a way that would reach the window at the same time with the same velocity; he refrained from doing so because he saw Joe's rock coming. We want Joe's throwing the rock to count as a cause of the window breaking; but if he hadn't thrown the rock, the window would have broken anyway (and in just the way it actually did). We have causation without counterfactual dependence.[24] But if we accept the transitivity of causation, we will get the desired causal claim as

such an approach would work only if the temporal restriction indirectly excludes common-cause counterfactuals somehow.

[23] If one wants events rather than facts in the cause or effect position, one can use counterfactuals about the occurrence of the events.

[24] One might try to save the counterfactual dependence story by taking the relevant counterfactual dependence to be this: the fact that the window broke *in just the way it did* counterfactually depends on the fact that Joe threw the rock *in just the way he did*. But if we suppose that had Joe thrown his rock differently from the way he actually threw it, Pete would have stopped Joe's rock and thrown his own rock in the way he was poised to do in the story (i.e. in a way that makes its final velocity and time

long as there are intermediate events that counterfactually depend on Joe's throw and on which the window's breaking counterfactually depends. And there are such, though we must be a bit careful in how to choose them.[25]

I'm sceptical, though, that the appeal to such intermediate events reflects our intuitive rationale for judging that Joe's throwing the rock was a cause of the window's shattering. The intuitive rationale, I think, involves *conditional* counterfactual dependence (rather than chains of unconditional counterfactual dependence): the intuitive rationale is that *holding fixed the fact that Pete didn't throw*, the window's shattering does depend counterfactually on Joe's throw.[26] If we can explain causation in terms of *conditional* counterfactual dependence, we don't need to transitivize. It seems to me that there is something quite odd about the use of transitivity to handle such examples of pre-emption, for such pre-emption examples seem intimately related to *failures* of transitivity: if Joe hadn't thrown, that would have caused Pete to throw, which would have caused the window to break; so transitivity tells us that Joe's not throwing would have caused the window to break! Moreover, there are many cases of pre-emption that invoking transitivity clearly won't solve (the various sorts of 'late pre-emption' discussed in Lewis 1986a), but many and perhaps all of them seem naturally handleable in terms of conditional dependence.[27] The

---

of arrival the same as on Joe's *actual* throw), there is no more a counterfactual dependence on Joe's manner of throwing than there is on his throwing.

[25] (1) If Pete's rock passing a certain point at a certain time (with a certain velocity) would have been a different event from Joe's rock passing that point at that time (with that velocity), then for any point and time on the final segment of the trajectory of Joe's rock, the event E_1 of the rock passing that point at that time counterfactually depends on Joe's throw, and the window's breaking in the way it did counterfactually depends (in the non-backtacking sense) on E_1. (2) Even without relying on the special assumption about event identity, we could rely on the fact that Pete can't have actually been in the path of Joe's rock (since if he had he would have been hit by it), so it would have taken him a certain amount of time to see that Joe wasn't throwing and to get into position to throw himself. So the window's shattering counterfactually depends on an event E_0 concerning the trajectory of a rock a microsecond before Pete would have had to throw, and of course E_0 depends on Joe's throw.

[26] When C, E, and A are true, saying that E counterfactually depends on C, holding A fixed, is simply to say that if A and not-C were the case then not-E would be the case. This is an ordinary non-backtracking counterfactual, though one whose antecedent involves multiple locations. (We need counterfactuals whose antecedents involve multiple locations for causal statements anyway, for cases where the cause involves what's going on at multiple locations.) Any apparent specialness in the particular multi-node counterfactuals here arises from the fact that, in the cases of interest, A is an effect of C. But a restriction on backtracking is best formalized by cutting the causal inputs to each node in the cause; and this way of formalizing it gives the results we want in the multi-node counterfactuals that we need here.

[27] Another kind of pre-emption ('trumping') is discussed in Schaffer (2000): the major and the sergeant shout the same order at the same time, and the private follows the common order; but it seems as if the major's order was the cause since had the two orders differed the private would have obeyed the major. It seems to me that any problem this raises for counterfactual theories is an artefact of using binary variables (major either giving order C or giving no order, and similarly for sergeant): a proper representation of the situation would allow the major and the sergeant each to give orders other than C, and this will show the counterfactual dependence on the major's order but not the sergeant's. (Indeed, the intuitive argument that the major's order was the cause already appealed to the possibility of orders other than C.)

suggestion that we use conditional dependence rather than transitivity to handle pre-emption is plausibly developed in Hitchcock (forthcoming). Hitchcock notes a different reason for finding the transitivity approach implausible: in cases (like the window case) where transitivity yields intuitively desirable results it is only by virtue of extremely carefully chosen intermediate variables (see note 25), so that the application of transitivity is unobvious; whereas in cases (like the Cartwright case) where it yields intuitively undesirable results, the fact that transitivity yields those results is plain to see. If transitivity is what is responsible for our intuitive judgements of causation, we ought to find causation obvious in the Cartwright case and much less obvious in the window case.

I don't mean to suggest that all problems about pre-emption are solved merely by adopting the conditional dependence approach. Collins (2000) presents an interesting group of puzzle cases that the approach doesn't seem to handle as it stands. Moreover, Cian Dorr has pointed out to me that with a clever choice of variables to hold fixed, many of the dubious cases of causation that are clearly licensed by transitivity can be argued to be licensed (though at least less obviously) by conditional dependence as well. Hitchcock (forthcoming) discusses this as well, and proposes a way to deal with it. A fuller discussion of the adequacy of his resolution or other possible resolutions would probably connect up with an issue from Russell with which I began: is causation a notion that has application only within an idealized model of the world, in which we simplify the causal history of an event by focusing on a few 'causal pathways' and ignore interactions among them and interventions from outside, or should we rather give an account that is sensitive to the fact that some features of every point in the past light cone of an event is causally relevant to that event? In addition to this issue, issues about independent complications in the account of causation, e.g. to handle symmetric overdetermination and causation under indeterminism, are sure to enter in. Such further discussion is far beyond the scope of this chapter.

4. THE DIRECTIONALITY OF CAUSATION

I now return to the issue of the directionality of causation. Lewis (1986b, d) claims that a main advantage of (his version of) the counterfactual account of causation over what he calls 'regularity analyses' is that the former can straightforwardly account for causal directionality. If we presuppose determinism and confine attention to causal claims where the cause statement C involves a certain instant of time t_1 and the effect statement E involves a certain distinct instant of time t_2, a simple 'regularity analysis' might say that C is a cause of E if and only if there is a minimal condition C^* involving t_1 that suffices for E given the basic physical laws, and C^* entails C. But unless we are willing to add the further requirement that t_1 precedes t_2, no account much like this can work in a two-way deterministic universe, since the right-hand side will be equally true when E is a cause of C.[28] And Lewis thinks it is a major defect in a theory of causation that it builds in the condition that the time of the cause precede that of the effect: that causes precede effects is something we ought to *explain*. A main advantage that he claims for his counterfactual theory is that it explains it.

Since Lewis explains causation in terms of counterfactual dependence, the issue for Lewis is how to explain the asymmetry of counterfactual dependence. If causation is explained in terms of counterfactual dependence, counterfactual dependence must be explained without use of the (full) notion of cause, and the objection to building a temporal precedence requirement into causation by fiat means that we can't simply rule out counterfactuals where the time of the antecedent is later than the time of the consequent by fiat. We're back to the issue of how to rule out backtrackers. (We have already observed that Lewis needs to count 'common cause' counterfactuals as backtrackers, even when the time of the antecedent precedes that of the consequent, so temporal fiat wouldn't directly suffice anyway, in the case of counterfactuals. But as I mentioned, such a fiat might be thought to rule out common-cause backtrackers indirectly.)

Lewis offers a very ingenious attempt to rule out backtrackers without temporal fiat, by an account of similarity among possible worlds. According to his basic account of counterfactuals, $\neg C \,\square\!\!\rightarrow \neg E$ is true iff there is a $\neg C$-world w (a possible world w where $\neg C$ holds) such that every possible $\neg C$-world that is at least as similar to the actual world as is w is a $\neg E$-world. He then proposes an account of similarity among worlds. If determinism holds in the actual world (as I will continue to assume for simplicity), then this account of similarity, taken together with familiar facts about the actual world, is supposed to have a dramatic consequence: that when C is a true event statement such that we might seriously entertain $\neg C$ as the antecedent of a counterfactual, there will be $\neg C$-worlds not too far from actuality, *and all of them will be like the actual world up until a time very shortly before the time of C.* At that point in any such world, a small miracle occurs, i.e. a small violation of the laws of the actual world, so as to allow $\neg C$ to hold; but then immediately afterwards, the laws of the actual world remain unviolated. This, I repeat, is supposed to follow (given contingent facts about the actual world) from an account of similarity *that doesn't rely on causal notions and doesn't build in a specific direction*

---

[28] Even with the requirement that t_1 precedes t_2, the condition *may* fail to rule out the possibility that C and E are effects of a common cause; I doubt that there is a problem here when the laws are like those of the actual universe (alleged examples, such as those of Bennett 1988: 45, fail to take account of how big determining conditions must be: see my n. 20), but there are imaginable laws for which the stipulation that t_1 precedes t_2 does not suffice.

of time. The similarity ordering of worlds that satisfies this account is the one we assume when we exclude backtrackers; for backtrackers there is a different similarity ordering, which we need not consider. So non-backtracking counterfactuals, Lewis claims, are simply counterfactuals that are to be evaluated by the standard similarity ordering.

Before discussing the main problem with this account, I'd like to note an immediate oddity about it. The oddity is that by avoiding temporal and causal notions in explaining backtracking, Lewis hasn't really *eliminated* backtracking in the normal sense (the sense where a true counterfactual of the form $\neg C \:\square\!\!\rightarrow\: \neg E$ where the time of E precedes the time of C is always a backtracker), but merely *limited* it. That is: assuming determinism, Lewis's account has it that it would have required a small miracle for Princeton not to have made the job offer to him that they in fact made, at some time t in 1969; and that the miracle would have had to occur at some point prior to t. It may not be determinate precisely which miracle would have occurred before t, but it is determinate that the world before t would have had to be a bit different somehow. So Lewis's account would seem to lead to the result that Princeton's offering him the job was a cause of some (highly conjunctive) effect just prior to it. (Lewis responds to this in Lewis 1981; for a counter-response, see Vihvelin 1991.) Indeed, for other counterfactuals, a price of keeping the miracle small is that the backtracking isn't limited to a very small time before (Bennett 1984): there are non-vacuous counterfactuals about what would have happened if Goldwater had won the 1964 election, but it is hard to see how a small miracle *a second or so before the time of the election* could have altered the outcome; there is a substantial period prior to the election that would have had to have been different for Goldwater to have won, and given Lewis's approach to backtracking some facts about this whole period would seem to come out as effects of Goldwater's losing. Anomalies like this seem to show that the prospects of explaining the intuitive distinction between backtrackers and non-backtrackers without appeal to either causation or a temporal direction are dim.

But a more fundamental worry about Lewis's account is that nothing in his account of similarity among worlds seems as if it can possibly explain why the 'small miracle' in the worlds most similar to the actual world must happen just prior to the time of the antecedent rather than just afterwards. (If it happened just afterwards, the possible worlds in question would be just like the actual world at later times, and differ drastically at times before, so that effects would mostly precede their causes rather than succeeding them.)

Lewis *appears* to address this point when he argues that when you take a possible world like ours in its initial stages, and introduce a small miracle in it at a time t_1, then if the world operates by the normal laws until a later time t_2, you will need a much bigger miracle at t_2 to bring the world back to coincidence with the actual world (because of the way that small differences get amplified over time). Lewis concludes that this illustrates a temporal asymmetry: because of something about what our world is like, 'convergence' miracles that bring worlds hitherto unlike ours into line with ours must be bigger than 'divergence miracles' that make worlds initially like ours start to differ. But this conclusion is too rash: the fact that you need a big miracle at t_2 to make a world that has diverged from the actual world at t_1 *reconverge* is really part of a temporally symmetric fact. The temporally symmetric fact that emerges from Lewis's discussion is that in a two-miracle world that is just like the actual world in both initial and final stages (and where there is a more than minuscule time between the two miracles), the miracles can't *both* be small; but the initial (divergence) miracle could be the big one.

The real issue for Lewis's account isn't the respective sizes of divergence miracles and *reconvergence* miracles; it's the respective sizes of (i) divergence miracles at a time $t_1 - \epsilon$ just prior to the actual time t_1 of C, in $\neg C$-worlds that are just like the actual world up until $t_1 - \epsilon$, but which may differ drastically after t; and (ii) convergence miracles at a time $t_1 + \epsilon$ just after the actual time of C, in $\neg C$-worlds that are just like the actual world after $t_1 + \epsilon$, but which may differ drastically before t. And (unless C is itself a temporally loaded claim) it is clear that the size of the miracle can be equally small in the two cases. Suppose, for instance, that C is a true claim about the position of one or more particles at t_1. One way to imagine a world that obeys the same laws as ours except for a minor miracle near t_1 is to suppose that the world is exactly like ours up until $t_1 - \epsilon$, but with shifted positions for these particles at t_1; the operation of the normal laws after t_1 will ensure that the world will become extremely different from ours at much later times. But just as easily, we can imagine that the world is exactly like ours after $t_1 + \epsilon$, but with shifted positions for these particles at t_1; the operation of the normal laws before t_1 will ensure that the world was extremely different from ours at much earlier times. There is simply no asymmetry here of the sort Lewis claims.[29]

Lewis's discussion of the asymmetry of traces may appear to provide an argument in the other direction. In our world, a stone dropping in a pond leaves many traces, in ripples proceeding outward and light waves being sent off into space and in the memories of those watching. What small miracle in a world where the stone didn't drop could have produced all these effects? It is important to realize that since the miracle-world need not (and cannot) be a *reconvergence* world, then in the period just prior to the miracle as well as in the period afterward, it can have misleading apparent traces of the stone having dropped: it needn't be the miracle that produces the misleading apparent traces. This removes a major intuitive obstacle to the miracle being small.

Even so, it may seem hard to conceive of what such a miracle-world would look like. But Elga (forthcoming) points out that if we assume the laws of physics to be time-reversal invariant, there is an easy way to conceive this. Take the time-reverse

---

[29] Something like this point is made in Price (1991), though in my view he concedes too much to Lewis.

of our world. (Roughly, the world that obeys the same physical laws as ours, and is now just like ours is now except with all particles having the opposite direction of travel.[30]) This world 'looks exactly like ours run backwards'; the concentric waves of water and light rush inward to converge on the stone as it reaches the surface of the water from below, propelling it upward. This seems an amazing and improbable coincidence; but the fact that it is compatible with basic physical laws, though statistically improbable, is uncontroversial. (The fact that cases like this never or virtually never happen, though their time-reverses are common, is a fact that Lewis calls 'Popper's asymmetry'; he is quite explicit that it is a matter of statistics only, not fundamental law.) It seems intuitively clear that a small miracle in the time-reversed world just before the stone was propelled upward (but after the incoming waves were noticeable) could have destroyed the delicate balance in initial conditions required for the stone to leave the surface. But the time-reverse of this is a world where the rock doesn't fall to the surface, but leaves the apparent traces of having done so.

Of course, it is clear that one-miracle worlds that are like ours in their final stages but not in their earlier ones will be extremely odd, in just the way that time-reversals of our world are odd: they will fail to accord with the 'statistical macro-laws' of the actual world (e.g. Popper's asymmetry), at the very least in the time surrounding the miracle and almost certainly in the pre-miracle part too.[31] Obviously statistical macro-laws are crucial to our judgements of what is an apparent trace of what. But Lewis is very explicit (1986b: 57) that such statistically based asymmetries should not be counted as matters of law, and he gives them no special weight in his account of similarity of worlds, so that he has no way to rule out of consideration worlds that violate them.[32] Lewis is offering an alternative to a statistical account of the direction of time, but there simply isn't the asymmetry he claims.

---

[30] Some further alterations, e.g. in the direction of magnetic fields, are required also.

[31] For instance, consider a world that obeys our laws except for a small miracle at $t + \epsilon$ in 1973 and is just like our world after the miracle, and in which at t, Nixon is pushing the button to launch missiles at the Soviet Union. In such a miracle-world, the apparent traces of Nixon not pressing the button would be illusory, which would require a failure of many macro-laws. Indeed, the failure of statistical macro-laws might be so drastic that a few minutes before t there is nothing recognizably a person that is continuous with the 'Nixon' that pushed the button at t, and nothing recognizably a button in the surroundings either. Given that we tend to identify objects across possible worlds by similarity in their initial segments rather than in their final segments, it may not be entirely appropriate to describe the miracle-world in the way that I did, as one in which Nixon was pushing the button. I don't think this shows anything of interest about the direction of causation; it merely shows that we tend to use counterfactuals whose antecedents are temporally loaded.

[32] Indeed, the problem of directionality would have lost a great deal of its initial punch if we had appealed at the start to statistical macro-laws such as the second law of thermodynamics. Such laws are evidently asymmetric and have a fundamentally different character in the forward direction than in the backward; indeed, even under the idealization that they are forward deterministic, they are not backward deterministic.

Lewis thinks that what underlies the (alleged) asymmetry of miracle size and of traces is a non-statistical fact about the world: an asymmetry of overdetermination. For the laws of our world to determine whether (say) Fisk hit a home run in a certain baseball game in 1975 on the basis of prior information (say, information about what happened at a moment on the previous day), one needs a *vast* amount of prior information; perhaps (as Latham 1987 argues convincingly) information about the entire cross-section of the past light cone at that prior moment. Given how much is required of the one determinant at that prior moment, there is no room for any other. But to determine whether Fisk hit the home run on the basis of *future* information, Lewis thinks that much less will do, and that there will be a great many of these smaller determinants: this is plausible (he says) given that there are many independent traces of Fisk's home run (in newspaper archives and TV clips and reminiscences of Red Sox fans). Of course, none of these traces by itself is literally *sufficient* given the laws for Fisk's home run: there are lots of ways that any given one could be a result of fakery or whatever. But fakery leaves its own traces, and reflection on this is supposed to make plausible that 'very many simultaneous disjoint combinations of traces of any present fact are determinants thereof; there is no lawful way for the combination to have come about in the absence of the fact' (1986d: 50).

In fact, however, while there is doubtless some sort of 'near-determination' of Fisk's home run by many diverse facts about a given future time t_2, I don't think it is at all plausible that there is overdetermination by facts about t_2, for I don't think that there can be complete determination of Fisk's home run by any collection of facts about t_2 that doesn't include facts about the entire cross-section of the future light cone. Certainly there is no obvious way to *prove* determination by anything less than this.

What of the fallback idea of an asymmetry of *near*-determination? It is doubtless true that there is some sort of 'near-determination' of Fisk's home run by many salient future facts, and that it is very unlikely that any *salient* facts about what happened before the home run (short of the state of an entire cross-section of the past light cone) give any 'near-determination' of it. But there are plenty of other cases that go in the opposite direction: in a system isolated between t_1 and t_3, if it is in equilibrium at the intermediate time t_2 then that 'nearly determines' its future state but not its past state. In any case, it should be clear that an analysis of 'near-determination' would make it dependent on statistical regularities of the universe. This is to bring in an element that goes beyond those that Lewis considered.

My own view is that while it would be hard to find an acceptable statistical account of the directional asymmetry based on an asymmetry of near-determination, still bringing in statistical macro-laws in one way or another is the way we need to go, for there simply is no directional asymmetry independent of them. (Lewis informs me that this is now his view as well.) In my opinion, the best account of directional asymmetry is the one mentioned earlier in connection with Spirtes,

Glymour, and Scheines' theory of causal graphs: it's simply a fact that the variables we find salient tend to be probabilistically related in such a way that you can draw causal graphs among them in accordance with Spirtes *et al.*'s constraints; and (around here anyway) what are causes on the causal graph criterion tend to precede their effects. This means that for systems too small for the statistical factors to show up, there is no 'intrinsic' difference between cause and effect: it's simply that the temporal relation of the cause to the effect in such small systems is the same as the temporal relation between causes and effects among salient variables in larger systems (at least, in larger systems around here) as determined by Spirtes *et al.*'s theory. This is doubtless at odds with our pre-theoretic conceptions about cause and effect, but those pre-theoretic conceptions cannot withstand what we have learned from physics. In this one regard at least, Russell was correct.

References

Arntzenius, Frank (1993). 'The Common Cause Principle', in D. Hull, M. Forbes, and K. Okruhlik (eds.), *PSA 1992*, vol. ii East Lansing, Mich.: Philosophy of Science Association, 227–37.

Bennett, Jonathan (1984). 'Counterfactuals and Temporal Direction'. *Philosophical Review*, 93: 57–91.

—— (1988). *Events and their Names*. Indianapolis: Hackett.

Cartwright, Nancy (1979). 'Causal Laws and Effective Strategies'. *Noûs*, 13: 419–38.

Collins, John (2000). 'Preemptive Prevention'. *Journal of Philosophy*, 97: 223–34.

Cushing, James, and Ernan McMullin (1989). *Philosophical Consequences of Quantum Theory*. Notre Dame, Ind.: University of Notre Dame.

Davidson, Donald (1967). 'Causal Relations'. *Journal of Philosophy*, 64: 691–703.

Earman, John (1976). 'Causation: A Matter of Life and Death'. *Journal of Philosophy*, 73: 5–25.

—— (1986). *A Primer on Determinism*. Dordrecht: Reidel.

Elga, Adam (forthcoming). 'Statistical Mechanics and the Asymmetry of Counterfactual Dependence'.

Hitchcock, Christopher (1993). 'A Generalized Probabilistic Theory of Causal Relevance'. *Synthese*, 97: 335–64.

—— (1995). 'The Mishap at Reichenbach Falls'. *Philosophical Studies*, 78: 257–91.

—— (forthcoming). 'The Intransitivity of Causation Revealed in Equations and Graphs'.

Horwich, Paul (1987). *Asymmetries in Time*. Cambridge, Mass.: MIT/Bradford.

Hume, David (1748). *An Enquiry concerning Human Understanding*. London.

Latham, Noa (1987). 'Singular Causal Statements and Strict Deterministic Laws'. *Pacific Philosophical Quarterly*, 68: 29–43.

Lewis, David (1973). 'Causation'. *Journal of Philosophy*, 70: 556–67. Repr. in Lewis (1986: 159–72).

—— (1981). 'Are we Free to Break the Laws?' *Theoria*, 47: 113–21. Repr. in Lewis (1986: 291–8).

—— (1986*a*). Postscript to 'Causation', in Lewis (1986*e*: 172–213).

—— (1986*b*). Postscript to 'Counterfactual Dependence and Time's Arrow', in Lewis (1986*e*: 52–66).

—— (1986c). 'Events', in Lewis (1986: 241–69).

—— (1986d). 'Counterfactual Dependence and Times Arrow', in Lewis (1986e: 291–8). First pub. in Noûs, 13: 455–76.

—— (1986e). Philosophical Papers, vol. ii. Oxford: Oxford University Press.

—— (2000). 'Causation as Influence'. Journal of Philosophy, 97: 182–97.

McDermott, Michael (1995a). 'Lewis on Causal Dependence'. Australasian Journal of Philosophy, 73: 129–39.

—— (1995b). 'Redundant Causation'. British Journal for the Philosophy of Science, 46: 523–44.

Mackie, John (1965). 'Causes and Conditions'. American Philosophical Quarterly, 2: 245–55.

Maudlin, Tim (1994). Quantum Non-Locality and Relativity. Oxford: Basil Blackwell.

Meek, Christopher, and Clark Glymour (1994). 'Conditioning and Intervening'. British Journal for the Philosophy of Science, 45: 1001–21.

Menzies, Peter (1989). 'Probabilistic Causation and Causal Processes: A Critique of Lewis'. Philosophy of Science, 56: 642–63.

Pearl, Judea (2000). Causality. Cambridge: Cambridge University Press.

Price, Huw (1986). 'Against Causal Decision Theory'. Synthese, 67: 195–212.

—— (1991). 'Agency and Probabilistic Causality'. British Journal for the Philosophy of Science, 42: 157–76.

—— (1992). 'Agency and Causal Asymmetry'. Mind, 101: 501–20.

Russell, Bertrand (1912–13). 'On the Notion of Cause'. Proceedings of the Aristotelian Society, 13: 1–26.

Schaffer, Jonathan (2000). 'Trumping Pre-emption'. Journal of Philosophy, 97: 165–81.

Sklar, Lawrence (1974). Space, Time and Spacetime. Berkeley: University of California Press.

Skyrms, Brian (1980). Causal Necessity. New Haven: Yale University Press.

Spirtes, Peter, Clark Glymour, and Richard Scheines (1993). Causation, Prediction and Search. New York: Springer-Verlag.

Vihvelin, Kadri (1991). 'Freedom, Causation and Counterfactuals'. Philosophical Studies, 64: 161–84.

CHAPTER 15

DISTILLING METAPHYSICS FROM QUANTUM PHYSICS

TIM MAUDLIN

METAPHYSICS is the theory of being, that is, the most generic account of what there is. As such, it must be informed by empirical science, since we can only discover the nature of the material world through our experience of it. The most general and fundamental account of material reality is provided by physics, hence physics is the scientific discipline most closely allied to (if not continuous with) metaphysics as a philosophical inquiry.

Modern physics has been an especially fertile source for astonishing suggestions about reality. No respectable inquiry into the nature of space and time, for example, can afford to ignore the Theory of Relativity, whose account of spatio-temporal structure would not have been discovered by any amount of armchair reflection. As truth is stranger than fiction, so is actual physical theory more conceptually challenging than a priori speculation.

This is not to say that as philosophers we should trade in our tools for those of the physicists. Physics provides theories which typically consist of a mathematical formalism and some procedures for applying that formalism to particular concrete situations. But both the formalism and the procedures may admit of alternative ontological *interpretations*. It may not be clear, for example, which part of the mathematics corresponds to real physical magnitudes and which is an artefact of arbitrary choices of units or gauges. It may not be clear which mathematical models represent real physical possibilities, and which do not. And it may not be clear which pairs of mathematical models represent the same physical situation. All of these problems confront even the philosopher who tries to take, for example, the Theory of Relativity 'at face value'.

These problems are magnified exponentially when one seeks to understand the ontological implications of quantum theory. There one finds a mathematical formalism and a set of practical procedures for using it, but no uniformity of opinion about how that formalism is to be interpreted. Further, there is almost nothing about which the alternative available interpretations agree, or which can be directly inferred from even the most surprising experimental phenomena.

If the ontological ramifications of quantum theory depend so critically on how the formalism is interpreted (or, in some details, on exactly what the formalism is), then the right way to address our topic would be to present the various interpretations in detail. Unfortunately, limitations of space make this impossible. A beautiful account of the interpretations can be found in David Albert's *Quantum Mechanics and Experience* (Albert 1992), and any philosopher with a serious interest in the subject should peruse that book. Instead of a proper explication, then, I shall here present only the merest sketch of the interpretations, along with a running tally of what each would imply about various metaphysical claims which have been made about quantum theory.

In order to be a version or interpretation of quantum theory at all, a theory must make use of a *quantum state* or *wavefunction*. If one begins with a classical theory, there are rules of thumb about how to produce a corresponding quantum theory, with different sorts of classical systems yielding different sorts of quantum states. Roughly speaking, a classical system of a given sort can, at any moment, be in one of a number of possible *configurations*: the configuration a system of particles is given by specifying the location of each particle; the configuration of a classical field is given by specifying the field's value at every point in space. If we think of each distinct configuration as a point in an abstract space, then the collection of all possible configurations forms the *configuration space* of the system.[1] A single point in configuration space specifies the complete instantaneous state of a classical system, and a trajectory through configuration space (parameterized by time) represents a complete physical history of the system.[2] The wavefunction of a system is typically a complex-valued function *on the configuration space*, i.e. a function which assigns a complex number to each possible configuration.

---

[1] There may be disputes about what ought to count as distinct configurations of a system (e.g. if all the particles in a system are moved by some fixed amount, is that a distinct configuration?), but I will ignore any such problems here.

[2] A configuration is the *instantaneous* state of a system, and so does not specify, for example, the velocities of particles, but only their positions. The velocities can of course be calculated if one is given a time-parameterized trajectory through configuration space.

If the system consists of a single classical particle, then a configuration of the system is just a specification of where the particle is, so the configuration space of the system is isomorphic to physical space (the collection of all the possible configurations of the system is given by the collection of all spatial locations, which is physical space). *In this case*, it is easy to fall into picturing the wavefunction of the particle as a kind of classical field, spread out in space, especially when thinking of, for example, the notorious two-slit experiment. But it can be severely misleading to assimilate wavefunctions in general to classical fields. If the system consists of two particles, then each point in the configuration space specifies the location of *both* the particles. One cannot, in this case, sensibly ask what the value of the wavefunction is *here* (indicating a point in physical space); one must rather ask what the value of the wavefunction is for the configuration in which one particle is here and the other at some other particular location. This feature of the wavefunction will be of paramount importance when we come to the issue of *entanglement*, but most of the issues I will examine can be illustrated using only a single particle as the system, and I will use this simple system wherever possible.

Although there are decent rules of thumb for quantizing many classical theories, two caveats should be kept in mind. First, not every classical theory has a straightforward quantum version, the General Theory of Relativity being the prime example. Secondly, not every quantum theory need be the quantized version of a classical theory: string theory, in particular, has been claimed to be a pure quantum theory, not obtainable by quantizing any classical system.

Incidentally, quantizing a theory, in this sense, means specifying a set of quantum states and associating certain mathematical operators with the classical quantities; it does not necessarily mean making classically continuous quantities discrete. It is true that certain quantized systems (e.g. the simple harmonic oscillator) have only a discrete set of allowable values for some quantities (e.g. energy) which can take a continuum of values in classical physics. But the position of a free quantum-mechanical particle is not 'quantized' in this sense: it can take any of a continuum of values.

All 'interpretations' of quantum theory, then, employ a quantum state or wavefunction. They all also agree on *part* of the dynamics for that wavefunction: the wavefunction at least usually develops in accord with a particular sort of deterministic linear equation of motion. The *Schrödinger* equation is used in the quantum theory of non-relativistic particles.[3] Again, if only a single particle is under consideration, the wavefunction can be visualized as a field in physical space, and the Schrödinger equation then specifies how that field changes with time. This gives rise to the usual (and somewhat misleading) picture of an electron 'smeared out in space' passing through both slits in the two-slit experiment and then (somehow)

---

[3] One uses a different equation, the Dirac equation, for Special Relativistic contexts, and there are other equations for field theories of various sorts.

giving rise to interference bands on the detection screen. But it is not that anything is smeared out in space; rather the wavefunction 'propagates' in configuration space in accord with the Schrödinger equation. All interpretations agree, though, that the state of the wavefunction depends on whether each slit is open or closed, and that this dependence on both slits plays a central role in accounting for the interference. There the agreement among interpretations ends.

The problem with positing *only* the wavefunction governed by Schrödinger evolution was pointed out long ago by Schrödinger himself, in his notorious example of the cat. A variation of the problem can be posed with polarized light. Suppose we have a polarized filter oriented in the vertical direction with a detector placed behind it. If we send a vertically polarized photon towards the filter, it will pass and the detector will fire. If we send a horizontally polarized photon, it will not pass and the detector will not fire. These plain physical facts are reflected in the behaviour of the wavefunction: starting with the quantum state of the vertically polarized photon and the detector in its ready state, Schrödinger evolution of the wavefunction yields a final state in which the only non-zero part of the wavefunction corresponds to the configuration in which the detector has fired. Similarly, the wavefunction of a horizontally polarized photon and the detector will evolve so the only non-zero part of the wavefunction corresponds to the detector not firing. But what if we send a *diagonally* polarized photon at the filter, as we can easily arrange?

The quantum state of a diagonally polarized photon is, as a mathematical object, a vector sum of the state of vertical polarization and the state of horizontal polarization. The *linearity* of the Schrödinger equation then implies that the end state of the wavefunction, after the interaction of the photon with the screen and the detector, will be a vector sum of a quantum state in which the detector has fired and a state in which it has not. The wavefunction in this case has a non-zero value for the detector firing and a non-zero value for the detector not firing, and those values may be made equal. The end state is, as we say, a superposition of a state in which the detector fires and one in which it does not. The central interpretative question of quantum theory is what we are to make of this state.

As a practical matter, physicists discovered long ago how to use this state for making predictions. Since, it seems, the actual detector either fires or fails to fire on any particular run, the final wavefunction should be used to assign *probabilities* to these two outcomes. The method for doing this is simple and uncontroversial: it goes by the name of *Born's rule*. Essentially, one takes the absolute square of the complex number that the wavefunction assigns to each of the configurations to be the likelihood that one will get that configuration on a given run. Every interpretation of quantum theory must vindicate Born's rule as providing at least a very good approximation of the chances for each outcome. But the *practical* utility of Born's rule for making predictions does nothing to solve the ontological problem we have been led into.

That problem is as follows. Irrespective of the use of Born's rule, the end quantum state given by Schrödinger evolution is neither one that simply represents a detector which has fired nor one that represents a detector which has not fired. But, it seems, the actual physical detector, at the end of the experiment, has either fired or not fired. Hence, as John Stewart Bell succinctly put it, 'Either the wavefunction, as given by the Schrödinger equation, is not everything, or it is not right' (Bell 1987: 201).

The idea that the wavefunction is not everything is the claim that the quantum state of a system does not provide a *complete physical description* of the system. Certain important aspects of a physical object may be captured by its wavefunction, but something at least as important is left out: whatever it is that makes a detector which has fired physically different from one which has not. Einstein, Podolsky, and Rosen raised the question 'Can quantum-mechanical description of reality be considered complete?' in an article with that very title, and concluded that it cannot (Einstein *et al.* 1935). Einstein, Podolsky, and Rosen did not themselves offer any explicit account of how the quantum-mechanical description was incomplete, or what it would take to complete it, or how to understand the wavefunction, but it is clear what sort of a job confronts the physicist who denies the completeness of the quantum state. If the wavefunction is not *everything*, then we need to know *what else there is*, and what is the *dynamics* of this extra stuff, and how the wavefunction comes into the story at all. Theories of this kind are commonly called *hidden-variables theories*, the 'hidden' variables being representations of whatever it is the quantum state leaves out of account. The term 'hidden variables' is particularly badly chosen, since these additional variables are supposed to represent whatever physical difference it is which distinguishes a detector which has fired from one which has not, and that difference, far from being hidden, is paradigmatically manifest. But in any case, the hidden-variables interpretations are free to regard the wavefunction, as given by the Schrödinger equation, as right but incomplete.[4]

The two questions which confront a hidden-variables theory, then, are 'What is there beside the wavefunction?' and 'What dynamical laws govern this additional ontology?' Several different such theories are currently on offer, the most famous being that originally suggested by Louis de Broglie and later developed by David Bohm. General algorithms for constructing hidden variables theories have been intensely studied by philosophers, often under the rubric of 'modal' interpretations (van Fraassen 1991; Bub 1998; Dickson 1998; Vermaas 1999). The term 'modal' traces back to the work of Bas van Fraassen, who got some of his ideas from analogies with modal logic, but the philosophical account of modality really plays little role in these theories. (Any incomplete physical description of a system can be considered

---

[4] A 'hidden variables' theory obviously *could* maintain that the wavefunction, as given by the Schrödinger equation, is *neither* right nor everything: one could both emend the linear evolution and add more variables. In practice, though, this has not been pursued, since the addition of the 'hidden' variables alone (with the right dynamics for them) can do the job.

'modal' in so far as it is consistent with various different completions, and so at best constrains how the system might be, but does not indicate exactly how it is.)

In Bohm's version of quantum *mechanics*, the additional variables are particle locations: particles, in this theory, always have exact locations, and hence form a single unique configuration, even when the wavefunction is spread out all over configuration space. The wavefunction always evolves in accord with Schrödinger's equation. The key to the theory is then a new equation, the *guidance equation*, which specifies how the positions of the particles evolve with time. The guidance equation makes use of the wavefunction: how a particular configuration will evolve is determined, in a simple way, by the form of the wavefunction.[5]

Hidden-variables theories seize the horn of Bell's dilemma which says that the wavefunction is not everything. The other horn is grasped by *collapse* theories. If the wavefunction is a complete representation of the physical world, then, it seems, it must evolve in such a way as to end up representing either a live cat or a dead cat, either a detector which has fired or one which has not. Schrödinger evolution, as we have seen, does not give this result, so the collapse theories must postulate that at least sometimes (if not always) the wavefunction does not evolve in accord with the Schrödinger equation. Of course, the exquisitely precise predictions of the quantum theory have all been derived by using the Schrödinger (or other appropriate linear) equation, and one doesn't want to throw out the baby with the bathwater. So the trick of a collapse theory is to come up with a new dynamics which at least closely mimics Schrödinger evolution for the sorts of small systems to which the quantum formalism can be applied and solved. Since the founders of the quantum orthodoxy, Bohr and Heisenberg, evidently meant to reject the incompleteness of the quantum state, they were committed (at least implicitly) to some such theory.

The most straightforward way to do this, exemplified by the classic account of von Neumann (1955), is to postulate pure Schrödinger evolution most of the time, punctuated by distinctly non-Schrödinger evolution (the 'collapse of the wavefunction') from time to time. The question which faces such a theory is *when* and *how* such collapses occur. The orthodoxy's first line of response is: (1) the collapse occurs when a measurement is made and (2) the state collapses, randomly, with the appropriate probabilities (provided by Born's rule), to a state in which the measured quantity has a definite value (a so-called *eigenstate* of the quantity). This response, though, is just a holding operation until some more rigorous account is provided of exactly what it takes for there to be a measurement, and what determines exactly which quantity is measured. It is here that some of the most extraordinary claims about the implications of quantum theory have been made, under the general rubric 'participation of the observer'. But we should note immediately that nothing in the logic

---

[5] There are many sources available with extensive discussions of Bohm's theory. Many topics are covered in Bohm and Hiley (1993). Important foundational issues concerning the role of probability in the theory are examined in Dürr *et al.* (1992).

of the physical problem requires a collapse theory to even mention measurements or observers. In the most rigorous formulated collapse theories, of Ghirardi, Rimini, and Weber (1986) and of Perle (1990), the *when* is answered: 'randomly, with fixed probability per unit time' and the *how* roughly 'to a state in which at least one particle has a much more sharply localized position'.[6] I will examine other possible answers to the 'when?' and 'how?' questions when I look at particular issues.

This brief overview of interpretations of the quantum formalism would not be complete without some mention of a notorious attempt to escape between the horns of Bell's dilemma. The idea is to reject both collapse in the dynamics of the wavefunction and the claim that the wavefunction is incomplete: the wavefunction given by pure Schrödinger evolution both is right and is everything. How then to understand the wavefunction of Schrödinger's cat, which has equal portions for the configuration of a live cat and for a dead one, or the wavefunction of our detector, split between regions of configuration space which correspond to the detector having fired and regions which correspond to no detection? The idea is that such a wavefunction represents *both* outcomes having occurred: the cat both survived and died; the detector both fired and did not. Why then does it seem to us that the cat is just plain alive, and that the detector failed to detect anything? Well, that is because the world has somehow split into two non-interacting parts, with different outcomes in each, and we are only aware (owing to the lack of interaction) of one part, the 'world' we now inhabit.

This is the so-called 'many-worlds' interpretation of quantum theory. The interpretation is often associated with the name of Hugh Everett, even though Everett himself never used the term, and, I think, never held the view. Everett called his interpretation the 'relative state' interpretation, and he paid particular attention to a mathematically well-defined object, the state of one part of an entangled system 'relative to' an *arbitrarily specified* state of another part of that system (Everett 1957). The relative state plays no central role in the many-worlds theory. Indeed, Everett's own interpretation is rather obscure on some central points, and so we will leave it out of account. But the many-worlds view deserves some attention.

I don't think that the many-worlds view, as just sketched, can be considered to be a viable interpretation of the quantum formalism-*cum*-practical-rules-of-thumb that we originally set out to understand. For that practical apparatus has, as a central feature, techniques for assigning *probabilities* to events, and it is the astonishing accuracy of those predictions that provide our grounds for taking the theory seriously. So any coherent interpretation which vindicates our use of the theory must hold that there is something those probabilistic predictions are *about*, and that those things have, in experiments, actual *frequencies* which closely

---

[6] In the continuous localization theories, the *when* for collapse becomes *all the time*, via a stochastic process which, for small systems, closely approximates Schrödinger evolution over normal laboratory timescales.

approximate the probabilities derived from the theory. In the hidden-variables approaches, the probabilities are ultimately about the actual values of the 'hidden' (i.e. manifest!) variables, which variables display some particular distribution over a series of experiments. For the collapse theories, the probabilities are for the collapses to occur in one way rather than another, and again there is, according to the theory, a fact about the frequencies with which various sorts of collapse occur. But on the many-worlds view, it is hard to see what the probabilities are probabilities *for*.

The probabilities are not for the 'hidden' variables to take on certain values, for there are none. They are not for the wavefunction to evolve one way rather than another, since it always evolves in accordance with the Schrödinger equation. According to this theory, what happens when a measurement takes place is that the world splits. But then what could it mean to assign, say, a 20 per cent probability to one outcome over the other, since both will surely occur, and in both there will equally be a descendant of the 'you' who started the experiment. The probabilities are calculated from the amplitude of the wavefunction, *but that amplitude does not play any metaphysical role in the theory.* If the world splits (assuming we can makes sense of that notion), it splits simply because the wavefunction is spread out a certain way in configuration space, and has nothing to do with *how much* of the wavefunction is in the different places.

Some people seem to equate the 'many worlds' talk simply with a no-collapse theory, i.e. they say that there are many worlds simply because the wavefunction is spread out. In this sense, all of the hidden-variables theories are many-worlds theories. But this usage of language is more likely to confuse than enlighten, for in the hidden-variables theory there is only one, unique distribution of values for the additional variables, which distribution corresponds to the world we see. Even when these variables are influenced by 'interfering' parts of the uncollapsed wavefunction, there is but one manifest world involved: the world of the additional variables. These theories have a physically dualist ontology: the physical world contains both the wavefunction and the additional variables, but of the two components it is the *wavefunction* which is hidden, its form and very presence made known only via its effect on the additional variables. So we will leave the many-worlds idea aside, as insufficiently clear to constitute an interpretation of the quantum formalism.[7]

Let's now turn to a series of ontological issues, and see how they come out according to various interpretations of the general form I have been examining.

---

[7] A somewhat more detailed discussion of the central interpretative problems confronting quantum theory can be found in Maudlin (1995). Remarks on the relation between the quantum formalism and the manifest world are amplified in Maudlin (1997).

1. Issue One: Determinism

Historically, the most widely remarked metaphysical innovation of quantum theory over classical physics is the rejection of determinism in favour of chance. Events such as the decay of a radioactive atom are typically held to be fundamentally random: there is no reason at all that the decay takes place at one time rather than another. Atoms that are physically identical in every respect may nonetheless behave differently. Einstein was resistant to the idea the God plays dice, and his insistence on determinism is taken to be a mark of a reactionary inability to accept the quantum theory.

Things are not quite so simple. Does either the pragmatic quantum formalism or the empirical result of any experiment require us to abandon determinism? No. The pragmatic formalism requires an interpretation, and some of the interpretations posit deterministic laws while others employ fundamentally stochastic dynamics. Further, little can be said in the way of generalization.

The Schrödinger equation itself is deterministic. So any interpretation which does not employ wave collapse at a fundamental level must find its indeterminism elsewhere (if it is to find it at all). As we have seen, theories which forgo collapse already have a problem to deal with: they need some additional physical stuff (beside the wavefunction) if they are to have any hope of modelling the world as we know it. The question of determinism for these theories becomes a question of the dynamics of this additional stuff, the 'hidden' variables.

The possibility of supplying the additional variables with a deterministic dynamics was demonstrated by the de Broglie–Bohm particle mechanics. The guidance equation in that theory is deterministic: given the initial state of the wavefunction of the universe and the initial configuration of the particles (in this case, their initial locations), the laws of the theory allow only one possible history for the universe. And since the theory makes the standard predictions, for example, the two-slit experiment and electron tunnelling and radioactive decay, these sorts of phenomena cannot assure us that the world operates by chance.

It is often thought that the whole *point* of Bohm's theory, and of 'hidden' variables in general, is to restore determinism (indeed, it is common to regard the purpose of the additional variables themselves as providing the hidden cause for an experiment to come out one way rather than another), but this is inaccurate on several counts. First, the main problem to be solved in these theories is not to give an *explanation* of why one result happened rather than another, but rather to have the theoretical resources to describe the experiment as having *had* one result rather than another. That problem is answered in the first place simply by having more than the wavefunction in the physical ontology, irrespective of the dynamics. *Most* hidden-variables theories, including the so-called modal interpretations, postulate *stochastic* dynamics for the additional variables. Bell, who was one of the great advocates of Bohm's theory, suggested a stochastic dynamics for his version of Bohmian field theory (Bell 1987, ch. 19), and Bohm himself was wont to speculate about an indeterministic 'sub-quantum' realm. The goal of Bohm's account was never determinism *per se*; it was clarity and precision in the theory.

What of collapse theories? Most of these do consider the non-Schrödinger evolution of the wavefunction to be fundamentally indeterministic. The original Spontaneous Collapse theory of Ghirardi, Rimini, and Weber (1986) made the collapses out to be discrete, unpredictable events which happen with some fixed probability per particle per unit time. But again, the question of determinism is only tangential to the motives of the enterprise. In moving from the discrete collapses to the 'continuous spontaneous reduction' model of Philip Perle, for example, the sudden reductions have been replaced by a coupling to a background 'white noise' which determines how the reduction occurs (Perle 1990). And what causes the white noise? The theory does not say (and does not need to, for the purposes at hand). It might be generated deterministically as well as stochastically. So we can't say that the quantum theory forces indeterminism on us. Furthermore, the whole issue looks more like a case of spoils to the victor than a fundamental point of contention: if some consideration militates in favour of a specific interpretation, the question of determinism will simply follow suit, and it seems very unlikely that determinism itself will be a decisive consideration. No one would unnecessarily complicate an interpretation either to instigate, or to avoid, deterministic dynamics.[8]

2. Issue Two: Determinateness

Allied to the question of determinism is a slightly different issue, which goes under the rubric 'determinateness of properties'. It is best illustrated by an example which can be raised only from within an interpretation. Suppose one rejects additional variables—the wavefunction is complete—and for simplicity suppose there is only one particle under consideration, so the wavefunction can be pictured without too much imprecision as a field in space. Further suppose, as will typically be the case, that the wavefunction is spread out, with non-zero values over a large region. What are we to say about the *position* of the particle in this situation?

---

[8] Ironically, mainstream physicists are at least as likely to attribute determinism as indeterminism to quantum theory. The so-called 'information-loss' paradox used in quantum cosmology is founded on the claim that quantum theory does not allow information about the physical state of a system ever to be lost, even if the system is tossed down a black hole. But if there is any fundamental indeterministic collapse of the wavefunction, information is lost all the time, whenever a collapse occurs.

The pragmatic apparatus (i.e. Born's rule) tells us what to predict in this circumstance if we should happen to *look for* the particle by means of, for example, a fluorescent screen. We could only make probabilistic predictions, with the probability for 'finding' the particle in a given location (i.e. the probability that a flash will occur on the screen in a given location) being equal to the squared amplitude of the wavefunction at that location. But what of the particle right before the flash? Did it have any particular position at all?

If the wavefunction is complete, then it obviously is incorrect to say that immediately before the flash the particle was in the vicinity of the part of the screen where the flash later occurred and not elsewhere. If the wavefunction was spread out over a large region, and if all physical facts are determined by the wavefunction, then the most one can say of the particle is that it was spread out. Hence in this sort of interpretation it is misleading to say that one 'found' the particle in a particular location, as if it had been there all along and its true location was merely *revealed* by the screen. According to this sort of theory, the observation does not reveal anything; it is rather an interaction which *creates* a more localized wavefunction from a less localized one. And before the observation, the right thing to say is that the particle had no determinate location at all.

Failure of determinateness in this sense is not the same as failure of determinism. Empedoclean atoms that sometimes randomly swerve in their trajectories are not deterministic, but seem to have, at all times, perfectly determinate properties. (They do not have perfectly determinate *propensities* since their future behaviour is unpredictable, but that failure is laid at the door of the dynamics.) What seems peculiar about the quantum particles is that they *sometimes* have determinate positions (after an observation using a screen, for example) but at other times do not.

But once one gets accustomed to the ontology of this sort of interpretation, this feature no longer seems at all mysterious. If the wavefunction of a particle is complete, then the only sense in which the particle can have a definite location is for the wavefunction to be localized, i.e. to be non-zero only in a relatively small region. That may happen, but even when it does, Schrödinger evolution guarantees that it won't last long. And once the wavefunction has spread out, the most one can say of the particle is that it is in a state which has the propensity, in varying degrees, to cause flashes on screens at various locations.

On the other hand, adopting a different interpretation can completely alter these conclusions. Bohmian particles, for example, always have exact determinate locations, no matter what the wavefunction is, and in Bohmian mechanics flashes on screens are caused by particles which were, immediately before the flash, in the vicinity of that part of the screen. The various 'modal' interpretations differ both on which properties are determinate at a given time and on what makes them determinate. In some interpretations,[9] what properties are determinate changes

---

[9] I refer to interpretations which use the polar decomposition theorem to pick out a preferred basis, such as Kochen (1985).

through time, depending on the wavefunction; in others it is fixed. If the interpretation is clear and coherent, it will posit a fundamental ontology, which is governed by some dynamical equations. It is then a relatively straightforward matter to analyse a given experimental procedure in terms of this ontology to discover whether the outcome of the experiment is a reliable indication of any pre-existing state of affairs. So once again, one cannot sensibly ask whether a given property of a system is determinate according to quantum theory; one must rather ask about the account of a particular experimental situation given by a particular interpretation of the theory. One has no reason to anticipate, though, that quantum systems will always be in states which assign determinate values to classical properties like position and momentum and energy.

3. Issue Three: The Role of the Observer

Perhaps the most metaphysically intriguing claim associated with quantum theory is the notion that it somehow introduces the observer, and irreducible subjectivity, back into physics at the most fundamental level. While classical physics aspired to a 'God's-eye view' of the universe, a purely objective and 'mechanistic' account of the world, we are sometimes told that quantum physics has rendered any such notion obsolete. At its most radical, this view suggests that it is only by the 'participation' of the conscious observer that the physical universe came into being at all, leaving us with the rather perplexing problem of how conscious observers themselves arose in the first place.[10] Perhaps unsurprisingly, the situation does not looks so dire when viewed through the lenses of our precise interpretations.

One way the observer might be thought to make an entrance into our story is via the so-called 'measurement problem'. A measurement, it is said, requires a measured system and a measuring system, and the measuring system must be some sort of observer, so without observers there are no measurements and so no measurement problem. Conversely, if there is a measurement problem, it must arise because of the presence of an observer.

It is true that some of the basic interpretational problems of quantum theory are often presented using measurement operations for illustrative purposes. Above, we

---

[10] Perhaps the most striking presentation of this view is not any explicit theory, but rather a picture which appears in John Wheeler's 'Law without Law' (Wheeler 1983a: 209). The illustration purports to show the universe as a 'self-excited circuit', in which observers who arise long after the big bang somehow impart 'tangible reality' to their own distant past by means of their observations.

considered what happens when a diagonally polarized photon is shot at a vertically oriented polarizer with a photodetector behind it. We saw that if the wavefunction does not collapse, the resulting quantum state will be a superposition of a state in which the detector fires and a state in which it does not, and we asked after the appropriate understanding of such a state. Since the laboratory operation we described constitutes what would normally be called a measurement of the vertical polarization of the photon, one might describe the problem of interpreting the superposition as the problem of understanding a measurement interaction, and hence a measurement problem.

But there are several things that must be immediately noted. The first is that problematic superpositions are not confined to the results of 'measurements'. Schrödinger's cat ends up in a problematic superposition if the wavefunction does not collapse, but the cat does not, in any straightforward sense, measure anything. As Philip Perle has put it, quantum theory does not so much have a measurement problem as a reality problem: we have to figure out how the quantum formalism represents anything at all as happening in the world, not just measurement interactions. Secondly, in order for the problem to arise, one does not need a *conscious* observer. The polarizer-cum-photodetector is not conscious, but would nonetheless normally be taken to constitute a measuring device. Thirdly, and most importantly, since interpretations such as Bohm's and Ghirardi, Rimini, and Weber's collapse theory are able to account for the behaviour of photodetectors and cats (as we take them to behave) without making any mention of consciousness, conscious observers do not need to be introduced in order to make sense of the mathematical formalism.

From the point of view of Bohm and Ghirardi *et al.*, 'measurement' interactions are simply a species of physical interaction like any other, governed by the same basic dynamical laws as everything else. If a system has a particular physical constitution, it may turn out to be a good indicator of something else. Measurement, as a physical matter, requires the existence of a sort of system (the measuring device) so constituted that, after interacting with a target system (the measured system), its state becomes *correlated* with that of the target system. This correlation means that after the interaction the state of the measuring device contains information about the measured system. None of this requires consciousness.

So how did consciousness, and the *human* observer, ever come into the discussion?[11] The only plausible account is that one may be driven to advert to consciousness as an act of desperation. Suppose one wants a collapse theory, and begins to consider under what conditions a collapse occurs. It *cannot* be that just any

---

[11] Even if consciousness somehow can get into the game, what's to say that it must be human consciousness? Einstein reportedly voiced his scepticism concerning the suppposed effects of conscious observation by saying that he couldn't believe that a mouse could bring about drastic changes in the universe simply by looking at it (this anecdote is recounted by Everett in his thesis; DeWitt and Graham 1973: 116).

interaction causes the wavefunction to collapse: that the wavefunction of an electron does not collapse whenever it interacts with another electron can be verified by experiment, since some observable interference effects depend on the interaction of both parts of the uncollapsed wavefunction. So one may naturally look for some special species of interaction which could cause collapse. In particular, one may naturally come to think that any interaction which can be understood as just electrons and protons and neutrons following the usual physical laws is *not* special, since the basic physics of such interactions does not require collapses to occur, as we have just seen.

At this point the following line of thought takes over. Let's consider, say, an electron which is fed through a Stern–Gerlach device, i.e. a device which 'measures' spin. In particular, consider an electron which is not in an eigenstate of x-spin and is fed into a device which measures x-spin, so that particles with x-spin up exit through the top of the device and particles with x-spin down exit through the bottom. Since our electron is not in an eigenstate, the wavefunction of the particle after the interaction will be a superposition of one in which the electron exits at the top and one in which it exits at the bottom. And we can *experimentally confirm* that at the moment the particle exits, the wavefunction has *not* collapsed into one or the other definite position by recombining the two beams and looking for interference effects (cf. Albert 1992, ch. 1). So interacting with a Stern–Gerlach device does not collapse the wavefunction.

If we do not recombine the beams, then the wavefunction of the electron is a superposition of states with different positions. Now suppose we decide to look for the electron by, say, putting up a fluorescent screen. The basic physics of the interaction of the electron with the screen, producing light, is well understood. There is nothing terribly exotic in this interaction, nothing fundamentally different from, say, the interaction of a single electron with another. So since merely interacting with an electron does not collapse the wavefunction, it is hard to see how interacting with the screen will. The screen should end up in a superposition of have excited electrons in one place and having excited electrons in another. And when the electrons return to their ground states, we should have light in a superposition of having flashed from one place and having flashed in another. And as we trace the career of the light, we understand how it will interact with the eye, and with the photoreceptors in the retina, and none of this require fundamentally new physics. So the retina of someone watching the screen should end up in a superposition of having one set of rods fire and having another set of rods fire.

Beyond this point, it is not accurate to say that we have a clear understanding of how things work. But we think that the passage of the neural signal down the optic nerve is a matter of simple chemistry, as is the way that the firing of one set of neurons causes the firing of another set. We think that all of this brain activity can more or less be understood in terms of chemistry, and that chemistry can more or less be understood in term of physics, and that although this gets very complicated it does not involve any fundamentally new physics, and so nothing which could do anything as dramatic as set off collapse of the wavefunction.

If one adheres to this line of thought, then the collapse can only be caused by something fundamentally new, by something that we don't have any idea, even more or less, how to understand in terms of the laws of physics and chemistry. And of course, there *is* something mysterious which fits this definition: the general relation between the physical state of the brain and conscious experience. Long before quantum theory, the mind–body problem was recognized as such an explanatory gap. So if we are looking for a trigger for wave collapse with the idea that the trigger must be some fundamentally new sort of interaction, and if we have already concluded that the interaction of mind and body is fundamentally unlike the interaction of body and body, then it is natural to locate the mysterious collapse process here. If we already have something we don't understand, then it seems economical to assimilate it to something else we don't understand. It is not that something about wave collapse could obviously explain consciousness, or that something about consciousness could obviously explain wave collapse, but rather that the explanatory gap between body and mind yawns wide enough to engulf the problem of collapse without so much as a tremble.

If this is what has led theorists to link quantum mechanics to consciousness, then two observations are in order. The first is that the whole line of argument is based on an unwarranted supposition. That supposition is that there must be some special kind of circumstance or interaction (a 'measurement' or 'observation') which 'triggers' collapse of the wavefunction. As the example of Ghirardi, Rimini, and Weber's theory shows, no such trigger is needed: in that theory, collapses happen at random, with a fixed probability, and are not particularly associated with any kind of interaction. The second is that even if one demands some particular circumstance for collapses, there is nothing in the *physics* which points to consciousness or mind as the key. All we know experimentally is that certain sorts of interactions do not collapse the wavefunction, but the differences between those interactions and typical 'measurement' interactions are manifold. Roger Penrose, for example, has speculated that collapses are tied not to consciousness but to *gravitation*: collapses occur when the superposed states differ enough in their gravitational structure (Penrose 1994: 339 ff.). In a way, this appeals to another explanatory gap: just as we don't have a good theory of the mind–body interaction, we don't have a good quantum theory of gravity. The point is that even if we accept that some special circumstance plays a role in collapse, there is absolutely nothing in the *phenomena* which points to consciousness rather than, say, gravity as the special ingredient. So unless one is already inclined to put the observer as the centre of one's theory, there is nothing in quantum physics to suggest that one do so.

Appeals to consciousness are not restricted to collapse theories. Non-collapse theories, as we have seen, must appeal to some ontology beyond the wavefunction in order to solve the measurement problem. The hallmark of these 'additional variables' is that they have determinate values even when the quantum state is not in an eigenstate of the corresponding operator. Probabilities appear in such theories as the likelihood, given the quantum state, that these additional variables take some particular value. In Bohmian mechanics, and Bohmian field theory, and the various 'modal' interpretations, the additional variables are purely physical: they have no intrinsic connection to consciousness. But in the Many-Minds theory of David Albert and Barry Loewer (1988), the additional variables, which always have determinate values, are conscious states. Like the variables in the modal interpretations[12] and in Bell's version of Bohmian field theory, the conscious states evolve indeterministically, giving a straightforward way to understand the probabilities of the theory.

It may come as a surprise that probabilities are easy to understand on the Many-Minds view given the argument above that the probabilities cannot be interpreted in the Many-Worlds view, rendering it unacceptable. It is important to note that the *source* of the multiplicity in each case is entirely different. The many 'worlds' are generated, as it were, by fission of a single parent world, so that no meaning can be ascribed to attaching different probabilities to the offspring, all of which are certain to be produced. In the Many-Minds theory, minds never fission: each mind has a single determinate history, such that we can ascribe definite frequencies to the apparent results of experiments (as perceived by the mind). Indeed, as far as the interpretation of probability goes, the multiplicity of minds plays no role whatsoever: the stochastic dynamics governs each single mind individually, and the so-called Single-Mind theory suffices for this purpose (Albert and Loewer 1988: 205). The reason to associate many minds rather than just one with each body concerns a desire to maintain something akin to the supervenience of the mental on the physical (although the conscious state of any particular mind does not supervene on the physical state of the associated body, and had better not, lest the wavefunction again become complete!), and with the desire to ensure that one is not typically misled into thinking that there are other minds with certain contents when there are none. Neither of these motivations come from physics *per se*, and so the multiplicity of minds plays no role in the interpretation of the purely physical aspects of the theory.

We can therefore say of the Many-Minds theory as we did of the collapse-inducing-consciousness theory that there are no *physical* considerations which militate in favour of appeals to consciousness here. The belief that consciousness should play a central role in an interpretation of quantum theory must ultimately rest on views about consciousness which are imported into the physics rather than being derived from it.

---

[12] This remark does not apply to van Fraassen's (1991) interpretation, where the dynamics for the additional variables (the 'value state') is not explicit.

4. Issue Four: Uncertainty and Complementarity

In light of the results of the first three issues, we can deal with this one expeditiously. All interpretations accept use of the wavefunction and Born's rule as a good device for making predictions about systems. These predictions are typically probabilistic, but for each observable characteristic, such as position or momentum, there are special states (the eigenstates for the observable) which allow one to predict with certainty what the outcome of an observation will be. It is a simple mathematical fact that the eigenstates, for example, the position of a particle in some dimension are not eigenstates for its momentum in that dimension, and vice versa. So there exist no quantum states which allow for certain prediction of both the outcome of a position measurement and the outcome of a momentum measurement. Furthermore, there is a quantifiable relation between the uncertainties associated with the measurements: the more certain one is about how one measurement will come out, the less certain one must be about the other. This is the Heisenberg Uncertainty Principle, and the relevant pairs of observables are called complementary.

The question which naturally arises is whether the Uncertainty Principle states a limitation on our *knowledge* or a more fundamental limitation on *the world itself.* For convenience, let's grant for the moment that all there is to having a determinate position or determinate momentum is to be disposed to produce a certain outcome in the appropriate experimental situation (a position or momentum measurement). Then the question is: is it possible for a particle to be disposed to give a particular result for both a position and momentum measurement, and so to have determinate values for both, but we just can't know of both dispositions simultaneously, or is it more fundamentally that no particle can have both dispositions at the same time?

Unsurprisingly, the answer depends on the interpretation one adopts. If the wavefunction is complete, then the more fundamental, ontological condition applies: no particle can have both dispositions at once. This is a consequence of the stochastic dynamics of the system, the fact that unless the system is in the appropriate eigenstate, nothing at all determines what the outcome of the experiment will be. In this case, the relevant uncertainty is uncertainty about how experiments will come out, but not uncertainty about the present state of the system: in knowing the wavefunction, one knows all there is about the system, and is not *ignorant* of anything. The Uncertainty Principle is then a limitation on one's knowledge of the present state of a system only in a Pickwickian sense: the limitation is in the facts to be known, not in our knowledge of any facts.

On the other hand, in a deterministic theory such as Bohm's, the Uncertainty Principle must be epistemic rather than ontic. Since the theory is deterministic, the outcome of any precisely specified experiment must be determined by the initial state of the system and apparatus, so if one knew enough about the system and apparatus one could predict with certainty how a particular position measurement or momentum measurement or any measurement would come out.[13] Conversely, our inability to predict the exact outcome of any experiment (as codified in Born's rule) must be a consequence of our ignorance of certain physically relevant facts about the system.

The natural question which then arises is why this sort of ignorance would be enforced on us, why we could not find out the relevant facts which would allow us to make predictions more precise than Born's rule allows. The surprisingly satisfying answer is that as physical objects ourselves, our ability to gather information about the world is constrained by physical laws. The very deterministic dynamics which ensures that there is a fact about how a particular particle would react to any possible experiment also precludes our coming to those facts by interacting with the system. Proving this requires a careful consideration of how one physical system can gather information about another, i.e. how the state of one can become correlated with the state of the other by means of a physical interaction (see Dürr *et al.* 1992). But it is exactly by taking observers seriously as *physical objects, subject to the laws of physics* (rather than as something outside or distinct from 'purely mechanical' physical systems), that Bohm's theory explains the Uncertainty Relations.

5. ISSUE FIVE: QUANTUM LOGIC

Perhaps the most intriguing claim about quantum theory is that it provides empirical grounds for revising *logic itself.* The general idea that logic could be become an empirical matter was advanced by Quine in 'Two Dogmas of Empiricism' (Quine 1951), and the more specific proposal to interpret the meet and join operation on the lattice of quantum propositions as the 'true' meaning of 'and' and 'or' traces back in the physics literature to Birkhoff and von Neumann (1936) and has been considered in the philosophical literature in Putnam (1969) among many others. The proposal is given precise meaning by associating quantum propositions with subspaces of Hilbert space, and understanding the 'conjunction' of two propositions as the intersection of the two spaces and the 'disjunction' of two propositions as their span. The physical state of the world is represented by a vector in the Hilbert space,

---

[13] One has to be a bit cautious here. The outcome of any precisely described experiment could be predicted; that does not mean that one could assign a value to every mathematically defined 'operator': in Bohm's theory, physically different experimental set-ups which would be associated with the same mathematical operator could evoke different outcomes. See Albert (1992: 153).

and a proposition is true just in case the vector lies in the subspace associated with the proposition. It immediately follows that a 'disjunction' can be true even though neither 'disjunct' is true, since a vector can lie in the span of two subspaces without lying in either subspace.

Even more striking is the failure of distributivity of the lattice of quantum propositions. Take any three non-collinear vectors A, B, and C such that C lies in the subspace spanned by A and B. Let '$\vee$' represent the join of two subspaces and '$\wedge$' represent the meet. Then $(A \vee B) \wedge C = C$, while $(A \wedge C) \vee (B \wedge C) = 0 \vee 0 = 0$. So if the vector which represents the state of the system is C, $(A \vee B) \wedge C$ is true while $(A \wedge C) \vee (B \wedge C)$ is not only false but necessarily false. Distributivity of meet over join fails. If we interpret meet and join as 'and' and 'or', then in this 'logic' de Morgan's law can fail. We are therefore outside the domain of classical logic.

A more intuitive presentation of the basic idea can be given by considering the standard two-slit experiment. Surely, it seems, any particle which gets to the screen must have passed through one slit or the other. But if it passed through the top slit, it might show up anywhere on the screen (a beam of particles shot through the top slit will not form interference bands), and if it passed through the bottom slit, it might show up anywhere on the screen (similar reasoning), but in fact there are places on the screen (the dark bands) where it will not show up. So it's not true that it went through the top slit and not true that it went through the bottom slit even though it is true that it went through the top or the bottom. Hence a disjunction can be true even though neither disjunct is true, so classical logic fails.

If a proposition is true just in case the quantum state is an eigenstate of the appropriate operator, then we can understand this result as follows: the wavefunction of the particle is not in an eigenstate of being located at the top slit (since not all of it passes through the top slit), nor is it in an eigenstate of being located at the bottom slit (for similar reasons), but it is in an eigenstate of being located at the union of the two slits. In this sense it passes through 'the top or the bottom' without passing through the top or passing through the bottom. So again, classical logic fails.

Or rather, it is now perfectly clear that classical logic does *not* fail. One would only think it did if one made the egregious mistake of thinking that the proposition that the particle passed through the *union* of two regions is the same as the disjunction of the proposition that it passed through the first with the proposition that it passed through the second. But the two are not equivalent. It may be true that the Rocky Mountains are located entirely in the union of the United States and Canada, but that is not the disjunction of the proposition that they are located entirely in the United States with the proposition that they are located entirely in Canada. Facts about unions are not just disjunctions of corresponding facts about the parts which comprise them.

In some cases, of course, facts about unions do correspond to disjunctions of facts about their parts. If a *pointlike* object is located in the union of the United States and Canada, then the object is either located in the United States or it is located in Canada. So if electrons were pointlike particles, always having a determinate position, then an electron could only pass though the union of the slits by passing through one slit or the other. But, as we have seen, if the wavefunction is complete, then the electron does not have a single determinate location, so one is not entitled to the inference.

Similarly, the right conclusion to draw from the non-distributivity of the lattice of quantum propositions is simple: the 'meet' and 'join' of two propositions on the lattice are not the conjunction and disjunction of those propositions. There may be circumstances in which the meet has the same truth-value as the conjunction, and the join the same truth-value as the disjunction, and indeed this might typically be so in circumstances where quantum effects are absent, but the very examples which are supposed to convince us that classical logic fails really only demonstrate that quantum 'logic' isn't *logic*, i.e. isn't an account of conjunction and disjunction. The two-slit experiment casts no more doubt on classical logic than do the Rocky Mountains.

What of theories in which the wavefunction is not complete? What, for example, of Bohm's theory, in which the electron *is* pointlike and always *does* have a single determinate location? In that theory it is true that each electron passes through the union of the two slits, but equally true that each electron passes through either the top slit or the bottom slit. Indeed, according to Bohm's theory one can tell which slit the particle passed through even though the collection forms interference bands on the screen: all the particles on the upper half of the screen passed through the upper slit and all of those on the lower half through the lower.[14]

But if each particle goes through one particular slit, why do interference bands form? After all, if we block off either slit, then the interference bands disappear, so *something* must be sensitive to the fact that both slits are open. If the particle only goes through one slit, how can it 'know' that both are open?

The answer, of course, is that the form of the *wavefunction* is different when only one of the slits is open rather than both. The wavefunction interacts with both slits even though the particle itself only passes through one. This requires thinking of the wavefunction as something different from the particle itself, but does not require any alteration in logic.

---

[14] Diagrams of the trajectories of Bohmian particles in this case have been produced; see, e.g. Bohm and Hiley (1993: 33).

6. ISSUE SIX: ENTANGLEMENT AND NON-LOCALITY

So far, the metaphysical results I have surveyed may seem disappointingly modest. There are essentially three points at which the ontology of an interpretation of quantum theory may depart from that of classical physics. One is in the acceptance of probabilistic dynamics at a fundamental level. This introduces objective chance into the theory, and therefore requires that one take dispositions seriously. The consequences of this are relatively straightforward, though interestingly constrained by the mathematical structure of the theory, as revealed in the Uncertainty Principle. We have also seen that this indeterminism is not forced on the theory directly by empirical results, since deterministic interpretations such as Bohm's can handle the archetypal quantum phenomena. A second point of ontological innovation may be introduced if one ties the collapse of the wavefunction or the nature of the additional variables to, for example, consciousness. But this sort of move is completely speculative, with no foundation in experiment at all. The third source of ontological innovation lies in the fact that the wavefunction of a system is a vector space defined on configuration space rather than on physical space. I will now turn to the implications of this circumstance.

The peculiar characteristics of the wavefunction are most easily illustrated by means of a particular state of two spin-$\frac{1}{2}$ particles (such as electrons), the so-called *singlet* state. The spin of a spin-$\frac{1}{2}$ particle can be measured by means of an inhomogeneous magnetic field oriented in a given direction (a Stern–Gerlach device): when passed through the field, the particle will be deflected in either one direction ('up') or the other ('down'). If we orient the field in the x-direction, then we measure x-spin, if in the y-direction, y-spin, and so on. A single particle can be in an eigenstate for spin in any direction, i.e. can be in a state in which it is disposed with certainty to be deflected in a certain way by the field. So among the quantum spin states available to a particle is a state in which it is certain to go up if the x-spin is measured, a state we represent by '$|x\uparrow\rangle$'. Similarly, a particle can be in the state $|x\downarrow\rangle$, in which an x-spin measurement will certainly deflect it down. It can be in the state $|z\uparrow\rangle$, in which it is certain to go up if spin in the z-direction is measured, and so on. It turns out to be a mathematical fact (in the usual representation) that $|z\rangle = \frac{1}{\sqrt{2}}|x\uparrow\rangle + \frac{1}{\sqrt{2}}|x\downarrow\rangle$, so a state with definite z-spin cannot have definite x-spin. In fact, if the z-spin can be predicted with certainty, the results of an x-spin measurement will be completely random. This is an example of an uncertainty relation.

If we have a pair of particles, then among the quantum states available are states where the first particle and the second particle each have given single-particle spin states, such as $|z\uparrow\rangle_1|z\uparrow\rangle_2$, $|z\uparrow\rangle_1|z\downarrow\rangle_2$, and $|z\uparrow\rangle_1|x\uparrow\rangle_2$ (in obvious notation). This is no surprise. But since the space of quantum states is a vector space, we can also form *superpositions* of states like these, by weighting different states by a (complex) coefficient and adding them. The particular state we will be concerned with, the singlet state, is a superposition of the state $|x\uparrow\rangle_1|x\downarrow\rangle_2$ and the state $|x\downarrow\rangle_1|x\uparrow\rangle_2$, namely:

$$\frac{1}{\sqrt{2}}|x\uparrow\rangle_1|x\downarrow\rangle_2 - \frac{1}{\sqrt{2}}|x\downarrow\rangle_1|x\uparrow\rangle_2.$$

What is this state like?

The singlet state is a superposition of two states in each of which the particles have opposite x-spins: in one, particle 1 has x-spin up and particle 2 x-spin down, and vice versa in the other. It is not surprising, then, that the quantum formalism makes a prediction with certainty: if x-spin is measured on both particles, one of the particles will have x-spin up and the other x-spin down. It is also not surprising that the quantum formalism does not predict with certainty *which* particle will be up and which down. Indeed, the formalism (Born's rule) ascribes a 50 per cent probability for each outcome, and hence a 50 per cent probability for either of the particles to display x-spin up if measured. Neither of these facts is surprising by itself, but taken together they are quite puzzling.

Suppose that the wavefunction is a complete physical description of the pair of particles. Then the pair can have opposite x-spins (i.e. be disposed with certainty to give opposite x-spin results if measured), even though neither particle has a determinate x-spin (i.e. a sure-fire disposition to react one way or another to an x-spin measurement). It sounds incoherent to say that neither particle has an x-spin but nonetheless their (non-existent?) x-spins are correlated, but the claim can be made clear sense of in terms of dispositions to respond to various measurements.

It is a mathematical fact that the singlet state

$$\frac{1}{\sqrt{2}}|x\uparrow\rangle_1|x\downarrow\rangle_2 - \frac{1}{\sqrt{2}}|x\downarrow\rangle_1|x\uparrow\rangle_2$$

can equally well be written in terms of z-spin as

$$\frac{1}{\sqrt{2}}|z\uparrow\rangle_1|z\downarrow\rangle_2 - \frac{1}{\sqrt{2}}|z\downarrow\rangle_1|z\uparrow\rangle_2.$$

So what was said for x-spin holds *mutatis mutandis* for z-spin: each particle has a 50 per cent chance of going up or going down if z-spin is measured, but if both z-spins are measured, the results for the two particles are sure to be opposite.

There are several curious features of this sort of *entangled* state of the two particles. From the perspective of fundamental metaphysics, the most important point is that the state seems to exhibit an irreducible form of *holism*. For if we consider, say, particle 1 on its own, and characterize how it is disposed to respond to spin measurements, we can say that is has a 50 per cent chance of going up or down if x-spin is measured, or if z-spin is measured, or indeed if spin in any direction is measured, and the same for particle 2. But knowing all there is to know about each particle individually (in this sense) does not suffice to tell us all there is to know about the pair. For it is a fact about the pair that they are disposed to give opposite results if spins in the same direction are measured, but this fact does not follow from the totality of dispositions of each particle taken separately. Formally, the quantum formalism would ascribe a particular *mixed state* to each particle, but knowing that each particle is in this mixed state is not enough to determine that the pair is in the singlet state.

The failure of the quantum state of the whole to supervene on the quantum states of the parts is most strikingly illustrated by the so-called $m = 0$ triplet state:

$$\frac{1}{\sqrt{2}}|x \uparrow\rangle_1 |x \uparrow\rangle_2 - \frac{1}{\sqrt{2}}|x \downarrow\rangle_1 |x \downarrow\rangle_2.$$

If one measures the x-spin of either particle in this state, again the quantum formalism ascribes a 50 per cent chance to each possible outcome, and similarly for z-spin, and spin in every other direction. That is, the mixed state ascribed to each particle in the $m = 0$ triplet state is *identical* to the mixed states ascribed to the particles in the singlet state. Nonetheless, the singlet differs from the $m = 0$ triplet. The difference, however, can only be revealed by a *global measurement* made on *both* particles, and not by any possible *local* measurement made on one particle. For if we measure the x-spins of both particles in the $m = 0$ triplet state, they are certain to give the *same* result rather than opposite results, although, of course, half the time they will both be spin up and half the time spin down. So the individual particles in the $m = 0$ triplet state are indistinguishable by any measurement from their counterparts in the singlet state: in so far as the individual particles have quantum states at all, they are identical. But the wholes of which they are parts are nonetheless in physically distinct states, as can be verified by a single global measurement. The quantum state of a whole therefore does not supervene on the states of its parts, exhibiting a form of holism.[15]

Here is another peculiarity about these entangled states. We have said that in the singlet state each particle has a 50 per cent disposition to go, for example, up if x-spin is measured. But suppose we measure the x-spin of particle 1 and it happens to go up. Since we are certain that x-spin measurements on *both* particles are certain to give opposite results, once we have measured particle 1 we can be certain that if the x-spin of particle 2 is measured, particle 2 will go down. That is, after the measurement performed on particle 1, the physical dispositions of particle 2 have changed. And, indeed, the measurement performed on particle 1 will change the *quantum state* assigned to particle 2 via the collapse of the wavefunction. Furthermore, this holds no matter how far apart the two particles are: measuring one will collapse the

15 A more detailed discussion of this point appears in Maudlin (1998).

wavefunction, and the collapse will change the quantum state ascribed to the other particle. This is what Einstein memorably called *spooky action-at-a-distance*.

All of our discussion so far has been conducted under the assumption that the wavefunction is a complete physical description of the pair of particles. We have already seen that any such theory must employ wave collapse to solve the measurement problem. What we are now seeing is that since the wavefunction is defined on the configuration space of the system, and since every configuration includes the states of all the parts of the system, the collapse can change the quantum states of all the parts, no matter where they are located. So if collapses can be triggered by interaction with single parts, those interactions can have global effects on all the parts, even those which seem to be distant and unconnected.

At this point the reader ought to feel that some very strong, and odd, metaphysical conclusions are being drawn from empirical results which seem fairly unremarkable. After all, all we have said is that if we prepare a bunch of pairs of particles in the singlet state, and then measure their x-spins, or their z-spins, or spins in any other direction, we will find the following two results:

(1) In the long term, the spin measurements in any direction will yield 'up' results half the time and 'down' results half the time.
(2) Whenever we measure spins in the same direction on a given pair, the results will be opposite.

It might well occur to one that this sort of empirical result can be easily obtained without any sort of metaphysical innovation at all. Suppose, for example, that there are really two sorts of pairs of particle produced when we perform the physical operation we call 'making a pair in the singlet state': sometimes we produce pairs in which particle 1 has x-spin up and particle 2 x-spin down (i.e. each particle always has a sure-fire disposition to react in a certain way to an x-spin measurement), and sometimes we produce pairs in which particle 1 is disposed to go down and particle 2 up.[16] If we happen to produce the first sort of pair about half the time and the second sort about half the time, then the empirical results will be as we have described, but no metaphysical funny business is needed. Each individual particle has a sure-fire disposition all along, and there is no 'spooky action-at-a-distance'. On this picture, 'collapse of the wavefunction' is a purely epistemic, rather than ontic, affair: when we measure the first particle, we simply *find out* whether we have created a pair of the first type or a pair of the second type. Our *knowledge* of the distant particle changes when we make a local measurement, but the particle itself is physically unchanged.

---

[16] I am describing these dispositions verbally rather than by using quantum states since we are not supposing that the true physical state of the particle can be captured by any quantum state. We don't want to assume, for example, that the true states are subject to the uncertainty relations.

This sort of explanation is so simple and prosaic that it seems at first glance perverse to stick to the idea that the wavefunction is complete. For all that we need to do to accept the prosaic explanation is to accept that the quantum state of the pair is not a complete physical description: quantum theory ascribes the same state to pairs of particles that are physically different, namely pairs where particle 1 is disposed to show x-spin up and particle 2 x-spin down, and pairs where it is the opposite. Einstein himself, of course, thought that the spooky action-at-a-distance was physically unacceptable, so that all of this talk about the collapse of the wavefunction just showed that the wavefunction could not be complete. As I mentioned above, the famous paper of Einstein, Podolsky, and Rosen is entitled 'Can quantum-mechanical description of reality be considered complete?', and their answer is, simply, no. From Einstein's point of view, the insistence on the completeness of the quantum state was perverse and unjustified in light of the attendant commitment to action-at-a-distance and the availability of alternative explanations that preserve contact action. And so things remained for thirty years.

The breakthrough in the debate occurred when John Stewart Bell proved his famous theorem. For although Einstein was right about the particular sorts of global measurements he considered—like the measurements considered above, they admit of a simple local explanation—Bell realized that there are other sorts of global measurements one can make. One can, for example, measure the x-spin of one particle and the z-spin of the other, or, more generally, one can measure the spins in arbitrary directions on each side. And what Bell showed is that if one considers the totality of these sorts of measurements, *no local theory can replicate the predictions of quantum mechanics*. That is, even if one denies the completeness of the wavefunction, one cannot get rid of the spooky action-at-a-distance and recover the quantum predictions.[17]

In Bohm's theory, for example, the wavefunction is not complete, and particles always have determinate locations, but still a measurement carried out on one particle can influence other entangled particles, no matter how distant. This influence is mediated by the wavefunction which, as we have seen, is irreducibly holistic. One must always bear in mind that even though Bohm's theory does not take the wavefunction to be complete, it does take it to represent a serious, irreducible part of reality. And even though the wavefunction in Bohm's theory does not itself collapse, its dynamical role allows it to underwrite action at a distance.

So the deepest metaphysical innovations of the quantum theory lie not in indeterminism, or in complementarity, or in the uncertainty relations, or in the role of observation, or in emendations to logic. The deepest metaphysical innovation lies in the holistic nature of the wavefunction, and the fact that the quantum state

[17] There are many accurate non-technical presentations of Bell's theorem in the literature, e.g. d'Espagnat (1979); Mermin (1981); Herbert (1985, ch. 12); Maudlin (1994, ch. 2).

of an entangled system cannot be recovered from the quantum states of its parts. Furthermore, the holism of the wavefunction, together with the dynamics that govern it (if one accepts collapses) or the dynamics it governs (in a hidden-variables theory), imply the existence of action-at-a-distance. And this action is not merely a theoretical posit: it has direct empirical consequences, namely violations of Bell's inequality, which cannot be predicted without it.

One might well wonder (as Einstein would have) whether this action-at-a-distance could be reconciled with Relativity, since the action has to act faster than light. This is an interesting question, and might even make a topic for a book (cf. Maudlin 1994).

REFERENCES

Albert, D. (1992). *Quantum Mechanics and Experience.* Cambridge, Mass.: Harvard University Press.

—— and B. Loewer (1988). 'Interpreting the Many-Worlds Interpretation'. *Synthese,* 77: 195–213.

Bell, J. S. (1987). *Speakable and Unspeakable in Quantum Mechanics.* Cambridge: Cambridge University Press.

—— (1990). 'Against "Measurement"', in A. I. Miller (ed.), *Sixty-Two Years of Uncertainty.* New York: Plenum Press, 17–31.

Birkhoff, G., and J. von Neumann (1936). 'The Logic of Quantum Mechanics'. *Annalen der Mathematik,* 37: 823.

Bohm, D., and B. J. Hiley (1993). *The Undivided Universe.* London: Routledge.

Bub, J. (1997). *Interpreting the Quantum World.* Cambridge: Cambridge University Press.

Cushing, J., and E. McMullin (eds.) (1989). *Philosophical Consequences of Quantum Theory.* Notre Dame, Ind.: Notre Dame University Press.

d'Espagnat, B. (1979). 'Quantum Theory and Reality'. *Scientific American,* 241: 158–70.

DeWitt, B., and N. Graham (eds.) (1973). *The Many-Worlds Interpretation of Quantum Mechanics.* Princeton: Princeton University Press.

Dickson, M. (1998). *Quantum Chance and Non-Locality.* Cambridge: Cambridge University Press.

Dürr, D., S. Goldstein, and N. Zhangi (1992). 'Quantum Equilibrium and the Origin of Absolute Uncertainty'. *Journal of Statistical Physics,* 67: 843–907.

Einstein, A., B. Podolsky, and N. Rosen (1935). 'Can Quantum-Mechanical Description of Reality be Considered Complete?' *Physical Review,* 47: 777–80. Repr. in Wheeler and Zurek (1981*b*).

Everett, H., III (1957). 'Relative State Formulation of Quantum Mechanics'. *Review of Modern Physics,* 29: 454–62. Repr. in Wheeler and Zurek (1981*b*).

Ghirardi, G. C., A. Rimini, and T. Weber (1986). 'Unified Dynamics for Microscopic and Macroscopic Physics'. *Physical Review,* D34: 470–91.

Healey, R., *The Philosophy of Quantum Mechanics: An Interactive Interpretation.* Cambridge: Cambridge University Press.

Herbert, N. (1985). *Quantum Reality.* New York: Anchor Press, Doubleday.

Hughes, R. (1989). *The Structure and Interpretation of Quantum Mechanics*. Cambridge, Mass.: Harvard University Press.

Kochen, S. (1985). 'A New Interpretation of Quantum Mechanics', in P. Lahti and P. Mittelstaedt (eds.), *Symposium on the Foundations of Modern Physics*. Singapore: World Scientific, 151–70.

Lockwood, M. (1989). *Mind, Brain and the Quantum*. Oxford: Oxford University Press.

Maudlin, T. (1994). *Quantum Non-Locality and Relativity*. Oxford: Basil Blackwell.

—— (1995). 'Three Measurement Problems'. *Topoi*, 14: 7–15 .

—— (1997). 'Descrying the World in the Wavefunction'. *The Monist*, 80: 2–23.

—— (1998). 'Part and Whole in Quantum Mechanics', in E. Castellani (ed.), *Interpreting Bodies*. Princeton: Princeton University Press, 46–60.

Mermin, D. (1981). 'Quantum Mysteries for Everyone'. *Journal of Philosophy*, 78: 397–408.

Miller, A. (ed.) (1990). *Sixty-Two Years of Uncertainty*. New York: Plenum Press.

Penrose, R. (1994). *Shadows of the Mind*. Oxford: Oxford University Press.

Perle, P. (1990). 'Toward a Relativistic Theory of Statevector Reduction', in A. I. Miller (ed.), *Sixty-Two Years of Uncertainty*. New York: Plenum Press, 193–214.

Putnam, H. (1969). 'Is Logic Empirical?' *Boston Studies in the Philosophy of Science*, 5: 199–215. Repr. as 'The Logic of Quantum Mechanics', in Putnam (1975: 174–97).

—— (1975). *Mathematics, Matter and Method*. Cambridge: Cambridge University Press.

Quine, W. (1951). 'Two Dogmas of Empiricism'. *Philosophical Review*, 60: 20–43.

Redhead, M. (1987). *Incompleteness, Nonlocality, and Realism*. Oxford: Clarendon Press.

van Fraassen, B. (1991). *Quantum Mechanics: An Empiricist View*. Oxford: Oxford University Press.

Vermaas, P. (1999). *A Philosopher's Understanding of Quantum Mechanics: Possibilities and Impossibilities of a Modal Interpretation*. Cambridge: Cambridge University Press.

von Neumann, J. (1955). *Mathematical Foundations of Quantum Mechanics*, trans. R. T. Beyer. Princeton: Princeton University Press.

Wheeler, J. (1981*a*). 'Law without Law', in Wheeler and Zurek, 182–213.

—— and W. Zurek (eds.) (1981*b*). *Quantum Theory and Measurement*. Princeton: Princeton University Press.

PART VI

PERSONS AND THE NATURE OF MIND

CHAPTER 16

MATERIAL PEOPLE

DEAN W. ZIMMERMAN

1. INTRODUCTION: SENSIBLE MATERIALISMS AND ENTIA SUCCESSIVA

1.1 The Varieties of 'Sensible Materialism'

DUALISM and materialism are competing answers to the question each of us may ask with the words 'What am I?' (spoken in a metaphysical tone of voice, with emphasis on the word 'am'). The following (admittedly somewhat stipulative) working definition of 'dualism' will suffice for present purposes: the doctrine that no human being is an object composed entirely of the kinds of physical stuff that make up rocks and trees and the bodies of animals, but that each of us is, instead, something quite different—a substance that has sensory experiences, thoughts, and emotions, but shares almost nothing in common (except, perhaps, spatial location) with the

I am grateful to audiences at Rutgers University, Queens University, the University of Rochester, MIT, University of Massachusetts–Amherst, and Syracuse University for useful comments and criticisms. Special thanks go to Lynne Rudder Baker, John G. Bennett, Phil Bricker, Alex Byrne, Earl Conee, Richard Feldman, Liz Harman, John Hawthorne, Eric Hiddleston, Leonard Katz, Henry Laycock, Kris McDaniel, Adele Mercier, Ted Sider, Judy Thomson, Peter van Inwagen, Brian Weatherson, and Stephen Yablo. Research leading up to this chapter was supported by a grant from the Pew Charitable Trusts; it was improved in workshops at Gordon College and Calvin College sponsored by the Council for Christian Colleges and Universities and the Calvin Center for Christian Scholarship; I thank participants in those meetings, including Alicia Finch, Greg Ganssle, William Hasker, Mike Murray, Tim O'Connor, Susan Papademetris, and, especially, Kevin Corcoran.

physical objects that surround us or with their fundamental constituents (electrons, quarks, and so on).[1] By 'materialism', I mean the doctrine that each human being *is* an object all of whose parts are, ultimately, made of the same kinds of physical substances as rocks and trees and the bodies of animals.

Dualism is not entirely lacking contemporary defenders, including some very able philosophers.[2] In this chapter, however, I confine my attention to materialist theories about human persons. As shall appear, I find dualism considerably less unbelievable once the materialist alternatives are clearly articulated. In fact, most days of the week I am a dualist myself. But in today's climate defending dualism is a Herculean, not to say Quixotic, task; for the moment, I leave it to others and adopt the assumption that some form of materialism must be true.

It would be an extreme understatement to say that, among philosophers, materialism is the more popular view. But there are many different versions of materialism, some just as unpopular as dualism. Descartes mentions some insane materialists who believe 'that their heads are made of earthenware, or that they are pumpkins, or made of glass' (Descartes 1984: 13). At least one otherwise sane contemporary philosopher has taken seriously the thesis that we are tiny physical particles lodged somewhere in our brains (see Chisholm 1998: 291–6 (reprints portions of Chisholm 1979); Quinn 1997). But more popular by far (and rightly so) are versions of what I will call 'sensible materialism'.

Some parts of living bodies have more or less natural boundaries: they fall under biological or functional kinds, such as *heart, cell, nervous system, brain, cerebrum, cerebral hemisphere, complete organism* (that 'part' that includes every other). Call the 'likely candidates' for being human persons those objects with natural boundaries that include *all* the parts upon which our ability to think most immediately depends. A couple of examples will help make this notion clearer. An 'object' composed of an arbitrary assortment of particles taken from toenail and eyelash and tongue does not count as a likely candidate, since it lacks natural boundaries. The kidneys, although they have natural boundaries, are ruled out by the discovery that our thinking is only *indirectly* dependent upon them and their parts; a human being can go on thinking without them, at least for a short time.

The likely candidates are, I take it, the only really satisfactory physical candidates for being a thinker such as I am. They include: the complete organism a person often refers to as 'my body', the entire nervous system within it, the brain,

---

[1] Dualism, as I have defined it, is a doctrine about how actual human beings and actual kinds of stuff are related. It should not be taken to imply that it is not possible for there to have been chemical atoms with atomic weights differing from any actual atoms, or that if there were such atoms then dualism would be true.

[2] Defenders of dualism include Swinburne (1997); Foster (1991); Robinson (1989); Hart (1988); Yandell (1995); Hasker (1999); and Harwood (1998). (All are at least defenders of *anti-materialism* about the self; Foster and Robinson are defenders of dualism by day, but the last of the idealists by night. For Foster's idealist tendencies revealed, see Foster 1982.)

the cerebrum, and perhaps one or the other single hemisphere of that cerebrum. *Sensible materialism*, then, will be the thesis that each human person is one of these likely candidates. (Note that identifying a human person with something having the boundaries of a human brain, or of a complete human organism, does not automatically imply that the person has purely biological persistence conditions— for example, it does not rule out the possibility of a person's 'switching bodies' by means of a 'brain state transfer' device.) Perhaps George Graham is right to think that we are in a state of 'strong ontic ignorance'—i.e. we do not know exactly what kind of thing we are.[3] But I suspect that, if there is good reason to reject all versions of sensible materialism, then one of the better dualisms is at least as likely to be true as any *non-sensible* materialism.

1.2 Chisholm's Entia Successiva Argument

Roderick Chisholm believed that one could answer few of the most interesting philosophical questions about persons without grappling with more general metaphysical questions.[4] Chisholm raised the following objection to the thesis that we are *entia successiva*—'successive entities', things that gain and lose parts over time.

The body that persists through time—the one I have been carrying with me, so to speak—is an *ens successivum*. That is to say, it is an entity made up of different things at different times. The set of things that make it up today is not identical with the set of things that made it up yesterday or with the set of things that made it up the day before. Now one could say that an *ens successivum* has different 'stand-ins' at different times and that these stand-ins do duty for the successive entity at the different times. Thus the thing that does duty for my body today is other than the thing that did duty for it yesterday and other than the thing that will do duty for it tomorrow. But what of me?

Am *I* an entity such that different things do duty for *me* at different days? Is it *one* thing that does my feeling depressed for me today and *another* thing that did it yesterday and still another thing that will do it tomorrow? If I happen to be feeling sad, then, surely, there is no *other* thing that is doing my feeling sad for me. We must reject the view that persons are thus *entia successiva*. (Chisholm 1979)

If Chisholm's argument is sound, then every form of sensible materialism must be rejected. For all the likely candidates are *entia successiva*.

Many have thought that Chisholm's argument is easily resisted. He seems to be presupposing that there is, in addition to the living body (or other *ens successivum* candidate for being me), yet another thing (a 'stand-in', as he calls it) made of the same parts as the body but incapable of surviving the gain and loss of parts. But why

---

[3] Graham (1999).

[4] The conviction was not so widely shared back in the 1960s and early 1970s as it is today. Compare Chisholm (1969, 1970, 1976).

suppose there is any such thing? Why not simply say that there is the living body, and a host of tiny particles that constitute the body, but no *extra* thing made of the same particles but differing from the living body in that it cannot acquire new particles or lose its present ones?

Chisholm takes it to be obvious that there are such extra things.[5] But not everyone finds them so obvious; and it would surely be a strike against such entities if countenancing them were to lead, as Chisholm's argument seems to show, to a quite bizarre conclusion. Chisholm's basic argument can, however, be further defended by appeal to the fact that *entia successiva*, such as artefacts and organisms, are made out of various kinds of material stuff; and that the stuff an artefact or organism is made of at one time is often not the same as the stuff it is made of at another. Mass terms—such as 'water', 'gold', 'cellular tissue', and the extremely general 'matter'— characterize kinds of stuff. And mass terms are used to form more complex terms that denote particular portions of stuff, or what some have called (following Locke 1985: II. xxvii[6]) 'masses' of stuff. I have in mind such singular terms as 'the water in the tub', 'the gold used to make my ring', 'the cellular tissue making up my liver', 'the matter of which my body is constituted'. Although some may doubt whether Chisholm's 'stand-ins' exist, we can hardly doubt that there are such things as these. We might argue about whether we should think of them as physical objects or as some other sort of thing; but we talk about them all the time, and surely much of what we say about them is true.

One truism about the water in the tub or the gold in the ring is that, if some of that water or gold were somehow destroyed, it would not be precisely the same water or gold that filled the tub or constituted the ring. Masses of stuff can, in general, undergo much less in the way of changes of parts than the *entia successiva* they constitute.[7] If drink destroys some of the cellular tissue in my liver, my liver is no longer made of the same cellular tissue; and, most importantly for our purposes, as new matter is assimilated by my body and old matter is sloughed off, *the matter of which I am constituted* changes. So, right now, one mass of matter or heap of stuff 'does duty for' the *ens successivum* that is my brain or body; and another will 'do duty for it' later. But then Chisholm's argument may be reinstated:

(P1)   If I am a thing that gains or loses parts, such as a brain or human body; then, each time I undergo a change of parts, there is another thing where I am, a mass of matter distinct from myself but having all the same intrinsic characteristics—e.g. size, shape, mass, and even mental states, like *feeling sad*.

---

[5] Kit Fine, Judith Jarvis Thomson, I, and many others agree with Chisholm about this (see Chisholm 1976; Fine 1994; Thomson 1998; Zimmerman 1995).

[6] I adopt this terminology in Zimmerman (1995).

[7] The relative mereological stability of constituting objects is exploited by Thomson in her definition of 'constitution'; cf. Thomson (1998).

(P2) But it is false that, where I am, there is something else with all the same intrinsic characteristics; there is only one thing here that feels sad, not two.

So I am neither a brain nor a human organism nor any other thing that changes parts—and therefore no version of sensible materialism can be true.

Accept the conclusion, and the only versions of materialism left are such outlandish theses as that I am a tiny particle lodged in my brain; or that I am some matter that is sad right now but that was and will soon be a non-conscious scattered thing, since the matter *now* in my body was spread throughout the biosphere and will soon be again. If materialism really is more plausible than dualism, then one of the premisses of this argument must be false. (One could, of course, accept the conclusion and reject both materialism and dualism; but only by doubting one's own existence—something even philosophers find difficult.)

What costs are associated with the various possible ways of denying one or the other premiss? The attempt to answer this question shall provide the structure of my survey of recent developments in materialist theories of human beings.

1.3 Warning: Criteria of Personal Identity not Included

There is a rich, well-known literature on personal identity stretching back to the middle of the last century, including important papers and books by Derek Parfit, David Lewis, Sydney Shoemaker, Richard Swinburne, John Perry, David Wiggins, Bernard Williams, Anthony Quinton, H. P. Grice, and many others;[8] and much of this debate is dominated by the propounding of competing 'criteria of personal identity', supported largely by appeal to intuitions about which sorts of mainly imaginary misadventures a person would or would not survive—what Mark Johnston (1987) has called 'the method of cases'. It is the method of John Locke (1985) in his famous chapter 'On Identity and Diversity', and a method that reaches its most sophisticated and sustained deployment in Peter Unger's *Identity, Consciousness, and Value* (Unger 1990).

By contrast, there will be almost no exploration, in this chapter, of competing criteria of personal identity—standardly subdivisible into 'psychological criteria' and 'physical criteria'. The rival materialisms I shall be surveying are on a higher level of abstraction than the alternatives in disputes pitting physical against psychological criteria. The target of the revised *entia successiva* argument is a very minimal materialism: that I am something with the boundaries of a brain or an organism (or some other likely candidate), something that

---

[8] For seminal papers by Quinton, Grice, Williams, Shoemaker, Perry, and Parfit, see Perry (1975). See also Wiggins (1971, 1980); papers by Lewis, Perry, Parfit, and Wiggins in Rorty (1976); and Shoemaker and Swinburne (1984).

can gain and lose parts. It makes no difference to the argument whether one supposes that the brain-shaped or body-shaped entity in question satisfies a psychological or a biological criterion of identity. I shall often write as though the materialist's best bet were to suppose that a human person is a human organism, a thing shaped like my body and satisfying persistence conditions not unlike those of other animals—whatever exactly those are. But nothing turns upon this.

Much of the recent metaphysical literature on persons has focused upon the basic ontology of persons, and not the details of their persistence conditions.[9] Peter van Inwagen's *Material Beings* (1990)—a watershed in recent discussions of the nature of persons—is typical of much recent work: it is a book predicated upon the assumption that it is impossible to answer very many of the most interesting philosophical questions about persons without taking sides in a host of purely metaphysical—indeed, ontological—debates. An impressive literature has been built up over the last twenty years that shares this assumption, much of it directly influenced by van Inwagen's way of framing the questions.[10]

1.4   To be Tender-Minded or Tough-Minded?

The fundamental puzzle about material persons that will be my focus is due simply to the fact that all the likely candidates for being me are things that gain and lose parts—something that ships and trees and dogs are generally thought to do as well.[11] (I shall sometimes call things that can gain and lose parts 'mereologically incontinent'; in organisms, artefacts, and the like, a certain amount of mereological incontinence is a good thing.) There is, then, great pressure to 'treat like cases alike'; to apply to persons whatever resolution one proposes to analogous problems for other mereologically incontinent objects—or, at the very least, to tell the same story about humans as one tells about non-human *organisms*.

---

[9] Recent years have also witnessed increasing scepticism about the results of 'the method of cases' concerning personal identity and in philosophy more generally. Bernard Williams's criticisms of psychological criteria of identity might be seen as the beginnings of this trend (Williams 1973). For recent developments, see Johnston (1987); Wilkes (1992); Rovane (1997); Gendler (2000).

[10] The papers collected in Rea (1997) are concerned with the more abstract ontological issues that have become the focus of much recent work about personal identity. The anthology serves as a splendid introduction to the debates I describe in this chapter. There is, of course, no sharp divide between the work I engage directly, and work concerned with specific criteria of personal identity; in fact, authors prominent in the latter debate—e.g. David Lewis, Sydney Shoemaker, and Derek Parfit—are among those most responsible for the 'metaphysical turn' the debate has taken.

[11] Several other difficulties concerning persistence through time of persons and other objects, and their potential resolutions, are explored in detail by Sally Haslanger in her contribution to this volume (Ch. 11).

Throughout my survey of approaches to the metaphysics of material persons, one should, therefore, consider whether reasons given for favouring or rejecting a view would have application to the metaphysics of plants and animals. Some of my objections to one or another version of materialism consist in pointing out counter-intuitive consequences for the thesis that *we* are such things as the view describes—consequences that would cause us little distress were the subject matter plants or 'dumb' animals. In the final section I sort these out, and call them 'personal' objections to sensible materialism. Those who would rely upon 'personal' considerations to support the view that we are special, metaphysically unlike non-human animals, will be charged with 'tender-mindedness'—and with reason. But these epistemological issues cannot be seriously explored, let alone resolved, within a mere survey of the metaphysical terrain.

2. Denying (P2)

2.1 The 'Too Many Minds' Objection

I begin by considering the case of materialisms that deny (P2). The problem with denying (P2) is that doing so introduces 'too many minds': if there are two or three thinkers here, then there are two or three pains that have to be taken into account in utilitarian calculations, for instance; and two thinkers thinking 'I am in pain'. And that certainly seems wrong.

There are at least two relatively distinct problems posed here under the heading 'too many minds'. First, denying (P2) seems to introduce two or more pains, feelings of melancholy, etc., one for each coincident entity, where intuitively there should be only one. Call this problem 'too many thoughts'. Secondly, there is the pressure to recognize two or three psychological subjects with first-person points of view, each subjectively just like the others, indiscernible 'from inside', unable to distinguish among themselves. Call this 'too many thinkers'.[12] Materialists who would reject the second premise must grapple with both aspects of the 'too many minds' objection.

---

[12] The second part of 'too many minds', what I call 'too many thinkers', is driven home with great force by Olson; see Olson (1997, esp. 106).

2.2 The Doctrine of Temporal Parts

One promising strategy for denying the second premiss presupposes the thesis that things have 'temporal parts'.[13] Consider the way a spatially three-dimensional object is generally thought to fill the region it occupies: namely, by having a different part filling each of the many subregions in the region occupied by the whole. My body, for example, fills the man-shaped region it does by having a part filling the head-shaped part of the region, two others filling the arm-shaped subregions, two others filling the leg-shaped subregions, and so on. Defenders of temporal parts claim that an object that lasts for a period of time is spread throughout that period in a similar fashion. For each instant, there is a distinct thing, a momentary 'temporal part' of the object, something that exists then and only then; and for each longer interval of time, there is a distinct *extended* temporal part of the object that exists just during that period and is composed of all the instantaneous temporal parts falling within the interval.[14] ('Perduring' and 'enduring' are often used to mean 'persisting by means of temporal parts' and 'persisting, but not by means of temporal parts', respectively.[15])

2.3 How Temporal Parts Help Block 'Too Many Thoughts'

'Too many thoughts' gets its bite from the conviction that, in some sense, there must be just *one* pain or pleasure located where I am, just one instance of each conscious experience I have. But how could that be if the mass of matter and I are intrinsically identical, each in pain—as the denier of (P2) admits? The friend of temporal parts can say that, strictly speaking, there is only one thing located *just* here and now: my present temporal part. I am in pain only in virtue of *its* being in pain. And the

[13] Many philosophers have used temporal parts to solve problems of coincident entities. Compare e.g. Quine (1960); Lewis (1976); Noonan (1989); Heller (1990); Hudson (2002); Sider (1997, 2001*b*). The doctrine of temporal parts is discussed in more detail by Haslanger in this volume (Ch. 11).

Warning: In the writings of contemporary philosophers, 'four-dimensionalism' sometimes means the doctrine of temporal parts, as in Sider (2001*b*); sometimes it stands for a thesis that is basically about the nature of truth—namely, that all truths are eternal truths; sometimes it means that presentism is false (e.g. in Michael Rea's contribution to this volume: Ch. 9); and sometimes it seems to mean a combination of these views.

[14] Though nothing here turns on the issue, one can affirm a general doctrine of temporal parts while denying the existence of literally instantaneous parts (see Zimmerman 1996*b*).

[15] There is a lively and ongoing debate about how best to make the distinction between perdurance and endurance. The moral of the debate seems to me to be that there are several 'packages' of metaphysical views that stand opposed to a temporal parts metaphysics, united by their opposition to perdurance but disagreeing about a sufficient number of substantive theses to make it hard to state a common positive view about persistence acceptable to all parties. Compare Merricks (1995, 1999); Sider (1997, 2001*b*); and Lombard (1999). (The use of 'perdurance' for persistence by means of temporal parts, 'endurance' for persistence without them, is due to Mark Johnston, and has been widely adopted.)

mass of matter now making me up is in pain in virtue of its *sharing* this selfsame part with me. If First Avenue and Seventh Street each develop a pothole, this may not add two potholes to the number the city must fill—for it might be the same pothole, in their intersection. Just so with my pain and that of my constituting matter.

The doctrine of temporal parts seems not only to provide the best way to resist (P2); it also seems to entail the denial of (P2). If I exist at a given time entirely in virtue of having a part that exists *only* then, the intrinsic properties I have at that time really ought to be confined to the ones that temporal part has. And if something has a certain temporal part at a time, the intrinsic properties it has then should be the same as those the temporal part has then. I assume that there are components of my present psychological state that are qualitative and intrinsic to me-as-I-am-now, states that would be shared by intrinsic duplicates of me that lasted no longer than the psychological states themselves.[16] If I have an independent contribution to make to the intrinsic characteristics I display, then I have a kind of independent presence here; there are two things here, I and my temporal part, and the contribution I make to what is happening here and now is different from that of my temporal part. Allowing that the intrinsic character of a thing at a time can be distinct from that of its temporal part at that time would lead directly to some of the apparent absurdities that bedevil the view I call 'coincidentalism' and discuss in detail below.

Some philosophers have doubted that any component of my psychology is intrinsic in this way. Some believe that my current phenomenal states are dependent upon the functional role played by physical states of my brain (a role often partly determined by extrinsic factors), or the aetiology of their causal roles.[17] It is unclear, to say the least, whether a physical state in a brief temporal part of me, e.g. a part lasting only one-hundredth of a second, should be said to play any sort of functional role in that fraction-of-a-second-long part in virtue of playing that role in longer temporal parts of me that contain it.

Although I do not find functionalism about the phenomenal to be very plausible, it is worth noting that temporal parts versions of such views entail the denial of (P2), nevertheless. There will be ever so many temporal parts of me that include the brief proper subject of a brief experience like my one-hundredth-of-a-second-long pain; and ever so many of these temporal parts will be long enough (lasting for hours or days or years before and after the experience) to allow the physical state that (supposedly) *is* this mental state to play its role—i.e. long enough for there to be a stable cognitive architecture intermediate between stimuli and behaviour in which this physical state is typically caused by so-and-so and typically causes

---

[16] Such a view would seem warranted by familiar arguments for anti-reductionism about qualia, e.g. those of Jackson (1982) and Chalmers (1996).

[17] For recent overviews of varieties of functionalism, see Block (1996) and Lewis (1996).

such-and-such. Denying that the phenomenal is intrinsic for broadly functionalist reasons does not, then, provide the temporal parts metaphysician with a way to avoid (P2).

2.4 Rejecting Temporal Parts and Introducing Shared 'Tropes'

One might attempt to divorce the number of pains or the amount of pain from the number of subjects feeling pain by supposing that pains are not individuated by their subjects, but are instead distinct individuals themselves—what D. C. Williams (1953) called 'tropes',[18] property instances that have a kind of independent existence. There might, then, be just one of these pain-individuals, indifferently related to however many subjects happen to be in its vicinity. Events, so conceived, must be at least somewhat independent of their subjects: they cannot be structured entities like Armstrong's facts or Jaegwon Kim's events, consisting simply of an object and a property it exemplifies (see Armstrong 1997; Kim 1976). If that were all there were to them, then the 'too many thoughts' dilemma would be as sharp as ever: either the person but not the aggregate is the subject-part of an event of something's being in pain, or vice versa (in either case the view amounts to a denial of (P1), not (P2)); or else each subject exemplifies pain and there are two events of something's being in pain. A metaphysics of shared property instances must add something to the mix besides subjects and properties.

Adopting a trope metaphysics may help with 'too many thoughts'. But it faces a dilemma: a trope metaphysics either (i) collapses into a temporal parts view, or (ii) posits a strange sort of bare particular. Take the first horn; suppose objects are bundles or sums of tropes—presumably, the tropes of their intrinsic properties. Objects like persons are changing nearly-continuously, which requires a near-continuous change of tropes. When an object is constituted by a batch of tropes at one time, and by entirely different batches of tropes at neighbouring times, is there any alternative but to say that it persists by means of temporal parts? I suppose one might say, of some object x, that it is the sum of tropes A, B, C, at one time, and tropes D, E, F, at another time; but that there does not exist a third and fourth thing, y and z, y being a sum of A, B, C that exists just at the first time, and z being a sum of D, E, F that exists just at the second time. But the view still has the smell of temporal parts about it; every object that changes continuously with respect to its intrinsic properties will be constituted, without remainder, by instantaneous items.

---

[18] Williams borrowed the term 'trope' from Santayana (1942); but Santayana used it to stand for universal essences of events, identical in their instances—a kind of entity Williams eliminates from his ontology by means of his more concrete, unrepeatable tropes. (For a detailed discussion of tropes, see Peter Simons's contribution to this volume: Ch. 12.)

If one takes the second horn, (ii), one must posit an underlying something or other in addition to the tropes; a thing that is red, say, in virtue of relations to its redness trope.[19] Since redness tropes are supposed themselves to be instances of red ('that redness over there'), the underlying thing is red because of its relations to a red thing—a thing that is red in some other, more direct fashion. Repeat this for all the intrinsic properties of a thing, and the nature of the underlying thing becomes quite mysterious.[20]

Even if a non-temporal-parts trope metaphysics could be made coherent, the use of shared mental tropes to cut down on the number of thoughts does not hold much promise as a resolution to 'too many thinkers', as indicated below. And, without temporal parts, the view becomes a version of coincidentalism, which will come in for a drubbing later on other grounds.

A plausible answer to 'too many thoughts' requires that there be a single instance of pain where I am. If a single trope of pain cannot be introduced as an independent extra entity for several subjects to share, the denier of (P2) must posit a single primary subject of pain in virtue of which the several subjects can all be (derivatively) in pain. So I confine my attention in the rest of this section to temporal parts metaphysics.

2.5 'Too Many Thinkers' and Too Many Temporal Parts

I turn now to 'too many thinkers'. The doctrine of temporal parts may have cut down on the number of sadnesses, pains, pleasures, and other mental states going on where I and my current mass of matter are located: there is really just one thing here, my current temporal part that experiences sadness, pain, or pleasure 'for itself', as it were. My experience, and that of the mass of matter, are 'borrowed' from the temporal part we share. But the cost for the reduction in the number of *local* subjects of experience is a lavish outlay in *persisting* subjects of experience. Every whole made of temporal parts that shares this one with me and my current stuff also shares our pains and pleasures. Consider: the temporal parts from my first thirty-seven years constitute a persisting thing that will cease to exist sooner than I; likewise for my

---

[19] This sort of trope theory is defended by C. B. Martin, who finds it in Locke's talk of substrata and modes. See Martin (1980).

[20] This 'bare substratum' objection to tropes-cum-underlying-subjects is quite different from the dubious 'bare substratum' objection typically lodged against traditional substance–attribute theories. Defenders of substance–attribute analyses of what it is for an object to be red will say that it is a matter of the object's standing in an exemplification relation to the property redness. But most will deny that the property redness is itself an instance of red, a red thing; and so they are not open to the 'bare substratum' objection I raise against tropes-cum-underlying-subjects. To insist that the substance–attribute philosopher posits a 'bare substratum', not 'red-in-itself' but only red 'in virtue of relations to something else', is simply to reject the proposed analysis.

temporal parts from this last year, or month, or day. In fact, there is a great host of beings here, each equally sad in virtue of sharing the one temporal part. Many strange consequences follow. As Eric Olson has emphasized, it is hard to see how I could be sure which one of them *I* am (see e.g. Olson 1997: 106–8). And it is odd that so many of the thinkers behave in seemingly irrational ways. When I make a small sacrifice now for a greater benefit to myself later, there are ever so many others who make the sacrifice with no hope of reward. The temporal parts metaphysics is borne down by the weight of this host of beings, each equally sad in virtue of sharing the one temporal part. Their existence leads to the absurd, or at least to things I find unbelievable.

To begin with, one should ask what the word 'I' means in the mouths of so many, and what it is that they refer to when they think first-person thoughts, such as they all do now when I say to myself, 'I am sad'. Does my present temporal part, the shortest one capable of thinking a single thought, say to itself that *it* is sad? And likewise for the longer ones, and the mass of matter as well? The friend of temporal parts had better deny this, or the game is up. To accept this result would be to populate the world with beings who share my subjective point of view precisely, who believe all the things about themselves that I believe about myself, but who are mostly wildly mistaken. I believe that I have been around for many years, and will probably live for many more, and that I am conscious more often than not; but, on the view now under consideration, many things *wrongly* think these things *about themselves*—such things as my present temporal part, and the sum of today's temporal parts, and the matter making up my body right now. But if I know that the vast majority of those who see the world just as I do now are terribly deceived, how could I possibly suppose that I know which one *I* am?

Not only should I be sceptical about my past and future, in such circumstances; I should be sceptical about what it is rational for me to do. Would not the mass of matter and today's temporal part behave differently if only they knew how short their conscious lives will be? My present temporal part, and the matter making up my body now, and the parts constituting just my first thirty-seven years have much less reason to undergo present hardship willingly for the sake of benefits *I* will reap later on. But, fortunately, each one mistakenly takes himself to be me, and behaves accordingly!

To avoid this dead end, the temporal parts metaphysician must insist that, when my current stage thinks the thought I would express by saying 'I am sad', each of the many things that share that stage with me attributes sadness to *me*, not to *itself*. That is just how the first-person pronoun works, she may say: when a temporal part uses the first person in thought or speech, it automatically refers to the whole *person* within which the temporal part falls, nothing larger or smaller. Now, when the friend of temporal parts asks herself whether she has been a conscious person for many years, she need not worry about whether she is one of the many hapless short-lived sums of temporal parts sharing this thought with her. '*I* cannot be one of them', she may reason, 'since it is just part of our conventions governing the use of "I" that its reference spreads to take in all and only temporal parts that belong to the *same person* as this current one.'

Does this strategy rid the world of hosts of irrational or at least strangely self-less beings; should it allay our sceptical fears? What prevents these many other subjects of experience from referring to themselves using the first person? Nothing but the conventions surrounding the English words 'I', 'me', 'myself', etc. Each *can* think thoughts that refer to itself; for instance, when I think that the mass of matter now constituting my body was once scattered over many miles, the mass of matter sharing that temporal part with me thinks a thought having *itself* for the subject. So, although it can refer to itself, it fails to care for its own fate; likewise, all the others allow their wills to be bent to mine. Perhaps an analogy will help convey the oddity of such passive behaviour. Suppose the emperor, hoping to encourage patriotism and self-sacrifice for the good of the empire, declares that first-person pronouns shall henceforth refer not to the speaker, but rather to the body politic—that is, to the citizens of the empire, collectively. The dutiful populace could obey the law without much trouble, at the expense of a bit of circumlocution. 'The part of me at the end of the counter needs a cup of coffee!' Now suppose that the new convention has its intended effect, rendering the individual subjects more willing to sacrifice themselves for the good of the whole. Would they have been given any *reason* to change their preferences in this way? The introduction of a new linguistic convention surely cannot by itself provide a reason for the change; it simply turned out to be a fact about the psychological laws governing these subjects that forcing them to talk in this funny way would make them more patriotic. Likewise, it is just a fact about the psychologies of short-lived temporal parts of humans, masses of matter overlapping with humans, and all the rest, that using 'I' according to present conventions prevents their taking any interest in themselves. There still seems to be a host of beings in the world who concern themselves entirely with my welfare, at the expense of their own.

Note that 'too many thinkers' makes trouble even for one who would deny (P2) and use tropes, not temporal parts, to answer 'too many thoughts'. Even if there is not an extra token thought when I think 'Which am I?', the question remains: Is the person or mass of matter the referent of 'I'? The token-thought trope belongs to both, so one must still ask whether the matter uses it to refer to itself, or to the person, or perhaps ambiguously (cf. Mills 1993; Ehring 1995). Admittedly, there need not be so many candidates, given coincident entities without temporal parts. However, there is still the oddity of a thinking thing that cares not for its own fate, though it can contemplate its future by thinking of itself as 'this portion of matter'. And it is hard to believe that I am constantly accompanied by beings with psychological points of view indiscernible from my own, but otherwise very different from me.

3. DENYING (P1)

3.1 Coincidentalism and Two-Category Theories

There are two radically different, initially plausible ways to deny the first premise. One might deny either that there are two things where I am, or that both are sad if one is. I begin discussion of the rejection of (P1) by considering theories that take the latter approach.

The person who recognizes two things here, the one thinking, the other not, has a choice. She *may* say that each is a physical object composed, in more or less the same sense, of material particles. Then I call her a 'coincidentalist': someone who posits coincident physical objects differing in their characteristics but made, at some level, of all the same parts arranged in the same way; and who rejects the doctrine of temporal parts.[21] But not everyone who recognizes two things where I am, with different properties, is what I call a coincidentalist; some say instead that either the human being or the matter is not *really* a physical object in the full-blooded sense of the word—that it does not have particles as literal parts, but 'contains' or 'includes' them in some other sense. Theories along these lines I will call 'two-category theories', since they imply that the coincident matter and person are really very different, belonging to radically different 'ontological categories'—for example, one but not the other might be said to be really an event or process, or a mathematical function from times to physical objects, or a set of particles. Two-category views are adopted to help make the coincidence of matter and person easier to swallow; the two things have properties that go by the same names but are really quite different. I criticize coincidentalism first.

3.2 Coincidentalism: 'The New Dualism'

On the coincidentalist view, the matter and the person do not share all their intrinsic characteristics. But, at the microphysical level, the two are intrinsically just alike. One might point out that one is a (mere) mass of matter while the other is a person or an organism. But why does the one get to be the one, the other the other, when they are so similar in every observable respect? What I find most puzzling is how things so alike in their *construction* could differ so radically in their *powers* and *potentialities*. The matter constituting a living body can survive being squashed by a steamroller, while the body cannot. The body can survive the gradual replacement of all its present constitutive atoms, while the mass of matter itself surely cannot.

---

[21] Coincidentalists abound. See e.g. Wiggins (1980); Shoemaker (1999); Johnston (1992); Lowe (1996); Doepke (1996); Simons (1987); Baker (2000, 2002, 2003); and Thomson (1997).

What explains these differences in abilities? Nothing other than the fact that the one is an organism, the other a mere mass of matter; but this is a fact one could never discover by examining their construction (cf. Burke 1992). (Note that this objection applies as much to a coincidentalism with shared mental tropes that denies (P1) as to a coincidentalism that denies (P2).)

Furthermore, it is unclear how the one can be thinking and the other not, given their structural similarity. Certainly both the matter in my body and the organism itself are disposed, right now, to produce the same observable behaviour in the same circumstances—to emit the same sounds when my skin is burned, for instance, and generally to cause the same motions of molecules. If the one is in pain while the other is not, it is hard to see how pain could in any sense be 'realized in' microphysical states, since these are shared. On the functionalist account of realization, for example, a physical state realizes pain in a creature because of its causal role with respect to stimuli, behaviour, and other internal states intermediate between stimuli and behaviour. And, right now, my constituting matter and I share internal states poised to produce, in both of us, the same behaviour upon the same stimulus (cf. Olson 1997: 106–8).

One might, however, question the claim that our shared internal states really do play the same causal roles in each of us; the grounds for doubt are similar to those given earlier to show that sufficiently short temporal parts of me can exemplify a physical state that plays the pain role in *me* without its playing the pain role in *them*. The matter now making up my body is not disposed to react in *precisely* the same ways I am to physical stimuli. Chop off my toe, and Zimmerman-the-person is disposed to become smaller, and to remove all of himself from the scene; but the matter constituting me is disposed not to become smaller but to become scattered, and to remove only *part* of itself from the scene.[22] But even though they are not precisely similarly disposed, matter and I are very similarly disposed *over the short term*; and the things the matter is disposed to 'do' and 'say' are very like paradigmatic displays of conscious behaviour. If the matter is not now capable of having states that, in it, play certain psychological roles, this will only be because it tends rather quickly to become too dispersed to qualify as the subject of a bodily action like running or sitting or speaking, despite the fact that *most* of the matter is still in my body, and is doing something *very much like* running or sitting or speaking.

I am willing to grant to the functionalist that the set of dispositions to behaviour that my constituting matter now exemplifies is much different from mine; and that many of my more complex mental states have causal roles that could not be played out in a thing that tended to scatter as quickly as a mere mass of matter does. But a thing need not have precisely *our* psychology to have psychological states; animals can feel pain and pleasure without many of the more complex dispositions we

---

[22] For discussion of this objection, I am grateful to Leonard Katz, Judy Thomson, Ted Sider, and John Hawthorne.

display. And, on the functionalist view of the mind, creatures much like terrestrial animals but who happen always to live very short lives ought also to be capable of psychological states such as pain and pleasure—so long as they react much as terrestrial animals do to similar stimuli, and have functionally similar inner states intermediate between stimulus and behaviour. But the matter constituting my body right now *is just such a creature!* So, coincident with me is another psychological subject—one that may have very different psychological states from mine, one that may be much more like a monkey than a man.

Of course, some materialists about persons will reject functionalism and other views according to which the mental is realized in physical states shared by person and mass of matter. One might, then, deny that the pain is realized in a shared microphysical state, insisting instead that the pain is some further, irreducible property exemplified by the organism but not the constituting matter. Even so, the pain is surely *caused by* microphysical events (located inside my head) that happen to both matter and organism. These events somehow fail to cause pain in the physically indiscernible mass of matter, within which they also occur. But again, how can they fail to do so, since the two are intrinsically exactly alike and located at the same place? There would have to be laws governing causal relations between microphysical events and emergent mental properties, laws that are sensitive to differences in microphysical duplicates—a puzzling result, to say the least.

Michael Burke (1997) has dubbed coincidentalism 'the New Dualism'. I agree with him that it is pretty much on a par with the old dualism.[23]

3.3 Two-Category Theories: Processes and Logical Constructions

Two-category theories, like coincidentalism, accept the existence of both the matter constituting my body, and me, the constituted person. Unlike coincidentalism, they affirm that person and matter belong to radically different ontological categories— categories so different that the sense in which the person is happy or in pain or heavy or cool will be quite different from the sense in which the matter is. Below, I describe a kind of two-category theory according to which the matter is not a physical whole at all, but rather a mere set of particles; the only physical whole with those particles as parts is the person. In this section I explore two-category views that do not take this route—theories that admit that the matter of which I am constituted is more than a mere set or collection of particles.

The problem these two-category views are meant to solve is explaining how there can be two things where there seems only one. The explanation is that one of the two

---

[23] I examine two versions of coincidentalism in more detail in Zimmerman (2003, forthcoming).

is of a less fundamental sort; it is a dependent or derivative thing that automatically shows up when the other thing takes a certain form, or is in certain circumstances; and it inherits its properties in a way that allows one to say that there are not really two instances of a person's mental states. The coincidence is rendered benign and unsurprising by displaying it as an instance of a broader, more familiar coincidence that we routinely regard as unproblematic. The only two-category theories of this sort on offer are ones that take the matter to be a physical object composed of the particles, and the material person (or other constituted entity) to be a categorially different kind of thing that somehow supervenes upon the behaviour of the various portions of matter constituting the person at different times.

What categories of thing are there that might be thought to supervene unproblematically upon the behaviour of various masses of matter? The only ones anyone has thought of that are significantly different from a whole made of parts (and so the only ones yielding a view that does not collapse into coincidentalism) are: (i) a *process* or *event* passing through various parcels of matter, just as a hurricane is a meteorological process passing through various masses of air and water, or a long war is a process involving different groups of people, weapons, and vehicles at different times; and (ii) a logical construction out of masses of matter, such as a mathematical function that takes different masses of matter for its values at different times.

Two-category theories try to explain away the problems associated with distinct but coincident entities by treating the mass of matter and the human being as very different kinds of things—so different that, for any property we should be loath to attribute to *both* of them, only *one* of them could have it in the most fundamental way, the other one either lacking it altogether or possessing it only derivatively.

Although I think process and logical construction theories deserve more attention than they have received, I shall say no more about them here. A few eminent philosophers have articulated theories of these sorts;[24] but, to my knowledge, they are without living defenders.[25] They lack the theoretical elegance of a temporal

---

[24] For process views, see Chisholm (1986: 66–7) and Broad (1925: 34–8). Grice was willing to describe a person as a series of mental events; but it is not clear what the rest of his metaphysics was like, and whether he recognized non-events to which mental events happen; see Grice (1941). Chisholm also offers an eliminative logical construction. The constructed mereologically incontinent entities, his *entia successiva*, are in fact fictions: all apparent quantification over tables, human bodies, and any other thing that can gain or lose parts is paraphrased away in favour of a language in which variables range only over objects characterized by a strict mereological essentialism. Cf. Chisholm (1976, ch. 3 and app. B). The 'Port-Royal Logic' of Arnauld and Nicole is also committed to the eliminative reduction of mereologically incontinent objects in terms of mereologically stable masses of matter. Cf. Arnauld and Nicole (1964, pt. 2, ch. 12). According to Richard E. Grandy, an ostensibly part-changing object 'is to be considered as a set of pairs consisting of bits of matter and times' (Grandy 1975: 224). See also Chandler (1971) and Montague (1979).

[25] Toomas Karmo, in his elegant two-page article 'Disturbances', affirms that living things are processes passing through various tracts of matter, just as storms are processes passing through various

parts metaphysics (a one-category theory, after all); they are open to most of the objections facing theories utilizing temporal parts, since there are ever so many distinct processes and functions involving the matter in my body now but different matter at other times; and they seem to make the matter that constitutes a person more fundamental than the person, so that it is unclear why the person should have *any* empirical properties in a fundamental or non-derivative fashion. On the other hand, process and logical construction theories seem to me to be much less problematic when applied to a ship or plant and its constituting matter; they only really begin to chafe when more complicated constituted creatures arrive upon the scene—particularly creatures with mental states among their local, empirical properties. The objections to two-category theories mainly fall, then, under the heading of what I shall call (in the final section) 'personal objections'.

3.4 No Such Things as Masses of Matter

Coincidentalism and the two-category views accept the part of (P1) that says there are two things where I am, but deny the part that says they are psychologically indiscernible. The other way to deny (P1) is to say that there is only *one* thing here; and since I am exploring sensible materialisms, that thing must be, not a mere mass of matter, but rather a human organism (or other likely candidate) that feels sad, say. There is simply no such thing as a mass of matter distinct from myself but present in the same location, threatening to feel sad if I do. This approach to problems of coincidence has been gaining steam of late. Since van Inwagen's influential *Material Beings* (1990), Michael Burke has published an impressive and original series of papers defending a rather different no-coincidents view (Burke 1992, 1994*a*,*b*, 1997); and, more recently, several younger metaphysicians—including Eric Olson (1997), Trenton Merricks (2001), and Michael Rea (1998, 2000)—have emerged as impressive defenders of views inspired by van Inwagen and Burke. But, given the obvious fact that there *is* matter in the universe, in this room, in my body, how can they deny that there is such a thing as the matter constituting my body now, something that was once scattered, and will soon be again?

At least this much seems undeniable: There are 'fundamental' (so far as we can tell now) particles (which may or may not persist 'identically' through time). To be made of some of this world's matter is, if these particles are ultimate, to be made of some batch of such particles; if they are not ultimate, but are in turn made of smaller, *truly* fundamental particles, then to be made of our kind of matter is to be made of a batch of these smaller things; and if what we now think of as 'fundamental particles' are made instead of some infinitely divisible stuff that comes pre-packaged

masses of gas and water (Karmo 1977). Although Karmo is alive and well, he has pursued a career outside philosophy.

as extremely tiny solids, then to be made of some earthly matter is to be made of some portion of *that* stuff. Can one deny the existence of a thing called 'the matter now constituting my body', without denying such truisms as these?

3.5 Van Inwagen's Theory, and a Modified Version

Peter van Inwagen offers one strategy for doing so. He points out that an expression can refer to some *things* without referring to some *thing*. On his view, 'the matter making up my body' does not refer to any *single thing*, not even a single *set* of things; it is, rather, a plural term referring to some particles, on the order of plural referring expressions like 'Larry, Moe, and Curly' or 'the Three Stooges' (Boolos 1998). Consequently, when ostensibly singular descriptions of the form 'the matter now constituting my body', 'the matter within a radius of 3 miles from the earth's centre of gravity', etc. succeed in picking out some matter, the way they do this is by referring to a number of fundamental particles but not by referring to a further thing, the set of those particles (van Inwagen 1990). This enables van Inwagen to deny that there is such a thing as the matter constituting this or that object, while respecting the truisms above. To say that there is matter in the universe, in my body, etc. is to say that there are particles in the universe, in my body, etc.

The appeal of van Inwagen's approach should be obvious to those who share his antipathy to coincidentalism—those who think that, at any one time, at most one object could be made out of a single collection of fundamental particles like those now in my body. Why not suppose that the one object, in the case of these particles, is my body—an organism which, according to sensible materialism, is identical to me? Granted, in some sense there is something else, namely the matter now constituting me. But why not simply say that 'the matter constituting my body now' refers collectively to some fundamental particles—all the particles in my body now? Why distinguish between these and the matter now constituting my body; why suppose that talk about matter is talk about a physical *object*?

Van Inwagen, then, offers us a way to deny (P1) *not* by denying that the mass of matter and the person are psychologically alike, but by denying that there are two things. Van Inwagen remains agnostic about whether, for every successful use of a term like 'the matter in my body' to refer collectively to some particles, there is also such a thing as the set of those particles. However, the implications of his theory are more easily explained on the assumption that there *are* such sets, and that 'the matter in my body' is as singular a term as its form suggests, referring to the set containing all and only the fundamental particles that are parts of my body. This modification of van Inwagen's view turns it into a two-category theory, one according to which there is such a thing as the matter now composing my body, a thing that belongs to a category of entity quite unlike the one to which persons belong: The matter in my body and the living body itself both 'contain' the same particles, but the former is a *set* with the particles as *members*, while the latter is a *physical object* with the particles (and other wholes made of those particles) as its *parts*. Those who find set theory unproblematic are not likely to have any complaints about the modification, and it makes no difference for my purposes. Wherever I ask 'Which set of things does "the matter constituting my body" refer to?', one might just as well ask 'Which *things* does "the matter constituting my body" refer to?' And the problems I find for answers to the former will be problems for answers to the latter.

A van Inwagen-inspired view handily dispatches all threatened doubling up of properties. The sense in which a plurality or a set can be said to have mass, shape, spatial location, electrical charge, and so on must be a highly derivative one.[26] Strictly speaking, sets are the wrong sorts of things to have weight, or mass, or shape, in the most fundamental way.[27] And the idea that a mere set could exemplify distinctively personal properties such as mentality sounds a bit ridiculous.[28]

3.6 Persons Made of Atomless Gunk

The problem with this rather appealing strategy is that its smooth application to all possible varieties of constituted persons depends upon a dubious assumption: that, necessarily, all constituted persons are ultimately composed of batches of simple atoms—i.e. partless particles, not divisible into any further particles or portions of stuff. To deny this assumption is to admit the possibility of what David Lewis has dubbed 'atomless gunk', matter of the sort postulated by Aristotle, Descartes, and perhaps even Newton.[29] Some philosophers have argued that, if three-dimensionally extended, solid objects are possible *at all*, then there must be some infinitely divisible,

---

[26] A set has a mass of 200 kg. derivatively—entirely in virtue of the fact that its members each have a mass and their individual masses add up to 200 kg. The idea should not seem puzzling or unfamiliar; consider the parts of my car. A certain set of parts came off widely separated assembly lines; those parts weighed 2 tons, altogether, even before they were assembled; and they now *still* weigh 2 tons while being coincident with a car that *also* weighs 2 tons. The parts do not constitute two objects, each weighing 2 tons; the set of parts only weighs 2 tons in virtue of having members that have individual weights that add up to this amount (members that do not overlap). For a more rigorous attempt to spell out a sense in which a set of objects can have a mass of *n* kg., see Zimmerman (1995: 59–60 n. 19).

[27] One might attempt to express the asymmetry by saying that, if no non-set had mass, no set would either; but a physical particle could have a mass even if there were no sets. Since set theory is, plausibly, necessarily true (if true at all), the latter claim is intended as a 'counter-possible'—so this way of putting things requires that counterfactuals with impossible antecedents are not all trivially true.

[28] Compare van Inwagen's insistence that, for psychological states, there must be a single subject (van Inwagen 1990: 194–210). The only philosopher I know to affirm, on the contrary, that a psychological state may be a relation exemplified by a plurality is Cian Dorr (see Dorr 2002; see also Dorr and Rosen 2002).

[29] Newton may have held that matter is infinitely divisible stuff that takes the form of extremely tiny extended spheres. This was Boscovich's interpretation, at any rate: Newtonian atoms are made of cohesive parts within parts within parts . . . and, though not divisible by any ordinary physical process,

atomless matter.[30] If they are right, denying the possibility of atomless matter would be tantamount to denying the very possibility of three-dimensional solids.

If atomless kinds of stuff are possible, as they seem to me to be, then there would seem to be no impossibility in there being living creatures made of atomless gunk—or at least in there being gunky things that are 'lifelike' in their macrophysical structure and behaviour. Surely such creatures would be constituted by different masses of matter at different times, just as we are. Call persons whose bodies are superficially like ours, but made of persisting portions of atomless gunk, 'mereologically incontinent humanoids'. (Call them 'humanoids' and not 'human beings', so as not to rule out the possibility that it is essential to humans that we be made of matter consisting of ultimate, indivisible particles.) If there were such creatures, there would still be a fact of the matter concerning whether one is made of the same matter as another, whether one has continued to be constituted by the same matter throughout a given period, and so on.

Given the possibility of atomless gunk, it is but a short step to recognition of the possibility of atomless gunk that is *infinitely malleable* in the following sense: for any size bit of it you like, a mereologically incontinent humanoid could be composed of a portion that size. The existence of organisms made of *our* sort of matter supervenes, presumably, upon the powers of and spatial relations among things like protons, neutrons, and electrons. Pretend, for the moment, that these are the only particles relevant to the existence of organisms. Now suppose that there are bits of gunky stuff that come in three shapes: e.g. pyramids, cubes, and spheres. And suppose that their behaviour relative to one another mirrors perfectly that of our protons, neutrons, and electrons—i.e. they have similar powers of attraction and repulsion, relative to one another, as measured from the geometrical centre of each particle. Would not such particles admit arrangements upon which the existence of organisms would supervene?[31] Once this is granted, the possibility of creatures of arbitrary size follows almost immediately—so long as the stuff is infinitely divisible, and the relative powers are proportionate to size. Where does the impossibility creep into this scenario, if not at the first step: the positing of infinitely divisible gunk?

But admitting such stuff lands a van Inwagen-style theory in severe difficulties.[32] A mereologically incontinent humanoid made of infinitely malleable gunk will

they are nonetheless divisible in principle—if only by a miracle. So conceived, a certain portion of Newtonian matter would be, not a set of atoms, but something that could survive the (miraculous) division of an atom.

[30] I argue for this conclusion in Zimmerman (1996c). My argument there is criticized in Sider (2000) and Mason (2000). Although I am not convinced by their objections, I am less impressed with my original argument than I once was. For discussion of others who have argued for this conclusion, see Zimmerman (1996a).

[31] Again, if one thinks, for some reason, that organisms are a natural kind that could not exist in the absence of our sort of matter, then call these 'organism-like creatures'.

[32] This difficulty is raised in Zimmerman (1995). For a similar criticism, see Sider (1993).

have parts that are not organisms.[33] The inorganic parts must themselves have parts—indeed, infinitely many, since there are no atoms. If the van Inwagen strategy is to be applied here, 'the matter constituting the humanoid now' must refer to a set of these inorganic parts. But which one? Given infinite malleability of the stuff, it does not matter how small the parts are that one picks to be in the set; there will still be trouble in supposing that 'the matter of which the humanoid's body is constituted at time t' refers to some set of parts.

Let S be any candidate set of parts to serve as 'the matter constituting the humanoid at t'. Every member of S is further decomposable into parts that could be rearranged so as to constitute or become a smaller mereologically incontinent living thing, with no gain or loss of matter. Suppose some member x does so at t^*. If the smaller living thing remains a part of the humanoid (e.g. if x comes to constitute a new cell within its body), then the humanoid may be constituted by the same matter at t^* despite the transformation of x. But then either x, the original inorganic part, would continue to exist after the change, coinciding with a new thing at t^*, an organism; or x would go out of existence. The former is not an option in this context, since we are exploring ways of rejecting (P2) by denying that an organism coincides with any other physical whole. So x would have to go out of existence by t^*. But then the original set S would no longer exist at t^* either, having lost a member—this despite the fact that the humanoid could still be constituted by the same matter at t^*. And if it is possible that the humanoid be constituted of the same matter at t and t^*, although S does not exist at both times, then the matter constituting the humanoid at t cannot simply be identified with S.

3.7 A More Complex Analysis of 'Consisting of the Same Matter'

Although *identifying* the matter with a certain set of parts does not work, there remains a promising strategy for analysing 'x is constituted at t by the same matter that constitutes y at t^*' in terms of shared sets of parts. The trick is to make use of sets of parts that *as a matter of fact* do not gain or lose any proper parts, while denying that any particular set of parts is the referent of a term like 'the matter constituting x at t'. One could be sure that an object x and an object y are made of the very same mass of matter if one knew that there were *some* set of parts S such that: (i) S constitutes both x and y, without remainder; and (ii) the members of S

[33] I assume the creature is not infinitely complex, with every part composed of further living creatures inside of living creatures, ad infinitum. Perhaps such things are possible, perhaps not; but, in any case, surely one could make a humanoid out of some kinds of atomless gunk without having to create infinitely many living creatures to serve as parts.

do not gain or lose any parts at all. The idea can be made more precise by appeal to the notion of a 'complete decomposition':

(D1) S is a complete decomposition of x at $t = _{df}$ At t, every member of S is a part of x, no members of S have any parts in common, and every part of x not in S has a part in common with some member of S.

(D2)   The matter constituting x at t is the same as the matter constituting y at $t^* = _{df}$ There is a set S such that: (i) S is a complete decomposition of x at t; (ii) S is a complete decomposition of y at t^*; and (iii) if $t \neq t^*$, then no member of S has gained or lost any parts during the period between t and t^*.

Restricting attention to objects made of matter that breaks down into partless atoms, (D2) implies that x is constituted by the same matter at t as constitutes y at t^* if and only if they share the same complete decomposition into atoms. So, absent worries about atomless gunk, there would be no problem with the original, van Inwagen-inspired theory about the referents of expressions like 'the matter that . . .'. If everything were, of necessity, constituted without remainder by partless particles, then the matter constituting something could be identified with a set of particles, and sameness of matter could be analysed in terms of identity of constituting sets. But atomism is not true of necessity (or so I believe); and the more complex analysis is necessary.

I also assume that nothing weaker than (D2) will suffice to ensure sameness of matter—i.e. that being constituted by the same matter requires that there be some set of parts that make up the whole of x and of y, and that have not been gaining and losing bits in between times.[34] So the difficulties I derive from the proposed analysis are, by my lights, unavoidable consequences of the possibility of atomless gunk.

3.8 Atomless Gunk Leads to Michael Burke's Theory

The matter constituting some object can outlast the object; more generally, it can continue to exist despite its not constituting anything at all, distinct from itself. This truism can be captured straightforwardly on the van Inwagen-inspired theory that identifies the matter with a single set of atoms: The set of particles constituting an object continues to exist while not constituting the object or any object at all. (D2) analyses 'is constituted by the same matter as' without identifying 'the matter' with anything in particular; so how is one to make use of this analysis and also make sense of the truism that the matter can exist without constituting anything? The answer is obvious: The matter continues to exist if there remains a set of parts of the

---

[34] In other words, I shall not take seriously the idea that 'constituted by the same matter as' is a primitive notion, implying nothing about the sharing of parts at sufficiently simple levels.

sort that, if they were to constitute an object, it would be an object constituted by the same matter as the original object, in the sense of (D2). It follows that, for any mereologically incontinent humanoid x constituted at t by some atomless matter, there must be a set S such that (a) S is a complete decomposition of x; and (b) as long as the matter now constituting x exists, the members of S continue to exist without change of parts.

But, given infinite malleability, each of the members could have come to constitute an organism. Presumably, an organism cannot exist before the beginning of its own organic life. So either the member of S would have come to coincide with a new object; or it would have been 'crowded out of existence', replaced by the organism when its parts were rearranged so as to form a living thing.[35] Neither option is a happy one. Van Inwagen dislikes coincidentalism for reasons like those I have given, and in any case the goal here is to discover a way to deny (P1) by denying that the matter is a physical whole. But supposing that a mere hunk of matter should go out of existence owing to rearrangement of parts is also a bit troubling.

A living thing can be destroyed by rearranging its parts so that it can no longer keep itself alive (e.g. damaging an animal's heart); an artefact can be destroyed by rearranging its parts so that it is no longer functional, and cannot be rebuilt (e.g. crushing an automobile into a cube of scrap metal). That one can destroy a mere hunk of matter simply by rearranging its parts seems less obvious.[36] But what is particularly odious about accepting this result is that a common way for some stuff to come to fully constitute an entity is for it to start out as a large part of an organism that shrinks; in which case, by destroying something that is merely attached to the mass of matter one causes it to cease to be. It seems especially hard to believe that the sorts of things in question here should go out of existence owing to extrinsic changes. The parts in S are not living things, nor are they artefacts; they are mere hunks of matter, devoid of any essential structure, and thus (it would seem) capable of surviving all sorts of rearrangements and changes in surroundings.

Van Inwagen himself rejects the possibility of things that cease to be owing to extrinsic change (van Inwagen 1990: 12–13). So he must either deny the possibility of infinitely malleable gunk, or hazard the following conjecture: that no bit of atomless inorganic matter could possibly become a whole organism just by having something

---

[35] I here ignore temporary identity or relative identity solutions to problems of constitution. The former is the view that the hunk of inorganic matter is temporarily identical with the organism after having been numerically distinct from it; the latter is the rejection of any such relation as numerical distinctness coupled with the thesis that the inorganic thing is the-same-matter-as but not the-same-organism-as the living thing. For defence of such 'devious' accounts of identity, see Gallois (1998) and Geach (1997). For criticism, see Sider (2001c) and John Hawthorne, Ch. 4 in this volume.

[36] Michael Burke finds this conclusion much less implausible than do I. See Burke (1994a: 138–9).

detached from itself. Then he could still hope to maintain that no *merely* extrinsic change (no mere 'Cambridge change') would ever result in a substantial change.[37]

But what restriction upon inorganic hunks of matter will prevent this seeming possibility from being realized? Van Inwagen might insist that a mere hunk of matter must *fill a connected region*; so that, as soon as a portion of inorganic matter is divided up into scattered bits, it ceases to be. A humanoid made of atomless gunk, if it is remotely like us in construction, has huge numbers of disconnected parts, and so has no part that is both a spatially connected mass of matter and anywhere nearly as big as itself. But if the only restriction on composition for inorganic hunks of matter is that the parts fill a connected region, then the above conjecture would require the impossibility of 'blobs', creatures that can survive the gain and loss of parts and can (at any time) be wholly constituted by a quantity of stuff that fills a connected region. Such blobs are not as far-out as one might at first think. If bodily fluids were genuinely continuous, filling up most of the space inside a creature's body (as was once believed to be the case), 'we' would have been blobs in this sense. Do we really want to offer a radically different ontological story about the persistence of such creatures? Or can we say with confidence that they are metaphysically impossible? Perhaps there is some more plausible restriction upon composition that will prevent mere hunks of stuff from ceasing to exist simply by virtue of coming to constitute the whole of a thing, after a part is detached. But it is not at all obvious what the restriction could be.

One might always reject the very possibility of infinitely malleable gunk, insisting that any type of substance that could constitute a living thing *must* consist, ultimately, of partless simples.[38] The denial of the possibility of infinitely divisible, atomless matter might seem rather far from anything we care about. Many philosophers will, nevertheless, be reluctant to solve a philosophical puzzle in this way. It implies that the physics of Aristotle, Descartes, and (on one reading) Newton are not merely empirically falsified but proven, by a priori philosophical argument from the metaphysician's armchair, to be *impossible*.

---

[37] This is how Arda Denkel puts the objection (see Denkel 1995). Joshua Hoffman and Gary Rosenkrantz have proposed a view that allows for both organisms and lumps of matter and rejects coincident entities. On their view, a lump has to be relatively rigid, so that the whole can be moved by pushing and pulling parts of it, though it need not be strictly connected, as on the view I am developing in the text to offer van Inwagen. They think that being a lump and being a living thing are incompatible, since living things have to have lots of loose parts (lots of parts that are quantities of various liquids, for one thing)—a strategy similar to the one suggested here. See Hoffmann and Rosenkrantz (1996); see also my review of their book (Zimmerman 1999b). Chisholm once held that the only wholes there are fill connected regions; see Chisholm (1976, app. B).

[38] See also Dorr and Rosen (2002), where the necessity of atomism is alleged to be an unproblematic consequence of the metaphysical thesis that only simples exist.

3.9 Michael Burke and the Case of
the Disappearing Matter

Atomless gunk was driving van Inwagen towards accepting objects that cease to
be owing to extrinsic changes. Michael Burke has developed a metaphysics that
embraces this result. Like van Inwagen, he denies (P1) by denying that 'the matter that now constitutes my body' refers to anything like a mere hunk of stuff—a
physical object that was widely scattered and shall be again. But what about other
cases, such as 'the matter that is located within 3 miles of the earth's centre of
gravity'? Michael Rea, who defends a view much like Burke's, is willing to allow
that expressions like 'the matter that . . .' fail to refer to mere masses of matter *only*
when there is danger of coincidence with something that is *not* a mere mass of
matter.[39] On this view, the matter within 3 miles of the earth's centre is a physical object exactly filling a spherical region of 3 miles radius at the earth's core—a
mere aggregate of material particles that can become scattered, once was scattered,
and cannot persist through the gain or loss of constituent bits of matter. Burke
himself is willing to grant, as a fallback position, that 'the matter within 3 miles of
the earth's centre', and other such expressions, refer to mere aggregates when the
matter in question constitutes nothing else. Officially, he would like mass terms
of this sort to be plural terms (as on van Inwagen's account); but he admits that
this cannot be a general solution to problems of coincidence, owing to atomless
stuff kinds; so he suggests that, although the atomless stuff constituting a thing
may not be a plurality, 'perhaps it is not *an* (one) object either' (Burke 1996: 14;
see also Burke 1994*a,b*). I have argued that he has no choice but to use his fallback position: expressions like 'the matter within 3 miles of the earth's centre'
typically refer to a mere aggregate that cannot survive gain or loss of any bits of
matter; they only fail to do so when admitting this would lead to coincident objects
(Zimmerman 1997).

  The matter that, though now scattered, will constitute my body in ten years' time
is a thing that is not in danger (now) of coinciding with a living thing; so there is
no block to 'the matter that will constitute my body in ten years' time' referring,
now, to a single thing—a mere mass of matter. But when ten years roll around,
and I am composed of the same matter as this now scattered mass of matter, how
can there be just one thing where I am? There would seem to be just two options.
(1) There are not two things there because the living body *is* the mass of matter, and
was scattered a short time ago and shall become scattered again—but that is not
a *sensible* materialism. (2) The once scattered matter that comes together to form
my living body literally *ceases to be* when, as we would normally say, 'it' comes to
constitute my body—and this is the alternative Burke accepts (when forced to accept

---

[39] See Rea (1998, 2000).

masses of matter) (Burke 1996: 15–16; Zimmerman 1997). When a mass of matter is about to take on the shape of a human being, it suddenly ceases to be, replaced by an organism.

Burke's picture has its problems. If the matter now constituting my body is not the same as the matter that ceased to be as it came to constitute me, what is it and where did it come from? Either there is really no such thing as the matter now constituting me; or else 'the matter now constituting my body' is just another name for my body, this human organism that can survive the gain and loss of parts.[40] On either alternative, to make something out of some matter is really to cause the matter to be replaced by something that is *not* constituted by *it*, since it is no more. On the face of it, neither alternative does justice to the obvious facts: that there is some matter constituting my body now and that this very matter does not have a human form at every time it exists.[41]

If Burke is to make sense of his position, it is imperative that he recover *some* sense in which the matter that just went out of existence because it came to constitute me can be said to be the same as the totality of the matter making up my body— some extended relation of 'same matter as' that is compatible with non-identity and that does not hold between that old matter and anything smaller or larger than the totality of my body now. (D2) can be used to provide Burke with a sense in which, though a mass of matter ceases to exist when it comes to constitute something, the new thing 'consists of the same matter as' the original mass of matter. But Burke's metaphysics still suffers from commitment to the thesis that, by rearranging the parts of a mere hunk of matter, or worse yet by simply detaching something from it and leaving it intrinsically unchanged, one can cause it to cease to exist.

4. Conclusion: An Argument for Dualism?

4.1 Exhausting the Ontological Options

The survey of responses to my revised version of Chisholm's *entia successiva* argument has elicited a finite number of possible views about the relation between objects that can change parts (i.e. are 'mereologically incontinent') and the various portions of matter (or, more generally, stuff, e.g. the ectoplasm of ghosts or merely

---

[40] This may be Burke's official view. See Burke (1996) and Zimmerman (1997).

[41] Perhaps, owing to the ephemerality of particles obeying quantum statistics, this matter only exists for an instant; but then, once again, it is not at all like the body it constitutes.

possible sorts of matter obeying different physical laws) that constitute them at different times. But is there reason to think that, for each way of denying the premises, the range of plausible views about the relation has been exhaustively surveyed, albeit at a very high level of generality? Here is an argument for the affirmative—for the conclusion that these are all of the even halfway plausible metaphysical theories about the constitution of material people.

How many ways are there to respond to the revised *entia successiva* argument? One may deny (P1) or (P2). To deny (P2) with any plausibility, the number of pains, pleasures, etc. must be kept down despite the admitted multiplicity of subjects that feel pain, pleasure, etc. Either there is a different instance of pain, pleasure, etc. for each subject, or there can be a single instance shared by many. The latter course offers individual 'tropes' of pain, pleasure, etc. that can be shared among coincident entities; adopting this strategy while eschewing temporal parts was considered and rejected. Those who take the former course, admitting instances for each subject, must reconcile the multiplicity of subjects, each feeling pain or pleasure, with the fact that, *really*, there is only one pain or pleasure. Temporal parts metaphysicians effect the reconciliation by identifying a primary subject of pain or pleasure (a temporal part that lasts just so long as the pain or pleasure in question), and ascribing feelings to the other subjects in virtue of their relations to it. But any view positing one primary subject and more than one secondary subject will face the sorts of objections I lodged against the temporal parts account. The possibility of doing without tropes, denying temporal parts, and simply positing more than one psychologically indiscernible subject was not considered; but such a view would inherit the defects of coincident objects metaphysics and temporal parts metaphysics, with none of the advantages. Since the doctrine of temporal parts entails the denial of (P2) (or so I argued), rejecting all attempts to deny (P2) means leaving temporal parts behind. There remain, then, only the various ways of rejecting (P1) without recourse to temporal parts.

Broadly speaking, there are only two ways out of (P1): denying that the matter and the organism (or other likely candidate) are two in number; or denying that they are psychologically similar. One who adopts the first strategy can hardly deny that there is a certain portion of the world's matter that has come to constitute my body and will soon cease to do so. One might claim that the 'portion' is not a real thing, and that 'the matter that just came to constitute my body' is a plural term for a bunch of particles. This is van Inwagen's official position; but it closely resembles the view that 'the matter that just came to constitute my body' is a singular term referring to the *set* of particles now 'in' my body—and the criticisms I lodged against that view apply to van Inwagen's official view as well. There is only one *other* way, so far as I can see, to affirm the existence of the organism while denying the existence of the portion of the world's matter which (obviously! in some sense!) constitutes it: Burke's strategy, which is to admit that there *was* such a thing, though it has been crowded out, for the time being, by the body it came to constitute. And so, to reject the first premiss by denying that there are two things, one must admit either: (i) that the matter, though not *one* thing, is many things; or (ii) that, though it does not exist, it *did* and is divisible into portions that continue to exist and jointly compose the body. And either approach was shown to lead to the problematic conclusion that masses of matter can go out of existence owing to merely extrinsic changes.

The other way to reject (P1)—accepting two things, but denying that they are psychologically similar—admits a richer variety of approaches, and it is harder to be sure that all have been catalogued. But here is why I suspect that the alternatives have been exhausted in this case as well.

A metaphysics of the material world will posit some paradigmatic, persisting macrophysical objects: space-occupying wholes persisting through time and made out of matter, whatever matter turns out to be like.[42] These paradigmatic physical objects should at least possess the *potential* to persist; with the doctrine of temporal parts out of the picture,[43] there should be no temptation to identify them with any instantaneous items. The paradigms, and anything else that is a complex persisting whole composed of physical parts, but not persisting by means of temporal parts, can rightly be said to belong to a common ontological category—call them 'enduring objects'.[44]

Some anti-temporal parts metaphysicians regard *organisms* as enduring objects. Some (or at least one—this one!) so regard *the matter* constituting an organism— together with the other portions of matter I have been calling 'masses of matter'.[45] And some metaphysicians regard *both* organisms *and* masses of matter as enduring objects. These are the coincidentalists. The alternative to coincidentalism is to regard either just the organism (or other likely candidate) or just the matter as belonging to the ontological category of enduring object. Since the only views remaining to be considered under the denial of (P1) admit the existence of both matter and organism, in either case something must be done about the less paradigmatic of the two persisting physical things—i.e. the one that is not an enduring object. How is it related to the object with which it shares its spatial location? What other ontological categories are there into which it might fall, besides *enduring object*?

[42] For every obvious truth, there is a philosopher who denies it; for the denial of the existence of composite objects of any sort, see Dorr (2002).

[43] Recall that the doctrine of temporal parts may be ignored when considering ways to reject (P1). I also neglect views according to which physical objects are not, strictly, *space-occupying* because they are to be identified with regions of space-time; such views are, for all intents and purposes, variations on the doctrine of temporal parts.

[44] There is no need to deny that this category may be further divisible along, broadly speaking, ontological lines—for instance, on the basis of the fact that some can gain or lose parts, and others cannot.

[45] As noted earlier, portions of matter might well be ephemeral, hardly persisting at all, because of contingent physical facts about the identity over time of particles; but, so long as the doctrine of temporal parts is in abeyance, masses of matter still belong in the same category as enduring objects, since masses of matter consisting of truly persisting bits would be enduring objects.

The alternatives I considered were these three: (i) sets of enduring objects; (ii) functions from enduring objects to times, or some other sort of 'logical construction' out of enduring objects; and (iii) physical events or processes happening to the enduring objects—'modes' of them, or 'tropes' inhering in them.

Although I have no proof that these are the only feasible candidates for being one or the other of the two physical things in question, I know of no other proposals for an alternative ontological category into which they might fit. One could always *posit* a further category; but, barring a conceptual revolution enabling us to see a category of physical entity to which our predecessors have been blind, to posit such a category would be to solve the problems of material persons by retreat into mystery.

These, then, are my reasons for thinking the metaphysical alternatives have been exhausted; that the *entia successiva* argument has driven out into the open the full range of ontological options for material people. This conclusion constitutes premiss 1 of the following argument—an expansion of the *entia successiva* argument. Of the remaining premisses, 3, 5, and 10 were ones I defended (with varying degrees of conviction) in the course of the chapter. And 7 strikes me as eminently plausible: it is the thesis that the metaphysics of humanoid–matter relations when the matter is gunky should not be radically different from the actual metaphysics of human–matter relations.

(1) Necessarily, if a mereologically incontinent object x is constituted by some matter y, then either:

    (a) x is a sum of temporal parts that shares temporal parts with many different masses of matter, including y;

    (b) x and y are both enduring complex physical objects (i.e. neither x nor y is a logical construction, process, set, or sum of temporal parts); and at some level of decomposition, x and y share all parts in common (that is, coincidentalism is true);

    (c) y is a set of parts, and the set is a complete decomposition of x;

    (d) x is a logical construction (e.g. a function from times to many masses of matter, with y as its present value);

    (e) x is a mode or process or disturbance passing through many different masses of matter, one that is now 'happening to' y; or

    (f) for x to be constituted by y is for y to cease to exist just as it is about to coincide with x.

(2) Necessarily, if x is a mereologically incontinent object similar to one of the 'likely candidates' (x is a 'humanoid') and x is constituted by a mass of atomless gunk y, then either: (a), (b), (c), (d), (e), or (f). (Instance of 1)

(3) It is not possible that there be a mereologically incontinent humanoid x that is constituted by a mass of atomless gunk y and either: (b), (c), or (f).

(4) So, necessarily, if a mereologically incontinent humanoid x is constituted by a mass of atomless gunk y, then either: (a) or (d) or (e). (2 & 3)

(5) It is possible that there be a mereologically incontinent humanoid constituted by a mass of atomless gunk.

(6) So it is possible that there be a mereologically incontinent humanoid x and a mass of atomless gunk y such that either: (a) or (d) or (e). (4 & 5)

(7) If it is possible that there be a mereologically incontinent humanoid x and a mass of atomless gunk y such that either: (a) or (d) or (e); then, necessarily, if x is instead one of the likely candidates, and y is the mass of matter constituting x, then either: (a) or (d) or (e).

(8) So, necessarily, if x is a mereologically incontinent likely candidate, and y is the mass of matter constituting x, then either: (a) or (d) or (e). (6 & 7)

(9) So, necessarily, if I am a mereologically incontinent likely candidate constituted by a mass of matter, then either:

   (a) I am a sum of temporal parts that shares temporal parts with many different masses of matter;

   (d) I am a logical construction, such as a function from times to masses of matter; or

   (e) I am a process passing through many different masses of matter. (Instance of 8)

(10) But I am not a logical construction or a process or a sum of temporal parts! (Stamp foot or pound fist)

So, I am not a mereologically incontinent likely candidate constituted by a mass of matter. (9 & 10)

I have divided the rejection of the various possibilities (a)–(f) into two stages (premisses 3 and 10) for a reason. The arguments I gave for rejecting (b), (c), and (f) were, in general, purely metaphysical in nature. These three alternatives were rejected because they were incompatible with various metaphysical theses. The arguments did not have anything much to do with preserving our self-conception; they were based instead upon modal claims concerning impersonal matters—the possibility of intrinsically identical objects with different persistence conditions, or the possibility of infinitely malleable atomless gunk, or the possibility of a hunk of matter's ceasing to be simply owing to rearrangement of its parts or changes in its surroundings. I believe premiss 3, if I do, because I trust my metaphysical instincts, my modal intuitions; so premiss 3 represents 'metaphysical objections' to sensible materialism. The reasons I gave for rejecting (a), (d), and (e), on the other hand, had more to do with preserving aspects of my self-conception: 'This time, it's personal!' I found it very hard to believe that I could be borrowing my mental states from other things that also had them, or that I could be psychologically just like a non-person who accompanies me. Premiss 10 represents the 'personal objections' to sensible materialism.

Perhaps my belief in premiss 10 is born of hubris. Why think I am so special, and not just one of many psychologically identical beings? On the other hand, perhaps my modal intuitions have been badly misfiring, and premiss 3 is false. In other words, perhaps atomless gunk, at least infinitely malleable gunk, is impossible after all; or perhaps there *can* be coincident objects which, though microphysically indiscernible, are nonetheless radically unlike one another; or perhaps there are portions of matter that can survive all sorts of radical rearrangements of parts, but sometimes go out of existence merely because of changes in their environment.

In any case, each premiss of the expanded *entia successiva* argument is, to one degree or another, defensible. To reject any would involve saying some hard things about persons or matter; or making some unintuitive, a priori claims about the nature of the physical world. Given the complexity of the trade-offs among these alternatives, debates about the metaphysics of material people are not likely to die down anytime soon.

REFERENCES

Armstrong, David M. (1997). *A World of States of Affairs*. Cambridge: Cambridge University Press.

Arnauld, Antoine, and Pierre Nicole (1964). *The Art of Thinking*, trans. James Dickoff and Patricia James. Indianapolis: Bobbs-Merrill.

Baker, Lynne Rudder (2000). *Persons and Bodies*. Cambridge: Cambridge University Press.

—— (2002). 'Replies'. *Philosophy and Phenomenological Research*, 64: 623–35.

—— (2003). 'On Making Things Up: Constitution and its Critics'. *Philosophical Topics*, 31.

Block, Ned (1996). 'Functionalism (2)', in Guttenplan (1996: 323–32).

Boolos, George (1998). 'To be is to be a Value of a Variable (Or to be Some Values of Some Variables)', in Boolos, *Logic, Logic, and Logic*. Cambridge, Mass.: Harvard University Press.

Broad, C. D. (1925). *Mind and its Place in Nature*. London: Routledge & Kegan Paul.

Burke, Michael B. (1992). 'Copper Statues and Pieces of Copper: A Challenge to the Standard Account'. *Analysis*, 52: 12–17.

—— (1994a). 'Dion and Theon: An Essentialist Solution to an Ancient Puzzle'. *Journal of Philosophy*, 91: 129–39.

—— (1994b). 'Preserving the Principle of One Object to a Place: A Novel Account of the Relations among Object, Sorts, Sortals, and Persistence Conditions'. *Philosophy and Phenomenological Research*, 54: 591–624.

—— (1996). 'Coinciding Objects: Reply to Lowe and Denkel'. *Analysis*, 57: 11–18.

—— (1997). 'Persons and Bodies: How to Avoid the New Dualism'. *American Philosophical Quarterly*, 34: 457–67.

Chalmers, David J. (1996). *The Conscious Mind: In Search of a Fundamental Theory*. New York: Oxford University Press.

Chandler, Hugh (1971). 'Constitutivity and Identity'. *Noûs*, 5: 313–19. Repr. in Rea (1997).

Chisholm, Roderick M. (1969). 'The Loose and Popular and the Strict and Philosophical Senses of Identity' and 'Reply', in Norman S. Care and Robert H. Grimm (eds.), *Perception and Personal Identity*. Cleveland: Case Western Reserve Press, 82–139.

—— (1970). 'Identity through Time', in Howard E. Kiefer and Milton K. Munitz (eds.), *Language, Belief, and Metaphysics*. Albany: State University of New York Press, 163–82.

—— (1976). *Person and Object*. LaSalle, Ill.: Open Court.

—— (1979). 'Is there a Mind–Body Problem?' *Philosophical Exchange*, 2: 25–34.

—— (1986). 'Self-Profile', in Radu J. Bogdan (ed.), *Roderick M. Chisholm*. Dordrecht: Reidel, 66–7.

—— (1998). 'Which Physical Thing am I? An Excerpt from "Is there a Mind–Body Problem?"', in Zimmerman and van Inwagen (1998: 291–6).

Denkel, Arda (1995). 'Theon's Tale: Does a Cambridge Change Result in a Substantial Change?' *Analysis*, 55: 166–70.

Descartes, René (1984). *Meditations on First Philosophy*, in Descartes, *The Philosophical Writings of Descartes*, vol. ii, trans. John Cottingham, Robert Stoothoff, and Dugald Murdoch. Cambridge: Cambridge University Press.

Doepke, Frederick C. (1996). *The Kinds of Things*. Chicago: Open Court.

Dorr, Cian Seán (2002). 'The Simplicity of Everything'. Ph.D. diss., Princeton University.

—— and Gideon Rosen (2002). 'Composition as a Fiction', in Richard Gale (ed.), *Blackwell Companion to Metaphysics*. Oxford: Basil Blackwell.

Ehring, Douglas (1995). 'Personal Identity and the R-Relation: Reconciliation through Cohabitation?' *Australasian Journal of Philosophy*, 73: 337–46.

Fine, Kit (1994). 'Compounds and Aggregates', *Noûs*, 28: 137–58.

Foster, John (1982). *The Case for Idealism*. London: Routledge & Kegan Paul.

—— (1991). *The Immaterial Self: A Defense of the Cartesian Dualist Conception of the Mind*. London: Routledge.

Gallois, André (1998). *Occasions of Identity*. Oxford: Oxford University Press.

Geach, Peter (1997). '*Reference and Generality* (Selections)', in Rea (1997: 305–12).

Gendler, Tamar (2000). *Thought Experiment: On the Power and Limits of Imaginary Cases*. New York: Garland.

Graham, George (1999). 'Self-Consciousness, Psychopathology, and Realism about the Self'. *Anthropology and Philosophy*, 3: 533–39.

Grandy, Richard E. (1975). 'Stuff and Things'. *Synthese*, 31: 479–85. Repr. in Pelletier (1979: 219–25).

Grice, H. P. (1941). 'Personal Identity'. *Mind*, 50: 330–50. Repr. in Perry (1975: 73–95).

Guttenplan, Samuel (ed.) (1996). *A Companion to the Philosophy of Mind*. Oxford: Basil Blackwell.

Hart, W. D. (1988). *The Engines of the Soul*. Cambridge: Cambridge University Press.

Harwood, Robin (1998). *The Survival of the Self*. Aldershot: Ashgate.

Hasker, William (1999). *The Emergent Self*. Ithaca, NY: Cornell University Press.

Heller, Mark (1990). *The Ontology of Physical Objects*. Cambridge: Cambridge University Press.

Hoffman, Joshua, and Gary S. Rosenkrantz (1996). *Substance: Its Nature and Existence*. London: Routledge.

Hudson, Hud (2002). *A Materialist Metaphysics of the Human Person*. Ithaca, NY: Cornell University Press.

Jackson, Frank (1982). 'Epiphenomenal Qualia'. *Philosophical Quarterly*, 32: 127–36.

Johnston, Mark (1987). 'Human Beings'. *Journal of Philosophy*, 84: 59–83.

—— (1992). 'Constitution is not Identity'. *Mind*, 101: 89–105.

Karmo, Toomas (1977). 'Disturbances'. *Analysis*, 37: 147–8.

Kim, Jaegwon (1976). 'Events as Property Exemplifications', in M. Brand and D. Walton (eds.), *Action Theory*. Dordrecht: Reidel, 159–77.

Korsgaard, Christine (1989). 'Personal Identity and the Unity of Agency: A Kantian Response to Parfit'. *Philosophy and Public Affairs*, 18: 103–31.

Laycock, Henry (forthcoming). *Words without Objects*.

Lewis, David (1976). 'Survival and Identity', in Rorty (1976: 17–40). Repr. with 'Postscripts to "Survival and Identity"', in Lewis, *Philosophical Papers*, vol. i. Oxford: Oxford University Press, 1983, 55–77.

—— (1986). 'Introduction', in Lewis, *Philosophical Papers*, vol. ii. Oxford: Oxford University Press.

—— (1996). 'David Lewis: Reduction of Mind', in Guttenplan (1996: 412–31).

Locke, John (1985). *An Essay concerning Human Understanding*, ed. P. H. Nidditch. Oxford: Clarendon Press.

Lombard, Lawrence (1999). 'On the Alleged Incompatibility of Presentism and Temporal Parts'. *Philosophia*, 27: 253–60.

Lowe, E. J. (1996). *The Subjects of Experience*. Cambridge: Cambridge University Press.

Martin, C. B. (1980). 'Substance Substantiated'. *Australasian Journal of Philosophy*, 58: 3–10.

Martin, Raymond (1991). 'Identity, Transformation, and What Matters in Survival', in D. Kolak and R. Martin (eds.), *Self and Identity: Contemporary Philosophical Issues*. New York: Macmillan.

Mason, Franklin (2000). 'How Not to Prove the Existence of "Atomless Gunk"'. *Ratio*, 13: 175–85.

Merricks, Trenton (1995). 'On the Incompatibility of Enduring and Perduring Entities'. *Mind*, 104: 523–31.

—— (1999). 'Persistence, Parts and Presentism'. *Noûs*, 33: 421–38.

—— (2001). *Objects and Persons*. Oxford: Oxford University Press.

Mills, Eugene (1993). 'Dividing without Reducing: Bodily Fission and Personal Identity'. *Mind*, 102: 37–51.

Montague, Richard (1979). 'The Proper Treatment of Mass Terms in English', in Pelletier (1979: 173–8).

Noonan, Harold (1989). *Personal Identity*. London: Routledge & Kegan Paul.

Olson, Eric T. (1997). *The Human Animal*. New York: Oxford University Press.

Parfit, Derek (1971). 'Personal Identity'. *Philosophical Review*, 80: 3–27.

—— (1984). *Reasons and Persons*. Oxford: Oxford University Press.

Pelletier, Francis Jeffry (ed.) (1979). *Mass Terms: Some Philosophical Problems*. Dordrecht: Reidel.

Perry, John (ed.) (1975). *Personal Identity*. Berkeley: University of California Press.

—— (1976). 'The Importance of being Identical', in Rorty (1976: 67–90).

Quine, W. V. O. (1960). *Word and Object*. Cambridge, Mass.: MIT Press.

Quinn, Philip L. (1997). 'Tiny Selves: Chisholm on the Simplicity of the Soul', in Lewis Hahn (ed.), *The Philosophy of Roderick M. Chisholm*. LaSalle, Ill.: Open Court, 55–67.

Quinton, Anthony (1962). 'The Soul'. *Journal of Philosophy*, 59: 393–409. Repr. in Perry (1975: 53–72).

Rea, Michael C. (ed.) (1997). *Material Constitution: A Reader*. Lanham, Md.: Rowman & Littlefield.

—— (1998). 'In Defense of Mereological Universalism'. *Philosophy and Phenomenological Research*, 58: 347–60.

—— (2000). 'Constitution and Kind Membership'. *Philosophical Studies*, 97: 169–93.

Robinson, Howard (1989). 'A Dualist Account of Embodiment', in J. R. Smythies and J. Beloff (eds.), *The Case for Dualism*. Charlottesville: University Press of Virginia, 43–57.

Rorty, Amélie, (ed.) (1976). *The Identities of Persons*. Berkeley: University of California Press.

Rovane, Carol (1997). *The Bounds of Agency: An Essay in Revisionary Metaphysics*. Princeton: Princeton University Press.

Santayana, George (1942). *Realms of Being*. New York: Scribners.

Shoemaker, Sydney (1967). *Self-Knowledge and Self-Identity*. Ithaca, NY: Cornell University Press.

—— (1971). 'Persons and their Pasts'. *American Philosophical Quarterly*, 7: 269–85.

—— (1999). 'Self, Body, and Coincidence'. *Proceedings of the Aristotelian Society*, suppl. vol. 73: 287–306.

—— and Richard Swinburne (1984). *Personal Identity*. Oxford: Basil Blackwell.

Sider, Theodore (1993). 'Van Inwagen and the Possibility of Gunk'. *Analysis*, 53: 285–9.

—— (1997). 'Four-Dimensionalism'. *Philosophical Review*, 106: 197–231.

—— (2000). 'Simply Possible'. *Philosophy and Phenomenological Research*, 60: 585–90.

—— (2001a). 'Criteria of Personal Identity and the Limits of Conceptual Analysis'. *Philosophical Perspectives*, 15: 189–209.

—— (2001b). *Four-Dimensionalism: An Ontology of Persistence and Time*. Oxford: Oxford University Press.

—— (2001c). Review of André Gallois, 'Occasions of Identity', *British Journal for the Philosophy of Science*, 52: 401–5.

Simons, Peter (1987). *Parts: A Study in Ontology*. Oxford: Oxford University Press.

Swinburne, Richard (1997). *The Evolution of the Soul*, 2nd edn. Oxford: Oxford University Press.

Thomson, Judith Jarvis (1997). 'People and their Bodies', in Jonathan Dancy (ed.), *Reading Parfit*. Oxford: Basil Blackwell, 202–29.

—— (1998). 'The Statue and the Clay'. *Noûs*, 32: 149–73.

Unger, Peter (1990). *Identity, Consciousness and Value*. New York: Oxford University Press.

van Inwagen, Peter (1990). *Material Beings*. Ithaca, NY: Cornell University Press.

Whiting, Jennifer (1986). 'Friends and Future Selves'. *Philosophical Review*, 95: 547–80.

Wiggins, David (1971). *Identity and Spatio-Temporal Continuity*. Oxford: Basil Blackwell.

—— (1980). *Sameness and Substance*. Cambridge, Mass.: Harvard University Press.

Wilkes, Kathleen V. (1992). *Real People: Personal Identity without Thought Experiments*. Oxford: Oxford University Press.

Williams, Bernard (1973). 'Imagination and the Self' (1966) and 'The Self and the Future' (1970), in Williams, *Problems of the Self*. Cambridge: Cambridge University Press.

Williams, D. C. (1953). 'On the Elements of Being: I and II'. *Review of Metaphysics*, 7: 3–18 and 171–92.

Yandell, Keith (1995). 'A Defense of Dualism.' *Faith and Philosophy*, 12: 548–66.

Zimmerman, Dean W. (1995). 'Theories of Masses and Problems of Constitution'. *Philosophical Review*, 104: 53–110.

—— (1996a). 'Indivisible Parts and Extended Objects: Some Philosophical Episodes from Topology's Prehistory'. *The Monist*, 79: 148–80.

—— (1996b). 'Persistence and Presentism'. *Philosophical Papers*, 25: 115–26.

—— (1996c). 'Could Extended Objects be made out of Simple Parts?' *Philosophy and Phenomenological Research*, 56: 1–29.

Zimmerman, Dean W. (1997). 'Coincident Objects: Could a "Stuff Ontology" Help?' *Analysis*, 57: 19–27.

—— (1998). 'Temporal Parts and Supervenient Causation: The Incompatibility of Two Humean Doctrines'. *Australasian Journal of Philosophy*, 76: 265–88.

—— (1999*a*). 'One Really Big Liquid Sphere: Reply to David Lewis'. *Australasian Journal of Philosophy*, 77: 213–15.

—— (1999*b*). Review of Joshua Hoffman and Gary S. Rosenkrantz, *Substance: Its Nature and Existence*. *Philosophical Review*, 108: 118–22.

—— (2002). 'Scala and the Spinning Sphere'. *Philosophy and Phenomenological Research*, 398–405.

—— (2003). 'The Constitution of Persons by Bodies: A Critique of Lynne Rudder Baker's Theory of Material Constitution'. *Philosophical Topics*.

—— (forthcoming). 'Shoemaker's Metaphysics of Minds, Bodies, and Properties'. *Philosophy and Phenomenological Research*.

—— and Peter van Inwagen (eds.) (1998). *Metaphysics: The Big Questions*. Malden, Mass.: Basil Blackwell.

CHAPTER 17

....

THE ONTOLOGY OF
THE MENTAL

....

HOWARD ROBINSON

1. INTRODUCTION

....

ONTOLOGY in the philosophy of mind can be divided into three sets of issues.

1. First, one can investigate the structure of those entities that constitute the content of the mind. Is the mind 'populated' by states, events, processes, or some combination of these?[1] Are these entities to be analysed in an *act–object*, an *adverbial*, or some other way and, if it is act–object, is the object to be construed internalistically or externalistically? Are there relevant differences in structure between perceptual or sensational 'states', on the one hand, and propositional attitudes, on the other?

2. Secondly, there is the issue of what binds these contents together. Is it some primitive co-mentality relation, or some other relation that does not make essential reference to a substantial owner, or is it their belonging to some one substance, or succession of substances?

3. The above issues can be characterized as formal ontology. In principle, the answer to these questions is neutral on the questions of dualism or materialism. So the third category of ontological issues concerns whether these contents and their uniting principle are material, immaterial, or something else.

---

[1] This issue, which I do not discuss below, is thoroughly examined in Steward (1997).

If one is to say anything worth-while about any of these issues, it is not possible to discuss them all in one chapter. My strategy will be to investigate the ontology of, first, sensory, and secondly, intellectual states, for these are the basic categories of mental state, with an eye to the consequences of what is said for the substantive metaphysical issue of materialism and dualism.[2]

2. The Ontology of Sensation and Perception

2.1 Sensation, Perception, and Naive Realism

The simplest conception of the ontology of perception is that it consists of an event involving a subject, an object, and an asymmetric relation between them of perceptual consciousness: as a result of this relation, the object, in the sense of *thing*, becomes an object-of-perceptual-consciousness, that is, an object in the grammatico-logical sense. If we call *how the world appears to the subject* the *content* of his experience, then, calling this theory 'naive realism', we can define it as follows:

> Naive realism = (df) that theory of perception according to which the content of experience is identical with, or constituted simply by, the thing which is the object-of-perceptual-consciousness.

The problems with such a form of naive realism are well known. First, the relation only holds between the subject and some part or aspect of the object, say the surface and its colour. This problem can be answered by identifying the content with the relevant features of the object. Secondly, and much more important, perception is never a perfect representation of the object as it is *in itself*, even regarding the appropriate features; the nature of the sensory mechanism and the conditions of perception always make a difference to the perceptual experience. A theory which pictures the mind as reaching out to the object, and leaves it at that, is obviously oversimplified. What I have called above the *content*, therefore, has to include something over and above the object and its properties. These as yet unaccounted for contents are the products of more than the nature of the object itself. The influences which produce this 'extra' content include conditions of the medium outside the subject as well as states of the subject's body. If these considerations refute naive

---

[2] I have discussed issues of materialism and dualism in various places, including Robinson (1982; 1994, ch. 5; 2003; forthcoming *a*).

realism in the very naive form in which I have defined it, its erstwhile protagonist might recoup under the banner of what I will call *direct realism*:[3]

> Direct realism = (df) that theory of perception according to which the content of experience is a mode of appearance of the object perceived, and not constituted by some other entity.

Direct realism preserves an important feature of naive realism, because it insists that there is no entity involved other than the external object we deem to be perceived, but it allows that there is a relation of *appearing* which is more than the simple apprehending of the object as it is, but the account of which remains so far unclear. This is to be contrasted with any theory that claims that the perceived object can do no more than *cause* the content of experience, as is the case with representative realism. These latter theories can be gathered under the label 'sense datum theories' and be defined as follows:

> Sense datum theory = (df) that theory of perception according to which the content of perception is identical with or is constituted by some entity which is a different entity from the external object we deem to be perceived.

One way of proving the sense datum theory, in controversion of direct realism, would be to show that the contents of perception are subjective, in the sense that they depend for their existence wholly on states of the perceiver and his body, not on the presence of the object deemed to be perceived. There is, in fact, an argument that proves this, as follows.

It would be unreasonable to doubt that, were the processes that are presently active in my head and associated with my seeing the room in which I am working, to be activated artificially, I would undergo visual experiences just like those I am now having. As in this second, hallucinatory, case, the contents would all be subjective— that is, no part of them could be treated in a direct realist way—then the same must be true for the real perception, for both conscious states have the same proximate cause, namely a certain brain process.

Put slightly more rigorously:

(1) It is theoretically possible, by activating some brain process which is involved in a particular type of perception, to cause a hallucination which exactly resembles that perception in its subjective character.

(2) It is necessary to give the same account of the contents of both hallucinating and perceptual experience *when they have the same neural cause*. Thus it is not, for example, plausible to say that the hallucination involves a mental

---

[3] My use of 'I will call' when introducing a familiar expression is not meant to be precious. Both 'naive realism' and 'direct realism' are common terms with generally but loosely understood senses. I am using them, I hope, in more than usually exact but not eccentric ways.

image or sense datum, but that the perception does not, if the two have the same proximate—that is, neural—cause.

(3) In the case of hallucination, the content of the experience is uncontroversially a subjective state, not a state of the external world.

Therefore,

(4) In the case of perception, there is a content of experience which is a subjective state, not a state of the external world.[4]

This argument refutes both naive and direct realism, but it does not say anything about the nature of the subjective contents: are they *objects* of awareness, like the ideas, impressions, and sense data of traditional empiricism, or are they *modes of the act* of sensing, as adverbialists claim? Indeed, if they are objects, are they just *intentional objects*, rather than genuine relata?

2.2 Adverbialism

What is at stake in these different theories? Jargon apart, it often seems difficult to see what is at issue. The key question is whether the subjective contents of sense actually instantiate the sensible qualities they seem to present. It is a matter of what I have elsewhere called the *phenomenal principle* (Robinson 1994: 32).

(PP) If there sensibly appears to a subject to be something which possesses a particular sensible quality, then there is something of which the subject is aware which does possess that quality.

The truth of (PP) is sufficient to guarantee that there is some entity of which we are aware in perception that is other than the external object we take ourselves to be perceiving. This would be sufficient to refute direct realism and to establish the sense datum theory, as defined above. But between those two theories there remains the option of admitting that contents of perception are subjective states—and so not appearances essentially of external objects—but to deny them status as *entities* which are objects of awareness.

There seem to be three motivations for trying to resist the objectual conception of content; one has its roots in the Wittgensteinian approach to the mind, one is metaphysical, and one epistemological. The Wittgensteinian rests on the anti-private language argument: if there are no private objects, then there cannot be an objectual account of content. I do not have the space to discuss this strategy

---

[4] I present this argument here without further discussion, but it is disputed, especially by those who defend the so-called 'disjunctive analysis' of perceptual awareness. They try to circumvent (2). For an extended discussion of this, see Robinson (1994, ch. 6).

here. Wittgenstein's arguments seem to me to be unsuccessful.[5] The metaphysical objection to the objectual theory is that it constitutes an unnecessary obstacle to physicalism. If, whenever I seem to see something red and square, there must be a red and square sense content before my mind, and if the mind and its contents are states of or events in the brain, then one ought to be able to find this red, square entity in the brain. Of course, such 'pictures' are not to be found in the brain, so physicalism must be false. If, however, one refuses to reify sense contents in this way—refuses to commit what is sometimes termed 'the phenomenological fallacy'—but rather treats such contents adverbially or intentionally, then physicalism lives to fight another day. The inadequacy of this argument is the assumption that treating content as adverbial or intentional renders it compatible with physicalism. Unless given some further reductive—for example, functional—treatment, sensing redly, with its attendant phenomenology, is no more a respectable physicalistic property than being aware of a red sense datum. And intentional objects, however mysterious they may be, are still real and not within the natural sciences.[6] The classic 'knowledge argument' against physicalism, for example, is in no way dependent on which analysis of sensory content is provided.[7]

It is the epistemological argument with which I shall mainly be concerned.

The epistemological reason for rejecting the sense datum account is that such data constitute a 'veil of perception' between the observer and the world. This both (a) creates a sense of alienation from the world—we do not perceive it, only 'pictures' of it—and, connectedly, (b) it leads to scepticism about the existence of the world. By contrast, the adverbial theory makes the subjective content into that feature of the perceptual act by which we perceive the world, not an object of awareness which stands surrogate for the world.

The fact is that adverbialism alienates the perceiver from the world, more, not less, than does the sense datum theory, so it is of no help to the perceptual realist. Adverbialism does this because, when combined with two other very plausible principles, it entails a conclusion which is both counter-intuitive, and, more relevantly, more remote from naive or direct realism than is the sense datum theory.

The first of these principles concerns the relations between physical objects and properties, on the one hand, and mental activities, on the other. It could hardly be disputed that the only way that physical objects and properties could enter into the content of a mental act would be as the object of such an act; it would make no sense for a perceptual realist to claim that a physical thing or a property of the sort that

---

[5] See Robinson (1994, ch. 4) for detailed argument.

[6] Though see later in this section for physicalist philosophers who seem to think that there is no issue of the ontological status of intentional objects.

[7] See Jackson (1982) for the classic source of the argument, and Balog (1999) for a recent list of readings. That the argument is independent of how sense contents are construed is argued convincingly by Crane (2000; see esp. 185).

are specifically properties of physical things could be a mode of mental activity.[8] For example, if I see a brown rectangular brick, neither its property of being a brick, not its rectangularity, not even its brownness could be regarded by a perceptual realist as modes of the subject's sensing. So this principle is that types of physical thing and physical properties are not modes of mental activity.

The second principle is that the content of perception is what is ostensively demonstrable, and, hence, such content is what makes possible the ostensive definition of words appropriately connected with the content. If I know that someone is currently seeming to see a red object, I can teach him the meaning of the word 'red', as the name for the colour that it now seems to him he is seeing. I can do this irrespective of whether the experience in question is a veridical perception, an illusory perception, or even a hallucination, so long as I know how it seems to him, for ostension of this sort depends only on the subjective content of the experience, not on further facts about the external world.

The defining claim of adverbialism is that the contents of sense experience are modes, not objects, of sensory activity. This can be put together with the two principles I have just explained to give the following argument.

(1)   The subjective content of experience is a mode of mental activity; no part of it is a genuine object of experience.

(2)   The subjective content of experience is—or includes—what is ostensively demonstrable and, hence, that of which the names can be ostensively defined.

Therefore,

(3)   What is ostensively demonstrable and definable is a mode of mental activity.

(4)   Types of physical objects and types of physical properties are not modes of mental activity.

Therefore,

(5)   No type of physical object or type of physical property is ostensively demonstrable or definable.

This conclusion is plainly inconsistent with direct realism. It is further removed from naive realism than is any common version of the sense datum theory. The sense datum theorist is either a representative realist or a phenomenalist (with whom we may, for present purposes, classify the idealist). A representative realist believes that at least some of the properties that are ostensively demonstrable in virtue of being exemplified in sense data are of the same kind as some of those exemplified in physical objects. And even of those that are not exemplified in bodies, he may

---

[8] This is not an objection to materialism. The point is not that mental acts could not be physical events, but that a naive realist could not claim that the physical objects in the manifest image of the world are modes of mental activity, as opposed to objects of it.

believe that it is logically possible that they should have been so exemplified. A Lockean, for example, who believes that bodies resemble sense data only in respect of primary qualities, could hold that bodies might, logically, have resembled them in respect of secondary qualities too. Or someone who held, with Russell of *Problems of Philosophy* (1912), that the physical world resembled the phenomenal only in abstract structure, could hold that it is contingent that it does not resemble it more fully. Even a phenomenalist believes that his phenomenal world resembles in all perceived respects the physical world in which the naive realist believes, so the ostensively demonstrable is not essentially different from the physical either as he, the phenomenalist, conceives the physical (for, to him, it is just a construction from the phenomenal), or as his principal opponent conceives it.

For the adverbialist the situation seems to be radically different, however. If only modes of sensing are ostensively available, and if the sorts of features bodies possess cannot be modes of mental activities, then it is a category mistake to entertain the possibility of any resemblance between what is ostensively available and properties of bodies. One could as sensibly say that an inert physical body could be proud, intelligent, or lazy, as that it could be red or square. Berkeley's maxim that nothing could be like an idea but an idea would be true, and have the modal force it is supposed to have.

There is only one strategy I can think of for resisting this argument. This is to deny that it is the adverbially construed content of experience which is ostensively demonstrable and which contains any sensible feature which can be ostensively defined. This is to deny the second plausible principle, or (2) in the formal argument above. As what is ostensively demonstrable is available in hallucination as well as perception, and as the adverbial account is supposed to apply to all content that is common to both, it is not easy to see how to achieve this objective. That which is ostensively demonstrable would have to be thought of as something over and above the content (that is, over and above that which is construed adverbially) while the content is held to be all that there is to a veridical-seeming hallucination. The thought would appear to be as follows:

> It is by the having of the content that one is aware of the object, but the object is intentionally inexistent and need be given no ontological status, whereas the content is adverbial and real.

Some philosophers do, indeed, seem to be prepared to say this; that is, they talk as if it is possible to allow the intentional object to cope with the phenomenology, and let the adverbial account specify the ontology, and say that the intentional object constitutes no ontological problem just because it is only intentional. So Lycan:

I take the view . . . that phenomenal individuals such as sense-data are intentional inexistents à la Brentano and Meinong. It is, after all, no surprise to be told that mental states have intentional objects that do not exist. So why should we not suppose that after-images and other sense-data are intentional objects that do not exist? If they do not exist then—*voilà*—they do not exist; there are in reality no such things. And that is why we can consistently admit that phenomenal-color properties qualify individuals without granting that there exist individuals that are the bearers of phenomenal-color properties. (Lycan 1987: 88)

Lycan combines this free-spirited attitude to intentional objects with adverbialism. I cannot see why, if the above attitude towards intentional objects were admissible, one should not stop there: mental contents are constituted by the non-existent, so we need not worry about them even though they are phenomenally real. This is, indeed Dretske's view. He says of perceptual and hallucinatory experience, 'the properties we are aware of in achieving this awareness (being universals) exist nowhere' (Dretske 2000: 160). He adds in a note:

I assume that universals (and, a fortiori, the universals one is aware of) are neither inside nor outside the head. Awareness of colors, shapes, and movements, when there is no external object that has the property one is aware of, is not, therefore, a violation of [the principle that experience involves no internal phenomenal properties]. A measuring instrument (a speedometer, for example) can (when malfunctioning) be 'aware of' (i.e., represent) a speed of 45 mph without any object's (inside or outside the instrument) having this magnitude.

The idea that a malfunctioning speedometer 'hallucinates' a speed in a sense close enough to that in which a person might hallucinate pink rats, for the comparison to be of any use in providing an account of conscious hallucination, is bizarre indeed: but the claim that one can ignore the ontological status of phenomenal objects simply because they are either intentional or abstract is hardly less so. The fact that Lycan feels obliged to give an account of experience in terms of what actually exists—the adverbial states—suggests that the *via negativa* alone is not adequate. The phenomena must be accounted for by what there is, not by what there is not.

The dilemma for the adverbialist is how he can insist that there is no more to the experience than the sensing, while not letting the sensing be identical with or contain that which is ostensively demonstrable in the experience (remember, this includes hallucinations as well as genuine perceptions): the genie must perform his magic while remaining in the lamp.[9]

Although these attempts to avoid phenomenal objects by manipulating the notions of the adverbial and the intentional seem to me doomed to failure, they do draw attention to an important point in perceptual experience, namely the way that it is two-layered. At the bottom there are the 'raw sense data' of sensation: at the top, experience which is conceptualized as perception of an external world. The adverbialist's intuition—I would say, his mistake—is to think that the

---

[9] I deal with this in more detail in Robinson (1994: 175–85). For the original statement of the best attempt at refuting adverbialism (as opposed to showing its incompatibility with direct realism), see Jackson (1975). For a brief and clear statement of the current situation with respect to such arguments, see Tye (1998).

sophisticated conceptualization requires that the preconceptual level be held to be non-objectual: if it is objectual, it somehow 'gets in the way'. I want now to look more closely at this traditional objection to the sense datum theory.[10]

2.3 The Objectual View and Common Sense

It is generally assumed that the sense datum theory and common-sense realism are incompatible: that the only form of realism available to the sense datum theorist is representative realism, and that this is not common sensical because it involves a 'veil of perception'.[11] This, I now think, is an oversimplification.

The core of the commonsensical theory of perception can be stated simply.

Common-sense realism. In perception, we are aware of physical objects themselves, and not merely of some surrogate.

---

[10] In this section I have talked almost interchangeably of *adverbialism* and *intentionalism*. In this I am following Chisholm (1957), who uses adverbialism to explain what it is for the object of experience to be intentional. More recently the theories have been treated as if they were entirely separate or incompatible (see Martin 2000; Crane 2001). In my view, this leaves the notion of intentional inexistence for perceptual objects unexplained unless something is put in the place of the adverbial explanation. Martin (2000: 222–3) says that intentional theories are popular when realism about the physical world is in fashion and the sense datum theory, based on the phenomenal principle, holds the day when scepticism or non-realist theories of the physical world are in vogue. The rationale for this is that *something* must instantiate sensible properties and, if physical reality cannot be relied upon to do the job, appearances must do it instead. Although there may be some truth in this, it commits what I believe to be the mistake of treating intentionalism and the sense datum theory as starting off as equally intuitively plausible accounts of phenomenal content, neither one more in need of explanation or defence than the other and to be chosen between on external grounds. In fact, the phenomenal principle gives a straightforward account of such content, namely the literal presence of the quality explains of the appearance. By contrast, intentionalism has the (so far unsolved) problem of trying to give a plausible account of intentional presence in perceptual experience, and, in particular, of saying how it differs from intentional presence in thought and belief. If when *x* seems to see something blue, nothing actually is blue, what *actual* thing constitutes that state and distinguishes it from seeming to see red or nothing at all? Tim Crane, like Martin, seems to think that intentional theories are essentially unproblematic, and the only way he distinguishes perception from pure belief is the presence of 'nonconceptual content', and of this he has only a negative characterization: 'we can say that a state with nonconceptual content is one of which the following is true:

(NCC) In order for subjects to be in a state with a content *p*, they do not have to possess the concepts which are canonical for *p*' (2001: 152).

(There is nothing mysterious about being *canonical*; these are just the concepts one would normally think of as being involved in the *belief* that *p*.) Given the unique role of perceptual experience in communicating the nature of empirical properties to us, is it likely that this is all that can be said about its distinguishing feature? The realization of sensible qualities in the experience, as in the sense datum theory and the phenomenal principle seems much more naturally to fit the bill, and to explain perceptual experience's role.

[11] This was, for example, my own view in Robinson (1994). According to Foster (2000: 196–243) this constitutes *the* 'problem of perception'.

Now common sense is not ignorant of the blatant fact that objects appear in different ways without themselves changing. To cope with this, the simple statement of the theory is augmented by:

> *The intentionality thesis.* (i) the subjective content of experience ('how the world seems') is not to be reified, so that (ii) even when an object seems other than the way it actually is, that object is still the direct object of awareness and the only thing of which we are aware.[12]

This theory—augmented common-sense realism—differs from direct realism because the intentionality thesis does not claim that perceptual variability ('illusion') is constituted by modes of appearance of the external object itself. It merely puts a constraint on the logic or grammar of how such phenomena are to be characterized. Nevertheless, it seems at first sight to be wholly at odds with the sense datum theory, for the sense datum theory reifies how the world seems and makes these reified objects into objects of awareness, which, it would seem, prevent one from being aware of physical objects directly. How could two theories be more in opposition? But perhaps this conflict is more illusory than real.

First, I want to draw attention to an interesting historical fact. The attack on the common-sense theory—under the label 'naive realism'—at the beginning of the twentieth century was largely based on the argument from illusion. That argument, in effect, said that common sense was incoherent, because it affirmed both the directness of perception and acknowledged the obvious fact that things look different when they have not changed intrinsically: this is inconsistent because you cannot both see something directly and not see it as it is in itself. The historical interest in this argument is that the philosophers who used it—Moore and Broad, for example—were at the forefront of the analytic attack on idealism; but the argumentative strategy of trying to show that our ordinary concepts—in this case, perception, commonsensically understood—have contradictions in them, is a strategy typical of the Hegelian idealists (see Moore 1918–19; Broad 1923). It is, for example, how Bradley tried to show that there cannot be relations, and McTaggart, that there cannot be time (Bradley 1930, ch. 3; McTaggart 1921–7, ch. 23). This in no way undermines the argument itself, but it does suggest that there ought to be another way of explicating our common-sense concept. The apparent antinomy that the argument from illusion exposes is, after all, far more obvious than those supposedly uncovered by Bradley or McTaggart. The intentionality thesis may seem to be a way of dissolving the problem, but we have seen that the appeal to intentional objects provides no clear alternative to the sense datum theory. Furthermore, I do

---

[12] The intentionality thesis can be taken as standing proxy for all those idioms which were appealed to by 'ordinary language' philosophers in their attempt to show that all phenomena can be characterized without resort to sense datum talk. The intentional idioms, such as 'seems', 'looks', 'appears', lie at the centre of this whole family.

not believe that the protagonist of common sense would wish to deny that there is a perfectly good sense in which, if one hallucinates a pink rat, or sees a white object looking pink, one is genuinely aware of pink. The challenge is not to set up the two theses of common sense as alternatives to the sense datum theory, but to reconcile them with it, as far as is possible.

We can begin from the fact that even the sense datum theorist accepts that taking our experience in the common-sense realist way is both natural and inevitable.[13] We can express this as follows.

> (1) Our sense data are naturally and inevitably conceptualized as—and, hence, interpreted as—appearances of a physical world, and this is the only way they can be made sense of and how they are 'meant' (by evolution, or God, or both) to be interpreted.

This commits us to speaking the language of perceptual realism, and, in so far as I am speaking of the physical world, when I report a hallucination there is nothing pink; there only seems to be. The same applies when the white wall looks pink. This gives us:

> (2) Within the scope of our common-sense realist interpretation of the sense data, the intentionality thesis holds. This thesis is at the core of the 'logic' of the perceptual realist interpretation of experience, which we cannot—and should not wish to—avoid.

But this does not constitute a reconciliation of common sense and sense data, for it is still unclear how we can be aware of objects in the physical world, not surrogates, and yet be aware of logically private sense data. Indeed, (1) and (2) above look more like an idealist attempt to explain how we construct a physical world out of our sense data, than a reconciliation with common sense. It is a common sense of a distinctly Berkeleian kind.

Although this is a conclusion to which I would be very sympathetic, I do not think that it is so easily reached. Let us call the interpretation of our sense data enshrined in (1) and (2) *the canonical interpretation*, because it expresses how the data are meant to be interpreted. If we are to understand how something like direct realism is to be infused into the canonical interpretation, we must look at what is involved when other cognitive states, such as thought and judgement, are taken to be directly and really *of* real objects in the world.

If I think about the Eiffel Tower, that it is in Paris, I think using words with meaning, but no one thinks that these vehicles of thought constitute some sort of veil between me and it. The thought is about the Eiffel Tower, *simpliciter*. (Those, who, like Locke, take thoughts to be images might have such a problem. Locke has no plausible doctrine of the intentionality of ideas, relying entirely on the probability of

---

[13] H. H. Price's (1932) account of *taking* or *acceptance* is a good case of this.

their having suitable resembling causes. As we shall see, that is not irrelevant to the present issue.) If we can take perception as being a form of judgement, represented not in language but sensorily, I do not see why it cannot be thought to be just as much *of* its object as is a verbal thought.

It is important to see how integrated the sense data and the judgement are. Consider the perceptual judgement involved in perceiving and recognizing that there is an armchair in front of me. What is the relation of the judgement to the phenomenal episode with which it is connected? It is tempting to think of them as accompanying each other—side by side, so to speak, or with the sense datum first, swiftly followed by the judgement. But it is also possible to think of them as synthesized into one event, with the phenomenal content contained within the judgement. Just as some judgements have words as their vehicle, perceptual ones have phenomenal contents. Now, the judgement is *about* the armchair, which is an object in the external world. This is no more a 'projection', in a sense that carries the derogatory overtones of illusion or unnoticed mistake, than it is in the case of the way the words, with their meanings, *refer* to the Eiffel Tower: the phenomenal features, when structured into a judgement, refer to the chair, in a way analogous to that in which the meaningful words refer.

Isn't this to relapse wholly into an intentional theory? No, because the sense data can be referred to in their own right: I can identify a pink, chair-shaped datum, as well as being able to judge perceptually that there is a physical object of a certain kind present. But must not the intentionalist say that when the perception is not veridical there is nothing referred to, for otherwise, are there not two competing objects of awareness, one a sense datum in private space, and the other a physical object in public space? This does appear to be the current dogma, but I can see no reason to accept it. Take, first, the claim that, when an experience is halluc- inatory, or a feature of experience non-veridical, there is no phenomenal object to be an object of reference.[14] The comparison with thought is instructive. When a thought fails of reference, there is no real proposition, but there is a meaningful sentence or thought with a certain character. If I try to refer to 'that star over there' when it is only a speck on the telescope lens, there may be no reference and no proposition, but there is a perfectly clear meaningful sentence, and we know, in the context, what the speaker is 'trying to say'. I can pick out and refer to the individual words and their meanings irrespective of whether the sentence succeeds in making a reference in the world, and say what would have to have been the case for there to have been a genuine proposition. What is more, without the meaningful words there would be no proposition thought (assuming the thoughts of this kind to be verbal, or dependent on words). The words and their meaning are identifiable independently of their specific contribution to that particular pro- position, if there is one; and, in an obvious sense, the word meanings are prior to

---

[14] This, for example, is the view in Snowdon (1982).

what is said by means of them in that individual case. Similarly, if I see a white wall looking yellow, or hallucinate my armchair altogether, the experience has a character and a content that I can individuate perfectly easily, and it involves the sense data, without which the judgement delivered by the canonical interpretation would not be possible.[15] The analogy with the relation between word meanings and their contribution to the content of a proposition shows why the sense datum in private space and the fully conceptualized experience of a public object are not in competition.

Does this mean that the traditional 'problem of perception', according to which acceptance of the arguments for sense data leads to a 'veil of perception', is misconceived? I think that it probably does, and that the traditional problem rests on the failure of the empiricists to have any understanding of thought and intentionality. When Locke stated in the introduction to the *Essay concerning Human Understanding* that he meant by *idea* 'whatever is meant by *phantasm, notion, species,* or *whatever it is that the mind is employed about in thinking*', he was not declaring *idea* to be a generic notion, but rather claiming that there was no serious theoretical difference between the various concepts that it was used to replace; in particular, that sense contents and intellectual contents are, *in re*, the same kind of thing. In fact, the assimilation is from the intellectual to the sensory, for both are mental images. Locke may have been less than clear what he was doing, but Berkeley and Hume understood.[16] For empiricism in general from that point on, thought was either the association of ideas (= images), or later, in, for example, the pragmatists and Ayer, the situating of those ideas in an appropriate behavioural or functional role.[17] The reconciliation I am proposing between the sense datum theory and common sense rests on taking the intentionality of thought to be as real and intrinsic a feature of perceptual judgement as is its phenomenal nature. Any theory which treats intentionality reductively, as a function of external relations of the data, cannot see it as an intrinsic part of the phenomenology, which is essential to saving common sense. In a sentence, my claim is that the apparent clash between representative realism and common sense derives mainly *not* from the role of sense data in the former, but from the crudity of empiricist accounts of judgement: repair this shortcoming and the conflict is much diminished, or even entirely avoided.

On the other hand, those traditions that revived intentionality and took it nonreductively seem to have believed that this involved avoiding reifying sense contents,

---

[15] I use the word 'character' in this context deliberately. Kaplan (1978) attributes 'character' to demonstratives even when they are failing to refer. This is the same for sense data, whether or not they are representing reality as it actually is.

[16] This interpretation of Locke, Berkeley, and Hume is challenged by Yolton (1984). He believes that *ideas* for the empiricists are fully intentional and that it was Reid who caused the misinterpretation. I think that this is utterly implausible and that Ayers (1991: 44–51) demonstrates this for Locke. If it cannot be maintained for Locke, it certainly cannot be maintained for Berkeley or Hume.

[17] See e.g. Ayer (1968, ch. 4) on Peirce's account of signs.

not merely in the context of the 'canonical interpretation', but altogether. Brentano, for example, maintains that if one treats phenomenal colour as existing, one would be obliged to do the same with other contents of possible thought, such as the round square. This is a quite bizarre non sequitur, which fails to allow for the wholly different nature of the presence of qualities in perceptual experience from their involvement in thought. Nevertheless, the prejudice carried over into Husserl and the phenomenological tradition, emerging back into 'analytical' philosophy in the form of 'percept' theory and Chisholm's adverbialism.[18]

I hope that this explains why I talk of saving 'common sense' but not of saving 'naive realism'. The theory called 'naive realism' is the classical empiricist attempt to express the common-sense view on perception. They articulate common belief as the claim that the sense data we perceive are themselves features—for example, surfaces—of objects. In the context of a theory that has only an imagistic conception of mental content, this is the best that can be done. A theory that takes intentionality seriously can, however, do better. In order for a cognitive act to be genuinely *of* its object it is not necessary (or, indeed, possible) for the mode of presentation to be identified with the thing itself, *simpliciter*. It is part of the logic of perceptual judgements that the appearance of an object is an appearance *of* that thing, but it is not part of that logic that the object is that way except as presented under those circumstances.

To return to the suspicion that idealism is lurking surreptitiously in my argument and that the *canonical interpretation* is an account of how we *construct* the world from sense data. This interpretation is available to the idealist, but it can also be treated as an account of how we construct our *sensory conception of the world*. The metaphysical nature of that world and how much it resembles our sensory conception of it are further issues which the fact that there are private objects involved in our sensing of it hardly affects. Indeed, it should not be thought that reconciling sense data and common sense solves any other philosophical problems. It does not arbitrate between idealism and physical realism or disprove scepticism: it only undermines arguments for these doctrines that rested solely on the 'veil of perception' doctrine. Nor does it of itself determine whether the content of our physical concepts can be adequately explained by reference to the contents of sense data, or, if they cannot, what other resources might be available.[19]

---

[18] For a further discussion of this, see Robinson (1994: 21–30).

[19] The theory that I propound in this section, bringing together a full-bodied sense datum theory and intentionalism, in defence of common sense, seems to me to be very little different from what H. H. Price defends under the lable 'perceptual acceptance'. As Michael Martin (2000: 210) points out, Price 'emphasises the intentionality of perceptual experience, which he calls perceptual acceptance— explicitly indicating that this is a belief-like state of mind, in the process alluding to the works of Reid and Husserl'. Perhaps a difference between Price's exposition and mine is that I emphasize the way in which judgements in general are directly *of* their objects, to show how experiential judgements can be so.

2.4 Conclusion: The Ontology of Perception

I think we can conclude that a sensation involves: a subject (whatever that may be) and a sense datum. And that, in the context of a perceptual type of experience, the sense datum is, via the canonical interpretation, incorporated into a judgement, which, if the experience is not hallucinatory, has an external thing as its object. In this case, the sense datum is experienced as the mode of presentation of that object. The sensation and the intentional structure must both be regarded as features of conscious experience, if this account is to work.

3. TRANSITIONAL REMARKS

I am assuming that no *reductive* physicalist accounts of sense data are available: that is, I am assuming that the qualia problem—the problem of 'what it is like', or the 'hard problem' as it has recently been called—has no solution of a strongly physicalist kind.[20] I believe that the same is true for thought. One reason for affirming this was given, by implication at least, at the end of the previous section. If the phenomenology of perception is to be taken in the way that brings it closest to common sense, its intentional structure must be part of the phenomenology, and thus part of 'what it is like', and, hence, of what is irreducible. It may be replied that this argument for irreducibility applies only to the intellectual component in perception itself, and not to conscious thought in general, and that non-perceptual thoughts can be treated reductively. Although it is not possible absolutely to disprove this here, a strong reason against it is that reductionism about thought is likely to involve epiphenomenalism, which is no more plausible in the case of thought than in the case of sensory consciousness. I say this for the following reason. A physicalist account of thought is likely to be computational. This treats the mind, in Dennett's phrase, as a syntactic, not a semantic engine (Dennett 1987, ch. 3). This means that when you are, for example, discussing philosophy, it is not your apprehension of the *meaning* of what your interlocutor says that determines what you say in response, but some process to which the semantics is an epiphenomenal add-on. When your interlocutor says something obscure, your sense that it is your struggling to *understand* what he says that makes you hesitant in constructing your response is an illusion: all that is really happening is that an unusual physical input is taking longer to connect with the response-generating mechanism. This is as mad, if not madder, than the suggestion that it is not the visual experience of the big red bus that makes you move out of the way, or the feeling of the pain that makes you cry out.

---

[20] David Chalmers hit upon this felicitous phrase (see Chalmers 1996).

Dretske denies that reductionism leads to epiphenomenalism (Dretske 2000, ch. 11). He accepts that the efficacy of any token internal state is independent of any external cause, and, hence, any informational content it may have. Looked at in that way, the engine is purely syntactic. That there *are* internal states of the relevant kind, however, is causally dependent on their sensitivity to a particular kind of external stimulus. Whereas, in an artefact, a designer places a 'representation' that will respond to some state of affairs the gadget is meant to discriminate, in nature evolution and conditioning or learning do the same thing. So the externally determined informational content of a state explains, not what it can do—that is explained by the purely physical properties—but why it is there at all. In that sense, 'what the state means' does have a causal explanatory role, by explaining why it is there in the first place.

This seems to me to be inadequate in two ways. First, it does not give any efficacy at the time of its occurrence to the meaning content of the occurrent thought, in the way that the example of philosophical argument shows it ought. Secondly, although what Dretske says about evolutionary development sounds plausible, it is not clear that it is a naturalistic explanation. Every natural generation of a state with a representational role can be explained without appeal to the fact that it has such a role. Standing back, we can see it as having such a role, but is not that imposing a scheme of interpretation that presupposes the presence of an interpreting mind? Dretske talks of 'a system that has a *need* for the information that *F*, a system whose *survival or well-being* depends on its doing *A* in conditions *F*' (Dretske 2000: 223; my italics), but, in systems that are not conscious of their own purposes, isn't this talk dependent on our choosing to give these objects a certain status? His evolutionary account, therefore, cannot be an account of the mentality it presupposes. The irreducible grasp of meaning is still present.[21]

It is a comment on the dogmatism with which many philosophers hold to the principle that the world is 'closed under physics' that they prefer to flirt with epiphenomenalism rather than admit that we simply do not understand how mind and body interact.

In what follows, therefore, a generally non-reductionist approach is presumed.[22]

---

[21] This is, of course, a familiar problem for all theories that insist on the role of interpretation—the intentional stance—in the creation of meaning. See the criticisms of Dennett in Hornsby (1997: 179–82) and Robinson (1993: 5–8).

There is a further reason which it would be difficult to give in sufficient detail in the body of the text. I agree with George Myro that there is an aspect of thought of which we are what he calls 'perfectly (!?) clear' and that this cannot be logically equivalent to anything externally accessible, such as words (abstracted from meaning), brain processes, or bits of behaviour. The upshot of Myro's argument is that the feature of thought given in consciousness is not a physical aspect of anything, even though it may be an aspect of something physical. See Myro (1993).

[22] It is quite normal to scoff at the idea that there might be something *sui generis* and irreducible about intellectual apprehension. See e.g. Putnam (1981: 51), where he sneers at what he calls 'Noetic rays' and says, 'such a view is obviously untenable. No present day philosopher would espouse such

4. The Ontology of Thought

4.1 The General Structure of Conscious Thought

Despite the absolute centrality of thought to mind, there has been much less discussion of it in recent philosophy than there has been of perception. This may seem a strange thing to say, given the amount of literature on propositional attitudes, the language of thought, and semantics as an aspect of the philosophy of mind. None of these, however, is directly concerned with the nature of conscious thought. They relate initially either to the philosophy of language, or to the computational conception of the mind, which indefinitely defers consideration of the role of consciousness, and is more directly relevant to the conditions necessary for the embodiment of thought than to the nature of thought itself.

My approach will be from a different angle, concerning thoughts as conscious events. Thought is concerned with grasping the intelligible aspects of the world. Plato's great insight was that a world with which we can engage intellectually cannot simply be a series of particulars, but must also contain things that are inherently treatable as universal. In Plato's jargon, this potentiality for universality is reified as Forms, which both participate in things and are also objects of mental activity. Using more modern terms, we can say that universals are Janus-faced: on the one hand, they are in things as properties, and, on the other, they are mentally realized as concepts. The general gist of this point does not depend on accepting realism—let alone a Platonic realism—about universals. It is enough to say that there are objective similarities in the world, at least some of the more salient ones of which the mind has the capacity to register. The metaphysical account of these similarities—the 'theory of universals'—need not bother us here, but their existence and the fact that we have a capacity to register them is the foundation of any cognitive contact with the world.[23]

With this in mind, we can characterize thought as follows.

(1) Thought is the ability (*a*) to grasp the intelligible form of actual and possible states of affairs, and, (*b*) to perform certain operations on them.

---

a view'. Kripke (1976: 51–4) is hardly more sympathetic. He seems to believe that grasping a sense would involve grasping its infinite extensions, as such. But, given the total failure of all reductive attempts to cope with qualia, would it be very surprising if something similar were true for our fundamental intellectual capacities?

[23] Sane readers might wonder what this rules out, but it is inconsistent with any Kantian view that thinks that all empirical discrimination is a function solely of the way our minds are constructed, such that none of our discriminations can be literally imputed to the world as it is in itself. This appears to be Putnam's position: '"Objects" do not exist independently of conceptual schemes. We cut up the world into objects when we introduce one or other scheme of description. Since the objects *and* the signs are alike *internal* to the scheme of description, it is possible to say what matches what' (Putnam 1981: 52).

(2) Performing these operations requires the existence of a syntactic structure, part of which corresponds to the structures of the states of affairs themselves (that is, to such things as objects, properties, and relations) and part of which concerns the operations of thought that can be performed on the expressions of states of affairs: these are the syncategorematic concepts formalized in logic, such as negation, conjunction, and implication.

(3) The ability to carry out the above normally requires the existence of some system of representations that correspond to the various components.

I want to add to these two further conditions that might seem to be in tension with one another.

(4) There is no reductive account possible of (1) in terms of operations on the representations referred to in (3), nor of the functional role of the same, nor of any other purely physical processes.

(5) Although thought is about grasping the intelligible form of things, it often merely *aspires* to this. Thoughts can be difficult to grasp or formulate, even when they are one's own.

These last two propositions are somewhat in tension with each other because the former is a firm rejection of physicalism, whereas the latter seems to be at odds with the Cartesian principle that mental contents are all 'clear and distinct'. I include (4) for the reasons I give in the transitional section above. (5) is included because it is true and it raises interesting issues for the non-reductionist.

If we reject a reductionist account, what illuminatingly can we say about thought? My opening remarks suggest that thoughts are the articulation of concepts, which are the intellectualized side of universals, properties, or objective similarities. What form does this intellectual realization take? One model is to take this as an irreducible grasping of an abstract entity of some sort—a property, universal, or meaning. The opposite pole is to treat the possession of a concept as essentially a dispositional state. The most straightforward version of the latter is a form of the reductionism that we have ruled out. Nevertheless, one could interpret the dispositional theory non-reductively, as involving an implicit awareness of the disposition and its natural unfolding. Understood in this way, it is not obviously different from the other conception.[24] The abstract entity that one grasps 'contemplatively' in being aware of a universal (etc.) is something the grasping of which has behavioural consequences: it is an *intensional* entity, that is, one which comprehends the possible objects that

---

[24] Peacocke (1992) accounts for our grasp of concepts in terms of our having the 'possession conditions' associated with them. These conditions are capacities, and, hence, broadly dispositional. My reservation about this account for my present purposes is that it does not seem to me to deal directly enough with the *experience* of understanding. When we think, we do in some way apprehend as a whole the conditions associated with a particular concept, even though we are only exercising some of them. It is here that there is irreducible mystery, as there is in our experience of qualia.

would be its instances, and, hence, has implications for how one should classify things. It is at this point that (5), which says that not all our apprehensions of thought contents are transparent, becomes relevant. The contemplative model, on a Cartesian, if not on a Platonic, conception, would lead one to expect that all thoughts were transparent.[25] But the dispositional account does not have this consequence, for the content of a disposition is open-ended, and someone might grasp its general 'sense of direction' without having a transparent conception of exactly what it includes. It is tempting to characterize the dispositional conception as teleological: it is possible to have a sense of what one is aiming at without being able to make it wholly explicit. It is also possible to believe that there is something one is aiming at when there is not.

So far, my concern has been with the relation between thought and general concepts. There is an important question, however, about the effect of reference to particulars on the ontology of thought. This is the issue of *externalism*, and it will preoccupy us for the rest of this section.

4.2 Does the Ontology of Thought Necessarily Involve the World?

Russell believed objects of reference were internal to thoughts, and drew the conclusion that we could only refer to things that were contents of our own minds, such as our sense data (Russell 1912: 73–4). This way he could combine the doctrine that objects are parts of thoughts with the natural assumption that thoughts are wholly internal to the mind. But, of course, there must be some account of how we can talk about, and, in some sense, refer to, external objects. Russell's account of this is his famous doctrine of definite descriptions. Unfortunately, this account is not intuitively satisfying.

Definite descriptions are too loose for purposes of reference, in the sense that, knowing that something is *the unique F*, of itself, still usually leaves one not knowing *which object it is* that is the unique *F*. What exactly is involved in knowing *which object* can seem puzzling: in a sense, if you know a uniquely identifying reference you know *which object*, namely the one and only one that satisfies that description. But it is clear that this is not intuitively adequate. This is brought out by the way it usually makes sense and is often quite natural to follow a definite description by an expression like 'whatever (or whoever) that may be'. For example, 'the first man to

---

[25] The Platonic conception, as shown, for example, in the *Meno* is both contemplative and allows for ignorance. Descartes does not seem to allow for this, but this is not simply an oversight. Descartes is attempting to say what it is for the mind to apprehend something, and he rightly tries to do this in terms of conscious understanding. This leaves oblique, unconscious, or incomplete understanding problematic.

climb Mount Everest, whoever that may be'. To respond to a request to know who did it by repeating the definite description would be a (bad) joke. In a way, looking for *which one* is just looking for more information about that individual, but this does not seem to be simply quantitative: there seems to be a point at which one pins down *which*, which is not simply a matter of quantity of information. What this point is, we shall see later.

This inadequacy has led more recent philosophers to be more daring. They have held on to Russell's claim that referential thoughts are impossible in the absence of their referents, while also retaining the common-sense belief that we can focus determinately on specific objects in the external world. This has the consequence that the objects to which we refer in the external world are parts of the thoughts by which we refer to them, and, consequently, that we could not have those very thoughts in the absence (in the sense of non-existence) of those particular objects. As we can never be absolutely sure of the existence of those external objects that we think exist, it may turn out that we are not thinking thoughts when we think we are. This is what I mean, in this context, by *externalism*.[26]

This version of the Russellian theory extended to take in external objects—generally known as the theory of *direct reference*—faces certain problems. Gareth Evans convincingly criticized what he called the *photographic model* of direct reference, according to which it is sufficient for a name to designate an object that there be an appropriate causal connection between the object and the use of the name (Evans 1982: 76–85). Evans maintained that Russell was right to insist that 'it is not possible for a person to have a thought about something unless he knows which particular individual in the world he is thinking about' (Evans 1982: 44), and a causal connection alone does not constitute such knowledge. This, Evans concludes, shows that Frege was right to think that names must have senses, which are 'modes of presentation' under which the thinker thinks of the object named. There is something disturbing here. According to this theory, an object's being presented under a sense consists of two components. These are an appropriate causal relation, and a sense, which is a true description of the thing. Evans thinks that the existence of a causal connection between object and thought is not enough to constitute a thinker's knowledge of the object: presumably because a brute causal connection does not constitute a genuine grasp on the object by the thinker: it is too external. But how can adding to this a sense, which is only a description of the object, and which, we have seen, is the kind of thing that provokes the response 'whichever that

---

[26] Of course, I am dealing here only with arguments for an externalist theory of *reference* I am not directly answering the claim that most or all empirical predicates, such as figure in non-referential descriptions, have externalistic meaning. The completely general version of the thesis, however, is closely associated with the theory that the inner workings are purely syntactic and all semantics is causal. This is a part of the kind of computational reductionism which I have tried to give reasons for rejecting. The specific case of natural kinds and externalism, however, I simply do not have the space to discuss.

may be', give real knowledge of the object? There is in the notion of sense the idea of a description which genuinely and adequately captures the thing itself. How can this be? To see how there might be an answer to this we must consider the notion of a *world map*.

4.3 World Maps and Reference

The theory of reference is an issue in both the philosophy of language and the philosophy of mind. When considered as a part of the philosophy of language, the tendency is to consider the logical and semantic properties of types of sentence or proposition taken in isolation. Thus one may anguish over how to understand the logical properties of sentences in which apparent references fail, such as 'The present king of France is bald'. In fact, people do not assert or think contents of this kind out of the blue and in isolation. If someone were to assert such a sentence, you would wonder what was going on in their minds—what the background beliefs and thoughts were that might give sense to such a strange utterance. It is more natural in the context of the philosophy of mind to approach the issue in this latter way. The idea that problems in this area must be approached with regard to the setting of language in the context of communication, epistemic situation, and, hence, the philosophy of mind has had its supporters. Strawson's approach to reference via the *making* of *statements*—that is, via utterances—was the initial move in this direction. But since 'On Referring' (Strawson 1950), Strawson, Grice, Lockwood, and Morris, and doubtless others, have tried to develop a different notion of what is involved in picking out a particular object. They were generally approaching this via problems with identity statements. Morris reports the positions as follows (Morris 1984: 59).

Strawson . . . has us picture to ourselves a sort of knowledge-map. . . . On this map are many dots, each representing what he calls a 'cluster of identifying knowledge'. . . . they each represent some propertied individual about whom we have some knowledge. . . . Any proper name by which we refer to an object is written on the map adjacent to the dot which represents its bearer. From each dot radiate lines bearing predicate expressions. These represent all the propositions we are able to affirm of each object within the scope of our knowledge.

Strawson (1974) uses another image. A person is, among other things, a machine for receiving and storing information. The machine contains 'one card for each cluster of identifying knowledge in his possession'. New knowledge is entered on the appropriate card, and an identity statement, if accepted, leads to two cards being amalgamated into one. Lockwood has a similar idea of what he calls 'mental files'.

The trouble with all these accounts is that they take the notion of information *about an individual* for granted. This is built into the various images used in these accounts: a dot, a card, or a mental file represents a putative individual. But the question of what it is for some such representation to be *of* a particular determinate individual in this way is not properly answered. The notion common to these alternative approaches is that of a *world map*. A complete world map would represent every spatio-temporal object that existed in the world and would track it—space-time worm fashion—throughout its history. Such a map would enable one to individuate objects with complete accuracy, in so far as the objects were themselves properly individuated—that is, did not overlap. Thus one could always tell whether the *F* at *p*, *t*, was the same *F* as that at *p′*, *t′*, by seeing whether they were part of the same space-time worm. And if someone responded to 'the first man to climb Everest' with the question 'Who was that?' and one replied by providing all the information about Sir Edmund Hillary (or it might be Sherpa Tensing), including relations, that are to be found on a complete world map, then it would make no sense to respond to *that* description with 'But who was he?'

Presumably, only God could have such a complete map of the world, but lesser beings might have lesser, but similar, maps. There are three ways in which a world map might be incomplete. First, it might be restricted in the region of space and/or time it covered. Secondly, though it might be unrestricted up to the present, it might fail to be complete by lacking the future. Thirdly, it might be patchy in its coverage of whatever region it encompassed. The world map of a human being would be restricted in all these ways, being a map of the environs, both spatially and temporally, of a particular individual, so being regionally restricted, and running only to the present, and with more gap than content for most of the objects represented in it. The primary information we possess about other objects is fragmentary, but, by augmenting this by common-sense assumptions about how the world works—for example, by assuming that the chair in the next room is not mysteriously replaced by an exact replica whenever I am not watching it—we can fill in many of the gaps. *This pragmatic and implicit completing of maps is essential to give determinacy of objects.* With these assumptions of spatio-temporal locality and common-sense extrapolation in construction, we can imagine how a normal finite subject could possess what might be called a *personally adequate* world map. Such a map is sufficient to give its owner enough information about the different objects with which he has to deal for him to know which of them is which, and to which of them new pieces of information relate. So we are not in danger of confusing the major dramatis personae in our lives, even including the historical ones that we know about only by report. Our map also enables us to recognize new information that did not apply to anything already in our map, but which was not inconsistent with what we already knew, as indicating the presence of an object not so far recorded. We can then start up a new file or life-track. Thus world maps solve the 'which object?' problem, for locating an object within such a map, in the standard case, individuates it adequately. It is no longer empty to say that we individuate objects by their dossiers, for now we have an account of what it is for a dossier to be *of* a particular object.

On one level—or, perhaps, in certain company—the postulation of such maps for subjects would seem obvious: it is difficult to see, for example, how any cognitive psychologist could manage without such an idea. But I am not sure how far it has been noticed that such an idea constitutes a threat to a traditional approach to reference. What I have claimed is that a subject's map, in respect to the regions and objects for which it is 'adequate', individuates objects, so that he is in a position to know which object he himself is speaking or thinking about, and, normally, which objects his interlocutors are referring to. Knowing *which object*, in an intuitively adequate sense, is a matter of being able to pick it out from the objects in one's map, or, if it is not already present, being able to set up a new 'dossier' or 'path', with a distinct identity. Does the existence of such maps depend on the existence of the objects they represent? That you cannot have reference without existence—that reference is an extensional, not intentional relation—is a dogma of analytic theory of reference, but there seems to be nothing in what I have said about the maps which requires that the world mapped be the actual world. Indeed, the notion of a complete map, with which I started, was equivalent to the description of any possible world; it seems very similar to what Plantinga (1974) calls a 'world book': or, perhaps, his world books are one possible form that a world map might take. There seems no reason why there should not be local maps and personally adequate maps of any world. There seems to be nothing to prevent the proverbial brain in a vat from having a personally adequate world map. Having just the same kind of putative information that we have, he will be able to individuate the putative objects in his notional world just as clearly as we can, and will know which of them to attribute new information to in just the same way as we do.[27] Given these possibilities, it would seem that these maps ought to consist of very complicated definite descriptions, with one for each entity, for such descriptions are not dependent on the entities they purportedly describe. But if descriptions lie at the root of all individuation in this way, does it not commit us to a descriptive theory of names, with all its notorious problems? The model of identificatory thought emerging, however, is not accurately represented as a set of definite descriptions. Although a map could be represented in this way at any given time, the dynamic process of its development must be conceived differently. If the map were thought of as consisting of descriptions through time, any new piece of information relating to an object already in the map would require that one identify the relevant description and 'reopen' it and add the information. The process of thought behind this could not be represented in Frege–Russell terms, for the subject would be recurring to the object anaphorically in a way that neither employed a logically proper name, nor was already within the scope of the brackets of the definite description. We must take a brief look at what may have gone wrong in modern theories of naming and reference. Indeed, is it not strange that reference is treated as extensional while propositional attitudes are intentional? It is allowed that one can believe in, worship, fear, or love Zeus, but one cannot refer to him. Surely, there must be a sense of 'pick out' in which one can pick him out

---

[27] It is important that I am assuming that descriptive content can be treated internalistically. See n. 30.

in order to do these other things, and is it not likely that this is, in our epistemological predicament in the world, more fundamental a form of reference than any other?[28]

4.4 Names, Background Descriptions, and Anaphora

The suggestion is that, in order to avoid a descriptive theory of names, some serious reinterpretation of the philosophy of language is required. To see how to begin on this, it is helpful to look at the way Mill's theory of names has been misused in modern controversy. Mill is treated as having held that proper names work semantically by direct reference, that is, by bringing their objects into the proposition. But in Mill's own writing the distinction between descriptive meaning and descriptive background gets blurred. Mill thought that a name, such as 'Dartmouth', had no connotation, that is, no descriptive meaning, but he did not think that one could think thoughts using it without a decent background knowledge of English geography. Proper names are mere labels, but they presuppose background information.

If, like the robber in the Arabian Nights, we make a mark with chalk on a house to enable us to know it again, the mark has a purpose, but it has not properly any meaning. . . . When we impose a proper name, we perform an operation in some degree analogous to what the robber intended in chalking the house. We put a mark, not indeed upon the object itself, but, so to speak, upon the idea of the object. A proper name is but an unmeaning mark which we connect in our minds with the idea of the object. . . . By [a name's] enabling [the hearer] to identify the individuals, we may connect them with information previously possessed by him; by saying This is York, we may tell him that it contains the Minster. But this is in virtue of what he had previously heard concerning York; not by any thing implied in the name. (Mill 1949: I. ii. 5, p. 22)

Those who cite Mill on this topic tend to emphasize the fact that names are marks with purpose but no meaning, and mere labels, and to ignore the claim that their role is to label the object *via the conception of that object the subject has,* and to connect new information with the information already held about the same object—in the more modern jargon, to put it into the right dossier. Emphasis on the labelling function tends to give support to the thought that there can be no naming in the absence of an object. But labelling only seems to require that one have *an idea* of the object, and so whether Millian names are directly referential will depend on

[28] The standard Fregean reply to this is that, in opaque contexts such as those created by propositional attitudes, one refers to the sense of an expression, not to its normal reference. But that is no help to extensionalists here. If one holds that the sense of a name is essentially a mode of presentation of the reference, then if there is no reference, there will be no sense, so this cannot help us in the case of Zeus. If, on the other hand, one treats the sense as not depending on the reference for its existence, it will be the same kind of thing as the descriptions that appear in the dossiers on objects that form the basis for the world maps discussed above.

whether one can have *an idea of an object* if there is no object. This depends, I claim, on whether we can answer the 'which object?' question in a way that avoids direct reference. I think that the ideas found above give us the materials to do so.

How has this misconception about Mill arisen? Mill does not think that names have meaning, but neither does he regard them as having the foundational role in the nature of language that Frege and Russell impute to them: there is nothing in Mill to suggest that '*Fa*', where '*a*' is a name, is the archetypal form of the sentence or the thought—indeed, there is no notion of 'the logical form' of sentences or thoughts. Proper names are just one type of word among many. It is only when Mill's theory of the meaninglessness of names is combined with the fundamentality of names that anything of ideological interest arises.

A Fregean semantics models the language on a domain. Only if the speaker is acquainted with the domain does he fully understand the language. If the domain is the positive integers, or one's own experience, then there is no problem, for the objects in the domain are given completely and, in a sense, a priori. But if the intended domain is the external world and if one's understanding of what is in the world is in a state of permanent development, then the domain of one's discourse is constantly changing. New names are introduced, but on the back of what had previously been descriptions.

Suppose that, at a certain point in the development of my world map, I get the information that there is something F at p, t. Later, as more information comes in, it becomes clear that this is not a phase of any of the other objects I have previously recognized, but is a new object of which I begin to build up a conception, and I finally reach a point at which it is natural to give it a name, say 'Fred'. (This situation might be one in which I am coming to recognize and individuate animals in a wild environment.) If we think of the accumulated description as 'the unique ϕ', we can say that:

the unique ϕ is ($=$) Fred.

But we say this as a way of introducing a new name and a newly grasped individual, not as a way of identifying the unique ϕ with something already given. But neither am I saying that 'Fred', like Evans's 'Julius', means *whoever* was the unique ϕ (Evans 1982: 31 ff.).[29] Objects are being discovered and names are being introduced on the backs of descriptions, but not just as going proxy for the descriptions, because the descriptive background is already enough to pick out the object on the speaker's map. It is not clear to me that this process of development can be captured within a Frege–Russell conception of language. The language is modifying its domain or model as it progresses: formally speaking, this looks like simply stopping and beginning again with a new language. The 'informal' but essential and rational pattern of thought

---

[29] Evans introduces the 'descriptive name' 'Julius' to designate *whoever* invented the zip.

that carries one through this process of necessary revision cannot be captured in modern formal logic.

In fact, descriptions are rarely used in a purely Russellian way, with a genuine agnosticism or openness about referential intent. Such expressions are usually employed either as explicitly relating to some dossier, or in anticipation of finding such an allocation, even if one does not yet know which, or suspects the appropriate one has not yet been set up. When the detective says 'The murderer (whoever he was, understood) was a cunning brute', this *may* just be a comment that there is a cunning, brutal murderer; but it is far more likely that this is an early move in building up an identifying picture. It is, in that sense, intended referentially. If this is the case, then definite descriptions are more like statements beginning 'Some F is . . .'—where this means 'Some (particular) F is . . .', and the 'particular F' invokes the appropriate dossier—than they are like quantified expressions. The force of the 'particular' in 'Some particular F is . . .' is as an expression of the possibility of taking up the reference to *that* object again, in a way that one cannot when a normal quantified expression has been closed. It is, that is, the expression of a kind of anaphora for which modern formal logic does not allow. This will also, of course, be true of the senses that present names. If some version of the 'dossier' or 'world map' theory of reference is the only way to answer the 'which object?' question, and if the component descriptions of a dossier have this identificatory form, as it seems they must if they are directed at a particular object, then it looks as if reference can only be understood within an Aristotelian theory of natural language, of the sort presented by Sommers (1982). This is, no doubt, too speculative a conclusion to be secure, or win many converts, but it remains the case that the modern approach to the form of language does not appear to capture the dynamic processes of thought.[30] Nor, as must be obvious, is this conclusion independent of the main purpose of this discussion, namely to show that we can produce a conception of an object which can be treated referentially without the truth of the reference being presupposed. It shows how a conception of an object can be built up from a descriptive kind of information, independently of whether anything actual satisfies it.

4.5 Causation and Reference

Before one takes seriously such suggestions for dramatic reforms in the theory of reference, one will first need to see a response to an obvious objection to any internalist theory of the kind that I am defending: namely that internalism ignores the role of

---

[30] Grice (1961) suggests that this process of identification is part of pragmatics, not of the semantics. This would save the orthodox semantics, but at the cost of making it exclude one of the fundamental features of our thought about objects and the development of our conception of them. I cannot discuss this issue properly here.

causation in determining reference. *Which object* one is referring to depends, at least in part, on which object stands in some appropriate causal relationship to one's act of thinking or referring. I argued in Section 4.3 that causal relation plus an ordinary description masquerading as a sense was not enough to give the thinker a proper knowledge of the object he was thinking about. I augmented the descriptive notion of sense with the richer conception that goes with placing an object within a world map. It does not follow that the brute causal element is eliminable. Evans (1985) argues that the existence of an accidental 'descriptive fit' between the information and some object in the world that had nothing to do with the causal origin of that information would not sustain reference to the object. He concludes that, because of this latter condition, if there is no object in the appropriate causal relation, then there is no referential act.

It seems to me that Evans makes a crucial mistake about the causal requirement. He sees it externalistically, as the requirement that the information in the dossier be in fact causally connected to an appropriate object. In fact the causal requirement is part of what is in the dossier: that is, when one thinks of an object referentially as *the thing that is F, G, H, etc.*, that that thing is responsible for our thinking of it in that way is taken for granted in the conception of it: that is, one thinks of it as *the thing that is F, G, H, etc. and which is responsible for our having the concept of something which is F, G, H etc.* It is part of our internal conception of the object of thought that our thought of it depends in some way (most naturally assumed to be causally) on it. That this is so is shown by the fact that the causal requirement is discoverable by philosophical analysis; it is built into our conception of what it is for something to be an object of referential thought. Evans is wrong, therefore, to think that the causal condition is some sort of a ground for externalism: it is part of our conception of thinking of something. So if A has a conception of *the thing which is F, G, H, etc. and is responsible for his having the concept of something which is F, G, H, etc.*, and if there is something corresponding to that conception (and so is, *ipso facto*, the cause of his having that conception), then the intentional object in the map and the object in the world are the same. But the existence of an adequately individuated object in the map does not depend on there being the actual object, for reasons that I gave when setting up the notion of a world map. Evans is confusing the extensionality (and externalism) of truth and of what is required for successful reference to an actual thing, with what is required for the existence of a genuine act of reference, with a well-defined intentional object.

The causal requirement does not, therefore, indicate any form of externalism.[31]

---

[31] Wiggins (1995) strengthens this conclusion. He argues that when a non-existent is referred to in an adequately full descriptive context, we do not have what Evans (1982, ch. 10) calls ' "as if" reference', but 'reference to an "as if" object'—which I take to be another way of saying that it is to a non-existent intentional object.

4.6 Conclusion: The Ontology of Thought

My very tentative conclusion is as follows. One cannot eliminate or analyse the notion that thought involves a grasp on entities essentially graspable as universal. Often this grasp is explicit, but in some cases it is more of an aspiration towards a concept. Representations and syntax are necessary to structure these apprehensions into thoughts, and a world map is needed to give it a grasp on empirical reality. Although real external things are usually the objects of such thoughts, they are not built into the thoughts, as externalists claim. The upshot of this chapter as a whole is that the traditional approaches to ontology in both perception and thought take for granted very dubious assumptions. In the case of perception, this is the assumption that common sense and moderate direct realism are incompatible with the sense datum theory; and in the case of thought, it is that reference is an external relation, not an intentional mental act. Those usually unquestioned assumptions deserve more examination than I have been able to give them here.

References

Ayer, A. J. (1968). *The Origins of Pragmatism*. London: Macmillan.

Ayers, M. (1991). *Locke*, i: *Epistemology*. London: Routledge.

Balog, K. (1999). 'Conceivability, Possibility, and the Mind–Body Problem'. *Philosophical Review*, 108: 497–528.

Bradley, F. H. (1930). *Appearance and Reality*. Oxford: Clarendon Press.

Broad, C. D. (1923). *Scientific Thought*. London: Paul, Trench, Trubner.

Chalmers, D. (1996). *The Conscious Mind*. New York: Oxford University Press.

Chisholm, R. (1957). *Perceiving: A Philosophical Study*. Ithaca, NY: Cornell University Press.

Crane, T. (2000). 'The Origins of Qualia', in Crane and Patterson (2000: 169–94).

—— (2001). *Elements of Mind*. Oxford: Oxford University Press.

—— and S. Patterson (eds.) (2000). *History of the Mind–Body Problem*. London: Routledge.

Davidson, D., and J. Hintikka (1969). *Words and Objections*. Dordrecht: Reidel.

Dennett, D. (1987). 'Three Kinds of Intentional Psychology', in Dennett, *The Intentional Stance*. Cambridge, Mass.: MIT Press, 43–81.

Dretske, F. (2000). *Perception, Knowledge and Belief*. Cambridge: Cambridge University Press.

Evans, G. (1982). *Varieties of References*, ed. John McDowell. Oxford: Clarendon Press.

—— (1985). 'The Causal Theory of Names', in Evans, *Collected Papers*. Oxford: Clarendon Press, 1–24.

Foster, J. (2000). *The Nature of Perception*. Oxford: Oxford University Press.

Grice, H. P. (1961). 'The Causal Theory of Perception'. *Proceedings of the Aristotelian Society*, suppl. vol. 35: 121–52.

—— (1969). 'Vacuous Names', in Davidson and Hintikka (1969: 118–45).

Hornsby, J. (1997). *Simple Mindedness*. Cambridge, Mass.: Harvard University Press.

Jackson, F. (1975). 'On the Adverbial Analysis of Visual Experience'. *Metaphilosophy*, 6: 127–35.

—— (1982). 'Epiphenomenal Qualia'. *Philosophical Quarterly*, 32: 127–36.

Kaplan, D. (1978). 'The Logic of Demonstratives'. *Journal of Philosophical Logic*, 8: 81–98.

Kripke, S. (1976). *Wittgenstein and Rule-Following*. Oxford: Clarendon Press.

Lockwood, M. (1971). 'Identity and Reference', in Munitz (1971: 19–211).

Lycan, W. G. (1987). *Consciousness*. Cambridge, Mass.: MIT Press.

Mace, C. A. (ed.) (1957). *British Philosophy in Mid-Century*. London: Allen & Unwin.

McTaggart, J. M. E. (1927). *The Nature of Existence*, vol. ii. Cambridge: Cambridge University Press.

Martin, M. G. F. (2000). 'Beyond Dispute: Sense-Data, Intentionality and the Mind–Body Problem', in Crane and Patterson (2000: 195–231).

Mill, J. S. (1949). *A System of Logic*. London: Longman.

Moore, G. E. (1957). 'Visual Sense-Data', in Mace (1957: 203–11).

Morris, T. V. (1984). *Understanding Identity Statements*. Aberdeen: Aberdeen University Press.

Munitz, M. (ed.) (1971). *Identity and Individuation*. New York: New York University Press.

Myro, G. (1993). 'Thinking', in Robinson (1993: 27–38).

Peacocke, C. (1992). *A Study of Concepts*. Cambridge, Mass.: MIT Press.

Plantinga, A. (1974). *The Nature of Necessity*. Oxford: Clarendon Press.

Price, H. H. (1932). *Perception*. London: Methuen.

Putnam, H. (1981). *Reason, Truth and History*. Cambridge: Cambridge University Press.

Robinson, H. (1982). *Matter and Sense*. Cambridge: Cambridge University Press.

—— (1989). 'A Dualist Account of Embodiment', in J. R. Smythies and J. Beloff (eds.), *The Case for Dualism*. Charlottesville: University Press of Virginia, 43–57.

—— (1993). *Objections to Physicalism*. Oxford: Clarendon Press.

—— (1994). *Perception*. London: Routledge.

—— (2003). 'Dualism', in S. Stich and T. Warfield (eds.), *The Blackwell Guide to the Philosophy of Mind*, 85–101.

—— (forthcoming *a*). 'Dualism', in *Stanford Encyclopaedia of Philosophy*.

Russell, B. (1905). 'On Denoting'. *Mind*, 14.

—— (1912). *The Problems of Philosophy*. Oxford: Oxford University Press.

Snowdon, P. (1982). 'Perception, Vision and Causation'. *Proceedings of the British Academy*, 68: 455–79.

Sommers, F. (1982). *The Logic of Natural Languages*. Oxford: Clarendon Press.

Steward, H. (1997). *The Ontology of Mind: Events, Processes and States*. Oxford: Clarendon Press.

Strawson, P. (1950). 'On Referring'. *Mind*, 59: 320–44.

—— (1974). *Subject and Predicate in Logic and Grammar*. London: Methuen.

Tye, M. (1998). 'Mental States, Adverbial Theory of', in E. Craig (ed.), *Routledge Encyclopaedia of Philosophy*. London: Routledge, i: 314–17.

Wiggins, D. (1995). 'The Kant–Frege–Russell View of Existence: Toward the Rehabilitation of the Second Level View', in W. Sinnot-Armstrong with D. Raffman and N. Asher (eds.), *Modality, Morality and Belief: Essays for Ruth Barcan Marcus*. New York: Cambridge University Press.

Yolton, J. (1984). *Perceptual Acquaintance from Descartes to Reid*. Oxford: Basil Blackwell.

CHAPTER 18

SUPERVENIENCE, EMERGENCE, REALIZATION, REDUCTION

JAEGWON KIM

1. INTRODUCTION

SUPERVENIENCE, emergence, realization, and reduction are among the concepts that have played—and continue to play—prominent roles in metaphysics during the past several decades, in particular in the debates over the mind–body problem and the status of the special sciences. One of their principal applications has been in characterizing the ways in which mental properties or phenomena are related to physical properties and processes. Thus, it has been claimed, and widely accepted, that the mentality of a creature is 'supervenient' on its physical nature in the sense that once a creature's physical nature is fixed, its mental nature is thereby fixed. It has also been suggested that consciousness and rationality are among the 'emergent' characteristics of complex organisms and systems in that these are 'novel' systemic properties that in some sense transcend the simpler properties of their constituent parts. Opposed to this emergentist view is reductionism, the position that mentality, and other higher-level features of complex systems, are reducible to, and explainable in terms of, their underlying physical–biological properties. Another relation that has been invoked in this connection is that of 'realization': it has been claimed, especially by those who hold the functional view of the mind, that psychological properties, though distinct from and irreducible to physical–biological properties, are nonetheless 'realized' or 'implemented' by them, rather like the way computational processes as characterized at the program level are realized, or implemented, by the electronic processes in an actual physical computer.

It is easily seen that these relations, supervenience, emergence, realization, and reduction, have applications beyond the mind–body problem. In fact, the notion of supervenience is generally thought to have made its first appearance in ethical theory,[1] in the idea that the moral character of a thing (an act, object, or agent) is fixed by its natural, or non-moral, character—or equivalently, it is not possible for two things to be exactly identical in all non-moral respects and yet differ in some moral respect (say, one is morally desirable but the other not). And it was an important implication of classical atomism that wholes that are alike in all atomic respects—that is, they are put together in the same way from identical atoms—must be alike overall. That is, the properties of a whole supervene on, or are determined by, the properties and relations holding for their atomic constituents. This is an instance of 'mereological supervenience'. According to British emergentists, like Samuel Alexander, C. Lloyd Morgan, and C. D. Broad, the phenomenon of emergence is not limited to mental properties; they claimed that even simple properties of chemical compounds, such as solubility in water or inflammability, were emergent properties since these properties could not, they thought, be inferred from the properties of a compound's constituent atoms or molecules. More famously, the emergentists claimed that life emerged out of physico-chemical processes, and that mentality emerged out of complex biological processes. These 'higher' phenomena were thought to emerge when, only when, appropriate 'basal' conditions are present, and yet they are not reducible to, or predictable from, information solely concerning these lower-level processes. The idea of realization also lends itself to generalization. Some believe in a hierarchy of realizations: chemical properties are realized by atomic–molecular properties and relations, biological properties are realized by physico-chemical properties, and mental properties are realized by neural–biological properties (Lycan 1987). Questions of reducibility have both a metaphysical dimension and a scientific-theoretical dimension. Are consciousness and intentionality reducible to brain processes or behaviour dispositions? Are biological functions reducible to physico-chemical

---

[1] It is standard to trace the idea of supervenience to G. E. Moore (1922) and the term 'supervenience' to R. M. Hare (1952). This, however, seems not entirely correct. C. Lloyd Morgan, a leading emergentist, was liberally using 'supervenience' and its cognates in Morgan (1923), roughly in its present philosophical sense. The Latin 'supervenire' was used by Leibniz in a similar sense, and even earlier uses of the core notion can be found. What is true, I believe, is that our current use of the concept is continuous with its use by Hare and others around the mid-20th century.

processes? These are metaphysical questions. And there are parallel questions about scientific theories: Are the psychological and cognitive sciences reducible to brain science? Are biological theories reducible to physics and chemistry?

What this shows is that supervenience, emergence, realization, and reduction are 'topic-neutral' relations that have applications to problems in various fields of philosophy. This is why it is an important task of metaphysics to clarify their natures and interrelationships. It is also important to investigate how these concepts are related to other concepts of central philosophical interest, such as causation and explanation, and my discussion will involve some consideration of these further concepts.

2. Supervenience

2.1 The Core Idea

One important attraction of the supervenience concept, which is responsible for the quick currency it has gained in the past three decades, is the fact that its core idea can be intuitively explained and easily grasped. Imagine a sculptor working on a statue. It is arduous physical work involving chiselling away at a large block of marble for weeks on end. When the physical work is finished, his work is finished; there is no *further* work of 'attaching' desired aesthetic properties, say elegance and expressiveness, to the finished piece of stone. The aesthetic character of a sculpture is wholly fixed once its physical properties are fixed; that is, *aesthetic properties supervene on physical properties.* If the sculptor is unhappy with the aesthetic quality of his creation and wishes to improve it, he must get out his chisel and hammer and do more physical work on the stone; it is only by changing its physical character that its aesthetic character can be improved or otherwise altered. Another idea, familiar from science fiction, is the idea of a replica of a person. Suppose some mad scientist wants to make a perfect replica of you, a creature who is indistinguishable from you in every respect, someone who is not only physically just like you but also exactly like you in all mental respects, that is, someone who has your memory and belief, your likes and dislikes, your life goals and projects. In order to accomplish this, all that the scientist needs to do is to make an exact *physical* replica of you; once a physical replica has been produced, it will also exhibit all of your psychological traits, dispositions, and capacities. Perhaps, creating an exact duplicate of your brain is the only conceivable way of creating a duplicate of your mind. If that is what we think, that is because we believe in mind–body supervenience, the thesis that the mentality of a person supervenes on, or is wholly determined, by the nature of his or her physical being.

It is convenient to think of supervenience as a relation between two families, or sets, of properties, supervenient family *A* and the base (or subvenient) family *B*. *A* could be a set of psychological properties and *B* a set of biological–physical properties; or *A* could be a set of moral properties and *B* a set of naturalistic, or non-moral, properties. The basic idea of supervenience can be explained in two ways: (i) things cannot differ in respect of *A*-properties (supervenient properties) unless they differ in respect of some *B*-properties (the base properties)—that is, indiscernibility in respect of *B*-properties entails indiscernibility in respect of *A*-properties. Thus, under the supervenience of moral on non-moral properties, two persons who are indiscernible in all non-moral respects cannot be unlike in some moral respect—say, one is a morally admirable person and the other not. Similarly, under mind–body supervenience, a person and her perfect physical replica cannot differ in some psychological respect, say in that one of them is experiencing a headache while the other isn't. (ii) A second way of explaining the core idea of supervenience is in terms of 'determination': if *A*-properties supervene on *B*-properties, any object's *B*-properties will determine all of its *A*-properties. The microphysical character of a world will determine the whole character of the world. The biological–physical character of an organism will determine its psychological character. 'Dependence' is a near enough converse of 'determination': thus, instead of saying that the biological–physical nature of a creature determines its mentality, we may say that its mentality 'depends' on its physical–biological nature.

2.2 Weak, Strong, and Global Supervenience

If the moral supervenes on the non-moral, then, as we saw, there could not be two persons who are exactly alike in all non-moral, or 'descriptive', respects and yet differ in some moral respect. This means that, given that St Francis was a good person, anyone who is just like St Francis in all non-moral respects (say, courage, generosity, benevolence, honesty, etc.) must also be a good person. In the familiar 'possible world' parlance, there is no possible world in which two things are alike in all non-moral respects and yet unlike in some moral respect.

This idea is now standardly called *weak* supervenience and can be defined thus:

> *A*-properties *weakly supervene* on *B*-properties just in case there is no possible world in which *B*-indiscernible things are *A*-discernible—or, equivalently, things that are alike in *B*-properties in any given world are alike in *A*-properties in that world.

Where *S* is any set of properties, we say that two things are '*S*-discernible' just in case there is some property in *S* such that one of the two has it while the other does not, and that they are 'S-indiscernible' just in case they are alike in respect of all properties in S.

The reason that the supervenience relation defined above is called 'weak' is that it is not robust enough to give us determination. We can easily see that it is not strong enough to express the idea that the moral goodness of a person is determined, or fixed, by that person's non-moral, or naturalistic, properties. For it is possible under supervenience as defined that St Francis, for all the worthy traits of character that he actually had (such as, say, benevolence, empathy, generosity, and honesty), might not have been a good person. Weak supervenience requires only that anyone who has the same non-moral properties (including the same traits of character) that St Francis had must be *like* St Francis in respect of being a good person, and *this leaves open the possibility that neither of them is a good person*. The weak supervenience of being a good person on traits of character only means that persons with the same character traits *must come out the same* in point of being a good person; so they could be both good or both not good, the only thing precluded being that one is good while the other isn't. This means that there is a possible world that is just like this world in all non-moral, descriptive, and factual respects but in which St Francis and others just like him are all morally reprehensible persons. Weak supervenience, therefore, is not strong enough to allow us to say that traits of character 'determine' whether a person is good or not good. For the same reason, if mentality only weakly supervenes on biological–physical properties, that would not warrant the assertion that a creature's physical–biological nature 'fixes' its psychological character. Weak mind–body supervenience only tells us that creatures that are physically alike must be psychologically alike.

To put this somewhat formally, weak supervenience allows the following possibility: object x has in world w the same B-properties that object y has in world w^*, and yet x has, in w, A-properties that y does not have in w^*. Under weak supervenience, therefore, the requirement 'Things that are B-alike must be A-alike' applies only *within* each possible world, not *across* different possible worlds. This means that weak supervenience lacks an important modal force required for the relation of determination or dependence: if traits of character determine whether or not a person is morally good, we expect that there are certain character traits such that anyone who has them *must* be a morally good person, that these traits *make* a person morally good. It cannot be that a person has all these 'good-making' characteristics and yet the question is still open as to whether that person is morally good.

Thus, we are led to a more strict supervenience relation, *strong* supervenience, which can be defined as follows:

> A-properties *strongly supervene* on B-properties just in case things that are alike in B-properties, *whether in the same or different possible worlds*, are alike in A-properties.

Another formulation of strong supervenience, which is equivalent to the foregoing under certain assumptions concerning property composition, is this:

> A-properties *strongly supervene* on B-properties just in case necessarily if anything x has an A-property, say F, then there is a B-property, say G, such that x has G, and *necessarily* anything that has G has F.[2]

The second formulation is useful in that it makes explicit the idea that when A-properties supervene on B-properties, each instance of an A-property, say, F, has a specific *subvenient base* property in B, say G, associated with it. So if pain supervenes on neural properties, a creature experiencing pain at a time must at that time instantiate some neural property such that anything instantiating this neural property must experience pain. Notice that this is consistent with multiple subvenient bases for any supervenient property. The subvenient base of pains in humans may be C-fibre activation; the base of pain in molluscs may be a quite different neural property, and we cannot a priori rule out the possibility of an inorganic base for pains in non-biological sentient systems. Similarly, it might be that someone is a good person because she is empathetic, generous, and kind, and another person is a good person because, though she lacks empathy and kindness, she is just, courageous, and honest. Thus, supervenience nicely accommodates the phenomenon sometimes called multiple realizability.

In the second formulation of strong supervenience the modal operator 'necessarily' occurs twice, and in any specific application the force of these operators needs to be made precise.[3] In particular, the interpretation of the second 'necessarily'—in 'necessarily anything that has G has F'—can be very important. Consider the mind–body case: If C-fibre stimulation is a subvenient base for pain, do we want to say that C-fibre stimulation is logically or metaphysically sufficient for pain, or that it is only nomologically sufficient for pain? Does mind–body supervenience hold with logical or metaphysical necessity (that is, in all possible worlds), or does it hold only with nomological (or, as some would put it, natural or physical) necessity (that is, in worlds that are like the reference world in its basic laws and ontology)? And on what basis can we decide which form of supervenience (if any) holds for the mental and the physical? These are among the most actively debated issues in current philosophy of mind (see e.g. Chalmers 1996).

It should be noted that weak supervenience, too, can be given a second definition along the lines of the second definition of strong supervenience, as follows:

> A-properties *weakly supervene* on B-properties if and only if necessarily if anything x has an A-property, say F, there is some B-property, say G, such that x has G, and anything that has G has F.

---

[2] For details, see Kim (1987) and McLaughlin (1995). Even if these two formulations are not equivalent in the strict sense, this is of little philosophical significance since there seem to be no interesting real-life applications in which one holds and the other doesn't.

[3] The same issues arise for the first formulation as well in the choice of the domain of possible worlds to be considered.

The only difference between strong and weak supervenience on these definitions is the fact that the definition of weak is lacking the second occurrence of 'necessarily' that appears in the definition of strong. The presence of this inner 'necessarily' in strong supervenience is what guarantees the stability of G–F covariance *across* possible worlds. Weak supervenience provides no such stability.

Another form of supervenience often employed in formulating physicalism is what is commonly called *global* supervenience. Weak and strong supervenience refer to individual objects, speaking of how their supervenient properties must covary with their subvenient properties. In contrast, global supervenience looks at whole worlds as units of comparison:

> A-properties *globally supervene* on B-properties if and only if worlds that are alike in B-properties must be alike in A-properties (or, as it is sometimes put, worlds in which the same B-facts hold must be alike in their A-facts).

Thus, physicalism has been stated as follows: Worlds that are physically indiscernible are psychologically indiscernible—in fact, physically indiscernible worlds are one and the same world (e.g. LePore and Loewer 1989; Jackson 1998).

There are various questions concerning the interpretation of global supervenience defined this way. For one thing, what does it mean to say that two worlds are alike in B-properties, say, physical properties? Consider a world that is like our world but which, in addition, contains non-physical spirits and ectoplasms (assuming that this world contains no such things). Should we say that this world and our world are physically alike (because as far as the physical portion is concerned they exactly coincide)? Or consider worlds that contain more or fewer physical things than our world but which are pretty much like ours in other physical respects (including basic physical laws). Should we say that they are physically different from this world just because they do not contain the same number of physical things (and so could be radically different mentally, even if global mind–body supervenience held)? However, for most purposes such questions can be set aside by only comparing worlds that have domains of the same cardinality or with the same individuals.[4]

2.3 Further Issues

It is evident that strong supervenience entails weak supervenience, but not conversely. We have already seen cases of weak supervenience that fail the requirements of strong supervenience. But what is the relation between strong supervenience and global supervenience?

---

[4] Horgan has proposed a further kind of supervenience, what he calls *superdupervenience* characterized as supervenience relations that have *naturalistically acceptable* explanations. See Horgan (1993b). However, there seems no need to think of this as a special supervenience relation; rather, it is best thought of as a variety of supervenience claims that meet a certain philosophical requirement (in Horgan's case a special reductive–naturalistic requirement).

It is easily seen that strong supervenience entails global supervenience (Kim 1984). But does global imply strong? It has sometimes been thought that the answer is no, that global supervenience is an essentially weaker relation than strong supervenience. The most salient apparent difference between them, which some philosophers have taken to be important, is this: while strong supervenience relates specific supervenient properties with specific base properties (so that every supervenient property has at least one base property that is sufficient for it), global supervenience appears more holistic in character and seems not to require property-to-property connections. For this reason, global supervenience has been favoured by those physicalists who think that strong supervenience is too close to physical reductionism, or that mental properties (especially, propositional attitudes) have a holistic dimension that precludes 'local' connections with physical properties (Chalmers 1996). However, the situation has turned out to be more complicated (Paull and Sider 1992; Kim 1993*b*; Stalnaker 1996). What is the case is this: global and strong supervenience are indeed equivalent if both the supervenient and base properties are restricted to intrinsic properties; or else if extrinsic properties are allowed in both sets of properties—in particular if, in addition to the usual Boolean operations, identity and quantification are allowed for property compositions (Barry Loewer, private communication; Paull and Sider 1992; Stalnaker 1996). The issues about the relationships between the three supervenience relations crucially depend on how we conceive of properties and modes of property composition (Bacon 1986; van Cleve 1989). Therefore, it is dubious at best that there is some kind of theoretical gain in using global rather than strong supervenience in formulating physicalism, or anything else. Global supervenience, however, provides us with a particularly succinct and striking way of expressing certain philosophical theses, including physicalism (Jackson 1998).

Supervenience is usually thought to include the idea of dependence or determination, and this has been my assumption. However, the foregoing definitions of the three supervenience relations make no reference to such metaphysical relations as determination or dependence. Rather, they only specify how two families of properties *covary* with each other—that is, how the distribution of one family of properties over the individuals of a world constrains, and is constrained by, the distribution of another family of properties. The relations as defined by these definitions are not asymmetric; they do not prohibit two families of properties from supervening, in any of the three senses, on each other, whereas we expect the relation of determination or dependence to be asymmetric. Nor does the intuitive idea of supervenience expressed by the slogan 'No difference in supervenient properties without a difference in subvenient properties' exclude mutual supervenience. As far as formal analysis is concerned, therefore, supervenience comes down strictly to relations of property covariance (Kim 1990). Where then does the idea of determination or dependence come from (Kim 1984; Grimes 1988; Post 1995)?

It is not likely that the idea of determination or dependence can somehow be coaxed out of property covariation alone. If we keep in mind the repeated failures to obtain causal dependence, or causal directionality, from property correlations alone, whether these are conceived as 'mere' Humean extensional correlations or modalized (e.g. 'lawlike') regularities, we should know better than to expect a 'deep' metaphysical relation like dependence to emerge from mere patterns of property covariation. This means that if you want to include a determination–dependence claim as part of a supervenience thesis, that claim must be explained and justified independently of the required pattern of property covariance. How such justification might proceed will of course depend on the specific supervenience claims at issue.

Consider, for example, normative supervenience—the supervenience of moral and other evaluative properties on non-moral, or descriptive–natural properties. Meta-ethical theories offer various possible explanations of why the supervenience holds, and in the process provide an account of the kind of dependence involved. Ethical naturalism, for example, says that moral properties are definable in terms of natural properties, and that is why the former supervene on the latter. Here the dependence involved would be definitional dependence (if that is a form of dependence). Ethical intuitionism would claim that the dependence here is apprehended by the special faculty of moral sense, and not further explainable; we morally intuit that, say, happiness optimization entails rightness, just as we directly sense colours and shapes. Some non-cognitivists would see supervenience as arising out of a certain consistency requirement on making recommendations and prescriptions. Or one might argue that normative supervenience is a consequence of the idea that normativity depends on evaluation, and that evaluation ultimately requires criteria stated in non-normative, non-evaluative terms.

That mental properties, especially the intrinsic ones,[5] covary with physical, in particular neural, properties has been widely recognized. But how do we explain mind–body covariations? Why is it that pain correlates with C-fibre activation, but not with neural processes of other kinds? Why is mentality manifested only in organisms with a complex neural system? Various mind–body theories on the scene can be thought of as responses to questions of this sort. Causal theorists—interactionists and epiphenomenalists—will explain mind–body regularities as grounded in causal regularities, and mind–body dependence as a form of causal dependence.[6] Emergentists will say that the emergence of the mental from the physical is in principle

---

[5] This qualification is motivated by considerations of 'wide-content' states, i.e. propositional attitudes like belief whose contents seemingly involve external objects and events, outside the subjects who hold these states. Mind–body supervenience can still be maintained by widening the supervenience base to include the physical environment of the subject.

[6] Serious interactionists will of course reject a pervasive one-way dependence of the mental on the physical. John Searle distinguishes between 'constitutive' and 'causal' supervenience, and regards mind–body supervenience as a case of causal supervenience (Searle 1992).

inexplicable, and that the dependence is not all one-way, there being 'downward' causation from the mental to the physical. Functionalists will say that mind–body supervenience is explained by the fact that mental properties, when they are realized, are physically realized, and that the dependence involved is one between a property and its realizers. We now turn to emergence and realization.

3. EMERGENCE AND MODELS OF REDUCTION

3.1 The Idea of Emergence

The idea of emergence is usually traced to John Stuart Mill's distinction between 'heteropathic' and 'homopathic' laws in *A System of Logic* (1843), but the term 'emergent' was introduced later by George Henry Lewes in his *Problems of Life and Mind* (1875) to mark off certain properties of complex systems that were regarded as specially noteworthy. The concept was further sharpened by British philosophers, like Samuel Alexander (1920), C. Lloyd Morgan (1923), and C. D. Broad (1925), and the doctrine of emergence, or emergentism, was propounded as a metaphysical view about the hierarchical structure of the natural world. Emergentism was also advanced by some as an overarching historical doctrine concerning the evolutionary developments of complex systems, like living organisms, with their 'novel' properties like life and mentality, from simpler and more basic physical systems and properties. In this chapter I will be chiefly concerned with the metaphysics of emergentism, not with its historical claims.[7]

Emergentists were probably the first to articulate what we may call a 'layered' model of reality. This model views the world as a hierarchically organized system stratified into 'levels' or 'orders' of entities and their properties, from the bottom level of the most basic bits of matter to higher levels consisting of increasingly complex structures composed of material particles. Thus, emergentism is a form of *ontological materialism* (or *physicalism*), the view that the contents of the world are exhausted by matter—bits of matter and complex systems wholly composed of bits of matter. When entities at the bottom level are configured into appropriate stable structures, atoms and molecules emerge. Living organisms and their 'vital' properties emerge when aggregates composed of atoms and molecules attain organizational complexity of an appropriate kind and degree. And in certain highly developed

---

[7] For an informative critical survey of British emergentism, see McLaughlin (1992).

organisms, sensations and consciousness emerge; and in still more complex organisms, thought and rationality emerge. According to the early emergentists, this is not only the picture of the world at a temporal cross-section, but it also depicts the actual evolutionary history of the world. There were some speculations about the direction in which the world is now headed—what higher emergent properties might be in store for us in the evolutionary future of the world (Alexander 1920; Morgan 1923).

A layered metaphysical scheme of the sort that the emergentists had in mind has become a ubiquitous assumption in contemporary philosophy, serving as an implicit backdrop for discussions of some central problems of philosophy of mind and philosophy of science. Expressions like 'levels of analysis', 'levels of description', and 'levels of explanation' are by now familiar idioms in primary scientific texts as well as philosophical writings. Commonly used terms like 'bottom-up', 'top-down', 'downward causation', 'higher-level', and 'lower-level' (as applied to concepts, laws, explanations, and the like) strongly suggest a ladder-like system of levels. The layered model, as noted, views reality as a structured hierarchy of levels, where each entity at any given level (higher than the bottom one) is taken to be wholly decomposable into entities belonging to the lower levels. Thus, the relation that generates the hierarchy is the mereological (or part–whole) relation. Parallel to this hierarchy of entities is another hierarchy, one of the properties of these entities. It is thought that each level has a set of properties that are characteristic of that level, namely the properties that make their first appearance at that level, like chemical properties at the level of molecules and biological properties at the level of cells and organisms. It is also commonly thought that physics is our basic science, in that it is in charge of the bottom level of basic physical particles and their properties, and that for each higher level there is a special science, perhaps more than one, that is responsible for investigating the entities and properties on that level.[8]

The most important metaphysical question about the layered model is how the properties characteristic of a given level are related to those at the adjacent levels, in particular those at the lower levels. A parallel question concerns the relationship between the sciences concerned with neighbouring levels. How are biological properties related to physico-chemical properties, and how is biology related to physics and chemistry? How are psychological properties related to biological and physico-chemical properties? And what is the relationship between the psychological–cognitive sciences and the neural–biological sciences? These are among the central questions currently debated in metaphysics, philosophy of mind, and philosophy of science.

---

[8] There are various questions and difficulties with the model as described, including the question whether the part–whole relation has the proper properties to generate hierarchies of the sort that the emergentists and others have in mind. For some discussion of these issues, see Kim (2002). See also Heil (2003). For a classic presentation of the layered scheme, from a global reductionist point of view, see Oppenheim and Putnam (1958).

3.2 Inter-Level Relationships: Supervenience, Emergence, and Reduction

Many will accept the supervenience of upper-level properties upon those at the lower levels in the following sense: the properties of any upper-level entity are entirely determined by its microproperties, that is, the properties of its constituents and the structural relationships that characterize them. In short, the character of a whole supervenes on its microstructure. This is the principle of *mereological supervenience* as applied to material systems.[9] The idea seems perfectly obvious and commonsensical: if you want to make a perfect duplicate of something, all you need to do is to put identical parts in identical structure. The principle is the metaphysical underpinning of industrial mass production; to make another '01 Ford Explorer, all you need to do is to assemble identical parts in identical structural configurations.

Supervenience, as we said, is widely accepted (see e.g. Horgan 1982, 1993*b*). But the question doesn't end there. As we saw, supervenience is not a 'deep' explanatory relation; it only indicates the presence of a dependence relation without telling us what it is. Emergentism is committed to supervenience: when the same basal conditions obtain, the same emergents must emerge. However, the heart of emergentism is the claim that some important upper-level properties are 'novel' properties over and above the properties at the lower levels, and that they are neither explainable nor predictable solely on the basis of information concerning their basal properties. This is what is thought to distinguish emergent properties from those that are 'resultant' or 'consequential'—properties of wholes that are derivable, and hence predictable, from properties of their parts (mass was often cited as an example). We may put all this in current terminology by saying that emergent properties are those that are not reducible to lower-level properties, whereas non-emergent, or resultant, properties are reducible. Emergentism and reductionism, then, are the two options with regard to the metaphysical question concerning the inter-level relationship of properties. To summarize, emergentism with respect to a given level is the claim that some of the properties characterizing entities of that level are irreducible to the properties at the lower levels. Reductionism denies this, claiming that all properties at that level are reducible. We can of course formulate reductionist and emergentist claims with regard to particular properties as well—for example, whether consciousness is an emergent property or it is reducible biologically or physically or computationally.

Much of the debate concerning the mind–body problem and, more broadly, the status of 'higher-level' properties and of the special sciences has centred on the reductionist versus emergentist (or anti-reductionist) controversy. Since around the late 1960s anti-reductionism has been predominant; it has arguably been the reigning orthodoxy on the nature of mentality and the status of the special sciences. This

---

[9] For further discussion, see Kim (1999) and Merricks (1998).

position is often called non-reductive materialism (or physicalism). It is materialist in that it accepts ontological materialism (the view that all that exists is material) and supervenience (the claim that physical facts determine all the facts), and yet in denying the reducibility of mental and other special-science properties to physical properties, it is anti-reductionist, embracing a dualism of mental and physical properties.[10] This entails a view about the nature of the special sciences: the higher-level sciences are autonomous and irreducible, in particular vis-à-vis basic physics.

But what is reduction? How do we reduce one set of properties to another? How are scientific theories reduced? Obviously, answers to these questions are crucial to the reductionist–emergentist debate. We now turn to the topic of reduction.

3.3 Bridge Law Reduction and Identity Reduction

Discussions of reduction and reductionism have long been dominated by the model of inter-theoretic reduction developed by Ernest Nagel in the 1950s (Nagel 1961). This model was intended as an analysis of *theory reduction*—the reduction of a scientific theory to another 'more basic' theory, such as the reduction of thermodynamics to statistical mechanics and of optics to electromagnetic theory. Nagel viewed such reductions basically as logical–mathematical derivations, in line with the then dominant view of scientific explanations as nomic derivations. Reduction, as Nagel conceived it, consists in the logical–mathematical derivation of the laws of the theory being reduced from the laws of the base theory. Since the base theory and the theory targeted for reduction must be expected to have their own proprietary vocabularies, Nagel thought that in order to enable the derivation, auxiliary premises are needed to coordinate the predicates of the two theories. These extra premises, standardly called *bridge laws*, are thought to be empirical and contingent correlations linking predicates of the two theories. This may be stated as a condition on Nagel reduction of theories:

> *The requirement of bridge laws.* If theory T is to be reduced to T^*, for each primitive predicate M of T there must be a bridge law of the form $M \leftrightarrow N$, providing M with a coextensive predicate N of T^*.

To take an ontological turn and speak of properties rather than the predicates, we can say that bridge laws, in a successful Nagel reduction, provide for each property in the theory being reduced with a nomologically coextensive property in the base domain. This means that the classificatory scheme of the reduced theory is absorbed

---

[10] Although this position is often characterized as property dualism, it is, more broadly speaking, property pluralism since it recognizes irreducible autonomous domains of properties other than mental properties. According to it, social-science properties, biological properties, and so forth are no more reducible than mental properties.

into that of the base theory, and we are supposed to be warranted in concluding that each property M in the reduced theory has been reduced to property N in the base domain with which it is connected by a bridge law. It is easily seen that the satisfaction of the bridge law requirement is not only necessary but also sufficient for Nagel reduction (Kim 1999).

Suppose we have determined empirically that the following correlation holds as a matter of law:

(L) Pain occurs to an organism at t ↔ the organism's C-fibres are stimulated at t.

This law could serve as a bridge law in a Nagel reduction of a psychological theory about pain to neurophysiological theory. Suppose such a reduction has been carried out. The question is whether we should, or could, regard this as sufficient for the reduction of pain to C-fibre stimulation. The answer, I believe, is in the negative, and this can be seen in at least two ways. First, the Nagel reducibility of mental properties is consistent with a whole group of obviously dualist theories, and it is in fact entailed by some of them. For, as we saw, Nagel reducibility is guaranteed if a pervasive system of mental–physical bridge laws is available, and the existence of such bridge laws is not only consistent with many dualist theories, including substance dualism, but it is entailed by theories like the double-aspect theory and the doctrine of pre-established harmony. It is reasonable, in fact mandatory, to expect mind–body reduction to exclude dualist theories of the mind. Another reason for regarding Nagel reduction as inadequate concerns the status of the bridge laws. When pain has been reduced to neural processes, we should expect to have achieved an understanding of why pain arises out of just these neural states. Why does pain, rather than itch or tickle, occur when C-fibres are stimulated? Why doesn't pain arise out of the stimulation of A-δ fibres instead? When consciousness has been reduced to brain processes, we should have an explanation of why and how consciousness arises out of, or correlates with, these brain processes. This means that in a reduction what we want to have explained is the bridge laws themselves. Some researchers think that phenomenal (or qualitative) consciousness correlates with a synchronized 40 hertz neural oscillation in the sensory areas of the brain cortex. Again, this correlation would guarantee Nagel reducibility of phenomenal consciousness to 40 hertz neural oscillation. But that can't be right: by assuming these and other bridge laws as unexplained auxiliary premises of reductive derivation, Nagel reduction is assuming as premises exactly what ought to be derived, and explained, in a genuine reduction.

A way of deflecting these criticisms is available, although it is not free of serious difficulties itself. This is to replace bridge laws with identities (Sklar 1967; Block and Stalnaker 1999). The proposal is that, instead of correlation law (L) above, the following identity be used as a bridging principle in the reductive derivation of pain theory from neurophysiology:

(I) Pain = C-fibre stimulation.

When Feigl and Smart (Feigl 1958; Smart 1959) first proposed the mind–body identity theory, or type physicalism as it is sometimes called, identities like (I) were thought to be not only empirical but also contingent. However, most philosophers have been persuaded by Kripke (1972) and Putnam (1975) that such identities, though empirical, cannot be contingent, and that they are necessarily true if true. The question exactly what difference, if any, is made by treating these identities as necessary rather than contingent in the context of reduction has not so far received much attention, and it is beyond the scope of the present chapter to explore this interesting and important issue. I will, however, have something more to say about whether identities like (I) can be regarded as necessary. We may call this strengthened model 'identity reduction' (to distinguish it from Nagel's original bridge law reduction).

In any case, the two objections raised earlier against Nagelian bridge law reduction are quickly dissipated by this move from correlations to identities. First, it is clear that an identity reduction using the likes of (I) excludes all forms of dualism; these mind–body identities take us straight to physicalism—in fact, the strongest form of reductionist physicalism. Second, the identification of pain with C-fibre stimulation seemingly neutralizes the emergentist demand for an explanation of why pain arises from, or correlates with, C-fibre stimulation (rather than some other neural process). They are one and the same, and the question why the one is the same as the other makes no sense. Questions like why we are warranted to identify pain with C-fibre stimulation, what the evidence for the identity is, and so forth make sense and we can perhaps answer them; but the question *why* pain is the same thing as C-fibre stimulation does not seem to make sense. Identities eliminate the logical space within which explanatory questions can be formulated. At least so it seems. This probably isn't the end of the story; however, it is clear that the move from bridge laws to identities provides a prima facie powerful response to the two objections.

The main difficulty—and I believe it is a critical one—with identity reduction concerns the availability of the identities. This is a point that is by now all too familiar, namely that many, perhaps all, special-science properties are 'multiply realizable', and for that reason, they cannot be identified with lower-level properties. Actually, the objection applies with equal force to Nagelian bridge laws; however, it was first raised as an objection to the Feigl–Smart-style mind–body identity theory (Putnam 1967). Putnam asked us to consider pain: pain may be realized by C-fibre stimulation in humans and other mammals, but we must expect that in organisms that are vastly different from us in their biology, say molluscs, we cannot expect pain's realizer to be C-fibre stimulation. It may well be that molluscs, and other pain-capable organisms, have no C-fibres at all! Think especially about all nomologically possible physical realizers of pain, and you will see that it is not possible to identify pain with any single biological or physical state. Putnam put this objection in terms of physical 'realizations', but that isn't crucial; the point can be put in a more neutral way by talking about physical or neural 'correlates' or 'substrates'. Putnam's argument was generalized by Fodor (1974) as an argument for the irreducibility of the special sciences and their proprietary properties.

The unavailability of these reduction-enabling identities does not necessarily show that the identity model of reduction is wrong. It might be argued that genuine reduction does require identities, and that their unavailability in a given case only goes to show that reduction cannot be had there. But it is also clear that when such cases multiply beyond reasonable bounds and the model in reality has no applications at all, that would cast serious doubt on its usefulness. Also, questions have been raised as to whether the phenomenon of multiple realization is really as pervasive as it has often been suggested.[11]

3.4 Functional Reduction

Recently an alternative model of reduction, *functional reduction*, has been proposed. The basic idea goes back to the early identity functionalists (Lewis 1966; Armstrong 1968), and more recently it has been present in the writings of Joseph Levine (1993) and David Chalmers (1996) among others. A fuller account is contained in Kim (1998, 1999). Here I will present it in brief but essential outlines.

Let us begin with an example: the reduction of the gene in molecular biology. To get the reduction going, we must first give a *functional interpretation* of the property of being a gene—that is, a definition of gene in terms of the causal work it performs—or somewhat more broadly in terms of its 'causal role'. Thus, being a gene is being a mechanism that encodes and transmits genetic information from parent to offspring. This means that whatever mechanism it is that performs this causal function in a given organism is a gene for that organism. This is our concept of the gene. The second stage in the reductive process is the actual scientific work of identifying the mechanism that performs this function, and it has turned out that DNA molecules execute the specified task, at least in terrestrial organisms. And we have a theory, molecular genetics, that explains just how DNA molecules manage to code and transmit genetic information.

To put all this schematically, let M be a property targeted for reduction:

Stage 1. Functionalize M—that is, give M a definition of the following form:

Having $M =$ def. having some property P such that P performs causal task C (or occupies causal role C).

Stage 2. Identify the 'realizers' of M (for systems under investigation)—that is, find actual properties, or mechanisms, that perform causal task C (in systems under study).

---

[11] On some of these issues, see Endicott (forthcoming).

Stage 3. Develop an explanatory theory that explains how the realizers of *M* perform causal task *C*.

Some philosophers, namely functionalists, have tried to give functional interpretations of mental properties. Being in pain, according to a proposed functional analysis, is being in a state (or exemplifying a property) that is standardly caused by tissue damage or trauma and that in turn causes winces, groans, and aversive behaviour. This is supposed to be a conceptual truth, a truth about the concept of being in pain, something that can be known a priori. Armed with this functional conception of pain, the researchers can look for its realizers (in humans, say) and find that C-fibre excitation is the mechanism that occupies the specified causal role: tissue damage and trauma cause C-fibres to be activated, and the activation of these neural fibres in turn causes winces, groans, and aversive behaviour. This would warrant, it seems, the reductive claim that pain, at least in humans, has been reduced to C-fibre activation.

It is worth while to point out that here there is no reference to bridge laws, and that functional reduction is entirely consistent with the phenomenon of multiple realization. In fact, Stage 2 above anticipates the existence of multiple lower-level realizers of the property being reduced. When scientists investigate the neural realizers of, say, pain, they would likely focus on a particular population of organisms, say humans or mammals, and try to identify pain's realizer, or realizers, for this population. In this sense, functional reductions are bound to be open-ended projects whose results come in only in a piecemeal fashion. No scientist is likely to attempt to identify pain's realizers for all actual and nomologically possible organisms or pain-capable systems; that is an impossible task. The functional model of reduction gives us a more realistic picture of actual scientific practices than the bridge law model, which portrays reduction as an all-or-nothing affair.

A second point to note is this: the fact that a given lower-level property or mechanism is a realizer of a functional property is not only empirical but also contingent. The reason is that the realization relation involves causal relations, and causal relations are in general contingent, not necessary. This is the case whether we think of causation as involving laws or counterfactuals. As may be recalled, the identity reduction of pain to C-fibre stimulation, on current understanding, holds that pain is *necessarily* C-fibre stimulation—that the association of pain and C-fibre stimulation holds across all possible worlds. In contrast, the functional reduction of pain to C-fibre stimulation (say, for mammals) does not involve a necessary association between the two. The fact that C-fibre stimulation realizes pain, namely that C-fibre stimulation is typically caused by tissue damage and typically causes winces and groans in humans, is a contingent fact that depends on the prevailing laws of this world. In worlds in which different laws hold, C-fibre stimulation may not have causal powers of this kind; in such worlds, other neural–physical mechanisms may be pain realizers, or perhaps there are no pain realizers at all.

If functional reduction of pain is used as a basis for restricted identities (e.g. human pain = C-fibre stimulation, reptilian pain = X-fibre stimulation, etc.), these identities will be metaphysically contingent, although they may be nomologically necessary (under a nomological conception of causality). This is a consequence of the fact that functionalized property designators are not 'rigid' in Kripke's sense; we might call them 'nomologically rigid' or 'semi-rigid' (Kim 1998).

3.5 Functional Reduction and Emergent Properties

Why does pain arise from C-fibre stimulation? Why doesn't a sensation of another sort, say an itch, arise? Why should any experience arise from C-fibre stimulation? Why is there such a thing as consciousness in a material world? These are the kinds of questions that the emergentists posed, and to which they despaired of finding answers. That is why emergentists take consciousness to be emergent and irreducible. Here is another way the emergentists framed their question: From complete knowledge of the neurophysiology of an organism, can we know what experience, if any, it is having or is capable of having? According to C. D. Broad, perhaps the most philosophically illuminating and astute of the British emergentist school, what divides emergentism and 'mechanism' (or physical reductionism in current terminology) is that a mechanist would answer this question in the affirmative whereas the emergentist answer, which Broad endorsed, is in the negative. From knowing all the physical–neural details of what is going in a person's brain, we cannot tell, on the basis of that information alone, what conscious experience that person is having, or whether any conscious experience is happening at all. Reduction must give us an understanding of the phenomena being reduced in terms of the underlying phenomena, and it must make it possible for us to predict them on the basis of information concerning the underlying phenomena.

How would an occurrence of pain be explained under a Nagel reduction of pain? We must expect such an explanation to take the following form:

> C-fibre stimulation is occurring in organism O at t.
> Pain occurs at t if and only if C-fibre stimulation occurs.
> Therefore, pain is occurring in organism O at t.

The second premiss of course is a Nagelian bridge law, and the derivation has the classic 'deductive-nomological' form. The problem with this explanation is that although there may be a sense in which it explains why O is having pain at t, the explanation is in no sense a *reductive* explanation; it does not explain why pain arises from C-fibre stimulation. On the contrary, the correlation between pain and C-fibre stimulation is assumed as an unexplained premiss; the explanation assumes exactly what is in need of explanation if reductive explanation of pain, or consciousness, is what is being sought. It is also easy to see why this derivation fails as a reductive prediction of pain. The use of the bridge law again is the reason for this failure: the predictive premisses already assume information about how pain correlates with a neural state; it is not a prediction of pain based *solely* on neural–physical information.

It is interesting to contrast this with the situation under an identity reduction. Consider:

> C-fibre stimulation is occurring in O at t.
> Pain $=$ C-fibre stimulation.
> Therefore, pain is occurring in O at t.

The deduction of course is valid; however, it cannot be viewed as an explanation of anything. The conclusion is a mere rewrite of the first premiss, and the two statements report one and the same fact. We can no more explain why Jones is having pain in terms of Jones's C-fibre stimulation than we can explain why Cicero is wise by pointing out that Tully is wise. This is consonant with the claim noted earlier that identities proscribe explanatory demands of the sorts the emergentists make, for example, why pains emerge from, or correlate with, C-fibre stimulation. We should note, though, that identity reductions are not able to meet the emergentists' predictive demand: the foregoing derivation, making use of substantial empirical information concerning pain in its second premiss, cannot serve as prediction of pain on the basis of physical–biological information alone.

Consider now a functional reduction of pain. Why is Jones experiencing pain at t? The following argument illustrates how a reductive explanation may go under functional reduction:

> Jones's C-fibres are being stimulated at t.
> Being in pain is $=$ $_{def.}$ being in a state that is caused by tissue damage and that in turn causes winces and groans.
> C-fibre stimulation is the state that, in Jones (and organisms like Jones), is caused by tissue damage and that causes winces and groans.
> Therefore, at t, Jones is experiencing pain.

This certainly looks like a reductive explanation of Jones's pain. Notice that unlike the Nagelian bridge explanation above, the explanans does not involve information about pains; the second premiss is a definition and is available a priori; if it is a truth about anything, it is a truth about the concept of pain, not about pains. It certainly is not an empirical and contingent bridge law as envisaged in Nagel reduction or an a posteriori necessary truth as required in identity reduction. But the explanans of the functional derivation, unlike the 'explanation' under identity reduction, does contain an empirical law in its third line.

It is also clear that, unlike the derivation under Nagelian or identity reduction, this derivation can be used to predict Jones's pain from neural–biological information alone. Again, note that the second premiss is a conceptual truth and available a priori; unlike the a posteriori identity 'pain = C-fibre stimulation', it represents no empirical information about pain.

Functional reduction, therefore, evidently satisfies both the explanatory and predictive requirements of reduction. This makes it plausible to define an *emergent* property as a *functionally irreducible* property. This construal of emergence gives a unified account of the emergentists' talk of the impossibility of explaining and predicting, or deducing, emergent phenomena from knowledge of their 'basal' conditions.

From a philosophical point of view, the crucial step in a functional reduction is the first stage, that of functionalizing the property to be reduced. Once a property is given a functional definition, the rest is up to science. Science is in charge of producing actual reductions; that surely cannot be a philosopher's job. Some might find it a bit surprising that reducibility, or the possibility of reduction, turns out, on this account, to be a purely conceptual affair. Suppose that M has been functionalized and that some object is found to have M. We know that this object has M because it instantiates a realizer of M. We know that a priori; we may not know what this realizer is but that makes no difference. Our best current science may not be able to help us at all in identifying the realizer involved, but we know that there must be a realizer of M instantiated here. And we know that this object's having M is—and is reducible to—its having a certain realizer of M. And that is all we need to know as philosophers concerning the reducibility of M. Reducibility in this sense may be a pretty trivial affair from a scientific point of view; the reducibility of M only means that there is some realizer or other of M. Will be it 'possible' to discover and identify this realizer? Depending on the sense of 'possible' involved, the answer may be yes or it may be no. But that is a scientific research question. Reducibility in the philosophical sense guarantees that there is a real scientific research project here. It is perhaps only natural that the possibility of reduction can be discussed at various stages and in various senses.

3.6 Emergence and 'Downward' Causation

Classic emergentists, like C. Lloyd Morgan (1923), and some contemporary emergentists, like Roger Sperry (1969), explicitly endorsed and promoted the idea of 'downward' causation.[12] This is the claim that emergent properties, having emerged from their basal conditions, acquire a causal life of their own, and can exert their own novel powers 'downward', that is, on events and processes at lower levels. To many emergentists this is a claim of critical importance; for what good is an emergent property unless it has its own distinctive causal powers to influence other events

---

[12] The term 'downward causation' is due to the biologist Donald Campbell (1974).

and phenomena of this world, including those at the lower levels? What can be more obvious than the fact that in virtue of the emergent mental properties that we possess, like consciousness and the capacity for thought and rationality, we have the power to build bridges and buildings, create works of art, and cause holes in the ozone layer? If you are an emergentist about mentality, you will almost certainly want downward causation.

But the idea of downward causation is not easily explained and defended, and there appear to be weighty considerations against it. One line of consideration goes as follows: emergentism conceives of emergent properties as supervenient on the properties from which they emerge. Suppose we take mental properties to be emergent, and suppose that a given mental property M 'downwardly' causes a physical property P.[13] *Ex hypothesi*, M has an emergence base (or 'basal condition') P^* on which it supervenes. This means that P^* is at least nomologically sufficient for M. Given this, it seems perfectly justified to say that P^* is a cause of P. Saying that does not in itself contradict the claim that M caused P; but it seriously weakens the claim that M can have *distinctive* and *novel* causal powers of its own, powers not had by lower-level events and processes from which it emerges (Kim 1993*a*; O'Connor 1994). In fact, arguments have been formulated that seem to show that emergent properties, if such exist, must be epiphenomenal—that is, they cannot have causal powers (Kim 1998). This point, however, remains controversial.

4. REALIZATION AND SUPERVENIENCE

4.1 Realization

The idea of realization, as far as I know, was first used by Hilary Putnam (1960), roughly in its current philosophical sense, in describing the relation between mathematically defined computers (e.g. Turing machines) and physical machines that carry out the actual computations in real time. One and the same computer in the abstract mathematical sense can be realized in many diverse physical devices, and the idea of multiple realizability had its origins in computer analogies of this kind. In any event, realization in this sense is a relation between mathematical–abstract entities on one hand and concrete physical entities and systems on the other (perhaps, if substance dualism is correct, there could be, as Putnam observed,

---

[13] When we talk of one property causing another, this is short for saying that an instance of the one causes the other to be instantiated.

immaterial realizations of Turing machines[14]), a relation akin to exemplification or instantiation.

But the idiom of realization soon caught on, and philosophers began using realization as a relation between properties, to indicate a certain way in which properties at different levels may be related to each other. Thus, it has been common to talk about psychological properties being realized by biological properties, which are in turn realized by physico-chemical properties. Some philosophers (Lycan 1987) think of what we have called the layered model in terms of a hierarchy of properties generated by the realization relation, with properties at a given level realizing properties at the level above it. This kind of thinking requires that both the realized and the realizers be ontologically homogeneous; if what is realized is an abstract object and its realizers are concrete things, the realization relation cannot generate a multi-level hierarchy of properties. The idiom of realization has by now taken firm hold in philosophy, especially in discussions of issues in philosophy of mind, metaphysics, and philosophy of science.

However, the concept of realization has received little analytical attention,[15] and it appears that most philosophers have used it on the basis of fairly loose computer analogies to refer to some unspecified relation between a property and its 'underlying' properties. Consider what LePore and Loewer (1989) say about realization:

The usual conception is that e's being P realizes e's being F iff e is P and there is a strong connection of some sort between P and F. We propose to understand this connection as a necessary connection which is explanatory. The existence of an explanatory connection between two properties is stronger than the claim that P → F is physically necessary since not every physically necessary connection is explanatory.

This characterization is incomplete in that it is not clear what this explanatory relation between a property and its realizers is supposed to be; but LePore and Loewer, I believe, may well be right in associating realization with explanation (recall reductive functional explanation above, which makes use of realizers to explain higher-level phenomena). In any case, one thing that LePore and Loewer make clear is that if P is a realizer of F, P is nomologically sufficient for F; that is, the conditional $P → F$ holds with physical (that is, nomological) necessity. What LePore and Loewer are saying is that the mere fact that $P → F$ is a law doesn't mean that P explains F. And that, too, must be right (recall our strictures on the use of Nagelian bridge laws in reductive explanations). All that we know is that the two

[14] At bottom, though, I do not believe this is a possibility. Any real-life computer must be a causal system, and there is real doubt as to whether immaterial things, if such existed, could enter into causal relations. See Kim (2001).

[15] Ronald Endicott is one philosopher who has devoted much effort to clarifying this concept. See especially Endicott (forthcoming).

properties covary in a certain way, and that alone cannot be regarded as constituting an explanatory relation.

Another point to keep in mind is that if P and F are two distinct properties without some ontological or constitutive relationship between them, it is difficult to see how they can be more intimately or interestingly related to each other than by mere covariation or correlation. They are different properties and it is a brute fact that the instantiation of one correlates with the instantiation of the other. The statement that P realizes F surely hints at a stronger relation than mere covariation; it includes the idea that F's instantiation in a given case holds *in virtue of* the fact that P is instantiated on that occasion, or perhaps something even stronger, that F's instantiation on a given occasion *consists in* P's instantiation on that occasion. When it is said that C-fibre stimulation realizes pain (in humans), the implication goes beyond saying that the two are correlated, or that whenever C-fibres are stimulated, pain occurs as a matter of law; it is to imply that pain is instantiated on a given occasion only because C-fibres are stimulated, that C-fibre stimulation is a means or mechanism that makes pain's instantiation possible. Even a stronger implication, which is tacitly accepted by many 'token' physicalists, is that, although pain as a kind is distinct from C-fibre stimulation, any instance of pain is identical with a specific instance of its neural realizer. When pain occurs in virtue of being realized by C-fibre stimulation, there is no event here distinct from, or 'over and above', the C-fibre stimulation. That is, realization arguably implies 'token' identity.

As the reader surely has noticed, we began using the terms 'realize', 'realization', and 'realizer' in connection with the functional model of reduction. It may be helpful to introduce the concept more formally, although this will involve some reiteration of the material presented earlier. Let D be a domain of 'first-order' properties—properties taken as the reference base in a given context; for example, in the mind–body discussion D would normally be taken as a set of physical properties including behavioural and neural–biological properties. 'Second-order' properties are defined as follows:[16]

> F is a *second-order property* over $D =$ def. F is the property of having some property ϕ in D such that $C(\phi)$, where C specifies a condition on members of D.

For example, let D be the set of chemical substances (or, more precisely, properties of being M, where M is a chemical substance), and let $C(\phi)$ be 'when ingested, ϕ causes sleep'. The second-order property defined by this C would be that of 'having dormitive power' or 'being a sleep-inducer'—the desired property of sleeping pills. When condition C over members of D is a causal condition, that is, when it is specified in terms of causal relations, we may speak of *functional properties*: functional

---

[16] This conception of second-order property comes from Putnam (1969).

properties are second-order properties defined by causal specifications—thus, they are 'causal roles'.

We may now define 'realizer': Let F be a second-order property defined over D by specification $C(\phi)$. We then say:

P is a realizer of $F =$ def. P satisfies condition C—that is, $C(P)$.

So P is an occupant of the causal role represented by F—some will say that F itself is a causal role. A couple of points are worth noting: first, second-order properties can have multiple realizers. Second, that a given property is a realizer of F can be an empirical and *contingent* fact; when F is a functional property, this will in general be a contingent fact. That is so because, as earlier noted, to say P realizes F is to say that P enters into a certain set of specified causal relations, and this will depend on the set of laws prevailing at a given world. The situation here is actually a little more complicated than that; what I have just said depends on viewing the identity of properties as independent—at least, largely independent—of their causal powers. But there is an approach to properties that closely associates properties with their causal powers; some may even define properties in terms of causal powers (e.g. Shoemaker 1980). On this extreme view, the second point above concerning realizers will not hold since if properties are identified with causal powers it would make no sense to speak of properties having different causal powers in other possible worlds. At least so it seems. There are complex questions here and we must set this issue aside.

4.2 Further Issues about Realization

There are some questions concerning the relationship between properties and their realizers that need to be addressed. As we will see, these questions are also relevant to a better understanding of functional reduction.

Let us begin with the question of the causal powers of functional properties. F is the property of having some property P such that P does causal work C. So by definition F has the power to perform C; that is to say, whenever F is instantiated, that instance of F performs causal work C. That much is clear. But a particular instance of F must be expected to have causal powers, or properties, in addition to performing C; a given instance of pain may touch off events like an anxiety reaction, an expletive, an involuntary jerking of the head, and so on—effects that go beyond those that all pains must by definition have. We must keep in mind the point that any given instance of F occurs in virtue of the instantiation of one of F's realizers, say, P: having F is, by definition, having some property with causal power C, and a certain entity x has F by having a particular realizer, P, of F. There is no more to x's having F on this occasion over and above x's having P on this occasion. In view of this, the following principle seems highly plausible—in fact, quite compelling:

> [*The causal inheritance principle.*] If a functional property F is realized on a given occasion in virtue of the instantiation of one of its realizers, P, the causal powers of this instance of F are identical with the causal powers of P. (Kim 1993*b*: 326–7)

If a pain occurs by being realized by C-fibre stimulation, the causal powers of this pain, according to this principle, are no more and no less than those of C-fibre stimulation (or, more precisely, the particular instance of C-fibre stimulation involved on this occasion). Pains cannot have causal powers beyond those they 'inherit' from their neural–physical realizers; if they did, that would be wholly magical. After all, on a functional conception of pain, having pain *is* identical with instantiating some property with a certain specified causal property, and on this occasion of pain's occurrence, the property instantiated is C-fibre stimulation. How could pain, on this conception, have causal powers, or any other property for that matter, that go beyond the causal powers of C-fibre stimulation?

What then is the relationship between a given instance of F and the instance of its realizer P in virtue of which F is instantiated on this occasion? Here, the only plausible option seems to be identity: this F-instance is identical with this P-instance. For one thing, this conclusion seems inescapable given the definitions: x's having F on this occasion is identical with x's having some property that has a certain causal property C, and as it happens this property is P. We must conclude, it seems, that x's having F on this occasion, namely this F-instance, is identical with x's having P on this occasion, namely this P-instance. Second, consider their causal powers: if the causal inheritance principle is accepted, the F-instance and the P-instance have identical causal powers. Given this, what useful purpose would be served by insisting on their distinctness? We are here reminded of Donald Davidson's criterion of event individuation: events are the same that have the same causes and same effects (Davidson 1969).

The picture, then, is this. Let F be a functional property with realizers $P_1, P_2, \ldots$ The class of F-instances partitions itself into mutually exclusive subclasses each of which represents one of F's realizers, P_i. To say that these P_is are diverse multiple realizers of F can only mean that they are causally and nomologically diverse—they have different causal powers and enter into different laws. For the only relevant sense of diversity in this context must be causal–nomological diversity. Accordingly, we must conclude that F itself is a causally–nomologically heterogeneous property. Multiply realizable functional properties are causally heterogeneous kinds. If mental properties have multiple diverse neural realizers, as many philosophers have claimed, it follows that mental properties are causally and nomologically heterogeneous properties and kinds. This raises the question whether a unitary and universal science of these properties, namely psychology or cognitive science valid for all creatures and systems with mentality and cognitive capacities, is a theoretical possibility (see Kim 1992; Block 1997; Fodor 1997; Antony and Levine 1997).

When we speak of a property, or a kind, a certain degree of homogeneity and uniformity, or 'similarity', is assumed for its instances. If no similarity or homogeneity of interest is present, there would hardly be any point in recognizing the presence of a kind or property. This is one standard reason for rejecting 'disjunctive' and 'negative' properties (for example, round and yellow things are *round or red*; so are square and red things). The absence of causal homogeneity in the case of functional properties, therefore, raises a serious question concerning the ontological status of such properties. True, instances of F, in spite of their causal–nomological diversity, do share one causal property, namely that of performing the causal task that defines F. In light of this, we may allow F as a disjunctive property, a disjunction of all its realizers, $P_1 \vee P_2 \vee \ldots$ Disjunctive properties like this are pretty 'thin' properties, and are too weak to support unrestricted inductions over their instances (Kim 1992). Another alternative is to abandon multiply realizable properties as properties, recognizing only functional *concepts* or *predicates* (Kim 1998). This would amount to a form of irrealism, and when applied to mental properties—if mental properties indeed are functional properties, which is far from certain (and probably false)—this would be a form of mental eliminativism. But it should be noted that if it is indeed a form of eliminativism, it differs crucially from the psychological eliminativism of the standard sort advocated by, say, Churchland (1981). 'Mental conceptualism' perhaps is a more appropriate and less deflationary term for this position.

But the irrealist implications of functional reduction should not surprise us. According to the views suggested in this chapter, functionalization amounts to reducibility, if not actual reduction, and if mental properties are functionalizable, they give way to the multiplicities of their realizers. The two options just sketched, namely disjunctivism and mental conceptualism, are in fact not so far apart. If mental conceptualism is a form of mental irrealism, we must remember that disjunctive properties are a target of scorn and disdain in some quarters. As noted, what may be a bit surprising is the fact that functionalizability entails reducibility, and that functional reducibility has these seemingly irrealist consequences. We should keep in mind that whether or not all mental properties are functional properties remains very much an open question, and that there are strong reasons for thinking that not all mental properties are functionally reducible. Some will say that intentional properties (the 'aboutness' of thoughts) are irreducible, while others will take the qualitative properties of consciousness ('qualia') as the prime examples that resist functionalization. What our discussion has made evident is the reductive and possibly irrealist consequences of the functionalist conception of mentality. It goes without saying that the point generalizes to all functional properties. Whether we are inclined towards reductionism or anti-reductionism (and there are pressures pointing to each direction), the picture presented here is something that we ought to keep in mind.

REFERENCES

Alexander, Samuel (1920). *Space, Time, and Deity*, 2 vols. London: Macmillan.

Antony, Louise, and Joseph Levine (1997). 'Reduction with Autonomy'. *Philosophical Perspectives*, 11: 83–105.

Armstrong, David (1968). *A Materialist Theory of Mind*. New York: Humanities Press.

Bacon, John (1986). 'Supervenience, Necessary Coextension, and Reducibility'. *Philosophical Studies*, 49: 163–76.

Beckermann, Ansgar, Hans Flohr, and Jaegwon Kim (1992). *Emergence or Reduction? Essays on the Prospects of Nonreductive Physicalism*. Berlin: De Gruyter.

Block, Ned (1997). 'Anti-Reductionist Slaps Back'. *Philosophical Perspectives*, 11: 107–32.

—— and Robert Stalnaker (1999). 'Conceptual Analysis, Dualism, and the Explanatory Gap'. *Philosophical Review*, 108: 1–46.

Broad, C. D. (1925). *The Mind and its Place in Nature*. London: Routledge & Kegan Paul.

Campbell, Donald T. (1974). ' "Downward Causation" in Hierarchically Organised Biological Systems', in F. J. Ayala and T. Dobzhansky (eds.), *Studies in the Philosophy of Biology*. Berkeley and Los Angeles: University of California Press, 179–86.

Chalmers, David (1996). *The Conscious Mind*. New York: Oxford University Press.

Churchland, Paul (1981). 'Eliminative Materialism and the Propositional Attitudes'. *Journal of Philosophy*, 78: 67–90.

Davidson, Donald (1969). 'The Individuation of Events', in Nicholas Rescher *et al.* (eds.), *Essays in Honor of Carl G. Hempel*. Dordrecht: Reidel, 216–34.

Endicott, Ronald (forthcoming). *The Book of Realization*.

Feigl, Herbert (1958). 'The "Mental" and the "Physical" ', in Herbert Feigl, Grover Maxwell, and Michael Scriven (eds.), *Minnesota Studies in the Philosophy of Science*, vol. ii. Minneapolis: University of Minnesota Press.

Fodor, Jerry A. (1974). 'Special Sciences; or, The Disunity of Science as a Working Hypothesis'. *Synthese*, 28: 77–115.

—— (1997). 'Special Sciences: Still Autonomous after All These Years'. *Philosophical Perspectives*, 11: 149–63.

Grimes, Thomas R. (1988). 'The Myth of Supervenience'. *Pacific Philosophical Quarterly*, 69: 152–60.

Hare, R. M. (1952). *Language of Morals*. Oxford: Clarendon Press.

Heil, John (2003). *From an Ontological Point of View*. Oxford: Clarendon Press.

Horgan, Terence (1982). 'Supervenience and Microphysics'. *Pacific Philosophical Quarterly*, 63: 29–43.

—— (1993a). 'Nonreductive Materialism and the Explanatory Autonomy of Psychology', in S. J. Wagner and R. Warner (eds.), *Naturalism: A Critical Appraisal*. Notre Dame, Ind.: Notre Dame University Press, 295–320.

—— (1993b). 'From Supervenience to Superdupervenience'. *Mind*, 102: 555–86.

Jackson, Frank (1998). *From Metaphysics to Ethics*. Oxford: Clarendon Press.

Kim, Jaegwon (1984). 'Concepts of Supervenience'. *Philosophy and Phenomenological Research*, 45: 153–76. Repr. in Kim (1993*b*).

—— (1987). '"Strong" and "Global" Supervenience Revisited'. *Philosophy and Phenomenological Research*, 48: 315–26. Repr. in Kim (1993*b*).

—— (1990). 'Supervenience as a Philosophical Concept'. *Metaphilosophy*, 21: 1–27.

—— (1992). 'Multiple Realization and the Metaphysics of Reduction'. *Philosophy and Phenomenological Research*, 52: 1–26.

—— (1993*a*). 'The Nonreductivist's Troubles with Mental Causation', in John Heil and Alfred Mele (eds.), *Mental Causation*. Oxford: Clarendon Press, 189–210.

—— (1993*b*). *Supervenience and Mind*. Cambridge: Cambridge University Press.

—— (1998). *Mind in a Physical World*. Cambridge, Mass.: MIT Press.

—— (1999). 'Making Sense of Emergence'. *Philosophical Studies*, 95: 3–36.

—— (2001). 'Lonely Souls: Substance Dualism and Causality', in Kevin Corcoran (ed.), *Soul, Body, and Survival*. Ithaca, NY: Cornell University Press, 30–43.

—— (2002). 'The Layered World: Metaphysical Considerations'. *Philosophical Explorations*, 5: 2–20.

Kripke, Saul (1972). '*Naming and Necessity*', in G. Harman and D. Davidson (eds.), *The Semantics of Natural Language*. Dordrecht: Reidel, 253–355. Repr. as *Naming and Necessity*. Cambridge, Mass.: Harvard University Press, 1980.

LePore, Ernest, and Barry Loewer (1989). 'More on Making Mind Matter'. *Philosophical Topics*, 17: 175–92.

Levine, Joseph (1993). 'On Leaving Out What it's Like', in Martin Davies and Glyn W. Humphreys (eds.), *Consciousness*. Oxford: Basil Blackwell, 121–36.

Lewis, David (1966). 'An Argument for the Identity Thesis'. *Journal of Philosophy*, 63: 17–25.

Lycan, William (1987). *Consciousness*. Cambridge, Mass.: MIT Press.

McLaughlin, Brian (1992). 'The Rise and Fall of British Emergentism', in Beckermann *et al.* (1992: 49–93).

—— (1995). 'Varieties of Supervenience', in Yalcin and Savellos (1995: 16–59).

Merricks, Trenton (1998). 'Against the Doctrine of Microphysical Supervenience'. *Mind*, 107: 59–71.

Moore, G. E. (1922). *Philosophical Studies*. London: Routledge & Kegan Paul.

Morgan, C. Lloyd (1923). *Emergent Evolution*. London: William & Norgate.

Nagel, Ernest (1961). *The Structure of Science*. New York: Harcourt, Brace, & World.

O'Connor, Timothy (1994). 'Emergent Properties'. *American Philosophical Quarterly*, 31: 91–104.

Oppenheim, Paul, and Hilary Putnam (1958). 'Unity of Science as a Working Hypothesis', in Herbert Feigl, Grover Maxwell, and Michael Scriven (eds.), *Minnesota Studies in the Philosophy of Science*, vol. ii. Minneapolis: University of Minnesota Press, 3–36.

Paull, Cranston, and Theodore Sider (1992). 'In Defense of Global Supervenience', *Philosophy and Phenomenological Research*, 52: 833–54.

Post, John (1995). '"Global" Supervenient Determination: Too Permissive?', in Yalcin and Savellos (1995: 73–100).

Putnam, Hilary (1960). 'Minds and Machines', in Sydney Hook (ed.), *Dimensions of Mind*. New York: New York University Press, 138–64.

—— (1967). 'The Nature of Mental States' (first pub. as 'Psychological Predicates'), in W. H. Capitan and D. D. Merrill (eds.), *Art, Mind, and Religion*. Pittsburgh: University of Pittsburgh Press, 37–48. Repr. in Putnam, *Philosophical Papers*, vol. ii. Cambridge: Cambridge University Press, 1975, 429–40.

Putnam, Hilary (1969). 'On Properties', in Nicholas Rescher *et al.* (eds.), *Essays in Honor of Carl G. Hempel*. Dordrecht: Reidel, 235–54.

——(1975). 'The Meaning of "Meaning"', in K. Gunderson (ed.), *Language, Mind, and Knowledge*. Minneapolis: University of Minnesota Press, 131–93. Repr. in Putnam, *Philosophical Papers*, vol. ii. Cambridge: Cambridge University Press, 1975, 215–71.

Searle, John (1992). *The Rediscovery of the Mind*. Cambridge, Mass.: MIT Press.

Shoemaker, Sydney (1980). 'Causality and Properties', in Peter van Inwagen (ed.), *Time and Cause*. Dordrecht: Reidel.

Sklar, Lawrence (1967). 'Types of Inter-Theoretic Reduction'. *British Journal for the Philosophy of Science*, 18: 109–24.

Smart, J. J. C. (1959). 'Sensations and Brain Processes'. *Philosophical Review*, 68: 141–56.

Sperry, Roger (1969). 'A Modified Concept of Consciousness'. *Psychological Review*, 76: 532–6.

Stalnaker, Robert (1996). 'Varieties of Supervenience'. *Philosophical Perspectives*, 10: 221–41.

Van Cleve, James (1989). 'Supervenience and Closure'. *Philosophical Studies*, 55: 225–38.

Yalcin, Umit, and Savellos, Elias (1995). *New Essays on Supervenience*. Cambridge: Cambridge University Press.

PART VII

FREEDOM OF THE WILL

CHAPTER 19

LIBERTARIANISM

CARL GINET

1. INTRODUCTION

THE term *libertarianism* is standardly used in philosophical discussions of free will to refer to a thesis composed of two parts: *incompatibilism* and *indeterminism*-in-the-right-places.

Incompatibilism is the claim that neither the existence of freely willed actions nor the existence of actions for which the agent is morally responsible is compatible with the truth of causal determinism. By a *freely willed* action (or, for short, a free action) I mean one such that it was open to the agent to take some alternative course instead of that action—to will a different action or to remain inactive—open in the sense that at the time nothing made it the case that the agent could not take the alternative course. An agent is *morally responsible* for her action (or for any other state of affairs) if and only if it would be right for those in a position to do so to hold her accountable for the action (or state of affairs). Causal *determinism* is the thesis that the causal laws that hold in this world plus complete information about the state of the world at a given time together entail every truth as to what happens after that time down to the smallest detail.

Indeterminism-in-the-right-places is the claim that on most of the occasions when it seems to us that we are freely choosing among alternative possible

I wish to thank John Fischer, Tim O'Connor, and David Widerker for helpful comments on an earlier draft.

actions then open to us, those alternatives are such that the causal laws and the antecedent state of the world do not determine which of them will occur: none of them has been ruled out by the antecedent state of the world plus the causal laws.

Whether indeterminism-in-the-right-places (hereafter referred to simply as indeterminism) is true is an empirical, not a philosophical, issue. Whether incompatibilism is true is, however, an a priori philosophical issue, and philosophical debate regarding libertarianism has for the most part really been about incompatibilism. This chapter will therefore confine its attention to incompatibilism.

There are current two versions of incompatibilism:

1. *Traditional incompatibilism.* The occurrence of free and responsible actions is incompatible with determinism because:

(*a*) having alternative possible courses of action (or inaction) open to one at a given time entails indeterminism-at-that-time-and-place, that is, it entails that the causal laws and the antecedent state of the world do not determine which of those alternative possibilities will then occur; and

(*b*) moral responsibility entails having alternative possibilities open, that is, an agent is morally responsible for a given action only if she had it open to her to avoid that action.

Claim (*b*) is often referred to as the principle of alternative possibilities, or PAP.

2. *Direct incompatibilism.* There are reasons to hold that responsibility entails indeterminism that are independent of whether PAP holds; so even if PAP is false, responsibility is still incompatible with indeterminism.

There are current two ways of opposing incompatibilism, i.e. two versions of compatibilism:

Traditional compatibilism. The (*b*) part of traditional incompatibilism, PAP, may be true but the (*a*) part is false: on a proper understanding of 'had it open to her', that an agent had it open to her to avoid acting as she did at a given time, does not entail indeterminism at that time and place; therefore, even though not having alternatives open may be incompatible with responsibility, determinism is not incompatible with it.

Semi-compatibilism. The (*a*) part of traditional incompatibilism may be true but the (*b*) part, PAP, is false: an agent's being morally responsible for an action does not entail that alternatives were open to the agent; therefore, even though having alternatives open may be incompatible with determinism, being responsible for an action is not.

2. Does having Alternatives Open Require Indeterminism?

Let us discuss first the (*a*) part of traditional incompatibilism, the claim that freedom of action is incompatible with determinism (this thesis has been defended in Ginet 1966, 1990; van Inwagen 1983; Fischer 1994; Widerker 1995*a*; Kane 1996; O'Connor 2000, among other places). One way to spell out this claim more exactly is as follows (which I will call *the incompatibility of freedom with determinism*, or IFD):

(IFD) For any person *S*, way of acting *A*, and time *T* such that *S* *A*-ed at time *T*: it was open to *S* at all times before *T* not to *A* at *T* only if no state of the world prior to *T* causally necessitated *S*'s *A*-ing at *T* (equivalently: it is not the case that complete information about the state of the world at some time before *T* and the causal laws entail that *S* *A*-ed at *T*).

The argument we can give for this claim will equally well support the corresponding claim about non-actions:

For any person *S*, way of acting *A*, and time *T* such that *S* did not *A* at time *T*: it was open to *S* at all times before *T* to *A* at *T* only if no state of the world prior to *T* causally necessitated *S* 's not *A*-ing at *T* (equivalently: it is not the case that complete information about the state of the world at some time before *T* and the causal laws entail that *S* did not *A* at *T*).

In stating the argument I will make use of the expression 'made it the case that' and take the meaning of this expression to be given by the following rule (see Ginet 1990: 98–101, for a fuller discussion of this locution):
S made it the case that *P* iff *P* and either:

(1) *P* is of the form '*S* acted in way *A* at *T*', or
(2) *S*'s acting in a certain way caused (or *S*'s not acting in a certain way allowed) it to be the case that *P*, or
(3) *P* is equivalent to a proposition of the form '*Q*-at-*T*1 and *R*-at-*T*2', *S* made it the case that *R*-at-*T*2, and '*Q*-at-*T*1' is a truth about what happened at a time *T*1 before *S* made it the case that *R*-at-*T*2.

Note that (3) allows it to be the case that *S* made it the case that *Q*-at-*T*1 and *R*-at-*T*2 even though *S* did not make it the case that *Q*-at-*T*1. Thus, for example, if I made it the case that my sidewalk was cleared of snow at noon (let this be *R*-at-*T*2) and I was the last one on my block to clear the snow from their sidewalk, then when I cleared my sidewalk I made it the case that every house on my block had its sidewalk cleared (*P*), even though I did not make it the case that the other sidewalks were cleared earlier (*Q*-at-*T*1).

The argument will assume two principles. The first, which might be dubbed *freedom to add to the given past* (or FAP), is this:

> (FAP) For any time earlier than T, Te, it was open to S at Te not to A at T only if, for any true proposition B about what happened before Te, it was open to S at Te to make it the case that: B and S did not A at T.

FAP says that freedom not to act in a certain way entails freedom to add one's not acting in that way to the given past, to make the world develop from its actual past so as to contain one's not acting in that way; and this seems evident: if it is open to me now to take a certain course of action or non-action after now, that surely means it is open to me now to make it the case that the world *as it has developed up until now* continues to develop after now in a certain way.

The other assumption, which can be dubbed *fixity of the laws* (or FL) is this:

> (FL) For any truth P such that P is entailed by the causal laws, it was never open to S to make it the case that not-P.

This says that the laws of nature constrain our actions, that it is never open to us to act in such a way that were we so to act, then we would make the case something that contradicts the laws. This seems to be something we quite readily assume in our reasoning about what is open to us. If we think that the laws of nature dictate that there is no combustion where there is no oxygen, then we think that it is not open to us to start a fire in a chamber from which all oxygen has been removed.

I will argue for IFD (the incompatibility of freedom and determinism) by showing that the above two assumptions and the antecedent of IFD ('It was open to S at all times before T not to A at T'—call this ANT) together entail the consequent of IFD ('No state of the world prior to T causally necessitated S's A-ing at T'—call this CON). Here is the argument:

Assume not-CON.
Not-CON *entails*

> (1) There is a truth B about what happened at some time before T such that the proposition 'If B then S A-ed at T' is entailed by the causal laws.

(1) and FL *entail*

> (2) It was never open to S to make it the case that: B and S did not A at T.

(2) and FAP *entail* not-ANT.
Therefore, if ANT, FL, and FAP, then CON.

This argument demonstrates that, if the two assumptions are true, then IFD is true: freedom of action is incompatible with determinism. Thus anyone wishing to reject IFD must reject at least one of the two assumptions. Each of them looks hard to deny, but for each of them an attempt to cast doubt on it has been made. Let us look at those attempts.

One might try to sow doubt about FAP with an example like the following (see Fischer 1994: 80–2). Suppose Henry sees his colleague Sam leave the office for home on a sunny afternoon carrying an umbrella. Henry asks their colleague Hilda why Sam is carrying an umbrella on such a nice day. Hilda says, 'It's because he heard on the early morning newscast that there was a 60 per cent chance of rain this afternoon. It's his policy to carry an umbrella when the chance of rain is greater than 50 per cent. If he had not taken his umbrella when he left the house, it would have been because he had not heard any such forecast of rain'. Later, in the course of discussing the free will problem, Hilda says, 'When Sam left the house this morning, it was open to him to act against his policy and not take his umbrella'. It seems wrong to suppose that in making this second remark Hilda was contradicting her earlier counterfactual conditional remark ('If Sam had not taken his umbrella, it would have been because he had not earlier heard a forecast of rain'), to suppose that there is any inconsistency between the two remarks. But FAP seems to entail that there is an inconsistency. For according to FAP, if it was open to Sam when he left the house not to take his umbrella (as Hilda's later assertion has it), then it was open to him then to make it the case that he did not take his umbrella even though he had earlier heard the forecast of rain. But how could this be if Hilda's earlier counterfactual were true? For that counterfactual says that if he had not taken his umbrella, then it would have been the case that he did not earlier hear the forecast of rain. And if that is right, then, it seems, it cannot have been open to him to make it the case that he did not take his umbrella *and* he heard the earlier forecast of rain: if he had made the first conjunct true then, according to that counterfactual, he would have made the second conjunct false.

The problem with this reasoning can be brought out by noting that in the context where Hilda says that it was open to Sam when he left the house to violate his policy and not take his umbrella, it would have been perfectly apt for her to put her point this way: 'It was open to him not to take his umbrella, and if he had not taken it he would have violated his policy (for he would have done so even though he had earlier heard a forecast of rain)'—that is, to make her point about what it was open to Sam to do in just the way that FAP licenses. The moral of the story is, not that it is hard to be consistent in one's remarks, but rather that the method for evaluating the truth of the counterfactual conditional 'If Sam had not taken his umbrella, then he would not have earlier heard a forecast of rain' is relative to the context in which it is being considered. In the context where what is in question is what it was open to Sam to do when he left his house, the appropriate method is to look at the nearest possible worlds where the antecedent is true and the past and the causal laws are the same as in the actual world, even if Sam's record of conforming to his umbrella-taking policy must be more blemished in those worlds. But in the context where what is in question is what explains Sam's having an umbrella with him this afternoon, it is appropriate to evaluate it by evaluating the consequent in possible worlds where the antecedent is true and the laws and Sam's record of conforming to his policy are the same as in the actual world, even if that means the past must be different in those worlds.

Now let's turn to the fixity of the laws. FL has been doubted on the ground that in cases where we seem to be relying on that principle in our reasoning, our inferences can be justified by a weaker principle, one that will not support the argument for incompatibilism, namely the following:

(FL-weak)   For any truth P such that P is entailed by the causal laws, it was never open to S to act (not act) in such a way that: either the proposition that S so acted (did not so act) would by itself entail that not-P, or a proposition reporting some event caused by S's so acting (not so acting) would by itself entail that not-P.

It is, some suggest (Lewis 1981; Fischer 1988), this weaker principle that expresses how we conceive the laws of nature to constrain our action. To take the example about combustion and oxygen given earlier, what we really assume here is that it is never open to anyone to perform an action that would cause something's igniting in the absence of oxygen. If, on the other hand, we suppose that it was open to S not to A at T despite the fact that some earlier state of the world B causally necessitated S's A-ing at T, we are not violating this weaker principle; for, although S's not A-ing at T would, in the sense I defined, have *made it the case* that there occurred a sequence of events that contradicts causal laws (namely, B and S's not A-ing at T), it would not *by itself* contradict causal laws or cause something that by itself contradicts causal laws.

FL-weak might suffice to explain the reasoning in the combustion-needs-oxygen example, but there are other examples where it is too weak to explain the inferences we are willing to make. If I think that causal laws dictate that the ingestion of a certain chemical is followed in five minutes by complete unconsciousness that lasts an hour, and that S has just now ingested this chemical, then I will conclude that it is not open to S to go for a walk ten minutes from now. But S's going for a walk ten minutes from now is not an action that would itself violate or cause a violation of that causal-law entailment; it is, however, an action that in the circumstances would *make it the case* that there was a violation of that entailment. So it seems that my inference relies on FL rather than FL-weak.

One might try another tack in resisting FL. One might say that the soundness of my inference in the preceding example depends, not only on the premiss that ingestion by S of the chemical at $T1$ causally necessitates S's not walking at $T1 + 10$ min., but on the additional, unstated assumption that the causal necessitation here does *not* go through S's motives and will in a certain way (the sort of way it might, for example, in a deterministic world in a case where S's having eaten a large amount ten minutes ago was S's reason for deciding not to go for a walk) (see Slote 1982 for a suggestion of this sort). The cases where we seem to be applying FL in our reasoning about what it was open to an agent S to bring about are always cases where it is safe to make this additional assumption; but, of course, in cases where what is in question is S's acting (or not acting) in a certain way—as in the argument for IFD given above—we cannot safely make this assumption and therefore cannot rely on FL.

The only way I can see to defend FL against this objection is to deny the suggestion about avoidability on which it is based—the suggestion that avoidability is not lost if one's action is nomically necessitated by one's motives and will in an appropriate way. This suggestion seems less plausible when one thinks about what it would be like really to know laws of nature governing the causing of particular actions by their agents' motives and to use this knowledge to manipulate agents. Suppose that we observe a man get out of his chair, go to the kitchen sink, and get a drink of water: an ordinary sequence of actions that appears to be freely undertaken at every step. But then we learn that this man's brain has been programmed and the environment arranged so that exactly those movements on his part would be causally necessitated by those antecedently arranged circumstances, and that all this was known in advance by those who did the arranging. They explain the relevant causal laws and show us how they can do the same thing with anybody. Our impression that here was an agent acting freely, with alternatives open to him, vanishes completely. And it would not be restored by our learning that during the episode the man had the normal impression of freedom, of having alternatives open to him, and his movements were the outcome of his perceptions and motives in the sort of way such things normally are. What we have learned would compel us to view him as not having it open to him (after the initial arrangements) to do other than what he did. And we would be compelled to this view via an inference of the form given in FL.

At this point someone might be tempted to say that what makes my latest example a case of unavoidable action—what is necessary to make it such a case—is that the antecedent state of the world that causally necessitates the action, through the agent's motivational states and processes in a natural way, did not itself come about in a natural way but rather by contrivance. The fact that that antecedent state was arranged by other agents with the intention of manipulating this agent, rather than having come about naturally, is what makes this a case of an unavoidable action.

This suggestion seems to me very implausible on its face. Why should the fact that manipulation-minded agents, rather than nature or blind chance, arranged the state of the world that causally necessitated this episode in this agent's life make any difference to the unavoidability of that episode by that agent? Suppose that we came to know of two cases—first, a case involving manipulators as described previously, and then later, another case where the very same sort of antecedent state of the world as the manipulators arranged in the first case happened to come about naturally—and we knew how such an antecedent state causally necessitates such an episode as was in fact experienced by both agents. We would surely find it no less compelling to say of the second, naturally occurring case that such an episode was unavoidable by the agent after the time of the antecedent state than to say this of the first, artificially arranged case. As soon as we learn about the naturally occurring case that there was here the same antecedent state of the world that causally necessitated the episode in the artificially arranged case, our impression that here was an agent with alternatives open to him will vanish completely. And it will not be restored by its being pointed out to us that here blind nature, rather than a designing agent, arranged the causally necessitating antecedent state.

3. TRADITIONAL COMPATIBILISM: THE REJECTION OF IFD

Traditional compatibilism denies claim (*a*), the part of traditional incompatibilism that I have just defended, holding that the proposition that an agent could have acted otherwise than she did (had alternatives open to her) *is* compatible with causal determinism. And it is so, on this view, because the proposition that *S could* have done *A* is equivalent to the proposition that *S would* have done *A if* she had willed or chosen to do *A*; and this latter proposition is clearly compatible with determinism: even if *S*'s willing or choosing to do *B* (rather than *A*), and as a result doing *B*, was causally necessitated by the state of the world before *S* was born, it may still be true that *if* (contrary to fact) *S had* chosen to do *A* then she would have done *A*.

A *locus classicus* of this view is Moore (1912), wherein Moore writes:

There are certainly good reasons for thinking that we *very often* mean by 'could' merely 'would, *if* so and so had chosen'. And if so, then we have a sense of the word 'could' in which the fact that we often *could* have done what we did not do, is perfectly compatible with the principle that everything has a cause . . . (Moore 1912: 131)

The view still has its defenders, for example Hillary Bok (1998). According to Bok, the counterfactual conditional analysis of having an alternative open is the right analysis for purposes of assessing agents' responsibility because it is the right analysis of what counts as an open alternative in the context of *deliberation*, that is, when one is deciding which among alternative actions to perform. She holds that (*a*) it is reasonable for a deliberator to take as among the alternatives to be considered in her deciding just those alternatives each of which is such that she is justified in thinking that she would do it if she chose (Bok 1998, ch. 3); and (*b*) it is correct to hold an agent responsible for any deliberated choice where there were alternatives it was reasonable for her to consider in making that choice (Bok 1998, ch. 4).

Both of these claims are questionable. Consider (*a*) first. This criterion for whether a deliberator should consider an alternative open to her (namely, that it is such that she is justified in thinking that she would do it if she chose) is both too wide and too narrow. It lets in too much because there can be cases where a possible action is such that the agent would do it if she chose to do it (and she knows this) but also such that the agent knows that, because the thought of doing it is so over-poweringly repulsive to her (e.g. eating what she knows to be excrement), she could not bring herself to choose to do it. It would not be reasonable for a deliberator to consider such an alternative as open to her. This sort of counter-example might be avoided by adding to the criterion that the subject does not believe that she cannot choose it. (Bok's remark that 'I can consider an action to be among my alternatives only if I do not know that it is impossible for me to perform it' (1998: 106), though not made in response to any such objection, suggests that she would endorse such an addition.)

But even with this modification the criterion would still be too narrow. It would exclude alternatives that it would be reasonable for a deliberator to consider, ones where 'I would do it if I chose' is false, but the deliberator does not know this. Suppose Bond knows that one of the two doors to the room he's in is unlocked but he doesn't know which; he suddenly learns that the room will fill with poisonous gas in thirty seconds; it's a large room and the doors are far apart, so he has only time enough to try one door; he knows that one of the two conditionals, 'If I were to choose to escape by door *A*, then I would escape by door *A*' and 'If I were to choose to escape by door *B*, then I would escape by door *B*' is true and the other is false, but he does not know which. In the circumstances, it would be reasonable for him (in deciding which door to try) to consider both alternatives, escaping via door *A* and escaping via door *B*, equally seriously, even though he knows that only one of them is open to him. Yet Bok's criterion would say that *neither* alternative is open to him *for purposes of deliberation*, because neither of those conditionals is such that Bond is justified in believing it to be true.

Further modification of the criterion might avoid this sort of counter-example also; so perhaps a satisfactory conditional, compatibilist criterion for 'open to the agent for purposes of deliberation' is achievable. But it would still remain a question whether (as claim (*b*) says) having an alternative open in this sense is sufficient for moral responsibility. One can be led to doubt this by considering (hypothetical) examples where a person's deliberative processes are manipulated by another. Take our Bond example again and change it a bit by supposing that, unknown to Bond, his thought processes are under the control of a powerful, evil neuroscientist (who has planted chips in Bond's brain for this purpose); this controller causes Bond to decide not to try either door but to remain in the room and be killed by the poisonous gas. Is Bond morally responsible in such a case for committing suicide (and abandoning his important mission)? Clearly not. In the relevant sense he had no alternative open to him. Yet in the sense of 'open for purposes of deliberation' given by Bok's criterion, he did have the alternative open of escaping through the unlocked door: he knew that if he chose to escape by that door then he would escape (and he believed that it was open to him to choose to escape by that door).

4. SEMI-COMPATIBILISM:
THE REJECTION OF PAP

The (*b*) part of traditional incompatibilism is the principle of alternative possibilities, PAP, which I have stated this way:

> An agent is morally responsible for a given action only if she had it open to her to avoid that action.

This simple statement of PAP can, without loss of plausibility, be generalized and strengthened.

One can be morally responsible for things other than one's actions. One can be responsible for one's failure to act in a certain way at a certain time (entailed by one's acting in some contrary way, or one's being inactive, at that time)—e.g. for not closing the door when one left the house. And one can be responsible for a consequence of one's action or of one's failure to act—e.g. for the mess on the floor (as a result of one's walking across it with muddy boots), or for the cat's getting outside (because of one's failure to close the door). We should formulate PAP so that it will apply to these other sorts of cases too. We can do this by having it talk about responsibility for its being the case that such-and-such:

> A person *S* is responsible for its being the case that *P* only if *S* could have avoided (i.e. had it open to her to avoid) its being the case that *P*.

Our original PAP is a special case falling under this more general principle, namely, the case where *P* is a proposition to the effect that *S* acted in a certain way at a certain time.

What needs to have obtained for it to be true that *S* could have avoided its being the case that *P*? There must have been something *S* could have done, or could have omitted doing, which would have led to its being not the case that *P*. More exactly, there must have been a time *T* such that: (i) if *S* had acted in a certain way at *T* that she did not act, then it would not have been the case that *P*, and up until *T* it was open to *S* to act in that way then; or (ii) if *S* had *not* acted at *T* in a certain way that she did act, then it would not have been the case that *P*, and up until *T* it was open to *S* not to act in that way then.

If it is plausible to hold that one's moral responsibility for a state of affairs requires that one was able to avoid it, it is equally plausible to hold that it requires something stronger, namely, that one was able to avoid it *by some means one knew about or should have known about.* More exactly, there must have been a time T such that: (i) if S had acted in a certain way at T that she did not act, then it would not have been the case that P, up until T it was open to S to act in that way then, *and S then knew or should have known those things;* or (ii) if S had *not* acted at T in a certain way that she did act, then it would not have been the case that P, up until T it was open to S not to act in that way then, *and S then knew or should have known those things.* So from now on let us take 'PAP' to refer to the following principle:

> A person S is responsible for its being the case that P *only if* S could have avoided its being the case that P by some means S knew about or should have known about.

Despite its plausibility, PAP is thought by many philosophers to be shown false by a certain sort of alleged counter-example introduced by Harry Frankfurt (1969). The basic idea in a Frankfurt-type example (an FTE) is that the circumstances that make it false that S could have avoided its being the case that P (by some means S knew about or should have known about: hereafter I will sometimes leave this qualification to be tacitly understood)—i.e. that make the necessary condition required by PAP fail to hold—are *not* among the circumstances that are responsible for S's failing to avoid its being the case that, P. The example is constructed by starting with an example where S brings it about, or allows it to be the case, that P in a way that satisfies PAP and all other requirements for S's being responsible for its being the case that P—an example about which it would be clear to everyone that S is responsible for its being the case that P—and then adding to the example circumstances that do not play any role in bringing it about that P but nevertheless do guarantee that S could not have avoided its being the case that P—for example, a mechanism that would bring it about that P if S were not to do so. The intuition that such an example is supposed to call forth is that, since those added circumstances play no role in bringing it about that P, S is just as responsible for its being the case that P as she would have been had those circumstances not been present and S could have avoided its being the case that, P. This is so, the reasoning goes, because it is true of the modified example that S *would* have brought it about (or allowed it to be the case) that P *even if* S could have avoided its being the case that P.

Should those of us who have found PAP intuitively plausible be persuaded to give it up by such an example? I think not. First, it should be noted that the principle relied on in an FTE to get from the facts of the example to the conclusion that it falsifies PAP, however plausible it may seem at first blush, can be shown to be invalid. This is the following principle:

> In a case where the circumstances making it true that S could not have avoided its being the case that P play no role in bringing it about that P, if it is also true that S *would* have brought it about (or allowed it to be the case) that P *even*

if S could have avoided its being the case that *P*, then *S* is responsible for its being the case that, *P*.

It is easy to come up with examples where this principle fails. Suppose *S* is in a room which, unbeknownst to *S*, has been locked from the outside to prevent *S* from going to warn someone of an imminent danger; *S* falsely believes she could leave the room and go to give the warning but decides not to do so and therefore makes no attempt to do so. Here *S* would not have left the room to give the warning (and for the same reasons) even if the room were not locked and *S* could have left it to give the warning, but clearly it does not follow, and is false, that *S* can be rightly blamed for its being the case that *S* did not leave the room to give the warning. All *S* can be blamed for here is its being the case that *S* did *not try* to leave the room to give the warning. (This example is inspired by one given in Locke 1894: II. xxi. 10; van Inwagen 1983, sect. 5.2, uses a similar example for a similar purpose.)

I confess that the only cases I can come up with that so incontrovertibly falsify the principle relied on in FTEs are ones where '*P*' says that *S* did *not* act in a certain way at a certain time. We should not, however, conclude from this that the principle must hold for other sorts of cases, at least not until we are given some reason to expect that cases of that sort but not others should be exceptions to the principle and I have seen no such reason offered. However, let us not just leave the matter there but instead examine cases of other sorts.

Consider cases where '*P*' represents a state of affairs which is, not *S*'s acting (or failing to act) in a certain way at a certain time, but rather a consequence of *S*'s action (or failure to act). Suppose, for example, that *S* and *R* wish to ruin their neighbour *M*'s elegant dinner party this evening; *R* has to be away this evening but *S* promises that he will see to it that their radio is playing extremely loud music during *M*'s party and he does so, and it is true that he could have avoided there being loud music ruining *M*'s dinner party (by means he knew about, namely, not turning on the radio). But now we add to the example a circumstance that falsifies this last condition, namely, that *R* does not trust *S* to remember to keep his promise and, unbeknownst to *S*, sets their radio to come on automatically at 8 p.m.; but *S* does keep his promise by turning on the radio to a high volume at 7.45 p.m. just before going out. About such cases a PAP-defender will find plausible a fairly simple counter-claim, namely, that *S* is *not* responsible for its being the case *that P* (in this example, that the radio is playing loudly during *M*'s party), since that is something *S* could not have avoided (by some means she knew about or should have known about), but that *S* *is* responsible for its being the case *that S brought it about that P*, which is something *S* could have avoided. (For an example where the radio's playing loudly during *M*'s party is a consequence of *S*'s *not* acting in a certain way, suppose that the radio is already on loud, but *R* has rigged it so that if *S* turns it off any time before 8 p.m., it will automatically come back on at 8 p.m. after *S* goes out.)

Next, consider cases where '*P*' says that *S* acted in a certain way at a certain time. (Later we will consider cases where '*P*' says that *S* did *not* act in a certain way at a certain time.) Let us take the act in question to be a *mental* act of *S*'s deciding at a certain time to do a certain thing. This will free us from distracting concerns about whether or not circumstances outside *S* provide opportunity for the action in question. So '*P*' is of the form '*S* decided at *T* to *A*'. ('*A*', for example, might be 'change her will so as to leave everything to her nephew *R*'.) Let '*T*' designate the precise (doubtless very short) period of time occupied by the decision event. (That is, every subinterval of *T* is occupied by part of the decision event and no interval before or after *T* is occupied by any part of the decision event.)

Following the recipe for constructing an FTE, we start with an example where it is true of every time up to *T* that at that time it was open to *S* to avoid its being the case that *S* decided at *T* to *A*. What can we add to the example that will make it *false* of every time up to *T* that *S* could have avoided that sort of decision event at *T* but that will play no part in bringing it about? We might try adding a device that monitors what goes on in *S*'s mind (or in *S*'s brain, whose processes realize or are the supervenience base of *S*'s mental processes) and, if during *T* it detects something other than (incompatible with) that sort of decision event's occurring at *T*, or if during some tiny early part of *T* it detects something other than the start of that sort of decision event, then it causes that sort of decision event to occur immediately (Stump 1999 makes such a move). But then, since the decision event that would have been caused by our device, had it been triggered, would have begun at some time after *T* began, we have failed to construct an example where it is false that *S* could have avoided making that sort of decision at *T*; we have got, rather, an example where it is false only that *S* could have avoided the less specific state of affairs of *S*'s making that sort of decision at some point within a certain larger interval that includes *T*. Being responsible for a given state of affairs does not entail being responsible for every less specific state affairs entailed by it: I am, let us suppose, responsible for its being the case that from 1 to 1.15 p.m. on 8 February 2001 I engaged in no running; it doesn't follow that I am responsible for its being the case that during at least part of February 2001 I engaged in no running: to hold me responsible for failing to run continuously throughout that month, on the ground that I was responsible for failing to run during a certain fifteen-minute part of it, would obviously be absurd. The PAP-sympathizer will find it plausible to think that *S* is *not* responsible for the less specific state of affairs of making a decision to *A* during a certain larger interval that includes *T*, because *S* could not have avoided it, but can be responsible at most only for the more specific state of affairs of deciding at *T* to *A*, which *S* could have avoided (and for which *S* is equally blameworthy, if *S* is responsible for it, as *S* would be for the less specific state of affairs were *S* responsible for it); nothing in the example gives the PAP-sympathizer reason to think otherwise.

(Some (for example, Fischer 1994, ch. 7) have argued that attempts to defend PAP against Frankfurt-type examples by specifying more precisely what the agent in such examples is responsible for end up appealing to alternative possibilities that should not count as genuine alternatives for the purpose of satisfying PAP. I cannot see how that charge has any plausibility against the foregoing defence of PAP. Consider the alternatives to deciding at T to A that are left open to S in the FTE just discussed. They include: at the beginning of T beginning to decide to do something else; or: at the beginning of T not beginning to make any decision at all (remaining inactive). I can see no reason why these should be thought to be not genuine alternatives for the purpose of justifying an attribution of responsibility. They are alternatives such that, had S taken one of them, S would have done so freely, and they are perfectly good answers to the question 'Well, if you blame S for deciding at T to A, what do you think S should have done instead?' What more could reasonably be required of a genuine alternative?)

Suppose, on the other hand, we try to design our back-up mechanism in such a way as to ensure that, if it were triggered, it would cause that sort of decision event to occur at precisely the same time T as it occurs in the actual sequence (where the device is not triggered). How could we do this, while at the same time ensuring that in the actual sequence S could not avoid the decision event at T? The only way, as far as I can see, is to make the device such that it is *not* triggered (it is 'neutralized') *only* if it detects before T some condition C which is such that the occurrence of C makes it the case that S could not avoid making that sort of decision at, T. Otherwise, if the device were designed to be neutralized by some development before T that fails to guarantee that S could not avoid such a decision at T, then there would be *nothing* in the example to make it the case that S could not avoid such a decision at T; and so the example would fail to be a counter-example to PAP. But now the recipe for constructing an FTE has been violated: we are not starting with an example which satisfies the PAP condition, where it is clear and indisputable that S is responsible for the decision, and then adding something that renders the decision unavoidable but plays no role in causing it; rather, we are starting with an example which already falsifies the PAP condition and about which the PAP-sympathizer will think that, for that reason, S is not responsible for the decision. And the addition to the example gives her no reason to think otherwise.

So the constructor of a Frankfurt-type example seems to be faced with a dilemma: either the added failsafe mechanism fails to make it the case that S could not have avoided deciding at T to A; or its making that decision event unavoidable depends on the event's being deterministically caused by prior conditions in the world; in which case the PAP-sympathizer can hardly be expected to agree that S was morally responsible for that event before the failsafe mechanism was added. (This sort of argument is made in Widerker 1995b; Ginet 1996.)

But Alfred Mele and David Robb (Mele and Robb 1998) claim to have found a way for an FTE-constructor to avoid this dilemma. They start with an example where

S's deciding at *T* to *A* is *indeterministically* caused, so that PAP is satisfied. (Because the causation was indeterministic it does not entail that *S* could not have avoided deciding at *T* to *A*.) Then they add to the example that there actually occurred right up to *T* a process that would have deterministically caused *S*'s deciding at *T* to *A* but for the fact that it was pre-empted by the other process that indeterministically caused that event. The upshot, they claim, is that we have an example where *S*'s deciding at *T* to *A* was something *S* could not have avoided (because of the presence of the deterministic process) but also something that was not deterministically caused (because the deterministic process was pre-empted by an indeterministic one); and since *S*'s deciding at *T* to *A* was not deterministically caused, there is no reason to hesitate to judge that *S* was responsible for her deciding at *T* to *A*. (Some PAP-sympathizers may be inclined to think that an agent cannot be responsible for an action that is indeterministically caused. I am not inclined to think this but, in any case, there is another problem with Mele's and Robb's argument.)

I doubt that the Mele–Robb example is coherent. Let me explain why. Let us give the label *E* to the event of *S*'s deciding to *A*. The short interval of time *T* occupied by the event *E* began, let us say, at instant T_1 and ended at instant T_2, i.e. *T* was the interval $[T_1–T_2]$. The final stages of both the deterministic process and the indeterministic process occur during an interval that is before and continuous with $[T_1–T_2]$, say $[T_0–T_1)$. Let us name those final stages of the deterministic and indeterministic processes *D-final* and *I-final*, respectively. What I doubt is that the following three claims that Mele–Robb make about the example can all be true:

(1) I-final pre-empts D-final as the immediate (most proximate) cause of *E* at $[T_1–T_2]$.

(2) If *E* had not been indeterministically caused by I-final, then D-final would have deterministically caused *E* to occur at precisely the same time as I-final caused it to occur, namely, precisely in the interval $[T_1–T_2]$.

(3) The occurrence of *E* at $[T_1–T_2]$ was unavoidable by *S*.

If (1) is true, then one or the other of the following two things must be true:

(1*a*) I-final's *causing E* (and nothing short of that) is what blocked D-final from causing *E*.

(1*b*) The *mere simultaneous presence* of I-final is what blocked D-final from causing *E*.

It is hard to see what other alternatives would make (1) true. But here's the rub: if (1*a*) is true, then (2) is false; and if, on other hand, (1*b*) is true, then (3) is false.

Suppose (1) is true in way (1*a*), i.e. what blocks D-final's causing *E* is that I-final *causes E*. Then D-final's causing *E* is not blocked (it is not determined that D-final will not cause *E*) until there occurs at least the beginning of I-final's causing *E*. But the process of I-final's causing *E* does not begin until *E* begins: since I-final's causing *E* is indeterministic, nature does not determine that I-final does produce

E until *E*'s being produced by I-final has begun to happen, and when *E*'s being produced has begun to happen so has *E*. This means that, in the counterfactual scenario, where, because I-final fails to cause *E*, D-final does, it is not determined that D-final *will* cause *E* until the interval $[T_1-T_2]$ has begun *without E*'s having begun, that is, until after T_1. In the counterfactual scenario D-final could not begin to cause *E* until after T_1, and therefore the *E*-type event that D-final causes in the counterfactual scenario must begin slightly later than it does in the actual scenario, contrary to what (2) says.

If, on the other hand, (1) is true in way (1*b*)—if what does the pre-empting of D-final is, not I-final's *causing E*, but just I-final's *occurring* simultaneously with D-final—then (3) must be false, i.e. *E*'s occurring at $[T_1-T_2]$ was avoidable by S. For to say that the mere simultaneous presence of I-final is what blocks D-final's efficacy is to say that D-final's being followed by *E* is nomologically necessary *only in the absence of simultaneous I-final*, that where D-final and I-final occur together, as in the actual scenario, they have the same real chance of not being followed by *E* as the chance that I-final will not indeterministically cause *E*. And that means that *E* at $[T_1-T_2]$ (*S*'s deciding at *T* to *A*) was no more unavoidable by *S* in the actual scenario than it would have been if the deterministic process had been absent. If it be insisted that D-final nomologically necessitates *E* whether or not I-final is present, then we have no reason to think that the presence of I-final *pre-empts* D-final, that D-final is not efficacious here. And a reason to think this is needed: we cannot just stipulate that it is so. If there is no such reason, then overdetermination of *E* by both D-final and I-final would seem the more plausible verdict (assuming that we have reason to think that I-final was also efficacious; if it's unclear what that reason might be, then an at least equally plausible verdict in this case is that D-final pre-empts I-final).

The upshot is that, since Mele–Robb's example cannot satisfy all of (1), (2), and (3), it cannot succeed in escaping the dilemma that thwarts success in attempts to construct a Frankfurt-type counter-example to PAP: either the example fails to make it the case that *S* could not have avoided deciding at *T* to *A* or it makes that event's unavoidability depend on its being deterministically caused.

Finally, consider cases where '*P*' says that *S* did *not* act in a certain way at a certain time. Again, let us take the act in question to be a mental act of deciding: '*P*' is of the form '*S* did not decide at *T* to *A*'. Here *T* can be any particular interval long enough to include such a decision event. Following the recipe for constructing an FTE, we begin with an example where it is clear to everyone that *S* was responsible for not deciding at *T* to *A*—including its being true that *S* could have avoided its being the case that *S* did not decide at *T* to *A* by deciding at *T* to *A*—and we add circumstances that make it false that *S* could have decided at *T* to *A* but that play no role in bringing it about that *S* did not decide at *T* to *A*. We add a device that monitors *S*'s mental activity during *T* and if at any time during that interval it were to detect that *S begins* to decide to *A*, it would prevent the decision process from going forward to completion, so that S would not have actually decided at T to A. But S never does during T begin to decide to A. So our added device plays no role in preventing S's so deciding; but its presence means that S could not so decide during T.

But it is also plain, I think, that S cannot be held responsible for not deciding at T to A, but only for not *trying* at T to decide to A. The case is quite analogous to the case considered earlier where S is in a room which, unbeknownst to S, has been locked from the outside to prevent S from going to warn someone of an imminent danger, and S, though believing she could leave the room and give the warning, chooses not to do so. In both cases, because external barriers render it impossible for S to act in the way in question, S is not responsible for not acting in that way but only for not trying to do so.

The upshot of all this is that the philosopher who, before becoming aware of Frankfurt-type examples, found PAP intuitively plausible should not find in such examples any convincing reason to abandon that principle.

Another sort of example that some (Wolf 1990; Stump 1996) have suggested shows the falsity of PAP is a case where one had no alternative to acting (or not acting) in a certain way because one had no motive at all for any alternative, no alternative had any appeal whatsoever, no alternative was recommended to any significant degree by any of one's desires or values. For example, on those occasions when I've been standing on a crowded subway platform watching a train come in, there is a sense in which I could have pushed the stranger next to me onto the track in front of the train: no external obstacle prevented it and it was within my physical capability. But in another sense I could *not* have done that: all my desires and values spoke against doing it and none spoke in favour: I was, one might say, motivationally incapable of doing it. Some would say that I was nevertheless morally responsible for not doing it. I deserve credit for not perpetrating that moral outrage despite the fact that I could not have done it.

I am inclined to disagree. It seems to me that to the degree it is doubtful whether I could have done it, doubtful whether there was for me the possibility of really *choosing* not to do it, it is equally doubtful that I merit any credit for not doing it. I see the case as in the same bag with one where we do not blame or reproach a person for failing to take bold action to ward off a danger if we think that panic or 'paralysing' fear prevented the person from considering such action as a serious option.

We must, by the way, distinguish such cases where we say a person could not do a certain thing, meaning that the person's psychological state blocked that alternative, from other cases where we might say a person could not do a certain thing and mean only that their moral principles, or their legal duty, or some authority it is their policy to obey, forbade it, cases where the forbidden option was tempting, had some appeal, to the person—it was a 'thinkable' option for them. (Certainly a child's 'I can't come out to play; my mother says I have to go to bed' is typically in this second category rather than the first. Probably also was Martin Luther's 'I can do no other', contrary to what some have suggested; e.g. Dennett 1984: 133.) In these latter cases, the person is morally responsible for not doing the thing but it is also true that in the relevant sense they *could* have done it: it was an option really open to them which they *chose* not to take.

5. Direct Incompatibilism

Direct incompatibilism is the view that there is reason to hold that determinism is incompatible with moral responsibility that is independent of whether PAP holds, or, in other words, that the incompatibility of moral responsibility with determinism can be shown directly, without reliance on PAP. (See van Inwagen 1980 for an early proposal of this view; see McKenna 2001 for a recent full discussion.) Here is one such direct argument.

We assume that the following principles express truths about moral responsibility. (In these principles the phrase '*S* is not responsible for . . .' is to be interpreted as meaning '*S* never was and never will be responsible for . . .'.)

(NRP) (non-responsibility for the past). For any agent *S* and truth *P* about what happened before *S* existed, *S* is not responsible for its being the case that *P*.

(NRL) (non-responsibility for the laws). For any agent *S* and truth *P* that is entailed by causal laws, *S* is not responsible for its being the case that *P*.

(NRA) (non-responsibility agglomerativity). For any true conjunction *P* & *Q*, if *S* is not responsible for its being the case that *P* and *S* is not responsible for its being the case that *Q*, then *S* is not responsible for its being the case that *P* & *Q*.

(NRT) (non-responsibility transfer). For any truths *P* and *Q*, if *P* logically entails *Q* and *S* is not responsible for its being the case that *P*, then *S* is not responsible for its being the case that *Q*.

Then we argue as follows.

If determinism is true, then, for any truth of the form '*S* does *A* at *T*', there is a truth *B* such that:

(1) *B* is entirely about how the world was before *S* existed and it follows from causal laws that if *B*, then *S* does *A* at *T*. (An obvious consequence of determinism)

(2) Therefore, S is not responsible for its being the case that: B & (if B then S does A at T). ((1), NRP, NRL, NRA)

(3) Therefore, S is not responsible for its being the case that S does A at T. ((2), NRT)

Therefore, if determinism is true, then, for any truth of the form 'S does A at T', S is not responsible for its being the case that S does A at T.

This argument demonstrates that, if our four NR principles hold, then in a deterministic world no one can be responsible for any of their actions. The only one of our four principles that has been questioned, or that seems at all open to question, is NRT, the principle that logical entailment transfers non-responsibility. I want to consider two different sorts of alleged counter-examples that have been suggested. (For still another sort, see Stump and Fischer 2000.)

The first sort involves causal pre-emption or causal overdetermination (Fischer and Ravizza 1998, ch. 6). In both pre-emption and overdetermination there occur two different conditions each of which is causally sufficient for a certain effect in the sense that, given the circumstances, each would have produced the effect had the other been absent. In pre-emption one of the sufficient conditions actually produces the effect and the other doesn't, either because the effective condition produces it before the other can (A and B each throws a rock towards a window with sufficient force to break it but A's rock gets there first) or because the effective condition interferes with the operation of the other condition (on its way to the window A's rock hits B's rock a glancing blow which is enough to change the trajectory of B's rock so that it would not hit the window). In overdetermination, neither sufficient condition pre-empts the other: there is as much reason to attribute the effect to the work of the one as to attribute it to the work of the other (A's and B's rocks strike the window at the same time each with enough force to break the window by itself).

According to some thinkers, an agent who is responsible for creating a causally sufficient condition for a certain effect is also responsible for that effect even if there is another sufficient condition for the same effect for which the agent is not responsible and which pre-empts the agent's sufficient condition or together with the agent's sufficient condition causally overdetermines the effect. Thus someone who thinks this will take the following to be a counter-example to NRT: Terrorist S plants a large bomb in the basement of a building with a timer attached set to cause the bomb to explode at noon; its explosion would be sufficient to destroy the building. But at 11.50 a.m. a powerful earthquake shakes the ground on which the building stands with sufficient force to cause its destruction moments before S's bomb would have caused it. (Or, for an overdetermination case, the earthquake shakes the building at just the same time as the bomb explodes.) We may suppose that long before the earthquake occurred there obtained a state of affairs that was causally sufficient to produce that earthquake at that time and place. S was not responsible for that state of affairs or for the consequence of the causal laws that if it occurred then the building would be destroyed at approximately noon. Yet, some would say, S was responsible for the destruction of the building. If their thought is right, then it follows that NRT does not hold.

But I find that thought counter-intuitive. While it is true that S is as much to blame as he would be had his bomb destroyed the building (or, in the overdetermination case, been the sole cause of its destruction), *what* S is to blame for is, not the destruction of the building, but knowingly creating a condition causally sufficient for the building's destruction (something equally reprehensible). So this sort of alleged counter-example to NRT is at best inconclusive.

Not so, however, the other sort. Suppose that S intentionally broke a front window of a house and then a violent windstorm broke a back window. S is not responsible for its being the case that a front window *and* a back window are broken, but he is responsible for its being the case that a front window is broken. Yet NRT dictates that if he is not responsible for the conjunctive state of affairs then he is not responsible for a logically entailed conjunct. NRT fails because the non-responsibility operator NR is not closed under conjunction elimination.

Can we rescue the argument by appealing to the following more specific version of NRT?

(NRT*) For any truths P and Q, if P is of the form 'B and it follows from causal laws that if B then Q' and S is not responsible either for its being the case that P or for its being the case that B, then S is not responsible for its being the case that Q.

I'm afraid not, as is shown by the following sort of example (for which I thank David Widerker, personal communication). Suppose that, during a November walk up a hill in the country, S moves a largish stone in order to see what is underneath it. A month later, after a snowstorm, R rides a sled down that hill and runs into that stone (which is concealed by the snow) and overturns. Suppose that, given certain circumstances C that were present and for which S was not responsible (including, among others, the circumstance that the stone was not moved between the time S moved it and the time of R's sled ride and the circumstance that R's sled took the precise route down the hill that it did), S's moving that stone was causally necessary for the sled's overturning: it follows from causal laws and the obtaining of C that, had the stone not been moved to its new location, nothing would have caused R's sled to overturn when and as it did. So it follows from causal laws that if R's sled overturned when and as it did and C obtained, then S moved the stone when and as she did. S was morally responsible for moving the stone but, since she neither knew nor should have known about R's later sled ride (S's ignorance of the fact that her moving the stone would result in a sled's overturning a month later was completely non-culpable), S is not morally responsible for the overturning of R's sled. If we take P to be the truth 'C obtained and R's sled overturned when and as it did, and it follows from causal laws that if C obtained and R's sled overturned when and as it did, then S moved the stone when and as she did' and Q to be the truth 'S moved the stone when and as she did', then we have a case where the antecedent of NRT* is true and its consequent is false.

We could avoid such counter-examples to NRT* by specifying it still further, to the following:

(NRT**)   For any truths P and Q, if P is of the form 'B and it follows from causal laws that if B then Q', Q reports an event or state that occurred later than the condition(s) reported by B, and S is not responsible either for its being the case that P or for its being the case that B, then S is not responsible for its being the case that Q.

I know of no (clear and non-controversial) counter-examples to NRT** and I am inclined to think it is true. If it is true, then appeal to it, instead of to NRT, in the argument above will give us a sound argument for incompatibilism and one that is independent of PAP. The only problem with NRT** that I see is that it is not as evident, as hard to deny, as our other NR assumptions, especially not to someone who is not already persuaded that determinism is incompatible with responsibility. The argument, even if sound, ends up being less conclusive than we might wish.

Some (Pereboom 1995, 2001; Stump 1996, 1999) have supposed that another direct argument for incompatibilism can be obtained from the assumption that the thing incompatible with determinism required by moral responsibility is, not that the agent have alternatives open, but rather that the agent be an *ultimate* or *originating* cause of that for which she is responsible. This will not be the case if determinism is true; for, given anything that has a causal source in me, determinism entails that there is a further-back causal source that lies outside me and that produced the causal source in me and therefore nothing in me can be an *ultimate* cause of anything, and for that reason I could not be responsible for anything. On the other hand, according to this line, if determinism is not true then I can, of course, be an ultimate cause of something and therefore responsible for it (assuming I knew I was causing it) even when it is also true that, if I had not caused that thing, then something else would have and therefore I could not have avoided its occurrence.

Philosophers who endorse PAP will doubt that this line actually has found a reason for incompatibilism that is independent of commitment to PAP. They will certainly agree that my being an ultimate cause of something is necessary for my being morally responsible for it, but will suggest that the reason for this is that only if I am the ultimate cause was it *wholly up to me* whether or not that thing occurred. In the special case where I was the ultimate cause of something, but it would have been caused by something else if I had not caused it, then it was *not* up to me whether that thing occurred and therefore it is not something for which I am responsible. What I *am* responsible for in such a case is, not the thing whose occurrence I could not avoid, but my causing that thing (or my contributing something sufficient to cause it), which is something I could have avoided: it was up to me whether I would cause it and so I am morally responsible for that—my causing it.

6. Agent Control

Traditional incompatibilism appears to be defensible, and perhaps more defensible than direct incompatibilism. There is, however, an alleged difficulty for incompatibilism of either sort that remains to be considered. Some have suggested (or worried) that, if an action is not causally determined, then it is a random event and not under the control of the agent, not something that the agent determines; and an event that is not under the control of, not determined by, the agent is surely not an event for which the agent is morally responsible (see, for example, Hobart 1934; Ayer 1959; Smart 1968; Double 1991; G. Strawson 1994).

Incompatibilists have (so far) come up with three different ways of denying this suggestion, three alternative ways of explaining how it can be that an agent controls or determines her causally undetermined action (see O'Connor 1993a). One is to say that the agent's control of her action consists in its being *indeterministically caused* by the motives or reasons the agent has that explain her performing that action (Clarke 1993, 1996; Kane 1996). One problem with this suggestion is that explanations of actions in terms of the agent's reasons (e.g. ones of the form 'S did A because she believed that she would thereby carry out her intention to B') do not require for their truth the truth of any causal laws, probabilistic or deterministic, connecting the reasons with the actions (see Ginet 1990, ch. 6, for a defence of this view), and so there can be responsible actions for reasons which are not indeterministically caused by those reasons. Another problem is that it does not seem to avoid the alleged difficulty but merely to relocate it. Consider a case where the agent has conflicting motives and the motive that ends up causing a corresponding action does so only indeterministically. If it is plausible to think that when an action is uncaused, nothing, not even the agent, determines or controls whether that action occurs, it should be plausible to think similarly that when one of a conflicting pair of motives indeterministically causes an action, nothing, not even the agent, determines which motive causes the action; and therefore the agent cannot be held responsible for which motive she acts on.

Another way of responding to the alleged difficulty is to say that the agent's control of her action consists, not in the obtaining of any causal relation between the action and prior events or states in the agent, but rather in the obtaining of a direct causal relation between the agent as such and the action (or some event internal to the action, so that the action consists in the agent's causing this event), that is, to posit a special *sui generis* causal relation where the relatum on the cause side is not any event in or state of the agent but just the agent herself, *qua* enduring entity: the agent controls or determines what she does by just agent-causing it, and these agent-causing events are not caused at all (though they typically will have reasons explanations) (see Chisholm 1966, 1969; Taylor 1966; Reid 1969; and especially O'Connor 2000). The main problem with this response is that it, too, seems just to relocate the alleged difficulty. Anyone who has the initial worry is likely to ask: How is it that *these agent-causing events* are determined or controlled by the agent if they are not in any way caused? If an action's being uncaused is a good reason to think that it is not determined or controlled by the agent, then it is hard to see how it really helps to allay the worry to say that the action *consists* in the agent's (or anything else's) causing something.

This brings us to the third way of responding to the difficulty, which is just to deny that an *action's* being uncaused is a reason to think that the agent lacked control over whether the action occurred. That is, we must deny what Robert Kane calls the 'pernicious assumption' that all control must be *antecedent* determining control (Kane 1996: 186–7). As Kane observes, if we were to discover that the brain processes underlying our seemingly free decisions involved antecedently undetermined events at the climactic points, we would not regard this as reason to deny that our decisions were not after all *made by us*, were not exercises of *our* wills but just chance events. It is, of course, true that if an event is *not* an action of mine, then I can make that event occur only by causing it, that is, by performing some action that causes it. But I make my own free, simple mental acts—my decisions and volitions—occur by simply performing them, by being their subject, by their being *my acts*. These are *ipso facto* determined by me, without need of any causal relation to me or anything else (provided that they are free, that is, not determined by something else, not causally necessitated by antecedent states and events). (The account of free agency in Chisholm (1976a; 1976b, ch. II) seems to agree, though one cannot be sure.) This simple sort of incompatibilist thinks that I am the ultimate cause of the things my free actions cause, simply because those things have their source in uncaused actions of mine.

REFERENCES

Albritton, R. (1985). 'Freedom of the Will and Freedom of Action'. *Proceedings and Addresses of the American Philosophical Association*, 59: 239–51.

Audi, R. (1978). 'Avoidability and Possible Worlds'. *Philosophical Studies*, 33: 413–21.

Ayer, A. J. (1959). 'Freedom and Necessity', in Ayer, *Philosophical Essays*. London: Macmillan, 271–84.

Berofsky, B. (1987). *Freedom from Necessity: The Metaphysical Basis of Responsibility*. New York: Routledge & Kegan Paul.

Bok, H. (1998). *Freedom and Responsibility*. Princeton: Princeton University Press.

Broad, C. D. (1952). 'Determinism, Indeterminism, and Libertarianism', in Broad, *Ethics and the History of Philosophy*. London: Routledge & Kegan Paul.

Campbell, C. A. (1951). 'Is "Free Will" a Pseudo-Problem?' *Mind*, 60: 441–65.

—— (1967). *In Defense of Free Will*. London: Allen & Unwin.

Chisholm, R. (1966). 'Freedom and Action', in Lehrer (1966: 11–44).

—— (1969). 'Some Puzzles about Agency', in K. Lambert (ed.), *The Logical Way of Doing Things*. New Haven: Yale University Press, 199–217.

—— (1976*a*). 'The Agent as Cause', in M. Brand and D. Walton (eds.), *Action Theory*. Dordrecht: Reidel, 199–211.

—— (1976*b*). *Person and Object*. LaSalle, Ill.: Open Court.

Clarke, R. (1993). 'Toward a Credible Agent Causal Account of Free Will'. *Noûs*, 27: 191–203.

—— (1995). 'Freedom and Determinism: Recent Work'. *Philosophical Books*, 36: 9–18.

—— (1996). 'Agent Causation and Event Causation in the Production of Free Action'. *Philosophical Topics*, 24: 19–48.

Dennett, D. (1984). *Elbow Room*. Cambridge, Mass.: MIT Press.

Double, R. (1991). *The Non-Reality of Free Will*. New York: Oxford University Press.

Duggan, T., and B. Gert (1979). 'Free Will as the Ability to Will'. *Noûs*, 13: 197–217.

Dworkin, G. (ed.) (1970). *Determinism, Free Will, and Moral Responsibility*. Englewood Cliffs, NJ: Prentice-Hall.

Fischer, J. M. (ed.) (1986). *Moral Responsibility*. Ithaca, NY: Cornell University Press.

—— (1988). 'Freedom and Miracles'. *Noûs*, 22: 235–52.

—— (1994). *The Metaphysics of Free Will: An Essay on Control*. Cambridge, Mass.: Basil Blackwell.

—— and M. Ravizza (eds.) (1993). *Perspectives on Moral Responsibility*. Ithaca, NY: Cornell University Press.

—— (1998). *Responsibility and Control: A Theory of Moral Responsibility*. New York: Cambridge University Press.

Frankfurt, H. (1969). 'Alternate Possibilities and Moral Responsibility'. *Journal of Philosophy*, 46: 829–39.

—— (1971). 'Freedom of the Will and the Concept of a Person'. *Journal of Philosophy*, 68: 5–20.

Ginet, C. (1966). 'Might we have No Choice?', in Lehrer (1966: 87–104).

—— (1983). 'In Defense of Incompatibilism'. *Philosophical Studies*, 44: 391–400.

—— (1990). *On Action*. New York: Cambridge University Press.

—— (1996). 'In Defense of the Principle of Alternative Possibilities: Why I don't Find Frankfurt's Argument Convincing', in J. E. Tomberlin (ed.), *Philosophical Perspectives. x: Metaphysics*. Atascadero, Calif.: Ridgeview, 403–17.

—— (1997). 'Freedom, Responsibility, and Agency'. *Journal of Ethics*, 1: 85–98.

Hill, C. (ed.) (1996). *Philosophical Topics: Free Will*. Fayetteville: University of Arkansas Press.

Hobart, R. E. (1934). 'Free-Will as Involving Determinism and Inconceivable without It'. *Mind*, 43: 1–27.

Honderich, T. (ed.) (1973). *Essays on Freedom of Action*. Boston: Routledge & Kegan Paul.

—— (1988). *A Theory of Determinism*. Oxford: Clarendon Press.

Hunt, D. (2000). 'Moral Responsibility and Avoidable Action'. *Philosophical Studies*, 97: 195–227.

James, W. (1921). 'The Dilemma of Determinism', in James, *The Will to Believe*. New York: Longmans, Green.

Kane, R. (1996). *The Significance of Free Will.* New York: Oxford University Press.

—— (ed.) (2002). *The Oxford Handbook on Free Will.* New York: Oxford University Press.

Lehrer, K. (ed.) (1966). *Freedom and Determinism.* New York: Random House.

—— (1968). 'Cans without Ifs'. *Analysis,* 29: 29–32.

—— (1976). ' "Can" in Theory and Practice: A Possible Worlds Analysis', in M. Brand and D. Walton (eds.), *Action Theory.* Dordrecht, Reidel: 241–70.

Lewis, D. (1981). 'Are we Free to Break the Laws?' *Theoria,* 47: 112–21.

Locke, J. (1894). *An Essay concerning Human Understanding.* Oxford: Clarendon Press.

Loewer, B. (1996). 'Freedom from Physics: Quantum Mechanics and Free Will'. *Philosophical Topics,* 24: 91–112.

McCann, H. (1998). *The Works of Agency.* Ithaca, NY: Cornell University Press.

McKenna, M. (2001). 'Source Incompatibilism, Ultimacy, and the Transfer of Non-Responsibility'. *American Philosophical Quarterly,* 38: 37–52.

Mele, A. (1995). *Autonomous Agents: From Self-Control to Autonomy.* New York: Oxford University Press.

—— and D. Robb (1998). 'Rescuing Frankfurt-Style Cases'. *Philosophical Review,* 107/1: 97–112.

Mill, J. S. (1867). 'On the Freedom of the Will', in Mill, *An Examination of Sir William Hamilton's Philosophy.* London: Longmans, Green, Reader, & Dyer.

—— (1873). 'Of Liberty and Necessity'. *A System of Logic.* New York: Harper, 547–52.

Moore, G. E. (1912). *Ethics.* New York: Oxford University Press.

Morgenbesser, S., and J. H. Walsh (eds.) (1962). *Free Will.* Englewood Cliffs, NJ: Prentice-Hall.

O'Connor, T. (1993a). 'Indeterminism and Free Agency: Three Recent Views'. *Philosophy and Phenomenological Research,* 53: 499–526.

—— (1993b). 'On the Transfer of Necessity'. *Noûs,* 27: 204–18.

—— (ed.) (1995). *Agents, Causes, and Events: Essays on Indeterminism and Free Will.* New York: Oxford University Press.

—— (2000). *Persons and Causes: The Metaphysics of Free Will.* New York: Oxford University Press.

Pereboom, D. (1995). 'Determinism al Dente'. *Noûs,* 29: 21–45.

—— (2001). *Living without Free Will.* Cambridge: Cambridge University Press.

Reid, T. (1969). *Essay on the Active Powers of the Human Mind.* Cambridge, Mass.: MIT Press.

Slote, M. (1982). 'Selective Necessity and the Free Will Problem'. *Journal of Philosophy,* 79: 5–24.

Smart, J. J. C. (1961). 'Free-Will, Praise and Blame'. *Mind,* 70: 291–306.

—— (1968). *Between Science and Philosophy.* New York: Random House.

Strawson, G. (1994). 'The Impossibility of Moral Responsibility'. *Philosophical Studies,* 75: 5–24.

Strawson, P. (1962). 'Freedom and Resentment'. *Proceedings of the British Academy,* 48: 1–25.

Stump, E. (1996). 'Libertarian Freedom and the Principle of Alternative Possibility', in D. Howard-Snyder and J. Jordan (eds.), *Faith, Freedom, and Responsibility: Essays in the Philosophy of Religion.* Lanham, M.: Rowman & Littlefield, 73–88.

—— (1999). 'Alternative Possibilities and Moral Responsibility: The Flicker of Freedom'. *Journal of Ethics,* 3/4: 299–324.

—— and J. M. Fischer (2000). 'Transfer Principles and Moral Responsibility', in Tomberlin (2000: 47–55).

Taylor, R. (1957). 'I Can'. *Philosophical Review,* 69: 78–89.

Taylor, R. (1966). *Action and Purpose.* Englewood Cliffs, NJ: Prentice-Hall.

Tomberlin, J. (ed.) (2000). *Philosophical Perspectives xiv: Action and Freedom.* New York: Basil Blackwell.

van Inwagen, P. (1978). 'Ability and Responsibility'. *Philosophical Review*, 87: 201–24.

—— (1980). 'The Incompatibility of Responsibility and Determinism', in M. Brady and M. Brand (eds.), *Action and Responsibility*. Bowling Green, Ohio: Bowling Green State University Press, ii. 30–7.

—— (1983). *An Essay on Free Will.* Oxford: Oxford University Press.

Wallace, R. J. (1994). *Responsibility and the Moral Sentiments.* Cambridge, Mass.: Harvard University Press.

Watson, G. (1975). 'Free Agency'. *Journal of Philosophy*, 72: 205–20.

—— (ed.) (1982). *Free Will.* Oxford: Oxford University Press.

—— (1999). 'Soft Libertarianism and Hard Compatibilism'. *Journal of Ethics*, 4/4: 351–65.

Widerker, D. (1987). 'On an Argument for Incompatibilism'. *Analysis*, 47: 37–41.

—— (1995a). 'Libertarian Freedom and the Avoidability of Decisions'. *Faith and Philosophy*, 12: 113–18.

—— (1995b). 'Libertarianism and Frankfurt's Attack on the Principle of Alternative Possibilities'. *Philosophical Review*, 104: 247–61.

—— (2000). 'Frankfurt's Attack on the Principle of Alternative Possibilities: A Further Look', in Tomberlin (2000: 181–201).

Wiggins, D. (1973). 'Towards a Reasonable Libertarianism', in Honderich (1973).

Wolf, S. (1980). 'Asymmetrical Freedom'. *Journal of Philosophy*, 77: 151–66.

—— (1990). *Freedom within Reason.* New York: Oxford University Press.

CHAPTER 20

COMPATIBILISM AND INCOMPATIBILISM: SOME ARGUMENTS

TED WARFIELD

COMPATIBILISTS think that metaphysical freedom ('freedom' for short) and causal determinism ('determinism' for short) are consistent. Determinism, according to this view, does not rule out the existence of freedom. Incompatibilists disagree, holding that every situation involving freedom is indeterministic. What is this disagreement about? What arguments exist for each main position in this debate? After trying to say what the disagreement is about, I will survey and discuss four arguments for compatibilism and three arguments for incompatibilism.

1. WHAT IS THIS DISAGREEMENT ABOUT?

Determinism is true in a world if and only if, at every time in the history of the world, the complete state of the world at that time conjoined with the world's laws

My work on this topic has been heavily influenced by Peter van Inwagen. I thank him for his unwavering support and friendship. In addition I thank others who have helped me think about freedom in recent years: Erik Carlson, Tom Crisp, Marian David, Alicia Finch, Barry Loewer, Bill Lycan, Tim O'Connor, Gordon Pettit, and Dean Zimmerman. Additionally, I thank Mike Loux and Christian Miller for helpful written comments on an earlier draft of this chapter.

of nature necessitate all future truths of the world. The picture looks something like this. The complete state of the world at a time includes all facts about stuff in the world and the properties of that stuff. The laws of a world 'operate on' the stuff as it makes its transitions from instant to instant. The world evolves in accordance with the laws of the world. A wholly deterministic world unfolds in the one precise way its laws permit. An indeterministic world has, for at least one instant in its history, multiple possible futures consistent with its state at that instant and its laws. An indeterministic world may, of course, have a lot more indeterminism than that, but the described condition is the minimal sufficient condition for a world's being indeterministic.

Though I was able to be fairly precise in explaining the thesis of determinism, it is more difficult to explain what metaphysical freedom is. A major part of this difficulty is that attempts to explain the core notion of freedom perhaps inevitably slide into theoretically controversial territory. So, for example, one might plausibly start out by suggesting that an action is free if and only if it is performed and it is or was genuinely open to the agent in question to refrain from performing the action (one would then presumably go on to try to explain the notion of what it is for something be 'genuinely open' to an agent). But, as we'll see, at least some compatibilists would take this initial suggestion to be question-begging because it presupposes that alternative possibilities are necessary for freedom. Perhaps they would be wrong to make this charge. Even if that is so, it would be nice to be able to include as many people as possible comfortably in the conversation about compatibilism and incompatibilism at this early stage.

A largely uninformative attempt to characterize freedom inclusively is this: one's action is free if and only if the action is performed and this performance is genuinely one's own. What is it for a performance to be genuinely one's own? And why think that this condition is sufficient for *free* action (rather than just for an action to be *my* action)? Once again I see no non-metaphorical way of answering these question without entering into theoretically disputed territory.

It might seem that we can do no better at this point than to say 'We know freedom when we see it.' This is too hasty a conclusion, however. Surely we can, at a minimum, agree on some core situations in which actions would *not* be free actions because they are not genuinely the issuance of the agent in question. So, for example, if Patrick is tossed out of the wrestling ring breaking a table, it is true, in some sense, that Patrick broke the table, but he did not freely break the table. Perhaps his activity did not even constitute an action; if it was an action, it certainly wasn't a free action because he did not genuinely govern or control the action. Similarly, if Shera is the victim of mind control during a period of time and is wholly guided in her activities during that time by the operation of the mind control device, then it seems clear that any actions she performs during that time are not free actions. There is more one might say to attempt initially to characterize the notion of freedom under debate, but as mentioned above, I fear that an attempt at greater precision will result in either begging the question of the compatibilism–incompatibilism debate or giving the appearance of doing so. The best course of action may well be to rely upon the common pre-theoretic understanding of this notion, perhaps guided by parts of the discussion of this section, and move on to a discussion of the positions and arguments for the positions. A closer look at various accounts of freedom and partial accounts of freedom will probably help us better understand the core notion of freedom under discussion.

2. ARGUMENTS FOR COMPATIBILISM

I will sketch and discuss four arguments for compatibilism. There are certainly other arguments that have been called 'arguments for compatibilism' and some of these arguments may even be arguments for compatibilism, but I will restrict my focus to four arguments that strike me as particularly important. The arguments all share the compatibilist conclusion that determinism and freedom are consistent. I will not exhaustively explore the historical or contemporary use or provenance of these arguments, nor will I fully document professional discussion of the arguments. My focus is exclusively on the arguments.

I begin with what I'll call the 'epistemic possibility' argument (a closely related argument is sometimes called the 'paradigm case' argument).[1] Building upon the idea that 'we recognize freedom when we see it', one might be tempted to argue as follows. I know that there are instances of free action, and I know this without knowing whether determinism is true. It seems to follow that the existence of freedom is independent of the question of determinism and that therefore freedom and determinism are compatible. One might reason similarly as follows. For all I know, determinism is true and for all I know determinism is false, but I know for sure that I'm free (or that *that*—demonstrating some apparently free action—is a free action). So free action must be independent of determinism.

I think that it is fair to formulate the reasoning in these overlapping lines of thought as follows:

(P1) I know that there are free actions.

(P2) I don't know whether or not determinism is true.

(C1) So, freedom and determinism are compatible.

[1] In ch. 4 of *An Essay on Free Will* (van Inwagen 1983) Peter van Inwagen discusses the 'paradigm case' argument in detail.

Unfortunately for defenders of this argument, it is invalid. At best, one might conclude from (P1) and (P2) that *for all I know* freedom and determinism are compatible. But the debate between compatibilists and incompatibilists is not a debate about anyone's knowledge. It is a debate about the consistency of two metaphysical theses.

That the epistemic possibility argument is invalid can be seen most clearly with a parallel argument. Imagine that Sara is an avid swimmer but does not know that water consists partly of hydrogen and indeed has no beliefs at all about hydrogen (she hasn't learned about it yet). If asked whether there could be water even if there is no hydrogen, Sara might reason as follows:

(P1) I know that there is water.
(P2) I don't know whether or not there is hydrogen.
(C1) So, there being water is consistent with there being no hydrogen.

This conclusion of course does not follow. Sara is at most entitled to conclude that for all she knows there being water is consistent with there being no hydrogen.

An alternative diagnosis of the failure of the epistemic possibility argument is available. When one claims confidently that one know that there are free actions, one must surely admit the fallibility of such claims. So, for example, if I demonstrate Michael's raising of his arm as a paradigm instance of free action, I need to recognize that the action may not really be a free action. Were I to learn that Michael's raising of his arm is being controlled not by Michael but instead by alien mind control (or hypnosis, or other unseen forces constraining his arm), I would conclude that the movement is not a free action. So, there are at least some possible further facts one could learn leading to one's withdrawal of any particular freedom ascription. Is the truth of causal determinism such a further fact? Perhaps it is and perhaps it isn't. The epistemic possibility argument requires for its success the claim that it isn't. Unfortunately for the compatibilist, no part of the argument even addresses this point. The argument is therefore at best incomplete. There are, I conclude, at least two serious problems facing the epistemic possibility argument.

I turn now to a type of argument that I call the 'here's an analysis' style of argument.[2] This type of argument has the following core structure. In the first step, compatibilists propose either an account of freedom or a sufficient condition for freedom and suggest that it is at least a plausible account. In the second step,

---

[2] Most instances of what I here call the 'here's an analysis' style of argument involve presentations of what are called 'conditional analyses of freedom'. Van Inwagen critically discusses this type of argument in van Inwagen (1983, ch. 4).

compatibilists argue directly that the satisfaction of the account in question is consistent with the truth of causal determinism. Compatibilists employing this type of argument therefore conclude that freedom and determinism are compatible.

It is quite ambitious for compatibilists to offer detailed accounts, or even just sufficient conditions, for the existence of free action. Compatibilists are to be congratulated for at least attempting this difficult project. Incompatibilists have, for the most part, been unable or unwilling to articulate fully any complete account of freedom (as we'll see later, incompatibilists typically provide only a necessary condition for freedom and argue that determinism undercuts the satisfaction of the necessary condition). Though compatibilists are to be congratulated for taking this direct approach towards defending their conclusion, it is unsurprising that this type of compatibilist argument is typically challenged in its first step. Let's look at a few instances of this type of argument.

Here's a simplistic compatibilist argument of this type. Freedom, according to this first proposal, is simply doing what one wants to do (alternatively: a sufficient condition for an action's being free is that the performer of the action is doing what she wants to do). Note, continues the argument, that even in a deterministic world one might do what one wants to do. Consider Alvin, who wants nothing more than to be mowing his lawn. Sure enough, in checking in with Alvin, we find him mowing his lawn, doing exactly what he wants to do. Alvin is free, according to this account of freedom, and it is obvious that Alvin's being free according to the account is completely independent of the question of determinism. So freedom, if this account is correct, is compatible with determinism.

One might fairly represent this argument as follows:

(P1)   If one is doing what one wants to do, then one's actions are free actions.
(P2)   Determinism is consistent with one doing what one wants to do.
(C1)   So, determinism is consistent with freedom.

The difficulty for this argument comes immediately in (P1). (P2) is quite plausible and the argument is (or would be after a bit more work) valid. But why would anyone think doing what one wants to do is sufficient for freedom? This might be a plausible necessary condition on free action (it might not even be that), but the success of the argument requires that it be a sufficient condition. This, objects the incompatibilist, it clearly is not. After all, one can be *forced* (again, via mind control, or unseen ropelike forces) to do exactly what one wants to do (and desires can be manipulated) and it seems that such compulsion is incompatible with freedom. If such compulsion is involved, it seems that the action in question is not a free action even if the agent wants to perform the action. Why not exactly? One promising and popular explanation here is that the action is not free because the agent lacks open alternative possibilities. Even if Alvin, for example, mowed his lawn and wanted to mow his lawn, if it was not open to him to refrain from mowing because of the compulsion of the mind control, it seems that Alvin's mowing is not free.

This suggests that an adequate analysis of freedom should incorporate at least some kind of 'open alternative possibilities' condition. The exact nature of this condition should be a matter open for serious discussion and debate.

Many (perhaps even all) compatibilists would agree that this first 'here's an analysis' type argument fails as an argument for compatibilism. Many would also accept the diagnosis of its failure offered above, acknowledging that some type of 'alternative possibilities' condition is necessary for free action. Perhaps this insight can be used in an attempt to provide a more sophisticated version of the 'here's an analysis' type argument. Let's look at a couple of attempts at doing this.

A compatibilist might attempt to accommodate the 'alternative possibilities' reasoning by supplementing the simplistic condition offered earlier. One might propose, for example, that one's action Z is free if (a) in doing Z one is doing what one wants to do *and* (b) if one wanted to refrain from Z one would so refrain. Clause (b) is a non-trivial attempt to incorporate an alternative possibilities condition into a compatibilist account of freedom. This is a compatibilist account of freedom because, it seems, the account could be satisfied even in a deterministic world. Consider once again Alvin mowing his lawn in a deterministic world. Consistent with this hypothesis are the following claims: (a) Alvin wants to mow his lawn and (b) If Alvin wanted to refrain from mowing his lawn, he would so refrain (that is, in the nearest world in which Alvin wants to refrain from mowing his lawn, he indeed refrains from doing so). Given that the world under consideration is deterministic, it's true in that world that Alvin is determined to mow his lawn and determined to want to mow his lawn. This, however, is consistent with Alvin's refraining from mowing in the nearest world in which that's what he wants to do. Of course, this nearest world would also have to be different in other ways. It would, of necessity, have a different past–laws combination and it may or may not be deterministic. These facts in no way undercut the point that the satisfaction of this second compatibilist analysis is consistent with determinism. The compatibilist can therefore claim with high confidence that this second proposed account of freedom can be satisfied consistent with the truth of determinism.

Unfortunately for the compatibilist, the trouble for this account again arises in an examination of the proposed account of freedom. Consider compulsive Alvin, who for deep psychological (or hidden physical) reasons is incapable of wanting to refrain from mowing. Compulsive Alvin, situated as is original Alvin above, will be mowing and will, when mowing, be doing exactly what he wants to do. It may also be true of compulsive Alvin that if he were to want to refrain from mowing, he would refrain from mowing (this would of course happen in a world in which compulsive Alvin lacks the relevant compulsion). According to the proposed account of freedom under discussion, compulsive Alvin is freely mowing, just as original Alvin is freely mowing (both are doing what they want and would refrain if they wanted). Compulsive Alvin, however, is not freely mowing. The attempt to cash out 'open alternative possibilities' by inclusion of the conditional clause is, it seems, a failure. With it fails this second 'here's an analysis' style argument for compatibilism.

Compatibilists might attempt further versions of the 'here's an analysis' type argument. Compatibilists wanting to do this would presumably either replace the second clause in the second proposal or would build on the second proposal with some third condition in an attempt to provide a sufficient condition for free action. Compatibilists attempting such a revision must of course be careful not to jeopardize the claim that the satisfaction of the proposed condition is consistent with the truth of determinism. I see no obvious way to do this (nor do I see any conclusive reason for thinking that it can't be done). Rather than explore possible further compatibilist proposals of this sort, let's move on to discuss a third argument for compatibilism.

I'll call this third argument the 'responsibility–freedom' argument. This argument is, most fundamentally, an attempt to argue for the compatibility of determinism and freedom via reflections on each individual concept and its link to moral responsibility.[3] It is quite common for metaphysicians to attempt to motivate interest in discussion of freedom by stressing a connection between the issue of freedom and questions of moral responsibility. Though the precise nature of this 'connection' is usually not explained, it is surely not outrageous to suggest that there is a link between the issues of freedom and responsibility. Some have suggested that this link exists because we are interested in whatever 'kind of freedom' is involved in attributions of moral responsibility.

Though one might be suspicious of this 'kinds of freedom' talk, it is not too difficult to see what philosophers who discuss the matter in this way must be getting at. The suggestion is likely this: moral responsibility requires freedom. One is morally responsible for an action only if one freely performed the action (alternatively, one is morally responsible for an outcome only if one freely produced the outcome). After all, it seems that a strong defence against a charge of responsibility for some action would be the reply that 'I didn't do it freely'. Though not all would do so, note that it is open to both compatibilists and incompatibilists alike to accept the claim that freedom is necessary for moral responsibility.

If freedom is indeed necessary for moral responsibility, one would have a sound argument for compatibilism if one could show that moral responsibility is consistent

---

[3] I don't know of anyone who has explicitly formulated and discussed this particular argument, but it is clear that something like this simple argument is lurking just beneath the surface of much of the contemporary literature on freedom and determinism. I know of no other way to explain the widely held presupposition of most participants in the contemporary debate that conclusions about the relationship between moral responsibility and causal determinism are somehow relevant to conclusions about the relationship between freedom and causal determinism. See Fischer (1986) for a sample of important discussion of the 'Frankfurt stories' I discuss in this section (the secondary literature on 'Frankfurt stories' is large and the discussion shows no signs of slowing down). I critically discuss the use of such stories in arguments for the compatibility of determinism and moral responsibility in Warfield (1996).

with determinism. For if *A* both implies *B* and is consistent with *C*, then *B* is consistent with *C*. The overall argument, to be clear, looks like this:

(P1) Moral responsibility requires freedom.
(P2) Moral responsibility is consistent with determinism.
(C1) So, freedom is compatible with determinism.

Do we have reason for thinking that moral responsibility is consistent with determinism? So-called 'Frankfurt stories' might be used in an attempt to argue for this thesis. Frankfurt stories are stories that strongly suggest that moral responsibility is consistent with a lack of alternative possibilities, and many think that determinism threatens moral responsibility by precluding alternative possibilities. If these claims are correct, then if Frankfurt stories show that moral responsibility is compatible with a lack of alternative possibilities, they provide evidence for thinking that moral responsibility is consistent with determinism.

One type of Frankfurt story goes like this. Larry pushes Freddy. Larry pushes Freddy because this is what Larry wants to do. Larry is in no way pressured into pushing Freddy. It seems quite plausible to say in this case that Larry is responsible for pushing Freddy. This is so even if we add to the story that Geoffrey was monitoring Larry's activities with his mind control device and stood ready and able to force Larry to push Freddy if Larry showed any inclination not to do so on his own. It is tempting to attribute moral responsibility to Larry in this situation because Geoffrey's intervention was not needed. Larry pushed Freddy 'on his own' and did so because he wanted to do so. It is also tempting to say in this case that Larry was going to push Freddy no matter what. There were no alternative possibilities in the situation described to Larry's pushing Freddy. Perhaps, then, this is a case of moral responsibility without alternative possibilities. As pointed out above, cases fitting this description are thought to provide evidence for the claim that moral responsibility is consistent with determinism. This, recall, in combination with the claim that such responsibility requires freedom, leads quickly to compatibilism about freedom and determinism.

The incompatibilist should raise three worries about this argument. First, the case described does, in at least one sense, involve alternative possibilities and so is not a case of responsibility without alternative possibilities. There are two ways for the pushing of Freddy by Larry to unfold. One possible alternative is for Larry to push Freddy on his own (as in the actual story), but another open alternative possibility exists in the story. In the alternative, Larry pushes Freddy only after showing signs of refraining from doing so and being forced to do so by Geoffrey's use of the mind control device.

Secondly, the incompatibilist should object that the story, even if it is a story involving responsibility but no alternative possibilities, does not provide evidence that responsibility can coexist with determinism. There being no alternative possibilities as described in the story does not entail determinism. And it does not appear that one can unproblematically stipulate that determinism obtains in the story about Larry, Freddy, and Geoffrey. If one tried to do this, adding that Larry's pushing of Freddy occurs in a deterministic setting, one must then question the claim that Geoffrey stands by on the sidelines ready, willing and able to intervene. For supposing Geoffrey to be able to do other than he does in a deterministic story is to suppose that compatibilism is true. But the story is supposed to be part of an argument for compatibilism and so this supposition would be inappropriate. It is therefore not clear how the story is supposed to support the compatibility of determinism and responsibility even if we grant that it is a case of responsibility without alternative possibilities.

Thirdly, if we are inclined to grant that this case is a case that somehow supports the compatibility of determinism and moral responsibility, we still shouldn't endorse the 'freedom–responsibility' argument because we should have doubts about the first premiss. Recall the initial description of Larry's behaviour in the story. He pushed Freddy, did so because he wanted to, and his doing so in no way involved the intervention of Geoffrey who was poised to intervene. If this really is a case in which Larry is responsible and doesn't have alternative possibilities, the incompatibilist should strongly suggest that we deny this is a case of moral responsibility *with freedom*. In other words, the incompatibilist should suggest that if this is a case of moral responsibility and 'no alternative possibilities' (as the compatibilist would have it), it is quite plausibly a case of moral responsibility without freedom. I will elaborate.

Why, after all, should we ascribe freedom to Larry in the story? Surely not because he's 'doing what he wants to do'—we've already seen that this is not a sufficient condition for freedom. A compatibilist may well be tempted to support Larry's freedom in the story by pointing out that the story seems to involve genuine alternative possibilities for Larry (he could either push Freddy on his own or show some sign of not doing this and then be forced into doing it by Geoffrey). But this plausible move just endorses the first incompatibilist criticism that I discussed. To point to alternative possibilities in the story is to give up on the claim that this story involves responsibility *without* alternative possibilities. The compatibilist therefore faces some non-trivial difficulties in this debate.

Rather than explore these difficulties further, I want to move on now to a fourth and final argument for compatibilism. Some compatibilists have claimed that freedom is not merely consistent with determinism: they have made the stronger claim that freedom actually requires determinism.[4] In brief, they have claimed this because they think we have convincing reasons for thinking that indeterminism rules out

---

[4] Versions of the argument under discussion in this section are defended most forcefully by Peter van Inwagen. In van Inwagen (1983, ch. 4) he discusses what he calls the 'Mind Argument'. See also his important paper 'The Mystery of Metaphysical Freedom' (van Inwagen 1998). For a critical discussion of the use of this type of argument in a defence of compatibilism, see Finch and Warfield (1998).

freedom. The claim that indeterminism excludes freedom is, of course, equivalent to the claim that freedom requires determinism. We will get to their reasons for thinking this in a minute. For now let me provide an initial, flawed, formulation of this argument. I call it the 'requirement' argument.

(P1) Freedom requires determinism (for reasons to be explained).
(C1) So, Freedom is consistent with determinism.

Note first that this argument is invalid. From 'A requires B' one cannot validly deduce that A is consistent with B. One needs an additional premiss. In this case 'freedom is possible' would, in combination with (P1), be enough, and the compatibilist could either offer support for this additional premiss or hope that interlocutors would grant at least that much for purposes of discussion (most no doubt would, though we'll return to this point in a substantive way shortly).

Let's formulate the revised argument:

(P1) Freedom requires determinism.
(P2) It's metaphysically possible that there is freedom.
(C1) So, freedom and determinism are compatible.

It is important in (P2) that the type of possibility be non-epistemic. If the claim were that 'For all we know it's possible that there's freedom', the conclusion would not validly follow from the premises. With that qualification noted, the argument is clearly valid. The second premiss tells us that there is at least some world, perhaps the actual world but perhaps not, where freedom exists. And the first premiss claims that every world with freedom is a deterministic world. These together imply the compatibilist conclusion.

What can be said in favour of the premises of the argument? We begin with the second premiss. Many incompatibilists (the 'libertarians') will quickly grant (P2). So against one primary opponent the compatibilist gets this premiss for free. In discussion with others (so-called 'hard determinists'), however, the compatibilist will need to defend the premiss. One way to argue that it's possible that there is freedom is to argue that there actually is freedom. Some would claim that widely shared intuitions about freedom offer credible support for the view that we are actually free agents. This type of reasoning was mentioned earlier in discussing the epistemic argument for compatibilism. Others would claim that the widely shared intuition that we are sometimes morally responsible agents together with the claim that responsibility requires freedom support the claim that freedom is actual and therefore possible. Of course, one might object that our intuitions about freedom (and/or responsibility) could be mistaken. As noted in discussion of the epistemic argument, we can imagine situations in which we have the intuitions but aren't free because of hidden factors.

This objection may, however, simply play into the hands of a compatibilist wanting to defend (P2). After all, defending the claim that freedom is actual is only one way to defend (P2). The compatibilist may well concede that we can imagine situations in which our intuitions about freedom fail us because of hidden factors. But if the appeal to possibly hidden factors is *needed* to undercut the evidential power of the intuitions about freedom, the compatibilist could simply point out that we can *also* imagine situations in which the hidden freedom-robbing factors are not present. Such situations might plausibly be thought to be situations in which freedom is present.

Turn to the argument's first premiss. How would the compatibilist support the claim that freedom requires determinism? Note first that this claim is equivalent to the claim that indeterminism rules out freedom. Compatibilists have tried to defend this claim in two ways. First, some compatibilists have asserted that indeterminism is straightforwardly equivalent to 'randomness', and have gone on to claim that randomness is incompatible with freedom. The idea here seems to be that a free act is one that is controlled by the agent and that random occurrences are inherently uncontrollable. Critics might or might not agree that random occurrences are thereby uncontrollable, but they should surely question the quick move to equate all indeterminism with randomness. I know of no argument for equating these notions.

A second compatibilist defence of (P1), related in some ways to the first, is perhaps more promising. Consider what is going on in any indeterministic world. In such a world the laws of nature 'operate on' the state of the world at one time to produce the state of the world at the next moment. Unlike a world with deterministic laws, an indeterministic world's evolution is not rigidly constrained by its past and laws. There are multiple ways an indeterministic world might unfold even given a total specification of its past and laws. This indeterministic evolution might be thought to conflict with freedom.

Consider an individual preparing to act in an indeterministic world.[5] Angie is preparing to walk. Consider the state of Angie's world millions of years before Angie was born. Angie clearly has and never had any control over that earlier time. And consider the path the world took to reach the present. Indeterministic laws (which Angie also did not choose and over which she has no control) operated on that long-ago state of the world producing the next state and then the next, and then the next, until now we reach the present where Angie is preparing to walk. Angie's walking or not walking, we stipulate, is left undetermined by the earlier state of the world and laws: it's 'part of' the indeterminism of the world. Assume that Angie indeed does walk. Her doing so is an indeterministic consequence of the earlier state of her world and the laws of that world. Can we correctly say that Angie

---

[5] By 'indeterministic' world I mean a world in which determinism does not obtain. Similarly, in later usage, by 'indeterministic laws' I mean laws which do not specify a unique possible 'output' for each possible 'input', and by 'indeterministic cause' I mean a cause which was not governed by a deterministic law.

freely walked? She surely had no control over the things from which her walking indeterministically followed, but did she freely walk?

In walking, Angie may well have been doing what she wanted to do, but that's not sufficient for making the action free. Furthermore, Angie's beliefs and desires may well have been leading her in the direction of a walk in the moments preceding the walk. Her walk therefore fits well with her psychological state at the time, and indeed, we can even add that her walk was indeterministically caused by these relevant psychological facts. Despite all of this, it is puzzling to say that Angie controlled her walking and freely walked, even though consistent with everything about Angie and her world just prior to the walk, the walk might not have happened. It seems that unless Angie could both make it the case that she walks and make it the case that she does not walk, the walking is not sufficiently up to Angie in a sense necessary for free action.

This worry generalizes to all possible agents in indeterministic possible worlds. If the worry is well founded, it seems that indeterminism undercuts freedom, and that therefore freedom requires determinism. Together with a successful defence of the premiss that freedom is possible, this claim would force a compatibilist resolution of the incompatibilism–compatibilism debate. How can incompatibilists reply? I'll discuss two replies: first, a reply to the reasoning offered, and, secondly, a question about the use of this reasoning in an argument for compatibilism.

I begin with a reply to the reasoning itself. However intuitively plausible the reasoning was on first presentation, it's surely worth asking just how the argument is supposed to go. The conclusion of the argument supporting the premiss is that indeterminism precludes freedom. The argument has us consider a generic situation involving Angie, action, and indeterminism, and invites us to agree that the action in question is not free. Why not? The argument seems to involve two key claims:

(1) Angie has no control over the past and indeterministic laws of nature.

and

(2) Angie has no control over whether her walking follows from the operation of the indeterministic laws on the past.

Because Angie has no control over these two things, it is at least plausible to suggest that she has no control over her walking (for it is out of her control that her walking follows from something she has no control over). In what sense does she have no control over these various things? The answer must be that she fails to have control in some unspecified sense necessary for freedom.

At a minimum we can fault the argument for failing to specify what this notion of 'control' is and why we should believe that it is necessary for freedom. We need to hear more here before becoming completely convinced by this argument, for it would be unwise to grant that all types of control are absent in indeterministic contexts. Consider, for example, Sara, who in her own indeterministic world shatters a window by throwing a ball at it. The shattering is an indeterministic consequence of Sara's toss (it was not necessitated by the past and laws of Sara's world). Who shattered the window? Sara did. Did she do so freely? It's at least not obvious that she didn't: merely noting that Sara's world is indeterministic doesn't instantly reveal to us that this wasn't a case of free action. Did she in any sense control the breaking of the window? Yes, she caused it with her intentional action of throwing the ball at it—though the window might not have shattered in that situation, but this doesn't show that Sara didn't, in at least some sense, control the breaking of the window. (Sara is surely responsible for breaking the window, and recall that one might plausibly suggest that responsibility entails freedom.) Some notion of control is surely present in this case. The defender of the compatibilist argument therefore needs to say more about just what notion of control is missing here because of the presence of indeterminism. The compatibilist must also say why this missing sense of 'control' is necessary for freedom.

I turn now to a worry about the use of this argument (concluding that indeterminism precludes freedom) within a larger overall argument for compatibilism. Assume for the sake of argument that we accept that the reasoning in question shows that indeterminism rules out freedom. Shouldn't we worry that this kind of reasoning might force us, after further inquiry, to reject the other premiss required for this overall compatibilist argument (the premiss that freedom is possible)? After all, reasoning closely paralleling the reasoning from indeterminism to a lack of freedom can be used to argue that determinism rules out freedom. I will examine this reasoning more carefully in the next section. For now, let's just quickly look at the parallel reasoning. This should be enough to highlight the worry about this argument for compatibilism.

Consider Angie preparing to walk, this time in a deterministic world. Just as in the indeterministic case, one might think that:

(1) Angie has no control over the distant past and the laws of nature of her world.

And closely paralleling the earlier argument, it seems to also be the case that

(2) Angie has no control over whether her walking follows from the deterministic laws and past of her world.

Indeed, if anything, this step seems more clearly correct than the corresponding step in the argument concerning indeterminism. So, by the same general reasoning offered in the indeterministic case, it seems that in this deterministic case Angie has no control over her walking. Once again nothing has been done to clarify this notion of control; it's left at an intuitive level. The relevant constraint is simply that the 'control' in question be necessary for freedom.

If this argument about determinism and freedom is at least as strong as the argument above concerning indeterminism and freedom, then the compatibilist will not be able to use this argument to establish compatibilism. If both determinism and indeterminism rule out freedom, then freedom is impossible and the compatibilist will not be able to employ successfully an argument taking freedom's possibility as a premiss.

This concludes my presentation and overview of some arguments for compatibilism. I turn now to arguments for incompatibilism.

3. Arguments for Incompatibilism

I will sketch and discuss three arguments for incompatibilism. There are, no doubt, other arguments that have been called 'arguments for incompatibilism', and some of them may even be arguments for incompatibilism. I will restrict my attention on this occasion to just three arguments. The three arguments share the conclusion that freedom and determinism are inconsistent. As in the section on compatibilist arguments, I will not fully explore historical and contemporary appearances of these arguments, nor will I survey professional discussion of the arguments. My focus remains on the arguments themselves.

I begin with a simple argument that I will call the 'alternative possibilities argument'.[6] In the discussion of the 'here's an analysis' argument above, we saw some reason for thinking that, for an agent to act freely, the agent must have available alternative possible courses of action. Freedom, in short, plausibly requires alternative possibilities. In a deterministic world only one future is consistent with the past and laws of the world. Determinism therefore seems to imply that the way things go is the only way they can go. Determinism, that is, plausibly rules out alternative possibilities. This suggests an argument for incompatibilism:

(P1) Necessarily, freedom requires alternative possibilities.
(P2) Necessarily, determinism precludes alternative possibilities.
(C1) So, necessarily, determinism precludes freedom.

If freedom requires something that determinism excludes, then incompatibilism follows.

What more can be said about the premisses of this argument? (P2) is fairly clear. The notion of determinism under discussion does provide a clear sense in which determinism rules out alternative possibilities. Resistance to the argument should focus on the phrase 'alternative possibilities' as it appears in the argument's first premiss. As we saw in Section 2, most would agree that in some sense it is true that

---

[6] For some helpful discussion of alternative possibilities and freedom, see Fischer (1994) and O'Connor (2000).

freedom requires alternative possibilities. This argument is valid only if 'alternative possibilities' is used univocally in the argument's two premisses, so let's explore whether this is so.

A clear sense has been assigned to the phrase 'alternative possibilities' as it appears in (P2). Unfortunately for the proponent of this argument, the support offered for (P1) that we encountered in the discussion of the 'here's an analysis' argument did not motivate any particular understanding of 'alternative possibilities'. Furthermore, as we also saw in that earlier section, compatibilists have attempted to address the apparent need for alternative possibilities in an account of freedom by offering understandings of 'alternative possibilities' that seem consistent with determinism (and therefore consistent with the absence of the 'alternative possibilities' ruled out by determinism). It isn't obvious that freedom requires alternative possibilities in the exact same sense in which determinism rules them out. It is also not obvious that determinism rules out alternative possibilities in a sense stronger than any sense of alternative possibilities required for freedom. At a minimum much more needs to be said in support of this incompatibilist argument. An incompatibilist victory cannot, therefore, be quickly achieved via this first argument.

I turn now to the second incompatibilist argument. In some ways, this second argument is an extension of the first. This argument might arise out of an incompatibilist attempt to respond to the worries expressed about the first argument.[7]

Consider what is true in a deterministic world in which I do not stand at noon on a given day. It must be true in such a world that the past and laws of nature imply that I not stand at noon on the day in question. This, plainly enough, implies that my standing at noon is not consistent with the past and laws of the world. In general then, for any action X,

(P1) Necessarily, if determinism is true and one doesn't do X, one's doing X is inconsistent with the past and laws.

Doesn't freedom to do something, however, require that my doing it be consistent with the past and laws?

For example, right now I'm going to remain seated. It seems quite plausible, however, that I'm free to stand. If I indeed am free to stand, then, says the incompatibilist, my doing so is at least logically consistent with the past and laws of nature. Why does the incompatibilist think this? The incompatibilist probably has something like this in mind: I am free only to add to the past consistent with the laws of nature. Surely all of the actions open to me are actions that, if performed, would add to the past of my world. And it's certainly the case that it is not open to me to add to the past in ways inconsistent with the laws of nature. So says the incompatibilist.

---

[7] An argument similar to the argument discussed in this section was discussed by Thomas Flint (1987). I discuss and defend a similar argument in Warfield (2000).

Here's an illustration an incompatibilist might offer to try to clarify this point. Consider a large book containing a list of all the true statements about my world up to the present moment. Imagine further that the book is continuously being updated. As I go about my daily business, what I do is add to the list of truths about my world. My actions add to the actual past in ways consistent with the laws of nature. My actions don't 'erase' earlier truths. And none of the additions my actions make are additions that involve my doing things in violation of natural law. This picture strongly suggests, or so incompatibilist proponents of this argument claim, that a necessary condition for my being free to do something is that my doing so be consistent with the actual past and laws. Combine this point with the earlier observation about determinism and we are led to our second argument:

(P1) Necessarily, if determinism is true and one doesn't do X, one's doing X is inconsistent with the past and laws.

(P2) Necessarily, if one is free to do X then one's doing X is consistent with the past and laws.

(C1) So, necessarily, if determinism is true, then one is not free to do anything other than what one does.

The first premiss is supported by reflections on the definition of determinism. The second is supported by reflection on how one's freedom to do various things must relate to the past and laws of one's world. Note that (C1), the conclusion of the argument so far, does not express the incompatibilist thesis that determinism and freedom are incompatible. The argument leaves open the compatibilist possibility that though one isn't free to do other than one does in a deterministic world, one still freely does at least some of what does in such a world. To reach the incompatibilist conclusion, the argument must go further, taking (C1) as simply a subconclusion along the way to the proper incompatibilist conclusion.

Here's the natural completion of this argument for incompatibilism.

(P3) Necessarily, if one is not free to do anything other than what one does, one is not free at all.

(C2) So, necessarily, if determinism is true, then one is not free at all.

We have already seen incompatibilist reasons for thinking that freedom requires alternative possibilities, and (P3) seems to be some kind of restatement of this idea. We have looked at what incompatibilists have to say in favour of this idea both in criticism of compatibilist arguments and in support of the first argument for incompatibilism. We also considered some compatibilist rejoinders. It has become increasingly clear that progress in this debate may well require significant work on the nature of the 'alternative possibilities' requirement on freedom. Rather than go further into this discussion or repeat the earlier discussion, I'll move on to examine the last of the three arguments for incompatibilism.

This final argument for incompatibilism, like the 'here's an analysis' argument for compatibilism, is really a family of arguments and not a single argument. This family is the family of arguments falling under the heading of 'the consequence argument'.[8] Here is one consequence argument:

(P1) Given determinism, the conjunction of the past and laws of nature strictly imply every future truth.

(P2) No one is free with respect to the actual past and laws of nature.

(P3) No one is free with respect to propositions strictly implied by true propositions that no one is free with respect to.

(C1) So, given determinism, no one is free with respect to any future truth.

The argument is valid and (P1) follows trivially from the definition of determinism under discussion. (P2) and (P3), however, require further discussion.

Both (P2) and (P3) employ the locution 'free with respect to'. Rather than fully defining this notion, an incompatibilist is likely to state just a necessary condition for being 'free with respect to' something. Here is one such suggestion that might be of use in the consequence argument sketched above: one is free with respect to a certain true proposition Q only if it is open to one to act in such a way that Q at least *might* be false. If, for example, I'm going to miss my lunch appointment and there's nothing I can now do that might get me to my lunch appointment, then I am not now free with respect to keeping the lunch appointment. With this understanding in place, the incompatibilist will suggest that (P2) and (P3) are quite plausible.

Surely, says the incompatibilist, the past and laws of nature are the way they are and there is nothing I can do that might render a proposition expressing that conjunction false. Furthermore, if P is true and it's not open to me to act so that P might be false, then surely this also applies to all propositions Q entailed by P. After all, if it was open to me, for some Q entailed by P, to act in some way that might bring about Q's falsity, that very action would also be an action that might bring about P's falsity (given that P entails Q). Given this plausible necessary condition on what it is to be free with respect to a true proposition, both (P2) and (P3) of the incompatibilist argument appear fairly strong. Furthermore, the argument is valid, and the conclusion seems quite relevant to the question of determinism's relation to freedom.

Some compatibilists are likely to protest that they do not know exactly what to say about this incompatibilist argument because the argument has not been adequately developed. The incompatibilist's partial unpacking of what it is to be free with respect to a true proposition is not, it might be protested, sufficiently developed for the compatibilist really to understand the incompatibilist argument. Similarly, the defences of (P2) and (P3) in the previous paragraph are little more than restatements

---

[8] The most important discussion of the consequence argument occurs in van Inwagen (1983, ch. 3). The secondary literature on this argument is enormous.

of the premisses with the partial understanding of 'free with respect to' substituted into the premisses. This, the compatibilist might claim, does not constitute sufficient argumentative support for the premisses of the argument.

Other compatibilists may challenge the argument on a different front. Consider once again the conclusion of the sample consequence argument above:

(C1) So, given determinism, no one is free with respect to any future truth.

This might appear to express the incompatibilist thesis that determinism is incompatible with freedom, but in fact it does so only if we understand the claim in a modally loaded way. What is needed to clearly express the incompatibilist thesis is the conclusion that:

(C2) *Necessarily*, given determinism, no one is free with respect to any future truth.

The consequence argument sketched above only delivers this stronger conclusion if each of its premisses expresses a necessary truth. (P1) is clearly a necessary truth. (P3) seems to express a perfectly general inference principle and is therefore necessary if true. But (P2) seems to express the contingent truth, if indeed it is a truth, that no one is free with respect to the past and laws of nature. It may well be the case that in the actual world (and many others) no one is free with respect to the laws of nature, but it seems at least not crazy to think that there are worlds in which powerful agents have power over the past and/or laws. The incompatibilist, it seems, either needs to deny that this is the case or needs in some other way to repair the consequence from this charge of modal fallacy. It is not obvious that the incompatibilist will have an easy time performing either of these possible repairs.

References

Finch, A., and T. Warfield (1998). 'The *Mind* Argument and Libertarianism'. *Mind*, 107: 515–28.

Fischer, J. M. (ed.) (1986). *Moral Responsibility*. Ithaca, NY: Cornell University Press.

——(1994). *The Metaphysics of Free Will*. Oxford: Basil Blackwell.

Flint, T. (1987). 'Compatibilism and the Argument from Unavoidability'. *Journal of Philosophy*, 84: 423–40.

O'Connor, T. (2000). *Persons and Causes*. Oxford: Oxford University Press.

van Inwagen, P. (1983). *An Essay on Free Will*. Oxford: Oxford University Press.

——(1998). 'The Mystery of Metaphysical Freedom', in D. Zimmerman and M. Loux (eds.), *Metaphysics: The Big Questions*. Oxford: Basil Blackwell, 365–74.

Warfield, T. (1996). 'Determinism and Moral Responsibility are Incompatible'. *Philosophical Topics*, 24: 215–26.

——(2000). 'Causal Determinism and Human Freedom are Incompatible: A New Argument for Incompatibilism'. *Philosophical Perspectives*, 14: 167–80.

PART VIII

ANTI-REALISM AND VAGUENESS

CHAPTER 21

REALISM AND ANTI-REALISM: DUMMETT'S CHALLENGE

MICHAEL J. LOUX

1. REALISM AND ANTI-REALISM

THE past three decades have seen a renewed interest among analytic philosophers in the topic of realism, an interest that has given rise to a significant body of literature at the intersection of metaphysics and the philosophy of language. Michael Dummett's contributions to this literature have been as influential as any. He first focused the attention of analytic philosophers on the topic in a series of papers in the late 1960s and early 1970s; and his continuing efforts to explore the issue of realism have shaped much of the discussion in the ensuing years.

Dummett's earliest writings on realism have a straightforward aim. The datum is the existence of a variety of disputes in which one party is called a realist.[1] Thus, we

---

[1] It is interesting that Dummett takes the debate about what is most frequently called realism—realism about universals—to have a structure different from the debates he actually characterizes. See Dummett (1978c: 147).

have scientific realism and a range of opposing views including operationalism and instrumentalism; realism about the psychological and behaviourism; realism about material objects and phenomenalism; realism or Platonism about mathematical objects and intuitionism. The obvious question is whether the common use of the term 'realism' points to some general pattern structuring these different disputes. Dummett thinks it does, and his project is to delineate the pattern.

It is initially tempting to say that what ties all these disputes together is that each bears on the existence of a distinct category of entities; or moving to the formal mode, the claim would be that the disputes all bear on the referential force of certain expressions—the theoretical predicates of science, psychological expressions, and so on. Dummett, however, thinks that construing debates over realism in these terms has the consequence, first, that we overlook certain forms of realism (realism about the past or realism about the future, for example) where what divides realists from their opponents is not commitment to any distinctive class of entities and, secondly, that we misrepresent the debate over mathematical realism, where, following Kreisel, Dummett tells us the central issue is the objectivity of mathematical claims rather than the existence of a special category of abstract entities (Dummett 1978c: 146).

What Dummett recommends is that we understand these debates between realists and their opponents (for whom Dummett coins the generic term 'anti-realists') as debates about a disputed body of statements—the theoretical statements of science, statements about the mental, statements about physical objects, mathematical statements, statements about the past, statements about the future.[2] According to Dummett, the intuitive core of what, in each of these debates, is called realism is a pair of related themes: first, that statements in the disputed class are attempts to reflect or express a sector of a mind-independent world and, secondly, that whether those statements are true or false depends upon how that sector is; and, as Dummett sees it, this intuitive core gets expressed in the realist's claim that statements making up the disputed class are determinately either true or false and are such independently of whether it is possible for us to tell which they are. So the realist in any of these debates wants to say that statements in the disputed class have a determinate truth-value and that the concept of truth that applies to them is an epistemically unconstrained notion. As Dummett typically puts it, the realist construes the notion

---

[2] A difficulty in Dummett's terminology is presented by his use of the word 'statement'. There is an ambiguity here that can prove frustrating. Sometimes he uses the word as synonymous with 'assertoric sentence' (as when he speaks of the meaning of a statement); and sometimes he uses it to refer to what gets asserted by the use of such a sentence (as when he speaks of the assertion or denial of a statement). It is easy enough to disambiguate some of Dummett's uses of the term, but for others this is well nigh impossible. Where it is clear that 'statement' is being used as equivalent to 'assertoric sentence', I use some variant of the latter; and where 'statement' has its Strawsonian use as what is asserted by the utterance of a sentence, I use 'statement'. Where it is not clear how the term is being used, I typically use 'statement', thereby preserving Dummett's ambiguity. But I have allowed the demands of a free-flowing style to override these general rules. Where accuracy in the use of the term would result in jarring switches from 'sentence' to 'statement' in a single context, I typically stick with a single word, despite the risk of inaccuracy.

of truth applicable to statements in the disputed class as verification-transcendent: it is a property a statement can have even if it is in principle impossible for us to establish conclusively that the statement has it.

By contrast, the opponent of realism in each of these debates—the anti-realist— denies that the concept of truth which applies to statements in the disputed class is, in this sense, verification-transcendent. According to Dummett, the anti-realist insists that the concepts of truth and falsehood are epistemically constrained. For the anti-realist, truth is just warranted or justified assertability.[3] The result is that only statements for which we can conclusively establish that their assertion (or denial) is warranted are true (or false). Given this characterization of the realist and anti-realist, it is no surprise that Dummett takes their opposition to focus on those statements in the relevant disputed class for which it is, in principle, impossible for us to have the warrant requisite for assertion or denial. These statements (the verification- or falsification-transcendent statements) Dummett calls undecidables; and he tells us that the realist in each of our debates insists that the relevant undecidables all have a determinate truth-value, whereas the anti-realist denies this. The upshot, Dummett claims, is that the principle of bivalence (the semantic principle that every statement is either true or false) provides 'a crucial test' (Dummett 1978c: 155) for determining whether one endorses a realist or anti-realist account of a particular body of discourse. Provided the body includes statements that are undecidable, we can say that whereas a realist interpretation will insist that bivalence holds for the body of discourse, an anti-realist interpretation will deny this.[4]

One is, however, likely to object that few of the historical debates Dummett seeks to characterize have gone the way he claims. The debate between Platonists and intuitionists may have taken the principle of bivalence or the related principle of the excluded middle (the non-semantic principle that either S or not-S) as its focus, but it is unique in this regard. We do not find scientific realists and operationalists debating bivalence for the theoretical statements of science; behaviourists typically do not question the assignment of truth-values to statements about the mental; nor do phenomenalists want to scuttle bivalence for statements about material objects. Dummett concedes that, in fact, the debates in question have not had the structure he outlines; but he insists that while the anti-realists in these debates have

---

[3] A frequently cited difficulty in interpreting Dummett bears on the status of the anti-realist's claim here. Is the anti-realist rejecting the notion of truth in favour of some substitute notion, or is it that the anti-realist means to be proposing an alternative analysis of the notion of truth? On the first reading, truth is what the realist says it is; the anti-realist finds this notion problematic and recommends that we invoke some other notion to play some of the roles that truth plays. On the second reading, there is a single pre-philosophical notion, and we have two different philosophical analyses of it—the realist analysis and the anti-realist analysis. Although it is possible to find texts that support both readings, Dummett's considered view is better captured by the second reading; or so it seems to me. Accordingly, throughout I interpret Dummett's anti-realist as someone giving an analysis of truth that is meant to be a competitor to the realist's analysis.

[4] But Dummett is often more cautious here. See e.g. Dummett (1993a: 467). Some of the reasons for the caution are discussed in Sect. 4.

typically not questioned the applicability of the principle of bivalence to statements of the disputed class, they should have done so (Dummett 1993*b*: 467). As he sees it, they all occupied a theoretical position from which this principle should have been problematic; for the deep lying insights motivating the various forms of anti-realism in these debates imply scepticism about, if not outright rejection of, the principle of bivalence in the case of those statements from the disputed class that are undecidable.

What Dummett wants to claim is that, in each of our debates, the dispute is ultimately about the kind of meaning associated with statements in the disputed class (Dummett 1978*c*: 155). The realist in each debate holds that a statement from the disputed class gets its sense or meaning from being correlated with a state of affairs, one whose obtaining might well transcend our ability to detect or recognize it. That state of affairs is, of course, the one whose obtaining is both a necessary and sufficient condition for the truth of the correlated statement. The anti-realist rejects the realist's transcendent states of affairs and insists that we understand the statements in the disputed class in terms of the recognizable features of our experience that count as evidence for those statements. Thus, the behaviourist rejects the private mental states of the psychological realist and insists that the content of a psychological statement is given by way of the overt behaviour that justifies our making such a statement. In the same way, the phenomenalist rejects the unobservable material objects of the realist and parses claims about ordinary objects in terms of the sense data or sensory experiences that warrant those claims, and the operationalist tells us that the meaning of a theoretical statement consists not in some inaccessible state of affairs, but in the operations, tests, or measurements that constitute evidence for the assertion of the statement. Notoriously, these claims have all been made within the context of a reductionist account of statements from the various disputed classes; but Dummett insists that the reductionism is an unfortunate and irrelevant addendum to the deep-lying insight at work in the various forms of anti-realism—the idea that the meaning of a statement from the disputed class is given by identifying the evidential base that provides warrant for the assertion of that statement (Dummett 1993*b*: 470–1; 1978*c*: 157).

It is because they endorse this idea that the anti-realists in our debates reject the account of truth defended by their realist opponents. Anti-realists reject the realist's transcendent states of affairs and insist that the content of statements from the various disputed classes is exhausted by what constitutes the evidence warranting the assertion or denial of those statements; but, then, the only thing that could count as truth-makers for those statements are the recognizable situations that warrant their assertion. So, for the anti-realist, truth has to be something like warranted or justified assertability.

Now, what Dummett argues is that this account of truth involves a commitment that anti-realists in our debates have seldom, if ever, appreciated—a commitment to the view that the principle of bivalence fails for undecidables. Pretty clearly, a statement can have a truth-value only if there is something that makes it true or false (Dummett 1978e: 14–17). As we have seen, the only thing that can play this role in the anti-realist's account is the sort of recognizable item that provides warrant for the assertion or denial of the statement in question. But, then, when there is no such item, the condition required for the statement's having a truth-value is missing. And, of course, there is no such item in the case of undecidable or verification-transcendent statements. Accordingly, what the anti-realists in our debates should have said is that the principle of bivalence fails for undecidables.

2. THE TRUTH-CONDITIONAL THEORY

It is, however, important to note how this line of response transforms Dummett's original project. The original aim was to identify a pattern structuring certain historical debates; but what began life as characters in historical debates have come to float free of their historical anchors. The realist and the anti-realist have become something like philosophical archetypes whose views Dummett feels free to stipulate. Furthermore, whereas we began with a series of properly metaphysical disputes, what we now confront is an opposition within the philosophy of language. Debate over a mind-independent reality constraining our statements and beliefs has been displaced by debate over the proper account of the meaning of assertoric sentences. For Dummett, the generalized form of the latter debate comes to be identified with the debate over realism. And the project gets altered in a further way. The initial aim was simply a characterization of two philosophical perspectives; but what started out as a neutral characterization of realism and anti-realism comes to take on a progressively more partisan cast. Dummett tries to expose weaknesses in the 'received view'—the realist's account of meaning—and to explore the strategies required to displace that account with the sort of theory of meaning proposed by the anti-realist.[5] So we leave the historical debates behind; we move from metaphysics to the philosophy of language; and we become something like apologists for an anti-realist theory of meaning.

Realism, we have said, is at bottom the view that an assertoric sentence gets its meaning from being correlated with a certain state of affairs, the state of affairs

---

[5] For the idea that the realist's account of meaning is the 'received view', see Dummett (1993f: 34). Although it is difficult not to see Dummett as something like an apologist for an anti-realist theory of meaning, he is himself more cautious in his characterization of his 'research programme'. See e.g. Dummett (1993b: 463–4).

that obtains just in case the sentence is true. Dummett calls the view the truth-conditional theory of meaning. On this view, to understand an assertoric statement, S, is to grasp the truth-condition for S; it is to know how the world must be for S to be true; and to assert a statement is to assert that its truth-condition obtains. This view, we have said, is the 'received view,' and Dummett thinks there are good reasons for its having that status. The view has deep intuitive appeal. We take it that, for any assertoric statement, S, 'S' is equivalent in content to 'It is true that S'; and, as Dummett puts it, that equivalence suggests that truth is precisely the notion to play the central role in the theory of meaning (Dummett 1993f: 42).

Now, according to Dummett, a theory of meaning for a language, L, is supposed to provide a theoretical representation of what a speaker of L knows in virtue of understanding the sentences of L—what Dummett calls a 'model of meaning' (Dummett 1978a: 217). For 'the received view'—truth-conditional semantics—the relevant model is provided by the sort of Tarskian theory of truth we meet in the work of Donald Davidson; and, as Dummett sees it, what the truth-conditional theory is recommending is that knowledge of something like that theory for language, L, be ascribed to a speaker of L.[6]

But in what sense is it that a speaker of a language knows the theory of truth for that language? If there is knowledge here, it cannot be propositional knowledge of an explicit or verbalizable sort. The idea that more than a handful of speakers of English could actually formulate anything remotely resembling a Tarskian theory for even a modest fragment of English is preposterous. But apart from that, the claim that an English speaker's knowledge of the truth-conditions for all the English sentences he or she understands is explicit or verbalizable seems to involve either circularity or a regress (Dummett 1993f: 45; 1978a: 217). Take any sentence, 'S', whose meaning our speaker grasps. Since the truth-conditional theorist is supposing that the speaker's knowledge of its meaning is explicit, the theorist is committed to the idea that the speaker could display his or her understanding by actually stating the truth-condition for 'S'. But how will our speaker do that? Either by using 'S' itself or by using some other sentence/s. If the former, then the truth-conditional theorist can be sure that we have the required display only if the theorist assumes in advance what needs to be shown—that our speaker's use of 'S' involves a knowledge of its meaning (that is, its truth-condition). If the latter, then the theorist can be sure that we have a display of the speaker's knowledge of the truth-condition of 'S' only if the theorist can be sure that our speaker knows the meaning (that is, the truth-condition) of the sentence/s used in the explanation of the truth-condition of 'S'. But, then, the same problem arises in the case of that sentence (or those sentences), and the truth-conditional theorist faces once again a choice between circularity and regress.

---

[6] But the assumption has a peculiar status. It is not to be understood as a psychological hypothesis, but as 'an analysis of the complex skill which constitutes mastery of a language' (Dummett 1993c: 37).

So defenders of the truth-conditional theory will need to deny that speakers of a language have explicit or verbalizable knowledge of the truth-conditions of all the sentences of the language. They will need to hold that, for at least some sentences (presumably, the sentences comprising the most primitive parts of the language), speakers have only an implicit knowledge of their meaning and, hence, their truth-conditions. Dummett, however, thinks that truth-conditional theorists face difficulties in their attempt to make sense of this attribution of implicit knowledge, difficulties so serious as to call into question the whole truth-conditional approach to meaning.

The truth-conditional theorist tells us that there are sentences whose truth-conditions speakers are unable to formulate explicitly, but know, nonetheless. The claim is that they know the truth-conditions of those sentences implicitly. Dummett's question is: what is it to grasp a truth-condition implicitly? The talk of knowledge suggests that the truth-conditional theorist is ascribing to speakers a state that is properly epistemic, but is, nonetheless ineffable; and that, in turn, suggests that, for the truth-conditional theorist, something like a private language underlies our understanding of public language. Dummett takes the notion of a private epistemic state to be incoherent; and he insists that if truth-conditional theorists are to avoid commitment to such states, they need to construe a speaker's implicit knowledge of a truth-condition as something like a practical skill or ability that gets manifested or displayed in a publicly accessible pattern of behaviour. Indeed, he tells us that if there is to be any content or meaning at all to the truth-conditional theorist's attribution of implicit knowledge, there must be some observable pattern of behaviour that could count as a manifestation of that knowledge (Dummett 1978a: 217).

Now, Dummett concedes that for any statement, S, such that it is impossible for its truth-condition to obtain without a speaker's recognition of that fact, it is easy to identify something that counts as a manifestation of the speaker's implicit knowledge of the truth-condition for S. The speaker's assent to S in the presence of the relevant truth-condition is sufficient manifestation to give content to the attribution of implicit knowledge. Unfortunately, there are very few statements whose truth-conditions cannot obtain without a speaker's recognizing that fact. 'I have a headache' and 'I am thinking' are, perhaps, like that; but the vast majority of sentences coming out of a speaker's mouth are such that their truth-conditions can obtain without the speaker's recognizing that fact. For many such sentences, however, there exists an effective procedure for verifying the sentence, a procedure following which a speaker is in a position to recognize the obtaining of the sentence's truth-condition whenever it obtains. 'It is snowing' and 'The grass is green' are, for most speakers at least, like this; and for a sentence like either of these, Dummett concedes, a speaker's ability to employ the relevant procedure to arrive at a verdict on the sentence is sufficient behavioural manifestation to give content to an ascription to the speaker of implicit knowledge of the sentence's truth-condition. For other sentences, there may now be no such effective decision procedure; but it is at least possible that there be one. A sentence like 'There is water 50 miles beneath the Martian equator' is, perhaps, an example. As things stand, there is nothing that counts as a behavioural manifestation of a speaker's grasp of the truth-condition for a sentence like this; but it is at least in principle possible that there be such a manifestation; and that, Dummett would allow, is sufficient to give meaning or content to an attribution of implicit knowledge of truth-conditions (see Dummett 1993f: 45–6).[7]

But, as Dummett points out, there are many sentences for which not even this sort of in principle possibility of effective decision procedure exists. He routinely lists three different operations that can generate such sentences: the use of the subjunctive conditional, reference to remote regions of time and space, and quantification over infinite or unsurveyable totalities. These operations generate sentences like 'If Clinton had been born in New York, he would never have become president', 'The triangle was Hannibal's favourite figure', and 'A city will never be built on this spot', all of which Dummett takes to be undecidable. He denies that it is even in principle possible that there be a generally effective decision procedure for any of them, a procedure following which we could conclusively establish or verify the sentence in any situation where it is true. But, then, there is no practical ability mastery of which constitutes a behavioural manifestation of the implicit knowledge of the truth-condition that is to be identified with understanding the meaning of the sentence, and that means that any ascription of such knowledge is without content or meaning. The upshot is that the truth-conditional theorist posits epistemic conditions for understanding sentences such that it is not even meaningful to suppose that they obtain.

For obvious reasons, this line of criticism has come to be known as the 'manifestation argument.' Dummett frequently supplements this argument with a related line of reasoning that has come to be known as the 'acquisition argument'. The argument seeks to show that if the truth-conditional theory were true, no speaker could ever learn the meaning of an undecidable or verification-transcendent sentence (Dummett 1978a: 217–18). According to Dummett, we learn a language by being trained to assent to sentences in certain situations and to deny them in others; but the situations in question need to be ones that a language-learner can recognize as obtaining whenever they obtain. This requirement presents no problems for the truth-conditional theorist's account of a decidable sentence; for, in its case, the truth-condition the theorist will insist a language-learner needs to grasp in order to learn its meaning is a state of affairs for which there exists an effective procedure enabling the learner to put himself or herself in a position to recognize its obtaining whenever it obtains; but with an undecidable sentence it is otherwise. The state

---

[7] Crispin Wright gives a more detailed account of in principle decidability than any we find in Dummett. See Wright (1987d: 30–2; 1987b: 180–3).

of affairs the truth-conditional theorist tells us we need to grasp if we are to learn the meaning of an undecidable sentence is not one whose obtaining the language-learner can be brought to recognize or detect whenever it obtains. But, then, if the truth-conditional theory is true, none of us could ever have done what we all have, in fact, done—learned the meaning of verification-transcendent sentences, and proof that we do grasp their meaning is just that we recognize them to be verification-transcendent.

The two arguments are closely related. The manifestation argument contends that nothing in a language-user's behaviour can ever show that he or she had an apprehension of a transcendent truth-condition; and the acquisition argument contends that there is no way a language-learner could ever have come by such an apprehension; and both arguments seek to undermine the truth-conditional theory by pointing out that these facts entail things that are pretty clearly not the case—that we never learn the meanings of verification-transcendent sentences and that we can never display our mastery of such sentences in our linguistic behaviour.

Both arguments rely on a cluster of related themes from the work of the later Wittgenstein—that meaning is use, that there can be no private language, that linguistic understanding is always a practical skill. What Dummett's arguments seek to show is that when truth-conditional theorists confront undecidable sentences, they are forced to repudiate these themes. Thus, Dummett explains the Wittgensteinian claim that meaning is use by telling us that 'the meaning of a . . . statement determines and is exhaustively determined by its use. The meaning of such a statement cannot be or contain as an ingredient anything which is not manifest in the use made of it, lying solely in the mind of the individual who apprehends the meaning' (1978a: 216). But if Dummett's arguments are on target, the truth-conditional theorist must reject this sort of Wittgensteinian account of a speaker's understanding of a verification-transcendent sentence and endorse instead a Cartesian model for characterizing our understanding of undecidables, where that understanding turns out to be a private state, the acquisition of which is a complete mystery and the subsequent possession of which there can be no manifestation in overt linguistic behaviour.

3. Dummett's Positive Programme

Dummett assumes that the spectre of these Cartesian commitments will motivate us to search for an alternative to the truth-conditional theory; and if the relevant Wittgensteinian themes are to provide constraints, the alternative theory of meaning will be one that construes linguistic understanding as a properly practical skill—more precisely, as a discriminatory or recognitional ability. On this sort of view, to understand a statement is to know how to use it properly; and to know that is to have the ability to recognize when the assertion of that statement would be correct. Dummett encapsulates this insight in the proposal that we replace the concept of truth-conditions with that of assertability conditions. To know the meaning of a statement is to know (in the sense of 'to be able to recognize') the conditions under which a speaker would be conclusively justified or warranted in asserting the statement; and to assert a statement is to assert that the conditions required for the statement to have conclusive warrant obtain. Such conditions are those in which the statement is verified. Accordingly, Dummett frequently calls his proposed alternative to the truth-conditional theory verificationist semantics.[8]

So the notion of an assertability condition is to be the central concept in our semantical theory. That concept, however, needs clarification. When the focus is the correctness or appropriateness of an assertion, we need to distinguish the demands of conversational etiquette and its social graces from the properly epistemic demands placed on assertion. It is only the latter that Dummett has in mind when he speaks of assertability conditions. But even when we keep this distinction in mind, there is an ambiguity in talk of assertability conditions. Talk of the epistemic conditions justifying assertion can be a reference to the situations or states of affairs in the world to which a speaker responds in assertion or to the states of response to such situations or states of affairs on the part of the speaker doing the asserting. For some statements, to be sure, there is no such distinction: the relevant states of affairs just are states of the speaker. First-person psychological statements are the obvious case; but the case is exceptional. More typical is the case where we can distinguish between what a speaker responds to and the state of the speaker doing the responding. Unfortunately, Dummett is not clear just which he has in mind when he speaks of conditions justifying assertion. Nor is there agreement among those who are sympathetic with Dummett's proposal of an assertability-conditional account of meaning. Thus, Crispin Wright seems to endorse an objectivist reading when, following a suggestion of Dummett's, he tells us that, for decidable statements, the truth-conditions of the 'received view' constitute a subspecies of assertability conditions (Wright 1987d: 242); whereas, John Skorupski seems to be proposing a subjectivist account when he tells us that we can understand assertability conditions as states of information, where these are states of the speaker doing the asserting (Skorupski 1988: 513; 1997: 41). Just as Wright's reading can find its inspiration in

---

[8] The most extended discussion of the topic is found in Dummett (1993f: 62 ff). As examples of what we might call evidentiary theories of meaning (or, following Skorupski 1988, 1993, epistemic theories of meaning), Dummett mentions both verificationism and falsificationism, where the latter tells us that to know the meaning is to know (in the sense, again, of 'to be able to recognize') what would falsify it. But while he even occasionally suggests a preference for a falsificationist theory (see Dummett 1993f: 93), he typically pits the truth-conditional theory against verificationism and talks as though a verificationist theory is the theory that most naturally expresses the Wittgensteinian themes just mentioned.

Dummett, Skorupski's understanding of assertability conditions seems to be what Dummett has in mind when he tells us that, for an observation statement, the conditions warranting assertion are the appropriate sense experiences on the part of the speaker.

But whichever interpretation is endorsed, the resulting conception of an assertability condition precludes the possibility that the meaning of a statement might involve some factor that transcends the 'detective' powers of someone who understands the statement. According to Dummett, whether or not a statement is one whose assertion has conclusive warrant or justification is something that, by the very nature of the case, is in principle detectable by a speaker. Contemporary epistemologists sometimes associate different senses with the terms 'warrant' and 'justification'. (See, for example, Plantinga 1993: 43–6.) They tell us that whereas the fact that an individual has justification for a particular belief or statement is, in principle, transparent to the individual, this is not so with warrant. Dummett, by contrast, uses the two terms interchangeably and so construes them that it is impossible for there to be conclusive warrant or justification for the assertion of a statement unless that fact is one that can be recognized by those speaking the language. A consequence, Dummett thinks, is that the assertability theorist has no difficulty handling the statements that are problematic for the truth-conditional view—the verification-transcendent or undecidable statements. One might suppose that this is not so, arguing that since there may be no conditions under which we are warranted in asserting these statements (they are, after all, verification-transcendent), the verificationist is no better off in giving an account of our grasp of their meaning than the truth-conditional theorist. But, according to Dummett, there is a confusion here. Knowing the meaning of a statement, he tells us, is a matter not of actually having the justification requisite for correct assertion, but rather of having an ability, the ability to recognize, if presented with it, the condition that would conclusively warrant the assertion of the statement; and that, Dummett wants to claim, is something one can have even in the absence of a grasp of the statement's truth-condition (Dummett 1993f: 70).

But Dummett thinks that if we are going to reject the truth-conditional theory of meaning in favour of an assertability-conditional approach, we will want to reject as well the theory of truth associated with that problematic theory of meaning. Dummett does not give us much argument to support this view. Indeed, it often seems that he takes the truth-conditional theory of meaning and the associated theory of truth to constitute a single package, neither component of which survives the demise of the other (see, for example, Dummett 1978c: 146, 155). But if pressed for argument, Dummett would likely claim that it is only because truth-conditional theorists subscribe to an account which makes truth epistemically unconstrained that they run into the problems Dummett delineates; for, Dummett would argue, it is only when they conjoin the truth-conditional theory with that sort of account of truth that those theorists find themselves forced to suppose that speakers have the problematic idea of verification-transcendent truth-conditions. Truth, Dummett concludes, cannot be a property that is capable of eluding our power to detect it.[9] It must be a property such that it is at least in principle possible for us to determine whether or not a statement has it. Having conclusive warrant or justification is just such a property, so Dummett concludes that truth is something like warranted or justified assertability.

An important consequence of Dummett's epistemic account of truth and the associated evidentiary conception of meaning is epistemological. It provides Dummett with a response to the stock arguments of the sceptic.[10] The sceptic calls into question our claim to have knowledge by arguing that it is possible that most of our familiar beliefs are false. The arguments have a standard form. The sceptic takes some familiar statement, S, and argues that the best evidence we could have for asserting S is compatible with the falsehood of S. Arguments of this form, however, just assume something like the 'received view' of meaning and truth. The sceptic needs to assume that the meaning of S is given by a verification-transcendent state of affairs and that warranted assertability and truth can come apart; but if Dummett is right, both claims are false. We can have no conception of the sceptic's verification-transcendent state of affairs; and if our evidence is sufficient to warrant the assertion of a statement, that statement is *eo ipso* true.

In any case, we have an epistemic theory of truth; and we are now back where we began our discussion of realism and anti-realism. If truth is epistemically constrained, then it is not clear that the principle of bivalence will hold across the board. If there are verification-transcendent or undecidable statements, then neither their assertion nor their denial will be warranted; and given an epistemically constrained notion of truth and falsehood, that means that there are statements which have no truth-value at all. Of course, the defender of the 'received view' will want to insist that the principle of bivalence holds across the board. So we have our original opposition. The realist—now construed as the defender of a truth-conditional theory of meaning and an epistemically unconstrained conception of truth—endorses the principle of bivalence for undecidables; and the anti-realist—now depicted as the proponent of verificationist semantics and an epistemically constrained conception of truth—denies that verification-transcendent statements have a determinate truth-value.

So Dummett's anti-realist rejects the principle of bivalence, the semantic principle that for any statement, S, either S is true or S is false; but Dummett denies that bivalence is the only classical logical principle his anti-realist is committed

---

[9] The general structure of argument in Dummett (1993*f*) confirms this reading of Dummett's intentions here.

[10] This feature of an epistemically constrained conception of truth is pressed in Putnam (1981, ch. 2); but Dummett is fully aware of the idea as well. See Dummett (1978*c*: 153). I am indebted here and elsewhere to Marian David, who helped me with the epistemological dimensions of the realism–anti-realism debate.

to rejecting. He thinks that a repudiation of the principle of the excluded middle (the non-semantic principle that S or not-S) is likewise implicit in the anti-realist's assertability-conditional semantics (see, for example, Dummett 1978e: 17–18; 1993f: 69–70).

The truth-conditional account explains the connectives by showing the truth-values of the complex sentences formed by the use of the connectives to be a function of the truth-values of the sentences that are their constituents. The assertability theorist, however, insists that the realist's notion of truth is to be replaced by the notion of assertability. Accordingly, Dummett tells us, the explanation of the connectives will proceed by construing the complex sentences into which they enter as having assertability conditions that are a function of the assertability conditions of their constituent sentences. Thus, the assertability theorist will explain the connective 'or' by saying something like the following: we have conclusive warrant for asserting a statement of the form 'A or B' just in case we have conclusive warrant for asserting A or we have conclusive warrant for asserting B.[11] The upshot is that where 'A' is an undecidable statement, the classical principle 'A or not-A' fails; for if 'A' is effectively undecidable, then we have conclusive warrant for asserting neither 'A' nor its negation, so we lack the warrant requisite for asserting the disjunction 'A or not-A'. What the verificationist theory delivers is an account of the connectives of the sort at work in intuitionist theories, where truth gets replaced by provability, itself a species of warranted assertability—the sort of warranted assertability associated with the statements of mathematics. And Dummett makes much of the connection between intuitionism and verificationist semantics. The latter, he suggests, can be understood as a generalization of the sort of theory of meaning the intuitionist provides for mathematical statements (see, for example, Dummett 1993f: 70).

4. Problems with Dummett's Account of Realism

To review: I began with Dummett's early claim that, in the disputes he addresses, what separates realist from anti-realist is the former's endorsement of the principle of bivalence for verification-transcendent or undecidable statements. That separation, we saw, is supposed to rest on a prior contrast in the theory of meaning—the contrast between a truth-conditional theory and an assertability-conditional theory. That contrast, we have seen, becomes the focus of Dummett's overarching research

[11] And there will be familiar differences as well in the assertability theorist's introduction of the quantifiers. See e.g. Dummett (1978f: 231).

programme in the philosophy of language. The programme has both a negative and positive side. On the negative side Dummett seeks to undermine the truth-conditional theory by invoking the Wittgensteinian insights expressed in the manifestation and acquisition arguments. On the positive side he is anxious to display verificationist semantics as a genuine alternative to the 'received view'. According to Dummett, the verificationist approach to meaning commits us to a rejection of the realist's conception of truth in favour of an epistemically constrained notion of truth that makes it something like justified or warranted assertion. We get the result that the anti-realist rejects the principle of bivalence in just the way Dummett's early analysis had claimed; and as we have just seen, we get as well the result that the connectives (and the quantifiers) are to be understood in intuitionist terms, so that classical principles like excluded middle fail.

Virtually every step in this complicated analysis has been challenged. Focusing first on Dummett's early attempt to characterize the opposition between realists and anti-realists, we meet with widespread scepticism about Dummett's claims to have identified the core intuition of realism in the idea that the principle of bivalence holds for undecidables. Some critics challenge the claim that acceptance of bivalence is a necessary condition for realism. They point out that there are grounds for denying bivalence that do not imply a move away from realism. One might, for example, question bivalence because one follows Frege and Strawson in denying truth-values to statements made by way of non-referring singular terms; but endorsing that analysis hardly makes one an anti-realist.[12] Likewise, one might deny truth-value to some statements involving the use of vague terms; but that strategy would not seem to preclude a realist account of the subject matter of vague discourse (see Vision 1988: 180; Wright 1987d: 4. For Dummett's response, see Dummett 1993b: 468). And there are the semantic paradoxes, where, whatever their metaphysical orientation, semantic theorists seem to have no alternative but to deny a truth-value (see, for example, Vision 1988: 181).

But as the critics themselves concede, these objections to Dummett's analysis do not undermine the fundamental insights at work in Dummett's analysis; they merely point to the need for suitable qualifications in its formulation.[13] More serious are concerns about Dummett's emphasis on the role of verification-transcendent statements in debates between realists and anti-realists. As we have seen, Dummett takes it to be constitutive of the realist outlook to insist on truth-values for effectively undecidable statements; but, as Crispin Wright points out, that stipulation has the consequence that it is impossible to be a genuine realist about bodies of discourse that include no verification-transcendent statements. Thus, there couldn't be

---

[12] Dummett himself deals with these problems in Dummett (1978b).

[13] And, in fairness to Dummett, his attribution of the principle of bivalence and the principle of excluded middle to the realist was almost always formulated cautiously. See Dummett (1978c: 155) and the detailed discussions in Dummett (1993a, c).

such a thing as realism about effectively decidable mathematical statements, moral discourse, or, more generally, any 'domain of states of affairs over which human cognitive powers are sovereign' (Wright 1987*d*: 3). But, as Wright goes on to argue, any such domain is one where realism 'ought to seem least problematic and it is where Dummett's anti-realist, at least, proposes to leave it alone' (1987*d*: 3).

So there can be forms of realism that do not bear on verification-transcendent statements. Following Wright, I mentioned moral realism as an example. Wright suggests that there is another way in which the debate over moral realism constitutes a counter-example to Dummett's account of disputes between realists and anti-realists. According to Dummett, the disagreement about bivalence for undecidables hinges on a more fundamental disagreement about the nature of truth; the anti-realist rejects the realist's idea that truth is epistemically unconstrained and identifies truth with something like warranted assertability. But, as Wright notes, nothing like this happens in the confrontation between moral realists and anti-realists. Instead, we have one of two quite different patterns (Wright 1992: 9–10). Some moral anti-realists—those who are called 'error theorists'—concede the applicability of realist truth-values to moral statements, but insist that since there are no genuinely ethical facts to make those statements true, moral statements are one and all false. By contrast, other moral anti-realists—emotivists, expressivists, projectionists—simply deny that moral sentences are statemental and so deny that any notion of truth-value, whether realist or not, applies to them.

Dummett himself concedes that his characterization of disputes between realists and anti-realists does not help us understand the case of ethics (Dummett 1993*b*: 466); but he insists that it holds for the cases he originally sought to capture (1993*b*: 468–71). However, critics have found even this claim problematic (see Devitt 1984: 261–7; Hale 1997: 284–5; Alston 1996: 130–1). Their difficulty with Dummett's analysis is one of principle rather than detail. What Dummett proposes is that we understand disputes between realists and anti-realists as disputes about language, truth, and meaning. The philosophers involved in the debates that interest Dummett, however, would almost certainly reject this linguistic reading of their views in favour of a more explicitly metaphysical characterization. And it surely seems natural to interpret the debates as the actual parties to those debates would themselves understand them. Scientific realists and operationalists, it seems, were arguing about whether there really are things like electrons, protons, and quarks. Phenomenalists were denying the existence of matter and material objects; and psychological realists and behaviourists were debating the reality of private, intrinsically mental states and episodes.

Dummett recognizes that his account of the realism issue is likely to evince this sort of response; he appreciates that he will be charged with changing the subject. What he wants to claim, however, is that unless the traditional debates are understood as he proposes, there will not be any propositional claims for the traditional realist and anti-realist to be disagreeing about. As Dummett sees it, when they are understood in the traditional metaphysical idiom, the various forms of realism and anti-realism are no better than metaphors or pictures (Dummett 1978*f*, p. xl; 1978*a*: 228–9; 1993*b*: 465). He takes his linguistic reading of the relevant views to transform poetic images into literal claims that can submit to argument and counter-argument. His view of metaphysical sentences is not much different from that of the old-line positivists: taken at face value, metaphysical sentences cannot be assertoric. The positivists had argued that since they are either assertoric or meaningless, metaphysical sentences turn out to be nonsense. Dummett parts company with the positivists at this point. Conceding that metaphysical sentences cannot have the literal force they seem to have, Dummett refuses to deny them cognitive content. He recommends instead that we construe them as disguised semantic claims. So it is because he is an anti-realist (or, perhaps, an irrealist) about metaphysical claims as traditionally understood that Dummett gives his own linguistic reading of disputes between realists and anti-realists.

And this anti-realism about ontological claims comes out in Dummett's response to questions about the metaphysical force of the anti-realist semantics he seeks to develop. He implies that such questions call not for an answer but for a further picture or image. He tells us that the picture need not be that of the subjective idealist who pictures the world as something we make. We can instead picture to ourselves a world that is not of our making, but that somehow springs into existence as we investigate it (Dummett 1978*e*: 18–19). Here, it is tempting to side with Crispin Wright, who associates with the anti-realist theory of meaning the more restrained picture of a world which exists independently of our investigatory efforts, but which is constituted by properties whose instantiation is, in principle at least, necessarily detectable by us or by beings whose conceptual abilities would represent a finite extension of our own (Wright 1987*b*: 181). But if we prefer the less colourful story Wright tells, we need to understand that, as Dummett sees it, our preference is merely a preference for a picture, image, or metaphor. The disagreement is not a factual disagreement. There are no properly metaphysical facts to disagree about. From the assertoric or propositional perspective, the anti-realist semantics is the bottom line; it does not have any metaphysical underpinnings because there are no such things.

5. Problems with the Negative Programme

Dummett's negative programme challenges defenders of truth-conditional semantics to show how a speaker could acquire and display a knowledge of transcendent truth-conditions. Rather than meet them head on, some critics have tried to show that Dummett's challenges rest on problematic assumptions. We have already noted, for example, that both the acquisition argument and the manifestation argument take as their backdrop a package of related Wittgensteinian themes—the use theory of meaning, the rejection of private mental states, the interpretation of linguistic understanding as a practical, discriminatory ability. Dummett provides nothing like a general defence of this package. Telling us that he finds Wittgenstein's attack on privacy 'incontrovertible' (Dummett 1978f: p. xxxiii), he merely reiterates the claim that since they are communicable, meanings must be public. Critics have seized on this lacuna in the argument. What the Wittgensteinian view assumes is that success-ful communication is possible only if one speaker knows what another means to communicate. It is because knowledge is thought to be required that we are admon-ished to dispense with private meanings in favour of items on public display. As Dummett puts it, we can communicate only what we can be *observed* to commun-icate (Dummett 1978a: 216). Critics have challenged the demand for knowledge here. They argue that successful communication requires only the weaker condition that speakers have *true beliefs* about each other. That condition would, however, be satisfied in a world where meanings are private, but we all operate with a very general, yet true, hypothesis about the similarity of human beings—the hypothesis that we are so constituted that, by and large, we have similar experiences in similar circumstances and react in similar ways when presented with similar experiences (Craig 1982: 552 ff; Strawson 1977: 19). As we have seen, Dummett's arguments seek to show that the only model for understanding a speaker's grasp of transcendent truth-conditions is one where meanings are private; but, then, if the critic is right that the relevant privacy is compatible with successful communication, Dummett's case against truth-conditional semantics breaks down.

Another problematic assumption of Dummett's negative programme is the idea that a speaker's apprehension of a truth-condition must be a state that gets mani-fested in a single way—in the speaker's recognition that the truth-condition obtains whenever it does. Defenders of holist and functionalist interpretations of men-tal states have objected to the idea that grasping a truth-condition is a state with a single canonical form of manifestation that can be identified independently of any reference to other mental states (McGinn 1980: 30–2; Skorupski 1988: 509–13). The objection is rooted in the familiar idea that the identity of a mental state involves more than behavioural outputs; it hinges as well on the place the mental state occupies in a network of related mental states. The claim is that the differ-ent items involved in the identification of a mental state interact organically, so that there is no such thing as *the* behavioural manifestation of a mental state. How, on any occasion, a mental state gets expressed depends upon the other mental states an individual happens to be in on that occasion. Grasping a truth-condition, then, is not simply a matter of behavioural response; and, in any case, there is no single pattern of response, whether narrowly recognitional or not, that counts as the manifestation of a speaker's apprehension of the truth-condition of a statement.

And there is a related assumption about linguistic understanding that critics have found problematic. Dummett seems to suppose that linguistic understanding is simply a matter of pairing sentences, one by one, with observable situations. Thus, his acquisition argument assumes that learning the meaning of a sentence is learning to correlate it with the appropriate observable state of affairs. Critics, however, argue that we learn the meanings of very few sentences in the way Dummett suggests. Were that not so, they claim, there would be no accounting for the fact that speakers of a language grasp the meanings of an infinity of different sentences. The claim is that we learn the meanings of most sentences by learning the meanings of their constituent terms and by learning the modes of composition or combination that tie those terms together (Hale 1997: 279–280; Alston 1996: 113–14); and critics of the acquisition argument insist that this is true for undecidable sentences no less than decidables. But, then, unless it is just stipulated that grasping the meaning of a sentence is not a matter of grasping its truth-condition, there is no reason to think that there is any special problem about acquiring a grasp of the truth-condition of a verification-transcendent sentence.

And similar remarks hold about the manifestation of linguistic understanding. Dummett assumes that the only way we can display our understanding of a statement is by expressing assent when presented with the evidentially appropriate state of affairs; but while critics concede that is one way to display understanding of the meaning of a statement, they insist it is not the only way. We can also display our understanding of a statement simply by displaying our mastery of the linguistic skills ingredient in making the statement. And this is true both for decidables and for undecidables. Thus, Anthony Appiah suggests that it counts as evidence that speakers understand the verification-transcendent statement that it rained on the earth 1 million years ago 'that they use "rain" properly in sentences about present rain, that they can count to a million, know how long a year is, and display a grasp of the past tense in relation to the recent past' (Appiah 1986: 80). But if this is right, then, again, it is only if we stipulate that knowing the meaning of a statement is not a matter of grasping its truth-condition that we have any reason to suppose that we cannot grasp the truth-condition of a verification-transcendent sentence.[14]

A rather different response to Dummett's negative programme is to attempt to show that the truth-conditional theorist has the resources to meet the challenges implicit in the manifestation and acquisition arguments. Thus, conceding that linguistic understanding needs to be a recognitional ability, one might argue that this reading of linguistic understanding is compatible with the idea that grasping the meaning of a sentence is grasping its truth-condition (Appiah 1986: 23–4 and

---

[14] Kirkham disagrees. See Kirkham (1992: 259–60).

passim). On this view, the claim that understanding is a recognitional ability does not entail that understanding a sentence is the ability to recognize its truth-condition. The claim will be that it can be that—as it is in the case of decidables; but while conceding that our understanding of a verification-transcendent statement cannot consist in the ability to recognize its truth-condition, the proponent of this response will deny that this fact precludes understanding's being recognitional. The claim will be, first, that grasping a truth-condition enables one to do precisely the things the assertability theorist talks about—to recognize what counts as evidence for the relevant statement and to recognize the epistemic relations between the statement and other statements[15] and, secondly, that evidence that we can do these things is evidence that we grasp the appropriate truth-condition.

In the same way, we find defenders of truth-conditional semantics responding to the acquisition argument by trying to construct accounts that show how we might come to possess a conception of verification-transcendent states of affairs. One strategy here is to look to familiar cases where we arrive at conceptions that take us beyond the observable (see, for example, Vision 1988: 206–11; McGinn 1980: 27–9). There are, for example, the ideas at work in theoretical science (like that of a muon or quark) and concepts involving idealization (like that of a perfectly straight line). The claim will be that our acquisition of concepts like these rests on a whole battery of perfectly acceptable conceptual moves including extrapolation, hypothetical inference, the appeal to analogy, and explanation by way of postulation. Those same moves, the claim will be, are sufficient to legitimize our ideas of other minds, inaccessible regions of space and time, infinite totalities, and so on. The response, of course, will be that the examples the realist appeals to include conceptions of precisely the sorts the anti-realist insists are open to question. In turn, the realist can reply that the anti-realist has cast the net too broadly. The claim will be that if we call into question the sorts of examples the realist invokes, few of our ongoing intellectual enterprises will remain untouched. What we face in this interchange is one of those burden of proof impasses that can be difficult to adjudicate, so even if the realist is satisfied with his line of response to the acquisition argument, the anti-realist will remain unconvinced that the challenge implicit in the argument has been met.

---

[15] Wright objects to this strategy for responding to the manifestation argument on the grounds that it involves postulating a grasp of truth-conditions to explain our ability to recognize evidence and inferential connections. He claims that the realist's account has no explanatory power whatsoever and that for verification-transcendent claims, we should dispense with an apprehension of truth-conditions and identify understanding directly with the recognitional abilities. See Wright (1987c: 241–2). Some realists (e.g. Vision 1988) may appeal to our grasp of truth-conditions to explain these recognitional abilities; but the realist need not be doing that. The realist I am thinking of is one who, like Appiah, endorses the truth-conditional theory because of its intuitive roots and then tries to meet the anti-realist's challenge of showing that our grasp of verification-transcendent truth-conditions has a recognitional manifestation.

To satisfy the anti-realist, the realist needs to construct a story that invokes no assumptions the anti-realist will question and shows how we could move from the evidential base the anti-realist insists on by way of principles the anti-realist would accept to a conception of a verification-transcendent state of affairs. One such story appeals to the fact that in learning a language we learn that the truth-values of some statements are systematically correlated with the truth-values of other statements. Consider the case of statements in the past-tense. Many such statements are in principle undecidable, so there ought to be a problem about the acquisition of the conception of such a claim's being true. Dummett, however, suggests a strategy the realist might invoke in dealing with this problem (Dummett 1978d: 363 ff). The realist can appeal to what Dummett calls the truth-value link between present-tense and past-tense statements. The idea is just that a past-tense statement of the form 'It was the case that p' is now true just in case the present-tense statement 'It is now the case that p' was true at the relevant time in the past. Now, grasping the idea at work in this principle is presumably something that non-problematically accompanies the learning of tensed language; but given that idea, all that we need if we are to acquire the idea of the present truth of a past-tense statement is the idea of the corresponding present-tense statement's being true. The idea of the obtaining of the truth-condition of a present-tense statement is, however, obviously one we can and do acquire. Accordingly, there should be no problem about our coming to grasp the truth-condition for a past-tense statement: we acquire that idea from our apprehension of the idea of a present-tense statement's being true together with our understanding of the truth-value link between present- and past-tense statements.

Now, if this suggestion works for the case of statements about the distant past, the appeal to the idea of a truth-value link holds out promise for dealing with other verification-transcendent claims (see McDowell 1978: 129–31). The suggestion generalizes to handle future-tense undecidables, and a similar strategy would seem to work for second- and third-person psychological statements. In the latter case, we have non-problematic self-ascriptions of psychological states and the principle that an ascription of a psychological state to another individual is true just in case that individual's self-ascription of the psychological state is or would have been true. So it seems that the acquisition of the idea of a second- or third-person psychological statement's being true is simply a matter of connecting the conception of a self-ascription's being true with the relevant principle.

One difficulty is that the truth-value link strategy is not applicable to all classes of undecidable statements. It does not, for example, work for the case of quantification over infinite domains (Wright 1987e: 89–90). Still, the cases it claims to handle are important; and if it is successful in those cases, the realist can claim genuine progress in explaining our acquisition of the idea of a transcendent truth-condition. Unfortunately, there are grounds for doubting the success of the strategy. The claim is that we come to grasp, for example, the truth-value link between past-tense and present-tense statements in the normal course of learning tensed language. But if that is so, then the normal course of learning tensed language seems to be open to the very challenge the appeal to the truth-value link was meant to answer. The aim is to show how we might have acquired the idea of a past-tense statement's being true. Towards realizing the aim, we say that a past-tense statement is now true just in case a present-tense statement *was* true; but if there was a general problem about our acquisition of the idea of a past-tense statement, we hardly answer it by appeal to that principle since it presupposes that we already have a conception of the past-tense. The same sort of difficulty arises for the case of second- and third-person psychological claims. The problem is one of coming to understand what it is for another person to be in a psychological state; the solution is to appeal to self-ascriptions and the principle that the ascription of a psychological state to a person, *P*, is true just in case *P*'s *self-ascription* of that state is or would have been true. But the principle makes reference to a psychological activity—self-ascription. How did we come by an understanding of another individual's engaging in that activity? (See McDowell 1978: 132–3; Wright 1987e: 91–3.)

The realist who appeals to truth-value links to answer the challenge set by the acquisition argument concedes that we never have immediate access to the states of affairs expressed by undecidable statements, but not all realists make that concession. John McDowell, for example, argues that there are occasions where we are directly confronted with the truth-condition for a second- or third-person psychological statement. These are situations where 'one can literally perceive, in another's facial expression or his behaviour, that he is in pain and not just infer that he is in pain from what one perceives' (McDowell 1978: 136). And McDowell thinks that something analogous holds for the past. On some occasions, McDowell claims, our knowledge of a past event is non-inferential. These are occasions when the perceptual impacts of a very recent event persist or, better, leave traces—immediate memory traces—of the event in the nervous system (1978: 136–7). Now, what McDowell argues is that these two sorts of situation are precisely those in which we get trained, respectively, to ascribe psychological states to others and to use the past-tense; and he insists that such situations provide a base that enables us to use these forms of language beyond the case where we are immediately presented with the truth-conditions for psychological claims and past-tense statements. We grasp that situations of the same kind as those that provide the materials for learning the ascription of psychological states or the past-tense can occur undetectably, so that the idea of a verification-transcendent psychological claim or an undecidable past-tense claim is just the idea of a statement whose truth-condition is a situation of the same sort or same kind as those involved in our training in psychological attributions or the use of the past-tense, but which obtains undetectably.

Critics have suggested that McDowell's use of the idea of 'the same kind' here is problematic. The claim seems to be that the property of undetectability imports a kind all its own, with the result that the suggestion that truth-conditions remain the same in kind while acquiring the property of undetectability is problematic (Hale 1997: 278). The notion of 'being the same in kind' is notoriously elusive, so it is difficult to know what to make of this criticism. If there is a problem for McDowell, it is the one pressed by Wright (Wright 1987e: 100–6). Wright is not convinced that the anti-realist needs to concede that, in the cases McDowell discusses, we actually have immediate or non-inferential access to the problematic truth-conditions. He points out that, in the psychological case, the relevant facial expressions and behaviour can occur without the corresponding psychological state. No matter how convincing an individual's expression or behaviour, it remains a possibility that the individual is deceiving us; and analogous claims hold for the case of our memory traces of the immediate past. Wright's point is just that if these allegedly privileged situations are not immune from familiar sceptical challenges, there is reason to doubt that they present us with cases where we are in immediate epistemic rapport with the problematic truth-conditions.

Before we conclude our discussion of Dummett's negative programme, we should note a potential problem that has not been discussed in the literature. Dummett's arguments are supposed to be perfectly general: their upshot is supposed to be that the idea of a state of affairs whose obtaining is verification-transcendent is unintelligible *simpliciter*: in no area of discourse can we make sense of the idea of a state of affairs that obtains undetectably. The difficulty is that Dummett tells us this sort of global anti-realism is likely incoherent (Dummett 1978d: 367–8). He tells us, for example, that one cannot be both a behaviourist and a phenomenalist. That is, one cannot coherently hold both that there are no transcendent mental states of affairs and that there are no transcendent physical or material states of affairs. The cost of being a phenomenalist is that one reject behaviourism; and vice versa. But if Dummett's arguments for anti-realism are so construed that if they hold at all, they hold across the board, then the fact that, by Dummett's own admission, they cannot have that kind of generality seems to entail that there is something wrong with those arguments.

6. PROBLEMS WITH THE POSITIVE PROGRAMME

Much in Dummett's positive programme is reminiscent of developments in old-line positivism. This is especially true of his theory of meaning, so it is no surprise that many of the criticisms of Dummett's verificationist semantics are familiar from the debates over positivist approaches to meaning.[16] Thus, Dummett's claim that each statement has an isolable set of verification conditions is met with the Quinean reply that 'our statements . . . face the tribunal of . . . experience not individually, but only as a corporate body' (Quine 1953: 40–1); and the upshot is supposed to be that the idea of a semantical theory that systematically identifies the verification conditions for statements taken individually represents a hopeless project.

Again, the suggestion that to understand the meaning of a statement is to grasp its verification conditions is countered by the claim that since we can determine which situations provide conclusive warrant for the assertion of a statement only if we know in advance what the statement says, the meaning of a statement must be something different from and epistemically prior to its verification conditions. The objection is meant to express some deep-lying, yet obvious intuitions about meaning. Closely related intuitions get expressed in the objection that if the assertability-conditional account of meaning is correct, we never manage to say what we want to say. Dummett's line is that the meaning of a sentence consists in its verification conditions; and Dummett explicitly tells us that to assert that p is to assert that p is capable of being conclusively established (Dummett 1993f: 76). But if that is right, then it turns out that to assert that p is to assert that one can conclusively establish that one can conclusively establish that p. Nor is this latter claim what it initially appears to be; for to assert it is to make some still more complicated claim involving a further iteration of the predicate 'is capable of being conclusively established'; and the same difficulty will arise for this new claim.[17] The content of our assertions seems to be perpetually elusive; and what is worse, no claim ever manages to be about what we intended it to be about. Suppose our original 'p' was the statement that grass is green. That statement would seem to be about grass; but it turns out that it is not; it is rather about what *we* are capable of conclusively establishing.[18]

The intuition underlying these objections—that meaning is something different from verification conditions—comes out in a still different way in a criticism of Strawson's. Strawson argues that statemental meaning cannot be identified with the conditions that warrant assertion since the latter can vary while meaning remains constant (Strawson 1977: 19–20). Strawson's example is the sentence 'Charles Stuart walked bareheaded to his place of execution'. He argues that despite the fact that the assertability conditions underlying the utterance of the sentence are very different

---

[16] For a number of such objections, see Alston (1996: 111 ff). The reference to Quine is found on p. 112.

[17] Alston denies that a related objection holds against Dummett (Alston 1996: 216–17); but it is less clear that the objection I state fails. Dummett does say that to assert that p is to assert that p is capable of being conclusively established. If we take the second phrase to be an analysis of the first, then we have a regress that is genuinely problematic. If, however, the equivalence is not meant to provide an analysis of asserting that p, then the regress is benign.

[18] See Johnston (1993) for a detailed discussion of this line of objection against verificationism.

for a witness to the execution and for someone in our day, the sentence means the same thing for both and its assertoric utterance by both involves the assertion of a single statement.

Although formulated as objections against verificationist semantics, the objections I have been considering apply to any account that identifies meaning with conditions of assertability; but Dummett's more particular claim that the assertability theorist should trade in verification conditions (that is, conditions that *conclusively* justify assertion) must face the objection that the resulting theory of meaning has precisely the difficulties Dummett takes to be the undoing of the truth-conditional theory. The claim is that to know the meaning of a statement is to know what would conclusively warrant its assertion; but statements that are in principle undecidable are such that there neither is nor can be anything that would conclusively justify their assertion or their denial. But, then, where is the strategic advantage of the assertability-conditional theory? As we have seen, Dummett tries to forestall this objection by identifying the apparently epistemic state with a practical, discriminatory ability—the ability to recognize, if presented with it, a condition which would justify assertion. But, of course, that is an ability that is in principle incapable of being exercised. And how is the attribution of that sort of ability any improvement on the truth-conditional theorist's attribution of epistemic states that can never get manifested?

But the verificationist's difficulties are not limited to the case of undecidables. Anyone who insists on verification conditions has to face the objection that very few empirical statements can be conclusively established or verified (see Appiah 1986: 35–53; Vision 1988: 183–9; Wright 1987c: 255 ff.). The evidence that grounds assertion is almost always defeasible. Now, it might seem that the moral of these two objections is that the assertability theorist has to give up talk of verification (and falsification) and replace it with talk of confirmation (and disconfirmation), so that what results is the view that to know the meaning of a statement is to be able to recognize the sorts of things that count as evidence confirming (disconfirming) the statement. Provided the assertability theorist is willing to supplement this talk of evidence with a reference to the full panoply of epistemic liaisons into which a statement enters, the resulting theory of meaning might have the resources for dealing with the first of our two objections—that bearing on undecidables.[19] But the defeasability of empirical claims continues to present problems, problems that cut in precisely the opposite direction from those associated with the first objection. The problems in question bear on Dummett's overarching project; for the fact that any piece of evidence for the assertion of an empirical statement is defeasible has

---

[19] I am assuming, first, that there can be broadly evidentiary conditions for and against undecidables and, secondly, that grasping those conditions together with the epistemic liaisons of an undecidable will provide a speaker with a sufficiently fine-grained understanding of the undecidable. For a discussion of these issues, see Wright (1987c: 241–3).

the consequence that, in the strict sense, that statement is verification-transcendent; and initially at least, that seems to be bad news for anyone who wants to endorse Dummett's anti-realist programme. The line, recall, is that there are serious difficulties in seeing how we could acquire and manifest a grasp of the truth-conditions for undecidable statements. The anti-realist, however, wants to concede that there is no difficulty understanding how we could come to possess and display an apprehension of the truth-conditions for ordinary empirical statements like 'It is raining out' and 'Grass is green'. But now these statements turn out to be verification-transcendent themselves; and that seems to imply that we can, after all, grasp the truth-conditions for verification-transcendent statements. So Dummett's concerns about statements involving the subjective conditional, quantification over infinite or unsurveyable totalities, or reference to remote regions of space and time begin to seem to have less urgency than we originally might have thought.

Dummett himself answers the objection that verification conditions cannot be assigned to statements taken one by one (Dummett 1991, ch. 10). He seems to concede that the understanding of verification conditions for any one statement might require a reference to the verification conditions for other statements in the same region of the language; but he claims that the criticism points to an in principle difficulty for verificationist semantics only if it is coupled with an extreme holism that makes it impossible to understand any one statement in a language without understanding all the others. But a holism that extreme, Dummett suggests, represents a threat not merely to verificationist semantics, but to every attempt to provide a systematic representation of what it is that a speaker understands in grasping the meaning of the statements of a language.

Crispin Wright addresses the sorts of objections that rest on the intuition that meaning and assertability conditions are different. He implies that the assertability theorist must reject Dummett's equation of the content of a statement with the content of the statement that its assertability conditions obtain. Wright tells us that a statement, S, and the statement that S is assertable differ in meaning. What the assertability theorist should say is that 'any situation which justifies assertion of S, even if defeasibly so, realizes the *truth-conditions* of "It is assertible that S" and hence provides a justification of the latter which is indefeasible' (Wright 1987d: 38). And Wright argues against Strawson that the fact that a statement's assertability conditions vary over time hardly shows that its meaning varies; for to know the meaning of a past-tense statement just is to know how the conditions of assertion are affected by the passage of time. As Wright puts it, 'grasping the meaning of past-tense statements involves grasping how their conditions of warranted assertion shift as one's temporal location shifts' (Wright 1987f: 78).

Dummett seems to recognize that the verificationist owes us an account of defeasibility, but he never provides the account. Again, we need to turn to Wright, who has much to say on the topic. The difficulty is that defeasibility seems to transform nearly every empirical statement into a verification-transcendent claim; and that calls into question the idea that Dummett's standard examples of undecidables should present any really interesting problems for the truth-conditional theorist. Wright, however, reads a quite different moral into the phenomenon of defeasibility (Wright 1987*f*: 264). We get a problem for Dummett only if we assume with him that, for the case of ordinary empirical claims, the notion of a truth-condition non-problematically applies. But Wright sees the near universality of defeasibility as showing that it is almost never right to understand assertoric sentences in truth-conditional terms. We need instead to suppose, first, that grasping the meaning of a statement is not a matter of grasping the conditions *conclusively* warranting its assertion, but is rather a matter of being able to recognize the sorts of things that count as defeasible evidence for the statement and, secondly, that in virtually no cases is that ability to be identified with an apprehension of truth-conditions.[20]

As we have seen, Dummett takes the assertability-conditional theorist to be committed to endorsing an epistemically constrained notion of truth; and Wright seems to agree. Like the associated theory of meaning, Dummett's account of truth has faced familiar objections. One such objection argues that the very notions that the anti-realist invokes in giving an account of truth as epistemically constrained are concepts that can be understood only in terms of realist truth (Vision 1988: 20–1, 97–101, 189–96).[21] The anti-realist speaks of evidence, justification, warrant, and the like in trying to provide an account of anti-realist truth; but while what counts as evidence for a statement may serve to underwrite the assertion of that statement, what makes it evidence is that it points to the *truth* of that statement. Likewise, the situations that confer justification or warrant on a statement may serve to justify or warrant the assertion of the statement; but they would not count as justification or warrant unless they increased the probability that the statement is *true*. The notion of truth at work here, the objection insists, cannot without circularity be the epistemic notion these concepts are being used to define. And a related objection seeks to show that no property like warranted assertability can be truth by pointing out that while the former is a property that a statement can lose or gain as our body of evidence alters, the latter is a permanent or abiding property of a statement. This second objection has, of course, been significant in traditional debates between realists and their opponents. It has traditionally been taken to show the need for refinements in the anti-realist's account of truth. Thus, it led Peirce to explain truth in terms of justification in the long run and Putnam to define truth as justification in epistemically ideal circumstances. More recently, it has led Crispin Wright to explain truth in terms of what he calls superassertability, where a statement is

---

[20] But Wright concedes that this move takes the anti-realist perilously close to idealism. See Wright (1987*c*: 264).

[21] Dummett thinks that the concept of correct assertion is prior to that of truth, and he wants to parse the concepts in question in terms of the former concept. See Dummett (1993*d*).

superassertable just in case its assertability has current warrant and will continue to have warrant no matter how our state of information gets improved.[22]

But not all those who defend an assertability approach to meaning agree that that sort of semantic account commits one to an anti-realist conception of truth as epistemically constrained. John Skorupski, for example, denies that assertability conditional semantics precludes the view that statements can be undetectably true or false (Skorupski 1988: 516 ff.). He thinks that what he calls the epistemic conception of meaning (the idea that grasping meaning is having the ability to recognize assertability conditions) and the epistemic conception of truth can be separated. Dummett fails to recognize this, Skorupski thinks, because his case for the epistemic theory of meaning hinges on his arguments to show that we could have no idea of undetectable truth or falsehood. But, Skorupski thinks those arguments fail since they presuppose a faulty conception of grasping a truth-condition as a 'single track ability to recognize the state of affairs when presented with it' (1988: 511). Skorupski, nonetheless, endorses the assertability approach and thinks we can derive it directly from the Wittgensteinian insight that understanding is a practical skill. That insight forces us to construe understanding in just the way the assertability theorist suggests, as a discriminatory ability. But, according to Skorupski, once we dissociate the epistemic theory of meaning from the manifestation and acquisition arguments, we have a theory of meaning that is neutral with regard to truth; it remains an open question whether there can be undetectably true or false statements.

Wright, I mentioned, disagrees and endorses both an epistemic theory of meaning and an epistemic theory of truth; but, unlike Dummett, Wright does not think that we are, thereby, committed to a rejection of classical logical principles. Dummett's argument that we must reject the principle of excluded middle is that we must give an assertability-functional account of the connectives. As we have seen, on such an account, we explain the connective 'or' by saying that a statement of the form 'A or B' is assertable just in case either 'A' is assertable or 'B' is assertable. But on this reading, the principle 'A or not-A' is not invariably assertable. Where 'A' is undecidable, neither 'A' nor its negation is assertable. Wright, however, objects to this conclusion. He suggests that it is clearly not in line with the general spirit of an assertability semantics. The central reason for endorsing Dummett's account of meaning is that it accords better than the truth-conditional theory with our ongoing linguistic practices; but, then, to be told that we have to reject excluded middle and with it the inferences it warrants is to be told that we need to revise our ongoing linguistic practices. The two counsels, Wright argues, are in clear tension. We can, however, relieve the tension. We need not and should not provide an account of the connectives that forces us to reject classical inference patterns. If we are to give an account that genuinely reflects our linguistic practices, that expresses the use we

---

[22] The objection and a reply are formulated in Putnam (1981: 54–6). For Wright's very interesting and important work on the notion of superassertability, see Wright (1992).

make of the language, we will express our account of 'or' by saying that 'A or B' is assertable not merely when either disjunct is assertable but also when 'B' is the negation of 'A' or a consequence of the negation of 'A' (Wright 1987a: 328).

7. DUMMETT AND POSITIVISM

When we step back from debate over the details of Dummett's project and focus on the project as a whole, we cannot fail to be impressed by the similarities between his views and those of the positivists of the 1930s and 1940s. I have already alluded to some of these similarities. Dummett himself makes no secret of his debt to the positivists in the theory of meaning. Indeed, he borrows their label and calls his version of the epistemic theory of meaning verificationist semantics; and although he is far more sensitive than any positivists were to the technical demands on a theory of meaning, his own verificationist semantics yields results not all that different from those associated with the famous positivist slogan that the meaning of a sentence is its method of verification. In the same way, Dummett's worries about a realist conception of truth have their positivist analogues. His doubts about the provenance of a verification-transcendent notion of truth are reminiscent of positivist worries about the empirical credentials of a 'metaphysical' notion of truth; and, like some of the positivists, he takes these problems about empirical derivation to motivate an epistemically constrained conception of truth. And, in both Dummett and the positivists we get the result that evidence-transcendent claims are problematic. According to the 'official history' of the movement, positivism took those claims to be without cognitive significance; whereas Dummett denies them a truth-value. Although we have different accounts of just what the problematic status of undecidables comes to, there is an undeniable analogy between the verification principle and the claim that verification-transcendent statements lack a truth-value, an analogy that comes out more forcefully when we note that the two theses are subject to parallel reflexivity problems. Just as there can be genuine doubts about the verifiability of the verification principle, there can be legitimate concerns about the in principle decidability of the statement that bivalence fails for undecidables. Furthermore, in the most interesting case of evidence-transcendent claims—metaphysical statements—Dummett's views turn out to be barely discernible from considered positivist thinking. Like the positivists, he is unwilling to take metaphysical claims to have the cognitive content traditionally associated with them. They are not what they seem to be—claims about the existence and nature of a material world, numbers, or minds. According to the story we all learned as undergraduates, the positivists construed metaphysical claims as nonsense; and certainly they may have sometimes said this. But they were not always comfortable with that verdict. Indeed, we are all familiar with the proposal to treat ontological claims as pseudo-material mode statements. So what the positivists offered us is a choice: take metaphysical 'claims' to be cognitively meaningless or take them to be disguised formal mode statements—statements about the syntactical properties of linguistic expressions. But Dummett likewise offers us a pair of options, and they are pretty close to the positivists' options: either construe metaphysical sentences as pictures or images—as something akin to poetry—or take them to be disguised statements about the semantics of a certain fragment of our language. And Dummett's characterization of particular disputes between realists and anti-realists does nothing so much as evoke a general sense of nostalgia for the good old days of logical positivism. Who, after all, are Dummett's anti-realists? They are phenomenalists about the material world, operationalists and instrumentalists in the philosophy of science, and behaviourists in the philosophy of mind; and when Dummett tries to identify a historical precedent for anti-realism about the past, the only philosopher he can cite is A. J. Ayer.

Why do I belabour these similarities between Dummett's views and those of the positivists? Because when we step back and attempt to get a fix on Dummett's overall approach to issues of realism and anti-realism, we find ourselves confronted not so much with a philosophical problem as with a historical question; for what most needs explanation, I think, is just the fact that there has been such a thing as the 'Dummett phenomenon'. On reflection, there is something genuinely puzzling in the fact that a view with such deep affinities to positivism should have received the hearing Dummett's views have enjoyed. What we need to remind ourselves is just how few philosophers from the past two or three decades have been sympathetic with the ideas of the positivists of the 1930s and 1940s. The nearly universal verdict of the philosophical community at large is that positivism has been thoroughly discredited. Philosophers seldom like to speak of the refutation of a view; but the vast majority of philosophers would agree that if any 'ism' stands refuted, it is positivism; and the alleged refutation claims as its victims theses from virtually every area in philosophy—epistemology, philosophy of science, ethics, metaphilosophy. Even to use the language in which positivists expressed their views—with its talk of protocol sentences, physicalist language, sense data, reduction sentences—is to evoke derisive smirks. And nowhere have positivist views been more roundly criticized than in the theory of meaning. The central target of attack here has been the verificationism that is so prominent in positivist writings, and the philosophical community is so convinced of the success of the attack that we often hear philosophers speaking of 'the verificationist fallacy'—the 'fallacy' of concluding that where evidence is, in principle lacking, there is no fact of the matter.

Of course, the philosophical community's assessment of the contributions of positivism might turn out to be a mere matter of intellectual fashion. It might turn out to be the expression of a prejudice that future generations of philosophers will manage to overcome. But what is significant is the fact that this negative verdict on positivism was part of the culture of Anglo-American philosophy in the 1970s, 1980s, and 1990s. If prejudice, it was deeply entrenched prejudice. How, then, was it that a bundle of claims so close to the central themes of logical positivism could have succeeded in finding the prominent place on the philosophical stage that Dummett's work occupied?

This is a difficult question. Towards answering it, one might point to features of Dummett's work that are independent of his attempt to develop a verificationist semantics. His analysis of debates between realists and their opponents provides us with one such set of themes. But so do his work on Frege, his account of the structure of a semantical theory, his criticism of semantic holism, and his views about the justification of logical principles. And, of course, there is the fact that Dummett himself seldom presents his claims in the theory of meaning as descendants of positivist thinking. As we have seen, he typically presents them in different dress— as consequences of the Wittgensteinian themes I have discussed. The claim would be that the Wittgensteinian lineage has done much to provide Dummett's epistemic theories of meaning and truth prima facie legitimacy.

But while there is something to these attempts to explain the 'Dummett phenomenon,' neither individually nor collectively do they give us a fully satisfactory account of the widespread attention his work has received. Philosophers have certainly been interested in his analysis of debates over realism, but what has drawn most attention are Dummett's views in the philosophy of language proper; and although his views about other issues in that area have been taken seriously, the lion's share of written work on Dummett focuses on his criticism of truth-conditional semantics and his attempt to develop epistemic theories of both meaning and truth. And while the Wittgensteinian flavour of his semantical theory might have given it an initial hearing, it is difficult to believe that their deference to the later Wittgenstein would have prevented philosophers from ultimately recognizing in Dummett's philosophy of language the very positivist views they had officially rejected; and in any case, interest in Dummett has not been limited to philosophers under the spell of the later Wittgenstein. The fact is, I think, that we do not as yet have a satisfactory resolution of the historical puzzle of the 'Dummett phenomenon'. It is a puzzle that future historians of twentieth-century Anglo-American philosophy will need to address.

References

Alston, W. (1996). *A Realist Conception of Truth*. Ithaca, NY: Cornell University Press.

Appiah, A. (1986). *For Truth in Semantics*. Oxford: Basil Blackwell.

Blackburn, S. (1984). *Spreading the Word*. Oxford: Oxford University Press.

—— (1987). 'Manifesting Realism', in P. French, T. Uehling, and H. Wettstein (eds.), *Midwest Studies in Philosophy*, xiv. Minneapolis: University of Minnesota Press, 29–42.

—— (1993). *Essays in Quasi-Realism*. Oxford: Oxford University Press.

Boolos, G. (1990). *Meaning and Method: Essays in Honor of Hilary Putnam*. Cambridge: Cambridge University Press.

Craig, E. (1982). 'Meaning, Use, and Privacy'. *Mind*, 91: 541–64.

Devitt, M. (1984). *Realism and Truth*. Oxford: Basil Blackwell.

Dummett, M. (1978*a*). 'The Philosophical Basis of Intuitionist Logic', in Dummett (1978*f*: 215–47).

—— (1978*b*). 'Presupposition', in Dummett (1978*f*: 25–8). First pub. in *Journal of Symbolic Logic*, 25 (1960), 336–9.

—— (1978*c*). 'Realism'. Paper presented to the Oxford Philosophical Society (1963), in Dummett (1978*f*: 145–65).

—— (1978*d*). 'The Reality of the Past', in Dummett (1978*f*: 358–74). First pub. in *Proceedings of the Aristotelian Society*, 69 (1969), 239–58.

—— (1978*e*). 'Truth', in Dummett (1978*f*: 1–24). First pub. in *Proceedings of the Aristotelian Society*, 59 (1959), 141–62.

—— (1978*f*). *Truth and Other Enigmas*. Cambridge, Mass.: Harvard University Press.

—— (1991). *The Logical Basis of Metaphysics*. Cambridge, Mass.: Harvard University Press.

—— (1993*a*). 'Realism', in Dummett (1993*c*: 230–77). First pub. in *Synthese*, 52 (1982), 55–112.

—— (1993*b*). 'Realism and Anti-Realism', in Dummett (1993*c*: 462–78).

—— (1993*c*). *The Seas of Language*. Oxford: Oxford University Press.

—— (1993*d*). 'The Source of the Concept of Truth', in Dummett (1993*c*: 188–201). First pub. in Boolos (1990: 1–15).

—— (1993*e*). 'What is a Theory of Meaning? (I)', in Dummett (1993*c*: 1–33). First pub. in Guttenplan (1974: 97–138).

—— (1993*f*). 'What is a Theory of Meaning? (II)', in Dummett (1993*c*: 34–93). First pub. in Evans and McDowell (1976: 67–137).

Evans, G., and J. McDowell (1976). *Truth and Meaning*. Oxford: Oxford University Press.

Guttenplan, S. (1974). *Mind and Language*. Oxford: Oxford University Press.

Haldane, J., and C. Wright (1992). *Reality, Representation, and Projection*. Oxford: Oxford University Press.

Hale, B. (1997). 'Realism and its Oppositions', in Hale and Wright (1997: 271–308).

—— and C. Wright (1997). *A Companion to the Philosophy of Language*. Oxford: Basil Blackwell.

Hookway, C., and P. Pettit (1978). *Action and Interpretation*. Cambridge: Cambridge University Press.

Horwich, P. (1982). 'Three Forms of Realism'. *Synthese*, 52: 181–202.

Johnston, M. (1993). 'Verificationism as Philosophical Narcissism'. *Philosophical Perspectives*, 7: 307–30.

Kirkham, R. (1992). *Theories of Truth*. Cambridge, Mass.: MIT Press.

McDowell, J. (1976). 'Truth Conditions, Bivalence, and Verificationism', in Evans and McDowell (1976: 42–66).

—— (1978). 'On "The Reality of the Past"', in Hookway and Pettit (1978: 127–44).

McGinn, C. (1979). 'An A Priori Argument for Realism'. *Journal of Philosophy*, 76: 111–33.

—— (1980). 'Truth and Use', in Platts (1980: 19–40).

—— (1982). 'Realist Semantics and Content Ascription'. *Synthese*, 52: 113–34.

Plantinga, A. (1993). *Warrant: The Current Debate*. Oxford: Oxford University Press.

Platts, M. (1980). *Reference, Truth, and Reality*. London: Routledge & Kegan Paul.

Putnam, H. (1981). *Reason, Truth, and History*. Cambridge: Cambridge University Press.

Quine, W. (1953). 'Two Dogmas of Empiricism', in Quine, *From a Logical Point of View*. Cambridge, Mass.: Harvard University Press, 20–46.

Scruton, R. (1976). 'Truth Conditions and Criteria'. *Proceedings of the Aristotelian Society*, suppl. vol. 50: 193–216.

Skorupski, J. (1988). 'Critical Study: *Realism, Meaning and Truth*'. *Philosophical Quarterly*, 38: 500–25.

——(1992). 'Anti-Realism, Inference, and the Logical Constants', in Haldane and Wright (1992: 133–64).

——(1997). 'Meaning, Use, Verification', in Hale and Wright (1997: 29–59).

Strawson, P. (1977). 'Scruton and Wright on Anti-Realism'. *Proceedings of the Aristotelian Society*, 77: 15–22.

Tennant, N. (1987). *Anti-Realism and Logic*. Oxford: Oxford University Press.

Vision, G. (1988). *Modern Anti-Realism and Manufactured Truth*. London: Routledge & Kegan Paul.

Wolterstorff, N. (1987). 'Are Concept-Users World-Makers?' *Philosophical Perspectives*, 1: 233–68.

Wright, C. (1987a). 'Anti-Realism and Revisionism', in Wright (1987d). First pub. in *Philosophical Quarterly*, 31 (1981).

——(1987b). 'Anti-Realism and Timeless Truth', in Wright (1987d: 176–203).

——(1987c). 'Anti-Realist Semantics', in Wright (1987d: 241–66). First pub. in *Philosophy*, suppl. vol. (1982), 225–48.

——(1987d). *Realism, Meaning, and Truth*. Oxford: Basil Blackwell.

——(1987e). 'Realism, Truth-Value Links, Other Minds and the Past', in Wright (1987d: 85–106). First pub. in *Ratio*, 22 (1980), 111–32.

——(1987f). 'Strawson on Anti-Realism', in Wright (1987d: 70–84). First pub. in *Synthese*, 40 (1979), 283–300.

——(1992). *Truth and Objectivity*. Cambridge, Mass.: Harvard University Press.

CHAPTER 22

ONTOLOGICAL AND CONCEPTUAL RELATIVITY AND THE SELF

ERNEST SOSA

THIS chapter takes up, in six sections, issues of realism and of ontological and conceptual relativity.[1] Section 1 briefly lays out the kind of absolutist realism of interest in what follows. Section 2 considers arguments against ordinary common-sense entities such as bodies, and for the view that subjects enjoy a superior ontological position. No such argument is found persuasive. I find no good argument against ordinary bodies or other common-sense entities, nor any good argument that subjects enjoy any ontological superiority. Section 3 lays out three options in ontology, opts for a kind of conceptual relativism, and takes up three problems for

---

This chapter is a supplement to my 'Subjects among Other Things: Persons and Other Beings' (Sosa 1987). Some of the ideas used here are developed further in Sosa (1999a,b, 2000).

[1] I'm afraid this will further substantiate Dean Zimmerman's clerihew:

> The metaphysics of Ernie Sosa
> has little in common with that of Spinoza,
> except for this: both claim to show
> all things are like a ball of snow.

the proposed view. Section 4 then offers a compromise position based on a kind of existential relativity meant to accommodate our most settled beliefs about what there is, while retaining a fundamentally realist and objectivist ontology. The main argument of that section relies on a distinction between (*a*) semantical relativity and (*b*) ontological relativity. Section 5 defends my use of the semantical–ontological distinction against objections to it in the recent literature. Section 6, in conclusion, takes up arguments for the view that, as subjects of consciousness and thought, we must after all occupy a special ontological position in objective reality, one whose status remains mysterious.

1. FORMULATIONS OF REALISM

Here is one way to understand realism:

> *Realism.* Tokens of most common-sense, and scientific, physical types objectively exist independently of the mental.[2]

This, however, can be variously interpreted; here is just one possibility:

> *Realism 1.* Most physical types commonly postulated by humanity have tokens that exist as such independently of the mental: i.e. these tokens might have existed and might have been of their respective types even had there been nothing mental.

One problem with this is that the truth of realism would require that there be humanity and that it postulate types, indeed physical types. Surely the philosophical doctrine of realism is not specifically about humanity and what humanity does or does not postulate. So we try again.

> *Realism 2.* Consider the physical types commonly postulated by humanity, and the statements, about each of these, that its tokens exist independently of the mental. Realism is the doctrine that most of these statements are true.

This is a realist doctrine all right. But so is the doctrine about the first physical type mentioned in the Bible and the statement that its tokens exist independently of the mental. And there are indefinitely many 'realist' doctrines of a similar cast, all of which seem inappropriately tied to the vagaries of human postulation. Why should realism be restricted to *these* statements, or, worse, to *most* of them?

---

[2] In Devitt (1997) Michael Devitt formulates realism along these lines.

For a doctrine less tied thus to humanity, consider this:

Realism 3. There are tokens independent of the mental in that they might have existed and have been of their respective types even had there been nothing mental.

This is indeed a kind of realism, but it is compatible with a Kantian doctrine of a noumenal reality beyond our ability to know or even to comprehend, and with the view that ordinary common-sense reality is dependent on human construction through conceptualization. So realism 3 is a rather weak doctrine. According to a stronger version:

Realism 4. The world of common-sense reality exists as it is thought to exist by at least the main lines of common sense, and this it does largely independently of the mental, in that it might have existed propertied and interrelated much as it is in fact propertied and interrelated even in the absence of anything mental.

Here 'common-sense reality' is the world as we commonsensically believe it to be, composed of things large and small, along with the medium-sized dry goods of daily commerce. For Kant such common-sense reality has only 'phenomenal' reality, constituted by human construction. Beyond this there is the 'noumenal', in-itself reality independent of human construction. But this is inaccessible to human cognition. Unlike Kant, more recent constructivists appeal to conceptual schemes distinctive of a particular culture. (Here Wittgenstein may be an exception, but his views are elusive: Is there a human form of life, unlike that of the lion, or is there more than one human form of life?)

Note how brief reflection has led us back to the aspect of realism 1 that I found initially off-putting. The problem is that once we abstract from humanity and its postulations, we are left with too thin a notion of realism, one compatible with a Kantian view: an inaccessible noumenal reality along with a constructivist account of our ordinary world. A more interesting realism does after all apparently require reference to ourselves and our common-sense postulations.

Many and varied are the constructivist heirs of Kant in more recent times.[3] For Nelson Goodman we make stars through our 'versions'.[4] According to Hilary Putnam's 'internal realism' the world is somehow internal to our conceptual scheme. As Benjamin Whorf would have it, language is itself our main world-making tool.

---

[3] Helpful reviews of much such literature may be found in Devitt (1997) and in Wolterstorff (1987).

[4] According to Goodman (1984: 29), 'What there is consists of what we make; everything ... is an artefact.' Also: 'We do not make stars as we make bricks; not all making is a matter of molding mud. The worldmaking mainly in question here is making not with hands but with minds, or rather with languages or other symbol systems. Yet when I say that worlds are made, I mean it literally; and what I mean should be clear from what I have already said. Surely we make versions, and right versions make worlds' (1984: 42).

For Thomas Kuhn different thinkers live in different worlds, each defined by its own theoretical ontology.[5] Many other varieties of anti-realism and relativism are now on the market, moreover, to the point of irrational exuberance.[6]

On the face of it, then, opposition to realism 4 has gained strength, starting with Kant's phenomenalism of ordinary reality, and spreading in powerful movements during the course of the twentieth century and up to the present. What arguments might be offered for so implausible a view? Given our limits, we can hardly do justice to the rich variety of such arguments, even in recent decades and much less as they figure in the imposing Kantian construction. Nevertheless, let us try to penetrate beneath the surface of a broad survey to consider some sample arguments in greater depth.

2. Are Subjects Ontologically Fundamental?

It is often assumed that if we restrict ourselves to a fundamental level of facts, we lose nothing substantial in our description of reality. Substances (or individual substances) are said to occupy that level, and have been thought to include perhaps subjects, physical atoms, and nothing else. For convenience I will refer to that basic level as that of the 'basic facts'.

Against the thesis that bodies are real, individually substantial entities, here now are two arguments. Consider first a principle of supervenience according to which: *if all true statements expressed at level L are entailed analytically or a priori by true statements at level L', then L adds no information, no descriptive power to L': all those facts can be stated at level L'.* Based on such a principle, it can now be argued that since, first, all true statements expressed at the level of ordinary bodies follow analytically from true statements at lower levels, and since, secondly, no loss of information derives from descent to lower levels, therefore, with the possible exception of atoms, we need no reference to bodies in a full description of the facts. Ontological descent need never stop until the basic facts are reached, at which point we have lost no real information even though now we refer only to simples and to no ordinary bodies.

That sort of argument, with its underlying principle, is question-begging against a layered ontology, whose advocates can agree that the upper layers derive from the lower, and may do so 'analytically or a priori', in a way that a well enough informed

---

[5] See Putnam (1981, 1983); Whorf (1956); Kuhn (1970).
[6] Thus the wilder excesses of postmodernists and their fellow travellers, and of warriors in the science wars.

and powerful enough intelligence could understand. This does not deny reality to the upper levels, or so they would argue; it does not entail that only the basic level is real. What is more, how do we know that there *is* a level of basic facts? How can we know any such thing ahead of a final physics? What rules out that reality be infinitely layered? If that is a possibility, it has implications for the argument against common sense. Under that possibility there is no assurance that we can ever dispense with reference to non-simple non-atoms in *any* full description of reality. At least there is no such assurance until we rule out the possibility that bodies occupy every level in the infinite hierarchy descending from the macro to lower and lower orders of the micro. Since I see no way to rule that out from the armchair, I remain unpersuaded by the argument from analytical supervenience.

Here is a further way to press the argument. Even if in fact, contingently, there is a fundamental level of items and/or fields and/or properties, nevertheless there *might not* have been such a level. But if supervenient derivation entails irreality, this presumably is not just contingent, but necessary. But consider now this interesting consequence. If there had been nothing fundamental, which is apparently granted on all sides to be a possibility, then there would have been nothing at all. But one does know that there is *something*, surely, namely that one does oneself exist. But in that case we do after all know that there is something fundamental, and we know it from the armchair. But how can we have such knowledge of what reality is deeply like, with no benefit of physical experiment or theory?

A form of the doctrine of ontological supervenience, Humean supervenience, has been persistently defended by David Lewis, who claims that

in a world like ours, the fundamental relations are exactly the spatiotemporal relations: distance relations, both spacelike and timelike, and perhaps also occupancy relations between point-sized things and spacetime points. And [in such a world] . . . the fundamental properties are local qualities: perfectly natural intrinsic properties of points, or of point-sized occupants of points. Therefore . . . all else supervenes on the spatiotemporal arrangement of local qualities throughout all of history, past and present and future. (Lewis 1999: 225–6).

But what does it mean to say that a property is 'fundamental'? What is the dimension involved in the postulated fundamentality? If the dimension's ordering relation is some 'in virtue of' relation, then it is not easy to foreclose a priori the possibility that there be no set of properties than which no set is more fundamental. Should we just include all properties altogether, or all those below a certain level of fundamentality, and be done with it? All truths would then still supervene on the properties thus designated as 'fundamental'. That would be a cheap 'fundamentality' by arbitrary stipulation: A proper subset of that set might then still be more fundamental than it: each of the properties in the less fundamental set would be exemplified, when it was exemplified, in virtue of the exemplification of one or more of the properties in the more fundamental set. How do we rule out that in this sense there be no fundamental set whatever? Any given set would always contain a different set more fundamental than it. And there might be lots of natural properties without any being fundamental (in the sense of being a member of a fundamental set). For surely there might be laws and causality and resemblance in such a universe, an open possibility despite infinite depth in the hierarchy of properties. These reflections raise the question of the extent to which Humean supervenience can survive rejection of ontological fundamentalism, especially rejection of any such doctrine held a priori. In fact nothing in our reasoning precludes its postulate that there is a level of physical properties, by the lights of current physics, such that all truths proper to our folk theories and special sciences are made true, somehow, by the pattern of instantiation of the properties on that level. This would seem to capture much of the content of the doctrine.

Some go further, however, than just embracing Humean supervenience. They question the literal or serious truth of our folk stances, by claiming that reality is constituted at best by the more fundamental properties. What if the more fundamental level itself supervenes, however, on levels deeper yet? How then can it be declared a level where reality *is* really to be found? Should it not, in fairness, receive the same treatment as the folk levels? It will be unclear, moreover, why there can't be *causality* and *resemblance* at levels well above the level of physics. If the levels deeper than that of current physics would not deprive that level of its proper causality and resemblance, how then can it deprive the levels above it? But if causality and resemblance can after all reside at the higher levels, then the natural would seem to rise above the level of physics. If so, where do we stop it? These questions press once we lose any reality-determining distinction in terms of absolute fundamentality. So it is far from clear how Humean supervenience or any similar doctrine would affect at least the main elements of our common-sense picture of things.

A further argument against ordinary bodies derives from an alleged failure of counterfactual identity, which is said to fail for ordinary, non-atomic bodies. This in turn is said to entail that there really are no such bodies, at least not in the basic facts. Supposing *arguendo* that there is a level of basic facts, let us now consider such reasoning from the failure of counterfactual identity. According to the first relevant insight now invoked, ordinary bodies enjoy no very precise criteria of existence and persistence. For example, it is easy to create puzzles as to how much a thing might vary in the respects of criterial relevance while remaining ontologically the same. True reality cannot be vague, and cannot be governed by criteria that permit vagueness, so ships, for example, should not be accepted as real. If there is a physical layer of reality, then, it would have to contain entities dependent on no vague criteria, hence all simple and fundamental.

How does this insight bear on subjects as opposed to bodies? Clearly that depends on the criteria of existence and persistence proper to subjects. At this point it would seem question-begging to assume that subjects are complex. To assume that they are all simple, however, would seem equally question-begging. More neutrally we might assume only that subjects have psychological life histories, just as bodies have physical trajectories. The possible alternative physical trajectories of ordinary bodies would seem plausibly delimited by criteria. But something similar would then hold for subjects. Are there no limits on how widely someone's life history could have diverged from the actual? Could all actual subjects have come into existence with zero degrees of consciousness, for example? And could each have remained in that state throughout eternity while different from everyone else? It may be replied that any subject must have some minimal degree of consciousness or at least some minimal potential for consciousness. But if subjects could be arrayed along some dimension in respect of such potential, this invites vagueness. Who could draw a consciousness line or a potential-for-consciousness line any more plausibly than a line in the sand separating dunes from non-dunes, or an exact specification of how much a ship would have to share with the actual one in order to be the very same ship?

So far I have discussed the vagueness insight. There is, however, a further, independent insight before us: namely, that numerical identity is cross-world transitive whereas its criteria, even if sharp, would be cross-world intransitive. Take a single time slice in the history of four possible worlds W_1–W_4, at which time a three-link chain is created. So we are supposing that four possible worlds, W_1–W_4, develop up to a time t, and at that time in each possible world some three-link chain comes into existence. And let's suppose our criteria for cross-world identity of such three-link chains to be the sharing of at least two links. Then clearly each of the four chains could be identical to its immediate cross-world neighbour(s), but to no other chains, and cross-world transitivity would fail, impossible though this appears.

This problem will not affect subjects if they are simple, but physical atoms will be equally safe, being equally simple. Therefore, subjects will not have been shown to hold an ontological advantage over the physical generally. But have they not been shown at least better off than ordinary bodies? No, that is not clear. True, subjects are now seen to be better off than ordinary bodies in the respect that these, because they are complex and ontologically dependent on their parts, are affected by certain problems of vagueness and of cross-world intransitivity of criteria. By contrast, because they are simple, subjects will not face *these* problems. Nor will atoms, being equally simple. Besides, that does not save subjects from all problems of a similar sort. We have seen already how the problem of vagueness of criteria enters with criteria themselves, regardless of whether these are compositional. And the same goes for the problem of cross-world transitivity of identity. Intransitivity of the criteria of existence will induce the problem of cross-world transitivity, regardless of whether the criteria are compositional.[7] The insights driving the argument from

---

[7] Advocates of a layered reality must face this problem as well as the problem of vague criteria. One might be tempted by the idea that existence claims are contextually world-bound, and to argue, for example, as follows: 'In world W_1 (the actual world) one can say correctly "C_2 would be the same chain as C_1 is". And in world W_2 one could say correctly "C_3 would be the same chain that C_2 is". But one cannot disquote and invoke transitivity in order to say correctly in W_1: "C_3 would be the same chain that C_1 is".' However, the fact remains that assuming W_2 is the actual world, one can correctly say both

bodily failure of counterfactual identity must therefore be shown restrictable to the case of ordinary complex bodies. For, on the basis of similar features of their criteria of existence and persistence, subjects seem open to similar objections.

We do not yet have any persuasive argument against ordinary bodies and other common-sense entities, nor have we any persuasive argument that subjects enjoy a distinctive ontological position. Section 3 now lays out three ontological options, one of which is a kind of conceptual relativity that tries to accommodate our most settled beliefs about what there is, while retaining a fundamentally realist and objectivist ontology. Section 3 will then consider three main problems for such conceptual relativism, and Section 4 will propose a compromise between conceptual relativism and absolutism.

3. THREE OPTIONS IN ONTOLOGY

According to our first option, any snowball B is constituted by a piece of snow P, which also then constitutes a snowdiscall D. Snowball B and snowdiscall D differ in their respective constitutive forms. Snowballs must be round, whereas snowdiscalls can be but need not be round; they can be anywhere between round and disc-shaped. Now B is distinct (a different entity) from P, since P would survive squashing and B would not. By similar reasoning, D also is distinct from P. And, again by similar reasoning, B must also be distinct from D, since enough partial flattening of P will destroy B but not D. Now, there are infinitely many shapes between roundness and flatness of a piece of snow, and, for any such shape, having a shape anywhere between flatness and that specific shape would give the form of a distinctive kind of entity to be compared with snowballs and snowdiscalls. Whenever a piece of snow constitutes a snowball, it thus constitutes infinitely many entities all sharing its place with it. Under a broadly Aristotelian conception, therefore, the smallest change will create and destroy infinitely many things, and ordinary reality suffers a sort of 'explosion'. This makes our first option quite implausible.

Does conceptual relativism enable us to escape this 'explosion'? Perhaps snowballs do exist relative to all actual conceptual schemes ever, but not relative to all conceivable conceptual schemes. Just as we do not countenance the existence of snowdiscalls, just so another culture might fail to admit snowballs. What does it mean to say that we do not 'countenance' snowdiscalls? Just this: that our conceptual scheme denies the snowdiscall form (being in shape between round and

that C_1 would be the same thing that C_2 is, and that C_3 would be the same thing that C_2 is, while it would be wrong to say that C_3 would be the same thing that C_1 would be.

disc-shaped) the status required for it to be a proper constitutive form of a separate sort of entity. The explosion of reality is blocked thereby, but at the cost of existential relativity. Constituted entities do not just exist or not in themselves, free of any dependence on or relativity to conceptual scheme. On the contrary, something may exist relative to one conceptual scheme while it does not exist relative to another. A sort of entity will exist relative to a conceptual scheme only if that conceptual scheme countenances the correlated constituent form as one that may appropriately constitute a distinctive sort of entity.

It may be objected that we are thus led to a vicious circle. For the existence even of the conceptual scheme itself and of its framers and users would now seem also relative to that conceptual scheme. But then the users of the scheme exist only relative to the scheme, which they do only in virtue of the scheme's countenancing their constituent form-cum-matter. But to say that the scheme countenances this form-cum-matter seems just a way of saying that the *users* of that scheme do so. And yet the users would seem themselves dependent in turn on the scheme for their existence!

That objection is based on a confusion. Existence *relative* to a conceptual scheme is *not* equivalent to existence *in virtue* of that conceptual scheme. Relative to scheme C the users of C exist *in virtue* of their constitutive matter and form, and how these satisfy certain criteria for existence and perdurance of such subjects (the users). There is hence no vicious circularity. So we seem to have here a defensible second option, conceptual relativism, defensible at least against a certain familiar and seemingly devastating objection.

Our third option, finally, is a disappearance or elimination theory. This option refuses to countenance supervenient, constituted objects, so that most if not all of ordinary reality will be lost, which makes this option particularly uninviting. Accordingly, what follows will first develop and defend our middle, relativist, option; but we shall be led eventually to a compromise position.

Here first are three problems for conceptual relativism.

> *First problem.* Our conceptual scheme encompasses criteria of existence and of persistence for the sorts of objects that it recognizes. Shall we say now that a sort of object O exists (has existed, exists now, or will exist) relative to a scheme C at t iff, at t, C recognizes sort O by allowing the corresponding criteria? But surely there are sorts of objects that our present conceptual scheme does not recognize, such as artefacts yet uninvented and particles yet undiscovered, to take only two obvious examples. Of course we allow there might be and probably are many such things. Not that there could be any such entities relative to our *present* conceptual scheme, however, for by hypothesis it does not recognize them. So are there sorts of objects—constituted sorts among them, as are the artefacts at least—such that they exist but not relative to our present scheme C? But then we are back to our problem. What is it for there

to be such objects? Is it just the in-itself satisfaction of constitutive forms by constitutive matters? That yields the explosion of reality.

Perhaps a constituted, supervenient sort of object O exists relative to our present scheme C if and only if O is recognized by C directly or recognized by it indirectly through being recognized by some predecessor or successor scheme. No, surely there might be sorts of particles that always go undiscovered by us, and sorts of artefacts in long-disappeared cultures unknown to us, whose conceptual schemes are not predecessors of ours. Perhaps then what exists relative to our present scheme C is what it recognizes directly, what it recognizes indirectly through its predecessors or successors, and what it *would* recognize if we had developed appropriately or were to do so now, and had been or were to be appropriately situated? This seems on the right track, but we shall need some account of the relevant 'appropriateness'. So this must remain a problem for further work.

> *Second problem.* Apparently, for conceptual relativism things *can* exist prior to our development of a conceptual scheme, as seems to have been granted through the distinction between existence in virtue of a conceptual scheme and existence relative to a conceptual scheme. But is that not to concede that things exist 'out there, in themselves', independently of conceptual schemes altogether, that things exist 'in themselves'. But then reality itself manages somehow to cut the cookies unaided by humans. What can be left of existential relativity after this has been granted?

If I say 'California is more than a mile away', my utterance is true, but the sentence I utter is true only relative to my present position. If I had uttered that sentence elsewhere, then I might well have said something false. So my sentence is true relative to my spatial position, but it is not true or false just on its own, independently of such context. And, in a sense, that California is more than a mile away is true relative to my present position but false relative to many other positions. However, it is not so that California is more than a mile from here *in virtue of* my present position. California would have been more than a mile from here even had I been located elsewhere.

Existential relativity can be viewed as a doctrine rather like the relativity involved in the evaluation of the truth of indexical sentences or thoughts. So when someone says or thinks that Os exist, this is to be evaluated relative to the position of the speaker or thinker in 'ontological space'. Relative to one conceptual scheme, it may be true that Os exist, even if it is not true relative to others. Relative to a given conceptual scheme, what determines whether or not it is true to say 'Os exist' would be that scheme's criteria of existence (or individuation). And these are specifications of the appropriate pairings of kinds of individuals with properties or relations, appropriate in the account of that conceptual scheme. (As will emerge shortly, no constructivism follows from this.)

According to existential relativity, then, the truth-value of 'Os exist' must be determined relative to the conceptual scheme of the speaker or thinker, to one's 'conceptual position', including its criteria of existence. But, again, it does not follow that 'Os exist' only *in virtue* of one's conceptual position, in that if one had not existed with some such conceptual scheme, or at least if no one had existed with some such conceptual scheme, then there would have been 'no Os in existence'. This no more follows than it follows from the relativity of the truth of my statement 'California is more than a mile away' that California is that far from here as a result of *my* being here (even if I am the speaker or thinker). Despite the relativity of the truth of my statement, California *would have been* exactly where it is, which is more than a mile from here, even if I had not been here. Similarly, even if no one had existed to occupy my (our) conceptual position, Os might have existed relative to this position.

> *Third problem.* Are we precluded from supposing that there might be or, even, that there definitely is, or, more yet, that there must be, some noumenal reality constituted in itself, with no relativity to categories or criteria of individuation and/or persistence contributed by the mind or by the culture? It is not easy to see why we should be. When we say that there are atoms, the truth of our affirmation seems independent of our point of view. The existence of atoms gives no sign of being relative to our ontological position. If some alien culture fails to recognize atoms, they would just be missing something real.

True enough, but perhaps we can do justice to this fact from within existential relativity. Compare this. The fact that Boston is near me now is a fact that someone else far away and in the future might still grasp even though it would be grasped, not by means of that very perspectival proposition but by some appropriately coordinated one. Someone with a snowdiscall ontology could perhaps grasp a fact that I grasp by saying 'There are snowballs' but only by means of a coordinated proposition such as, perhaps, 'There are non-disc-shaped snowdiscalls'. We may be able to move to a level on which our schemes coincide: for example, we may both believe in chunks of snow while we both have a grasp of the properties of roundness and of being disc-shaped, etc. But the same issues will recur for any level that recognizes items, be they particles or fields or whatever, if these items are viewed in terms of the matter–form model, with entailed criteria of individuation and persistence. Every level might still allow for agreement or disagreement determined by coordinated, perspectival propositions. Such coordination among propositions is then to be understood in terms of some deeper ontological level, deeper in a sense suggested as follows. When I think 'Boston is near to where I am now', a fact makes that true, one involving two entities and a distance between them. It may not be possible for us to state non-perspectivally the fact in virtue of which my thought 'Boston is nearby' is true. But that need not prevent us from supposing that a fact *is* stated and could be stated by any one of a large number of coordinated propositions, which would be used by different, appropriately positioned subjects; a fact, moreover, that is not mind-dependent, since its being a fact is independent of its being grasped by anyone, in any of the various perspectival ways in which it might be grasped. If challenged to say what that fact might be, the right response may well be: 'The fact that Boston is nearby'. Even if I have no way to state it except perspectivally, so that the truth of the thought or proposition that I thereby state is not objective or mind-independent, it simply does not follow that the fact itself must therefore be mind-dependent. A mind-independent fact may be approachable only from a perspective, from any of indefinitely many perspectives, and statable only in the corresponding, mutually coordinated perspectival ways. Such statements and thoughts are of course mind-dependent, at least in the sense that they are truth-evaluable only relative to their users. However, that does not entail that no mind-independent fact is thereby stated, even if our access to that fact must be perspectivally mind-dependent.

4. A Via Media?

We are pulled in several directions at once, as is typical of a paradox. *On the one hand,* when a certain combination $(m + l)$ of a piece of metal m and a piece of lead l is used both as a writing instrument and occasionally as a paperweight, it constitutes both that writing instrument and that paperweight. Are there then three things there: first, $(m + l)$; secondly, the writing instrument; and, thirdly, the paperweight? Are these distinct entities, occupying the same location? One is drawn here to say that really there is just $(m + l)$, which might be used as a writing instrument, or used as a paperweight, or both. *On the other hand,* why stop with $(m + l)$? Why not say that what really exists in that situation is just m and l severally, which, if properly joined, can be used for writing, for pointing, etc. But why stop even there? After all, m itself will be a combination of certain molecules, each in turn a combination of certain atoms, etc. Where does it all stop? What is the bottom? How indeed can we know that there *is* a bottom? How, again, do we know that there is a level that does not itself derive from some underlying level of reality in the way the paperweight derives from $(m + l)$'s having a certain use, or in the way $(m + l)$ derives from m and l severally, when the two are relevantly joined, or the way m derives from certain molecules being arrayed a certain way? Et cetera.

Science, so far as I can tell, itself postulates no such bottom. Science reaches a level where it infers the truth of certain claims, including theories, based on their explanatory and predictive success. Does the scientist *qua* scientist ever say in addition that there will never be any deeper explanation of the truth of his theory? It is hard to see how such a claim could be justified, how it could be justified scientifically. Only philosophers seem to venture such claims. Scientists may aspire to arrive at a complete theory. However, what would the claim of completeness mean and how could it be established scientifically? Would such a claim be just a metaphysical dogma?

Consider now the eliminativism that rejects the entities at any given level ontologically derivative from an underlying level. To avoid the ontological nihilism for which there is absolutely nothing ever anywhere, such eliminativism must commit itself to the existence of an ontological bottom level. But, again, this seems little better than dogma. However, if one does therefore admit a layered reality, with ontological levels derived from underlying levels, what governs such derivation? The most general characterization of the way in which ontologically derivative particulars derive from an underlying reality would seem to be our Aristotelian conception according to which a sequence of particulars (matters) at the underlying level exemplifies a property or relation (form), giving rise thereby to a distinctive object at the higher, derived level. But now our earlier questions recur: One would want to know what restrictions if any there might be on matter–form pairs that constitute derived entitites. Why rule out entities of the sort of $(m + l)$ or properties of the form: having such and such a function (writing, holding papers down, etc.)? Why rule these out as ways of constituting entities? Perhaps then a distinctive entity can be constituted not only by a piece of snow as matter and approximate roundness as form, but also by a piece of snow as matter, and a shape anywhere between roundness and being disc-shaped as form. But then we seem driven to the explosion. Where does it all stop?

Interestingly relative to context is the claim that a certain irregularly shaped figure f drawn on a surface is 'shapeless'. This claim might be true iff figure f has no shape whatever, in which case it would of course be false, since f does have some shape or other, however irregular. Yet it might alternatively be evaluated as true iff f lacks any of the shapes in some restricted set of shapes, with the specific restriction somehow set by the context of utterance. A certain irregular shape may thus rate as highly significant within a given religious context, wherein items with that shape would not count as 'shapeless', while in other contexts they would. Compare now a contextual relativism of *existential* claims. Here, analogously, objects on the derived level relevant to semantic evaluation of an existential claim are those in some contextually restricted set. Consider 'There is nothing in that box'. (What about the air?)

Here then, apparently, are our choices:

1. An *eliminativism* according to which supposed derived entities are unreal. However, on pain of nihilism, this carries a commitment to an ontological bottom, one that seems inadequately evidenced from the armchair.

2. An *absolutism* that rejects eliminativism, while placing no restrictions on how an object might be constituted from given matter(s) and form.[8] *Any* matter–form combination whatever will determine a corresponding entity at the next higher level, which entails the 'explosion' of reality.

3. An *unrestricted absolutism* that accepts absolutism as defined, while affirming that existential claims must always be assessed for truth or falsity relative to all objects and properties without restriction.

4. A *conceptual relativism* that again accepts absolutism as defined, but rejects unrestricted absolutism, by adding that existential claims are true or false only relative to the context of speech or thought, which restricts the sorts of objects relevant to the assessment, in ways governed by various pragmatic or theoretical considerations.

Our conceptual *relativism* is thus moderate and irenic. Its objective metaphysics is absolutist and latitudinarian, given our inability to find any well-motivated objective restriction on the matter–form pairs that constitute derived entities. Its relativism applies only to the truth or falsity of existential and other ontologically committed claims. It is here that a restriction is imposed by the conceptual scheme of the claimant speaker or thinker. But the restriction is as harmless and even trivial as is that involved in a claim that some selected figure *f* is 'shapeless' made in full awareness that *f* does have some specific shape, however irregular. Analogously, the claim that there are only snowballs at location *L* may rely on some context-driven restriction of the totality of objects which, in full strictness, one *would* recognize at that location. Loosely and popularly it may be said that there are only snowballs there, even if strictly and philosophically one would recognize as present at that location much that remains undreamed of in our ordinary talk.

Have we a robust intuition that snowballs are a different order of entity, somehow less a product of conceptual artifice, than snowdiscalls, or a robust intuition that paperweights, or even mechanical pencils, are too dependent on the vagaries of human convenience and convention to count as distinctive kinds of entities, artificial though they may be? And if paperweights do not count, how or why can pencils count, or, for that matter, houses? Et cetera. Can we hold out for animals and elements as somehow ontologically superior? But what exactly enables us to distinguish the distinguished classes of entities favoured as objectively real, by contrast with the artificial or shadowy snowdiscalls, pencils, paperweights, snowballs, and even cars? Here I have tried to frame that question in a context that rejects eliminativism on one side, and questions the explosion on the other. But in the end the latitudinarian 'explosion' does seem preferable, since eliminativism is even less inviting on one side, and since there are no attractive and well-motivated restrictions on allowable matter–form pairs on the other. But the vast history of the issue and the subtle and

---

[8] Again, the reference should be, more strictly, to 'matter(s)–form' pairs, so as to allow plural constitution.

intricate contemporary discussions of it would give anyone reasonable pause. Our strategy in what follows will be to accommodate, through a kind of metalinguistic or metaconceptual ascent, the intuitions that drive the desire for restriction. This gives rise to a kind of conceptual relativism.

5. DOES SEMANTIC RELATIVITY LEAD TO ONTOLOGICAL RELATIVITY?[9]

1. Consider for comparison our vocabulary of indexicals and the associated perspectival concepts of oneself and of the temporal present. It may well be that these are important and ineliminable components of any adequate conceptual scheme (adequate for us limited humans, anyhow). Suppose that our *concepts* and our *conceptual scheme* are thus importantly perspectival, that the semantical values of our speech acts and even of our thoughts are thus context-dependent. Would it follow that reality itself must be similarly dependent on conceptual context? This seems incredible in light of the following.

Take a world W defined by two people (Tom and Dick) and the height of each, such that, in W, Tom is under 6 feet tall and Dick is over 6 feet tall. In W, therefore, the sentence 'I am under 6 feet tall' is true relative to Tom, but false relative to Dick. And, more generally: whatever is true and whatever is false in a certain world, relative to a certain perspective, has its truth-value in that world as a necessary consequence of how things are in that world absolutely and non-perspectivally.

Our talk and even, granted, our *thought* is largely perspectival. Perhaps the perspectival character of our thought is not even eliminable. But from the fundamentally and ineliminably perspectival character of our thought it would not follow that reality itself is fundamentally perspectival. Everything that is true relative to a perspective and everything that is false relative to a perspective may *still, in spite of that*, be thus true or thus false, as a necessary consequence of the absolute and non-perspectival character of things. That is left wide open. Although we use indexicals to talk about ourselves and the things around us, so that the truth of what we then say is relative to the context of speech, this does not entail that the things around us and their states of being and their interrelations are also somehow, in some sense, also relative to context. This further relativity does not follow even if our use of indexicals is essential and not optional. It is still left open that things might have been propertied and interrelated pretty much as they are in fact propertied and

[9] Lynch (1998) says yes, I say no, and we aired our disagreement at an American Philosophical Association session on the book (Dec. 2000).

interrelated, even if we had not been around to use our indexicals, and even if no other indexical-users had taken our place. What is more, our successful perspectival references and truths might still be seen to derive necessarily from absolute and unperspectival reality, in the sense that when we do refer through an indexical or affirm something true thereby, our successful reference or true affirmation may derive its success in part from how things stand in non-perspectival reality. Thus when Tom says 'I am under 6 feet tall' and thereby succeeds in saying something true about himself, this derives at least in part from the non-perspectival fact, concerning a certain body (Tom's), that its head-to-heels length is under 6 feet.

Again, that a height of 5 feet falls short of my current height is true relative to the height I now have but false relative to other heights I have had or might have had. However, it is not so that 5 feet falls short of my current height *in virtue of* my now having that height. Five feet would have fallen short of my current height even if I had been under 5 feet tall. How tall I am does not determine the relation between a height of 5 feet and this height that I now have.

A kind of existential relativity is rather like the relativity involved in the evaluation of the truth of indexical sentences or thoughts. In effect, 'existence claims' can be viewed as implicitly indexical, and that is what our existential relativist is now suggesting. So when someone says or thinks that Os exist, this is to be evaluated relative to the position of the speaker or thinker in 'ontological space'. Relative to the conceptual scheme thus distinguished, it might be that Os do exist, although this is not true relative to many other conceptual schemes.

But what is it about a 'conceptual scheme' that determines whether or not it is true to say that 'Os exist'? Whether 'there are' constituted entities of a certain sort relative to a certain conceptual scheme would be determined at least in part by that scheme's criteria of existence (or individuation). When one says or thinks 'Os exist', then, according to existential relativity this is not true or false absolutely. Its truth-value must be determined relative to one's conceptual scheme, to one's 'conceptual position', including its criteria of existence and persistence. Suppose one's claim that 'Os exist' must be evaluated relative to one's conceptual position, so that it can be very naturally said that 'Os exist' relative to one's conceptual position (in that sense). Even so, it does not follow that 'Os exist' only *in virtue* of one's conceptual position, in that if one had not existed with some such conceptual scheme, or at least if no one had existed with some such conceptual scheme, then there would have been 'no Os in existence'. This inference is no more valid than is the inference from (*a*) the contextual relativity of the truth of my utterance 'Chicago is over 500 miles from here', to (*b*) the conclusion that Chicago is that far from here as a result of *my* being here (even if I am the utterer). Despite the relativity of the truth of my statement, Chicago *would have been* exactly where it is, over 500 miles from here, even if I had not been here. Similarly, Os might have existed relative to my (our) conceptual position, even if no one had existed to occupy this position.

2. Consider the equivalence, E, that:

> relative to our conceptual scheme, a is white, iff, there is an existing entity consisting of that snowball a and the colour property whiteness, where a exemplifies whiteness independently of anyone's thought or speech or conceptual scheme.

How does realism fare if we grant that no one could possibly *state* any such equivalence as E independently of conceptual scheme, since the concept of exemplification is just as conceptually relative as are the concepts of truth, existence, object, etc. Here we do have an apparent problem for realism, which let us now explore.

For the sake of the example let us assume a Newtonian world of things absolutely spread out in space and in time. This assumption is compatible, moreover, with the possibility that we humans can refer to particular places or times only through indexical terms or concepts such as those of oneself and of the present time. We may have no way to 'anchor' our thought referentially to any particular places or times except by way of such concepts. But this still would not preclude that there be a world of things spread out absolutely in space and time.

The analogous idea of existential relativity is that our claims of 'existence' are similarly relative to a background position that implicitly delimits the possible existents through the commitments inherent in our conceptual scheme. But the really possible existents are said to outrun any such delimitation. And, unfortunately, this is what now seems incoherent. What are we saying when we allow that 'there are' possible existents beyond the ones admitted within our delimitation? A restricted quantifier may not coherently be used to range beyond its restriction.

When we say that there is nothing in a certain box, we are speaking within an implicit delimitation that rules out air molecules. When we say that a certain mark on a sheet of paper is shapeless, our implicit delimitation rules out irregular shapes or the like. But we can of course retreat to contexts where such restrictions are dropped and we allow air molecules, and even perhaps volumes of empty space, as entities, and allow all shapes, including the irregular. So we can drop delimitations or restrictions. A similar move may enable us to escape the supposed incoherence in existential relativity. Perhaps we can abstract away from the object delimitations normally presupposed in our ordinary speech and thought. Thus we could allow a much wider set of possible objects that include not only those ordinarily countenanced by ordinary criteria of existence and persistence, but also weird ones that would be countenanced by sufficiently liberal criteria. If we allow that move, however, then in what sense are our ordinary criteria of existence and persistence constitutive of our *conceptual scheme*? Granted, 'conceptual scheme' may be unfortunate terminology, if one thinks of such a scheme as including not only concepts of features of our surroundings but also concepts of substantial continuants, with corresponding criteria of existence and persistence.

At least the terminology seems unfortunate if we view these concepts as absolute and non-contextual.

My proposal is, again, to view such basic concepts, including those of existence and of object, as indexical, with application conditions relative to context. Thus when one speaks of what 'exists', and of how many 'objects' there are in a certain location, certain features of the speech context will determine the truth of what one says, or will determine the absolute conditions that must be satisfied for one's affirmation to be true. And something similar would seem to hold for thought as for speech. Here I do not mean just the contribution made by the fact that one is speaking English. Over and above the contribution made by the linguistic meanings of the words one uses, there is the further contribution made by contextual parameters whose relevance to the semantic value of one's utterance is determined precisely by those already given or presupposed linguistic meanings.

We escape the supposed incoherence, finally, if we do not require *delimitation* for occupancy of a position in conceptual space, if we require only *specification*, which could take the form of delimitation but might also take the form of the most abstract and liberal specification, for which, ontologically, anything goes, or at least anything is possible. Existential claims and claims about objects within such a liberal, fully abstract, context would not be bound by any delimitation. So these might be the contexts in which even the volumes of space count as occupants of the box (on our Newtonian background assumption), and even the irregular squiggles would not be ruled shapeless.

3. On such a radical version of conceptual relativism, then, the truth or falsity of our existential and other ontological claims will be relative to the context of speech or thought, in the sense that their truth or falsity will be assessed relative to a universe of discourse supplied by the context. Some features of such contexts will be widely shared in a given culture, but might not be shared in other cultures. And even within a given culture there may be contextual differences that derive not from the culture but from interests distinctive of the particular context of discussion or reflection within which an existential claim is made. Thus in ordinary, practical contexts, we may affirm, correctly, affirmative or negative existentials that would be false if affirmed in more theoretical or philosophical contexts.

It is this sort of context-relativity that enables us, in a philosophical context, to countenance the possibility that *in fact there be* lots of things propertied and interrelated in a great many ways, where in no sense is this state of things *relative* to humans or their conceptual schemes. In fact, the things thus admitted as possible might even go beyond the sort of delimitation imposed by our own normal delimiting criteria, our ordinary criteria of existence and persistence. We can say this because in our present, philosophical context, we are *not* delimiting the things that *there might be* in any way, and so not in any way provided by our ordinary criteria of existence and persistence. We are allowing here that ontologically anything goes. So we can allow in our present, liberal context that there might be plenty of things beyond the delimitations imposed by ontological criteria imposed *in ordinary, practical contexts* (for example), though these are not delimitations we impose right now as we reflect more abstractly and theoretically about what there is, all things considered, and what there might be.

4. In any case, finally, without even attributing to ourselves the ability to abstract from all delimitations in our ontological theorizing, we can still define a way in which the relativity of the world does not follow from the relativity of our thought and speech. Here again the analogy with indexical thought and speech is suggestive. Suppose that, in order to think about the world, I must at some depth depend on reference to myself and to the now (or so let us suppose for the sake of the analogy). Suppose, that is to say, that our thought and speech about the contingent world is at some level inevitably contextual and perspectival, in the sense that the truth or falsity of such thought or speech is assessable only relative to the context of thought or speech. Take, for example, my present claim that I am now standing, or, better, that my body is now upright. This is of course perspectival, and the truth or falsity of my affirmation must be assessed relative to the context of affirmation. But from this it does not follow this body's postural state is also perspectival. Ironically, we can perspectivally affirm the non-perspectival character of that state in reality, as follows: This body of mine might have been now upright even if I had not taken note of that fact, even if I had been permanently unconscious now, and even if, through some cataclysm, the universe had been for ever more bereft of any consciousness anywhere. We can thus make use of perspectival concepts, and of contextually relative claims, in order to lay out the view that reality itself is *not* perspectival, that reality is not dependent on our use of any such concepts, or indeed on our use of any concepts at all. Reality may be propertied and interrelated in ways that we can specify only through the use of perspectival concepts and context-dependent claims, even though reality might have been thus propertied and interrelated forever undescribed by humans or any other finite intelligent beings. Reality might thus have enjoyed its own intrinsic character and existence quite beyond the scope of any such intelligent knowledge or conceptualization of its intrinsic character or existence.

6. ARE PERSONS ONTOLOGICALLY SPECIAL?

Here I will assume that a person is wholly constituted neither by a soul nor by a body.[10] If one is neither a soul nor a body (nor an aggregate), however, what then

---

10 This is argued for in Sosa (1987).

could one possibly be? Perhaps intractable directly, this question is best approached through some preliminary questions: What constitutes one's existing at a time and one's lasting through a period? What do one's existing at a time and one's lasting through a period consist in? And now we must ask: what constitutes constituting? What is involved in something's constituting a state of affairs or fact, such as one's existing at a time or lasting through a period? How would one complete this schema: *S is constituted by (consists in) C iff* . . . ? Here we need to distinguish between two different ways in which S might be constituted by C: by being *sufficiently* constituted and by being *necessarily and sufficiently* constituted.

Thus my wallet may contain ten dollars and its doing so may be sufficiently constituted by its containing ten dollar bills, or by its containing two fives, etc. Here is a way to understand all this.

> S is *sufficiently constituted* by C iff S ontologically derives from C by the two obtaining at the same time while S obtains in virtue of C's obtaining but not in virtue of the obtaining of any proper content of C (i.e. any state C' such that C necessarily implies C' but not conversely).

> S is *necessarily and sufficiently constituted* by A iff (x) { {x is contingent and Necessarily (x obtains & x sufficiently constitutes S)} only if x is a member of A}

What then sufficiently constitutes one's existence at a time and one's lasting through a period?

Since one normally might have had a very different inner life and a very different psychological development more generally, therefore even if one's life is in fact sufficiently constituted by a certain sequence of psychological profiles, one might have had a life constituted by a different sequence. Therefore, either person P cannot be identified with P's life or P's life cannot be identified with any particular sequence of psychological profiles. Therefore, *either* we do not yet know what P's life is, in which case even if P could not have had a different 'life', we still do not know what P is (since we do not even know what P's life is); *or* we do know what P's life is (since it is either the life of a certain body, or else a certain stream of psychological profiles), but then we do not know what P is, since P might have had a different life.

Compare the simpler case of snowballs, in hopes that it will admit relatively simple answers that will cast light on the more complex and controversial case of persons. Oversimplifying somewhat, let's suppose that in order to be a snowball an entity must consist of snow and must be round. May we now say that a particular snowball S is just a particular quantity of snow N that is round? No, that seems in conflict with some plain facts: (*a*) Squashing N would destroy S but would only reshape N. (*b*) (If the snowball S had been placed on the kitchen counter rather than in the refrigerator) S might have been much smaller now, unlike N.

If the snowball S is not just the round quantity of snow N, what then could it possibly be? This question now seems intractable directly, and perhaps best approached through related questions: what sufficiently constitutes the existing of S at a time and S's lasting through a period (or, alternatively, what do these latter states consist in)? Why not answer that S's existence at a time is bound to be sufficiently constituted by the being round of a certain quantity of snow N at that time, and the 'life' of a snowball S over a period is bound to consist in a sequence of such states, each related to its successor by relevant causal relations. Even if this answer proves right, however, that still does not tell us what a snowball is. After all, S might have been differently embodied at various stages. So, even if the life of snowball S is sufficiently constituted by the history of a certain quantity of snow N, S's history might have been sufficiently constituted by a sequence of states of different quantities of snow.

Our question concerning what S is becomes more daunting yet given that (a) S is essentially round, and could not have been flat or cubical or any other shape; whereas (b) when we consider the quantity of snow N whose being round sufficiently constitutes the existence of S, we see that N is not essentially round but might have been cubical or flat. Given that much, a problem now arises from the fact that the modal properties of an entity—its might-have-beens, would-have-beens, has-to-bes, etc.—would seem to derive from its actual, non-modal properties via modal principles.

The problem concerns a property like roundness, a property shared by a snowball and its constituting quantity of snow, two different things, one of which exemplifies that property necessarily while the other does not. How then are we to explain that property's being *necessarily* exemplified by the entity that has it essentially? What distinguishes the snowball from the quantity of snow, enabling us to explain why it is that, although both are round, only one is so necessarily? Might the difference reside precisely in S's property of *being a snowball*? No, that would be an empty answer. After all, what it is to be a snowball has been defined through essential or necessary possession of roundness. If our answer is to have more content, therefore, we must define in some other way what it is to be a snowball. Why then is snowball S necessarily round? If we are to give a non-vacuous answer in terms of S's being a snowball, we must not in turn use *essential or* necessary roundness in our account of what ontologically constitutes a snowball.

Still, the appeal to *de re* necessity seems essential: we cannot properly define what it is to be a snowball merely in terms of the non-modal properties of being round and composed of snow. For, again, quantity of snow N has those properties without being itself a snowball. Perhaps what we need is a notion of formal constitution to go along with our notion of material composition. Thus, we might define a snowball as an entity formally constituted by roundness and materially constituted by a certain quantity of snow. This would be constitutional definition. Thus x is a snowball iff x is materially constituted of a quantity of snow n and formally constituted by roundness. *How* might n and roundness constitute x? By n and roundness coming together in the way such a quantity of matter and property ontologically come together; namely, by n *having* roundness.

In that case, a snowball would seem to be an ontologically complex structure of the form [*Fx*], such that it exists, when it does, in virtue of *x*'s having *F*, where *x* is a quantity of snow and *F* is roundness. If so, we can then explain why snowballs are necessarily round by appeal to the ontological constitution of snowballs. And that seems essentially on the right track, even if a snowball cannot be defined in terms of a particular quantity of snow, since a rather different quantity of snow might have constituted the very same snowball at the time in question. However, that requires only a complication in the defining structure. The snowball has a 'life', and it can change its material composition through its life, so we must distinguish among its stages and say that certain structures make up its life by obtaining in a certain sequence while appropriately interrelated causally.

A further step is required, however, since, as we have seen, at any stage the snowball might have been constituted by a quite different quantity of snow, but the very sequence of structures that makes up its life could not possibly have contained any different structure at any of its stages. So we must appeal to a tree of structures, whose branches would constitute alternative possible snowball lives. Such a tree may now be said to tree-constitute a snowball. For a snowball to exist in some possible world is for exactly one branch of its tree to be actualized (in that world). What explains the essential roundness of a snowball is now the fact that at every node of every branch the constitutive structure of its tree includes roundness.

How now could we possibly tell which compound we are referring to at any stage, or which compound we have in mind? Call this the 'problem of specific reference'. With enough understanding and information, one could simply distinguish these compounds in detail, of course. One would just spell out the tree, stage by stage. Since we do not normally have such understanding of ordinary items in our surroundings, we can't refer thus to a particular snowball or compound. Perhaps, therefore, what we pick out in ordinary speech or thought is not particular compounds but particular constitutive structures, and we then in effect make a general commitment to there being at least one appropriate compound containing the selected structure. Thus ⟨*This* compound is *F*⟩ would be tantamount to ⟨There is a compound sufficiently constituted at the present stage by this particular structure, and it is *F*⟩.

Suppose, however, that, no person is either (i) a Cartesian ego, monad, or soul—a fundamental subject of consciousness existing separately from any physical entities, or (ii) a mere quantity of matter, or any aggregate of physical entities, since even if *P*'s existence at *t* consists in the having of certain properties or interrelations by certain physical entities, still *P*'s existence might have consisted in *other* physical entities being thus propertied and interrelated. And suppose further that no one is identical to (iii) the particular sequence of psychological and/or physical states that constitute the stages of *P*'s life, since *P* might have lived a somewhat different life, or even a *very* different life.

What then *is* this person *P*? And how can this person be essentially endowed with personhood, with the psychological properties and/or potentials or capacities proper to a person? What explains its essential possession of such properties and/or potentials, especially when it shares such properties and potentials with a certain body containing a complex nervous system just as a snowball shares its roundness with a certain quantity of snow, though the former has it essentially, with *de re* necessity, while the latter does not? The answer to these questions about persons must now differ only in details from the corresponding answers about snowballs or compounds. Persons are ontologically more complex beings because of our more elaborate formal constitution, involving a rich psychological profile, et cetera, whereas snowballs have mostly just roundness for their formal constitution. Otherwise the answers are bound to agree in essentials, persons being complex trees of person-structures.

Our hypothesis of two paragraphs ago loses plausibility, however, when applied to persons. I speculated that perhaps we pick out, in ordinary speech or thought, not particular compounds but particular constitutive structures, and we then commit to there being at least one compound containing the selected structure. So our supposed reference to a certain snowball, for example, would be no such thing, as it would express only a general commitment to there being a snowball sufficiently constituted at its present stage by *this* particular structure, where we would specify a particular quantity of snow, one that figured in the structure that sufficiently constitutes some snowball at the present stage.

Regardless of whether this proposal works for snowballs and other artefacts, it seems wrong for persons. You are yourself surely able to refer to yourself easily enough, to think that you think, for example, or that you exist. And what one refers to here is precisely the very person who is then oneself. If one is *a certain modal tree structure*, accordingly, *that* is then the object of one's reference when one thinks that one thinks and exists. But we have seen how implausible it is that one should have the ability to refer to any such modal tree structure, given for one thing one's ignorance of the full panoply of possibilities associated with one's life from birth to the moment of reference.

Perhaps the solution is that we are reversing proper order. One manages to refer to oneself by the first-person concept because this is a concept whose condition of reference is this: *exercises of that concept necessarily refer to the user.* It does not matter what sort of entity the user may be, whether soul, body, or Aristotelian substance of whatever sort, including our modal trees. So here is a way to secure specific reference to a modal tree: *by being identical with that tree and exercising the first-person concept.* However, there is a worse problem than just the fact that one seems unable to pick out a specific tree in which one ontologically consists. Worse yet is the fact that our criteria of existence and persistence seem insufficiently full to *determine* a unique tree. So if we are ignorant of the full panoply, it is perhaps because there *is* no unique such.

Besides, our solution for the first person does not solve the problem of how one could refer to *others*. So here is a problem of other minds: If we are modal trees, then how could any of us refer to anyone else in particular? We are unable to specify a single modal tree, except possibly in that very special case in which one is oneself identical with that modal tree. Our reference to other contingent particulars must be general and indeterminate, taking perhaps the form of a general reference to all modal trees that contain a particular perceived or otherwise singled-out structure. But in that case our reference to others must be similarly general and indeterminate. When I refer to 'you', I pick out a particular structure consisting of a body with certain characteristics that it exemplifies in actuality, and I refer in general, indeterminate terms to modal trees that contain that structure in actuality as a proper constituent. And this of course fails to secure reference to yourself specifically; at best it secures reference to an infinite set of modal trees, all sharing the specific selected structure as a proper constituent.

That is one unpleasant and counter-intuitive consequence of the present account. Even if it should turn out, contrary to appearances, that our criteria of existence and persistence are determinative enough to determine unique trees, so that we could after all enjoy identity with some such, we would still suffer alienation from one another, through a chasm unbridgeable even in thought. For, even if in fact there are such criteria, who will be bold enough to claim knowledge of them in their full determinacy? Absent such knowledge, however, we do not use such criteria to secure unique reference, even supposing them to exist. So we cannot be saved from alienation even by determinative criteria, if they remain thus elusive. If we naturally shrink from this alienating conclusion, it is only to be gripped once again by paradox.[11]

References

Devitt, Michael (1997). *Realism and Truth* (1984), 2nd edn. with new afterword. Princeton: Princeton University Press.

Goodman, Nelson (1978). *Ways of Worldmaking*. Indianapolis: Hackett.

—— (1984). *Of Mind and Other Matters*. Cambridge, Mass.: Harvard University Press.

---

[11] And there are other problems in addition for my view. One might reasonably wonder, for example, what could possibly unify a modal tree. Is it a matter of how an underlying entity might have developed through alternative properties and relations as we trace its life from coming into being to passing away? And what of the underlying entity? It too is presumably a modal tree. What unifies it? Can it be underlying entities to infinite depth? But if we do not understand any contingent entity except as a modal tree, can it be modal trees to infinite depth? Can possibility space enjoy fundamental ontological status? Please note that it is not just self-founding, abstract, necessary possibilities that seem puzzling here. Such self-founding abstract possibilities seem comparatively easy to accept by comparison with self-founding *contingent* possibilities. Nevertheless, why should this be any more puzzling than future or past existents ontologically irreducible to the present?

Hirsch, Eli (1993). *Dividing Reality*. Oxford: Oxford University Press.

Kuhn, Thomas S. (1970). *The Structure of Scientific Revolutions* (1962), 2nd edn. Chicago: Chicago University Press.

Latour, Bruno, and Steve Woolgar (1986). *Laboratory Life: The Construction of Scientific Facts* (1979), 2nd edn. Princeton: Princeton University Press.

Lewis, David (1999). *Papers in Metaphysics and Epistemology*. Cambridge: Cambridge University Press.

Lynch, Michael (1998). *Truth in Context: An Essay in Pluralism and Objectivity*. Cambridge, Mass.: MIT Press.

McCormick, Peter J. (1996). *Starmaking: Realism, Anti-Realism, and Irrealism*. Cambridge, Mass.: MIT Press.

Putnam, Hilary (1981). *Reason, Truth and History*. Cambridge: Cambridge University Press.

—— (1983). *Realism and Reason, Philosophical Papers*, vol. iii. Cambridge: Cambridge University Press.

Rorty, Richard (1979). *Philosophy and the Mirror of Nature*. Princeton: Princeton University Press.

Sosa, Ernest (1987). 'Subjects among Other Things: Persons and Other Beings'. *Philosophical Perspectives*, 1 (1987), 155–89. Repr. in Michael Rea (ed.), *Material Constitution: A Reader*. Lanham, Md.: Rowman & Littlefield, 1997, 63–89.

—— (1999*a*). 'The Essentials of Persons'. *Dialectica*, 53: 227–41.

—— (1999*b*). 'Existential Relativity', in P. French, T. Uehling, and H. Wettstein (eds.), *Midwest Studies in Philosophy*, xxiii. Minneapolis: University of Minnesota Press, 132–43.

—— (2000). Review of David Lewis, Papers in *Metaphysics and Epistemology. Journal of Philosophy*, 97: 301–7.

Whorf, Benjamin Lee (1956). *Language, Thought, and Reality*, ed. and introd. John B. Carroll. Cambridge, Mass.: MIT Press.

Wolterstorff, Nicholas (1987). 'Are Concept-Users World-Makers?', in J. E. Tomterlin (ed.), *Philosophical Perspectives, x: Metaphysics*. Atascadero, Calif.: Ridgeview, 233–67.

CHAPTER 23

VAGUENESS IN REALITY

TIMOTHY WILLIAMSON

1. INTRODUCTION

WHEN I take off my glasses, the world looks blurred. When I put them back on, it looks sharp-edged. I do not think that the world really was blurred; I know that what changed was my relation to the distant physical objects ahead, not those objects themselves. I am more inclined to believe that the world really is and was sharp-edged. Is that belief any more reasonable than the belief that the world really is and was blurred? I see more accurately with my glasses on than off, so visual appearances when they are on have some cognitive priority over visual appearances when they are off. If I must choose which kind of visual appearance to take at face value, I will choose the sharp-edged look. But what should I think when I see a mist, which looks very blurred however well I am seeing? Indeed, why choose to take any of the looks at face value? Why not regard all the choices as illegitimate projections of ways of seeing the world onto the world itself?

Such questions arise for thought and language as well as for perception. They concern vagueness, susceptibility to borderline cases in which a judgement is neither

Thanks to Dorothy Edgington, Delia Graff, Dean Zimmerman, and an audience in Oxford for comments on an earlier draft.

clearly correct nor clearly incorrect. For example, Mount Everest has vague boundaries: some rocks are neither clearly part of Everest nor clearly not part of Everest.
Is Everest therefore a vague object? Or is only the name 'Everest' vague? If the name
is vague, is it a vague object, since names are objects too? In what sense, if any, is all
vagueness mind-dependent?

Raised in a theoretical vacuum, such questions quickly produce confusion. We
make more progress by teasing out the metaphysical consequences of vagueness
within a systematic framework for reasoning with vague concepts. Sections 2 and 3
explain two main proposals for accommodating vagueness by modifying the traditional dichotomy between truth and falsity and consequently rethinking logic:
fuzzy logic and supervaluationism. Within these frameworks, we wish to ask 'Is
reality vague?' What does that mean? Section 4 uses the idea of a state of affairs
to clarify the question. Sections 5 and 6 show how supervaluationism and fuzzy
logic embody opposite answers to it. Of course, a semantic theory alone cannot
answer the question, because it is not a question about language, but it can say what
reality must be like for our claims about vagueness to be true. Section 7 considers
whether objects, properties, and relations can be vague. Section 8 concerns the special case of vague identity. Section 9 introduces an epistemic theory of vagueness as
an alternative perspective on all these questions.

This chapter is not intended as a general introduction to the philosophy of vagueness, much of which falls within the philosophy of language and epistemology rather
than metaphysics.[1] Instead, the aim is to elucidate the metaphysical significance of
some subtle issues in the logic of vagueness.

2. FUZZY SEMANTICS

A common proposal is to adjust logic to vagueness by smoothing out the classical
dichotomy of truth and falsity into a continuum of degrees of truth. On this view,
as the sun sets, 'It is dark' starts off definitely false, gradually increases in degree
of truth, and ends up definitely true. For convenience, degrees of truth are usually
identified with the continuum of real numbers between 0 and 1 inclusive: 0 is definite
falsity, 1 is definite truth. When 'It is dark' has degree of truth 0.5, it is just as true as
false. This is the basis of fuzzy logic.[2] What distinguishes the fuzzy approach is not
merely that it postulates degrees of truth, for proponents of other approaches such

---

[1] For vagueness in general, see Graff and Williamson (2002); Keefe and Smith (1996); Keefe (2000);
and Williamson (1994).

[2] Goguen (1969) is an early example of this approach. See also Forbes (1983; 1985: 164–74).

as supervaluationism can postulate them too (see Section 3). Rather, fuzzy semantics is distinctive because it gives degrees of truth the same structural role as truth and falsity play in standard truth-conditional semantics. In particular, just as standard semantics gives the meaning of a logical connective by stating how the truth-value of a complex sentence composed from simpler sentences with that connective depends on the truth-values of those simpler sentences, so fuzzy semantics gives the meaning of the connective by stating how the degree of truth of the complex sentence depends on the degrees of truth of the simpler sentences.

Since we want to express generalizations as well as particular claims, we shall need a language with variables as well as constants. As in classical semantics, variables refer not absolutely but relative to assignments of appropriate values.[3] Call the referent of an expression e relative to an assignment a of values to all variables 'Ref$_a(e)$'. If e is a variable, Ref$_a(e)$ is simply $a(e)$, the value a assigns to e. If e is a constant, Ref$_a(e)$ is independent of a. Call the degree of truth of a formula α relative to an assignment a 'Val$_a(\alpha)$'.

In an atomic sentence $Ft_1, \ldots, t_n$, F is an n-place predicate and $t_1, \ldots, t_n$ are singular terms. We call the referents of singular terms 'objects' without prejudice to their nature. In two-valued semantics, an n-place predicate maps each n-tuple of objects to a truth-value. Thus the two-place predicate 'kisses' maps the ordered pair $\langle$John, Mary$\rangle$ to truth if John kisses Mary and to falsity otherwise. Likewise in fuzzy semantics, an n-place predicate maps each n-tuple of objects to a degree of truth; for example, 'kisses' might map $\langle$John, Mary$\rangle$ to 0.5 if Mary draws back before it is clear whether John has succeeded in kissing her. Thus the degree of truth of the atomic sentence relative to an assignment a is the value to which the function Ref$_a(F)$ maps the n-tuple of objects $\langle$Ref$_a(t_1), \ldots,$ Ref$_a(t_n)\rangle$. Formally:

(FUZZYatom) $\text{Val}_a(Ft_1 \ldots t_n) = \text{Ref}_a(F)(\text{Ref}_a(t_1), \ldots, \text{Ref}_a(t_n))$.

Classical semantics treats a logical operator such as negation ($\sim$), conjunction (&), or disjunction ($\vee$) as truth-functional: the truth-value of a complex sentence consisting of such an operator applied to one or more simpler sentences is a function of the truth-values of those simpler sentences, displayed by the truth-table for that operator. Similarly, fuzzy semantics treats those operators as degree-functional: the degree of truth of the complex sentence is a function of the degrees of truth of the simpler sentences. For negation the obvious proposal is:

(FUZZY$\sim$) $\text{Val}_a(\sim\alpha) = 1 - \text{Val}_a(\alpha)$.

---

[3] For simplicity, we ignore other relativizations: to circumstances of evaluation (possible worlds and times) for modal and temporal operators, to contexts of utterance for indexicals. These complications would not harm the argument of this chapter. Possibility and time are dimensions orthogonal to vagueness. Context-shifting has been argued to play a major role in one of the main manifestations of vagueness, sorites paradoxes (Kamp 1981), but pragmatic effects are not of primary interest for the metaphysics of vagueness.

If α is definitely false, it has degree of truth 0, so $\sim\alpha$ has degree of truth 1 and is definitely true. If α is definitely true, it has degree of truth 1, so $\sim\alpha$ has degree of truth 0 and is definitely false. Thus, if we equate truth and falsity with degree of truth 1 and 0 respectively, the classical truth-table for $\sim$ emerges as a special case of FUZZY$\sim$. But as 'It is dark' gradually increases in degree of truth, so 'It is not dark' gradually decreases. At the halfway point, both statements have degree of truth 0.5; they characterize the situation equally well. The case is perfectly borderline.

So far, degrees of truth look formally just like probabilities (the probability of $\sim\alpha$ is 1 minus the probability of α). Not so for other operators. The probability of a conjunction is not determined by the probabilities of its conjuncts. For if both conjuncts have probability 0.5, the probability of the conjunction may be anywhere between 0 and 0.5. For a fair coin on a given toss, the conjunction 'The coin will come up heads and the coin will come up tails' has probability 0 while both its conjuncts have probability 0.5; the repetitive conjunction 'The coin will come up heads and the coin will come up heads' has probability 0.5 while both its conjuncts have probability 0.5 too. But fuzzy semantics calculates the degree of truth of a conjunction from the degrees of truth of its conjuncts. The standard proposal is that it is their minimum:

(FUZZY&) $\mathrm{Val}_a(\alpha \,\&\, \beta) = \min\{\mathrm{Val}_a(\alpha), \mathrm{Val}_a(\beta)\}.$

The classical truth-table for & emerges as a special case of FUZZY&, for it implies that the conjunction has degree of truth 1 if both conjuncts have degree of truth 1 and degree of truth 0 if at least one conjunct has degree of truth 0. FUZZY& has intuitively attractive features. It implies that adding a conjunct never increases the degree of truth of a conjunction (the expanded conjunction entails the original one), that increasing the degree of truth of a conjunct never decreases the degree of truth of a conjunction, and that repeating a conjunct makes no difference to the degree of truth of a conjunction. One can easily show that FUZZY& gives the *only* function from the degrees of truth of the conjuncts to the degree of truth of the conjunction that satisfies those desiderata.

Nevertheless, FUZZY& has counter-intuitive consequences. Suppose, for example, that the twins Jack and Mack are balding in the same way. Their scalps are in exactly the same state; they are bald to exactly the same degree. However far the process has gone, the claim 'Jack is bald and Mack isn't' ($Bj \,\&\, \sim Bm$) is not perfectly balanced between truth and falsity; intuitively, it is false, or at least much closer to falsity than to truth. The conjunction is not merely conversationally mis-leading, by not speaking symmetrically of the twins, for the conditional 'If Jack is bald, then Mack is bald' does not speak of them symmetrically but is intuitively correct. $Bj \,\&\, \sim Bm$ should receive a degree of truth less than 0.5 at every point of the synchronized balding processes. At the halfway point, Bj has degree of truth 0.5. So has Bm, for Jack and Mack are in the same state; so has $\sim Bm$ by FUZZY$\sim$. There-fore, FUZZY& assigns $Bj \,\&\, \sim Bm$ degree of truth 0.5, the wrong result. A similar argument shows that FUZZY& assigns the contradiction $Bj \& \sim Bj$ degree of truth 0.5 at the halfway point. Yet, intuitively, the contradiction is closer to falsity than to truth. If fuzzy semanticists attempt to avoid these results by using a different function to compute the degrees of truth of conjunctions, they violate the intuitive desiderata that only FUZZY& satisfies. The problem is not in the choice of function from the degrees of truth of the conjuncts to the degree of truth of the conjunction but in the very idea that there is such a function. This kind of objection has long been familiar under the terminology of 'penumbral connections' (Fine 1975: 269–70; Kamp 1975: 131; Williamson 1994: 135–8). Fuzzy logicians have never found a convincing response. We should remember this dark cloud over fuzzy logic as we continue to discuss the approach.

Just as the classical truth-tables assign a conjunction the lowest truth-value of its conjuncts, so they assign a disjunction the highest truth-value of its disjuncts. Just as fuzzy logicians generalize to the minimum degree of truth for conjunctions, so they generalize to the maximum degree of truth for disjunctions:

(FUZZY∨) $\mathrm{Val}_a(\alpha \vee \beta) = \max\{\mathrm{Val}_a(\alpha), \mathrm{Val}_a(\beta)\}.$

Conjunction and disjunction raise similar issues. Note that FUZZY∨ makes the law of excluded middle a half-truth. When α has degree of truth 0.5, so has $\sim\alpha$; thus by FUZZY∨ so too has $\alpha \vee \sim\alpha$.

What of the quantifiers? A universal generalization resembles the conjunction of its instances. Since some objects lack names, the instances need not correspond to distinct sentences in the language; the conjunction is not to be understood substitutionally. Rather, $\forall v\alpha$ (where α may contain the variable v) is equivalent to the conjunction of α itself under all assignments to v (while the assignments to other variables are held fixed). That is as in classical semantics. Given FUZZY&, one might therefore expect the degree of truth of a universal generalization to be the minimum of the degrees of truth of its instances. However, there is a technical hitch, for if it has infinitely many instances, there may be no minimum degree of truth. For example, the set $\{0.99, 0.909, 0.9009, \ldots\}$ has no least member. Nevertheless, although 0.9 is not a member of that set, it is its greatest lower bound (glb): the greatest number not greater than any member of the set. Every set of degrees of truth has a unique greatest lower bound. Accordingly, the proper generalization of FUZZY& is:

(FUZZY∀) $\mathrm{Val}_a(\forall v\alpha) = \mathrm{glb}\{\mathrm{Val}_{a^*}(\alpha)$: a^* an assignment differing from a at most on $v\}$.

Similarly, we extend FUZZY∨ to a rule for the existential quantifier using the analogy between existential generalization and disjunction. As greatest lower bounds replace minima, so least upper bounds (lubs) replace maxima:

(FUZZY∃) $\mathrm{Val}_a(\exists v\alpha) = \mathrm{lub}\{\mathrm{Val}_{a^*}(\alpha)$: a^* an assignment differing from a at most on $v\}$.

So far, we cannot talk *about* vagueness in the formal language. We might want to say that Jack is a borderline case of baldness, neither definitely bald nor definitely not bald. To do so, we introduce the operator Δ, 'definitely'. $\sim\!\Delta Bj$ & $\sim\!\Delta\!\sim\!Bj$ says roughly that Jack is neither definitely bald nor definitely not bald. Δ means 'it is definite that' rather than 'it is definite whether', so $\Delta\alpha$ is false if α is false. The obvious rule is that $\Delta\alpha$ is definitely true when α is definitely true and definitely false otherwise. Since definite truth is degree of truth 1, that amounts to:

$$(\text{FUZZY}\Delta)\quad \text{Val}_a(\Delta\alpha) = 1 \text{ if } \text{Val}_a(\alpha) = 1$$
$$\text{Val}_a(\Delta\alpha) = 0 \text{ otherwise.}$$

Fuzzy logicians generally use classical meta-logic when reasoning in the meta-language. Thus they accept the metalinguistic instance of the law of excluded middle that either $\text{Val}_a(\alpha) = 1$ or $\text{Val}_a(\alpha) \neq 1$. Consequently, either $\text{Val}_a(\Delta\alpha) = 1$ or $\text{Val}_a(\Delta\alpha) = 0$. Therefore, $\Delta\Delta\alpha \lor \Delta\!\sim\!\Delta\alpha$ always has degree of truth 1, so $\Delta\alpha$ is not itself vague. Thus nobody is a borderline case of definite baldness. That is counter-intuitive. As Jack gradually goes bald, it is no clearer when he becomes definitely bald than it is when he becomes bald. It is sometimes unclear whether he is bald; it is sometimes unclear whether he is definitely bald. This is the problem of higher-order vagueness. If first-order borderline cases should be assigned interme-diate degrees of truth, so should second-order borderline cases. No modification of FUZZYΔ by itself would help, for within fuzzy semantics FUZZYΔ defines a perfectly good operator that intuitively is vague. To redefine Δ is to change the subject, not solve the problem. One major unmet challenge facing fuzzy logic is to give an adequate treatment of higher-order vagueness. Presumably, that would involve the recognition that the meta-language is vague too, and therefore requires a fuzzy semantics given the fuzzy approach to vagueness. But since fuzzy semantics is supposed to invalidate classical logic (for example, the law of excluded middle), fuzzy logicians' use of classical meta-logic would be illegitimate.

Fuzzy logic is a special case of many-valued logic, where logical operators act truth-functionally on more than two truth-values (degrees of truth). Many theo-rists have applied a three-valued logic of truth, falsity, and neutrality to vagueness, although it is unclear why a threefold classification should work if a twofold clas-sification does not. Higher-order vagueness is a pressing problem for many-valued logic quite generally.[4] The earlier problem of penumbral connections is also dam-aging for any many-valued approach with a neutral value that a sentence shares with its negation, as in standard three-valued logics. A natural response to these problems is supervaluationism.

---

[4] Tye (1990, 1994) and Horgan (1994) discuss higher-order vagueness in a three-valued context, but their remarks neither constitute a systematic metalogical treatment nor show how to construct one. See also Williamson (1994: 127–31).

3. SUPERVALUATIONIST SEMANTICS

According to supervaluationism, a vague language admits a range of different clas-sical assignments of referents to terms and truth-values to sentences. [5] Some but not all classical assignments are in some sense compatible with speakers' use of vague terms, the context of utterance and the extralinguistic facts; they are the *admissi-ble valuations* (speakers themselves may be incapable of completely specifying such valuations). For example, each admissible valuation assigns an extension to 'bald', containing everybody who is definitely bald, nobody who is definitely not bald, and anybody as bald as somebody whom it contains. If Jack is borderline, he is in the extension of 'bald' on some admissible valuations and not on others, depending on where they put the cut-off point. Each (declarative) sentence is true or false on each valuation. A borderline sentence is true on some admissible valuations, false on others.

Consider a language with the same expressions as in Section 2. Supervaluationists relativize reference to a valuation V in addition to an assignment a of values to variables. If e is a variable, $\text{Ref}_{V,a}(e)$ is simply $a(e)$, the value a assigns to e, which is independent of V. If e is a constant, $\text{Ref}_{V,a}(e)$ is independent of a, but varies with V if e is vague. For example, the vague name 'Everest' refers to objects with slightly different spatio-temporal boundaries according to different admissible valuations. As in classical semantics, an n-place predicate refers to a function from n-tuples of objects to truth-values (truth or falsity). Since classical semantics emerges as a special case of fuzzy semantics when degrees of truth are restricted to 1 and 0 (now conceived as truth and falsity), we can write the clauses for the standard logical operators as in Section 2, with the extra valuation parameter V:

(SUPERatom) $\text{Val}_{V,a}(Ft_1 \ldots t_n) = \text{Ref}_{V,a}(F)(\text{Ref}_{V,a}(t_1), \ldots, \text{Ref}_{V,a}(t_n))$

(SUPER$\sim$) $\text{Val}_{V,a}(\sim\alpha) = 1 - \text{Val}_{V,a}(\alpha)$

(SUPER&) $\text{Val}_{V,a}(\alpha \,\&\, \beta) = \min\{\text{Val}_{V,a}(\alpha), \text{Val}_{V,a}(\beta)\}$

(SUPER$\vee$) $\text{Val}_{V,a}(\alpha \vee \beta) = \max\{\text{Val}_{V,a}(\alpha), \text{Val}_{V,a}(\beta)\}$

(SUPER$\forall$) $\text{Val}_{V,a}(\forall v\alpha) = \text{glb}\{\text{Val}_{V,a^*}(\alpha)$: a^* an assignment differing from a at most on $v\}$

(SUPER$\exists$) $\text{Val}_{V,a}(\exists v\alpha) = \text{lub}\{\text{Val}_{V,a^*}(\alpha)$: a^* an assignment differing from a at most on $v\}$.

---

[5] Fine (1975) and Kamp (1975) exemplify the supervaluationist approach; for discussion see also Williamson (1994: 142–64) and Keefe (2000).

Here the non-classical effect of the fuzzy clauses disappears because the super-valuationist Val delivers only 0 and 1 as values. The only non-classical feature of these clauses is the parameter V, which so far is doing no work.

Supervaluationists use classical meta-logic. Thus for each sentence α, valuation V, and assignment a, either $\mathrm{Val}_{V,a}(\alpha)$ is 1 or $\mathrm{Val}_{V,a}(\sim\alpha)$ is 1 by SUPER$\sim$; either way, by SUPER$\vee$, $\mathrm{Val}_{V,a}(\alpha \vee \sim\alpha)$ is 1. Thus the law of excluded middle holds, even for borderline sentences. More generally, every theorem of classical logic is true on each valuation. Similarly, on each valuation modus ponens and other classical rules preserve truth.[6]

Supervaluationist semantics elegantly solves the problem of penumbral connections on which fuzzy semantics came to grief. If Jack and Mack are borderline for baldness, Bj and Bm are true on some admissible valuations and false on others. But since they have qualitatively identical scalps, no admissible valuation evaluates Bj and Bm differently; $\mathrm{Val}_{V,a}(Bj)$ and $\mathrm{Val}_{V,a}(Bm)$ are both 1 or both 0; either way, $\mathrm{Val}_{V,a}(Bj \,\&\, \sim Bm)$ is 0. Thus $Bj \,\&\, \sim Bm$ is false on every valuation, as it should be; likewise for the contradiction $Bj \,\&\, \sim Bj$.

On traditional versions of supervaluationism, α is true absolutely if and only if α is true (has value 1) on every admissible valuation ('supertruth'); α is false absolutely if and only if α is false (has value 0) on every admissible valuation ('superfalsity'). Thus the principle of bivalence fails: borderline sentences are neither true nor false (absolutely), even though they satisfy the law of excluded middle. The true disjunction $\alpha \vee \sim\alpha$ has no true disjunct when α is borderline. Equally, the false conjunction $\alpha \,\&\, \sim\alpha$ then has no false conjunct. Similarly, a true existential generalization may have no true instance, for example 'For some number n, a man with n hairs is bald and a man with $n + 1$ hairs is not bald'. Again, a false universal generalization may have no false instance, for example 'For every number n, either a man with n hairs is not bald or a man with $n + 1$ hairs is bald'. Every valuation specifies a cut-off, but it varies across valuations.

If supervaluationists reject the principle of bivalence, they must also reject Tarskian biconditionals such as these:

(TARSKI) 'Jack is bald' is true if and only if Jack is bald.
        'Jack is not bald' is true if and only if Jack is not bald.

For since they accept that Jack is either bald or not bald, accepting TARSKI would commit them by their classical meta-logic (and their assumption that α is false if $\sim\alpha$ is true) to the conclusion that 'Jack is bald' is either true or false, which they reject. To combine acceptance of excluded middle with rejection of bivalence they must reject TARSKI.

---

[6] Some versions of supervaluationism do not validate classical rules involving the discharge of premises, such as conditional proof and *reductio ad absurdum* (Fine 1975: 290; Williamson 1994: 150–3).

Supervaluationism enables us to introduce another truth predicate T that does satisfy Tarski's constraints (Fine 1975: 296). As usual, we give the meaning of an expression by specifying its reference relative to each valuation. Since T is a one-place predicate, its referent maps objects to truth-values. Relative to any valuation V and assignment a, T refers to a function that maps an object o to truth if o is a true sentence of the original language relative to V and a, and otherwise maps o to falsity. Consequently, for any sentence α of the original language, the Tarskian biconditional $T\ulcorner\alpha\urcorner \equiv \alpha$ is true on any valuation. Since those biconditionals are central to the inferential role that we expect a truth predicate to play, why do traditional supervaluationists take 'supertrue' rather than T to express truth? The sentence $T\ulcorner\alpha\urcorner$ is just as vague as α itself; they vary in truth-value across admissible valuations in exactly the same way. Perhaps the original idea was to avoid using T in analysing vagueness because T is vague, and therefore a poor theoretical instrument. Supervaluationists sought to formulate a precise analysis of vagueness by using 'supertrue'. But that motivation is misconceived, for it neglects higher-order vagueness. 'Supertrue' is vague too, for 'admissible' is vague. One can readily check that by trying to see where on the colour spectrum 'That shade is red' passes from supertrue to unsupertrue, and where it passes from unsuperfalse to superfalse; it is as hopeless as trying to see where red passes into non-red. Some shades are neither definitely red nor definitely not red; sometimes 'That shade is red' is neither definitely supertrue nor definitely not supertrue. Thus the identification of truth with supertruth does not compensate for the loss of the Tarski biconditionals by any gain of precision (Williamson 1994: 162–4). More recent versions of supervaluationism therefore tend to avoid the identification, or at least to claim that 'true' is ambiguous between supertruth and Tarskian truth (McGee and McLaughlin 1995; for discussion see also Andjelković and Williamson 2000).

Whether truth is supertruth or Tarskian truth, supervaluationists can characterize borderline cases within the object language using the 'definitely' operator Δ. The idea is that $\Delta\alpha$ is true when α is true on all admissible valuations. Thus Δ functions like a universal quantifier, but varies the valuation rather than the assignment. A complication is that since 'admissible' is vague, it too must be relativized to a valuation; we write 'admissible by V'. Each valuation makes a ruling as to which valuations count as admissible. To emphasize the analogy with $\forall$, we state the rule for Δ thus:

(SUPERΔ) $\mathrm{Val}_{V,a}(\Delta\alpha) = \mathrm{glb}\{\mathrm{Val}_{V^*,a}(\alpha)\colon V^*$ a valuation admissible by $V\}$.

$\Delta\alpha$ is true on V if α is true on every valuation admissible by V, and false on V otherwise. If we omitted the relativization 'by V' from SUPERΔ, $\Delta\alpha$ would be true on all valuations or on none, so $\Delta\Delta\alpha \vee \Delta\mathord\sim\Delta\alpha$ would be true on all valuations; that formula forbids borderline status to $\Delta\alpha$, thereby denying higher-order vagueness. Formally, SUPERΔ works like standard possible worlds semantics for the necessity operator $\Box$, where necessity is truth in all possible worlds. Possible worlds become admissible valuations; contingency becomes borderline status. Just as a relation of admissibility between valuations permits higher-order vagueness, so a relation of possibility ('accessibility') between worlds permits contingent necessity or possibility in modal logics weaker than the system S5. For simplicity, we ignore higher-order vagueness where it is peripheral to the discussion (but see Fine 1975: 287–98; Williamson 1994: 156–61; 1999a).

SUPERΔ gives Δ nice features. In particular, it makes definiteness closed under logical consequence: if the argument from the premises $\alpha_1, \ldots, \alpha_n$ to the conclusion β is valid (truth-preserving on all valuations and assignments), so is the argument from $\Delta\alpha_1, \ldots, \Delta\alpha_n$ to $\Delta\beta$. Furthermore, on the reasonable assumption that every admissible valuation rules itself admissible, definiteness is factive: the argument from $\Delta\alpha$ to α is valid.

Problematic supervaluationist claims based on the identification of truth with supertruth correspond to less problematic claims about definiteness. For example, a disjunction can be definite even though no disjunct is definite; if α is borderline, $\Delta(\alpha \vee \sim\alpha)$ is true but $\Delta\alpha \vee \Delta\sim\alpha$ false. Similarly, an existential generalization can be definite even though no instance is definite; if Bn says that a man with n hairs is bald, $\Delta\exists n(Bn \& \sim Bn + 1)$ is true but $\exists n\Delta(Bn \& \sim Bn + 1)$ false.

Supervaluationists can even postulate a scale of degrees of truth; such degrees are not the preserve of fuzzy logic (Kamp 1975: 137–45; Williamson 1994: 154–6). For, given a suitable notion of proportion, we can define the degree of truth of α as the proportion of admissible valuations on which α is true. Thus $\Delta\alpha$ gives α degree of truth 1 and $\Delta\sim\alpha$ gives it degree of truth 0. Like probabilities, and unlike degrees of truth in fuzzy semantics, supervaluationist degrees of truth falsify degree-functionality; the supervaluationist degree of truth of a conjunction or disjunction is no function of the degrees of truth of its conjuncts or disjuncts.

4. BORDERLINE STATES OF AFFAIRS

Vagueness is articulated by the 'definitely' operator (as in $\Delta\alpha$) and its derivative 'it is vague whether' (as in $\sim\Delta\alpha \& \sim\Delta\sim\alpha$). They operate on sentences (such as α). Vagueness concerns borderline cases; in a borderline case (for example, when it is vague whether Jack is bald) there is a judgement to be hesitated over (the judgement that Jack is bald); the expression of a judgement is in a sentence ('Jack is bald'). For simplicity, let us suppose that expressions of different grammatical categories are all correlated with different elements of reality, their *ontological correlates*. The ontological correlate of a sentence is a state of affairs, just as the ontological correlate of a singular term is an object and the ontological correlate of a predicate is a property or relation. We should therefore expect the question of vagueness in reality to arise primarily for states of affairs, not for objects or even properties and relations. 'Is reality vague?' is not to be paraphrased as 'Are there vague objects?' or 'Are there vague properties and relations?'

What is a state of affairs? For any object o and any property P, there is the state of affairs that o has P; it obtains if and only if o has P. For any objects o_1 and o_2 and any binary relation R, there is the state of affairs that o_1 has R to o_2; it obtains if and only if o_1 has R to o_2.[7] There are doubtless many other kinds of states of affairs. For present purposes, we need not take the ontology of states of affairs wholly seriously. Once we have the items that determine them (such as objects, properties, and relations), we could speak of those items directly. But the notion of a state of affairs is convenient, because it enables us to generalize without surveying the items that compose states of affairs.

States of affairs can be individuated in coarse-grained or fine-grained ways. On a fine-grained conception, states of affairs are structured items, with objects, properties, and relations as constituents; S and S^* may be distinct states of affairs because they are differently constituted even if, necessarily, S obtains if and only if S^* obtains. On a less fine-grained conception, S and S^* are identical if and only if, necessarily, S obtains if and only if S^* obtains. Such states of affairs might be identified with classes of possible worlds. Formally, it would be simplest to use a *very* coarse-grained conception, on which states of affairs are simply truth-values or degrees of truth, for those are the items correlated with sentences by the extensional semantic theories in Sections 2 and 3. Truth obtains and falsity does not; a degree of truth obtains to that very degree. Although the phrase 'state of affairs' becomes rather misleading when applied to truth-values or degrees of truth, what matters is that sentences stand to them in a relation something like reference. Once modal and temporal operators are introduced, sentences might be treated as referring to functions from possible worlds and times to truth-values or degrees of truth; such functions are more naturally conceived as formal versions of states of affairs. In any case, the arguments below do not require the coarse-grained conception; they run on any reasonable standard of individuation.

Since states of affairs are the ontological correlates of sentences, the most natural way to generalize over states of affairs is by quantifying into sentence position. Indeed, in a metaphysically deeper discussion, we might *explain* apparent quantification over states of affairs as a crude rendering into a natural language of quantification into sentence position. For example, to say that some state of affairs does not obtain, we write $\exists S \sim S$. In English we have the noun phrase 'state of affairs' and must use the verb 'obtain' to construct a corresponding sentence; but that is an artefact of the difficulty of expressing quantification into anything but noun phrase

---

[7] An ordering of the argument places of R is assumed.

position unambiguously in natural language. The formal language achieves the desired effect more economically. This quantification into sentence position should not be understood substitutionally. Just as some objects may lack names, so some states of affairs may lack sentences to express them. Rather, the quantification should be understood in the normal way, by variation in the assignment to the relevant variable ('S'). Any state of affairs may be assigned to a variable in sentence position.

'. . .' expresses a borderline case if and only if it is vague whether . . . We therefore define a state of affairs S to be borderline if and only if it is vague whether S obtains. Reality is vague if and only if at least one state of affairs is borderline. For if reality is vague, it is vague how things are, so for some way it is vague whether things are that way; thus, for some state of affairs S, it is vague whether S obtains. Conversely, if for some state of affairs S it is vague whether S obtains, for some way it is vague whether things are that way, so it is vague how things are; thus reality is vague. Reality is precise if and only if it is not vague: no state of affairs is borderline; every one either definitely obtains or definitely fails to obtain.[8] Again, the formal language expresses the idea more economically. To say that reality is vague, that some state of affairs neither definitely obtains nor definitely fails to obtain, we write:

(1) $\exists S(\sim \Delta S \, \& \, \sim \Delta \sim S)$.

To say that reality is precise, we write the negation of (1), or equivalently $\forall S(\Delta S \vee \Delta \sim S)$.

5. Supervaluationist States of Affairs

Does the account in Section 4 trivialize the claim that reality is vague? Everyone agrees that it is vague whether this (I point) is a heap. Thus it is vague whether the state of affairs that this is a heap obtains. Therefore, apparently, of at least one state of affairs (that this is a heap) it is vague whether it obtains, so at least one state of affairs is borderline, so reality is vague. That conclusion looks cheap; the case is paradigmatically one in which we want to locate the vagueness in our words or concepts.

The argument is fallacious. It moves from 'It is vague whether the state of affairs that this is a heap obtains' to 'Of the state of affairs that this is a heap, it is vague

---

[8] For the contrasting proposal that the world is vague if and only if vague matters do not supervene on precise ones, see Peacocke (1981: 132–3), criticized by Hyde (1998); for relevant discussion, see Williamson (1994: 201–4) and McLaughlin (1997). Sainsbury (1995) finds no substance to the question whether the world is vague; he looks in the wrong place.

whether it obtains'. That is no more valid than the fallacious move from 'It is contingent whether the number of planets is even' to 'Of the number of planets, it is contingent whether it is even' (it is contingent how many planets there are, but not whether a given number is even). In the premiss, a definite description ('the state of affairs that this is a heap', 'the number of planets') is in the scope of an operator ('it is vague whether', 'it is contingent whether'); in the conclusion their scopes have been illegitimately reversed. Just as for no number n is it necessary that there are exactly n planets, so perhaps for no state of affairs S is it definite that S obtains if and only if this is a heap. Thus reality may be precise even though it is vague whether this is a heap.

Supervaluationism realizes this possibility in a natural way. It is vague whether this is a heap (Ht):

(2) $\sim\!\Delta Ht$ & $\sim\!\Delta\!\sim\!Ht$.

The question is whether (2) entails (1), perhaps by existential introduction. As quantification into sentence position is comparatively unfamiliar, we may start by assessing separate existentially generalizations into name and predicate position in (2):

(1*) $\exists X \exists x (\sim\!\Delta Xx$ & $\sim\!\Delta\!\sim\!Xx)$.

According to (1*), for some property and object it is vague whether the latter has the former. It will emerge that, under supervaluationism, (1*) is false and does not follow from (2). By an extension of the argument, (1) is false and does not follow from (2).

First consider (2). Since H and t are constants rather than variables, we can ignore the assignment a. In this context we may treat the singular term t ('this') as precise; for some object o, its referent $\mathrm{Ref}_{V,a}(t)$ is o for every admissible valuation V. But the predicate H ('is a heap') is vague; its extension contains o on some but not all admissible valuations. For some admissible valuations V, by SUPERatom, $\mathrm{Val}_{V,a}(Ht) = \mathrm{Ref}_{V,a}(H)(o) = 1$, so $\Delta\!\sim\!Ht$ is false. For other admissible valuations V, $\mathrm{Val}_{V,a}(Ht) = \mathrm{Ref}_{V,a}(H)(o) = 0$, so ΔHt is false. Thus (2) is true. That is the standard supervaluationist treatment of a borderline case: the sentence varies in truth-value across admissible valuations.

Now take (1*). Consider the truth-value of Xx. By SUPERatom, $\mathrm{Val}_{V,a}(Xx) = \mathrm{Ref}_{V,a}(X)(\mathrm{Ref}_{V,a}(x))$. Since X and x are variables, their referents are just what a assigns to them; $\mathrm{Ref}_{V,a}(X) = a(X)$ and $\mathrm{Ref}_{V,a}(x) = a(x)$. Consequently, $\mathrm{Val}_{V,a}(Xx) = a(X)(a(x))$. Xx is true if the object assigned to x is in the extension assigned to X and false otherwise. The crucial point is that $a(X)(a(x))$ depends on a but not on V. Consequently, for any given assignment, Xx is true on all valuations or none. Thus $\sim\!\Delta Xx$ & $\sim\!\Delta \sim Xx$ is false on all assignments, so by SUPER$\exists$ (1*) is false too. Thus (1*) does not follow from (2). On this treatment, it cannot be vague whether an object has a property.

The argument against (1*) works because variables are not vague. It therefore extends to an argument against (1). The simplest extension treats S as a zero-place predicate variable. By SUPERatom, $\mathrm{Val}_{V,a}(S)$ would be $a(S)(\langle\rangle)$, where $a(S)$ is a function from zero-tuples (of which there is only one) to truth-values and $\langle\rangle$ is the zero-tuple; this is tantamount to having a assign S a truth-value. There are more complex possibilities too. What matters is that there is no more room for the truth-value of S to depend on the valuation V than there was for the truth-value of Xx to do so, because the assignment alone fixes the value of the variable. For any given assignment, S is true on all valuations or none. Thus $\sim\!\Delta S$ & $\sim\!\Delta\!\sim\!S$ is false on any assignment, so (1) is false and $\forall S(\Delta S \vee \Delta\!\sim\!S)$ true. Thus (1) does not follow from (2). On this supervaluationist treatment, it cannot be vague whether a state of affairs obtains. Reality is guaranteed to be precise.

Under supervaluationism, one can existentially generalize into the scope of Δ only if the expression on which one generalizes refers precisely. For the singular term t, the condition is $\exists x\Delta x = t$; for the predicate H, it is $\exists X\Delta\forall x(Xx \equiv Hx)$; for the sentence Ht, it is $\exists S\Delta(S \equiv Ht)$. Those conditions for H and Ht are not met here. Supervaluationists grant the weaker conditions $\Delta\exists X\forall x(Xx \equiv Hx)$ and $\Delta\exists S(S \equiv Ht)$, but they do not suffice for existential generalization.

The key to the falsification of (1) and (1*) is that variables are precise: on a given assignment, their reference is constant across valuations. One might therefore suppose that supervaluationists could verify (1) and (1*) simply by having assignments assign values to variables relative to valuations. But that change collapses a distinction crucial to supervaluationists. They admit that, definitely, there is a cut-off point for a vague predicate F ($\Delta\exists n(Fn$ & $\sim\!Fn+1)$), since every admissible valuation has such a point. But they insist that F is still vague because no point is definitely the cut-off ($\sim\!\exists n\Delta(Fn$ & $\sim\!Fn+1)$); the point varies across valuations. If the assignment of values to variables were relativized to valuations, $\Delta(Fn$ & $\sim\!Fn+1)$ would be true when, relative to each valuation, the variable n was assigned the cut-off number for that valuation; thus, by SUPER$\exists$, $\exists n\Delta(Fn$ & $\sim\!Fn + 1)$ would be evaluated as true and the supervaluationist claim of indefiniteness would disappear. The precision of variables is no technical accident. It is crucial to supervaluationists' articulation of their main idea. To focus on states of affairs rather than our ways of referring to them, we generalize with variables whose reference is fixed to one states of affairs across valuations; in doing so, we eliminate vagueness. If vagueness is variation across admissible valuations, then reality is precise.

Many theorists of vagueness accept the metaphysics of supervaluationism but reject its semantics. Like supervaluationists, they conceive vague thought and language as related only indirectly to an underlying reality (typically, one described by popular physics), but disagree on the semantic consequences of that shared conception. Nihilists, for instance, take vague terms to suffer reference failure, and therefore vague predications to be truth-valueless or false; although they may share the supervaluationists' view of what there is to be referred to, they take a harsher view of the semantic consequences of indecision between potential referents. Under nihilism too, reality is precise.[9]

6. Fuzzy States of Affairs

Section 4 explicated the claim that reality is vague. Section 5 asked whether that explication makes the claim trivially true, and answered no by showing that it makes the claim false given a standard form of supervaluationism. But that easy argument raises the opposite question: does the explication make the claim trivially false? By showing that it makes the claim true given a standard form of fuzzy logic, this section will answer no to that question too. On whether reality is vague, supervaluationism and fuzzy logic stand opposed.

As before, the issue is whether a banal statement of a borderline case, for example (2), that it is vague whether this is a heap, entails (1), that reality is vague. And, as before, it is easiest to start by asking whether (2) entails the more specific claim (1*), that for some property and some object, it is vague whether the latter has the former. Can we existentially generalize into the scope of 'it is vague whether' and therefore of Δ? The semantics of those operators is more straightforward under fuzzy logic than under supervaluationism. Indeed, Δ is as much of a degree-function (the analogue of a truth-function) as negation is on the fuzzy semantics; quantifying into the scope of Δ is no more problematic than quantifying into the scope of negation. In classical semantics, the predicate variable X can be assigned any function from objects to truth-values; likewise, in fuzzy semantics, it can be assigned any function from objects to degrees of truth, in particular that to which the predicate H refers. Similarly, the variable x can be assigned any object, in particular that to which the singular term t refers. Thus by FUZZY∃ (1*) is a straightforward consequence of (2). For analogous reasons, (1) is also a straightforward consequence of (2). The extension of the argument is simplest if we regard S as a zero-place predicate variable, but holds on more complex interpretations too. In fuzzy logic, *every* borderline case, however 'linguistic' in appearance, makes reality vague.

At first sight the result is disconcerting. On reflection, however, it presents a problem for fuzzy logic, not for the explication of the claim that reality is vague. Given FUZZYΔ, the degree of truth of $\Delta\alpha$ depends only on the degree of truth of α,

---

⁹ For nihilist arguments of varying degrees of extremism, see Heller (1988, 1990); Horgan (1995); Unger (1979*a,b,c*, 1980; contrast 1990: 321–3); Wheeler (1975, 1979). For discussion, see Abbott (1983); Grim (1982, 1983, 1984); Sanford (1979); Williamson (1994: 165–84).

just as the degree of truth of $\sim\alpha$ depends only on the degree of truth of α; $\Delta\alpha$ is just as much about what α is about as $\sim\alpha$ is. Δ does not represent any kind of semantic ascent to a metalinguistic level. Thus vagueness in whether this is a heap is straightforward vagueness in how things are. By contrast, SUPERΔ makes Δ a kind of universal quantifier over admissible valuations, which is a kind of semantic ascent. Of course, it is natural to object to FUZZYΔ that it makes vagueness in reality come far too cheap. Perhaps there is no single state of affairs that this is a heap but many states of affairs concerning the exact number and arrangement of grains. But that suggestion is more congenial to supervaluationism than to fuzzy logic. For FUZZYatom relates 'This is a heap' to reality as directly as it does sentences concerning the exact number and arrangement of grains. To take the fuzzy semantics at face value is to treat vagueness in whether this is a heap as simply vagueness in how things are. If it is not vagueness in how things are, then something is wrong with the fuzzy semantics.

According to supervaluationism, no borderline case makes reality vague. According to fuzzy semantics, any borderline case makes reality vague. Of course, there will be no end of mixed views, perhaps embodying elements of both supervaluationism and fuzzy semantics, according to which some but not all borderline cases make reality vague. Some may even insist on applying 'supervaluationism' or 'fuzzy logic' as a label to such a mixed view. We cannot survey all the possible combinations here. Nevertheless, we may wonder whether an account of vagueness can distinguish in any principled way between some borderline cases that make reality vague and others that do not. At any rate, it has become obvious that the question 'Is reality vague?' must eventually be answered by comparing theories of vagueness overall.

7. VAGUE OBJECTS, PROPERTIES, AND RELATIONS

'Is reality vague?' and 'Are there vague objects?' are often treated as the same question.[10] That conflation is symptomatic of a tendency to conceive reality as merely a collection of objects, as though one could describe it fully by listing them, without having to specify their properties and relations. The tendency has been elevated to an explicit claim, the truthmaker principle, according to which (in its unqualified form) for every truth an object exists whose existence is sufficient for that truth.

---

[10] For some discussion of relevant issues, see Akiba (2000); Burgess (1990); Lewis (1993); Lowe (1995); Quine (1981); Rolf (1980); Sainsbury (1989, 1995); Sanford (1993); Sorensen (1998); Tye (1990, 1995, 1996).

Once we take quantification into predicate and sentence position seriously in its own right, the truthmaker principle looks unmotivated, for it assigns a metaphysically privileged status to quantification into name position (over objects). It derives ontology from linguistic prejudice (Williamson 1999*b*).

Although 'Are there vague objects?' is not equivalent to 'Is reality vague?', the former question might be interesting on its own terms. What could it mean to call an object 'vague'? Objects are the referents of names and other singular terms; vagueness is characterized by operators on sentences. Of course, a word is an object and can be vague in the ordinary sense; but it is vague because there are or could be cases in which it is vague whether it applies. 'It applies' is a sentence, not a singular term, and application has no obvious analogue for objects other than expressions and concepts.

In many ordinary cases it is tempting to say that there is a vague object. Where, for example, are the boundaries of Mount Everest? Of some spatial points, it is vague whether Everest includes them; for some rocks, it is vague whether they are part of Everest. We might conclude that Everest is a vague object. But what, if anything, is special about the relations of location and parthood? And what justifies the move from vagueness expressed at the level of the sentences 'Everest includes those points' and 'Those rocks are part of Everest' to vagueness expressed at the level of the name 'Everest'?

Supervaluationists can significantly ascribe vagueness to referring expressions of any syntactic category. The test is whether they vary in reference across admissible valuations. Thus the name 'Everest' is vague if on two such valuations it refers to different mountainous objects. But that is not vagueness in the objects referred to. As argued in Section 5, supervaluationism implies that it is never vague how things are. For example, either 'is part of' is vague or it is not. If it is vague, for some objects o and o^* it is vague whether o is part of o^*, but we are not justified in attributing the vagueness to o or o^*. If 'is part of' is precise, then for no objects o and o^* is it vague whether o is part of o^*. Either way, under supervaluationism, we have no basis for classifying objects as vague.

What of fuzzy semantics? 'Is part of' refers to a function that maps the ordered pair of Everest and a peripheral rock to an intermediate degree of truth. On the face of it, that is vagueness in the function, not in the objects. The fuzzy approach seems to provide a natural notion of vagueness for the referents of predicates (which we may call 'properties' and 'relations'), as the capacity to yield intermediate degrees for some objects, but no natural notion of vagueness for objects, the referents of singular terms. Could fuzzy logicians define an object o to be vague if and only if for some object o^* it is vague whether o^* is part of o (o^* is part of o to an intermediate degree)? That would be a more or less arbitrary stipulation, without natural grounding in the fuzzy semantics. Why should vagueness in whether o^* is part of o be attributed to o rather than to o^* or to parthood? Indeed, the admission of vague objects would undermine the original conception of vague properties and relations, for why should vague objects not have precise properties (such as having mass exactly *m*) or relations (such as having exactly the same mass) to intermediate degrees? Even granted a notion of a precise object, we cannot determine whether a property is vague by asking whether it applies to precise objects to intermediate degrees, for the degree to which any precise object has the intuitively vague property of being a very vague red object is 0. Such difficulties for the conception of vague objects generalize beyond fuzzy logic.

We have no good reason to enter the maze created by the conception of vague objects. It depends on the attempt to attribute vagueness at the level of subsentential expressions. Without a theory of vagueness, we should not assume that the attempt is sensible. After all, it would be foolish to attribute *falsity* at the level of subsentential expressions, to ask whether the falsity of 'Cats bark' should be blamed on falsity in 'cats' or cats or on falsity in 'barks' or barking. We need some reason to suppose that vagueness distributes in a way in which falsity does not. Fuzzy logic supplies no such reason. Although supervaluationism provides a reason, its way of distributing vagueness among subsentential expressions forbids its projection onto their referents. Such considerations suggest that we should abandon the question 'Are there vague objects?' We can do so the more easily because we do not thereby abandon the question 'Is reality vague?'

8. VAGUE IDENTITY

Much of the literature on vague objects focuses on whether it can be vague of objects whether they are identical. Problem cases of identity might suggest a positive answer. If it is unclear whether the person who emerges from drastic brain surgery is the same as the one who was pushed into the operating theatre, perhaps the earlier person and the later one are objects of which it is vague whether they are identical. However, Gareth Evans (1978) proposed a general argument to show that it cannot be vague whether objects are identical. In brief, suppose that it is vague whether o is o^*; since it is not vague whether o^* is o^*, something holds of o that does not hold of o^* (that it is vague whether it is o^*); but Leibniz's law of identity states that if o is o^*, then whatever holds of o holds of o^*; therefore o is not o^*.[11] That is not yet a straight contradiction. However, by an extension of the argument, from the definiteness of its premiss we can infer the definiteness of its conclusion: given that it is *definitely* vague whether o is o^*, it follows that *definitely* o is not o^*, and therefore that it is

---

[11] For a similar argument, see Salmon (1982: 243–6; 1984; 1986: 110–14).

not vague whether o is o^*. But given that it is definitely vague whether o is o^*, it also follows that it *is* vague whether o is not o^*. Thus at least the supposition that it is definitely vague whether o is o^* seems to yield a contradiction. Many defenders of vagueness in reality or of vague objects have felt obliged to find a fallacy in Evans's argument, although it is not obvious why the more general issues should be thought to turn on the very special relation of identity.[12]

For most supervaluationists, '=' has the same extension on every admissible valuation; it is uniquely identified by its structural characteristics (its extension contains the ordered pair of each object with itself and is a subclass of every class with that property). Thus the sentence $t = t^*$ varies in truth-value across admissible valuations only if at least one of the singular terms t and t^* varies in reference across such valuations. Consequently, we cannot quantify into $\sim\Delta t = t^*$ & $\sim\Delta\sim t = t^*$ to conclude that for some objects it is vague whether they are identical (Thomason 1982). That is consistent with Evans's idea that the formula defeats itself on the assumption that t and t^* refer precisely to objects between which identity is vague (Lewis 1988). His intended conclusion is supervaluationistically correct, as the argument of Section 5 implies.

Evans's argument is more interesting in a fuzzy context, where existential generalization holds. Suppose that, relative to some assignment, $x = x^*$ is true to some intermediate degree. Thus $\sim\Delta x = x^*$ is true to degree 1. But $x = x$ is also true to degree 1, as therefore is $\Delta x = x$. Consequently, the argument from $\Delta x = x$ and $\sim\Delta x = x^*$ to $\sim x = x^*$ has premises true to degree 1 and a conclusion true to a degree less than 1: it does not preserve definite truth in fuzzy logic, even though it has the form of an argument from $\varphi(x)$ and $\sim\varphi(x^*)$ to $\sim x = x^*$. Strictly speaking, what fails is not Leibniz's law (from $x = x^*$ and $\varphi(x)$ to $\varphi(x^*)$) but a contraposed variant (Parsons 1987). Nevertheless, the contraposed variant is fundamental to our thinking about identity. If what we know is that this man is of blood group O and that John is not of blood group O, how else are we to conclude that this man is not John? Moreover, even the uncontraposed Leibniz's law fails to preserve intermediate degrees of truth. Under the same supposition as before, the argument from $x = x^*$ and $\Delta x = x$ to $\Delta x = x^*$ has both premises true to a degree greater than 0 and a conclusion true to degree 0.

The natural suspicion is that fuzzy logicians permit degrees of identity only by losing their grip on the notion of identity. Consider the classical meta-logic on which fuzzy logicians rely. Since they take vague terms to require non-classical logic, they

---

[12] On vague identity, see also Broome (1984); Burgess (1989, 1990); Cook (1986); Copeland (1995, 1997); Cowles (1994); Cowles and White (1991); Engel (1991: 196–8, 213–15); French and Krause (1995); Garrett (1988, 1991); Gibbins (1982); Hawley (1998); Heck (1998); Hirsch (1999); Howard-Snyder (1991); Johnsen (1989); Keefe (1995); Lowe (1994, 1997); McGee and McLaughlin (1995); Noonan (1982, 1984, 1990, 1995); Over (1984, 1989); Parsons (1987, 2000); Parsons and Woodruff (1995); Pelletier (1984, 1989); Priest (1991, 1998); Rasmussen (1986); Stalnaker (1988); Tye (1990), van Inwagen (1988, 1990); Wiggins (1986); Williamson (1996a, 2002); Zemach (1991).

are treating the meta-language as precise, its sentences true to degree 1 or 0. Since '=' figures in the meta-language, $x = x^*$ is true in the meta-language to degree 1 or 0 relative to any assignment. Unless $x = x^*$ is true in the object language to the same degree relative to the same assignment, '=' is not being interpreted as identity. Consequently, fuzzy logicians should assign intermediate degrees of truth to identity sentences only if they adopt a non-classical meta-logic. The same goes for other forms of many-valued logic.

Opponents of Evans's argument often claim to show that it is fallacious or question-begging by constructing many-valued models that invalidate one or more of its steps within the framework of a classical meta-logic (van Inwagen 1988; Parsons and Woodruff 1995; Priest 1998). The foregoing considerations show this method to be unsound, for it depends on interpreting '=' in the object language as meaning something other than identity. After all, we can construct a formal model in which $t = t^*$ and Ft are true and Ft^* is false by interpreting '=' to mean distinctness. To claim on those grounds that Leibniz's law is fallacious or question-begging would be silly. The purported many-valued counter-models to Evans's argument make the same mistake, albeit in a far subtler form (Williamson 2002). No adequate treatment of Evans's argument within a systematically fuzzy or many-valued meta-logic has been provided. Moreover, the earlier problem of penumbral connections gives us ample reason to reject approaches based on fuzzy or many-valued logic.

9. Epistemicism

Section 3 argued that supervaluationists' rejection of Tarskian constraints on truth and falsity is poorly motivated. But if they accept those constraints, they must also accept the principle of bivalence: 'This is a heap' is either true or false, although we have no way of knowing which. Thus supervaluationism threatens to collapse into an epistemic view of vagueness (Williamson 1995; 1997: 216–17). Rather than examine the putative collapse, let us consider epistemicism in its own right. On this view, truth is Tarskian and logic is classical. Vagueness consists in a special kind of irremediable ignorance in borderline cases.[13]

What prevents us from knowing whether this is a heap? Suppose that it is in fact a heap. I might judge, truly, 'This is a heap'. But, in a borderline case, I could

---

[13] For development and defence of epistemicism, and references to earlier epistemicist and anti-epistemicist writings, see Williamson (1994, 1995, 1996b, 1997). Keefe (2000) contains a recent critique of epistemicism. For technical issues relevant to both epistemicism and supervaluationism, see Andjelković and Williamson (2001) and Williamson (1999a).

easily have judged 'This is a heap' even if the factors that determine the reference of my word 'heap' had differed slightly, making me express a different and false proposition. In that sense I cannot discriminate the counterfactual assignment of reference to my words from the actual assignment; the two semantic valuations are indiscriminable for me. Our powers of discrimination are limited; we cannot make our judgements perfectly sensitive to all the reference-determining factors. Thus my actual judgement is unreliably based; even if true, it does not constitute knowledge. That, in outline, is an epistemicist explanation of our irremediable ignorance.

At least in its simplest form, epistemicism can take over and reinterpret the formal apparatus of supervaluationism, with a Tarskian conception of truth. To say that a valuation V^* is admissible by a valuation V is now to say that V^* is indiscriminable from V in the sense indicated. Since Δ now has an epistemic sense, we can read it as 'clearly' rather than 'definitely'.

If epistemicism has the same formal structure as supervaluationism, it too implies that reality is precise. Suppose that it is vague whether this rock is part of Everest and that 'this rock' and 'is part of' are precise. Then both supervaluationists and epistemicists deny that Everest is an object of which it is vague whether this rock is part of it. They assert that Everest is an object of which it is vague whether it is Everest (for no object is the referent of 'Everest' on all admissible valuations), although it is not vague whether Everest is Everest. For epistemicists, this simply reflects our limited capacity to discriminate between situations in which the name 'Everest' refers to Everest and situations in which it refers to entities that coincide with Everest only approximately; in particular, some differ from Everest in whether they include this rock. Yet when we ask ourselves 'Is this rock part of Everest?', 'Everest' refers to a unique object. Consider an analogy in which we prescind from vagueness. Let the name 'Es' refer to England if there is life in other galaxies and to Scotland otherwise. We know that Cumbria is part of England and not part of Scotland. Not knowing whether there is life in other galaxies, we know neither that Es is England nor that Es is Scotland. We do not know whether Cumbria is part of Es. Yet when we ask ourselves 'Is Cumbria part of Es?', 'Es' refers to a unique object, perhaps England, perhaps Scotland.

The epistemic point that no object is clearly Everest does not at all undermine the metaphysical point that some object is uniquely Everest. By contrast, although supervaluationists grudgingly admit that, definitely, some object is uniquely Everest, they take their admission to be somehow metaphysically unserious because no object is definitely Everest; no object is definitely the unique referent of 'Everest'. Supervaluationists conceive their relativization of reference to valuations as making the relation between language and reality somehow less direct than it is in classical truth-conditional semantics. For epistemicists, the relativization has no such effect: it is simply a technical device within classical truth-conditional semantics to handle an epistemic operator. Consequently, epistemicism does not involve the second-guessing of our vague metaphysical beliefs that is characteristic of supervaluationism.

How can it be epistemically vague which object is Everest? Surely a mountaineer can look at Everest, say 'That mountain is Everest', and thereby express knowledge, of Everest, that it is Everest. Visual acquaintance provides a paradigm of such *de re* knowledge. But if it is known, of Everest, that it is Everest, how can it also be epistemically vague, of Everest, that it is Everest? In situations indiscriminable from the actual one, the visual demonstrative 'that mountain' and the name 'Everest' refer to something slightly different from Everest, but still maintain coreference; in saying 'That mountain is Everest' the mountaineer would still express a truth, although a slightly different one. The *de dicto* knowledge that the mountain is Everest is unthreatened. Moreover, *de dicto* knowledge entails *de dicto* clarity; it is not epistemically vague whether the mountain is Everest. But *de re* knowledge may not entail *de re* clarity. Unlike *de re* clarity, *de re* knowledge may not require perfect discrimination of the object. The notion of knowing something of an object has everyday uses because we are willing to apply it to subjects who do not meet a perfectionist standard for discriminating the object. By contrast, the Δ operator is a theoretical instrument for analysing vagueness; in that project, slight failures of discrimination are just what we are interested in. Thus it can be epistemically vague of Everest whether it is Everest even though it is known of Everest that it is Everest. Our self-attribution of *de re* knowledge in such borderline cases helps to explain our temptation to attribute the vagueness to the objects themselves.

Under epistemicism, each state of affairs either clearly obtains or clearly fails to obtain. One might therefore conclude that the source of any vagueness is our way of conceptualizing the state of affairs, not the state of affairs itself. For example, suppose that it is vague whether 17 is small (for a natural number). For some natural number n, 'small' refers in this context to the property of being less than n. Some numeral, say '18', refers to n. On some reasonable conceptions of states of affairs, the state of affairs that 17 is small is the state of affairs that 17 is less than 18. It is not vague whether 17 is less than 18. That it is vague whether 17 is small shows that the state of affairs that 17 is small *can* be conceptualized as borderline, not that it *must* be.

Are all borderline cases like that, given epistemicism? That every state of affairs can be conceptualized precisely is not obvious. Perhaps heaphood cannot be conceptualized precisely. But complete precision may be unnecessary. Suppose that 'This is a heap' (Ht) is borderline. Define artificial predicates $H+$ and $H-$ to have the same extension as H in all non-actual worlds; in the actual world, $H+x$ is equivalent to $Hx \lor x = t$ and $H-x$ to $Hx \ \& \sim x = t$. If Ht is true, $H+$ is necessarily coextensive with H, so Ht and $H+t$ arguably express the same state of affairs; but $H+t$ ($Ht \lor t = t$) is clearly true. If Ht is false, $H-t$ is necessarily coextensive with H, so Ht and $H-t$ arguably express the same state of affairs; but $H-t(Ht \ \& \sim t = t)$ is clearly false. Since Ht is either true or false, the state of affairs that this is a heap can be conceptualized as non-borderline, unless states of affairs are so fine-grained that the additional logical structure in the new predicates makes them express new states of affairs.

Perhaps any state of affairs that can be conceptualized as borderline can also be conceptualized as non-borderline. But that might require highly artificial methods of conceptualization. Some states of affairs may be 'naturally' conceptualizable only as borderline. That property would distinguish those states of affairs from others, and it might reflect underlying intrinsic differences between the states of affairs.

Identity states of affairs illustrate the point (see also Williamson 2002). Suppose that it is vague whether Everest is Schmeverest. If the identity holds, 'Everest is Schmeverest' expresses the same state of affairs as 'Everest is Everest'; it is clear that Everest is Everest. But if the identity fails, the two sentences express different states of affairs; perhaps the state of affairs that Everest is Schmeverest cannot be 'naturally' conceptualized as non-borderline.

Epistemicism provides only an aetiolated sort of metaphysical vagueness, constitutively dependent on thinkers' epistemological limitations. That may be as much metaphysical vagueness as we have any reason to expect. Common sense insists that it is vague whether this rock is part of Everest, that this rock and Everest are genuine objects and that parthood is a genuine relation; it leaves the underlying nature of the vagueness for theory to determine. Under epistemicism, common sense may be straightforwardly correct.

References

Abbott, W. (1983). 'A Note on Grim's Sorites Argument'. *Analysis*, 43: 161–4.

Akiba, K. (2000). 'Vagueness as a Modality'. *Philosophical Quarterly*, 50: 359–70.

Andjelković, M., and T. Williamson (2000). 'Truth, Falsity and Borderline Cases'. *Philosophical Topics*, 28: 211–44.

Broome, J. (1984). 'Indefiniteness in Identity'. *Analysis*, 44: 6–12.

Burgess, J. A. (1989). 'Vague Identity: Evans Misrepresented'. *Analysis*, 49: 112–19.

—— (1990). 'Vague Objects and Indefinite Identity'. *Philosophical Studies*, 59: 263–87.

Cook, M. (1986). 'Indeterminacy of Identity'. *Analysis*, 46: 179–86.

Copeland, B. J. (1995). 'On Vague Objects, Fuzzy Logic, and Fractal Boundaries'. *Southern Journal of Philosophy*, suppl. vol. 33: 83–96.

—— (1997). 'Vague Identity and Fuzzy Logic'. *Journal of Philosophy*, 94: 514–34.

Cowles, D. (1994). 'On van Inwagen's Defense of Vague Identity'. *Philosophical Perspectives*, 8: 137–58.

—— and M. White, (1991). 'Vague Objects for those who Want Them'. *Philosophical Studies*, 63: 203–16.

Engel, P. (1991). *The Norm of Truth*. London: Harvester Wheatsheaf.

Evans, G. (1978). 'Can there be Vague Objects?' *Analysis*, 38: 208.

Fine, K. (1975). 'Vagueness, Truth and Logic'. *Synthese*, 30: 265–300.

Forbes, G. (1983). 'Thisness and Vagueness'. *Synthese*, 54: 235–59.

—— (1985). The *Metaphysics of Modality*. Oxford: Clarendon Press.

French, S., and D. Krause (1995). 'Vague Identity and Quantum Indeterminacy'. *Analysis*, 55: 20–6.

Garrett, B. (1988). 'Vagueness and Identity'. *Analysis*, 48: 130–4.

—— (1991). 'Vague Identity and Vague Objects'. *Noûs*, 25: 341–51.

Gibbins, P. (1982). 'The Strange Modal Logic of Indeterminacy'. *Logique et Analyse*, 25: 443–6.

Goguen, J. (1969). 'The Logic of Inexact Concepts'. *Synthese*, 19: 325–73.

Graff, D., and T. Williamson (eds.) (2002). *Vagueness*. Aldershot: Ashgate.

Grim, P. (1982). 'What won't Escape Sorites Arguments'. *Analysis*, 42: 38–43.

—— (1983). 'Is this a Swizzle Stick which I See before Me?'. *Analysis*, 43: 164–6.

—— (1984). 'Taking Sorites Arguments Seriously: Some Hidden Costs'. *Philosophia*, 14: 251–72.

Hawley, K. (1998). 'Indeterminism and Indeterminacy'. *Analysis*, 58: 101–6.

Heck, R. (1998). 'That there might be Vague Objects (so far as concerns Logic)'. *The Monist*, 81: 274–96.

Heller, M. (1988). 'Vagueness and the Standard Ontology'. *Noûs*, 22: 109–31.

—— (1990). *The Ontology of Physical Objects: Four-Dimensional Hunks of Matter*. Cambridge: Cambridge University Press.

Hirsch, E. (1999). 'The Vagueness of Identity'. *Philosophical Topics*, 26: 139–58.

Horgan, T. (1994). 'Robust Vagueness and the Forced-March Sorites Paradox'. *Philosophical Perspectives*, 8: 159–88.

—— (1995). 'Transvaluationism: A Dionysian Approach to Vagueness'. *Southern Journal of Philosophy*, 33: 97–126.

Howard-Snyder, F. (1991). '*De Re* Modality Entails *De Re* Vagueness'. *Pacific Philosophical Quarterly*, 72: 101–12.

Hyde, D. (1998). 'Vagueness, Ontology and Supervenience'. *The Monist*, 81: 297–312.

Johnsen, B. (1989). 'Is Vague Identity Incoherent?' *Analysis*, 49: 103–12.

Kamp, H. (1975). 'Two Theories about Adjectives', in E. Keenan (ed.), *Formal Semantics of Natural Language*. Cambridge: Cambridge University Press.

—— (1981). 'The Paradox of the Heap', in U. Mönnich (ed.), *Aspects of Philosophical Logic*. Dordrecht: Reidel.

Keefe, R. (1995). 'Contingent Identity and Vague Identity'. *Analysis*, 55: 183–90.

—— (2000). *Theories of Vagueness*. Cambridge: Cambridge University Press.

—— and P. Smith (eds.) (1996). *Vagueness: A Reader*. Cambridge, Mass: MIT Press.

Lewis, D. (1988). 'Vague Identity: Evans Misunderstood'. *Analysis*, 48: 128–30.

—— (1993). 'Many, but almost One', in J. Bacon, K. Campbell, and L. Reinhardt (eds.), *Ontology, Causality and Mind: Essays in Honour of D. M. Armstrong*. Cambridge: Cambridge University Press.

Lowe, E. J. (1994). 'Vague Identity and Quantum Indeterminacy'. *Analysis*, 54: 110–14.

—— (1995). 'The Problem of the Many and the Vagueness of Constitution'. *Analysis*, 55: 179–82.

—— (1997). 'Reply to Noonan on Vague Identity'. *Analysis*, 57: 88–91.

McGee, V., and B. McLaughlin (1995). 'Distinctions without a Difference'. *Southern Journal of Philosophy*, 33: 203–51.

McLaughlin, B. (1997). 'Supervenience, Vagueness and Determination'. *Philosophical Perspectives*, 11: 209–30.

Noonan, H. (1982). 'Vague Objects'. *Analysis*, 42: 3–6.

—— (1984). 'Indefinite Identity: A Reply to Broome'. *Analysis*, 44: 117–21.

—— (1990). 'Vague Identity Yet Again'. *Analysis*, 50: 157–62.

—— (1995). 'E. J. Lowe on Vague Identity and Quantum Indeterminacy'. *Analysis*, 55: 14–19.

Over, D. (1984). 'The Consequences of Direct Reference'. *Philosophical Books*, 25: 1–7.

—— (1989). 'Vague Objects and Identity'. *Analysis*, 49: 97–9.

Parsons, T. (1987). 'Entities without Identity'. *Philosophical Perspectives*, 1: 1–19.

—— (2000). *Indeterminate Identify: Metaphysics and Semantics* Oxford: Clarendon Press.

—— and P. Woodruff (1995). 'Worldly Indeterminacy of Identity'. *Proceedings of the Aristotelian Society*, 95: 171–91.

Peacocke, C. (1981). 'Are Vague Predicates Incoherent?' *Synthese*, 46: 121–41.

Pelletier, F. (1984). 'The Not-So-Strange Modal Logic of Indeterminacy'. *Logique et Analyse*, 27: 415–22.

—— (1989). 'Another Argument against Vague Objects'. *Journal of Philosophy*, 86: 481–92.

Priest, G. (1991). 'Sorites and Identity'. *Logique et Analyse*, 34: 293–6.

—— (1998). 'Fuzzy Identity and Local Validity'. *The Monist*, 81: 331–42.

Quine, W. V. O. (1981). 'What Price Bivalence?' *Journal of Philosophy*, 78: 90–5.

Rasmussen, S. (1986). 'Vague Identity'. *Mind*, 95: 81–91.

Rolf, B. (1980). 'A Theory of Vagueness'. *Journal of Philosophical Logic*, 9: 315–25.

Sainsbury, R. M. (1989). 'What is a Vague Object?'. *Analysis*, 49: 99–103.

—— (1995). 'Why the World cannot be Vague'. *Southern Journal of Philosophy*, 33, suppl. vol. 33: 63–81.

Salmon, N. (1982). *Reference and Essence*. Oxford: Basil Blackwell.

—— (1984). 'Fregean Theory and the Four Worlds Paradox: A Reply to David Over'. *Philosophical Books*, 25: 7–11.

—— (1986). 'Modal Paradox: Parts and Counterparts, Points and Counterpoints'. in P. French, T. Uehling, and H. Wettstein (eds.), *Midwest Studies in Philosophy*, xi. Minneapolis: University of Minnesota Press, 75–120.

Sanford, D. (1979). 'Nostalgia for the Ordinary: Comments on Papers by Unger and Wheeler'. *Synthese*, 41: 175–84.

—— (1993). 'The Problem of the Many, Many Composition Questions, and Naive Mereology'. *Noûs*, 27: 219–28.

Sorensen, R. (1998). 'Sharp Boundaries for Blobs'. *Philosophical Studies*, 91: 275–95.

Stalnaker, R. (1988). 'Vague Identity', in D. Austin (ed.), *Philosophical Analysis: A Defense by Example*. Dordrecht: Kluwer.

Thomason, R. (1982). 'Identity and Vagueness'. *Philosophical Studies*, 42: 329–32.

Tye, M. (1990). 'Vague Objects'. *Mind*, 99: 535–57.

—— (1994). 'Sorites Paradoxes and the Semantics of Vagueness'. *Philosophical Perspectives*, 8: 189–206.

—— (1995). 'Vagueness: Welcome to the Quicksand'. *Southern Journal of Philosophy*, suppl. vol. 33: 1–22.

—— (1996). 'Fuzzy Realism and the Problem of the Many'. *Philosophical Studies*, 81: 215–25.

Unger, P. (1979a). 'I do not Exist', in G. Macdonald (ed.), *Perception and Identity*. London: Macmillan.

—— (1979b). 'There are no Ordinary Things'. *Synthese*, 41: 117–54.

—— (1979c). 'Why there are No People', in *Midwest Studies in Philosophy*, iv: *Studies in Metaphysics*. Minneapolis: University of Minnesota Press, 177–222.

—— (1980). 'The Problem of the Many'. *Midwest Studies in Philosophy*, v: Minneapolis: University of Minnesota Press, 411–67.

—— (1990). *Identity, Consciousness and Value*. Oxford: Oxford University Press.

van Inwagen, P. (1988). 'How to Reason about Vague Objects'. *Philosophical Topics*, 16: 255–84.

—— (1990). *Material Beings*. Ithaca, NY: Cornell University Press.

Wheeler, S. (1975). 'Reference and Vagueness'. *Synthese*, 30: 367–79.

—— (1979). 'On that which is Not'. *Synthese* 41: 155–73.

Wiggins, D. (1986). 'On Singling out an Object Determinately', in P. Pettit and J. McDowell (eds.), *Subject, Thought and Context*. Oxford: Oxford University Press.

Williamson, T. (1994). *Vagueness*. London: Routledge.

—— (1995). 'Definiteness and Knowability'. *Southern Journal of Philosophy*, suppl. vol. 33: 171–91.

—— (1996a). 'The Necessity and Determinacy of Distinctness', in S. Lovibond and S. Williams (eds.), *Essays for David Wiggins: Identity, Truth and Value*. Oxford: Basil Blackwell.

—— (1996b). 'What Makes it a Heap?' *Erkenntnis*, 44: 327–39.

—— (1997). 'Imagination, Stipulation and Vagueness'. *Philosophical Issues*, 8: 215–28.

—— (1999a). 'On the Structure of Higher-Order Vagueness'. *Mind*, 108: 127–43.

—— (1999b). 'Truthmakers and the Converse Barcan Formula'. *Dialectica*, 53: 253–70.

—— (2002). 'Vagueness, Identity and Leibniz's Law', in P. Giaretta, A. Bottani, and M. Carrara (eds.), *Individuals, Essence, and Identity: Themes of Analytic Metaphysics*. Dordrecht: Kluwer.

Zemach, E. (1991). 'Vague Objects'. *Noûs*, 25: 323–40.

INDEX

....